W9-AVO-981

P_f	Price of good in foreign country
P_h	Price of good in home country
P_N	A stock's horizon, or terminal, value
P/E	Price/earnings ratio
PM	Profit margin
PMT	Payment of an annuity
PPP	Purchasing power parity
PV	Present value
PVA_N	Present value of an annuity for N years
Q	Quantity produced or sold
Q_{BE}	Breakeven quantity
r	(1) A percentage discount rate, or cost of capital; also denoted by i
	(2) Nominal risk-adjusted required rate of return
$\bar{r}$	"r bar," historic, or realized, rate of return
$\hat{r}$	"r hat," an expected rate of return
r^*	Real risk-free rate of return
r_d	Before-tax cost of debt
r_e	Cost of new common stock (outside equity)
r_f	Interest rate in foreign country
r_h	Interest rate in home country
r_i	Required return for an individual firm or security
r_M	Return for "the market" or for an "average" stock
r_{NOM}	Nominal rate of interest; also denoted by i_{NOM}
r_{ps}	(1) Cost of preferred stock
	(2) Portfolio's return
r_{PER}	Periodic rate of return
r_{RF}	Rate of return on a risk-free security
r_s	(1) Required return on common stock
	(2) Cost of current outstanding common stock
ρ	Correlation coefficient (lowercase rho); also denoted by R when using historical data
ROA	Return on assets
ROE	Return on equity
RP	Risk premium
RP_M	Market risk premium
RR	Retention rate
S	(1) Sales
	(2) Estimated standard deviation for sample data
	(3) Intrinsic value of stock (i.e., all common equity)
SML	Security Market Line
Σ	Summation sign (uppercase sigma)
σ	Standard deviation (lowercase sigma)
σ^2	Variance
t	Time period
T	Marginal income tax rate
TV_N	A stock's horizon, or terminal, value
TIE	Times interest earned
V	Variable cost per unit
V_B	Bond value
V_L	Total market value of a levered firm
V_{op}	Value of operations
V_{ps}	Value of preferred stock
V_U	Total market value of an unlevered firm
VC	Total variable costs
w	Proportion or weight
w_d	Weight of debt
w_{ps}	Weight of preferred stock
w_s	Weight of common equity raised internally by retaining earnings
WACC	Weighted average cost of capital
X	Exercise price of option
YTC	Yield to call
YTM	Yield to maturity

Financial Management

Southern New Hampshire University

FIN 500

Eugene F. Brigham | Michael C. Ehrhardt

CENGAGE
Learning·

Australia • Brazil • Japan • Korea • Mexico • Singapore • Spain • United Kingdom • United States

Financial Management: Southern New Hampshire University, FIN 500

Eugene F. Brigham | Michael C. Ehrhardt

Financial Management: Theory & Practice, 14th Edition
Eugene F. Brigham | Michael C. Ehrhardt
© 2014, 2011, 2008 and 2005 Cengage Learning. All rights reserved.

Senior Project Development Manager:
 Linda deStefano

Market Development Manager:
 Heather Kramer

Senior Production/Manufacturing Manager:
 Donna M. Brown

Production Editorial Manager:
 Kim Fry

Sr. Rights Acquisition Account Manager:
 Todd Osborne

ALL RIGHTS RESERVED. No part of this work covered by the copyright herein may be reproduced, transmitted, stored or used in any form or by any means graphic, electronic, or mechanical, including but not limited to photocopying, recording, scanning, digitizing, taping, Web distribution, information networks, or information storage and retrieval systems, except as permitted under Section 107 or 108 of the 1976 United States Copyright Act, without the prior written permission of the publisher.

For product information and technology assistance, contact us at
Cengage Learning Customer & Sales Support, 1-800-354-9706

For permission to use material from this text or product,
submit all requests online at **cengage.com/permissions**
Further permissions questions can be emailed to
permissionrequest@cengage.com

This book contains select works from existing Cengage Learning resources and was produced by Cengage Learning Custom Solutions for collegiate use. As such, those adopting and/or contributing to this work are responsible for editorial content accuracy, continuity and completeness.

Compilation © 2013 Cengage Learning
ISBN-13: 978-1-285-92222-5

ISBN-10: 1-285-92222-0
Cengage Learning
5191 Natorp Boulevard
Mason, Ohio 45040
USA

Cengage Learning is a leading provider of customized learning solutions with office locations around the globe, including Singapore, the United Kingdom, Australia, Mexico, Brazil, and Japan. Locate your local office at:
international.cengage.com/region.
Cengage Learning products are represented in Canada by Nelson Education, Ltd.
For your lifelong learning solutions, visit **www.cengage.com/custom.**
Visit our corporate website at **www.cengage.com.**

Printed in the United States of America

Brief Contents

Web Chapters   Web Chapter 27: Providing and Obtaining Credit

                 Web Chapter 28: Advanced Issues in Cash Management and
                 Inventory Control

                 Web Chapter 29: Pension Plan Management

                 Web Chapter 30: Financial Management in Not-for-Profit
                 Businesses

PART **1**

The Company and Its Environment

© lulu/fotolia.com

© Adalberto Rios Szalay/Sexto Sol/Getty Images

CHAPTER 1

An Overview of Financial Management and the Financial Environment

W W W

See money.cnn.com/ magazines/fortune for updates on the ranking.

I n a global beauty contest for companies, the winner is ... Apple Computer.

Or at least Apple is the most admired company in the world, according to *Fortune* magazine's annual survey. The others in the global top ten are Google, Berkshire Hathaway, Southwest Airlines, Procter & Gamble, Coca-Cola, Amazon.com, FedEx, Microsoft, and McDonald's. What do these companies have that separates them from the rest of the pack?

According to a survey of executives, directors, and security analysts, these companies have very high average scores across nine attributes: (1) innovativeness, (2) quality of management, (3) long-term investment value, (4) social responsibility, (5) employee talent, (6) quality of products and services, (7) financial soundness, (8) use of corporate assets, and (9) effectiveness in doing business globally. After culling weaker companies, the final rankings are then determined by over 3,700 experts from a wide variety of industries.

What do these companies have in common? First, they have an incredible focus on using technology to understand their customers, reduce costs, reduce inventory, and speed up product delivery. Second, they continually innovate and invest in ways to differentiate their products. Some are known for game-changing products, such as Apple's iPad. Others continually introduce small improvements, such as Southwest Airlines's streamlined boarding procedures.

In addition to their acumen with technology and customers, they are also on the leading edge when it comes to training employees and providing a workplace in which people can thrive.

Prior to the global economic crisis, these companies maintained reasonable debt levels and avoided overpaying for acquisitions. This allowed them to weather the crisis and position themselves for stronger subsequent performance than many of their competitors.

In a nutshell, these companies reduce costs by having innovative production processes, they create value for customers by providing high-quality products and services, and they create value for employees by training and fostering an environment that allows employees to utilize all of their skills and talents. As you will see throughout this book, the resulting cash flow and superior return on capital also create value for investors.

3

GLOBAL ECONOMIC CRISIS

© uniquely india/Getty Images

The Global Economic Crisis

The global economic crisis is like a guest at a party who has one drink and is very interesting and entertaining but who then has many more drinks, gets sick, and lingers on after everyone else has left. At the risk of oversimplification, this is what happened during the past decade: Many of the world's individuals, financial institutions, and governments borrowed too much money and used those borrowed funds to make speculative investments. Those investments turned out to be worth less than the amounts owed by the borrowers, forcing widespread bankruptcies, buyouts, and restructurings for both borrowers and lenders. This in turn reduced the supply of available funds that

financial institutions normally lent to creditworthy individuals, manufacturers, and retailers. Without access to credit, consumers bought less, manufacturers produced less, and retailers sold less—all of which led to layoffs. According to the National Bureau of Economic Research, the resulting recession lasted from December 2007 through June 2009. But as we write this chapter in 2012, the U.S. economy is still not growing very quickly. As we progress through this chapter and the rest of the book, we will discuss different aspects of the crisis. For real-time updates, go to the Global Economic Watch (GEW) Resource Center at **www.cengage.com/thewatch**.

resource

The textbook's Web site has tools for teaching, learning, and conducting financial research.

This chapter should give you an idea of what financial management is all about, including an overview of the financial markets in which corporations operate. Before going into details, let's look at the big picture. You're probably in school because you want an interesting, challenging, and rewarding career. To see where finance fits in, here's a five-minute MBA.

1-1 The Five-Minute MBA

Okay, we realize you can't get an MBA in five minutes. But just as an artist quickly sketches the outline of a picture before filling in the details, we can sketch the key elements of an MBA education. The primary objective of an MBA program is to provide managers with the knowledge and skills they need to run successful companies, so we start our sketch with some common characteristics of successful companies. In particular, all successful companies are able to accomplish two main goals:

1. All successful companies identify, create, and deliver products or services that are highly valued by customers—so highly valued that customers choose to purchase from them rather than from their competitors.
2. All successful companies sell their products/services at prices that are high enough to cover costs and to compensate owners and creditors for the use of their money and their exposure to risk.

It's easy to talk about satisfying customers and investors, but it's not so easy to accomplish these goals. If it were, then all companies would be successful, and you wouldn't need an MBA!

1-1a The Key Attributes of Successful Companies

First, *successful companies have skilled people* at all levels inside the company, including leaders, managers, and a capable workforce.

Second, *successful companies have strong relationships* with groups outside the company. For example, successful companies develop win–win relationships with suppliers and excel in customer relationship management.

Third, *successful companies have enough funding* to execute their plans and support their operations. Most companies need cash to purchase land, buildings, equipment, and materials. Companies can reinvest a portion of their earnings, but most growing companies also must raise additional funds externally by some combination of selling stock and/or borrowing in the financial markets.

Just as a stool needs all three legs to stand, a successful company must have all three attributes: skilled people, strong external relationships, and sufficient capital.

1-1b The MBA, Finance, and Your Career

WWW

Consult **www.careers-in-finance.com** for an excellent site containing information on a variety of business career areas, listings of current jobs, and other reference materials.

To be successful, a company must meet its first main goal: identifying, creating, and delivering highly valued products and services to customers. This requires that it possess all three of the key attributes mentioned above. Therefore, it's not surprising that most of your MBA courses are directly related to these attributes. For example, courses in economics, communication, strategy, organizational behavior, and human resources should prepare you for a leadership role and enable you to manage your company's workforce effectively. Other courses, such as marketing, operations management, and information technology, increase your knowledge of specific disciplines, enabling you to develop the efficient business processes and strong external relationships your company needs. Portions of *this* finance course will address raising the capital your company needs to implement its plans. In short, your MBA courses will give you the skills you need to help a company achieve its first goal: producing goods and services that customers want.

Recall, though, that it's not enough just to have highly valued products and satisfied customers. Successful companies must also meet their second main goal, which is generating enough cash to compensate the investors who provided the necessary capital. To help your company accomplish this second goal, you must be able to evaluate any proposal, whether it relates to marketing, production, strategy, or any other area, and implement only the projects that add value for your investors. For this, you must have expertise in finance, no matter your major. Thus, finance is a critical part of an MBA education, and it will help you throughout your career.

SELF-TEST

What are the goals of successful companies?

What are the three key attributes common to all successful companies?

How does expertise in finance help a company become successful?

1-2 The Corporate Life Cycle

Many major corporations, including Apple and Hewlett-Packard, began life in a garage or basement. How is it possible for such companies to grow into the giants we see today? No two companies develop in exactly the same way, but the following sections describe some typical stages in the corporate life cycle.

Columbus Was Wrong—the World Is Flat! And Hot! And Crowded!

© Rob Webb/Getty Images

In his best-selling book *The World Is Flat*, Thomas L. Friedman argues that many of the barriers that long protected businesses and employees from global competition have been broken down by dramatic improvements in communication and transportation technologies. The result is a level playing field that spans the entire world. As we move into the information age, any work that can be digitized will flow to those able to do it at the lowest cost, whether they live in San Jose's Silicon Valley or Bangalore, India. For physical products, supply chains now span the world. For example, raw materials might be extracted in South America, fabricated into electronic components in Asia, and then used in computers assembled in the United States, with the final product being sold in Europe.

Similar changes are occurring in the financial markets, as capital flows across the globe to those who can best use it. Indeed, China and Hong Kong raised more through initial public offerings in 2011 than both Europe and the United States together.

Unfortunately, a dynamic world can bring runaway growth, which can lead to significant environmental problems and energy shortages. Friedman describes these problems in another bestseller, *Hot, Flat, and Crowded*. In a flat world, the keys to success are knowledge, skills, and a great work ethic. In a flat, hot, and crowded world, these factors must be combined with innovation and creativity to deal with truly global problems.

1-2a Starting Up as a Proprietorship

Many companies begin as a **proprietorship**, which is an unincorporated business owned by one individual. Starting a business as a proprietor is easy—one merely begins business operations after obtaining any required city or state business licenses. The proprietorship has three important advantages: (1) it is easily and inexpensively formed, (2) it is subject to few government regulations, and (3) its income is not subject to corporate taxation but is taxed as part of the proprietor's personal income.

However, the proprietorship also has three important limitations: (1) It may be difficult for a proprietorship to obtain the capital needed for growth. (2) The proprietor has unlimited personal liability for the business's debts, which can result in losses that exceed the money invested in the company (creditors may even be able to seize a proprietor's house or other personal property!). (3) The life of a proprietorship is limited to the life of its founder. For these three reasons, sole proprietorships are used primarily for small businesses. In fact, proprietorships account for only about 13% of all sales, based on dollar values, even though about 80% of all companies are proprietorships.

1-2b More Than One Owner: A Partnership

Some companies start with more than one owner, and some proprietors decide to add a partner as the business grows. A **partnership** exists whenever two or more persons or entities associate to conduct a noncorporate business for profit. Partnerships may operate under different degrees of formality, ranging from informal, oral understandings to formal agreements filed with the secretary of the state in which the partnership was formed. Partnership agreements define the ways any profits and losses are shared between partners. A partnership's advantages and disadvantages are generally similar to those of a proprietorship.

Regarding liability, the partners potentially can lose all of their personal assets, even assets not invested in the business, because under partnership law, each partner is liable for the business's debts. Therefore, in the event the partnership goes bankrupt, if any partner is unable to meet his or her pro rata liability, then the remaining partners must make good on the unsatisfied claims, drawing on their personal assets to the extent necessary. To avoid this, it is possible to limit the liabilities of some of the partners by establishing a **limited partnership**, wherein certain partners are designated **general partners** and others **limited partners**. In a limited partnership, the limited partners can lose only the amount of their investment in the partnership, while the general partners have unlimited liability. However, the limited partners typically have no control—it rests solely with the general partners—and their returns are likewise limited. Limited partnerships are common in real estate, oil, equipment leasing ventures, and venture capital. However, they are not widely used in general business situations because usually no partner is willing to be the general partner and thus accept the majority of the business's risk, and no partners are willing to be limited partners and give up all control.

In both regular and limited partnerships, at least one partner is liable for the debts of the partnership. However, in a **limited liability partnership (LLP)**, sometimes called a **limited liability company (LLC)**, all partners enjoy limited liability with regard to the business's liabilities, and their potential losses are limited to their investment in the LLP. Of course, this arrangement increases the risk faced by an LLP's lenders, customers, and suppliers.

1-2c Many Owners: A Corporation

Most partnerships have difficulty attracting substantial amounts of capital. This is generally not a problem for a slow-growing business, but if a business's products or services really catch on, and if it needs to raise large sums of money to capitalize on its opportunities, then the difficulty in attracting capital becomes a real drawback. Thus, many growth companies, such as Hewlett-Packard and Microsoft, began life as a proprietorship or partnership, and at some point their founders decided to convert to a corporation. On the other hand, some companies, in anticipation of growth, actually begin as corporations. A **corporation** is a legal entity created under state laws, and it is separate and distinct from its owners and managers. This separation gives the corporation three major advantages: (1) *unlimited life*—a corporation can continue after its original owners and managers are deceased; (2) *easy transferability of ownership interest*—ownership interests are divided into shares of stock, which can be transferred far more easily than can proprietorship or partnership interests; and (3) *limited liability*—losses are limited to the actual funds invested.

To illustrate limited liability, suppose you invested $10,000 in a partnership that then went bankrupt and owed $1 million. Because the owners are liable for the debts of a partnership, you could be assessed for a share of the company's debt, and you could be held liable for the entire $1 million if your partners could not pay their shares. On the other hand, if you invested $10,000 in the stock of a corporation that went bankrupt, your potential loss on the investment would be limited to your $10,000 investment.[1] Unlimited life, easy transferability of ownership interest, and limited liability make it much easier for corporations than proprietorships or partnerships to raise money in the financial markets and grow into large companies.

---

[1] In the case of very small corporations, the limited liability may be fiction because lenders frequently require personal guarantees from the stockholders.

The corporate form offers significant advantages over proprietorships and partnerships, but it also has two disadvantages: (1) Corporate earnings may be subject to double taxation—the earnings of the corporation are taxed at the corporate level, and then earnings paid out as dividends are taxed again as income to the stockholders. (2) Setting up a corporation involves preparing a charter, writing a set of bylaws, and filing the many required state and federal reports, which is more complex and time-consuming than creating a proprietorship or a partnership.

The **charter** includes the following information: (1) name of the proposed corporation, (2) types of activities it will pursue, (3) amount of capital stock, (4) number of directors, and (5) names and addresses of directors. The charter is filed with the secretary of the state in which the firm will be incorporated, and when it is approved, the corporation is officially in existence.[2] After the corporation begins operating, quarterly and annual employment, financial, and tax reports must be filed with state and federal authorities.

The **bylaws** are a set of rules drawn up by the founders of the corporation. Included are such points as (1) how directors are to be elected (all elected each year or perhaps one-third each year for 3-year terms); (2) whether the existing stockholders will have the first right to buy any new shares the firm issues; and (3) procedures for changing the bylaws themselves, should conditions require it.

There are several different types of corporations. Professionals such as doctors, lawyers, and accountants often form a **professional corporation (PC)** or a **professional association (PA)**. These types of corporations do not relieve the participants of professional (malpractice) liability. Indeed, the primary motivation behind the professional corporation was to provide a way for groups of professionals to incorporate in order to avoid certain types of unlimited liability yet still be held responsible for professional liability.

Finally, if certain requirements are met, particularly with regard to size and number of stockholders, owners can establish a corporation but elect to be taxed as if the business were a proprietorship or partnership. Such firms, which differ not in organizational form but only in how their owners are taxed, are called **S corporations**.

1-2d Growing and Managing a Corporation

Once a corporation has been established, how does it evolve? When entrepreneurs start a company, they usually provide all the financing from their personal resources, which may include savings, home equity loans, or even credit cards. As the corporation grows, it will need factories, equipment, inventory, and other resources to support its growth. In time, the entrepreneurs usually deplete their own resources and must turn to external financing. Many young companies are too risky for banks, so the founders must sell stock to outsiders, including friends, family, private investors (often called angels), or venture capitalists. If the corporation continues to grow, it may become successful enough to attract lending from banks, or it may even raise additional funds through an **initial public offering (IPO)** by selling stock to the public at large. After an IPO, corporations support their growth by borrowing from banks, issuing debt, or selling additional shares of stock. In short, a corporation's ability to grow depends on its interactions with the financial markets, which we describe in much more detail later in this chapter.

For proprietorships, partnerships, and small corporations, the firm's owners are also its managers. This is usually not true for a large corporation, which means that large firms'

---

[2]More than 60% of major U.S. corporations are chartered in Delaware, which has, over the years, provided a favorable legal environment for corporations. It is not necessary for a firm to be headquartered, or even to conduct operations, in its state of incorporation, or even in its country of incorporation.

stockholders, who are its owners, face a serious problem. What is to prevent managers from acting in their own best interests, rather than in the best interests of the stockholder/ owners? This is called an **agency problem**, because managers are hired as agents to act on behalf of the owners. Agency problems can be addressed by a company's **corporate governance**, which is the set of rules that control the company's behavior towards its directors, managers, employees, shareholders, creditors, customers, competitors, and community. We will have much more to say about agency problems and corporate governance throughout the book, especially in Chapters 13, 14, and 15.

SELF-TEST

What are the key differences between proprietorships, partnerships, and corporations?

Describe some special types of partnerships and corporations, and explain the differences among them.

1-3 The Primary Objective of the Corporation: Value Maximization

Shareholders are the owners of a corporation, and they purchase stocks because they want to earn a good return on their investment without undue risk exposure. In most cases, shareholders elect directors, who then hire managers to run the corporation on a day-to-day basis. Because managers are supposed to be working on behalf of shareholders, they should pursue policies that enhance shareholder value. Consequently, throughout this book we operate on the assumption that management's primary objective should be *stockholder wealth maximization.*

The **market price** is the stock price that we observe in the financial markets. We later explain in detail how stock prices are determined, but for now it is enough to say that a company's market price incorporates the information available to investors. If the market price reflects all *relevant* information, then the observed price is the **intrinsic price**, also called the **fundamental price**.

However, investors rarely have all relevant information. Companies report most major decisions, but they may withhold selected information to prevent competitors from gaining strategic advantages. In addition, managers may take actions that boost bonuses linked to higher current earnings yet actually decrease future cash flows, such as reducing scheduled maintenance. As we show in Chapter 7, short-term focus can reduce the intrinsic price but might actually increase the market price if such actions are difficult for investors to discern immediately. Thus, the market price can deviate from the intrinsic price. In this example, the market price initially would go up relative to the intrinsic price, but it would then fall in the future as the company experienced production problems due to poorly maintained equipment.

Therefore, when we say management's objective should be to maximize stockholder wealth, we really mean it is to *maximize the fundamental price of the firm's common stock,* not just the current market price. Firms do, of course, have other objectives; in particular, the managers who make the actual decisions are interested in their own personal satisfaction, in their employees' welfare, and in the good of their communities and society at large. Still, for the reasons set forth in the following sections, *maximizing intrinsic stock value should be the most important objective for most corporations.*

Ethics for Individuals and Businesses

© Rob Webb/Getty Images

A firm's commitment to business ethics can be measured by the tendency of its employees, from the top down, to adhere to laws, regulations, and moral standards relating to product safety and quality, fair employment practices, fair marketing and selling practices, the use of confidential information for personal gain, community involvement, and illegal payments to obtain business.

Ethical Dilemmas

When conflicts arise between profits and ethics, sometimes legal and ethical considerations make the choice obvious. At other times the right choice isn't clear. For example, suppose Norfolk Southern's managers know that its trains are polluting the air, but the amount of pollution is within legal limits and further reduction would be costly, causing harm to their shareholders. Are the managers ethically bound to reduce pollution? Aren't they also ethically bound to act in their shareholders' best interests? This is clearly a dilemma.

Ethical Responsibility

Over the past few years, illegal ethical lapses have led to a number of bankruptcies, which have raised this question: Were the *companies* unethical, or was it just a few of their *employees*? Arthur Andersen, an accounting firm, audited Enron, WorldCom, and several other companies that committed accounting fraud. The U.S. Justice Department concluded that Andersen itself was guilty because it fostered a climate in which unethical behavior was permitted, and it built an incentive system that made such behavior profitable to both the perpetrators and the firm itself. As a result, Andersen went out of business. Andersen was later judged to be not guilty, but by the time the judgment was rendered the company was already out of business. People simply did not want to deal with a tainted accounting firm.

Protecting Ethical Employees

If employees discover questionable activities or are given questionable orders, should they obey their bosses' orders, refuse to obey those orders, or report the situation to a higher authority, such as the company's board of directors, its auditors, or a federal prosecutor? In 2002 Congress passed the Sarbanes-Oxley Act, with a provision designed to protect "whistle-blowers." If an employee reports corporate wrongdoing and later is penalized, he or she can ask the Occupational Safety and Health Administration to investigate the situation. If the employee was improperly penalized, the company can be required to reinstate the person, along with providing back pay and a sizable penalty award. Several big awards have been handed out since the act was passed.

1-3a Intrinsic Stock Value Maximization and Social Welfare

WWW

The Investment Company Institute is a great source of information. For updates on mutual fund ownership, see **www.ici.org/ research#fact_books**.

If a firm attempts to maximize its intrinsic stock value, is this good or bad for society? In general, it is good. Aside from such illegal actions as fraudulent accounting, exploiting monopoly power, violating safety codes, and failing to meet environmental standards, *the same actions that maximize intrinsic stock values also benefit society*. Here are some of the reasons:

1. **Most individuals have a stake in the stock market.** Seventy-five years ago this was not true, because most stock ownership was concentrated in the hands of a relatively small segment of society consisting of the wealthiest individuals. More than 44% of all U.S. households now own mutual funds, as compared with only 4.6% in 1980. When direct stock ownership and indirect ownership through pension funds are also considered, many members of society now have an important stake in the stock market, either directly or indirectly. Therefore, when a manager takes actions to maximize the stock price, this improves the quality of life for millions of ordinary citizens.

2. **Consumers benefit.** Stock price maximization requires efficient, low-cost businesses that produce high-quality goods and services at the lowest possible cost. This means that companies must develop products and services that consumers want and need, which leads to new technology and new products. Also, companies that maximize their stock price must generate growth in sales by creating value for customers in the form of efficient and courteous service, adequate stocks of merchandise, and well-located business establishments.

    People sometimes argue that firms, in their efforts to raise profits and stock prices, increase product prices and gouge the public. In a reasonably competitive economy, which we have, prices are constrained by competition and consumer resistance. If a firm raises its prices beyond reasonable levels, it will simply lose market share. Even giant firms such as Dell and Coca-Cola lose business to domestic and foreign competitors if they set prices above the level necessary to cover production costs plus a "normal" profit. Of course, firms *want* to earn more, and they constantly try to cut costs, develop new products, and so on, and thereby earn above-normal profits. Note, though, that if they are indeed successful and do earn above-normal profits, those very profits will attract competition, which will eventually drive prices down. So again, the main long-term beneficiary is the consumer.

3. **Employees benefit.** In some situations a stock increases when a company announces plans to lay off employees, but viewed over time this is the exception rather than the rule. In general, companies that successfully increase stock prices also grow and add more employees, thus benefiting society. Note, too, that many governments across the world, including U.S. federal and state governments, are privatizing some of their state-owned activities by selling these operations to investors. Perhaps not surprisingly, the sales and cash flows of recently privatized companies generally improve. Moreover, studies show that newly privatized companies tend to grow and thus require more employees when they are managed with the goal of stock price maximization.

1-3b Managerial Actions to Maximize Shareholder Wealth

What types of actions can managers take to maximize shareholder wealth? To answer this question, we first need to ask, "What determines a firm's value?" In a nutshell, it is *a company's ability to generate cash flows now and in the future.*

    We address different aspects of this in detail throughout the book, but we can lay out three basic facts now: (1) Any financial asset, including a company's stock, is valuable only to the extent that it generates cash flows. (2) The timing of cash flows matters—cash received sooner is better. (3) Investors are averse to risk, so all else equal, they will pay more for a stock whose cash flows are relatively certain than for one whose cash flows are more risky. Therefore, managers can increase their firm's value by increasing the size of the expected cash flows, by speeding up their receipt, and by reducing their risk.

    The cash flows that matter are called **free cash flows (FCF)**, not because they are free, but because they are available (or free) for distribution to all of the company's investors, including creditors and stockholders. You will learn how to calculate free cash flows in Chapter 2, but for now you should know that free cash flow is:

$$FCF = \frac{Sales}{revenues} - \frac{Operating}{costs} - \frac{Operating}{taxes} - \frac{Required\ investments}{in\ new\ operating\ capital}$$

Corporate Scandals and Maximizing Stock Price

© Rob Webb/Getty Images

The list of corporate scandals seems to go on forever: Sunbeam, Enron, ImClone, WorldCom, Tyco, Adelphia.... At first glance, it's tempting to say, "Look what happens when managers care only about maximizing stock price." But a closer look reveals a much different story. In fact, if these managers were trying to maximize stock price, they failed dismally, given the resulting values of these companies.

Although details vary from company to company, a few common themes emerge. First, managerial compensation was linked to the *short-term* performance of the stock price via poorly designed stock option and stock grant programs. This provided managers with a powerful incentive to drive up the stock price at the option vesting date without worrying about the future. Second, it is virtually impossible to take *legal and ethical* actions that drive up the stock price in the short term without harming it in the long term because the value of a company is based on all of its future free cash flows and not just cash flows in the immediate future. Because legal and ethical actions to quickly drive up the stock price didn't

exist (other than the old-fashioned ones, such as increasing sales, cutting costs, or reducing capital requirements), these managers began bending a few rules. Third, as they initially got away with bending rules, it seems that their egos and hubris grew to such an extent that they felt they were above all rules, so they began breaking even more rules.

Stock prices did go up, at least temporarily, but as Abraham Lincoln said, "You can't fool all of the people all of the time." As the scandals became public, the stocks' prices plummeted, and in some cases the companies were ruined.

There are several important lessons to be learned from these examples. First, people respond to incentives, and poorly designed incentives can cause disastrous results. Second, ethical violations usually begin with small steps, so if stockholders want managers to avoid large ethical violations, then they shouldn't let them make the small ones. Third, there is no shortcut to creating lasting value. It takes hard work to increase sales, cut costs, and reduce capital requirements, but this is the formula for success.

Brand managers and marketing managers can increase sales (and prices) by truly understanding their customers and then designing goods and services that customers want. Human resource managers can improve productivity through training and employee retention. Production and logistics managers can improve profit margins, reduce inventory, and improve throughput at factories by implementing supply chain management, just-in-time inventory management, and lean manufacturing. In fact, all managers make decisions that can increase free cash flows.

One of the financial manager's roles is to help others see how their actions affect the company's ability to generate cash flow and, hence, its intrinsic value. Financial managers also must decide *how to finance the firm*. In particular, they must choose the mix of debt and equity to use and the specific types of debt and equity securities to issue. They also must decide what percentage of current earnings to retain and reinvest rather than pay out as dividends. Along with these financing decisions, the general level of interest rates in the economy, the risk of the firm's operations, and stock market investors' overall attitude toward risk determine the rate of return required to satisfy a firm's investors. This rate of return from an investor's perspective is a cost from the company's point of view. Therefore, the rate of return required by investors is called the **weighted average cost of capital (WACC)**.

The following equation defines the relationship between a firm's fundamental value, its free cash flows, and its cost of capital:

$$\text{Value} = \frac{\text{FCF}_1}{(1+\text{WACC})^1} + \frac{\text{FCF}_2}{(1+\text{WACC})^2} + \frac{\text{FCF}_3}{(1+\text{WACC})^3} + \cdots + \frac{\text{FCF}_\infty}{(1+\text{WACC})^\infty} \quad (1\text{-}1)$$

We will explain how to use this equation in later chapters, but for now note that (1) a growing firm often needs to raise external funds in the financial markets, and (2) the actual price of a firm's stock is determined in those markets. The rest of this chapter focuses on financial markets.

SELF-TEST

What should be management's primary objective?

How does maximizing the fundamental stock price benefit society?

Free cash flow depends on what three factors?

How is a firm's fundamental value related to its free cash flows and its cost of capital?

1-4 An Overview of the Capital Allocation Process

Businesses often need capital to implement growth plans; governments require funds to finance building projects; and individuals frequently want loans to purchase cars, homes, and education. Where can they get this money? Fortunately, there are some individuals and firms with incomes greater than their expenditures. In spite of William Shakespeare's advice, most individuals and firms are both borrowers and lenders. For example, an individual might borrow money with a car loan or a home mortgage but might also lend money through a bank savings account. In the aggregate, individuals are net savers and provide most of the funds ultimately used by nonfinancial corporations. Although most nonfinancial corporations own some financial securities, such as short-term Treasury bills, nonfinancial corporations are net borrowers in the aggregate. In the United States federal, state, and local governments are also net borrowers in the aggregate, although many foreign governments, such as those of China and oil-producing countries, are actually net lenders. Banks and other financial corporations raise money with one hand and invest it with the other. For example, a bank might raise money from individuals in the form of a savings account and then lend most of that money to business customers. In the aggregate, financial corporations borrow slightly more than they lend.

Transfers of capital between savers and those who need capital take place in three different ways. Direct transfers of money and securities, as shown in Panel 1 of Figure 1-1, occur when a business (or government) sells its securities directly to savers. The business delivers its securities to savers, who in turn provide the firm with the money it needs. For example, a privately held company might sell shares of stock directly to a new shareholder, or the U.S. government might sell a Treasury bond directly to an individual investor.

As shown in Panel 2, indirect transfers may go through an **investment banking house** such as Goldman Sachs, which *underwrites* the issue. An underwriter serves as a middleman and facilitates the issuance of securities. The company sells its stocks or bonds to the investment bank, which in turn sells these same securities to savers. Because new securities are involved and the corporation receives the proceeds of the sale, this is a "primary" market transaction.

Transfers also can be made through a **financial intermediary** such as a bank or mutual fund, as shown in Panel 3. Here the intermediary obtains funds from savers in exchange for its own securities. The intermediary then uses this money to purchase and then hold businesses' securities. For example, a saver might give dollars to a bank and receive a certificate of deposit, and then the bank might lend the money to a small business, receiving in exchange a signed loan. Thus, intermediaries literally create new types of securities.

FIGURE 1-1

Diagram of the Capital Allocation Process

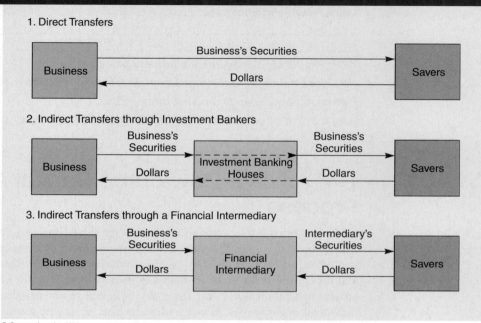

© Cengage Learning 2014

There are three important characteristics of the capital allocation process. First, new financial securities are created. Second, financial institutions are often involved. Third, allocation between providers and users of funds occurs in financial markets. The following sections discuss each of these characteristics.

SELF-TEST

Identify three ways that capital is transferred between savers and borrowers.

Distinguish between the roles played by investment banking houses and financial intermediaries.

1-5 Financial Securities

The variety of financial securities is limited only by human creativity, ingenuity, and governmental regulations. At the risk of oversimplification, we can classify most financial securities by the type of claim and the time until maturity. In addition, some securities actually are created from packages of other securities. We discuss the key aspects of financial securities in this section.

You can access current and historical interest rates and economic data from the Federal Reserve Economic Data (FRED) site at **www.stls.frb.org/fred**.

1-5a Type of Claim: Debt, Equity, or Derivatives

Financial securities are simply pieces of paper with contractual provisions that entitle their owners to specific rights and claims on specific cash flows or values. Debt instruments typically have specified payments and a specified maturity. For example, an Alcoa bond might promise to pay 10% interest for 30 years, at which time it promises to make a $1,000 principal payment. If debt matures in more than a year, it is called a *capital market security*. Thus, the Alcoa bond in this example is a capital market security.

If the debt matures in less than a year, it is a *money market security*. For example, Home Depot might expect to receive $300,000 in 75 days, but it needs cash now. Home Depot might issue commercial paper, which is essentially an IOU. In this example, Home Depot might agree to pay $300,000 in 75 days in exchange for $297,000 today. Thus, commercial paper is a money market security.

Equity instruments are a claim upon a residual value. For example, Alcoa's stockholders are entitled to the cash flows generated by Alcoa after its bondholders, creditors, and other claimants have been satisfied. Because stock has no maturity date, it is a capital market security.

resource

For an overview of derivatives, see **Web Extension 1A** *on the textbook's Web site.*

Notice that debt and equity represent claims upon the cash flows generated by real assets, such as the cash flows generated by Alcoa's factories and operations. In contrast, **derivatives** are securities whose values depend on, or are *derived* from, the values of some other traded assets. For example, options and futures are two important types of derivatives, and their values depend on the prices of other assets. An option on Alcoa stock or a futures contract to buy pork bellies are examples of derivatives. We discuss options in Chapter 8 and in **Web Extension 1A**, which provides a brief overview of options and other derivatives.

Some securities are a mix of debt, equity, and derivatives. For example, preferred stock has some features like debt and some like equity, while convertible debt has both debt-like and option-like features.

We discuss these and other financial securities in detail later in the book, but Table 1-1 provides a summary of the most important conventional financial securities. We discuss rates of return later in this chapter, but notice now in Table 1-1 that interest rates tend to increase with the maturity and risk of the security.

Some securities are created from packages of other assets, a process called *securitization*. The misuse of securitized assets is one of the primary causes of the global financial crisis, so every manager needs to understand the process of securitization.

1-5b The Process of Securitization

Many types of assets can be securitized, but we will focus on mortgages because they played such an important role in the global financial crisis. At one time, most mortgages were made by **savings and loan associations (S&Ls)**, which took in the vast majority of their deposits from individuals who lived in nearby neighborhoods. The S&Ls pooled these deposits and then lent money to people in the neighborhood in the form of fixed-rate mortgages, which were pieces of paper signed by borrowers promising to make specified payments to the S&L. The new homeowners paid principal and interest to the S&L, which then paid interest to its depositors and reinvested the principal repayments in other mortgages. This was clearly better than having individuals lend directly to aspiring homeowners, because a single individual might not have enough money to finance an entire house or the expertise to know if the borrower was creditworthy. Note that the S&Ls were government-chartered institutions. They obtained money in the form of immediately withdrawable deposits and then invested most of it in the form of mortgages with fixed interest rates and on individual homes. Also, initially the S&Ls were not permitted to have branch operations—they were limited to one office to maintain their local orientation.

These restrictions had important implications. First, in the 1950s there was a massive migration of people to the west, so there was a strong demand for funds

TABLE 1-1

Summary of Major Financial Instruments

Instrument	Major Participants	Risk	Original Maturity	Rates of Return on 1/24/12[a]
U.S. Treasury bills	Sold by U.S. Treasury	Default-free	91 days to 1 year	0.07%
Bankers' acceptances	A firm's promise to pay, guaranteed by a bank	Low if strong bank guarantees	Up to 180 days	0.28%
Commercial paper	Issued by financially secure firms to large investors	Low default risk	Up to 270 days	0.15%
Negotiable certificates of deposit (CDs)	Issued by major banks to large investors	Depends on strength of issuer	Up to 1 year	0.37%
Money market mutual funds	Invest in short-term debt; held by individuals and businesses	Low degree of risk	No specific maturity (instant liquidity)	0.51%
Eurodollar market time deposits	Issued by banks outside the United States	Depends on strength of issuer	Up to 1 year	0.20%
Consumer credit loans	Loans by banks/credit unions/finance companies	Risk is variable	Variable	Variable
Commercial loans	Loans by banks to corporations	Depends on borrower	Up to 7 years	Tied to prime rate (3.25%) or LIBOR (0.56%)[b]
U.S. Treasury notes and bonds	Issued by U.S. government	No default risk, but price falls if interest rates rise	2 to 30 years	3.15%
Mortgages	Loans secured by property	Risk is variable	Up to 30 years	4.11%
Municipal bonds	Issued by state and local governments to individuals and institutions	Riskier than U.S. government bonds, but exempt from most taxes	Up to 30 years	4.08%
Corporate bonds	Issued by corporations to individuals and institutions	Riskier than U.S. government debt; depends on strength of issuer	Up to 40 years[c]	5.33%
Leases	Similar to debt; firms lease assets rather than borrow and then buy them	Risk similar to corporate bonds	Generally 3 to 20 years	Similar to bond yields
Preferred stocks	Issued by corporations to individuals and institutions	Riskier than corporate bonds	Unlimited	6% to 9%
Common stocks[d]	Issued by corporations to individuals and institutions	Riskier than preferred stocks	Unlimited	9% to 15%

[a]Data are from *The Wall Street Journal* (**online.wsj.com**) or the *Federal Reserve Statistical Release* (**www.federalreserve.gov/releases/H15/update**). Bankers' acceptances assume a 3-month maturity. Money market rates are for the Merrill Lynch Ready Assets Trust. The corporate bond rate is for AAA-rated bonds.
[b]The prime rate is the rate U.S. banks charge to good customers. LIBOR (London Interbank Offered Rate) is the rate that U.K. banks charge one another.
[c]A few corporations have issued 100-year bonds; however, most have issued bonds with maturities of less than 40 years.
[d]Common stocks are expected to provide a "return" in the form of dividends and capital gains rather than interest. Of course, if you buy a stock, your *actual* return may be considerably higher or lower than your *expected* return.

© Cengage Learning 2014

in that area. However, the wealthiest savers were in the east. That meant that mortgage interest rates were much higher in California and other western states than in New York and the east. This created disequilibrium in the financial markets, something that can't last forever.

Second, note that the S&Ls' assets consisted mainly of long-term, fixed-rate mortgages, but their liabilities were in the form of deposits that could be withdrawn immediately. The combination of long-term assets and short-term liabilities created another problem. If the overall level of interest rates increased, the S&Ls would have to increase the rates they paid on deposits or else savers would take their money elsewhere. However, the S&Ls couldn't increase the rates on their outstanding mortgages because these mortgages had fixed interest rates. This problem came to a head in the 1960s, when the Vietnam War led to inflation, which pushed up interest rates. At this point, the "money market fund" industry was born, and it literally sucked money out of the S&Ls, forcing many of them into bankruptcy.

The government responded by giving the S&Ls broader lending powers, permitting nationwide branching and allowing them to obtain funds as long-term debt in addition to immediately withdrawable deposits. Unfortunately, these changes had another set of unintended consequences. S&L managers who had previously dealt with a limited array of investments and funding choices in local communities could suddenly expand their scope of operations. Many of these inexperienced S&L managers made poor business decisions and the result was disastrous—virtually the entire S&L industry collapsed, with many S&Ls going bankrupt or being acquired in shotgun mergers with commercial banks.

The demise of the S&Ls created another financial disequilibrium—a higher demand for mortgages than the supply of available funds from the mortgage lending industry. Savings were accumulating in pension funds, insurance companies, and other institutions, not in S&Ls and banks, the traditional mortgage lenders.

This situation led to the development of "mortgage securitization," a process whereby banks, the remaining S&Ls, and specialized mortgage-originating firms would originate mortgages and then sell them to investment banks, which would bundle them into packages and then use these packages as collateral for bonds that could be sold to pension funds, insurance companies, and other institutional investors. Thus, individual loans were bundled and then used to back a bond—a "security"—that could be traded in the financial markets.

Congress facilitated this process by creating two stockholder-owned but government-sponsored entities, the Federal National Mortgage Association (Fannie Mae) and the Federal Home Loan Mortgage Corporation (Freddie Mac). Fannie Mae and Freddie Mac were financed by issuing a relatively small amount of stock and a huge amount of debt.

To illustrate the securitization process, suppose an S&L or bank is paying its depositors 5% but is charging its borrowers 8% on their mortgages. The S&L can take hundreds of these mortgages, put them in a pool, and then sell the pool to Fannie Mae. The mortgagees can still make their payments to the original S&L, which will then forward the payments (less a small handling fee) to Fannie Mae.

Consider the S&L's perspective. First, it can use the cash it receives from selling the mortgages to make additional loans to other aspiring homeowners. Second, the S&L is no longer exposed to the risk of owning mortgages. The risk hasn't disappeared—it has been transferred from the S&L (and its federal deposit insurers) to Fannie Mae. This is clearly a better situation for aspiring homeowners and, perhaps, also for taxpayers.

Fannie Mae can take the mortgages it just bought, put them into a very large pool, and sell bonds backed by the pool to investors. The homeowner will pay the S&L, the S&L will forward the payment to Fannie Mae, and Fannie Mae will use the funds to pay interest on the bonds it issued, to pay dividends on its stock, and to buy additional mortgages from

S&Ls, which can then make additional loans to aspiring homeowners. Notice that the mortgage risk has been shifted from Fannie Mae to the investors who now own the mortgage-backed bonds.

How does the situation look from the perspective of the investors who own the bonds? In theory, they own a share in a large pool of mortgages from all over the country, so a problem in a particular region's real estate market or job market won't affect the whole pool. Therefore, their expected rate of return should be very close to the 8% rate paid by the home-owning mortgagees. (It will be a little less due to handling fees charged by the S&L and Fannie Mae and to the small amount of expected losses from the homeowners who could be expected to default on their mortgages.) These investors could have deposited their money at an S&L and earned a virtually risk-free 5%. Instead, they chose to accept more risk in hopes of the higher 8% return. Note, too, that mortgage-backed bonds are more liquid than individual mortgage loans, so the securitization process increases liquidity, which is desirable. The bottom line is that risk has been reduced by the pooling process and then allocated to those who are willing to accept it in return for a higher rate of return.

Thus, in theory it is a win–win–win situation: More money is available for aspiring homeowners, S&Ls (and taxpayers) have less risk, and there are opportunities for investors who are willing to take on more risk to obtain higher potential returns. Although the securitization process began with mortgages, it is now being used with car loans, student loans, credit card debt, and other loans. The details vary for different assets, but the processes and benefits are similar to those with mortgage securitization: (1) increased supplies of lendable funds; (2) transfer of risk to those who are willing to bear it; and (3) increased liquidity for holders of the debt.

Mortgage securitization was a win–win situation in theory, but as practiced in the last decade it has turned into a lose–lose situation. We will have more to say about securitization and the global economic crisis later in this chapter, but first let's take a look at the cost of money.

1-6 The Cost of Money

In a free economy, capital from those with available funds is allocated through the price system to users who have a need for funds. The interaction of the providers' supply and the users' demand determines the cost (or price) of money, which is the rate users pay to providers. For debt, we call this price the **interest rate**. For equity, we call it the **cost of equity**, and it consists of the dividends and capital gains stockholders expect. Keep in mind that the "price" of money is a cost from a user's perspective but a return from the provider's point of view.

Notice in Table 1-1 that a financial instrument's rate of return generally increases as its maturity and risk increase. We will have much more to say about the relationships among an individual security's features, risk, and return later in the book, but first we will examine some fundamental factors and economic conditions that affect all financial instruments.

1-6a Fundamental Factors That Affect the Cost of Money

The four most fundamental factors affecting the cost of money are (1) **production opportunities,** (2) **time preferences for consumption,** (3) **risk,** and (4) **inflation.** By production opportunities, we mean the ability to turn capital into benefits. If a business raises capital, the benefits are determined by the expected rates of return on its production opportunities. If a student borrows to finance his or her education, the benefits are higher expected future salaries (and, of course, the sheer joy of learning!). If a homeowner borrows, the benefits are the pleasure from living in his or her own home, plus any expected appreciation in the value of the home. Observe that the expected rates of return on these "production opportunities" put an upper limit on how much users can pay to providers.

Providers can use their current funds for consumption or saving. By saving, they give up consumption now in the expectation of having more consumption in the future. If providers have a strong preference for consumption now, then it takes high interest rates to induce them to trade current consumption for future consumption. Therefore, the time preference for consumption has a major impact on the cost of money. Notice that the time preference for consumption varies for different individuals, for different age groups, and for different cultures. For example, people in Japan have a lower time preference for consumption than those in the United States, which partially explains why Japanese families tend to save more than U.S. families even though interest rates are lower in Japan.

If the expected rate of return on an investment is risky, then providers require a higher expected return to induce them to take the extra risk, which drives up the cost of money. As you will see later in this book, the risk of a security is determined by market conditions and the security's particular features.

Inflation also leads to a higher cost of money. For example, suppose you earned 10% one year on your investment but inflation caused prices to increase by 20%. This means you can't consume as much at the end of the year as when you originally invested your money. Obviously, if you had expected 20% inflation, you would have required a higher rate of return than 10%.

1-6b Economic Conditions and Policies That Affect the Cost of Money

Economic conditions and policies also affect the cost of money. These include: (1) Federal Reserve policy; (2) the federal budget deficit or surplus; (3) the level of business activity; and (4) international factors, including the foreign trade balance, the international business climate, and exchange rates.

W W W

*The home page for the Board of Governors of the Federal Reserve System can be found at **www. federalreserve.gov**. You can access general information about the Federal Reserve, including press releases, speeches, and monetary policy.*

FEDERAL RESERVE POLICY

If the Federal Reserve Board wants to stimulate the economy, it most often uses open market operations to purchase Treasury securities held by banks. Because banks are selling some of their securities, the banks will have more cash, which increases their supply of loanable funds, which in turn makes banks willing to lend more money at lower interest rates. In addition, the Fed's purchases represent an increase in the demand for Treasury securities. As with anything for sale, increased demand causes Treasury securities' prices to go up and interest rates to go down. The net result is a reduction in interest rates, which stimulates the economy by making it less costly for companies to borrow for new projects or for individuals to borrow for major purchases or other expenditures.

When banks sell their holdings of Treasury securities to the Fed, the banks' reserves go up, which increases the money supply. A larger money supply ultimately leads to an increase in expected inflation, which eventually pushes interest rates up. Thus, the Fed can stimulate the economy in the short term by driving down interest rates and increasing the money supply, but this creates longer-term inflationary pressures. This is exactly the dilemma facing the Fed in mid-2012.

On the other hand, if the Fed wishes to slow down the economy and reduce inflation, the Fed reverses the process. Instead of purchasing Treasury securities, the Fed sells Treasury securities to banks, which causes an increase in short-term interest rates but a decrease in long-term inflationary pressures.

BUDGET DEFICITS OR SURPLUSES

WWW

For today's cumulative total federal debt (the total public debt), check out the Current Daily Treasury Statement at **www.fms. treas.gov/dts/index.html**.

If the federal government spends more than it takes in from tax revenues, then it runs a deficit, and that deficit must be covered either by borrowing or by printing money (increasing the money supply). The government borrows by issuing new Treasury securities. All else held equal, this creates a greater supply of Treasury securities, which leads to lower security prices and higher interest rates. Other federal government actions that increase the money supply also increase expectations for future inflation, which drives up interest rates. Thus, the larger the federal deficit, other things held constant, the higher the level of interest rates. As shown in Figure 1-2, the federal government has run deficits in 15 of the past 19 years. Annual deficits in the mid-1990s were in the $250 billion range, but they have ballooned to well over a trillion dollars in recent years. These huge deficits have contributed to the cumulative federal debt, which in early 2012 stood at more than $15 trillion.

FIGURE 1-2

Federal Budget Surplus/Deficits and Trade Balances (Billions of Dollars)

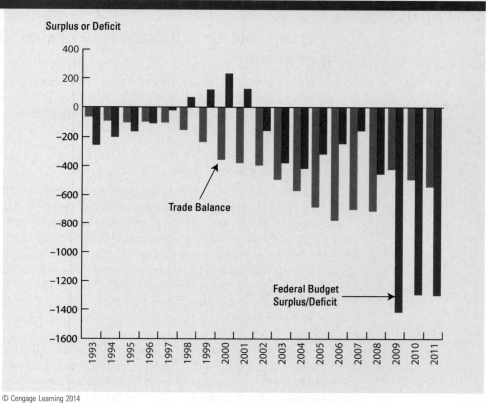

© Cengage Learning 2014

BUSINESS ACTIVITY

Figure 1-3 shows interest rates, inflation, and recessions. Notice that interest rates and inflation typically rise prior to a recession and fall afterward. There are several reasons for this pattern.

Consumer demand slows during a recession, keeping companies from increasing prices, which reduces price inflation. Companies also cut back on hiring, which reduces wage inflation. Less disposable income causes consumers to reduce their purchases of homes and automobiles, reducing consumer demand for loans. Companies reduce investments in new operations, which reduce their demand for funds. The cumulative effect is downward pressure on inflation and interest rates. The Federal Reserve is also active during recessions, trying to stimulate the economy by driving down interest rates.

INTERNATIONAL TRADE DEFICITS OR SURPLUSES

Businesses and individuals in the United States buy from and sell to people and firms in other countries. If we buy more than we sell (that is, if we import more than we export), we are said to be running a *foreign trade deficit*. When trade deficits occur, they must be financed, and the main source of financing is debt. In other words, if we

FIGURE 1-3

Business Activity, Interest Rates, and Inflation

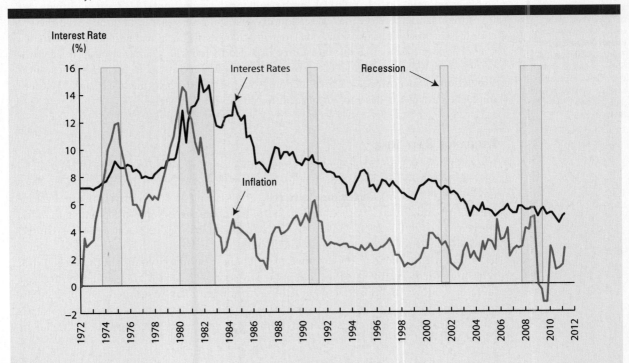

Notes:

1. Tick marks represent January 1 of the year.
2. The shaded areas designate business recessions as defined by the National Bureau of Economic Research; see **www.nber.org/cycles**.
3. Interest rates are for AAA corporate bonds; see the St. Louis Federal Reserve Web site: **http://research.stlouisfed.org/fred**. These rates reflect the average rate during the month ending on the date shown.
4. Inflation is measured by the annual rate of change for the Consumer Price Index (CPI) for the preceding 12 months; see **http://research.stlouisfed.org/fred**.

© Cengage Learning 2014

import $200 billion of goods but export only $90 billion, we run a trade deficit of $110 billion, and we will probably borrow the $110 billion.[3] Therefore, the larger our trade deficit, the more we must borrow, and the increased borrowing drives up interest rates. Also, international investors are willing to hold U.S. debt if and only if the risk-adjusted rate paid on this debt is competitive with interest rates in other countries. Therefore, if the Federal Reserve attempts to lower interest rates in the United States, causing our rates to fall below rates abroad (after adjustments for expected changes in the exchange rate), then international investors will sell U.S. bonds, which will depress bond prices and result in higher U.S. rates. Thus, if the trade deficit is large relative to the size of the overall economy, it will hinder the Fed's ability to reduce interest rates and combat a recession.

The United States has been running annual trade deficits since the mid-1970s; see Figure 1-2 for recent years. The cumulative effect of trade deficits and budget deficits is that the United States has become the largest debtor nation of all time. As noted earlier, this federal debt exceeds *$15 trillion!* As a result, our interest rates are influenced by interest rates in other countries around the world.

INTERNATIONAL COUNTRY RISK

W W W

Transparency International provides a ranking of countries based on their levels of perceived corruption. See **www.transpar ency.org/policy_research/ surveys_indices/cpi/2010**. *The U.S. Department of State provides thorough descriptions of countries' business climates at* **www. state.gov/e/eb/rls/othr/ics/ 2011**.

International risk factors may increase the cost of money that is invested abroad. **Country risk** is the risk that arises from investing or doing business in a particular country, and it depends on the country's economic, political, and social environment. Countries with stable economic, social, political, and regulatory systems provide a safer climate for investment and therefore have less country risk than less stable nations. Examples of country risk include the risk associated with changes in tax rates, regulations, currency conversion, and exchange rates. Country risk also includes the risk that (1) property will be expropriated without adequate compensation; (2) the host country will impose new stipulations concerning local production, sourcing, or hiring practices; and (3) there might be damage or destruction of facilities due to internal strife.

EXCHANGE RATE RISK

International securities frequently are denominated in a currency other than the dollar, which means that the value of an investment depends on what happens to exchange rates. This is known as **exchange rate risk**. For example, if a U.S. investor purchases a Japanese bond, interest probably will be paid in Japanese yen, which must then be converted to dollars if the investor wants to spend his or her money in the United States. If the yen weakens relative to the dollar, then the yen will buy fewer dollars when it comes time for the investor to convert the Japanese bond's payout. Alternatively, if the yen strengthens relative to the dollar, the investor will earn higher dollar returns. It therefore follows that the effective rate of return on a foreign investment will depend on both the performance of the foreign security in its home market and on what happens to exchange rates over the life of the investment. We discuss exchange rates in detail in Chapter 17.

---

[3]The deficit could also be financed by selling assets, including gold, corporate stocks, entire companies, and real estate. The United States has financed its massive trade deficits through all of these means in recent years, but the primary method has been by borrowing from foreigners.

SELF-TEST

What four fundamental factors affect the cost of money?

Name some economic conditions that influence interest rates, and explain their effects.

1-7 Financial Institutions

When raising capital, direct transfers of funds from individuals to businesses are most common for small businesses or in economies where financial markets and institutions are not well developed. Businesses in developed economies usually find it more efficient to enlist the services of one or more financial institutions to raise capital. Most financial institutions don't compete in a single line of business but instead provide a wide variety of services and products, both domestically and globally. The following sections describe the major types of financial institutions and services, but keep in mind that the dividing lines among them are often blurred. Also, note that the global financial crisis we are now going through is changing the structure of our financial institutions, and new regulations are certain to affect those that remain. Finance today is dynamic, to say the least!

1-7a Investment Banks and Brokerage Activities

Investment banking houses help companies raise capital. Such organizations underwrite security offerings, which means they (1) advise corporations regarding the design and pricing of new securities, (2) buy these securities from the issuing corporation, and (3) resell them to investors. Although the securities are sold twice, this process is really one primary market transaction, with the investment banker acting as a facilitator to help transfer capital from savers to businesses. An investment bank often is a division or subsidiary of a larger company. For example, JPMorgan Chase & Co. is a very large financial services firm, with over $2 *trillion* in managed assets. One of its holdings is J.P. Morgan, an investment bank.

In addition to security offerings, investment banks also provide consulting and advisory services, such as merger and acquisition (M&A) analysis and investment management for wealthy individuals.

Most investment banks also provide brokerage services for institutions and individuals (called "retail" customers). For example, Merrill Lynch (acquired in 2008 by Bank of America) has a large retail brokerage operation that provides advice and executes trades for its individual clients. Similarly, J.P. Morgan helps execute trades for institutional customers, such as pension funds.

At one time, most investment banks were partnerships, with income generated primarily by fees from their underwriting, M&A consulting, asset management, and brokering activities. When business was good, investment banks generated high fees and paid big bonuses to their partners. When times were tough, investment banks paid no bonuses and often fired employees. In the 1990s, however, most large investment banks were reorganized into publicly traded corporations (or were acquired and then operated as subsidiaries of public companies). For example, in 1994 Lehman Brothers sold some of its own shares of stock to the public via an IPO. Like most corporations, Lehman Brothers was financed by a combination of equity and debt. A relaxation of regulations in the 2000s allowed investment banks to undertake much riskier activities than at any time since the Great Depression. The new regulations allowed investment banks to use an unprecedented amount of debt to finance their activities—Lehman used roughly $30 of debt for every dollar of equity. In addition to their fee-generating activities, most investment banks also began trading securities for their own accounts. In other words, they took the borrowed money and invested it in financial securities. If you are earning 12% on your investments while paying 8% on your borrowings, then the more money you borrow, the more profit you make. But if you are leveraged 30 to 1 and your investments decline in value by even 3.33%, your business will fail. This is exactly what happened to Bear Stearns, Lehman Brothers, and Merrill Lynch in the fall of 2008. In short, they borrowed money, used it to make risky investments, and then failed when the investments turned out to be worth less than the amount they owed. Note that it was not their traditional investment banking activities that caused the failure, but the fact that they borrowed so much and used those funds to speculate in the market.

1-7b Deposit-Taking Financial Intermediaries

Some financial institutions take deposits from savers and then lend most of the deposited money to borrowers. Following is a brief description of such intermediaries.

SAVINGS AND LOAN ASSOCIATIONS (S&Ls)

As we explained in Section 1.5, S&Ls originally accepted deposits from many small savers and then loaned this money to home buyers and consumers. Later, they were allowed to make riskier investments, such as investing in real estate development. **Mutual savings banks (MSBs)** are similar to S&Ls, but they operate primarily in the northeastern states. Today, most S&Ls and MSBs have been acquired by banks.

CREDIT UNIONS

Credit unions are cooperative associations whose members have a common bond, such as being employees of the same firm or living in the same geographic area. Members' savings are lent only to other members, generally for auto purchases, home-improvement loans, and home mortgages. Credit unions are often the cheapest source of funds available to individual borrowers.

COMMERCIAL BANKS

Commercial banks raise funds from depositors and by issuing stock and bonds to investors. For example, someone might deposit money in a checking account. In return, that person can write checks, use a debit card, and even receive interest on the deposits. Those who buy the banks' stocks expect to receive dividends and interest payments. Unlike nonfinancial corporations, most commercial banks are highly leveraged in the sense that they owe much more to their depositors and creditors than they raised from stockholders. For example, a typical bank has about $90 of debt for every $10 of stockholders' equity. If the bank's assets are worth $100, we can calculate its equity capital by subtracting the $90 of liabilities from the $100 of assets: Equity capital = $100 − $90 = $10. But if the assets drop in value by 5% to $95, the equity drops to $5 = $95 − $90, a 50% decline.

Banks are vitally important for a well-functioning economy, and their highly leveraged positions make them risky. As a result, banks are more highly regulated than nonfinancial firms. Given the high risk, banks might have a hard time attracting and retaining deposits unless the deposits were insured, so the Federal Deposit Insurance Corporation (FDIC), which is backed by the U.S. government, insures up to $250,000 per depositor. As a result of the global economic crisis, this insured amount was increased from $100,000 in 2008 to reassure depositors.

Without such insurance, if depositors believed that a bank was in trouble, they would rush to withdraw funds. This is called a "bank run," which is exactly what happened in the United States during the Great Depression, causing many bank failures and leading to the creation of the FDIC in an effort to prevent future bank runs. Not all countries have their own versions of the FDIC, so international bank runs are still possible. In fact, a bank run occurred in September 2008 at the U.K. bank Northern Rock, leading to its nationalization by the government.

Most banks are small and locally owned, but the largest banks are parts of giant financial services firms. For example, JPMorgan Chase Bank, commonly called Chase Bank, is owned by JPMorgan Chase & Co., and Citibank is owned by Citicorp (at the time we write this, but perhaps not when you read this—the financial landscape changes daily).

1-7c Investment Funds

At some financial institutions, savers have an ownership interest in a pool of funds rather than owning a deposit account. Examples include mutual funds, hedge funds, and private equity funds.

MUTUAL FUNDS

Mutual funds are corporations that accept money from savers and then use these funds to buy financial instruments. These organizations pool funds, which allows them to reduce risks by diversification and achieve economies of scale in analyzing securities, managing portfolios, and buying/selling securities. Different funds are designed to meet the objectives of different types of savers. Hence, there are bond funds for those who desire safety and stock funds for savers who are willing to accept risks in the hope of higher returns. There are literally thousands of different mutual funds with dozens of different goals and purposes. Some funds are actively managed, with their managers trying to find under-valued securities, while other funds are passively managed and simply try to minimize expenses by matching the returns on a particular market index.

Money market funds invest in short-term, low-risk securities, such as Treasury bills and commercial paper. Many of these funds offer interest-bearing checking accounts with rates that are greater than those offered by banks, so many people invest in money market funds as an alternative to depositing money in a bank. Note, though, that money market funds are not required to be insured and so are riskier than bank deposits.[4]

Most traditional mutual funds allow investors to redeem their share of the fund only at the close of business. A special type of mutual fund, the **exchange traded fund (ETF)**, allows investors to sell their share at any time during normal trading hours. ETFs usually have very low management expenses and are rapidly gaining in popularity.

HEDGE FUNDS

Hedge funds raise money from investors and engage in a variety of investment activities. Unlike typical mutual funds, which can have thousands of investors, hedge funds are limited to institutional investors and a relatively small number of high-net-worth individuals. Because these investors are supposed to be sophisticated, hedge funds are much less regulated than mutual funds. The first hedge funds literally tried to hedge their bets by forming portfolios of conventional securities and derivatives in such a way as to limit their potential losses without sacrificing too much of their potential gains. Many hedge funds

---

[4]The U.S. Treasury sold deposit insurance to eligible money market funds between September 2008 and September 2009 to help stabilize the markets during the height of the financial crisis.

had spectacular rates of return during the 1990s. This success attracted more investors, and thousands of new hedge funds were created. Much of the low-hanging fruit had already been picked, however, so the hedge funds began pursuing much riskier (and unhedged) strategies, including the use of high leverage in unhedged positions. Perhaps not surprisingly (at least in retrospect), some funds have produced spectacular losses. For example, many hedge fund investors suffered huge losses in 2007 and 2008 when large numbers of sub-prime mortgages defaulted.

Private Equity Funds

Private equity funds are similar to hedge funds in that they are limited to a relatively small number of large investors. They differ in that they own stock (equity) in other companies and often control those companies, whereas hedge funds usually own many different types of securities. In contrast to a mutual fund, which might own a small percentage of a publicly traded company's stock, a private equity fund typically owns virtually all of a company's stock. Because the company's stock is not traded in the public markets, it is called "private equity." In fact, private equity funds often take a public company (or subsidiary) and turn it private, such as the 2007 privatization of Chrysler by Cerberus. (Fiat is now the majority owner.) The general partners who manage private equity funds usually sit on the companies' boards and guide their strategies with the goal of later selling the companies for a profit. For example, The Carlyle Group, Clayton Dubilier & Rice, and Merrill Lynch Global Private Equity bought Hertz from Ford on December 22, 2005, and then sold shares of Hertz in an IPO less than a year later.

Many private equity funds experienced high rates of return in the last decade, and those returns attracted enormous sums from investors. A few funds, most notably The Blackstone Group, actually went public themselves through an IPO. Just as with hedge funds, the performance of many private equity funds faltered. For example, shortly after its IPO in June 2007, Blackstone's stock price was over $31 per share; by early 2009, it had fallen to about $4. By early 2012 the stock price was about $15, still well short of its IPO price.

1-7d Life Insurance Companies and Pension Funds

Life insurance companies take premiums, invest these funds in stocks, bonds, real estate, and mortgages, and then make payments to beneficiaries. Life insurance companies also offer a variety of tax-deferred savings plans designed to provide retirement benefits.

Traditional **pension funds** are retirement plans funded by corporations or government agencies. Pension funds invest primarily in bonds, stocks, mortgages, hedge funds, private equity, and real estate. Most companies now offer self-directed retirement plans, such as 401(k) plans, as an addition to or substitute for traditional pension plans. In traditional plans, the plan administrators determine how to invest the funds; in self-directed plans, all individual participants must decide how to invest their own funds. Many companies are switching from traditional plans to self-directed plans, partly because this shifts the risk from the company to the employee.

1-7e Regulation of Financial Institutions

In 1933, the Glass-Steagall Act was passed with the intent of preventing another great depression. In addition to creating the FDIC to insure bank deposits, the law imposed constraints on banking activities and separated investment banking from commercial banking. The regulatory environment of the post-Depression era included a prohibition on nationwide branch banking, restrictions on the types of assets the institutions could buy, ceilings on the interest rates they could pay, and limitations on the types of services they could provide. Arguing that these regulations impeded the free flow of capital and hurt the efficiency of our capital markets, policymakers took several steps from the 1970s to the 1990s to deregulate financial services companies, culminating with the Gramm–Leach–Bliley Act of 1999, which "repealed" Glass-Steagall's separation of commercial and investment banking.

One result of deregulation was the creation of huge financial services corporations, which own commercial banks, S&Ls, mortgage companies, investment-banking houses, insurance companies, pension plan operations, and mutual funds. Many are now global banks with branches and operations across the country and around the world.

For example, Citigroup combined one of the world's largest commercial banks (Citibank), a huge insurance company (Travelers), and a major investment bank (Smith Barney), along with numerous other subsidiaries that operate throughout the world. Bank of America also made numerous acquisitions of many different financial companies, including Merrill Lynch, with its large brokerage and investment banking operations, and mortgage giant Countrywide Financial.

These conglomerate structures are similar to those of major institutions in Europe, Japan, and elsewhere around the globe. Though U.S. banks grew dramatically as a result of recent mergers, they are still relatively small by global standards. Among the world's largest world banks, based upon total assets, only three—Bank of America, Citigroup, and JPMorgan Chase—are headquartered in the United States.

The financial crisis of 2008–2009 and the continuing global economic crisis are causing regulators and financial institutions to rethink the wisdom of deregulating conglomerate financial services corporations. To address some of these concerns, the Dodd-Frank Wall Street Reform and Consumer Protection Act was passed in 2010. We discuss Dodd-Frank and other regulatory changes in Section 1.13, where we explain the events leading up to the global economic crisis.

W W W

For current bank rankings, go to Global Finance Magazine's Web site, **www.gfmag.com**, and use the Tools tab.

SELF-TEST

What is the difference between a pure commercial bank and a pure investment bank?

List the major types of financial institutions, and briefly describe the original purpose of each.

What are some important differences between mutual funds and hedge funds? How are they similar?

1-8 Financial Markets

Financial markets bring together people and organizations needing money with those having surplus funds. There are many different financial markets in a developed economy. Each market deals with a somewhat different type of instrument, customer, or geographic location. Here are some ways to classify markets:

1. **Physical asset markets** (also called "tangible" or "real" asset markets) are those for such products as wheat, autos, real estate, computers, and machinery. **Financial asset markets**, on the other hand, deal with stocks, bonds, notes, mortgages, derivatives, and other **financial instruments**.
2. **Spot markets** and **futures markets** are markets where assets are being bought or sold for "on-the-spot" delivery (literally, within a few days) or for delivery at some future date, such as 6 months or a year into the future.

3. **Money markets** are the markets for short-term, highly liquid debt securities, while **capital markets** are the markets for corporate stocks and debt maturing more than a year in the future. The New York Stock Exchange is an example of a capital market. When describing debt markets, "short term" generally means less than 1 year, "intermediate term" means 1 to 5 years, and "long term" means more than 5 years.

4. **Mortgage markets** deal with loans on residential, agricultural, commercial, and industrial real estate, while **consumer credit markets** involve loans for autos, appliances, education, vacations, and so on.

5. **World**, **national**, **regional**, and **local markets** also exist. Thus, depending on an organization's size and scope of operations, it may be able to borrow or lend all around the world, or it may be confined to a strictly local, even neighborhood, market.

6. **Primary markets** are the markets in which corporations raise new capital. If Microsoft were to sell a new issue of common stock to raise capital, this would be a primary market transaction. The corporation selling the newly created stock receives the proceeds from such a transaction. The **initial public offering (IPO) market** is a subset of the primary market. Here firms "go public" by offering shares to the public for the first time. For example, Google had its IPO in 2004. Previously, founders Larry Page and Sergey Brin, other insiders, and venture capitalists owned all the shares. In many IPOs, the insiders sell some of their shares and the company sells newly created shares to raise additional capital. **Secondary markets** are markets in which existing, already outstanding securities are traded among investors. Thus, if you decided to buy 1,000 shares of Aeropostale stock, the purchase would occur in the secondary market. The New York Stock Exchange is a secondary market, because it deals in outstanding (as opposed to newly issued) stocks. Secondary markets also exist for bonds, mortgages, and other financial assets. The corporation whose securities are being traded is not involved in a secondary market transaction and, thus, does not receive any funds from such a sale.

7. **Private markets**, where transactions are worked out directly between two parties, are differentiated from **public markets**, where standardized contracts are traded on organized exchanges. Bank loans and private placements of debt with insurance companies are examples of private market transactions. Because these transactions are private, they may be structured in any manner that appeals to the two parties. By contrast, securities that are issued in public markets (for example, common stock and corporate bonds) are ultimately held by a large number of individuals. Public securities must have fairly standardized contractual features because public investors cannot afford the time to study unique, nonstandardized contracts. Hence private market securities are more tailor-made but less liquid, whereas public market securities are more liquid but subject to greater standardization.

You should recognize the big differences among types of markets, but keep in mind that the distinctions are often blurred. For example, it makes little difference if a firm borrows for 11, 12, or 13 months and thus whether such borrowing is a "money" or "capital" market transaction.

SELF-TEST

Distinguish between (1) physical asset markets and financial asset markets, (2) spot and futures markets, (3) money and capital markets, (4) primary and secondary markets, and (5) private and public markets.

1-9 Trading Procedures in Financial Markets

A huge volume of trading occurs in the secondary markets. Although there are many secondary markets for a wide variety of securities, we can classify their trading procedures along two dimensions: location and method of matching orders.

1-9a Physical Location versus Electronic Network

A secondary market can be either a **physical location exchange** or a **computer/telephone network**. For example, the New York Stock Exchange, the American Stock Exchange (AMEX), the Chicago Board of Trade (the CBOT trades futures and options), and the Tokyo Stock Exchange are all physical location exchanges. In other words, the traders actually meet and trade in a specific part of a specific building.

In contrast, NASDAQ, which trades a number of U.S. stocks, is a network of linked computers. Other network examples are the markets for U.S. Treasury bonds and foreign exchange, which operate via telephone and/or computer networks. In these electronic markets, the traders never see one another except maybe for cocktails after work.

By their very nature, networks are less transparent than physical location exchanges. For example, credit default swaps are traded directly between buyers and sellers, and there is no easy mechanism for recording, aggregating, and reporting the transactions or the net positions of the buyers and sellers.

1-9b Matching Orders: Auctions, Dealers, and ECNs

The second dimension is the way orders from sellers and buyers are matched. This can occur through an open outcry **auction** system, through dealers, or by automated order matching. An example of an outcry auction is the CBOT, where traders actually meet in a pit and sellers and buyers communicate with one another through shouts and hand signals.

In a **dealer market**, there are "market makers" who keep an inventory of the stock (or other financial instrument) in much the same way that any merchant keeps an inventory. These dealers list bid quotes and ask quotes, which are the prices at which they are willing to buy or sell. Computerized quotation systems keep track of all bid and asked prices, but they don't actually match buyers and sellers. Instead, traders must contact a specific dealer to complete the transaction. NASDAQ (U.S. stocks) is one such market, as is the London SEAQ (U.K. stocks).

The third method of matching orders is through an **electronic communications network (ECN)**. Participants in an ECN post their orders to buy and sell, and the ECN automatically matches orders. For example, someone might place an order to buy 1,000 shares of IBM stock—this is called a "market order" because it is to buy the stock at the current market price. Suppose another participant had placed an order to sell 1,000 shares of IBM, but only at a price of $91 per share, and this was the lowest price of any "sell" order. The ECN would automatically match these two orders, execute the trade, and notify both participants that the trade has occurred. The $91 sell price was a "limit order" as opposed to a market order because the action was limited by the seller. Note that orders can also be limited with regard to their duration. For example, someone might stipulate that they are willing to buy 1,000 shares of IBM at $90 per share if the price falls that low during the next two hours. In other words, there are limits on the price and/or the duration of the order. The ECN will execute the limit order only if both conditions are met.

Life in the Fast Lane: High-Frequency Trading!

© Rob Webb/Getty Images

In the time it takes to blink an eye, a high-frequency trader's computer could have made hundreds of bids, canceled all but one, purchased shares of stock, and then sold them for a profit of less than a penny. It may sound like a lot of work for such a small profit, but a million similar trades a day add up to big bucks. In fact, high-frequency trading (HFT) firms made about $7.2 billion total profit in 2009.

Who are these traders? First, there are only about 400 HTF firms out of the 20,000 or so institutional traders, so there really aren't very many of them. Second, many of their employees have math and computer science backgrounds rather than trading experience. Third, they have access to the very best computer technology. Their demand for speed is so great that Hibernia Atlantic plans to lay a new underwater cable along a slightly shorter route from the U.K. to Canada in order to cut the transmission time from 65 to 60 milliseconds!

Despite the relatively small number of HFT firms, they have a huge impact on the market, accounting for over 60% of the stock trading volume and over 40% of the foreign exchange volume. But are HFT firms good or bad for markets and other investors? The answer is not clear. On the one hand, other investors can trade much more quickly now, with execution time dropping from 10.1 seconds in 2005 to 0.7 seconds in 2010. The cost of trading, as measured by the spread in bid and ask prices, has also shrunk dramatically. On the other hand, some critics say that high-frequency trading distorts prices and makes markets less stable. As we write this in early 2012, the Securities and Exchange Commission is considering placing restrictions on high-frequency trading. One thing is for sure: Electronic trading will continue to have a big impact on financial markets.

Sources: Doug Cameron and Jacob Bunge, "Underwater Options? Ocean Cable Will Serve High-Frequency Traders," *The Wall Street Journal*, October 1, 2010, p. C-3; and Kambiz Foroohar, "Speed Geeks," *Bloomberg Markets,* November 2010, pp. 111–122.

Two of the largest ECNs for trading U.S. stocks are INET (owned by NASDAQ) and Arca (owned by NYSE Euronext). Other large ECNs include Eurex (an ECN for derivatives, owned by the Deutsche Börse) and SETS (a stock exchange owned by the SIX Swiss Exchange). Notice that most "conventional" exchanges also operate ECNs.

SELF-TEST

What are the major differences between physical location exchanges and computer/telephone networks?

What are the differences among open outcry auctions, dealer markets, and ECNs?

W W W

For updates on IPO activity, see www.renaissance capital.com/IPOHome/ MarketWatch.aspx. *The* Wall Street Journal *also provides IPO data in its Year-End Review of Markets & Finance at* online.wsj.com. *See Professor Jay Ritter's Web site for additional IPO data and analysis,* http://bear.cba.ufl.edu/ ritter/ipodata.htm.

1-10 Types of Stock Market Transactions

Because the primary objectives of financial management are to maximize the firm's intrinsic value and then help ensure that the current stock price equals that value, knowledge of the stock market is important to anyone involved in managing a business. We can classify stock market transactions into three distinct types: (1) initial public offerings, (2) seasoned equity offerings, and (3) secondary market transactions.

Whenever stock is offered to the public for the first time, the company is said to be **going public**. This primary market transaction is called the initial public offering (IPO) market. If a company later decides to sell (i.e., issue) additional shares to raise new equity capital, this is still a primary market, but it is called a **seasoned equity offering**. Trading in the outstanding shares of established, publicly owned companies are secondary market transactions. For example, if the owner of 100 shares of publicly held stock sells his or her stock, the trade is said to have occurred in the secondary market. Thus, the market for outstanding shares, or used shares, is the secondary market. The company receives no new money when sales occur in this market.

Here is a brief description of recent IPO activity. There were 1,285 total global IPOs in 2011, with total proceeds of $168 billion. China and Hong Kong together represented over 40% of the total. The biggest IPO was the $10 billion raised by Glencore International, a Swiss mining company.

In the United States, the average first-day return was around 13% in 2011. However, some firms had spectacular first-day price run-ups, such as LinkedIn's 109% gain on its first day of trading. Not all companies fared so well—indeed, FriendFinder fell by over 21% on its first trading day.

For 2011, some IPOs had big gains for the year, such as Imperva's 92.5% return. Others had big annual losses; HCA Holdings fell by over 26%. In fact, the average IPO lost over 13% during 2011.

Even if you are able to identify a "hot" issue, it is often difficult to purchase shares in the initial offering. In strong markets, these deals generally are oversubscribed, which means that the demand for shares at the offering price exceeds the number of shares issued. In such instances, investment bankers favor large institutional investors (who are their best customers), and small investors find it hard, if not impossible, to get in on the ground floor. They can buy the stock in the aftermarket, but evidence suggests that if you do not get in on the ground floor, the average IPO underperforms the overall market over the long run.[5]

Before you conclude that it isn't fair to let only the best customers have the stock in an initial offering, think about what it takes to become a best customer. Best customers are usually investors who have done lots of business in the past with the investment banking firm's brokerage department. In other words, they have paid large sums as commissions in the past, and they are expected to continue doing so in the future. As is so often true, there is no free lunch—most of the investors who get in on the ground floor of an IPO have, in fact, paid for this privilege.

resource

For more on issuing stock, see **Web Extension 1B** on the textbook's Web site.

SELF-TEST

Differentiate between an IPO, a seasoned equity offering, and a secondary transaction.

Why is it often difficult for the average investor to make money during an IPO?

1-11 The Secondary Stock Markets

The two leading U.S. stock markets today are the New York Stock Exchange and the NASDAQ stock market.

1-11a The New York Stock Exchange

WWW

You can access the home pages of the major U.S. stock markets at **www.nyse.com** and **www.NASDAQ.com**. These sites provide background information as well as the opportunity to obtain individual stock quotes.

Before March of 2006, the **New York Stock Exchange (NYSE)** was a privately held firm owned by its members. It then merged with Archipelago, a publicly traded company that was one of the world's largest ECNs. NYSE members received approximately 70% of the shares in the combined firm, with Archipelago shareholders receiving 30%. The combined firm, which also owned the Pacific Exchange, was known as The NYSE Group, Inc., and

[5]See Jay R. Ritter, "The Long-Run Performance of Initial Public Offerings," *Journal of Finance*, March 1991, pp. 3–27.

was traded publicly under the ticker symbol NYX. It continued to operate the New York Stock Exchange (a physical location exchange located on Wall Street) and Arca (comprising the Pacific Exchange and the ECN formerly known as Archipelago). In 2007 the NYSE Group merged with Euronext, a European company that operates stock exchanges (called bourses) in Paris, Amsterdam, Brussels, and Lisbon. The combined company is called NYSE Euronext.

resource

For more on stock markets, see **Web Extension 1B** on the textbook's Web site.

The NYSE still has over 300 member organizations, which are corporations, partnerships, or LLCs. Membership prices were as high as $4 million in 2005, and the last sale before the Euronext merger was $3.5 million. Member organizations are registered broker-dealers, but they may not conduct trading on the floor of the exchange unless they also hold a trading license issued by the NYSE. Before going public, the equivalent to the trading license was called a "seat," although there was very little sitting on the floor of the exchange. Trading licenses are now leased by member organizations from the exchange, with an annual fee of $40,000 for 2012. The NYSE has leased most of its 1,500 available trading licenses.

Most of the larger investment banking houses operate *brokerage departments* and are members of the NYSE with leased trading rights. The NYSE is open on all normal working days, and members meet in large rooms equipped with electronic equipment that enables each member to communicate with his or her firm's offices throughout the country. For example, Merrill Lynch (now owned by Bank of America) might receive an order in its Atlanta office from a customer who wants to buy shares of Procter & Gamble stock. Simultaneously, Edward Jones' St. Louis office might receive an order from a customer wishing to sell shares of P&G. Each broker communicates electronically with the firm's representative on the NYSE. Other brokers throughout the country also communicate with their own exchange members. The exchange members with *sell orders* offer the shares for sale, and members with *buy orders* bid for them. Thus, the NYSE operates as an *auction market*.[6]

However, trading on the NYSE floor has declined in importance. In addition to the trading of NYSE stocks on its own ECN, Arca, hundreds of private ECNs and brokers trade NYSE stocks. In 2010, about 79% of the trading volume for NYSE-listed stocks occurred on these private networks.

1-11b The NASDAQ Stock Market

The **National Association of Securities Dealers (NASD)** is a self-regulatory body that licenses brokers and oversees trading practices. The computerized network used by the NASD is known as the NASD Automated Quotation System, or NASDAQ. NASDAQ started as a quotation system, but it has grown to become an organized securities market with its own listing requirements. NASDAQ lists about 5,000 stocks, although not all trade through the same NASDAQ system. For example, the NASDAQ National Market

---

[6]The NYSE is actually a modified auction market, wherein people (through their brokers) bid for stocks. Originally—about 200 years ago—brokers would literally shout, "I have 100 shares of Erie for sale; how much am I offered?" and then sell to the highest bidder. If a broker had a buy order, he or she would shout, "I want to buy 100 shares of Erie; who'll sell at the best price?" The same general situation still exists, although the exchanges now have members known as specialists who facilitate the trading process by keeping an inventory of shares of the stocks in which they specialize. If a buy order comes in at a time when no sell order arrives, the specialist will sell off some inventory. Similarly, if a sell order comes in, the specialist will buy and add to inventory. The specialist sets a bid price (the price the specialist will pay for the stock) and an asked price (the price at which shares will be sold out of inventory). The bid and asked prices are set at levels designed to keep the inventory in balance. If many buy orders start coming in because of favorable developments or sell orders come in because of unfavorable events, the specialist will raise or lower prices to keep supply and demand in balance. Bid prices are somewhat lower than asked prices, with the difference, or spread, representing the specialist's profit margin.

Measuring the Market

© Rob Webb/Getty Images

A *stock index* is designed to show the performance of the stock market. Here we describe some leading indexes.

Dow Jones Industrial Average

Begun in 1896, the Dow Jones Industrial Average (DJIA) now includes 30 widely held stocks that represent almost one-fifth of the market value of all U.S. stocks. See **www. dowjones.com** for more information.

S&P 500 Index

Created in 1926, the S&P 500 Index is widely regarded as the standard for measuring large-cap U.S. stocks' market performance. It is value weighted, so the largest companies (in terms of value) have the greatest influence. The S&P 500 Index is used as a comparison benchmark by 97% of all U.S. money managers and pension plan sponsors. See **www2. standardandpoors.com** for more information.

NASDAQ Composite Index

The NASDAQ Composite Index measures the performance of all common stocks listed on the NASDAQ stock market. Currently, it includes more than 3,200 companies, many of which are in the technology sector. Microsoft, Cisco Systems, and Intel account for a high percentage of the index's value-weighted market capitalization. For this reason, substantial movements in the same direction by these three companies can move the entire index. See **www.NASDAQ.com** for more information.

NYSE Composite Index

The NYSE Composite Index measures the performance of all common stocks listed on the NYSE. It is a value-weighted index and is based on just over 2,000 stocks that represent 77% of the total market capitalization of all publicly traded companies in the United States. See **www.nyse.com** for more information.

Trading the Market

Through the use of exchange traded funds (ETFs), it is now possible to buy and sell the market in much the same way as an individual stock. For example, the Standard & Poor's depository receipt (SPDR) is a share of a fund that holds the stocks of all the companies in the S&P 500. SPDRs trade during regular market hours, making it possible to buy or sell the S&P 500 any time during the day. There are hundreds of other ETFs, including ones for the NASDAQ, the Dow Jones Industrial Average, gold stocks, utilities, and so on.

Recent Performance

Go to the Web site **finance.yahoo.com**. Enter the symbol for any of the indexes (^DJI for the Dow Jones, ^GSPC for the S&P 500, ^IXIC for the NASDAQ, and ^NYA for the NYSE) and then click GO. This will bring up the current value of the index, shown in a table. Click Basic Chart in the panel on the left, which will bring up a chart showing the historical performance of the index. Directly above the chart is a series of buttons that allows you to choose the number of years and to plot the relative performance of several indexes on the same chart. You can even download the historical data in spreadsheet form by clicking Historical Prices in the left panel.

lists the larger NASDAQ stocks, such as Microsoft and Intel, while the NASDAQ Small-Cap Market lists smaller companies with the potential for high growth. NASDAQ also operates the NASDAQ OTC Bulletin Board, which lists quotes for stocks registered with the Securities and Exchange Commission (SEC) but not listed on any exchange, usually because the company is too small or not sufficiently profitable.[7] Finally, NASDAQ

[7]OTC stands for over-the-counter. Before NASDAQ, the quickest way to trade a stock that was not listed at a physical location exchange was to find a brokerage firm that kept shares of that stock in inventory. The stock certificates were kept in a safe and were literally passed over the counter when bought or sold. Today the certificates for almost all listed stocks and bonds in the United States are stored in a vault, beneath Manhattan, that is operated by the Depository Trust and Clearing Corporation (DTCC). Most brokerage firms have an account with the DTCC, and most investors leave their stocks with their brokers. Thus, when stocks are sold, the DTCC simply adjusts the accounts of the brokerage firms that are involved, and no stock certificates are actually moved.

operates the Pink Sheets, which provide quotes on companies that are not registered with the SEC.

"Liquidity" is the ability to trade quickly at a net price (i.e., after any commissions) that is close to the security's recent market price. In a dealer market, such as NASDAQ, a stock's liquidity depends on the number and quality of the dealers who make a market in the stock. NASDAQ has more than 400 dealers, most of whom make markets in a large number of stocks. The typical stock has about 10 market makers, but some stocks have more than 50 market makers. Obviously, there are more market makers, and hence more liquidity, for the NASDAQ National Market than for the SmallCap Market. Stocks listed on the OTC Bulletin Board or the Pink Sheets have much less liquidity.

1-11c Competition in the Secondary Markets

W W W

For updates, see **www.world-exchanges.org/statistics/time-series/market-capitalization** *at the* World Federation of Exchanges.

There is intense competition between the NYSE, NASDAQ, and other international stock exchanges—they all want the larger, more profitable companies to list on their exchange. Because most of the largest U.S. companies trade on the NYSE, the market capitalization of NYSE-traded stocks is much higher than for stocks traded on NASDAQ (about $13.4 trillion compared with $3.9 trillion at the end of 2010). However, reported volume (number of shares traded) is often larger on NASDAQ, and more companies are listed on NASDAQ.[8] For comparison, the market capitalizations for global exchanges are $3.8 trillion in Tokyo, $3.6 trillion in London, $2.7 trillion in Shanghai, $2.7 trillion in Hong Kong, $1.4 trillion in Germany, and $1.6 trillion in Bombay.

Interestingly, many high-tech companies such as Microsoft and Intel have remained on NASDAQ even though they easily meet the listing requirements of the NYSE. At the same time, however, other high-tech companies such as Iomega have left NASDAQ for the NYSE. Despite these defections, NASDAQ's growth over the past decade has been impressive. In an effort to become even more competitive with the NYSE and with international markets, NASDAQ acquired one of the leading ECNs, Instinet, in 2005. NASDAQ subsequently acquired the Nordic exchange OMX, giving it an international presence. The combined company is the NASDAQ OMX Group.

Despite the shifting ownerships of exchanges, one thing is clear—there will be a continued consolidation in the securities exchange industry, with a blurring of the lines between physical location exchanges and electronic exchanges.

SELF-TEST

What are some major differences between the NYSE and the NASDAQ stock market?

1-12 Stock Market Returns

During the period 1968–2011, the average annual return for the stock market, as measured by total returns (dividends plus capital gains) on the S&P 500 index, was about 10.9%, but this average does not reflect the considerable annual variation. Notice in Panel A of Figure 1-4 that the market was relatively flat in the 1970s, increased somewhat in the 1980s, and has been a roller coaster ever since. In fact, the market in early 2009 dipped to a level last seen in 1995. Panel B highlights the year-to-year risk by showing annual returns. Notice that stocks have had positive returns in most years, but there have been

---

[8]One transaction on NASDAQ generally shows up as two separate trades (the buy and the sell). This "double counting" makes it difficult to compare the volume between stock markets.

several years with large losses. Stocks lost more than 40% of their value during 1973–1974 and again during 2000–2002, and they lost 37% of their value in 2008 alone. We will examine risk in more detail later in the book, but even a cursory glance at Figure 1-4 shows just how risky investing in stocks can be!

U.S. stocks amount to only about 40% of the world's stocks, and this is prompting many U.S. investors to also hold foreign stocks. Analysts have long touted the benefits of investing overseas, arguing that foreign stocks improve diversification and provide good

FIGURE 1-4

S&P 500 Stock Index Performance

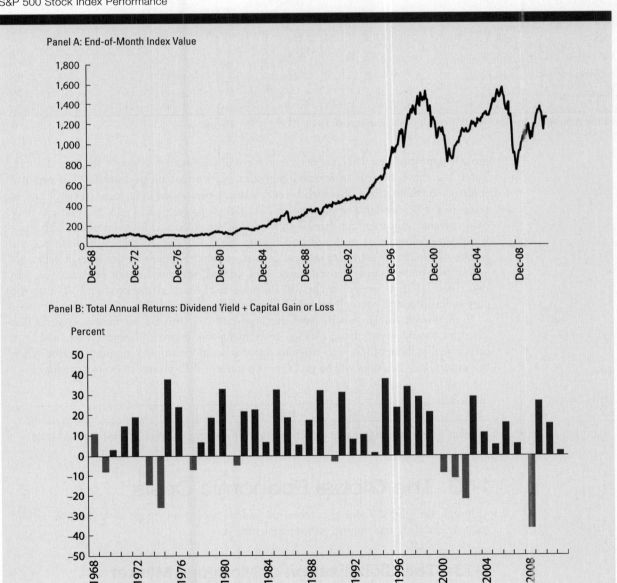

Panel A: End-of-Month Index Value

Panel B: Total Annual Returns: Dividend Yield + Capital Gain or Loss

Sources: Returns data are from various issues of *The Wall Street Journal*, "Investment Scoreboard" section; the index level is from **http://finance.yahoo.com**.

TABLE 1-2

2011 Performance of Selected Dow Jones Global Stock Indexes, Ranked Highest to Lowest

Country	U.S. Dollars	Local Currency	Country	U.S. Dollars	Local Currency
Qatar	4.0%	4.0%	France	−19.3%	−16.6%
Iceland	0.6	7.4	Germany	−19.9	−17.3
Ireland	−1.1	2.2	China	−20.2	−20.3
U.K.	−6.7	−6.0	Russia	−21.0	−16.9
Switzerland	−9.0	−8.7	Hong Kong	−23.5	−23.6
South Korea	−11.6	−10.3	Brazil	−24.2	−14.8
Japan	−14.3	−18.7	Chile	−24.9	−16.6
Canada	−14.3	−12.2	India	−39.1	−27.7
Mexico	−14.7	−3.5	Greece	−58.3	−56.9
Spain	−17.2	−14.4			

Source: Adapted from *The Wall Street Journal,* January 3, 2012, R17.

growth opportunities. This has been true for many years, but it wasn't the case in 2011. Table 1-2 shows returns in selected countries. Notice that most countries had negative returns. The table shows how each country's stocks performed in its local currency and in terms of the U.S. dollar. For example, in 2011 German stocks had a −17.3% return in their own currency, but that translated into a −19.9% return to a U.S. investor; the difference was due to depreciation in the euro relative to the U.S. dollar. As this example shows, the results of foreign investments depend in part on what happens in the foreign economy and in part on movements in exchange rates. Indeed, when you invest overseas, you face two risks: (1) that foreign stocks will decrease in their local markets, and (2) that the currencies in which you will be paid will fall relative to the dollar.

Even though foreign stocks have exchange-rate risk, this by no means suggests that investors should avoid them. Foreign investments do improve diversification, and it is inevitable that there will be years when foreign stocks outperform U.S. domestic stocks. When this occurs, U.S. investors will be glad they put some of their money in overseas markets.

SELF-TEST

Explain how exchange rates affect the rate of return on international investments.

1-13 The Global Economic Crisis

Although the global economic crisis has many causes, mortgage securitization in the 2000s is certainly one culprit, so we begin with it.

1-13a The Globalization of Mortgage Market Securitization

A national TV program ran a documentary on the travails of Norwegian retirees resulting from defaults on Florida mortgages. Your first reaction might be to wonder how Norwegian retirees became financially involved with risky Florida mortgages. We will break the answer to that question into two parts. First, we will identify the different links in the financial chain between the retirees and mortgagees. Second, we will explain why there were so many weak links.

In the movie *Jerry Maguire,* Tom Cruise said, "Show me the money!" That's a good way to start identifying the financial links, starting with a single home purchase in Florida.

1. HOME PURCHASE

In exchange for cash, a seller in Florida turned over ownership of a house to a buyer.

2. MORTGAGE ORIGINATION

To get the cash used to purchase the house, the buyer signed a mortgage loan agreement and gave it to an "originator." Years ago the originator would probably have been an S&L or a bank, but more recently the originators have been specialized mortgage brokers, as in this case. The broker gathered and examined the borrower's credit information, arranged for an independent appraisal of the house's value, handled the paperwork, and received a fee for these services.

3. SECURITIZATION AND RESECURITIZATION

In exchange for cash, the originator sold the mortgage to a securitizing firm. For example, Merrill Lynch's investment banking operation was a major player in securitizing loans. It would bundle large numbers of mortgages into pools and then create new securities that had claims on the pools' cash flows. Some claims were simple, such as a proportional share of a pool; some were more complex, such as a claim on all interest payments during the first 5 years or a claim on only principal payments. More complicated claims were entitled to a fixed payment, while other claims would receive payments only after the "senior" claimants had been paid. These slices of the pool were called "tranches," which comes from a French word for slice.

Some of the tranches were themselves re-combined and then re-divided into securities called collateralized debt obligations (CDOs), some of which were themselves combined and subdivided into other securities, commonly called CDOs-squared. For example, Lehman Brothers often bought different tranches, split them into CDOs of differing risk, and then had the different CDOs rated by an agency like Moody's or Standard & Poor's.

There are three very important points to notice. First, the process didn't change the *total amount of risk* embedded in the mortgages, but it did make it possible to create some securities that were less risky than average and some that were more risky. Second, the complexity of the CDOs spread a little bit of each mortgage's risk to very many different investors, making it difficult for investors to determine the aggregate risk of a particular CDO. Third, each time a new security was created or rated, fees were being earned by the investment banks and rating agencies.

4. THE INVESTORS

In exchange for cash, the securitizing firms sold the newly created securities to individual investors, hedge funds, college endowments, insurance companies, and other financial institutions, including a pension fund in Norway. Keep in mind that financial institutions are funded by individuals, so cash begins with individuals and flows through the system until it is eventually received by the seller of the home. If all goes according to plan, payments on the mortgages eventually return to the individuals who originally provided the cash. But in this case, the chain was broken by a wave of mortgage defaults, resulting in problems for Norwegian retirees.

Students and managers often ask, "What happened to all the money?" The short answer is, "It went from investors to home sellers, with fees being skimmed off all along the way."

Although the process is complex, in theory there is nothing inherently wrong with it. In fact, it should, in theory, provide more funding for U.S. home purchasers, and it should allow risk to be shifted to those best able to bear it. Unfortunately, this isn't the end of the story.

1-13b The Dark Side of Securitization: The Sub-Prime Mortgage Meltdown

What caused the financial crisis? Entire books have been written on this subject, but we can identify a few of the culprits.

REGULATORS APPROVED SUB-PRIME STANDARDS

In the 1980s and early 1990s, regulations did not permit a nonqualifying mortgage to be securitized, so most originators mandated that borrowers meet certain requirements, including having at least a certain minimum level of income relative to the mortgage payments and a minimum down payment relative to the size of the mortgage. But in the mid-1990s, Washington politicians wanted to extend home ownership to groups that traditionally had difficulty obtaining mortgages. To accomplish this, regulations were relaxed so that nonqualifying mortgages could be securitized. Such loans are commonly called sub-prime or Alt-A mortgages. Thus, riskier mortgages were soon being securitized and sold to investors. Again, there was nothing inherently wrong, provided the two following questions were being answered in the affirmative: One, were home buyers making sound decisions regarding their ability to repay the loans? And two, did the ultimate investors recognize the additional risk? We now know that the answer to both questions is a resounding "no." Homeowners were signing mortgages that they could not hope to repay, and investors treated these mortgages as if they were much safer than they actually were.

THE FED HELPED FUEL THE REAL ESTATE BUBBLE

With more people able to get a mortgage, including people who should not have obtained one, the demand for homes increased. This alone would have driven up house prices. However, the Fed also slashed interest rates to historic lows after the terrorist attacks of 9/11 to prevent a recession, and it kept them low for a long time. These low rates made mortgage payments lower, which made home ownership seem even more affordable, again contributing to an increase in the demand for housing. Figure 1-5 shows that the combination of lower mortgage qualifications and lower interest rates caused house prices to skyrocket. Thus, the Fed contributed to an artificial bubble in real estate.

HOME BUYERS WANTED MORE FOR LESS

Even with low interest rates, how could sub-prime borrowers afford the mortgage payments, especially with house prices rising? First, most sub-prime borrowers chose an adjustable rate mortgage (ARM) with an interest rate based on a short-term rate, such as that on 1-year Treasury bonds, to which the lender added a couple of percentage points. Because the Fed had pushed short-term rates so low, the initial rates on ARMs were very low.

With a traditional fixed-rate mortgage, the payments remain fixed over time. But with an ARM, an increase in market interest rates triggers higher monthly payments, so an ARM is riskier than a fixed-rate mortgage. However, many borrowers chose an *even*

FIGURE 1-5

The Real Estate Boom: Housing Prices and Mortgage Rates

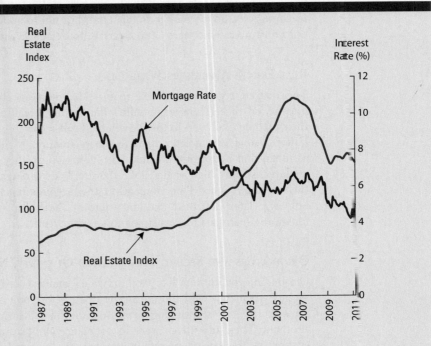

Notes:

1. The real estate index is the Case-Shiller composite index for house prices in 10 real estate markets, not seasonally adjusted, available at **www.standardandpoors.com/indices/sp-case-shiller-home-price-indices/en/us/?indexId=spusa-cashpidff-p-us——**.

2. Interest rates are for 30-year conventional fixed-rate mortgages, available from the St. Louis Federal Reserve: **http://research.stlouisfed.org/fred2/series/MORTG/downloaddata?cid=114**.

© Cengage Learning 2014

riskier mortgage, the "option ARM," where the borrower can choose to make such low payments during the first couple of years that they don't even cover the interest, causing the loan balance to actually increase each month! At a later date, the payments would be reset to reflect both the current market interest rate and the higher loan balance. For example, in some cases a monthly payment of $948 for the first 32 months was reset to $2,454 for the remaining 328 months. (We provide the calculations for this example in Chapter 4.)

Why would anyone who couldn't afford to make a $2,454 monthly payment choose an option ARM? Here are three possible reasons. First, some borrowers simply didn't understand the situation and were victims of predatory lending practices by brokers eager to earn fees regardless of the consequences. Second, some borrowers thought that the home price would go up enough to allow them to sell at a profit or else refinance with another low-payment loan. Third, some people were simply greedy and shortsighted, and they wanted to live in a better home than they could afford.

MORTGAGE BROKERS DIDN'T CARE

Years ago, S&Ls and banks had a vested interest in the mortgages they originated because they held them for the life of the loan—up to 30 years. If a mortgage went bad, the bank or S&L would lose money, so they were careful to verify that the borrower would be able to repay the loan. In the bubble years, though, over 80% of mortgages were arranged by independent mortgage brokers who received a commission. Thus, the broker's incentive was to complete deals even if the borrowers couldn't make the payments after the soon-to-come reset. So it's easy to understand (but not to approve!) why brokers pushed deals onto borrowers who were almost certain to default eventually.

REAL ESTATE APPRAISERS WERE LAX

The relaxed regulations didn't require the mortgage broker to verify the borrower's income, so these loans were called "liar loans" because the borrowers could overstate their income. But even in these cases the broker had to get an appraisal showing that the house's value was greater than the loan amount. Many real estate appraisers simply assumed that house prices would keep going up, so they were willing to appraise houses at unrealistically high values. Like the mortgage brokers, they were paid at the time of their service. Other than damage to their reputations, they weren't concerned if the borrower later defaulted and the value of the house turned out to be less than the remaining loan balance, causing a loss for the lender.

ORIGINATORS AND SECURITIZERS WANTED QUANTITY, NOT QUALITY

Originating institutions like Countrywide Financial and New Century Mortgage made money when they sold the mortgages, long before any of the mortgages defaulted. The same is true for securitizing firms such as Bear Stearns, Merrill Lynch, and Lehman Brothers. Their incentives were to generate volume through originating loans, not to ensure that the loans were safe investments. This started at the top—CEOs and other top executives received stock options and bonuses based on their firms' profits, and profits depended on volume. Thus, the top officers pushed their subordinates to generate volume, those subordinates pushed the originators to write more mortgages, and the originators pushed the appraisers to come up with high values.

RATING AGENCIES WERE LAX

Investors who purchased the complicated mortgage-backed securities wanted to know how risky they were, so they insisted on seeing the bonds' "ratings." The securitizing firms paid rating agencies to investigate the details of each bond and to assign a rating that reflected the security's risk. For example, Lehman Brothers hired Moody's to rate some of its CDOs. Indeed, the investment banks would actually pay for advice from the rating agencies as they were designing the securities. The rating and consulting activities were extremely lucrative for the agencies, which ignored the obvious conflict of interest: The investment bank wanted a high rating, the rating agency got paid to help design securities that would qualify for a high rating, and high ratings led to continued business for the raters.

INSURANCE WASN'T INSURANCE

To provide a higher rating and make these mortgage-backed securities look even more attractive to investors, the issuers would frequently purchase a type of insurance policy on the security called a **credit default swap**. For example, suppose you had wanted to purchase a CDO from Lehman Brothers but worried about the risk. What if Lehman Brothers had agreed to pay an annual fee to an insurance company such as AIG, which would guarantee the CDO's payments if the underlying mortgages defaulted? You probably would have felt confident enough to buy the CDO.

But any similarity to a conventional insurance policy ends here. Unlike home insurance, where there is a single policyholder and a single insurer, totally uninvolved speculators can also make bets on your CDO by either selling or purchasing credit default swaps on the CDO. For example, a hedge fund could buy a credit default swap on your CDO if it thinks the CDO will default; or an investment bank like Bear Stearns could sell a swap, betting that the CDO won't default. In fact, the International Swaps and Derivatives Association estimates that in mid-2008 there was about $54 trillion in credit default swaps. This staggering amount was approximately 7 times the value of all U.S. mortgages, was over 4 times the level of the U.S. national debt, and was over twice the value of the entire U.S. stock market.

Another big difference is that home insurance companies are highly regulated, but there was virtually no regulation in the credit default swap market. The players traded directly among themselves, with no central clearinghouse. It was almost impossible to tell how much risk any of the players had taken on, making it impossible to know whether or not counterparties like AIG would be able to fulfill their obligations in the event of a CDO default. And that made it impossible to know the value of CDOs held by many banks, which in turn made it impossible to judge whether or not those banks were de facto bankrupt.

ROCKET SCIENTISTS HAD POOR REARVIEW MIRRORS AND RISK MANAGERS DROVE BLIND

Brilliant financial experts, often trained in physics and hired from rocket science firms, built elegant models to determine the value of these new securities. Unfortunately, a model is only as good as its inputs. The experts looked at the high growth rates of recent real estate prices (see Figure 1-5) and assumed that future growth rates also would be high. These high growth rates caused models to calculate very high CDO prices. Perhaps more surprisingly, many risk managers simply did not insist on seeing scenarios in which housing prices fell.

INVESTORS WANTED MORE FOR LESS

In the early 2000s, low-rated debt (including mortgage-backed securities), hedge funds, and private equity funds produced great rates of return. Many investors jumped into this debt to keep up with the Joneses. As shown in Chapter 4 when we discuss bond ratings and bond spreads, investors began lowering the premium they required for taking on extra risk. Thus, investors focused primarily on returns and largely ignored risk. In fairness, some investors assumed the credit ratings were accurate, and they trusted the representatives of the investment banks selling the securities. In retrospect, however, Warren Buffett's maxim that "I only invest in companies I understand" seems wiser than ever.

THE EMPEROR HAS NO CLOTHES

In 2006, many of the option ARMs began to reset, borrowers began to default, and home prices first leveled off and then began to fall. Things got worse in 2007 and 2008, and by early 2009, almost 1 out of 10 mortgages was in default or foreclosure, resulting in displaced families and virtual ghost towns of new subdivisions. As homeowners defaulted on their mortgages, so did the CDOs backed by the mortgages. That brought down the counterparties like AIG who had insured the CDOs via credit default swaps. Virtually overnight, investors realized that mortgage-backed security default rates were headed higher and that the houses used as collateral were worth less than the mortgages. Mortgage-backed security prices plummeted, investors quit buying newly securitized mortgages, and liquidity in the secondary market disappeared. Thus, the investors who owned these securities were stuck with pieces of paper that were substantially lower than the values reported on their balance sheets.

1-13c From Sub-Prime Meltdown to Liquidity Crisis to Economic Crisis

Like the Andromeda strain, the sub-prime meltdown went viral, and it ended up infecting almost all aspects of the economy. But why did a burst bubble in one market segment, sub-prime mortgages, spread across the globe?

First, securitization allocated the sub-prime risk to many investors and financial institutions. The huge amount of credit default swaps linked to sub-prime-backed securities spread the risk to even more institutions. Unlike previous downturns in a single market, such as the dot-com bubble in 2002, the decline in the sub-prime mortgage values affected many, if not most, financial institutions.

Second, banks were more vulnerable than at any time since the 1929 Depression. Congress had "repealed" the Glass-Steagall Act in 1999, allowing commercial banks and investment banks to be part of a single financial institution. The SEC compounded the problem in 2004 when it allowed large investment banks' brokerage operations to take on much higher leverage. Some, like Bear Stearns, ended up with $33 of debt for every dollar of its own equity. With such leverage, a small increase in the value of its investments would create enormous gains for the equity holders and large bonuses for the managers; conversely a small decline would ruin the firm.

When the sub-prime market mortgages began defaulting, mortgage companies were the first to fall. Many originating firms had not sold all of their sub-prime mortgages, and they failed. For example, New Century declared bankruptcy in 2007, IndyMac was placed under FDIC control in 2008, and Countrywide was acquired by Bank of America in 2008 to avoid bankruptcy.

Securitizing firms also crashed, partly because they kept some of the new securities they created. For example, Fannie Mae and Freddie Mac had huge losses on their portfolio assets, causing them to be virtually taken over by the Federal Housing Finance Agency in 2008. In addition to big losses on their own sub-prime portfolios, many investment banks also had losses related to their positions in credit default swaps. Thus, Lehman Brothers was forced into bankruptcy, Bear Stearns was sold to JPMorgan Chase, and Merrill Lynch was sold to Bank of America, with huge losses to stockholders.

Because Lehman Brothers defaulted on some of its commercial paper, investors in the Reserve Primary Fund, a big money market mutual fund, saw the value of its investments "break the buck," dropping to less than a dollar per share. To avoid panic and a total lockdown in the money markets, the U.S. Treasury agreed to insure some investments in money market funds.

AIG was the largest backer of credit default swaps, and it operated worldwide. In 2008 it became obvious that AIG could not honor its commitments as a counterparty, so the Fed effectively nationalized AIG to avoid a domino effect in which AIG's failure would topple hundreds of other financial institutions.

In normal times, banks provide liquidity to the economy and funding for creditworthy businesses and individuals. These activities are crucial for a well-functioning economy. However, the financial contagion spread to commercial banks because some owned mortgage-backed securities, some owned commercial paper issued by failing institutions, and some had exposure to credit default swaps. As banks worried about their survival in the fall of 2008, they stopped providing credit to other banks and businesses. The market for commercial paper dried up to such an extent that the Fed began buying new commercial paper from issuing companies.

Prior to the sub-prime meltdown, many nonfinancial corporations had been rolling over short-term financing to take advantage of low interest rates on short-term lending. When the meltdown began, banks began calling in loans rather than renewing them. In

GLOBAL ECONOMIC CRISIS

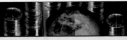

© uniquely india/Getty Images

Anatomy of a Toxic Asset

Consider the dismal history of one particular toxic asset named "GSAMP TRUST 2006-NC2." This toxic asset began life as 3,949 individual mortgages issued by New Century in 2006 with a total principal of about $881 million. Almost all were adjustable rate mortgages, half were concentrated in just two states (California and Florida), and many of the borrowers had previous credit problems. Goldman Sachs bought the mortgages, pooled them into a trust, and divided the trust into 16 "debt" tranches called mortgage-backed securities (MBS). The tranches had different provisions regarding distribution of payments should there be any defaults, with senior tranches getting paid first and junior tranches getting paid only if funds were available. Despite the mortgages' poor quality and the pool's lack of diversification, Moody's and Standard & Poor's gave most tranches good ratings, with over 79% rated AAA.

Five years later, in July 2011, about 36% of the underlying mortgages were behind in payments, defaulted, or even foreclosed. Not surprisingly, the market prices of the mortgage-backed securities had plummeted. These were very toxic assets indeed!

The story doesn't end here. Fannie Mae and Freddie Mac had purchased some of these toxic assets and taken a beating. In September, 2011, the Federal Housing Finance Agency (now the conservator of Fannie Mae and Freddie Mac) sued Goldman Sachs, alleging that Goldman Sachs had knowingly overstated the value of the securities in the prospectuses. The FHFA also alleges that at the very same time Goldman Sachs was selling these and other mortgage-backed securities to Fannie and Freddie, Goldman was: (1) trying to get rid of the mortgages by "putting" them back to New Century, and (2) was "betting" against the mortgages in the credit default swap market. As of early 2012, this suit has not yet been settled, but it is safe to say that these toxic assets will continue to poison our economy for many more years.

Source: Adam B. Ashcraft and Til Schuermann, *Understanding the Securitization of Subprime Mortgage Credit*, Federal Reserve Bank of New York Staff Reports, no. 318, March 2008; John Cassidy, *How Markets Fail* (New York: Farrar, Straus and Giroux, 2009), pp. 260–272; and the Federal Housing Finance Agency, **www.fhfa.gov/webfiles/22589/ FHFA%20v%20Goldman%20Sachs.pdf**.

response, many companies began throttling back their plans. Consumers and small businesses faced a similar situation: With credit harder to obtain, consumers cut back on spending and small businesses cut back on hiring. Plummeting real estate prices caused a major contraction in the construction industry, putting many builders and suppliers out of work.

What began as a slump in housing prices caused enormous distress for commercial banks, not just mortgage companies. Commercial banks cut back on lending, which caused difficulties for nonfinancial business and consumers. Similar scenarios played out all over the world, resulting in the worst recession in the U.S. since 1929.

1-13d Responding to the Economic Crisis

Unlike the beginning of the 1929 Depression, the U.S. government did not take a hands-off approach in the most recent crisis. In late 2008 Congress passed the Troubled Asset Relief Plan (TARP), which authorized the U.S. Treasury to purchase mortgage-related assets from financial institutions. The intent was to simultaneously inject cash into the banking system and get these toxic assets off banks' balance sheets. The Emergency Economic Stabilization Act of 2008 (EESA) allowed the Treasury to purchase preferred stock in banks (whether they wanted the investment or not). Again, this injected cash into the banking system. Several very large banks have already paid back the funding they received from the TARP and EESA financing, although it is doubtful whether all recipients will be able to do so. It is almost certain that some financial institutions, such as AIG, will leave taxpayers bearing the burden of their bailouts.

Although TARP and EESA were originally intended for financial institutions, they were subsequently modified so that the Treasury was able to make loans to GM and Chrylser in 2008 and early 2009 so that they could stave off immediate bankruptcy. Both GM and Chrysler went into bankruptcy in the summer of 2009 despite government loans, but quickly emerged as stronger companies. Although the U.S. government is still a shareholder, there is a possibility that GM and Chrysler will pay back the government's investment.

The government also used traditional measures, such as stimulus spending, tax cuts, and monetary policy: (1) The American Recovery and Reinvestment Act of 2009 provided over $700 billion in direct stimulus spending for a variety of federal projects and aid for state projects. (2) In 2010 the government also temporarily cut Social Security taxes from 6.2% to 4.2%. (3) The Federal Reserve has purchased around $2 trillion in assets, including long-term bonds, from financial institutions, a process called "quantitative easing."

Has the response worked? You will have a better answer at the time you read this than we had when we wrote this in early 2012, but here is our answer: The economy is better now than at the worst of the crisis, with the unemployment rate down to 8.5% from its 2009 high of 10%, and GDP is growing rather than contracting. Whether or not it was due to the government's response, it does not appear likely that the economy will soon fall into another Great Depression, something that we could not write in 2009. On the other hand, it is likely that it will take years, if not a full decade, for the economy and stock markets to fully recover.[9]

1-13e Preventing the Next Crisis

Can the next crisis be prevented? Congress passed the Dodd-Frank Wall Street Reform and Consumer Protection Act in 2010 as an attempt to do just that. As we write this in 2012, many provisions have not yet been enacted. Following is a brief summary of some major elements in the Act.

PROTECT CONSUMERS FROM PREDATORS AND THEMSELVES

Dodd-Frank established the Consumer Financial Protection Bureau, whose objectives include ensuring that borrowers fully understand the terms and risks of the mortgage contracts, that mortgage originators verify borrower's ability to repay, and that originators maintain an interest in the borrowers by keeping some of the mortgages they originate. The Bureau will also oversee credit cards, debit cards, payday loans, and other areas in which consumers might have been targets of predatory lending practices. As of early 2012, the Bureau has been established, but it has done very little.

SEPARATE BANKING FROM SPECULATING

The act's "Volker Rule," named after former Fed chairman Paul Volcker, would greatly limit a bank's proprietary trading, such as investing the banks' own funds into hedge funds. The basic idea is to prevent banks from making highly leveraged

---

[9]For a comparison of this crisis with 15 previous banking crises, see Serge Wind, "A Perspective on 2000's Illiquidity and Capital Crisis: Past Banking Crises and their Relevance to Today's Credit Crisis," *Review of Business*, Volume 31, Number 1, Fall 2010, pp. 68–83. Based on these previous crises, Professor Wind estimates it will take 10 years for equity markets to reach the pre-crisis high.

bets on risky assets. The Volcker Rule has not been implemented as of early 2012, although Goldman Sachs and Morgan Stanley have cut back their proprietary trading operations.

INCREASE TRANSPARENCY

The act calls for regulation and transparency in the now-private derivatives markets, including the establishment of a trading exchange. It also provides for more oversight of hedge funds and credit rating agencies in an effort to spot potential landmines before they explode. Not much has been accomplished as of early 2012.

HEAD OFF AND REIN IN SYSTEMIC FAILURES AT TOO-BIG-TO-FAIL BANKS

When a bank gets extremely large and has business connections with many other companies, it can be very dangerous to the rest of the economy if the institution fails and goes bankrupt, as the 2008 failure of Lehman Brothers illustrates. In other words, a bank or other financial institution can become "too big to fail." Systemic risk is defined as something that affects most companies. When there are a large number of too-big-to-fail institutions and systemic shock hits, the entire world can be dragged into a recession, as we saw in 2008.

Dodd-Frank gives regulators more oversight of too-big-to-fail institutions, including all banks with $50 billion in assets and any other financial institutions that regulators deem systemically important. This oversight includes authority to require additional capital or reductions in leverage if conditions warrant. In addition, these institutions must prepare "transition" plans that would make it easier for regulators to liquidate the institution should it fail. In other words, this provision seeks to reduce the likelihood that a giant financial institution will fail and to minimize the damage if it does fail. Not much has been implemented as of early 2012.

SELF-TEST

Briefly describe some of the mistakes that participants in the sub-prime mortgage process made.

1-14 The Big Picture

Finance has vocabulary and tools that might be new to you. To help you avoid getting bogged down in the trenches, Figure 1-6 presents the big picture. A manager's primary job is to increase the company's intrinsic value, but how exactly does one go about doing that? The equation in the center of Figure 1-6 shows that intrinsic value is the present value of the firm's expected free cash flows, discounted at the weighted average cost of capital. Thus, there are two approaches for increasing intrinsic value: Improve FCF or reduce the WACC. Observe that several factors affect FCF and several factors affect the WACC. In the rest of the book's chapters, we will typically focus on only one of these factors, systematically building the vocabulary and tools that you will use after graduation to improve your company's intrinsic value. It is true that every manager needs to understand financial vocabulary and be able to apply financial tools, but successful managers also understand how their decisions affect the big picture. So as you read this book, keep in mind where each topic fits into the big picture.

FIGURE **1-6**

The Determinants of Intrinsic Value: The Big Picture

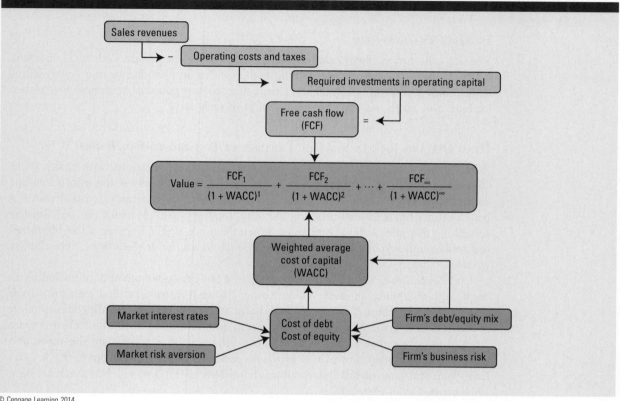

© Cengage Learning 2014

1-15 e-Resources

The textbook's Web site contains several types of files that will be helpful to you:

r e s o u r c e

1. It contains *Excel* files, called **Tool Kits** that provide well-documented models for almost all of the text's calculations. Not only will these **Tool Kits** help you with this finance course, they also will serve as tool kits for you in other courses and in your career.
2. There are problems at the end of the chapters that require spreadsheets, and the Web site contains the models you will need to begin work on these problems.

W W W

When we think it might be helpful for you to look at one of the Web site's files, we'll show an icon in the margin like the one shown here.

THOMSON REUTERS

Other resources are also on the Web site, including Cyberproblems and problems that use the Thomson ONE—Business School Edition Web site. The textbook's Web site also contains an electronic library that contains Adobe PDF files for "extensions" to many chapters that cover additional useful material related to the chapter.

SUMMARY

- The three main forms of business organization are the **proprietorship**, the **partnership**, and the **corporation**. Although each form of organization offers advantages and disadvantages, *corporations conduct much more business than the other forms.*

- The primary objective of management should be to *maximize stockholders' wealth*, and this means *maximizing the company's* **fundamental**, or **intrinsic, stock price**. Legal actions that maximize stock prices usually increase social welfare.

- **Free cash flows (FCFs)** are the cash flows available for distribution to all of a firm's investors (shareholders and creditors) after the firm has paid all expenses (including taxes) and has made the required investments in operations to support growth.

- The **weighted average cost of capital (WACC)** is the average return required by all of the firm's investors. It is determined by the firm's *capital structure* (the firm's relative amounts of debt and equity), *interest rates,* the firm's *risk,* and the *market's attitude toward risk.*

- The value of a firm depends on the size of the firm's free cash flows, the timing of those flows, and their risk. A **firm's fundamental**, or **intrinsic, value** is defined by

$$\text{Value} = \frac{FCF_1}{(1 + \text{WACC})^1} + \frac{FCF_2}{(1 + \text{WACC})^2} + \frac{FCF_3}{(1 + \text{WACC})^3} + \ldots + \frac{FCF_\infty}{(1 + \text{WACC})^\infty}$$

- Transfers of capital between borrowers and savers take place (1) by **direct transfers** of money and securities; (2) by transfers through **investment banking houses**, which act as go-betweens; and (3) by transfers through **financial intermediaries**, which create new securities.

- Four fundamental factors affect the cost of money: (1) **production opportunities**, (2) **time preferences for consumption**, (3) **risk**, and (4) **inflation**.

- **Derivatives**, such as options, are claims on other financial securities. In **securitization**, new securities are created from claims on packages of other securities.

- Major financial institutions include **commercial banks, savings and loan associations, mutual savings banks, credit unions, pension funds, life insurance companies, mutual funds, money market funds, hedge funds**, and **private equity funds**.

- **Spot markets** and **futures markets** are terms that refer to whether the assets are bought or sold for "on-the-spot" delivery or for delivery at some future date.

- **Money markets** are the markets for debt securities with maturities of less than a year. **Capital markets** are the markets for long-term debt and corporate stocks.

- **Primary markets** are the markets in which corporations raise new capital. **Secondary markets** are markets in which existing, already outstanding securities are traded among investors.

- Orders from buyers and sellers can be matched in one of three ways: (1) in an open outcry **auction**, (2) through **dealers**, and (3) automatically through an **electronic communications network (ECN)**.

- There are two basic types of markets—the physical location exchanges (such as the NYSE) and computer/telephone networks (such as NASDAQ).

- *Web Extension 1A* discusses derivatives, and *Web Extension 1B* provides additional coverage of stock markets.

QUESTIONS

(1-1)   Define each of the following terms:

    a. Proprietorship; partnership; corporation
    b. Limited partnership; limited liability partnership; professional corporation
    c. Stockholder wealth maximization
    d. Money market; capital market; primary market; secondary market
    e. Private markets; public markets; derivatives
    f. Investment banker; financial services corporation; financial intermediary

g. Mutual fund; money market fund

h. Physical location exchanges; computer/telephone networks

i. Open outcry auction; dealer market; electronic communications network (ECN)

j. Production opportunities; time preferences for consumption

k. Foreign trade deficit

(1-2) What are the three principal forms of business organization? What are the advantages and disadvantages of each?

(1-3) What is a firm's fundamental, or intrinsic, value? What might cause a firm's intrinsic value to be different from its actual market value?

(1-4) Edmund Enterprises recently made a large investment to upgrade its technology. Although these improvements won't have much of an impact on performance in the short run, they are expected to reduce future costs significantly. What impact will this investment have on Edmund Enterprises's earnings per share this year? What impact might this investment have on the company's intrinsic value and stock price?

(1-5) Describe the ways in which capital can be transferred from suppliers of capital to those who are demanding capital.

(1-6) What are financial intermediaries, and what economic functions do they perform?

(1-7) Is an initial public offering an example of a primary or a secondary market transaction?

(1-8) Differentiate between dealer markets and stock markets that have a physical location.

(1-9) Identify and briefly compare the two leading stock exchanges in the United States today.

MINI CASE

Assume that you recently graduated and have just reported to work as an investment advisor at the brokerage firm of Balik and Kiefer Inc. One of the firm's clients is Michelle DellaTorre, a professional tennis player who has just come to the United States from Chile. DellaTorre is a highly ranked tennis player who would like to start a company to produce and market apparel she designs. She also expects to invest substantial amounts of money through Balik and Kiefer. DellaTorre is very bright, and she would like to understand in general terms what will happen to her money. Your boss has developed the following set of questions you must answer to explain the U.S. financial system to DellaTorre.

a. Why is corporate finance important to all managers?

b. Describe the organizational forms a company might have as it evolves from a start-up to a major corporation. List the advantages and disadvantages of each form.

c. How do corporations go public and continue to grow? What are agency problems? What is corporate governance?

d. What should be the primary objective of managers?

(1) Do firms have any responsibilities to society at large?

(2) Is stock price maximization good or bad for society?

(3) Should firms behave ethically?

e. What three aspects of cash flows affect the value of any investment?

f. What are free cash flows?

g. What is the weighted average cost of capital?

h. How do free cash flows and the weighted average cost of capital interact to determine a firm's value?

i. Who are the providers (savers) and users (borrowers) of capital? How is capital transferred between savers and borrowers?

j. What do we call the price that a borrower must pay for debt capital? What is the price of equity capital? What are the four most fundamental factors that affect the cost of money, or the general level of interest rates, in the economy?

k. What are some economic conditions (including international aspects) that affect the cost of money?

l. What are financial securities? Describe some financial instruments.

m. List some financial institutions.

n. What are some different types of markets?

o. How are secondary markets organized?

   (1) List some physical location markets and some computer/telephone networks.

   (2) Explain the differences between open outcry auctions, dealer markets, and electronic communications networks (ECNs).

p. Briefly explain mortgage securitization and how it contributed to the global economic crisis.

© Adalberto Rios Szalay/Sexto Sol/Getty Images

CHAPTER 2

Financial Statements, Cash Flow, and Taxes

E ven in today's era of financial crises, $12.6 billion is a lot of money. This is the amount of cash flow that Hewlett-Packard (HP) generated in 2011. The ability to generate cash flow is the lifeblood of a company and the basis for its fundamental value. How did HP use this cash flow? HP invested for the future by making over $10 billion in acquisitions.

Other companies also generated large cash flows from operations in 2011, but they used the money differently. For example, Walgreens generated over $3.6 billion from its operations and used over $1.2 billion for capital expenditures, much of it on new stores and the purchase of worksite health centers.

Procter & Gamble generated $13.2 billion. The company made relatively small capital expenditures and returned the lion's share (almost $13 billion) to shareholders as dividends or through stock repurchases.

Apple generated over $37 billion but made relatively small capital expenditures, acquisitions, or distributions to shareholders. Instead, it put about $32 billion into short-term financial securities like T-bills.

These four well-managed companies used their operating cash flows in four different ways: HP made acquisitions, Walgreens spent on a mix of internal and external growth, P&G returned cash to shareholders, and Apple saved for a rainy day. Which company made the right choice? Only time will tell, but keep these companies and their different cash flow strategies in mind as you read this chapter.

Intrinsic Value, Free Cash Flow, and Financial Statements

© Rob Webb/Getty Images

In Chapter 1, we told you that managers should strive to make their firms more valuable and that a firm's intrinsic value is determined by the present value of its free cash flows (FCF) discounted at the weighted average cost of capital (WACC). This chapter focuses on FCF, including its calculation from financial statements and its interpretation when evaluating a company and manager.

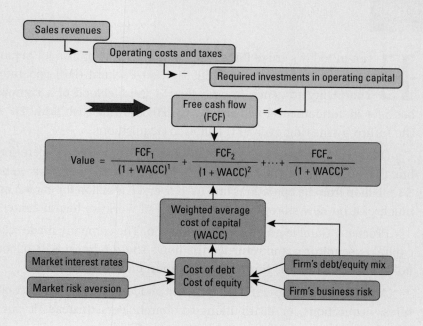

© Cengage Learning 2014

r e s o u r c e

The textbook's Web site contains an Excel file that will guide you through the chapter's calculations. The file for this chapter is **Ch02 Tool Kit.xls,** and we encourage you to open the file and follow along as you read the chapter.

The stream of cash flows a firm is expected to generate in the future determines its fundamental value (also called intrinsic value). But how does an investor go about estimating future cash flows, and how does a manager decide which actions are most likely to increase cash flows? The first step is to understand the financial statements that publicly traded firms must provide to the public. Thus, we begin with a discussion of financial statements, including how to interpret them and how to use them. Value depends on after-tax cash flows, so we provide an overview of the federal income tax system and highlight differences between accounting income and cash flow.

2-1 Financial Statements and Reports

A company's **annual report** usually begins with the chairperson's description of the firm's operating results during the past year and a discussion of new developments that will affect future operations. The annual report also presents four basic financial statements— the *balance sheet*, the *income statement*, the *statement of stockholders' equity,* and the *statement of cash flows.*

W W W

See the Securities and Exchange Commission's (SEC) Web site for quarterly reports and more detailed annual reports that provide breakdowns for each major division or subsidiary. These reports, called 10-Q and 10-K reports, are available on the SEC's Web site at **www.sec.gov** under the heading "EDGAR."

The quantitative and written materials are equally important. The financial statements report *what has actually happened* to assets, earnings, dividends, and cash flows during the past few years, whereas the written materials attempt to explain why things turned out the way they did.

SELF-TEST

What is the annual report, and what two types of information does it present?

What four types of financial statements does the annual report typically include?

2-2 The Balance Sheet

resource

See **Ch02 Tool Kit.xls** for details.

For illustrative purposes, we use a hypothetical company, MicroDrive Inc., which produces memory components for computers and smartphones. Figure 2-1 shows MicroDrive's most recent **balance sheets**, which represent "snapshots" of its financial position on the last day of each year. Although most companies report their balance sheets only on the last day of a given period, the "snapshot" actually changes daily as inventories are bought and sold, as fixed assets are added or retired, or as loan balances are increased or paid down. Moreover, a retailer will have larger inventories before Christmas than later in the spring, so balance sheets for the same company can look quite different at different times during the year.

FIGURE 2-1

MicroDrive Inc.: December 31 Balance Sheets (Millions of Dollars)

	A	B	C	D	E	F	G
						2013	2012
30	*Assets*						
31	Cash and equivalents					$ 50	$ 60
32	Short-term investments					-	40
33	Accounts receivable					500	380
34	Inventories					1,000	820
35	Total current assets					$ 1,550	$ 1,300
36	Net plant and equipment					2,000	1,700
37	Total assets					$ 3,550	$ 3,000
38							
39	*Liabilities and Equity*						
40	Accounts payable					$ 200	$ 190
41	Notes payable					280	130
42	Accruals					300	280
43	Total current liabilities					$ 780	$ 600
44	Long-term bonds					1,200	1,000
45	Total liabilities					$ 1,980	$ 1,600
46	Preferred stock (1,000,000 shares)					100	100
47	Common stock (50,000,000 shares)					500	500
48	Retained earnings					970	800
49	Total common equity					$ 1,470	$ 1,300
50	Total liabilities and equity					$ 3,550	$ 3,000

The balance sheet begins with assets, which are the "things" the company owns. Assets are listed in order of "liquidity," or length of time it typically takes to convert them to cash at fair market values. The balance sheet also lists the claims that various groups have against the company's value; these are listed in the order in which they must be paid. For example, suppliers may have claims called "accounts payable" that are due within 30 days, banks may have claims called "notes payable" that are due within 90 days, and bond-holders may have claims that are not due for 20 years or more.

Stockholders' claims represent ownership (or equity) and need never be "paid off." These are residual claims in the sense that stockholders may receive payments only if there is value remaining after other claimants have been paid. The nonstockholder claims are liabilities from the stockholders' perspective. The amounts shown on the balance sheets are called **book values** because they are based on the amounts recorded by book-keepers when assets are purchased or liabilities are issued. As you will see throughout this textbook, book values may be very different from **market values**, which are the current values as determined in the marketplace.

The following sections provide more information about specific asset, liability, and equity accounts.

2-2a Assets

Cash, short-term investments, accounts receivable, and inventories are listed as current assets because MicroDrive is expected to convert them into cash within a year. All assets are stated in dollars, but only cash represents actual money that can be spent. Some marketable securities mature very soon, and these can be converted quickly into cash at prices close to their book values. Such securities are called "cash equivalents" and are included with cash. Therefore, MicroDrive could write checks for a total of $50 million. Other types of marketable securities have a longer time until maturity, and their market values are less predictable. These securities are classified as "short-term investments."

When MicroDrive sells its products to a customer but doesn't demand immediate payment, the customer then has an obligation called an "account receivable." The $500 million shown in accounts receivable is the amount of sales for which MicroDrive has not yet been paid.

Inventories show the dollars MicroDrive has invested in raw materials, work-in-process, and finished goods available for sale. MicroDrive uses the **FIFO (first-in, first-out)** method to determine the inventory value shown on its balance sheet ($1 billion). It could have used the **LIFO (last-in, first-out)** method. During a period of rising prices, by taking out old, low-cost inventory and leaving in new, high-cost items, FIFO will produce a higher balance sheet inventory value but a lower cost of goods sold on the income statement. (FIFO is used strictly for accounting purposes; companies actually use older items first.) Because MicroDrive uses FIFO and because inflation has been occurring: (1) its balance sheet inventories are higher than they would have been had it used LIFO, (2) its cost of goods sold is lower than it would have been under LIFO, and (3) its reported profits are therefore higher. In MicroDrive's case, if the company had elected to switch to LIFO, then its balance sheet would have had inventories of $850 million rather than $1 billion, and its pre-tax earnings (discussed in the next section) would have been reduced by $50 million. Thus, the inventory valuation method can have a significant effect on financial statements, which is important to know when comparing companies.

Rather than treat the entire purchase price of a long-term asset (such as a factory, plant, or equipment) as an expense in the purchase year, accountants "spread" the purchase cost over the asset's useful life.[1] The amount they charge each year is called the **depreciation** expense. Some companies report an amount called "gross plant and equipment," which is the total cost of the long-term assets they have in place, and another amount called "accumulated depreciation," which is the total amount of depreciation that has been charged on those assets. Some companies, such as MicroDrive, report only net plant and equipment, which is gross plant and equipment less accumulated depreciation. Chapter 11 provides a more detailed explanation of depreciation methods.

2-2b Liabilities and Equity

Accounts payable, notes payable, and accruals are listed as current liabilities because MicroDrive is expected to pay them within a year. When MicroDrive purchases supplies but doesn't immediately pay for them, it takes on an obligation called an account payable. Similarly, when MicroDrive takes out a loan that must be repaid within a year, it signs an IOU called a note payable. MicroDrive doesn't pay its taxes or its employees' wages daily, and the amount it owes on these items at any point in time is called an "accrual" or an "accrued expense." Long-term bonds are also liabilities because they, too, reflect a claim held by someone other than a stockholder.

Preferred stock is a hybrid, or a cross between common stock and debt. In the event of bankruptcy, preferred stock ranks below debt but above common stock. Also, the preferred dividend is fixed, so preferred stockholders do not benefit if the company's earnings grow. Most firms do not use much, if any, preferred stock, so "equity" usually means "common equity" unless the words "total" or "preferred" are included.

When a company sells shares of stock, it records the proceeds in the common stock account.[2] Retained earnings are the cumulative amount of earnings that have not been paid out as dividends. The sum of common stock and retained earnings is called "common equity," or just "equity." If a company could actually sell its assets at their book value, and if the liabilities and preferred stock were actually worth their book values, then a company could sell its assets, pay off its liabilities and preferred stock, and the remaining cash would belong to common stockholders. Therefore, common equity is sometimes called **net worth**—it's the assets minus (or "net of") the liabilities.

SELF-TEST

What is the balance sheet, and what information does it provide?

What determines the order of the information shown on the balance sheet?

Why might a company's December 31 balance sheet differ from its June 30 balance sheet?

A firm has $8 million in total assets. It has $3 million in current liabilities, $2 million in long-term debt, and $1 million in preferred stock. What is the total value of common equity? **($2 million)**

---

[1]This is called *accrual accounting*, which attempts to match revenues to the periods in which they are earned and expenses to the periods in which the effort to generate income occurred.

[2]Companies sometimes break the total proceeds into two parts, one called "par" and the other called "paid-in capital" or "capital surplus." For example, if a company sells shares of stock for $10, it might record $1 of par and $9 of paid-in capital. For most purposes, the distinction between par and paid-in capital is not important, and most companies use no-par stock.

GLOBAL ECONOMIC CRISIS

© uniquely india/Getty Images

The Global Economic Crisis

Let's Play Hide-and-Seek!

In a shameful lapse of regulatory accountability, banks and other financial institutions were allowed to use "structured investment vehicles" (SIVs) to hide assets and liabilities and simply not report them on their balance sheets. Here's how SIVs worked and why they subsequently failed. The SIV was set up as a separate legal entity that the bank owned and managed. The SIV would borrow money in the short-term market (backed by the credit of the bank) and then invest in long-term securities. As you might guess, many SIVs invested in mortgage-backed securities. When the SIV paid only 3% on its borrowings but earned 10% on its investments, the managing bank was able to report fabulous earnings, especially if it also earned fees for creating the mortgage securities that went into the SIV.

But this game of hide-and-seek didn't have a happy ending. Mortgage-backed securities began defaulting in 2007 and 2008, causing the SIVs to pass losses through to the banks. SunTrust, Citigroup, Bank of America, and Northern Rock are just a few of the many banks that reported enormous losses in the SIV game. Investors, depositors, and the government eventually found the hidden assets and liabilities, but by then the assets were worth a lot less than the liabilities.

In a case of too little and too late, regulators are closing these loopholes, and it doesn't look like there will be any more hidden SIVs in the near future. But the damage has been done, and the entire financial system was put at risk in large part because of this high-stakes game of hide-and-seek.

2-3 The Income Statement

Figure 2-2 shows the **income statements** and selected additional information for MicroDrive. Income statements can cover any period of time, but they are usually prepared monthly, quarterly, and annually. Unlike the balance sheet, which is a snapshot of a firm at a point in time, the income statement reflects performance during the period.

resource

See *Ch02 Tool Kit.xls* for details.

Net sales are the revenues less any discounts or returns. Depreciation and amortization reflect the estimated costs of the assets that wear out in producing goods and services. To illustrate depreciation, suppose that in 2010 MicroDrive purchased a $100,000 machine with a life of 5 years and zero expected salvage value. This $100,000 cost is not expensed in the purchase year but is instead spread out over the machine's 5-year depreciable life. In straight-line depreciation, which we explain in Chapter 11, the depreciation charge for a full year would be $100,000/5 = $20,000. The reported depreciation expense on the income statement is the sum of all the assets' annual depreciation charges. Depreciation applies to tangible assets, such as plant and equipment, whereas amortization applies to intangible assets such as patents, copyrights, trademarks, and goodwill.[3]

---

[3]The accounting treatment of goodwill resulting from mergers has changed in recent years. Rather than an annual charge, companies are required to periodically evaluate the value of goodwill and reduce net income only if the goodwill's value has decreased materially ("become impaired," in the language of accountants). For example, in 2002 AOL Time Warner wrote off almost $100 billion associated with the AOL merger. It doesn't take too many $100 billion expenses to really hurt net income!

FIGURE 2-2

MicroDrive Inc.: Income Statements for Years Ending December 31 (Millions of Dollars, Except for Per Share Data)

	A	B	C	D	E	F	G
59						2013	2012
60	Net sales					$ 5,000	$ 4,760
61	Costs of goods sold except depreciation					3,800	3,560
62	Depreciation and amortization					200	170
63	Other operating expenses					500	480
64	Earnings before interest and taxes (EBIT)					$ 500	$ 550
65	Less interest					120	100
66	Pre-tax earnings					$ 380	$ 450
67	Taxes					152	180
68	Net Income before preferred dividends					$ 228	$ 270
69	Preferred dividends					8	8
70	Net Income available to common stockholders					$ 220	$ 262
71							
72	*Additional Information*						
73	Common dividends					$ 50	$ 48
74	Addition to retained earnings					$ 170	$ 214
75	Number of common shares					50.00	50.00
76	Stock price per share					$27.00	$40.00
77							
78	*Per Share Data*						
79	Earnings per share, EPS[b]					$4.40	$5.24
80	Dividends per share, DPS[c]					$1.00	$0.96
81	Book value per share, BVPS[d]					$29.40	$26.00

Notes:

[a]MicroDrive has no amortization charges.

$$^b EPS = \frac{\text{Net income available to common stockholders}}{\text{Common shares outstanding}}$$

$$^c DPS = \frac{\text{Dividends to common stockholders}}{\text{Common shares outstanding}}$$

$$^d BVPS = \frac{\text{Total common equity}}{\text{Common shares outstanding}}$$

The cost of goods sold (COGS) includes labor, raw materials, and other expenses directly related to the production or purchase of the items or services sold in that period. The COGS includes depreciation, but we report depreciation separately so that analysis later in the chapter will be more transparent. Subtracting COGS (including depreciation) and other operating expenses results in earnings before interest and taxes (EBIT).

Many analysts add back depreciation to EBIT to calculate **EBITDA**, which stands for earnings before interest, taxes, depreciation, and amortization. Because neither depreciation nor amortization is paid in cash, some analysts claim that EBITDA is a better measure of financial strength than is net income. MicroDrive's EBITDA is

$$EBITDA = EBIT + Depreciation$$

$$= \$500 + \$200 = \$700 \text{ million}$$

Alternatively, EBITDA's calculation can begin with sales:

$$EBITDA = Sales - COGS \text{ excluding depreciation} - \text{Other expenses}$$

$$= \$5,000 - \$3,800 - \$500 = \$700$$

However, as we show later in the chapter, EBITDA is not as useful to managers and analysts as free cash flow, so we usually focus on free cash flow instead of EBITDA.

The net income available to common shareholders, which equals revenues less expenses, taxes, and preferred dividends (but before paying common dividends), is generally referred to as **net income**. Net income is also called **accounting profit**, **profit**, or **earnings**, particularly in financial news reports. Dividing net income by the number of shares outstanding gives earnings per share (EPS), often called "the bottom line." Throughout this book, unless otherwise indicated, net income means net income available to common stockholders.[4]

SELF-TEST

What is an income statement, and what information does it provide?

What is often called "the bottom line?"

What is EBITDA?

How does the income statement differ from the balance sheet with regard to the time period reported?

A firm has $2 million in earnings before taxes. The firm has an interest expense of $300,000 and depreciation of $200,000; it has no amortization. What is its EBITDA? **($2.5 million)**

2-4 Statement of Stockholders' Equity

Changes in stockholders' equity during the accounting period are reported in the **statement of stockholders' equity**. Figure 2-3 shows that MicroDrive earned $220 million during 2013, paid out $50 million in common dividends, and plowed $150 million back into the business. Thus, the balance sheet item "Retained earnings" increased from $800 million at year-end 2012 to $970 million at year-end 2013.[5] The last column shows the beginning stockholders' equity, any changes, and the end-of-year stockholders' equity.

Note that "retained earnings" does not represent assets but is instead a *claim against assets*. In 2013, MicroDrive's stockholders allowed it to reinvest $170 million instead of distributing the money as dividends, and management spent this money on new assets.

resource

See Ch02 Tool Kit.xls for details.

---

[4]Companies also report "comprehensive income," which is the sum of net income and any "comprehensive" income item, such as the change in market value of a financial asset. For example, a decline in a financial asset's value would be recorded as a loss even though the asset has not been sold. We assume that there are no comprehensive income items in our examples.

Some companies also choose to report "pro forma income." For example, if a company incurs an expense that it doesn't expect to recur, such as the closing of a plant, it might calculate pro forma income as though it had not incurred the one-time expense. There are no hard-and-fast rules for calculating pro forma income, so many companies find ingenious ways to make pro forma income higher than traditional income. The SEC and the Public Company Accounting Oversight Board (PCAOB) are taking steps to reduce deceptive uses of pro forma reporting.

[5]If they had been applicable, then columns would have been used to show "Additional Paid-in Capital" and "Treasury Stock." Also, additional rows would have contained information on such things as new issues of stock, treasury stock acquired or reissued, stock options exercised, and unrealized foreign exchange gains or losses.

FIGURE 2-3

MicroDrive Inc.: Statement of Stockholders' Equity, December 31, 2012

	A	B	C	D	E	F	G	H
				Preferred Stock	Common Shares	Common Stock	Retained Earnings	Total Equity
103								
104	Balances, Dec. 31, 2012			$100	50	$500	$800	$1,400
105	Changes during year:							
106	Net income						$220	$220
107	Cash dividends						(50)	(50)
108	Issuance/repurchase of stock			0	0	0		
109	Balances, Dec. 31, 2013			$100	50	$500	$970	$1,570
110								
111	*Note:* In financial statements, parentheses denote a negative number.							

Thus, retained earnings, as reported on the balance sheet, does not represent cash and is not "available" for the payment of dividends or anything else.[6]

SELF-TEST

What is the statement of stockholders' equity, and what information does it provide?

Why do changes in retained earnings occur?

Explain why the following statement is true: "The retained earnings reported on the balance sheet does not represent cash and is not available for the payment of dividends or anything else."

A firm had a retained earnings balance of $3 million in the previous year. In the current year, its net income is $2.5 million. If it pays $1 million in common dividends in the current year, what is its resulting retained earnings balance? **($4.5 million)**

2-5 Statement of Cash Flows

Even if a company reports a large net income during a year, the *amount of cash* reported on its year-end balance sheet may be the same or even lower than its beginning cash. The reason is that the company can use its net income in a variety of ways, not just keep it as cash in the bank. For example, the firm may use its net income to pay dividends, to increase inventories, to finance accounts receivable, to invest in fixed assets, to reduce debt, or to buy back common stock. Indeed, many factors affect a company's *cash position* as reported on its balance sheet. The **statement of cash flows** separates a company's activities into three categories—operating, investing, and financing— and summarizes the resulting cash balance.

---

[6]The amount reported in the retained earnings account is *not* an indication of the amount of cash the firm has. Cash (as of the balance sheet date) is found in the cash account, an asset account. A positive number in the retained earnings account indicates only that the firm earned some income in the past, but its dividends paid were less than its earnings. Even if a company reports record earnings and shows an increase in its retained earnings account, it still may be short of cash.

The same situation holds for individuals. You might own a new BMW (no loan), lots of clothes, and an expensive stereo and hence have a high net worth. But if you have only 23 cents in your pocket plus $5 in your checking account, you will still be short of cash.

Financial Analysis on the Web

© Rob Webb/Getty Images

A wide range of valuable financial information is available on the Web. With just a couple of clicks, an investor can easily find the key financial statements for most publicly traded companies. Here's a partial (by no means a complete) list of places you can go to get started.

- One of the very best sources of financial information is Thomson Financial. Go to the textbook's Web site and follow the directions to access Thomson ONE—Business School Edition. An especially useful feature is the ability to download up to 10 years of financial statements in spreadsheet form. First, enter the ticker for a company and click Go. From the menu at left (in dark blue), select Financials. A new menu (in light blue) will expand, and selecting Thomson Financials under the Financial Statements heading will reveal Balance Sheets, Income Statements, and Cash Flow Statements items. Select any of these, and a menu item for 5YR and 10YR statements will pop up. Select the 10YR item, and 10 years of the selected financial statements will be displayed. To download the financial statements into a spreadsheet, click on the *Excel* icon toward the right of the light blue row at the top of the Thomson ONE panel. This will bring up a dialog box that lets you download the *Excel* file to your computer.
- Try Yahoo! Finance's Web site, **finance.yahoo.com**. Here you will find updated market information along with links to a variety of interesting research sites. Enter a stock's ticker symbol, click Get Quotes, and you will see the stock's current price along with recent news about the company. The panel on the left has links to key statistics and to the company's income statement, balance sheet, statement of cash flows, and more. The Web site also has a list of insider transactions, so you can tell if a company's CEO and other key insiders are buying or selling their company's stock. In addition, there is a message board where investors share opinions about the company, and there is a link to the company's filings with the SEC. Note that, in most cases, a more complete list of the SEC filings can be found at **www.sec.gov**.
- Other sources for up-to-date market information are **money.cnn.com** and **www.zacks.com**. These sites also provide financial statements in standardized formats.
- Both **www.bloomberg.com** and **www.marketwatch.com** have areas where you can obtain stock quotes along with company financials, links to Wall Street research, and links to SEC filings.
- If you are looking for charts of key accounting variables (for example, sales, inventory, depreciation and amortization, and reported earnings), as well as financial statements, take a look at **www.smartmoney.com**.
- Another good place to look is **www.reuters.com**. Here you can find links to analysts' research reports along with the key financial statements.

In addition to this information, you may be looking for sites that provide opinions regarding the direction of the overall market and views regarding individual stocks. Two popular sites in this category are The Motley Fool's Web site, **www.fool.com**, and the Web site for The Street.com, **www.thestreet.com**.

2-5a Operating Activities

As the name implies, the section for operating activities focuses on the amount of cash generated (or lost) by the firm's operating activities. The section begins with the reported net income before paying preferred dividends and makes several adjustments, beginning with noncash activities.

NONCASH ADJUSTMENTS

Some revenues and expenses reported on the income statement are not received or paid in cash during the year. For example, depreciation and amortization reduce reported net income but are not cash payments.

Reported taxes often differ from the taxes that are paid, resulting in an account called deferred taxes, which is the cumulative difference between the taxes that are reported and those that are paid. Deferred taxes can occur in many ways, including the use of accelerated depreciation for tax purposes but straight-line depreciation for financial reporting. This increases reported taxes relative to actual tax payments in the early years of an asset's life, causing the resulting net income to be lower than the true cash flow. Therefore, increases in deferred taxes are added to net income when calculating cash flow, and decreases are subtracted from net income.

Another example of noncash reporting occurs if a customer purchases services or products that extend beyond the reporting date, such as a 3-year extended warranty for a computer. Even if the company collects the cash at the time of the purchase, it will spread the reported revenues over the life of the purchase. This causes income to be lower than cash flow in the first year and higher in subsequent years, so adjustments must be made when calculating cash flow.

Changes in Working Capital

Increases in current assets other than cash (such as inventories and accounts receivable) decrease cash, whereas decreases in these accounts increase cash. For example, if inventories are to increase, then the firm must use cash to acquire the additional inventory. Conversely, if inventories decrease, this generally means the firm is selling inventories and not replacing all of them, hence generating cash. Here's how we keep track of whether a change in assets increases or decreases cash flow: If the amount we own goes up (like getting a new laptop computer), it means we have spent money and our cash goes down. On the other hand, if something we own goes down (like selling a car), our cash goes up.

Now consider a current liability, such as accounts payable. If accounts payable increase then the firm has received additional credit from its suppliers, which saves cash; but if payables decrease, this means it has used cash to pay off its suppliers. Therefore, increases in current liabilities such as accounts payable increase cash, whereas decreases in current liabilities decrease cash. To keep track of the cash flow's direction, think about the impact of getting a student loan. The amount you owe goes up and your cash goes up. Now think about paying off the loan: The amount you owe goes down, but so does your cash.

2-5b Investing Activities

Investing activities include transactions involving fixed assets or short-term financial investments. For example, if a company buys new IT infrastructure, its cash goes down at the time of the purchase. On the other hand, if it sells a building or T-bill, its cash goes up.

2-5c Financing Activities

Financing activities include raising cash by issuing short-term debt, long-term debt, or stock. Because dividend payments, stock repurchases, and principal payments on debt reduce a company's cash, such transactions are included here.

2-5d Putting the Pieces Together

The statement of cash flows is used to help answer questions such as these: Is the firm generating enough cash to purchase the additional assets required for growth? Is the firm generating any extra cash it can use to repay debt or to invest in new products? Such

resource

See *Ch02 Tool Kit.xls* for details.

information is useful both for managers and investors, so the statement of cash flows is an important part of the annual report.

Figure 2-4 shows MicroDrive's statement of cash flows as it would appear in the company's annual report. The top section shows cash generated by and used in operations—for MicroDrive, operations provided net cash flows of $158 million. This subtotal is in many respects the most important figure in any of the financial statements. Profits as reported on the income statement can be "doctored" by such tactics as depreciating assets too slowly, not recognizing bad debts promptly, and the like. However, it is far more difficult to simultaneously doctor profits and the working capital accounts. Therefore, it is not

FIGURE 2-4

MicroDrive Inc.: Statement of Cash Flows for 2013 (Millions of Dollars)

	A	B	C	D	E	F
123	*Operating Activities*					**2013**
124	Net Income before preferred dividends					$ 228
125	*Noncash adjustments*					
126	Depreciation[a]					200
127	*Working capital adjustments*					
128	Increase in accounts receivable[b]					(120)
129	Increase in inventories					(180)
130	Increase in accounts payable					10
131	Increase in accruals					20
132	Net cash provided (used) by operating activities					$ 158
133						
134	*Investing Activities*					
135	Cash used to acquire fixed assets[c]					$ (500)
136	Sale of short-term investments					40
137	Net cash provided (used) by investing activities					$ (460)
138						
139	*Financing Activities*					
140	Increase in notes payable					$ 150
141	Increase in bonds					200
142	Payment of common and preferred dividends					(58)
143	Net cash provided (used) by financing activities					$ 292
144						
145	*Summary*					
146	Net change in cash and equivalents					$ (10)
147	Cash and securities at beginning of the year					60
148	Cash and securities at end of the year					$ 50

Notes:

[a]Depreciation is a noncash expense that was deducted when calculating net income. It must be added back to show the correct cash flow from operations.

[b]An increase in a current asset decreases cash. An increase in a current liability increases cash. For example, inventories increased by $180 million and therefore reduced cash by the same amount.

[c]The net increase in fixed assets is $300 million; however, this net amount is after a deduction for the year's depreciation expense. Depreciation expense must be added back to find the increase in gross fixed assets. From the company's income statement, we see that the year's depreciation expense is $200 million; thus, expenditures on fixed assets were actually $500 million.

Filling in the GAAP

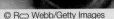

© Ric Webb/Getty Images

While U.S. companies adhere to "generally accepted accounting principles," or GAAP, when preparing financial statements, most other developed countries use "International Financial Reporting Standards," or IFRS. The U.S. GAAP system is rules-based, with thousands of instructions, or "guidances," for how individual transactions should be reported in financial statements. IFRS, on the other hand, is a principles-based system in which detailed instructions are replaced by overall guiding principles.

For example, whereas GAAP provides extensive and detailed rules about when to recognize revenue from any conceivable activity, IFRS provides just four categories of revenue and two overall principles for timing recognition. This means that even the most basic accounting measure, revenue, is different under the two standards—Total Revenue, or Sales, under GAAP won't typically equal Total Revenue under IFRS. Thus, financial statements prepared under GAAP cannot be compared directly to IFRS financial statements, making comparative financial analysis of U.S. and international companies difficult. Perhaps more problematic is that the IFRS principles allow for more company

discretion in recording transactions. This means that two different companies may treat an identical transaction differently when using IFRS, which makes company-to-company comparisons more difficult.

The U.S. Financial Accounting Standards Board (FASB) and the International Accounting Standards Board (IASB) have been working to merge the two sets of standards since 2002. If the current timetable holds, the joint standards will be completed by the end of 2013, with adoption by U.S. firms possibly by 2015.

What does this mean for you? There will still be an income statement, a balance sheet, and an equivalent to the statement of cash flows. Line item summary measures may change a bit, and the technical details about how to record individual transactions will certainly change. Accounting systems will be reprogrammed, accounting texts will be rewritten, and CPAs will have to retrain. The end result, though, will be a better ability to compare U.S. and international companies' financial statements.

To keep abreast of developments in IFRS/GAAP convergence, visit the IASB Web site at **www.iasb.org** and the FASB Web site at **www.fasb.org**.

uncommon for a company to report positive net income right up to the day it declares bankruptcy. In such cases, however, the net cash flow from operations almost always began to deteriorate much earlier, and analysts who kept an eye on cash flow could have predicted trouble. Therefore, if you are ever analyzing a company and are pressed for time, look first at the trend in net cash flow provided by operating activities, because it will tell you more than any other single number.

The second section shows investing activities. MicroDrive purchased fixed assets totaling $500 million and sold $40 million of short-term investments, for a net cash flow from investing activities of *minus* $460 million.

The third section, financing activities, includes borrowing from banks (notes payable), selling new bonds, and paying dividends on common and preferred stock. MicroDrive raised $350 million by borrowing, but it paid $58 million in preferred and common dividends. Therefore, its net inflow of funds from financing activities was $292 million.

In the summary, when all of these sources and uses of cash are totaled, we see that MicroDrive's cash outflows exceeded its cash inflows by $10 million during 2013; that is, its net change in cash was a *negative* $10 million.

MicroDrive's statement of cash flows should be worrisome to its managers and to outside analysts. The company had $5 billion in sales but generated only $158 million from operations, not nearly enough to cover the $500 million it spent on fixed assets and the $58 million it paid in dividends. It covered these cash outlays by borrowing heavily and by liquidating short-term investments. Obviously, this situation cannot continue year after year, so MicroDrive managers will have to make changes. We will return to MicroDrive throughout the textbook to see what actions its managers are planning.

SELF-TEST

What types of questions does the statement of cash flows answer?

Identify and briefly explain the three categories of activities in the statement of cash flows.

A firm has inventories of $2 million for the previous year and $1.5 million for the current year. What impact does this have on net cash provided by operations? **(Increase of $500,000)**

2-6 Net Cash Flow

In addition to the cash flow from operations as defined in the statement of cash flows, many analysts use also calculate **net cash flow**, which is defined as:

$$\text{Net cash flow} = \text{Net income} - \text{Noncash revenues} + \text{Noncash expenses} \qquad (2\text{-}1)$$

where net income is the net income available for distribution to common shareholders. Depreciation and amortization usually are the largest noncash items, and in many cases the other noncash items roughly net out to zero. For this reason, many analysts assume that net cash flow equals net income plus depreciation and amortization:

$$\text{Net cash flow} = \text{Net income} + \text{Depreciation and amortization} \qquad (2\text{-}2)$$

We will generally assume that Equation 2-2 holds. However, you should remember that Equation 2-2 will not accurately reflect net cash flow when there are significant noncash items other than depreciation and amortization.

We can illustrate Equation 2-2 with 2013 data for MicroDrive taken from Figure 2-2:

$$\text{Net cash flow} = \$220 + \$200 = \$420 \text{ million}$$

You can think of net cash flow as the profit a company would have if it did not have to replace fixed assets as they wear out. This is similar to the net cash flow from operating activities shown on the statement of cash flows, except that the net cash flow from operating activities also includes the impact of working capital. Net income, net cash flow, and net cash flow from operating activities each provide insight into a company's financial health, but none is as useful as the measures we discuss in the next section.

SELF-TEST

Differentiate between net cash flow and accounting profit.

A firm has net income of $5 million. Assuming that depreciation of $1 million is its only noncash expense, what is the firm's net cash flow? **($6 million)**

2-7 Free Cash Flow: The Cash Flow Available for Distribution to Investors

So far in the chapter we have focused on financial statements as presented in the annual report. When you studied income statements in accounting, the emphasis was probably on the firm's net income. However, the intrinsic value of a company's operations is determined by the stream of cash flows that the operations will generate now and in the future. To be more specific, the value of operations depends on all the future expected **free cash flows (FCF)**, defined as after-tax operating profit minus the amount of new investment in working capital and fixed assets necessary to sustain the business. *Therefore, the way for managers to make their companies more valuable is to increase free cash flow now and in the future.*

Notice that FCF is the cash flow *available for distribution to all the company's investors after the company has made all investments necessary to sustain ongoing operations.* How successful were MicroDrive's managers in generating FCF? In this section, we will calculate MicroDrive's FCF and evaluate the performance of MicroDrive's managers.

Figure 2-5 shows the five steps in calculating free cash flow. As we explain each individual step in the following sections, refer back to Figure 2-1 to keep the big picture in mind.

2-7a Net Operating Profit after Taxes (NOPAT)

If two companies have different amounts of debt, thus different amounts of interest charges, they could have identical operating performances but different net incomes—the one with more debt would have a lower net income. Net income is important, but it

FIGURE **2-5**

Calculating Free Cash Flow

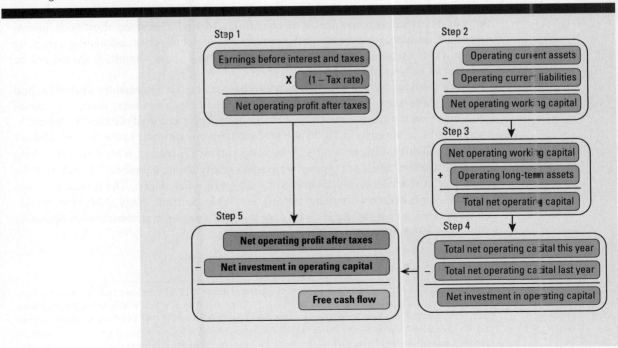

© Cengage Learning 2014

does not always reflect the true performance of a company's operations or the effectiveness of its managers. A better measure for comparing managers' performance is **net operating profit after taxes**, or **NOPAT**, which is the amount of profit a company would generate if it had no debt and held no financial assets. NOPAT is defined as follows:[7]

$$NOPAT = EBIT(1 - \text{Tax rate}) \qquad (2\text{-}3)$$

Using data from the income statements of Figure 2-2, MicroDrive's 2013 NOPAT is

$$NOPAT = \$500(1 - 0.4) = \$500(0.6) = \$300 \text{ million}$$

This means MicroDrive generated an after-tax operating profit of $300 million, less than its previous NOPAT of $550(0.6) = $330 million.

2-7b Net Operating Working Capital

Most companies need some current assets to support their operating activities. For example, all companies must carry some cash to "grease the wheels" of their operations. Companies continuously receive checks from customers and write checks to suppliers, employees, and so on. Because inflows and outflows do not coincide perfectly, a company must keep some cash in its bank account. In other words, it must have some cash to conduct operations. The same is true for most other current assets, such as inventory and accounts receivable, which are required for normal operations. The short-term assets normally used in a company's operating activities are called **operating current assets**.

Not all current assets are operating current assets. For example, holdings of short-term marketable securities generally result from investment decisions made by the treasurer and not as a natural consequence of operating activities. Therefore, short-term investments are **nonoperating assets** and normally are excluded when calculating operating current assets. A useful rule of thumb is that if an asset pays interest, it should not be classified as an operating asset.

In this textbook we will always distinguish between the cash needed for operations and the marketable securities held as short-term investments. However, many companies don't make such a clean distinction. For example, Apple reported almost $10 billion in cash for 2011, in addition to $16 billion in short-term investments. Apple certainly doesn't need $10 billion in cash to run its business operations. Therefore, if we were calculating operating current assets for Apple, we would classify about $2 billion as cash and the remainder as short-term investments: $10 − $2 + $16 = $24 billion. The reverse situation is possible, too, where a company reports very little cash but many short-term investments. In such a case we would classify some of the short-term investments as operating cash when calculating operating current assets.

---

[7]For firms with a more complicated tax situation, it is better to define NOPAT as follows: NOPAT = (Net income before preferred dividends) + (Net interest expense)(1 − Tax rate). Also, if a firm is able to defer paying some taxes, perhaps by the use of accelerated depreciation, then it needs to adjust NOPAT to reflect the taxes it actually paid on operating income. See P. Daves, M. Ehrhardt, and R. Shrieves, *Corporate Valuation: A Guide for Managers and Investors* (Mason, OH: Thomson South-Western, 2004) for a detailed explanation of these and other adjustments.

Some current liabilities—especially accounts payable and accruals—arise in the normal course of operations. Such short-term liabilities are called **operating current liabilities**. Not all current liabilities are operating current liabilities. For example, consider the current liability shown as notes payable to banks. The company could have raised an equivalent amount as long-term debt or could have issued stock, so the choice to borrow from the bank was a financing decision and not a consequence of operations. Again, the rule of thumb is that if a liability charges interest, it is not an operating liability.

If you are ever uncertain about whether an item is an operating asset or operating liability, ask yourself whether the item is a natural consequence of operations or if it is a discretionary choice, such as a particular method of financing or an investment in a particular financial asset. If it is discretionary, then the item is not an operating asset or liability.

Notice that each dollar of operating current liabilities is a dollar that the company does not have to raise from investors in order to conduct its short-term operating activities. Therefore, we define **net operating working capital (NOWC)** as operating current assets minus operating current liabilities. In other words, net operating working capital is the working capital acquired with investor-supplied funds. Here is the definition in equation form:

$$\text{Net operating working capital} = \text{Operating current assets} - \text{Operating current liabilities} \tag{2-4}$$

We can apply these definitions to MicroDrive, using the balance sheet data given in Figure 2-1. Here is its net operating working capital at year-end 2013:

$$\begin{aligned}\text{NOWC} &= \text{Operating current assets} - \text{Operating current liabilities}\\ &= (\text{Cash} + \text{Accounts receivable} + \text{Inventories})\\ &\quad - (\text{Accounts payable} + \text{Accruals})\\ &= (\$50 + \$500 + \$1,000) - (\$200 + \$300)\\ &= \$1,050 \text{ million}\end{aligned}$$

For the previous year, net operating working capital was

$$\begin{aligned}\text{NOWC} &= (\$60 + \$380 + \$820) - (\$190 + \$280)\\ &= \$790 \text{ million}\end{aligned}$$

2-7c Total Net Operating Capital

In addition to working capital, most companies also use long-term assets to support their operations. These include land, buildings, factories, equipment, and the like. **Total net operating capital** is the sum of NOWC and operating long-term assets:

$$\text{Total net operating capital} = \text{NOWC} + \text{Operating long-term assets} \tag{2-5}$$

Because MicroDrive's operating long-term assets consist only of net plant and equipment, its total net operating capital at year-end 2013 was

$$\begin{aligned}\text{Total net operating capital} &= \$1,050 + \$2,000\\ &= \$3,050 \text{ million}\end{aligned}$$

For the previous year, its total net operating capital was

$$\text{Total net operating capital} = \$790 + \$1,700$$
$$= \$2,490 \text{ million}$$

Notice that we have defined total net operating capital as the sum of net operating working capital and operating long-term assets. In other words, our definition is in terms of operating assets and liabilities. However, we can also calculate total net operating capital by looking at the sources of funds. **Total investor-supplied capital** is defined as the total of funds provided by investors, such as notes payable, long-term bonds, preferred stock, and common equity. For most companies, total investor-supplied capital is:

$$\begin{matrix} \text{Total investor-supplied} \\ \text{capital} \end{matrix} = \begin{matrix} \text{Notes} \\ \text{payable} \end{matrix} + \begin{matrix} \text{Long-term} \\ \text{bonds} \end{matrix} + \begin{matrix} \text{Preferred} \\ \text{stock} \end{matrix} + \begin{matrix} \text{Common} \\ \text{equity} \end{matrix} \qquad \textbf{(2-6)}$$

For MicroDrive, the total capital provided by investors at year-end 2012 was $130 + $1,000 + $100 + $1,300 = $2,530 million. Of this amount, $40 million was tied up in short-term investments, which are not directly related to MicroDrive's operations. Therefore, we define **total investor-supplied operating capital** as:

$$\begin{matrix} \text{Total investor-supplied} \\ \text{operating capital} \end{matrix} = \begin{matrix} \text{Total investor-supplied} \\ \text{operating capital} \end{matrix} - \begin{matrix} \text{Short-term} \\ \text{investments} \end{matrix} \qquad \textbf{(2-7)}$$

MicroDrive had $2,530 − $40 = $2,490 million of investor-supplied operating capital. Notice that this is exactly the same value as calculated before. Therefore, we can calculate total net operating capital either from net operating working capital and operating long-term assets or from the investor-supplied funds. We usually base our calculations on operating data because this approach allows us to analyze a division, factory, or work center. In contrast, the approach based on investor-supplied capital is applicable only for the entire company.

The expression "total net operating capital" is a mouthful, so we often call it *operating capital* or even just *capital.* Also, unless we specifically say "investor-supplied capital," we are referring to total net operating capital.

2-7d Net Investment in Operating Capital

As calculated previously, MicroDrive had $2,490 million of total net operating capital at the end of 2012 and $3,050 million at the end of 2013. Therefore, during 2013, it made a **net investment in operating capital** of

$$\text{Net investment in operating capital} = \$3,050 - \$2,490 = \$560 \text{ million}$$

Most of this investment was made in net operating working capital, which rose from $790 million to $1,050 million, or by $260 million. This 33% increase in net operating working capital, in view of a sales increase of only 5% (to $5 billion from $4.76 billion), should set off warning bells in your head: Why did MicroDrive tie up so much additional cash in working capital? Is the company gearing up for a big increase in sales, or are inventories not moving and receivables not being collected? We will address these questions in detail in Chapter 3, when we cover ratio analysis.

2-7e Calculating Free Cash Flow

Free cash flow is defined as

$$\text{FCF} = \text{NOPAT} - \text{Net investment in operating capital} \qquad (2\text{-}8)$$

MicroDrive's free cash flow in 2013 was

$$\begin{aligned} \text{FCF} &= \$300 - (\$3{,}050 - \$2{,}490) \\ &= \$300 - \$560 \\ &= -\$260 \text{ million} \end{aligned}$$

Although we prefer this approach to calculating FCF, sometimes the financial press calculates FCF differently:

$$\text{FCF} = \begin{bmatrix} \text{EBIT}(1-\text{T}) \\ + \text{Depreciation} \end{bmatrix} - \begin{bmatrix} \text{Gross investment} \\ \text{in fixed assets} \end{bmatrix} - \begin{bmatrix} \text{Investment} \\ \text{NOWC} \end{bmatrix} \qquad (2\text{-}9)$$

For MicroDrive, this calculation is:

$$\text{FCF} = (\$300 + \$200) - \$500 - (\$1{,}050 - \$790) = -\$260$$

Notice that the results are the same for either calculation. To see this, substitute NOPAT into the first bracket of Equation 2-9 and substitute the definition for net investment in fixed assets into the second bracket:

$$\text{FCF} = \begin{bmatrix} \text{NOPAT} \\ + \text{Depreciation} \end{bmatrix} - \begin{bmatrix} \text{Net investment} \\ \text{in fixed assets} \\ + \text{Depreciation} \end{bmatrix} - \begin{bmatrix} \text{Investment} \\ \text{NOWC} \end{bmatrix} \qquad (2\text{-}9a)$$

Both the first and second brackets have depreciation, so depreciation can be cancelled out, leaving

$$\text{FCF} = \text{NOPAT} - \begin{bmatrix} \text{Net investment} \\ \text{in fixed assets} \end{bmatrix} - \begin{bmatrix} \text{Investment} \\ \text{NOWC} \end{bmatrix} \qquad (2\text{-}9b)$$

The last two bracketed terms are equal to the net investment in operating capital, so Equation 2-9b simplifies to Equation 2-8. We usually use Equation 2-8 because it saves us the step of adding depreciation both to NOPAT and to the net investment in fixed assets.

2-7f The Uses of FCF

Recall that free cash flow (FCF) is the amount of cash that is available for distribution to all investors, including shareholders and debtholders. There are five good uses for FCF:

1. Pay interest to debtholders, keeping in mind that the net cost to the company is the after-tax interest expense.
2. Repay debtholders; that is, pay off some of the debt.

Sarbanes-Oxley and Financial Fraud

© Rob Webb/Getty Images

Investors need to be cautious when they review financial statements. Although companies are required to follow generally accepted accounting principles (GAAP), managers still use a lot of discretion in deciding how and when to report certain transactions. Consequently, two firms in the same operating situation may report financial statements that convey different impressions about their financial strength. Some variations may stem from legitimate differences of opinion about the correct way to record transactions. In other cases, managers may choose to report numbers in a way that helps them present either higher earnings or more stable earnings over time. As long as they follow GAAP, such actions are not illegal, but these differences make it harder for investors to compare companies and gauge their true performances.

Unfortunately, there have also been cases in which managers reported fraudulent statements. Indeed, a number of high-profile executives have faced criminal charges because of their misleading accounting practices. For example, in June 2002 it was discovered that WorldCom (now called MCI) had committed the most massive accounting fraud of all time by recording over $7 billion of ordinary operating costs as capital expenditures, thus overstating net income by the same amount.

WorldCom's published financial statements fooled most investors, who bid the stock price up to $64.50; and banks and other lenders provided the company with more than $30 billion of loans. Arthur Andersen, the firm's auditor, was faulted for not detecting the fraud. WorldCom's CFO and CEO were convicted, and Arthur Andersen went bankrupt. But these consequences didn't help the investors who relied on the published financial statements.

In response to these and other abuses, Congress passed the Sarbanes-Oxley Act of 2002. One of its provisions requires both the CEO and the CFO to sign a statement certifying that the "financial statements and disclosures fairly represent, in all material respects, the operations and financial condition" of the company. This will make it easier to haul off in handcuffs a CEO or CFO who has been misleading investors. Whether this will prevent future financial fraud remains to be seen.

3. Pay dividends to shareholders.
4. Repurchase stock from shareholders.
5. Buy short-term investments or other nonoperating assets.

Consider MicroDrive, with its FCF of −$260 million in 2013. How did MicroDrive use the FCF?

MicroDrive's income statement shows an interest expense of $120 million. With a tax rate of 40%, the after-tax interest payment for the year is

$$\text{After-tax interest payment} = \$120(1 - 40\%) = \$72 \text{ million}$$

The net amount of debt that is repaid is equal to the amount at the beginning of the year minus the amount at the end of the year. This includes notes payable and long-term debt. If the amount of ending debt is less than the beginning debt, the company paid down some of its debt. But if the ending debt is greater than the beginning debt, the company actually borrowed additional funds from creditors. In that case, it would be a negative use of FCF. For MicroDrive, the net debt repayment for 2012 is equal to the amount at the beginning of the year minus the amount at the end of the year:

$$\text{Net debt repayment} = (\$130 + \$1,000) - (\$280 + \$1,200) = -\$350 \text{ million}$$

This is a "negative use" of FCF because it increased the debt balance. This is typical of most companies because growing companies usually add debt each year.

MicroDrive paid $8 million in preferred dividends and $50 in common dividends for a total of

$$\text{Dividend payments} = \$8 + \$50 = \$58 \text{ million}$$

The net amount of stock that is repurchased is equal to the amount at the beginning of the year minus the amount at the end of the year. This includes preferred stock and common stock. If the amount of ending stock is less than the beginning stock, then the company made net repurchases. But if the ending stock is greater than the beginning stock, the company actually made net issuances. In that case, it would be a negative use of FCF. Even though MicroDrive neither issued nor repurchased stock during the year, many companies use FCF to repurchase stocks as a replacement for or supplement to dividends, as we discuss in Chapter 14.

The amount of net purchases of short-term investments is equal to the amount at the end of the year minus the amount at the beginning of the year. If the amount of ending investments is greater than the beginning investments, then the company made net purchases. But if the ending investments are less than the beginning investments, the company actually sold investments. In that case, it would be a negative use of FCF. MicroDrive's net purchases of short-term investments in 2013 are:

$$\text{Net purchases of short-term investments} = \$0 - \$40 = -\$40 \text{ million}$$

Notice that this is a "negative use" because MicroDrive sold short-term investments instead of purchasing them.

We combine these individual uses of FCF to find the total uses.

1. After-tax interest: $ 72
2. Net debt repayments: −350
3. Dividends: 58
4. Net stock repurchases: 0
5. Net purchases of ST investments: −40
      Total uses of FCF: −$260

As it should be, the −$260 total for uses of FCF is identical to the value of FCF from operations that we calculated previously.

Observe that a company does not use FCF to acquire operating assets, because the calculation of FCF already takes into account the purchase of operating assets needed to support growth. Unfortunately, there is evidence to suggest that some companies with high FCF tend to make unnecessary investments that don't add value, such as paying too much to acquire another company. Thus, high FCF can cause waste if managers fail to act in the best interests of shareholders. As discussed in Chapter 1, this is called an agency cost, because managers are hired as agents to act on behalf of stockholders. We discuss agency costs and ways to control them in Chapter 13, where we discuss value-based management and corporate governance, and in Chapter 15, where we discuss the choice of capital structure.

2-7g FCF and Corporate Value

Free cash flow is the amount of cash available for distribution to investors; so the fundamental value of a company to its investors depends on the present value of its expected future FCFs, discounted at the company's weighted average cost of capital (WACC). Subsequent chapters will develop the tools needed to forecast FCFs and evaluate their risk. Chapter 12 ties all this together with a model used to calculate the value of a company. Even though you do not yet have all the tools to apply the model, you must understand this basic concept: *FCF is the cash flow available for distribution to investors. Therefore, the fundamental value of a firm depends primarily on its expected future FCF.*

SELF-TEST

What is net operating working capital? Why does it exclude most short-term investments and notes payable?

What is total net operating capital? Why is it important for managers to calculate a company's capital requirements?

Why is NOPAT a better performance measure than net income?

What is free cash flow? Why is it important?

A firm's total net operating capital for the previous year was $2 million. For the current year, its total net operating capital is $2.5 million and its NOPAT is $1.2 million. What is its free cash flow for the current year? **($700,000)**

2-8 Performance Evaluation

Because free cash flow has such a big impact on value, managers and investors can use FCF and its components to measure a company's performance. The following sections explain three performance measures: return on invested capital, market value added, and economic value added.

2-8a The Return on Invested Capital

Even though MicroDrive had a positive NOPAT, its very high investment in operating assets caused a negative FCF. Is a negative free cash flow always bad? The answer is, "Not necessarily; it depends on why the free cash flow is negative." It's a bad sign if FCF is negative because NOPAT is negative, which probably means the company is experiencing operating problems. However, many high-growth companies have positive NOPAT but negative FCF because they are making large investments in operating assets to support growth. For example, Under Armour's sales grew by 38% in 2011 and its NOPAT grew by 42%; however, it made large capital investments to support that growth and ended the year with a FCF of *negative* $148 million.

There is nothing wrong with value-adding growth, even if it causes negative free cash flows, but it is vital to determine whether growth is actually adding value. For this we use the **return on invested capital (ROIC)**, which shows how much NOPAT is generated by each dollar of operating capital:

$$ROIC = \frac{NOPAT}{Operating\ capital} \tag{2-10}$$

As shown in Figure 2-6, in 2013 MicroDrive's ROIC is $300/$3,050 = 9.83%. To determine whether this ROIC is high enough to add value, compare it to the weighted average cost of capital (WACC). Chapter 9 explains how to calculate the WACC; for now accept that the WACC considers a company's individual risk as well as overall market conditions. Figure 2-6 shows that MicroDrive's 9.84% ROIC is less than its 11% WACC. Thus, MicroDrive did not generate a sufficient rate of return to compensate its investors for the risk they bore in 2013. This is markedly different from the previous year, in which MicroDrive's 13.25% ROIC was greater than its 10.5% WACC. Not only is the current ROIC too low, but the trend is in the wrong direction.

resource

*See **Ch02 Tool Kit.xls** for details.*

Although not the case for MicroDrive, in many situations a negative FCF is not necessarily bad. For example, Under Armour had a negative FCF in 2011, but its ROIC was about 16.2%. Because its WACC was only 12%, Under Armour's growth was adding

FIGURE 2-6

Calculating Performance Measures for MicroDrive Inc. (Millions of Dollars)

	A	B	C	D	E	F	G
						2013	2012
349							
350	*Calculating NOPAT*						
351	EBIT					$500	$550
352	x (1 – Tax rate)					60%	60%
353	NOPAT = EBIT(1 – T)					$300	$330
354							
355	*Calculating Net Operating Working Capital (NOWC)*						
356	Operating current assets					$1,550	$1,260
357	– Operating current liabilities					$500	$470
358	NOWC					$1,050	$790
359							
360	*Calculating Total Net Operating Capital*						
361	NOWC					$1,050	$790
362	+ Net plant and equipment					$2,000	$1,700
363	Total net operating capital					$3,050	$2,490
364							
365	*Calculating Return on Invested Capital (ROIC)*						
366	NOPAT					$300	$330
367	÷ Total net operating capital					$3,050	$2,490
368	ROIC = NOPAT/Total net operating capital					9.84%	13.25%
369	Weighted average cost of capital (WACC)					11.00%	10.50%
370							
371	*Calculating Market Value Added (MVA)*						
372	Price per share					$27	$40
373	x Number of shares (millions)					50	50
374	Market value of equity = P x (# of shares)					$1,350	$2,000
375	– Book value of equity					$1,470	$1,300
376	MVA = Market value – Book value					–$120	$700
377							
378	*Calculating Economic Value Added (EVA)*						
379	Total net operating capital					$3,050.0	$2,490.0
380	x Weighted average cost of capital (WACC)					11.0%	10.5%
381	Dollar cost of capital					$335.5	$261.5
382							
383	NOPAT					$300.0	$330.0
384	– Dollar cost of capital					$335.5	$261.5
385	EVA = NOPAT – Dollar cost of capital					–$35.5	$68.6

value.[8] At some point Under Armour's growth will slow, and it will not require such large capital investments. If Under Armour maintains a high ROIC, then its FCF will become positive and very large as growth slows.

Neither traditional accounting data nor return on invested capital incorporates stock prices, even though the primary goal of management should be to maximize the firm's intrinsic stock price. In contrast, Market Value Added (MVA) and Economic Value Added (EVA) do attempt to compare intrinsic measures with market measures.[9]

2-8b Market Value Added (MVA)

One measure of shareholder wealth is the *difference* between the market value of the firm's stock and the cumulative amount of equity capital that was supplied by shareholders. This difference is called the **Market Value Added (MVA)**:

$$
\begin{aligned}
\text{MVA} &= \text{Market value of stock–Equity capital supplied by shareholders} \\
&= (\text{Shares outstanding})(\text{Stock price})-\text{Total common equity}
\end{aligned}
\tag{2-11}
$$

For an updated estimate of Coca-Cola's MVA, go to **finance.yahoo.com**, enter KO, and click GO. This shows the market value of equity, called Mkt Cap. To get the book value of equity, select Balance Sheet from the left panel.

To illustrate, consider Coca-Cola. In February 2012, its total market equity value, commonly called market capitalization, was $157 billion, while its balance sheet showed that stockholders had put up only $32 billion. Thus, Coca-Cola's MVA was $157 − $32 = $125 billion. This $125 billion represents the difference between the money that Coca-Cola's stockholders have invested in the corporation since its founding—including indirect investment by retaining earnings—and the cash they could get if they sold the business. The higher its MVA, the better the job management is doing for the firm's shareholders.

Sometimes MVA is defined as the total market value of the company minus the total amount of investor-supplied capital:

$$
\begin{aligned}
\text{MVA} &= \text{Total market value} - \text{Total investor-supplied capital} \\
&= (\text{Market value of stock} + \text{Market value of debt}) \\
&\quad - \text{Total investor-supplied capital}
\end{aligned}
\tag{2-11a}
$$

For most companies, the total amount of investor-supplied capital is the sum of equity, debt, and preferred stock. We can calculate the total amount of investor-supplied capital directly from their reported values in the financial statements. The total market value of a company is the sum of the market values of common equity, debt, and preferred stock. It is easy to find the market value of equity because stock prices are readily available, but it is not always easy to find the market value of debt. Hence, many analysts use the value of debt reported in the financial statements, which is the debt's book value, as an estimate of the debt's market value.

---

[8]If g is the growth rate in capital, then with a little (or a lot of!) algebra, free cash flow is

$$
\text{FCF} = \text{Capital}\left(\text{ROIC} - \frac{g}{1+g}\right)
$$

This shows that when the growth rate gets almost as high as ROIC, then FCF will be negative.

[9]The concepts of EVA and MVA were developed by Joel Stern and Bennett Stewart, co-founders of the consulting firm Stern Stewart & Company. Stern Stewart copyrighted the terms "EVA" and "MVA," so other consulting firms have given other names to these values. Still, EVA and MVA are the terms most commonly used in practice.

For Coca-Cola, the total amount of reported debt was about $29 billion; Coca-Cola had no preferred stock. Using the debt's book value as an estimate of the debt's market value, Coke's total market value was $157 + $29 = $186 billion. The total amount of investor-supplied funds was $32 + $29 = $61 billion. Using these total values, the MVA was $186 − $61 = $125 billion. Note that this is the same answer as when we used the previous definition of MVA. Both methods will give the same result if the market value of debt is approximately equal to its book value.

Figure 2-6 shows that MicroDrive has 50 million shares of stock and a stock price of $27, giving it a market value of equity equal to $1,350 million. MicroDrive has $1,470 in book equity, so its MVA is $1,350 − $1,470 = −$120. In other words, MicroDrive's current market value is less than the cumulative amount of equity that its shareholders have invested during the company's life.

2-8c Economic Value Added (EVA)

Whereas MVA measures the effects of managerial actions since the inception of a company, **Economic Value Added (EVA)** focuses on managerial effectiveness in a given year. The EVA formula is:

$$\text{EVA} = \frac{\text{Net operating profit}}{\text{after taxes}} - \frac{\text{After-tax dollar cost of capital}}{\text{used to support operations}} \qquad (2\text{-}12)$$

$$= \text{NOPAT} - (\text{Total net operating capital})(\text{WACC})$$

Economic Value Added is an estimate of a business's true economic profit for the year, and it differs sharply from accounting profit.[10] EVA represents the residual income that remains after the cost of *all* capital, including equity capital, has been deducted, whereas accounting profit is determined without imposing a charge for equity capital. As we discuss in Chapter 9, equity capital has a cost because shareholders give up the opportunity to invest and earn returns elsewhere when they provide capital to the firm. This cost is an *opportunity cost* rather than an *accounting cost,* but it is real nonetheless.

Note that when calculating EVA we do not add back depreciation. Although it is not a cash expense, depreciation is a cost because worn-out assets must be replaced, and it is therefore deducted when determining both net income and EVA. Our calculation of EVA assumes that the true economic depreciation of the company's fixed assets exactly equals the depreciation used for accounting and tax purposes. If this were not the case, adjustments would have to be made to obtain a more accurate measure of EVA.

Economic Value Added measures the extent to which the firm has increased shareholder value. Therefore, if managers focus on EVA, they will more likely operate in a manner consistent with maximizing shareholder wealth. Note too that EVA can be determined for divisions as well as for the company as a whole, so it provides a useful basis for determining managerial performance at all levels. Consequently, many firms include EVA as a component of compensation plans.

---

[10]The most important reason EVA differs from accounting profit is that the cost of equity capital is deducted when EVA is calculated. Other factors that could lead to differences include adjustments that might be made to depreciation, to research and development costs, to inventory valuations, and so on. These other adjustments also can affect the calculation of investor-supplied capital, which affects both EVA and MVA. See G. Bennett Stewart, III, *The Quest for Value,* (New York: HarperCollins Publishers, Inc., 1991).

We can also calculate EVA in terms of ROIC:

$$\text{EVA} = (\text{Total net operating capital})(\text{ROIC} - \text{WACC}) \qquad (2\text{-}13)$$

As this equation shows, a firm adds value—that is, has a positive EVA—if its ROIC is greater than its WACC. If WACC exceeds ROIC, then growth can actually reduce a firm's value.

Using Equation 2-12, Figure 2-6 shows that MicroDrive's EVA is

$$\text{EVA} = \$300 - (\$3,050)(11\%) = \$300 - \$335.5 = -\$35.5 \text{ million}$$

This negative EVA reinforces our earlier conclusions that MicroDrive lost value in 2013 due to an erosion in its operating performance. In Chapter 12 we will determine MicroDrive's intrinsic value and explore ways in which MicroDrive can reverse its downward trend.

2-8d Intrinsic Value, MVA, and EVA

We will have more to say about both MVA and EVA later in the book, but we can close this section with two observations. First, there is a relationship between MVA and EVA, but it is not a direct one. If a company has a history of negative EVAs, then its MVA will probably be negative; conversely, its MVA probably will be positive if the company has a history of positive EVAs. However, the stock price, which is the key ingredient in the MVA calculation, depends more on expected future performance than on historical performance. Therefore, a company with a history of negative EVAs could have a positive MVA, provided investors expect a turnaround in the future.

The second observation is that when EVAs or MVAs are used to evaluate managerial performance as part of an incentive compensation program, EVA is the measure that is typically used. The reasons are: (1) EVA shows the value added during a given year, whereas MVA reflects performance over the company's entire life, perhaps even including times before the current managers were born, and (2) EVA can be applied to individual divisions or other units of a large corporation, whereas MVA must be applied to the entire corporation.

SELF-TEST

A company's NOPAT is $12 million and its total net operating capital is $100 million. What is the ROIC? **(12%)**

Define Market Value Added (MVA) and Economic Value Added (EVA).

How does EVA differ from accounting profit?

A firm has $100 million in total net operating capital. Its return on invested capital is 14%, and its weighted average cost of capital is 10%. What is its EVA? **($4 million)**

2-9 The Federal Income Tax System

The value of any financial asset (including stocks, bonds, and mortgages), as well as most real assets such as plants or even entire firms, depends on the after-tax stream of cash flows produced by the asset. The following sections describe the key features of corporate and individual taxation.

TABLE 2-1

Corporate Tax Rates as of January 2012

If a Corporation's Taxable Income Is	It Pays This Amount on the Base of the Bracket	Plus This Percentage on the Excess Over the Base	Average Tax Rate at Top of Bracket
Up to $50,000	$0	15%	15.0%
$50,000–$75,000	$7,500	25	18.3
$75,000–$100,000	$13,750	34	22.3
$100,000–$335,000	$22,250	39	34.0
$335,000–$10,000,000	$113,900	34	34.0
$10,000,000–$15,000,000	$3,400,000	35	34.3
$15,000,000–$18,333,333	$5,150,000	38	35.0
Over $18,333,333	$6,416,667	35	35.0

© Cengage Learning 2014

2-9a Corporate Income Taxes

The corporate tax structure, shown in Table 2-1, is relatively simple. The **marginal tax rate** is the rate paid on the last dollar of income, while the **average tax rate** is the average rate paid on all income. To illustrate, if a firm had $65,000 of taxable income, its tax bill would be

$$\text{Taxes} = \$7,500 + 0.25(\$65,000 - \$50,000)$$
$$= \$7,500 + \$3,750 = \$11,250$$

Its marginal rate would be 25%, and its average tax rate would be $11,250/$65,000 = 17.3%. Note that corporate income above $18,333,333 has an average and marginal tax rate of 35%.

INTEREST AND DIVIDEND INCOME RECEIVED BY A CORPORATION

Interest income received by a corporation is taxed as ordinary income at regular corporate tax rates. However, *70% of the dividends received by one corporation from another are excluded from taxable income, while the remaining 30% are taxed at the ordinary tax rate.*[11] Thus, a corporation earning more than $18,333,333 and paying a 35% marginal tax rate would pay only (0.30)(0.35) = 0.105 = 10.5% of its dividend income as taxes, so its effective tax rate on dividends received would be 10.5%. If this firm had $10,000 in pre-tax dividend income, then its after-tax dividend income would be $8,950:

$$\text{After-tax income} = \text{Before-tax income} - \text{Taxes}$$
$$= \text{Before-tax income} - (\text{Before-tax income})(\text{Effective tax rate})$$
$$= \text{Before-tax income}(1 - \text{Effective tax rate})$$
$$= \$10,000[1 - (0.30)(0.35)]$$
$$= \$10,000(1 - 0.105) = \$10,000(0.895) = \$8,950.$$

---

[11]The size of the dividend exclusion actually depends on the degree of ownership. Corporations that own less than 20% of the stock of the dividend-paying company can exclude 70% of the dividends received; firms that own more than 20% but less than 80% can exclude 80% of the dividends; and firms that own more than 80% can exclude the entire dividend payment. We will, in general, assume a 70% dividend exclusion.

If the corporation pays its own after-tax income out to stockholders as dividends, then the income is ultimately subject to *triple taxation:* (1) the original corporation is first taxed, (2) the second corporation is then taxed on the dividends it received, and (3) the individuals who receive the final dividends are taxed again. This is the reason for the 70% exclusion on intercorporate dividends.

If a corporation has surplus funds that can be invested in marketable securities, the tax treatment favors investment in stocks, which pay dividends, rather than in bonds, which pay interest. For example, suppose Home Depot had $100,000 to invest, and suppose it could buy either bonds that paid interest of $8,000 per year or preferred stock that paid dividends of $7,000. Home Depot is in the 35% tax bracket; therefore, its tax on the interest, if it bought bonds, would be 0.35($8,000) = $2,800, and its after-tax income would be $5,200. If it bought preferred (or common) stock, its tax would be 0.35[(0.30)($7,000)] = $735, and its after-tax income would be $6,265. Other factors might lead Home Depot to invest in bonds, but the tax treatment certainly favors stock investments when the investor is a corporation.[12]

Interest and Dividends Paid by a Corporation

A firm's operations can be financed with either debt or equity capital. If the firm uses debt, then it must pay interest on this debt, but if the firm uses equity, then it is expected to pay dividends to the equity investors (stockholders). The interest *paid* by a corporation is deducted from its operating income to obtain its taxable income, but dividends paid are not deductible. Therefore, a firm needs $1 of pre-tax income to pay $1 of interest, but if it is in the 40% federal-plus-state tax bracket, it must earn $1.67 of pre-tax income to pay $1 of dividends:

$$\text{Pre-tax income needed to pay \$1 of dividends} = \frac{\$1}{1 - \text{Tax rate}} = \frac{\$1}{0.60} = \$1.67$$

Working backward, if a company has $1.67 in pre-tax income, it must pay $0.67 in taxes: (0.4)($1.67) = $0.67. This leaves the firm with after-tax income of $1.00.

Of course, it is generally not possible to finance exclusively with debt capital, and the risk of doing so would offset the benefits of the higher expected income. Still, *the fact that interest is a deductible expense has a profound effect on the way businesses are financed: Our corporate tax system favors debt financing over equity financing.* This point is discussed in more detail in Chapters 9 and 15.

Corporate Capital Gains

Before 1987 corporate long-term capital gains were taxed at lower rates than corporate ordinary income, so the situation was similar for corporations and individuals. Under current law, however, corporations' capital gains are taxed at the same rates as their operating income.

---

[12]This illustration demonstrates why corporations favor investing in lower-yielding preferred stocks over higher-yielding bonds. When tax consequences are considered, the yield on the preferred stock, [1 − 0.35(0.30)](7.0%) = 6.265%, is higher than the yield on the bond, (1 − 0.35)(8.0%) = 5.2%. Also, note that corporations are restricted in their use of borrowed funds to purchase other firms' preferred or common stocks. Without such restrictions, firms could engage in *tax arbitrage,* whereby the interest on borrowed funds reduces taxable income on a dollar-for-dollar basis while taxable income is increased by only $0.30 per dollar of dividend income. Thus, current tax laws reduce the 70% dividend exclusion in proportion to the amount of borrowed funds used to purchase the stock.

When It Comes to Taxes, History Repeats and Repeals Itself!

© Rob Webb/Getty Images

Prior to 1987, many large corporations such as General Electric and Boeing paid no federal income taxes even though they reported profits. How could this happen? Some expenses, especially depreciation, were defined differently for calculating taxable income than for reporting earnings to stockholders. So some companies reported positive profits to stockholders but losses—hence no taxes—to the Internal Revenue Service. Also, some companies that otherwise would have paid taxes were able used various tax credits to avoid paying taxes.

The Tax Reform Act of 1986 eliminated many loopholes and tightened up provisions in the corporate Alternative Minimum Tax (AMT) code so that companies would not be able to utilize tax credits and accelerated depreciation to such an extent that their federal taxes fell below a certain minimum level.

Fast forward to the present. According to a report published in late 2011, General Electric and Boeing paid no federal income taxes in 2008, 2009, or 2010 even though they reported profits in each year. In fact, 30 companies with an average profit of over $1.7 billion per year paid no taxes during the 3-year study period. Of the 280 companies in the study, 97 paid 10% or less of their reported profit as federal income taxes. The average effective rate was less than 19%, much lower than the 35% rate shown in the corporate tax table. Only 25% of the companies in the study paid more than 30%. How did history repeat itself?

Over the years Congress gradually repealed many of the 1986 tax reforms and weakened the AMT, adding more and more loopholes and credits. Some of these breaks were for all firms, such as the 2008 acceleration of depreciation intended to stimulate corporate investment in the wake of the global economic crisis. Others were for specific industries, such as tax breaks for ethanol production that might help reduce reliance on imported oil. However, some of the changes appear difficult to justify, such as the 2010 tax breaks given to NASCAR track owners.

The net result is a complicated tax system in which corporations with shrewd accountants and well-connected lobbyists pay substantially less than other companies. As we write this in 2012, President Obama and leaders in Congress are calling for corporate tax reform.

Sources: Adapted from Robert S. McIntyre, Matthew Gardner, Rebecca J. Wilkins, and Richard Phillips "Corporate Taxpayers & Corporate Tax Dodgers 2008–10," *Joint Project of Citizens for Tax Justice & the Institute on Taxation and Economic Policy,* November 2011; see **www.ctj.org/corporatetaxdodgers/ CorporateTaxDodgers Report.pdf**.

CORPORATE LOSS CARRYBACK AND CARRYFORWARD

Ordinary corporate operating losses can be carried back (**carryback**) to each of the preceding 2 years and forward (**carryforward**) for the next 20 years and thus be used to offset taxable income in those years. For example, an operating loss in 2013 could be carried back and used to reduce taxable income in 2011 and 2012 as well as carried forward, if necessary, to reduce taxes in 2014, 2015, and so on, to the year 2033. After carrying back 2 years, any remaining loss is typically carried forward first to the next year, then to the one after that, and so on, until losses have been used up or the 20-year carryforward limit has been reached.

To illustrate, suppose Apex Corporation had $2 million of *pre-tax* profits (taxable income) in 2011 and 2012, and then, in 2013, Apex lost $12 million. Also, assume that Apex's federal-plus-state tax rate is 40%. As shown in Table 2-2, the company would use the carryback feature to recalculate its taxes for 2011, using $2 million of the 2013 operating losses to reduce the 2011 pre-tax profit to zero. This would permit it to recover the taxes paid in 2011. Therefore, in 2013 Apex would receive a refund of its 2011 taxes because of the loss experienced in 2013. Because $10 million of the unrecovered losses would still be available, Apex would repeat this procedure for 2012. Thus, in 2013 the

TABLE 2-2

Apex Corporation: Calculation of $12 Million Loss Carryback and Amount Available for Carryforward

	Past Year 2011	Past Year 2012	Current Year 2013
Original taxable income	$2,000,000	$2,000,000	–$12,000,000
Carryback credit	2,000,000	2,000,000	
Adjusted profit	$ 0	$ 0	
Taxes previously paid (40%)	800,000	800,000	
Difference = Tax refund due	$ 800,000	$ 800,000	
Total tax refund received			$ 1,600,000
Amount of loss carryforward available			
Current loss			–$12,000,000
Carryback losses used			4,000,000
Carryforward losses still available			–$ 8,000,000

© Cengage Learning 2014

company would pay zero taxes for 2013 and also would receive a refund for taxes paid in 2011 and 2012. Apex would still have $8 million of unrecovered losses to carry forward, subject to the 20-year limit. This $8 million could be used to offset future taxable income. The purpose of this loss treatment is to avoid penalizing corporations whose incomes fluctuate substantially from year to year.

resource

See *Ch02 Tool Kit.xls* for details.

IMPROPER ACCUMULATION TO AVOID PAYMENT OF DIVIDENDS

Corporations could refrain from paying dividends and thus permit their stockholders to avoid personal income taxes on dividends. To prevent this, the Tax Code contains an **improper accumulation** provision that states that earnings accumulated by a corporation are subject to penalty rates *if the purpose of the accumulation is to enable stockholders to avoid personal income taxes.* A cumulative total of $250,000 (the balance sheet item "retained earnings") is by law exempted from the improper accumulation tax for most corporations. This is a benefit primarily to small corporations.

The improper accumulation penalty applies only if the retained earnings in excess of $250,000 are *shown by the IRS to be unnecessary to meet the reasonable needs of the business.* A great many companies do indeed have legitimate reasons for retaining more than $250,000 of earnings. For example, firms may retain and use earnings to pay off debt, finance growth, or provide the corporation with a cushion against possible cash drains caused by losses. How much a firm should be allowed to accumulate for uncertain contingencies is a matter of judgment. We shall consider this matter again in Chapter 14, which deals with corporate dividend policy.

CONSOLIDATED CORPORATE TAX RETURNS

If a corporation owns 80% or more of another corporation's stock, then it can aggregate income and file one consolidated tax return; thus, the losses of one company can be used to offset the profits of another. (Similarly, one division's losses can be used to offset another division's profits.) No business ever wants to incur losses (you can go broke losing $1 to save 35¢ in taxes), but tax offsets do help make it more feasible for large, multi-divisional corporations to undertake risky new ventures or ventures that will suffer losses during a developmental period.

TAXES ON OVERSEAS INCOME

Many U.S. corporations have overseas subsidiaries, and those subsidiaries must pay taxes in the countries where they operate. Often, foreign tax rates are lower than U.S. rates. As long as foreign earnings are reinvested overseas, no U.S. tax is due on those earnings. However, when foreign earnings are repatriated to the U.S. parent, they are taxed at the applicable U.S. rate, less a credit for taxes paid to the foreign country. As a result, U.S. corporations such as IBM, Coca-Cola, and Microsoft have been able to defer billions of dollars of taxes. This procedure has stimulated overseas investments by U.S. multinational firms—they can continue the deferral indefinitely, but only if they reinvest the earnings in their overseas operations.[13]

2-9b Taxation of Small Businesses: S Corporations

The Tax Code provides that small businesses that meet certain restrictions may be set up as corporations and thus receive the benefits of the corporate form of organization—especially limited liability—yet still be taxed as proprietorships or partnerships rather than as corporations. These corporations are called **S corporations**. ("Regular" corporations are called C corporations.) If a corporation elects S corporation status for tax purposes, then all of the business's income is reported as personal income by its stockholders, on a pro rata basis, and thus is taxed at the rates that apply to individuals. This is an important benefit to the owners of small corporations in which all or most of the income earned each year will be distributed as dividends, because then the income is taxed only once, at the individual level.

2-9c Personal Taxes

Web Extension 2A provides a more detailed treatment of individual taxation, but the key elements are presented here. **Ordinary income** consists primarily of wages or profits from a proprietorship or partnership, plus investment income. For the 2012 tax year, individuals with less than $8,700 of taxable income are subject to a federal income tax rate of 10%. For those with higher income, tax rates increase and go up to 35%, depending on the level of income. This is called a **progressive tax**, because the higher one's income, the larger the percentage paid in taxes.

resource

See Web Extension 2A on the textbook's Web site for details concerning personal taxation.

As noted before, individuals are taxed on investment income as well as earned income, but with a few exceptions and modifications. For example, interest received from most state and local government bonds, called **municipals** or **munis**, is not subject to federal taxation. However, interest earned on most other bonds or lending is taxed as ordinary income. This means that a lower-yielding muni can provide the same after-tax return as a higher-yielding corporate bond. For a taxpayer in the 35% marginal tax bracket, a muni yielding 5.5% provides the same after-tax return as a corporate bond with a pre-tax yield of 8.46%: 8.46%(1 − 0.35) = 5.5%.

---

[13]This is a contentious political issue. U.S. corporations argue that our tax system is similar to systems in the rest of the world, and if they were taxed immediately on all overseas earnings then they would be at a competitive disadvantage vis-à-vis their global competitors. Others argue that taxation encourages overseas investments at the expense of domestic investments, contributing to the jobs-outsourcing problem and also to the federal budget deficit.

Assets such as stocks, bonds, and real estate are defined as capital assets. If you own a capital asset and its price goes up, then your wealth increases, but you are not liable for any taxes on your increased wealth until you sell the asset. If you sell the asset for more than you originally paid, the profit is called a **capital gain**; if you sell it for less, then you suffer a **capital loss**. The length of time you owned the asset determines the tax treatment. If held for less than 1 year, then your gain or loss is simply added to your other ordinary income. If held for more than a year, then gains are called *long-term capital gains* and are taxed at a lower rate. See *Web Extension 2A* for details, but the long-term capital gains rate is 15% for most situations.

Under the 2003 tax law changes, dividends are now taxed as though they are capital gains. As stated earlier, corporations may deduct interest payments but not dividends when computing their corporate tax liability, which means that dividends are taxed twice, once at the corporate level and again at the personal level. This differential treatment motivates corporations to use debt relatively heavily and to pay small (or even no) dividends. The 2003 tax law did not eliminate the differential treatment of dividends and interest payments from the corporate perspective, but it did make the tax treatment of dividends more similar to that of capital gains from investors' perspectives. To see this, consider a company that doesn't pay a dividend but instead reinvests the cash it could have paid. The company's stock price should increase, leading to a capital gain, which would be taxed at the same rate as the dividend. Of course, the stock price appreciation isn't actually taxed until the stock is sold, whereas the dividend is taxed in the year it is paid, so dividends will still be more costly than capital gains for many investors.

Finally, note that the income of S corporations *and* noncorporate businesses is reported as income by the firms' owners. Because there are far more S corporations, partnerships, and proprietorships than C corporations (which are subject to the corporate tax), individual tax considerations play an important role in business finance.

SELF-TEST

Explain what is meant by this statement: "Our tax rates are progressive."

If a corporation has $85,000 in taxable income, what is its tax liability? **($17,150)**

Explain the difference between marginal tax rates and average tax rates.

What are municipal bonds, and how are these bonds taxed?

What are capital gains and losses, and how are they taxed?

How does the federal income tax system treat dividends received by a corporation versus those received by an individual?

What is the difference in the tax treatment of interest and dividends paid by a corporation? Does this factor favor debt or equity financing?

Briefly explain how tax loss carryback and carryforward procedures work.

SUMMARY

- The four basic statements contained in the **annual report** are the balance sheet, the income statement, the statement of stockholders' equity, and the statement of cash flows.
- The **balance sheet** shows assets and liabilities and equity, or claims against assets. The balance sheet may be thought of as a snapshot of the firm's financial position at a particular point in time.

- The **income statement** reports the results of operations over a period of time, and it shows earnings per share as its "bottom line."
- The **statement of stockholders' equity** shows the change in stockholders' equity, including the change in retained earnings, between balance sheet dates. Retained earnings represent a claim against assets, not assets per se.
- The **statement of cash flows** reports the effect of operating, investing, and financing activities on cash flows over an accounting period.
- **Net cash flow** differs from **accounting profit** because some of the revenues and expenses reflected in accounting profits may not have been received or paid out in cash during the year. Depreciation is typically the largest noncash item, so net cash flow is often expressed as net income plus depreciation.
- **Operating current assets** are the current assets that are used to support operations, such as cash, inventory, and accounts receivable. They do not include short-term investments.
- **Operating current liabilities** are the current liabilities that occur as a natural consequence of operations, such as accounts payable and accruals. They do not include notes payable or any other short-term debts that charge interest.
- **Net operating working capital** is the difference between operating current assets and operating current liabilities. Thus, it is the working capital acquired with investor-supplied funds.
- **Operating long-term assets** are the long-term assets used to support operations, such as net plant and equipment. They do not include any long-term investments that pay interest or dividends.
- **Total net operating capital** (which means the same as **operating capital** and **net operating assets**) is the sum of net operating working capital and operating long-term assets. It is the total amount of capital needed to run the business.
- **NOPAT** is net operating profit after taxes. It is the after-tax profit a company would have if it had no debt and no investments in nonoperating assets. Because NOPAT excludes the effects of financial decisions, it is a better measure of operating performance than is net income.
- **Return on Invested Capital (ROIC)** is equal to NOPAT divided by total net operating capital. It measures the rate of return that the operations are generating. It is the best measure of operating performance.
- **Free cash flow (FCF)** is the amount of cash flow remaining after a company makes the asset investments necessary to support operations. In other words, FCF is the amount of cash flow available for distribution to investors, so *the value of a company is directly related to its ability to generate free cash flow*. FCF is defined as NOPAT minus the net investment in operating capital.
- **Market Value Added (MVA)** represents the difference between the total market value of a firm and the total amount of investor-supplied capital. If the market values of debt and preferred stock equal their values as reported on the financial statements, then MVA is the difference between the market value of a firm's stock and the amount of equity its shareholders have supplied.
- **Economic Value Added (EVA)** is the difference between after-tax operating profit and the total dollar cost of capital, including the cost of equity capital. EVA is an estimate of the value created by management during the year, and it differs substantially from accounting profit because no charge for the use of equity capital is reflected in accounting profit.

- Interest income received by a corporation is taxed as **ordinary income**; however, 70% of the dividends received by one corporation from another are excluded from **taxable income**.
- Because interest paid by a corporation is a **deductible expense** whereas dividends are not, our tax system favors debt over equity financing.
- Ordinary corporate operating losses can be **carried back** to each of the preceding 2 years and **carried forward** for the next 20 years in order to offset taxable income in those years.
- **S corporations** are small businesses that have the limited-liability benefits of the corporate form of organization yet are taxed as partnerships or proprietorships.
- In the United States, tax rates are **progressive**—the higher one's income, the larger the percentage paid in taxes.
- Assets such as stocks, bonds, and real estate are defined as **capital assets**. If a capital asset is sold for more than its cost, the profit is called a **capital gain**; if the asset is sold for a loss, it is called a **capital loss**. Assets held for more than a year provide **long-term gains** or **losses**.
- Dividends are taxed as though they were capital gains.
- **Personal taxes** are discussed in more detail in **Web Extension 2A**.

QUESTIONS

(2-1) Define each of the following terms:

   a. Annual report; balance sheet; income statement
   b. Common stockholders' equity, or net worth; retained earnings
   c. Statement of stockholders' equity; statement of cash flows
   d. Depreciation; amortization; EBITDA
   e. Operating current assets; operating current liabilities; net operating working capital; total net operating capital
   f. Accounting profit; net cash flow; NOPAT; free cash flow; return on invested capital
   g. Market Value Added; Economic Value Added
   h. Progressive tax; taxable income; marginal and average tax rates
   i. Capital gain or loss; tax loss carryback and carryforward
   j. Improper accumulation; S corporation

(2-2) What four statements are contained in most annual reports?

(2-3) If a "typical" firm reports $20 million of retained earnings on its balance sheet, can the firm definitely pay a $20 million cash dividend?

(2-4) Explain the following statement: "Whereas the balance sheet can be thought of as a snapshot of the firm's financial position *at a point in time,* the income statement reports on operations *over a period of time.*"

(2-5) What is operating capital, and why is it important?

(2-6) Explain the difference between NOPAT and net income. Which is a better measure of the performance of a company's operations?

(2-7) What is free cash flow? Why is it the most important measure of cash flow?

(2-8) If you were starting a business, what tax considerations might cause you to prefer to set it up as a proprietorship or a partnership rather than as a corporation?

SELF-TEST PROBLEM   Solution Appears in Appendix A

(ST-1)

Net Income, Cash Flow, and EVA

Last year Cole Furnaces had $5 million in operating income (EBIT). The company had a net depreciation expense of $1 million and an interest expense of $1 million; its corporate tax rate was 40%. The company has $14 million in operating current assets and $4 million in operating current liabilities; it has $15 million in net plant and equipment. It estimates that it has an after-tax cost of capital of 10%. Assume that Cole's only noncash item was depreciation.

a. What was the company's net income for the year?
b. What was the company's net cash flow?
c. What was the company's net operating profit after taxes (NOPAT)?
d. Calculate net operating working capital and total net operating capital for the current year.
e. If total net operating capital in the previous year was $24 million, what was the company's free cash flow (FCF) for the year?
f. What was the return on invested capital?
g. What was the company's Economic Value Added (EVA)?

PROBLEMS   Answers Appear in Appendix B

Note: By the time this book is published, Congress may have changed rates and/or other provisions of current tax law as noted in the chapter, as such changes occur fairly often. Work all problems on the assumption that the information in the chapter is applicable.

Easy Problems 1–6

(2-1)

Personal After-Tax Yield

An investor recently purchased a corporate bond that yields 9%. The investor is in the 36% combined federal and state tax bracket. What is the bond's after-tax yield?

(2-2)

Personal After-Tax Yield

Corporate bonds issued by Johnson Corporation currently yield 8%. Municipal bonds of equal risk currently yield 6%. At what tax rate would an investor be indifferent between these two bonds?

(2-3)

Income Statement

Molteni Motors Inc. recently reported $6 million of net income. Its EBIT was $13 million, and its tax rate was 40%. What was its interest expense? (*Hint:* Write out the headings for an income statement, and then fill in the known values. Then divide $6 million net income by $1 - T = 0.6$ to find the pre-tax income. The difference between EBIT and taxable income must be the interest expense. Use this procedure to work some of the other problems.)

(2-4)

Income Statement

Talbot Enterprises recently reported an EBITDA of $8 million and net income of $2.4 million. It had $2.0 million of interest expense, and its corporate tax rate was 40%. What was its charge for depreciation and amortization?

(2-5)

Net Cash Flow

Kendall Corners Inc. recently reported net income of $3.1 million and depreciation of $500,000. What was its net cash flow? Assume it had no amortization expense.

(2-6)

Statement of Retained Earnings

In its most recent financial statements, Del-Castillo Inc. reported $70 million of net income and $900 million of retained earnings. The previous retained earnings were $855 million. How much in dividends did the firm pay to shareholders during the year?

(2-7)
Corporate Tax Liability

The Talley Corporation had a taxable income of $365,000 from operations after all operating costs but before (1) interest charges of $50,000, (2) dividends received of $15,000, (3) dividends paid of $25,000, and (4) income taxes. What are the firm's income tax liability and its after-tax income? What are the company's marginal and average tax rates on taxable income?

(2-8)
Corporate Tax Liability

The Wendt Corporation had $10.5 million of taxable income.

a. What is the company's federal income tax bill for the year?

b. Assume the firm receives an additional $1 million of interest income from some bonds it owns. What is the tax on this interest income?

c. Now assume that Wendt does not receive the interest income but does receive an additional $1 million as dividends on some stock it owns. What is the tax on this dividend income?

(2-9)
Corporate After-Tax Yield

The Shrieves Corporation has $10,000 that it plans to invest in marketable securities. It is choosing among AT&T bonds, which yield 7.5%, state of Florida muni bonds, which yield 5% (but are not taxable), and AT&T preferred stock, with a dividend yield of 6%. Shrieves's corporate tax rate is 35%, and 70% of the dividends received are tax exempt. Find the after-tax rates of return on all three securities.

(2-10)
Net Cash Flows

The Moore Corporation has operating income (EBIT) of $750,000. The company's depreciation expense is $200,000. Moore is 100% equity financed, and it faces a 40% tax rate. What is the company's net income? What is its net cash flow?

(2-11)
Income and Cash Flow Analysis

The Berndt Corporation expects to have sales of $12 million. Costs other than depreciation are expected to be 75% of sales, and depreciation is expected to be $1.5 million. All sales revenues will be collected in cash, and costs other than depreciation must be paid for during the year. Berndt's federal-plus-state tax rate is 40%. Berndt has no debt.

a. Set up an income statement. What is Berndt's expected net cash flow?

b. Suppose Congress changed the tax laws so that Berndt's depreciation expenses doubled. No changes in operations occurred. What would happen to reported profit and to net cash flow?

c. Now suppose that Congress changed the tax laws such that, instead of doubling Berndt's depreciation, it was reduced by 50%. How would profit and net cash flow be affected?

d. If this were your company, would you prefer Congress to cause your depreciation expense to be doubled or halved? Why?

(2-12)
Free Cash Flows

Using Rhodes Corporation's financial statements (shown below), answer the following questions.

a. What is the net operating profit after taxes (NOPAT) for 2013?

b. What are the amounts of net operating working capital for both years?

c. What are the amounts of total net operating capital for both years?

d. What is the free cash flow for 2013?

e. What is the ROIC for 2013?

f. How much of the FCF did Rhodes use for each of the following purposes: after-tax interest, net debt repayments, dividends, net stock repurchases, and net purchases of short-term investments? (*Hint:* Remember that a net use can be negative.)

Rhodes Corporation: Income Statements for Year Ending December 31 (Millions of Dollars)

	2013	2012
Sales	$11,000	$10,000
Operating costs excluding depreciation	9,360	8,500
Depreciation and amortization	380	360
Earnings before interest and taxes	$ 1,260	$ 1,140
Less interest	120	100
Pre-tax income	$ 1,140	$ 1,040
Taxes (40%)	456	416
Net income available to common stockholders	$ 684	$ 624
Common dividends	$ 220	$ 200

Rhodes Corporation: Balance Sheets as of December 31 (Millions of Dollars)

	2013	2012
Assets		
Cash	$ 550	$ 500
Short-term investments	110	100
Accounts receivable	2,750	2,500
Inventories	1,650	1,500
Total current assets	$5,060	$4,600
Net plant and equipment	3,850	3,500
Total assets	$8,910	$8,100
Liabilities and Equity		
Accounts payable	$1,100	$1,000
Accruals	550	500
Notes payable	384	200
Total current liabilities	$2,034	$1,700
Long-term debt	1,100	1,000
Total liabilities	$3,134	$2,700
Common stock	4,312	4,400
Retained earnings	1,464	1,000
Total common equity	$5,776	$5,400
Total liabilities and equity	$8,910	$8,100

(2-13)
Loss Carryback and Carryforward
The Bookbinder Company has made $150,000 before taxes during each of the last 15 years, and it expects to make $150,000 a year before taxes in the future. However, in 2013 the firm incurred a loss of $650,000. The firm will claim a tax credit at the time it files its 2013 income tax return, and it will receive a check from the U.S. Treasury. Show how it calculates this credit, and then indicate the firm's tax liability for each of the next 5 years. Assume a 40% tax rate on *all* income to ease the calculations.

SPREADSHEET PROBLEMS

(2-14)

Build a Model:
Financial
Statements, EVA,
and MVA

resource

Begin with the partial model in the file *Ch02 P14 Build a Model.xls* on the textbook's *Web site.*

a. The 2013 sales of Cumberland Industries were $455,000,000; operating costs (excluding depreciation) were equal to 85% of sales; net fixed assets were $67,000,000; depreciation amounted to 10% of net fixed assets; interest expenses were $8,550,000; the state-plus-federal corporate tax rate was 40%; and Cumberland paid 25% of its net income out in dividends. Given this information, construct Cumberland's 2013 income statement. Also calculate total dividends and the addition to retained earnings. (*Hint:* Start with the partial model in the file and report all dollar figures in thousands to reduce clutter.)

b. The partial balance sheets of Cumberland Industries are shown below. Cumberland issued $10,000,000 of new common stock in 2013. Using this information and the results from part a, fill in the missing values for common stock, retained earnings, total common equity, and total liabilities and equity.

Cumberland Industries: Balance Sheets as of December 31 (Thousands of Dollars)

	2013	2012
Assets		
Cash	$ 91,450	$ 74,625
Short-term investments	11,400	15,100
Accounts receivable	108,470	85,527
Inventories	38,450	34,982
Total current assets	$249,770	$210,234
Net fixed assets	67,000	42,436
Total assets	$316,770	$252,670
Liabilities and Equity		
Accounts payable	$ 30,761	$ 23,109
Accruals	30,405	22,656
Notes payable	12,717	14,217
Total current liabilities	$ 73,883	$ 59,982
Long-term debt	80,263	63,914
Total liabilities	$154,146	$123,896
Common stock	?	$ 90,000
Retained earnings	?	38,774
Total common equity	?	$128,774
Total liabilities and equity	?	$252,670

c. Construct the statement of cash flows for 2013.

(2-15)

Build a Model: Free
Cash Flows, EVA,
and MVA

r e s o u r c e

Begin with the partial model in the file *Ch02 P15 Build a Model.xls* on the textbook's Web site.

a. Using the financial statements shown below for Lan & Chen Technologies, calculate net operating working capital, total net operating capital, net operating profit after taxes, free cash flow, and return on invested capital for 2013. (*Hint:* Start with the partial model in the file and report all dollar figures in thousands to reduce clutter.)

b. Assume there were 15 million shares outstanding at the end of 2013, the year-end closing stock price was $65 per share, and the after-tax cost of capital was 8%. Calculate EVA and MVA for 2013.

Lan & Chen Technologies: Income Statements for Year Ending December 31 (Thousands of Dollars)

	2013	2012
Sales	$945,000	$900,000
Expenses excluding depreciation and amortization	812,700	774,000
EBITDA	$132,300	$126,000
Depreciation and amortization	33,100	31,500
EBIT	$ 99,200	$ 94,500
Interest expense	10,470	8,600
Pre-tax earnings	$ 88,730	$ 85,900
Taxes (40%)	35,492	34,360
Net income	$ 53,238	$ 51,540
Common dividends	$ 43,300	$ 41,230
Addition to retained earnings	$ 9,938	$ 10,310

Lan & Chen Technologies: December 31 Balance Sheets

	2013	2012
Assets		
Cash and cash equivalents	$ 47,250	$ 45,000
Short-term investments	3,800	3,600
Accounts receivable	283,500	270,000
Inventories	141,750	135,000
Total current assets	$476,300	$453,600
Net fixed assets	330,750	315,000
Total assets	$807,050	$768,600
Liabilities and Equity		
Accounts payable	$ 94,500	$ 90,000
Accruals	47,250	45,000
Notes payable	26,262	9,000
Total current liabilities	$168,012	$144,000
Long-term debt	94,500	90,000
Total liabilities	$262,512	$234,000
Common stock	444,600	444,600
Retained earnings	99,938	90,000
Total common equity	$544,538	$534,600
Total liabilities and equity	$807,050	$768,600

THOMSON ONE Business School Edition Problem

THOMSON REUTERS   Use the Thomson ONE—Business School Edition online database to work this chapter's questions.

Exploring Starbucks's Financial Statements with Thomson ONE—Business School Edition

Over the past decade, Starbucks coffee shops have become an increasingly familiar part of the urban landscape. The Thomson ONE—Business School Edition online database can provide a wealth of financial information for companies such as Starbucks. Begin by entering the company's ticker symbol, SBUX, and then selecting GO. The opening screen includes a summary of what Starbucks does, a chart of its recent stock price, EPS estimates, some recent news stories, and a list of key financial data and ratios.

For recent stock price performance, look at the top of the Stock Price Chart and click on the section labeled Interactive Chart. From this point, we are able to obtain a chart of the company's stock price performance relative to the overall market, as measured by the S&P 500. To obtain a 10-year chart, go to Time Frame, click on the down arrow, and select 10 years. Then click on Draw, and a 10-year price chart should appear.

You can also find Starbucks's recent financial statements. On the left side of your screen, click on the Financials tab to find the company's balance sheet, income statement, and statement of cash flows for the past 5 years. Clicking on the Microsoft *Excel* icon downloads these statements directly to a spreadsheet.

Thomson ONE—BSE Discussion Questions

1. Looking at the most recent year available, what is the amount of total assets on Starbucks's balance sheet? What percentage is fixed assets, such as plant and equipment, and what percentage is current assets? How much has the company grown over the years shown?
2. Does Starbucks have a lot of long-term debt? What are Starbucks's primary sources of financing?
3. Looking at the statement of cash flows, what factors can explain the change in the company's cash position over the last couple of years?
4. Looking at the income statement, what are the company's most recent sales and net income? Over the past several years, what has been the sales growth rate? What has been the growth rate in net income?

MINI CASE

Jenny Cochran, a graduate of the University of Tennessee with 4 years of experience as an equities analyst, was recently brought in as assistant to the chairman of the board of Computron Industries, a manufacturer of computer components.

The company doubled its plant capacity, opened new sales offices outside its home territory, and launched an expensive advertising campaign. Computron's results were not satisfactory, to put it mildly. Its board of directors, which consisted of its president and vice president plus its major stockholders (who were all local businesspeople), was most upset when directors learned how the expansion was going. Suppliers were being paid late and were unhappy, and the bank was complaining about the deteriorating situation and threatening to cut off credit. As a result, Robert Edwards, Computron's president, was informed that changes would have to be made—and quickly—or he would be fired. At the board's insistence, Jenny Cochran was given the job of assistant to Gary Meissner, a retired banker who was Computron's chairman and largest stockholder. Meissner agreed to give up a few of his golfing days and to help nurse the company back to health, with Cochran's assistance.

Cochran began by gathering financial statements and other data. Note: these are available in the file *Ch02 Tool Kit.xls* in the *Mini Case* tab.

	2012	2013
Balance Sheets		
Assets		
Cash	$ 9,000	$ 7,282
Short-term investments	48,600	20,000
Accounts receivable	351,200	632,160
Inventories	715,200	1,287,360
Total current assets	$1,124,000	$1,946,802
Gross fixed assets	491,000	1,202,950
Less: Accumulated depreciation	146,200	263,160
Net fixed assets	$ 344,800	$ 939,790
Total assets	$1,468,800	$2,886,592
Liabilities and Equity		
Accounts payable	$ 145,600	$ 324,000
Notes payable	200,000	720,000
Accruals	136,000	284,960
Total current liabilities	$ 481,600	$1,328,960
Long-term debt	323,432	1,000,000
Common stock (100,000 shares)	460,000	460,000
Retained earnings	203,768	97,632
Total equity	$ 663,768	$ 557,632
Total liabilities and equity	$1,468,800	$2,886,592

	2012	2013
Income Statements		
Sales	$3,432,000	$ 5,834,400
Cost of goods sold	2,864,000	4,980,000
Other expenses	340,000	720,000
Depreciation and amortization	18,900	116,960
Total operating costs	$3,222,900	$ 5,816,960
EBIT	$ 209,100	$ 17,440
Interest expense	62,500	176,000
Pre-tax earnings	$ 146,600	($ 158,560)
Taxes (40%)	58,640	(63,424)
Net income	$ 87,960	($ 95,136)

Other Data		2012		2013
Stock price	$	8.50	$	6.00
Shares outstanding		100,000		100,000
EPS	$	0.880	($	0.951)
DPS	$	0.220	$	0.110
Tax rate		40%		40%

	2013
Statement of Cash Flows	
Operating Activities	
Net income	($ 95,136)
Adjustments:	
Noncash adjustments:	
Depreciation and amortization	116,960
Changes in working capital:	
Change in accounts receivable	(280,960)
Change in inventories	(572,160)
Change in accounts payable	178,400
Change in accruals	148,960
Net cash provided (used) by operating activities	($ 503,936)
Investing Activities	
Cash used to acquire fixed assets	($ 711,950)
Change in short-term investments	28,600
Net cash provided (used) by investing activities	($ 683,350)
Financing Activities	
Change in notes payable	$ 520,000
Change in long-term debt	676,568
Change in common stock	—
Payment of cash dividends	(11,000)
Net cash provided (used) by financing activities	$1,185,568
Summary	
Net change in cash	($ 1,718)
Cash at beginning of year	9,000
Cash at end of year	$ 7,282

Assume that you are Cochran's assistant and that you must help her answer the following questions for Meissner.

a. What effect did the expansion have on sales and net income? What effect did the expansion have on the asset side of the balance sheet? What effect did it have on liabilities and equity?

b. What do you conclude from the statement of cash flows?

c. What is free cash flow? Why is it important? What are the five uses of FCF?

    d. What is Computron's net operating profit after taxes (NOPAT)? What are operating current assets? What are operating current liabilities? How much net operating working capital and total net operating capital does Computron have?

    e. What is Computron's free cash flow (FCF)? What are Computron's "net uses" of its FCF?

    f. Calculate Computron's return on invested capital. Computron has a 10% cost of capital (WACC). Do you think Computron's growth added value?

    g. Cochran also has asked you to estimate Computron's EVA. She estimates that the after-tax cost of capital was 10% in both years.

    h. What happened to Computron's Market Value Added (MVA)?

    i. Assume that a corporation has $100,000 of taxable income from operations plus $5,000 of interest income and $10,000 of dividend income. What is the company's federal tax liability?

    j. Assume that you are in the 25% marginal tax bracket and that you have $5,000 to invest. You have narrowed your investment choices down to California bonds with a yield of 7% or equally risky ExxonMobil bonds with a yield of 10%. Which one should you choose and why? At what marginal tax rate would you be indifferent to the choice between California and ExxonMobil bonds?

© Adalberto Rios Szalay/Sexto Sol/Getty Images

CHAPTER **3**

Analysis of Financial Statements

Macy's, a large department store retailer, announced its fourth quarter 2011 results of $1.74 earnings per share (EPS). According to Zacks .com's Earnings Scorecard, Macy's EPS came in a little higher than analysts' estimates of $1.65. Perhaps not surprisingly, Macy's stock return during the 5-day period centered on its announcement date was positive: Macy's had a 5% return, much greater than the S&P 500's 0.6% return. Macy's announcement also provided guidance for its expected 2012 EPS of $3.25 to $3.30.

Should a company provide earnings guidance estimates to investors? Virtually no one disputes that investors need as much information as possible to evaluate a company, and academic studies show that companies with greater transparency have higher valuations. However, greater disclosure often brings the possibility of lawsuits if investors have reason to believe that the disclosure is fraudulent. In addition, the Security and Exchange Commission's Reg FD (Regulation Fair Disclosure) prevents companies from disclosing information only to select groups, such as analysts. Reg FD led many companies to begin providing quarterly earnings forecasts directly to the public. In fact, a survey by the National Investors Relations Institute showed that 95% of respondents in 2006 provided either annual or quarterly earnings forecasts, up from 45% in 1999.

Two trends have emerged. First, the number of companies reporting quarterly earnings forecasts is falling, but the number reporting annual forecasts is increasing. Second, many companies are providing other types of forward-looking information, including key operating ratios plus qualitative information about the company and its industry. Ratio analysis can help investors use such information, so keep that in mind as you read this chapter.

Sources: Adapted from Macy's press release: **http://phx.corporate-ir.net/phoenix.zhtml?c=84477&p=RssLanding&cat=news&id=1663112**; Zacks's Earnings Scorecard: **www.zacks.com/stock/news/70862/Earnings+Scorecard%3A+Macy's**; Joseph McCafferty, "Guidance Lite," *CFO*, June 2006, 16–17; and William F. Coffin and Crocker Coulson, "Is Earnings Guidance Disappearing in 2006?" 2006, White Paper, available at **www.ccgir.com/ccgir/white_papers/pdf/Earnings%20Guidance%202006.pdf**.

Intrinsic Value and Analysis of Financial Statements

© Rob Webb/Getty Images

The intrinsic value of a firm is determined by the present value of the expected future free cash flows (FCF) when discounted at the weighted average cost of capital (WACC). This chapter explains how to use financial statements to evaluate a company's profitability, required capital investments, business risk, and mix of debt and equity.

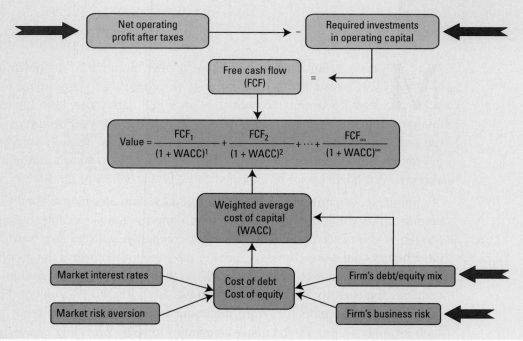

$$Value = \frac{FCF_1}{(1 + WACC)^1} + \frac{FCF_2}{(1 + WACC)^2} + \cdots + \frac{FCF_\infty}{(1 + WACC)^\infty}$$

© Cengage Learning 2014

r e s o u r c e

The textbook's Web site contains an Excel *file that will guide you through the chapter's calculations. The file for this chapter is* **Ch03 Tool Kit.xls,** *and we encourage you to open the file and follow along as you read the chapter.*

Financial statement analysis involves (1) comparing a firm's performance with that of other firms in the same industry, and (2) evaluating trends in the firm's financial position over time. Managers use financial analysis to identify situations needing attention, potential lenders use financial analysis to determine whether a company is creditworthy, and stockholders use financial analysis to help predict future earnings, dividends, and free cash flow. This chapter will explain the similarities and differences among these uses.

3-1 Financial Analysis

When we perform a financial analysis, we conduct the following steps.

3-1a Gather Data

W W W

See **www.zacks.com** *for a source of standardized financial statements.*

The first step in financial analysis is to gather data. As discussed in Chapter 2, financial statements can be downloaded from many different Web sites. One of our favorites is Zacks Investment Research, which provides financial statements in a standardized format.

If you cut and paste financial statements from Zacks into a spreadsheet and then perform a financial analysis, you can quickly repeat the analysis on a different company by pasting that company's financial statements into the same cells of the spreadsheet. In other words, you do not need to reinvent the wheel each time you analyze a company.

3-1b Examine the Statement of Cash Flows

Some financial analysis can be done with virtually no calculations. For example, we always look to the statement of cash flows first, particularly the net cash provided by operating activities. Downward trends or negative net cash flow from operations almost always indicate problems. The statement of cash flows section on investing activities shows whether the company has made a big acquisition, especially when compared with the prior years' net cash flows from investing activities. A quick look at the section on financing activities also reveals whether a company is issuing debt or buying back stock; in other words, is the company raising capital from investors or returning it to them?

3-1c Calculate and Examine the Return on Invested Capital and Free Cash Flow

After examining the statement of cash flows, we calculate the free cash flow (FCF) and return on invested capital (ROIC) as described in Chapter 2. The ROIC provides a vital measure of a firm's overall performance. If the ROIC is greater than the company's weighted average cost of capital (WACC), then the company usually is adding value. If the ROIC is less than the WACC, then the company usually has serious problems. No matter what the ROIC tells us about overall performance, it is important to examine specific activities, and to do that we use financial ratios.

3-1d Begin Ratio Analysis

Financial ratios are designed to extract important information that might not be obvious simply from examining a firm's financial statements. For example, suppose Firm A owes $5 million in debt while Firm B owes $50 million. Which company is in a stronger financial position? It is impossible to answer this question without first standardizing each firm's debt relative to total assets, earnings, and interest. Such standardized comparisons are provided through *ratio analysis*.

We will calculate the 2013 financial ratios for MicroDrive Inc. using data from the balance sheets and income statements given in Figure 3-1. We will also evaluate the ratios in relation to the industry averages. Note that dollar amounts are in millions.

3-2 Liquidity Ratios

r e s o u r c e

See **Ch03 Tool Kit.xls** *for all calculations.*

As shown in Figure 3-1, MicroDrive has current liabilities of $780 million that it must pay off within the coming year. Will it have trouble satisfying those obligations? **Liquidity ratios** attempt to answer this type of question. We discuss two commonly used liquidity ratios in this section.

3-2a The Current Ratio

Calculate the **current ratio** by dividing current assets by current liabilities:

$$\text{Current ratio} = \frac{\text{Current assets}}{\text{Current liabilities}}$$

$$= \frac{\$1,550}{\$780} = 2.0$$

Industry average $= 2.2$

FIGURE 3-1

MicroDrive Inc.: Balance Sheets and Income Statements for Years Ending December 31 (Millions of Dollars, Except for Per Share Data)

	A	B	C	D	E
23	**Balance Sheets**			**2013**	**2012**
24	*Assets*				
25	Cash and equivalents			$ 50	$ 60
26	Short-term investments			-	40
27	Accounts receivable			500	380
28	Inventories			1,000	820
29	Total current assets			$ 1,550	$ 1,300
30	Net plant and equipment			2,000	1,700
31	Total assets			$ 3,550	$ 3,000
32					
33	*Liabilities and Equity*				
34	Accounts payable			$ 200	$ 190
35	Notes payable			280	130
36	Accruals			300	280
37	Total current liabilities			$ 780	$ 600
38	Long-term bonds			1,200	1,000
39	Total liabilities			$ 1,980	$ 1,600
40	Preferred stock (400,000 shares)			100	100
41	Common stock (50,000,000 shares)			500	500
42	Retained earnings			970	800
43	Total common equity			$ 1,470	$ 1,300
44	Total liabilities and equity			$ 3,550	$ 3,000
45					
46	**Income Statements**			**2013**	**2012**
47	Net sales			$ 5,000	$ 4,760
48	Costs of goods sold except depreciation			3,800	3,560
49	Depreciation			200	170
50	Other operating expenses			500	480
51	Earnings before interest and taxes (EBIT)			$ 500	$ 550
52	Less interest			120	100
53	Pretax earnings			$ 380	$ 450
54	Taxes (40%)			152	180
55	Net Income before preferred dividends			$ 228	$ 270
56	Preferred dividends			8	8
57	Net Income available to common stockholders			$ 220	$ 262
58	**Other Data**				
59	Common dividends			$50	$48
60	Addition to retained earnings			$170	$214
61	Lease payments			$28	$28
62	Bonds' required sinking fund payments			$20	$20
63	Common stock price per share			$27	$40

Current assets normally include cash, marketable securities, accounts receivable, and inventories. Current liabilities consist of accounts payable, short-term notes payable, current maturities of long-term debt, accrued taxes, and other accrued expenses.

MicroDrive has a slightly lower current ratio than the average for its industry. Is this good or bad? Sometimes the answer depends on who is asking the question. For example, suppose a supplier is trying to decide whether to extend credit to MicroDrive. In general, creditors like to see a high current ratio. If a company starts to experience financial difficulty, it will begin paying its bills (accounts payable) more slowly and borrowing more from its bank, so its current liabilities will be increasing. If current liabilities are rising faster than current assets, then the current ratio will fall, and this could spell trouble. Because the current ratio provides the best single indicator of the extent to which the claims of short-term creditors are covered by assets that are expected to be converted to cash fairly quickly, it is the most commonly used measure of short-term solvency.

Now consider the current ratio from a shareholder's perspective. A high current ratio could mean that the company has a lot of money tied up in nonproductive assets, such as excess cash or marketable securities. Or perhaps the high current ratio is due to large inventory holdings, which might become obsolete before they can be sold. Thus, shareholders might not want a high current ratio.

An industry average is not a magic number that all firms should strive to maintain—in fact, some well-managed firms will be above the average, while other good firms will be below it. However, if a firm's ratios are far from the averages for its industry, this is a red flag, and analysts should be concerned about why the variance occurs. For example, suppose a low current ratio is traced to low inventories. Is this a competitive advantage resulting from the firm's mastery of just-in-time inventory management, or is it an Achilles' heel that is causing the firm to miss shipments and lose sales? Ratio analysis doesn't answer such questions, but it does point to areas of potential concern.

3-2b The Quick, or Acid Test, Ratio

The **quick ratio**, also called the **acid test ratio**, is calculated by deducting inventories from current assets and then dividing the remainder by current liabilities:

$$\text{Quick ratio} = \frac{\text{Current assets} - \text{Inventories}}{\text{Current liabilities}}$$

$$= \frac{\$1,550 - \$1,000}{\$780} = 7.0$$

Industry average $= 0.8$

A **liquid asset** is one that trades in an active market, so it can be converted quickly to cash at the going market price. Inventories are typically the least liquid of a firm's current assets; hence they are the current assets on which losses are most likely to occur in a bankruptcy. Therefore, a measure of the firm's ability to pay off short-term obligations without relying on the sale of inventories is important.

MicroDrive's quick ratio is close to the industry average. However, both are below 1.0, which means that inventories would have to be liquidated in order to pay off current liabilities should the need arise.

How does MicroDrive compare to S&P 500 companies? There has been a steady decline in the average liquidity ratios of S&P 500 companies during the past decade. As we write this in 2012, the average current and quick ratios are well below 1.0, so MicroDrive and its industry peers are more liquid than the typical S&P 500 company.

SELF-TEST

Identify two ratios to use to analyze a firm's liquidity position, and write out their equations.

What are the characteristics of a liquid asset? Give some examples.

Which current asset is typically the least liquid?

A company has current liabilities of $800 million, and its current ratio is 2.5. What is its level of current assets? **($2,000 million)** *If this firm's quick ratio is 2, how much inventory does it have?* **($400 million)**

3-3 Asset Management Ratios

Asset management ratios measure how effectively a firm is managing its assets. If a company has excessive investments in assets, then its operating capital is unduly high, which reduces its free cash flow and ultimately its stock price. On the other hand, if a company does not have enough assets, then it may lose sales, which would hurt profitability, free cash flow, and the stock price. Therefore, it is important to have the *right* amount invested in assets. Ratios that analyze the different types of assets are described in this section.

3-3a Evaluating Total Assets: The Total Assets Turnover Ratio

The **total assets turnover ratio** measures the dollars in sales that are generated for each dollar that is tied up in assets:

$$\text{Total assets turnover ratio} = \frac{\text{Sales}}{\text{Total assets}}$$

$$= \frac{\$5,000}{\$3,550} = 1.4$$

$$\text{Industry average} = 1.8$$

MicroDrive's ratio is somewhat below the industry average, indicating that the company is not generating as much business (relative to its peers) given its total asset investment. In other words, MicroDrive uses its assets relatively inefficiently. The following ratios can be used to identify the specific asset classes that are causing this problem.[1]

---

[1]Sales occur throughout the year, but assets are reported at end of the period. For a growing company or a company with seasonal variation, it would be better to use *average* assets held during the year when calculating turnover ratios. However, we use year-end values for all turnover ratios so that we are more comparable with most reported industry averages.

3-3b Evaluating Fixed Assets: The Fixed Assets Turnover Ratio

The **fixed assets turnover ratio** measures how effectively the firm uses its plant and equipment. It is the ratio of sales to net fixed assets:

$$\text{Fixed assets turnover ratio} = \frac{\text{Sales}}{\text{Net fixed assets}}$$

$$= \frac{\$5,000}{\$2,000} = 2.5$$

$$\text{Industry average} = 3.0$$

MicroDrive's ratio of 2.5 is a little below the industry average, indicating that the firm is not using its fixed assets as intensively as are other firms in its industry.

Inflation can cause problems when interpreting the fixed assets turnover ratio because fixed assets are reported using the historical costs of the assets instead of current replacement costs that may be higher due to inflation. Therefore, a mature firm with fixed assets acquired years ago might well have a higher fixed assets turnover ratio than a younger company with newer fixed assets that are reported at inflated prices relative to the historical prices of the older assets. However, this would reflect the difficulty accountants have in dealing with inflation rather than inefficiency on the part of the new firm. You should be alert to this potential problem when evaluating the fixed assets turnover ratio.

3-3c Evaluating Receivables: The Days Sales Outstanding

Days sales outstanding (DSO), also called the "average collection period" (ACP), is used to appraise accounts receivable, and it is calculated by dividing accounts receivable by average daily sales to find the number of days' sales that are tied up in receivables. Thus, the DSO represents the average length of time that the firm must wait after making a sale before receiving cash, which is the average collection period. MicroDrive's DSO is 37, above the 36-day industry average:

$$\text{DSO} = \frac{\text{Days sales}}{\text{outstanding}} = \frac{\text{Receivables}}{\text{Average sales per day}} = \frac{\text{Receivables}}{\text{Annual sales}/365}$$

$$= \frac{\$500}{\$5,000/365} = \frac{\$500}{\$13.7} = 36.5 \text{ days} \approx 37 \text{ days}$$

$$\text{Industry average} = 30 \text{ days}$$

MicroDrive's sales terms call for payment within 30 days. The fact that 37 days of sales are outstanding indicates that customers, on average, are not paying their bills on time. As with inventory, high levels of accounts receivable cause high levels of NOWC, which hurts FCF and stock price.

A customer who is paying late may be in financial trouble, which means MicroDrive may have a hard time collecting the receivable. Therefore, if the trend in DSO has been rising unexpectedly, steps should be taken to review credit standards and to expedite the collection of accounts receivable.

3-3d Evaluating Inventories: The Inventory Turnover Ratio

The **inventory turnover ratio** is defined as costs of goods sold (COGS) divided by inventories.[2] The previous ratios use sales instead of COGS. However, sales revenues include costs and profits, whereas inventory usually is reported at cost. Therefore, it is better to compare inventory with costs rather than sales.

The income statement in Figure 3-1 separately reports depreciation and the portion of costs of goods sold that is not comprised of depreciation, which is helpful when calculating cash flows. However, we need the total COGS for calculating the inventory turnover ratio. For MicroDrive, virtually all depreciation is associated with producing its products, so its COGS is:

$$COGS = \text{Costs of goods sold except depreciation} + \text{Depreciation}$$

$$= \$3,800 + \$200 = \$4,000 \text{ million}$$

We can now calculate the inventory turnover:

$$\text{Inventory turnover ratio} = \frac{COGS}{\text{Inventories}}$$

$$= \frac{\$3,800 + \$200}{\$1,000} = 4.0$$

$$\text{Industry average} = 5.0$$

As a rough approximation, each item of MicroDrive's inventory is sold out and restocked, or "turned over," 4 times per year.[3]

MicroDrive's turnover of 4 is lower than the industry average of 5. This suggests that MicroDrive is holding too much inventory. High levels of inventory add to net operating working capital (NOWC), which reduces FCF, which leads to lower stock prices. In addition, MicroDrive's low inventory turnover ratio makes us wonder whether the firm is holding obsolete goods not worth their stated value.

In summary, MicroDrive's low fixed asset turnover ratio, high DSO, and low inventory turnover ratio each cause MicroDrive's total assets turnover ratio to be lower than the industry average.

---

[2]In previous editions, we defined the inventory turnover ratio using sales instead of COGS because some compilers of financial ratio statistics, such as Dun & Bradstreet, use the ratio of sales to inventories. However, most sources now report the turnover ratio using COGS, so we have changed our definition to conform to the majority of reporting organizations.

[3]"Turnover" is derived from the old Yankee peddler who would load up his wagon with goods and then go off to peddle his wares. If he made 10 trips per year, stocked 100 pans, and made a gross profit of $5 per pan, his annual gross profit would be $(100)(\$5)(10) = \$5,000$. If he "turned over" (i.e., sold) his inventory faster and made 20 trips per year, then his gross profit would double, other things held constant. So, his turnover directly affected his profits.

GLOBAL ECONOMIC CRISIS

© uniquely india/Getty Images

The Global Economic Crisis

The Price Is Right! (Or Wrong!)

How much is an asset worth if no one is buying or selling? The answer to that question matters because an accounting practice called "mark to market" requires that some assets be adjusted on the balance sheet to reflect their "fair market value." The accounting rules are complicated, but the general idea is that if an asset is available for sale, then the balance sheet would be most accurate if it showed the asset's market value. For example, suppose a company purchased $100 million of Treasury bonds and the value of those bonds later fell to $90 million. With mark to market, the company would report the bonds' value on the balance sheet as $90 million, not the original purchase price of $100 million. Notice that marking to market can have a significant impact on financial ratios and thus on investors' perception of a firm's financial health.

But what if the assets are mortgage-backed securities that were originally purchased for $100 million? As defaults increased during 2008, the value of such securities fell rapidly, and then investors virtually stopped trading them. How should the company report

them? At the $100 million original price? At a $60 million price that was observed before the market largely dried up? At $25 million when a hedge fund in desperate need for cash to avoid a costly default sold a few of these securities? At $0, because there are no current quotes? Or should they be reported at a price generated by a computer model or in some other manner?

The answer to this is especially important during times of economic stress. Congress, the SEC, FASB, and the U.S. Treasury all are working to find the right answers. If they come up with a price that is too low, it could cause investors mistakenly to believe that some companies are worth much less than their intrinsic values, and this could trigger runs on banks and bankruptcies for companies that might otherwise survive. But if the price is too high, some "walking dead" or "zombie" companies could linger on and later cause even larger losses for investors, including the U.S. government, which is now the largest investor in many financial institutions. Either way, an error in pricing could perhaps trigger a domino effect that might topple the entire financial system. So let's hope the price is right!

SELF-TEST

Identify four ratios that measure how effectively a firm is managing its assets, and write out their equations.

What problem might arise when comparing firms' fixed assets turnover ratios?

A firm has $200 million annual sales, $180 million costs of goods sold, $40 million of inventory, and $60 million of accounts receivable. What is its inventory turnover ratio? **(4.5)** *What is its DSO based on a 365-day year?* **(109.5 days)**

3-4 Debt Management Ratios

The extent to which a firm uses debt financing is called **financial leverage**. Here are three important implications: (1) Stockholders can control a firm with smaller investments of their own equity if they finance part of the firm with debt. (2) If the firm's assets generate a higher pre-tax return than the interest rate on debt, then the shareholders' returns are magnified, or "leveraged." Conversely, shareholders' losses are also magnified if assets generate a pre-tax return less than the interest rate. (3) If a company has high leverage, even a small decline in performance might cause the firm's value to fall below the amount it owes to creditors. Therefore, a creditor's position becomes riskier as leverage increases. Keep these three points in mind as you read the following sections.

3-4a How the Firm Is Financed: Leverage Ratios

MicroDrive's two primary types of debt are notes payable and long-term bonds, but more complicated companies also might report the portion of long-term debt due within a year, the value of capitalized leases, and other types of obligations that charge interest. For MicroDrive, total debt is:

$$\text{Total debt} = \text{Notes payable} + \text{Long-term bonds}$$

$$= \$280 + \$1,200 = \$1,480 \text{ million}$$

Is this too much debt, not enough, or the right amount? To answer this question, we begin by calculating the percentage of MicroDrive's assets that are financed by debt. The ratio of total debt to total assets is called the **debt-to-assets ratio**. It is sometimes shortened to the **debt ratio**.[4] Total debt is the sum of all short-term debt and long-term debt; it does not include other liabilities. MicroDrive's debt ratio is:

$$\text{Debt-to-assets ratio} = \text{Debt ratio} = \frac{\text{Total debt}}{\text{Total assets}}$$

$$= \frac{\$280 + \$1,200}{\$3,550} = \frac{\$1,480}{\$3,550} = 41.7\%$$

$$\text{Industry average} = 25.0\%$$

MicroDrive's debt ratio is 41.7%, which is substantially higher than the 25% industry average.

The debt-to-equity ratio is defined as:[5]

$$\text{Debt-to-equity ratio} = \frac{\text{Total debt}}{\text{Total common equity}}$$

$$= \frac{\$280 + \$1,200}{\$1,470} = \frac{\$1,480}{\$1,470} = 1.01$$

$$\text{Industry average} = 0.46$$

The debt-to-equity ratio shows that MicroDrive has $1.01 of debt for every dollar of equity, whereas the debt ratio shows that 41.7% of MicroDrive's assets are financed by debt. We find it more intuitive to think about the percentage of the firm that is financed with debt, so we usually use the debt ratio. However, the debt-to-equity ratio is also widely used, so you should know how to interpret it as well.

Be sure you know how a ratio is defined before you use it. Some sources define the debt ratio using only long-term debt instead of total debt; others use investor-supplied capital instead of total assets. Some sources make similar changes in the debt-to-equity ratio, so be sure to check your source's definition.

[4]In previous editions we defined the debt ratio as total liabilities divided by total assets. For better comparability with Web-based reporting sources, we have changed our definition to total debt divided by total assets.
[5]In previous editions we defined the debt-to-equity ratio as total liabilities divided by total common equity. For better comparability with Web-based reporting sources, we have changed our definition to total debt divided by total common equity.

Sometimes it is useful to express debt ratios in terms of market values. It is easy to calculate the market value of equity, which is equal to the stock price multiplied by the number of shares. MicroDrive's market value of equity is $27(50) = $1,350. Often it is difficult to estimate the market value of debt, so many analysts use the debt reported in the financial statements. The market debt ratio is defined as:

$$\text{Market debt ratio} = \frac{\text{Total debt}}{\text{Total debt} + \text{Market value of equity}}$$

$$= \frac{\$280 + \$1,200}{(\$280 + \$1,200) - (\$27 \times 50)} = \frac{\$1,480}{\$1,480 + \$1,350}$$

$$= 52.3\%$$

$$\text{Industry average} = 20.0\%$$

MicroDrive's market debt ratio in the previous year was 36.1%. The big increase was due to two major factors: Debt increased and the stock price fell. The stock price reflects a company's prospects for generating future cash flows, so a decline in stock price indicates a likely decline in future cash flows. Thus, the market debt ratio reflects a source of risk that is not captured by the conventional debt ratio.

Finally, the ratio of total liabilities to total assets shows the extent to which a firm's assets are not financed by equity. The **liabilities-to-assets ratio** is defined as:

$$\text{Liabilities-to-assets ratio} = \frac{\text{Total liabilities}}{\text{Total assets}}$$

$$= \frac{\$1,980}{\$3,550} = 55.8\%$$

$$\text{Industry average} = 45.0\%$$

For all the ratios we examined, MicroDrive has more leverage than its industry peers. The next section shows how close MicroDrive might be to serious financial distress.

3-4b Ability to Pay Interest: Times-Interest-Earned Ratio

The **times-interest-earned (TIE) ratio,** also called the **interest coverage ratio,** is determined by dividing earnings before interest and taxes (EBIT in Figure 3-1) by the interest expense:

$$\text{Times-interest-earned (TIE) ratio} = \frac{\text{EBIT}}{\text{Interest expense}}$$

$$= \frac{\$500}{\$120} = 4.2$$

$$\text{Industry average} = 10.0$$

The TIE ratio measures the extent to which operating income can decline before the firm is unable to meet its annual interest costs. Failure to meet this obligation can bring legal action by the firm's creditors, possibly resulting in bankruptcy. Note that earnings before interest and taxes, rather than net income, is used in the numerator. Because interest is paid with pre-tax dollars, the firm's ability to pay current interest is not affected by taxes.

MicroDrive's interest is covered 4.2 times, which is well above 1, the point at which EBIT isn't sufficient to pay interest. The industry average is 10, so even though MicroDrive has enough EBIT to pay interest expenses, it has a relatively low margin of safety compared to its peers. Thus, the TIE ratio reinforces the conclusion from our analysis of the debt ratio that MicroDrive might face difficulties if it attempts to borrow additional funds.

3-4c Ability to Service Debt: EBITDA Coverage Ratio

The TIE ratio is useful for assessing a company's ability to meet interest charges on its debt, but this ratio has two shortcomings: (1) Interest is not the only fixed financial charge—companies must also reduce debt on schedule, and many firms lease assets and thus must make lease payments. Failure to repay debt or meet lease payments may force them into bankruptcy. (2) EBIT (earnings before interest and taxes) does not represent all the cash flow available to service debt, especially if a firm has high depreciation and/or amortization charges. A better coverage ratio would take into account the "cash" earnings and the other financial charges.

MicroDrive had $500 million of EBIT and $200 million in depreciation, for an EBITDA (earnings before interest, taxes, depreciation, and amortization) of $700 million. Also, lease payments of $28 million were deducted while calculating EBIT. That $28 million was available to meet financial charges; hence it must be added back, bringing the total available to cover fixed financial charges to $728 million. Fixed financial charges consisted of $120 million of interest, $20 million of sinking fund payments, and $28 million for lease payments, for a total of $168 million.[6]

MicroDrive's **EBITDA coverage ratio** is:[7]

$$\text{EBITDA coverage ratio} = \frac{\text{EBITDA} + \text{Lease payments}}{\text{Interest} + \text{Principal payments} + \text{Lease payments}}$$

$$= \frac{(\$500 + 200) + \$28}{\$120 + \$20 + \$28} = \frac{\$728}{\$168} = 4.3$$

$$\text{Industry average} = 12.0$$

MicroDrive covered its fixed financial charges by 4.3 times. MicroDrive's ratio is well below the industry average, so again the company seems to have a relatively high level of debt.

The EBITDA coverage ratio is most useful for relatively short-term lenders such as banks, which rarely make loans (except real estate-backed loans) for longer than about 5 years. Over a relatively short period, depreciation-generated funds can be used to service debt. Over a longer time, those funds must be reinvested to maintain the plant and equipment or else the company cannot remain in business. Therefore, banks and other relatively short-term lenders focus on the EBITDA coverage ratio, whereas long-term bondholders focus on the TIE ratio.

---

[6]A sinking fund is a required annual payment designed to reduce the balance of a bond or preferred stock issue.
[7]Different analysts define the EBITDA coverage ratio in different ways. For example, some omit the lease payment information; others "gross up" principal payments by dividing them by 1 − T because these payments are not tax deductions and so must be made with after-tax cash flows. We included lease payments because for many firms they are quite important, and failing to make them can lead to bankruptcy as surely as can failure to make payments on "regular" debt. We did not gross up principal payments because, if a company is in financial difficulty, then its tax rate will probably be zero; hence the gross up is not necessary whenever the ratio is really important.

SELF-TEST

How does the use of financial leverage affect current stockholders' control position?

Name six ratios that are used to measure the extent to which a firm uses financial leverage, and write out their equations.

A company has EBITDA of $600 million, interest payments of $60 million, lease payments of $40 million, and required principal payments (due this year) of $30 million. What is its EBITDA coverage ratio? **(4.9)**

3-5 Profitability Ratios

Profitability is the net result of a number of policies and decisions. The ratios examined thus far provide useful clues as to the effectiveness of a firm's operations, but the **profitability ratios** go on to show the combined effects of liquidity, asset management, and debt on operating results.

3-5a Net Profit Margin

The **net profit margin**, also called the **profit margin on sales**, is calculated by dividing net income by sales. It gives the profit per dollar of sales:

$$\text{Net profit margin} = \frac{\text{Net income available to common stockholders}}{\text{Sales}}$$

$$= \frac{\$220}{\$5,000} = 4.4\%$$

$$\text{Industry average} = 6.2\%$$

MicroDrive's net profit margin is below the industry average of 6.2%, but why is this so? Is it due to inefficient operations, high interest expenses, or both?

Instead of just comparing net income to sales, many analysts also break the income statement into smaller parts to identify the sources of a low net profit margin. For example, the **operating profit margin** is defined as

$$\text{Operating profit margin} = \frac{\text{EBIT}}{\text{Sales}}$$

The operating profit margin identifies how a company is performing with respect to its operations before the impact of interest expenses is considered.

Some analysts drill even deeper by breaking operating costs into their components. For example, the **gross profit margin** is defined as

$$\text{Gross profit margin} = \frac{\text{Sales} - \text{Cost of goods sold}}{\text{Sales}}$$

The gross profit margin identifies the gross profit per dollar of sales before any other expenses are deducted.

Rather than calculate each type of profit margin here, later in the chapter we will use common size analysis and percent change analysis to focus on different parts of the

The World Might Be Flat, but Global Accounting Is Bumpy! The Case of IFRS versus FASB

© Rob Webb/Getty Images

In a flat world, distance is no barrier. Work flows to where it can be done most efficiently, and capital flows to where it can be invested most profitably. If a radiologist in India is more efficient than one in the United States, then images will be e-mailed to India for diagnosis; if rates of return are higher in Brazil, then investors throughout the world will provide funding for Brazilian projects. One key to "flattening" the world is agreement on common standards. For example, there are common Internet standards so that users throughout the world are able to communicate.

A glaring exception to standardization is in accounting. The Securities and Exchange Commission (SEC) in the United States requires firms to comply with standards set by the Financial Accounting Standards Board (FASB). But the European Union requires all EU-listed companies to comply with the International Financial Reporting Standards (IFRS) as defined by the International Accounting Standards Board (IASB).

IFRS tends to rely on general principles, whereas FASB standards are rules-based. As the recent accounting scandals demonstrate, many U.S. companies have been able to comply with U.S. rules while violating the principle, or intent, underlying the rules. The United States is likely to adopt IFRS, or a slightly modified IFRS, but the question is "When?" The SEC estimated that a large company is likely to incur costs of up to $32 million when switching to IFRS. So even though a survey by the accounting firm KPMG indicates that most investors and analysts favor adoption of IFRS, the path to adoption is likely to be bumpy.

Sources: See the Web sites of the IASB and the FASB, **www .iasb.org.uk** and **www.fasb.org**. Also see David M. Katz and Sarah Johnson, "Top Obama Advisers Clash on Global Accounting Standards," January 15, 2009, at **www.cfo.com**; and "Survey Favors IFRS Adoption," February 3, 2009, at **www.webcpa.com**.

income statement. In addition, we will use the DuPont equation to show how the ratios interact with one another.

Sometimes it is confusing to have so many different types of profit margins. To simplify the situation, we will focus primarily on the net profit margin throughout the book and call it the "profit margin."

3-5b Basic Earning Power (BEP) Ratio

The **basic earning power (BEP) ratio** is calculated by dividing earnings before interest and taxes (EBIT) by total assets:

$$\text{Basic earning power (BEP ratio)} = \frac{\text{EBIT}}{\text{Total assets}}$$

$$= \frac{\$500}{\$3,550} = 14.1\%$$

$$\text{Industry average} = 20.2\%$$

This ratio shows the earning power of the firm's assets before the influence of taxes and leverage, and it is useful for comparing firms with different tax situations and different degrees of financial leverage. Because of its low turnover ratios and low profit margin on sales, MicroDrive is not getting as high a return on its assets as is the average company in its industry.

3-5c Return on Total Assets

The ratio of net income to total assets measures the **return on total assets (ROA)** after interest and taxes. This ratio is also called the **return on assets** and is defined as follows:

$$\text{Return on total assets} = \text{ROA} = \frac{\text{Net income available to common stockholders}}{\text{Total assets}}$$

$$= \frac{\$220}{\$3,550} = 6.2\%$$

$$\text{Industry average} = 11.0\%$$

MicroDrive's 6.2% return is well below the 9% average for the industry. This low return is due to (1) the company's low basic earning power, and (2) high interest costs resulting from its above-average use of debt. Both of these factors cause MicroDrive's net income to be relatively low.

3-5d Return on Common Equity

The ratio of net income to common equity measures the **return on common equity (ROE)**:

$$\text{Return on common equity} = \text{ROE} = \frac{\text{Net income available to common stockholders}}{\text{Common equity}}$$

$$= \frac{\$220}{\$1,470} = 15.0\%$$

$$\text{Industry average} = 19.0\%$$

Stockholders invest to earn a return on their money, and this ratio tells how well they are doing in an accounting sense. MicroDrive's 15% return is below the 19% industry average, but not as far below as its return on total assets. This somewhat better result is due to the company's greater use of debt, a point that we explain in detail later in the chapter.

SELF-TEST

Identify and write out the equations for four profitability ratios.

Why is the basic earning power ratio useful?

Why does the use of debt lower ROA?

What does ROE measure?

A company has $200 billion of sales and $10 billion of net income. Its total assets are $100 billion, financed half by debt and half by common equity. What is its profit margin? **(5%)** *What is its ROA?* **(10%)** *What is its ROE?* **(20%)** *Would ROA increase if the firm used less leverage?* **(Yes)** *Would ROE increase?* **(No)**

3-6 Market Value Ratios

Market value ratios relate a firm's stock price to its earnings, cash flow, and book value per share. Market value ratios are a way to measure the value of a company's stock relative to that of another company.

3-6a Price/Earnings Ratio

The **price/earnings (P/E) ratio** shows how much investors are willing to pay per dollar of reported profits. MicroDrive has $220 million in net income and 50 million shares, so its earnings per share (EPS) is $4.40 = $220/50. MicroDrive's stock sells for $27, so its P/E ratio is:

$$\text{Price/earnings (P/E) ratio} = \frac{\text{Price per share}}{\text{Earnings per share}}$$

$$= \frac{\$27.00}{\$4.40} = 6.1$$

$$\text{Industry average} = 10.5$$

Price/earnings ratios are higher for firms with strong growth prospects, other things held constant, but they are lower for riskier firms. Because MicroDrive's P/E ratio is below the average, this suggests that the company is regarded as being somewhat riskier than most, as having poorer growth prospects, or both. In early 2012, the average P/E ratio for firms in the S&P 500 was 13.4, indicating that investors were willing to pay $13.40 for every dollar of earnings.

3-6b Price/Cash Flow Ratio

Stock prices depend on a company's ability to generate cash flows. Consequently, investors often look at the **price/cash flow ratio**, where cash flow is defined as net income plus depreciation and amortization:

$$\text{Price/cash flow ratio} = \frac{\text{Price per share}}{\text{Cash flow per share}}$$

$$= \frac{\$27.00}{(\$220 + \$200)/50} = 3.2$$

$$\text{Industry average} = 6.8$$

MicroDrive's price/cash flow ratio is also below the industry average, once again suggesting that its growth prospects are below average, its risk is above average, or both.

The **price/EBITDA ratio** is similar to the price/cash flow ratio, except the price/EBITDA ratio measures performance before the impact of interest expenses and taxes, making it a better measure of operating performance. MicroDrive's EBITDA per share is ($500 + $200)/50 = $14, so its price/EBITDA is $27/$14 = 1.9. The industry average price/EBITDA ratio is 4.0, so we see again that MicroDrive is below the industry average.

Note that some analysts look at other multiples as well. For example, depending on the industry, some may look at measures such as price/sales or price/customers. Ultimately, though, value depends on free cash flows, so if these "exotic" ratios do not forecast future free cash flow, they may turn out to be misleading. This was true in the case of the dot-com retailers before they crashed and burned in 2000, costing investors many billions.

3-6c Market/Book Ratio

The ratio of a stock's market price to its book value gives another indication of how investors regard the company. Companies with relatively high rates of return on equity generally sell at higher multiples of book value than those with low returns. First, we find MicroDrive's book value per share:

$$\text{Book value per share} = \frac{\text{Total common equity}}{\text{Shares outstanding}}$$

$$= \frac{\$1,470}{50} = \$29.4$$

Now we divide the market price by the book value to get a **market/book (M/B) ratio**:

$$\text{Market/book ratio} = \text{M/B} = \frac{\text{Market price per share}}{\text{Book value per share}}$$

$$= \frac{\$27.00}{\$29.40} = 0.9$$

$$\text{Industry average} = 1.8$$

Investors are willing to pay relatively little for a dollar of MicroDrive's book value.

The book value is a record of the past, showing the cumulative amount that stockholders have invested, either directly by purchasing newly issued shares or indirectly through retaining earnings. In contrast, the market price is forward-looking, incorporating investors' expectations of future cash flows. For example, in early 2012 Bank of America had a market/book ratio of only 0.4, reflecting the financial services industry's problems, whereas Apple's market/book ratio was 5.6, indicating that investors expected Apple's past successes to continue.

Table 3-1 summarizes selected ratios for MicroDrive. As the table indicates, the company has many problems.

SELF-TEST

Describe three ratios that relate a firm's stock price to its earnings, cash flow, and book value per share, and write out their equations.

What does the price/earnings (P/E) ratio show? If one firm's P/E ratio is lower than that of another, what are some factors that might explain the difference?

How is book value per share calculated? Explain why book values often deviate from market values.

A company has $6 billion of net income, $2 billion of depreciation and amortization, $80 billion of common equity, and 1 billion shares of stock. If its stock price is $96 per share, what is its price/earnings ratio? (16) Its price/cash flow ratio? (12) Its market/book ratio? (1.2)

TABLE 3-1

MicroDrive Inc.: Summary of Selected Financial Ratios (Millions of Dollars)

Ratio	Formula	Calculation	Ratio	Industry Average	Comment
Liquidity					
Current	$\dfrac{\text{Current assets}}{\text{Current liabilities}}$	$\dfrac{\$1,550}{\$780} =$	2.0	2.2	Poor
Quick	$\dfrac{\text{Current assets} - \text{Inventories}}{\text{Current liabilities}}$	$\dfrac{\$1,550}{\$780} =$	0.7	0.8	Poor
Asset Management					
Total assets turnover	$\dfrac{\text{Sales}}{\text{Total assets}}$	$\dfrac{\$5,000}{\$3,550} =$	1.4	1.8	Poor
Fixed assets turnover	$\dfrac{\text{Sales}}{\text{Net fixed assets}}$	$\dfrac{\$5,000}{\$2,000} =$	2.5	3.0	Poor
Days sales outstanding (DSO)	$\dfrac{\text{Receivables}}{\text{Annual sales}/365}$	$\dfrac{\$500}{\$13.7} =$	36.5	30.0	Poor
Inventory turnover	$\dfrac{\text{COGS}}{\text{Inventories}}$	$\dfrac{\$4,000}{\$1,000} =$	4.0	5.0	Poor
Debt Management					
Debt-to-assets ratio	$\dfrac{\text{Total debt}}{\text{Total assets}}$	$\dfrac{\$1,480}{\$3,550} =$	41.7%	25.0%	High (risky)
Times-interest-earned (TIE)	$\dfrac{\text{Earnings before interest and taxes (EBIT)}}{\text{Interest charges}}$	$\dfrac{\$500}{\$120} =$	4.2	10.0	Low (risky)
Profitability					
Profit margin on sales	$\dfrac{\text{Net income available to common stockholders}}{\text{Sales}}$	$\dfrac{\$220}{\$5,000} =$	4.4%	6.2%	Poor
Basic earning power (BEP)	$\dfrac{\text{Earnings before interest and taxes (EBIT)}}{\text{Total assets}}$	$\dfrac{\$500}{\$3,550} =$	14.1%	20.2%	Poor
Return on total assets (ROA)	$\dfrac{\text{Net income available to common stockholders}}{\text{Total assets}}$	$\dfrac{\$220}{\$3,550} =$	6.2%	11.0%	Poor
Return on common equity (ROE)	$\dfrac{\text{Net income available to common stockholders}}{\text{Common equity}}$	$\dfrac{\$220}{\$1,470} =$	15.0%	19.0%	Poor
Market Value					
Price/earnings (P/E)	$\dfrac{\text{Price per share}}{\text{Earnings per share}}$	$\dfrac{\$27.00}{\$4.40} =$	6.1	10.5	Low
Market/book (M/B)	$\dfrac{\text{Market price per share}}{\text{Book value per share}}$	$\dfrac{\$27.00}{\$29.40} =$	0.9	1.8	Low

© Cengage Learning 2014

3-7 Trend Analysis, Common Size Analysis, and Percentage Change Analysis

Trends give clues as to whether a firm's financial condition is likely to improve or deteriorate. To do a **trend analysis**, you examine a ratio over time, as shown in Figure 3-2. This graph shows that MicroDrive's rate of return on common equity has been declining since 2011, in contrast to the industry average. All the other ratios could be analyzed similarly.

In a **common size analysis**, all income statement items are divided by sales, and all balance sheet items are divided by total assets. Thus, a common size income statement shows each item as a percentage of sales, and a common size balance sheet shows each item as a percentage of total assets.[8] The advantage of common size analysis is that it facilitates comparisons of balance sheets and income statements over time and across companies.

Common size statements are easy to generate if the financial statements are in a spreadsheet. In fact, if you obtain your data from a source that uses standardized financial statements, then it is easy to cut and paste the data for a new company over your original company's data, and all of your spreadsheet formulas will be valid for the new company. We generated Figure 3-3 in the *Excel* file ***Ch03 Tool Kit.xls.*** Figure 3-3 shows MicroDrive's 2012 and 2013 common size income statements, along with the composite statement for the industry. (*Note:* Rounding may cause addition/subtraction differences in Figures 3-3, 3-4, and 3-5.) MicroDrive's EBIT is slightly below average, and its interest expenses are slightly above average. The net effect is a relatively low profit margin.

FIGURE 3-2

MicroDrive, Inc.: Trend Analysis of Rate of Return on Common Equity

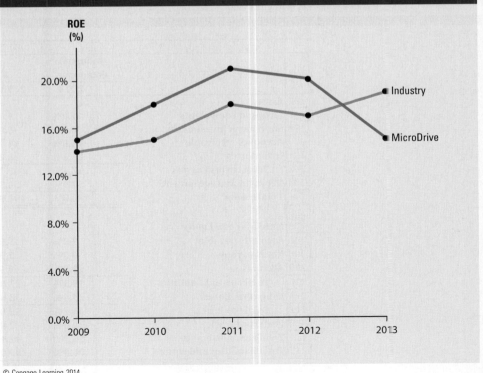

© Cengage Learning 2014

---

[8]Some sources of industry data, such as Risk Management Associates (formerly known as Robert Morris Associates), are presented exclusively in common size form.

FIGURE 3-3

MicroDrive Inc.: Common Size Income Statement

	A	B	C	Industry Composite	MicroDrive	
175				2013	2013	2012
176						
177	Net sales			100.0%	100.0%	100.0%
178	Costs of goods sold except depreciation			75.5%	76.0%	74.8%
179	Depreciation			3.0%	4.0%	3.6%
180	Other operating expenses			10.0%	10.0%	10.1%
181	Earnings before interest and taxes (EBIT)			11.5%	10.0%	11.6%
182	Less interest			1.2%	2.4%	2.1%
183	Pretax earnings			10.4%	7.6%	9.5%
184	Taxes (40%)			4.1%	3.0%	3.8%
185	Net Income before preferred dividends			6.2%	4.6%	5.7%
186	Preferred dividends			0.0%	0.2%	0.2%
187	Net Income available to common stockholders			6.2%	4.4%	5.5%

FIGURE 3-4

MicroDrive Inc.: Common Size Balance Sheet

	A	B	Industry Composite	MicroDrive	
195			2013	2013	2012
196					
197	Assets				
198	Cash and equivalents		1.8%	1.4%	2.0%
199	Short-term investments		0.0%	0.0%	1.3%
200	Accounts receivable		14.0%	14.1%	12.7%
201	Inventories		26.3%	28.2%	27.3%
202	Total current assets		42.1%	43.7%	43.3%
203	Net plant and equipment		57.9%	56.3%	56.7%
204	Total assets		100.0%	100.0%	100.0%
205					
206	Liabilities and Equity				
207	Accounts payable		7.0%	5.6%	6.3%
208	Notes payable		0.0%	7.9%	4.3%
209	Accruals		12.3%	8.5%	9.3%
210	Total current liabilities		19.3%	22.0%	20.0%
211	Long-term bonds		25.4%	33.8%	33.3%
212	Total liabilities		44.7%	55.8%	53.3%
213	Preferred stock		0.0%	2.8%	3.3%
214	Total common equity		55.3%	41.4%	43.3%
215	Total liabilities and equity		100.0%	100.0%	100.0%

FIGURE 3-5

MicroDrive Inc.: Income Statement Percentage Change Analysis

	A	B	C	D
225	Base year = 2012			Percent
226				Change in 2013
227	Net sales			5.0%
228	Costs of goods sold except depreciation			6.7%
229	Depreciation			17.6%
230	Other operating expenses			4.2%
231	Earnings before interest and taxes (EBIT)			(9.1%)
232	Less interest			20.0%
233	Pretax earnings			(15.6%)
234	Taxes (40%)			(15.6%)
235	Net Income before preferred dividends			(15.6%)
236	Preferred dividends			0.0%
237	Net income available to common stockholders			(16.0%)

See *Ch03 Tool Kit.xls* for details.

resource

Figure 3-4 shows MicroDrive's common size balance sheets along with the industry composite. Its accounts receivable are significantly higher than the industry average, its inventories are significantly higher, and it uses much more debt than the average firm.

In **percentage change analysis**, growth rates are calculated for all income statement items and balance sheet accounts relative to a base year. To illustrate, Figure 3-5 contains MicroDrive's income statement percentage change analysis for 2013 relative to 2012. Sales increased at a 5% rate during 2013, but EBIT fell by 9.1%. Part of this decline was due to an increase in depreciation, which is a noncash expense, but the cost of goods sold also increased by a little more than the growth in sales. In addition, interest expenses grew by 20%. We apply the same type of analysis to the balance sheets (see the file *Ch03 Tool Kit.xls*), which shows that inventories grew at a whopping 22% rate and accounts receivable grew over 31%. With only a 5% growth in sales, the extreme growth in receivables and inventories should be of great concern to MicroDrive's managers.

SELF-TEST

What is a trend analysis, and what information does it provide?

What is common size analysis?

What is percentage change analysis?

3-8 Tying the Ratios Together: The DuPont Equation

In ratio analysis, it is sometimes easy to miss the forest for all the trees. In particular, how do managerial actions affecting a firm's profitability, asset efficiency, and financial leverage interact to determine the return on equity, a performance measure that is important for investors? The extended **DuPont equation** provides just such a framework.

The DuPont equation uses two ratios we covered previously, the profit margin and the total asset turnover ratio, as measures of profitability and asset efficiency. But it also uses a new measure of financial leverage, the *equity multiplier,* which is the ratio of assets to common equity:

$$\text{Equity multiplier} = \frac{\text{Total assets}}{\text{Common equity}} \qquad (3\text{-}1)$$

Using this new definition of financial leverage, the extended DuPont equation is:

$$\text{ROE} = \frac{\text{Net income}}{\text{Sales}} = \frac{\text{Net income}}{\text{Sales}} \times \frac{\text{Sales}}{\text{Total assets}} \times \frac{\text{Total assets}}{\text{Common equity}} \qquad (3\text{-}2)$$

$$= (\text{Profit margin})(\text{Total assets turnover})(\text{Equity multiplier})$$

As calculated previously, MicroDrive's 2013 profit margin is 4.4% and its total assets turnover ratio is 1.41. MicroDrive's equity multiplier is:

$$\text{Equity multiplier} = \frac{\$3,550}{\$1,470} = 2.415$$

Applying the DuPont equation to MicroDrive, its return on equity is:

$$\text{ROE} = (4.4\%)(1.41)(2.415) = 15\%$$

Sometimes it is useful to focus just on asset profitability and financial leverage. Firms that have a lot of financial leverage (i.e., a lot of liabilities or preferred stock) have a high equity multiplier because the assets are financed with a relatively smaller amount of equity. Therefore, the return on equity (ROE) depends on the ROA and the use of leverage:

$$\text{ROE} = \text{ROA} \times \text{Equity multiplier}$$

$$= \frac{\text{Net income}}{\text{Total assets}} \times \frac{\text{Total assets}}{\text{Common equity}} \qquad (3\text{-}3)$$

Using Equation 3-3, we see that MicroDrive's ROE is 15.0%, the same value given by the DuPont equation:

$$\text{ROE} = 6.20\% \times 2.415 = 15\%$$

The insights provided by the DuPont model are valuable, and the model can be used for "quick and dirty" estimates of the impact that operating changes have on returns. For example, holding all else equal, if MicroDrive can implement lean production techniques and increase to 1.8 its ratio of sales to total assets, then its ROE will improve to (4.4%)(1.8)(2.415) = 19.1%.

For a more complete "what if" analysis, most companies use a forecasting model such as the one described in Chapter 12.

SELF-TEST

Explain how the extended, or modified, DuPont equation can be used to reveal the basic determinants of ROE.

What is the equity multiplier?

A company has a profit margin of 6%, a total asset turnover ratio of 2, and an equity multiplier of 1.5. What is its ROE? **(18%)**

3-9 Comparative Ratios and Benchmarking

Ratio analysis involves comparisons. A company's ratios are compared with those of other firms in the same industry—that is, with industry average figures. However, like most firms, MicroDrive's managers go one step further: they also compare their ratios with those of a smaller set of the leading computer companies. This technique is called **benchmarking**, and the companies used for the comparison are called **benchmark companies**. For example, MicroDrive benchmarks against five other firms that its management considers to be the best-managed companies with operations similar to its own.

Many companies also benchmark various parts of their overall operation against top companies, whether they are in the same industry or not. For example, MicroDrive has a division that sells hard drives directly to consumers through catalogs and the Internet. This division's shipping department benchmarks against Amazon, even though they are in different industries, because Amazon's shipping department is one of the best. MicroDrive wants its own shippers to strive to match Amazon's record for on-time shipments.

Comparative ratios are available from a number of sources, including *Value Line*, Dun and Bradstreet (D&B), and the *Annual Statement Studies* published by Risk Management Associates, which is the national association of bank loan officers. Table 3-2 reports selected ratios from Reuters for Apple and its industry, revealing that Apple has a much higher profit margin and lower debt ratio than its peers.

Each data-supplying organization uses a somewhat different set of ratios designed for its own purposes. For example, D&B deals mainly with small firms, many of which are proprietorships, and it sells its services primarily to banks and other lenders. Therefore, D&B is concerned largely with the creditor's viewpoint, and its ratios emphasize current assets and liabilities, not market value ratios. So, when you select a comparative data source, you should be sure that your own emphasis is similar to that of the agency whose ratios you plan to use. Additionally, there are often definitional differences in the ratios presented by different sources, so before using a source, be sure to verify the exact definitions of the ratios to ensure consistency with your own work.

SELF-TEST

Compare and contrast trend analysis and comparative ratio analysis.

Explain benchmarking.

TABLE 3-2

Comparative Ratios for Apple Inc., the Computer Hardware Industry, and the Technology Sector

Ratio	Apple	Computer Hardware Industry[a]	Technology Sector[b]
P/E ratio	15.53	13.69	20.92
Market to book	5.64	2.22	3.6
Net profit margin	21.48	22.48	23.48
Quick ratio	1.55	1.19	1.06
Current ratio	1.58	1.5	2.72
Total debt-to-equity	0.00	56.48	21.7
Interest coverage (TIE)[c]	--	3.38	1.3
Return on assets	29.26	7.06	13.13
Return on equity	35.28	36.28	37.28
Inventory turnover	69.42	15.4	466.83
Asset turnover	1.13	1.45	1.02

[a]The computer hardware industry is composed of 50 firms, including IBM, Dell, Apple, Sun Microsystems, Gateway, and Silicon Graphics.
[b]The technology sector contains 11 industries, including communications equipment, computer hardware, computer networks, semiconductors, and software and programming.
[c]Apple had more interest income than interest expense.

Source: Adapted from **www.reuters.com**, March 10, 2012. Select Market, Stocks, and enter the ticker symbol for Apple, AAPL. Select Financials to see updated data.

3-10 Uses and Limitations of Ratio Analysis

Ratio analysis provides useful information concerning a company's operations and financial condition, but it has limitations that necessitate care and judgment. Some potential problems include the following.

1. Many large firms operate different divisions in different industries, and for such companies it is difficult to develop a meaningful set of industry averages. Therefore, industry averages are more meaningful for small, narrowly focused firms than for large, multidivisional ones.
2. To set goals for high-level performance, it is best to benchmark on the industry *leaders'* ratios rather than the industry *average* ratios.
3. Inflation may badly distort firms' balance sheets—reported values are often substantially different from "true" values. Further, because inflation affects depreciation charges and inventory costs, reported profits are also affected. Thus, inflation can distort a ratio analysis for one firm over time or a comparative analysis of firms of different ages.
4. Seasonal factors can distort a ratio analysis. For example, the inventory turnover ratio for a food processor will be radically different if the balance sheet figure used for inventory is the one just before versus the one just after the close of the canning season. This problem can be minimized by using monthly averages for inventory (and receivables) when calculating turnover ratios.

Ratio Analysis on the Web

© Rob Webb/Getty Images

A great source for comparative ratios is **www .reuters.com**. Enter a company's ticker at the top of the page. This brings up a table with the stock quote, company information, and additional links. Select Financials, which brings up a page with a detailed ratio analysis for the company and includes comparative ratios for other companies in the same sector, the same industry, and the S&P 500. (Note: You may have to register to get extra features, but registration is free.)

5. Firms can employ **"window dressing" techniques** to make their financial statements look stronger. To illustrate, suppose a company takes out a 2-year loan in late December. Because the loan is for more than 1 year, it is not included in current liabilities even though the cash received through the loan is reported as a current asset. This improves the current and quick ratios and makes the year-end balance sheet look stronger. If the company pays the loan back in January, then the transaction was strictly window dressing.

6. Companies' choices of different accounting practices can distort comparisons. For example, choices of inventory valuation and depreciation methods affect financial statements differently, making comparisons among companies less meaningful. As another example, if one firm leases a substantial amount of its productive equipment, then its assets may appear low relative to sales (because leased assets often do not appear on the balance sheet) and its debt may appear low (because the liability associated with the lease obligation may not be shown as debt).[9]

In summary, conducting ratio analysis in a mechanical, unthinking manner is dangerous. But when ratio analysis is used intelligently and with good judgment, it can provide useful insights into a firm's operations and identify the right questions to ask.

SELF-TEST

List several potential problems with ratio analysis.

3-11 Looking Beyond the Numbers

Sound financial analysis involves more than just calculating and comparing ratios—qualitative factors must be considered. Here are some questions suggested by the American Association of Individual Investors (AAII).

1. To what extent are the company's revenues tied to one key customer or to one key product? To what extent does the company rely on a single supplier? Reliance on single customers, products, or suppliers increases risk.

2. What percentage of the company's business is generated overseas? Companies with a large percentage of overseas business are exposed to risk of currency exchange volatility and political instability.

3. What are the probable actions of current competitors and the likelihood of additional new competitors?

---

[9]This may change when FASB and IASB complete their joint project on leasing. As of mid-2012, the estimated project completion date was not certain. For the current status of the project, go to **www.fasb.org** and select the tab for Projects.

4. Do the company's future prospects depend critically on the success of products currently in the pipeline or on existing products?

5. How does the legal and regulatory environment affect the company?

SELF-TEST

What qualitative factors should analysts consider when evaluating a company's likely future financial performance?

SUMMARY

This chapter explained techniques investors and managers use to analyze financial statements. The key concepts covered are listed below.

- **Liquidity ratios** show the relationship of a firm's current assets to its current liabilities and thus its ability to meet maturing debts. Two commonly used liquidity ratios are the **current ratio** and the **quick**, or **acid test**, **ratio**.

- **Asset management ratios** measure how effectively a firm is managing its assets. These ratios include **inventory turnover**, **days sales outstanding**, **fixed assets turnover**, and **total assets turnover**.

- **Debt management ratios** reveal (1) the extent to which the firm is financed with debt, and (2) its likelihood of defaulting on its debt obligations. They include the **debt-to-assets ratio** (also called the **debt ratio**), the **debt-to-equity ratio**, the **times-interest-earned ratio**, and the **EBITDA coverage ratio**.

- **Profitability ratios** show the combined effects of liquidity, asset management, and debt management policies on operating results. They include the **net profit margin** (also called the **profit margin on sales**), the **basic earning power ratio**, the **return on total assets**, and the **return on common equity**.

- **Market value ratios** relate the firm's stock price to its earnings, cash flow, and book value per share, thus giving management an indication of what investors think of the company's past performance and future prospects. These include the **price/earnings ratio**, the **price/cash flow ratio**, and the **market/book ratio**.

- **Trend analysis**, in which one plots a ratio over time, is important because it reveals whether the firm's condition has been improving or deteriorating over time.

- The **DuPont system** is designed to show how the profit margin on sales, the assets turnover ratio, and the use of debt all interact to determine the rate of return on equity. The firm's management can use the Du Pont system to analyze ways of improving performance.

- **Benchmarking** is the process of comparing a particular company with a group of similar successful companies.

Ratio analysis has limitations, but when used with care and judgment it can be very helpful.

QUESTIONS

(3-1)   Define each of the following terms:

a. *Liquidity ratios:* current ratio; quick, or acid test, ratio

b. Asset management ratios: inventory turnover ratio; days sales outstanding (DSO); fixed assets turnover ratio; total assets turnover ratio

  c. *Financial leverage ratios:* debt ratio; times-interest-earned (TIE) ratio; coverage
     ratio
  d. *Profitability ratios:* profit margin on sales; basic earning power (BEP) ratio; return
     on total assets (ROA); return on common equity (ROE)
  e. Market value ratios: price/earnings (P/E) ratio; price/cash flow ratio; market/book
     (M/B) ratio; book value per share
  f. Trend analysis; comparative ratio analysis; benchmarking
  g. DuPont equation; window dressing; seasonal effects on ratios

(3-2)   Financial ratio analysis is conducted by managers, equity investors, long-term creditors,
            and short-term creditors. What is the primary emphasis of each of these groups in
            evaluating ratios?

(3-3)   Over the past year, M. D. Ryngaert & Co. has realized an increase in its current ratio and a
            drop in its total assets turnover ratio. However, the company's sales, quick ratio, and fixed
            assets turnover ratio have remained constant. What explains these changes?

(3-4)   Profit margins and turnover ratios vary from one industry to another. What differences
            would you expect to find between a grocery chain such as Safeway and a steel company?
            Think particularly about the turnover ratios, the profit margin, and the Du Pont equation.

(3-5)   How might (a) seasonal factors and (b) different growth rates distort a comparative ratio
            analysis? Give some examples. How might these problems be alleviated?

(3-6)   Why is it sometimes misleading to compare a company's financial ratios with those of
            other firms that operate in the same industry?

SELF-TEST PROBLEMS   Solutions Appear in Appendix A

(ST-1)   Argent Corporation has $60 million in current liabilities, $150 million in total liabilities,
Debt Ratio   and $210 million in total common equity; Argent has no preferred stock. Argent's total
                 debt is $120 million. What is the debt-to-assets ratio? What is the debt-to-equity ratio?

(ST-2)   The following data apply to Jacobus and Associates (millions of dollars):

Ratio Analysis

Cash and marketable securities	$ 100.00
Fixed assets	$ 283.50
Sales	$ 1,000.00
Net income	$ 50.00
Quick ratio	2.0
Current ratio	3.0
DSO	40.55 days
ROE	12%

Jacobus has no preferred stock—only common equity, current liabilities, and long-term
debt. Find Jacobus's (1) accounts receivable, (2) current liabilities, (3) current assets, (4) total
assets, (5) ROA, (6) common equity, and (7) long-term debt.

PROBLEMS   Answers Appear in Appendix B

(3-1)
Days Sales
Outstanding

Greene Sisters has a DSO of 20 days. The company's average daily sales are $20,000. What is the level of its accounts receivable? Assume there are 365 days in a year.

(3-2)
Debt Ratio

Vigo Vacations has $200 million in total assets, $5 million in notes payable, and $25 million in long-term debt. What is the debt ratio?

(3-3)
Market/Book Ratio

Winston Washers's stock price is $75 per share. Winston has $10 billion in total assets. Its balance sheet shows $1 billion in current liabilities, $3 billion in long-term debt, and $6 billion in common equity. It has 800 million shares of common stock outstanding. What is Winston's market/book ratio?

(3-4)
Price/Earnings Ratio

Reno Revolvers has an EPS of $1.50, a cash flow per share of $3.00, and a price/cash flow ratio of 8.0. What is its P/E ratio?

(3-5)
ROE

Needham Pharmaceuticals has a profit margin of 3% and an equity multiplier of 2.0. Its sales are $100 million and it has total assets of $50 million. What is its ROE?

(3-6)
Du Pont Analysis

Gardial & Son has an ROA of 12%, a 5% profit margin, and a return on equity equal to 20%. What is the company's total assets turnover? What is the firm's equity multiplier?

(3-7)
Current and Quick
Ratios

Ace Industries has current assets equal to $3 million. The company's current ratio is 1.5, and its quick ratio is 1.0. What is the firm's level of current liabilities? What is the firm's level of inventories?

(3-8)
Profit Margin and
Debt Ratio

Assume you are given the following relationships for the Haslam Corporation:

Sales/total assets	1.2
Return on assets (ROA)	4%
Return on equity (ROE)	7%

Calculate Haslam's profit margin and liabilities-to-assets ratio. Suppose half its liabilities are in the form of debt. Calculate the debt-to-assets ratio.

(3-9)
Current and Quick
Ratios

The Nelson Company has $1,312,500 in current assets and $525,000 in current liabilities. Its initial inventory level is $375,000, and it will raise funds as additional notes payable and use them to increase inventory. How much can Nelson's short-term debt (notes payable) increase without pushing its current ratio below 2.0? What will be the firm's quick ratio after Nelson has raised the maximum amount of short-term funds?

(3-10)
Times-Interest-
Earned Ratio

The Morris Corporation has $600,000 of debt outstanding, and it pays an interest rate of 8% annually. Morris's annual sales are $3 million, its average tax rate is 40%, and its net profit margin on sales is 3%. If the company does not maintain a TIE ratio of at least 5 to 1, then its bank will refuse to renew the loan and bankruptcy will result. What is Morris's TIE ratio?

(3-11)
Balance Sheet
Analysis

Complete the balance sheet and sales information in the table that follows for J. White Industries using the following financial data:

Total assets turnover: 1.5
Gross profit margin on sales: (Sales − Cost of goods sold)/Sales = 25%
Total liabilities-to-assets ratio: 40%
Quick ratio: 0.80
Days sales outstanding (based on 365-day year): 36.5 days
Inventory turnover ratio: 3.75

Partial Income	**Statement Information**		
Sales	_____		
Cost of goods sold	_____		
Balance Sheet			
Cash	_____	Accounts payable	_____
Accounts receivable	_____	Long-term debt	50,000
Inventories	_____	Common stock	_____
Fixed assets	_____	Retained earnings	100,000
Total assets	$400,000	Total liabilities and equity	_____

(3-12)
Comprehensive Ratio Calculations

The Kretovich Company had a quick ratio of 1.4, a current ratio of 3.0, a days sales outstanding of 36.5 days (based on a 365-day year), total current assets of $810,000, and cash and marketable securities of $120,000. What were Kretovich's annual sales?

(3-13)
Comprehensive Ratio Analysis

Data for Lozano Chip Company and its industry averages follow.

a. Calculate the indicated ratios for Lozano.
b. Construct the extended Du Pont equation for both Lozano and the industry.
c. Outline Lozano's strengths and weaknesses as revealed by your analysis.

Lozano Chip Company: Balance Sheet as of December 31, 2013 (Thousands of Dollars)

Cash	$ 225,000	Accounts payable	$ 601,866
Receivables	1,575,000	Notes payable	326,634
Inventories	1,125,000	Other current liabilities	525,000
Total current assets	$2,950,000	Total current liabilities	$1,453,500
Net fixed assets	1,350,000	Long-term debt	1,068,750
		Common equity	1,752,750
Total assets	$4,275,000	Total liabilities and equity	$4,275,000

Lozano Chip Company: Income Statement for Year Ended December 31, 2013 (Thousands of Dollars)

Sales	$ 7,500,000
Cost of goods sold	6,375,000
Selling, general, and administrative expenses	825,000
Earnings before interest and taxes (EBIT)	$ 300,000
Interest expense	111,631
Earnings before taxes (EBT)	$ 188,369
Federal and state income taxes (40%)	75,348
Net income	$ 113,022

Ratio	Lozano	Industry Average
Current assets/Current liabilities	_____	2.0
Days sales outstanding (365-day year)	_____	35.0 days
COGS/Inventory	_____	6.7
Sales/Fixed assets	_____	12.1
Sales/Total assets	_____	3.0
Net income/Sales	_____	1.2%
Net income/Total assets	_____	3.6%
Net income/Common equity	_____	9.0%
Total debt/Total assets	_____	30.0%
Total liabilities/Total assets	_____	60.0%

(3-14)
Comprehensive Ratio Analysis

The Jimenez Corporation's forecasted 2014 financial statements follow, along with some industry average ratios. Calculate Jimenez's 2014 forecasted ratios, compare them with the industry average data, and comment briefly on Jimenez's projected strengths and weaknesses.

Jimenez Corporation: Forecasted Balance Sheet as of December 31, 2014

Assets

Cash	$ 72,000
Accounts receivable	439,000
Inventories	894,000
Total current assets	$ 1,405,000
Fixed assets	431,000
Total assets	$ 1,836,000

Liabilities and Equity

Accounts payable	$ 332,000
Notes payable	100,000
Accruals	170,000
Total current liabilities	$ 602,000
Long-term debt	404,290
Common stock	575,000
Retained earnings	254,710
Total liabilities and equity	$ 1,836,000

Jimenez Corporation: Forecasted Income Statement for 2014

Sales	$4,290,000
Cost of goods sold	3,580,000
Selling, general, and administrative expenses	370,320
Depreciation and amortization	159,000
Earnings before taxes (EBT)	$ 180,680
Taxes (40%)	72,272
Net income	$ 108,408

Per Share Data

EPS	$	4.71
Cash dividends per share	$	0.95
P/E ratio		5.0
Market price (average)	$	23.57
Number of shares outstanding		23,000

Industry Financial Ratios (2013)[a]

Quick ratio	1.0
Current ratio	2.7
Inventory turnover[b]	7.0
Days sales outstanding[c]	32.0 days
Fixed assets turnover[b]	13.0
Total assets turnover[b]	2.6
Return on assets	9.1%
Return on equity	18.2%
Profit margin on sales	3.5%
Debt-to-assets ratio	21.0%
Liabilities-to-assets ratio	50.0%
P/E ratio	6.0
Price/Cash flow ratio	3.5
Market/Book ratio	3.5

[a]Industry average ratios have been constant for the past 4 years.
[b]Based on year-end balance sheet figures.
[c]Calculation is based on a 365-day year.

SPREADSHEET PROBLEMS

(3-15)
Build a Model: Ratio Analysis

Start with the partial model in the file *Ch03 P15 Build a Model.xls* from the textbook's Web site. Joshua & White (J&W) Technologies's financial statements are also shown below. Answer the following questions. (*Note:* Industry average ratios are provided in *Ch03 P15 Build a Model.xls.*)

resource

a. Has J&W's liquidity position improved or worsened? Explain.
b. Has J&W's ability to manage its assets improved or worsened? Explain.
c. How has J&W's profitability changed during the last year?
d. Perform an extended DuPont analysis for J&W for 2012 and 2013. What do these results tell you?
e. Perform a common size analysis. What has happened to the composition (that is, percentage in each category) of assets and liabilities?
f. Perform a percentage change analysis. What does this tell you about the change in profitability and asset utilization?

Joshua & White Technologies: December 31 Balance Sheets
(Thousands of Dollars)

Assets	2013	2012	Liabilities & Equity	2013	2012
Cash	$ 21,000	$ 20,000	Accounts payable	$ 33,600	$ 32,000
Short-term investments	3,759	3,240	Accruals	12,600	12,000
Accounts receivable	52,500	48,000	Notes payable	19,929	6,480
Inventories	84,000	56,000	Total current liabilities	$ 66,129	$ 50,480
Total current assets	$161,259	$127,240	Long-term debt	67,662	58,320
Net fixed assets	218,400	200,000	Total liabilities	$133,791	$108,800
Total assets	$379,659	$327,240	Common stock	183,793	178,440
			Retained earnings	62,075	40,000
			Total common equity	$245,868	$218,440
			Total liabilities & equity	$379,659	$327,240

Joshua & White Technologies December 31 Income Statements
(Thousands of Dollars)

	2013	2012
Sales	$420,000	$400,000
COGS excluding depr. & amort.	300,000	298,000
Depreciation and amortization	19,660	18,000
Other operating expenses	27,600	22,000
EBIT	$ 72,740	$ 62,000
Interest expense	5,740	4,460
EBT	$ 67,000	$ 57,540
Taxes (40%)	26,800	23,016
Net income	$ 40,200	$ 34,524
Common dividends	$ 18,125	$ 17,262

Other Data	2012	2011
Year-end stock price	$ 90.00	$ 96.00
Number of shares (thousands)	4,052	4,000
Lease payment (thousands of dollars)	$ 20,000	$ 20,000
Sinking fund payment (thousands of dollars)	$ 5,000	$ 5,000

 THOMSON REUTERS

Use the Thomson ONE—Business School Edition online database to work this chapter's questions.

Analysis of Ford's Financial Statements with Thomson ONE—Business School Edition

Use Thomson ONE to analyze Ford Motor Company. Enter Ford's ticker symbol (F) and select GO. By selecting the menu at left labeled Financials, you can find Ford's key financial statements for the past several years. Under the Financial Ratios heading, select Thomson Ratios and then Annual Ratios to see an in-depth summary of Ford's various ratios over the past 5 years.

Click on the Comparables menu at left and scroll down to find the submenu items for Key Financials and Key Financial Ratios for Ford and a few of its peers. If you scroll up, still in the Comparables menu, you can select a different list of peer firms to be included in the analysis. The default group is "Peers by SIC code."

Thomson ONE—BSE Discussion Questions

1. What has happened to Ford's liquidity position over the past 3 years? How does Ford's liquidity compare with its peers? (*Hint:* You may use both the peer key financial ratios and liquidity comparison to answer this question.)

2. Look at Ford's inventory turnover ratio. How does this ratio compare with its peers? Have there been any interesting changes over time in this measure? Do you consider Ford's inventory management to be a strength or a weakness?

3. Construct a simple DuPont analysis for Ford and its peers. What are Ford's strengths and weaknesses relative to its competitors?

MINI CASE

The first part of the case, presented in Chapter 2, discussed the situation of Computron Industries after an expansion program. A large loss occurred in 2013, rather than the expected profit. As a result, its managers, directors, and investors are concerned about the firm's survival.

Jenny Cochran was brought in as assistant to Gary Meissner, Computron's chairman, who had the task of getting the company back into a sound financial position. Computron's 2012 and 2013 balance sheets and income statements, together with projections for 2014, are shown in the following tables. The tables also show the 2012 and 2013 financial ratios, along with industry average data. The 2014 projected financial statement data represent Cochran's and Meissner's best guess for 2014 results, assuming that some new financing is arranged to get the company "over the hump."

Balance Sheets

	2012	2013	2014E
Assets			
Cash	$ 9,000	$ 7,282	$ 14,000
Short-term investments	48,600	20,000	71,632
Accounts receivable	351,200	632,160	878,000
Inventories	715,200	1,287,360	1,716,480
Total current assets	$ 1,124,000	$1,946,802	$2,680,112
Gross fixed assets	491,000	1,202,950	1,220,000
Less: Accumulated depreciation	146,200	263,160	383,160
Net fixed assets	$ 344,800	$ 939,790	$ 836,840
Total assets	$ 1,468,800	$2,886,592	$3,516,952
Liabilities and Equity			
Accounts payable	$ 145,600	$ 324,000	$ 359,800
Notes payable	200,000	720,000	300,000
Accruals	136,000	284,960	380,000
Total current liabilities	$ 481,600	$1,328,960	$1,039,800
Long-term debt	323,432	1,000,000	500,000
Common stock (100,000 shares)	460,000	460,000	1,680,936
Retained earnings	203,768	97,632	296,216
Total equity	$ 663,768	$ 557,632	$1,977,152
Total liabilities and equity	$ 1,468,800	$2,886,592	$3,516,952

Note: "E" denotes "estimated"; the 2014 data are forecasts.

Income Statements

	2012	2013	2014E
Sales	$ 3,432,000	$5,834,400	$7,035,600
Cost of goods sold except depr.	2,864,000	4,980,000	5,800,000
Depreciation and amortization	18,900	116,960	120,000
Other expenses	340,000	720,000	612,960
Total operating costs	$ 3,222,900	$5,816,960	$6,532,960
EBIT	$ 209,100	$ 17,440	$ 502,640
Interest expense	62,500	176,000	80,000
EBT	$ 146,600	($ 158,560)	$ 422,640
Taxes (40%)	58,640	(63,424)	169,056
Net income	$ 87,960	($ 95,136)	$ 253,584

Other Data

Stock price	$ 8.50	$ 6.00	$ 12.17
Shares outstanding	100,000	100,000	250,000
EPS	$ 0.880	($ 0.951)	$ 1.014
DPS	$ 0.220	0.110	0.220
Tax rate	40%	40%	40%
Book value per share	$ 6.638	$ 5.576	$ 7.909
Lease payments	$ 40,000	$ 40,000	$ 40,000

Note: "E" denotes "estimated"; the 2014 data are forecasts.

Ratio Analysis

	2012	2013	2014E	Industry Average
Current	2.3	1.5	_____	2.7
Quick	0.8	0.5	_____	1.0
Inventory turnover	4.0	4.0	_____	6.1
Days sales outstanding	37.3	39.6	_____	32.0
Fixed assets turnover	10.0	6.2	_____	7.0
Total assets turnover	2.3	2.0	_____	2.5
Debt ratio	35.6%	59.6%	_____	32.0%
Liabilities-to-assets ratio	54.8%	80.7%	_____	50.0%
TIE	3.3	0.1	_____	6.2
EBITDA coverage	2.6	0.8	_____	8.0
Profit margin	2.6%	−1.6%	_____	3.6%
Basic earning power	14.2%	0.6%	_____	17.8%
ROA	6.0%	−3.3%	_____	9.0%
ROE	13.3%	−17.1%	_____	17.9%
Price/Earnings (P/E)	9.7	−6.3	_____	16.2
Price/Cash flow	8.0	27.5	_____	7.6
Market/Book	1.3	1.1	_____	2.9

Note: "E" denotes "estimated."

Cochran must prepare an analysis of where the company is now, what it must do to regain its financial health, and what actions to take. Your assignment is to help her answer the following questions. Provide clear explanations, not yes or no answers.

a. Why are ratios useful? What three groups use ratio analysis and for what reasons?
b. Calculate the 2014 current and quick ratios based on the projected balance sheet and income statement data. What can you say about the company's liquidity position in 2012, 2013, and as projected for 2014? We often think of ratios as being useful (1) to managers to help run the business, (2) to bankers for credit analysis, and (3) to stockholders for stock valuation. Would these different types of analysts have an equal interest in the liquidity ratios?

c. Calculate the 2014 inventory turnover, days sales outstanding (DSO), fixed assets turnover, and total assets turnover. How does Computron's utilization of assets stack up against that of other firms in its industry?

d. Calculate the 2014 debt ratio, liabilities-to-assets ratio, times-interest-earned, and EBITDA coverage ratios. How does Computron compare with the industry with respect to financial leverage? What can you conclude from these ratios?

e. Calculate the 2014 profit margin, basic earning power (BEP), return on assets (ROA), and return on equity (ROE). What can you say about these ratios?

f. Calculate the 2014 price/earnings ratio, price/cash flow ratio, and market/book ratio. Do these ratios indicate that investors are expected to have a high or low opinion of the company?

g. Perform a common size analysis and percentage change analysis. What do these analyses tell you about Computron?

h. Use the extended DuPont equation to provide a summary and overview of Computron's financial condition as projected for 2014. What are the firm's major strengths and weaknesses?

i. What are some potential problems and limitations of financial ratio analysis?

j. What are some qualitative factors that analysts should consider when evaluating a company's likely future financial performance?

SELECTED ADDITIONAL CASES

The following cases from CengageCompose cover many of the concepts discussed in this chapter and are available at **compose.cengage.com**.

Klein-Brigham Series:
Case 35, "Mark X Company (A)," illustrates the use of ratio analysis in the evaluation of a firm's existing and potential financial positions; Case 36, "Garden State Container Corporation," is similar in content to Case 35; Case 51, "Safe Packaging Corporation," updates Case 36; Case 68, "Sweet Dreams Inc.," also updates Case 36; and Case 71, "Swan-Davis, Inc.," illustrates how financial analysis—based on both historical statements and forecasted statements—is used for internal management and lending decisions.

© lulu/fotolia.com

PART **2**

Fixed Income Securities

© Adalberto Rios Szalay/Sexto Sol/Getty Images

CHAPTER 4

Time Value of Money

When you graduate and go to work, your compensation package will almost certainly include either a *defined benefit (DB)* or a *defined contribution (DC)* pension plan. Under a DB plan, the company will put funds for you into its pension fund, which will then invest in stocks, bonds, real estate, and so forth and then use those funds to make the promised payments after you retire. Under a DC plan, the company will put money into your 401(k) plan (which is essentially a mutual fund), you will decide what type of assets to buy, and you will withdraw money after you retire. The analysis required to set up a good retirement program is based on the subject of this chapter, the time value of money (TVM).

How do you suppose a stock market crash like we had in 2008, with the average stock down about 40%, will affect DB and DC retirement plans? If you have a 401(k) plan that holds stocks, as most people do, TVM analysis would show clearly that you will have to work longer than you expected, reduce your post-retirement standard of living, or both.

With a DB plan, a stock market decline reduces the value of the investments set aside for you by the company. If there is also a decline in interest rates, as there was in 2008, TVM analysis shows that the amount of money the company should set aside for you goes up. Thus, the company's pension funding status, which is the difference between the value of the pension plan's investments and the amount the plan should have on hand to cover the future obligations, becomes severely underfunded if the market crashes *and* interest rates fall. This can even lead to bankruptcy, in which case you might end up with retirement payments from the government instead of from the company, with the government's payments a lot lower than those promised by the company's plan. If you don't believe us, ask someone who recently retired from a bankrupt airline or auto company.

Corporate Valuation and the Time Value of Money

© Rob Webb/Getty Images

In Chapter 1 we explained (1) that managers should strive to make their firms more valuable, and (2) that the value of a firm is determined by the size, timing, and risk of its free cash flows (FCF). Recall from Chapter 2 that free cash flows are the cash flows available for distribution to all of a firm's investors (stockholders and creditors). We explain how to calculate the weighted average cost of capital (WACC) in Chapter 9, but it is enough for now to think of the WACC as the average rate of return required by all of the firm's investors. The intrinsic value of a company is given by the following diagram. Note that central to this value is discounting the free cash flows at the WACC in order to find the value of the firm. This discounting is one aspect of the time value of money. We discuss time value of money techniques in this chapter.

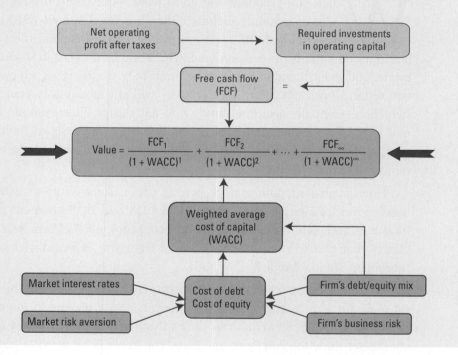

© Cengage Learning 2014

In Chapter 1, we saw that the primary objective of financial management is to maximize the intrinsic value of a firm's stock. We also saw that stock values depend on the timing of the cash flows investors expect from an investment—a dollar expected sooner is worth more than a dollar expected further in the future. Therefore, it is essential for financial managers to understand the time value of money and its impact on stock prices. In this chapter we will explain exactly how the timing of cash flows affects asset values and rates of return.

The principles of time value analysis have many applications, including retirement planning, loan payment schedules, and decisions to invest (or not) in new equipment. *In fact, of all the concepts used in finance, none is more important than the* **time value of money (TVM)**, *also called* **discounted cash flow (DCF) analysis**. Time value concepts are used throughout the remainder of the book, so it is vital that you understand the material in this chapter and be able to work the chapter's problems before you move on to other topics.

4-1 Time Lines

The first step in a time value analysis is to set up a **time line** to help you visualize what's happening in the particular problem. To illustrate, consider the following diagram, where PV represents $100 that is in a bank account today and FV is the value that will be in the account at some future time (3 years from now in this example):

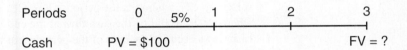

r e s o u r c e

The textbook's Web site contains an Excel file that will guide you through the chapter's calculations. The file for this chapter is **Ch04 Tool Kit.xls**, *and we encourage you to open the file and follow along as you read the chapter.*

The intervals from 0 to 1, 1 to 2, and 2 to 3 are time periods such as years or months. Time 0 is today, and it is the beginning of Period 1; Time 1 is one period from today, and it is both the end of Period 1 and the beginning of Period 2; and so on. In our example, the periods are years, but they could also be quarters or months or even days. Note again that each tick mark corresponds to both the *end* of one period and the *beginning* of the next one. Thus, if the periods are years, the tick mark at Time 2 represents both the end of Year 2 and the beginning of Year 3.

Cash flows are shown directly below the tick marks, and the relevant interest rate is shown just above the time line. Unknown cash flows, which you are trying to find, are indicated by question marks. Here the interest rate is 5%; a single cash outflow, $100, is invested at Time 0; and the Time-3 value is unknown and must be found. In this example, cash flows occur only at Times 0 and 3, with no flows at Times 1 or 2. We will, of course, deal with situations where multiple cash flows occur. Note also that in our example the interest rate is constant for all 3 years. The interest rate is generally held constant, but if it varies, then in the diagram we show different rates for the different periods.

Time lines are especially important when you are first learning time value concepts, but even experts use them to analyze complex problems. Throughout the book, our procedure is to set up a time line to show what's happening, provide an equation that must be solved to find the answer, and then explain how to solve the equation with a regular calculator, a financial calculator, and a computer spreadsheet.

SELF-TEST

Do time lines deal only with years, or could other periods be used?

Set up a time line to illustrate the following situation: You currently have $2,000 in a 3-year certificate of deposit (CD) that pays a guaranteed 4% annually. You want to know the value of the CD after 3 years.

4-2 Future Values

A dollar in hand today is worth more than a dollar to be received in the future—if you had the dollar now you could invest it, earn interest, and end up with more than one dollar in the future. The process of going forward, from **present values (PVs)** to **future values (FVs)**, is called **compounding**. To illustrate, refer back to our 3-year time line and assume that you have $100 in a bank account that pays a guaranteed 5% interest each year. How much would you have at the end of Year 3? We first define some terms, and then we set up a time line and show how the future value is calculated.

> PV = Present value, or beginning amount. In our example, PV = $100.
>
> FV_N = Future value, or ending amount, in the account after N periods. Whereas PV is the value *now*, or the *present value*, FV_N is the value N periods into the *future*, after interest earned has been added to the account.
>
> CF_t = Cash flow. Cash flows can be positive or negative. For a borrower, the first cash flow is positive and the subsequent cash flows are negative, and the reverse holds for a lender. The cash flow for a particular period is often given a subscript, CF_t, where t is the period. Thus, CF_0 = PV = the cash flow at Time 0, whereas CF_3 would be the cash flow at the end of Period 3. In this example the cash flows occur *at the ends* of the periods, but in some problems they occur at the beginning.
>
> I = Interest rate earned per year. (Sometimes a lowercase i is used.) Interest earned is based on the balance at the beginning of each year, and we assume that interest is paid at the end of the year. Here I = 5% or, expressed as a decimal, 0.05. Throughout this chapter, we designate the interest rate as I (or I/YR, for interest rate per year) because that symbol is used on most financial calculators. Note, though, that in later chapters we use the symbol "r" to denote the rate because r (for *rate* of return) is used more often in the finance literature. Also, in this chapter we generally assume that interest payments are guaranteed by the U.S. government and hence are riskless (i.e., certain). In later chapters we will deal with risky investments, where the rate actually earned might be different from its expected level.
>
> INT = Dollars of interest earned during the year = (Beginning amount) × I. In our example, INT = $100(0.05) = $5 for Year 1, but it rises in subsequent years as the amount at the beginning of each year increases.
>
> N = Number of periods involved in the analysis. In our example, N = 3. Sometimes the number of periods is designated with a lowercase n, so both N and n indicate number of periods.

We can use four different procedures to solve time value problems.[1] These methods are described next.

4-2a Step-by-Step Approach

The time line itself can be modified and used to find the FV of $100 compounded for 3 years at 5%, as shown below:

Time	0	5%	1	2	3
Amount at beginning of period	$100.00 →		$105.00 →	$110.25 →	$115.76

---

[1]A fifth procedure is called the *tabular approach*, which uses tables that provide "interest factors;" this procedure was used before financial calculators and computers became available. Now, though, calculators and spreadsheets such as *Excel* are programmed to calculate the specific factor needed for a given problem, which is then used to find the FV. This is much more efficient than using the tables. Also, calculators and spreadsheets can handle fractional periods and fractional interest rates. For these reasons, tables are not used in business today; hence we do not discuss them in the text. However, because some professors cover the tables for pedagogical purposes, we discuss them in **Web Extension 4A**, on the textbook's Web site.

We start with $100 in the account, which is shown at t = 0. We then multiply the initial amount, and each succeeding beginning-of-year amount, by $(1 + I) = (1.05)$.

- You earn $100(0.05) = $5 of interest during the first year, so the amount at the end of Year 1 (or at t = 1) is

$$
\begin{aligned}
FV_1 &= PV + INT \\
&= PV + PV(I) \\
&= PV(1 + I) \\
&= \$100(1 + 0.05) = \$100(1.05) = \$105
\end{aligned}
$$

- We begin the second year with $105, earn 0.05($105) = $5.25 on the now larger beginning-of-period amount, and end the year with $110.25. Interest during Year 2 is $5.25, and it is higher than the first year's interest, $5, because we earned $5(0.05) = $0.25 interest on the first year's interest. This is called "compounding," and interest earned on interest is called "compound interest."
- This process continues, and because the beginning balance is higher in each successive year, the interest earned each year increases.
- The total interest earned, $15.76, is reflected in the final balance, $115.76.

The step-by-step approach is useful because it shows exactly what is happening. However, this approach is time-consuming, especially if the number of years is large and you are using a calculator rather than *Excel*, so streamlined procedures have been developed.

4-2b Formula Approach

In the step-by-step approach, we multiplied the amount at the beginning of each period by $(1 + I) = (1.05)$. Notice that the value at the end of Year 2 is

$$
\begin{aligned}
FV_2 &= FV_1(1 + I) \\
&= PV(1 + I)(1 + I) \\
&= PV(1 + I)^2 \\
&= 100(1.05)^2 = \$110.25
\end{aligned}
$$

If N = 3, then we multiply PV by $(1 + I)$ three different times, which is the same as multiplying the beginning amount by $(1 + I)^3$. This concept can be extended, and the result is this key equation:

$$
FV_N = PV(1 + I)^N \tag{4-1}
$$

We can apply Equation 4-1 to find the FV in our example:

$$
FV_3 = \$100(1.05)^3 = \$115.76
$$

Equation 4-1 can be used with any calculator, even a nonfinancial calculator that has an exponential function, making it easy to find FVs no matter how many years are involved.

4-2c Financial Calculators

Financial calculators were designed specifically to solve time value problems. First, note that financial calculators have five keys that correspond to the five variables in the basic time value equations. Equation 4-1 has only four variables, but we will shortly deal with situations where a fifth variable (a set of periodic additional payments) is involved. We show the inputs for our example above their keys in the following diagram, and the output, which is the FV, below its key. Because there are no periodic payments in this example, we enter 0 for PMT. We describe the keys in more detail below the diagram.

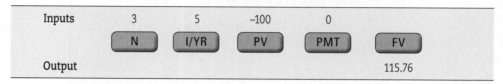

N = Number of periods = 3. Some calculators use n rather than N.

I/YR = Interest rate per period = 5. Some calculators use i or I rather than I/YR. Calculators are programmed to automatically convert the 5 to the decimal 0.05 before doing the arithmetic.

PV = Present value = 100. In our example we begin by making a deposit, which is an outflow of 100, so the PV is entered with a negative sign. On most calculators you must enter the 100, then press the +/− key to switch from +100 to −100. If you enter −100 directly, this will subtract 100 from the last number in the calculator, which will give you an incorrect answer unless the last number was zero.

PMT = Payment. This key is used if we have a series of equal, or constant, payments. Because there are no such payments in our current problem, we enter PMT = 0. We will use the PMT key later in this chapter.

FV = Future value. In our example, the calculator automatically shows the FV as a positive number because we entered the PV as a negative number. If we had entered the 100 as a positive number, then the FV would have been negative. Calculators automatically assume that either the PV or the FV must be negative.

As noted in our example, you first enter the four known values (N, I/YR, PV, and PMT) and then press the FV key to get the answer, FV = 115.76.[2]

4-2d Spreadsheets

r e s o u r c e

*See **Ch04 Tool Kit.xls** for all calculations.*

Spreadsheets are ideally suited for solving many financial problems, including those dealing with the time value of money.[2] Spreadsheets are obviously useful for calculations, but they can also be used like a word processor to create exhibits like our Figure 4-1, which includes text, drawings, and calculations. We use this figure to show that four methods can be used to find the FV of $100 after 3 years at an interest rate of 5%. The time line on Rows 36 to 37 is useful for visualizing the problem, after which the spreadsheet calculates the required answer. Note that the letters across the top designate columns, the numbers down the left column designate rows, and the rows and columns jointly designate cells. Thus, cell C32 shows the amount of the investment, $100, and it is given a minus sign because it is an outflow.

---

[2]The file **Ch04 Tool Kit.xls** on the book's Web site does the calculations in the chapter using *Excel*. We *highly recommend* that you study the models in this **Tool Kit**. Doing so will give you practice with *Excel*, and that will help you tremendously in later courses, in the job market, and in the workplace. Also, going through the models will improve your understanding of financial concepts.

Hints on Using Financial Calculators

© Rob Webb/Getty Images

When using a financial calculator, make sure your machine is set up as indicated below. Refer to your calculator manual or to our calculator tutorial on the textbook's Web site for information on setting up your calculator.

- **One payment per period.** Many calculators "come out of the box" assuming that 12 payments are made per year; that is, they assume monthly payments. However, in this book we generally deal with problems in which only one payment is made each year. *Therefore, you should set your calculator at one payment per year and leave it there. See our tutorial or your calculator manual if you need assistance.* We will show you how to solve problems with more than 1 payment per year in Section 4-15.
- **End mode.** With most contracts, payments are made at the *end* of each period. However, some contracts call for payments at the *beginning* of each period. You can switch between "End Mode" and "Begin Mode" depending on the problem you are solving. *Because most of the problems in this book call for end-of-period payments, you should return your calculator to End Mode after you work a problem in which payments are made at the beginning of periods.*
- **Negative sign for outflows.** When first learning how to use financial calculators, students often forget that one cash flow must be negative. Mathematically, financial calculators solve a version of this equation:

$$PV(1 + I)^N + FV_N = 0 \qquad (4\text{-}2)$$

Notice that for reasonable values of I, either PV or FV_N must be negative, and the other one must be positive to make the equation equal 0. This is reasonable because, in all realistic situations, one cash flow is an outflow (which should have a negative sign) and one is an inflow (which should have a positive sign). For example, if you make a deposit (which is an outflow, and hence should have a negative sign) then you will expect to make a later withdrawal (which is an inflow with a positive sign). *The bottom line is that one of your inputs for a cash flow must be negative and one must be positive. This generally means typing the outflow as a positive number and then pressing the +/− key to convert from + to − before hitting the Enter key.*

- **Decimal places.** When doing arithmetic, calculators allow you to show from 0 to 11 decimal places on the display. When working with dollars, we generally specify two decimal places. When dealing with interest rates, we generally specify two places if the rate is expressed as a percentage like 5.25%, but we specify four places if the rate is expressed as a decimal like 0.0525.
- **Interest rates.** *For arithmetic operations with a nonfinancial calculator, the rate 5.25% must be stated as a decimal, .0525. However, with a financial calculator you must enter 5.25, not .0525, because financial calculators are programmed to assume that rates are stated as percentages.*

It is useful to put all inputs in a section of the spreadsheet designated "INPUTS." In Figure 4-1, we put the inputs in the aqua-colored range of cells. Rather than enter fixed numbers into the model's formulas, we enter the cell references for the inputs. This makes it easy to modify the problem by changing the inputs and then automatically use the new data in the calculations.

Time lines are important for solving finance problems because they help us visualize what's happening. When we work a problem by hand we usually draw a time line, and when we work a problem with *Excel*, we set the model up as a time line. For example, in Figure 4-1, Rows 36 to 37 are indeed a time line. It's easy to construct time lines with *Excel*, with each column designating a different period on the time line.

FIGURE **4-1**

Alternative Procedures for Calculating Future Values

	A	B	C	D	E	F	G
31	**INPUTS:**						
32	**Investment = CF_0 = PV =**		**−$100.00**				
33	**Interest rate = I =**		**5%**				
34	**No. of periods = N =**		**3**				
35							
36	**Time Line**		**Periods:**	**0**	**1**	**2**	**3**
37			**Cash flow:**	**−$100.00**	**0**	**0**	**FV = ?**
38							
39	**1. Step-by-Step: Multiply by (1 + I) each step**			**$100.00 →**	**$105.00 →**	**$110.25 →**	**$115.76**
40							
41	**2. Formula: $FV_N = PV(1+I)^N$**				**$FV_3 = $100(1.05)^3$**	**=**	**$115.76**
42							
43		**Inputs:**	**3**	**5**	**−100**	**0**	
44	**3. Financial Calculator:**		**N**	**I/YR**	**PV**	**PMT**	**FV**
45	**Output:**						**$115.76**
46							
47	**4. *Excel* Spreadsheet:**		**FV function:**	**FV_N =**	**=FV(I,N,0,PV)**		
48			**Fixed inputs:**	**FV_N =**	**=FV(0.05,3,0,−100) =**		**$115.76**
49			**Cell references:**	**FV_N =**	**=FV(C33,C34,0,C32) =**		**$115.76**
50	**In the *Excel* formula, the terms are entered in this sequence: interest, periods, 0 to indicate no periodic cash flows, and then the PV. The data can be entered as fixed numbers or, better yet, as**						
51	**cell references.**						

On Row 39, we use *Excel* to go through the step-by-step calculations, multiplying the beginning-of-year values by (1 + I) to find the compounded value at the end of each period. Cell G39 shows the final result of the step-by-step approach.

We illustrate the formula approach in Row 41, using *Excel* to solve Equation 4-1 to find the FV. Cell G41 shows the formula result, $115.76. As it must, it equals the step-by-step result.

Rows 43 to 45 illustrate the financial calculator approach, which again produces the same answer, $115.76.

The last section, in Rows 47 to 49, illustrates *Excel*'s future value (FV) function. You can access the function wizard by clicking the f_x symbol in *Excel*'s formula bar. Then select the category for Financial functions, and then the FV function, which is =**FV(I,N,0,PV)**, as shown in Cell E47.[3] Cell E48 shows how the formula would look with numbers as inputs; the actual function itself is entered in Cell G48, but it shows up in the table as the answer, $115.76. If you access the model and put the pointer on Cell G48,

---

[3] All functions begin with an equal sign. The third entry is zero in this example, which indicates that there are no periodic payments. Later in this chapter we will use the FV function in situations where we have nonzero periodic payments. Also, for inputs we use our own notation, which is similar but not identical to *Excel*'s notation.

you will see the full formula. Finally, Cell E49 shows how the formula would look with cell references rather than fixed values as inputs, with the actual function again in Cell G49. We generally use cell references as function inputs because this makes it easy to change inputs and see how those changes affect the output. This is called "sensitivity analysis." Many real-world financial applications use sensitivity analysis, so it is useful to form the habit of setting up an input data section and then using cell references rather than fixed numbers in the functions.

When entering interest rates in *Excel*, you can use either actual numbers or percentages, depending on how the cell is formatted. For example, we first formatted Cell C33 to Percentage, and then typed in 5, which showed up as 5%. However, *Excel* uses 0.05 for the arithmetic. Alternatively, we could have formatted C33 as a Number, in which case we would have typed "0.05." If a cell were formatted to Number and you entered 5, then *Excel* would think you meant 500%. Thus, *Excel*'s procedure is different from the convention used in financial calculators.

Sometimes students are confused about the sign of the initial $100. We used +$100 in Rows 39 and 41 as the initial investment when calculating the future value using the step-by-step method and the future value formula, but we used −$100 with a financial calculator and the spreadsheet function in Rows 43 and 48. When must you use a positive value and when must you use a negative value? The answer is that whenever you set up a time line and use either a financial calculator's time value functions or *Excel's* time value functions, you must enter the signs that correspond to the "direction" of the cash flows. Cash flows that go out of your pocket (outflows) are negative, but cash flows that come into your pocket (inflows) are positive. In the case of the FV function in our example, if you invest $100 (an outflow, and therefore negative) at Time 0 then the bank will make available to you $115.76 (an inflow, and therefore positive) at Time 3. In essence, the FV function on a financial calculator or *Excel* answers the question "If I invest this much now, how much will be available to me at a time in the future?" The investment is an outflow and negative, and the amount available to you is an inflow and positive. If you use algebraic formulas then you must keep track of whether the value is an outflow or an inflow yourself. When in doubt, refer back to a correctly constructed time line.

4-2e Comparing the Procedures

The first step in solving any time value problem is to understand what is happening and then to diagram it on a time line. Woody Allen said that 90% of success is just showing up. With time value problems, 90% of success is correctly setting up the time line.

After you diagram the problem on a time line, your next step is to pick one of the four approaches shown in Figure 4-1 to solve the problem. Any one approach may be used, but your choice will depend on the particular situation.

All business students should know Equation 4-1 by heart and should also know how to use a financial calculator. So, for simple problems such as finding the future value of a single payment, it is generally easiest and quickest to use either the formula approach or a financial calculator. However, for problems that involve several cash flows, the formula approach usually is time-consuming, so either the calculator or spreadsheet approach would generally be used. Calculators are portable and quick to set up, but if many calculations of the same type must be done, or if you want to see how changes in an input such as the interest rate affect the future value, then the spreadsheet approach is generally more efficient. If the problem has many irregular cash flows, or if you want to analyze alternative scenarios using different cash flows or interest rates, then the spreadsheet approach definitely is the most efficient procedure.

Spreadsheets have two additional advantages over calculators. First, it is easier to check the inputs with a spreadsheet because they are visible; with a calculator the inputs are buried somewhere in the machine. Thus, you are less likely to make a mistake in a complex problem when you use the spreadsheet approach. Second, with a spreadsheet, you can make your analysis much more transparent than you can when using a calculator. This is not necessarily important when all you want is the answer, but if you need to present your calculations to others, like your boss, it helps to be able to show intermediate steps, which enables someone to go through your exhibit and see exactly what you did. Transparency is also important when you must go back, sometime later, and reconstruct what you did.

You should understand the various approaches well enough to make a rational choice, given the nature of the problem and the equipment you have available. In any event, you must understand the concepts behind the calculations, and you also must know how to set up time lines in order to work complex problems. This is true for stock and bond valuation, capital budgeting, lease analysis, and many other types of financial problems.

4-2f Graphic View of the Compounding Process

Figure 4-2 shows how a $100 investment grows (or declines) over time at different interest rates. Interest rates are normally positive, but the "growth" concept is broad enough to include negative rates. We developed the curves by solving Equation 4-1 with different values for N and I. The interest rate is a growth rate: If money is deposited and earns 5% per year, then your funds will grow by 5% per year. Note also that time value concepts can be applied to anything that grows—sales, population, earnings per share, or your future salary. Also, as noted before, the "growth rate" can be negative, as was sales growth for a number of auto companies in recent years.

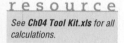

resource

See *Ch04 Tool Kit.xls* for all calculations.

FIGURE **4-2**

Growth of $100 at Various Interest Rates and Time Periods

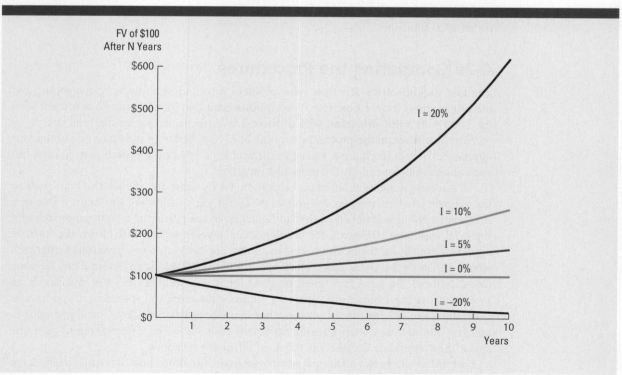

© Cengage Learning 2014

4-2g Simple Interest versus Compound Interest

As explained earlier, when interest is earned on the interest earned in prior periods, we call it **compound interest**. If interest is earned only on the principal, we call it **simple interest**. The total interest earned with simple interest is equal to the principal multiplied by the interest rate times the number of periods: PV(I)(N). The future value is equal to the principal plus the interest: FV = PV + PV(I)(N). For example, suppose you deposit $100 for 3 years and earn simple interest at an annual rate of 5%. Your balance at the end of 3 years would be:

$$FV = PV + PV(I)(N)$$
$$= \$100 + \$100(5\%)(3)$$
$$= \$100 + \$15 = \$115$$

Notice that this is less than the $115.76 we calculated earlier using compound interest. Most applications in finance are based on compound interest, but you should be aware that simple interest is still specified in some legal documents.

SELF-TEST

Explain why this statement is true: "A dollar in hand today is worth more than a dollar to be received next year, assuming interest rates are positive."

What is compounding? What would the future value of $100 be after 5 years at 10% compound interest? **($161.05)**

Suppose you currently have $2,000 and plan to purchase a 3-year certificate of deposit (CD) that pays 4% interest, compounded annually. How much will you have when the CD matures? **($2,249.73)** *How would your answer change if the interest rate were 5%, or 6%, or 20%? (Hint: With a calculator, enter N = 3, I/YR = 4, PV = –2000, and PMT = 0, then press FV to get 2,249.73. Then, enter I/YR = 5 to override the 4% and press FV again to get the second answer. In general, you can change one input at a time to see how the output changes.)* **($2,315.25; $2,382.03; $3,456.00)**

A company's sales in 2012 were $100 million. If sales grow by 8% annually, what will they be 10 years later? **($215.89 million)** *What would they be if they decline by 8% per year for 10 years?* **($43.44 million)**

How much would $1, growing at 5% per year, be worth after 100 years? **($131.50)** *What would FV be if the growth rate were 10%?* **($13,780.61)**

4-3 Present Values

Suppose you have some extra money and want to make an investment. A broker offers to sell you a bond that will pay a guaranteed $115.76 in 3 years. Banks are currently offering a guaranteed 5% interest on 3-year certificates of deposit (CDs), and if you don't buy the bond you will buy a CD. The 5% rate paid on the CD is defined as your **opportunity cost**, or the rate of return you would earn on an alternative investment of similar risk if you don't invest in the security under consideration. Given these conditions, what's the most you should pay for the bond?

4-3a Discounting a Future Value to Find the Present Value

First, recall from the future value example in the last section that if you invested $100 at 5% in a CD, it would grow to $115.76 in 3 years. You would also have $115.76 after 3 years if you bought the bond. Therefore, the most you should pay for the bond is

It's a Matter of Trust

© Rob Webb/Getty Images

One of our Founding Fathers, Benjamin Franklin, wanted to make a donation to the cities of Boston and Philadelphia, but he didn't want the cities to squander the money before it had grown enough to make a big impact. His solution was the "Methuselah Trust." When Franklin died in 1790, his will left £1,000, at that time about $4,550, to Philadelphia and to Boston, but on the condition that it would be invested for 100 years, after which some the proceeds were to be used for the public projects (primarily trade schools and water works) and the rest invested for another 100 years. Depending on interest rates, this strategy could generate quite a bit of money! For example, if half of his bequest, $2,275, remained invested at 5% compound interest for the entire 200 years, the value in 1990 would be $39.3 million! The ultimate payout, however, was only about $7 million, because substantial amounts were eaten up by trustee fees, taxes, and legal battles. Franklin certainly would have been disappointed!

In 1936 an eccentric investor and New York lawyer, Jonathan Holden, decided to expand on Franklin's idea by donating a series of 500-year and 1,000-year trusts to Hartwick College and several other recipients. By 2008 Hartwick College's trust had grown in value to about $9 million; if invested at 5% for the remaining 928 years of its planned life, its value would grow to ($9 million)$(1.05)^{928}$ = 4.15×10^{26}. That is a lot of dollars by any measure! For example, million-dollar bills (if they existed by then) would paper the earth 10,000 times over, or laid end to end would reach the nearest star, Alpha Centauri, more than 1,000 times. In a move that surely would have disappointed Holden, Hartwick College was able to convert the trust into annual cash flows of about $450,000 a year.

The trusts of Franklin and Holden didn't turn out exactly as they had planned—Franklin's trust didn't grow adequately, and Holden's trust was converted into annual cash flows. This goes to show that you can't always trust a trust!

Sources: Jake Palmateer, "On the Bright Side: Hartwick College Receives $9 million Trust," *The Daily Star,* *Oneonta, NY,* January 22, 2008, **http://thedailystar.com/local/ x112892349/On-The-Bright-Side-Hartwick-College-receives- 9M-trust/print**; Lewis H. Lapham, "Trust Issues," *Lapham's Quarterly,* Friday December 2, 2011, **www.laphamsquarterly. org/essays/trust-issues.php?page=1.**

$100—this is its "fair price," which is also its intrinsic, or fundamental, value. If you could buy the bond for *less than* $100, then you should buy it rather than invest in the CD. Conversely, if its price were *more than* $100, you should buy the CD. If the bond's price were exactly $100, you should be indifferent between the bond and the CD.

The $100 is defined as the present value, or PV, of $115.76 due in 3 years when the appropriate interest rate is 5%. In general, *the present value of a cash flow due N years in the future is the amount which, if it were on hand today, would grow to equal the given future amount.* Because $100 would grow to $115.76 in 3 years at a 5% interest rate, $100 is the present value of $115.76 due in 3 years at a 5% rate.

Finding present values is called **discounting**, and as previously noted, it is the reverse of compounding: If you know the PV, you can compound it to find the FV, or if you know the FV, you can discount it to find the PV. Indeed, we simply solve Equation 4-1, the formula for the future value, for the PV to produce the present value equation as follows.

Compounding to find future values: Future value = $FV_N = PV(1 + I)^N$ (4-1)

Discounting to find present values: Present value = $PV = \dfrac{FV_N}{(1 + I)^N}$ (4-3)

The top section of Figure 4-3 shows inputs and a time line for finding the present value of $115.76 discounted back for 3 years. We first calculate the PV using the step-by-step approach. When we found the FV in the previous section, we worked from left to right, *multiplying* the initial amount and each subsequent amount by $(1 + I)$. To find present values, we work backward, or from right to left, *dividing* the future value and each subsequent amount by $(1 + I)$, with the present value of $100 shown in Cell D105. The step-by-step procedure shows exactly what's happening, and that can be quite useful when you are working complex problems or trying to explain a model to others. However, it's inefficient, especially if you are dealing with more than a year or two.

A more efficient procedure is to use the formula approach in Equation 4-3, simply dividing the future value by $(1 + I)^N$. This gives the same result, as we see in Figure 4-3, Cell G107.

Equation 4-2 is actually programmed into financial calculators. As shown in Figure 4-3, Rows 109 to 111, we can find the PV by entering values for N = 3, I/YR = 5, PMT = 0, and FV = 115.76, and then pressing the PV key to get −100.

resource

See ChO4 Tool Kit.xls for all calculations.

FIGURE 4-3

Alternative Procedures for Calculating Present Values

	A	B	C	D	E	F	G
97	INPUTS:						
98	Future payment = CF_N = FV =		$115.76				
99	Interest rate = I =		5.00%				
100	No. of periods = N =		3				
101							
102	Time Line		Periods:	0	1	2	3
103			Cash flow:	PV = ?	0	0	$115.76
104							
105	1. Step-by-Step:			$100.00	← $105.00	← $110.25	← $115.76
106							
107	2. Formula: $PV_N = FV/(1+I)^N$			PV = $115.76/(1.05)^3		=	$100.00
108							
109	Inputs:		3	5		0	115.76
110	3. Financial Calculator:		N	I/YR	PV	PMT	FV
111	Output:				−$100.00		
112							
113	4. *Excel* Spreadsheet:		PV function:	PV =	=PV(I,N,0,FV)		
114			Fixed inputs:	PV =	=PV(0.05,3,0,115.76) =		−$100.00
115			Cell references:	PV =	=PV(C99,C100,0,C98) =		−$100.00
116							
117	In the *Excel* formula, the terms are entered in this sequence: interest, periods, 0 to indicate no periodic cash flows, and then the FV. The data can be entered as fixed numbers or, better yet, as cell references.						

Excel also has a function that solves Equation 4-3—this is the PV function, and it is written as **=PV(I,N,0,FV).**[4] Cell E113 shows the inputs to this function. Next, Cell E114 shows the *Excel* function with fixed numbers as inputs, with the actual function and the resulting −$100 in Cell G114. Cell E115 shows the *Excel* function using cell references, with the actual function and the resulting −$100 in Cell G115.

As with the future value calculation, students often wonder why the result of the present value calculation is sometimes positive and sometimes negative. In the algebraic calculations in Rows 105 and 107, the result is +$100, while the result of the calculation using a financial calculator or *Excel's* function in Rows 111 and 114 is −$100. Again, the answer is in the signs of a correctly constructed time line. Outflows are negative and inflows are positive. The PV function for *Excel* and a financial calculator answer the question "How much must I invest today in order to have available to me a certain amount of money in the future?" If you want to have $115.76 available in 3 years (an inflow to you, and therefore positive), then you must invest $100 today (an outflow, and therefore negative). If you use the algebraic functions as in Rows 105 and 107, you must keep track of whether the results of your calculations are inflows or outflows.

The fundamental goal of financial management is to maximize the firm's intrinsic value, and the intrinsic value of a business (or any asset, including stocks and bonds) is the *present value* of its expected future cash flows. Because present value lies at the heart of the valuation process, we will have much more to say about it in the remainder of this chapter and throughout the book.

4-3b Graphic View of the Discounting Process

Figure 4-4 shows that the present value of a sum to be received in the future decreases and approaches zero as the payment date is extended farther and farther into the future; it also shows that, the higher the interest rate, the faster the present value falls. At relatively high rates, funds due in the future are worth very little today, and even at relatively low rates present values of sums due in the very distant future are quite small. For example, at a 20% discount rate, $100 due in 40 years would be worth less than 7 cents today. (However, 1 cent would grow to almost $1 million in 100 years at 20%.)

r e s o u r c e

See *Ch04 Tool Kit.xls* for all calculations.

SELF-TEST

What is "discounting," and how is it related to compounding? How is the future value equation (4-1) related to the present value equation (4-3)?

How does the present value of a future payment change as the time to receipt is lengthened? As the interest rate increases?

Suppose a risk-free bond promises to pay $2,249.73 in 3 years. If the going risk-free interest rate is 4%, how much is the bond worth today? **($2,000)** *How much is the bond worth if it matures in 5 rather than 3 years?* **($1,849.11)** *If the risk-free interest rate is 6% rather than 4%, how much is the 5-year bond worth today?* **($1,681.13)**

How much would $1 million due in 100 years be worth today if the discount rate were 5%? **($7,604.49)** *What if the discount rate were 20%?* **($0.0121)**

---

[4]The third entry in the PV function is zero to indicate that there are no intermediate payments in this example.

FIGURE **4-4**

Present Value of $100 at Various Interest Rates and Time Periods

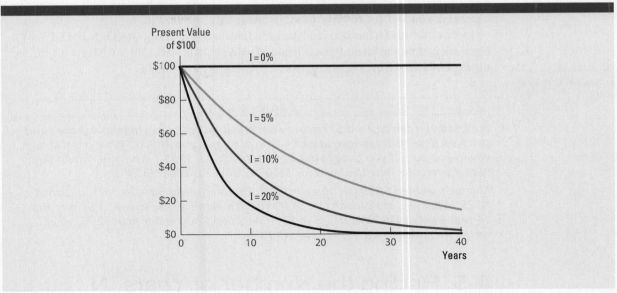

© Cengage Learning 2014

4-4 Finding the Interest Rate, I

We have used Equations 4-1, 4-2, and 4-3 to find future and present values. Those equations have four variables, and if we know three of them, then we (or our calculator or *Excel*) can solve for the fourth. Thus, if we know PV, I, and N, we can solve Equation 4-1 for FV, or if we know FV, I, and N, we can solve Equation 4-3 to find PV. That's what we did in the preceding two sections.

Now suppose we know PV, FV, and N, and we want to find I. For example, suppose we know that a given security has a cost of $100 and that it will return $150 after 10 years. Thus, we know PV, FV, and N, and we want to find the rate of return we will earn if we buy the security. Here's the solution using Equation 4-1 (with FV on the right side of the formula):

$$PV(1 + I)^N = FV$$
$$\$100(1 + I)^{10} = \$150$$
$$(1 + I)^{10} = \$150/\$100$$
$$(1 + I)^{10} = 1.5$$
$$(1 + I) = 1.5^{(1/10)}$$
$$1 + I = 1.0414$$
$$I = 0.0414 = 4.14\%$$

Finding the interest rate by solving the formula takes a little time and thought, but financial calculators and spreadsheets find the answer almost instantly. Here's the calculator setup:

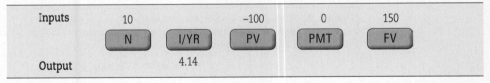

Enter N = 10, PV = −100, PMT = 0 (because there are no payments until the security matures), and FV = 150. Then, when you press the I/YR key, the calculator gives the answer, 4.14%. Notice that the PV is a negative value because it is a cash outflow (an investment) and the FV is positive because it is a cash inflow (a return of the investment). If you enter both PV and FV as positive numbers (or both as negative numbers), you will get an error message rather than the answer.

In *Excel*, the **RATE** function can be used to find the interest rate: =**RATE(N,PMT,PV,FV)**. For this example, the interest rate is found as =**RATE(10,0,−100,150)** = 0.0414 = 4.14%. See the file *Ch04 Tool Kit.xls* on the textbook's Web site for an example.

resource

See *Ch04 Tool Kit.xls* for all calculations.

SELF-TEST

Suppose you can buy a U.S. Treasury bond that makes no payments until the bond matures 10 years from now, at which time it will pay you $1,000.[5] What interest rate would you earn if you bought this bond for $585.43? **(5.5%)** *What rate would you earn if you could buy the bond for $550?* **(6.16%)** *For $600?* **(5.24%)***

Microsoft earned $0.33 per share in 1997. Fourteen years later, in 2011, it earned $2.75. What was the growth rate in Microsoft's earnings per share (EPS) over the 14-year period? **(16.35%)** *If EPS in 2011 had been $2.00 rather than $2.75, what would the growth rate have been?* **(13.73%)***

4-5 Finding the Number of Years, N

We sometimes need to know how long it will take to accumulate a specific sum of money, given our beginning funds and the rate we will earn. For example, suppose we now have $500,000 and the interest rate is 4.5%. How long will it be before we have $1 million?

Here's Equation 4-1, showing all the known variables.

$$\$1,000,000 = \$500,000(1 + 0.045)^N \tag{4-1}$$

We need to solve for N, and we can use three procedures: a financial calculator, *Excel* (or some other spreadsheet), or by working with natural logs. As you might expect, the calculator and spreadsheet approaches are easier.[6] Here's the calculator setup:

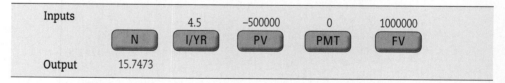

Enter I/YR = 4.5, PV = −500000, PMT = 0, and FV = 1000000. We press the N key to get the answer, 15.7473 years. In *Excel*, we would use the **NPER** function: =**NPER(I,PMT,PV,FV)**. Inserting data, we have =**NPER(0.045,0,−500000,1000000)** = 15.7473. The chapter's tool kit, *Ch04 Tool Kit.xls,* shows this example.

---

[5]This is a STRIP bond, which we explain in Chapter 5.
[6]Here's the setup for the log solution. First, transform Equation 4-1 as indicated, then find the natural logs using a financial calculator, and then solve for N:

$$\$1,000,000 = \$500,000(1 + 0.045)^N$$
$$2 = (1 + 0.045)^N$$
$$\ln(2) = N[\ln(1.045)]$$
$$N = 0.6931/0.0440 = 15.7473 \text{ years}$$

SELF-TEST

How long would it take $1,000 to double if it were invested in a bank that pays 6% per year? **(11.9 years)** *How long would it take if the rate were 10%?* **(7.27 years)**

A company's 2013 earnings per share were $2.75, and its growth rate during the prior 14 years was 16.35% per year. If that growth rate were maintained, how long would it take for EPS to double? **(4.58 years)**

4-6 Perpetuities

The previous sections examined the relationship between the present value and future value of a single payment at a fixed point in time. However, some securities promise to make payments forever. For example, preferred stock, which we discuss in Chapter 7, promises to pay a dividend forever. Another "forever" security originated in the mid-1700s when the British government issued some bonds that never matured and whose proceeds were used to pay off other British bonds. Because this action consolidated the government's debt, the new bonds were called "consols." The term stuck, and now any bond that promises to pay interest perpetually is called a **consol**, or a perpetuity. The interest rate on the consols was 2.5%, so a consol with a face value of £1,000 would pay £25 per year in perpetuity (£ is the currency symbol for a British pound).

A consol, or **perpetuity**, is simply an annuity whose promised payments extend out forever. Since the payments go on forever, you can't apply the step-by-step approach. However, it's easy to find the PV of a perpetuity with the following formula:[7]

$$\text{PV of a perpetuity} = \frac{\text{PMT}}{\text{I}} \qquad (4\text{-}4)$$

We can use Equation 4-4 to find the value of a British consol with a face value of £1,000 that pays £25 per year in perpetuity. The answer depends on the interest rate being earned on investments of comparable risk at the time the consol is being valued. Originally, the "going rate" as established in the financial marketplace was 2.5%, so originally the consol's value was £1,000:

$$\text{Consol's value}_{\text{Originally}} = £25/0.025 = £1,000$$

The annual payment is still £25 today, but the going interest rate has risen to about 5.2%, causing the consol's value to fall to £480.77:

$$\text{Consol's value}_{\text{Today}} = £25/0.052 = £480.77$$

Note, though, that if interest rates decline in the future, say to 2%, then the value of the consol will rise to £1,250.00:

$$\text{Consol's value if rates decline to 2\%} = £25/0.02 = £1,250.00$$

---

[7]Here is an intuitive explanation for Equation 4-4. Suppose you deposit an amount equal to PV in a bank that pays an interest rate of I. Each year you would be able to withdraw an amount equal to I × PV. If you left your deposit in forever, you could withdraw a payment of I × PV forever: PMT = I × PV. Rearranging, we get Equation 4-4. This is only an intuitive explanation, so see **Web Extension 4B** on the textbook's Web site for a mathematical derivation of the perpetuity formula.

These examples demonstrate an important point: *When interest rates change, the prices of outstanding bonds also change, but inversely to the change in rates. Thus, bond prices **decline** if rates **rise**, and prices **increase** if rates **fall**. This holds for all bonds, both consols and those with finite maturities.* We discuss this point in more detail in Chapter 5, where we cover bonds in depth.

SELF-TEST

What is the present value of a perpetuity that pays £1,000 per year, beginning 1 year from now, if the appropriate interest rate is 5%? **(£20,000)** *What would the value be if the perpetuity began its payments immediately?* **(£21,000)** *(Hint: Just add the £1,000 to be received immediately to the formula value of the annuity.)*

Do bond prices move directly or inversely with interest rates—that is, what happens to the value of a bond if interest rates increase or decrease?

4-7 Annuities

Thus far, we have dealt with single payments, or "lump sums." However, assets such as bonds provide a series of cash inflows over time, and obligations such as auto loans, student loans, and mortgages call for a series of payments. If the payments are equal and are made at fixed intervals, then we have an **annuity**. For example, $100 paid at the end of each of the next 3 years is a 3-year annuity.

If payments occur at the *end* of each period, then we have an **ordinary** (or **deferred**) **annuity**. Payments on mortgages, car loans, and student loans are generally made at the ends of the periods and thus are ordinary annuities. If the payments are made at the *beginning* of each period, then we have an **annuity due**. Rental lease payments, life insurance premiums, and lottery payoffs (if you are lucky enough to win one!) are examples of annuities due. Ordinary annuities are more common in finance, so when we use the term "annuity" in this book, you may assume that the payments occur at the ends of the periods unless we state otherwise.

Next we show the time lines for a $100, 3-year, 5%, ordinary annuity and for the same annuity on an annuity due basis. With the annuity due, each payment is shifted back (to the left) by 1 year. In our example, we assume that a $100 payment will be made each year, so we show the payments with minus signs.

Ordinary Annuity:

Periods	0		1	2	3
		5%			
Payments			−$100	−$100	−$100

Annuity Due:

Periods	0		1	2	3
		5%			
Payments	−$100		−$100	−$100	

As we demonstrate in the following sections, we can find an annuity's future value, present value, the interest rate built into the contracts, how long it takes to reach a financial goal using the annuity, and, if we know all of those values, the size of the annuity payment. Keep in mind that annuities must have *constant payments* and a *fixed number of periods*. If these conditions don't hold, then the series is not an annuity.

SELF-TEST

What's the difference between an ordinary annuity and an annuity due?

Why should you prefer to receive an annuity due with payments of $10,000 per year for 10 years than an otherwise similar ordinary annuity?

4-8 Future Value of an Ordinary Annuity

Consider the ordinary annuity whose time line was shown previously, where you deposit $100 at the *end* of each year for 3 years and earn 5% per year. Figure 4-5 shows how to calculate the **future value of the annuity**, FVA_N, using the same approaches we used for single cash flows.

FIGURE 4-5

Summary: Future Value of an Ordinary Annuity

	A	B	C	D	E	F	G
243	INPUTS:						
244	Payment amount = PMT =		−$100				
245	Interest rate = I =		5.00%				
246	No. of periods = N =		3				
247							
248	1. Step-by-Step:	Periods:	0	1	2	3	
249		Cash flow:		−$100	−$100	−$100	
250				↓	↓	↓	
251				↓	↓	$100.00	
252	Multiply each payment by			↓	↳→→	$105.00	
253	$(1+I)^{N-t}$ and sum these FVs to			↳→→→→→→→→→		$110.25	
254	find FVA_N:					$315.25	
255							
256	2. Formula:						
257							
258		FVA_N	$= PMT \times \left(\dfrac{(1+I)^N}{I} - \dfrac{1}{I} \right) =$			$315.25	
259							
260							
261		Inputs:	3	5	0	−100	
262	3. Financial Calculator:		N	I/YR	PV	PMT	FV
263		Output:					$315.25
264							
265	4. *Excel* Spreadsheet:		FV function:	FVA_N =	=FV(I,N,PMT,PV)		
266			Fixed inputs:	FVA_N =	=FV(0.05,3,-100,0)	=	$315.25
267			Cell references:	FVA_N =	=FV(C245,C246,C244,0)	=	$315.25

As shown in the step-by-step section of Figure 4-5, we compound each payment out to Time 3, and then sum those compounded values in Cell F254 to find the annuity's FV, $FVA_3 = \$315.25$. The first payment earns interest for two periods, the second for one period, and the third earns no interest because it is made at the end of the annuity's life. This approach is straightforward, but if the annuity extends out for many years, it is cumbersome and time-consuming.

As you can see from the time line diagram, with the step-by-step approach we apply the following equation with $N = 3$ and $I = 5\%$:

$$FVA_N = PMT(1 + I)^{N-1} + PMT(1 + I)^{N-2} + PMT(1 + I)^{N-3}$$
$$= \$100(1.05)^2 + \$100(1.05)^1 + \$100(1.05)^0$$
$$= \$315.25$$

For the general case, the future value of an annuity is

$$FVA_N = PMT(1 + I)^{N-1} + PMT(1 + I)^{N-2} + PMT(1 + I)^{N-3} + \cdots + PMT(1 + I)^0$$

As shown in **Web Extension 4B** on the textbook's Web site, the future value of an annuity can be written as follows:[8]

$$FVA_N = PMT\left[\frac{(1 + I)^N}{I} - \frac{1}{I}\right] \qquad (4\text{-}5)$$

Using Equation 4-5, the future value of the annuity is found to be \$315.25:

$$FVA_3 = \$100\left[\frac{(1 + 0.05)^3}{0.05} - \frac{1}{0.05}\right] = \$315.25$$

As you might expect, annuity problems can be solved easily using a financial calculator or a spreadsheet, most of which have the following formula built into them:

$$PV(1 + I)^N + PMT\left[\frac{(1 + I)^N}{I} - \frac{1}{I}\right] + FV = 0 \qquad (4\text{-}6)$$

The procedure when dealing with annuities is similar to what we have done thus far for single payments, but the presence of recurring payments means that we must use the PMT key. Here's the calculator setup for our illustrative annuity:

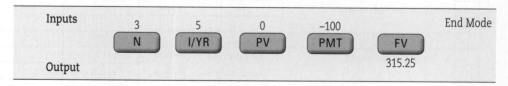

[8]Section 4-6 shows that the present value of an infinitely long annuity, called a perpetuity, is equal to PMT/I. The cash flows of an ordinary annuity of N periods are equal to the cash flows of a perpetuity minus the cash flows of a perpetuity that begins at year N+1. Therefore, the future value of an N-period annuity is equal to the future value (as of year N) of a perpetuity minus the value (as of year N) of a perpetuity that begins at year N+1. See **Web Extension 4B** on the textbook's Web site for details regarding derivations of Equation 4-5.

The Power of Compound Interest

© Rob Webb/Getty Images

Assume that you are 26 and just received your MBA. After reading the introduction to this chapter, you decide to start investing in the stock market for your retirement. Your goal is to have $1 million when you retire at age 65. Assuming you earn 10% annually on your stock investments, how much must you invest at the end of each year in order to reach your goal?

The answer is $2,491, but this amount depends critically on the return your investments earn. If your return drops to 8%, the required annual contribution would rise to $4,185. On the other hand, if the return rises to 12%, you would need to put away only $1,462 per year.

What if you are like most 26-year-olds and wait until later to worry about retirement? If you wait until age 40, you will need to save $10,168 per year to reach your $1 million goal, assuming you can earn 10%, but $13,679 per year if you earn only 8%. If you wait until age 50 and then earn 8%, the required amount will be $36,830 per year!

Although $1 million may seem like a lot of money, it won't be when you get ready to retire. If inflation averages 5% a year over the next 39 years, then your $1 million nest egg would be worth only $149,148 in today's dollars. If you live for 20 years after retirement and earn a real 3% rate of return, your annual retirement income in today's dollars would be only $9,733 before taxes. So, after celebrating your graduation and new job, start saving!

We enter PV = 0 because we start off with nothing, and we enter PMT = −100 because we will deposit this amount in the account at the end of each of the 3 years. The interest rate is 5%, and when we press the FV key we get the answer, $FVA_3 = 315.25$.

Because this is an ordinary annuity, with payments coming at the *end* of each year, we must set the calculator appropriately. As noted earlier, most calculators "come out of the box" set to assume that payments occur at the end of each period—that is, to deal with ordinary annuities. However, there is a key that enables us to switch between ordinary annuities and annuities due. For ordinary annuities, the designation "End Mode" or something similar is used, while for annuities due the designator is "Begin," "Begin Mode," "Due," or something similar. If you make a mistake and set your calculator on Begin Mode when working with an ordinary annuity, then each payment will earn interest for 1 extra year, which will cause the compounded amounts, and thus the FVA, to be too large.

The spreadsheet approach uses *Excel*'s FV function, **=FV(I,N,PMT,PV)**. In our example, we have **=FV(0.05,3,−100,0)**, and the result is again $315.25.

resource

*See **Ch04 Tool Kit.xls** for all calculations.*

SELF-TEST

For an ordinary annuity with 5 annual payments of $100 and a 10% interest rate, for how many years will the first payment earn interest, and what is the compounded value of this payment at the end? **(4 years, $146.41)** *Answer these questions for the fifth payment.* **(0 years, $100)**

Assume that you plan to buy a condo 5 years from now, and you estimate that you can save $2,500 per year toward a down payment. You plan to deposit the money in a bank that pays 4% interest, and you will make the first deposit at the end of this year. How much will you have after 5 years? **($13,540.81)** *How would your answer change if the bank's interest rate were increased to 6%, or decreased to 3%?* **($14,092.73; $13,272.84)**

4-9 Future Value of an Annuity Due

Because each payment occurs one period earlier with an annuity due, the payments will all earn interest for one additional period. Therefore, the FV of an annuity due will be greater than that of a similar ordinary annuity.

If you followed the step-by-step procedure, you would see that our illustrative annuity due has a FV of $331.01 versus $315.25 for the ordinary annuity. See **Ch04 Tool Kit.xls** on the textbook's Web site for a summary of future value calculations.

With the formula approach, we first use Equation 4-5, but because each payment occurs one period earlier, we multiply the Equation 4-5 result by $(1 + I)$:

$$FVA_{due} = FVA_{ordinary}(1 + I)$$ (4-7)

Thus, for the annuity due, $FVA_{due} = \$315.25(1.05) = \$331.01$, which is the same result as found with the step-by-step approach.

With a calculator, we input the variables just as we did with the ordinary annuity, but we now set the calculator to Begin Mode to get the answer, $331.01.

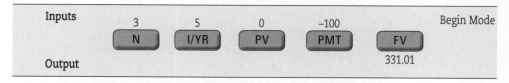

r e s o u r c e

See **Ch04 Tool Kit.xls** for all calculations.

In *Excel*, we still use the FV function, but we must indicate that we have an annuity due. The function is **=FV(I,N,PMT,PV,Type)**, where "Type" indicates the type of annuity. If Type is omitted, then *Excel* assumes that it is 0, which indicates an ordinary annuity. For an annuity due, Type = 1. As shown in **Ch04 Tool Kit.xls**, the function is **=FV(0.05,3,−100,0,1)** = $331.01.

SELF-TEST

Why does an annuity due always have a higher future value than an ordinary annuity?

If you know the value of an ordinary annuity, explain why you could find the value of the corresponding annuity due by multiplying by (1+I).

Assume that you plan to buy a condo 5 years from now and that you need to save for a down payment. You plan to save $2,500 per year, with the first payment being made immediately and deposited in a bank that pays 4%. How much will you have after 5 years? **($14,082.44)** *How much would you have if you made the deposits at the end of each year?* **($13,540.81)**

4-10 Present Value of Ordinary Annuities and Annuities Due

The present value of any annuity, PVA_N, can be found using the step-by-step, formula, calculator, or spreadsheet methods. We begin with ordinary annuities.

4-10a Present Value of an Ordinary Annuity

See Figure 4-6 for a summary of the different approaches for calculating the present value of an ordinary annuity.

resource

*See **Ch04 Tool Kit.xls** for all calculations.*

As shown in the step-by-step section of Figure 4-6, we discount each payment back to Time 0, and then sum those discounted values to find the annuity's PV, $PVA_3 = \$272.32$. This approach is straightforward, but if the annuity extends out for many years, it is cumbersome and time-consuming.

The time line diagram shows that with the step-by-step approach we apply the following equation with $N = 3$ and $I = 5\%$:

$$PVA_N = PMT/(1 + I)^1 + PMT/(1 + I)^2 + \cdots + PMT/(1 + I)^N$$

FIGURE 4-6

Summary: Present Value of an Ordinary Annuity

	A	B	C	D	E	F	G
313	INPUTS:						
314	Payment amount = PMT =		−$100				
315	Interest rate = I =		5.00%				
316	No. of periods = N =		3				
317							
318	1. Step-By-Step:	Periods:	0	1	2	3	
319		Cash flow:		−$100	−$100	−$100	
320				↓	↓	↓	
321			$95.24	←←↵	↓	↓	
322	Divide each payment by		$90.70	←←←←←← ←←↵	↓	↓	
323	$(1+I)^t$ and sum these PVs to		$86.38	←←←←←← ←←←←←←	←←↵	↓	
324	find PVA_N:		$272.32				
325							
326	2. Formula:						
327							
328	PVA_N	$= PMT \times \left(\dfrac{1}{I} - \dfrac{1}{I\,(1+I)^N} \right) =$				$272.32	
329							
330							
331							
332		Inputs:	3	5		−100	0
333	3. Financial Calculator:		N	I	PV	PMT	FV
334		Output:			272.32		
335							
336	4. *Excel* Spreadsheet:		PV function:	$PVA_N =$	=PV(I,N,PMT,FV)		
337			Fixed inputs:	$PVA_N =$	=PV(0.05,3,-100,0) =		$272.32
338			Cell references:	$PVA_N =$	=PV(C315,C316,C314,0) =		$272.32

The present value of an annuity can be written as[9]

$$PVA_N = PMT\left[\frac{1}{I} - \frac{1}{I(1+I)^N}\right] \qquad (4\text{-}8)$$

For our example annuity, the present value is

$$PVA_3 = PMT\left[\frac{1}{0.05} - \frac{1}{0.05(1+0.05)^3}\right] = \$272.32$$

Financial calculators are programmed to solve Equation 4-6, so we input the variables and press the PV key, *first making sure the calculator is set to End Mode*. The calculator setup is shown below:

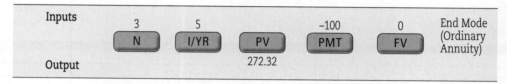

r e s o u r c e

*See **Ch04 Tool Kit.xls** for all calculations.*

The last section of Figure 4-6 shows the spreadsheet solution using *Excel*'s built-in PV function: **=PV(I,N,PMT,FV)**. In our example, we have **=PV(0.05,3,−100,0)** with a resulting value of $272.32.

4-10b Present Value of Annuities Due

Because each payment for an annuity due occurs one period earlier, the payments will all be discounted for one less period. Therefore, the PV of an annuity due must be greater than that of a similar ordinary annuity.

If you went through the step-by-step procedure, you would see that our example annuity due has a PV of $285.94 versus $272.32 for the ordinary annuity. See ***Ch04 Tool Kit.xls*** for this and the other calculations.

With the formula approach, we first use Equation 4-8 to find the value of the ordinary annuity and then, because each payment now occurs one period earlier, we multiply the Equation 4-8 result by $(1 + I)$:

$$PVA_{due} = PVA_{ordinary}(1 + I) \qquad (4\text{-}9)$$

$$PVA_{due} = \$272.32(1.05) = \$285.94$$

With a financial calculator, the inputs are the same as for an ordinary annuity, except you must set the calculator to Begin Mode:

Inputs		3	5		−100	0	Begin Mode (Annuity Due)
		N	I/YR	PV	PMT	FV	
Output				285.94			

---

[9]See ***Web Extension 4B*** on the textbook's Web site for details of this derivation.

Variable Annuities: Good or Bad?

© Rob Webb/Getty Images

Retirees appreciate stable, predictable income, so they often buy annuities. Insurance companies have been the traditional suppliers, using the payments they receive to buy high-grade bonds, whose interest is then used to make the promised payments. Such annuities were quite safe and stable and provided returns of around 7.5%. However, returns on stocks (dividends plus capital gains) have historically exceeded bonds' returns (interest). Therefore, some insurance companies in the 1990s began to offer *variable annuities*, which were backed by stocks instead of bonds. If stocks earned in the future as much as they had in the past, then variable annuities could offer returns of about 9%; this is better than the return on fixed-rate annuities. If stock returns turned out to be lower in the future than they had been in the past (or even had negative returns), then the variable annuities promised a *guaranteed minimum payment* of about 6.5%. Variable annuities appealed to many retirees, so companies that offered them had a significant competitive advantage.

The insurance company that pioneered variable annuities, The Hartford Financial Services Group, tried to hedge its position with derivatives that paid off if stocks went down. But like so many other derivatives-based risk management programs, this one went awry in 2008 because stock losses exceeded the assumed worst-case scenario. The Hartford, which was founded in 1810 and was one of the oldest and largest U.S. insurance companies at the beginning of 2008, saw its stock price fall from $85.54 per share to $4.16. Because of the general stock market crash, investors feared that The Hartford would be unable to make good on its variable annuity promises, and this would lead to bankruptcy. The company was bailed out by the economic stimulus package, but this 203-year-old firm will never be the same again.

Source: Leslie Scism and Liam Pleven, "Hartford Aims to Take Risk Out of Annuities," *Online Wall Street Journal*, January 13, 2009.

resource

See *Ch04 Tool Kit.xls* for all calculations.

In *Excel*, we again use the PV function, but now we must indicate that we have an annuity due. The function is now =PV(I,N,PMT,FV,Type), where "Type" is the type of annuity. If Type is omitted then *Excel* assumes that it is 0, which indicates an ordinary annuity; for an annuity due, Type = 1. As shown in *Ch04 Tool Kit.xls*, the function for this example is =PV(0.05,3,−100,0,1) = $285.94.

SELF-TEST

Why does an annuity due have a higher present value than an ordinary annuity?

If you know the present value of an ordinary annuity, what's an easy way to find the PV of the corresponding annuity due?

What is the PVA of an ordinary annuity with 10 payments of $100 if the appropriate interest rate is 10%? **($614.46)** *What would the PVA be if the interest rate were 4%?* **($811.09)** *What if the interest rate were 0%?* **($1,000.00)** *What would the PVAs be if we were dealing with annuities due?* **($675.90, $843.53, and $1,000.00)**

Assume that you are offered an annuity that pays $100 at the end of each year for 10 years. You could earn 8% on your money in other equally risky investments. What is the most you should pay for the annuity? **($671.01)** *If the payments began immediately, then how much would the annuity be worth?* **($724.69)**

4-11 Finding Annuity Payments, Periods, and Interest Rates

In the three preceding sections we discussed how to find the FV and PV of ordinary annuities and annuities due, using these four methods: step-by-step, formula, financial calculator, and *Excel*. Five variables are involved—N, I, PMT, FV, and PV—and if you know any four, you can find the fifth by solving either Equation 4-4 (4-6 for annuities due) or 4-7 (4-8 for annuities due). However, a trial-and-error procedure is generally required to find N or I, and that can be quite tedious. Therefore, we discuss only the financial calculator and spreadsheet approaches for finding N and I.

4-11a Finding Annuity Payments, PMT

We need to accumulate $10,000 and have it available 5 years from now. We can earn 6% on our money. Thus, we know that FV = 10,000, PV = 0, N = 5, and I/YR = 6. We can enter these values in a financial calculator and then press the PMT key to find our required deposits. However, the answer depends on whether we make deposits at the end of each year (ordinary annuity) or at the beginning (annuity due), so the mode must be set properly. Here are the results for each type of annuity:

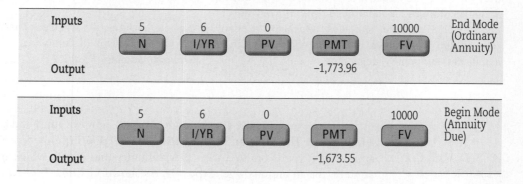

Thus, you must put away $1,773.96 per year if you make payments at the *end* of each year, but only $1,673.55 if the payments begin *immediately*. Finally, note that the required payment for the annuity due is the ordinary annuity payment divided by (1 + I): $1,773.96/1.06 = $1,673.55.

   Excel can also be used to find annuity payments, as shown below for the two types of annuities. For end-of-year (ordinary) annuities, "Type" can be left blank or a 0 can be inserted. For beginning-of-year annuities (annuities due), the same function is used but now Type is designated as 1. Here is the setup for the two types of annuities.

r e s o u r c e

See *Ch04 Tool Kit.xls* for all calculations.

Function:	= PMT(I,N,PV,FV,Type)	
Ordinary annuity:	= PMT(0.06,5,0,10000)	= − $1,773.96
Annuity due:	= PMT(0.06,5,0,10000,1)	= − $1,673.55

4-11b Finding the Number of Periods, N

Suppose you decide to make end-of-year deposits, but you can save only $1,200 per year. Again assuming that you would earn 6%, how long would it take you to reach your $10,000 goal? Here is the calculator setup:

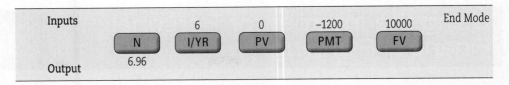

With these smaller deposits, it would take 6.96 years, not 5 years, to reach the $10,000 target. If you began the deposits immediately, then you would have an annuity due and N would be slightly less, 6.63 years.

resource

See **Ch04 Tool Kit.xls** for all calculations.

With *Excel*, you can use the NPER function: **=NPER(I,PMT,PV,FV,Type).** For our ordinary annuity example, Type is left blank (or 0 is inserted) and the function is **=NPER(0.06,−1200,0,10000)** = 6.96. If we put in 1 for Type, we would find N = 6.63.

4-11c Finding the Interest Rate, I

Now suppose you can save only $1,200 annually, but you still need to have the $10,000 in 5 years. What rate of return would you have to earn to reach your goal? Here is the calculator setup:

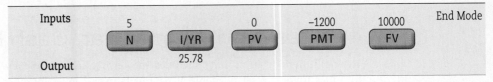

Thus, you would need to earn a whopping 25.78%! About the only way to earn such a high return would be either to invest in speculative stocks or head to a Las Vegas casino. Of course, speculative stocks and gambling aren't like making deposits in a bank with a guaranteed rate of return, so there would be a high probability that you'd end up with nothing. So, you should probably save more, lower your $10,000 target, or extend your time horizon. It might be appropriate to seek a somewhat higher return, but trying to earn 25.78% in a 6% market would involve speculation, not investing.

In *Excel*, you can use the RATE function: **=RATE(N,PMT,PV,FV,Type).** For our example, the function is **=RATE(5,−1200,0,10000)** = 0.2578 = 25.78%. If you decide to make the payments beginning immediately then the required rate of return would decline sharply, to 17.54%.

SELF-TEST

You just inherited $100,000 and invested it at 7% per year. How large a withdrawal could you make at the end of each of the next 10 years and end up with zero? **($14,237.75)** *How would your answer change if you made withdrawals at the beginning of each year?* **($13,306.31)**

If you have $100,000 that is invested at 7% and you wanted to withdraw $10,000 at the end of each year, how long will your funds last? **(17.8 years)** *How long would they last if you earned 0%?* **(10 years)** *How long would they last if you earned the 7% but limited your withdrawals to $7,000 per year?* **(forever)**

Your uncle named you as the beneficiary of his life insurance policy. The insurance company gives you a choice of $100,000 today or a 12-year annuity of $12,000 at the end of each year. What rate of return is the insurance company offering? **(6.11%)**

You just inherited an annuity that will pay you $10,000 per year for 10 years, and you receive the first payment today. A professional investor offers to give you $60,000 for the annuity. If you sell it to him, what rate of return will he earn on the investment? **(13.70%)** *If you think a "fair" rate of return would be 6%, how much should you ask for the annuity?* **($78,016.92)**

Using the Internet for Personal Financial Planning

© Rob Webb/Getty Images

How good are your financial planning skills? For example, should you buy or lease a car? How much and how soon should you begin to save for your children's education? How expensive a house can you afford? Should you refinance your home mortgage? How much must you save each year if you are to retire comfortably? The answers to these questions are often complicated and depend on a number of factors, such as projected housing and education costs, interest rates, inflation, expected family income, and stock market returns.

Fortunately, you should be able to use time value of money concepts and online resources to begin developing your financial plan. In addition to the online data sources described in Chapter 2, an excellent source of information is available at **www.smartmoney.com**. *Smartmoney* is a personal finance magazine produced by the publishers of *The Wall Street Journal*. If you go to *Smartmoney*'s Web site, you will find a section entitled "Tools." This section has a number of financial calculators, spreadsheets, and descriptive materials that cover a wide range of personal finance issues.

4-12 Uneven, or Irregular, Cash Flows

The definition of an annuity includes the term *constant payment,* which suggests that annuities involve a set of identical payments over a given number of periods. Although many financial decisions do involve constant payments, many others involve cash flows that are **uneven** or **irregular**. For example, the dividends on common stocks are typically expected to increase over time, and the investments that companies make in new products, expanded production capacity, and replacement machinery almost always generate cash flows that vary from year to year. Throughout the book, we use the term *payment* (PMT) in situations where the cash flows are constant and thus an annuity is involved; if different cash flows occur in different time periods, t, then we use the term CF_t to designate the *cash flow* in period t.

There are two important classes of uneven cash flows: (1) those in which the cash flow stream consists of a series of annuity payments plus an additional final lump sum in Year N, and (2) all other uneven streams. Bonds are an instance of the first type, while stocks and capital investments illustrate the second type. Here's an example of each type.

Stream 1. Annuity plus an additional final payment:

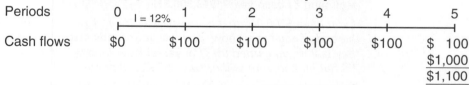

Stream 2. Irregular cash flow stream:

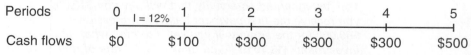

Equation 4-10 can be used, following the step-by-step procedure, to find the PV of either stream. However, as we shall see, the solution process differs significantly for the two types.

$$PV = \frac{CF_1}{(1+I)^1} + \frac{CF_2}{(1+I)^2} + \cdots + \frac{CF_N}{(1+I)^N} = \sum_{t=1}^{N} \frac{CF_t}{(1+I)^t} \qquad (4\text{-}10)$$

4-12a Annuity Plus Additional Final Payment

First, consider Stream 1 and notice that it is a 5-year, 12%, ordinary annuity plus a final payment of $1,000. We can find the PV of the annuity, find the PV of the final payment, and then sum them to get the PV of the stream. Financial calculators are programmed to do this for us—we use all five time value of money (TVM) keys, entering the data for the four known values as shown below, and then pressing the PV key to get the answer, $927.90:

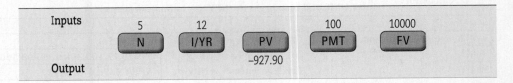

Similarly, we could use *Excel*'s PV function: **=PV(I,N,PMT,FV) = PV(0.12,5,100,1000) =** −$927.90. Note that the process is similar to that for annuities, except we now have a nonzero value for FV.

4-12b Irregular Cash Flow Stream

Now consider the irregular stream, which is analyzed in Figure 4-7. The top section shows the basic time line, which contains the inputs, and we first use the step-by-step approach to find PV = $1,016.35. Note that we show the PV of each cash flow directly below the cash flow, and then we sum these PVs to find the PV of the stream. This setup saves space as compared with showing the individual PVs in a column, and it is also transparent and thus easy to understand.

Now consider the financial calculator approach. The cash flows don't form an annuity, so you can't use the annuity feature on the calculator. You could, of course, use the calculator in the step-by-step procedure, but financial calculators have a feature—the cash flow register—that allows you to find the present value more efficiently. First, you input the individual cash flows, in chronological order, into the cash flow register.[10] Cash flows are designated CF_0, CF_1, CF_2, CF_3, and so on, up to the last cash flow, CF_N. Next, you enter the interest rate, I/YR. At this point, you have substituted in all the known values of Equation 4-10, so when you press the NPV key you get the PV of the stream. The calculator finds the PV of each cash flow and sums them to find the PV of the entire stream. To input the cash flows for this problem, enter 0 (because $CF_0 = 0$), 100, 300, 300, 300, and 500 in that order into the cash flow register, enter I/YR = 12, and then press NPV to obtain the answer, $1,016.35.

r e s o u r c e

*See **Ch04 Tool Kit.xls** for all calculations.*

Two points should be noted. First, when dealing with the cash flow register, the calculator uses the term "NPV" rather than "PV." The N stands for "net," so NPV is the abbreviation for "net present value," which is simply the net present value of a series of positive and negative cash flows, including any cash flow at time zero. The NPV

---

[10]These instructions are for the HP 10bII+, but most other financial calculators work in a similar manner.

FIGURE 4-7

Present Value of an Irregular Cash Flow Stream

	A	B	C	D	E	F	G
466	**INPUTS:**						
467		**Interest rate = I =**	**12%**				
468							
469	**1. Step-by-step:**						
470	**Periods:**	**0**	**1**	**2**	**3**	**4**	**5**
471	**Cash Flows:**	**$0.00**	**$100.00**	**$300.00**	**$300.00**	**$300.00**	**$500.00**
472	**PVs of the CFs:**		**$89.29**	**$239.16**	**$213.53**	**$190.66**	**$283.71**
473							
474	**PV of the Irregular CF Stream = Sum of the Individual PVs =**			**$1,016.35**			
475							
476							
477	**2. Calculator:**	**You could enter the cash flows into the cash flow register of a financial calculator, enter I/YR, and then press the NPV key to find the answer.**					**$1,016.35**
478							
479	**3. *Excel* Spreadsheet:**		**NPV Function:**	**NPV =**	**= NPV(I,CFs)**		
480			**Fixed inputs:**	**NPV =**	**=NPV(0.12,100,300,300,300,500)**		**$1,016.35**
481			**Cell references:**	**NPV =**	**=NPV(C467,C471:G471)**		**$1,016.35**
482							
483	**The *Excel* formula ignores the initial cash flow (in Year 0). When entering a cash flow range, *Excel* assumes that**						
484	**the first value occurs at the <u>end</u> of the first year. As we will see later, if there is an initial cash flow, it must be**						
485	**added separately to complete the NPV formula result. Notice too that you can enter cash flows one-by-one, but if the cash flows appear in consecutive cells, you can enter the cell range, as we did here.**						

function will be used extensively when we get to capital budgeting, where CF_0 is generally the cost of the project.

The second point to note is that repeated cash flows with identical values can be entered into the cash flow register more efficiently on some calculators by using the Nj key. In this illustration, you would enter $CF_0 = 0$, $CF_1 = 100$, $CF_2 = 300$, Nj = 3 (which tells the calculator that the 300 occurs 3 times), and $CF_5 = 500$.[11] Then enter I = 12, press the NPV key, and 1,016.35 will appear in the display. Also, note that numbers entered into the cash flow register remain in the register until they are cleared. Thus, if you previously worked a problem with eight cash flows and then moved to one with only four cash flows, the calculator would simply add the cash flows from the second problem to those of the first problem, and you would get an incorrect answer. Therefore, you must be sure to clear the cash flow register before starting a new problem.

Spreadsheets are especially useful for solving problems with uneven cash flows. You enter the cash flows in the spreadsheet as shown in Figure 4-7 on Row 471. To find the PV of these cash flows without going through the step-by-step process, you would use the NPV function. First put the cursor on the cell where you want the answer to appear, Cell G481, click the function wizard, choose Financial, scroll down to NPV, and click OK to

---

[11]On some calculators, instead of entering $CF_5 = 500$, you enter $CF_3 = 500$, because this is the next cash flow *different* from 300.

get the dialog box. Then enter C467 (or 0.12) for Rate and enter either the individual cash flows or the range of cells containing the cash flows, C471:G471, for Value 1. Be very careful when entering the range of cash flows. With a financial calculator, you begin by entering the Time-0 cash flow. With *Excel*, you do *not* include the Time-0 cash flow; instead, you begin with the Time-1 cash flow. Now when you click OK, you get the PV of the stream, $1,016.35. Note that you can use the PV function if the payments are constant, but you must use the NPV function if the cash flows are not constant. Finally, note that *Excel* has a major advantage over financial calculators in that you can see the cash flows, which makes it easy to spot data-entry errors. With a calculator, the numbers are buried in the machine, making it harder to check your work.

SELF-TEST

Could you use Equation 4-3, once for each cash flow, to find the PV of an uneven stream of cash flows?

What is the present value of a 5-year ordinary annuity of $100 plus an additional $500 at the end of Year 5 if the interest rate is 6%? **($794.87)** *What would the PV be if the $100 payments occurred in Years 1 through 10 and the $500 came at the end of Year 10?* **($1,015.21)**

What is the present value of the following uneven cash flow stream: $0 at Time 0, $100 at the end of Year 1 (or at Time 1), $200 at the end of Year 2, $0 at the end of Year 3, and $400 at the end of Year 4—assuming the interest rate is 8%? **($558.07)**

Would a "typical" common stock provide cash flows more like an annuity or more like an uneven cash flow stream?

4-13 Future Value of an Uneven Cash Flow Stream

The future value of an uneven cash flow stream (sometimes called the **terminal**, or **horizon**, **value**) is found by compounding each payment to the end of the stream and then summing the future values:

$$FV = CF_0(1+I)^N + CF_1(1+I)^{N-1} + CF_2(1+I)^{N-2} + \cdots + CF_{N-1}(1+I) + CF_N$$
$$= \sum_{t=0}^{N} CF_t(1+I)^{N-t} \tag{4-11}$$

The future value of our illustrative uneven cash flow stream is $1,791.15, as shown in Figure 4-8.

Most financial calculators have a net future value (NFV) key, which, after the cash flows and interest rate have been entered, can be used to obtain the future value of an uneven cash flow stream. If your calculator doesn't have the NFV feature, you can first find the net present value of the stream, and then find its net future value as $NFV = NPV(1+I)^N$. In the illustrative problem, we find PV = 1,016.35 using the cash flow register and I = 12. Then we use the TVM register, entering N = 5, I = 12, PV = −1016.35, and PMT = 0. When we press FV, we find FV = 1,791.15, which is the same as the value shown on the time line in Figure 4-8. As Figure 4-8 also shows, the same procedure can be used with *Excel*.

SELF-TEST

What is the future value of this cash flow stream: $100 at the end of 1 year, $150 after 2 years, and $300 after 3 years, assuming the appropriate interest rate is 15%? **($604.75)**

FIGURE 4-8

Future Value of an Irregular Cash Flow Stream

	A	B	C	D	E	F	G
498	INPUTS:						
499		Interest rate = I =	12%				
500							
501	1. Step-by-step:						
502	Periods:	0	1	2	3	4	5
503	Cash flows:	$0.00	$100.00	$300.00	$300.00	$300.00	$500.00
504	FVs of the CFs:		$157.35	$421.48	$376.32	$336.00	$500.00
505							
506	PV of the Irregular CF Stream = Sum of the Individual PVs =			$1,791.15			
507							
508							
509	2. Calculator:	You could enter the cash flows into the cash flow register of a financial calculator, enter I/YR, and then press the NFV key to find the answer.					$1,791.15
510							
511	3. *Excel* Spreadsheet		Step 1. Find NPV:		=NPV(C499,C503:G503)		$1,016.35
512			Step 2. Compound NPV to find NFV:		=FV(C499,G502,0,-G511)		$1,791.15

4-14 Solving for I with Irregular Cash Flows

Before financial calculators and spreadsheets existed, it was *extremely difficult* to find I if the cash flows were uneven. However, with spreadsheets and financial calculators it's easy to find I. If you have an *annuity plus a final lump sum*, you can input values for N, PV, PMT, and FV into the calculator's TVM registers and then press the I/YR key. Here's the setup for Stream 1 from Section 4-12, assuming we must pay $927.90 to buy the asset:

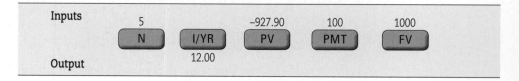

The rate of return on the $927.90 investment is 12%.

Finding the interest rate for an *irregular cash flow stream* with a calculator is a bit more complicated. Figure 4-9 shows Stream 2 from Section 4-12, assuming a required investment of $CF_0 = -\$1,000$. First, note that there is no simple step-by-step method for finding the rate of return—finding the rate for this investment requires a trial-and-error process, which is terribly time-consuming. Therefore, we really need a financial calculator or a spreadsheet. With a calculator, we would enter the CFs into the cash flow register and then press the IRR key to get the answer. IRR stands for "internal rate of return," and it is the rate of return the investment provides. The investment is the cash flow at Time 0, and it must be entered as a negative number. When we enter those cash flows in the calculator's cash flow register and press the IRR key, we get the rate of return on the $1,000 investment, 12.55%. Finally, note that once you have entered the cash flows in the calculator's register,

FIGURE 4-9

IRR of an Uneven Cash Flow Stream

	A	B	C	D	E	F	G
545	Periods:	0	1	2	3	4	5
546	Cash flows:	-$1,000	$100	$300	$300	$300	$500
547							
548	1. Calculator:	You could enter the cash flows into the cash flow register of a financial calculator and then press the IRR key to find the answer.					12.55%
549							
550	2. *Excel* IRR Function:		Cell references:	IRR =	=IRR(B546:G546)		12.55%

you can find both the investment's net present value (NPV) and its internal rate of return. For investment decisions, we typically want both of these numbers. Therefore, we generally enter the data once and then find both the NPV and the IRR.

You would get the same answer using *Excel*'s IRR function, as shown in Figure 4-9. Notice that when using the IRR—unlike using the NPV function—you must include all cash flows, including the Time-0 cash flow.

SELF-TEST

An investment costs $465 now and is expected to produce cash flows of $100 at the end of each of the next 4 years, plus an extra lump-sum payment of $200 at the end of the fourth year. What is the expected rate of return on this investment? **(9.05%)**

An investment costs $465 and is expected to produce cash flows of $100 at the end of Year 1, $200 at the end of Year 2, and $300 at the end of Year 3. What is the expected rate of return on this investment? **(11.71%)**

4-15 Semiannual and Other Compounding Periods

In most of our examples thus far, we assumed that interest is compounded once a year, or annually. This is **annual compounding**. Suppose, however, that you put $1,000 into a bank that pays a 6% annual interest rate but credits interest each 6 months. This is **semiannual compounding**. If you leave your funds in the account, how much would you have at the end of 1 year under semiannual compounding? Note that you will receive $60 of interest for the year, but you will receive $30 of it after only 6 months and the other $30 at the end of the year. You will earn interest on the first $30 during the second 6 months, so you will end the year with more than the $60 you would have had under annual compounding. You would be even better off under quarterly, monthly, weekly, or daily compounding. Note also that virtually all bonds pay interest semiannually; most stocks pay dividends quarterly; most mortgages, student loans, and auto loans involve monthly payments; and most money fund accounts pay interest daily. Therefore, it is essential that you understand how to deal with nonannual compounding.

4-15a Types of Interest Rates

When we move beyond annual compounding, we must deal with the following four types of interest rates:

- Nominal annual rates, given the symbol I_{NOM}
- Annual percentage rates, termed **APR** rates
- Periodic rates, denoted as I_{PER}
- Effective annual rates, given the symbol **EAR** or **EFF%**

NOMINAL (OR QUOTED) RATE, I_{NOM}[12]

This is the rate quoted by banks, brokers, and other financial institutions. So, if you talk with a banker, broker, mortgage lender, auto finance company, or student loan officer about rates, the nominal rate is the one he or she will normally quote you. However, to be meaningful, the quoted nominal rate must also include the number of compounding periods per year. For example, a bank might offer you a CD at 6% compounded daily, while a credit union might offer 6.1% compounded monthly.

Note that the nominal rate is never shown on a time line, and it is never used as an input in a financial calculator (except when compounding occurs only once a year). If more frequent compounding occurs, you must use periodic rates.

PERIODIC RATE, I_{PER}

This is the rate charged by a lender or paid by a borrower each period. It can be a rate per year, per 6 months (semiannually), per quarter, per month, per day, or per any other time interval. For example, a bank might charge 1.5% per month on its credit card loans, or a finance company might charge 3% per quarter on installment loans.

We find the periodic rate as follows:

$$\text{Periodic rate } I_{PER} = I_{NOM}/M \qquad (4\text{-}12)$$

where I_{NOM} is the nominal annual rate and M is the number of compounding periods per year. Thus, a 6% nominal rate with semiannual payments results in a periodic rate of

$$\text{Periodic rate } I_{PER} = 6\%/2 = 3.00\%$$

If only one payment is made per year then M = 1, in which case the periodic rate would equal the nominal rate: 6%/1 = 6%.

The periodic rate is the rate shown on time lines and used in calculations.[13] To illustrate, suppose you invest $100 in an account that pays a nominal rate of 12%, compounded

---

[12]The term nominal rate as used here does not have the same meaning as it did in Chapter 1. There, nominal interest rates referred to stated market rates as opposed to real (zero-inflation) rates. In this chapter, the term nominal rate means the stated, or quoted, annual rate as opposed to the effective annual rate, which we explain later. In both cases, though, nominal means stated, or quoted, as opposed to some sort of adjusted rate.

[13]The only exception is in cases where (1) annuities are involved and (2) the payment periods do not correspond to the compounding periods. In such cases—for example, if you are making quarterly payments into a bank account to build up a specified future sum but the bank pays interest on a daily basis—then the calculations are more complicated. For such problems, the simplest procedure is to determine the periodic (daily) interest rate by dividing the nominal rate by 365 (or by 360 if the bank uses a 360-day year), then compound each payment over the exact number of days from the payment date to the terminal point, and then sum the compounded payments to find the future value of the annuity. This is a simple process with a computer.

quarterly, or 3% per period. How much would you have after 2 years if you leave the funds on deposit? First, here is the time line for the problem:

Quarters 0   1   2   3   4   5   6   7   8
3%
−$100   FV=?

To find the FV, we would use this modified version of Equation 4-1:

$$FV_N = PV(1 + I_{PER})^{\text{Number of periods}} = PV\left(1 + \frac{I_{NOM}}{M}\right)^{MN} \tag{4-13}$$

$$= \$100\left(1 + \frac{0.12}{4}\right)^{4 \times 2} = \$100(1 + 0.03)^8 = \$126.68.$$

With a financial calculator, we find the FV using these inputs: N = 4 × 2 = 8, I = 12/4 = 3, PV = −100, and PMT = 0. The result is again FV = $126.68.[14]

Inputs	8	3	−100	0	
	N	I/YR	PV	PMT	FV
Output					126.68

EFFECTIVE (OR EQUIVALENT) ANNUAL RATE (EAR OR EFF%)

This is the annual (interest once a year) rate that produces the same final result as compounding at the periodic rate for M times per year. The EAR, also called EFF% (for effective percentage rate), is found as follows:[15]

$$EAR = EFF\% = (1 + I_{PER})^M - 1.0$$
$$= \left(1 + \frac{I_{NOM}}{M}\right)^M - 1.0 \tag{4-14}$$

Here I_{NOM}/M is the periodic rate, N is the number of years, and M is the number of periods per year. If a bank would lend you money at a nominal rate of 12%, compounded quarterly, then the EFF% rate would be 12.5509%:

Rate on bank loan: EFF% $= (1 + 0.03)^4 - 1.0 = (1.03)^4 - 1.0$

$$= 1.125509 - 1.0 = 0.125509 = 12.5509\%$$

---

[14]Most financial calculators have a feature that allows you to set the number of payments per year and then use the nominal annual interest rate. However, students tend to make fewer errors when using the periodic rate with their calculators set for one payment per year (i.e., per period), so this is what we recommend. Note also that you cannot use a normal time unless you use the periodic rate.

[15]You could also use the "interest conversion feature" of a financial calculator. Most financial calculators are programmed to find the EFF% or, given the EFF%, to find the nominal rate; this is called "interest rate conversion." You enter the nominal rate and the number of compounding periods per year, and then press the EFF% key to find the effective annual rate. However, we generally use Equation 4-14 because it's easy and because using the equation reminds us of what we are really doing. If you do use the interest rate conversion feature on your calculator, don't forget to reset your settings afterward. Interest conversion is discussed in our calculator tutorials.

Truth in Lending: What Loans Really Cost

© Rob Webb/Getty Images

Congress passed the Consumer Credit Protection Act in 1968. The Truth in Lending provisions in the Act require banks and other lenders to disclose the **annual percentage rate (APR)** they are charging. For example, suppose you plan to buy a fancy TV set that costs $3,000, and the store offers you credit for 1 year at an "add-on" quoted rate of 8%. Here we first find the total dollars of interest by multiplying the $3,000 you are borrowing times 8%, resulting in $240. Add the interest to the $3,000 cost of the TV, for a total loan of $3,240. Then divide the total loan by 12 to get the monthly payments: $3,240/12 = $270 per month, with the first payment made at the time of purchase. Therefore, we have a 12-month annuity due with payments of $270. Is your cost really the 8% that you were quoted?

To find the APR, set your calculator to Begin Mode, then enter N = 12, PV = 3000, PMT = –270, and FV = 0. Then, when you press the I/YR key, you get the periodic rate, 1.4313%. You then multiply by 12 to get the APR, 17.1758%. You could also find the EFF%, which is 18.5945%. We show these calculations using both the calculator and *Excel*, along with a time line that helps us visualize what's happening, in the chapter's *Excel Tool Kit*.

The 17.1758% APR that the dealer is required to report is a much better indicator of the loan's cost than the 8% nominal rate, but it still does not reflect the true cost, which is the 18.5945% effective annual rate. Thus, buying the TV on time would really cost you 18.5945%. If you don't know what's happening when you buy on time or borrow, you may pay a lot more than you think!

To see the importance of the EFF%, suppose that—as an alternative to the bank loan—you could borrow on a credit card that charges 1% per month. Would you be better off using the bank loan or credit card loan? *To answer this question, the cost of each alternative must be expressed as an EFF%.* We just saw that the bank loan's effective cost is 12.5509%. The cost of the credit card loan, with monthly payments, is slightly higher, 12.6825%:

$$\text{Credit card loan: EFF\%} = (1 + 0.01)^{12} - 1.0 = (1.01)^{12} - 1.0$$

$$= 1.126825 - 1.0 = 0.126825 = 12.6825\%$$

This result is logical: Both loans have the same 12% nominal rate, yet you would have to make the first payment after only 1 month on the credit card versus 3 months under the bank loan.

The EFF% rate is rarely used in calculations. *However, it must be used to compare the effective costs of different loans or rates of return on different investments when payment periods differ,* as in our example of the credit card versus a bank loan.

4-15b The Result of Frequent Compounding

What would happen to the future value of an investment if interest were compounded annually, semiannually, quarterly, or some other less-than-annual period? Because interest will be earned on interest more often, you should expect higher future values the more frequently compounding occurs. Similarly, you should expect the effective annual rate to increase with more frequent compounding. As Figure 4-10 shows, these results do occur —the future value and the EFF% do increase as the frequency of compounding increases. Notice that the biggest increase in FV (and in EFF%) occurs when compounding goes from annual to semiannual, and notice also that moving from monthly to daily compounding has a relatively small impact. Although Figure 4-10 shows daily compounding as the smallest interval, it is possible to compound even more frequently. At the limit, compounding can occur **continuously**. This is explained in *Web Extension 4C* on the textbook's Web site.

FIGURE 4-10

Effect on $100 of Compounding More Frequently Than Once a Year

	A	B	C	D	E	F	G
568	Frequency of Compounding	Nominal Annual Rate	Number of Periods per Year (M)[a]	Periodic Interest Rate (I_{PER})	Effective Annual Rate (EFF%)[b]	Future Value[c]	Percentage Increase in FV
569	Annual	12%	1	12.0000%	12.0000%	$112.00	
570	Semiannual	12%	2	6.0000%	12.3600%	$112.36	0.32%
571	Quarterly	12%	4	3.0000%	12.5509%	$112.55	0.17%
572	Monthly	12%	12	1.0000%	12.6825%	$112.68	0.12%
573	Daily	12%	365	0.0329%	12.7475%	$112.75	0.06%

Notes:

[a] We used 365 days per year in the calculations.
[b] The EFF% is calculated as $(1 + I_{PER})^M$.
[c] The Future value is calculated as $100(1 + EFF\%)$.

SELF-TEST

Would you rather invest in an account that pays a 7% nominal rate with annual compounding or with monthly compounding? If you borrowed at a nominal rate of 7%, would you rather make annual or monthly payments? Why?

What is the future value of $100 after 3 years if the appropriate interest rate is 8%, compounded annually? **($125.97)** *Compounded monthly?* **($127.02)**

What is the present value of $100 due in 3 years if the appropriate interest rate is 8%, compounded annually? **($79.38)** *Compounded monthly?* **($78.73)**

Define the following terms: annual percentage rate (APR), effective annual rate (EFF%), and nominal interest rate (I_{NOM}).

A bank pays 5% with daily compounding on its savings accounts. Should it advertise the nominal or effective rate if it is seeking to attract new deposits?

Credit card issuers must by law print their annual percentage rate on their monthly statements. A common APR is 18%, with interest paid monthly. What is the EFF% on such a loan? **(19.56%)**

Some years ago banks weren't required to reveal the rate they charged on credit cards. Then Congress passed a "truth in lending" law that required them to publish their APR rate. Is the APR rate really the most truthful rate, or would the EFF% be even more truthful?

4-16 Fractional Time Periods[16]

So far we have assumed that payments occur at either the beginning or the end of periods, but not *within* periods. However, we occasionally encounter situations that require compounding or discounting over fractional periods. For example, suppose you deposited $100 in a bank

[16]This section is interesting and useful, but relatively technical. It can be omitted, at the option of the instructor, without loss of continuity.

that pays a nominal rate of 10%, compounded daily, based on a 365-day year. How much would you have after 9 months? The answer of $107.79 is found as follows:[17]

$$\text{Periodic rate} = I_{PER} = 0.10/365 = 0.000273973 \text{ per day}$$

$$\text{Number of days} = (9/12)(365) = 0.75(365)$$

$$= 273.75 \text{ days, rounded to } 274$$

$$\text{Ending amount} = \$100(1.000273973)^{274} = \$107.79$$

Now suppose that instead you borrow $100 at a nominal rate of 10% per year and are charged *simple interest*, which means that interest is not charged on interest. If the loan is outstanding for 274 days (or 9 months), how much interest would you have to pay? The interest owed is equal to the principal multiplied by the interest rate times the number of periods. In this case, the number of periods is equal to a fraction of a year: N = 274/365 = 0.7506849.

$$\text{Interest owed} = \$100(10\%)(0.7506849) = \$7.51$$

Another approach would be to use the daily rate rather than the annual rate and thus to use the exact number of days rather than the fraction of the year:

$$\text{Interest owed} = \$100(0.000273973)(274) = \$7.51$$

You would owe the bank a total of $107.51 after 274 days. This is the procedure most banks use to calculate interest on loans, except that they generally require borrowers to pay the interest on a monthly basis rather than after 274 days; this more frequent compounding raises the EFF% and thus the total amount of interest paid.

SELF-TEST

Suppose a company borrowed $1 million at a rate of 9%, using simple interest, with interest paid at the end of each month. The bank uses a 360-day year. How much interest would the firm have to pay in a 30-day month? **($7,500.00)** *What would the interest be if the bank used a 365-day year?* **($7,397.26)**

Suppose you deposited $1,000 in a credit union that pays 7% with daily compounding and a 365-day year. What is the EFF%? **(7.250098%)** *How much could you withdraw after 7 months, assuming this is 7/12 of a year?* **($1,041.67)**

4-17 Amortized Loans

An extremely important application of compound interest involves loans that are paid off in installments over time. Included are automobile loans, home mortgage loans, student

---

[17]We assume that these 9 months constitute 9/12 of a year. Also, bank deposit and loan contracts specifically state whether they are based on a 360-day or a 365-day year. If a 360-day year is used, then the daily rate is higher, so the effective rate is also higher. Here we assumed a 365-day year. Finally, note that banks use software with built-in calendars, so they calculate the exact number of days.

Note also that banks often treat such loans as follows: (1) They require monthly payments, and they calculate the interest for the month by multiplying the periodic rate by the beginning-of-month balance times the number of days in the month. This is called "simple interest." (2) The interest for the month is either added to the next beginning of month balance, or the borrower must actually pay the earned interest. In this case, the EFF% is based on 12 compounding periods, not 365 as is assumed in our example.

What You Know Is What You Get: Not in Payday Lending

© Rob Webb/Getty Images

When money runs low toward the end of a month, many individuals turn to payday lenders. If a borrower's application is approved, the payday lender makes a short-term loan, which will be repaid on with the next paycheck. In fact, on the next payday the lender actually transfers the repayment from the borrower's bank account. This repayment consists of the amount borrowed plus a fee.

How costly are payday loans? The lender charges a fee of about $15 to $17 per $100 borrowed. A typical loan is for about $350, so the typical fee is about $56. A typical borrower gets paid about every two weeks, so the loan is for a very short amount of time. With a big fee and a short time until repayment, the typical payday loan has an APR of over 400%.

How informed are borrowers? Two professors at the University of Chicago set out to answer this question. When loans are approved, borrowers receive a form to sign that shows the APR. However, subsequent telephone surveys of borrowers show that over 40% of borrowers thought their APR was around 15%; perhaps not coincidentally, these are similar numerals to the fee schedules that are posted prominently in the lender's office.

The professors then did an experiment (with the agreement of 77 payday loan stores) in which they provided more information than just the APR. One group of borrowers received information about the APR of the payday loan as compared to the APRs of other loans, such as car loans. A second group received information about the dollar cost of the payday loan as compared to the dollar cost of other loans, such as car loans. A third group received information about how long it takes most payday borrowers to repay their loans (which is longer than the next payday; borrowers tend to extend the loan for additional pay periods, accruing additional fees).

Compared to a control group with no additional information, the results show that some borrowers with additional information decided not to take the loan; other borrowers reduced the amount that they borrow. These findings suggest that better information helps borrowers make less costly decisions. The more you know, the less you get, at least when it comes to costly payday loans.

Source: Marianne Bertrand and Adair Morse, "Information Disclosure, Cognitive Biases, and Payday Borrowing," *Journal of Finance*, Vol. 66, No. 6, December 2011, pp. 1865–1893.

loans, and many business loans. A loan that is to be repaid in equal amounts on a monthly, quarterly, or annual basis is called an **amortized loan.**[18]

4-17a Payments

Suppose a company borrows $100,000, with the loan to be repaid in 5 equal payments at the end of each of the next 5 years. The lender charges 6% on the balance at the beginning of each year.

Here's a picture of the situation:

0		1	2	3	4	5
$100,000	I = 6%	PMT	PMT	PMT	PMT	PMT

Our task is to find the amount of the payment, PMT, such that the sum of their PVs equals the amount of the loan, $100,000:

$$\$100,000 = \frac{PMT}{(1.06)^1} + \frac{PMT}{(1.06)^2} + \frac{PMT}{(1.06)^3} + \frac{PMT}{(1.06)^4} + \frac{PMT}{(1.06)^5} = \sum_{t=1}^{5} \frac{PMT}{(1.06)^t}$$

---

[18]The word *amortized* comes from the Latin *mors*, meaning "death," so an amortized loan is one that is "killed off" over time.

It is possible to solve the annuity formula, Equation 4-8, for PMT, but it is much easier to use a financial calculator or spreadsheet. With a financial calculator, we insert values as shown below to get the required payments, $23,739.64.

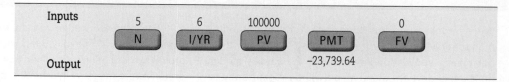

With *Excel*, you would use the PMT function: **=PMT(I,N,PV,FV) = PMT(0.06,5,100000,0) =** −$23,739.64. Thus, we see that the borrower must pay the lender $23,739.64 per year for the next 5 years.

4-17b Amortization Schedules

Each payment will consist of two parts—part interest and part repayment of principal. This breakdown is shown in the **amortization schedule** given in Figure 4-11. The interest component is relatively high in the first year, but it declines as the loan balance decreases. For tax purposes, the borrower would deduct the interest component while the lender would report the same amount as taxable income. Over the 5 years, the lender will earn 6% on its investment and also recover the amount of its investment.

FIGURE 4-11

Loan Amortization Schedule, $100,000 at 6% for 5 Years

	A	B	C	D	E	F
675	INPUTS:					
676		Amount borrowed:	$100,000			
677		Years:	5			
678		Rate:	6%			
679	Intermediate calculation:					
680		PMT:	$23,739.64	=PMT(C678,C677,−C676)		
681	Year	Beginning Amount (1)	Payment (2)	Interest[a] (3)	Repayment of Principal[b] (2) − (3) = (4)	Ending Balance (1) − (4) = (5)
682	1	$100,000.00	$23,739.64	$6,000.00	$17,739.64	$82,260.36
683	2	$82,260.36	$23,739.64	$4,935.62	$18,804.02	$63,456.34
684	3	$63,456.34	$23,739.64	$3,807.38	$19,932.26	$43,524.08
685	4	$43,524.08	$23,739.64	$2,611.44	$21,128.20	$22,395.89
686	5	$22,395.89	$23,739.64	$1,343.75	$22,395.89	$0.00

Notes:

[a] Interest in each period is calculated by multiplying the loan balance at the beginning of the year by the interest rate. Therefore, interest in Year 1 is $100,000(0.06) = $6,000; in Year 2 it is $82,260.36(0.06) = $4,935.62; and so on.

[b] Repayment of principal is the $23,739.64 annual payment minus the interest charge for the year, $17,739.64 for Year 1.

4-17c Mortgage Interest Payments

Now consider a 30-year home mortgage of $250,000 at an annual rate of 6%. How much interest will the borrower pay over the life of the loan? How much in the first year?

Begin by finding the monthly payment. The financial calculator inputs are shown below (notice that N and I/YR are adjusted to reflect monthly payments):

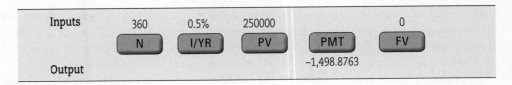

The total amount of payments is 360($1,498.8763) ≈ $539,595. The borrower pays back the borrowed $250,000 over the life of the loan, so the total interest paid is $539,595 − $250,000 = $289,595.

To find the amount of interest paid in the first year, begin by finding the amount the borrower owes at the end of the first year. We know the number of remaining payments (360 − 12 = 348) and the amount of each payment ($1,498.88), so we can solve for the PV:

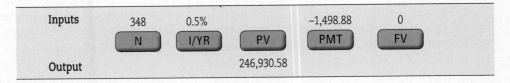

The amount of principal repaid in the first year is $250,000 − $246,930.58 = $3,069.42. The total payments during the year are 12($1,498.88) = $17,986.56. So the total interest paid in the year is $17,986.56 − $3,069.42 = $14,917.14. Almost 83% of the payments in the first year go to interest!

Now consider a 15-year mortgage. To compare apples to apples, assume the interest rate stays at 6%, although it probably would be a bit lower. Changing N to 180, the new payment is $2,109.6421. The total amount of payments is 180($2,109.6421) ≈ $379,736 and the total interest paid is $379,736 − $250,000 = $129,736, a big decrease from the $289,595 paid on the 30-year mortgage. As this example shows, increasing the monthly payment can dramatically reduce the total interest paid and the time required to pay off the mortgage.

SELF-TEST

Consider again the example in Figure 4-11. If the loan were amortized over 5 years with 60 equal monthly payments, how much would each payment be, and how would the first payment be divided between interest and principal? **(Each payment would be $1,933.28; the first payment would have $500 of interest and $1,433.28 of principal repayment.)**

Suppose you borrowed $30,000 on a student loan at a rate of 8% and now must repay it in three equal installments at the end of each of the next 3 years. How large would your payments be, how much of the first payment would represent interest and how much would be principal, and what would your ending balance be after the first year? **(PMT = $11,641.01; interest = $2,400; principal = $9,241.01; balance at end of Year 1 = $20,758.99)**

GLOBAL ECONOMIC CRISIS

© uniquely india/Getty Images

An Accident Waiting to Happen: Option Reset Adjustable Rate Mortgages

Option reset adjustable rate mortgages (ARMs) give the borrower some choices regarding the initial monthly payment. One popular option ARM allowed borrowers to make a monthly payment equal to only half of the interest due in the first month. Because the monthly payment was less than the interest charge, the loan balance grew each month. When the loan balance exceeded 110% of the original principal, the monthly payment was reset to fully amortize the now-larger loan at the prevailing market interest rates.

Here's an example. Someone borrows $325,000 for 30 years at an initial rate of 7%. The interest accruing in the first month is (7%/12)($325,000) = $1,895.83. Therefore, the initial monthly payment is 50%($1,895.83) = $947.92. Another $947.92 of deferred interest is added to the loan balance, taking it up to $325,000 + $947.92 = $325,947.82. Because the loan is now larger, interest in the second month is higher, and both interest and the loan balance will continue to rise each month. The first month after the loan balance exceeds 110%($325,000) = $357,500, the contract calls for the payment to be reset so as to fully amortize the loan at the then-prevailing interest rate.

First, how long would it take for the balance to exceed $357,500? Consider this from the lender's perspective: The lender initially pays out $325,000, receives $947.92 each month, and then would receive a payment of $357,500 if the loan were payable when the balance hit that amount, with interest accruing at a 7% annual rate and with monthly compounding. We enter these values into a financial calculator: I = 7%/12,

PV = −325000, PMT = 947.92, and FV = 357500. We solve for N = 31.3 months, rounded up to 32 months. Thus, the borrower will make 32 payments of $947.92 before the ARM resets.

The payment after the reset depends upon the terms of the original loan and the market interest rate at the time of the reset. For many borrowers, the initial rate was a lower-than-market "teaser" rate, so a higher-than-market rate would be applied to the remaining balance. For this example, we will assume that the original rate wasn't a teaser and that the rate remains at 7%. Keep in mind, though, that for many borrowers the reset rate was higher than the initial rate. The balance after the 32nd payment can be found as the future value of the original loan and the 32 monthly payments, so we enter these values in the financial calculator: N = 32, I = 7%/12, PMT = 947.92, PV = −325000, and then solve for FV = $358,242.84. The number of remaining payments to amortize the $358,424.84 loan balance is 360 − 32 = 328, so the amount of each payment is found by setting up the calculator as: N = 328, I = 7%/12, PV = 358242.84, and FV = 0. Solving, we find that PMT = $2,453.94.

Even if interest rates don't change, the monthly payment jumps from $947.92 to $2,453.94 and would increase even more if interest rates were higher at the reset. This is exactly what happened to millions of American homeowners who took out option reset ARMS in the early 2000s. When large numbers of resets began in 2007, defaults ballooned. The accident caused by option reset ARMs didn't wait very long to happen!

4-18 Growing Annuities[19]

Normally, an annuity is defined as a series of *constant* payments to be received over a specified number of periods. However, the term **growing annuity** is used to describe a series of payments that grow at a constant rate.

4-18a Example 1: Finding a Constant Real Income

Growing annuities are often used in the area of financial planning, where a prospective retiree wants to determine the maximum constant *real*, or *inflation-adjusted*, withdrawals that he or

---

[19]This section is interesting and useful, but relatively technical. It can be omitted, at the option of the instructor, without loss of continuity.

she can make over a specified number of years. For example, suppose a 65-year-old is contemplating retirement. The individual expects to live for another 20 years, has a $1 million nest egg, expects the investments to earn a nominal annual rate of 6%, expects inflation to average 3% per year, and wants to withdraw a constant *real* amount annually over the next 20 years so as to maintain a constant standard of living. If the first withdrawal is to be made today, what is the amount of that initial withdrawal?

This problem can be solved in three ways. (1) Set up a spreadsheet model that is similar to an amortization table, where the account earns 6% per year, withdrawals rise at the 3% inflation rate, and *Excel*'s Goal Seek function is used to find the initial inflation-adjusted withdrawal. A zero balance will be shown at the end of the twentieth year. (2) Use a financial calculator, where we first calculate the real rate of return, adjusted for inflation, and use it for I/YR when finding the payment for an annuity due. (3) Use a relatively complicated and obtuse formula to find this same amount.[20] We will focus on the first two approaches.

r e s o u r c e

*See **Ch04 Tool Kit.xls** for all calculations.*

We illustrate the spreadsheet approach in the chapter model, ***Ch04 Tool Kit.xls.*** The spreadsheet model provides the most transparent picture, because it shows the value of the retirement portfolio, the portfolio's annual earnings, and each withdrawal over the 20-year planning horizon—especially if you include a graph. A picture is worth a thousand numbers, and graphs make it easy to explain the situation to people who are planning their financial futures.

To implement the calculator approach, we first find the expected *real* rate of return, where r_r is the real rate of return and r_{NOM} the nominal rate of return. The real rate of return is the return that we would see if there were no inflation. We calculate the real rate as:

$$\text{Real rate} = r_r = [(1 + r_{NOM})/(1 + \text{Inflation})] - 1.0 \tag{4-15}$$

$$= [1.06/1.03] - 1.0 = 0.029126214 = 2.9126214\%$$

Using this real rate of return, we solve the annuity due problem exactly as we did earlier in the chapter. We set the calculator to Begin Mode, after which we input N = 20, I/YR = real rate = 2.9126214, PV = −1000000, and FV = 0; then we press PMT to get $64,786.88. This is the amount of the initial withdrawal at Time 0 (today), and future withdrawals will increase at the inflation rate of 3%. These withdrawals, growing at the inflation rate, will provide the retiree with a constant real income over the next 20 years—provided the inflation rate and the rate of return do not change.

In our example, we assumed that the first withdrawal would be made immediately. The procedure would be slightly different if we wanted to make end-of-year withdrawals. First, we would set the calculator to End Mode. Second, we would enter the same inputs into the calculator as just listed, including the real interest rate for I/YR. The calculated PMT would be $66,673.87. However, that value is in beginning-of-year terms, and because inflation of 3% will occur during the year, we must make the following adjustment to find the inflation-adjusted initial withdrawal:

---

[20]For example, the formula used to find the payment of a growing annuity due is shown below. If g = annuity growth rate and r = nominal rate of return on investment, then

PVIF of a growing annuity due = $PVIFGA_{Due} = \{1 - [(1 + g)/(1 + r)]^N\}[(1 + r)/(r - g)]$

$PMT = PV/PVIFGA_{Due}$

where PVIF denotes "present value interest factor." Similar formulas are available for growing ordinary annuities.

$$\text{Initial end-of-year withdrawal} = \$66,673.87(1 + \text{Inflation})$$
$$= \$66,673.87(1.03)$$
$$= \$68,674.09$$

Thus, the first withdrawal at the *end* of the year would be $68,674.09; it would grow by 3% per year; and after the 20th withdrawal (at the end of the 20th year), the balance in the retirement fund would be zero.

We also demonstrate the solution for this end-of-year payment example in *Ch04 Tool Kit.xls.* There we set up a table showing the beginning balance, the annual withdrawals, the annual earnings, and the ending balance for each of the 20 years. This analysis confirms the $68,674.09 initial end-of-year withdrawal derived previously.

4-18b Example 2: Initial Deposit to Accumulate a Future Sum

As another example of growing annuities, suppose you need to accumulate $100,000 in 10 years. You plan to make a deposit in a bank now, at Time 0, and then make 9 more deposits at the beginning of each of the following 9 years, for a total of 10 deposits. The bank pays 6% interest, you expect inflation to be 2% per year, and you plan to increase your annual deposits at the inflation rate. How much must you deposit initially? First, we calculate the real rate:

$$\text{Real rate} = r_r = [1.06/1.02] - 1.0 = 0.0392157 = 3.9215686\%$$

Next, because inflation is expected to be 2% per year, in 10 years the target $100,000 will have a real value of

$$\$100,000/(1 + 0.02)^{10} = \$82,034.83$$

Now we can find the size of the required initial payment by setting a financial calculator to the Begin Mode and then inputting N = 10, I/YR = 3.9215686, PV = 0, and FV = 82034.83. Then, when we press the PMT key, we get PMT = −6,598.87. Thus, a deposit of $6,598.87 made at time 0 and growing by 2% per year will accumulate to $100,000 by Year 10 if the interest rate is 6%. Again, this result is confirmed in the chapter's *Tool Kit.* The key to this analysis is to express I/YR, FV, and PMT in real, not nominal, terms.

SELF-TEST

Differentiate between a "regular" and a "growing" annuity.

What three methods can be used to deal with growing annuities?

If the nominal interest rate is 10% and the expected inflation rate is 5%, what is the expected real rate of return? **(4.7619%)**

SUMMARY

Most financial decisions involve situations in which someone makes a payment at one point in time and receives money later. Dollars paid or received at two different points in time are different, and this difference is dealt with using *time value of money (TVM) analysis.*

- **Compounding** is the process of determining the **future value (FV)** of a cash flow or a series of cash flows. The compounded amount, or future value, is equal to the beginning amount plus interest earned.
- Future value of a single payment = $FV_N = PV(1 + I)^N$.
- **Discounting** is the process of finding the **present value (PV)** of a future cash flow or a series of cash flows; discounting is the reciprocal, or reverse, of compounding.
- Present value of a payment received at the end of Time $N = PV = \dfrac{FV_N}{(1+I)^N}$.
- An **annuity** is defined as a series of equal periodic payments (PMT) for a specified number of periods.
- An annuity whose payments occur at the *end* of each period is called an **ordinary annuity**.
- Future value of an (ordinary) annuity $FVA_N = PMT\left[\dfrac{(1 + I)^N}{I} - \dfrac{1}{I}\right]$.

- Present value of an (ordinary) annuity $PVA_N = PMT\left[\dfrac{1}{I} - \dfrac{1}{I(1 + I)^N}\right]$.

- If payments occur at the *beginning* of the periods rather than at the end, then we have an **annuity due**. The PV of each payment is larger, because each payment is discounted back one year less, so the PV of the annuity is also larger. Similarly, the FV of the annuity due is larger because each payment is compounded for an extra year. The following formulas can be used to convert the PV and FV of an ordinary annuity to an annuity due:

$$PVA_{due} = PVA_{ordinary}(1 + I)$$
$$FVA_{due} = FVA_{ordinary}(1 + I)$$

- **A perpetuity** is an annuity with an infinite number of payments.

$$\text{Value of a perpetuity} = \frac{PMT}{I}$$

- To find the PV or FV of an uneven series, find the PV or FV of each individual cash flow and then sum them.
- If you know the cash flows and the PV (or FV) of a cash flow stream, you can **determine its interest rate**.
- When compounding occurs more frequently than once a year, the nominal rate must be converted to a periodic rate, and the number of years must be converted to periods:

$$\text{Periodic rate}(I_{PER}) = \text{Nominal annual rate} \div \text{Periods per year}$$
$$\text{Number of Periods} = \text{Years} \times \text{Periods per year}$$

The periodic rate and number of periods is used for calculations and is shown on time lines.
- If you are comparing the costs of alternative loans that require payments more than once a year, or the rates of return on investments that pay interest more than once a year, then the comparisons should be based on **effective** (or **equivalent**) **rates** of return. Here is the formula:

$$EAR = EFF\% = (1 + I_{PER})^M - 1.0 = \left(1 + \frac{I_{NOM}}{M}\right)^M - 1.0$$

- The general equation for finding the future value of a current cash flow (PV) for any number of compounding periods per year is

$$FV_N = PV(1 + I_{PER})^{\text{Number of periods}} = PV\left(1 + \frac{I_{NOM}}{M}\right)^{MN}$$

where

I_{NOM} = Nominal quoted interest rate
M = Number of compounding periods per year
N = Number of years

- An **amortized loan** is paid off with equal payments over a specified period. An **amortization schedule** shows how much of each payment constitutes interest, how much is used to reduce the principal, and the unpaid balance at the end of each period. The unpaid balance at Time N must be zero.
- A "**growing annuity**" is a stream of cash flows that grows at a constant rate for a specified number of years. The present and future values of growing annuities can be found with relatively complicated formulas or, more easily, with an *Excel* model.
- *Web Extension 4A* explains the **tabular approach**.
- *Web Extension 4B* provides derivations of the annuity formulas.
- *Web Extension 4C* explains **continuous compounding**.

QUESTIONS

(4-1) Define each of the following terms:

a. PV; I; INT; FV_N; PVA_N; FVA_N; PMT; M; I_{NOM}
b. Opportunity cost rate
c. Annuity; lump-sum payment; cash flow; uneven cash flow stream
d. Ordinary (or deferred) annuity; annuity due
e. Perpetuity; consol
f. Outflow; inflow; time line; terminal value
g. Compounding; discounting
h. Annual, semiannual, quarterly, monthly, and daily compounding
i. Effective annual rate (EAR or EFF%); nominal (quoted) interest rate; APR; periodic rate
j. Amortization schedule; principal versus interest component of a payment; amortized loan

(4-2) What is an *opportunity cost rate?* How is this rate used in discounted cash flow analysis, and where is it shown on a time line? Is the opportunity rate a single number that is used to evaluate all potential investments?

(4-3) An *annuity* is defined as a series of payments of a fixed amount for a specific number of periods. Thus, $100 a year for 10 years is an annuity, but $100 in Year 1, $200 in Year 2, and $400 in Years 3 through 10 does *not* constitute an annuity. However, the entire series *does contain* an annuity. Is this statement true or false?

(4-4) If a firm's earnings per share grew from $1 to $2 over a 10-year period, the *total growth* would be 100%, but the *annual growth rate* would be *less than* 10%. True or false? Explain.

(4-5) Would you rather have a savings account that pays 5% interest compounded semiannually or one that pays 5% interest compounded daily? Explain.

SELF-TEST PROBLEMS   Solutions Appear in Appendix A

(ST-1)
Future Value

Assume that 1 year from now you plan to deposit $1,000 in a savings account that pays a nominal rate of 8%.

    a. If the bank compounds interest annually, how much will you have in your account 4 years from now?

    b. What would your balance be 4 years from now if the bank used quarterly compounding rather than annual compounding?

    c. Suppose you deposited the $1,000 in 4 payments of $250 each at the end of Years 1, 2, 3, and 4. How much would you have in your account at the end of Year 4, based on 8% annual compounding?

    d. Suppose you deposited 4 equal payments in your account at the end of Years 1, 2, 3, and 4. Assuming an 8% interest rate, how large would each of your payments have to be for you to obtain the same ending balance as you calculated in part a?

(ST-2)
Time Value of Money

Assume that 4 years from now you will need $1,000. Your bank compounds interest at an 8% annual rate.

    a. How much must you deposit 1 year from now to have a balance of $1,000 at Year 4?

    b. If you want to make equal payments at the end of Years 1 through 4 to accumulate the $1,000, how large must each of the 4 payments be?

    c. If your father were to offer either to make the payments calculated in part b ($221.92) or to give you a lump sum of $750 one year from now, which would you choose?

    d. If you will have only $750 at the end of Year 1, what interest rate, compounded annually, would you have to earn to have the necessary $1,000 at Year 4?

    e. Suppose you can deposit only $186.29 each at the end of Years 1 through 4, but you still need $1,000 at the end of Year 4. What interest rate, with annual compounding, is required to achieve your goal?

    f. To help you reach your $1,000 goal, your father offers to give you $400 one year from now. You will get a part-time job and make 6 additional deposits of equal amounts each 6 months thereafter. If all of this money is deposited in a bank that pays 8%, compounded semiannually, how large must each of the 6 deposits be?

    g. What is the effective annual rate being paid by the bank in part f?

(ST-3)
Effective Annual Rates

Bank A pays 8% interest, compounded quarterly, on its money market account. The managers of Bank B want its money market account's effective annual rate to equal that of Bank A, but Bank B will compound interest on a monthly basis. What nominal, or quoted, rate must Bank B set?

PROBLEMS   Answers Appear in Appendix B

Easy Problems 1–8

(4-1)
Future Value of a Single Payment

If you deposit $10,000 in a bank account that pays 10% interest annually, how much will be in your account after 5 years?

(4-2)
Present Value of a Single Payment

What is the present value of a security that will pay $5,000 in 20 years if securities of equal risk pay 7% annually?

(4-3)
Interest Rate on a Single Payment

Your parents will retire in 18 years. They currently have $250,000, and they think they will need $1 million at retirement. What annual interest rate must they earn to reach their goal, assuming they don't save any additional funds?

(4-4)
Number of Periods of a Single Payment

If you deposit money today in an account that pays 6.5% annual interest, how long will it take to double your money?

(4-5)
Number of Periods for an Annuity

You have $42,180.53 in a brokerage account, and you plan to deposit an additional $5,000 at the end of every future year until your account totals $250,000. You expect to earn 12% annually on the account. How many years will it take to reach your goal?

(4-6)
Future Value: Ordinary Annuity versus Annuity Due

What is the future value of a 7%, 5-year ordinary annuity that pays $300 each year? If this were an annuity due, what would its future value be?

(4-7)
Present and Future Value of an Uneven Cash Flow Stream

An investment will pay $100 at the end of each of the next 3 years, $200 at the end of Year 4, $300 at the end of Year 5, and $500 at the end of Year 6. If other investments of equal risk earn 8% annually, what is this investment's present value? Its future value?

(4-8)
Annuity Payment and EAR

You want to buy a car, and a local bank will lend you $20,000. The loan would be fully amortized over 5 years (60 months), and the nominal interest rate would be 12%, with interest paid monthly. What is the monthly loan payment? What is the loan's EFF%?

Intermediate
Problems 9–29

(4-9)
Present and Future Values of Single Cash Flows for Different Periods

Find the following values, *using the equations,* and then work the problems using a financial calculator to check your answers. Disregard rounding differences. (*Hint:* If you are using a financial calculator, you can enter the known values and then press the appropriate key to find the unknown variable. Then, without clearing the TVM register, you can "override" the variable that changes by simply entering a new value for it and then pressing the key for the unknown variable to obtain the second answer. This procedure can be used in parts b and d, and in many other situations, to see how changes in input variables affect the output variable.)

a. An initial $500 compounded for 1 year at 6%
b. An initial $500 compounded for 2 years at 6%
c. The present value of $500 due in 1 year at a discount rate of 6%
d. The present value of $500 due in 2 years at a discount rate of 6%

(4-10)
Present and Future Values of Single Cash Flows for Different Interest Rates

Use both the TVM equations and a financial calculator to find the following values. See the Hint for Problem 4-9.

a. An initial $500 compounded for 10 years at 6%
b. An initial $500 compounded for 10 years at 12%
c. The present value of $500 due in 10 years at a 6% discount rate
d. The present value of $500 due in 10 years at a 12% discount rate

(4-11)
Time for a Lump Sum to Double

To the closest year, how long will it take $200 to double if it is deposited and earns the following rates? [*Notes:* (1) See the Hint for Problem 4-9. (2) This problem cannot be solved exactly with some financial calculators. For example, if you enter PV = −200, PMT = 0, FV = 400, and I = 7 in an HP-12C and then press the N key, you will get 11 years for part a. The correct answer is 10.2448 years, which rounds to 10, but the calculator rounds up. However, the HP10BII gives the exact answer.]

a. 7%
b. 10%
c. 18%
d. 100%

(4-12)
Future Value of an
Annuity

Find the *future value* of the following annuities. The first payment in these annuities is made at the *end* of Year 1, so they are *ordinary annuities*. (*Notes:* See the Hint to Problem 4-9. Also, note that you can leave values in the TVM register, switch to Begin Mode, press FV, and find the FV of the annuity due.)

a. $400 per year for 10 years at 10%
b. $200 per year for 5 years at 5%
c. $400 per year for 5 years at 0%
d. Now rework parts a, b, and c assuming that payments are made at the *beginning* of each year; that is, they are *annuities due.*

(4-13)
Present Value of an
Annuity

Find the *present value* of the following *ordinary annuities* (see the *Notes* to Problem 4-12).

a. $400 per year for 10 years at 10%
b. $200 per year for 5 years at 5%
c. $400 per year for 5 years at 0%
d. Now rework parts a, b, and c assuming that payments are made at the *beginning* of each year; that is, they are *annuities due.*

(4-14)
Uneven Cash Flow
Stream

a. Find the present values of the following cash flow streams. The appropriate interest rate is 8%. (*Hint:* It is fairly easy to work this problem dealing with the individual cash flows. However, if you have a financial calculator, read the section of the manual that describes how to enter cash flows such as the ones in this problem. This will take a little time, but the investment will pay huge dividends throughout the course. Note that, when working with the calculator's cash flow register, you must enter CF0 = 0. Note also that it is quite easy to work the problem with *Excel*, using procedures described in the Chapter 4 *Tool Kit.*)

Year	Cash Stream A	Cash Stream B
1	$100	$300
2	400	400
3	400	400
4	400	400
5	300	100

b. What is the value of each cash flow stream at a 0% interest rate?

(4-15)
Effective Rate of
Interest

Find the interest rate (or rates of return) in each of the following situations.

a. You *borrow* $700 and promise to pay back $749 at the end of 1 year.
b. You *lend* $700 and receive a promise to be paid $749 at the end of 1 year.
c. You borrow $85,000 and promise to pay back $201,229 at the end of 10 years.
d. You borrow $9,000 and promise to make payments of $2,684.80 at the end of each of the next 5 years.

(4-16)
Future Value for
Various
Compounding
Periods

Find the amount to which $500 will grow under each of the following conditions.

a. 12% compounded annually for 5 years
b. 12% compounded semiannually for 5 years
c. 12% compounded quarterly for 5 years
d. 12% compounded monthly for 5 years

(4-17)
Present Value
for Various
Compounding
Periods

Find the present value of $500 due in the future under each of the following conditions.

a. 12% nominal rate, semiannual compounding, discounted back 5 years
b. 12% nominal rate, quarterly compounding, discounted back 5 years
c. 12% nominal rate, monthly compounding, discounted back 1 year

(4-18)
Future Value of an
Annuity for Various
Compounding
Periods

Find the future values of the following ordinary annuities.

a. FV of $400 each 6 months for 5 years at a nominal rate of 12%, compounded semiannually
b. FV of $200 each 3 months for 5 years at a nominal rate of 12%, compounded quarterly
c. The annuities described in parts a and b have the same total amount of money paid into them during the 5-year period, and both earn interest at the same nominal rate, yet the annuity in part b earns $101.75 more than the one in part a over the 5 years. Why does this occur?

(4-19)
Effective versus
Nominal Interest
Rates

Universal Bank pays 7% interest, compounded annually, on time deposits. Regional Bank pays 6% interest, compounded quarterly.

a. Based on effective interest rates, in which bank would you prefer to deposit your money?
b. Could your choice of banks be influenced by the fact that you might want to withdraw your funds during the year as opposed to at the end of the year? In answering this question, assume that funds must be left on deposit during an entire compounding period in order for you to receive any interest.

(4-20)
Amortization
Schedule

a. Set up an amortization schedule for a $25,000 loan to be repaid in equal installments at the end of each of the next 5 years. The interest rate is 10%.
b. How large must each annual payment be if the loan is for $50,000? Assume that the interest rate remains at 10% and that the loan is still paid off over 5 years.
c. How large must each payment be if the loan is for $50,000, the interest rate is 10%, and the loan is paid off in equal installments at the end of each of the next 10 years? This loan is for the same amount as the loan in part b, but the payments are spread out over twice as many periods. Why are these payments not half as large as the payments on the loan in part b?

(4-21)
Growth Rates

Sales for Hanebury Corporation's just-ended year were $12 million. Sales were $6 million 5 years earlier.

a. At what rate did sales grow?
b. Suppose someone calculated the sales growth for Hanebury in part a as follows: "Sales doubled in 5 years. This represents a growth of 100% in 5 years; dividing 100% by 5 results in an estimated growth rate of 20% per year." Explain what is wrong with this calculation.

(4-22)
Expected Rate of
Return

Washington-Pacific invested $4 million to buy a tract of land and plant some young pine trees. The trees can be harvested in 10 years, at which time W-P plans to sell the forest at an expected price of $8 million. What is W-P's expected rate of return?

(4-23)
Effective Rate of
Interest

A mortgage company offers to lend you $85,000; the loan calls for payments of $8,273.59 at the end of each year for 30 years. What interest rate is the mortgage company charging you?

(4-24)
Required Lump-Sum
Payment

To complete your last year in business school and then go through law school, you will need $10,000 per year for 4 years, starting next year (that is, you will need to withdraw the first $10,000 one year from today). Your uncle offers to put you through school, and he will deposit in a bank paying 7% interest a sum of money that is sufficient to provide the 4 payments of $10,000 each. His deposit will be made today.

a. How large must the deposit be?

b. How much will be in the account immediately after you make the first withdrawal? After the last withdrawal?

(4-25)
Repaying a Loan

While Mary Corens was a student at the University of Tennessee, she borrowed $12,000 in student loans at an annual interest rate of 9%. If Mary repays $1,500 per year, then how long (to the nearest year) will it take her to repay the loan?

(4-26)
Reaching a Financial Goal

You need to accumulate $10,000. To do so, you plan to make deposits of $1,250 per year—with the first payment being made a year from today—into a bank account that pays 12% annual interest. Your last deposit will be less than $1,250 if less is needed to round out to $10,000. How many years will it take you to reach your $10,000 goal, and how large will the last deposit be?

(4-27)
Present Value of a Perpetuity

What is the present value of a perpetuity of $100 per year if the appropriate discount rate is 7%? If interest rates in general were to double and the appropriate discount rate rose to 14%, what would happen to the present value of the perpetuity?

(4-28)
PV and Effective Annual Rate

Assume that you inherited some money. A friend of yours is working as an unpaid intern at a local brokerage firm, and her boss is selling securities that call for 4 payments of $50 (1 payment at the end of each of the next 4 years) plus an extra payment of $1,000 at the end of Year 4. Your friend says she can get you some of these securities at a cost of $900 each. Your money is now invested in a bank that pays an 8% nominal (quoted) interest rate but with quarterly compounding. You regard the securities as being just as safe, and as liquid, as your bank deposit, so your required effective annual rate of return on the securities is the same as that on your bank deposit. You must calculate the value of the securities to decide whether they are a good investment. What is their present value to you?

(4-29)
Loan Amortization

Assume that your aunt sold her house on December 31, and to help close the sale she took a second mortgage in the amount of $10,000 as part of the payment. The mortgage has a quoted (or nominal) interest rate of 10%; it calls for payments every 6 months, beginning on June 30, and is to be amortized over 10 years. Now, 1 year later, your aunt must inform the IRS and the person who bought the house about the interest that was included in the two payments made during the year. (This interest will be income to your aunt and a deduction to the buyer of the house.) To the closest dollar, what is the total amount of interest that was paid during the first year?

Challenging Problems 30–34

(4-30)
Loan Amortization

Your company is planning to borrow $1 million on a 5-year, 15%, annual payment, fully amortized term loan. What fraction of the payment made at the end of the second year will represent repayment of principal?

(4-31)
Nonannual Compounding

a. It is now January 1. You plan to make a total of 5 deposits of $100 each, one every 6 months, with the first payment being made *today*. The bank pays a nominal interest rate of 12% but uses *semiannual* compounding. You plan to leave the money in the bank for 10 years. How much will be in your account after 10 years?

b. You must make a payment of $1,432.02 in 10 years. To get the money for this payment, you will make 5 equal deposits, beginning today and for the following 4 quarters, in a bank that pays a nominal interest rate of 12% with *quarterly compounding*. How large must each of the 5 payments be?

(4-32)
Nominal Rate of Return

Anne Lockwood, manager of Oaks Mall Jewelry, wants to sell on credit, giving customers 3 months to pay. However, Anne will have to borrow from her bank to carry the accounts receivable. The bank will charge a nominal rate of 15% and will compound monthly.

Anne wants to quote a nominal rate to her customers (all of whom are expected to pay on time) that will exactly offset her financing costs. What nominal annual rate should she quote to her credit customers?

(4-33)
Required Annuity Payments

Assume that your father is now 50 years old, plans to retire in 10 years, and expects to live for 25 years after he retires—that is, until age 85. He wants his first retirement payment to have the same purchasing power at the time he retires as $40,000 has today. He wants all of his subsequent retirement payments to be equal to his first retirement payment. (Do not let the retirement payments grow with inflation: Your father realizes that if inflation occurs the real value of his retirement income will decline year by year after he retires.) His retirement income will begin the day he retires, 10 years from today, and he will then receive 24 additional annual payments. Inflation is expected to be 5% per year from today forward. He currently has $100,000 saved and expects to earn a return on his savings of 8% per year with annual compounding. To the nearest dollar, how much must he save during each of the next 10 years (with equal deposits being made at the end of each year, beginning a year from today) to meet his retirement goal? (*Note:* Neither the amount he saves nor the amount he withdraws upon retirement is a growing annuity.)

(4-34)
Growing Annuity Payments

You want to accumulate $1 million by your retirement date, which is 25 years from now. You will make 25 deposits in your bank, with the first occurring *today*. The bank pays 8% interest, compounded annually. You expect to receive annual raises of 3%, which will offset inflation, and you will let the amount you deposit each year also grow by 3% (i.e., your second deposit will be 3% greater than your first, the third will be 3% greater than the second, etc.). How much must your first deposit be if you are to meet your goal?

SPREADSHEET PROBLEM

(4-35)
Build a Model: The Time Value of Money

resource

1. Start with the partial model in the file ***Ch04 P35 Build a Model.xls*** from the textbook's Web site. Answer the following questions, using a spreadsheet model to do the calculations.
   a. Find the FV of $1,000 invested to earn 10% annually 5 years from now. Answer this question first by using a math formula and then by using the *Excel* function wizard.
   b. Now create a table that shows the FV at 0%, 5%, and 20% for 0, 1, 2, 3, 4, and 5 years. Then create a graph with years on the horizontal axis and FV on the vertical axis to display your results.
   c. Find the PV of $1,000 due in 5 years if the discount rate is 10% per year. Again, first work the problem with a formula and then by using the function wizard.
   d. A security has a cost of $1,000 and will return $2,000 after 5 years. What rate of return does the security provide?
   e. Suppose California's population is 30 million people and its population is expected to grow by 2% per year. How long would it take for the population to double?
   f. Find the PV of an ordinary annuity that pays $1,000 at the end of each of the next 5 years if the interest rate is 15%. Then find the FV of that same annuity.
   g. How would the PV and FV of the above annuity change if it were an annuity due rather than an ordinary annuity?
   h. What would the FV and PV for parts a and c be if the interest rate were 10% with *semiannual* compounding rather than 10% with *annual* compounding?

i. Find the PV and FV of an investment that makes the following end-of-year payments. The interest rate is 8%.

Year	Payment
1	$100
2	200
3	400

j. Suppose you bought a house and took out a mortgage for $50,000. The interest rate is 8%, and you must amortize the loan over 10 years with equal end-of-year payments. Set up an amortization schedule that shows the annual payments and the amount of each payment that repays the principal and the amount that constitutes interest expense to the borrower and interest income to the lender.

  (1) Create a graph that shows how the payments are divided between interest and principal repayment over time.
  (2) Suppose the loan called for 10 years of monthly payments, 120 payments in all, with the same original amount and the same nominal interest rate. What would the amortization schedule show now?

MINI CASE

Assume that you are nearing graduation and have applied for a job with a local bank. The bank's evaluation process requires you to take an examination that covers several financial analysis techniques. The first section of the test addresses discounted cash flow analysis. See how you would do by answering the following questions.

a. Draw time lines for (1) a $100 lump sum cash flow at the end of Year 2, (2) an ordinary annuity of $100 per year for 3 years, and (3) an uneven cash flow stream of −$50, $100, $75, and $50 at the end of Years 0 through 3.

b. (1) What's the *future value* of an initial $100 after 3 years if it is invested in an account paying 10% annual interest?
   (2) What's the *present value* of $100 to be received in 3 years if the appropriate interest rate is 10%?

c. We sometimes need to find out how long it will take a sum of money (or something else, such as earnings, population, or prices) to grow to some specified amount. For example, if a company's sales are growing at a rate of 20% per year, how long will it take sales to double?

d. If you want an investment to double in 3 years, what interest rate must it earn?

e. What's the difference between an ordinary annuity and an annuity due? What type of annuity is shown below? How would you change the time line to show the other type of annuity?

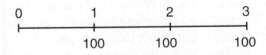

f. (1) What's the future value of a 3-year ordinary annuity of $100 if the appropriate interest rate is 10%?
   (2) What's the present value of the annuity?
   (3) What would the future and present values be if the annuity were an annuity due?

g. What is the present value of the following uneven cash flow stream? The appropriate interest rate is 10%, compounded annually.

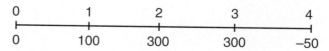

h. (1) Define the stated (quoted) or nominal rate I_{NOM} as well as the periodic rate I_{PER}.
   (2) Will the future value be larger or smaller if we compound an initial amount more often than annually—for example, every 6 months, or *semiannually*—holding the stated interest rate constant? Why?
   (3) What is the future value of $100 after 5 years under 12% annual compounding? Semiannual compounding? Quarterly compounding? Monthly compounding? Daily compounding?
   (4) What is the effective annual rate (EAR or EFF%)? What is the EFF% for a nominal rate of 12%, compounded semiannually? Compounded quarterly? Compounded monthly? Compounded daily?

i. Will the effective annual rate ever be equal to the nominal (quoted) rate?
j. (1) Construct an amortization schedule for a $1,000, 10% annual rate loan with 3 equal installments.
   (2) During Year 2, what is the annual interest expense for the borrower, and what is the annual interest income for the lender?

k. Suppose that on January 1 you deposit $100 in an account that pays a nominal (or quoted) interest rate of 11.33463%, with interest added (compounded) daily. How much will you have in your account on October 1, or 9 months later?

l. (1) What is the value at the end of Year 3 of the following cash flow stream if the quoted interest rate is 10%, compounded semiannually?

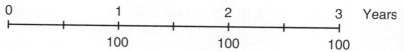

   (2) What is the PV of the same stream?
   (3) Is the stream an annuity?
   (4) An important rule is that you should never show a nominal rate on a time line or use it in calculations unless what condition holds? (*Hint:* Think of annual compounding, when I_{NOM} = EFF% = I_{PER}.) What would be wrong with your answers to parts (1) and (2) if you used the nominal rate of 10% rather than the periodic rate, $I_{NOM}/2$ = 10%/2 = 5%?

m. Suppose someone offered to sell you a note calling for the payment of $1,000 in 15 months. They offer to sell it to you for $850. You have $850 in a bank time deposit that pays a 6.76649% nominal rate with daily compounding, which is a 7% effective annual interest rate, and you plan to leave the money in the bank unless you buy the note. The note is not risky—you are sure it will be paid on schedule. Should you buy the note? Check the decision in three ways: (1) by comparing your future value if you buy the note versus leaving your money in the bank; (2) by comparing the PV of the note with your current bank account; and (3) by comparing the EFF% on the note with that of the bank account.

© Adalberto Rios Szalay/Sexto Sol/Getty Images

CHAPTER 5

Bond, Bond Valuation, and Interest Rates

A lot of bonds have been issued in the United States, and we mean a *lot!* According to the Federal Reserve, at the beginning of 2012 there were about $10.4 trillion of outstanding U.S. Treasury securities, more than $3.7 trillion of municipal securities, $4.9 trillion of corporate bonds, and more than $1.7 trillion of foreign bonds held in the United States. Not only is the dollar amount mind-boggling, but so is the variety.

Bonds aren't the only way to borrow. In addition to their bonds, corporations owe $2.9 trillion in short-term debt. Noncorporate businesses, which include small businesses, owe $3.8 trillion. Interestingly, small business borrowing is down from $4.1 trillion from the beginning of 2009, reflecting the reluctance of many banks to make loans during the financial crisis.

Let's not ignore households, which owe $2.5 trillion in consumer debt, such as car loans and credit cards. This works out to about $22,000 per household, and this doesn't even include the $10.3 trillion (about $90,000 per household) in federal debt.

Given the enormous amount of debt in the modern world, it is vital for everyone to understand debt and interest rates.

Sources: "Flow of Funds Accounts of the United States, Section L.2, Credit Market Debt Owed by Nonfinancial Sectors," **www.federalreserve.gov/releases/Z1/current/**; **http://quickfacts. census.gov/qfd/states/00000.html**.

Intrinsic Value and the Cost of Debt

© Rob Webb/Getty Images

This chapter explains bond pricing and bond risk, which affect the return demanded by a firm's bondholders. A bondholder's return is a cost from the company's point of view. This cost of debt affects the firm's weighted average cost of capital (WACC), which in turn affects the company's intrinsic value. Therefore, it is important for all managers to understand the cost of debt, which we explain in this chapter.

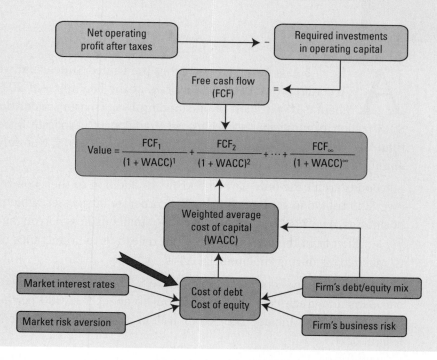

© Cengage Learning 2014

Growing companies must acquire land, buildings, equipment, inventory, and other operating assets. The debt markets are a major source of funding for such purchases. Therefore, every manager should have a working knowledge of the types of bonds that companies and government agencies issue, the terms that are contained in bond contracts, the types of risks to which both bond investors and issuers are exposed, and procedures for determining the values of and rates of return on bonds.

resource

*The textbook's Web site contains an Excel file that will guide you through the chapter's calculations. The file for this chapter is **Ch05 Tool Kit.xls**, and we encourage you to open the file and follow along as you read the chapter.*

5-1 Who Issues Bonds?

A **bond** is a long-term contract under which a borrower agrees to make payments of interest and principal, on specific dates, to the holders of the bond. For example, on January 5, 2013, MicroDrive Inc. issued $200 million of bonds. For convenience, we assume that MicroDrive sold 200,000 individual bonds for $1,000 each. Actually, it could have sold one $200 million bond, 10 bonds with a $20 million face value, or any other combination that totals to $200 million. In exchange for $200 million, MicroDrive promised to make annual interest payments and to repay the $200 million on a specified maturity date.

Investors have many choices when investing in bonds, but bonds are classified into four main types: Treasury, corporate, municipal, and foreign. Each type differs with respect to expected return and degree of risk.

Treasury bonds, sometimes referred to as *government bonds,* are issued by the U.S. federal government.[1] It is reasonable to assume that the federal government will make good on its promised payments, so these bonds have almost no default risk. However, Treasury bond prices decline when interest rates rise, so they are not free of all risks.

Federal agencies and other government-sponsored entities (GSEs) include the Tennessee Valley Authority, the Small Business Administration, Fannie Mae, Freddie Mac, and the Federal Home Loan Bank System, among others. **Agency debt** and **GSE debt** are not officially backed by the full faith and credit of the U.S. government, but investors assume that the government implicitly guarantees this debt, so these bonds carry interest rates only slightly higher than Treasury bonds. In 2008, the implicit guarantee became much more explicit as the government placed several GSEs into conservatorship, including Fannie Mae and Freddie Mac.

Corporate bonds, as the name implies, are issued by corporations. Unlike Treasury bonds, corporate bonds are exposed to default risk—if the issuing company gets into trouble, it may be unable to make the promised interest and principal payments. Different corporate bonds have different levels of default risk, depending on the issuing company's characteristics and the terms of the specific bond. Default risk is often referred to as "credit risk," and the larger the credit risk, the higher the interest rate the issuer must pay.

Municipal bonds, or "munis," are issued by state and local governments. Like corporate bonds, munis have default risk. However, munis offer one major advantage: The interest earned on most municipal bonds is exempt from federal taxes and also from state taxes if the holder is a resident of the issuing state. Consequently, municipal bonds carry interest rates that are considerably lower than those on corporate bonds with the same default risk.

Foreign bonds are issued by foreign governments or foreign corporations. Foreign corporate bonds are, of course, exposed to default risk, and so are some foreign government bonds. An additional risk exists if the bonds are denominated in a currency other than that of the investor's home currency. For example, if a U.S. investor purchases a corporate bond denominated in Japanese yen, and if the yen subsequently falls relative to the dollar, then the investor will lose money even if the company does not default on its bonds.

SELF-TEST

What is a bond?

What are the four main types of bonds?

Why are U.S. Treasury bonds not riskless?

To what types of risk are investors of foreign bonds exposed?

---

[1]The U.S. Treasury actually issues three types of securities: bills, notes, and bonds. A bond makes an equal payment every 6 months until it matures, at which time it makes an additional lump-sum payment. If the maturity at the time of issue is less than 10 years, the security is called a note rather than a bond. A T-bill has a maturity of 52 weeks or less at the time of issue, and it makes no payments at all until it matures. Thus, T-bills are sold initially at a discount to their face, or maturity, value.

GLOBAL ECONOMIC CRISIS

© uniquely india/Getty Images

The Global Economic Crisis

Betting With or Against the U.S. Government: The Case of Treasury Bond Credit Default Swaps

It might be hard to believe, but there is actually a market for U.S. Treasury bond insurance. In July 2011, investors worried that Congress would not extend the debt ceiling, inducing defaults in Treasury securities. At that time a credit default swap (CDS) on a 5-year T-bond was selling for 63.5 basis points (a basis point is 1/100 of a percentage point). This means that you could pay $6.35 a year to a counterparty who would promise to insure $1,000 of T-bond principal against default. Considering that the T-bond was yielding an amount equal to about $15 a year,

the insurance would eat up a lot of the annual return for an investor who owned the bond. However, most of the trading in this CDS is by speculators and hedgers who don't even own the T-bond but are simply betting for or against the financial soundness of the U.S. government.

But it does make you wonder: "If the United States fails, who will be around to pay off the CDS?"

Note: For updates on the 5-year CDS, go to **www. bloomberg.com** and enter a quote for CT786896:IND.

5-2 Key Characteristics of Bonds

Although all bonds have some common characteristics, they do not always have identical contractual features, as described below.

W W W

An excellent site for information on many types of bonds is the FINRA Web page, **http://cxa.marketwatch.com/ finra/bondcenter/default .aspx.** *The site has a great deal of information about corporates, municipals, Treasuries, and bond funds. It includes free bond searches, through which the user specifies the attributes desired in a bond and then the search returns the publicly traded bonds meeting the criteria.*

5-2a Par Value

The **par value** is the stated face value of the bond; for illustrative purposes, we generally assume a par value of $1,000. In practice, some bonds have par values that are multiples of $1,000 (for example, $5,000) and some have par values of less than $1,000 (Treasury bonds can be purchased in multiples of $100). The par value generally represents the amount of money the firm borrows and promises to repay on the maturity date.

5-2b Coupon Interest Rate

MicroDrive's bonds require the company to pay a fixed number of dollars of interest every year (or, more typically, every 6 months). When this **coupon payment**, as it is called, is divided by the par value, the result is the **coupon interest rate**. For example, MicroDrive's bonds have a $1,000 par value, and they pay $90 in interest each year. The bond's coupon interest is $90, so its coupon interest rate is $90/$1,000 = 9%. The coupon payment, which is fixed at the time the bond is issued, remains in force during the life of the bond.[2] Typically, at the time a bond is issued, its coupon payment is set at a level that will enable the bond to be issued at or near its par value.

---

[2]At one time, bonds literally had a number of small coupons attached to them, and on each interest payment date the owner would clip off the coupon for that date and either cash it at the bank or mail it to the company's paying agent, who would then mail back a check for the interest. For example, a 30-year, semiannual bond would start with 60 coupons. Today, most new bonds are *registered*—no physical coupons are involved, and interest checks automatically are mailed to the registered owners or directly deposited in their bank accounts.

In some cases, a bond's coupon payment will vary over time. For these **floating-rate bonds**, the coupon rate is set for, say, the initial 6-month period, after which it is adjusted every 6 months based on some market rate. Some corporate issues are tied to the Treasury bond rate; other issues are tied to other rates, such as LIBOR (the London Interbank Offered Rate). Many additional provisions can be included in floating-rate issues. For example, some are convertible to fixed-rate debt, whereas others have upper and lower limits ("caps" and "floors") on how high or low the rate can go.

Floating-rate debt is popular with investors who are worried about the risk of rising interest rates, because the interest paid on such bonds increases whenever market rates rise. This stabilizes the market value of the debt, and it also provides institutional buyers, such as banks, with income that is better geared to their own obligations. Banks' deposit costs rise with interest rates, so the income on floating-rate loans they have made rises at the same time as their deposit costs rise. The savings and loan industry was almost destroyed as a result of its former practice of making fixed-rate mortgage loans but borrowing on floating-rate terms. If you earn 6% fixed but pay 10% floating (which they were), you will soon go bankrupt (which they did). Moreover, floating-rate debt appeals to corporations that want to issue long-term debt without committing themselves to paying a historically high interest rate for the entire life of the loan.

resource

For more on zero coupon bonds, including U.S. Treasury STRIP bonds, see **Web Extension 5A** on the textbook's Web site.

Some bonds pay no coupons at all but are offered at a substantial discount below their par values and hence provide capital appreciation rather than interest income. These securities are called **zero coupon bonds** ("zeros"). Most zero coupon bonds are Treasury bonds, although a few corporations, such as Coca-Cola, have zero coupon bonds outstanding. Some bonds are issued with a coupon rate too low for the bond to be issued at par, so the bond is issued at a price less than its par value. In general, any bond originally offered at a price significantly below its par value is called an **original issue discount (OID) bond**.

Some bonds don't pay cash coupons but pay coupons consisting of additional bonds (or a percentage of an additional bond). These are called **payment-in-kind bonds**, or just **PIK bonds**. PIK bonds are usually issued by companies with cash flow problems, which makes them risky.

Some bonds have a step-up provision: If the company's bond rating is downgraded, then it must increase the bond's coupon rate. Step-ups are more popular in Europe than in the United States, but that is beginning to change. Note that a step-up is quite dangerous from the company's standpoint. The downgrade means that it is having trouble servicing its debt, and the step-up will exacerbate the problem. This combination has led to a number of bankruptcies.

5-2c Maturity Date

Bonds generally have a specified **maturity date** on which the par value must be repaid. MicroDrive bonds issued on January 5, 2013, will mature on January 5, 2028; thus, they have a 15-year maturity at the time they are issued. Most bonds have **original maturities** (the maturity at the time the bond is issued) ranging from 10 to 40 years, but any maturity is legally permissible.[3] Of course, the effective maturity of a bond declines each year after it has been issued. Thus, MicroDrive's bonds have a 15-year original maturity, but in 2014, a year later, they will have a 14-year maturity, and so on.

---

[3]In July 1993, Walt Disney Co., attempting to lock in a low interest rate, issued the first 100-year bonds to be sold by any borrower in modern times. Soon after, Coca-Cola became the second company to stretch the meaning of "long-term bond" by selling $150 million of 100-year bonds.

5-2d Provisions to Call or Redeem Bonds

Most corporate bonds contain a **call provision**, which gives the issuing corporation the right to call the bonds for redemption.[4] The call provision generally states that the company must pay the bondholders an amount greater than the par value if they are called. The additional sum, which is termed a **call premium**, is often set equal to 1 year's interest if the bonds are called during the first year, and the premium declines at a constant rate of INT/N each year thereafter (where INT = annual interest and N = original maturity in years). For example, the call premium on a $1,000 par value, 10-year, 10% bond would generally be $100 if it were called during the first year, $90 during the second year (calculated by reducing the $100, or 10%, premium by one-tenth), and so on. However, bonds are often not callable until several years (generally 5 to 10) after they are issued. This is known as a **deferred call**, and the bonds are said to have **call protection**.

Suppose a company sold bonds when interest rates were relatively high. Provided the issue is callable, the company could sell a new issue of low-yielding securities if and when interest rates drop. It could then use the proceeds of the new issue to retire the high-rate issue and thus reduce its interest expense. This process is called a **refunding operation**.

A call provision is valuable to the firm but potentially detrimental to investors. If interest rates go up, the company will not call the bond, and the investor will be stuck with the original coupon rate on the bond, even though interest rates in the economy have risen sharply. However, if interest rates fall, the company *will* call the bond and pay off investors, who then must reinvest the proceeds at the current market interest rate, which is lower than the rate they were getting on the original bond. In other words, the investor loses when interest rates go up but doesn't reap the gains when rates fall. To induce an investor to take this type of risk, a new issue of callable bonds must provide a higher coupon rate than an otherwise similar issue of noncallable bonds.

Bonds that are **redeemable at par** at the holder's option protect investors against a rise in interest rates. If rates rise, the price of a fixed-rate bond declines. However, if holders have the option of turning their bonds in and having them redeemed at par, then they are protected against rising rates. If interest rates have risen, holders will turn in the bonds and reinvest the proceeds at a higher rate.

Event risk is the chance that some sudden event will occur and increase the credit risk of a company, hence lowering the firm's bond rating and the value of its outstanding bonds. Investors' concern over event risk means that those firms deemed most likely to face events that could harm bondholders must pay extremely high interest rates. To reduce this interest rate, some bonds have a covenant called a **super poison put**, which enables a bondholder to turn in, or "put," a bond back to the issuer at par in the event of a takeover, merger, or major recapitalization.

Some bonds have a **make-whole call provision**. This allows a company to call the bond, but it must pay a call price that is essentially equal to the market value of a similar noncallable bond. This provides companies with an easy way to repurchase bonds as part of a financial restructuring, such as a merger.

5-2e Sinking Funds

Some bonds include a **sinking fund provision** that facilitates the orderly retirement of the bond issue. On rare occasions the firm may be required to deposit money with a trustee, which invests the funds and then uses the accumulated sum to retire the bonds when they

---

[4]A majority of municipal bonds also contain call provisions. Although the U.S. Treasury no longer issues callable bonds, some past Treasury issues were callable.

mature. Usually, though, the sinking fund is used to buy back a certain percentage of the issue each year. A failure to meet the sinking fund requirement throws the bond into default, which may force the company into bankruptcy.

In most cases, the firm is given the right to administer the sinking fund in either of two ways.

1. The company can call in for redemption (at par value) a certain percentage of the bonds each year; for example, it might be able to call 5% of the total original amount of the issue at a price of $1,000 per bond. The bonds are numbered serially, and those called for redemption are determined by a lottery administered by the trustee.
2. The company may buy the required number of bonds on the open market.

The firm will choose the least-cost method. If interest rates have risen, causing bond prices to fall, then it will buy bonds in the open market at a discount; if interest rates have fallen, it will call the bonds. Note that a call for sinking fund purposes is quite different from a refunding call as discussed previously. A sinking fund call typically requires no call premium, but only a small percentage of the issue is normally callable in any one year.[5]

Although sinking funds are designed to protect bondholders by ensuring that an issue is retired in an orderly fashion, you should recognize that sinking funds also can work to the detriment of bondholders. For example, suppose that the bond carries a 10% interest rate but that yields on similar bonds have fallen to 7.5%. A sinking fund call at par would require an investor to give up a bond that pays $100 of interest and then to reinvest in a bond that pays only $75 per year. This obviously harms those bondholders whose bonds are called. On balance, however, bonds that have a sinking fund are regarded as being safer than those without such a provision, so at the time they are issued sinking fund bonds have lower coupon rates than otherwise similar bonds without sinking funds.

5-2f Other Provisions and Features

Owners of **convertible bonds** have the option to convert the bonds into a fixed number of shares of common stock. Convertibles offer investors the chance to share in the upside if a company does well, so investors are willing to accept a lower coupon rate on convertibles than on an otherwise identical but nonconvertible bond.

Warrants are options that permit the holder to buy stock at a fixed price, thereby providing a gain if the price of the stock rises. Some bonds are issued with warrants. As with convertibles, bonds with warrants have lower coupon rates than straight bonds.

An **income bond** is required to pay interest only if earnings are high enough to cover the interest expense. If earnings are not sufficient, then the company is not required to pay interest and the bondholders do not have the right to force the company into bankruptcy. Therefore, from an investor's standpoint, income bonds are riskier than "regular" bonds.

Indexed bonds, also called **purchasing power bonds**, first became popular in Brazil, Israel, and a few other countries plagued by high inflation rates. The interest payments and maturity payment rise automatically when the inflation rate rises, thus protecting the bondholders against inflation. In January 1997, the U.S. Treasury began issuing indexed bonds called TIPS, short for Treasury Inflation-Protected Securities. Later in this chapter we show how TIPS can be used to estimate the risk-free rate.

---

[5]Some sinking funds require the issuer to pay a call premium.

5-2g Bond Markets

Corporate bonds are traded primarily in electronic/telephone markets rather than in organized exchanges. Most bonds are owned by and traded among a relatively small number of very large financial institutions, including banks, investment banks, life insurance companies, mutual funds, and pension funds. Although these institutions buy and sell very large blocks of bonds, it is relatively easy for bond dealers to arrange transactions because there are relatively few players in this market as compared with stock markets.

Information on bond trades is not widely published, but a representative group of bonds is listed and traded on the bond division of the NYSE and is reported on the bond market page of *The Wall Street Journal*. The most useful Web site (as of mid-2012) is provided by the Financial Industry Regulatory Authority (FINRA) at **http://cxa.marketwatch.com/finra/bondcenter/default.aspx**.

SELF-TEST

Define "floating-rate bonds" and "zero coupon bonds."

Why is a call provision advantageous to a bond issuer?

What are the two ways a sinking fund can be handled? Which method will be chosen by the firm if interest rates have risen? If interest rates have fallen?

Are securities that provide for a sinking fund regarded as being riskier than those without this type of provision? Explain.

What are income bonds and indexed bonds?

Why do convertible bonds and bonds with warrants have lower coupons than similarly rated bonds that do not have these features?

5-3 Bond Valuation

The value of any financial asset—a stock, a bond, a lease, or even a physical asset such as an apartment building or a piece of machinery—is simply the present value of the cash flows the asset is expected to produce. The cash flows from a specific bond depend on its contractual features. The following section shows the time line and cash flows for a bond.

5-3a Time Line, Cash Flows, and Valuation Formulas for a Bond

For a standard coupon-bearing bond, the cash flows consist of interest payments during the life of the bond plus the amount borrowed when the bond matures (usually a $1,000 par value):

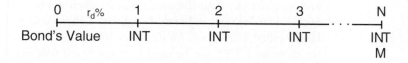

The notation in the time line is explained below.

r_d = The bond's required rate of return, which is the market rate of interest for that type of bond. This is the discount rate that is used to calculate the present value of the bond's cash flows. It is also called the "yield" or "going rate of interest." Note that r_d is *not* the coupon interest rate. It is equal to the coupon rate only if (as in this case) the bond is selling at par. Generally, most coupon bonds are issued at par, which implies that the coupon rate is set at r_d. Thereafter, interest rates, as measured by r_d, will fluctuate, but the coupon rate is fixed, so r_d will equal the coupon rate only by chance. We use the term "i" or "I" to designate the interest rate for many calculations because those terms are used on financial calculators, but "r," with the subscript "d" to designate the rate on a debt security, is normally used in finance.

N = Number of years until the bond matures. Note that N declines each year after the bond was issued, so a bond that had a maturity of 15 years when it was issued (original maturity = 15) will have N = 14 after 1 year, N = 13 after 2 years, and so on. Note also that for the sake of simplicity we assume the bond pays interest once a year, or annually, so N is measured in years. We consider bonds with semiannual payment bonds later in the chapter.

INT = Dollars of interest paid each year = (Coupon rate)(Par value). For a bond with a 9% coupon and a $1,000 par value, the annual interest is 0.09($1,000) = $90. In calculator terminology, INT = PMT = 90. If the bond had been a semiannual payment bond, the payment would have been $45 every 6 months.

M = Par, or maturity, value of the bond. This amount must be paid off at maturity, and it is often equal to $1,000.

The following general equation, written in several forms, can be used to find the value of any bond, V_B:

$$
\begin{aligned}
V_B &= \frac{INT}{(1 + r_d)^1} + \frac{INT}{(1 + r_d)^2} + \cdots + \frac{INT}{(1 + r_d)^N} + \frac{M}{(1 + r_d)^N} \\[2mm]
&= \sum_{t=1}^{N} \frac{INT}{(1 + r_d)^t} + \frac{M}{(1 + r_d)^N} \\[2mm]
&= INT \left[\frac{1}{r_d} - \frac{1}{r_d(1 + r_d)^N} \right] + \frac{M}{(1 + r_d)^N}
\end{aligned}
\tag{5-1}
$$

Observe that the cash flows consist of an annuity of N years plus a lump-sum payment at the end of Year N. Equation 5-1 can be solved by using (1) a formula, (2) a financial calculator, or (3) a spreadsheet.

5-3b Solving for the Bond Price

Recall that MicroDrive issued a 15-year bond with an annual coupon rate of 9% and a par value of $1,000. To find the value of MicroDrive's bond by using a formula, insert values for MicroDrive's bond into Equation 5-1:

$$V_B = \sum_{t=1}^{15} \frac{\$90}{(1+0.09)^t} + \frac{\$1,000}{(1+0.09)^{15}}$$

$$= \$100\left[\frac{1}{0.09} - \frac{1}{0.09(1+0.09)^{15}}\right] + \frac{\$1,000}{(1+0.09)^{15}} \qquad (5\text{-}1a)$$

$$= \$725.46 + \$274.54 = \$1,000$$

You could use the first line of Equation 5-1a to discount each cash flow back to the present and then sum these PVs to find the bond's value of $1,000; see Figure 5-1. This procedure is not very efficient, especially if the bond has many years to maturity.

Alternatively, you could use the formula in the second line of Equation 5-1a with a simple or scientific calculator. As shown in the third line of Equation 5-1a, the total bond value of $1,000 is the sum of the coupons' present values ($725.46) and the par value's present value ($274.54). This is easier than the step-by-step approach, but it is still somewhat cumbersome.

A financial calculator is ideally suited for finding bond values. Here is the setup for MicroDrive's bond:

See *Ch05 Tool Kit.xls* on the textbook's Web site.

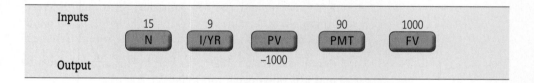

Input N = 15, I/YR = r_d = 9, INT = PMT = 90, and M = FV = 1000; then press the PV key to find the value of the bond, $1,000. Because the PV is an outflow to the investor, it is shown with a negative sign. The calculator is programmed to solve Equation 5-1: It finds the PV of an annuity of $100 per year for 15 years, discounted at 10%, then it finds the PV of the $1,000 maturity payment, and then it adds these two PVs to find the value of the bond. Notice that even though the bond has a total cash flow of $1,090 at Year 15, you should *not* enter FV = 1090! When you entered N = 15 and PMT = 90, you told the calculator that there is a $90 payment at Year 15. Thus, setting FV = 1000 accounts for any *extra* payment at Year 15, above and beyond the $90 payment.

See *Ch05 Tool Kit.xls* on the textbook's Web site.

With *Excel*, it is easiest to use the PV function: =PV(I,N,PMT,FV,0). For MicroDrive's bond, the function is =PV(0.09,15,90,1000,0) with a result of −$1,000. Like the financial calculator solution, the bond value is negative because PMT and FV are positive.

Excel also provides specialized functions for bond prices based on actual dates. For example, in *Excel* you could find the MicroDrive bond value as of the date it was issued by using the function wizard to enter this formula:

= PRICE(DATE(2013,1,5),DATE(2028,1,5),9%,9%,100,1,1)

The first two arguments in the function are *Excel*'s DATE function. The DATE function takes the year, month, and day as inputs and converts them into a date. The first argument is the date on which you want to find the price, and the second argument is the maturity date. The third argument in the PRICE function is the bond's coupon rate, followed by the required return on the bond, r_d. The fifth argument, 100, is the redemption value of the bond at maturity per $100 of face value; entering "100" means that the bond pays 100% of its face value when it matures. The sixth argument is the number of

FIGURE 5-1

Finding the Value of MicroDrive's Bond (V_B)

	A	B	C	D	E	F	G
19	INPUTS:						
20	Years to maturity = N =		15				
21	Coupon payment = INT =		$90				
22	Par value = M =		$1,000				
23	Required return = r_d =		9%				
24							
25	1. Step-by-Step: Divide each cash flow by $(1 + r_d)^t$						
26	Year (t)	Coupon Payment	PV of Coupon Payment	Par Value	PV of Par Value		
27	1	$90	$82.57				
28	2	$90	$75.75				
29	3	$90	$69.50				
30	4	$90	$63.76				
31	5	$90	$58.49				
32	6	$90	$53.66				
33	7	$90	$49.23				
34	8	$90	$45.17				
35	9	$90	$41.44				
36	10	$90	$38.02				
37	11	$90	$34.88				
38	12	$90	$32.00				
39	13	$90	$29.36				
40	14	$90	$26.93				
41	15	$90	$24.71	$1,000	$274.54		
42		Total =	$725.46				
43							
44	V_B = PV of all coupon payments + PV of par value =			$1,000.00			
45							
46	Inputs:		15	0		90	1,000
47	2. Financial Calculator:		N	I/YR	PV	PMT	FV
48	Output:				−$1,000.00		
49							
50	3. Excel:		PV function:	PV_N =	=PV(9%,15,90,1000)		
51			Fixed inputs:	PV_N =	=PV(9%,15,90,1000) =	−$1,000.00	
52			Cell references:	PV_N =	=PV(C23,C20,C21,C22) =	−$1,000.00	

payments per year. The last argument, 1, tells the program to base the price on the actual number of days in each month and year. This function produces a result based upon a face value of $100. In other words, if the bond pays $100 of face value at maturity, then the PRICE function result is the price of the bond. Because MicroDrive's bond pays $1,000 of face value at maturity, we must multiply the PRICE function's result by 10. In this example, the PRICE function returns a result of $100. When we multiply it by 10, we get the actual price of $1,000. This function is essential if a bond is being evaluated between coupon payment dates. See **Ch05 Tool Kit.xls** on the textbook's Web site for an example.[6]

5-3c Interest Rate Changes and Bond Prices

In this example, MicroDrive's bond is selling at a price equal to its par value. Whenever the going market rate of interest, r_d, is equal to the coupon rate, a *fixed-rate* bond will sell at its par value. Normally, the coupon rate is set at the going rate when a bond is issued, causing it to sell at par initially.

The coupon rate remains fixed after the bond is issued, but interest rates in the market move up and down. Looking at Equation 5-1, we see that an *increase* in the market interest rate (r_d) will cause the price of an outstanding bond to *fall*, whereas a *decrease* in rates will cause the bond's price to *rise*. For example, if the market interest rate on MicroDrive's bond increased by 5 percentage points to 14% immediately after it was issued, we would recalculate the price with the new market interest rate as follows:

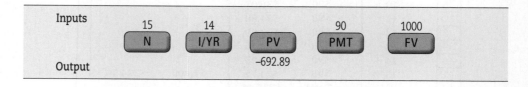

The price would fall to $692.89. Notice that the bond would then sell at a price below its par value. Whenever the going rate of interest *rises above* the coupon rate, a fixed-rate bond's price will *fall below* its par value, and it is called a **discount bond**.

On the other hand, bond prices rise when market interest rates fall. For example, if the market interest rate on MicroDrive's bond decreased by 5 percentage points to 4%, then we would once again recalculate its price:

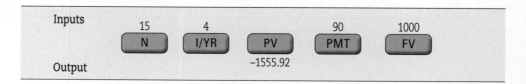

In this case, the price rises to $1,555.92. In general, whenever the going interest rate *falls below* the coupon rate, a fixed-rate bond's price will *rise above* its par value, and it is called a **premium bond**.

---

[6]The bond prices quoted by brokers are calculated as described. However, if you bought a bond between interest payment dates, you would have to pay the basic price plus accrued interest. Thus, if you purchased a MicroDrive bond 6 months after it was issued, your broker would send you an invoice stating that you must pay $1,000 as the basic price of the bond plus $45 interest, representing one-half the annual interest of $90. The seller of the bond would receive $1,045. If you bought the bond the day before its interest payment date, you would pay $1,000 + (364/365)($90) = $1,089.75. You would receive an interest payment of $90 at the end of the next day.

S E L F - T E S T

Why do the prices of fixed-rate bonds fall if expectations for inflation rise?

What is a discount bond? A premium bond?

A bond that matures in 6 years has a par value of $1,000, an annual coupon payment of $80, and a market interest rate of 9%. What is its price? **($955.14)**

A bond that matures in 18 years has a par value of $1,000, an annual coupon of 10%, and a market interest rate of 7%. What is its price? **($1,301.77)**

5-4 Changes in Bond Values Over Time

At the time a coupon bond is issued, the coupon is generally set at a level that will cause the market price of the bond to equal its par value. If a lower coupon were set, investors would not be willing to pay $1,000 for the bond, and if a higher coupon were set, investors would clamor for the bond and bid its price up over $1,000. Investment bankers can judge quite precisely the coupon rate that will cause a bond to sell at its $1,000 par value.

A bond that has just been issued is known as **a new issue**. (Investment bankers classify a bond as a new issue for about a month after it has first been issued. New issues are usually actively traded and are called "on-the-run" bonds.) Once the bond has been on the market for a while, it is classified as an **outstanding bond**, also called a **seasoned issue**. Newly issued bonds generally sell very close to par, but the prices of seasoned bonds vary widely from par. Except for floating-rate bonds, coupon payments are constant, so when economic conditions change, a 9% coupon bond with a $90 coupon that sold at par when it was issued will sell for more or less than $1,000 thereafter.

MicroDrive's bonds with a 9% coupon rate were originally issued at par. If r_d remained constant at 9%, what would the value of the bond be 1 year after it was issued? Now the term to maturity is only 14 years—that is, N = 14. With a financial calculator, just override N = 15 with N = 14, press the PV key, and you find a value of $1,000. If we continued, setting N = 13, N = 12, and so forth, we would see that the value of the bond will remain at $1,000 as long as the going interest rate remains equal to the coupon rate, 9%.

Now suppose interest rates in the economy fell after the MicroDrive bonds were issued and, as a result, r_d *fell below the coupon rate*, decreasing from 9% to 4%. Both the coupon interest payments and the maturity value remain constant, but now 4% would have to be used for r_d in Equation 5-1. The value of the bond at the end of the first year would be $1,494.93:

$$V_B = \sum_{t=1}^{14} \frac{\$90}{(1 + 0.04)^t} + \frac{\$1,000}{(1 + 0.04)^{14}}$$

$$= \$100 \left[\frac{1}{0.04} - \frac{1}{0.04(1 + 0.04)^{14}} \right] + \frac{\$1,000}{(1 + 0.04)^{14}}$$

$$= \$1,528.16$$

With a financial calculator, just change r_d = I/YR from 9 to 4, and then press the PV key to get the answer, $1,528.16. Thus, if r_d fell *below* the coupon rate, the bond would sell *above* par, or at a **premium**.

The arithmetic of the bond value increase should be clear, but what is the logic behind it? Because r_d has fallen to 4%, with $1,000 to invest you could buy new bonds like MicroDrive's (every day some 10 to 12 companies sell new bonds), except that these new bonds would pay $40 of interest each year rather than $90. Naturally, you would prefer $90 to $40, so you would be willing to pay more than $1,000 for a MicroDrive bond to obtain its higher coupons. All investors would react similarly; as a result, the MicroDrive bonds would be bid up in price to $1,528.16, at which point they would provide the same 4% rate of return to a potential investor as the new bonds.

Assuming that interest rates remain constant at 4% for the next 14 years, what would happen to the value of a MicroDrive bond? It would fall gradually from $1,528.16 to $1,000 at maturity, when MicroDrive will redeem each bond for $1,000. This point can be illustrated by calculating the value of the bond 1 year later, when it has 13 years remaining to maturity. With a financial calculator, simply input the values for N, I/YR, PMT, and FV, now using N = 13, and press the PV key to find the value of the bond, $1,499.28. Thus, the value of the bond will have fallen from $1,528.16 to $1,499.28, or by $28.88. If you were to calculate the value of the bond at other future dates, the price would continue to fall as the maturity date approached.

Note that if you purchased the bond at a price of $1,528.16 and then sold it 1 year later with r_d still at 4%, you would have a capital loss of 28.88, or a total dollar return of $90.00 − $28.88 = $61.12. Your percentage rate of return would consist of the rate of return due to the interest payment (called the **current yield**) and the rate of return due to the price change (called the **capital gains yield**). This total rate of return is often called the bond yield, and it is calculated as follows:

$$\text{Interest, or current, yield} = \$90/\$1,528.16 = 0.0589 = 5.89\%$$
$$\text{Capital gains yield} = -\$28.88/\$1,528.16 = -0.0189 = \underline{-1.89\%}$$
$$\text{Total rate of return, or yield} = \$61.12/\$1,528.16 = 0.0400 = \underline{\underline{4.00\%}}$$

Had interest rates risen from 9% to 14% during the first year after issue (rather than falling from 9% to 4%), then you would enter N = 14, I/YR = 14, PMT = 90, and FV = 1000, and then press the PV key to find the value of the bond, $699.90. In this case, the bond would sell below its par value, or at a discount. The total expected future return on the bond would again consist of an expected return due to interest and an expected return due to capital gains or capital losses. In this situation, the capital gains yield would be *positive*. The total return would be 14%. To see this, calculate the price of the bond with 13 years left to maturity, assuming that interest rates remain at 14%. With a calculator, enter N = 13, I/YR = 15, PMT = 90, and FV = 1000; then press PV to obtain the bond's value, $707.88.

Note that the capital gain for the year is the difference between the bond's value at Year 2 (with 13 years remaining) and the bond's value at Year 1 (with 14 years remaining), or $707.88 − $699.90 = $7.98. The interest yield, capital gains yield, and total yield are calculated as follows:

$$\text{Interest, or current, yield} = \$90/\$699.90 = 0.1286 = 12.86\%$$
$$\text{Capital gains yield} = \$7.98/\$699.90 = 0.0114 = \underline{1.14\%}$$
$$\text{Total rate of return, or yield} = \$97.98/\$699.90 = 0.1400 = \underline{\underline{14.00\%}}$$

Figure 5-2 graphs the value of the bond over time, assuming that interest rates in the economy (1) remain constant at 9%, (2) fall to 4% and then remain constant at that level, or (3) rise to 14% and remain constant at that level. Of course, if interest rates do *not* remain constant, then the price of the bond will fluctuate. However, regardless of what future interest rates do, the bond's price will approach $1,000 as it nears the maturity date (barring bankruptcy, which might cause the bond's value to fall dramatically).

FIGURE 5-2

Time Path of the Value of a 9% Coupon, $1,000 Par Value Bond When Interest Rates Are 4%, 9%, and 14%

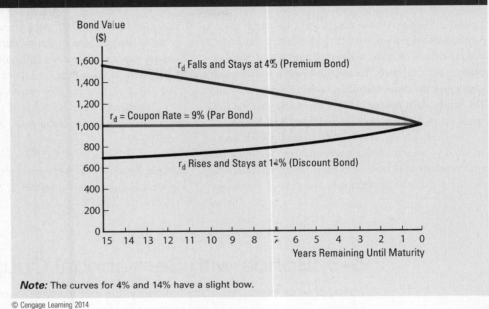

Note: The curves for 4% and 14% have a slight bow.

© Cengage Learning 2014

resource

See **Ch05 Tool Kit.xls** for all calculations.

Figure 5-2 illustrates the following key points.

1. Whenever the going rate of interest, r_d, is equal to the coupon rate, a *fixed-rate* bond will sell at its par value. Normally, the coupon rate is set equal to the going rate when a bond is issued, causing it to sell at par initially.
2. Interest rates do change over time, but the coupon rate remains fixed after the bond has been issued. Whenever the going rate of interest *rises above* the coupon rate, a fixed-rate bond's price will *fall below* its par value. Such a bond is called a discount bond.
3. Whenever the going rate of interest *falls below* the coupon rate, a fixed-rate bond's price will *rise above* its par value. Such a bond is called a premium bond.
4. Thus, an *increase* in interest rates will cause the prices of outstanding bonds to *fall,* whereas a *decrease* in rates will cause bond prices to *rise*.
5. The market value of a bond will always approach its par value as its maturity date approaches, provided the firm does not go bankrupt.

These points are very important, for they show that bondholders may suffer capital losses or make capital gains depending on whether interest rates rise or fall after the bond is purchased.

SELF-TEST

What is meant by the terms "new issue" and "seasoned issue"?

Last year, a firm issued 30-year, 8% annual coupon bonds at a par value of $1,000. (1) Suppose that 1 year later the going rate drops to 6%. What is the new price of the bonds, assuming that they now have 29 years to maturity? **($1,271.81)** *(2) Suppose instead that 1 year after issue the going interest rate increases to 10% (rather than dropping to 6%). What is the price?* **($812.61)**

Drinking Your Coupons

© Rob Webb/Getty Images

In 1996, Jonathan Maltus was looking for some cash to purchase additional vines and to modernize production facilities at Chateau Teyssier, a vineyard and winery in the Bordeaux region of France. The solution? With the assistance of a leading underwriter, Matrix Securities, the vineyard issued 375 bonds, each costing 2,650 British pounds. The issue raised nearly 1 million pounds, or roughly $1.5 million.

What makes these bonds interesting is that, instead of paying with something boring like money, they paid their investors back with wine. Each June until 2002, when the bond matured, investors received their "coupons."

Between 1997 and 2001, each bond provided six cases of the vineyard's rosé or claret. Starting in 1998 and continuing through maturity in 2002, investors also received four cases of its prestigious Saint Emilion Grand Cru. Then, in 2002, they got their money back.

The bonds were not without risk. Maltus acknowledged that the quality of the wine "is at the mercy of the gods."

Source: Steven Irvine, "My Wine Is My Bond, and I Drink My Coupons," *Euromoney,* July 1996, p. 7.

5-5 Bonds with Semiannual Coupons

Although some bonds pay interest annually, the vast majority actually pay interest semiannually. To evaluate semiannual payment bonds, we must modify the valuation model as follows.

1. Divide the annual coupon interest payment by 2 to determine the dollars of interest paid every 6 months.
2. Multiply the years to maturity, N, by 2 to determine the number of semiannual periods.
3. Divide the nominal (quoted) interest rate, r_d, by 2 to determine the periodic (semiannual) interest rate.

By making these changes, we obtain the following equation for finding the value of a bond that pays interest semiannually:

$$V_B = \sum_{t=1}^{2N} \frac{INT/2}{(1 + r_d/2)^t} + \frac{M}{(1 + r_d/2)^{2N}} \qquad (5\text{-}2)$$

To illustrate, assume now that MicroDrive's bonds pay $45 interest every 6 months rather than $90 at the end of each year. Each semiannual interest payment is only half as large, but there are twice as many of them. The nominal, or quoted, coupon rate is "9%, semiannual payments."[7]

---

[7]In this situation, the coupon rate of "9% paid semiannually" is the rate that bond dealers, corporate treasurers, and investors generally would discuss. Of course, if this bond were issued at par, then its *effective annual rate* would be higher than 9%:

$$EAR = EFF\% = \left(1 + \frac{r_{NOM}}{M}\right)^M - 1 = \left(1 + \frac{0.09}{2}\right)^2 - 1 = (1.045)^2 - 1 = 9.20\%$$

Because 9.20% with annual payments is quite different from 9% with semiannual payments, we have assumed a change in effective rates in this section from the situation described in Section 5-3, where we assumed 9% with annual payments.

When the going (nominal) rate of interest is 4% with semiannual compounding, the value of this 15-year bond is found as follows:

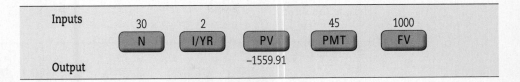

Inputs	30	2		45	1000
	N	I/YR	PV	PMT	FV
Output			−1559.91		

Enter N = 30, r_d = I/YR = 2, PMT = 45, FV = 1000, and then press the PV key to obtain the bond's value, $1,559.91. The value with semiannual interest payments is slightly larger than $1,552.92, the value when interest is paid annually. This higher value occurs because interest payments are received somewhat sooner under semiannual compounding.

SELF-TEST

Describe how the annual bond valuation formula is changed to evaluate semiannual coupon bonds. Write out the revised formula.

A bond has a 25-year maturity, an 8% annual coupon paid semiannually, and a face value of $1,000. The going nominal annual interest rate (r_d) is 6%. What is the bond's price? **($1,257.30)**

5-6 Bond Yields

Unlike the coupon interest rate, which is fixed, the bond's *yield* varies from day to day depending on current market conditions. Moreover, the yield can be calculated in three different ways, and three "answers" can be obtained. These different yields are described in the following sections.

5-6a Yield to Maturity

Suppose 1 year after it was issued, you could buy MicroDrive's 14-year, 9% annual coupon, $1,000 par value bond at a price of $1,528.16. What rate of interest would you earn on your investment if you bought the bond and held it to maturity? This rate is called the bond's **yield to maturity (YTM)**, and it is the interest rate generally discussed by investors when they talk about rates of return. The yield to maturity is usually the same as the market rate of interest, r_d. To find the YTM for a bond with annual interest payments, you must solve Equation 5-1 for r_d:[8]

$$\text{Bond price} = \sum_{t=1}^{N} \frac{\text{INT}}{(1 + \text{YTM})^t} + \frac{M}{(1 + \text{YTM})^N} \qquad \text{(5-3)}$$

For MicroDrive's yield, you must solve this equation:

$$\$1,528.16 = \frac{\$90}{(1 + r_d)^1} + \cdots + \frac{\$90}{(1 + r_d)^{14}} + \frac{\$1,000}{(1 + r_d)^{14}}$$

---

[8]If the bond has semiannual payments, you must solve Equation 5-2 for r_d.

You could substitute values for r_d until you found a value that "works" and forces the sum of the PVs on the right side of the equal sign to equal $1,528.16, but this would be tedious and time-consuming.[9] As you might guess, it is much easier with a financial calculator. Here is the setup:

Simply enter N = 14, PV = −1,528.16, PMT = 90, and FV = 1000, and then press the I/YR key for the answer of 4%.

resource
*See **Ch05 Tool Kit.xls** on the textbook's Web site.*

You could also find the YTM with a spreadsheet. In *Excel,* you would use the RATE function for this bond, inputting N = 14, PMT = 90, PV = −1528.16, FV = 1000, 0 for Type, and leave Guess blank: **=RATE(14,90,−1528.16,1000,0)**. The result is 4%. The RATE function works only if the current date is immediately after either the issue date or a coupon payment date. To find bond yields on other dates, use *Excel*'s YIELD function. See the **Ch05 Tool Kit.xls** file for an example.

The yield to maturity can be viewed as the bond's *promised rate of return,* which is the return that investors will receive if all the promised payments are made. However, the yield to maturity equals the *expected rate of return* only if (1) the probability of default is zero and (2) the bond cannot be called. If there is some default risk or if the bond may be called, then there is some probability that the promised payments to maturity will not be received, in which case the calculated yield to maturity will differ from the expected return.

The YTM for a bond that sells at par consists entirely of an interest yield, but if the bond sells at a price other than its par value, then the YTM will consist of the interest yield plus a positive or negative capital gains yield. Note also that a bond's yield to maturity changes whenever interest rates in the economy change, and this is almost daily. If you purchase a bond and hold it until it matures, you will receive the YTM that existed on the purchase date, but the bond's calculated YTM will change frequently between the purchase date and the maturity date.[10]

5-6b Yield to Call

If you purchased a bond that was callable and the company called it, you would not have the option of holding the bond until it matured. Therefore, the yield to maturity would not be earned. For example, if MicroDrive's 9% coupon bonds were callable and if interest rates fell from 9% to 4%, then the company could call in the 9% bonds, replace them with 4% bonds, and save $90 − $40 = $50 interest per bond per year. This would be good for the company but not for the bondholders.

---

[9]Alternatively, you can substitute values of r_d into the third form of Equation 5-1 until you find a value that works.
[10]We often are asked by students if the purchaser of a bond will receive the YTM if interest rates subsequently change. The answer is definitely "yes" provided the question means "Is the realized rate of return on the investment in the bond equal to the YTM?" This is because the realized rate of return on an investment is by definition the rate that sets the present value of the realized cash flows equal to the price. If instead the question means "Is the realized rate of return on the investment in the bond and the subsequent reinvestment of the coupons equal to the YTM?" then the answer is definitely "no." Thus, the question really is one about strategy and timing. The bond, in combination with a reinvestment strategy, is really two investments, and clearly the realized rate on this combined strategy depends on the reinvestment rate (see **Web Extension 5C** for more on investing for a target future value). For the rest of the book, we assume that an investment in a bond is only an investment in the bond, and not a combination of the bond and a reinvestment strategy; this means the investor earns the expected YTM if the bond is held to maturity.

If current interest rates are well below an outstanding bond's coupon rate, then a callable bond is likely to be called, and investors will estimate its expected rate of return as the **yield to call (YTC)** rather than as the yield to maturity. To calculate the YTC, solve this equation for r_d:

$$\text{Price of callable bond} = \sum_{t=1}^{N} \frac{\text{INT}}{(1 + r_d)^t} + \frac{\text{Call price}}{(1 + r_d)^N} \tag{5-4}$$

Here N is the number of years until the company can call the bond, r_d is the YTC, and "Call price" is the price the company must pay in order to call the bond (it is often set equal to the par value plus 1 year's interest).

To illustrate, suppose MicroDrive's bonds had a provision that permitted the company, if it desired, to call the bonds 10 years after the issue date at a price of $1,100. Suppose further that 1 year after issuance the going interest rate had declined, causing the price of the bonds to rise to $1,528.16. Here is the time line and the setup for finding the bond's YTC with a financial calculator:

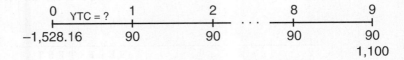

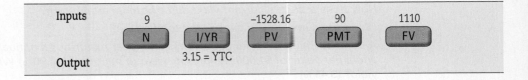

The YTC is 3.15%—this is the return you would earn if you bought the bond at a price of $1,528.16 and it was called 9 years from today. (The bond could not be called until 10 years after issuance, and 1 year has gone by, so there are 9 years left until the first call date.)

Do you think MicroDrive *will* call the bonds when they become callable? MicroDrive's actions depend on the going interest rate when the bonds become callable. If the going rate remains at $r_d = 4\%$, then MicroDrive could save 9% − 4% = 5%, or $50 per bond per year, by calling them and replacing the 9% bonds with a new 4% issue. There would be costs to the company to refund the issue, but the interest savings would probably be worth the cost, so MicroDrive would probably refund the bonds. Therefore, you would probably earn YTC = 3.15% rather than YTM = 4% if you bought the bonds under the indicated conditions.

In the balance of this chapter, we assume that bonds are not callable unless otherwise noted. However, some of the end-of-chapter problems deal with yield to call.

5-6c Current Yield

If you examine brokerage house reports on bonds, you will often see reference to a bond's **current yield**. The current yield is the annual interest payment divided by the bond's current price. For example, if MicroDrive's bonds with a 9% coupon were currently selling at $985, then the bond's current yield would be $90/$985 = 0.0914 = 9.14\%$.

Unlike the yield to maturity, the current yield does not represent the rate of return that investors should expect on the bond. The current yield provides information regarding the amount of cash income that a bond will generate in a given year, but it does not provide an accurate measure of the bond's total expected return, the yield to maturity. In fact, here is the relation between current yield, capital gains yield (which can be negative for a capital loss), and the yield to maturity:

$$\text{Current yield} + \text{Capital gains yield} = \text{Yield to maturity} \qquad (5\text{-}5)$$

5-6d The Cost of Debt and Intrinsic Value

The "Intrinsic Value Box" at the beginning of this chapter highlights the cost of debt, which affects the weighted average cost of capital (WACC), which in turn affects the company's intrinsic value. The pre-tax cost of debt from the company's perspective is the required return from the debtholder's perspective. Therefore, the pre-tax cost of debt is the yield to maturity (or the yield to call if a call is likely). But why do different bonds have different yields to maturity? The following sections answer this question.

SELF-TEST

Explain the difference between the yield to maturity and the yield to call.

How does a bond's current yield differ from its total return?

Could the current yield exceed the total return?

A bond currently sells for $850. It has an 8-year maturity, an annual coupon of $80, and a par value of $1,000. What is its yield to maturity? **(10.90%)** *What is its current yield?* **(9.41%)**

A bond currently sells for $1,250. It pays a $110 annual coupon and has a 20-year maturity, but it can be called in 5 years at $1,110. What are its YTM and its YTC? **(8.38%, 6.85%)** *Is the bond likely to be called if interest rates don't change?*

5-7 The Pre-Tax Cost of Debt: Determinants of Market Interest Rates

Until now we have given you r_d, the going market rate. But as we showed in Chapter 1, different debt securities often have very different market rates. What explains these differences? In general, the quoted (or nominal) interest rate on a debt security, r_d, is composed of a real risk-free rate of interest, r^*, plus several premiums that reflect inflation, the risk of the security, and the security's marketability (or liquidity). A conceptual framework is shown below:

$$\begin{aligned}\text{Quoted market interest rate} = r_d &= r^* + IP + DRP + LP + MRP \\ &= r_{RF} + DRP + LP + MRP\end{aligned} \qquad (5\text{-}6)$$

Here are definitions of the variables in Equation 5-6:

r_d = Quoted, or nominal, rate of interest on a given security.[11] There are many different securities and hence many different quoted interest rates.

r^* = Real risk-free rate of interest. Pronounced "r-star," r^* is the rate on a riskless security if zero inflation were expected.

IP = Inflation premium, which is equal to the average expected inflation rate over the life of the security. The expected future inflation rate is not necessarily equal to the current inflation rate, so IP is not necessarily equal to current inflation.

r_{RF} = r^* + IP, and it is the quoted risk-free rate of interest on a security such as a U.S. Treasury bill, which is very liquid and also free of most risks. Note that r_{RF} includes the premium for expected inflation because $r_{RF} = r^* + IP$.

DRP = Default risk premium. This premium reflects the possibility that the issuer will not pay interest or principal at the stated time and in the stated amount. The DRP is zero for U.S. Treasury securities, but it rises as the riskiness of issuers increases.

LP = Liquidity, or marketability, premium. This is a premium charged by lenders to reflect the fact that some securities cannot be converted to cash on short notice at a "reasonable" price. The LP is very low for Treasury securities and for securities issued by large, strong firms, but it is relatively high on securities issued by very small firms.

MRP = Maturity risk premium. Changes in market interest rates can cause large changes in the prices of long-term bonds, even Treasury bonds. Lenders charge a maturity risk premium to reflect this risk.

We discuss the components whose sum makes up the quoted, or nominal, rate on a given security in the following sections.

W W W

See **www.bloomberg.com** and select MARKETS. Then select RATES AND BONDS for a partial listing of indexed Treasury bonds and their interest rates. See **online.wsj.com** for a complete set of Treasury quotes. See **www.treasury direct.gov/indiv/products/ products.htm** for a complete listing of all Treasury securities.

SELF-TEST

Write out an equation for the nominal interest rate on any debt security.

5-8 The Real Risk-Free Rate of Interest, r*

The **real risk-free rate of interest, r***, is defined as the interest rate that would exist on a riskless security if no inflation were expected, and it may be thought of as the rate of interest on *short-term* U.S. Treasury securities in an inflation-free world. The real risk-free

---

[11]The term *nominal* as used here means the *stated* rate as opposed to the *real* rate, which is adjusted to remove inflation effects. Suppose you bought a 10-year Treasury bond with a quoted, or nominal, rate of about 4.6%. If inflation averages 2.5% over the next 10 years, then the real rate would be about 4.6% − 2.5% = 2.1%. To be technically correct, we should find the real rate by solving for r^* in the following equation: $(1 + r^*)(1 + 0.025) = (1 + 0.046)$. Solving the equation, we find $r^* = 2.05\%$. Because this is very close to the 2.1% just calculated, we will continue to approximate the real rate in this chapter by subtracting inflation from the nominal rate.

rate is not static—it changes over time depending on economic conditions, especially (1) the rate of return corporations and other borrowers expect to earn on productive assets, and (2) people's time preferences for current versus future consumption.[12]

In addition to its regular bond offerings, in 1997 the U.S. Treasury began issuing **indexed bonds**, with payments linked to inflation. These bonds are called **TIPS**, short for **Treasury Inflation-Protected Securities**. (For details on how TIPS are adjusted to protect against inflation, see *Web Extension 5B* on the textbook's Web site.) Because the payments (including the principal) are tied to inflation, the yield on a TIPS with 1 year until maturity is a good estimate of the real risk-free rate. In theory, we would like an even shorter maturity to estimate the real risk-free rate, but short-term TIPS are thinly traded and the reported yields are not as reliable.

Historically, the real interest rate has averaged around 1.5% to 2.5%. In March 2012, the TIPS with about 1 year remaining until maturity had a *−2.00%* yield. Although unusual, negative real rates are possible. In spring 2008, the combination of stagnant economic growth, a high level of investor uncertainty, fears of inflation, and the Federal Reserve's reduction in nominal short-term interest rates caused the real rate to fall below zero, as measured by negative yields on several short-term TIPS. The yields on short-term TIPS have remained low since then. Negative real rates are possible, but negative nominal rates are impossible (or at least extraordinarily rare) because investors would just hold cash instead of investing in a negative-yield bond.

SELF-TEST

What security provides a good estimate of the real risk-free rate?

5-9 The Inflation Premium (IP)

Inflation has a major effect on interest rates because it erodes the purchasing power of the dollar and lowers the real rate of return on investments. To illustrate, suppose you invest $3,000 in a default-free zero coupon bond that matures in 1 year and pays a 5% interest rate. At the end of the year, you will receive $3,150—your original $3,000 plus $150 of interest. Now suppose that the inflation rate during the year is 10% and that it affects all items equally. If gas had cost $3 per gallon at the beginning of the year, it would cost $3.30 at the end of the year. Therefore, your $3,000 would have bought $3,000/$3 = 1,000 gallons at the beginning of the year but only $3,150/$3.30 = 955 gallons at the end. In *real terms,* you would be worse off—you would receive $150 of interest, but it would not be sufficient to offset inflation. You would thus be better off buying 1,000 gallons of gas (or some other storable asset) than buying the default-free bond.

Investors are well aware of inflation's effects on interest rates, so when they lend money, they build in an **inflation premium (IP)** equal to the average expected inflation rate over the life of the security. For a short-term, default-free U.S. Treasury bill, the

---

[12]The real rate of interest as discussed here is different from the *current* real rate as often discussed in the press. The current real rate is often estimated as the current interest rate minus the current (or most recent) inflation rate, whereas the real rate, as used here (and in the fields of finance and economics generally) without the word "current," is the current interest rate minus the *expected future* inflation rate over the life of the security. For example, suppose the current quoted rate for a 1-year Treasury bill is 5%, inflation during the previous year was 2%, and inflation expected for the coming year is 4%. Then the *current* real rate would be approximately 5% − 2% = 3%, but the *expected* real rate would be approximately 5% − 4% = 1%.

actual interest rate charged, $r_{T\text{-bill}}$, would be the real risk-free rate, r^*, plus the inflation premium (IP):

$$r_{T\text{-bill}} = r_{RF} = r^* + IP$$

Therefore, if the real short-term risk-free rate of interest were $r^* = 0.6\%$ and if inflation were expected to be 1.0% (and hence IP = 1.0%) during the next year, then the quoted rate of interest on 1-year T-bills would be 0.6% + 1.0% = 1.6%.

It is important to note that the inflation rate built into interest rates is *the inflation rate expected in the future,* not the rate experienced in the past. Thus, the latest reported figures might show an annual inflation rate of 2%, but that is for the *past* year. If people on average expect a 6% inflation rate in the future, then 6% would be built into the current interest rate.

Note also that the inflation rate reflected in the quoted interest rate on any security is the *average rate of inflation expected over the security's life.* Thus, the inflation rate built into a 1-year bond is the expected inflation rate for the next year, but the inflation rate built into a 30-year bond is the average rate of inflation expected over the next 30 years. If I_t is the expected inflation during year t, then the inflation premium for an N-year bond's yield (IP_N) can be approximated as

$$IP_N = \frac{I_1 + I_2 + \cdots + I_N}{N} \qquad \textbf{(5-7)}$$

For example, if investors expect inflation to average 3% during Year 1 and 5% during Year 2, then the inflation premium built into a 2-year bond's yield can be approximated by[13]

$$IP_2 = \frac{I_1 + I_2}{2} = \frac{3\% + 5\%}{2} = 4\%$$

In the previous section, we saw that the yield on an inflation-indexed Treasury bond (TIPS) is a good estimate of the real interest rate. We can also use TIPS to estimate inflation premiums. For example, in early 2012 the yield on a 5-year nonindexed T-bond was 1.21% and the yield on a 5-year TIPS was − 1.05%. Thus, the 5-year inflation premium was 1.21% − (−1.05%) = 2.26%, implying that investors expected inflation to average 2.26% over the next 5 years.[14] Similarly, the rate on a 20-year nonindexed T-bond was 2.97% and the rate on a 20-year indexed T-bond was 0.58%. Thus, the 20-year inflation premium was approximately 2.97% − 0.58% = 2.39%, implying that investors expected inflation to average 2.39% over the long term.[15] These calculations are summarized below:

---

[13]To be mathematically correct, we should take the *geometric average*: $(1 + IP_2)^2 = (1 + I_1)(1 + I_2)$. In this example, we have $(1 + IP_2)^2 = (1 + 0.03)(1 + 0.05)$. Solving for IP_2 yields 3.9952, which is close to our approximation of 4%.

[14]As we noted in the previous footnote, the mathematically correct approach is to use a *geometric average* and solve the following equation: $(1 + IP)(1 + −0.0105) = 1 + .0121$. Solving for IP gives IP = 2.28%, which is very close to our approximation.

Note, though, that the difference in yield between a T-bond and a TIPS of the same maturity reflects both the expected inflation *and* any risk premium for bearing inflation risk. So the difference in yields is really an upper limit on the expected inflation.

[15]There are several other sources for the estimated inflation premium. The Congressional Budget Office regularly updates the estimates of inflation that it uses in its forecasted budgets; see **www.cbo.gov**; select Economic Projections. A second source is the University of Michigan's Institute for Social Research, which regularly polls consumers regarding their expectations for price increases during the next year; see **www.sca.isr.umich.edu** for the survey.

We prefer using inflation premiums derived from indexed and nonindexed Treasury securities, as described in the text, because these are based on how investors actually spend their money, not on theoretical models or opinions.

Yields	Maturity		
	1 Year	5 Years	20 Years
Nonindexed U.S. Treasury Bond	0.23%	1.21%	2.97%
TIPS	−2.00%	−1.05%	0.58%
Inflation premium	2.23%	2.26%	2.39%

Expectations for future inflation are closely, but not perfectly, correlated with rates experienced in the recent past. Therefore, if the inflation rate reported for last month increases, people often raise their expectations for future inflation, and this change in expectations will cause an increase in interest rates.

Note that Germany, Japan, and Switzerland have, over the past several years, had lower inflation rates than the United States, so their interest rates have generally been lower than ours. South Africa, Brazil, and most South American countries have experienced higher inflation, which is reflected in their interest rates.

SELF-TEST

Explain how a TIPS and a nonindexed Treasury security can be used to estimate the inflation premium.

The yield on a 15-year TIPS is 3% and the yield on a 15-year Treasury bond is 5%. What is the inflation premium for a 15-year security? **(2%)**

5-10 The Nominal, or Quoted, Risk-Free Rate of Interest, r_{RF}

The **nominal**, or **quoted, risk-free rate, r_{RF}**, is the real risk-free rate plus a premium for expected inflation: $r_{RF} = r^* + IP$. To be strictly correct, the risk-free rate should mean the interest rate on a totally risk-free security—one that has no risk of default, no maturity risk, no liquidity risk, no risk of loss if inflation increases, and no risk of any other type. There is no such security, so there is no observable truly risk-free rate. When the term "risk-free rate" is used without either the modifier "real" or the modifier "nominal," people generally mean the quoted (nominal) rate, and we will follow that convention in this book. Therefore, when we use the term "risk-free rate, r_{RF}," we mean the nominal risk-free rate, which includes an inflation premium equal to the average expected inflation rate over the life of the security. In general, we use the T-bill rate to approximate the short-term risk-free rate and use the T-bond rate to approximate the long-term risk-free rate (even though it also includes a maturity premium). So, whenever you see the term "risk-free rate," assume that we are referring either to the quoted U.S. T-bill rate or to the quoted T-bond rate.

Because $r_{RF} = r^* + IP$, we can express the quoted rate as

$$\text{Nominal, or quoted, rate} = r_d = r_{RF} + DRP + LP + MRP \qquad (5\text{-}8)$$

SELF-TEST

What security is a good approximation of the nominal risk-free rate?

5-11 The Default Risk Premium (DRP)

If the issuer defaults on a payment, investors receive less than the promised return on the bond. The quoted interest rate includes a default risk premium (DRP)—the greater the default risk, the higher the bond's yield to maturity.[16] The default risk on Treasury securities is virtually zero, but default risk can be substantial for corporate and municipal bonds. In this section, we consider some issues related to default risk.

5-11a Bond Contract Provisions That Influence Default Risk

Default risk is affected by both the financial strength of the issuer and the terms of the bond contract, especially whether collateral has been pledged to secure the bond. Several types of contract provisions are discussed next.

BOND INDENTURES

An **indenture** is a legal document that spells out the rights of both bondholders and the issuing corporation. A **trustee** is an official (usually a bank) who represents the bondholders and makes sure the terms of the indenture are carried out. The indenture may be several hundred pages in length, and it will include **restrictive covenants** that cover such points as the conditions under which the issuer can pay off the bonds prior to maturity, the levels at which certain ratios must be maintained if the company is to issue additional debt, and restrictions against the payment of dividends unless earnings meet certain specifications.

The Securities and Exchange Commission (1) approves indentures and (2) makes sure that all indenture provisions are met before allowing a company to sell new securities to the public. A firm will have different indentures for each of the major types of bonds it issues, but a single indenture covers all bonds of the same type. For example, one indenture will cover a firm's first mortgage bonds, another its debentures, and a third its convertible bonds.

MORTGAGE BONDS

A corporation pledges certain assets as security for a **mortgage bond**. The company might also choose to issue *second-mortgage bonds* secured by the same assets that were secured by a previously issued mortgage bond. In the event of liquidation, the holders of these second mortgage bonds would have a claim against the property, but only after the first mortgage bondholders had been paid off in full. Thus, second mortgages are sometimes called *junior mortgages* because they are junior in priority to the claims of *senior mortgages,* or *first-mortgage bonds.* All mortgage bonds are subject to an indenture that usually limits the amount of new bonds that can be issued.

DEBENTURES AND SUBORDINATED DEBENTURES

A **debenture** is an unsecured bond, and as such it provides no lien against specific property as security for the obligation. Debenture holders are, therefore, general creditors whose claims are protected by property not otherwise pledged.

---

[16]Suppose two bonds have the same promised cash flows, coupon rate, maturity, liquidity, and inflation exposure, but one bond has more default risk than the other. Investors will naturally pay less for the bond with the greater chance of default. As a result, bonds with higher default risk will have higher interest rates.

GLOBAL ECONOMIC CRISIS

© uniquely india/Getty Images

The Global Economic Crisis

Insuring with Credit Default Swaps: Let the Buyer Beware!

A credit default swap (CDS) is like an insurance policy. The purchaser of the CDS agrees to make annual payments to a counterparty that agrees to pay if a particular bond defaults. During the 2000s, investment banks often would purchase CDS for the mortgage-backed securities (MBS) they were creating in order to make the securities more attractive to investors. But how good was this type of insurance? As it turned out, not very. For example, Lehman Brothers might have bought a CDS from AIG in order to sell a Lehman-created MBS to an investor. But when the MBS began defaulting, neither Lehman nor AIG was capable of making full restitution to the investor.

The term *subordinate* means "below" or "inferior to"; thus, in the event of bankruptcy, subordinated debt has claims on assets only after senior debt has been paid off. **Subordinated debentures** may be subordinated either to designated notes payable (usually bank loans) or to all other debt. In the event of liquidation or reorganization, holders of subordinated debentures cannot be paid until all senior debt, as named in the debentures' indentures, has been paid.

DEVELOPMENT BONDS

Some companies may be in a position to benefit from the sale of either **development bonds** or **pollution control bonds**. State and local governments may set up both *industrial development agencies* and *pollution control agencies*. These agencies are allowed, under certain circumstances, to sell **tax-exempt bonds** and then make the proceeds available to corporations for specific uses deemed (by Congress) to be in the public interest. For example, a Detroit pollution control agency might sell bonds to provide Ford with funds for purchasing pollution control equipment. Because the income from the bonds would be tax exempt, the bonds would have relatively low interest rates. Note, however, that these bonds are guaranteed by the corporation that will use the funds, not by a governmental unit, so their rating reflects the credit strength of the corporation using the funds.

MUNICIPAL BOND INSURANCE

Municipalities can have their bonds insured, which means that an insurance company guarantees to pay the coupon and principal payments should the issuer default. This reduces risk to investors, who will thus accept a lower coupon rate for an insured bond than for a comparable but uninsured one. Even though the municipality must pay a fee to have its bonds insured, its savings due to the lower coupon rate often make insurance cost-effective. Keep in mind that the insurers are private companies, and the value added by the insurance depends on the creditworthiness of the insurer. The larger insurers are strong companies, and their own ratings are AAA.

5-11b Bond Ratings

Since the early 1900s, bonds have been assigned quality ratings that reflect their probability of going into default. The three major rating agencies are Moody's Investors Service (Moody's), Standard & Poor's Corporation (S&P), and Fitch Ratings. As shown in Columns (3) and (4) of Table 5-1, triple-A and double-A bonds are extremely safe, rarely

TABLE 5-1

Bond Ratings, Default Risk, and Yields

Rating Agency[a]		Percent Defaulting Within:[b]		Median Ratios[c]		Percent Upgraded or Downgraded in 2011[b]		
S&P and Fitch (1)	Moody's (2)	1 year (3)	5 years (4)	Return on capital (5)	Total debt/ Total capital (6)	Down (7)	Up (8)	Yield[d] (9)
Investment-grade bonds								
AAA	Aaa	0.00%	0.00%	27.6%	12.4%	0.00%	NA	4.11%
AA	Aa	0.03	0.12	27.0	28.3	29.24	0.00	3.38
A	A	0.09	0.74	17.5	37.5	7.79	0.00	3.37
BBB	Baa	0.23	2.54	13.4	42.5	3.29	2.95	6.24
Junk bonds								
BB	Ba	1.17	6.91	11.3	53.7	4.82	8.13	6.28
B	B	2.14	9.28	8.7	75.9	3.48	7.59	7.02
CCC	Caa	24.47	35.23	3.2	113.5	16.67	20.00	9.98

Notes: [a]The ratings agencies also use "modifiers" for bonds rated below triple-A. S&P and Fitch use a plus and minus system; thus, A+ designates the strongest A-rated bonds and A− the weakest. Moody's uses a 1, 2, or 3 designation, with 1 denoting the strongest and 3 the weakest; thus, within the double-A category, Aa1 is the best, Aa2 is average, and Aa3 is the weakest.
[b]Default data are from Fitch Ratings Global Corporate Finance 2011 Transition and Default Study, March 16, 2012: see **www.fitchratings.com/creditdesk/reports/report_frame.cfm?rpt_id=669829**.
[c]Median ratios are from Standard & Poor's 2006 Corporate Ratings Criteria, April 23, 2007: see **www2.standardandpoors. com/spf/pdf/fixedincome/Corporate_Ratings_2006.pdf**.
[d]Composite yields for 10-year AAA, AA, A, and BBB bonds can be found at **www.bondsonline.com/Todays_Market/ Composite_Bond_Yields_table.php**. Representative yields for 10-year BB, B, and CCC bonds can be found using the bond screener at **http://cxa.marketwatch.com/finra/bondcenter/AdvancedScreener.aspx**. Thin markets cause the AAA rate to be unusually high.

defaulting even within 5 years of being assigned a rating. Single-A and triple-B bonds are also strong enough to be called **investment-grade bonds**, and they are the lowest-rated bonds that many banks and other institutional investors are permitted by law to hold. Double-B and lower bonds are speculative bonds and are often called **junk bonds**. These bonds have a significant probability of defaulting.

5-11c Bond Rating Criteria, Upgrades, and Downgrades

Bond ratings are based on both quantitative and qualitative factors, as we describe below.

1. **Financial Ratios.** Many ratios potentially are important, but the return on invested capital, debt ratio, and interest coverage ratio are particularly valuable for predicting financial distress. For example, Columns (1), (5), and (6) in Table 5-1 show a strong relationship between ratings and the return on capital and the debt ratio.
2. **Bond Contract Terms.** Important provisions for determining the bond's rating include whether the bond is secured by a mortgage on specific assets, whether the bond is subordinated to other debt, any sinking fund provisions, guarantees by some other party with a high credit ranking, and *restrictive covenants* such as requirements that the

firm keep its debt ratio below a given level or that it keep its times interest earned ratio above a given level.

3. **Qualitative Factors.** Included here would be such factors as sensitivity of the firm's earnings to the strength of the economy, how it is affected by inflation, whether it is having or is likely to have labor problems, the extent of its international operations (including the stability of the countries in which it operates), potential environmental problems, potential antitrust problems, and so on. Today (2012), a critical factor is exposure to sub-prime loans, including the difficulty of determining the extent of this exposure owing to the complexity of the assets backed by such loans.

Rating agencies review outstanding bonds on a periodic basis and re-rate if necessary. Columns (7) and (8) in Table 5-1 show the percentages of companies in each rating category that were downgraded or upgraded in 2011 by Fitch Ratings. The year 2011 was a difficult one, as more bonds were downgraded than upgraded.

Over the long run, ratings agencies have done a reasonably good job of measuring the average credit risk of bonds and of changing ratings whenever there is a significant change in credit quality. However, it is important to understand that ratings do not adjust immediately to changes in credit quality, and in some cases there can be a considerable lag between a change in credit quality and a change in rating. For example, Enron's bonds still carried an investment-grade rating on a Friday in December 2001, but the company declared bankruptcy two days later, on Sunday. Many other abrupt downgrades occurred in 2007 and 2008, leading to calls by Congress and the SEC for changes in rating agencies and the way they rate bonds. Clearly, improvements can be made, but there will always be occasions when completely unexpected information about a company is released, leading to a sudden change in its rating.

5-11d Bond Ratings and the Default Risk Premium

Why are bond ratings so important? First, most bonds are purchased by institutional investors rather than individuals, and many institutions are restricted to investment-grade securities. Thus, if a firm's bonds fall below BBB, it will have a difficult time selling new bonds because many potential purchasers will not be allowed to buy them. Second, many bond covenants stipulate that the coupon rate on the bond automatically increases if the rating falls below a specified level. Third, because a bond's rating is an indicator of its default risk, the rating has a direct, measurable influence on the bond's yield. Column (9) of Table 5-1 shows that an AA bond has a yield of 3.38% and that yields increase as the rating falls. In fact, an investor would earn 9.98% on a CCC bond if it didn't default.

A **bond spread** is the difference between a bond's yield and the yield on some other security of the same maturity. Unless specified differently, the term "spread" generally means the difference between a bond's yield and the yield on a Treasury bond of similar maturity.

Figure 5-3 shows the spreads between an index of AAA bonds and a 10-year Treasury bond; it also shows spreads for an index of BBB bonds relative to the T-bond. Figure 5-3 illustrates three important points. First, the BAA spread always is greater than the AAA spread. This is because a BAA bond is riskier than an AAA bond, so BAA investors require extra compensation for their extra risk. The same is true for other ratings: Lower-rated bonds have higher yields.

Second, the spreads are not constant over time. For example, look at the AAA spread. It was exceptionally low during the boom years of 2005–2007 but rose dramatically as the economy declined in 2008 and 2009.

Third, the difference between the BAA spread and the AAA spread isn't constant over time. The two spreads were quite close to one another in early 2000 but were very far

GLOBAL ECONOMIC CRISIS

© uniquely india/Getty Images

The Global Economic Crisis

U.S. Treasury Bonds Downgraded!

The worsening recession that began at the end of 2007 led Congress to pass a huge economic stimulus package in early 2009. The combination of the stimulus package and the government's bailouts of financial institutions caused the U.S. government to increase its borrowing substantially. The current (March 2012) level of public debt is $10.4 trillion, about 68% of gross domestic product (GDP). The Congressional Budget Office long-term projections show this percentage growing to 70% to 90%, depending on the assumptions. Any way you look at it, this is a lot of money, even by Washington standards!

With so much debt outstanding and enormous annual deficits continuing, in mid-2011 Congress was faced with the need to increase the amount of debt the federal government is allowed to issue. Although Congress had increased the debt ceiling 74 times previously, and 10 times since 2001, partisan and heated debate seriously delayed approval of the measure and brought the federal government to the brink of default on its obligations by August. At the last minute, Congress approved a debt ceiling increase, narrowly avoiding a partial government shutdown. However, the deficit reduction package that accompanied the legislation was small, doing little to address the structural revenue and spending imbalance the federal government faces going forward.

On August 5, 2011, the combination of a dysfunctional political process apparently incapable of reliably performing basic financial housekeeping chores, and the lack of a clear plan to address future deficits, raised enough questions about the U.S. government's financial stability to induce Standard & Poor's (S&P), the credit rating agency, to downgrade U.S. public debt from AAA to AA+, effectively removing it from its list of risk-free investments. Financial markets quickly responded to this dark assessment with the Dow Jones Industrial Average plunging some 13% over the next week. Moody's and Fitch, the other two major rating agencies, however, kept their ratings of U.S. public debt at their highest levels. With 2 out of 3 agencies rating U.S. debt at the highest level, is the yield on U.S. debt still a proxy for the riskless rate? Only time will tell.

apart in early 2009. In other words, BAA investors didn't require much extra return over that of an AAA bond to induce them to take on that extra risk most years, but in 2009 they required a very large risk premium.

Not only do spreads vary with the rating of the security, they also usually increase as maturity increases. This should make sense. If a bond matures soon, investors are able to forecast the company's performance fairly well. But if a bond has a long time until it matures, investors have a difficult time forecasting the likelihood that the company will fall into financial distress. This extra uncertainty creates additional risk, so investors demand a higher required return.

SELF-TEST

Differentiate between mortgage bonds and debentures.

Name the major rating agencies, and list some factors that affect bond ratings.

What is a bond spread?

How do bond ratings affect the default risk premium?

A 10-year T-bond has a yield of 6%. A 10-year corporate bond with a rating of AA has a yield of 7.5%. If the corporate bond has excellent liquidity, what is an estimate of the corporate bond's default risk premium? **(1.5%)**

FIGURE 5-3

Bond Spreads

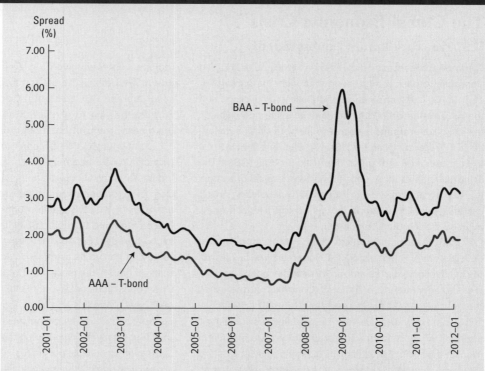

Note: All data are from the Federal Reserve Bank of St. Louis's Economic Database, FRED: **research.stlouisfed.org/fred2**. The spreads are defined as the yield on the risky bond (AAA or BAA) minus the yield on a 10-year Treasury bond.

5-12 The Liquidity Premium (LP)

A "liquid" asset can be converted to cash quickly and at a "fair market value." Financial assets are generally more liquid than real assets. Because liquidity is important, investors include **liquidity premiums (LPs)** when market rates of securities are established. Although liquidity premiums are difficult to measure accurately, a differential of at least 2 percentage points (and perhaps up to 4 or 5 percentage points) exists between the least liquid and the most liquid financial assets of similar default risk and maturity. Corporate bonds issued by small companies are traded less frequently than those issued by large companies, so small-company bonds tend to have a higher liquidity premium.

For example, liquidity in the market for mortgage-backed securities evaporated in 2008 and early 2009. The few transactions that occurred were priced such that the yields on these MBS were extremely high, which was partially due to a much higher liquidity premium caused by the extremely low liquidity of MBS.

SELF-TEST

Which bond usually will have a higher liquidity premium: one issued by a large company or one issued by a small company?

The Few, the Proud, the... AAA-Rated Companies!

© Rob Webb/Getty Images

AAA-rated companies are members of an elite group. Over the last 20 years, this cream of the crop has included such powerhouses as 3M, Abbott Labs, BellSouth, ExxonMobil, GE, Kellogg, Microsoft, and UPS. Only large companies with stable cash flows make it into this group, and for years they guarded their AAA ratings vigilantly. In recent years, however, the nonfinancial AAA-rated corporation has become a vanishing breed. In March 2012, the major ratings agencies (Fitch, S&P, and Moody's) only agreed on the highest rating for three nonfinancial companies without government backing: ExxonMobil, XTO Energy (a subsidiary of ExxonMobil), and Johnson & Johnson. When the list is expanded to more than just nonfinancials, it is interesting to note that many of the powerhouses are not-for-profits. For example, Saddleback Valley Community Church, a megachurch located in Southern California, has a top rating, as do MIT and Princeton University.

Why do so few companies have AAA ratings? One reason may be that the recent financial crisis and recession have hurt the creditworthiness of even large, stable companies. A more likely explanation, however, is that in recent years large, stable companies have increased their debt levels to take greater advantage of the tax savings that they afford. With higher debt levels, these companies are no longer eligible for the highest rating. In essence, they have sacrificed their AAA rating for lower taxes. Does this sound like a good tradeoff to you? We will discuss how companies choose the level of debt in Chapter 15.

Source: **www.finra.org/Investors/InvestmentChoices/Bonds**

5-13 The Maturity Risk Premium (MRP)

All bonds, even Treasury bonds, are exposed to two additional sources of risk: interest rate risk and reinvestment risk. The net effect of these two sources of risk upon a bond's yield is called the **maturity risk premium, MRP**. The following sections explain how interest rate risk and reinvestment risk affect a bond's yield.

5-13a Interest Rate Risk

Interest rates go up and down over time, and an increase in interest rates leads to a decline in the value of outstanding bonds. This risk of a decline in bond values due to rising interest rates is called **interest rate risk.** To illustrate, suppose you bought some 9% MicroDrive bonds at a price of $1,000, and then interest rates rose in the following year to 14%. As we saw earlier, the price of the bonds would fall to $692.89, so you would have a loss of $307.11 per bond.[17] Interest rates can and do rise, and rising rates cause a loss of value for bondholders. Thus, bond investors are exposed to risk from changing interest rates.

This point can be demonstrated by showing how the value of a 1-year bond with a 10% annual coupon fluctuates with changes in r_d and then comparing these changes with those on a 25-year bond. The 1-year bond's value for $r_d = 5\%$ is shown below:

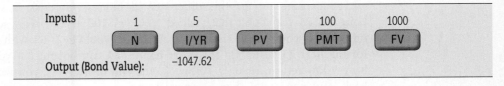

Inputs	1	5		100	1000
	N	I/YR	PV	PMT	FV
Output (Bond Value):		−1047.62			

---

[17]You would have an *accounting* (and tax) loss only if you sold the bond; if you held it to maturity, you would not have such a loss. However, even if you did not sell, you would still have suffered a *real economic loss in an opportunity cost sense* because you would have lost the opportunity to invest at 14% and would be stuck with a 9% bond in a 14% market. In an economic sense, "paper losses" are just as bad as realized accounting losses.

GLOBAL ECONOMIC CRISIS

© uniquely india/Getty Images

The Global Economic Crisis

Fear and Rationality

The graph below shows two measures of fear. One is the "Hi-Yield" spread between the yields on junk bonds and Treasury bonds. The second is the **TED spread**, which is the difference between the 3-month LIBOR rate and the 3-month T-bill rate. Both are measures of risk aversion. The Hi-Yield spread measures the amount of extra compensation investors need to induce them to take on risky junk bonds. The TED spread measures the extra compensation that banks require to induce them to lend to one another. Observe that the yields were very low from mid-2003 through the end of 2007. During these boom years, investors and bankers had a voracious appetite for risk and simply didn't require much extra return for additional risk. But as the economy began to deteriorate in 2008, investors and bankers reversed course and became extremely risk averse, with spreads skyrocketing. Interestingly, the pre-financial crisis appetite for risk has returned seems to have returned, with spreads again very low. It is hard to

reconcile such drastic changes in risk aversion with careful, deliberate, and rational behavior!

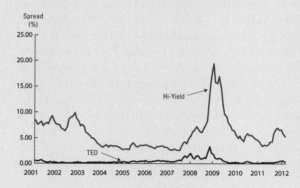

Source: The Hi-Yield spread is the average monthly value of the BofA Merrill Lynch US High Yield Master II Effective Yield minus the 10-year T-bond yield. TED is the difference between the 3-month LIBOR rate and the 3-month T-bill rate. All data are from the Federal Reserve Bank of St. Louis's Economic Database, FRED: **http://research.stlouisfed.org/fred2**.

Using either a calculator or a spreadsheet, you could calculate the bond values for a 1-year and a 25-year bond at several current market interest rates; these results are plotted in Figure 5-4. Note how much more sensitive the price of the 25-year bond is to changes in interest rates. At a 10% interest rate, both the 25-year and the 1-year bonds are valued at $1,000. When rates rise to 15%, the 25-year bond falls to $676.79 but the 1-year bond falls only to $956.52.

For bonds with similar coupons, this differential sensitivity to changes in interest rates always holds true: The longer the maturity of the bond, the more its price changes in response to a given change in interest rates. Thus, even if the risk of default on two bonds is exactly the same, the one with the longer maturity is exposed to more risk from a rise in interest rates.

The explanation for this difference in interest rate risk is simple. Suppose you bought a 25-year bond that yielded 10%, or $100 a year. Now suppose interest rates on bonds of comparable risk rose to 15%. You would be stuck with only $100 of interest for the next 25 years. On the other hand, had you bought a 1-year bond, you would have a low return for only 1 year. At the end of the year, you would get your $1,000 back, and you could then reinvest it and receive a 15% return ($150) for the next year. Thus, interest rate risk reflects the length of time one is committed to a given investment.

In addition to maturity, interest rate sensitivity reflects the size of coupon payments. Intuitively, this is because more of a high-coupon bond's value is received sooner than

r e s o u r c e

See Ch05 Tool Kit.xls.

FIGURE 5-4

Value of Long- and Short-Term 10% Annual Coupon Bonds at Different Market Interest Rates

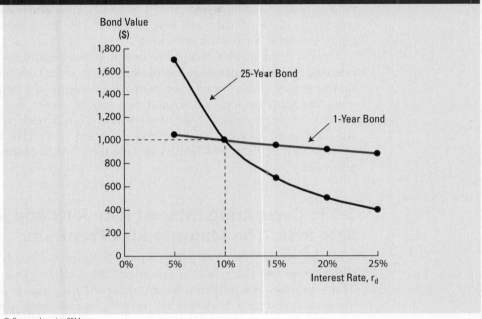

© Cengage Learning 2014

that of a low-coupon bond of the same maturity This intuitive concept is measured by "duration," which finds the average number of years that the bond's PV of cash flows (coupons and principal payments) remains outstanding; see **Web Extension 5C** and **Ch05 Tool Kit.xls** for the exact calculation. A zero coupon bond, which has no payments until maturity, has a duration equal to its maturity. Coupon bonds have durations that are shorter than maturity, and the higher the coupon rate, the shorter the duration.

Duration measures a bond's sensitivity to interest rates in the following sense: Given a change in interest rates, the percentage change in a bond's price is proportional to its duration:[18]

$$\% \text{ change in } V_B = (\% \text{ change in } 1 + r_d)(-\text{Duration})$$

Excel's DURATION function provides an easy way to calculate a bond's duration. See **Web Extension 5C** and **Ch05 Tool Kit.xls** for more discussion of duration and its use in measuring and managing interest rate risk.

5-13b Reinvestment Rate Risk

As we saw in the preceding section, an *increase* in interest rates will hurt bondholders because it will lead to a decline in the value of a bond portfolio. But can a *decrease* in interest rates also hurt bondholders? The answer is "yes," because if interest rates fall then a bondholder may suffer a reduction in his or her income. For example, consider a retiree

resource

*For more on bond risk, including duration analysis, see **Web Extension 5C** on the textbook's Web site.*

---

[18]This is true for the case in which the term structure (which we discuss in Section 5-14) is flat and can only shift up and down. However, other duration measures can be developed for other term structure assumptions.

who has a portfolio of bonds and lives off the income they produce. The bonds, on average, have a coupon rate of 10%. Now suppose that interest rates decline to 5%. The short-term bonds will mature, and when they do, they will have to be replaced with lower-yielding bonds. In addition, many of the remaining long-term bonds may be called, and as calls occur, the bondholder will have to replace 10% bonds with 5% bonds. Thus, our retiree will suffer a reduction of income.

The risk of an income decline due to a drop in interest rates is called **reinvestment rate risk**. Reinvestment rate risk is obviously high on callable bonds. It is also high on short-maturity bonds, because the shorter the maturity of a bond, the fewer the years when the relatively high old interest rate will be earned and the sooner the funds will have to be reinvested at the new low rate. Thus, retirees whose primary holdings are short-term securities, such as bank CDs and short-term bonds, are hurt badly by a decline in rates, but holders of long-term bonds continue to enjoy their old high rates.

5-13c Comparing Interest Rate Risk and Reinvestment Rate Risk: The Maturity Risk Premium

Note that interest rate risk relates to the *value* of the bonds in a portfolio, while reinvestment rate risk relates to the *income* the portfolio produces. If you hold long-term bonds then you will face a lot of interest rate risk, because the value of your bonds will decline if interest rates rise; but you will not face much reinvestment rate risk, so your income will be stable. On the other hand, if you hold short-term bonds, you will not be exposed to much interest rate risk because the value of your portfolio will be stable, but you will be exposed to considerable reinvestment rate risk because your income will fluctuate with changes in interest rates. We see, then, that no fixed-rate bond can be considered totally riskless—even most Treasury bonds are exposed to both interest rate risk and reinvestment rate risk.[19]

Bond prices reflect the trading activities of the marginal investors, defined as those who trade often enough and with large enough sums to determine bond prices. Although one particular investor might be more averse to reinvestment risk than to interest rate risk, the data suggest that the marginal investor is more averse to interest rate risk than to reinvestment risk. To induce the marginal investor to take on interest rate risk, long-term bonds must have a higher expected rate of return than short-term bonds. Holding all else equal, this additional return is the maturity risk premium (MRP).

SELF-TEST

Differentiate between interest rate risk and reinvestment rate risk.

To which type of risk are holders of long-term bonds more exposed? Short-term bondholders?

Assume that the real risk-free rate is r* = 3% and that the average expected inflation rate is 2.5% for the foreseeable future. The DRP and LP for a bond are each 1%, and the applicable MRP is 2%. What is the bond's yield? **(9.5%)**

---
[19]Although indexed Treasury bonds are almost riskless, they pay a relatively low real rate. Note also that risks have not disappeared—they have simply been transferred from bondholders to taxpayers.

5-14 The Term Structure of Interest Rates

The **term structure of interest rates** describes the relationship between long-term and short-term rates. The term structure is important both to corporate treasurers deciding whether to borrow by issuing long-term or short-term debt and to investors who are deciding whether to buy long-term or short-term bonds.

Interest rates for bonds with different maturities can be found in a variety of publications, including *The Wall Street Journal* and the *Federal Reserve Bulletin*, as well as on a number of Web sites, including Bloomberg, Yahoo!, CNN Financial, and the Federal Reserve Board. Using interest rate data from these sources, we can determine the term structure at any given point in time. For example, Figure 5-5 presents interest rates for different maturities on three different dates. The set of data for a given date, when plotted on a graph such as Figure 5-5, is called the **yield curve** for that date.

As the figure shows, the yield curve changes both in position and in slope over time. In March 1980, all rates were quite high because high inflation was expected. However, the rate of inflation was expected to decline, so the inflation premium (IP) was larger for short-term bonds than for long-term bonds. This caused short-term yields to be higher than long-term yields, resulting in a *downward-sloping* yield curve. By February 2000, inflation had indeed declined and thus all rates were lower. The yield curve had become **humped**—medium-term rates were higher than either short- or long-term rates. In March 2012, all rates were below the 2000 levels. Because short-term rates had dropped below long-term rates, the yield curve was *upward sloping*.

Historically, long-term rates are generally higher than short-term rates owing to the maturity risk premium, so the yield curve usually slopes upward. For this reason, people often call an upward-sloping yield curve a **"normal" yield curve** and a yield curve that

FIGURE 5-5

U.S. Treasury Bond Interest Rates on Different Dates

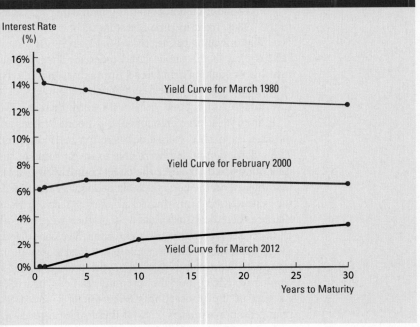

© Cengage Learning 2014

slopes downward an **inverted**, or **"abnormal," curve**. Thus, in Figure 5-5 the yield curve for March 1980 was inverted, whereas the yield curve in March 2012 was normal. As stated above, the February 2000 curve was humped.

resource

For a discussion of the expectations theory, see **Web Extension 5D** on the textbook's Web site.

A few academics and practitioners contend that large bond traders who buy and sell securities of different maturities each day dominate the market. According to this view, a bond trader is just as willing to buy a 30-year bond to pick up a short-term profit as to buy a 3-month security. Strict proponents of this view argue that the shape of the yield curve is therefore determined only by market expectations about future interest rates, a position that is called the **pure expectations theory**, or sometimes just the **expectations theory**. If this were true, then the maturity risk premium (MRP) would be zero and long-term interest rates would simply be a weighted average of current and expected future short-term interest rates. See **Web Extension 5D** for a more detailed discussion of the expectations theory.

SELF-TEST

What is a yield curve, and what information would you need to draw this curve?

Distinguish among the shapes of a "normal" yield curve, an "abnormal" curve, and a "humped" curve.

If the interest rates on 1-, 5-, 20-, and 30-year bonds are (respectively) 4%, 5%, 6%, and 7%, then how would you describe the yield curve? How would you describe it if the rates were reversed?

5-15 Financing with Junk Bonds

Recall that bonds rated less than BBB are noninvestment-grade debt, also called junk bonds or high-yield debt. There are two ways that a bond can become a junk bond. First, the bond might have been investment-grade debt when it was issued but its rating declined because the issuing corporation had fallen on hard times. Such bonds are called "fallen angels," and there are many such bonds as we write this in 2012.

Some bonds are junk bonds at the time they are issued, but this was not always true. Prior to the 1980s, fixed-income investors such as pension funds and insurance companies were generally unwilling to buy risky bonds, so it was almost impossible for risky companies to raise capital in the public bond markets. Then, in the late 1970s, Michael Milken of the investment banking firm Drexel Burnham Lambert, relying on historical studies that showed risky bonds yielded more than enough to compensate for their risk, convinced institutional investors that junk bond yields were worth their risk. Thus was born the junk bond market.

In the 1980s, large investors like T. Boone Pickens and Henry Kravis thought that certain old-line, established companies were run inefficiently and were financed too conservatively. These corporate raiders were able to invest some of their own money, borrow the rest via junk bonds, and take over the target company, usually taking the company private. The fact that interest on the bonds was tax deductible, combined with the much higher debt ratios of the restructured firms, increased after-tax cash flows and helped make the deals feasible. Because these deals used lots of debt, they were called **leveraged buyouts (LBOs)**.

In recent years, private equity firms have conducted transactions similar to the LBOs of the 1980s, taking advantage of historically low junk-bond rates to help finance their purchases. For example, in 2007 the private equity firm Kohlberg Kravis Roberts and Company (KKR) took the discount retailer Dollar General private in a $6.9 billion deal. As part of the transaction, Dollar General issued $1.9 billion in junk bonds. So KKR financed approximately 73% of the deal with its own cash (coming from its own equity and from money it had borrowed on its own account) and about 27% of the deal with money that Dollar General raised, for a net investment of about $5 billion. In late 2009, KKR took Dollar General public again at $21 per share with a resulting market value of equity of $7.1 billion and a very tidy gain!

SELF-TEST

What are junk bonds?

5-16 Bankruptcy and Reorganization

A business is *insolvent* when it does not have enough cash to meet its interest and principal payments. When this occurs, either the creditors or the company may file for bankruptcy in the United States Bankruptcy Court. After hearing from the creditors and the company's managers, a federal bankruptcy court judge decides whether to dissolve the firm through *liquidation* or to permit it to *reorganize* and thus stay alive. Chapter 7 of the federal bankruptcy statutes addresses liquidation and Chapter 11 addresses reorganization.

The decision to force a firm to liquidate versus permit it to reorganize depends on whether the value of the reorganized firm is likely to be greater than the value of the firm's assets if they are sold off piecemeal. In a reorganization, the firm's creditors negotiate with management on the terms of a potential reorganization. The reorganization plan may call for a *restructuring* of the firm's debt, in which case the interest rate may be reduced, the term to maturity may be lengthened, or some of the debt may be exchanged for equity. The point of the restructuring is to reduce the financial charges to a level that the firm's cash flows can support. Of course, the common stockholders also have to give up something: They often see their position diluted as a result of additional shares being given to debtholders in exchange for accepting a reduced amount of debt principal and interest. In fact, the original common stockholders often end up with nothing. The court may appoint a trustee to oversee the reorganization, but usually the existing management is allowed to retain control.

Liquidation occurs if the company is deemed to be too far gone to be saved—if it is worth more dead than alive. If the bankruptcy court orders liquidation, then assets are sold off and the cash obtained is distributed as specified in Chapter 7 of the Bankruptcy Act. Here is the priority of claims: (1) past-due property taxes; (2) secured creditors who are entitled to the proceeds from the sale of collateral; (3) the trustee's costs of administering and operating the bankrupt firm; (4) expenses incurred after bankruptcy was filed; (5) wages due workers, up to a limit of $2,000 per worker; (6) claims for unpaid contributions to employee benefit plans (with wages and claims not to exceed $2,000 per worker); (7) unsecured claims for customer deposits up to $900 per customer; (8) federal, state, and local taxes due; (9) unfunded pension plan liabilities (although some limitations exist); (10) general unsecured creditors; (11) preferred stockholders (up to the par value of their stock); and (12) common stockholders (although usually nothing is left for them).

The key points for you to know are: (1) the federal bankruptcy statutes govern both reorganization and liquidation, (2) bankruptcies occur frequently, and (3) a priority of the specified claims must be followed when distributing the assets of a liquidated firm.

SELF-TEST

Differentiate between a Chapter 7 liquidation and a Chapter 11 reorganization.

List the priority of claims for the distribution of a liquidated firm's assets.

SUMMARY

This chapter described the different types of bonds that governments and corporations issue, explained how bond prices are established, and discussed how investors estimate the rates of return they can expect to earn. The rate of return required by debtholders is the company's pre-tax cost of debt, and this rate depends on the risk that investors face when they buy bonds.

- A **bond** is a long-term promissory note issued by a business or governmental unit. The issuer receives money in exchange for promising to make interest payments and to repay the principal on a specified future date.
- Some special types of long-term financing include **zero coupon bonds**, which pay no annual interest but are issued at a discount; see *Web Extension 5A* for more on zero coupon bonds. Other types are **floating-rate debt**, whose interest payments fluctuate with changes in the general level of interest rates; and **junk bonds**, which are high-risk, high-yield instruments issued by firms that use a great deal of financial leverage.
- A **call provision** gives the issuing corporation the right to redeem the bonds prior to maturity under specified terms, usually at a price greater than the maturity value (the difference is a **call premium**). A firm will typically call a bond if interest rates fall substantially below the coupon rate.
- A **sinking fund** is a provision that requires the corporation to retire a portion of the bond issue each year. The purpose of the sinking fund is to provide for the orderly retirement of the issue. A sinking fund typically requires no call premium.
- The **value of a bond** is found as the present value of an **annuity** (the interest payments) plus the present value of a lump sum (the **principal**). The bond is evaluated at the appropriate periodic interest rate over the number of periods for which interest payments are made.
- The equation used to find the value of an annual coupon bond is

$$V_B = \sum_{t=1}^{N} \frac{INT}{(1 + r_d)^t} + \frac{M}{(1 + r_d)^N}$$

- An adjustment to the formula must be made if the bond pays interest **semiannually**: divide INT and r_d by 2, and multiply N by 2.
- The expected rate of return on a bond held to maturity is defined as the bond's **yield to maturity (YTM)**:

$$\text{Bond price} = \sum_{t=1}^{N} \frac{INT}{(1 + YTM)^t} + \frac{M}{(1 + YTM)^N}$$

- The expected rate of return on a callable bond held to its call date is defined as the **yield to call (YTC)**.
- The **nominal** (or **quoted**) **interest rate** on a debt security, r_d, is composed of the real risk-free rate, r^*, plus premiums that reflect inflation (IP), default risk (DRP), liquidity (LP), and maturity risk (MRP):

$$r_d = r^* + IP + DRP + LP + MRP$$

- The **risk-free rate of interest** r_{RF}, is defined as the real risk-free rate, r^*, plus an inflation premium, IP: $r_{RF} = r^* + IP$.
- **Treasury Inflation-Protected Securities (TIPS)** are U.S. Treasury bonds that have no inflation risk. See *Web Extension 5B* for more discussion of TIPS.

- The longer the maturity of a bond, the more its price will change in response to a given change in interest rates; this is called **interest rate risk**. However, bonds with short maturities expose investors to high **reinvestment rate risk**, which is the risk that income from a bond portfolio will decline because cash flows received from bonds will be rolled over at lower interest rates.
- **Duration** is a measure of interest rate risk. See *Web Extension 5C* for a discussion of duration.
- Corporate and municipal bonds have **default risk**. If an issuer defaults, investors receive less than the promised return on the bond. Therefore, investors should evaluate a bond's default risk before making a purchase.
- Bonds are assigned **ratings** that reflect the probability of their going into default. The highest rating is AAA, and they go down to D. The higher a bond's rating, the lower its risk and therefore its interest rate.
- The relationship between the yields on securities and the securities' maturities is known as the **term structure of interest rates**, and the **yield curve** is a graph of this relationship.
- The shape of the yield curve depends on two key factors: (1) *expectations about future inflation* and (2) *perceptions about the relative risk of securities with different maturities*.
- The yield curve is normally **upward sloping**—this is called a **normal yield curve**. However, the curve can slope downward (an **inverted yield curve**) if the inflation rate is expected to decline. The yield curve also can be **humped**, which means that interest rates on medium-term maturities are higher than rates on both short- and long-term maturities.
- The **expectations theory** states that yields on long-term bonds reflect expected future interest rates. *Web Extension 5D* discusses this theory.

QUESTIONS

(5-1)   Define each of the following terms:

     a. Bond; Treasury bond; corporate bond; municipal bond; foreign bond
     b. Par value; maturity date; coupon payment; coupon interest rate
     c. Floating-rate bond; zero coupon bond; original issue discount bond (OID)
     d. Call provision; redeemable bond; sinking fund
     e. Convertible bond; warrant; income bond; indexed, or purchasing power, bond
     f. Premium bond; discount bond
     g. Current yield (on a bond); yield to maturity (YTM); yield to call (YTC)
     h. Indentures; mortgage bond; debenture; subordinated debenture
     i. Development bond; municipal bond insurance; junk bond; investment-grade bond
     j. Real risk-free rate of interest, r^*; nominal risk-free rate of interest, r_{RF}
     k. Inflation premium (IP); default risk premium (DRP); liquidity; liquidity premium (LP)
     l. Interest rate risk; maturity risk premium (MRP); reinvestment rate risk
     m. Term structure of interest rates; yield curve
     n. "Normal" yield curve; inverted ("abnormal") yield curve

(5-2)   "Short-term interest rates are more volatile than long-term interest rates, so short-term bond prices are more sensitive to interest rate changes than are long-term bond prices." Is this statement true or false? Explain.

(5-3)   The rate of return on a bond held to its maturity date is called the bond's yield to maturity. If interest rates in the economy rise after a bond has been issued, what will happen to the bond's price and to its YTM? Does the length of time to maturity affect the extent to which a given change in interest rates will affect the bond's price? Why or why not?

(5-4)   If you buy a *callable* bond and interest rates decline, will the value of your bond rise by as much as it would have risen if the bond had not been callable? Explain.

(5-5)   A sinking fund can be set up in one of two ways. Discuss the advantages and disadvantages of each procedure from the viewpoint of both the firm and its bondholders.

SELF-TEST PROBLEM   Solution Appears in Appendix A

(ST-1)
Bond Valuation

The Pennington Corporation issued a new series of bonds on January 1, 1990. The bonds were sold at par ($1,000), had a 12% coupon, and matured in 30 years on December 31, 2019. Coupon payments are made semiannually (on June 30 and December 31).

a. What was the YTM on the date the bonds were issued?
b. What was the price of the bonds on January 1, 1995 (5 years later), assuming that interest rates had fallen to 10%?
c. Find the current yield, capital gains yield, and total yield on January 1, 1995, given the price as determined in part b.
d. On July 1, 2013 (6.5 years before maturity), Pennington's bonds sold for $916.42. What are the YTM, the current yield, and the capital gains yield for that date?
e. Now assume that you plan to purchase an outstanding Pennington bond on March 1, 2013, when the going rate of interest given its risk is 15.5%. How large a check must you write to complete the transaction? (*Hint:* Don't forget the accrued interest.)

PROBLEMS   Answers Appear in Appendix B

(5-1)
Bond Valuation with Annual Payments

Jackson Corporation's bonds have 12 years remaining to maturity. Interest is paid annually, the bonds have a $1,000 par value, and the coupon interest rate is 8%. The bonds have a yield to maturity of 9%. What is the current market price of these bonds?

(5-2)
Yield to Maturity for Annual Payments

Wilson Wonders's bonds have 12 years remaining to maturity. Interest is paid annually, the bonds have a $1,000 par value, and the coupon interest rate is 10%. The bonds sell at a price of $850. What is their yield to maturity?

(5-3)
Current Yield for Annual Payments

Heath Foods's bonds have 7 years remaining to maturity. The bonds have a face value of $1,000 and a yield to maturity of 8%. They pay interest annually and have a 9% coupon rate. What is their current yield?

(5-4)
Determinant of Interest Rates

The real risk-free rate of interest is 4%. Inflation is expected to be 2% this year and 4% during the next 2 years. Assume that the maturity risk premium is zero. What is the yield on 2-year Treasury securities? What is the yield on 3-year Treasury securities?

(5-5)
Default Risk Premium

A Treasury bond that matures in 10 years has a yield of 6%. A 10-year corporate bond has a yield of 9%. Assume that the liquidity premium on the corporate bond is 0.5%. What is the default risk premium on the corporate bond?

(5-6)
Maturity Risk Premium

The real risk-free rate is 3%, and inflation is expected to be 3% for the next 2 years. A 2-year Treasury security yields 6.3%. What is the maturity risk premium for the 2-year security?

(5-7)
Bond Valuation with Semiannual Payments

Renfro Rentals has issued bonds that have a 10% coupon rate, payable semiannually. The bonds mature in 8 years, have a face value of $1,000, and a yield to maturity of 8.5%. What is the price of the bonds?

(5-8)
Yield to Maturity and Call with Semiannual Payments

Thatcher Corporation's bonds will mature in 10 years. The bonds have a face value of $1,000 and an 8% coupon rate, paid semiannually. The price of the bonds is $1,100. The bonds are callable in 5 years at a call price of $1,050. What is their yield to maturity? What is their yield to call?

(5-9)
Bond Valuation and Interest Rate Risk

The Garraty Company has two bond issues outstanding. Both bonds pay $100 annual interest plus $1,000 at maturity. Bond L has a maturity of 15 years, and Bond S has a maturity of 1 year.

a. What will be the value of each of these bonds when the going rate of interest is (1) 5%, (2) 8%, and (3) 12%? Assume that there is only one more interest payment to be made on Bond S.
b. Why does the longer-term (15-year) bond fluctuate more when interest rates change than does the shorter-term bond (1 year)?

(5-10)
Yield to Maturity and Required Returns

The Brownstone Corporation's bonds have 5 years remaining to maturity. Interest is paid annually, the bonds have a $1,000 par value, and the coupon interest rate is 9%.

a. What is the yield to maturity at a current market price of (1) $829 or (2) $1,104?
b. Would you pay $829 for one of these bonds if you thought that the appropriate rate of interest was 12%—that is, if $r_d = 12\%$? Explain your answer.

(5-11)
Yield to Call and Realized Rates of Return

Seven years ago, Goodwynn & Wolf Incorporated sold a 20-year bond issue with a 14% annual coupon rate and a 9% call premium. Today, G&W called the bonds. The bonds originally were sold at their face value of $1,000. Compute the realized rate of return for investors who purchased the bonds when they were issued and who surrender them today in exchange for the call price.

(5-12)
Bond Yields and Rates of Return

A 10-year, 12% semiannual coupon bond with a par value of $1,000 may be called in 4 years at a call price of $1,060. The bond sells for $1,100. (Assume that the bond has just been issued.)

a. What is the bond's yield to maturity?
b. What is the bond's current yield?
c. What is the bond's capital gain or loss yield?
d. What is the bond's yield to call?

(5-13)
Yield to Maturity and Current Yield

You just purchased a bond that matures in 5 years. The bond has a face value of $1,000 and has an 8% annual coupon. The bond has a current yield of 8.21%. What is the bond's yield to maturity?

(5-14)
Current Yield with Semiannual Payments

A bond that matures in 7 years sells for $1,020. The bond has a face value of $1,000 and a yield to maturity of 10.5883%. The bond pays coupons semiannually. What is the bond's current yield?

(5-15)
Yield to Call, Yield to Maturity, and Market Rates

Absalom Motors's 14% coupon rate, semiannual payment, $1,000 par value bonds that mature in 30 years are callable 5 years from now at a price of $1,050. The bonds sell at a price of $1,353.54, and the yield curve is flat. Assuming that interest rates in the economy are expected to remain at their current level, what is the best estimate of the nominal interest rate on new bonds?

(5-16)
Interest Rate Sensitivity

A bond trader purchased each of the following bonds at a yield to maturity of 8%. Immediately after she purchased the bonds, interest rates fell to 7%. What is the percentage change in the price of each bond after the decline in interest rates? Fill in the following table:

	Price @ 8%	Price @ 7%	Percentage Change
10-year, 10% annual coupon	_____	_____	_____
10-year zero	_____	_____	_____
5-year zero	_____	_____	_____
30-year zero	_____	_____	_____
$100 perpetuity	_____	_____	_____

(5-17)
Bond Value as Maturity Approaches

An investor has two bonds in his portfolio. Each bond matures in 4 years, has a face value of $1,000, and has a yield to maturity equal to 9.6%. One bond, Bond C, pays an annual coupon of 10%; the other bond, Bond Z, is a zero coupon bond. Assuming that the yield to maturity of each bond remains at 9.6% over the next 4 years, what will be the price of each of the bonds at the following time periods? Fill in the following table:

t	Price of Bond C	Price of Bond Z
0	_____	_____
1	_____	_____
2	_____	_____
3	_____	_____
4	_____	_____

(5-18)
Determinants of Interest Rates

The real risk-free rate is 2%. Inflation is expected to be 3% this year, 4% next year, and then 3.5% thereafter. The maturity risk premium is estimated to be $0.0005 \times (t - 1)$, where t = number of years to maturity. What is the nominal interest rate on a 7-year Treasury security?

(5-19)
Maturity Risk Premiums

Assume that the real risk-free rate, r*, is 3% and that inflation is expected to be 8% in Year 1, 5% in Year 2, and 4% thereafter. Assume also that all Treasury securities are highly liquid and free of default risk. If 2-year and 5-year Treasury notes both yield 10%, what is the difference in the maturity risk premiums (MRPs) on the two notes; that is, what is MRP_5 minus MRP_2?

(5-20)
Inflation Risk Premiums

Because of a recession, the inflation rate expected for the coming year is only 3%. However, the inflation rate in Year 2 and thereafter is expected to be constant at some level above 3%. Assume that the real risk-free rate is r* = 2% for all maturities and that there are no maturity premiums. If 3-year Treasury notes yield 2 percentage points more than 1-year notes, what inflation rate is expected after Year 1?

Suppose Hillard Manufacturing sold an issue of bonds with a 10-year maturity, a $1,000 par value, a 10% coupon rate, and semiannual interest payments.

   a. Two years after the bonds were issued, the going rate of interest on bonds such as these fell to 6%. At what price would the bonds sell?

   b. Suppose that 2 years after the initial offering, the going interest rate had risen to 12%. At what price would the bonds sell?

   c. Suppose that 2 years after the issue date (as in part a) interest rates fell to 6%. Suppose further that the interest rate remained at 6% for the next 8 years. What would happen to the price of the bonds over time?

Arnot International's bonds have a current market price of $1,200. The bonds have an 11% annual coupon payment, a $1,000 face value, and 10 years left until maturity. The bonds may be called in 5 years at 109% of face value (call price = $1,090).

   a. What is the yield to maturity?

   b. What is the yield to call if they are called in 5 years?

   c. Which yield might investors expect to earn on these bonds, and why?

   d. The bond's indenture indicates that the call provision gives the firm the right to call them at the end of each year beginning in Year 5. In Year 5, they may be called at 109% of face value, but in each of the next 4 years the call percentage will decline by 1 percentage point. Thus, in Year 6 they may be called at 108% of face value, in Year 7 they may be called at 107% of face value, and so on. If the yield curve is horizontal and interest rates remain at their current level, when is the latest that investors might expect the firm to call the bonds?

Suppose you and most other investors expect the inflation rate to be 7% next year, to fall to 5% during the following year, and then to remain at a rate of 3% thereafter. Assume that the real risk-free rate, r^*, will remain at 2% and that maturity risk premiums on Treasury securities rise from zero on very short-term securities (those that mature in a few days) to a level of 0.2 percentage points for 1-year securities. Furthermore, maturity risk premiums increase 0.2 percentage points for each year to maturity, up to a limit of 1.0 percentage point on 5-year or longer-term T-notes and T-bonds.

   a. Calculate the interest rate on 1-, 2-, 3-, 4-, 5-, 10-, and 20-year Treasury securities, and plot the yield curve.

   b. Now suppose ExxonMobil's bonds, rated AAA, have the same maturities as the Treasury bonds. As an approximation, plot an ExxonMobil yield curve on the same graph with the Treasury bond yield curve. (*Hint:* Think about the default risk premium on ExxonMobil's long-term versus short-term bonds.)

   c. Now plot the approximate yield curve of Long Island Lighting Company, a risky nuclear utility.

SPREADSHEET PROBLEMS

Start with the partial model in the file *Ch05 P24 Build a Model.xls* on the textbook's Web site. A 20-year, 8% semiannual coupon bond with a par value of $1,000 may be called in 5 years at a call price of $1,040. The bond sells for $1,100. (Assume that the bond has just been issued.)

resource

a. What is the bond's yield to maturity?
b. What is the bond's current yield?
c. What is the bond's capital gain or loss yield?
d. What is the bond's yield to call?
e. How would the price of the bond be affected by a change in the going market interest rate? (*Hint:* Conduct a sensitivity analysis of price to changes in the going market interest rate for the bond. Assume that the bond will be called if and only if the going rate of interest *falls below* the coupon rate. This is an oversimplification, but assume it for purposes of this problem.)
f. Now assume the date is October 25, 2014. Assume further that a 12%, 10-year bond was issued on July 1, 2014, pays interest semiannually (on January 1 and July 1), and sells for $1,100. Use your spreadsheet to find the bond's yield.

MINI CASE

Sam Strother and Shawna Tibbs are vice presidents of Mutual of Seattle Insurance Company and co-directors of the company's pension fund management division. An important new client, the North-Western Municipal Alliance, has requested that Mutual of Seattle present an investment seminar to the mayors of the represented cities, and Strother and Tibbs, who will make the actual presentation, have asked you to help them by answering the following questions.

a. What are the key features of a bond?
b. What are call provisions and sinking fund provisions? Do these provisions make bonds more or less risky?
c. How does one determine the value of any asset whose value is based on expected future cash flows?
d. How is the value of a bond determined? What is the value of a 10-year, $1,000 par value bond with a 10% annual coupon if its required rate of return is 10%?
e. (1) What would be the value of the bond described in part d if, just after it had been issued, the expected inflation rate rose by 3 percentage points, causing investors to require a 13% return? Would we now have a discount or a premium bond?
   (2) What would happen to the bond's value if inflation fell and r_d declined to 7%? Would we now have a premium or a discount bond?
   (3) What would happen to the value of the 10-year bond over time if the required rate of return remained at 13%? If it remained at 7%? (*Hint:* With a financial calculator, enter PMT, I/YR, FV, and N, and then change N to see what happens to the PV as the bond approaches maturity.)
f. (1) What is the yield to maturity on a 10-year, 9% annual coupon, $1,000 par value bond that sells for $887.00? That sells for $1,134.20? What does the fact that a bond sells at a discount or at a premium tell you about the relationship between r_d and the bond's coupon rate?
   (2) What are the total return, the current yield, and the capital gains yield for the discount bond? (Assume the bond is held to maturity and the company does not default on the bond.)
g. How does the equation for valuing a bond change if semiannual payments are made? Find the value of a 10-year, semiannual payment, 10% coupon bond if the nominal r_d = 13%.

   h. Suppose a 10-year, 10% semiannual coupon bond with a par value of $1,000 is currently selling for $1,135.90, producing a nominal yield to maturity of 8%. However, the bond can be called after 5 years for a price of $1,050.
      (1) What is the bond's *nominal* yield to call (YTC)?
      (2) If you bought this bond, do you think you would be more likely to earn the YTM or the YTC? Why?
   i. Write a general expression for the yield on any debt security (r_d) and define these terms: real risk-free rate of interest (r^*), inflation premium (IP), default risk premium (DRP), liquidity premium (LP), and maturity risk premium (MRP).
   j. Define the nominal risk-free rate (r_{RF}). What security can be used as an estimate of r_{RF}?
   k. Describe a way to estimate the inflation premium (IP) for a t-year bond.
   l. What is a *bond spread* and how is it related to the default risk premium? How are bond ratings related to default risk? What factors affect a company's bond rating?
   m. What is *interest rate* (or *price*) *risk?* Which bond has more interest rate risk: an annual payment 1-year bond or a 10-year bond? Why?
   n. What is *reinvestment rate risk?* Which has more reinvestment rate risk: a 1-year bond or a 10-year bond?
   o. How are interest rate risk and reinvestment rate risk related to the maturity risk premium?
   p. What is the term structure of interest rates? What is a yield curve?
   q. Briefly describe bankruptcy law. If a firm were to default on its bonds, would the company be liquidated immediately? Would the bondholders be assured of receiving all of their promised payments?

SELECTED ADDITIONAL CASES

The following cases from CengageCompose cover many of the concepts discussed in this chapter and are available at **compose.cengage.com.**
Klein-Brigham Series:
Case 3, "Peachtree Securities, Inc. (B)"; Case 72, "Swan Davis"; and Case 78, "Beatrice Peabody."
Brigham-Buzzard Series:
Case 3, "Powerline Network Corporation (Bonds and Preferred Stock)."

© lulu/fotolia.com

© lulu/fotolia.com

PART 3

Stocks and Options

© Adalberto Rios Szalay/Sexto Sol/Getty Images

CHAPTER **6**

Risk and Return

What a difference a year makes! At the beginning of 2011, many investors purchased shares of stock in the NASDAQ companies Pharmasset and YRC Worldwide. But by year end, Pharmasset had gone up by 488% while YRC Worldwide had fallen by 99.1% (yet still remained listed on NASDAQ). Big gains and losses weren't limited to small companies. Investors in McDonald's were lovin' it, with a 31% gain for the year. At the other extreme, Bank of America's stock went down by over 58%.

Did investors in YRC Worldwide and BofA make bad decisions? Before you answer, suppose you were making the decision back in January 2011, with the information available then. You now know the decision's *outcome* was poor, but that doesn't mean the decision itself was badly made. Investors must have known these stocks were risky, with a chance of a gain or a loss. But given the information available to them, they certainly invested with the expectation of a gain. What about the investors in Pharmasset and McDonald's? They also realized the stock prices could go down or up, but were probably pleasantly surprised that the stocks went up so much.

These examples show that what you expect to happen and what actually happens are often very different—the world is risky! Therefore, it is vital that you understand risk and the ways to manage it. As you read this chapter and think about risk, keep the examples of McDonald's and BofA in mind.

Intrinsic Value, Risk, and Return

© Rob Webb/Getty Images

The intrinsic value of a company is the present value of its expected future free cash flows (FCF) discounted at the weighted average cost of capital (WACC). This chapter shows you how to measure a firm's risk and the rate of return expected by shareholders, which affects the WACC. All else held equal, higher risk increases the WACC, which reduces the firm's value.

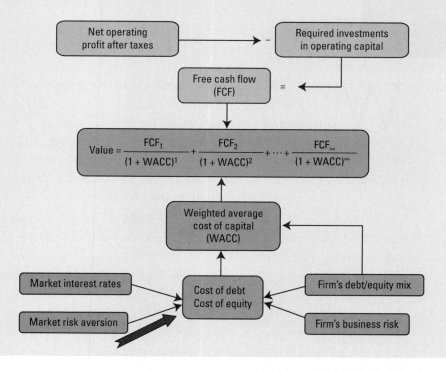

© Cengage Learning 2014

In this chapter, we start from the basic premise that investors like returns and dislike risk; this is called **risk aversion**. Therefore, people will invest in relatively risky assets only if they expect to receive relatively high returns—the higher the perceived risk, the higher the expected rate of return an investor will demand. In this chapter, we define exactly what the term *risk* means as it relates to investments, we examine procedures used to measure risk, and we discuss more precisely the relationship between risk and required returns. In later chapters, we extend these relationships to show how risk and return interact to determine security prices. Managers must understand and apply these concepts as they plan the actions that will shape their firms' futures, and investors must understand them in order to make appropriate investment decisions.

resource

The textbook's Web site contains an Excel file that will guide you through the chapter's calculations. The file for this chapter is ***Ch06 Tool Kit.xls*** *and we encourage you to open the file and follow along as you read the chapter.*

6-1 Investment Returns and Risk

With most investments, an individual or business spends money today with the expectation of earning even more money in the future. However, most investments are risky. Following are brief definitions of return and risk.

6-1a Returns on Investments

The concept of *return* provides investors with a convenient way to express the financial performance of an investment. To illustrate, suppose you buy 10 shares of a stock for $1,000. The stock pays no dividends, but at the end of 1 year you sell the stock for $1,100. What is the return on your $1,000 investment?

One way to express an investment's return is in *dollar terms:*

$$\text{Dollar return} = \text{Amount to be received} - \text{Amount invested}$$
$$= \$1,100 - \$1,000$$
$$= \$100$$

If instead at the end of the year you sell the stock for only $900, your dollar return will be −$100.

Although expressing returns in dollars is easy, two problems arise: (1) To make a meaningful judgment about the return, you need to know the scale (size) of the investment; a $100 return on a $100 investment is a great return (assuming the investment is held for 1 year), but a $100 return on a $10,000 investment would be a poor return. (2) You also need to know the timing of the return; a $100 return on a $100 investment is a great return if it occurs after 1 year, but the same dollar return after 20 years is not very good.

The solution to these scale and timing problems is to express investment results as *rates of return,* or *percentage returns.* For example, the rate of return on the 1-year stock investment, when $1,100 is received after 1 year, is 10%:

$$\text{Rate of return} = \frac{\text{Amount received} - \text{Amount invested}}{\text{Amount invested}}$$

$$= \frac{\text{Dollar return}}{\text{Amount invested}} = \frac{\$100}{\$1,000}$$

$$= 0.10 = 10\%$$

The rate of return calculation "standardizes" the dollar return by considering the annual return per unit of investment. Although this example has only one outflow and one inflow, the annualized rate of return can easily be calculated in situations where multiple cash flows occur over time by using time value of money concepts as discussed in Chapter 4.

6-1b Stand-Alone Risk versus Portfolio Risk

Risk is defined in *Webster's* as "a hazard; a peril; exposure to loss or injury." Thus, risk refers to the chance that some unfavorable event will occur. For an investment in financial assets or in new projects, the unfavorable event is ending up with a lower return than you expected. An asset's risk can be analyzed in two ways: (1) on a stand-alone basis, where the asset is considered in isolation; and (2) on a portfolio basis, where the asset is held as one of a number of assets in a portfolio. Thus, an asset's **stand-alone risk** is the risk an investor would face if she held only this one asset. Most assets are held in portfolios, but it is necessary to understand stand-alone risk in order to understand risk in a portfolio context.

SELF-TEST

Differentiate between dollar returns and rates of return.

*Why are rates of return superior to dollar returns when comparing different potential investments? (*Hint: *Think about size and timing.)*

If you pay $500 for an investment that returns $600 in 1 year, what is your annual rate of return? **(20%)**

6-2 Measuring Risk for Discrete Distributions

Political and economic uncertainty affect stock market risk. For example, in the summer of 2011, the market fell sharply when Congress debated whether or not to raise the debt ceiling. Investors were unsure whether Congress would solve the crisis, come up with a temporary solution, or let the U.S. government default on Treasury securities and fall short on obligations to Social Security and Medicare. At the risk of oversimplification, these outcomes represented three distinct (or discrete) scenarios for the market, with each scenario having a very different market return.

Risk can be a complicated topic, so we begin with a simple example that has discrete possible outcomes.[1]

6-2a Probability Distributions for Discrete Outcomes

An event's *probability* is defined as the chance that the event will occur. For example, a weather forecaster might state: "There is a 40% chance of rain today and a 60% chance that it will not rain." If all possible events, or outcomes, are listed, and if a probability is assigned to each event, then the listing is called a **probability distribution**. (Keep in mind that the probabilities must sum to 1.0, or 100%.)

Suppose an investor is facing a situation similar to the debt ceiling crisis and believes there are three possible outcomes for the market as a whole: (1) Best case, with a 30% probability; (2) Most Likely case, with a 40% probability; and (3) Worst case, with a 30% probability. The investor also believes the market would go up by 37% in the Best scenario, go up by 11% in the Most Likely scenario, and go down by 15% in the Worst scenario.

Figure 6-1 shows the probability distribution for these three scenarios. Notice that the probabilities sum to 1.0 and that the possible returns are dispersed around the Most Likely scenario's return.

FIGURE 6-1

Discrete Probability Distribution for Three Scenarios

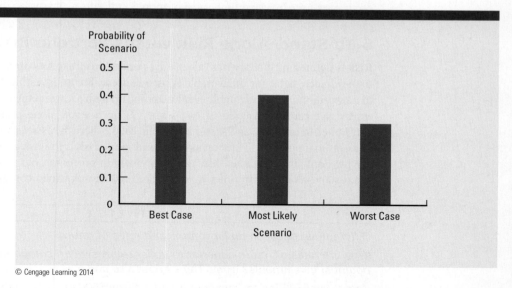

© Cengage Learning 2014

---

[1]The following discussion of risk applies to all random variables, not just stock returns.

We can calculate expected return and risk using the probability distribution, as we illustrate in the next sections.

6-2b Expected Rate of Return for Discrete Distributions

The rate-of-return probability distribution is shown in the "Inputs" section of Figure 6-2; see Columns (1) and (2). This portion of the figure is called a *payoff matrix* when the outcomes are cash flows or returns.

If we multiply each possible outcome by its probability of occurrence and then sum these products, as in Column (3) of Figure 6-2, the result is a *weighted average* of outcomes. The weights are the probabilities, and the weighted average is the **expected rate of return, $\hat{r}$**, called "r-hat."[2] The expected rate of return is 11%, as shown in cell D66 in Figure 6-2.[3]

The calculation for expected rate of return can also be expressed as an equation that does the same thing as the payoff matrix table:

$$\text{Expected rate of return} = \hat{r} = p_1 r_1 + p_2 r_2 + \cdots + p_n r_n$$

$$= \sum_{i=1}^{n} p_i r_i$$

(6-1)

FIGURE 6-2

Calculating Expected Returns and Standard Deviations: Discrete Probabilities

	A	B	C	D	E	F	G
61	INPUTS:			Expected Return	Standard Deviation		
62	Scenario	Probability of Scenario (1)	Market Rate of Return (2)	Product of Probability and Return (1) x (2) = (3)	Deviation from Expected Return (2) – D66 = (4)	Squared Deviation (4)² = (5)	Sq. Dev. × Prob. (1) x (5) = (6)
63	Best Case	0.30	37%	11.1%	26%	6.8%	2.0%
64	Most Likely	0.40	11%	4.4%	0%	0.0%	0.0%
65	Worst Case	0.30	–15%	–4.5%	–26%	6.8%	2.0%
66		1.00	Exp. ret. =	Sum = 11.0%		Sum = Variance =	4.1%
67						Std. Dev. = Square root of variance =	20.1%

[2]In other chapters, we will use $\hat{r}_d$ and $\hat{r}_s$ to signify expected returns on bonds and stocks, respectively. However, this distinction is unnecessary in this chapter, so we just use the general term, $\hat{r}$, to signify the expected return on an investment.
[3]Don't worry about why there is an 11% expected return for the market. We discuss the market return in more detail later in the chapter.

Here r_i is the return if outcome i occurs, p_i is the probability that outcome i occurs, and n is the number of possible outcomes. Thus, $\hat{r}$ is a weighted average of the possible outcomes (the r_i values), with each outcome's weight being its probability of occurrence. Using the data for from Figure 6-2, we obtain the expected rate of return as follows:

$$\hat{r} = p_1(r_1) + p_2(r_2) + p_3(r_3)$$
$$= 0.3(37\%) + 0.4(11\%) + 0.3(-15\%)$$
$$= 11\%$$

6-2c Measuring Stand-Alone Risk: The Standard Deviation of a Discrete Distribution

For simple distributions, it is easy to assess risk by looking at the dispersion of possible outcomes—a distribution with widely dispersed possible outcomes is riskier than one with narrowly dispersed outcomes. For example, we can look at Figure 6-1 and see that the possible returns are widely dispersed. But when there are many possible outcomes and we are comparing many different investments, it isn't possible to assess risk simply by looking at the probability distribution—we need a quantitative measure of the tightness of the probability distribution. One such measure is the **standard deviation**, the symbol for which is σ, pronounced "sigma." A large standard deviation means that possible outcomes are widely dispersed, whereas a small standard deviation means that outcomes are more tightly clustered around the expected value.

To calculate the standard deviation, we proceed as shown in Figure 6-2, taking the following steps:

1. Calculate the expected value for the rate of return using Equation 6-1.
2. Subtract the expected rate of return ($\hat{r}$) from each possible outcome (r_i) to obtain a set of deviations about $\hat{r}$ as shown in Column 4 of Figure 6-2:

$$\text{Deviation}_i = r_i - \hat{r}$$

3. Square each deviation as shown in Column 5. Then multiply the squared deviations in Column 5 by the probability of occurrence for its related outcome; these products are shown in Column 6. Sum these products to obtain the **variance** of the probability distribution:

$$\text{Variance} = \sigma^2 = \sum_{i=1}^{n} (r_i - \hat{r})^2 p_i \qquad (6\text{-}2)$$

Thus, the variance is essentially a weighted average of the squared deviations from the expected value.

4. Finally, take the square root of the variance to obtain the standard deviation:

$$\text{Standard deviation} = \sigma = \sqrt{\sum_{i=1}^{n} (r_i - \hat{r})^2 p_i} \qquad (6\text{-}3)$$

resource

See **Ch06 Tool Kit.xls** on the textbook's Web site for all calculations.

The standard deviation provides an idea of how far above or below the expected value the actual value is likely to be. Using this procedure in Figure 6-2, our hypothetical investor believes that the market return has a standard deviation of about 20%.

SELF-TEST

What does "investment risk" mean?

Set up an illustrative probability distribution for an investment.

What is a payoff matrix?

How does one calculate the standard deviation?

An investment has a 20% chance of producing a 25% return, a 60% chance of producing a 10% return, and a 20% chance of producing a −15% return. What is its expected return? **(8%)** *What is its standard deviation?* **(12.9%)**

6-3 Risk in a Continuous Distribution

Investors usually don't estimate discrete outcomes in normal economic times but instead use the scenario approach during special situations, such as the debt ceiling crisis, the European bond crisis, oil supply threats, bank stress tests, and so on. Even in these situations, they would estimate more than 3 outcomes. For example, an investor might add more scenarios to our example; Figure 6-3 shows 15 scenarios for our original example.

We live in a complex world, with an infinite number of outcomes. But instead of adding more and more scenarios, most analysts turn to continuous distributions, with one of the most widely used being the **normal distribution**. With a normal distribution, the *actual* return will be within ±1 standard deviation of the *expected* return 68.26% of the time. Figure 6-4 illustrates this point, and it also shows the situation for ±2σ and ±3σ. For our 3-scenario example, $\hat{r} = 11\%$ and $\sigma = 20\%$. If returns come from a normal distribution with the same expected value and standard deviation rather than the discrete distribution,

FIGURE 6-3

Discrete Probability Distribution for 15 Scenarios

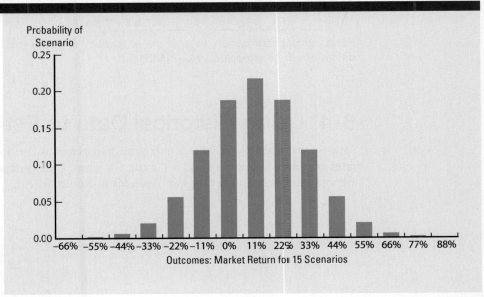

© Cengage Learning 2014

FIGURE 6-4

Probability Ranges for a Normal Distribution

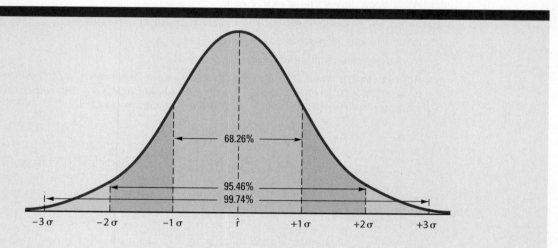

Notes:

[a]The area under the normal curve always equals 1.0, or 100%. Thus, the areas under any pair of normal curves drawn on the same scale, whether they are peaked or flat, must be equal.

[b]Half of the area under a normal curve is to the left of the mean, indicating that there is a 50% probability that the actual outcome will be less than the mean, and half is to the right of $\hat{r}$, indicating a 50% probability that it will be greater than the mean.

[c]Of the area under the curve, 68.26% is within ±1σ of the mean, indicating that the probability is 68.26% that the actual outcome will be within the range $\hat{r} - \sigma$ to $\hat{r} + \sigma$.

© Cengage Learning 2014

r e s o u r c e

*For more discussion of probability distributions, see **Web Extension 6A**, available on the textbook's Web site.*

there would be a 68.26% probability that the actual return would be in the range of 11% ± 20%, or from −9% to 31%.

When using a continuous distribution, it is common to use historical data to estimate the standard deviation, as we explain in the next section.

SELF-TEST

For a normal distribution, what is the probability of being within 1 standard deviation of the expected value? **(68.26%)**

6-4 Using Historical Data to Estimate Risk

Suppose that a sample of returns over some past period is available. These past **realized rates of return** are denoted as $\bar{r}_t$ ("r bar t"), where t designates the time period. The average annual return over the last T periods is denoted as $\bar{r}_{Avg}$:

$$\bar{r}_{Avg} = \frac{\displaystyle\sum_{t=1}^{T} \bar{r}_t}{T} \tag{6-4}$$

What Does Risk Really Mean?

© Rob Webb/Getty Images

As explained in the text, the probability of being within 1 standard deviation of the expected return is 68.26%, so the probability of being further than 1 standard deviation from the mean is 31.74%. There is an equal probability of being above or below the range, so there is a 15.87% chance of being more than one standard deviation below the mean, which is roughly equal to a 1 in 6 chance (1 in 6 is 16.67%).

For the average firm listed on the New York Stock Exchange, σ has been in the range of 35% to 40% in recent years, with an expected return of around 8% to 12%. One standard deviation below this expected return is about 10% − 35% = −25%. This means that, for a typical stock in a typical year, there is about a 1 in 6 chance of having a 25% loss. You might be thinking that 1 in 6 is a pretty low probability, but what if your chance of getting hit by a car when you crossed a street were 1 in 6? When put that way, 1 in 6 sounds pretty scary.

You might also correctly be thinking that there would be a 1 in 6 chance of getting a return higher than 1 standard deviation above the mean, which would be about 45% for a typical stock. A 45% return is great, but human nature is such that most investors would dislike a 25% loss a whole lot more than they would enjoy a 45% gain.

You might also be thinking that you'll be OK if you hold stock long enough. But even if you buy and hold a diversified portfolio for 10 years, there is still roughly a 10% chance that you will lose money. If you hold it for 20 years, there is about a 4% chance of losing. Such odds wouldn't be worrisome if you were engaged in a game of chance that could be played multiple times, but you have only one life to live and just a few rolls of the dice.

We aren't suggesting that investors shouldn't buy stocks; indeed, we own stock ourselves. But we do believe investors should understand more clearly how much risk investing entails.

The standard deviation of a sample of returns can then be estimated using this formula:[4]

$$\text{Estimated } \sigma = S = \sqrt{\frac{\sum_{t=1}^{T}(\bar{r}_t - \bar{r}_{Avg})^2}{T-1}} \qquad (6\text{-}5)$$

When estimated from past data, the standard deviation is often denoted by S.

6-4a Calculating the Historical Standard Deviation

To illustrate these calculations, consider the following historical returns for a company:

Year	Return
2011	15%
2012	−5%
2013	20%

Using Equations 6-4 and 6-5, the estimated average and standard deviation are, respectively,

---

[4]Because we are estimating the standard deviation from a sample of observations, the denominator in Equation 6-5 is "T − 1" and not just "T." Equations 6-4 and 6-5 are built into all financial calculators. For example, to find the sample standard deviation, enter the rates of return into the calculator and press the key marked S (or S_x) to get the standard deviation. See your calculator's manual for details.

$$\bar{r}_{Avg} = \frac{15\% - 5\% + 20\%}{3} = 10.0\%$$

$$\text{Estimated } \sigma \text{ (or S)} = \sqrt{\frac{(15\% - 10\%)^2 + (-5\% - 10\%)^2 + (20\% - 10\%)^2}{3-1}}$$

$$= 13.2\%$$

The average and standard deviation can also be calculated using *Excel*'s built-in functions, shown below using numerical data rather than cell ranges as inputs:

$$=\textbf{AVERAGE}(\textbf{0.15,}-\textbf{0.05,0.20}) = 10.0\%$$
$$=\textbf{STDEV}(\textbf{0.15,}-\textbf{0.05,0.20}) = 13.2\%$$

The historical standard deviation is often used as an estimate of future variability. Because past variability is often repeated, past variability may be a reasonably good estimate of future risk. However, it is usually incorrect to use $\bar{r}_{Avg}$ based on a past period as an estimate of $\hat{r}$, the expected future return. For example, just because a stock had a 75% return in the past year, there is no reason to expect a 75% return this year.

6-4b Calculating MicroDrive's Historical Standard Deviation

Figure 6-5 shows 48 months of recent stock returns for two companies, MicroDrive and SnailDrive; the actual data are in the *Excel* file ***Ch06 Tool Kit.xls.*** A quick glance is enough to determine that MicroDrive's returns are more volatile.

We could use Equations 6-4 and 6-5 to calculate the average return and standard deviation, but that would be quite tedious. Instead, we use *Excel's* AVERAGE and STDEV functions and find that MicroDrive's monthly average return was 1.22% and its monthly standard deviation was 14.19%. SnailDrive had an average monthly return of 0.72% and a standard deviation of 7.45%. These calculations confirm the visual evidence in Figure 6-5: MicroDrive had greater stand-alone risk than SnailDrive.

We often use monthly data to estimate averages and standard deviations, but we normally present data in an annualized format. Multiply the monthly average return by 12 to get MicroDrive's annualized average return of 1.22%(12) = 14.6%. As noted earlier, the past average return isn't a good indicator of the future return.

To annualize the standard deviation, multiply the monthly standard deviation by the square root of 12. MicroDrive's annualized standard deviation was 14.19%($\sqrt{12}$) = 49.2%.[5] SnailDrive's average annual return was 8.6% and its annualized standard deviation was 25.8%.

Notice that MicroDrive had higher risk than SnailDrive (a standard deviation of 49.2% versus 25.8%) and a higher average return (14.6% versus 8.6%) during the past 48 months. However, a higher return for undertaking more risk isn't guaranteed—if it were, then a riskier investment wouldn't really by risky!

The file ***Ch06 Tool Kit.xls*** calculates the annualized average return and standard deviation using just the most recent 12 months. Here are the results:

---

[5]If we had calculated the monthly variance, we would annualize it by multiplying it by 12, as intuition (and mathematics) suggests. Because standard deviation is the square root of variance, we annualize the monthly standard deviation by multiplying it by the square root of 12.

FIGURE 6-5

Historical Monthly Stock Returns for MicroDrive and SnailDrive

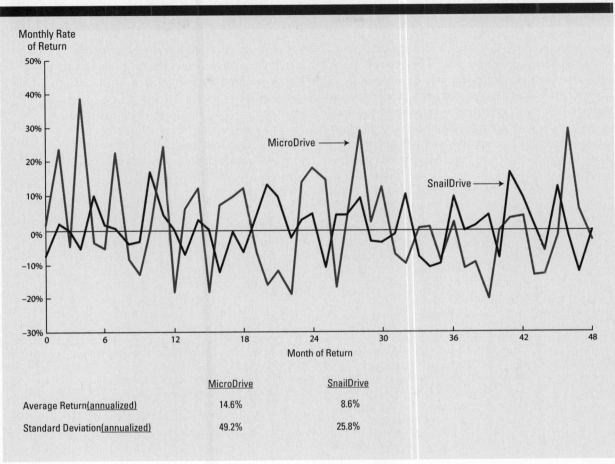

	MicroDrive	SnailDrive
Average Return(annualized)	14.6%	8.6%
Standard Deviation(annualized)	49.2%	25.8%

© Cengage Learning 2014

Results for Most Recent 12 Months	MicroDrive	SnailDrive
Average return (annual)	−29.3%	17.9%
Standard deviation (annual)	44.5%	28.8%

Even though MicroDrive's standard deviation remained well above that of SnailDrive during the last 12 months of the sample period, MicroDrive experienced an annualized average loss of over 29% while SnailDrive gained almost 18%.[6] MicroDrive's stockholders certainly learned that higher risk doesn't always lead to higher *actual* returns.

SELF-TEST

A stock's returns for the past 3 years were 10%, −15%, and 35%. What is the historical average return? **(10%)** What is the historical sample standard deviation? **(25%)**

---

[6]During the last 12 months, MicroDrive had an average monthly loss of 2.44%, but it had a compound loss for the year of over 30%. We discuss the difference between arithmetic averages and geometric averages (based on compound returns) in Chapter 9.

The Historic Trade-off between Risk and Return

© Rob Webb/Getty Images

The table accompanying this box summarizes the historical trade-off between risk and return for different classes of investments. The assets that produced the highest average returns also had the highest standard deviations and the widest ranges of returns. For example, small-company stocks had the highest average annual return, but their standard deviation of returns also was the highest. In contrast, U.S. Treasury bills had the lowest standard deviation, but they also had the lowest average return.

Note that a T-bill is riskless *if you hold it until maturity,* but if you invest in a rolling portfolio of T-bills and hold the portfolio for a number of years, then your investment income will vary depending on what happens to the level of interest rates in each year. You can be sure of the return you will earn on an individual T-bill, but you cannot be sure of the return you will earn on a portfolio of T-bills held over a number of years.

	Realized Returns, 1926–2011					
	Small-Company Stocks	Large-Company Stocks	Long-Term Corporate Bonds	Long-Term Government Bonds	U.S. Treasury Bills	Inflation
Average return	18.0%	11.8%	6.4%	6.1%	3.6%	3.1%
Standard deviation	38.9	20.3	8.4	9.8	3.1	4.2
Excess return over T-bonds[a]	11.9	5.7	0.3			

[a]The excess return over T-bonds is called the "historical risk premium." This excess return will also be the current risk premium that is reflected in security prices if and only if investors expect returns in the future to be similar to returns earned in the past.

Source: Based on *Stocks, Bonds, Bills, and Inflation: Valuation Edition 2012 Yearbook* (Chicago: Ibbotson Associates, 2012).

6-5 Risk in a Portfolio Context

Most financial assets are actually held as parts of portfolios. Banks, pension funds, insurance companies, mutual funds, and other financial institutions are required by law to hold diversified portfolios. Even individual investors—at least those whose security holdings constitute a significant part of their total wealth—generally hold portfolios, not the stock of only one firm.

6-5a Creating a Portfolio

A portfolio is a collection of assets. The weight of an asset in a portfolio is the percentage of the portfolio's total value that is invested in the asset. For example, if you invest $1,000 in each of 10 stocks, your portfolio has a value of $10,000, and each stock has a weight of $1,000/$10,000 = 10%. If instead you invest $5,000 in 1 stock and $1,000 apiece in 5 stocks, the first stock has a weight of $5,000/$10,000 = 50%, and each of the other 5 stocks has a weight of 10%. Usually it is more convenient to talk about an asset's weight in a portfolio rather than the dollars invested in the asset. Therefore, when we create a portfolio, we choose a weight (or a percentage) for each asset, with the weights summing to 1.0 (or the percentages summing to 100%).

Suppose we have a portfolio of n stocks. The actual return on a portfolio in a particular period is the weighted average of the actual returns of the stocks in the portfolio, with w_i denoting the weight invested in Stock i:

$$\bar{r}_p = w_1\bar{r}_1 + w_2\bar{r}_2 + \cdots + w_n\bar{r}_n$$
$$= \sum_{i=1}^{n} w_i\bar{r}_i \tag{6-6}$$

The average portfolio return over a number of periods is also equal to the weighted average of the stock's average returns:

$$\bar{r}_{Avg,p} = \sum_{i=1}^{n} w_1\bar{r}_{Avg,i}$$

Recall from the previous section that SnailDrive had an average annualized return of 8.6% during the past 48 months and MicroDrive had a 14.6% return. A portfolio with 75% invested in SnailDrive and 25% in MicroDrive would have had the following return:

$$\bar{r}_{Avg,p} = 0.75(8.6\%) + 0.25(14.6\%) = 10.1\%$$

Notice that the portfolio return of 10.1% is between the returns of SnailDrive (8.6%) and MicroDrive (14.6%), as you would expect.

Suppose an investor with stock only in SnailDrive came to you for advice, saying "I would like more return, but I hate risk!" How do you think the investor would react if you suggested taking 25% of the investment in the low-risk SnailDrive (with a standard deviation of 25.8%) and putting it into the high-risk MicroDrive (with a standard deviation of 49.2%)? As shown above, the return during the 48 month period would have been 10.1%, well above the return on SnailDrive. But what would have happened to risk?

The file **Ch06 Tool Kit.xls** calculates the portfolio return for each month (using Equation 6-6) and calculates the portfolio's standard deviation by applying *Excel's* STDEV function to the portfolio's monthly returns. Imagine the investor's surprise in learning that the portfolio's standard deviation is 21.8%, *less than* that of SnailDrive's 25.8% standard deviation. In other words, adding a risky asset to a safer asset can reduce risk!

How can this happen? MicroDrive sells high-end memory storage whereas SnailDrive sells low-end memory, including reconditioned hard drives. When the economy is doing well, MicroDrive has high sales and profits, but SnailDrive's sales lag because customers prefer faster memory. But when times are tough, customers resort to SnailDrive for low-cost memory storage. Take a look at Figure 6-5. Notice that SnailDrive's returns don't move in perfect lockstep with MicroDrive: Sometimes MicroDrive goes up and SnailDrive goes down, and vice versa.

6-5b Correlation and Risk for a Two-Stock Portfolio

The tendency of two variables to move together is called **correlation**, and the **correlation coefficient** measures this tendency. The symbol for the correlation coefficient is the Greek letter rho, ρ (pronounced roe). The correlation coefficient can range from +1.0, denoting that the two variables move up and down in perfect synchronization, to −1.0, denoting that the variables always move in exactly opposite directions. A correlation coefficient of zero indicates that the two variables are not related to each other at all—that is, changes in one variable are independent of changes in the other.

The estimate of correlation from a sample of historical data is often called "R." Here is the formula to estimate the correlation between stocks i and j ($\bar{r}_{i,t}$ is the actual return for Stock i in period t, and $\bar{r}_{i,Avg}$ is the average return during the T-period sample; similar notation is used for stock j):

$$\text{Estimated } \rho = R = \frac{\sum_{t=1}^{T}(\bar{r}_{i,t} - \bar{r}_{i,Avg})(\bar{r}_{j,t} - \bar{r}_{j,Avg})}{\sqrt{\left[\sum_{t=1}^{T}(\bar{r}_{i,t} - \bar{r}_{i,Avg})^2\right]\left[\sum_{t=1}^{T}(\bar{r}_{j,t} - \bar{r}_{j,Avg})^2\right]}} \tag{6-7}$$

Fortunately, it is easy to estimate the correlation coefficient with a financial calculator or *Excel*. With a calculator, simply enter the returns of the two stocks and then press a key labeled "r."[7] In *Excel*, use the CORREL function. See ***Ch06 Tool Kit.xls,*** where we calculate the correlation between the returns of MicroDrive and SnailDrive to be −0.10. The negative correlation means that when SnailDrive is having a poor return, MicroDrive tends to have a good return; when SnailDrive is having a good return, MicroDrive tends to have a poor return. In other words, adding some of MicroDrive's stock to a portfolio that only had SnailDrive's stock tends to reduce the volatility of the portfolio.

Here is a way to think about the possible benefit of diversification: *If a portfolio's standard deviation is less than the weighted average of the individual stocks' standard deviations, then diversification provides a benefit.* Does diversification always reduce risk? If so, by how much? And how does correlation affect diversification? Let's consider the full range of correlation coefficients, from −1 to +1.

If two stocks have a correlation of −1 (the lowest possible correlation), when one stock has a higher than expected return then the other stock has a lower than expected return, and vice versa. In fact, it would be possible to choose weights such that one stock's deviations from its mean return completely cancel out the other stock's deviations from its mean return.[8] Such a portfolio would have a zero standard deviation but would have an expected return equal to the weighted average of the stock's expected returns. In this situation, diversification can eliminate all risk: *For correlation of −1, the portfolio's standard deviation can be as low as zero if the portfolio weights are chosen appropriately.*

If the correlation were +1 (the highest possible correlation), the portfolio's standard deviation would be the weighted average of the stock's standard deviations. In this case, diversification doesn't help: *For correlation of +1, the portfolio's standard deviation is the weighted average of the stocks' standard deviations.*

For any other correlation, diversification reduces, but cannot eliminate, risk: *For correlation between −1 and +1, the portfolio's standard deviation is less than the weighted average of the stocks' standard deviations.*

---

[7]See your calculator manual for the exact steps. Also, note that the correlation coefficient is often denoted by the term "r." We use ρ here to avoid confusion with r, which is used to denote the rate of return.

[8]If the correlation between stocks 1 and 2 is equal to −1, then the weights for a zero-risk portfolio are $w_1 = \sigma_1/(\sigma_1 + \sigma_2)$ and $w_2 = \sigma_2/(\sigma_1 + \sigma_2)$.

The correlation between most pairs of companies is in the range of 0.2 to 0.3, so diversification reduces risk, but it doesn't completely eliminate risk.[9]

6-5c Diversification and Multi-Stock Portfolios

Figure 6-6 shows how portfolio risk is affected by forming larger and larger portfolios of randomly selected New York Stock Exchange (NYSE) stocks. Standard deviations are plotted for an average one-stock portfolio, an average two-stock portfolio, and so on, up to a portfolio consisting of all 2,000-plus common stocks that were listed on the NYSE at the time the data were plotted. The graph illustrates that, in general, the risk of a portfolio consisting of large-company stocks tends to decline and to approach some limit as the size of the portfolio increases. According to data from recent years, σ_1, the standard deviation of a one-stock portfolio (or an average stock), is approximately 35%. However, a portfolio consisting of all stocks, which is called the **market portfolio**, would have a standard deviation, σ_M, of only about 20%, which is shown as the horizontal dashed line in Figure 6-6.

Thus, *almost half of the risk inherent in an average individual stock can be eliminated if the stock is held in a reasonably well-diversified portfolio, which is one containing 40 or more stocks in a number of different industries.* The part of a stock's risk that *cannot* be eliminated is called *market risk,* while the part that *can* be eliminated is called *diversifiable risk.*[10] The fact that a large part of the risk of any individual stock can be eliminated is vitally important, because rational investors *will* eliminate it simply by holding many stocks in their portfolios and thus render it irrelevant.

Market risk stems from factors that systematically affect most firms: war, inflation, recessions, and high interest rates. Because most stocks are affected by these factors, market risk cannot be eliminated by diversification. **Diversifiable risk** is caused by such random events as lawsuits, strikes, successful and unsuccessful marketing programs, winning or losing a major contract, and other events that are unique to a particular firm. Because these events are random, their effects on a portfolio can be eliminated by diversification—bad events in one firm will be offset by good events in another.

SELF-TEST

Explain the following statement: "An asset held as part of a portfolio is generally less risky than the same asset held in isolation."

What is meant by perfect positive correlation, perfect negative correlation, *and* zero correlation?

In general, can the risk of a portfolio be reduced to zero by increasing the number of stocks in the portfolio? Explain.

---

[9]During the period 1968–1998, the average correlation coefficient between two randomly selected stocks was 0.28, while the average correlation coefficient between two large-company stocks was 0.33; see Louis K. C. Chan, Jason Karceski, and Josef Lakonishok, "On Portfolio Optimization: Forecasting Covariance and Choosing the Risk Model," *The Review of Financial Studies,* Vol. 12, No. 5, Winter 1999, pp. 937–974. The average correlation fell from around 0.35 in the late 1970s to less than 0.10 by the late 1990s; see John Y. Campbell, Martin Lettau, Burton G. Malkiel, and Yexiao Xu, "Have Individual Stocks Become More Volatile? An Empirical Exploration of Idiosyncratic Risk," *Journal of Finance,* February 2001, pp. 1–43.

[10]Diversifiable risk is also known as *company-specific risk* or *unsystematic risk.* Market risk is also known as *nondiversifiable risk* or *systematic risk;* it is the risk that remains after diversification.

FIGURE 6-6

Effects of Portfolio Size on Portfolio Risk for Average Stocks

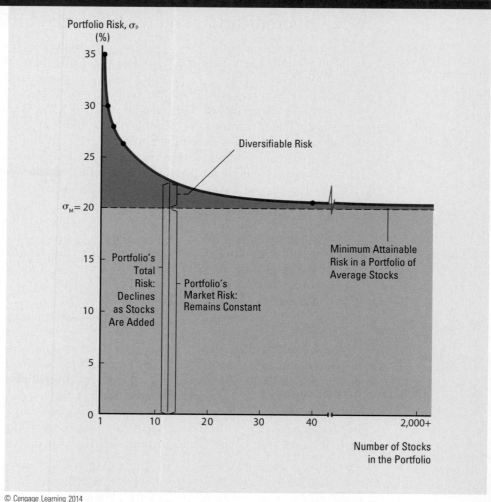

© Cengage Learning 2014

6-6 The Relevant Risk of a Stock: The Capital Asset Pricing Model (CAPM)

We assume that investors are risk averse and demand a premium for bearing risk; that is, the higher the risk of a security, the higher its expected return must be to induce investors to buy it or to hold it. All risk except that related to broad market movements can, and presumably will, be diversified away. After all, why accept risk that can be eliminated easily? This implies that investors are primarily concerned with the risk of their *portfolios* rather than the risk of the individual securities in the portfolio. How, then, should the risk of an individual stock be measured?

The **Capital Asset Pricing Model (CAPM)** provides one answer to that question. A stock might be quite risky if held by itself, but—because diversification eliminates about half of its risk—the stock's **relevant risk** is its *contribution to a well-diversified portfolio's risk,* which is much smaller than the stock's stand-alone risk.[11]

---

[11]Nobel Prizes were awarded to the developers of the CAPM, Professors Harry Markowitz and William F. Sharpe.

6-6a Contribution to Market Risk: Beta

A well-diversified portfolio has only market risk. Therefore, the CAPM defines the relevant risk of an individual stock as the amount of risk that the stock contributes to the market portfolio, which is a portfolio containing all stocks.[12] In CAPM terminology, ρ_{iM} is the correlation between Stock i's return and the market return, σ_i is the standard deviation of Stock i's return, and σ_M is the standard deviation of the market's return. The relevant measure of risk is called **beta**. The beta of Stock i, denoted by b_i, is calculated as:

$$b_i = \left(\frac{\sigma_i}{\sigma_M} \right) \rho_{iM} \qquad (6\text{-}8)$$

This formula shows that a stock with a high standard deviation, σ_i, will tend to have a high beta, which means that, other things held constant, the stock contributes a lot of risk to a well-diversified portfolio. This makes sense, because a stock with high stand-alone risk will tend to destabilize a portfolio. Note too that a stock with a high correlation with the market, ρ_{iM}, will also tend to have a large beta and hence be risky. This also makes sense, because a high correlation means that diversification is not helping much, with the stock performing well when the portfolio is also performing well, and the stock performing poorly when the portfolio is also performing poorly.

Suppose a stock has a beta of 1.4. What does that mean? To answer that question, we begin with an important fact: The beta of a portfolio, b_p, is the weighted average of the betas of the stocks in the portfolio, with the weights equal to the same weights used to create the portfolio. This can be written as:

$$b_p = w_1 b_1 + w_2 b_2 + \cdots + w_n b_n$$
$$= \sum_{i=1}^{n} w_i b_i \qquad (6\text{-}9)$$

For example, suppose an investor owns a $100,000 portfolio consisting of $25,000 invested in each of four stocks; the stocks have betas of 0.6, 1.2, 1.2, and 1.4. The weight of each stock in the portfolio is $25,000/$100,000 = 25%. The portfolio's beta will be $b_p = 1.1$:

$$b_p = 25\%(0.6) + 25\%(1.2) + 25\%(1.2) + 25\%(1.4) = 1.1$$

The second important fact is that the standard deviation of a well-diversified portfolio, σ_p, is approximately equal to the product of the portfolio's beta and the market standard deviation:

$$\sigma_p = b_p \sigma_M \qquad (6\text{-}10)$$

Equation 6-10 shows that (1) a portfolio with a beta greater than 1 will have a bigger standard deviation than the market portfolio; (2) a portfolio with a beta equal to 1 will have the same standard deviation as the market; and (3) a portfolio with a beta less than 1 will have a smaller standard deviation than the market. For example, suppose the market

---

[12]In theory, the market portfolio should contain all assets. In practice, it usually contains only stocks. Many analysts use returns on the S&P 500 Index to estimate the market return.

standard deviation is 20%. Using Equation 6-10, a well-diversified portfolio with a beta of 1.1 will have a standard deviation of 22%:

$$\sigma_p = 1.1(20\%) = 22\%$$

By substituting Equation 6-9 into 6-10, we can see the impact that each individual stock beta has on the risk of a well-diversified portfolio:

$$\sigma_p = (w_1 b_1 + w_2 b_2 + \cdots + w_n b_n)\sigma_M$$

$$= \sum_{i=1}^{n} w_i b_i \sigma_M$$

(6-11)

A well-diversified portfolio would have more than 4 stocks, but for the sake of simplicity suppose that the 4-stock portfolio in the previous example is well diversified. If that is the case, then Figure 6-7 shows how much risk each stock contributes to the portfolio.[13] Out of the total 22% standard deviation of the portfolio, Stock 1 contributes $w_1 b_1 \sigma_M$ = (25%)(0.6)(20%) = 3%. Stocks 2 and 3 have betas that are twice as big as Stock 1's beta, so Stock's 2 and 3 contribute twice as much risk as Stock 1. Stock 4 has the largest beta, and it contributes the most risk.

FIGURE 6-7

The Contribution of Individual Stocks to Portfolio Risk: The Effect of Beta

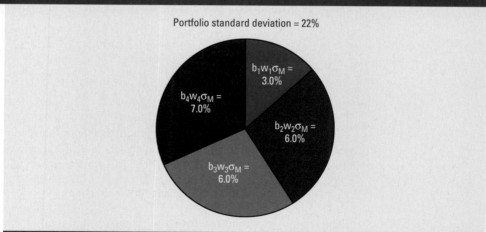

Portfolio standard deviation = 22%

$b_1 w_1 \sigma_M$ = 3.0%

$b_4 w_4 \sigma_M$ = 7.0%

$b_2 w_2 \sigma_M$ = 6.0%

$b_3 w_3 \sigma_M$ = 6.0%

Market standard deviation = σ_M = 20%

	Stock Beta: b_i	Weight in Portfolio: w_i	Contribution to Portfolio Beta: $b_i \times w_i$	Contribution to Portfolio Risk: $b_i \times w_i \times \sigma_M$
Stock 1	0.6	25.0%	0.150	3.0%
Stock 2	1.2	25.0%	0.300	6.0%
Stock 3	1.2	25.0%	0.300	6.0%
Stock 4	1.4	25.0%	0.350	7.0%
			b_p =1.100	σ_p = 22.0%

© Cengage Learning 2014

[13]If the portfolio isn't well diversified, then $b_p \sigma_M$ measures the amount of market risk in the portfolio, and $b_p w_i \sigma_M$ measures the amount of market risk that stock i contributes to the portfolio.

We demonstrate how to estimate beta in the next section, but here are some key points about beta. (1) Beta measures how much risk a stock contributes to a well-diversified portfolio. If all the stocks' weights in a portfolio are equal, then a stock with a beta that is twice as big as another stock's beta contributes twice as much risk. (2) The average of all stocks' betas is equal to 1; the beta of the market also is equal to 1. Intuitively, this is because the market return is the average of all the stocks' returns. (3) A stock with a beta greater than 1 contributes more risk to a portfolio than does the average stock, and a stock with a beta less than 1 contributes less risk to a portfolio than does the average stock. (4) Most stocks have betas that are between about 0.4 and 1.6.

6-6b Estimating Beta

The CAPM is an *ex ante* model, which means that all of the variables represent before-the-fact, *expected* values. In particular, the beta coefficient used by investors should reflect the relationship between a stock's expected return and the market's expected return during some *future* period. However, people generally calculate betas using data from some *past* period and then assume that the stock's risk will be the same in the future as it was in the past.

Most analysts use 4 to 5 years of monthly data, although some use 52 weeks of weekly data. Using the 4 years of monthly returns from *Ch06 Tool Kit.xls,* we can calculate the betas of MicroDrive and SnailDrive using Equation 6-8:

	Market	MicroDrive	SnailDrive
Standard deviation (annual):	20.0%	49.2%	25.8%
Correlation with the market:		0.582	0.465
$b_i = \rho_{iM}(\sigma_i/\sigma_M)$		1.43	0.60

Table 6-1 shows the betas for some well-known companies as provided by two different financial organizations, Value Line and Yahoo!Finance. Notice that their estimates of beta usually differ because they calculate it in slightly different ways. Given these differences, many analysts choose to calculate their own betas or else average the published betas.

Calculators and spreadsheets can calculate the components of Equation 6-8 (ρ_{iM}, σ_i, and σ_M), which can then be used to calculate beta, but there is another way.[14] The **covariance between Stock i and the market, COV$_{iM}$, is defined as**[15]

$$COV_{iM} = \rho_{iM}\sigma_i\sigma_M \qquad (6\text{-}12)$$

---

[14]For an explanation of computing beta with a financial calculator, see *Web Extension 6B* on the textbook's Web site.
[15]Using historical data, the sample covariance can be calculated as

$$\text{Sample covariance from historical data} = COV_{iM} = \frac{\sum_{t=1}^{T}(\bar{r}_{i,t} - \bar{r}_{i,Avg})(\bar{r}_{M,t} - \bar{r}_{M,Avg})}{n-1}$$

Calculating the covariance is somewhat easier than calculating the correlation. So if you have already calculated the standard deviations, it is easier to calculate the covariance and then calculate the correlation as $\rho_{iM} = COV_{iM}/(\sigma_i\sigma_M)$.

W W W

To see updated estimates, go to **www.valueline.com** and enter the ticker symbol. Or go to **http://finance .yahoo.com** and enter the ticker symbol. When the results page comes up, select Key Statistics from the left panel to find beta.

TABLE 6-1

Beta Coefficients for Some Actual Companies

Stock (Ticker Symbol)	Value Line	Yahoo! Finance
Amazon.com (AMZN)	1.05	0.69
Apple (AAPL)	1.05	1.00
Coca-Cola (KO)	0.60	0.42
Empire District Electric (EDE)	0.70	0.37
Energen Corp. (EGN)	1.15	1.26
General Electric (GE)	1.20	1.67
Google (GOOG)	0.90	1.19
Heinz (HNZ)	0.65	0.41
Microsoft Corp. (MSFT)	0.85	1.00
Procter &Gamble (PG)	0.60	0.35

Sources: **www.valueline.com** and **http://finance.yahoo.com**, April 2012.

Substituting Equation 6-12 into 6-8 provides another frequently used expression for calculating beta:

$$b_i = \frac{COV_{iM}}{\sigma_M^2} \qquad (6\text{-}13)$$

Suppose you plotted the stock's returns on the y-axis of a graph and the market portfolio's returns on the x-axis. The formula for the slope of a regression line is exactly equal to the formula for beta in Equation 6-13. Therefore, to estimate beta for a security, you can estimate a regression with the stock's returns on the y-axis and the market's returns on the x-axis. Figure 6-8 illustrates this approach. The blue dots represent each of the 48 data points, with the stock's returns on the y-axis and the market's returns on the x-axis. For reference purposes, the thick black line shows the plot of market versus market. Notice that MicroDrive's returns are generally above the market's returns (the black line) when the market is doing well but below the market when the market is doing poorly, suggesting that MicroDrive is risky.

We used the Trendline feature in *Excel* to show the regression equation and R^2 on the chart (these are colored red): MicroDrive has an estimated beta of 1.43, the same as we calculated earlier using Equation 6-8. It is also possible to use *Excel's* **SLOPE** function to estimate the slope from a regression: **=SLOPE(known_y's,known_x's)**. The **SLOPE** function is more convenient if you are going to calculate betas for many different companies; see *Ch06 Tool Kit.xls* for more details.

6-6c Interpreting the Estimated Beta

First, always keep in mind that beta cannot be observed, it can only be estimated. The R^2 value shown in the chart measures the degree of dispersion about the regression line. Statistically speaking, it measures the percentage of the variance that is explained by the regression equation. An R^2 of 1.0 indicates that all points lie exactly on the regression line

FIGURE **6-8**

Stock Returns of MicroDrive and the Market: Estimating Beta

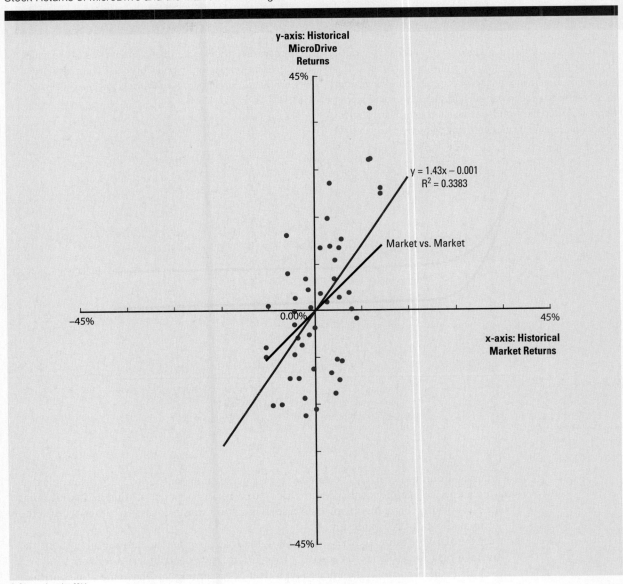

© Cengage Learning 2014

and hence that all of the variations in the y-variable are explained by the x-variable. MicroDrive's R^2 is about 0.34, which is similar to the typical stock's R^2 of 0.32. This indicates that about 34% of the variance in MicroDrive's returns is explained by the market return; in other words, much of MicroDrive's volatility is due to factors other than market gyrations. If we had done a similar analysis for a portfolio of 40 randomly selected stocks, then the points would probably have been clustered tightly around the regression line and the R^2 probably would have exceeded 0.90. Almost 100% of a well-diversified portfolio's volatility is explained by the market.

Ch06 Tool Kit.xls demonstrates how to use the *Excel* function LINEST to calculate the confidence interval for MicroDrive's estimated beta and shows that the 95% confidence

The Benefits of Diversifying Overseas

© Rob Webb/Getty Images

Figure 6-6 shows that an investor can significantly reduce portfolio risk by holding a large number of stocks. The figure accompanying this box suggests that investors may be able to reduce risk even further by holding stocks from all around the world, because the returns on domestic and international stocks are not perfectly correlated.

Sources: For further reading, see Kenneth Kasa, "Measuring the Gains from International Portfolio Diversification," *Federal Reserve Bank of San Francisco Weekly Letter,* no. 94–14 (April 8, 1994).

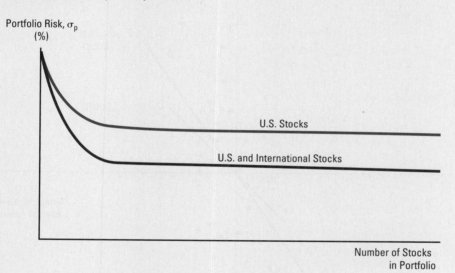

Portfolio Risk, σ_p (%)

U.S. Stocks

U.S. and International Stocks

Number of Stocks in Portfolio

© Cengage Learning 2014

interval around MicroDrive's estimated beta ranges from about 0.7 to 2.2. This means that we can be 95% confident that MicroDrive's true beta is between 0.7 and 2.2. Notice that this is a fairly big range, which is also typical for most stocks. In other words, the estimated beta truly is an estimate!

MicroDrive's estimated beta is about 1.4. What does that mean? By definition, the average beta for all stocks is equal to 1, so MicroDrive contributes 40% more risk to a well-diversified portfolio than does a typical stock (assuming they have the same portfolio weight). Notice also from Figure 6-8 that the slope of the estimated line is about 1.4, which is steeper than a slope of 1. When the market is doing well, a high beta stock like MicroDrive tends to do better than an average stock, and when the market does poorly, a high beta stock also does worse than an average stock. The opposite is true for a low beta stock: When the market soars, the low beta stock tends to go up by a smaller amount; when the market falls, the low beta stock tends to fall less than the market.

Finally, observe that the intercept shown in the regression equation on the chart is −0.001. This is a monthly return; the annualized value is 12(−0.1%) = −1.2%. This indicates that MicroDrive lost about 1.2% per year as a result of factors other than general market movements.

For more on calculating beta, take a look at *Ch06 Tool Kit.xls,* which shows how to download data for an actual company and calculate its beta.

What is the average beta? If a stock has a beta of 0.8, what does that imply about its risk relative to the market?

Why is beta the theoretically correct measure of a stock's risk?

If you plotted the returns on a particular stock versus those on the S&P 500 Index over the past five years, what would the slope of the regression line tell you about the stock's market risk?

What types of data are needed to calculate a beta coefficient for an actual company?

What does the R^2 measure? What is the R^2 for a typical company?

An investor has a three-stock portfolio with $25,000 invested in Dell, $50,000 invested in Ford, and $25,000 invested in Walmart. Dell's beta is estimated to be 1.20, Ford's beta is estimated to be 0.80, and Walmart's beta is estimated to be 1.0. What is the estimated beta of the investor's portfolio? **(0.95)**

6-7 The Relationship between Risk and Return in the Capital Asset Pricing Model

In the preceding section we saw that beta measures a stock's contribution to the risk of a well-diversified portfolio. The CAPM assumes that the marginal investors (i.e., the investors with enough cash to move market prices) hold well-diversified portfolios. Therefore, beta is the proper measure of a stock's relevant risk. However, we need to quantify how risk affects required returns: For a given level of risk as measured by beta, what rate of expected return do investors require to compensate them for bearing that risk? To begin, we define the following terms.

$\hat{r}_i$ = *Expected* rate of return on Stock i.

r_i = *Required* rate of return on Stock i. This is the minimum expected return that is required to induce an average investor to purchase the stock.

$\bar{r}$ = Realized, after-the-fact return.

r_{RF} = Risk-free rate of return. In this context, r_{RF} is generally measured by the expected return on long-term U.S. Treasury bonds.

b_i = Beta coefficient of Stock i.

r_M = Required rate of return on a portfolio consisting of all stocks, which is called the *market portfolio*.

RP_i = Risk premium on Stock i: $RP_i = b_i (RP_M)$.

RP_M = Risk premium on "the market." $RP_M = (r_M - r_{RF})$ is the additional return over the risk-free rate required to induce an average investor to invest in the market portfolio.

6-7a The Security Market Line (SML)

In general, we can conceptualize the required return on an individual stock as the risk-free rate plus the extra return (i.e., the risk premium) needed to induce the investor to hold the stock. The CAPM's **Security Market Line (SML)** formalizes this general concept by showing that a stock's risk premium is equal to the product of the stock's beta and the market risk premium:

$$\text{Required return on Stock i} = \text{Risk-free rate} + \begin{pmatrix} \text{Risk premium} \\ \text{for stock i} \end{pmatrix}$$

$$\text{Required return on Stock i} = \text{Risk-free rate} + \begin{pmatrix} \text{Beta of} \\ \text{stock i} \end{pmatrix}\begin{pmatrix} \text{Market risk} \\ \text{premium} \end{pmatrix} \qquad \text{(6-14)}$$

$$r_i = r_{RF} + b_i(RP_M)$$

$$= r_{RF} + (r_M - r_{RF})b_i$$

Let's take a look at the three components of required return (the risk-free rate, the market risk premium, and beta) to see how they interact in determining a stock's required return.

The Risk-Free Rate

Notice that a stock's required return begins with the risk-free rate. To induce an investor to take on a risky investment, the investor will need a return that is at least as big as the risk-free rate. The yield on long-term Treasury bonds is often used to measure the risk-free rate.

The Market Risk Premium

The **market risk premium, RP_M**, is the extra rate of return that investors require to invest in the stock market rather than purchase risk-free securities. The size of the market risk premium depends on the degree of risk aversion that investors have on average. When investors are very risk averse, the market risk premium is high; when investors are less concerned about risk, the market risk premium is low. For example, suppose that investors (on average) need an extra return of 5% before they will take on the stock market's risk. If Treasury bonds yield $r_{RF} = 6\%$, then the required return on the market, r_M, is 11%:

$$r_M = r_{RF} + RP_M = 6\% + 5\% = 11\%$$

If we had instead begun with an estimate of the required market return (perhaps through scenario analysis similar to the example in Section 6-2), then we can find the implied market risk premium. For example, if the required market return is estimated as 11%, then the market risk premium is:

$$RP_M = r_M - r_{RF} = 11\% - 6\% = 5\%$$

We discuss the market risk premium in detail in Chapter 9, but for now you should know now that a most analysts use a market risk premium in the range of 4% to 7%.

The Risk Premium for an Individual Stock

The CAPM shows that the **risk premium for an individual stock, RP_i**, is equal to the product of the stock's beta and the market risk premium:

$$\text{Risk premium for Stock i} = RP_i = b_i(RP_M) \qquad \text{(6-15)}$$

For example, consider a low-risk stock with $b_L = 0.5$. If the market risk premium is 5%, then the risk premium for the stock (RP_L) is 2.5%:

$$RP_L = (5\%)(0.5)$$
$$= 2.5\%$$

Using the SML in Equation 6-14, the required return for our illustrative low-risk stock is then found as follows:

$$r_L = 6\% + 5\%(0.5)$$
$$= 8.5\%$$

If a high-risk stock has $b_H = 2.0$, then its required rate of return is 16%:

$$r_H = 6\% + (5\%)2.0 = 16\%$$

An average stock, with $b_A = 1.0$, has a required return of 11%, the same as the market return:

$$r_A = 6\% + (5\%)1.0 = 11\% = r_M$$

Figure 6-9 shows the SML when $r_{RF} = 6\%$ and $RP_M = 5\%$. Note the following points:

1. Required rates of return are shown on the vertical axis, while risk as measured by beta is shown on the horizontal axis. This graph is quite different from the regression line shown in Figure 6-8, where the returns on individual stocks were plotted on the vertical axis and returns on the market index were shown on the horizontal axis. For the SML in Figure 6-9, the slope of the regression line from an analysis such as that conducted in Figure 6-8 is plotted as beta on the horizontal axis of Figure 6-9.
2. Riskless securities have $b_i = 0$; therefore, r_{RF} appears as the vertical axis intercept in Figure 6-9. If we could construct a portfolio that had a beta of zero, then it would have a required return equal to the risk-free rate.
3. The slope of the SML (5% in Figure 6-9) reflects the degree of risk aversion in the economy: The greater the average investor's aversion to risk, then (a) the steeper the slope of the line, (b) the greater the risk premium for all stocks, and (c) the higher the required rate of return on all stocks.[16]

6-7b The Impact on Required Return Due to Changes in the Risk-Free Rate, Risk Aversion, and Beta

The required return depends on the risk-free rate, the market risk premium, and the stock's beta. The following sections illustrate the impact of changes in these inputs.

THE IMPACT OF CHANGES IN THE RISK-FREE RATE

Suppose that some combination of an increase in real interest rates and in anticipated inflation causes the risk-free interest rate to increase from 6% to 8%. Such a change is

---

[16]Students sometimes confuse beta with the slope of the SML. The slope of any straight line is equal to the "rise" divided by the "run," or $(Y_1 - Y_0)/(X_1 - X_0)$. Consider Figure 6-9. If we let $Y = r$ and $X = $ beta and if we go from the origin to $b = 1.0$, then we see that the slope is $(r_M - r_{RF})/(b_M - b_{RF}) = (11\% - 6\%)/(1 - 0) = 5\%$. Thus, the slope of the SML is equal to $(r_M - r_{RF})$, the market risk premium. In Figure 6-9, $r_i = 6\% + 5\%(b_i)$, so an increase of beta from 1.0 to 2.0 would produce a 5-percentage-point increase in r_i.

FIGURE 6-9

The Security Market Line (SML)

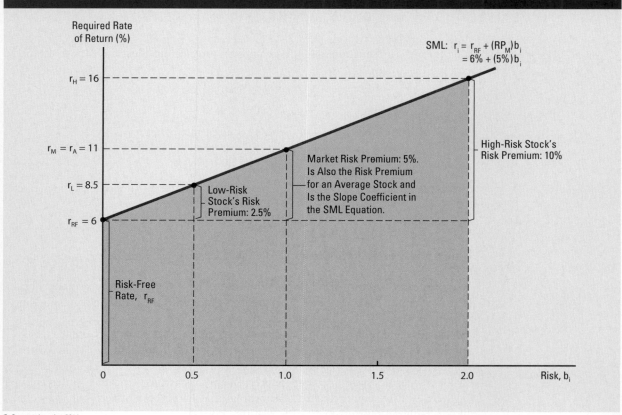

© Cengage Learning 2014

shown in Figure 6-10. A key point to note is that a change in r_{RF} will not necessarily cause a change in the market risk premium. Thus, as r_{RF} changes, so will the required return on the market, and this will, other things held constant, keep the market risk premium stable.[17] Notice that, under the CAPM, the increase in r_{RF} leads to an *identical* increase in the rate of return on all assets, because the same risk-free rate is built into the required rate of return on all assets. For example, the required rate of return on the market (and the average stock), r_M, increases from 11% to 13%. Other risky securities' returns also rise by 2 percentage points.

CHANGES IN RISK AVERSION

The slope of the Security Market Line reflects the extent to which investors are averse to risk: The steeper the slope of the line, the greater the average investor's aversion to risk. Suppose all investors were indifferent to risk—that is, suppose they were *not* risk averse.

---

[17]Think of a sailboat floating in a harbor. The distance from the ocean floor to the ocean surface is like the risk-free rate, and it moves up and down with the tides. The distance from the top of the ship's mast to the ocean floor is like the required market return: It too moves up and down with the tides. The distance from the mast-top to the ocean surface is like the market risk premium—it stays the same, even though tides move the ship up and down. Thus, other things held constant, a change in the risk-free rate also causes an identical change in the required market return, r_M, resulting in a relatively stable market risk premium, $r_M - r_{RF}$.

FIGURE **6-10**

Shift in the SML Caused by an Increase in the Risk-Free Rate

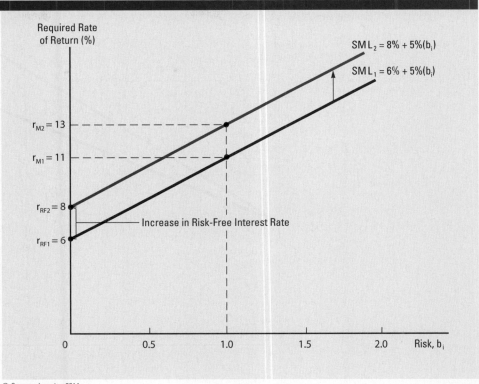

© Cengage Learning 2014

If r_{RF} were 6%, then risky assets would also provide an expected return of 6%, because if there were no risk aversion then there would be no risk premium, and the SML would be plotted as a horizontal line. As risk aversion increases, so does the risk premium, and this causes the slope of the SML to become steeper.

Figure 6-11 illustrates an increase in risk aversion. The market risk premium rises from 5% to 7.5%, causing r_M to rise from $r_{M1} = 11\%$ to $r_{M2} = 13.5\%$. The returns on other risky assets also rise, and the effect of this shift in risk aversion is greater for riskier securities. For example, the required return on a stock with $b_i = 0.5$ increases by only 1.25 percentage points, from 8.5% to 9.75%; that on a stock with $b_i = 1.0$ increases by 2.5 percentage points, from 11.0% to 13.5%; and that on a stock with $b_i = 1.5$ increases by 3.75 percentage points, from 13.5% to 17.25%.

CHANGES IN A STOCK'S BETA COEFFICIENT

Given risk aversion and a positively sloped SML as in Figure 6-9, the higher a stock's beta, the higher its required rate of return. As we shall see later in the book, a firm can influence its beta through changes in the composition of its assets and also through its use of debt: Acquiring riskier assets will increase beta, as will a change in capital structure that calls for a higher debt ratio. A company's beta can also change as a result of external factors such as increased competition in its industry, the expiration of basic patents, and the like. When such changes lead to a higher or lower beta, the required rate of return will also change.

FIGURE **6-11**

Shift in the SML Caused by Increased Risk Aversion

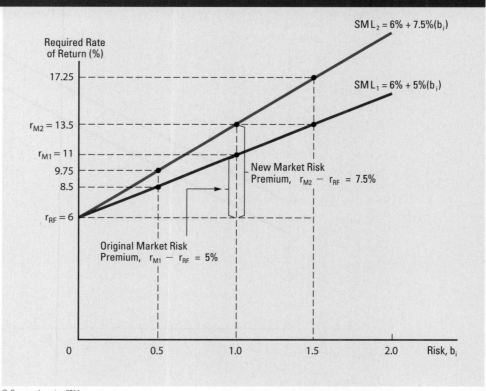

© Cengage Learning 2014

6-7c Portfolio Returns and Portfolio Performance Evaluation

The **expected return on a portfolio, $\hat{r}_p$,** is the weighted average of the expected returns on the individual assets in the portfolio. Suppose there are n stocks in the portfolio and the expected return on Stock i is $\hat{r}_i$. The expected return on the portfolio is

$$\hat{r}_p = \sum_{i=1}^{n} w_i \hat{r}_i \qquad (6\text{-}16)$$

The **required return on a portfolio, r_p,** is the weighted average of the required returns on the individual assets in the portfolio:

$$r_p = \sum_{i=1}^{n} w_i r_i \qquad (6\text{-}17)$$

We can also express the required return on a portfolio in terms of the portfolio's beta:

$$r_p = r_{RF} + b_p RP_M$$

(6-18)

Equation 6-18 means that we do not have to estimate the beta for a portfolio if we have already estimated the betas for the individual stocks. All we have to do is calculate the portfolio beta as the weighted average of the stock's betas (see Equation 6-9) and then apply Equation 6-18.

This is particularly helpful when evaluating portfolio managers. For example, suppose the stock market has a return for the year of 9% and a particular mutual fund has a 10% return. Did the portfolio manager do a good job or not? The answer depends on how much risk the fund has. If the fund's beta is 2, then the fund should have had a much higher return than the market, which means the manager did not do well. The key is to evaluate the portfolio manager's return against the return the manager should have made given the risk of the investments.

6-7d Required Returns versus Expected Returns: Market Equilibrium

We explained in Chapter 1 that managers should seek to maximize the value of their firms' stocks. We also emphasized the difference between the market price and intrinsic value. Intrinsic value incorporates all *relevant available* information about expected cash flows and risk. This includes information about the company, the economic environment, and the political environment. In contrast to intrinsic value, market prices are based on investors' *selection and interpretation* of information. To the extent that investors don't select all relevant information and don't interpret it correctly, market prices can deviate from intrinsic values. Figure 6-12 illustrates this relationship between market prices and intrinsic value.

When market prices deviate from their intrinsic values, astute investors have profitable opportunities. For example, recall from Chapter 5 that the value of a bond is the present value of its cash flows when discounted at the bond's required return, which reflects the bond's risk. This is the intrinsic value of the bond because it incorporates all relevant available information. Notice that the intrinsic value is "fair" in the sense that it incorporates the bond's risk and investors' required returns for bearing the risk.

What would happen if a bond's market price were lower than its intrinsic value? In this situation, an investor could purchase the bond and receive a rate of return in excess of the required return. In other words, the investor would get more compensation than justified by the bond's risk. If all investors felt this way, then demand for the bond would soar as investors tried to purchase it, driving the bond's price up. But recall from Chapter 5 that as the price of a bond goes up, its yield goes down. This means that an increase in price would reduce the subsequent return for an investor purchasing (or holding) the bond at the new price.[18] It seems reasonable to expect that investors' actions would continue to drive the price up until the expected return on the bond equaled its required return. After that point, the bond would provide just enough return to compensate its owner for the bond's risk.

---

[18]The original owner of the bond when it was priced too low would reap a nice benefit as the price climbs, but the subsequent purchasers would only receive the now-lower yield.

FIGURE 6-12

Determinants of Intrinsic Values and Market Prices

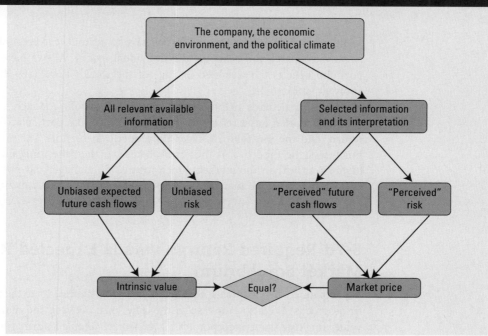

© Cengage Learning 2014

If the bond's price were too high compared to its intrinsic value, then investors would sell the bond, causing its price to fall and its yield to increase until its expected return equaled its required return.

A stock's future cash flows aren't as predictable as a bond's, but we show in the next chapter that a stock's intrinsic value is the present value of its expected future cash flows, just as a bond's intrinsic value is the present value of its cash flows. If the price of a stock is lower than its intrinsic value, then an investor would receive an expected return greater than the return required as compensation for risk. The same market forces we described for a mispriced bond would drive the mispriced stock's price up. If this process continues until its expected return equals it required return, then we say that there is **market equilibrium:**

Market equilibrium: Expected return = Required return

$$\hat{r} = r$$

We can also express market equilibrium in terms of prices:

Market equilibrium: Market price = Intrinsic value

New information about the risk-free rate, the market's degree of risk aversion, or a stock's expected cash flows (size, timing, or risk) will cause a stock's price to change. But other than periods in which prices are adjusting to new information, is the market usually in equilibrium? We address that question in the next section.

Another Kind of Risk: The Bernie Madoff Story

© Rob Webb/Getty Images

In the fall of 2008, Bernard Madoff's massive Ponzi scheme was exposed, revealing an important type of risk that's not dealt with in this chapter. Madoff was a money manager in the 1960s, and apparently through good luck he produced above-average results for several years. Madoff's clients then told their friends about his success, and those friends sent in money for him to invest. Madoff's actual returns then dropped, but he didn't tell his clients that they were losing money. Rather, he told them that returns were holding up well, and he used new incoming money to pay dividends and meet withdrawal requests. The idea of using new money to pay off old investors is called a Ponzi scheme, named after Charles Ponzi, a Bostonian who set up the first widely publicized such scheme in the early 1900s.

Madoff perfected the system, ran his scheme for about 40 years, and attracted about $50 billion of investors' funds. His investors ranged from well-known billionaires to retirees who invested their entire life savings. His advertising was strictly word of mouth, and clients telling potential clients about the many wealthy and highly regarded people who invested with him certainly helped. All of his investors assumed that someone else had done the "due diligence" and found the operation to be clean. A few investors who actually did some due diligence were suspicious and didn't invest with him, but for the most part, people just blindly followed the others.

All Ponzi schemes crash when something occurs that causes some investors to seek to withdraw funds in amounts greater than the incoming funds from new investors. Someone tries to get out, can't do it, tells others who worry and try to get out too, and almost overnight the scam unravels. That happened to Madoff in 2008, when the stock market crash caused some of his investors to seek withdrawals and few new dollars were coming in. In the end, his investors lost billions; some lost their entire life savings, and several have committed suicide.

SELF-TEST

Differentiate among the expected rate of return ($\hat{r}$), the required rate of return (r), and the realized, after-the-fact return ($\bar{r}$) on a stock. Which must be larger to get you to buy the stock, $\hat{r}$ or r? Would $\hat{r}$, r, and $\bar{r}$ typically be the same or different for a given company at a given point in time?

What are the differences between the relative returns graph (the regression line in Figure 6-8), where "betas are made," and the SML graph (Figure 6-9), where "betas are used"? Discuss how the graphs are constructed and the information they convey.

What happens to the SML graph in Figure 6-9 when inflation increases or decreases?

What happens to the SML graph when risk aversion increases or decreases? What would the SML look like if investors were completely indifferent to risk—that is, had zero risk aversion?

How can a firm's managers influence market risk as reflected in beta?

A stock has a beta of 0.8. Assume that the risk-free rate is 5.5% and that the market risk premium is 6%. What is the stock's required rate of return? **(10.3%)**

6-8 The Efficient Markets Hypothesis

The **Efficient Markets Hypothesis (EMH)** asserts that (1) stocks are always in equilibrium and (2) it is impossible for an investor to "beat the market" and consistently earn a higher rate of return than is justified by the stock's risk. In other words, a stock's market price is always equal to its intrinsic value. To put it a little more precisely, suppose a stock's market price is equal to the stock's intrinsic value but new information arrives that changes the stock's intrinsic value. The EMH asserts that the market price will adjust to the new intrinsic value so quickly that there isn't time for an investor to receive the new information, evaluate the information, take a position in the stock before the market price changes, and then profit from the subsequent change in price.

Here are three points to consider. First, almost every stock is under considerable scrutiny. With 100,000 or so full-time, highly trained, professional analysts and traders each following about 30 of the roughly 3,000 actively traded stocks (analysts tend to specialize in a specific industry), there are an average of about 1,000 analysts following each stock. Second, financial institutions, pension funds, money management firms, and hedge funds have billions of dollars available for portfolio managers to use in taking advantage of mispriced stocks. Third, SEC disclosure requirements and electronic information networks cause new information about a stock to become available to all analysts virtually simultaneously and almost immediately. With so many analysts trying to take advantage of temporary mispricing due to new information, with so much money chasing the profits due to temporary mispricing, and with such widespread dispersal of information, a stock's market price should adjust quickly from its pre-news intrinsic value to its post-news intrinsic value, leaving only a very short amount of time that the stock is "mispriced" as it moves from one equilibrium price to another. That, in a nutshell, is the logic behind the efficient markets hypothesis.

The following sections discuss forms of the efficient markets hypothesis and empirical tests of the hypothesis.

6-8a Forms of the Efficient Markets Hypothesis

There are three forms of the efficient markets hypothesis, and each focuses on a different type of information availability.

WEAK-FORM EFFICIENCY

The **weak form** of the EMH asserts that all information contained in past price movements is fully reflected in current market prices. If this were true, then information about recent trends in stock prices would be of no use in selecting stocks—the fact that a stock has risen for the past three days, for example, would give us no useful clues as to what it will do today or tomorrow. In contrast, **technical analysts**, also called "chartists," believe that past trends or patterns in stock prices can be used to predict future stock prices.

To illustrate the arguments supporting weak-form efficiency, suppose that after studying the past history of the stock market, a technical analyst identifies the following historical pattern: If a stock has fallen for three consecutive days, its price rose by 10% (on average) the following day. The technician would then conclude that investors could make money by purchasing a stock whose price has fallen three consecutive days.

Weak-form advocates argue that if this pattern truly existed then other investors would soon discover it, and if so, why would anyone be willing to sell a stock after it had fallen for three consecutive days? In other words, why sell if you know that the price is going to increase by 10% the next day? For example, suppose a stock had fallen three consecutive days to $40. If the stock were really likely to rise by 10% to $44 tomorrow, then its price *today, right now,* would actually rise to somewhere close to $44, thereby eliminating the trading opportunity. Consequently, weak-form efficiency implies that any information that comes from past stock prices is too rapidly incorporated into the current stock price for a profit opportunity to exist.

SEMISTRONG-FORM EFFICIENCY

The **semistrong form** of the EMH states that current market prices reflect all *publicly available* information. Therefore, if semistrong-form efficiency exists, it would do no good to pore over annual reports or other published data because market prices would have adjusted to any good or bad news contained in such reports back when the news came out. With semistrong-form efficiency, investors should expect to earn returns commensurate with risk, but they should not expect to do any better or worse other than by chance.

Another implication of semistrong-form efficiency is that whenever information is released to the public, stock prices will respond only if the information is different from what had been expected. For example, if a company announces a 30% increase in earnings and if that increase is about what analysts had been expecting, then the announcement should have little or no effect on the company's stock price. On the other hand, the stock price would probably fall if analysts had expected earnings to increase by more than 30%, but it probably would rise if they had expected a smaller increase.

STRONG-FORM EFFICIENCY

The **strong form** of the EMH states that current market prices reflect all pertinent information, whether publicly available or privately held. If this form holds, even insiders would find it impossible to earn consistently abnormal returns in the stock market.

6-8b Is the Stock Market Efficient? The Empirical Evidence

Empirical studies are joint tests of the EMH and an asset pricing model, such as the CAPM. They are joint tests in the sense that they examine whether a particular strategy can beat the market, where "beating the market" means earning a return higher than that predicted by the particular asset pricing model. Before addressing tests of the particular forms of the EMH, let's take a look at market bubbles.

MARKET BUBBLES

The history of finance is marked by numerous instances in which (1) prices climb rapidly to heights that would have been considered extremely unlikely before the run-up; (2) the volume of trading is much higher than past volume; (3) many new investors (or speculators?) eagerly enter the market; and (4) prices suddenly fall precipitously, leaving many of the new investors with huge losses. These instances are called market bubbles.

The stock market bubbles that burst in 2000 and 2008 suggest that, at the height of these booms, the stocks of many companies—especially in the technology sector in 2000 and the financial sector in 2008—vastly exceeded their intrinsic values, which should not happen if markets are always efficient. Two questions arise. First, how are bubbles formed? Behavioral finance, which we discuss in Section 6-10, provides some possible answers. Second, why do bubbles persist when it is possible to make a fortune when they burst? For example, hedge fund manager Mark Spitznagel reputedly made billions for his Universa funds by betting against the market in 2008. The logic underlying market equilibrium suggests that everyone would bet against an overvalued market, and that their actions would cause market prices to fall back to intrinsic values fairly quickly. To understand why this doesn't happen, let's examine the strategies for profiting from a falling market: (1) Sell stocks (or the market index itself) short; (2) purchase a put option or write a call option; or (3) take a short position in a futures contract on the market index. Following is an explanation for how these strategies work (or fail).

Loosely speaking, selling a stock short means that you borrow a share from a broker and sell it. You get the cash (subject to collateral requirements required by the broker) but you owe a share of stock. For example, suppose you sell a share of Google short at a current price of $500. If the price falls to $400, you can buy a share of the stock at the now-lower $400 market price and return the share to the broker, pocketing the $100 difference between the higher price ($500) when you went short and the lower price ($400) when you closed the position. Of course, if the price goes up, say to $550, you lose $50 because you must replace the share you borrowed (at $500) with one that is now more costly ($550). Even if your broker doesn't require you to close out your position when the price goes up, your broker certainly will require that you put in more collateral.

Recall from Chapter 1 that a put option gives you the option to sell a share at a fixed strike price. For example, suppose you buy a put on Google for $60 with a strike price of $500. If the stock price falls below the strike price, say to $400, you can buy a share at the low price ($400) and sell it at the higher strike price ($500), making a net $40 profit from the decline in the stock price: $40 = −$60 −$400 + $500. However, if the put expires before the stock price falls below the strike price, you lose the $60 you spent buying the put. You can also use call options to bet on a decline. For example, if you write a call option, you receive cash in return for an obligation to sell a share at the strike price. Suppose you write a call option on Google with a strike price of $500 and receive $70. If Google's price stays below the $500 strike price, you keep the $70 cash you received from writing the call. But if Google goes up to $600 and the call you wrote is exercised, you must buy a share at the new high price ($600) and sell it at the lower strike price ($500), for a net loss of $30: $70 −$600 + $500 = −$30.[19]

With a short position in a futures contract on the market index (or a particular stock), you are obligated to sell a share at a fixed price. If the market price falls below the specified price in the futures contract, you make money because you can buy a share in the market and sell it at the higher price specified in the futures contract. But if the market price increases, you lose money because you must buy a share at the now higher price and sell it at the price fixed in the futures contract.[20]

Each of these strategies allows an investor to make a lot of money. And if all investors tried to capitalize on an overvalued market, their actions would soon drive the market back to equilibrium, preventing a bubble from forming. But here is the problem with these strategies. Even if the market is overvalued, it might takes months (or even years) before the market falls to its intrinsic value. During this period, an investor would have to spend a lot of cash maintaining the strategies described above, including margin calls, settling options, and daily marking to market for futures contracts. These negative cash flows could easily drive an investor into bankruptcy before the investor was eventually proven correct. Unfortunately, there aren't any low risk strategies for puncturing a market bubble.

Notice that the problem of negative cash flows doesn't exist for the opposite situation of an undervalued market in which the intrinsic value is greater than the market price. Investors can simply buy stock at the too-low market price and hold it until the market price eventually increases to the intrinsic value. Even if the market price continues to go down before eventually rising, the investor experiences only paper losses and not actual negative cash flows. Thus, we would not expect "negative" bubbles to persist very long.

---

[19]Options are usually settled by cash rather than by actually buying and selling shares of stock.
[20]Recall from Chapter 1 that futures contracts are actually settled daily and that they are usually settled for cash rather than the actual shares.

TESTS OF WEAK-FORM EFFICIENCY

Most studies suggest that the stock market is highly efficient in the weak form, with two exceptions. The first exception is for long-term reversals, with studies showing that portfolios of stocks with poor past long-term performance (over the past five years, for example) tend to do slightly better in the long-term future than the CAPM predicts, and vice versa. The second is momentum, with studies showing that stocks with strong performance in the short-term past (over the past six to nine months, for example) tend to do slightly better in the short-term future than the CAPM predicts, and likewise for weak performance.[21] Strategies based on taking advantage of long-term reversals or short-term momentum produce returns that are in excess of those predicted by the CAPM. However, the excess returns are small, especially when transaction costs are considered.

TESTS OF SEMISTRONG-FORM EFFICIENCY

Most studies show that markets are reasonably efficient in the semistrong form: It is difficult to use publicly available information to create a trading strategy that consistently has returns greater than those predicted by the CAPM. In fact, the professionals who manage mutual fund portfolios, on average, do not outperform the overall stock market as measured by an index like the S&P 500 and tend to have returns lower than predicted by the CAPM, possibly because many mutual funds have high fees.[22]

However, there are two well-known exceptions to semistrong-form efficiency. The first is for small companies, which have had historical returns greater than predicted by the CAPM. The second is related to book-to-market ratios (B/M), defined as the book value of equity divided by the market value of equity (this is the inverse of the market-to-book ratio defined in Chapter 3). Companies with high B/M ratios have had higher returns than predicted by the CAPM. We discuss these exceptions in more detail in Section 6-9.

TESTS OF STRONG-FORM EFFICIENCY

The evidence suggests that the strong form EMH does not hold, because those who possessed inside information could and have (illegally) make abnormal profits. On the other hand, many insiders have gone to jail, so perhaps there is indeed a trade-off between risk and return!

SELF-TEST

What is the Efficient Markets Hypothesis (EMH)?

What are the differences among the three forms of the EMH?

Why is it difficult to puncture a market bubble?

What violations of the EMH have been demonstrated?

What is short-term momentum? What are long-term reversals?

---

[21]For example, see N. Jegadeesh and S. Titman, "Returns to Buying Winners and Selling Losers: Implications for Stock Market Efficiency," *Journal of Finance,* March 1993, pp. 69–91, and W. F. M. DeBondt and R. H. Thaler, "Does the Stock Market Overreact?" *Journal of Finance,* July 1985, pp. 793–808.

[22]For a discussion of the performance of actively managed funds, see Jonathan Clements, "Resisting the Lure of Managed Funds," *The Wall Street Journal,* February 27, 2001, p. C1.

6-9 The Fama-French Three-Factor Model[23]

Take a look at Table 6-2, which reports the returns for 25 portfolios formed by Professors Eugene Fama and Kenneth French. The Fama-French portfolios are based on the company's size as measured by the market value of its equity (MVE) and the company's book-to-market ratio (B/M), defined as the book value of equity divided by the market value of equity. Each row shows portfolios with similarly sized companies; each column shows portfolios whose companies have similar B/M ratios. Notice that if you look across each row, the average return tends to increase as the B/M ratio increases. In other words, stocks with high B/M ratios have higher returns. If you look up each column (except for the column with the lowest B/M ratios), stock returns tend to increase: Small companies have higher returns.

This pattern alone would not be a challenge to the CAPM if small firms and high B/M firms had large betas (and thus higher returns). However, even after adjusting for their betas, the small-stock portfolios and the high B/M portfolios earned returns higher than predicted by the CAPM. This indicates that (1) markets are inefficient or (2) the CAPM isn't the correct model to describe required returns.

In 1992, Fama and French published a study hypothesizing that the SML should have three factors rather than just beta as in the CAPM.[24] The first factor is the stock's CAPM beta, which measures the market risk of the stock. The second is the size of the company, measured by the market value of its equity (MVE). The third factor is the book-to-market ratio (B/M).

When Fama and French tested their hypotheses, they found that small companies and companies with high B/M ratios had higher rates of return than the average stock, just as

TABLE 6-2

Average Annual Returns for the Fama-French Portfolios Based on Size and Book Equity to Market Equity, 1927–2011

Size	Book Equity to Market Equity				
	Low	2	3	4	High
Small	11.3%	17.3%	18.4%	19.9%	25.2%
2	10.3	15.4	16.9	16.6	18.1
3	11.3	14.2	15.5	15.8	18.2
4	11.6	12.4	13.6	15.0	16.6
Big	10.3	11.9	12.1	12.8	15.7

Source: Professor Kenneth French, **mba.tuck.dartmouth.edu/pages/faculty/ken.french/data_library.html**. These are equal-weighted annual returns. Following is a description from Professor French's Web site describing the construction of the portfolios: "The portfolios, which are constructed at the end of each June, are the intersections of 5 portfolios formed on size (market equity, ME) and 5 portfolios formed on the ratio of book equity to market equity (BE/ME). The size breakpoints for year t are the NYSE market equity quintiles at the end of June of t. BE/ME for June of year t is the book equity for the last fiscal year end in t − 1 divided by ME for December of t − 1. The BE/ME breakpoints are NYSE quintiles. The portfolios for July of year t to June of t + 1 include all NYSE, AMEX, and NASDAQ stocks for which we have market equity data for December of t − 1 and June of t, and (positive) book equity data for t − 1."

---

[23]This section may be omitted with no loss in continuity.
[24]See Eugene F. Fama and Kenneth R. French, "The Cross-Section of Expected Stock Returns," *Journal of Finance*, Vol. 47, 1992, pp. 427–465.

they hypothesized. Somewhat surprisingly, however, they found that beta was not useful in explaining returns. After taking into account the returns due to the company's size and B/M ratio, high-beta stocks did not have higher than average returns and low-beta stocks did not have lower than average returns.

In 1993, Fama and French developed a three-factor model based on their previous results.[25] The first factor in the **Fama-French three-factor model** is the market risk premium, which is the market return, $\bar{r}_M$, minus the risk-free rate, $\bar{r}_{RF}$. Thus, their model begins like the CAPM, but they go on to add a second and third factor.[26] To form the second factor, they ranked all actively traded stocks by size and then divided them into two portfolios, one consisting of small stocks and one consisting of big stocks. They calculated the return on each of these two portfolios and created a third portfolio by subtracting the return on the big portfolio from that of the small one. They called this the SMB (small minus big) portfolio. This portfolio is designed to measure the variation in stock returns that is caused by the size effect.

To form the third factor, they ranked all stocks according to their book-to-market ratios (B/M). They placed the 30% of stocks with the highest ratios into a portfolio they called the H portfolio (for high B/M ratios) and placed the 30% of stocks with the lowest ratios into a portfolio called the L portfolio (for low B/M ratios). Then they subtracted the return of the L portfolio from that of the H portfolio to derive the HML (high minus low) portfolio. Their resulting model is shown here:

$$(\bar{r}_{i,t} - \bar{r}_{RF,t}) = a_i + b_i(\bar{r}_{M,t} - \bar{r}_{RF,t}) + c_i(\bar{r}_{SMB,t}) + d_i(\bar{r}_{HML,t}) + e_{i,t} \qquad \text{(6-19)}$$

where

$\bar{r}_{i,t}$ = Historical (realized) rate of return on Stock i in period t.

$\bar{r}_{RF,t}$ = Historical (realized) rate of return on the risk-free rate in period t.

$\bar{r}_{M,t}$ = Historical (realized) rate of return on the market in period t.

$\bar{r}_{SMB,t}$ = Historical (realized) rate of return on the small-size portfolio minus the big-size portfolio in period t.

$\bar{r}_{HML,t}$ = Historical (realized) rate of return on the high-B/M portfolio minus the low-B/M portfolio in period t.

a_i = Vertical axis intercept term for Stock i.

$b_i, c_i,$ and d_i = Slope coefficients for Stock i.

$e_{i,t}$ = Random error, reflecting the difference between the actual return on Stock i in period t and the return as predicted by the regression line.

When this model is applied to actual stock returns, the "extra" return disappears for portfolios based on a company's size or B/M ratio. In fact, the extra returns for the long-term

---

[25]See Eugene F. Fama and Kenneth R. French, "Common Risk Factors in the Returns on Stocks and Bonds," *Journal of Financial Economics,* Vol. 33, 1993, pp. 3–56.
[26]Although our description captures the essence of their process for forming factors, the actual procedure is a little more complicated. The interested reader should see their 1993 paper, cited in footnote 25.

stock reversals that we discussed in Section 6-8 also disappear. Thus, the Fama-French model accounts for the major violations of the EMH that we described earlier.

Because the Fama-French model explains so well a stock's actual return given the return on the market, the SMB portfolio, and the HML portfolio, the model is very useful in identifying the market's reaction to news about a company.[27] For example, suppose a company announces that it is going to include more outsiders on its board of directors. If the company's stock falls by 2% on the day of the announcement, does that mean investors don't want outsiders on the board? We can answer that question by using the Fama-French model to decompose the actual return of the company on the announcement day into the portion that is explained by the environment (i.e., the market and the SMB and HML portfolios) and the portion due to the company's announcement.

To do this, we gather a sample of data ($\bar{r}_{i,t}$, $\bar{r}_{RF,t}$, $\bar{r}_{M,t}$, $\bar{r}_{SMB,t}$, and $\bar{r}_{HML,t}$) for T periods prior to the announcement date and then run a regression using Equation 6-20. (This is similar to the way in which we estimated beta in Section 6-6 except we are estimating more than one slope coefficient in a multiple regression.) Suppose the estimated coefficients are: $a_i = 0.0$, $b_i = 0.9$, $c_i = 0.2$, and $d_i = 0.3$. On the day of the announcement, the stock market had a return of −3%, the r_{SMB} portfolio had a return of −1%, and the r_{HML} portfolio had a return of −2%. The annual risk-free rate was 6%, so the daily rate is 6%/365 = 0.01%, which is so small that it can be ignored. The predicted value of the error term in the Fama-French model, $e_{i,t}$, is by definition equal to zero. Based on these assumptions, the predicted return on the announcement day using the Fama-French three-factor model is:

$$\begin{aligned} \text{Predicted return} &= a_i + b_i(\bar{r}_{M,t}) + c_i(\bar{r}_{SMB,t}) + d_i(\bar{r}_{HML,t}) \\ &= 0.0 + 0.9(-3\%) + 0.2(-1\%) + 0.3(-2\%) \\ &= -3.5\% \end{aligned} \tag{6-20}$$

The unexplained return is equal to the actual return less the predicted return:

$$\text{Unexplained return} = 2.0\% - (-3.5\%) = 1.5\%$$

Although the stock price went down by 2% on the announcement day, the Fama-French model predicted that the price should have gone down by 3.5%. Thus, the stock had a positive 1.5% reaction on the announcement day. This is just one company, but if we repeated this process for many companies that made similar announcements and calculated the average unexplained reaction, we could draw a conclusion regarding the market's reaction to adding more outside directors. As this example shows, the model is very useful in identifying actions that affect a company's value.

There is no question that the Fama-French three-factor model does a good job in explaining *actual* returns, but how well does it perform in explaining *required* returns? In other words, does the model define a relationship between risk and compensation for bearing risk?

Advocates of the model suggest that size and B/M are related to risk. Small companies have less access to capital markets than do large companies, which subjects small companies to greater risk in the event of a credit crunch—such as the one that occurred

[27]Because the Fama-French model doesn't seem to explain short-term momentum, many researchers also use the 4-factor model which includes a factor for momentum; see Mark Carhart, "On Persistence in Mutual Fund Performance," *Journal of Finance*, Vol. 52, No. 1. (Mar), pp. 57–82.

during the global economic crisis that began in 2007. With greater risk, investors would require a higher expected return to induce them to invest in small companies.

Similar arguments apply for companies with high B/M ratios. If a company's prospects are poor, then the company will have a low market value, which causes a high B/M ratio. Lenders usually are reluctant to extend credit to a company with poor prospects, so an economic downturn can cause such a company to experience financial distress. In other words, a stock with a high B/M ratio might be exposed to the risk of financial distress, in which case investors would require a higher expected return to induce them to invest in such a stock.

If a company's sensitivity to the size factor and the B/M factor are related to financial distress risk, then the Fama-French model would be an improvement on the CAPM regarding the relationship between risk and required return. However, the evidence is mixed as to whether financially distressed firms do indeed have higher expected returns as compensation for their risk. In fact, some studies show financially distressed firms actually have *lower* returns instead of higher returns.[28]

A number of other studies suggest that the size effect no longer influences stock returns, that there never was a size effect (the previous results were caused by peculiarities in the data sources), that the size effect doesn't apply to most companies, and that the book-to-market effect is not as significant as first supposed.[29]

In summary, the Fama-French model is very useful in identifying the unexplained component of a stock's return. However, the model is less useful when it comes to estimating the required return on a stock because the model does not provide a well-accepted link between risk and required return.

SELF-TEST

What are the factors in the Fama-French model?

How can the model be used to estimate the predicted return on a stock?

Why isn't the model widely used by managers at actual companies?

*An analyst has modeled the stock of a company using a Fama-French three-factor model and has estimate that $a_i = 0$, $b_i = 0.7$, $c_i = 1.2$, and $d_i = 0.7$. Suppose that the daily risk-free rate is approximately equal to zero, the market return is 11%, the return on the SMB portfolio is 3.2%, and the return on the HML portfolio is 4.8% on a particular day. The stock had an actual return of 16.9% on that day. What is the stock's predicted return for that day? **(14.9%)** What is the stock's unexplained return for the day? **(2%)***

---

[28]For studies supporting the relationship between risk and return as related to size and the B/M ratio, see Nishad Kapadia, "Tracking Down Distress Risk," *Journal of Financial Economics*, Vol. 102, 2011, pp. 167–182; Thomas J. George, "A Resolution of the Distress Risk and Leverage Puzzles in the Cross Section of Stock Returns," *Journal of Financial Economics*, Vol. 96, 2010, pp. 56–79; and Lorenzo Garlappi and Hong Yan, "Financial Distress and the Cross-section of Equity Returns," *Journal of Finance*, June, 2011, pp. 789–822. For studies rejecting the relationship, see John Y. Campbell, Jens Hilscher, and Jan Szilagyi, "In Search of Distress Risk," *Journal of Finance*, December 2008, pp. 2899–2940; and Ilia D. Dichev, "Is the Risk of Bankruptcy a Systematic Risk?" *Journal of Finance*, June 1998, pp. 1131–1147.

[29]See Peter J. Knez and Mark J. Ready, "On the Robustness of Size and Book-to-Market in the Cross-Sectional Regressions," *Journal of Finance*, September 1997, pp. 1355–1382; Dongcheol Kim, "A Reexamination of Firm Size, Book-to-Market, and Earnings Price in the Cross-Section of Expected Stock Returns," *Journal of Financial and Quantitative Analysis*, December 1997, pp. 463–489; and Tyler Shumway and Vincent A. Warther, "The Delisting Bias in CRSP's Nasdaq Data and Its Implications for the Size Effect," *Journal of Finance*, December 1999, pp. 2361–2379; and Tim Loughran, "Book-to-Market across Firm Size, Exchange, and Seasonality: Is There an Effect?" *Journal of Financial and Quantitative Analysis*, September 1997, pp. 249–268.

6-10 Behavioral Finance[30]

A large body of evidence in the field of psychology shows that people often behave irrationally, but in predictable ways. The field of behavioral finance focuses on irrational, but predictable, financial decisions. The following sections examine applications of behavioral finance to market bubbles and to other financial decisions.

6-10a Market Bubbles and Behavioral Finance

We showed in Section 6-8 that strategies for profiting from a punctured bubble expose an investor to possible large negative cash flows if it takes a long time for the bubble to burst. That explains why a bubble can persist, but it doesn't explain how a bubble is created. There are no definitive explanations, but the field of behavioral finance offers some possible reasons, including overconfidence, anchoring bias, and herding.

Many psychological tests show that people are overconfident with respect to their own abilities relative to the abilities of others, which is the basis of Garrison Keillor's joke about a town where all the children are above average. Professor Richard Thaler and his colleague Nicholas Barberis address this phenomenon as it applies to finance:

> "Overconfidence may in part stem from two other biases, self-attribution bias and hindsight bias. Self-attribution bias refers to people's tendency to ascribe any success they have in some activity to their own talents, while blaming failure on bad luck, rather than on their ineptitude. Doing this repeatedly will lead people to the pleasing but erroneous conclusion that they are very talented. For example, investors might become overconfident after several quarters of investing success [Gervais and Odean (2001)[31]]. Hindsight bias is the tendency of people to believe, after an event has occurred, that they predicted it before it happened. If people think they predicted the past better than they actually did, they may also believe that they can predict the future better than they actually can."[32]

Psychologists have learned that many people focus too closely on recent events when predicting future events, a phenomenon called **anchoring bias**. Therefore, when the market is performing better than average, people tend to think it will continue to perform better than average. When anchoring bias is coupled with overconfidence, investors can become convinced that their prediction of an increasing market is correct, thus creating even more demand for stocks. This demand drives stock prices up, which serves to reinforce the overconfidence and move the anchor even higher.

There is another way that an increasing market can reinforce itself. Studies have shown that gamblers who are ahead tend to take on more risks (i.e., they are playing with the house's money), whereas those who are behind tend to become more conservative. If this is true for investors, we can get a feedback loop: when the market goes up, investors have gains, which can make them less risk averse, which increases their demand for stock, which leads to higher prices, which starts the cycle again.

Herding behavior occurs when groups of investors emulate other successful investors and chase asset classes which are doing well. For example, high returns in mortgage-backed securities during 2004 and 2005 enticed other investors to move into that asset class. Herding behavior can create excess demand for asset classes that have done well,

---

[30]This section may be omitted with no loss of continuity.

[31]See Terrance Odean and Simon Gervais, "Learning to Be Overconfident," *Review of Financial Studies,* Spring 2001, pp. 1–27.

[32]See page 1066 in an excellent review of behavioral finance by Nicholas Barberis and Richard Thaler, "A Survey of Behavioral Finance," in *Handbook of the Economics of Finance,* George Constantinides, Milt Harris, and René Stulz, eds. (Amsterdam: Elsevier/North-Holland, 2003), Chapter 18.

causing price increases which induce additional herding behavior. Thus, herding behavior can inflate rising markets.

Sometimes herding behavior occurs when a group of investors assumes that other investors are better informed—the herd chases the "smart" money. But in other cases herding can occur even when those in the herd suspect that prices are overinflated. For example, consider the situation of a portfolio manager who believes that bank stocks are overvalued even though many other portfolios are heavily invested in such stocks. If the manager moves out of bank stocks and they subsequently fall in price, then the manager will be rewarded for her judgment. But if the stocks continue to do well, the manager may well lose her job for missing out on the gains. If instead the manager follows the herd and invests in bank stocks, then the manager will do no better or worse than her peers. Thus, if the penalty for being wrong is bigger than the reward for being correct, it is rational for portfolio managers to herd even if they suspect the herd is wrong.

Researchers have shown that the combination of overconfidence and biased self-attribution can lead to overly volatile stock markets, short-term momentum, and long-term reversals.[33] We suspect that overconfidence, anchoring bias, and herding can contribute to market bubbles.

6-10b Other Applications of Behavioral Finance

Psychologists Daniel Kahneman and Amos Tversky show that individuals view potential losses and potential gains very differently.[34] If you ask an average person whether he or she would rather have $500 with certainty or flip a fair coin and receive $1,000 if it comes up heads and nothing if it comes up tails, most would prefer the certain $500 gain, which suggests an aversion to risk—a *sure* $500 gain is better than a risky *expected* $500 gain. However, if you ask the same person whether he or she would rather pay $500 with certainty or flip a coin and pay $1,000 if it's heads and nothing if it's tails, most would indicate that they prefer to flip the coin, which suggests a preference for risk—a risky *expected* $500 loss is better than a *sure* $500 loss. In other words, losses are so painful that people will make irrational choices to avoid sure losses. This phenomenon is called "loss aversion."

One way that people avoid a loss is by not admitting that they have actually had a loss. For example, in many people's mental bookkeeping, a loss isn't really a loss until the losing investment is actually sold. Therefore, they tend to hold risky losers instead of accepting a certain loss, which is a display of loss aversion. Of course, this leads investors to sell losers much less frequently than winners even though this is suboptimal for tax purposes.[35]

Many corporate projects and mergers fail to live up to their expectations. In fact, most mergers end up destroying value in the acquiring company. Because this is well known, why haven't companies responded by being more selective in their investments? There are many possible reasons, but research by Ulrike Malmendier and Geoffrey Tate suggests that overconfidence leads managers to overestimate their abilities and the quality of their projects.[36] In other words, managers might know that the average decision to merge destroys value, but they are certain that their decision is above average.

---

[33]See Terrance Odean, "Volume, Volatility, Price, and Profit When All Traders Are Above Average," *Journal of Finance,* December 1998, pp. 1887–1934; and Kent Daniel, David Hirshleifer, and Avanidhar Subrahmanyam, "Investor Psychology and Security Market Under- and Overreactions," *Journal of Finance,* December 1998, pp. 1839–1885.

[34]Daniel Kahneman and Amos Tversky, "Prospect Theory: An Analysis of Decision under Risk," *Econometrica,* March 1979, pp. 263–292.

[35]See Terrance Odean, "Are Investors Reluctant to Realize Their Losses?" *Journal of Finance,* October 1998, pp. 1775–1798.

[36]See Ulrike Malmendier and Geoffrey Tate, "CEO Overconfidence and Corporate Investment," *Journal of Finance,* December 2005, pp. 2661–2700.

Finance is a quantitative field, but good managers in all disciplines must also understand human behavior.[37]

What is behavioral finance?

What is anchoring bias? What is herding behavior? How can these contribute to market bubbles?

6-11 The CAPM and Market Efficiency: Implications for Corporate Managers and Investors

A company is like a portfolio of projects: factories, retail outlets, R&D ventures, new product lines, and the like. Each project contributes to the size, timing, and risk of the company's cash flows, which directly affect the company's intrinsic value. This means that *the relevant risk and expected return of any project must be measured in terms of its effect on the stock's risk and return.* Therefore, all managers must understand how stockholders view risk and required return in order to evaluate potential projects.

Stockholders should not expect to be compensated for the risk they can eliminate through diversification, but only for the remaining market risk. The CAPM provides an important tool for measuring the remaining market risk and goes on to show how a stock's required return is related to the stock's market risk. It is for this reason that the CAPM is widely used to estimate the required return on a company's stock and, hence, the required returns that projects must generate to provide the stock's required return. We describe this process in more detail in Chapters 7 and 9, which cover stock valuation and the cost of capital. We apply these concepts to project analysis in Chapters 10 and 11.

Is the CAPM perfect? No. First, we cannot observe beta but must instead estimate beta. As we saw in Section 6-6, estimates of beta are not precise. Second, we saw that small stocks and stocks with high B/M ratios have returns higher than the CAPM predicts. This could mean that the CAPM is the wrong model, but there is another possible explanation. If the composition of a company's assets were changing over time with respect to the mix of physical assets and growth opportunities (involving, e.g., R&D or patents), then this would be enough to make it *appear* as though there were size and B/M effects. In other words, even if the returns on the individual assets conform to the CAPM, changes in the mix of assets would cause the firm's beta to change over time in such a way that the firm would appear to have size and book-to-market effects.[38] Recent research supports this hypothesis, and we will use the CAPM in subsequent chapters.[39]

Regarding market efficiency, our understanding of the empirical evidence suggests it is very difficult, if not impossible, to beat the market by earning a return that is higher than justified by the investment's risk. This suggests that markets are reasonably efficient for

---

[37]Excellent reviews of behavioral finance are by Richard H. Thaler, Editor, *Advances in Behavioral Finance* (New York: Russell Sage Foundation, 1993); and Andrei Shleifer, *Inefficient Markets: An Introduction to Behavioral Finance* (New York: Oxford University Press, 2000).

[38]See Jonathan B. Berk, Richard C. Green, and Vasant Naik, "Optimal Investment, Growth Options, and Security Returns," *Journal of Finance,* October 1999, pp. 1553–1608.

[39]See Zhi Da, Re-Jin Guo, and Ravi Jagannathan, "CAPM for Estimating the Cost of Equity Capital: Interpreting the Empirical Evidence," *Journal of Financial Economics,* Vol. 103, 2012, pp. 204–220.

most assets for most of the time. However, we believe that market bubbles do occur and that it is very difficult to implement a low-risk strategy for profiting when they burst.

SELF-TEST

Explain the following statement: "The stand-alone risk of an individual corporate project may be quite high, but viewed in the context of its effect on stockholders' risk, the project's true risk may be much lower."

SUMMARY

This chapter focuses on the trade-off between risk and return. We began by discussing how to estimate risk and return for both individual assets and portfolios. In particular, we differentiated between stand-alone risk and risk in a portfolio context, and we explained the benefits of diversification. We introduced the CAPM, which describes how risk affects rates of return.

- **Risk** can be defined as exposure to the chance of an unfavorable event.
- The risk of an asset's cash flows can be considered on a **stand-alone basis** (each asset all by itself) or in a **portfolio context**, in which the investment is combined with other assets and its risk is reduced through **diversification**.
- Most rational investors hold **portfolios of assets**, and they are more concerned with the risk of their portfolios than with the risk of individual assets.
- The **expected return** on an investment is the mean value of its probability distribution of returns.
- The **greater the probability** that the actual return will be far below the expected return, the **greater the asset's stand-alone risk.**
- The average investor is **risk averse**, which means that he or she must be compensated for holding risky assets. Therefore, riskier assets have higher required returns than less risky assets.
- An asset's risk has two components: (1) **diversifiable risk**, which can be eliminated by diversification, and (2) **market risk**, which cannot be eliminated by diversification.
- Market risk is measured by the standard deviation of returns on a well-diversified portfolio, one that consists of all stocks traded in the market. Such a portfolio is called the **market portfolio**.
- The **CAPM** defines the **relevant risk** of an individual asset as its contribution to the risk of a well-diversified portfolio. Because market risk cannot be eliminated by diversification, investors must be compensated for bearing it.
- A stock's **beta coefficient, b,** measures how much risk a stock contributes to a well-diversified portfolio.
- A stock with a beta greater than 1 has stock returns that tend to be higher than the market when the market is up but tend to be below the market when the market is down. The opposite is true for a stock with a beta less than 1.
- The **beta of a portfolio** is a **weighted average** of the betas of the individual securities in the portfolio.
- The CAPM's **Security Market Line (SML)** equation shows the relationship between a security's market risk and its required rate of return. The return required for any security i is equal to the **risk-free rate** plus the **market risk premium** multiplied by the security's **beta:** $r_i = r_{RF} + (RP_M)b_i$.

- In equilibrium, the expected rate of return on a stock must equal its required return. However, a number of things can happen to cause the required rate of return to change: (1) **the risk-free rate can change** because of changes in either real rates or expected inflation, (2) **a stock's beta can change,** and (3) **investors' aversion to risk can change.**
- Because returns on assets in different countries are not perfectly correlated, **global diversification** may result in lower risk for multinational companies and globally diversified portfolios.
- The **intrinsic value** (also called the **fundamental value**) of a financial asset is the present value of an asset's expected future cash flows, discounted at the appropriate risk-adjusted rate. The intrinsic value incorporates all *relevant available* information about the asset's expected cash flows and risk.
- **Equilibrium** is the condition under which the expected return on a security as seen by the marginal investor is just equal to its required return, $\hat{r} = r$. Also, the stock's intrinsic value must be equal to its market price.
- The **Efficient Markets Hypothesis (EMH)** holds that (1) stocks are always in equilibrium and (2) it is impossible for an investor who does not have inside information to consistently "beat the market." Therefore, according to the EMH, stocks are always fairly valued and have a required return equal to their expected return.
- The **Fama-French three-factor model** has one factor for the **market return**, a second factor for the **size effect**, and a third factor for the **book-to-market effect**.
- **Behavioral finance** assumes that investors don't always behave rationally. **Anchoring bias** is the human tendency to "anchor" too closely on recent events when predicting future events. **Herding** is the tendency of investors to follow the crowd. When combined with overconfidence, anchoring and herding can contribute to market bubbles.
- Two Web extensions accompany this chapter: *Web Extension 6A* provides a discussion of **continuous probability distributions**, and *Web Extension 6B* shows how to calculate beta with a financial calculator.

QUESTIONS

(6-1)   Define the following terms, using graphs or equations to illustrate your answers where feasible.

    a. Risk in general; stand-alone risk; probability distribution and its relation to risk
    b. Expected rate of return, $\hat{r}$
    c. Continuous probability distribution
    d. Standard deviation, σ; variance, σ^2
    e. Risk aversion; realized rate of return, $\bar{r}$
    f. Risk premium for Stock i, RP_i; market risk premium, RP_M
    g. Capital Asset Pricing Model (CAPM)
    h. Expected return on a portfolio, $\hat{r}_p$; market portfolio
    i. Correlation as a concept; correlation coefficient, ρ
    j. Market risk; diversifiable risk; relevant risk
    k. Beta coefficient, b; average stock's beta
    l. Security Market Line (SML); SML equation
    m. Slope of SML and its relationship to risk aversion
    n. Equilibrium; Efficient Markets Hypothesis (EMH); three forms of EMH
    o. Fama-French three-factor model
    p. Behavioral finance; herding; anchoring

(6-2) The probability distribution of a less risky return is more peaked than that of a riskier return. What shape would the probability distribution have for (a) completely certain returns and (b) completely uncertain returns?

(6-3) Security A has an expected return of 7%, a standard deviation of returns of 35%, a correlation coefficient with the market of −0.3, and a beta coefficient of −1.5. Security B has an expected return of 12%, a standard deviation of returns of 10%, a correlation with the market of 0.7, and a beta coefficient of 1.0. Which security is riskier? Why?

(6-4) If investors' aversion to risk *increased*, would the risk premium on a high-beta stock increase by more or less than that on a low-beta stock? Explain.

(6-5) If a company's beta were to double, would its expected return double?

SELF-TEST PROBLEMS   Solutions Appear in Appendix A

(ST-1)
Realized Rates of
Return

Stocks A and B have the following historical returns:

Year	$\bar{r}_A$	$\bar{r}_B$
2009	−18%	−24%
2010	44	24
2011	−22	−4
2012	22	8
2013	34	56

a. Calculate the average rate of return for each stock during the 5-year period. Assume that someone held a portfolio consisting of 50% of Stock A and 50% of Stock B. What would have been the realized rate of return on the portfolio in each year? What would have been the average return on the portfolio for the 5-year period?
b. Now calculate the standard deviation of returns for each stock and for the portfolio. Use Equation 6-5.
c. Looking at the annual returns data on the two stocks, would you guess that the correlation coefficient between returns on the two stocks is closer to 0.8 or to −0.8?
d. If you added more stocks at random to the portfolio, which of the following is the most accurate statement of what would happen to σ_p?

(1) σ_p would remain constant.
(2) σ_p would decline to somewhere in the vicinity of 20%.
(3) σ_p would decline to zero if enough stocks were included.

(ST-2)
Beta and Required
Rate of Return

ECRI Corporation is a holding company with four main subsidiaries. The percentage of its business coming from each of the subsidiaries, and their respective betas, are as follows:

Subsidiary	Percentage of Business	Beta
Electric utility	60%	0.70
Cable company	25	0.90
Real estate	10	1.30
International/special projects	5	1.50

a. What is the holding company's beta?
b. Assume that the risk-free rate is 6% and that the market risk premium is 5%. What is the holding company's required rate of return?
c. ECRI is considering a change in its strategic focus: It will reduce its reliance on the electric utility subsidiary so that the percentage of its business from this subsidiary will be 50%. At the same time, ECRI will increase its reliance on the international/special projects division, and the percentage of its business from that subsidiary will rise to 15%. What will be the shareholders' required rate of return if management adopts these changes?

PROBLEMS   Answers Appear in Appendix B

Easy Problems 1–4

(6-1)
Portfolio Beta

Your investment club has only two stocks in its portfolio. $20,000 is invested in a stock with a beta of 0.7, and $35,000 is invested in a stock with a beta of 1.3. What is the portfolio's beta?

(6-2)
Required Rate of Return

AA Industries's stock has a beta of 0.8. The risk-free rate is 4% and the expected return on the market is 12%. What is the required rate of return on AA's stock?

(6-3)
Required Rates of Return

Suppose that the risk-free rate is 5% and that the market risk premium is 7%. What is the required return on (1) the market, (2) a stock with a beta of 1.0, and (3) a stock with a beta of 1.7? Assume that the risk-free rate is 5% and that the market risk premium is 7%.

(6-4)
Fama-French Three-Factor Model

An analyst has modeled the stock of a company using the Fama-French three-factor model. The risk-free rate is 5%, the market return is 10%, the return on the SMB portfolio (r_{SMB}) is 3.2%, and the return on the HML portfolio (r_{HML}) is 4.8%. If $a_i = 0$, $b_i = 1.2$, $c_i = -0.4$, and $d_i = 1.3$, what is the stock's predicted return?

Intermediate
Problems 5–10

(6-5)
Expected Return:
Discrete Distribution

A stock's return has the following distribution:

Demand for the Company's Products	Probability of This Demand Occurring	Rate of Return If This Demand Occurs (%)
Weak	0.1	−50%
Below average	0.2	−5
Average	0.4	16
Above average	0.2	25
Strong	0.1	60
	1.0	

Calculate the stock's expected return and standard deviation.

(6-6)
Expected Returns:
Discrete Distribution

The market and Stock J have the following probability distributions:

Probability	r_M	r_J
0.3	15%	20%
0.4	9	5
0.3	18	12

a. Calculate the expected rates of return for the market and Stock J.
b. Calculate the standard deviations for the market and Stock J.

(6-7)
Required Rate of
Return

Suppose r_{RF} = 5%, r_M = 10%, and r_A = 12%.

a. Calculate Stock A's beta.
b. If Stock A's beta were 2.0, then what would be A's new required rate of return?

(6-8)
Required Rate of
Return

As an equity analyst you are concerned with what will happen to the required return to Universal Toddler Industries's stock as market conditions change. Suppose r_{RF} = 5%, r_M = 12%, and b_{UTI} = 1.4.

a. Under current conditions, what is r_{UTI}, the required rate of return on UTI stock?
b. Now suppose r_{RF} (1) increases to 6% or (2) decreases to 4%. The slope of the SML remains constant. How would this affect r_M and r_{UTI}?
c. Now assume r_{RF} remains at 5% but r_M (1) increases to 14% or (2) falls to 11%. The slope of the SML does not remain constant. How would these changes affect r_{UTI}?

(6-9)
Portfolio Beta

Your retirement fund consists of a $5,000 investment in each of 15 different common stocks. The portfolio's beta is 1.20. Suppose you sell one of the stocks with a beta of 0.8 for $5,000 and use the proceeds to buy another stock whose beta is 1.6. Calculate your portfolio's new beta.

(6-10)
Portfolio Required
Return

Suppose you manage a $4 million fund that consists of four stocks with the following investments:

Stock	Investment	Beta
A	$ 400,000	1.50
B	600,000	-0.50
C	1,000,000	1.25
D	2,000,000	0.75

If the market's required rate of return is 14% and the risk-free rate is 6%, what is the fund's required rate of return?

Challenging
Problems 11–14

(6-11)
Portfolio Beta

You have a $2 million portfolio consisting of a $100,000 investment in each of 20 different stocks. The portfolio has a beta of 1.1. You are considering selling $100,000 worth of one stock with a beta of 0.9 and using the proceeds to purchase another stock with a beta of 1.4. What will the portfolio's new beta be after these transactions?

(6-12)
Required Rate of
Return

Stock R has a beta of 1.5, Stock S has a beta of 0.75, the expected rate of return on an average stock is 13%, and the risk-free rate is 7%. By how much does the required return on the riskier stock exceed that on the less risky stock?

(6-13)
Historical Realized
Rates of Return

You are considering an investment in either individual stocks or a portfolio of stocks. The two stocks you are researching, stocks A and B, have the following historical returns:

Year	$\bar{r}_A$	$\bar{r}_B$
2009	-20.00%	-5.00%
2010	42.00	15.00
2011	20.00	-13.00
2012	-8.00	50.00
2013	25.00	12.00

a. Calculate the average rate of return for each stock during the 5-year period.
b. Suppose you had held a portfolio consisting of 50% of Stock A and 50% of Stock B. What would have been the realized rate of return on the portfolio in each year? What would have been the average return on the portfolio during this period?
c. Calculate the standard deviation of returns for each stock and for the portfolio.
d. If you are a risk-averse investor, then, assuming these are your only choices, would you prefer to hold Stock A, Stock B, or the portfolio? Why?

(6-14)
Historical Returns:
Expected and
Required Rates of
Return

You have observed the following returns over time:

Year	Stock X	Stock Y	Market
2009	14%	13%	12%
2010	19	7	10
2011	−16	−5	−12
2012	3	1	1
2013	20	11	15

Assume that the risk-free rate is 6% and the market risk premium is 5%.

a. What are the betas of Stocks X and Y?
b. What are the required rates of return on Stocks X and Y?
c. What is the required rate of return on a portfolio consisting of 80% of Stock X and 20% of Stock Y?

SPREADSHEET PROBLEM

(6-15)

resource

Evaluating Risk and
Return

Start with the partial model in the file *Ch06 P15 Build a Model.xls* on the textbook's Web site. The file contains hypothetical data for working this problem. Goodman Industries's and Landry Incorporated's stock prices and dividends, along with the Market Index, are shown below. Stock prices are reported for December 31 of each year, and dividends reflect those paid during the year. The market data are adjusted to include dividends.

	Goodman Industries		Landry Incorporated		Market Index
Year	Stock Price	Dividend	Stock Price	Dividend	Includes Dividends
2013	$25.88	$1.73	$73.13	$4.50	17,495.97
2012	22.13	1.59	78.45	4.35	13,178.55
2011	24.75	1.50	73.13	4.13	13,019.97
2010	16.13	1.43	85.88	3.75	9,651.05
2009	17.06	1.35	90.00	3.38	8,403.42
2008	11.44	1.28	83.63	3.00	7,058.96

a. Use the data given to calculate annual returns for Goodman, Landry, and the Market Index, and then calculate average annual returns for the two stocks and the index. (*Hint:* Remember, returns are calculated by subtracting the beginning price from the ending price to get the capital gain or loss, adding the dividend to the capital gain or loss, and then dividing the result by the beginning price. Assume that dividends are already included in the index. Also, you cannot calculate the rate of return for 2008 because you do not have 2007 data.)

b. Calculate the standard deviations of the returns for Goodman, Landry, and the Market Index. (*Hint:* Use the sample standard deviation formula given in the chapter, which corresponds to the STDEV function in *Excel.*)

c. Construct a scatter diagram graph that shows Goodman's returns on the vertical axis and the Market Index's returns on the horizontal axis. Construct a similar graph showing Landry's stock returns on the vertical axis.

d. Estimate Goodman's and Landry's betas as the slopes of regression lines with stock return on the vertical axis (y-axis) and market return on the horizontal axis (x-axis). (*Hint:* Use *Excel*'s SLOPE function.) Are these betas consistent with your graph?

e. The risk-free rate on long-term Treasury bonds is 6.04%. Assume that the market risk premium is 5%. What is the required return on the market? Now use the SML equation to calculate the two companies' required returns.

f. If you formed a portfolio that consisted of 50% Goodman stock and 50% Landry stock, what would be its beta and its required return?

g. Suppose an investor wants to include some Goodman Industries stock in his portfolio. Stocks A, B, and C are currently in the portfolio, and their betas are 0.769, 0.985, and 1.423, respectively. Calculate the new portfolio's required return if it consists of 25% Goodman, 15% Stock A, 40% Stock B, and 20% Stock C.

THOMSON ONE   Business School Edition Problem

 THOMSON REUTERS   Use the Thomson ONE—Business School Edition online database to work this chapter's questions.

Using Past Information to Estimate Required Returns

In the Capital Asset Pricing Model (CAPM) discussion, beta is identified as the correct measure of risk for diversified shareholders. Recall that beta measures the extent to which the returns of a given stock move with the stock market. When using the CAPM to estimate required returns, we would ideally like to know how the stock will move with the market in the future, but because we don't have a crystal ball we generally use historical data to estimate this relationship.

As noted in the chapter, beta can be estimated by regressing the individual stock's returns against the returns of the overall market. As an alternative to running our own regressions, we can instead rely on reported betas from a variety of sources. These published sources make it easy to obtain beta estimates for most large publicly traded corporations. However, a word of caution is in order. Beta estimates can often be quite sensitive to the time period in which the data are estimated, the market index used, and the frequency of the data used. Therefore, it is not uncommon to find a wide range of beta estimates among the various published sources. Indeed, Thomson ONE reports multiple beta estimates. These multiple estimates reflect the fact that Thomson ONE puts together data from a variety of different sources.

Thomson ONE—BSE Discussion Questions

1. Begin by taking a look at the historical performance of the overall stock market. If you want to see, for example, the performance of the S&P 500, select INDICES and enter S&PCOMP.

Click on PERFORMANCE and you will immediately see a quick summary of the market's performance in recent months and years. How has the market performed over the past year? The past 3 years? The past 5 years? The past 10 years?

2. Now let's take a closer look at the stocks of four companies: Colgate Palmolive (CL), Procter & Gamble (PG), Heinz (HNZ), and Microsoft (MSFT). Before looking at the data, which of these companies would you expect to have a relatively high beta (greater than 1.0), and which of these companies would you expect to have a relatively low beta (less than 1.0)?

3. Select one of the four stocks listed in question 2 by selecting COMPANIES, entering the company's ticker symbol, and clicking on GO. On the overview page, you should see a chart that summarizes how the stock has done relative to the S&P 500 over the past 6 months. Has the stock outperformed or underperformed the overall market during this time period?

4. Return to the overview page for the stock you selected. If you scroll down the page you should see an estimate of the company's beta. What is the company's beta? What was the source of the estimated beta?

5. Click on the tab labeled PRICES. What is the company's current dividend yield? What has been its total return to investors over the past 6 months? Over the past year? Over the past 3 years? (Remember that total return includes the dividend yield plus any capital gains or losses.)

6. What is the estimated beta on this page? What is the source of the estimated beta? Why might different sources produce different estimates of beta?

7. Assume that the risk-free rate is 5% and that the market risk premium is 6%. What is the required return on the company's stock?

8. Repeat the same exercise for each of the three remaining companies. Do the reported betas confirm your earlier intuition? In general, do you find that the higher-beta stocks tend to do better in up markets and worse in down markets? Explain.

MINI CASE

Assume that you recently graduated and landed a job as a financial planner with Cicero Services, an investment advisory company. Your first client recently inherited some assets and has asked you to evaluate them. The client presently owns a bond portfolio with $1 million invested in zero coupon Treasury bonds that mature in 10 years.[40] The client also has $2 million invested in the stock of Blandy, Inc., a company that produces meat-and-potatoes frozen dinners. Blandy's slogan is "Solid food for shaky times."

Unfortunately, Congress and the President are engaged in an acrimonious dispute over the budget and the debt ceiling. The outcome of the dispute, which will not be resolved until the end of the year, will have a big impact on interest rates one year from now. Your first task is to determine the risk of the client's bond portfolio. After consulting with the economists at your firm, you have specified five possible scenarios for the resolution of the dispute at the end of the year. For each scenario, you have estimated the probability of the scenario occurring and the impact on interest rates and bond prices if the scenario occurs. Given this information, you have calculated the rate of return on 10-year zero coupon for each scenario. The probabilities and returns are shown below:

---
[40]The total par value at maturity is $1.79 million and yield to maturity is about 6%, but that information is not necessary for this mini case.

Scenario	Probability of Scenario	Return on a 10-Year Zero Coupon Treasury Bond During the Next Year
Worst Case	0.10	−14%
Poor Case	0.20	−4%
Most Likely	0.40	6%
Good Case	0.20	16%
Best Case	0.10	26%
	1.00	

You have also gathered historical returns for the past 10 years for Blandy, Gourmange Corporation (a producer of gourmet specialty foods), and the stock market.

	Historical Stock Returns		
Year	Market	Blandy	Gourmange
1	30%	26%	47%
2	7	15	−54
3	18	−14	15
4	−22	−15	7
5	−14	2	−28
6	10	−18	40
7	26	42	17
8	−10	30	−23
9	−3	−32	−4
10	38	28	75
Average return:	8.0%	?	9.2%
Standard deviation:	20.1%	?	38.6%
Correlation with the market:	1.00	?	0.678
Beta:	1.00	?	1.30

The risk-free rate is 4% and the market risk premium is 5%.

a. What are investment returns? What is the return on an investment that costs $1,000 and is sold after 1 year for $1,060?

b. Graph the probability distribution for the bond returns based on the 5 scenarios. What might the graph of the probability distribution look like if there were an infinite number of scenarios (i.e., if it were a continuous distribution and not a discrete distribution)?

c. Use the scenario data to calculate the expected rate of return for the 10-year zero coupon Treasury bonds during the next year.

d. What is stand-alone risk? Use the scenario data to calculate the standard deviation of the bond's return for the next year.

e. Your client has decided that the risk of the bond portfolio is acceptable and wishes to leave it as it is. Now your client has asked you to use historical returns to estimate the standard deviation of Blandy's stock returns. (*Note:* Many analysts use 4 to 5 years of monthly returns to estimate risk and many use 52 weeks of weekly returns;

some even use a year or less of daily returns. For the sake of simplicity, use Blandy's 10 annual returns.)

f. Your client is shocked at how much risk Blandy stock has and would like to reduce the level of risk. You suggest that the client sell 25% of the Blandy stock and create a portfolio with 75% Blandy stock and 25% in the high-risk Gourmange stock. How do you suppose the client will react to replacing some of the Blandy stock with high-risk stock? Show the client what the proposed portfolio return would have been in each of year of the sample. Then calculate the s average return and standard deviation using the portfolio's annual returns. How does the risk of this two-stock portfolio compare with the risk of the individual stocks if they were held in isolation?

g. Explain correlation to your client. Calculate the estimated correlation between Blandy and Gourmange. Does this explain why the portfolio standard deviation was less than Blandy's standard deviation?

h. Suppose an investor starts with a portfolio consisting of one randomly selected stock. As more and more randomly selected stocks are added to the portfolio, what happens to the portfolio's risk?

i. (1) Should portfolio effects influence how investors think about the risk of individual stocks? (2) If you decided to hold a one-stock portfolio and consequently were exposed to more risk than diversified investors, could you expect to be compensated for all of your risk; that is, could you earn a risk premium on that part of your risk that you could have eliminated by diversifying?

j. According to the Capital Asset Pricing Model, what measures the amount of risk that an individual stock contributes to a well-diversified portfolio? Define this measurement.

k. What is the Security Market Line (SML)? How is beta related to a stock's required rate of return?

l. Calculate the correction coefficient between Blandy and the market. Use this and the previously calculated (or given) standard deviations of Blandy and the market to estimate Blandy's beta. Does Blandy contribute more or less risk to a well-diversified portfolio than does the average stock? Use the SML to estimate Blandy's required return.

m. Show how to estimate beta using regression analysis.

n. (1) Suppose the risk-free rate goes up to 7%. What effect would higher interest rates have on the SML and on the returns required on high- and low-risk securities? (2) Suppose instead that investors' risk aversion increased enough to cause the market risk premium to increase to 8%. (Assume the risk-free rate remains constant.) What effect would this have on the SML and on returns of high- and low-risk securities?

o. Your client decides to invest $1.4 million in Blandy stock and $0.6 million in Gourmange stock. What are the weights for this portfolio? What is the portfolio's beta? What is the required return for this portfolio?

p. Jordan Jones (JJ) and Casey Carter (CC) are portfolio managers at your firm. Each manages a well-diversified portfolio. Your boss has asked for your opinion regarding their performance in the past year. JJ's portfolio has a beta of 0.6 and had a return of 8.5%; CC's portfolio has a beta of 1.4 and had a return of 9.5%. Which manager had better performance? Why?

q. What does market equilibrium mean? If equilibrium does not exist, how will it be established?

r. What is the Efficient Markets Hypothesis (EMH) and what are its three forms? What evidence supports the EMH? What evidence casts doubt on the EMH?

SELECTED ADDITIONAL CASES

The following cases from CengageCompose cover many of the concepts discussed in this chapter and are available at **compose.cengage.com**.

Klein-Brigham Series:

Case 2, "Peachtree Securities, Inc. (A)."

Brigham-Buzzard Series:

Case 2, "Powerline Network Corporation (Risk and Return)."

© Adalberto Rios Szalay/Sexto Sol/Getty Images

CHAPTER 7

Valuation of Stocks and Corporations

S
tock brokerage companies, mutual fund companies, financial services institutions, pension funds, and financial advisory firms are among the many companies that employ security analysts to estimate the value and risk of stocks.

"Sell side" analysts work for investment banks and brokerages. They write reports that are distributed to investors, generally through brokers. "Buy side" analysts work for mutual funds, hedge funds, pension funds, and other institutional investors. Those institutions obtain information from the buy-side analysts, but they also do their own research and ignore the buy side if they disagree.

The analysts on both sides generally focus on specific industries, and many of them were hired as analysts after working for a time in the industry they cover. Physics PhDs are often electronics analysts, biologists analyze biotech stocks, and so on. The analysts pore over financial statements and *Excel* models, but they also go on the road and talk with company officials, companies' customers, and their suppliers. The analysts' primary objective is to predict corporate earnings, dividends, and free cash flow—and thus stock prices.

Stock prices are volatile, so it is difficult to estimate a stock's value. However, some analysts are better than others, and the material in this chapter can help you be better than average.

How much is a company worth? What can managers do to make a company more valuable? Why are stock prices so volatile? This chapter addresses those questions through the application of two widely used valuation models: the dividend growth model and the free cash flow valuation model. But before plunging into stock valuation, we begin with a closer look at what it means to be a stockholder.

Corporate Valuation and Stock Prices

© Rob Webb/Getty Images

Free cash flows (FCF) are the cash flows that are available for distribution to all of a company's investors; the weighted average cost of capital is the overall return required by all of a company's investors. So the present value of a company's free cash flows, discounted by the company's weighted average cost of capital, is the total value of the company to all its investors. It is called the value of operations because operating activities generate the FCF.

We can use this approach to estimate the stock price, but we can do this more directly in some circumstances. Recall that one use of FCF is to pay dividends, which are distributed to stockholders. Chapter 6 showed how to estimate stockholders' required return. Therefore, discounting the cash flows to stockholders (the dividends) at the rate required by stockholders determines the stock's value.

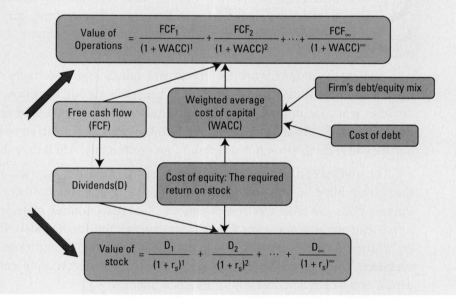

$$\text{Value of Operations} = \frac{FCF_1}{(1 + WACC)^1} + \frac{FCF_2}{(1 + WACC)^2} + \cdots + \frac{FCF_\infty}{(1 + WACC)^\infty}$$

Free cash flow (FCF)

Weighted average cost of capital (WACC)

Firm's debt/equity mix

Cost of debt

Dividends(D)

Cost of equity: The required return on stock

$$\text{Value of stock} = \frac{D_1}{(1 + r_s)^1} + \frac{D_2}{(1 + r_s)^2} + \cdots + \frac{D_\infty}{(1 + r_s)^\infty}$$

© Cengage Learning 2014

resource

The textbook's Web site contains an Excel file that will guide you through the chapter's calculations. The file for this chapter is **Ch07 Tool Kit.xls,** and we encourage you to open the file and follow along as you read the chapter.

7-1 Legal Rights and Privileges of Common Stockholders

Common stockholders are the *owners* of a corporation, and as such they have certain rights and privileges as discussed in this section.

7-1a Control of the Firm

A firm's common stockholders have the right to elect its directors, who, in turn, elect the officers who manage the business. In a small firm, the largest stockholder typically serves as president and chairperson of the board. In a large, publicly owned firm, the managers typically have some stock, but their personal holdings are generally insufficient to give them voting control. Thus, the managers of most publicly owned firms can be removed by the stockholders if the management team is not effective.

Corporations must hold periodic elections to select directors, usually once a year, with the vote taken at the annual meeting. At some companies, all directors are elected each year for a 1-year term. At other companies, the terms are staggered. For example, one-third of the directors are elected each year for a 3-year term.

Each share of stock has one vote, so the owner of 1,000 shares has 1,000 votes for each director.[1] Stockholders can appear at the annual meeting and vote in person, but typically they transfer their right to vote to another party by means of a **proxy**. Management always solicits stockholders' proxies and usually gets them. However, if earnings are poor and stockholders are dissatisfied, an outside group may solicit the proxies in an effort to overthrow management and take control of the business. This is known as a **proxy fight**. Proxy fights are discussed in detail in Chapter 13.

7-1b The Preemptive Right

Common stockholders often have the right, called the **preemptive right**, to purchase any additional shares sold by the firm. In some states, the preemptive right is automatically included in every corporate charter; in others, it is used only if it is specifically inserted into the charter.

W W W

Note that **http://finance .yahoo.com** *provides an easy way to find stocks meeting specified criteria. Under the Investing tab, select Stocks and then Stock Screener. To find the largest companies in terms of market value, for example, choose More Preset Screens, then select Largest Market Cap. You can also create custom screens to find stocks meeting other criteria.*

The preemptive right enables current stockholders to maintain control, and it also prevents a transfer of wealth from current stockholders to new stockholders. If not for this safeguard, the management of a corporation could issue additional shares at a low price and purchase these shares itself. Management could thereby seize control of the corporation and steal value from the current stockholders. For example, suppose 1,000 shares of common stock, each with a price of $100, were outstanding, making the total market value of the firm $100,000. If an additional 1,000 shares were sold at $50 a share, or for $50,000, this would raise the total market value to $150,000. When total market value is divided by new total shares outstanding, a value of $75 a share is obtained. The old stockholders thus lose $25 per share, and the new stockholders have an instant profit of $25 per share. Thus, selling common stock at a price below the market value would dilute its price and transfer wealth from the present stockholders to those who were allowed to purchase the new shares. The preemptive right prevents such occurrences.

SELF-TEST

What is a proxy fight?

What are the two primary reasons for using preemptive rights?

7-2 Types of Common Stock

Although most firms have only one type of common stock, in some instances companies use **classified stock** to meet special needs. Generally, when special classifications are used, one type is designated *Class A*, another *Class B*, and so on. Small, new companies seeking funds from outside sources frequently use different types of common stock. For example, when Genetic Concepts went public, its Class A stock was sold to the public and paid a dividend, but this stock had no voting rights for 5 years. Its Class B stock, which the firm's organizers retained, had full voting rights for 5 years, but the legal terms stated that the company could not pay dividends on the Class B stock until it had established its earning

---

[1]In the situation described, a 1,000-share stockholder could cast 1,000 votes for each of three directors if there were three contested seats on the board. An alternative procedure that may be prescribed in the corporate charter calls for *cumulative voting*. Here the 1,000-share stockholder would get 3,000 votes if there were three vacancies, and he or she could cast all of them for one director. Cumulative voting helps minority stockholders (i.e., those who do not own a majority of the shares) get representation on the board.

power and built up retained earnings to a designated level. The use of classified stock thus enabled the public to take a position in a conservatively financed growth company without sacrificing income, while the founders retained absolute control during the crucial early stages of the firm's development. At the same time, outside investors were protected against excessive withdrawals of funds by the original owners. As is often the case in such situations, the Class B stock was called **founders' shares**.[2]

As these examples illustrate, the right to vote is often a distinguishing characteristic between different classes of stock. Suppose two classes of stock differ in only one respect: One class has voting rights but the other does not. As you would expect, the stock with voting rights would be more valuable. In the United States, which has a legal system with fairly strong protection for minority stockholders (that is, noncontrolling stockholders), voting stock typically sells at a price 4% to 6% above that of otherwise similar nonvoting stock. Thus, if a stock with no voting rights sold for $50, then one with voting rights would probably sell for $52 to $53. In countries with legal systems that provide less protection for minority stockholders, the right to vote is far more valuable. For example voting stock in Israel sells for 45% more on average than nonvoting stock, and voting stock in Italy has an 82% higher value than nonvoting stock.

Some companies have multiple lines of business, with each line having different growth prospects. Because cash flows for all business lines are mingled on financial statements, some companies worry that investors are not able to value the high-growth business lines correctly. To separate the cash flows and to allow separate valuations, occasionally a company will have classes of stock with dividends tied to a particular part of a company. This is called **tracking stock**, or **target stock**. For example, in 2006 Liberty Media Corporation, a conglomerate that owned such entertainment assets as the Starz movie channel and investments in Time Warner, issued two different tracking stocks to track its two different business lines. One of these, Liberty Interactive tracking stock, was designed to track the performance of its QVC home shopping network and other high-growth Internet-based interactive assets. The other, Liberty Capital Group, comprised slower-growth holdings like the Starz Entertainment Group. The idea was that investors would assign a higher value to the high growth portion of the company if it traded separately.

However, many analysts are skeptical as to whether tracking stock increases a company's total market value. Companies still report consolidated financial statements for the entire company and have considerable leeway in allocating costs, deploying capital, and reporting the financial results for the various divisions, even those with tracking stock. Thus, a tracking stock is far from identical to the stock of an independent, stand-alone company.

SELF-TEST

What are some reasons why a company might use classified stock?

7-3 Stock Market Reporting

Fifty years ago, investors who wanted real-time information would sit in brokerage firms' offices watching a "ticker tape" go by that displayed prices of stocks as they were traded. Those who did not need current information could find the previous day's prices from the business section of a daily newspaper like *The Wall Street Journal*. Today, though, one can get quotes

---

[2]Note that the terms "Class A," "Class B," and so on have no standard meanings. Most firms have no classified shares, but a firm that does could designate its Class B shares as founders' shares and its Class A shares as those sold to the public; another firm might reverse these designations.

FIGURE **7-1**

Stock Quote and Other Key Data for GE, February 24, 2012

Source: **http://finance.yahoo.com**.

throughout the day from many different Internet sources, including Yahoo!.[3] Figure 7-1 shows the quote for General Electric, which is traded on the NYSE under the symbol GE, on February 24, 2012. GE ended the regular trading day (4 p.m. EST) at $19.24, down $0.07, which was a 0.36% decrease from the previous day. However, in after-hours trading the stock fell by an additional 3 cents. The data also show that GE opened the day at $19.36 and traded in a range from $19.14 to $19.37. If this quote had been obtained during trading hours, it would also have provided current information about the quotes at which the stock could be bought (the Ask quote) or sold (the Bid quote). During past 52 weeks, the price hit a high of $21.17 and a low of $14.02. A total of 23.93 million GE shares traded that day, which was below the average trading volume of 58.20 million shares during the past 3 months.

The screen with the stock quote information also gives the total market value of GE's common stock (the Market Cap), the dividend, the dividend yield, the most recent "ttm" ("trailing twelve months") EPS and P/E ratios, and a graph showing the stock's performance during the day. (However, the graph can be changed to show the stock's performance over a number of time periods up to and including 5 years.) In addition to this information, the Web page has links to financial statements, research reports, historical ratios, analysts' forecasts of EPS and EPS growth rates, and a wealth of other data.

S E L F - T E S T

What information is provided on the Internet in addition to the stock's latest price?

7-4 Valuing Common Stocks

Common stocks are expected to provide a stream of future cash flows, and a stock's value is found the same way as the values of other financial assets—namely, as the present value of its expected future cash flow stream. In later sections we will show how to estimate a

---

[3]Most free sources actually provide quotes that are delayed by 20 minutes, but if you subscribe to a paid site like *The Wall Street Journal*'s online service, or if you have a brokerage account, you can generally get real-time quotes online.

stock's value as part of a company's total value, but we begin here by directly valuing a stock's cash flows to shareholders.

7-4a Definitions of Terms Used in Stock Valuation Models

It's obvious why an investor needs a stock valuation model, but why does a manager also need a valuation model? For the reasons given in Chapter 1, a manager should seek to maximize the intrinsic value of her firm's stock. To do this, a manager needs to know how her actions are likely to affect the stock's value. In other words, managers need a stock valuation model just as much as investors do.

We begin by defining key terms:

D_t = Dividend the stockholder *expects* to receive at the end of Year t. D_0 is the most recent dividend, which has already been paid; D_1 is the first dividend expected, which will be paid at the end of this year; D_2 is the dividend expected at the end of Year 2; and so forth. D_1 represents the first cash flow that a new purchaser of the stock will receive, because D_0 has just been paid. D_0 is known with certainty, but all future dividends are expected values.[4]

P_0 = Actual **market price** of the stock today.

$\hat{P}_1$ = Expected price of the stock at the end of each Year t (pronounced "P hat t"). $\hat{P}_0$ is estimated value of the stock today as seen by the particular investor doing the analysis; $\hat{P}_1$ is the price expected at the end of 1 year; and so on.

D_1/P_0 = Expected **dividend yield** during the coming year. For example, if a stock to pay a dividend of $D_1 = \$1$ during the next 12 months and if its current price is $P_0 = \$10$, then the expected dividend yield is $\$1/\$10 = 0.10 = 10\%$.

$\frac{\hat{P}_1 - P_0}{P_0}$ = Expected **capital gains yield** during the coming year. If the stock sells for $10 today and if it is expected to rise to $10.50 at the end of one year, then the expected capital gain is $\hat{P}_1 - P_0 = \$10.50 - \$10.00 = \$0.50$, and the expected capital gains yield is $\$0.50/\$10 = 0.05 = 5\%$.

g = Expected **growth rate** in dividends as predicted by a marginal investor.

r_s = The **required rate of return** on the stock. As shown in Chapter 6, the primary determinants of r_s include the risk-free rate and adjustments for the stock's risk.

$\hat{r}_s$ = **Expected rate of return** that an investor who buys the stock expects to receive in the future. $\hat{r}_s$ (pronounced "r hat s") could be above or below r_s, but one would buy the stock only if $\hat{r}_s \geq r_s$. Note that the expected return($\hat{r}_s$) is equal to the expected dividend yield (D_1/P_0) plus

---

[4]Stocks generally pay dividends quarterly, so theoretically we should evaluate them on a quarterly basis. However, in stock valuation, most analysts work on an annual basis because the data generally are not precise enough to warrant refinement to a quarterly model. For additional information on the quarterly model, see Robert Brooks and Billy Helms, "An N-Stage, Fractional Period, Quarterly Dividend Discount Model," *Financial Review*, November 1990, pp. 651–657.

the expected capital gains yield ($[\hat{P}_1 - P_0]/P_0$). In our example, $\hat{r}_s = 10\% + 5\% = 15\%$.

$\bar{r}_s =$ **Actual**, or **realized**, *after-the-fact* **rate of return**, pronounced "r bar s." For a risky security, the actual return can differ considerably from the expected return.

7-4b Expected Dividends as the Basis for Stock Values

Like all financial assets, the value of a stock is estimated by finding the present value of a stream of expected future cash flows. What are the cash flows that corporations are expected to provide to their stockholders? First, think of yourself as an investor who buys a stock with the intention of holding it (in your family) forever. In this case, all that you (and your heirs) will receive is a stream of dividends, and the value of the stock today is calculated as the present value of an infinite stream of dividends:

$$
\begin{aligned}
\text{Value of stock} = \hat{P}_0 &= \text{PV of expected future dividends} \\
&= \frac{D_1}{(1 + r_s)^1} + \frac{D_2}{(1 + r_s)^2} + \cdots + \frac{D_\infty}{(1 + r_s)^\infty} \\
&= \sum_{t=1}^{\infty} \frac{D_t}{(1 + r_s)^t}
\end{aligned}
\tag{7-1}
$$

What about the more typical case, where you expect to hold the stock for a finite period and then sell it—what is the value of $\hat{P}_0$ in this case? Unless the company is likely to be liquidated or sold and thus to disappear, *the value of the stock is again determined by Equation 7-1*. To see this, recognize that for any individual investor, the expected cash flows consist of expected dividends plus the expected sale price of the stock. However, the sale price a current investor receives will depend on the dividends some future investor expects. Therefore, for all present and future investors in total, expected cash flows must be based on expected future dividends. Put another way, unless a firm is liquidated or sold to another concern, the cash flows it provides to its stockholders will consist only of a stream of dividends. Therefore, the value of a share of its stock must be the present value of that expected dividend stream.

The general validity of Equation 7-1 can also be confirmed by solving the following problem. Suppose I buy a stock and expect to hold it for 1 year. I will receive dividends during the year plus the value $\hat{P}_1$ when I sell at the end of the year. But what will determine the value of $\hat{P}_1$? The answer is that it will be determined as the present value of the dividends expected during Year 2 plus the stock price at the end of that year, which, in turn, will be determined as the present value of another set of future dividends and an even more distant stock price. This process can be continued ad infinitum, and the ultimate result is Equation 7-1.[5]

---

[5]It is ironic that investors periodically lose sight of the long-run nature of stocks as investments and forget that, in order to sell a stock at a profit, one must find a buyer who will pay the higher price. If you analyze a stock's value in accordance with Equation 7-1, conclude that the stock's market price exceeds a reasonable value, and then buy the stock anyway, you would be following the "bigger fool" theory of investment—you think that you may be a fool to buy the stock at its excessive price, but you think that when you get ready to sell it, you can find someone who is an even bigger fool. Many investors might have been following the bigger fool theory during the big stock run-ups prior to the bursting bubbles in 2000 and 2007.

What are the two components of most stocks' expected total return?

How does one calculate the capital gains yield and the dividend yield of a stock?

If $D_1 = \$3.00$, $P_0 = \$50$, and $\hat{P}_1 = \$52$, what are the stock's expected dividend yield, expected capital gains yield, and expected total return for the coming year? **(6%, 4%, 10%)**

7-5 Valuing a Constant Growth Stock

Equation 7-1 is a generalized stock valuation model in that the time pattern of D_t can be anything: D_t can be rising, falling, fluctuating randomly, or even zero for several years, yet Equation 7-1 will still hold. With a computer spreadsheet we can easily use this equation to find a stock's value for any pattern of dividends, up to the limit of the computer's memory. However, if future dividends are expected to grow at a constant rate, we can use the constant growth model.

7-5a The Constant Growth Model

In the long run, dividends can't grow faster than earnings. A dollar used to pay dividends can't be used for reinvestment in the firm or to pay down debt, so everything else equal, higher dividends must be associated either with declining earnings growth due to a lack of reinvestment or with increasing debt levels. Growth in dividends can be supported by increasing debt for a while, but to avoid unacceptably high levels of debt, long-term dividend growth must be limited to long-term earnings growth.

Long-term earnings per share (EPS) growth depends on economy-wide factors (such as recessions and inflation), industry-wide factors (such as technological innovations), and firm-specific factors (management skill, brand identity, patent protection, etc.). For a firm to grow faster than the economy, either the industry must become a bigger part of the economy or the firm must take market share from its competitors. But as markets mature, competition and market saturation will tend to limit EPS growth to a constant long-term rate, approximately equal to the sum of population growth and inflation.

Some companies are in growing industries and won't hit their long-term constant growth rate for many years, but some mature firms in saturated industries are already at their constant long-term growth rate. We will address valuation of faster-growing firms later in the chapter, but for a mature company whose dividends are growing at a constant rate, Equation 7-1 can be rewritten as follows:

resource

The last term in Equation 7-2 is derived in **Web Extension 7A** *on the textbook's Web site.*

$$
\begin{aligned}
\hat{P}_0 &= \frac{D_0\,(1+g)^1}{(1+r_s)^1} + \frac{D_0\,(1+g)^2}{(1+r_s)^2} + \cdots + \frac{D_0\,(1+g)^\infty}{(1+r_s)^\infty} \\[2mm]
&= D_0 \sum_{t=1}^{\infty} \frac{(1+g)^t}{(1+r_s)^t} \\[2mm]
&= \frac{D_0(1+g)}{r_s - g} = \frac{D_1}{r_s - g}
\end{aligned}
\tag{7-2}
$$

The last term of Equation 7-2 is called the **constant growth model**, or the **Gordon model**, after Myron J. Gordon, who did much to develop and popularize it.

A necessary condition for the validity of Equation 7-2 is that r_s be greater than g. Look back at the second form of Equation 7-2. If g is larger than r_s, then $(1 + g)^t/(1 + r_s)^t$ must always be greater than 1. In this case, the second line of Equation 7-2 is the sum of an infinite number of terms, with each term being larger than 1. Therefore, if g were constant and greater than r_s, the resulting stock price would be infinite! Because no company is worth an infinite amount, it is impossible to have a constant growth rate that is greater than r_s forever. Unfortunately, a student will occasionally plug a value for g that is greater than r_s into the last form of Equation 7-2 and report a negative stock price. Always keep in mind that the last form of Equation 7-2 is valid only when g is less than r_s. *If g is greater than r_s then the constant growth model cannot be used, and the answer you would get from using Equation 7-2 would be wrong and misleading.*

7-5b Illustration of a Constant Growth Stock

Assume that R&R Enterprises just paid a dividend of $1.15 (that is, $D_0 = \$1.15$). Its stock has a required rate of return, r_s, of 13.4%, and investors expect the dividend to grow at a constant 8% rate in the future. The estimated dividend 1 year hence would be $D_1 = \$1.15$ $(1.08) = \$1.24$; D_2 would be $1.34; and the estimated dividend 5 years hence would be $1.69:

$$D_t = D_0(1 + g)^t = \$1.15(1.08)^5 = \$1.69$$

We could use this procedure to estimate each future dividend and then use Equation 7-1 to determine the current stock value, $\hat{P}_0$. In other words, we could find each expected future dividend, calculate its present value, and then sum all the present values to find the estimated value of the stock.

Such a process would be time-consuming, but we can take a shortcut—just insert the illustrative data into Equation 7-2 to find the stock's estimated value:

$$\hat{P}_0 = \frac{\$1.15(1.08)}{0.134 - 0.08} = \frac{\$1.242}{0.054} = \$23.00$$

The concept underlying the valuation process for a constant growth stock is graphed in Figure 7-2. Dividends are growing at the rate g = 8%, but because r_s > g, the present value of each future dividend is declining. For example, the dividend in Year 1 is $D_1 = D_0(1 + g)^1 = \$1.15(1.08) = \$1.242$. However, the present value of this dividend, discounted at 13.4%, is $PV(D_1) = \$1.242/(1.134)^1 = \$1.095$. The dividend expected in Year 2 grows to $1.242(1.08) = \$1.341$, but the present value of this dividend falls to $1.043. Continuing, $D_3 = \$1.449$ and $PV(D_3) = \$0.993$, and so on. Thus, the expected dividends are growing, but the present value of each successive dividend is declining, because the dividend growth rate (8%) is less than the rate used for discounting the dividends to the present (13.4%).

If we summed the present values of each future dividend, this summation would be the value of the stock, $\hat{P}_0$. When g is a constant, this summation is equal to $D_1/(r_s - g)$, as shown in Equation 7-2. Therefore, if we extend the lower step-function curve in Figure 7-2 on out to infinity and add up the present values of each future dividend, the summation would be identical to the value given by Equation 7-2, $23.00.

Although Equation 7-2 assumes there are *infinite* time periods, most of the value is based on dividends during a *finite* time period. In our example, 70% of the value is attributed to the first 25 years, 91% to the first 50 years, and 99.4% to the first 100 years. This means that companies don't have to survive forever to justify using the Gordon growth model.

FIGURE 7-2

Present Value of Dividends of a Constant Growth Stock Where $D_0 = \$1.15$, $g = 8\%$, and $r_s = 13.4\%$

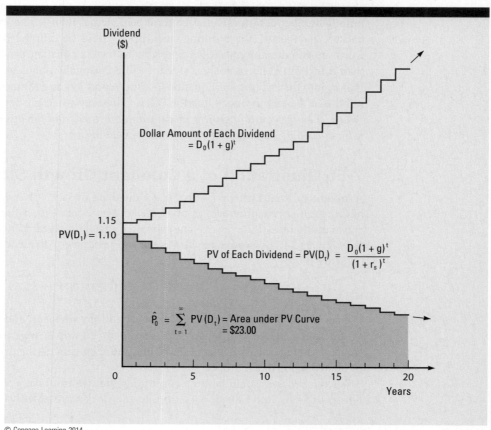

© Cengage Learning 2014

W W W

*The popular Motley Fool Web site **www.fool.com** provides a good description of benefits and drawbacks of a few of the more commonly used valuation procedures. Select Investing Commentary tab, choose Basics, then "How to Value Stocks."*

7-5c Do Stock Prices Reflect Long-Term or Short-Term Events?

Managers often complain that the stock market is shortsighted and that investors care only about conditions over the next few years. Let's use the constant growth model to test this assertion. R&R's most recent dividend was $1.15, and it is expected to grow at a rate of 8% per year. Because we know the growth rate, we can forecast the dividends for each of the next 5 years and then find their present values:

$$PV = \frac{D_0(1+g)^1}{(1+r_s)^1} + \frac{D_0(1+g)^2}{(1+r_s)^2} + \frac{D_0(1+g)^3}{(1+r_s)^3} + \frac{D_0(1+g)^4}{(1+r_s)^4} + \frac{D_0(1+g)^5}{(1+r_s)^5}$$

$$= \frac{\$1.15(1.08)^1}{(1.134)^1} + \frac{\$1.15(1.08)^2}{(1.134)^2} + \frac{\$1.15(1.08)^3}{(1.134)^3} + \frac{\$1.15(1.08)^4}{(1.134)^4} + \frac{\$1.15(1.08)^5}{(1.134)^5}$$

$$= \frac{\$1.242}{(1.134)^1} + \frac{\$1.341}{(1.134)^2} + \frac{\$1.449}{(1.134)^3} + \frac{\$1.565}{(1.134)^4} + \frac{\$1.690}{(1.134)^5}$$

$$= 1.095 + 1.043 + 0.993 + 0.946 + 0.901$$

$$\approx \$5.00$$

Recall that R&R's stock price is $23.00. Therefore, only $5.00, or $5/$23 = 0.22 = 22%, of the $23.00 stock price is attributable to short-term cash flows. This means that R&R's managers will affect the stock price more by working to increase long-term cash flows than by focusing on short-term flows. This situation holds for most companies. Indeed, a number of professors and consulting firms have used actual company data to show that more than 80% of a typical company's stock price is due to cash flows expected farther than 5 years in the future.

This brings up an interesting question. If most of a stock's value is due to long-term cash flows, then why do managers and analysts pay so much attention to quarterly earnings? Part of the answer lies in the information conveyed by short-term earnings. For example, when actual quarterly earnings are lower than expected not because of fundamental problems but only because a company has increased its research and development (R&D) expenditures, studies have shown that the stock price probably won't decline and may actually increase. This makes sense, because R&D should increase future cash flows. On the other hand, if quarterly earnings are lower than expected because customers don't like the company's new products, then this new information will have negative implications for future values of g, the long-term growth rate. As we show later in this chapter, even small changes in g can lead to large changes in stock prices. Therefore, short-term quarterly earnings themselves might not contribute a large portion to a stock's price, but the information they convey about future prospects can be extremely important.

Another reason many managers focus on short-term earnings is that some firms pay managerial bonuses on the basis of current earnings rather than stock prices (which reflect future earnings). For these managers, the concern with quarterly earnings is not due to their effect on stock prices—it's due to their effect on bonuses. Many apparent puzzles in finance can be explained either by managerial compensation systems or by peculiar features of the Tax Code. So, if you can't explain a firm's behavior in terms of economic logic, look to compensation procedures or taxes as possible explanations.

7-5d Stock Price Volatility

Recall from Chapter 6 that a typical company's stock returns are very volatile. Indeed, many stocks declined by 80% or more during 2012, and some enjoyed gains of over 100%. At the risk of understatement, the stock market is volatile! To see why stock prices are volatile, we estimate R&R's stock value after making small changes to the inputs of the constant growth model, as shown in Table 7-1. The estimated price is $23 for the original

TABLE 7-1

Estimated Stock Value of R&R Enterprise for Different Inputs of Growth and Required Return (D_0 = $1.15)

Growth Rate: g	Required Return: r_s				
	11.4%	12.4%	13.4%	14.4%	15.4%
6%	$22.57	$19.05	$16.47	$14.51	$12.97
7%	$27.97	$22.79	$19.23	$16.63	$14.65
8%	$36.53	$28.23	$23.00	$19.41	$16.78
9%	$52.23	$36.87	$28.49	$23.21	$19.59
10%	$90.36	$52.71	$37.21	$28.75	$23.43

© Cengage Learning 2014

inputs, shown in the boxed cell. Notice that even small changes in the required return or estimated growth rate cause large changes in the estimated stock value.

What might cause investors to change their expectations about the growth rate or risk of future dividends? It could be new information about the company, such as preliminary results for an R&D program, initial sales of a new product, or the discovery of harmful side effects from the use of an existing product. Or new information that will affect many companies could arrive, such as the collapse of the credit markets in 2008. Given the existence of computers and telecommunications networks, new information hits the market on an almost continuous basis, and it causes frequent and sometimes large changes in stock prices. In other words, *ready availability of information causes stock prices to be volatile.*

If a stock's price is stable, this probably means that little new information is arriving. But if you think it's risky to invest in a volatile stock, imagine how risky it would be to invest in a company that rarely releases new information about its sales or operations. It may be bad to see your stock's price jump around, but it would be a lot worse to see a stable quoted price most of the time and then to see huge moves on the rare days when new information is released.[6] Fortunately, in our economy timely information is readily available, and evidence suggests that stocks—especially those of large companies—adjust rapidly to new information.

7-5e Expected Rate of Return on a Constant Growth Stock

When using Equation 7-2, we first estimated D_1 and r_s, the *required* rate of return on the stock; then we solved for the stock's intrinsic value, which we compared to its actual market price. We can also reverse the process, observing the actual stock price, substituting it into Equation 7-2, and solving for the rate of return. In doing so, we are finding the *expected* rate of return (recall from Chapter 6 that if the market is in equilibrium, the expected return will equal the *required* rate of return, $\hat{r}_s = r_s$):

$$
\begin{aligned}
\hat{r}_s = \begin{matrix} \text{Expected rate} \\ \text{of return} \end{matrix} &= \begin{matrix} \text{Expected} \\ \text{dividend yield} \end{matrix} + \begin{matrix} \text{Expected capital} \\ \text{gains yield} \end{matrix} \\[2ex]
&= \begin{matrix} \text{Expected} \\ \text{dividend yield} \end{matrix} + \begin{matrix} \text{Expected} \\ \text{growth rate} \end{matrix} \\[2ex]
&= \frac{D_1}{P_0} + g
\end{aligned}
\tag{7-3}
$$

Thus, if you buy a stock for a price $P_0 = \$23$, and if you expect the stock to pay a dividend $D_1 = \$1.242$ in a year and to grow at a constant rate $g = 8\%$ in the future, then your expected rate of return will be 13.4%:

$$
\hat{r}_s = \frac{\$1.242}{\$23} + 8\% = 5.4\% + 8\% = 13.4\%
$$

In this form, we see that $\hat{r}_s$ is the *expected total return* and that it consists of an *expected dividend yield*, $D_1/P_0 = 5.4\%$, plus an *expected growth rate* (which is also the *expected capital gains yield*) of $g = 8\%$.

---

[6]Note, however, that if information came out infrequently, stock prices would probably be stable for a time and then experience large price swings when news did come out. This would be a bit like not having a lot of little earthquakes (frequent new information) that relieve stress along the fault and instead building up stress for a number of years before a massive earthquake.

Suppose that the current price, P_0, is equal to $23 and that the Year-1 expected dividend, D_1, is equal to $1.242. What is the expected price at the end of the first year, immediately after D_1 has been paid? First, we can estimate the expected Year-2 dividend as $D_2 = D_1(1 + g) = \$1.242(1.08) = \$1.3414$. Then we can apply a version of Equation 7-2 that is shifted ahead by 1 year, using D_2 instead of D_1 and solving for $\hat{P}_1$ instead of $\hat{P}_0$:

$$\hat{P}_1 = \frac{D_2}{r_s - g} = \frac{\$1.3414}{0.134 - 0.08} = \$24.84$$

Even easier, notice that $\hat{P}_1$ must be 8% larger than $23, the price found 1 year earlier for P_0:

$$\$23(1.08) = \$24.84$$

Either way, we expect a capital gain of $24.84 - $23.00 = $1.84 during the year, which is a capital gains yield of 8%:

$$\text{Capital gains yield} = \frac{\text{Capital gain}}{\text{Beginning price}} = \frac{\$1.84}{\$23.00} = 0.08 = 8\%$$

We could extend the analysis, and in each future year the expected capital gains yield would always equal g, the expected dividend growth rate.

The dividend yield during the year could be estimated as follows:

$$\text{Dividend yield} = \frac{D_2}{\hat{P}_1} = \frac{\$1.3414}{\$24.84} = 0.054 = 5.4\%$$

The dividend yield for the following year could also be calculated, and again it would be 5.4%. Thus, *for a constant growth stock*, the following conditions must hold:

1. The dividend is expected to grow forever at a constant rate, g.
2. The stock price will also grow at this same rate.
3. The expected dividend yield is constant.
4. The expected capital gains yield is also constant and is equal to g, the dividend (and stock price) growth rate.
5. The expected total rate of return, $\hat{r}_s$, is equal to the expected dividend yield plus the expected growth rate: $\hat{r}_s$ = dividend yield + g.

SELF-TEST

Write out and explain the valuation formula for a constant growth stock.

Are stock prices affected more by long-term or short-term performance? Explain.

Why doesn't a volatile stock price necessarily imply irrational pricing?

What conditions must hold in order for a stock to be evaluated using the constant growth model?

A stock is expected to pay a dividend of $2 at the end of the year. The required rate of return is r_s = 12%. What would the stock's price be if the constant growth rate in dividends were 4%? **($25.00)** *What would the price be if g = 0%?* **($16.67)**

If D_0 = $4.00, r_s = 9%, and g = 5% for a constant growth stock, what are the stock's expected dividend yield and capital gains yield for the coming year? **(4%, 5%)**

7-6 Valuing Nonconstant Growth Stocks

For many companies, it is not appropriate to assume that dividends will grow at a constant rate. Firms typically go through *life cycles*. During their early years, their growth is much faster than that of the economy as a whole; then they match the economy's growth; and finally their growth is slower than that of the economy. Automobile manu-facturers in the 1920s, software companies such as Microsoft in the 1990s, and technology firms such as Cisco in the 2000s are examples of firms in the early part of the cycle; these firms are called **supernormal**, or **nonconstant**, **growth** firms.

Suppose R&R, the company from the previous section, was not yet in its constant growth phase but was expected to grow at a 30% rate for the first year, 20% for the second year, 10% for the third year, after which the growth rate is expected to fall to 8% and remain there. Chapters 12 and 14 explain how to forecast dividends, but for now just accept the forecasts for R&R. Figure 7-3 illustrates this pattern of nonconstant growth and also compares it with normal growth, zero growth, and negative growth.[7]

The value of R&R is the present value of its expected future dividends as determined by Equation 7-1. When D_t is growing at a constant rate, we simplify Equation 7-1 to $\hat{P}_0 = D_1/(r_s - g)$. In the nonconstant case, however, the expected growth rate is not a constant during the first 3 years, so we cannot apply the constant growth formula during these years.

Because Equation 7-2 requires a constant growth rate, we obviously cannot use it at Year 0 to value stocks that subsequently have nonconstant growth. However, assuming a company currently experiencing nonconstant growth will eventually slow down and become a constant growth stock, we can use Equation 7-2 to help find the stock's value.

FIGURE 7-3

Illustrative Dividend Growth at Different Rates

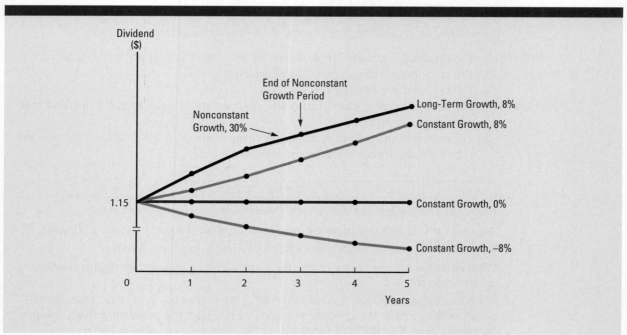

© Cengage Learning 2014

[7]A negative growth rate indicates a declining company. A mining company whose profits are falling because of a declining ore body is an example. Someone buying such a company would expect its earnings, and consequently its dividends and stock price, to decline each year, and this would lead to capital losses rather than capital gains. Obviously, a declining company's stock price will be relatively low, and its dividend yield must be high enough to offset the expected capital loss and still produce a competitive total return. Students sometimes argue that they would never be willing to buy a stock whose price was expected to decline. However, if the annual dividends are large enough to *more than offset* the falling stock price, the stock could still provide a fair return.

First, we assume that the dividend will grow at nonconstant rates (generally at relatively high rates) for N periods, after which it will grow at a constant rate, g_L. Often N is called the **horizon date** or the **terminal date**.

Recall that a stock's current estimated value, $\hat{P}_0$, is the present value of all dividends after Time 0, discounted back to Time 0. Similarly, the estimated value of a stock at Time N is the present value of all dividends beyond Time N, discounted back to Time N. When dividends beyond Time N are expected to grow at a constant long-term rate of g_L, we can use a variation of the constant growth formula, Equation 7-2, to estimate the stock's intrinsic value at Time N. The estimated value at Time N is often called the **horizon value** or the **terminal value**. For stocks, $\hat{P}_N$, denotes the horizon value of the expected stock price at Time N:

$$\text{Horizon value for stock} = \hat{P}_N = \frac{D_{N+1}}{r_s - g_L} = \frac{D_N(1 + g_L)}{r_s - g_L} \tag{7-4}$$

A stock's estimated value today, $\hat{P}_0$, is the present value of the dividends during the nonconstant growth period plus the present value of the dividends after the horizon date:

$$\hat{P}_0 = \underbrace{\frac{D_1}{(1+r_s)^1} + \frac{D_2}{(1+r_s)^2} + \cdots + \frac{D_N}{(1+r_s)^N}}_{\substack{\text{PV of dividends during the} \\ \text{nonconstant growth period} \\ t = 1 \text{ to } N}} + \underbrace{\frac{D_{N+1}}{(1+r_s)^{N+1}} + \cdots + \frac{D_\infty}{(1+r_s)^\infty}}_{\substack{\text{PV of dividends during the} \\ \text{constant growth period} \\ t = N+1 \text{ to } \infty}}$$

The horizon value is the value of all dividends beyond Time N discounted back to Time N. Discounting the horizon value from Time N to Time 0 provides an estimate of the present value of all dividends beyond the nonconstant growth period. Thus, the stock's current estimated value is the present value of all dividends during the nonconstant growth period plus the present value of the horizon value:

$$\hat{P}_0 = \left[\frac{D_1}{(1+r_s)^1} + \frac{D_2}{(1+r_s)^2} + \cdots + \frac{D_N}{(1+r_s)^N} \right] + \frac{\hat{P}_N}{(1+r_s)^N}$$

$$= \left[\frac{D_1}{(1+r_s)^1} + \frac{D_2}{(1+r_s)^2} + \cdots + \frac{D_N}{(1+r_s)^N} \right] + \frac{\left[(D_{N+1})/(r_s - g_L) \right]}{(1+r_s)^N} \tag{7-5}$$

To implement Equation 7-5, we go through the following three steps.

1. Estimate the expected dividends for each year during the period of nonconstant growth.
2. Find the expected price of the stock at the end of the nonconstant growth period, at which point it has become a constant growth stock.
3. Find the present values of the expected dividends during the nonconstant growth period and the present value of the expected stock price at the end of the nonconstant growth period. Their sum is the estimated value of the stock, $\hat{P}_0$.

Figure 7-4 illustrates the process for valuing a nonconstant growth stock. Notice that the dividends are projected using the appropriate growth rate for each year. The estimated horizon value, $\hat{P}_3$, is the value of all dividends from Year 4 through infinity, discounted back to Year 3 by application of the constant growth model at Year 3. The horizon value is actually the value a split-second after D_3 has been paid. Therefore, the estimated value at Time 0 is the present value of the first three dividends plus the present value of $\hat{P}_3$, for an estimated current value of $31.13. A detailed explanation is set forth in the steps below the diagram.

SELF-TEST

Explain how to find the value of a nonconstant growth stock.

Explain what is meant by the terms "horizon (terminal) date" and "horizon (terminal) value."

Suppose D_0 = $5.00 and r_s = 10%. The expected growth rate from Year 0 to Year 1 (g_1) = 20%, the expected growth rate from Year 1 to Year 2 (g_2) = 10%, and the constant growth rate beyond Year 2 is g_L = 5%. What are the expected dividends for Year 1 and Year 2? **($6.00 and $6.60)** *What is the expected horizon value price at Year 2 ($\hat{P}_3$)?* **($138.60)** *What is $\hat{P}_0$?* **($125.45)**

7-7 The Free Cash Flow Valuation Model

As stated earlier, managers should estimate and evaluate the impact of alternative strategies on their firms' values, which means that managers need a valuation model. The dividend growth model provides many meaningful insights, such as (1) the relative importance of long-term cash flows versus short-term cash flows and (2) the reason stock prices are so volatile. However, the dividend growth model is unsuitable in many situations.

For example, suppose a start-up company is formed to develop and market a new product. Its managers will focus on product development, marketing, and raising capital. They will probably be thinking about an eventual IPO, or perhaps the sale of the company to a larger firm; for example, Google, Cisco, Microsoft, Intel, IBM, or another of the industry leaders buy hundreds of successful new companies each year. For the managers of such a start-up, the decision to initiate dividend payments in the foreseeable future will be totally off the radar screen. Thus, the dividend growth model is not useful for valuing most start-up companies.

Also, many established firms pay no dividends. Investors may expect them to pay dividends sometime in the future—but when, and how much? As long as internal opportunities and acquisitions are so attractive, the initiation of dividends will be postponed, and this makes the dividend growth model of little use. Even Apple, one of the world's most successful companies, paid no dividends from 1995 until 2012, when it initiated quarterly dividend payments.

Finally, the dividend growth model is generally of limited use for internal management purposes, even for a dividend-paying company. If the firm consisted of just one big asset and if that asset produced all of the cash flows used to pay dividends, then alternative strategies could be judged through the use of the dividend growth model. However, most firms have several different divisions with many assets, so the corporation's value depends on the cash flows from many different assets and on the actions of many managers. These managers need a way to measure the effects of

FIGURE 7-4

Process for Finding the Value of a Nonconstant Growth Stock

	A	B	C	D	E	F	G	H
217	INPUTS:							
218	$D_0 =$	$1.15	Last dividend the company paid.					
219	$r_s =$	13.4%	Stockholders' required return.					
220	$g_{0,1} =$	30%	Growth rate for Year 1 only.					
221	$g_{1,2} =$	20%	Growth rate for Year 2 only.					
222	$g_{2,3} =$	10%	Growth rate for Year 3 only.					
223	$g_L =$	8%	Constant long-run growth rate for all years after Year 3.					
224								
225	Growth rate		30%	20%	10%	8%	8%	
226	Year	0	1	2	3	4		∞
227	Dividends		$1.4950	$1.7940	$1.9734	$2.1313		
228			↓	↓	↓	↓		
229			D_1	D_2	D_3	↓		
230						↓		
231			$(1+r_s)^1$	$(1+r_s)^2$	$(1+r_s)^3$	↓		
232			↓	↓	↓	↓		
233			↓	↓	↓	↳→		D_4
234		$1.318	←⤶	↓	↓			$= \hat{P}_3$
235	PVs of dividends	$1.395	←←←←	←⤶	↓			$(r_s - g_L)$
236		$1.353	←←←←	←←←←	←⤶			↓
237	PV of HV$_3$	$27.065	←←←		$39.468	↖		$2.131
238			↓	⤶ ←←←←←	$=\dfrac{}{}$		$39.468 =$	$= \hat{P}_3$
239	$\hat{P}_0 =$	$31.132			$(1+r_s)^3$		5.40%	

Notes:

Step 1. Calculate the dividends expected at the end of each year during the nonconstant growth period. Calculate the first dividend, $D_1 = D_0(1 + g_{0,1}) =$ $1.15(1.30) = 1.4950. Here $g_{0,1}$ is the growth rate (30%) during the first year of the nonconstant growth period. Show the $1.4950 on the time line as the cash flow at Year 1. Then calculate $D_2 = D_1(1 + g_{1,2}) = $1.4950(1.20) = 1.7940 and then $D_3 = D_2(1 + g_{2,3}) = $1.7940(1.10) = 1.9734. (The figure shows the values rounded to four decimal places, but all calculations used nonrounded values.) Show these values on the time line as the cash flows at Year 2 and Year 3. Note that D_0 is used only to calculate D_1.

Step 2. At Year 3, the stock becomes a constant growth stock. Therefore, we can use the constant growth formula to find $\hat{P}_3$, which is the PV of the dividends from Year 4 to infinity as evaluated at Year 3. First we determine $D_4 = $1.9734(1.08) = 2.1313 for use in the formula, and then we calculate $\hat{P}_3$ as follows:

$$\hat{P}_3 = \frac{D_4}{r_s - g_L} = \frac{$2.1313}{0.134 - 0.08} = $39.4680$$

We show this $39.468 on the time line as a second cash flow at Year 3. The $39.468 is a Year-3 cash flow in the sense that the owner of the stock could sell it for $39.468 at Year 3 and also in the sense that $39.468 is the value at Year 3 of the dividend cash flows from Year 4 to infinity.

Step 3. Now that the cash flows have been placed on the time line, we can discount each cash flow at the required rate of return, $r_s = 13.4\%$. This produces the PVs shown to the left below the time line, and the sum of the PVs is the value of the nonconstant growth stock, $31.13.

In the figure we show the setup for an *Excel* solution. With a financial calculator, you could use the cash flow (CFLO) register of your calculator. Enter 0 for CF_0 because you get no cash flow at Time 0, $CF_1 = 1.495$, $CF_2 = 1.7940$, and $CF_3 = 1.9734 + 39.468 = 41.4414$. Then enter I/YR = 13.4 and press the NPV key to find the value of the stock, $31.1315.

resource

See Ch07 Tool Kit.xls on the textbook's Web site.

their decisions on corporate value, but the discounted dividend model isn't very useful because individual divisions don't pay dividends.

Fortunately, the free cash flow valuation model does not depend on dividends, and it can be applied to divisions and subunits as well as to the entire firm.

7-7a Sources of Value and Claims on Value

Companies have two primary sources of value, the value of operations and the value of nonoperating assets. There are three major types of claims on this value: debt, preferred stock, and common stock. Following is a description of these sources and claims.

SOURCES OF VALUE

Recall from Chapter 2 that free cash flow (FCF) is the cash flow available for distribution to *all* of a company's investors. The weighted average cost of capital (WACC) is the overall return required by *all* of a company's investors. Because FCF is generated by a company's operations, the present value of expected FCF when discounted by the WACC is equal to the value of a company's operations, V_{op}:

$$V_{op} = \frac{FCF_1}{(1 + WACC)^1} + \frac{FCF_2}{(1 + WACC)^2} + \cdots + \frac{FCF_\infty}{(1 + WACC)^\infty}$$

$$= \sum_{t=1}^{\infty} \frac{FCF_t}{(1 + WACC)^t}$$

(7-6)

The primary source of value for most companies is the value of operations. A secondary source of value comes from nonoperating assets (also called financial assets). There are two major types of nonoperating assets: (1) marketable securities, which are short-term securities (like T-bills) that are over and above the amount of cash needed to operate the business; (2) other nonoperating assets, which often are investments in other businesses. For example, Ford Motor Company's automotive operation held about $14.2 billion in marketable securities at the end of December 2010, and this was in addition to $6.3 billion in cash. Second, Ford also had $2.4 billion of investments in other businesses, which were reported on the asset side of the balance sheet as "Equity in Net Assets of Affiliated Companies." In total, Ford had $14.2 + $2.4 = $16.6 billion of nonoperating assets, amounting to 26% of its $64.6 billion of total automotive assets. For most companies, the percentage is much lower. For example, as of the end of October 2010, Walmart's percentage of nonoperating assets was less than 1%, which is more typical.

We see, then, that for most companies operating assets are far more important than nonoperating assets. Moreover, companies can influence the values of their operating assets, whereas the values of nonoperating assets are largely beyond their direct control.

CLAIMS ON VALUE

For a company that is a going concern, debtholders have the first claim on value in the sense that interest and scheduled principal payments must be paid before any preferred or common dividends can be paid. Preferred stockholders have the next claim because preferred dividends must be paid before common dividends. Common shareholders come last in this pecking order and have a residual claim on the company's value.

7-7b Estimating the Value of Operations

The free cash flow (FCF) model is analogous to the dividend growth model, except the FCF valuation model (1) discounts free cash flows instead of dividends and (2) the discount rate is the weighted average cost of capital (WACC) instead of the required return on stock. Free cash flow is generated by operations, FCF is the cash flow available for all investors, and the WACC is the overall required return of all investors; therefore, the result of the FCF model is the total value of operations, not just the value of the stock.

We will illustrate the FCF valuation model using MagnaVision Inc., which produces optical systems for use in medical photography. Growth has been rapid in the past, but the market is becoming saturated, so the sales growth rate is projected to decline from 21% in 2013 to a sustainable rate of 5% in 2016 and beyond. Profit margins are expected to improve as the production process becomes more efficient and because MagnaVision will no longer be incurring marketing costs associated with the introduction of a major product. All items on the financial statements are projected to grow at a 5% rate after 2016.

Chapter 2 explained how to calculate FCF if you have historical financial statements; however, you need *forecasted* financial statements to apply the FCF valuation model. To better focus on the free cash flow valuation model in this example, we provide MagnaVision's projected free cash flows in Figure 7-5 and defer forecasting until Chapter 12.[8] We also provide MagnaVision's weighted average cost of capital, 10.84%; we will explain how to estimate the cost of capital in Chapter 9. All calculations in Figure 7-5 are explained in the following paragraphs.

resource

*See **Ch07 Tool Kit.xls** on the textbook's Web site.*

Notice that MagnaVision has negative free cash flows in the first two projected years. Negative free cash flow in early years is typical for young, high-growth companies. Even though net operating profit after taxes (NOPAT) may be positive, free cash flow often is negative due to investments in operating assets during the high-growth years. As growth slows, free cash flow will become positive and eventually grow at a constant rate.

FIGURE 7-5

MagnaVision's Value of Operations (Millions of Dollars)

	A	B	C	D	E	F	G	H
263	INPUTS:							
264	g_L =	5.00%						
265	WACC =	10.84%	Projections					
266	Year	2012	2013	2014	2015	2016		
267	FCF		−$18.00	−$23.00	$46.40	$49.00	→↴	
268			↓	↓	↓	↓	↓	
269			FCF_{2013}	FCF_{2014}	FCF_{2015}	FCF_{2016}	↓	
270							↓	
271			$(1+WACC)^1$	$(1+WACC)^2$	$(1+WACC)^3$	$(1+WACC)^4$	$HV = V_{op(12/31/16)}$	
272			↓	↓	↓	↓	↓	
273			↓	↓	↓	↓	$\frac{FCF_{2016}(1+g_L)}{(WACC-g_L)}$	
274		−$16.240	←↵	↓	↓	↓		
275	PVs of FCFs	−$18.721	←←←←	←↵	↓	↓		
276		$34.074	←←←←	←←←←	←↵	↓		↓
277		$32.465	←←←←	←←←←	←←←←	←↵		↓
278	PV of HV	$583.696				$880.993	↰	$51.450
279		↓				= ———	↲	= ———
280	V_{op} =	$615.27				$(1+WACC)^4$		5.84%

[8]We have provided MagnaVision's projected statements and calculations of projected FCF in a worksheet in ***Ch07 Tool Kit.xls***.

To estimate MagnaVision's value of operations, we use an approach similar to the nonconstant dividend growth model for stocks and proceed as follows.

1. Recognize that growth after Year N will be constant, so we can use a constant growth formula to find the firm's value at Year N. The value at Year N is the sum of the PVs of FCF for year N + 1 and all subsequent years, discounted back to Year N.
2. Find the PV of the free cash flows for each of the N nonconstant growth years. Also, find the PV of the firm's value at Year N.
3. Now sum all the PVs, those of the annual free cash flows during the nonconstant period plus the PV of the Year-N value, to find the firm's value of operations.

A variant of the constant growth dividend model is shown in Equation 7-7, in which FCF replaces dividends and the WACC replaces r_s. This equation can be used to find the value of MagnaVision's operations at time N, when its free cash flows stabilize and begin to grow at a constant rate. This is the value of all FCFs beyond time N, discounted back to time N (which is 2016 for MagnaVision):

$$V_{op\,(\text{at time N})} = \sum_{t=N+1}^{\infty} \frac{FCF_t}{(1+WACC)^{t-N}}$$

$$= \frac{FCF_{N+1}}{WACC - g_L} = \frac{FCF_N(1+g_L)}{WACC - g_L} \qquad (7\text{-}7)$$

Based on a 10.84% cost of capital, $49 million of free cash flow in 2016, and a 5% growth rate, the value of MagnaVision's operations as of December 31, 2016, is estimated to be $880.99 million:

$$V_{op\,(12/31/16)} = \frac{FCF_{12/31/16}(1+g_L)}{WACC - g_L}$$

$$= \frac{\$49(1+0.05)}{0.1084 - 0.05} = \frac{\$51.45}{0.1084 - 0.05} = \$880.99 \qquad (7\text{-}7a)$$

This $880.99 million figure is called the company's horizon value because it is the value at the end of the forecast period. It is also sometimes called a continuing value or terminal value. It is the amount that MagnaVision could expect to receive if it sold its operating assets on December 31, 2016.

Figure 7-5 shows the free cash flow for each year during the nonconstant growth period along with the horizon value of operations in 2016. To find the value of operations as of "today," December 31, 2012, we find the PV of the horizon value and each annual free cash flow in Figure 7-5, discounting at the 10.84% cost of capital:

$$V_{op\,(12/31/12)} = \frac{-\$18.00}{(1+0.1084)^1} + \frac{-\$23.00}{(1+0.1084)^2} + \frac{\$46.40}{(1+0.1084)^3}$$

$$+ \frac{\$49.00}{(1+0.1084)^4} + \frac{\$880.99}{(1+0.1084)^4}$$

$$= \$615.27$$

The sum of the PVs is approximately $615 million, and it represents an estimate of the price MagnaVision could expect to receive if it sold its operating assets "today," December 31, 2012.

7-7c Estimating the Price per Share

In addition to the value of operations, we need to know the value of MagnaVision's nonoperating assets, claims on value (such as debt and preferred stock), and the number of shares. Those values are shown in the INPUTS section of Figure 7-6. The other calculations in Figure 7-6 are explained as follows.

resource

See Ch07 Tool Kit.xls on the textbook's Web site.

Think of a company's value as though it were a pie whose size is determined by the value of operations and the value of any financial (nonoperating) assets. The first piece of pie belongs to debtholders, the second to preferred stockholders, and the remaining piece (if there is one) to common shareholders. In other words, common shareholders have a residual claim.

On December 31, 2012, MagnaVision reported owning $63 million of marketable securities. We don't need to calculate a present value for marketable securities because short-term financial assets as reported on the balance sheet are at (or close to) their market value. Therefore, MagnaVision's total value on December 31, 2012, is $615.27 + $63 = $678.27 million.

The value of common equity is the remaining value after other claims. Figure 7-6 shows that MagnaVision has $247 million in debt and $62 million in preferred stock.[9] Therefore, the value left for common stockholders is $678.27 − $247 − $62 = $369.27 million.[10]

Figure 7-7 illustrates the sources of and claims on MagnaVision's value.

FIGURE 7-6

Estimating the Value of MagnaVision's Stock Price (Millions, Except for Per Share Data)

	A	B	C	D	E
289	**INPUTS:**				
290			Value of operations =		$615.27
291			Value of nonoperating assets =		$63.00
292			All debt =		$247.00
293			Preferred stock =		$62.00
294			Number of shares of common stock =		100.00
295	**Estimating Price Per Share**				
296			Value of operations		$615.27
297			+ Value of nonoperating assets		63.00
298			Total estimated value of firm		$678.27
299			− Debt		247.00
300			− Preferred stock		62.00
301			Estimated value of equity		$369.27
302			÷ Number of shares		100.00
303			Estimated stock price per share =		$3.69

[9]Accounts payable and accruals were part of the calculation of FCF, so their impact on value is already incorporated into the valuation of the company's operations. It would be double-counting to subtract them now from the value of operations.

[10]When estimating the intrinsic market value of equity, it would be better to subtract the market values of debt and preferred stock rather than their book values. However, in most cases (including this one), the book values of fixed-income securities are close to their market values. When this is true, one can simply use book values.

FIGURE 7-7

MagnaVision's Sources of Value and Claims on Value (Millions of Dollars)

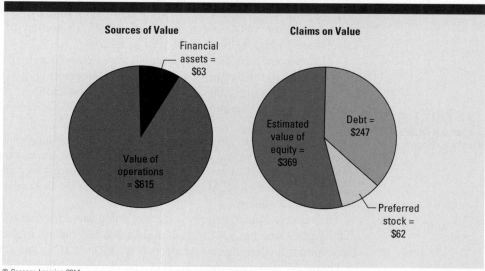

© Cengage Learning 2014

As shown in Figure 7-6, MagnaVision has 100 million shares outstanding. Its estimated equity value is $369.27 million. Therefore, the estimated value of a single share is $369.27/ 100 = $3.69.

7-7d Comparing the Free Cash Flow Valuation and Dividend Growth Models

In Chapter 12 we show that the free cash flow valuation model and the dividend growth model give the same estimated stock price if you are very careful to be consistent with the implicit assumptions underlying the projections of free cash flows and dividends.[11] Which model should you use, as they both give the same answer? If you were a financial analyst estimating the value of a mature company whose dividends are expected to grow steadily in the future, it would probably be more efficient to use the dividend growth model. In this case you would need to estimate only the growth rate in dividends, not the entire set of forecasted financial statements.

However, if a company is paying a dividend but is still in the high-growth stage of its life cycle, you would need to project the future financial statements before you could make a reasonable estimate of future dividends. After you have estimated future financial statements, it would be a toss-up as to whether the corporate valuation model or the dividend growth model would be easier to apply. If you were trying to estimate the value of a company that has never paid a dividend, a private company (including companies nearing an IPO), or a division of a company, then there would be no choice: You would have to estimate future financial statements and use the corporate valuation model.

---

[11]For a more detailed explanation of corporate valuation and forecasting financial statements, see P. Daves, M. Ehrhardt, and R. Shrieves, *Corporate Valuation: A Guide for Managers and Investors* (Mason, OH: Thomson/ South-Western, 2004).

Why is the free cash flow valuation model applicable in more circumstances than the dividend growth model?

Write out the equation for the value of operations.

What is the horizon value? Why is it also called the terminal value or continuing value?

Explain how to estimate the price per share using the corporate free cash flow valuation model.

A company expects FCF of –$10 million at Year 1 and FCF of $20 million at Year 2; after Year 2, FCF is expected to grow at a 5% rate. If the WACC is 10%, then what is the horizon value of operations, $V_{op(Year\ 2)}$? **($420 million)** *What is the current value of operations, $V_{op(Year\ 0)}$?* **($354.55 million)**

A company has a current value of operations of $800 million, and it holds $100 million in short-term investments. If the company has $400 million in debt and has 10 million shares outstanding, what is the estimated price per share? **($50.00)**

7-8 Market Multiple Analysis

Some analysts use **market multiple analysis** to estimate a company's value. The analyst chooses a metric for the firm—say, its EPS—and then multiplies the company's EPS by a market-determined multiple such as the average P/E ratio for a sample of similar companies. This would give an estimate of the stock's intrinsic value. Market multiples can also be applied to total net income, to sales, to book value, or to number of subscribers for businesses such as cable TV or cellular telephone systems. Whereas the discounted dividend method applies valuation concepts by focusing on expected cash flows, market multiple analysis is more judgmental.

To illustrate the concept, suppose Tapley Products is a privately held firm whose forecasted earnings per share are $7.70, and suppose the average price/earnings (P/E) ratio for a set of similar publicly traded companies is 12. To estimate the intrinsic value of Tapley's stock we would simply multiply its $7.70 EPS by the multiple 12, obtaining the value $7.70(12) = $92.40.

Another commonly used metric is *earnings before interest, taxes, depreciation, and amortization (EBITDA)*. The EBITDA *multiple* is the total value of a company (the market value of its equity plus that of its debt) divided by EBITDA. This multiple is based on total value, since EBITDA is used to compensate the firm's stockholders and bondholders. Therefore, it is called an **entity multiple**. The EBITDA market multiple is the average EBITDA multiple for a group of similar publicly traded companies. This procedure gives an estimate of the company's total value, and to find the estimated intrinsic value of the stock we would subtract the value of the debt from total value and then divide by the shares of stock outstanding.

As suggested previously, in some businesses, such as cable TV and cellular telephone, a critical factor is the number of customers the company has. For example, when a telephone company acquires a cellular operator, it might pay a price that is based on the number of customers. Managed care companies such as HMOs have applied similar logic in acquisitions, basing valuations primarily on the number of people insured. Some Internet companies have been valued by the number of "eyeballs," which is the number of hits on the site.

What is market multiple analysis?

What is an entity multiple?

7-9 Preferred Stock

Preferred stock is a *hybrid*—it's similar to bonds in some respects and to common stock in others. Like bonds, preferred stock has a par value, and a fixed amount of dividends must be paid on it before dividends can be paid on the common stock. However, if the preferred dividend is not earned, the directors can omit (or "pass") it without throwing the company into bankruptcy. So, although preferred stock has a fixed payment like bonds, a failure to make this payment will not lead to bankruptcy.

The dividends on preferred stock are fixed, and if they are scheduled to go on forever, the issue is a perpetuity whose value is found as follows:

$$V_{ps} = \frac{D_{ps}}{r_{ps}} \tag{7-8}$$

V_{ps} is the value of the preferred stock, D_{ps} is the preferred dividend, and r_{ps} is the required rate of return. Notice that Equation 7-8 is just a special case of the constant dividend growth model for which growth is zero.

MicroDrive has preferred stock outstanding that pays a dividend of $8 per year. If the required rate of return on this preferred stock is 8%, then its value is $100:

$$V_{ps} = \frac{\$8.00}{0.8} = \$100.00$$

If we know the current price of a preferred stock and its dividend, we can transpose terms and solve for the expected rate of return as follows:

$$\hat{r}_{ps} = \frac{D_{ps}}{V_{ps}} \tag{7-9}$$

Some preferred stock has a stated maturity, say, 50 years. If a firm's preferred stock matures in 50 years, pays a $8 annual dividend, has a par value of $100, and has a required return of 6%, then we can find its price using a financial calculator: Enter N = 50, I/YR = 6, PMT = 8, and FV = 100. Then press PV to find the price, $V_{ps} = \$131.52$. If you know the price of a share of preferred stock, you can solve for I/YR to find the expected rate of return, $\hat{r}_{ps}$.

Most preferred stock pays dividends quarterly. This is true for MicroDrive, so we could find the effective rate of return on its preferred stock as follows:

$$EFF\% = EAR = \left(1 + \frac{r_{NOM}}{M}\right)^M - 1 = \left(1 + \frac{0.08}{4}\right)^4 - 1 = 8.24\%$$

If an investor wanted to compare the returns on MicroDrive's bonds and its preferred stock, it would be best to convert the nominal rates on each security to effective rates and then compare these "equivalent annual rates."

SELF-TEST

Explain the following statement: "Preferred stock is a hybrid security."

Is the equation used to value preferred stock more like the one used to evaluate perpetual bonds or the one used for common stock? Explain.

A preferred stock has an annual dividend of $5. The required return is 8%. What is the V_{ps}? **($62.50)**

SUMMARY

Corporate decisions should be analyzed in terms of how alternative courses of action are likely to affect a firm's value. However, it is necessary to know how stock prices are established before attempting to measure how a given decision will affect a firm's value. This chapter showed how stock values are determined and also how investors go about estimating the rates of return they expect to earn. The key concepts covered are listed below.

- A **proxy** is a document that gives one person the power to act for another, typically the power to vote shares of common stock. A **proxy fight** occurs when an outside group solicits stockholders' proxies in an effort to overthrow the current management.

- Stockholders often have the right to purchase any additional shares sold by the firm. This right, called the **preemptive right**, protects the present stockholders' control and prevents dilution of their value.

- Although most firms have only one type of common stock, in some instances **classified stock** is used to meet the special needs of the company. One type is **founders' shares**. This is stock owned by the firm's founders that carries sole voting rights but restricted dividends for a specified number of years.

- The equation used to find **estimated value of a constant growth stock** is

$$\hat{P}_0 = \frac{D_1}{r_s - g}$$

Web Extension 7A provides a derivation of this formula.

- The **expected total rate of return** from a stock consists of an **expected dividend yield** plus an **expected capital gains yield**. For a constant growth firm, both the dividend yield and the capital gains yield are expected to remain constant in the future.

- The equation for $\hat{r}_s$, the **expected rate of return on a constant growth stock**, is

$$\hat{r}_s = \frac{D_1}{P_0} + g$$

- A **zero growth stock** is one whose future dividends are not expected to grow at all. A **nonconstant growth stock** is one whose earnings and dividends are expected to grow much faster than the economy as a whole over some specified time period and then to grow at a sustainable long-term rate.

- To estimate the **present value of a nonconstant growth stock**, (1) forecast the dividends expected during the nonconstant growth period, (2) estimate the projected price of the stock at the end of the nonconstant growth period, (3) discount the dividends and the projected price back to the present, and (4) sum these PVs to find the current estimated value of the stock, $\hat{P}_0$.

- The **horizon (terminal) date** is the date when individual dividend forecasts are no longer made because the dividend growth rate is assumed to be constant thereafter.

- The **horizon value** for a stock is the present value of all dividends *after* the horizon date discounted back to horizon date:

$$\hat{P}_N = \frac{D_{N+1}}{r_s - g}$$

- **Preferred stock** is a hybrid security having some characteristics of debt and some of equity.

- The **value of a share of perpetual preferred stock** is found as the dividend divided by the required rate of return:

$$V_{ps} = \frac{D_{ps}}{r_{ps}}$$

- **Preferred stock** that has a finite maturity is evaluated with a formula that is identical in form to the bond value formula.

- The **value of operations** is the present value of all the future free cash flows expected from operations when discounted at the weighted average cost of capital:

$$V_{op\,(at\,time\,0)} = \sum_{t=1}^{\infty} \frac{FCF_t}{(1 + WACC)^t}$$

- **Nonoperating assets** include **financial assets** such as investments in marketable securities and noncontrolling interests in the stock of other companies.

- The **value of nonoperating assets** is usually close to the figure reported on the balance sheet.

- The **horizon value** of operations is the value of operations at the end of the explicit forecast period. It is also called the **terminal value** or **continuing value**, and it is equal to the present value of all free cash flows beyond the forecast period, discounted back to the end of the forecast period at the weighted average cost of capital:

$$\text{Continuing value} = V_{op(at\,time\,N)} = \frac{FCF_{N+1}}{WACC - g} = \frac{FCF_N(1 + g)}{WACC - g}$$

- The **free cash flow model** can be used to calculate the total value of a company by finding the value of operations plus the value of nonoperating assets.

- The estimate **value of equity** is the total value of the company minus the value of the debt and preferred stock. The intrinsic **price per share** is the total value of the equity divided by the number of shares.

QUESTIONS

(7-1)   Define each of the following terms:

a. Proxy; proxy fight; preemptive right; classified stock; founders' shares

b. Estimated value ($\hat{P}_0$); market price (P_0)

    c. Required rate of return, r_s; expected rate of return, $\hat{r}_s$; actual, or realized, rate of return, $\bar{r}_s$

    d. Capital gains yield; dividend yield; expected total return

    e. Constant growth; nonconstant growth; zero growth stock

    f. Preferred stock

    g. Nonoperating assets

    h. Value of operations; horizon value; free cash flow valuation model

(7-2) Two investors are evaluating General Electric's stock for possible purchase. They agree on the expected value of D_1 and also on the expected future dividend growth rate. Further, they agree on the risk of the stock. However, one investor normally holds stocks for 2 years and the other normally holds stocks for 10 years. On the basis of the type of analysis done in this chapter, they should both be willing to pay the same price for General Electric's stock. True or false? Explain.

(7-3) A bond that pays interest forever and has no maturity date is a perpetual bond, also called a perpetuity or a consol. In what respect is a perpetual bond similar to (1) a no-growth common stock and (2) a share of preferred stock?

(7-4) Explain how to use the corporate valuation model to find the price per share of common equity.

SELF-TEST PROBLEMS   Solutions Appear in Appendix A

(ST-1)
Constant Growth
Stock Valuation

Ewald Company's current stock price is $36, and its last dividend was $2.40. In view of Ewald's strong financial position and its consequent low risk, its required rate of return is only 12%. If dividends are expected to grow at a constant rate g in the future, and if r_s is expected to remain at 12%, then what is Ewald's expected stock price 5 years from now?

(ST-2)
Nonconstant Growth
Stock Valuation

Snyder Computer Chips Inc. is experiencing a period of rapid growth. Earnings and dividends are expected to grow at a rate of 15% during the next 2 years, at 13% in the third year, and at a constant rate of 6% thereafter. Snyder's last dividend was $1.15, and the required rate of return on the stock is 12%.

    a. Calculate the value of the stock today.

    b. Calculate $\hat{P}_1$ and $\hat{P}_2$.

    c. Calculate the dividend yield and capital gains yield for Years 1, 2, and 3.

(ST-3)
Free Cash Flow
Valuation Model

Watkins Inc. has never paid a dividend, and when the firm might begin paying dividends is not known. Its current free cash flow is $100,000, and this FCF is expected to grow at a constant 7% rate. The weighted average cost of capital is WACC = 11%. Watkins currently holds $325,000 of nonoperating marketable securities. Its long-term debt is $1,000,000, but it has never issued preferred stock. Watkins has 50,000 shares of stock outstanding.

    a. Calculate Watkins's value of operations.

    b. Calculate the company's total value.

    c. Calculate the estimated value of common equity.

    d. Calculate the estimated per share stock price.

PROBLEMS   Answers Appear in Appendix B

Easy Problems 1–7

(7-1)
DPS Calculation
Thress Industries just paid a dividend of $1.50 a share (i.e., $D_0 = \$1.50$). The dividend is expected to grow 5% a year for the next 3 years and then 10% a year thereafter. What is the expected dividend per share for each of the next 5 years?

(7-2)
Constant Growth
Valuation
Boehm Incorporated is expected to pay a $1.50 per share dividend at the end of this year (i.e., $D_1 = \$1.50$). The dividend is expected to grow at a constant rate of 6% a year. The required rate of return on the stock, r_s, is 13%. What is the estimated value per share of Boehm's stock?

(7-3)
Constant Growth
Valuation
Woidtke Manufacturing's stock currently sells for $22 a share. The stock just paid a dividend of $1.20 a share (i.e., $D_0 = \$1.20$), and the dividend is expected to grow forever at a constant rate of 10% a year. What stock price is expected 1 year from now? What is the estimated required rate of return on Woidtke's stock (assume the market is in equilibrium with the required return equal to the expected return)?

(7-4)
Preferred Stock
Valuation
Nick's Enchiladas Incorporated has preferred stock outstanding that pays a dividend of $5 at the end of each year. The preferred sells for $50 a share. What is the stock's required rate of return (assume the market is in equilibrium with the required return equal to the expected return)?

(7-5)
Nonconstant Growth
Valuation
A company currently pays a dividend of $2 per share ($D_0 = \$2$). It is estimated that the company's dividend will grow at a rate of 20% per year for the next 2 years, and then at a constant rate of 7% thereafter. The company's stock has a beta of 1.2, the risk-free rate is 7.5%, and the market risk premium is 4%. What is your estimate of the stock's current price?

(7-6)
Value of Operations
of Constant Growth
Firm
EMC Corporation has never paid a dividend. Its current free cash flow of $400,000 is expected to grow at a constant rate of 5%. The weighted average cost of capital is WACC = 12%. Calculate EMC's estimated value of operations.

(7-7)
Horizon Value
Current and projected free cash flows for Radell Global Operations are shown below. Growth is expected to be constant after 2015, and the weighted average cost of capital is 11%. What is the horizon (continuing) value at 2016 if growth from 2015 remains constant?

| | Actual | Projected | | |
	2013	2014	2015	2016
Free cash flow (millions of dollars)	$606.82	$667.50	$707.55	$750.00

Intermediate
Problems 8–17

(7-8)
Constant Growth
Rate, g
A stock is trading at $80 per share. The stock is expected to have a year-end dividend of $4 per share ($D_1 = \$4$), and it is expected to grow at some constant rate g throughout time. The stock's required rate of return is 14% (assume the market is in equilibrium with the required return equal to the expected return). What is your forecast of g?

(7-9)
Constant Growth
Valuation
Crisp Cookware's common stock is expected to pay a dividend of $3 a share at the end of this year ($D_1 = \$3.00$); its beta is 0.8; the risk-free rate is 5.2%; and the market risk premium is 6%. The dividend is expected to grow at some constant rate g, and the stock currently sells for $40 a share. Assuming the market is in equilibrium, what does the market believe will be the stock's price at the end of 3 years (i.e., what is $\hat{P}_3$)?

(7-10)

Preferred Stock Rate of Return

What is the required rate of return on a preferred stock with a $50 par value, a stated annual dividend of 7% of par, and a current market price of (a) $30, (b) $40, (c) $50, and (d) $70 (assume the market is in equilibrium with the required return equal to the expected return)?

(7-11)

Declining Growth Stock Valuation

Brushy Mountain Mining Company's coal reserves are being depleted, so its sales are falling. Also, environmental costs increase each year, so its costs are rising. As a result, the company's earnings and dividends are declining at the constant rate of 4% per year. If $D_0 = 6 and $r_s = 14\%$, what is the estimated value of Brushy Mountain's stock?

(7-12)

Nonconstant Growth Stock Valuation

Assume that the average firm in your company's industry is expected to grow at a constant rate of 6% and that its dividend yield is 7%. Your company is about as risky as the average firm in the industry, but it has just successfully completed some R&D work that leads you to expect that its earnings and dividends will grow at a rate of 50% [$D_1 = D_0(1 + g) = D_0(1.50)$] this year and 25% the following year, after which growth should return to the 6% industry average. If the last dividend paid (D_0) was $1, what is the estimated value per share of your firm's stock?

(7-13)

Nonconstant Growth Stock Valuation

Simpkins Corporation does not pay any dividends because it is expanding rapidly and needs to retain all of its earnings. However, investors expect Simpkins to begin paying dividends, with the first dividend of $0.50 coming 3 years from today. The dividend should grow rapidly—at a rate of 80% per year—during Years 4 and 5. After Year 5, the company should grow at a constant rate of 7% per year. If the required return on the stock is 16%, what is the value of the stock today (assume the market is in equilibrium with the required return equal to the expected return)?

(7-14)

Preferred Stock Valuation

Several years ago, Rolen Riders issued preferred stock with a stated annual dividend of 10% of its $100 par value. Preferred stock of this type currently yields 8%. Assume dividends are paid annually.

a. What is the estimated value of Rolen's preferred stock?
b. Suppose interest rate levels have risen to the point where the preferred stock now yields 12%. What would be the new estimated value of Rolen's preferred stock?

(7-15)

Return on Common Stock

You buy a share of The Ludwig Corporation stock for $21.40. You expect it to pay dividends of $1.07, $1.1449, and $1.2250 in Years 1, 2, and 3, respectively, and you expect to sell it at a price of $26.22 at the end of 3 years.

a. Calculate the growth rate in dividends.
b. Calculate the expected dividend yield.
c. Assuming that the calculated growth rate is expected to continue, you can add the dividend yield to the expected growth rate to obtain the expected total rate of return. What is this stock's expected total rate of return (assume the market is in equilibrium with the required return equal to the expected return)?

(7-16)

Constant Growth Stock Valuation

Investors require a 13% rate of return on Brooks Sisters's stock ($r_s = 13\%$).

a. What would the estimated value of Brooks's stock be if the previous dividend were $D_0 = \$3.00$ and if investors expect dividends to grow at a constant annual rate of (1) −5%, (2) 0%, (3) 5%, and (4) 10%?
b. Using data from part a, what is the constant growth model's estimated value for Brooks Sisters's stock if the required rate of return is 13% and the expected growth rate is (1) 13% or (2) 15%? Are these reasonable results? Explain.
c. Is it reasonable to expect that a constant growth stock would have $g > r_s$?

(7-17)

Value of Operations

Kendra Enterprises has never paid a dividend. Free cash flow is projected to be $80,000 and $100,000 for the next 2 years, respectively; after the second year, FCF is expected to grow at a constant rate of 8%. The company's weighted average cost of capital is 12%.

a. What is the terminal, or horizon, value of operations? (*Hint:* Find the value of all free cash flows beyond Year 2 discounted back to Year 2.)

b. Calculate the value of Kendra's operations.

(7-18)
Free Cash Flow
Valuation

Dozier Corporation is a fast-growing supplier of office products. Analysts project the following free cash flows (FCFs) during the next 3 years, after which FCF is expected to grow at a constant 7% rate. Dozier's weighted average cost of capital is WACC = 13%.

	Year		
	1	2	3
Free cash flow ($ millions)	–$20	$30	$40

a. What is Dozier's terminal, or horizon, value? (*Hint:* Find the value of all free cash flows beyond Year 3 discounted back to Year 3.)

b. What is the current value of operations for Dozier?

c. Suppose Dozier has $10 million in marketable securities, $100 million in debt, and 10 million shares of stock. What is the intrinsic price per share?

Challenging
Problems 19–21

(7-19)
Constant Growth
Stock Valuation

You are analyzing Jillian's Jewlery (JJ) stock for a possible purchase. JJ just paid a dividend of $1.50 *yesterday*. You expect the dividend to grow at the rate of 6% per year for the next 3 years; if you buy the stock, you plan to hold it for 3 years and then sell it.

a. What dividends do you expect for JJ stock over the next 3 years? In other words, calculate D_1, D_2, and D_3. Note that D_0 = $1.50.

b. JJ's stock has a required return of 13% and so this is the rate you'll use to discount dividends. Find the present value of the dividend stream; that is, calculate the PV of D_1, D_2, and D_3, and then sum these PVs.

c. JJ stock should trade for $27.05 3 years from now (i.e., you expect $\hat{P}_3$ = $27.05). Discounted at a 13% rate, what is the present value of this expected future stock price? In other words, calculate the PV of $27.05.

d. If you plan to buy the stock, hold it for 3 years, and then sell it for $27.05, what is the most you should pay for it?

e. Use the constant growth model to calculate the present value of this stock. Assume that g = 6% and is constant.

f. Is the value of this stock dependent on how long you plan to hold it? In other words, if your planned holding period were 2 years or 5 years rather than 3 years, would this affect the value of the stock today, $\hat{P}_0$? Explain your answer.

(7-20)
Nonconstant Growth
Stock Valuation

Reizenstein Technologies (RT) has just developed a solar panel capable of generating 200% more electricity than any solar panel currently on the market. As a result, RT is expected to experience a 15% annual growth rate for the next 5 years. By the end of 5 years, other firms will have developed comparable technology, and RT's growth rate will slow to 5% per year indefinitely. Stockholders require a return of 12% on RT's stock. The most recent annual dividend (D_0), which was paid yesterday, was $1.75 per share.

a. Calculate RT's expected dividends for t = 1, t = 2, t = 3, t = 4, and t = 5.

b. Calculate the estimated intrinsic value of the stock today, $\hat{P}_0$. Proceed by finding the present value of the dividends expected at t = 1, t = 2, t = 3, t = 4, and t = 5 plus the present value of the stock price that should exist at t = 5, $\hat{P}_5$. The $\hat{P}_5$ stock price can be found by using the constant growth equation. Note that to find $\hat{P}_5$ you use the dividend expected at t = 6, which is 5% greater than the t = 5 dividend.

   c. Calculate the expected dividend yield ($D_1/\hat{P}_0$), the capital gains yield expected during the first year, and the expected total return (dividend yield plus capital gains yield) during the first year. (Assume that $\hat{P}_0 = P_0$, and recognize that the capital gains yield is equal to the total return minus the dividend yield.) Also calculate these same three yields for t = 5 (e.g., $D_6/\hat{P}_5$).

(7-21)
Nonconstant Growth
Stock Valuation

Conroy Consulting Corporation (CCC) has been growing at a rate of 30% per year in recent years. This same nonconstant growth rate is expected to last for another 2 years ($g_{0,1} = g_{1,2} = 30\%$).

   a. If $D_0 = \$2.50$, $r_s = 12\%$, and $g_L = 7\%$, then what is CCC's stock worth today? What are its expected dividend yield and capital gains yield at this time?

   b. Now assume that CCC's period of nonconstant growth is to last another 5 years rather than 2 years ($g_{0,1} = g_{1,2} = g_{2,3} = g_{3,4} = g_{4,5} = 30\%$). How would this affect its price, dividend yield, and capital gains yield? Answer in words only.

   c. What will CCC's dividend yield and capital gains yield be once its period of nonconstant growth ends? (*Hint:* These values will be the same regardless of whether you examine the case of 2 or 5 years of nonconstant growth, and the calculations are very easy.)

   d. Of what interest to investors is the relationship over time between dividend yield and capital gains yield?

SPREADSHEET PROBLEMS

(7-22)
Build a Model:
Nonconstant Growth
and Corporate
Valuation

Start with the partial model in the file **Ch07 P22 Build a Model.xls** on the textbook's Web site. Hamilton Landscaping's dividend growth rate is expected to be 30% in the next year, drop to 15% from Year 1 to Year 2, and drop to a constant 5% for Year 2 and all subsequent years. Hamilton has just paid a dividend of $2.50, and its stock has a required return of 11%.

resource

   a. What is Hamilton's estimated stock price today?

   b. If you bought the stock at Year 0, what are your expected dividend yield and capital gains for the upcoming year?

   c. What are your expected dividend yield and capital gains for the second year (from Year 1 to Year 2)? Why aren't these the same as for the first year?

(7-23)
Build a Model: Free
Cash Flow Valuation
Model

Start with the partial model in the file **Ch07 P23 Build a Model.xls** on the textbook's Web site. Selected data for the Derby Corporation are shown below. Use the data to answer the following questions.

resource

   a. Calculate the estimated horizon value (i.e., the value of operations at the end of the forecast period immediately after the Year-4 free cash flow).

   b. Calculate the present value of the horizon value, the present value of the free cash flows, and the estimated Year-0 value of operations.

   c. Calculate the estimated Year-0 price per share of common equity.

INPUTS (In Millions)		Year			
	Current		Projected		
	0	1	2	3	4
Free cash flow		–$20.0	$20.0	$80.0	$84.0
Marketable securities	$40				
Notes payable	$100				
Long-term bonds	$300				
Preferred stock	$50				
WACC	9.00%				
Number of shares of stock	40				

THOMSON ONE Business School Edition Problem

 THOMSON REUTERS

Use the Thomson ONE—Business School Edition online database to work this chapter's questions.

Estimating ExxonMobil's Intrinsic Stock Value with Thomson ONE—Business School Edition

In this chapter we described the various factors that influence stock prices and the approaches analysts use to estimate a stock's intrinsic value. By comparing these intrinsic value estimates to the current price, an investor can assess whether it makes sense to buy or sell a particular stock. Stocks trading at a price far below their estimated intrinsic values may be good candidates for purchase, whereas stocks trading at prices far in excess of their intrinsic value may be good stocks to avoid or sell.

Although estimating a stock's intrinsic value is a complex exercise that requires reliable data and good judgment, we can use the data available in Thomson ONE to arrive at a quick "back of the envelope" calculation of intrinsic value.

Thomson ONE—BSE Discussion Questions

1. For the purposes of this exercise, let's take a closer look at the stock of ExxonMobil Corporation (XOM). Looking at the Company Overview, we can immediately see the company's current stock price and its performance relative to the overall market in recent months. What is ExxonMobil's current stock price? How has the stock performed relative to the market over the past few months?

2. Click on the "News" tab to see the recent news stories for the company. Have there been any recent events affecting the company's stock price, or have things been relatively quiet?

3. To provide a starting point for gauging a company's relative valuation, analysts often look at a company's price-to-earnings (P/E) ratio. Returning to the Company Overview page, you can see XOM's current P/E ratio. To put this number in perspective, it is useful to compare this ratio with other companies in the same industry and to take a look at how this ratio has changed over time. If you want to see how XOM's P/E ratio stacks up to its peers, click on the tab labeled Comparables, then select Key Financial Ratios.

Toward the bottom of the table you should see information on the P/E ratio in the section titled Market Value Ratios. Toward the top, you should see an item that says Click Here To Select New Peer Set—do this if you want to compare XOM to a different set of firms.

For the most part, is XOM's P/E ratio above or below that of its peers? Off the top of your head, can these factors explain why XOM's P/E ratio differs from its peers?

4. To see how XOM's P/E ratio has varied over time, return to the Company Overview page. Next click Financials—Growth Ratios and then select Worldscope—Income Statement Ratios. Is XOM's current P/E ratio well above or well below its historical average? If so, do you have any explanation for why the current P/E deviates from its historical trend? On the basis of this information, does XOM's current P/E suggest that the stock is undervalued or overvalued? Explain.

5. In the text, we discussed using the dividend growth model to estimate a stock's intrinsic value. To keep things as simple as possible, let's assume at first that XOM's dividend is expected to grow at some constant rate over time. Then its intrinsic value would equal D_1 / $(r_s - g)$, where D_1 is the expected annual dividend 1 year from now, r_s is the stock's required rate of return, and g is the dividend's constant growth rate. To estimate the dividend growth rate, it's helpful first to look at XOM's dividend history. Staying on the current Web page (Worldscope—Income Statement Ratios), you should immediately find the company's annual dividend for the past several years. On the basis of this information, what has been the average annual dividend growth rate? Another way to obtain estimates of dividend growth rates is to look at analysts' forecasts for future dividends, which can be found on the Estimates tab, which should bring up the Thomson Estimated Tearsheet. Scrolling down the page, you should see an area marked Consensus Estimates; select Thomson Forecast Reports and a tab under Available Measures. Here you click on the down arrow key and select Dividends Per Share (DPS). What is the median year-end dividend forecast? You can use this as an estimate of D_1 in your measure of intrinsic value. You can also use this forecast along with the historical data to arrive at a measure of the forecasted dividend growth rate, g.

6. The required return on equity, r_s, is the final input needed to estimate intrinsic value. For our purposes you can either assume a number (say, 8% or 9%) or use the CAPM to calculate an estimated cost of equity using the data available in Thomson ONE. (For more details, see the Thomson ONE exercise for Chapter 6.) Having decided on your best estimates for D_1, r_s, and g, you can then calculate XOM's intrinsic value. How does this estimate compare with the current stock price? Does your preliminary analysis suggest that XOM is undervalued or overvalued? Explain.

7. Often it is useful to perform a sensitivity analysis, in which you show how your estimate of intrinsic value varies according to different estimates of D_1, r_s, and g. To do so, recalculate your intrinsic value estimate for a range of different estimates for each of these key inputs. One convenient way to do this is to set up a simple data table in *Excel*. Refer to the *Excel* tutorial accessed through the textbook's Web site for instructions on data tables. On the basis of this analysis, what inputs justify the current stock price?

8. On the basis of the dividend history you uncovered in question 5 and your assessment of XOM's future dividend payout policies, do you think it is reasonable to assume that the constant growth model is a good proxy for intrinsic value? If not, how would you use the available data in Thomson ONE to estimate intrinsic value using the nonconstant growth model?

9. Finally, you can also use the information in Thomson ONE to value the entire corporation. This approach requires that you estimate XOM's annual free cash flows. Once you estimate the value of the entire corporation, you subtract the value of debt and preferred stock to arrive at an estimate of the company's equity value. Divide this number by the number of shares of common stock outstanding, which yields an alternative estimate of the stock's intrinsic value. This approach may take some more time and involve more judgment concerning forecasts of future free cash flows, but you can use the financial statements and growth. forecasts in Thomson ONE as useful starting points. Go to Worldscope's Cash Flow Ratios Report (which you find by clicking on Financials, Fundamental Ratios, and Worldscope Ratios) to find an estimate of "free cash flow per share." Although this number is useful, Worldscope's definition of free cash flow subtracts out dividends per share; therefore, to make it comparable to the measure used in this text, you must add back dividends. To see Worldscope's definition of free cash flow (or any term), click on Search For Companies from the left toolbar and then select the Advanced Search tab. In the middle of your screen, on the right-hand side, you will see a dialog box with terms. Use the down arrow to scroll through the terms, highlighting the term for which you would like to see a definition. Then, click on the Definition button immediately below the dialog box.

MINI CASE

.Your employer, a mid-sized human resources management company, is considering expansion into related fields, including the acquisition of Temp Force Company, an employment agency that supplies word processor operators and computer programmers to businesses with temporary heavy workloads. Your employer is also considering the purchase of a Biggerstaff & Biggerstaff (B&B), a privately held company owned by two brothers, each with 5 million shares of stock. B&B currently has free cash flow of $24 million, which is expected to grow at a constant rate of 5%. B&B's financial statements report marketable securities of $100 million, debt of $200 million, and preferred stock of $50 million. B&B's WACC is 11%. Answer the following questions.

a. Describe briefly the legal rights and privileges of common stockholders.
b. (1) Write out a formula that can be used to value any stock, regardless of its dividend pattern.
    (2) What is a constant growth stock? How are constant growth stocks valued?
    (3) What happens if a company has a constant g that exceeds its r_s? Will many stocks have expected $g > r_s$ in the short run (i.e., for the next few years)? In the long run (i.e., forever)?
c. Assume that Temp Force has a beta coefficient of 1.2, that the risk-free rate (the yield on T-bonds) is 7.0%, and that the market risk premium is 5%. What is the required rate of return on the firm's stock?
d. Assume that Temp Force is a constant growth company whose last dividend (D_0, which was paid yesterday) was $2.00 and whose dividend is expected to grow indefinitely at a 6% rate.
    (1) What is the firm's current estimated intrinsic stock price?
    (2) What is the stock's expected value 1 year from now?
    (3) What are the expected dividend yield, the expected capital gains yield, and the expected total return during the first year?

e. Suppose Temp Force's stock price is selling for $30.29. Is the stock price based more on long-term or short-term expectations? Answer this by finding the percentage of Temp Force's current stock price that is based on dividends expected during Years 1, 2, and 3.

f. Why are stock prices volatile? Using Temp Force as an example, what is the impact on the estimated stock price if g falls to 5% or rises to 7%? If r_s changes to 12%% or to 14%?

g. Now assume that the stock is currently selling at $30.29. What is its expected rate of return?

h. Now assume that Temp Force's dividend is expected to experience nonconstant growth of 30% from Year 0 to Year 1, 25% from Year 1 to Year 2, and 15% from Year 2 to Year 3. After Year 3, dividends will grow at a constant rate of 6%. What is the stock's intrinsic value under these conditions? What are the expected dividend yield and capital gains yield during the first year? What are the expected dividend yield and capital gains yield during the fourth year (from Year 3 to Year 4)?

i. What is free cash flow (FCF)? What is the weighted average cost of capital? What is the free cash flow valuation model?

j. Use a pie chart to illustrate the sources that comprise a hypothetical company's total value. Using another pie chart, show the claims on a company's value. How is equity a residual claim?

k. Use B&B's data and the free cash flow valuation model to answer the following questions.
   (1) What is its estimated value of operations?
   (2) What is its estimated total corporate value?
   (3) What is its estimated intrinsic value of equity?
   (4) What is its estimated intrinsic stock price per share?

l. You have just learned that B&B has undertaken a major expansion that will change its expected free cash flows to –$10 million in 1 year, $20 million in 2 years, and $35 million in 3 years. After 3 years, free cash flow will grow at a rate of 5%. No new debt or preferred stock was added; the investment was financed by equity from the owners. Assume the WACC is unchanged at 11% and that there are still 10 million shares of stock outstanding.
   (1) What is the company's horizon value (i.e., its value of operations at Year 3)? What is its current value of operations (i.e., at Time 0)?
   (2) What is its estimated intrinsic value of equity on a price-per-share basis?

m. Compare and contrast the free cash flow valuation model and the dividend growth model.

n. What is market multiple analysis?

o. What is preferred stock? Suppose a share of preferred stock pays a dividend of $2.10 and investors require a return of 7%. What is the estimated value of the preferred stock?

SELECTED ADDITIONAL CASES

The following cases from CengageCompose cover many of the concepts discussed in this chapter and are available at **compose.cengage.com**.

Klein-Brigham Series:
Case 3, "Peachtree Securities, Inc. (B)"; Case 71, "Swan Davis"; Case 78, "Beatrice Peabody"; and Case 101, "TECO Energy."
Brigham-Buzzard Series:
Case 4, "Powerline Network Corporation (Stocks)."

© Adalberto Rios Szalay/Sexto Sol/Getty Images

CHAPTER **8**

Financial Options and Applications in Corporate Finance

I n 2012, Cisco had over 621 million outstanding employee stock options and about 5.4 billion outstanding shares of stock. If all these options are exercised, then the option holders will own about 10% of Cisco's stock: $0.621/(5.4 + 0.621) = 0.10$. Many of these options may never be exercised, but any way you look at it, 621 million is a lot of options. Cisco isn't the only company with mega-grants: Pfizer, Time Warner, Ford, and Bank of America are among the many companies that have granted to their employees options to buy more than 100 million shares. Whether your next job is with a high-tech firm, a financial services company, or a manufacturer, you will probably receive stock options, so it's important that you understand them.

In a typical grant, you receive options allowing you to purchase shares of stock at a fixed price, called the strike price or exercise price, on or before a stated expiration date. Most plans have a vesting period, during which you can't exercise the options. For example, suppose you are granted 1,000 options with a strike price of $50, an expiration date 10 years from now, and a vesting period of 3 years. Even if the stock price rises above $50 during the first 3 years, you can't exercise the options because of the vesting requirement. After 3 years, if you are still with the company, you have the right to exercise the options. For example, if the stock goes up to $110, you could pay the company $50(1,000) = $50,000 and receive 1,000 shares of stock worth $110,000. However, if you don't exercise the options within 10 years, they will expire and thus be worthless.

Even though the vesting requirement prevents you from exercising the options the moment they are granted to you, the options clearly have some immediate value. Therefore, if you are choosing between different job offers where options are involved, you will need a way to determine the value of the alternative options. This chapter explains how to value options, so read on.

The Intrinsic Value of Stock Options

© Rob Webb/Getty Images

In previous chapters we showed that the intrinsic value of an asset is the present value of its cash flows. This time value of money approach works well for stocks and bonds, but we must use another approach for options and derivatives. If we can find a portfolio of stocks and risk-free bonds that replicates an option's cash flows, then the intrinsic value of the option must be identical to the value of the replicating portfolio.

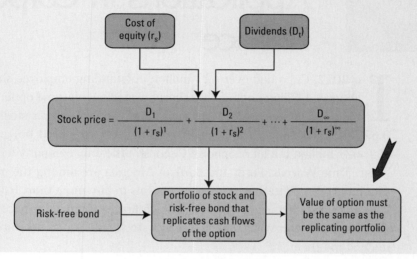

© Cengage Learning 2014

There are two fundamental approaches to valuing assets. The first is the *discounted cash flow* (DCF) approach, which we covered in previous chapters: An asset's value is the present value of its cash flows. The second is the *option pricing* approach. It is important that every manager understands the basic principles of option pricing for the following reasons. First, many projects allow managers to make strategic or tactical changes in plans as market conditions change. The existence of these "embedded options" often means the difference between a successful project and a failure. Understanding basic financial options can help you manage the value inherent in these real options. Second, many companies use derivatives to manage risk; many derivatives are types of financial options, so an understanding of basic financial options is necessary before tackling derivatives. Third, option pricing theory provides insights into the optimal debt/equity choice, especially when convertible securities are involved. And fourth, knowing about financial options will help you understand any employee stock options that you receive.

r e s o u r c e

*The textbook's Web site contains an Excel file that will guide you through the chapter's calculations. The file for this chapter is **Ch08 Tool Kit.xls**, and we encourage you to open the file and follow along as you read the chapter.*

8-1 Overview of Financial Options

In general, an **option** is a contract that gives its owner the right to buy (or sell) an asset at some predetermined price within a specified period of time. However, there are many types of options and option markets.[1] Consider the options reported in Table 8-1, which

---

[1]For an in-depth treatment of options, see Don M. Chance and Robert Brooks, *An Introduction to Derivatives and Risk Management,* 8th ed. (Mason, OH: South-Western, Cengage Learning, 2010), or John C. Hull, *Options, Futures, and Other Derivatives,* 8th ed. (Upper Saddle River, NJ: Prentice-Hall, 2012).

TABLE 8-1

Listed Options Quotations for January 7, 2013

		CALLS—LAST QUOTE			PUTS—LAST QUOTE		
Closing Price	Strike Price	February	March	May	February	March	May
General Computer Corporation (GCC)							
53.50	50	4.25	4.75	5.50	0.65	1.40	2.20
53.50	55	1.30	2.05	3.15	2.65	r	4.50
53.50	60	0.30	0.70	1.50	6.65	r	8.00

Note: r means not traded on January 7.

© Cengage Learning 2014

is an extract from a Listed Options Quotations table as it might appear on a Web site or in a daily newspaper. The first column reports the closing stock price. For example, the table shows that General Computer Corporation's (GCC) stock price closed at $53.50 on January 7, 2013.

A **call option** gives its owner the right to *buy* a share of stock at a fixed price, which is called the **strike price** (sometimes called the **exercise price** because it is the price at which you exercise the option). A **put option** gives its owner the right to *sell* a share of stock at a fixed strike price. For example, the first row in Table 8-1 is for GCC's options that have a $50 strike price. Observe that the table has columns for call options and for put options with this strike price.

Each option has an **expiration date,** after which the option may not be exercised. Table 8-1 reports data for options that expire in February, March, and May.[2] If the option can be exercised any time before the expiration, it is called an **American option;** if it can be exercised only on its expiration date, it is a **European option.** All of GCC's options are American options. The first row shows that GCC has a call option with a strike price of $50 that expires on May 17 (the third Saturday in May 2013 is the 18th). The quoted price for this option is $5.50.[3]

When the current stock price is greater than the strike price, the option is **in-the-money.** For example, GCC's $50 (strike) May call option is in-the-money by $53.50 − $50 = $3.50. Thus, if the option were immediately exercised, it would have a payoff of $3.50. On the other hand, GCC's $55 (strike) May call is **out-of-the-money** because the current $53.50 stock price is below the $55 strike price. Obviously, you currently would not want to exercise this option by paying the $55 strike price for a share of stock selling for $53.50. Therefore, the **exercise value,** which is any profit from immediately exercising an option, is[4]

---

[2]At its Web site, **www.cboe.com/learncenter/glossary.aspx**, the CBOE defines the expiration date as follows: "The day on which an option contract becomes void. The expiration date for listed stock options is the Saturday after the third Friday of the expiration month. Holders of options should indicate their desire to exercise, if they wish to do so, by this date." The CBOE also defines the expiration time as: "The time of day by which all exercise notices must be received on the expiration date. Technically, the expiration time is currently 5:00PM on the expiration date, but public holders of option contracts must indicate their desire to exercise no later than 5:30PM on the business day preceding the expiration date. The times are Eastern Time."

[3]Option contracts are generally written in 100-share multiples, but to reduce confusion we focus on the cost and payoffs of a single option.

[4]MAX means choose the maximum. For example, MAX[15, 0] = 15 and MAX[−10, 0] = 0.

$$\text{Exercise value} = \text{MAX}[\text{Current price of the stock} - \text{Strike price}, 0] \qquad \textbf{(8-1)}$$

An American option's price always will be greater than (or equal to) its exercise value. If the option's price were less, you could buy the option and immediately exercise it, reaping a sure gain. For example, GCC's May call with a $50 strike price sells for $5.50, which is greater than its exercise value of $3.50. Also, GCC's out-of-the-money May call with a strike price of $55 sells for $3.15 even though it would be worthless if it had to be exercised immediately. An option always will be worth more than zero as long as there is still any chance it will end up in-the-money: Where there is life, there is hope! The difference between the option's price and its exercise value is called the **time value** because it represents the extra amount over the option's immediate exercise value that a purchaser will pay for the chance the stock price will appreciate over time.[5] For example, GCC's May call with a $50 strike price sells for $5.50 and has an exercise value of $3.50, so its time value is $5.50 − $3.50 = $2.00.

Suppose you bought GCC's $50 (strike) May call option for $5.50 and then the stock price increased to $60. If you exercised the option by purchasing the stock for the $50 strike price, you could immediately sell the share of stock at its market price of $60, resulting in a payoff of $60 − $50 = $10. Notice that the stock itself had a return of 12.1% = ($60 − $53.50)/$53.50, but the option's return was 81.8% = ($10 − $5.50)/$5.50. Thus, the option offers the possibility of a higher return.

However, if the stock price fell to $50 and stayed there until the option expired, the stock would have a return of −6.5% = ($50.00 − $53.50)/$53.50, but the option would have a 100% loss (it would expire worthless). As this example shows, call options are a lot riskier than stocks. This works to your advantage if the stock price goes up but to your disadvantage if the stock price falls.

Suppose you bought GCC's May put option (with a strike price of $50) for $2.20 and then the stock price fell to $45. You could buy a share of stock for $45 and exercise the put option, which would allow you to sell the share of stock at its strike price of $50. Your payoff from exercising the put would be $5 = $50 − $45. Stockholders would lose money because the stock price fell, but a put holder would make money. In this example, your rate of return would be 127.3% = ($5 − $2.20)/$2.20. So if you think a stock price is going to fall, you can make money by purchasing a put option. On the other hand, if the stock price doesn't fall below the strike price of $50 before the put expires, you would lose 100% of your investment in the put option.[6]

Options are traded on a number of exchanges, with the Chicago Board Options Exchange (CBOE) being the oldest and the largest. Existing options can be traded in the secondary market in much the same way that existing shares of stock are traded in secondary markets. But unlike new shares of stock that are issued by corporations, new options can be "issued" by investors. This is called **writing** an option.

For example, you could write a call option and sell it to some other investor. You would receive cash from the option buyer at the time you wrote the option, but you would be obligated to sell a share of stock at the strike price if the option buyer later

---

[5]Among traders, an option's market price is also called its "premium." This is particularly confusing because for all other securities the word *premium* means the excess of the market price over some base price. To avoid confusion, we will not use the word *premium* to refer to the option price.

[6]Most investors don't actually exercise an option prior to expiration. If they want to cash in the option's profit or cut its losses, they sell the option to some other investor. As you will see later in the chapter, the cash flow from selling an American option before its expiration is always greater than (or equal to) the profit from exercising the option.

decided to exercise the option.[7] Thus, each option has two parties, the writer and the buyer, with the CBOE (or some other exchange) acting as an intermediary. Other than commissions, the writer's profits are exactly opposite those of the buyer. An investor who writes call options against stock held in his or her portfolio is said to be selling **covered options.** Options sold without the stock to back them up are called **naked options.**

W W W

The Chicago Board Options Exchange provides 20-minute delayed quotes for equity, index, and LEAPS options at **www.cboe.com**.

In addition to options on individual stocks, options are also available on several stock indexes such as the NYSE Index and the S&P 100 Index. Index options permit one to hedge (or bet) on a rise or fall in the general market as well as on individual stocks.

The leverage involved in option trading makes it possible for speculators with just a few dollars to make a fortune almost overnight. Also, investors with sizable portfolios can sell options against their stocks and earn the value of the option (less brokerage commissions) even if the stock's price remains constant. Most important, though, options can be used to create *hedges* that protect the value of an individual stock or portfolio.[8]

Conventional options are generally written for 6 months or less, but a type of option called a **Long-Term Equity AnticiPation Security (LEAPS)** is different. Like conventional options, LEAPS are listed on exchanges and are available on both individual stocks and stock indexes. The major difference is that LEAPS are long-term options, having maturities of up to almost 3 years. One-year LEAPS cost about twice as much as the matching 3-month option, but because of their much longer time to expiration, LEAPS provide buyers with more potential for gains and offer better long-term protection for a portfolio.

Corporations on whose stocks the options are written have nothing to do with the option market. Corporations do not raise money in the option market, nor do they have any direct transactions in it. Moreover, option holders do not vote for corporate directors or receive dividends. There have been studies by the SEC and others as to whether option trading stabilizes or destabilizes the stock market and whether this activity helps or hinders corporations seeking to raise new capital. The studies have not been conclusive, but research on the impact of option trading is ongoing.

SELF-TEST

What is an option? A call option? A put option?

Define a call option's exercise value. Why is the market price of a call option usually above its exercise value?

Brighton Memory's stock is currently trading at $50 a share. A call option on the stock with a $35 strike price currently sells for $21. What is the exercise value of the call option? **($15.00)** *What is the time value?* **($6.00)**

---

[7]Your broker would require collateral to ensure that you kept this obligation.

[8]Insiders who trade illegally generally buy options rather than stock because the leverage inherent in options increases the profit potential. However, it is illegal to use insider information for personal gain, and an insider using such information would be taking advantage of the option seller. Insider trading, in addition to being unfair and essentially equivalent to stealing, hurts the economy: Investors lose confidence in the capital markets and raise their required returns because of an increased element of risk, and this raises the cost of capital and thus reduces the level of real investment.

Financial Reporting for Employee Stock Options

© Rob Webb/Getty Images

When granted to executives and other employees, options are a "hybrid" form of compensation. At some companies, especially small ones, option grants may be a substitute for cash wages: Employees are willing to take lower cash salaries if they have options. Options also provide an incentive for employees to work harder. Whether issued to motivate employees or to conserve cash, options clearly have value at the time they are granted, and they transfer wealth from existing shareholders to employees to the extent that they do not reduce cash expenditures or increase employee productivity enough to offset their value at the time of issue.

Companies like the fact that an option grant requires no immediate cash expenditure, although it might dilute shareholder wealth if it is exercised later. Employees, and especially CEOs, like the potential wealth they receive when they are granted options. When option grants were relatively small, they didn't show up on investors' radar screens. However, as the high-tech sector began making mega-grants in the 1990s, and as other industries followed suit, stockholders began to realize that large grants were making some CEOs filthy rich at the stockholders' expense.

Before 2005, option grants were barely visible in companies' financial reports. Even though such grants are clearly a wealth transfer to employees, companies were required only to footnote the grants and could ignore them when reporting their income statements and balance sheets. The Financial Accounting Standards Board now requires companies to show option grants as an expense on the income statement. To do this, the value of the options is estimated at the time of the grant and then expensed during the vesting period, which is the amount of time the employee must wait before being allowed to exercise the options. For example, if the initial value is $100 million and the vesting period is 2 years, the company would report a $50 million expense for each of the next 2 years. This approach isn't perfect, because the grant is not a cash expense; nor does the approach take into account changes in the option's value after the initial grant. However, it does make the option grant more visible to investors, which is a good thing.

8-2 The Single-Period Binomial Option Pricing Approach

We can use a model like the Capital Asset Pricing Model (CAPM) to calculate the required return on a stock and then use that required return to discount its expected future cash flows to find its value. No such model exists for the required return on options, so we must use a different approach to find an option's value. In Section 8-5 we describe the Black-Scholes option pricing model, but in this section we explain the binomial option pricing model. The idea behind this model is different from that of the DCF model used for stock valuation. Instead of discounting cash flows at a required return to obtain a price, as we did with the stock valuation model, we will use the option, shares of stock, and the risk-free rate to construct a portfolio whose value we already know and then deduce the option's price from this portfolio's value.

The following sections describe and apply the binomial option pricing model to Western Cellular, a manufacturer of cell phones. Call options exist that permit the holder to buy 1 share of Western at a strike price, X, of $35. Western's options will expire at the end of 6 months (t is the number of years until expiration, so t = 0.5 for Western's options). Western's stock price, P, is currently $40 per share. Given this background information, we will use the binomial model to determine the call option's value. The first step is to determine the option's possible payoffs, as described in the next section.

8-2a Payoffs in a Single-Period Binomial Model

In general, the time until expiration can be divided into many periods, with n denoting the number of periods. But in a single-period model, which we describe in this section, there is only one period. We assume that, at the end of the period, the stock's price can take on only one of two possible values, so this is called the **binomial approach.** For this example, Western's stock will either go up (u) by a factor of 1.25 or go down (d) by a factor of 0.80. If we were considering a riskier stock, then we would have assumed a wider range of ending prices; we will show how to estimate this range later in the chapter. If we let u = 1.25 and d = 0.80, then the ending stock price will be either P(u) = $40(1.25) = $50 or P(d) = $40(0.80) = $32. Figure 8-1 illustrates the stock's possible price paths and contains additional information about the call option that is explained in the text that follows.

resource

*See **Ch08 Tool Kit.xls** on the textbook's Web site.*

When the option expires at the end of the year, Western's stock will sell for either $50 or $32. As shown in Figure 8-1, if the stock goes up to $50 then the option will have a payoff, C_u, of $15 at expiration because the option is in-the-money: $50 − $35 = $15. If the stock price goes down to $32, then the option's payoff, C_d, will be zero because the option is out-of-the-money.

8-2b The Hedge Portfolio Approach

Suppose we created a portfolio by writing 1 call option and purchasing 1 share of stock. As Figure 8-1 shows, if the stock price goes up then our portfolio's stock will be worth $50 but we will owe $15 on the option, so our portfolio's net payoff is $35 = $50 − $15. If the stock price goes down then our portfolio's stock will be worth only $32, but the amount we owe on the written option also will fall to zero, leaving the portfolio's net payoff at $32. The portfolio's end-of-period price range is smaller than if we had just owned the stock, so writing the call

FIGURE 8-1

Binomial Payoffs from Holding Western Cellular's Stock or Call Option

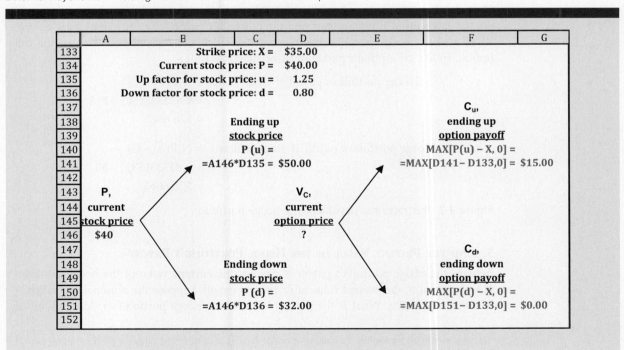

option reduces the portfolio's price risk. Taking this further: Is it possible for us to choose the number of shares held by our portfolio so that it will have the same net payoff whether the stock goes up or down? If so, then our portfolio is hedged and will have a riskless payoff when the option expires. Therefore, it is called a **hedge portfolio.**

We are not really interested in investing in the hedge portfolio, but we want to use it to help us determine the value of the option. Notice that if the hedge portfolio has a riskless net payoff when the option expires, then we can find the present value of this payoff by discounting it at the risk-free rate. Our current portfolio value must equal this present value, which allows us to determine the option's value. The following example illustrates the steps in this approach.

1. FIND N_s, THE NUMBER OF SHARES OF STOCK IN THE HEDGE PORTFOLIO

We want the portfolio's payoff to be the same whether the stock goes up or down. If we write 1 call option and buy N_s shares of stock, then the portfolio's stock will be worth $N_s(P)(u)$ should the stock price go up, so its net payoff will be $N_s(P)(u) - C_u$. The portfolio's stock will be worth $N_s(P)(d)$ if the stock price goes down, so its net payoff will be $N_s(P)(d) - C_d$. Setting these portfolio payoffs equal to one another and then solving for N_s yields

$$N_s = \frac{C_u - C_d}{P(u) - P(d)} = \frac{C_u - C_d}{P(u - d)} \qquad (8\text{-}2)$$

For Western, the hedge portfolio has 0.83333 share of stock:[9]

$$N_s = \frac{C_u - C_d}{P(u) - P(d)} = \frac{\$15 - \$0}{\$50 - \$32} = 0.83333$$

2. FIND THE HEDGE PORTFOLIO'S PAYOFF

Our next step is to find the hedge portfolio's payoff when the stock price goes up (you will get the same result if instead you find the portfolio's payoff when the stock goes down). Recall that the hedge portfolio has N_s shares of stock and that we have written the call option, so the call option's payoff must be subtracted:

$$\text{Hedge portfolio's payoff if stock is up} = N_sP(u) - C_u$$
$$= 0.83333(\$50) - \$15$$
$$= \$26.6665$$

$$\text{Hedge portfolio's payoff if stock is down} = N_sP(d) - C_d$$
$$= 0.83333(\$32) - \$0$$
$$= \$26.6665$$

Figure 8-2 illustrates the payoffs of the hedge portfolio.

3. FIND THE PRESENT VALUE OF THE HEDGE PORTFOLIO'S PAYOFF

Because the hedge portfolio's payoff is riskless, the current value of the hedge portfolio must be equal to the present value of its riskless payoff. Suppose the nominal annual risk-free rate, r_{RF}, is 8%. What is the present value of the hedge portfolio's riskless payoff of

[9]An easy way to remember this formula is to notice that N_s is equal to the range in possible option payoffs divided by the range in possible stock prices.

FIGURE 8-2

Hedge Portfolio with Riskless Payoffs

	A	B	C	D	E	F
180					Strike price: X =	$35.00
181					Current stock price: P =	$40.00
182					Up factor for stock price: u =	1.25
183					Down factor for stock price: d =	0.80
184					Up option payoff: C_u = MAX[0,P(u)-X] =	$15.00
185					Down option payoff: C_d =MAX[0,P(d)-X] =	$0.00
186			Number of shares of stock in portfolio: N_s = (C_u - C_d) / P(u-d) =			0.83333
187						
188				Stock price = P (u) =	$50.00	
189	P,			Portfolio's stock payoff: = P(u)(N_s) =		$41.67
190	current			Subtract option's payoff: C_u =		$15.00
191	stock price			Portfolio's net payoff = P(u)N_s - C_u =		$26.67
192	$40					
193						
194						
195						
196				Stock price = P (d) =	$32.00	
197				Portfolio's stock payoff: = P(d)(N_s) =		$26.67
198				Subtract option's payoff: C_d =		$0.00
199				Portfolio's net payoff = P(d)N_s - C_d =		$26.67
200						

$26.6665 in 6 months? Recall from Chapter 4 that the present value depends on how frequently interest is compounded. Let's assume that interest is compounded daily.[10] We can use a financial calculator to find the present value of the hedge portfolio's payoff by entering N = 0.5(365), because there are 365 days in a year and the contract expires in half a year; I/YR = 8/365, because we want a daily interest rate; PMT = 0; and FV = −$26.6665, because we want to know the amount we would take today in exchange for giving up the payoff when the option expires. Using these inputs, we solve for PV = $25.6210, which is the present value of the hedge portfolio's payoff.[11]

resource

See **ChO8 Tool Kit.xls** on the textbook's Web site.

4. FIND THE OPTION'S VALUE

The current value of the hedge portfolio is the value of the stock, N_s(P), less the value of the call option we wrote:

$$\text{Current value of hedge portfolio} = N_s(P) - V_C$$

Because the payoff is riskless, the current value of the hedge portfolio must also equal the present value of the riskless payoff:

$$\text{Current value of hedge portfolio} = \text{Present value of riskless payoff}$$

---

[10]Option pricing models usually assume continuous compounding, which we discuss in **Web Extension 4C** on the textbook's Web site, but daily compounding works well. We will apply continuous compounding in Sections 8-3 and 8-4.
[11]We could also solve for the present value using the present value equation with the daily periodic interest rate and the number of daily periods: PV = $26.6665/(1 + 0.08/365)^{0.5(365)}$ = $25.6210.

Substituting for the current value of the hedge portfolio, we get:

$$N_s(P) - V_C = \frac{\text{Present value of}}{\text{riskless payoff}}$$

Solving for the call option's value, we get

$$V_C = N_s(P) - \frac{\text{Present value of}}{\text{riskless payoff}}$$

For Western's option, this is

$$V_C = 0.83333(\$40) - \$25.621$$
$$= \$7.71$$

8-2c Hedge Portfolios and Replicating Portfolios

In our previous derivation of the call option's value, we combined an investment in the stock with writing a call option to create a risk-free investment. We can modify this approach and create a portfolio that replicates the call option's payoffs. For example, suppose we formed a portfolio by purchasing 0.83333 shares of Western's stock and borrowing \$25.621 at the risk-free rate (this is equivalent to selling a T-bill short). In 6 months, we would repay the future value of a \$25.621, compounded daily at the risk-free rate. Using a financial calculator, input N = 0.5(365), I/YR = 8/365, PV = −\$25.621, and solve for FV = \$26.6665.[12] If the stock goes up, our net payoff would be 0.83333(\$50) − \$26.6665 = \$15.00. If the stock goes down, our net payoff would be 0.83333(\$32) − \$26.6665 = \$0. The portfolio's payoffs are exactly equal to the option's payoffs as shown in Figure 8-1, so our portfolio of 0.83333 shares of stock and the \$25.621 that we borrowed would exactly replicate the option's payoffs. Therefore, this is called a **replicating portfolio.** Our cost to create this portfolio is the cost of the stock less the amount we borrowed:

$$\text{Cost of replicating portfolio} = 0.83333(\$40) - \$25.621 = \$7.71$$

If the call option did not sell for exactly \$7.71, then a clever investor could make a sure profit. For example, suppose the option sold for \$8. The investor would write an option, which would provide \$8 of cash now but would obligate the investor to pay either \$15 or \$0 in 6 months when the option expires. However, the investor could use the \$8 to create the replicating portfolio, leaving the investor with \$8 − \$7.71 = \$0.29. In 6 months, the replicating portfolio will pay either \$15 or \$0. Thus, the investor isn't exposed to any risk—the payoffs received from the replicating portfolio exactly offset the payoffs owed on the option. The investor uses none of his own money, has no risk, has no net future obligations, but has \$0.29 in cash. This is **arbitrage,** and if such an arbitrage opportunity existed then the investor would scale it up by writing thousands of options.[13]

Such arbitrage opportunities don't persist for long in a reasonably efficient economy because other investors will also see the opportunity and will try to do the same thing. With so many investors trying to write (i.e., sell) the option, its price will fall; with so many investors trying to purchase the stock, its price will increase. This will continue until the option and replicating portfolio have identical prices. And because our financial markets are really quite efficient, you would never observe the derivative security and the replicating portfolio trading for different prices—they would always have the same price and there would be no arbitrage opportunities. What this means is that, by finding

---

[12]Alternatively, use the present value equation with daily compounding: $\$25.621(1 + 0.08/365)^{365(0.5/1)} = \$26.6665$.

[13]If the option sold for less than the replicating portfolio, the investor would raise cash by shorting the portfolio and use the cash to purchase the option, again resulting in arbitrage profits.

the price of a portfolio that replicates a derivative security, we have also found the price of the derivative security itself!

SELF-TEST

Describe how a risk-free hedge portfolio can be created using stocks and options.

How can such a portfolio be used to help estimate a call option's value?

What is a replicating portfolio, and how is it used to find the value of a derivative security?

What is arbitrage?

Lett Incorporated's stock price is now $50, but it is expected either to rise by a factor of 1.5 or fall by a factor of 0.7 by the end of the year. There is a call option on Lett's stock with a strike price of $55 and an expiration date 1 year from now. What are the stock's possible prices at the end of the year? ($75 or $35) What is the call option's payoff if the stock price goes up? ($20) If the stock price goes down? ($0) If we sell 1 call option, how many shares of Lett's stock must we buy to create a riskless hedged portfolio consisting of the option position and the stock? (0.5) What is the payoff of this portfolio? ($17.50) If the annual risk-free rate is 6%, then how much is the riskless portfolio worth today (assuming daily compounding)? ($16.48) What is the current value of the call option? ($8.52)

8-3 The Single-Period Binomial Option Pricing Formula[14]

The hedge portfolio approach works well if you only want to find the value of one type of option with one period until expiration. But in all other situations, the step-by-step approach becomes tedious very quickly. The following sections describe a formula that replaces the step-by-step approach.

8-3a The Binomial Option Pricing Formula

With a little (or a lot!) of algebra, we can derive a single formula for a call option. Instead of using daily compounding, we use continuous compounding to make the binomial formula consistent with the Black-Scholes formula in Section 8-5.[15] Here is the resulting binomial option pricing formula:

$$V_C = \frac{C_u\left[\dfrac{e^{r_{RF}(t/n)} - d}{u - d}\right] + C_d\left[\dfrac{u - e^{r_{RF}(t/n)}}{u - d}\right]}{e^{r_{RF}(t/n)}} \tag{8-3}$$

After programming it into *Excel*, which we did for this chapter's **Tool Kit**, it is easy to change inputs and determine the new value of a call option. Here is the binomial option pricing formula:

---

[14]The material in this section is relatively technical, and some instructors may choose to skip it with no loss in continuity.

[15]With continuous compounding, the present value is equal to the future value divided by $(1 + r_{RF}/365)^{365(0.5/1)}$. With continuous compounding, the present value is $e^{-r_{RF}(t/n)}$. See **Web Extension 4C** on the textbook's Web site for more discussion of continuous compounding.

We can apply this formula to Western's call option:

$$V_C = \frac{\$15\left[\dfrac{e^{0.08(0.5/1)}-0.80}{1.25-0.80}\right] + \$0\left[\dfrac{1.25-e^{0.08(0.5/1)}}{1.25-0.80}\right]}{e^{0.08(0.5/1)}}$$

$$= \frac{\$15(0.5351) + \$0(0.4649)}{1.04081} = \$7.71$$

Notice that this is the same value that resulted from the step-by-step process shown earlier.

The binomial option pricing formula in Equation 8-3 does not include the actual probabilities that the stock will go up or down, nor does it include the expected stock return, which is not what one might expect. After all, the higher the stock's expected return, the greater the chance that the call will be in-the-money at expiration. Note, however, that the stock's expected return is already indirectly incorporated into the stock price.

8-3b Primitive Securities and the Binomial Option Pricing Formula

If we want to value other Western call options or puts that expire in 6 months, then we can use Equation 8-3, but there is a time-saving approach. Notice that for options with the same time left until expiration, C_u and C_d are the only variables that depend on the option itself. The other variables depend only on the stock process (u and d), the risk-free rate, the time until expiration, and the number of periods until expiration. If we group these variables together, we can then define π_u and π_d as

$$\pi_u = \frac{\left[\dfrac{e^{r_{RF}(t/n)}-d}{u-d}\right]}{e^{r_{RF}(t/n)}} \tag{8-4}$$

and

$$\pi_d = \frac{\left[\dfrac{u-e^{r_{RF}(t/n)}}{u-d}\right]}{e^{r_{RF}(t/n)}} \tag{8-5}$$

By substituting these values into Equation 8-3, we obtain an option pricing model that can be applied to all of Western's 6-month options:

$$V_C = C_u\pi_u + C_d\pi_d \tag{8-6}$$

In this example, π_u and π_d are

$$\pi_u = \frac{\left[\dfrac{e^{0.08(0.5/1)}-0.80}{1.25-0.80}\right]}{e^{0.08(0.5/1)}} = 0.5142$$

and

$$\pi_d = \frac{\left[\dfrac{1.25 - e^{0.08(0.5/1)}}{1.25 - 0.80} \right]}{e^{0.08(0.5/1)}} = 0.4466$$

Using Equation 8-6, the value of Western's 6-month call option with a strike price of $35 is

$$V_c = C_u\pi_u + C_d\pi_d$$
$$= \$15(0.5142) + \$0(0.4466)$$
$$= \$7.71$$

Sometimes these π's are called *primitive securities* because π_u is the price of a simple security that pays $1 if the stock goes up and nothing if it goes down; π_d is the opposite. This means that we can use these π's to find the price of any 6-month option on Western. For example, suppose we want to find the value of a 6-month call option on Western but with a strike price of $30. Rather than reinvent the wheel, all we have to do is find the payoffs of this option and use the same values of π_u and π_d in Equation 8-6. If the stock goes up to $50, the option will pay $50 − $30 = $20; if the stock falls to $32, the option will pay $32 − $30 = $2. The value of the call option is:

$$\text{Value of 6-month call with \$30 strike price} = C_u\pi_u + C_d\pi_d$$
$$= \$20(0.5141) + \$2(0.4466)$$
$$= \$11.18$$

It is a bit tedious initially to calculate π_u and π_d, but once you save them, it is easy to find the value of any 6-month call or put option on the stock. In fact, you can use these π's to find the value of any security with payoffs that depend on Western's 6-month stock prices, which makes them a very powerful tool.

S E L F - T E S T

Yegi's Fine Phones has a current stock price of $30. You need to find the value of a call option with a strike price of $32 that expires in 3 months. Use the binomial model with one period until expiration. The factor for an increase in stock price is u = 1.15; the factor for a downward movement is d = 0.85. What are the possible stock prices at expiration? **($34.50 or $25.50)** *What are the option's possible payoffs at expiration?* **($2.50 or $0)** *What are π_u and π_d?* **(0.5422 and 0.4429)** *What is the current value of the option (assume each month is 1/12 of a year)?* **($1.36)**

8-4 The Multi-Period Binomial Option Pricing Model[16]

Clearly, the one-period example is simplified. Although you could duplicate buying 0.8333 share and writing one option by buying 8,333 shares and writing 10,000 options, the stock price assumptions are unrealistic—Western's stock price could be

---

[16]The material in this section is relatively technical, and some instructors may choose to skip it with no loss in continuity.

almost anything after 6 months, not just \$50 or \$32. However, if we allowed the stock to move up or down more often, then a more realistic range of ending prices would result. In other words, dividing the time until expiration into more periods would improve the realism of the resulting prices at expiration. The key to implementing a multi-period binomial model is to keep the stock return's annual standard deviation the same no matter how many periods you have during a year. In fact, analysts typically begin with an estimate of the annual standard deviation and use it to determine u and d. The derivation is beyond the scope of a financial management textbook, but the appropriate equations are

$$u = e^{\sigma\sqrt{t/n}} \tag{8-7}$$

$$d = \frac{1}{u} \tag{8-8}$$

where σ is the annualized standard deviation of the stock's return, t is the time in years until expiration, and n is the number of periods until expiration.

The standard deviation of Western's stock returns is 31.5573%, and application of Equations 8-7 and 8-8 confirms the values of u and d that we used previously:

$$u = e^{0.315573\sqrt{0.5/1}} = 1.25 \quad \text{and} \quad d = \frac{1}{1.25} = 0.80$$

Now suppose we allow stock prices to change every 3 months (which is 0.25 years). Using Equations 8-7 and 8-8, we estimate u and d to be

$$u = e^{0.31573\sqrt{0.5/2}} = 1.1709 \quad \text{and} \quad d = \frac{1}{1.1709} = 0.8540$$

At the end of the first 3 months, Western's price would either rise to \$40(1.1709) = \$46.84 or fall to \$40(0.8540) = \$34.16. If the price rises in the first 3 months to \$46.84, then it would either go up to \$46.84(1.1709) = \$54.84 or go down to \$46.84(0.8540) = \$40 at expiration. If instead the price initially falls to \$40(0.8540) = \$34.16 during the first 3 months, then it would either go up to \$34.16(1.1709) = \$40 or go down to \$34.16(0.8540) = \$29.17 by expiration. This pattern of stock price movements is called a **binomial lattice** and is shown in Figure 8-3.

Because the interest rate and the volatility (as defined by u and d) are constant for each period, we can calculate π_u and π_d for any period and apply these same values for each period:[17]

$$\pi_u = \frac{\left[\dfrac{e^{0.08(0.5/2)} - 0.80}{1.25 - 0.80}\right]}{e^{0.08(0.5/2)}} = 0.51400$$

$$\pi_d = \frac{\left[\dfrac{1.25 - e^{0.08(0.5/1)}}{1.25 - 0.80}\right]}{e^{0.08(0.5/1)}} = 0.46620$$

These values are shown in Figure 8-3.

---

[17]These values were calculated in *Excel*, so there may be small differences due to rounding in intermediate steps.

FIGURE **8-3**

Two-Period Binomial Lattice and Option Valuation

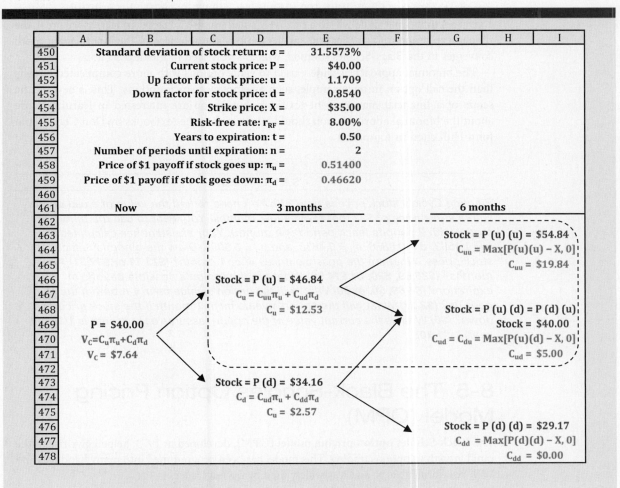

	A	B	C	D	E	F	G	H	I
450		Standard deviation of stock return: σ =			31.5573%				
451		Current stock price: P =			$40.00				
452		Up factor for stock price: u =			1.1709				
453		Down factor for stock price: d =			0.8540				
454		Strike price: X =			$35.00				
455		Risk-free rate: r_{RF} =			8.00%				
456		Years to expiration: t =			0.50				
457		Number of periods until expiration: n =			2				
458		Price of $1 payoff if stock goes up: π_u =			0.51400				
459		Price of $1 payoff if stock goes down: π_d =			0.46620				

The lattice for periods Now, 3 months, and 6 months shows:

Now:
P = $40.00
$V_C = C_u \pi_u + C_d \pi_d$
V_C = $7.64

3 months (up):
Stock = P (u) = $46.84
$C_u = C_{uu}\pi_u + C_{ud}\pi_d$
C_u = $12.53

3 months (down):
Stock = P (d) = $34.16
$C_d = C_{ud}\pi_u + C_{dd}\pi_d$
C_u = $2.57

6 months (up-up):
Stock = P (u) (u) = $54.84
$C_{uu} = Max[P(u)(u) - X, 0]$
C_{uu} = $19.84

6 months (up-down):
Stock = P (u) (d) = P (d) (u)
Stock = $40.00
$C_{ud} = C_{du} = Max[P(u)(d) - X, 0]$
C_{ud} = $5.00

6 months (down-down):
Stock = P (d) (d) = $29.17
$C_{dd} = Max[P(d)(d) - X, 0]$
C_{dd} = $0.00

r e s o u r c e

*See ChO8 Tool Kit.xls on
the textbook's Web site.*

The lattice shows the possible stock prices at the option's expiration and we know the strike price, so we can calculate the option payoffs at expiration. Figure 8-3 also shows the option payoffs at expiration. If we focus only on the upper right portion of the lattice shown inside the dotted lines, then it is similar to the single-period problem we solved in Section 8-3. In fact, we can use the binomial option pricing model from Equation 8-6 to determine the value of the option in 3 months given that the stock price increased to $46.84. As shown in Figure 8-3, the option will be worth $12.53 in 3 months if the stock price goes up to $46.84. We can repeat this procedure on the lower right portion of Figure 8-3 to determine the call option's value in 3 months if the stock price falls to $34.16; in this case, the call's value would be $2.57. Finally, we can use Equation 8-6 and the 3-month option values just calculated to determine the current price of the option, which is $7.64. Thus, we are able to find the current option price by solving three simple binomial problems.

If we broke the year into smaller periods and allowed the stock price to move up or down more often, then the lattice would have an even more realistic range of possible ending stock prices. Of course, estimating the current option price would require solving lots of binomial problems within the lattice, but each problem is simple and computers can solve them rapidly. With more outcomes, the resulting estimated option price is more accurate. For example, if we divide the year into 15 periods then the estimated price is $7.42. With 50 periods, the price is $7.39. With 100 periods it is still $7.39, which shows that the solution converges to its final value within a relatively small number of steps. In fact, as we break the time to expiration into smaller and smaller periods, the solution for the binomial approach converges to the Black-Scholes solution, which is described in the next section.

The binomial approach is widely used to value options with more complicated payoffs than the call option in our example, such as employee stock options. This is beyond the scope of a financial management textbook, but if you are interested in learning more about the binomial approach, you should take a look at the textbooks by Don Chance and John Hull cited in footnote 1.

SELF-TEST

*Ringling Cycle's stock price is now $20. You need to find the value of a call option with a strike price of $22 that expires in 2 months. You want to use the binomial model with 2 periods (each period is a month). Your assistant has calculated that $u = 1.1553$, $d = 0.8656$, $\pi_u = 0.4838$, and $\pi_d = 0.5095$. Draw the binomial lattice for stock prices. What are the possible prices after 1 month? **($23.11 or $17.31)** After 2 months? **($26.69, $20, or $14.99)** What are the option's possible payoffs at expiration? **($4.69, $0, or $0)** What will the option's value be in 1 month if the stock goes up? **($2.27)** What will the option's value be in 1 month if the stock price goes down? **($0)** What is the current value of the option (assume each month is 1/12 of a year)? **($1.10)***

8-5 The Black-Scholes Option Pricing Model (OPM)

The **Black-Scholes option pricing model (OPM),** developed in 1973, helped give rise to the rapid growth in options trading. This model has been programmed into many handheld and Web-based calculators, and it is widely used by option traders.

8-5a OPM Assumptions and Results

For a Web-based option calculator, see **www.cboe .com/LearnCenter/ OptionCalculator.aspx**.

In deriving their model to value call options, Fischer Black and Myron Scholes made the following assumptions.

1. The stock underlying the call option provides no dividends or other distributions during the life of the option.
2. There are no transaction costs for buying or selling either the stock or the option.
3. The short-term, risk-free interest rate is known and is constant during the life of the option.
4. Any purchaser of a security may borrow any fraction of the purchase price at the short-term, risk-free interest rate.
5. Short selling is permitted, and the short seller will receive immediately the full cash proceeds of today's price for a security sold short.
6. The call option can be exercised only on its expiration date.
7. Trading in all securities takes place continuously, and the stock price moves randomly.

The derivation of the Black-Scholes model rests on the same concepts as the binomial model, except time is divided into such small increments that stock prices change continuously. The Black-Scholes model for call options consists of the following three equations:

$$V_C = P[N(d_1)] - Xe^{-r_{RF}t}[N(d_2)] \qquad (8\text{-}9)$$

$$d_1 = \frac{\ln(P/X) + [r_{RF} + (\sigma^2/2)]t}{\sigma\sqrt{t}} \qquad (8\text{-}10)$$

$$d_2 = d_1 - \sigma\sqrt{t} \qquad (8\text{-}11)$$

The variables used in the Black-Scholes model are explained below.

W W W

Robert's Online Option Pricer can be accessed at **www.intrepid.com/robertl/index.html**. *The site provides a financial service over the Internet to small investors for option pricing, giving anyone a means to price option trades without having to buy expensive software and hardware.*

V_C = Current value of the call option.

P = Current price of the underlying stock.

$N(d_i)$ = Probability that a deviation less than d_i will occur in a standard normal distribution. Thus, $N(d_1)$ and $N(d_2)$ represent areas under a standard normal distribution function.

X = Strike price of the option.

$e \approx 2.7183$.

r_{RF} = Risk-free interest rate.[18]

t = Time until the option expires (the option period).

$\ln(P/X)$ = Natural logarithm of P/X.

σ = Standard deviation of the rate of return on the stock.

The value of the option is a function of five variables: (1) P, the stock's price; (2) t, the option's time to expiration; (3) X, the strike price; (4) σ, the standard deviation of the underlying stock; and (5) r_{RF}, the risk-free rate. We do not derive the Black-Scholes model—the derivation involves some extremely complicated mathematics that go far beyond the scope of this text. However, it is not difficult to use the model. Under the assumptions set forth previously, if the option price is different from the one found by Equation 8-9, then this would provide the opportunity for arbitrage profits, which would force the option price back to the value indicated by the model. As we noted earlier, the Black-Scholes model is widely used by traders because actual option prices conform reasonably well to values derived from the model.

---

[18]The correct process to estimate the risk-free rate for use in the Black-Scholes model for an option with 6 months to expiration is to find the annual nominal rate (compounded continuously) that has the same effective annual rate as a 6-month T-bill. For example, suppose a 6-month T-bill is yielding a 6-month periodic rate of 4.081%. The risk-free rate to use in the Black-Scholes model is $r_{RF} = \ln(1 + 0.0408)/0.5 = 8\%$. Under continuous compounding, a nominal rate of 8% produces an effective rate of yields $e^{0.08} - 1 = 8.33\%$. This is the same effective rate yielded by the T-bill: $(1+0.0408)^2 - 1 = 8.33\%$. The same approach can be applied for options with different expiration periods. We will provide the appropriate risk-free rate for all problems and examples.

8-5b Application of the Black-Scholes Option Pricing Model to a Call Option

The current stock price (P), the exercise price (X), and the time to maturity (t) can all be obtained from a newspaper, such as *The Wall Street Journal*, or from the Internet, such as the CBOE's Web site. The risk-free rate (r_{RF}) is the yield on a Treasury bill with a maturity equal to the option expiration date. The annualized standard deviation of stock returns (σ) can be estimated from daily stock prices. First, find the stock return for each trading day for a sample period, such as each trading day of the past year. Second, estimate the variance of the daily stock returns. Third, multiply this estimated daily variance by the number of trading days in a year, which is approximately 250.[19] Take the square root of the annualized variance, and the result is an estimate of the annualized standard deviation.

We will use the Black-Scholes model to estimate Western's call option that we discussed previously. Here are the inputs:

$$P = \$40$$
$$X = \$35$$
$$t = 6 \text{ months (0.5 years)}$$
$$r_{RF} = 8.0\% = 0.080$$
$$\sigma = 31.557\% = 0.31557$$

resource

*See **Ch08 Tool Kit.xls** on the textbook's Web site for all calculations.*

Given this information, we first estimate d_1 and d_2 from Equations 8-10 and 8-11:

$$d_1 = \frac{\ln(\$40/\$35) + [0.08 + ((0.31557^2)/2)](0.5)}{0.31557\sqrt{0.5}}$$

$$= \frac{0.13353 + 0.064896}{0.22314} = 0.8892$$

$$d_2 = d_1 - 0.31557\sqrt{0.5} = 0.6661$$

Note that $N(d_1)$ and $N(d_2)$ represent areas under a standard normal distribution function. The easiest way to calculate this value is with *Excel*. For example, we can use the function =**NORMSDIST(0.8892),** which returns a value of $N(d_1)$ = N(0.8892) = 0.8131. Similarly, the **NORMSDIST** function returns a value of $N(d_2)$ = 0.7473.[20] We can use those values to solve Equation 6-9:

$$V_C = \$40[N(0.8892)] \$35e^{-(0.08)(0.5)}[N(0.6661)]$$

$$= \$7.39$$

Thus, the value of the option is $7.39. This is the same value we found using the binomial approach with 100 periods in the year.

---

[19]If stocks traded every day of the year, then each return covers a 24-hour period; you would simply estimate the variance of the 1-day returns with your sample of daily returns and then multiply this estimate by 365 for an estimate of the annual variance. However, stocks don't trade every day because of weekends and holidays. If you measure returns from the close of one trading day until the close of the next trading day (called "trading-day returns"), then some returns are for 1 day (such as Thursday close to Friday close) and some are for longer periods, like the 3-day return from Friday close to Monday close. It might seem reasonable that the 3-day returns have 3 times the variance of a 1-day return and should be treated differently when estimating the daily return variance, but that is not the case. It turns out that the 3-day return over a weekend has only slightly higher variance than a 1-day return (perhaps because of less new information on non-weekdays), and so it is reasonable to treat all of the trading-day returns the same. With roughly 250 trading days in a year, most analysts take the estimate of the variance of daily returns and multiply by 250 (or 252, depending on the year, to be more precise) to obtain an estimate of the annual variance.

[20]If you do not have access to *Excel*, then you can use the table in Appendix A. For example, the table shows that the value for d_1 = 0.88 is 0.5000 + 0.3106 = 0.8106 and that the value for d_1 = 0.89 is 0.5000 + 0.3133 = 0.8133, so N(0.8892) lies between 0.8106 and 0.8133. You could interpolate to find a closer value, but we suggest using *Excel* instead.

FIGURE 8-4

Western Cellular's Call Options with a Strike Price of $35

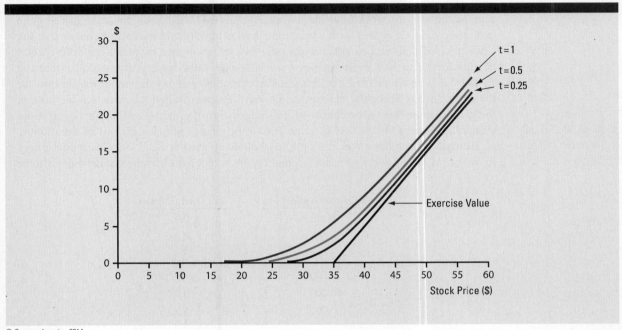

© Cengage Learning 2014

8-5c The Five Factors That Affect Call Option Prices

resource

See **Ch08 Tool Kit.xls** on
the textbook's Web site.

The Black-Scholes model has five inputs, so there are five factors that affect call option prices. As we will see in the next section, these five inputs also affect put option prices. Figure 8-4 shows how three of Western Cellular's call options are affected by Western's stock price (all three options have a strike price of $35). The three options expire in 1 year, in 6 months (0.5 years, like the option in our example), and in 3 months (or 0.25 years), respectively.

Figure 8-4 offers several insights regarding option valuation. Notice that for all stock prices in the Figure, the call option prices are always above the exercise value. If this were not true, then an investor could purchase the call and immediately exercise it for a quick profit.[21]

Also, when the stock price falls far below the strike price, call option prices fall toward zero. In other words, calls lose value as they become more and more out-of-the-money. When the stock price greatly exceeds the strike price, call option prices fall toward the exercise value. Thus, for very high stock prices, call options tend to move up and down by about the same amount as does the stock price.

Call option prices increase if the stock price increases. This is because the strike price is fixed, so an increase in stock price increases the chance that the option will be in-the-money at expiration. Although we don't show it in the figure, an increase in the strike price would obviously cause a decrease in the call option's value because higher strike prices mean a lower chance of being in-the-money at expiration.

---

[21]More precisely, this statement is true for all American call options (which can be exercised before expiration) and for European call options written on stocks that pay no dividends. Although European options may not be exercised prior to expiration, investors could earn a riskless profit if the call price were less than the exercise value by selling the stock short, purchasing the call, and investing at the risk-free rate an amount equal to the present value of the strike price. The vast majority of call options are American options, so the call price is almost always above the exercise value.

The 1-year call option always has a greater value than the 6-month call option, which always has a greater value than the 3-month call option; thus, the longer a call option has until expiration, the greater its value. Here is the intuition for that result. With a long time until expiration, the stock price has a chance to increase well above the strike price by the expiration date. Of course, with a long time until expiration, there is also a chance that the stock price will fall far below the strike price by expiration. But there is a big difference in payoffs for being well in-the-money versus far out-of-the-money. Every dollar that the stock price is above the strike price means an extra dollar of payoff, but no matter how far the stock price is below the strike price, the payoff is zero. When it comes to a call option, the gain in value due to the chance of finishing well in-the-money with a big payoff more than compensates for the loss in value due to the chance of being far out-of-the money.

How does volatility affect call options? Following are the Black-Scholes model prices for Western's call option with the original inputs except for different standard deviations:

resource

*See **Ch08 Tool Kit.xls** for all calculations.*

Standard Deviation (σ)	Call Option Price
0.001%	$ 6.37
10.000	6.38
31.557	7.39
40.000	8.07
60.000	9.87
90.000	12.70

The first row shows the option price if there is very little stock volatility.[22] Notice that as volatility increases, so does the option price. Therefore, the riskier the underlying security, the more valuable the option. To see why this makes sense, suppose you bought a call option with a strike price equal to the current stock price. If the stock had no risk (which means σ = 0), then there would be a zero probability of the stock going up, hence a zero probability of making money on the option. On the other hand, if you bought a call option on a higher-volatility stock, there would be a higher probability that the stock would increase well above the strike price by the expiration date. Of course, with higher volatility there also would be a higher probability that the stock price would fall far below the strike price. But as we previously explained, an increase in the price of the stock helps call option holders more than a decrease hurts them: The greater the stock's volatility, the greater the value of the option. This makes options on risky stocks more valuable than those on safer, low-risk stocks. For example, an option on Cisco should have a greater value than an otherwise identical option on Kroger, the grocery store chain.

---

[22]With such a low standard deviation, the current stock price of $40 is unlikely to change very much before expiration, so the option will be in-the-money at expiration and the owner will certainly pay the strike price and exercise the option at that time. This means that the present value of the strike price is the cost of exercising expressed in today's dollars. The present value of a stock's expected cash flows is equal to the current stock price. So the value of the option today is approximately equal to the current stock price of $40 less the present value of the strike price that must be paid when the stock is exercised at expiration. If we assume daily compounding, then the current option price should be:

$$V_C(\text{for } \sigma = 0.001\%) \approx \$40 - \frac{\$35}{\left(1 + \frac{0.08}{365}\right)^{365(0.5)}} = \$6.37$$

Observe that this is the same value given by the Black-Scholes model, even though we calculated it more directly. This approach only works if the volatility is almost zero.

Taxes and Stock Options

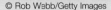

© Rob Webb/Getty Images

If an employee stock option grant meets certain conditions, it is called a "tax-qualifying grant" or sometimes an "Incentive Stock Option"; otherwise, it is a "nonqualifying grant." For example, suppose you receive a grant of 1,000 options with an exercise price of $50. If the stock price goes to $110 and you exercise the options, you must pay $50 (1,000) = $50,000 for stock that is worth $110,000, which is a sweet deal. But what is your tax liability? If you receive a nonqualifying grant, then you are liable for ordinary income taxes on 1,000($110 − $50) = $60,000 when you exercise the option. But if it is a tax-qualified grant, you owe no regular taxes when exercised. By waiting at least a year and then selling the stock for, say, $150, you would have a long-term capital gain of 1,000($150 − $50) = $100,000, which would be taxed at the lower capital gains rate.

Before you gloat over your newfound wealth, you had better consult your accountant. Your "profit" when you exercise the tax-qualified options isn't taxable under the regular tax code, but it is under the Alternative Minimum Tax (AMT) code. With an AMT tax rate of up to 28%, you might owe as much as 0.28($110 − $50)(1,000) = $16,800. Here's where people get into trouble. The AMT tax isn't due until the following April, so you might think about waiting until then to sell some stock to pay your AMT tax (so that the sale will qualify as a long-term capital gain).

But what happens if the stock price falls to $5 by next April? You can sell your stock, which raises only $5(1,000) = $5,000 in cash. Without going into the details, you will have a long-term capital loss of 1,000 ($50 − $5) = $45,000 but IRS regulations limit your net capital loss in a single year to $3,000. In other words, the cash from the sale and the tax benefit from the capital loss aren't nearly enough to cover the AMT tax. You may be able to reduce your taxes in future years because of the AMT tax you pay this year and the carryforward of the remaining long-term capital loss, but that doesn't help right now. You lost $45,000 of your original $50,000 investment, you now have very little cash, and—adding insult to injury—the IRS will insist that you also pay the $16,800 AMT tax.

This is exactly what happened to many people who made paper fortunes in the dot-com boom only to see them evaporate in the ensuing bust. They were left with worthless stock but multimillion-dollar AMT tax obligations. In fact, many still have IRS liens garnishing their wages until they eventually pay their AMT tax. So if you receive stock options, we congratulate you. But unless you want to be the next poster child for poor financial planning, we advise you to settle your AMT tax when you incur it.

resource

See **Ch08 Tool Kit.xls** for all calculations.

The risk-free rate also has a relatively small impact on option prices. Shown below are the prices for Western's call option with the original inputs except for the risk-free rate, which is allowed to vary.

Risk-free rate (r_{RF})	Call option price
0%	$6.41
4	6.89
8	7.39
12	7.90
20	8.93

As the risk-free rate increases, the value of the option increases. The principal effect of an increase in r_{RF} is to reduce the present value of the exercise price, which increases the current value of the option. Option prices in general are not very sensitive to interest rate changes, at least not to changes within the ranges normally encountered.

Myron Scholes and Robert Merton (who also was a pioneer in the field of options) were awarded the 1997 Nobel Prize in Economics, and Fischer Black would have been a co-recipient had he still been living. Their work provided analytical tools and methodologies that are widely used to solve many types of financial problems, not just option pricing. Indeed, the entire field of modern risk management is based primarily on their contributions. Although the Black-Scholes model was derived for a European option that can be exercised only on its maturity date, it also applies to American options that don't pay any dividends prior to expiration. The textbooks by Don Chance and John Hull (cited in footnote 1) show adjusted models for dividend-paying stocks.

SELF-TEST

What is the purpose of the Black-Scholes option pricing model?

Explain what a "riskless hedge" is and how the riskless hedge concept is used in the Black-Scholes OPM.

Describe the effect of a change in each of the following factors on the value of a call option: (1) stock price, (2) exercise price, (3) option life, (4) risk-free rate, and (5) stock return standard deviation (i.e., risk of stock).

Using an Excel *worksheet, what is the value of a call option with these data: P = \$35, X = \$25, r_{RF} = 6%, t = 0.5 (6 months), and σ = 0.6?* **(\$12.05)**

8-6 The Valuation of Put Options

A put option gives its owner the right to sell a share of stock. Suppose a stock pays no dividends and a put option written on the stock can be exercised only upon its expiration date. What is the put's value? Rather than reinventing the wheel, we can establish the price of a put relative to the price of a call.

8-6a Put-Call Parity

Consider the payoffs for two portfolios at expiration date T, as shown in Table 8-2. The first portfolio consists of a put option and a share of stock; the second has a call option (with the same strike price and expiration date as the put option) and some cash. The amount of cash is equal to the present value of the strike price discounted at the continuously compounded risk-free rate, which is $Xe^{-r_{RF}t}$. At expiration, the value of this cash will equal the strike price, X.

TABLE 8-2

Portfolio Payoffs

		Payoff at Expiration If:	
		$P_T < X$	$P_T \geq X$
Put		$X - P_T$	0
Stock		P_T	P_T
	Portfolio 1:	X	P_T
Call		0	$P_T - X$
Cash		X	X
	Portfolio 2:	X	P_T

© Cengage Learning 2014

If P_T, the stock price at expiration date T, is less than X, the strike price, when the option expires, then the value of the put option at expiration is $X - P_T$. Therefore, the value of Portfolio 1, which contains the put and the stock, is equal to X minus P_T plus P_T, or just X. For Portfolio 2, the value of the call is zero at expiration (because the call option is out-of-the-money), and the value of the cash is X, for a total value of X. Notice that both portfolios have the same payoffs if the stock price is less than the strike price.

What if the stock price is greater than the strike price at expiration? In this case, the put is worth nothing, so the payoff of Portfolio 1 is equal to P_T, the stock price at expiration. The call option is worth $P_T - X$, and the cash is worth X, so the payoff of Portfolio 2 is P_T. Hence the payoffs of the two portfolios are equal regardless of whether the stock price is below or above the strike price.

If the two portfolios have identical payoffs, then they must have identical values. This is known as the **put–call parity relationship:**

$$\text{Put option} + \text{Stock} = \text{Call option} + \text{PV of exercise price.}$$

If V_C is the Black-Scholes value of the call option, then the value of a put is[23]

$$\text{Put option} = V_C - P + Xe^{-r_{RF}t} \tag{8-12}$$

For example, consider a put option written on the stock discussed in the previous section. If the put option has the same exercise price and expiration date as the call, then its price is

$$\text{Put option} = \$7.39 - \$40 + \$35\,e^{-0.08\,(0.5)}$$

$$= \$7.39 - \$40 + \$33.63 = \$1.02$$

It is also possible to modify the Black-Scholes call option formula to obtain a put option formula:

$$\text{Put option} = P[N(d_1)-1] - Xe^{-r_{RF}t}[N(d_2)-1] \tag{8-13}$$

The only difference between this formula for puts and the formula for calls is the subtraction of 1 from $N(d_1)$ and $N(d_2)$ in the call option formula.

8-6b The Five Factors That Affect Put Option Prices

Just like with call options, the exercise price, the underlying stock price, the time to expiration, the stock's standard deviation, and the risk-free rate affect the price of a put option. Because a put pays off when the stock price declines below the exercise price, the impact of the underlying stock price and exercise price and risk-free rate on the put are opposite that of the call option. That is, put prices are higher when the stock price is lower and when the exercise price is higher. Put prices are also lower when the risk-free rate is higher, mostly because a higher risk-free rate reduces the present value of the exercise price, which for a put is a payout to the option holder when the option is exercised.

---

[23]This model cannot be applied to an American put option or to a European option on a stock that pays a dividend prior to expiration. For an explanation of valuation approaches in these situations, see the books by Chance and Hull cited in footnote 1.

On the other hand, put options are affected by the stock's standard deviation just like call options. Both put and call option prices are higher when the stock's standard deviation is higher. This is true for put options because the higher the standard deviation, the bigger the chance of a large stock price decline and a large put payoff. The effect of the time to maturity on the put option price is indeterminate. A call option is more valuable the longer the maturity, but some puts are more valuable the longer to maturity, and some are less valuable. For example, consider an in-the-money put option (the stock price is below the exercise price) on a stock with a low standard deviation. In this case a longer maturity put option is less valuable than a shorter maturity put option because the longer the time to maturity, the more likely the stock is to grow and erode the put's payoff. But if the stock's standard deviation is high, then the longer maturity put option will be more valuable because the likelihood of the stock declining even more and resulting in a high payoff to the put is greater.

SELF-TEST

In words, what is put–call parity?

A put option written on the stock of Taylor Enterprises (TE) has an exercise price of $25 and 6 months remaining until expiration. The risk-free rate is 6%. A call option written on TE has the same exercise price and expiration date as the put option. TE's stock price is $35. If the call option has a price of $12.05, then what is the price (i.e., value) of the put option? ($1.31)

Explain why both put and call options are worth more if the stock return standard deviation is higher, but put and call options are affected oppositely by the stock price.

8-7 Applications of Option Pricing in Corporate Finance

Option pricing is used in four major areas of corporate finance: (1) real options analysis for project evaluation and strategic decisions, (2) risk management, (3) capital structure decisions, and (4) compensation plans.

8-7a Real Options

Suppose a company has a 1-year proprietary license to develop a software application for use in a new generation of wireless cellular telephones. Hiring programmers and marketing consultants to complete the project will cost $30 million. The good news is that if consumers love the new cell phones, there will be a tremendous demand for the software. The bad news is that if sales of the new cell phones are low, the software project will be a disaster. Should the company spend the $30 million and develop the software?

Because the company has a license, it has the option of waiting for a year, at which time it might have a much better insight into market demand for the new cell phones. If demand is high in a year, then the company can spend the $30 million and develop the software. If demand is low, it can avoid losing the $30 million development cost by simply letting the license expire. Notice that the license is analogous to a call option: It gives the company the right to buy something (in this case, software for the new cell phones) at a fixed price ($30 million) at any time during the next year. The license gives the company a **real option,** because the underlying asset (the software) is a real asset and not a financial asset.

There are many other types of real options, including the option to increase capacity at a plant, to expand into new geographical regions, to introduce new products, to switch inputs (such as gas versus oil), to switch outputs (such as producing sedans versus SUVs), and to abandon a project. Many companies now evaluate real options with techniques that are similar to those described earlier in the chapter for pricing financial options.

8-7b Risk Management

Suppose a company plans to issue $400 million of bonds in 6 months to pay for a new plant now under construction. The plant will be profitable if interest rates remain at current levels, but if rates rise then it will be unprofitable. To hedge against rising rates, the company could purchase a put option on Treasury bonds. If interest rates go up then the company would "lose" because its bonds would carry a high interest rate, but it would have an offsetting gain on its put options. Conversely, if rates fall then the company would "win" when it issues its own low-rate bonds, but it would lose on the put options. By purchasing puts, the company has hedged the risk due to possible interest rate changes that it would otherwise face.

Another example of risk management is a firm that bids on a foreign contract. For example, suppose a winning bid means that the firm will receive a payment of 12 million euros in 9 months. At a current exchange rate of $1.57 per euro, the project would be profitable. But if the exchange rate falls to $1.10 per euro, the project would be a loser. To avoid exchange rate risk, the firm could take a short position in a forward contract that allows it to convert 12 million euros into dollars at a fixed rate of $1.50 per euro in 9 months, which would still ensure a profitable project. This eliminates exchange rate risk if the firm wins the contract, but what if the firm loses the contract? It would still be obligated to sell 12 million euros at a price of $1.50 per euro, which could be a disaster. For example, if the exchange rate rises to $1.75 per euro, then the firm would have to spend $21 million to purchase 12 million euros at a price of $1.75/€ and then sell the euros for $18 million = ($1.50/€)(€12 million), a loss of $3 million.

To eliminate this risk, the firm could instead purchase a currency put option that allows it to sell 12 million euros in 9 months at a fixed price of $1.50 per euro. If the company wins the bid, it will exercise the put option and sell the 12 million euros for $1.50 per euro if the exchange rate has declined. If the exchange rate hasn't declined, then it will sell the euros on the open market for more than $1.50 and let the option expire. On the other hand, if the firm loses the bid, it has no reason to sell euros and could let the option contract expire. Note, however, that even if the firm doesn't win the contract, it still is gambling on the exchange rate because it owns the put; if the price of euros declines below $1.50, the firm will still make some money on the option. Thus, the company can lock in the future exchange rate if it wins the bid and can avoid any net payment at all if it loses the bid. The total cost in either scenario is equal to the initial cost of the option. In other words, the cost of the option is like insurance that guarantees the exchange rate if the company wins the bid and guarantees no net obligations if it loses the bid.

Many other applications of risk management involve futures contracts and other complex derivatives rather than calls and puts. However, the principles used in pricing derivatives are similar to those used earlier in this chapter for pricing options. Thus, financial options and their valuation techniques play key roles in risk management.

8-7c Capital Structure Decisions

Decisions regarding the mix of debt and equity used to finance operations are quite important. One interesting aspect of the capital structure decision is based on option pricing. For example, consider a firm with debt requiring a final principal payment of $60 million in 1 year. If the company's value 1 year from now is $61 million, then it can pay off the debt and have $1 million left for stockholders. If the firm's value is less than $60 million, then it may well file for bankruptcy and turn over its assets to creditors, resulting in stockholders' equity of zero. In other words, the value of the stockholders' equity is analogous to a call option: The equity holders have the right to buy the assets for $60 million (which is the face value of the debt) in 1 year (when the debt matures).

Suppose the firm's owner-managers are considering two projects. One project has very little risk, and it will result in an asset value of either $59 million or $61 million. The other has high risk, and it will result in an asset value of either $20 million or $100 million. Notice that the equity will be worth zero if the assets are worth less than $60 million, so the stockholders will be no worse off if the assets end up at $20 million than if they end up at $59 million. On the other hand, the stockholders would benefit much more if the assets were worth $100 million rather than $61 million. Thus, the owner-managers have an incentive to choose risky projects, which is consistent with an option's value rising with the risk of the underlying asset. Potential lenders recognize this situation, so they build covenants into loan agreements that restrict managers from making excessively risky investments.

Not only does option pricing theory help explain why managers might want to choose risky projects (consider, for example, the cases of Enron, Lehman Brothers, and AIG) and why debtholders might want restrictive covenants, but options also play a direct role in capital structure choices. For example, a firm could choose to issue convertible debt, which gives bondholders the option to convert their debt into stock if the value of the company turns out to be higher than expected. In exchange for this option, bondholders charge a lower interest rate than for nonconvertible debt. Because owner-managers must share the wealth with convertible-bond holders, they have a smaller incentive to gamble with high-risk projects.

8-7d Compensation Plans

Many companies use stock options as a part of their compensation plans. It is important for boards of directors to understand the value of these options before they grant them to employees. We discuss compensation issues associated with stock options in more detail in Chapter 13.

SELF-TEST

Describe four ways that option pricing is used in corporate finance.

SUMMARY

In this chapter we discussed option pricing topics, which included the following.

- **Financial options** are instruments that (1) are created by exchanges rather than firms, (2) are bought and sold primarily by investors, and (3) are of importance to both investors and financial managers.
- The two primary types of financial options are (1) **call options,** which give the holder the right to purchase a specified asset at a given price (the **exercise,** or **strike**, **price**) for a given period of time, and (2) **put options,** which give the holder the right to sell an asset at a given price for a given period of time.

- A call option's **exercise value** is defined as the maximum of zero or the current price of the stock less the strike price.
- The **Black-Scholes option pricing model (OPM)** or the **binomial model** can be used to estimate the value of a call option.
- The five inputs to the Black-Scholes model are (1) P, the current stock price; (2) X, the strike price; (3) r_{RF}, the risk-free interest rate; (4) t, the remaining time until expiration; and (5) σ, the standard deviation of the stock's rate of return.
- A call option's value increases if P increases, X decreases, r_{RF} increases, t increases, or σ increases.
- The **put–call parity relationship** states that

$$\text{Put option} + \text{Stock} = \text{Call option} + \text{PV of exercise price.}$$

Questions

(8-1)   Define each of the following terms:

     a. Option; call option; put option
     b. Exercise value; strike price
     c. Black-Scholes option pricing model

(8-2)   Why do options sell at prices higher than their exercise values?

(8-3)   Describe the effect on a call option's price that results from an increase in each of the following factors: (1) stock price, (2) strike price, (3) time to expiration, (4) risk-free rate, and (5) standard deviation of stock return.

SELF-TEST PROBLEMS   Solutions Appear in Appendix A

(ST-1)
Binomial Option
Pricing

The current price of a stock is $40. In 1 year, the price will be either $60 or $30. The annual risk-free rate is 5%. Find the price of a call option on the stock that has an exercise price of $42 and that expires in 1 year. (*Hint:* Use daily compounding.)

(ST-2)
Black-Scholes Model

Use the Black-Scholes Model to find the price for a call option with the following inputs: (1) current stock price is $22, (2) strike price is $20, (3) time to expiration is 6 months, (4) annualized risk-free rate is 5%, and (5) standard deviation of stock return is 0.7.

PROBLEMS   Answers Appear in Appendix B

Easy Problems 1–2

(8-1)
Options

A call option on the stock of Bedrock Boulders has a market price of $7. The stock sells for $30 a share, and the option has a strike price of $25 a share. What is the exercise value of the call option? What is the option's time value?

(8-2)
Options

The exercise price on one of Flanagan Company's options is $15, its exercise value is $22, and its time value is $5. What are the option's market value and the price of the stock?

Intermediate
Problems 3–4

(8-3)
Black-Scholes Model

Assume that you have been given the following information on Purcell Industries:

Current stock price = $15	Strike price of option = $15
Time to maturity of option = 6 months	Risk-free rate = 6%
Variance of stock return = 0.12	
$d_1 = 0.24495$	$N(d_1) = 0.59675$
$d_2 = 0.00000$	$N(d_2) = 0.50000$

According to the Black-Scholes option pricing model, what is the option's value?

(8-4)
Put–Call Parity

The current price of a stock is $33, and the annual risk-free rate is 6%. A call option with a strike price of $32 and with 1 year until expiration has a current value of $6.56. What is the value of a put option written on the stock with the same exercise price and expiration date as the call option?

Challenging
Problems 5–7

(8-5)
Black-Scholes Model

Use the Black-Scholes Model to find the price for a call option with the following inputs: (1) current stock price is $30, (2) strike price is $35, (3) time to expiration is 4 months, (4) annualized risk-free rate is 5%, and (5) variance of stock return is 0.25.

(8-6)
Binomial Model

The current price of a stock is $20. In 1 year, the price will be either $26 or $16. The annual risk-free rate is 5%. Find the price of a call option on the stock that has a strike price of $21 and that expires in 1 year. (*Hint:* Use daily compounding.)

(8-7)
Binomial Model

The current price of a stock is $15. In 6 months, the price will be either $18 or $13. The annual risk-free rate is 6%. Find the price of a call option on the stock that has a strike price of $14 and that expires in 6 months. (*Hint:* Use daily compounding.)

SPREADSHEET PROBLEM

(8-8)
Build a Model: Black-
Scholes Model

Start with the partial model in the file **Ch08 P08 Build a Model.xls** on the textbook's Web site. You have been given the following information for a call option on the stock of Puckett Industries: P = $65.00, X = $70.00, t = 0.50, r_{RF} = 5.00% and σ = 50.00%.

r e s o u r c e

a. Use the Black-Scholes option pricing model to determine the value of the call option.

b. Suppose there is a put option on Puckett's stock with exactly the same inputs as the call option. What is the value of the put?

MINI CASE

Assume that you have just been hired as a financial analyst by Triple Play Inc., a mid-sized California company that specializes in creating high-fashion clothing. Because no one at Triple Play is familiar with the basics of financial options, you have been asked to prepare a brief report that the firm's executives can use to gain a cursory understanding of the topic.

To begin, you gathered some outside materials on the subject and used these materials to draft a list of pertinent questions that need to be answered. In fact, one possible approach to the report is to use a question-and-answer format. Now that the questions have been drafted, you have to develop the answers.

a. What is a financial option? What is the single most important characteristic of an option?

b. Options have a unique set of terminology. Define the following terms:

(1) Call option
(2) Put option
(3) Strike price or exercise price
(4) Expiration date
(5) Exercise value
(6) Option price
(7) Time value
(8) Writing an option
(9) Covered option
(10) Naked option
(11) In-the-money call
(12) Out-of-the-money call
(13) LEAPS

c. Consider Triple Play's call option with a $25 strike price. The following table contains historical values for this option at different stock prices:

Stock Price	Call Option Price
$25	$ 3.00
30	7.50
35	12.00
40	16.50
45	21.00
50	25.50

(1) Create a table that shows (a) stock price, (b) strike price, (c) exercise value, (d) option price, and (e) the time value, which is the option's price less its exercise value.
(2) What happens to the time value as the stock price rises? Why?

d. Consider a stock with a current price of P = $27. Suppose that over the next 6 months the stock price will either go up by a factor of 1.41 or down by a factor of 0.71. Consider a call option on the stock with a strike price of $25 that expires in 6 months. The risk-free rate is 6%.

(1) Using the binomial model, what are the ending values of the stock price? What are the payoffs of the call option?
(2) Suppose you write one call option and buy N_s shares of stock. How many shares must you buy to create a portfolio with a riskless payoff (i.e., a hedge portfolio)? What is the payoff of the portfolio?
(3) What is the present value of the hedge portfolio? What is the value of the call option?
(4) What is a replicating portfolio? What is arbitrage?

e. In 1973, Fischer Black and Myron Scholes developed the Black-Scholes option pricing model (OPM).

   (1) What assumptions underlie the OPM?
   (2) Write out the three equations that constitute the model.
   (3) According to the OPM, what is the value of a call option with the following characteristics?

   Stock price = $27.00
   Strike price = $25.00
   Time to expiration = 6 months = 0.5 years
   Risk-free rate = 6.0%
   Stock return standard deviation = 0.49

f. What impact does each of the following parameters have on the value of a call option?
   (1) Current stock price
   (2) Strike price
   (3) Option's term to maturity
   (4) Risk-free rate
   (5) Variability of the stock price

g. What is put–call parity?

© lulu/fotolia.com

PART 4

Projects and Their Valuation

Adalberto Rios Szalay/Sexto Sol/Getty Images

CHAPTER 9

The Cost of Capital

When companies consider investing in new projects, the cost of capital plays a major role. Sunny Delight Beverage Co. is making big investments to upgrade its juice factories, but would this happen if low interest rates had not driven down the cost of capital? According to CEO Billy Cyr, "When the cost of capital goes up, it is harder to justify an equipment purchase." The opposite is true when the cost of capital goes down.

Among its businesses, Phoenix Stamping Group LLC produces components for equipment used in agriculture and transportation. After modernizing two factories, Phoenix President Brandyn Chapman said, "The cost of capital certainly helps that decision."

For these and many other companies, the historically low cost of capital is making possible major investments in machinery, equipment, and technology. Many of these investments are designed to increase productivity, which will lead to lower prices for consumers and higher cash flows for shareholders. On the other hand, productivity gains mean not as many employees are needed to run the business.

Think about these issues as you read this chapter.

Source: Adapted from Timothy Aeppel, "Man vs. Machine, a Jobless Recovery—Companies Are Spending to Upgrade Factories but Hiring Lags; Robots Pump Out Sunny Delight," *The Wall Street Journal,* January 17, 2012, B1.

Corporate Valuation and the Cost of Capital

© Rob Webb/Getty Images

In Chapter 1, we told you that managers should strive to make their firms more valuable and that the value of a firm is determined by the size, timing, and risk of its free cash flows (FCF). Indeed, a firm's intrinsic value is estimated as the present value of its FCFs, discounted at the weighted average cost of capital (WACC). In previous chapters, we examined the major sources of financing (stocks, bonds, and preferred stock) and the costs of those instruments. In this chapter, we put those pieces together and estimate the WACC that is used to determine intrinsic value.

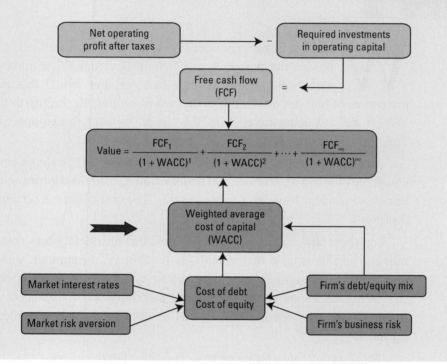

© Cengage Learning 2014

resource

The textbook's Web site contains an Excel file that will guide you through the chapter's calculations. The file for this chapter is **Ch09 Tool Kit.xls**, *and we encourage you to open the file and follow along as you read the chapter.*

Businesses require capital to develop new products, build factories and distribution centers, install information technology, expand internationally, and acquire other companies. For each of these actions, a company must estimate the total investment required and then decide whether the expected rate of return exceeds the cost of the capital. The cost of capital is also a factor in compensation plans, with bonuses dependent on whether the company's return on invested capital exceeds the cost of that capital. This cost is also a key factor in choosing the firm's mixture of debt and equity and in decisions to lease rather than buy assets. As these examples illustrate, the cost of capital is a critical element in many business decisions.[1]

---

[1]The cost of capital is also an important factor in the regulation of electric, gas, and water companies. These utilities are natural monopolies in the sense that one firm can supply service at a lower cost than could two or more firms. Because it has a monopoly, an unregulated electric or water company could exploit its customers. Therefore, regulators (1) determine the cost of the capital investors have provided the utility and then (2) set rates designed to permit the company to earn its cost of capital, no more and no less.

9-1 The Weighted Average Cost of Capital

The value of a company's operations is the present value of the expected free cash flows (FCF) discounted at the weighted average cost of capital (WACC):

$$V_{op} = \sum_{t=1}^{\infty} \frac{FCF_1}{(1 + WACC)^t} \qquad (9\text{-}1)$$

We defined free cash flows (FCF) in Chapter 2, explained how to find present values in Chapter 4, and used the valuation equation in Chapter 7. Now we define the **weighted average cost of capital (WACC):**

$$WACC = w_d r_d (1 - T) + w_{std} r_{std} (1 - T) + w_{ps} r_{ps} + w_s r_s \qquad (9\text{-}2)$$

Some of these variables should be familiar to you from previous chapters, but some are new. All are defined as follows:

r_d = Coupon rate on new long-term debt being issued by the firm. Recall from Chapter 5 that r_d is the required return on a bond; for previously issued bonds, r_d, is equal to the bond's yield to maturity.

T = The firm's effective marginal tax rate.

r_{std} = Interest rate on short-term debt, such as notes payable.

r_{ps} = Required return on preferred stock, as defined in Chapter 7.

r_s = Required return on common stock, as defined in Chapter 7.

w = w_d, w_{std}, w_{ps}, and w_s, = weights of long-term debt, short-term debt, preferred stock, and common stock in the firm's target capital structure. The weights are the percentages of the different sources of capital the firm plans to use on a regular basis, with the percentages based on the market values of those sources of capital in the target capital structure.

In the following sections we explain how to estimate the WACC of a specific company, MicroDrive, Inc., but let's begin with a few general concepts. First, companies are financed by several sources of investor-supplied capital, which are called **capital components**. We have included short-term debt and preferred stock because some companies use them as sources of funding, but most companies only use two major sources of investor-supplied capital, long-term debt, and common stock.

Second, investors providing the capital components require rates of return (r_d, r_{std}, r_{ps}, and r_s) commensurate with the risks of the components in order to induce them to make the investments. Previous chapters defined those required returns from an investor's view, but those returns are costs from a company's viewpoint. This is why we call the WACC a *cost* of capital.

Third, recall that FCF is the cash flow available for distribution to all investors. Therefore, the free cash flows must provide an overall rate of return sufficient to compensate investors for their exposure to risk. Intuitively, it makes sense that this overall return should be a weighted average of the capital components' required returns. This intuition is confirmed by applying algebra to the definitions of required returns, free cash flow, and the value of operations: The discount rate used in Equation 9-1 is equal to the WACC as defined in Equation 9-2. In other words, the correct rate for estimating the present value of a company's (or project's) cash flows is the *weighted* average cost of capital.

S E L F - T E S T

Identify a firm's major capital structure components and give the symbols for their respective costs and weights.

What is a component cost?

9-2 Choosing Weights for the Weighted Average Cost of Capital

Figure 9-1 selected data for MicroDrive, Inc., including: (1) liabilities and equity (L&E) from the balance sheets; (2) percentages of total L&E comprised by each liability or equity account; (3) book values (as reported on the balance sheets) and percentages of financing from investor-supplied capital; (4) current market values and percentages of financing from investor-supplied capital; and (5) target capital structure weights.

Notice that we exclude accounts payable and accruals from capital structure weights. Capital is provided by *investors*—interest-bearing debt, preferred stock, and common equity. Accounts payable and accruals arise from operating decisions, not from financing decisions. Recall that the impact of payables and accruals is incorporated into a firm's free cash flows and a project's cash flows rather than into the cost of capital. Therefore, we consider only investor-supplied capital when discussing capital structure weights.

Figure 9-1 reports percentages of financing based on book values, market values, and target weights. Book values are a record of the cumulative amounts of capital supplied by investors over the life of the company. For equity, stockholders have supplied capital directly when MicroDrive issued stock, but they have also supplied capital indirectly when MicroDrive retained earnings instead of paying bigger dividends. The WACC is used to find the present value of *future* cash flows, so it would be inconsistent to use weights based on the *past* history of the company.

Stock prices are volatile, so current market values of total common equity often change dramatically from day to day. Companies certainly don't try to maintain the weights in their capital structures daily by issuing stock, repurchasing stock, issuing debt, or repaying debt in response to changes in their stock price. Therefore, the capital structure weights based on the current market values might not be a good estimate of the capital structure that the company will have on average during the future.

The target capital structure is defined as the average capital structure weights (based on market values) that a company will have during the future. MicroDrive has chosen a target capital structure composed of 2% short-term debt, 28% long-term debt, 3% preferred stock, and 67% common equity. MicroDrive presently has more debt in its actual capital structure (using either book values or market values), but it intends to move towards its target capital structure in the near future. We explain how firms choose their capital structures in Chapter 15, but for now just accept the given target weights for MicroDrive.

The following sections explain how to estimate the required returns for the capital structure components.

FIGURE 9-1

MicroDrive, Inc.: Selected Capital Structure Data (Millions of Dollars, December 31, 2013)

	A	B	C	D	E	F	G	H	I	J
30						Investor-Supplied Capital				
31						Book		Market		Target
32				Percent	Book	Percent	Market	Percent		Capital
33	*Liabilities and Equity*			of Total	Value	of Total	Value	of Total		Structure
34	Accounts payable		$ 200	5.6%						
35	Notes payable		280	7.9%	$ 280	9.2%	$ 280	9.9%	W_{std} =	2%
36	Accruals		300	8.5%						
37	Total C.L.		$ 780	22.0%						
38	Long-term debt		1,200	33.8%	1,200	39.3%	1,200	42.4%	W_d =	28%
39	Total liabilities		$1,980	55.8%						
40	Preferred stock		100	2.8%	100	3.3%	100	3.5%	W_{ps} =	3%
41	Common stock		500	14.1%						
42	Retained earnings		970	27.3%						
43	Total common equity		$1,470	41.4%	$1,470	48.2%	$1,250	44.2%	W_s =	67%
44	Total L&E		$3,550	100.0%	$3,050	100.0%	$2,830	100.0%		100%
45										
46	Other Data (Millions, except per share data):									
47	Number of common shares outstanding =			50						
48	Price per share of common stock =			$25.00						
49	Number of preferred shares outstanding =			1						
50	Price per share of preferred stock =			$100.00						

Notes:

1. The market value of the notes payable is equal to the book value. Some of the long-term bonds sell at a discount and some sell at a premium, but their aggregate market value is approximately equal to their aggregate book value.

2. The common stock price is $25 per share. There are 50 million shares outstanding, for a total market value of equity of $25(50) = $1,250 million.

3. The preferred stock price is $100 per share. There are 1 million shares outstanding, for a total market value of preferred stock of $100(1) = $100 million.

SELF-TEST

What is a target capital structure?

9-3 After-Tax Cost of Debt: $r_d(1 - T)$ and $r_{std}(1 - T)$

The first step in estimating the cost of debt is to determine the rate of return lenders require.

9-3a The Before-Tax Cost of Short-Term Debt: r_{std}

Short-term debt should be included in the capital structure only if it is a permanent source of financing in the sense that the company plans to continually repay and refinance the short-term debt. This is the case for MicroDrive, whose bankers charge 10% on notes payable. Therefore, MicroDrive's short-term lenders have a required return of $r_{std} = 10\%$, which is MicroDrive's before-tax cost of short-term debt.

Some large companies use commercial paper as a source of short-term financing. We discuss this in Chapter 16.

9-3b The Before-Tax Cost of Long-Term Debt: r_d

For long-term debt, estimating r_d is conceptually straightforward, but some problems arise in practice. Companies use both fixed- and floating-rate debt, both straight and convertible debt, both long- and short-term debt, as well as debt with and without sinking funds. Each type of debt may have a somewhat different cost.

It is unlikely that the financial manager will know at the beginning of a planning period the exact types and amounts of debt that will be used during the period. The type or types used will depend on the specific assets to be financed and on capital market conditions as they develop over time. Even so, the financial manager does know what types of debt are typical for his firm. For example, MicroDrive typically issues 15-year bonds to raise long-term debt used to help finance its capital budgeting projects. Because the WACC is used primarily in capital budgeting, MicroDrive's treasurer uses the cost of 15-year bonds in her WACC estimate.

Assume that it is January 2014 and that MicroDrive's treasurer is estimating the WACC for the coming year. How should she calculate the component cost of debt? Most financial managers begin by discussing current and prospective interest rates with their investment bankers. Assume MicroDrive's bankers believe that a new, 15-year, noncallable, straight bond issue would require a 9% coupon rate with semiannual payments. It can be offered to the public at its $1,000 par value. Therefore, their estimate of r_d is 9%.[2]

Note that 9% is the cost of **new**, or **marginal**, **debt**, and it will probably not be the same as the average rate on MicroDrive's previously issued debt, which is called the **historical,** or **embedded, rate**. The embedded cost is important for some decisions but not for others. For example, the average cost of all the capital raised in the past and still outstanding is used by regulators when they determine the rate of return that a public utility should be allowed to earn. However, in financial management the WACC is used primarily to make investment decisions, and these decisions hinge on projects' expected future returns versus the cost of the new, or marginal, capital that will be used to finance those projects. *Thus, for our purposes, the relevant cost is the marginal cost of new debt to be raised during the planning period.*

MicroDrive has issued debt in the past and the bonds are publicly traded. The financial staff can use the market price of the bonds to find the yield to maturity (or yield to call, if the bonds sell at a premium and are likely to be called). This yield is the rate of return that current bondholders expect to receive, and it is also a good estimate of r_d, the rate of return that new bondholders will require.

MicroDrive's outstanding bonds were recently issued and have a 9% coupon, paid semiannually. The bonds mature in 15 years and have a par value of $1,000. These bonds are trading at $1,000. We can find the yield to maturity by using a financial calculator with these inputs: $N = 30$, $PV = -1000$, $PMT = 45$, and $FV = 1000$. Solving for the rate, we find $I/YR = 4.5\%$. This is a semiannual periodic rate, so the nominal annual rate is 9.0%. This is consistent with the investment bankers' estimated rate, so 9% is a reasonable estimate for r_d.

---

[2]Because it is a semiannual bond, the effective annual rate is $(1 + 0.09/2)^2 - 1 = 9.2\%$, but MicroDrive and most other companies use nominal rates for all component costs.

MicroDrive's outstanding bonds are trading at par, so the yield is equal to the coupon rate. But consider a hypothetical example for which the market price isn't par but instead is $923.14. We can find the yield to maturity by using a financial calculator with these inputs: N = 30, PV = −923.14, PMT = 45, and FV = 1000. Solving for the rate, we find I/YR = 5%, which implies a hypothetical nominal annual rate of 10%. As this hypothetical example illustrates, it is not necessary for the bond to trade at par in order to estimate the cost of debt.

Even if MicroDrive had no publicly traded debt, its staff could still look at the yields on publicly traded debt of similar firms for a reasonable estimate of r_d.

Be alert to situations in which there is a significant probability that the company will default on its debt. In such a case, the yield to maturity (whether calculated from market prices of an outstanding bond or taken as the coupon rate on a newly issued bond) overstates the investor's expected return and hence the company's expected cost. For example, let's reconsider MicroDrive's 15-year semiannual bonds that can be issued at par if the coupon rate is 9%. As shown previously, the nominal annual yield to maturity is 9%. But suppose investors believe there is a significant chance that MicroDrive will default. To keep the example simple, suppose investors believe that the bonds will default in 14 years and that the recovery rate on the par value will be 70%. Here are the new inputs: N = 2(14) = 28, PV = −1000, PMT = 45, and FV = 0.70(1000) = 700. Solving for the rate, we find I/YR = 3.9%, implying an annual expected return of 7.8%. This is an extremely simple example, but it illustrates that the expected return on a bond is less than the yield to maturity as it is normally calculated. For bonds with a relatively low expected default rate, we recommend using the yield to maturity. But for bonds with high expected default rates, it would be necessary to do a scenario analysis (such as the one in Section 6.2) to estimate the bond's expected return.

9-3c The After-Tax Cost of Debt: $r_d(1 - T)$ and $r_{std}(1 - T)$

The required return to debtholders, r_d, is not equal to the company's cost of debt because interest payments are deductible, which means the government in effect pays part of the total cost. As a result, the weighted average cost of capital is calculated using the **after-tax cost of debt**, $r_d(1 - T)$, which is the interest rate on debt, r_d, less the tax savings that result because interest is deductible. Here T is the firm's marginal tax rate.[3]

$$\begin{aligned} \text{After–tax component cost of debt} &= \text{Interest rate} - \text{Tax savings} \\ &= r_d - r_d T \\ &= r_d(1 - T) \end{aligned} \qquad (9\text{-}3)$$

If we assume that MicroDrive's marginal federal-plus-state tax rate is 40%, then its after-tax cost of debt is 5.4%:[4]

---

[3]The federal tax rate for most corporations is 35%. However, most corporations are also subject to state income taxes, so the marginal tax rate on most corporate income is about 40%. For illustrative purposes, we assume that the effective federal-plus-state tax rate on marginal income is 40%. The effective tax rate is *zero* for a firm with such large current or past losses that it does not pay taxes. In this situation, the after-tax cost of debt is equal to the pre-tax interest rate.

[4]Strictly speaking, the after-tax cost of debt should reflect the *expected* cost of debt. Although MicroDrive's bonds have a promised return of 9%, there is some chance of default and so its bondholders' expected return (and consequently MicroDrive's cost) is a bit less than 9%. However, for a relatively strong company such as MicroDrive, this difference is quite small.

How Effective Is the Effective Corporate Tax Rate?

© Rob Webb/Getty Images

The statutory U.S. federal corporate tax rate is 35%. With Japan cutting its tax rate in 2012, U.S. corporations face the highest combined federal and state taxes in the world. Or do they? The following chart shows the actual federal corporate tax receipts as a percentage of domestic economic profits. Notice that the effective tax rate averaged around 25% for about 15 years after the tax reforms of 1986, but that it has gyrated wildly since 2000, dropping to an all-time low of 12.1% in 2011, probably due to temporary changes in the tax code made to stimulate the economy in response to the recession. International comparisons are difficult due to data availability and complexity (and due to the analysts' political leanings), but the average effective tax rate on corporations in developed countries usually is around 25%.

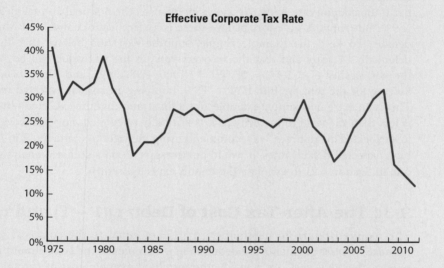

Effective Corporate Tax Rate

Source: Adapted from the Congressional Budget Office report on January 19, 2012, *The Budget and Economic Outlook: Fiscal Years 2012 to 2022.* To see the report, go to **www.cbo.gov/publication/42905**. To get the data in an *Excel* workbook, select Data Underlying Figures.

$$r_d(1-T) = 9\%(1.0-0.4)$$
$$= 9\%(0.6)$$
$$= 5.4\%$$

For MicroDrive's short-term debt, the after-tax cost is 6%: $r_{std}(1-T) = 10\%(1.0-0.4) = 6\%$.

9-3d Flotation Costs and the Cost of Debt

Most debt offerings have very low flotation costs, especially for privately placed debt. Because flotation costs are usually low, most analysts ignore them when estimating the after-tax cost of debt. However, the following example illustrates the procedure for incorporating flotation costs as well as their impact on the after-tax cost of debt.

Suppose MicroDrive can issue 30-year debt with an annual coupon rate of 9%, with coupons paid semiannually. The flotation costs, F, are equal to 1% of the value of the issue. Instead of finding the pre-tax yield based upon pre-tax cash flows and then adjusting it to reflect taxes, as we did before, we can find the after-tax, flotation-adjusted cost by using this formula:

$$M(1-F) = \sum_{t=1}^{N} \frac{INT(1-T)}{[1 + r_d(1-T)]^t} + \frac{M}{[1 - r_d(1-T)]^N} \qquad (9\text{-}4)$$

Here M is the bond's maturity (or par) value, F is the **percentage flotation cost** (i.e., the percentage of proceeds paid to the investment bankers), N is the number of payments, T is the firm's tax rate, INT is the dollars of interest per period, and $r_d(1 - T)$ is the after-tax cost of debt adjusted for flotation costs. With a financial calculator, enter N = 60, PV = −1000(1 − 0.01) = −990, PMT = 45(1 − 0.40) = 27, and FV = 1000. Solving for I/YR, we find I/YR = $r_d(1 - T)$ = 2.73%, which is the semiannual after-tax component cost of debt. The nominal after-tax cost of debt is 5.46%. Note that this is quite close to the original 5.40% after-tax cost, so in this instance adjusting for flotation costs doesn't make much difference.[5]

However, the flotation adjustment would be higher if F were larger or if the bond's life were shorter. For example, if F were 10% rather than 1%, then the nominal annual flotation-adjusted $r_d(1 - T)$ would be 6.13%. With N at 1 year rather than 30 years and F still equal to 1%, the nominal annual $r_d(1 - T)$ = 6.45%. Finally, if F = 10% and N = 1, then the nominal annual $r_d(1 - T)$ = 16.67%. In all of these cases, the effect of flotation costs would be too large to ignore.

As an alternative to adjusting the cost of debt for flotation costs, in some situations it makes sense to instead adjust the project's cash flows. For example, **project financing** is a special situation in which a large project, such as an oil refinery, is financed with debt plus other securities that have a specific claim on the project's cash flows. This is different from the usual debt offering, in which the debt has a claim on all of the corporation's cash flows. Because project financing is funded by securities with claims tied to a particular project, the flotation costs can be included with the project's other cash flows when evaluating the project's value. However, project financing is relatively rare, so when we incorporate the impact of flotation costs, we usually do so by adjusting the component cost of the new debt.

SELF-TEST

Why is the after-tax cost of debt, rather than its before-tax cost, used to calculate the weighted average cost of capital?

Is the relevant cost of debt when calculating the WACC the interest rate on already outstanding debt or the rate on new debt? Why?

A company has outstanding long-term bonds with a face value of $1,000, a 10% coupon rate, 25 years remaining until maturity, and a current market value of $1,214.82. If it pays interest semiannually, then what is the nominal annual pre-tax cost of debt? (8%) If the company's tax rate is 40%, what is the after-tax cost of debt? (4.8%)

---

[5]Equation 9-4 produces the correct after-tax cost of debt only for bonds issued at par. For bonds with a price other than par, the after-tax cash flows must be adjusted to take into account the actual taxation of the discount or premium. See *Web Extension 5A* on the textbook's Web site for a discussion of the taxation of original issue discount bonds. Also, we ignored the tax shield due to amortization of flotation costs because it has very little effect on the cost of debt; see *Ch09 Tool Kit.xls* for an example that incorporates the amortization tax shield.

9-4 Cost of Preferred Stock, r_{ps}

Many firms (including MicroDrive) use, or plan to use, preferred stock as part of their financing mix. Preferred dividends are not tax deductible, so the company bears their full cost. Therefore, *no tax adjustment is used when calculating the cost of preferred stock.* Some preferred stocks are issued without a stated maturity date, but today most have a sinking fund that effectively limits their life. Finally, although it is not mandatory that preferred dividends be paid, firms generally have every intention of doing so, because otherwise (1) they cannot pay dividends on their common stock, (2) they will find it difficult to raise additional funds in the capital markets, and (3) in some cases preferred stockholders can take control of the firm.

The **component cost of preferred stock**, r_{ps}, is the cost used in the WACC calculation. For preferred stock with a stated maturity date, we use the same approach as in the previous section for the cost of debt, keeping in mind that a firm has no tax savings with preferred stock. For preferred stock without a stated maturity date, r_{ps} is

$$\text{Component cost of preferred stock} = r_{ps} = \frac{D_{ps}}{P_{ps}(1-F)} \qquad (9\text{-}5)$$

Here D_{ps} is the preferred dividend, P_{ps} is the preferred stock price, and F is the flotation cost as a percentage of proceeds.

To illustrate the calculation, assume MicroDrive has preferred stock that pays an $8 dividend per share and sells for $100 per share. If MicroDrive issued new shares of preferred, then it would incur an underwriting (or flotation) cost of 2.5%, or $2.50 per share, so it would net $97.50 per share. Therefore, MicroDrive's cost of preferred stock is 8.2%:

$$r_{ps} = \$8/\$97.50 = 8.2\%$$

If we had not incorporated flotation costs, we would have incorrectly estimated r_{ps} = $8/$100 = 8.0%, which is too big a difference to ignore. Therefore, analysts usually include flotation costs when estimating the firm's cost of preferred stock.

Although preferred stock is riskier than debt, MicroDrive's preferred stock has a lower return to investors than does its debt: 8% versus 9%. However, recall that most preferred stock is held by other companies, which are allowed to exclude 70% of preferred stocks' dividends from taxation. Thus, the after-tax return to these investors is higher for preferred stock than for debt, which is consistent with preferred stock being riskier than debt.

SELF-TEST

Does the component cost of preferred stock include or exclude flotation costs? Explain.

Why is no tax adjustment made to the cost of preferred stock?

A company's preferred stock currently trades for $50 per share and pays a $3 annual dividend. Flotation costs are equal to 3% of the gross proceeds. If the company issues preferred stock, what is the cost of that stock? **(6.19%)**

9-5 Cost of Common Stock: The Market Risk Premium, RP_M

Before addressing the required return for an individual stock, let's start with the big picture, which is the required return for the entire stock market. In other words, how much return do investors require to induce them to invest in stocks? It often is more convenient to focus on the extra return that investors require to induce them to invest in risky equities over and beyond the return on a Treasury bond. As Chapter 6 explained, this extra return is called the market risk premium, RP_M. Sometimes this is called the **equity risk premium**, or just the **equity premium**.

Unfortunately, the required return on the market, and hence the equity premium, is not directly observable. Three approaches may be used to estimate the market risk premium: (1) calculate historical premiums and use them to estimate the current premium; (2) survey experts; and (3) use the current value of the market to estimate forward-looking premiums. Following are descriptions of each approach.

9-5a Historical Risk Premium

Historical risk premium data for U.S. securities, updated annually, are available from many sources, including Ibbotson Associates.[6] Using data from 1926 through the most recent year, Ibbotson calculates the actual realized rate of return each year for the stock market and for long-term government bonds. Ibbotson defines the annual equity risk premium as the difference between the historical realized returns on stocks and the historical yields to maturity on long-term T-bonds.[7] Ibbotson recently reported a 6.6% arithmetic average historical risk premium.[8] How should these data be used?

First, stock returns are quite volatile, which leads to low statistical confidence in estimated averages. For example, the estimated historical average premium is 6.6%, but based on the market return's standard deviation of around 20%, the 95% confidence interval ranges about plus or minus 3% from 6.6%. In other words, the historical average is helpful in deciding whether the risk premium is on the order of 6% or 20%, but it isn't very helpful in deciding whether the premium should be 4% or 6%.

Second, the historical average is extremely sensitive to the period over which it is calculated. For example, we provide annual data for the period 1968–2011 in the file **Ch09 Tool Kit.xls.** For this period, the estimated historic risk premium is just 3.9%.

Third, changes in the risk premium can occur if investors' tolerance for risk changes. This causes problems in interpreting historical returns because a change in the required risk premium causes an *opposite change in the observed* premium. For example, an increase in the required premium means that investors have become more risk averse and require a higher return on stocks. But applying a higher discount rate to a stock's future cash flows causes a decline in stock price. Thus, an *increase* in the required premium causes a simultaneous *decrease* in the observed premium. Part of the market's precipitous decline in 2008 and 2009 surely was due to investors' increased risk aversion.

---

[6]See *Ibbotson Stocks, Bonds, Bills, and Inflation: 2012 Valuation Yearbook* (Chicago: Morningstar, Inc., 2012) for the most recent estimates.

[7]The risk premium should be defined using the yield on T-bonds. As a proxy for yield, Ibbotson uses the return on 20-year T-bonds that is due to coupons. This underestimates yield for discount bonds and overstates yield for premium bonds, but the error probably averages out to zero in most years.

[8]The arithmetic average often is used as an estimate of next year's risk premium; this is most appropriate if investor risk aversion had actually been constant during the sample period. On the other hand, the geometric average would be most appropriate to estimate the longer-term risk premium, say, for the next 20 years. The geometric average for this time period is 4.7%, which is less than the arithmetic average.

9-5b Surveys of Experts

What do the experts think about the market risk premium? Two professors at Duke University, John Graham and Campbell Harvey (working in conjunction with *CFO* magazine), have surveyed CFOs quarterly beginning in 2000.[9] One survey question asks CFOs what they expect the S&P 500 return to be over the next 10 years; the CFOs are also given the yield on a 10-year T-bond. Their average response in the March 2012 survey implied an average expected risk premium of about 4.35%.

Professor Fernando Fernandez of the IESE Business School regularly surveys professors, analysts, and companies.[10] For 2011, based on the average U.S. responses, professors recommend a premium of 5.7%, analysts recommend 5.0%, and companies recommend 5.5%.

In summary, in 2011–2012, experts predicted a premium within the range of about 4.35% to 5.7%.

9-5c Forward-Looking Risk Premiums

An alternative to the historical risk premium is the forward-looking, or ex ante, risk premium. As shown in Chapter 7, if we assume that the market dividend will grow at a constant rate and that the firms that make up the market pay out as dividends all the funds available for distribution (i.e., the firms make no stock repurchases or purchases of short-term investments), then the expected market rate of return, $\hat{r}_M$ is:

$$\hat{r}_M = \frac{D_1}{P_0} + g \qquad (9\text{-}6)$$

If we also assume that the market is in equilibrium, then required return on the market, r_M, is equal to the expected return, $\hat{r}_M$, found by using Equation 9-6. Thus, the required return on the market can be estimated as the sum of the market's expected dividend yield plus the expected constant growth rate in dividends.

SIMPLIFIED ILLUSTRATION OF ESTIMATING A FORWARD-LOOKING RISK PREMIUM

resource

*For current estimates, see instructions in **Ch09 Tool Kit.xls**.*

Following is an illustration for how to use Equation 9-6 to estimate the required return on the market. First, you need an estimate of the expected dividend. In April 2012, Standard & Poor's Web site reported a projected dividend yield of 2.16% for the S&P 500, based on declared dividends. Second, you need an estimate of the constant dividend growth rate, g. One approach is to use the historical average growth rate in dividends for the S&P 500, which is about 4.4% (for 1926–2011). Using these estimates produces an estimate of the required market return:

$$r_M = \hat{r}_M = \frac{D_1}{P_0} + g$$
$$= 2.16\% + 4.4\%$$
$$= 6.56\%$$

---

[9]See John Graham and Campbell Harvey, "The Equity Risk Premium in 2012," Working Paper, Duke University, 2012. For periodic updates, see Professor Graham's Web site, **http://faculty.fuqua.duke.edu/~jgraham/resume. html**, and look for the section on Permanent Working Papers.

[10]See Pablo Fernández, "Market Risk Premium Used in 56 Countries in 2011: A Survey with 6,014 Answers," at SSRN: **ssrn.com/abstract=1822192**.

At the time we estimated r_M, the 10-year T-bond yield was 2.19%. Using the previously estimated r_M of 6.56%, the estimated forward-looking market risk premium is:

$$RP_M = r_M - r_{RF}$$
$$= 6.56\% - 2.19\%$$
$$= 4.37\%$$

COMPLICATIONS WHEN ESTIMATING A FORWARD-LOOKING RISK PREMIUM

We made numerous simplifying assumptions in the previous example regarding three complications that arise in practice. First, the growth rate in dividends probably will not be constant in the near future but might instead take many years before leveling out. Second, the historical average growth rate in dividends might not be a good estimate of the expected long-term dividend growth rate. Long-term growth in dividends is probably related to long-term sales and profits, which in turn depend on inflation (which affects reported dollar value of sales), population growth (which affects the unit volume of sales), and productivity (which affects profits). Third, the model is based on dividends per share, but it ignores the impact of stock repurchases on the number of outstanding shares (which then changes the growth rate of dividends per share).

Fortunately, there are ways to address these technical issues, including the use of a multistage growth model. The interested reader should see *Web Extension 9A* and the corresponding worksheet, *Web 9A*, in *Ch9 Tool Kit.xls*.

9-5d Our View on the Market Risk Premium

After reading the previous sections, you might well be confused about the best way to estimate the market risk premium. Here's our opinion: The risk premium is driven primarily by investors' attitudes toward risk, and there are good reasons to believe that investors' risk aversion changes over time. The introduction of pension plans, Social Security, health insurance, and disability insurance over the last 50 years means that people today can take more chances with their investments, which should make them less risk averse. Moreover, many households have dual earners, allowing households to take more chances. Therefore, we think the risk premium is lower now than it was 50 years ago.

In our consulting, we currently (spring 2012) use a risk premium of about 5% to 6%, but we would have a hard time arguing with someone who used a risk premium anywhere in the range of 3% to 7%. We believe that investors' aversion to risk is relatively stable much of the time, but it is not absolutely constant from year to year and is certainly not constant during periods of great stress, such as during the 2008–2009 financial crisis. When stock prices are relatively high, investors feel less risk averse, so we use a risk premium at the low end of our range. Conversely, when prices are depressed, we use a premium at the high end of the range. The bottom line is that there is no way to prove that a particular risk premium is either right or wrong, though we'd be suspicious of an estimated market premium that is less than 3% or greater than 7%.

SELF-TEST

Explain both the historical and the forward-looking approaches to estimating the market risk premium.

9-6 Using the CAPM to Estimate the Cost of Common Stock, r_s

Before estimating the return required by MicroDrive's shareholders, r_s, it is worth considering the two ways that a company can raise common equity: (1) Sell newly issued shares to the public. (2) Reinvest (retain) earnings by not paying out all net income as dividends.

Does new equity capital raised by reinvesting earnings have a cost? The answer is a resounding "yes!" If earnings are reinvested, then stockholders will incur an **opportunity cost**—the earnings could have been paid out as dividends or used to repurchase stock, and in either case stockholders would have received funds that they could reinvest in other securities. *Thus, the firm should earn on its reinvested earnings at least as much as its stockholders could earn on alternative investments of equivalent risk.*

What rate of return could stockholders expect to earn on equivalent-risk investments? The answer is r_s, because they could presumably earn that return by simply buying the stock of the firm in question or that of a similar firm. *Therefore, r_s is the cost of common equity raised internally as reinvested earnings.* If a company can't earn at least r_s on reinvested earnings, then it should pass those earnings on to its stockholders as dividends and let them invest the money themselves in assets that do yield r_s.

9-6a The Capital Asset Pricing Model

To estimate the cost of common stock using the Capital Asset Pricing Model as discussed in Chapter 6, we proceed as follows.

1. Estimate the risk-free rate, r_{RF}.
2. Estimate the current market risk premium, RP_M, which is the required market return in excess of the risk-free rate.
3. Estimate the stock's beta coefficient, b_i, which measures the stock's relative risk. The subscript i signifies Stock i's beta.
4. Use these three values to estimate the stock's required rate of return:

$$r_s = r_{RF} + (RP_M)b_i \qquad (9\text{-}7)$$

Equation 9-7 shows that the CAPM estimate of r_s begins with the risk-free rate, r_{RF}. We then add a risk premium that is equal to the risk premium on the market, RP_M, scaled up or down to reflect the particular stock's risk as measured by its beta coefficient. The following sections explain how to implement this four-step process.

9-6b Estimating the Risk-Free Rate, r_{RF}

The starting point for the CAPM cost-of-equity estimate is r_{RF}, the risk-free rate. There is no such thing as a truly riskless asset in the U.S. economy. Treasury securities are essentially free of default risk; however, nonindexed long-term T-bonds will suffer capital losses if interest rates rise, indexed long-term bonds will decline if the real rate rises, and a portfolio of short-term T-bills will provide a volatile earnings stream because the rate earned on T-bills varies over time.

Because we cannot, in practice, find a truly riskless rate upon which to base the CAPM, what rate should we use? Keep in mind that our objective is to estimate the cost of capital, which will be used to discount a company's free cash flows or a project's cash flows. Free cash flows occur over the life of the company and many projects last for many years.

W W W

To find the rate on a T-bond, go to www.federal reserve.gov. Select "Economic Research & Data" and then select "Statistical Releases andHistorical Data." Click on "Daily" for "H.15: Selected Interest Rates."

Because the cost of capital will be used to discount relatively long-term cash flows, it seems appropriate to use a relatively long-term risk-free rate, such as the yield on a 10-year Treasury bond. Indeed, a survey of highly regarded companies shows that about two-thirds of them use the rate on 10-year Treasury bonds.[11]

T-bond rates can be found in *The Wall Street Journal*, the *Federal Reserve Bulletin*, or on the Internet. Although most analysts use the yield on a 10-year T-bond as a proxy for the risk-free rate, yields on 20- or 30-year T-bonds are also reasonable proxies.

9-6c Estimating the Market Risk Premium, RP_M

We described three approaches for estimating the market risk premium, RP_M, in Section 9.5: (1) use historical averages, (2) survey experts, and (3) estimate forward-looking expected market returns. All three approaches provide estimates in the same ballpark, around 3% to 7%. The final choice really boils down to judgment informed by the current state of the market and the estimates provided by the three approaches. We will use a market risk premium of 6% in this example.

9-6d Estimating Beta, b_i

W W W

To find an estimate of beta, go to www.valueline.com and then enter the ticker symbol for a stock quote. Or go to Thomson ONE— Business School Edition. Beta is shown in the Key Fundamentals section.

Recall from Chapter 6 a stock's beta, b_i, can be estimated as:

$$b_i = \left(\frac{\sigma_i}{\sigma_M} \right) \rho_{iM} \qquad (9\text{-}8)$$

where ρ_{iM} is the correlation between Stock i's return and the market return, σ_i is the standard deviation of Stock i's return, and σ_M is the standard deviation of the market's return. This definition is also equal to the estimated slope coefficient in a regression, with the company's stock returns on the y-axis and market returns on the x-axis.

It is easy to gather historical returns from the Web and then estimate your own beta, as we show in the Chapter 6 **Tool Kit**. Also, many Web sources provide estimates of beta. The good news is that there is no shortage of beta estimates; the bad news is that many estimates differ from one another. We will discuss this in the next section.

9-6e An Illustration of the CAPM Approach: MicroDrive's Cost of Equity, r_s

Following is an application of the CAPM approach to MicroDrive. As estimated in Chapter 6, MicroDrive's beta, b_j, is 1.43. We assume that the market risk premium, RP_M, is about 6%. For this example, assume that the risk-free rate, r_{RF}, is 5%. Using Equation 9-7, we estimate MicroDrive's required return as about 13.6%:

$$
\begin{aligned}
r_s &= 5\% + (6\%)(1.43) \\
&= 5\% + 8.58\% \\
&= 13.58\% \approx 13.6\%
\end{aligned}
$$

---

[11]See Robert E. Bruner, Kenneth M. Eades, Robert S. Harris, and Robert C. Higgins, "Best Practices in Estimating the Cost of Capital: Survey and Synthesis," *Financial Practice and Education*, Spring/Summer 1998, pp. 13–28.

This estimate of 13.6% is a required return from an investor's point of view, but it is a cost of equity from a company's perspective.

Always keep in mind that the estimated cost of equity is indeed an estimate, for several reasons. First, the yield on any long-term T-bond would be an appropriate estimate of the risk-free rate, and different yields would lead to different estimates of r_s. Second, no one truly knows the correct market risk premium. We can narrow the estimated RP_M down to a fairly small range, but different estimates in this range would lead to different estimates of r_s. Third, estimates of beta are inexact. In addition to a large range of the confidence interval around an estimated beta, using slightly different time periods to estimate beta can lead to rather large differences in the estimated beta.

Still, in our judgment, it is possible to develop "reasonable" estimates of the required inputs, and we believe that the CAPM can be used to obtain reasonable estimates of the cost of equity. Indeed, despite the difficulties we have noted, surveys indicate that the CAPM is by far the most widely used method. Although most firms use more than one method, almost 74% of respondents in one survey (and 85% in another) used the CAPM.[12] This is in sharp contrast to a 1982 survey, which found that only 30% of respondents used the CAPM.[13]

SELF-TEST

What are the two primary sources of equity capital?

Explain why there is a cost to using reinvested earnings; that is, why aren't reinvested earnings a free source of capital?

Which is generally considered the more appropriate estimate of the risk-free rate: the yield on a short-term T-bill or the yield on a 10-year T-bond?

A company's beta is 1.4, the yield on a 10-year T-bond is 4%, and the market risk premium is 4.5%. What is r_s? **(10.3%)**

9-7 Dividend-Yield-Plus-Growth-Rate, or Discounted Cash Flow (DCF), Approach

In Chapter 7, we saw that if an investor expects dividends to grow at a constant rate and if the company makes all payouts in the form of dividends (the company does not repurchase stock), then the price of a stock can be found as follows:

$$\hat{P}_0 = \frac{D_1}{r_s - g} \qquad (9\text{-}9)$$

---

[12]See John R. Graham and Campbell Harvey, "The Theory and Practice of Corporate Finance: Evidence from the Field," *Journal of Financial Economics,* 2001, pp. 187–243, and the paper cited in footnote 10. It is interesting that a growing number of firms (about 34%) also are using CAPM-type models with more than one factor. Of these firms, over 40% include factors for interest rate risk, foreign exchange risk, and business cycle risk (proxied by gross domestic product). More than 20% of these firms include a factor for inflation, size, and exposure to particular commodity prices. Less than 20% of these firms make adjustments due to distress factors, book-to-market ratios, or momentum factors.

[13]See Lawrence J. Gitman and Vincent Mercurio, "Cost of Capital Techniques Used by Major U.S. Firms: Survey Analysis of *Fortune's* 1000," *Financial Management,*1982, pp. 21–29.

Here $\hat{P}_0$ is the intrinsic value of the stock for the investor, D_1 is the dividend expected to be paid at the end of Year 1, g is the expected growth rate in dividends, and r_s is the required rate of return. For the marginal investor, the required return is equal to the expected return. If this investor is the marginal investor then $\hat{P}_0 = P_0$, the market price of the stock, and we can solve for r_s to obtain the required rate of return on common equity:

$$\hat{r}_s = r_s = \frac{D_1}{P_0} + \text{Expected g} \tag{9-10}$$

Thus, investors expect to receive a dividend yield, D_1/P_0, plus a capital gain, g, for a total expected return of $\hat{r}_s$. In equilibrium this expected return is also equal to the required return, r_s. This method of estimating the cost of equity is called the **discounted cash flow,** or **DCF, method**. Henceforth, we will assume that markets are at equilibrium (which means that $r_s = \hat{r}_s$), and this permits us to use the terms r_s and $\hat{r}_s$ interchangeably.

9-7a Estimating Inputs for the DCF Approach

Three inputs are required to use the DCF approach: the current stock price, the current dividend, and the marginal investor's expected dividend growth rate. The stock price and the dividend are easy to obtain, but the expected growth rate is difficult to estimate, as we will see in the following sections.

HISTORICAL GROWTH RATES

If earnings and dividend growth rates have been relatively stable in the past, and if investors expect these trends to continue, then the past realized growth rate may be used as an estimate of the expected future growth rate. Unfortunately, such situations occur only at a handful of very mature, slow-growing companies, which precludes the usefulness of historical growth rates as predictors of future growth rates for most companies.

RETENTION GROWTH MODEL

Most firms pay out some of their net income as dividends and reinvest, or retain, the rest. The more they retain, and the higher the earned rate of return on those retained earnings, the larger their growth rate. This is the idea behind the retention growth model.

The **payout ratio** is the percent of net income that the firm pays out in dividends, and the **retention ratio** is the complement of the payout ratio: Retention ratio = (1 − Payout ratio). To illustrate, consider Aldabra Corporation, a mature company. Aldabra's payout ratio has averaged 63% over the past 15 years, so its retention rate has averaged $1.0 - 0.63 = 0.37 = 37\%$. Also, Aldabra's return on equity (ROE) has averaged 14.5% over the past 15 years. We know that, other things held constant, the earnings growth rate depends on the amount of income the firm retains and the rate of return it earns on those retained earnings, and the **retention growth equation** can be expressed as follows:

$$g = \text{ROE(Retention ratio)} \tag{9-11}$$

Using Aldabra's 14.5% average ROE and its 37% retention rate, we can use Equation 9-11 to find the estimated g:

$$g = 14.5\%(0.37) = 5.365 \approx 5.4\%$$

Although easy to implement, this approach requires four major assumptions: (1) the payout rate, and thus the retention rate, remain constant; (2) the ROE on new investments remains constant and equal to the ROE on existing assets; (3) the firm is not expected to repurchase or issue new common stock, or, if it does, this new stock will be sold at a price equal to its book value; and (4) future projects are expected to have the same degree of risk as the firm's existing assets. Unfortunately, these assumptions apply in very few situations, limiting the usefulness of the retention growth model.

ANALYSTS' FORECASTS

A third technique calls for using security analysts' forecasts. As we discussed earlier, analysts publish earnings' growth rate estimates for most of the larger publicly owned companies. For example, *Value Line* provides such dividend forecasts on about 1,700 companies. Several sources compile analysts' earnings forecasts on a regular basis, and these earnings growth rates can be used as proxies for dividend growth rates.

However, analysts usually forecast nonconstant growth, which limits the usefulness of the constant growth model. Instead, a multistage model must be used. See **Web Extension 9A** on the textbook's Web site for an explanation of multistage approach; all calculations are in the worksheet **Web 9A** in the file **Ch9 Tool Kit.xls.**

9-7b An Illustration of the DCF Approach

To illustrate the DCF approach, suppose Aldabra's stock sells for $32, its next expected dividend is $1.82, and its expected constant growth rate is 5.4%. Aldabra is not expected to repurchase any stock. Aldabra's stock is thought to be in equilibrium, so its expected and required rates of return are equal. Based on these assumptions, its estimated DCF cost of common equity is 11.1%:

$$\hat{r}_s = r_s = \frac{\$1.82}{\$32.00} + 5.4\%$$
$$= 5.7\% + 5.4\%$$
$$= 11.1\%$$

As previously noted, it is difficult to apply the DCF approach because dividends do not grow at a constant rate for most companies. Surveys show that 16% of responding firms use the DCF approach, down from 31% in 1982.[14]

SELF-TEST

What inputs are required for the DCF method?

What are three ways to estimate the expected dividend growth rate?

A company's estimated growth rate in dividends is 6%, its current stock price is $40, and its expected annual dividend is $2. Using the DCF approach, what is the firm's r_s? **(11%)**

[14]See the sources cited in footnotes 12 and 13.

9-8 The Weighted Average Cost of Capital (WACC)

As we mentioned earlier in this chapter (and as we discuss in more detail in Chapter 15), each firm has an optimal capital structure, which is defined as the mix of debt, preferred stock, and common equity that maximizes its stock price. Therefore, a value-maximizing firm must attempt to find its *target (or optimal) capital structure* and then raise new capital in a manner that will keep the actual capital structure on target over time. In this chapter, we assume that the firm has identified its optimal capital structure, that it uses this optimum as the target, and that it finances so as to remain constantly on target. How the target is established is examined in Chapter 15. The target proportions of debt, preferred stock, and common equity, along with the component costs of capital, are used to calculate the WACC, as shown previously in Equation 9-2:

$$\text{WACC} = w_d r_d (1 - T) + w_{std} r_{std} (1 - T) + w_{ps} r_{ps} + w_s r_s \qquad (9\text{-}2)$$

Here w_d, w_{std}, w_{ps}, and w_s are the target weights for long-term debt, short-term debt, preferred stock, and common equity, respectively.

To illustrate, we first note that MicroDrive has a target capital structure calling for 28% long-term debt, 2% short-term debt, 3% preferred stock, and 67% common equity. Before-tax cost of long-term debt, r_d, is 9%; before-tax cost of short-term debt, r_{std}, is 10%; cost of preferred stock, r_{ps}, is 8.16%; cost of common equity, r_s, is 13.58%; and marginal tax rate is 40%. We can now calculate MicroDrive's weighted average cost of capital as follows:

$$
\begin{aligned}
\text{WACC} &= 0.28(9.0\%)(1 - 0.4) + 0.02(10.0\%)(1 - 0.4) + 0.03(8.16\%) + 0.67(13.58\%) \\
&= 11\%
\end{aligned}
$$

Three points should be noted. First, the WACC is the cost the company would incur to raise each new, or *marginal*, dollar of capital—it is not the average cost of dollars raised in the past. Second, the percentages of each capital component, called *weights,* should be based on management's target capital structure, not on the particular sources of financing in any single year. Third, the target weights should be based on market values and not on book values. The following sections explain these points.

9-8a Marginal Rates versus Historical Rates

The required rates of return for a company's investors, whether they are new or old, are always marginal rates. For example, a stockholder might have invested in a company last year when the risk-free interest rate was 6% and the required return on equity was 12%. If the risk-free rate subsequently falls and is now 4%, then the investor's required return on equity is now 10% (holding all else constant). This is the same required rate of return that a new equity holder would have, whether the new investor bought stock in the secondary market or through a new equity offering. In other words, whether the shareholders are already equity holders or are brand-new equity holders, they all have the same required rate of return, which is the current required rate of return on equity. The same reasoning applies for the firm's bondholders. All bondholders, whether old or new, have a required rate of return equal to today's yield on the firm's debt, which is based on current market conditions.

Because investors' required rates of return are based on *current* market conditions, not on market conditions when they purchased their securities, it follows that the cost of capital depends on current conditions and not on past market conditions.

9-8b Target Weights versus Annual Financing Choices

We have heard managers (and students!) say, "Our debt has a 5% after-tax cost versus a 10% WACC and a 14% cost of equity. Therefore, because we will finance only with debt this year, we should evaluate this year's projects at a 5% cost." There are two flaws in this line of reasoning.

First, suppose the firm exhausts its capacity to issue low-cost debt this year to take on projects with after-tax returns as low as 5.1% (which is slightly higher than the after-tax cost of debt). Then next year, when the firm must finance with common equity, it will have to turn down projects with returns as high as 13.9% (which is slightly lower than the cost of equity). To avoid this problem, a firm that plans to remain in business indefinitely should evaluate all projects using the 10% WACC.

Second, both existing and new investors have claims on *all* future cash flows. For example, if a company raises debt and also invests in a new project that same year, the new debtholders don't have a specific claim on that specific project's cash flows (assuming it is not non-recourse project financing). In fact, new debtholders receive a claim on the cash flows being generated by existing as well as new projects, while old debtholders (and equity holders) have claims on both new and existing projects. Thus, the decision to take on a new project should depend on the project's ability to satisfy all of the company's investors, not just the new debtholders, even if only debt is being raised that year.

9-8c Weights for Component Costs: Book Values versus Market Values versus Targets

Our primary reason for calculating the WACC is to use it in capital budgeting or corporate valuation. In particular, we need to compare the expected returns on projects and stocks with investors' required returns to determine whether investors are compensated fairly for the risk they bear. The total amount of required compensation depends both on the *rate of required return* and the *amount* investors have at stake.

Regarding the rate of return required by investors, the previous sections showed that investors require a rate of return equal to the current rate they could get on alternative investments of equivalent risk. In other words, the required rate is the opportunity cost.

Regarding the amount that investors have at stake, we again apply the "opportunity" concept. Investors have the opportunity to sell their investment at the market value, so this is the amount that investors have at stake. Notice that the amount at stake is not equal to the book values as reported on the financial statements. Book values are a record of historical investments, not the current market value of the investment. Because the WACC is used to discount future cash flows, the weights should be based on the market value weights expected on average in the future, not necessarily the current weights based on current market values.

In summary, the weights should not be based on book values but instead should be based on the market-value weights in the target capital structure. Obviously, the target capital structure must be realistic—companies can't take on so much debt that they will almost certainly go bankrupt. Also, a company must try to adjust its market value weights toward the target weights; otherwise the average weights over time might differ significantly from those in the target capital structure. We discuss capital structures, including how fast companies adjust their weights, in Chapter 15.

Global Variations in the Cost of Capital

© Rob Webb/Getty Images

For U.S. firms to be competitive with foreign companies, they must have a cost of capital no greater than that faced by their international competitors. In the past, many experts argued that U.S. firms were at a disadvantage. In particular, Japanese firms enjoyed a very low cost of capital, which lowered their total costs and thus made it hard for U.S. firms to compete with them. Recent events, however, have considerably narrowed cost-of-capital differences between U.S. and Japanese firms. In particular, the U.S. stock market has outperformed the Japanese market in recent years, which has made it easier and cheaper for U.S. firms to raise equity capital.

As capital markets become increasingly integrated, cross-country differences in the cost of capital are declining. Today, most large corporations raise capital throughout the world; hence, we are moving toward one global capital market instead of distinct capital markets in each country. Government policies and market conditions can affect the cost of capital within a given country, but this primarily affects smaller firms that do not have access to global capital markets, and even these differences are becoming less important as time passes. What matters most is the risk of the individual firm, not the market in which it raises capital.

SELF-TEST

How is the weighted average cost of capital calculated? Write out the equation.

Should the weights used to calculate the WACC be based on book values, market values, or something else? Explain.

A firm has the following data: target capital structure of 25% debt, 10% preferred stock, and 65% common equity; tax rate = 40%; r_d = 7%; r_{ps} = 7.5%; and r_s = 11.5%. Assume the firm will not issue new stock. What is this firm's WACC? **(9.28%)**

9-9 Adjusting the Cost of Equity for Flotation Costs

Few firms with moderate or slow growth issue new shares of common stock through public offerings.[15] In fact, less than 2% of all new corporate funds come from the external public equity market, for two very good reasons, negative signaling and direct costs. We discuss signaling in Chapter 15, but we address direct costs here.

The direct costs of new issuance are called **flotation costs**. Table 9-1 shows the average flotation costs for debt and equity U.S. corporations issued in the 1990s. Notice that flotation costs, as a *percentage* of capital raised, fall as the *amount* of capital raised increases. The common stock flotation costs are for non-IPO issues. For IPOs, flotation costs are higher—about 17% higher if less than $10 million is raised and higher still as issue size increases. The data in Table 9-1 include both utility and nonutility companies; if utilities had been excluded, the reported flotation costs would have been higher. Table 9-1 shows that flotation costs are significantly higher for equity than for debt. One reason for higher equity flotation costs is that corporate debt is sold mainly in large blocks to institutional investors, whereas common

---

[15]A few companies issue new shares through new-stock dividend reinvestment plans, which we discuss in Chapter 14. Many companies sell stock to their employees, and companies occasionally issue stock to finance huge projects or mergers. Also, some utilities regularly issue common stock.

TABLE 9-1

Average Flotation Costs for Debt and Equity

Amount of Capital Raised (Millions of Dollars)	Average Flotation Cost for Common Stock (% of Total Capital Raised)	Average Flotation Cost for New Debt (% of Total Capital Raised)
2–9.99	13.28%	4.39%
10–19.99	8.72	2.76
20–39.99	6.93	2.42
40–59.99	5.87	2.32
60–79.99	5.18	2.34
80–99.99	4.73	2.16
100–199.99	4.22	2.31
200–499.99	3.47	2.19
500 and up	3.15	1.64

Source: "The Costs of Raising Capital," Inmoo Lee, Scott Lochhead, Jay Ritter, and Quanshui Zhao. Copyright © 1996 by *The Journal of Financial Research.* Reproduced with permission of John Wiley & Sons, Ltd.

stock is sold in smaller amounts to many different investors; this imposes higher costs on the investment banks, which pass these costs on to the issuing company. Also, stock values are harder to estimate than debt values, which make selling stock more difficult, again leading to higher costs for the investment banks.

For companies that do issue new common stock, the **cost of new common equity, r_e,** or external equity, is higher than the cost of equity raised internally by reinvesting earnings, r_s, because of the flotation costs involved in issuing new common stock. What rate of return must be earned on new investments to make issuing stock worthwhile? Put another way, what is the cost of new common stock?

> r_e = component cost of *external equity*, or common equity raised by issuing new stock. As we will see, r_e is equal to r_s plus a factor that reflects the cost of issuing new stock.

The answer, for a constant growth firm, is found by applying this formula:

$$r_e = \hat{r}_e = \frac{D_1}{P_0(1-F)} + g \qquad \text{(9-12)}$$

In Equation 9-12, F is the percentage flotation cost incurred in selling the new stock, so $P_0(1 - F)$ is the net price per share received by the company.

Here is an example. In Section 9.7b, we estimated Aldabra's cost of common equity using the DCF approach as 11.1%, assuming Aldabra didn't issue new equity. Now assume that Aldabra must issue new equity with a flotation cost of 12.5%. The cost of new outside equity is calculated as follows:

$$r_e = \frac{\$1.82}{\$32(1-0.125)} + 5.4\%$$

$$= 6.5\% + 5.4\% = 11.9\%$$

Because of flotation costs, Aldabra must earn 11.9% on the new equity capital in order to provide shareholders the 11.1% they require.

As we noted previously, most analysts use the CAPM to estimate the cost of equity. How would the analyst incorporate flotation costs into a CAPM cost estimate? If application of the DCF methodology gives a cost of internally generated equity of 11.1% but a cost of 11.9% when flotation costs are involved, then the flotation costs add 0.8 percentage points to the cost of equity. To incorporate flotation costs into the CAPM estimate, we would simply add 0.8% to the CAPM estimate.

As an alternative to adjusting the cost of equity for flotation costs, many companies simply include the flotation costs as a negative cash flow when they perform project analysis. See Chapter 11 for a description of cash flow estimation for projects.

SELF-TEST

What are flotation costs?

Why are flotation costs higher for stock than for debt?

A firm has common stock with D_1 = \$3.00; P_0 = \$30; g = 5%; and F = 4%. If the firm must issue new stock, what is its cost of external equity, r_e? **(15.42%)**

9-10 Privately Owned Firms and Small Businesses

So far our discussion of the cost of capital has been focused on publicly owned corporations. Privately owned firms and small businesses have different situations calling for slightly different approaches.

9-10a Estimating the Cost of Stock by the Comparison Approach

When we estimated the rate of return required by public stockholders, we use stock returns to estimate beta as an input for the CAPM approach and stock prices as input data for the DCF method. But how can one measure the cost of equity for a firm whose stock is not traded? Most analysts begin by identifying one or more publicly traded firms that are in the same industry and that are approximately the same size as the privately owned firm.[16] The analyst then estimates the betas for these publicly traded firms and uses their average beta as an estimate of the beta of the privately owned firm.

9-10b Own-Bond-Yield-Plus-Judgmental-Risk-Premium Approach

From Chapter 5, we know that a company's cost of debt is above the risk-free rate due to the default risk premium. We also know that a company's cost of stock should be greater than its cost of debt because equity is riskier than debt. Therefore, some

---

[16]In Chapter 15, we show how to adjust if these comparison firms have differences in capital structures.

analysts use a subjective, ad hoc procedure to estimate a firm's cost of common equity: They simply add a judgmental risk premium of 3% to 5% to the cost of debt. In this approach,

$$r_s = r_d + \text{Judgmental risk premium} \tag{9-13}$$

For example, consider a privately held company with a 10% cost of debt. Using 4% as the judgmental risk premium (because it is the mid-point of the 3%–5% range), the estimated cost of equity is 14%:

$$r_s = 10\% + 4\% = 14\%$$

9-10c Adjusting for Lack of Liquidity

The stock of a privately held firm is less liquid than that of a publicly held firm. As we explained in Chapter 5, investors require a liquidity premium on thinly traded bonds. Therefore, many analysts make an ad hoc adjustment to reflect this lack of liquidity by adding 1 to 3 percentage points to the firm's cost of equity. This rule of thumb is not theoretically satisfying because we don't know exactly how large the liquidity premium should be, but it is logical and is also a common practice.

9-10d Estimating Consistent Weights in the Capital Structure

Suppose a privately held firm is concerned that its current capital structure weights are appropriate. The first step for a publicly traded company would be to estimate the capital structure weights based on current market values. However, a privately held firm can't directly observe its market value, so it can't directly observe its market value weights.

To resolve this problem, many analysts begin by making a trial guess as to the value of the firm's equity. The analysts then use this estimated value of equity to estimate the cost of capital, next use the cost of capital to estimate the value of the firm, and finally complete the circle by using the estimated value of the firm to estimate the value of its equity. If this newly estimated equity value is different from their trial guess, analysts repeat the process but start the iteration with the newly estimated equity value as the trial value of equity. After several iterations, the trial value of equity and the resulting estimated equity value usually converge. Although somewhat tedious, this process provides consistent estimates of the weights, the cost of capital, and the value of the firm.

SELF-TEST

Identify problems that occur when estimating the cost of capital for a privately held firm. What are some solutions to these problems?

Explain the reasoning behind the bond-yield-plus-judgmental-risk-premium approach.

*A company's bond yield is 7%. If the appropriate own-bond-yield risk premium is 3.5%, then what is r_s? (**10.5%**)*

9-11 Managerial Issues and the Cost of Capital

We describe several managerial issues in this section, starting with how managerial decisions affect the cost of capital.

9-11a How Managerial Decisions Affect the Cost of Capital

The cost of capital is affected by some factors that are under a firm's control and some that are not.

FOUR FACTORS THE FIRM CANNOT CONTROL

Four factors are beyond managerial control: (1) interest rates, (2) credit crises, (3) the market risk premium, and (4) tax rates.

Interest Rates.   Interest rates in the economy affect the costs of both debt and equity, but they are beyond a manager's control. Even the Fed can't control interest rates indefinitely. For example, interest rates are heavily influenced by inflation, and when inflation hit historic highs in the early 1980s, interest rates followed. Rates trended mostly down for 25 years through the recession accompanying the 2008 financial crisis. Strong actions by the federal government in the spring of 2009 brought rates even lower, which contributed to the official ending of the recession in June 2009. These actions encouraged investment, and there is little doubt that they will eventually lead to stronger growth. However, many observers fear that the government's actions will also reignite long-run inflation, which would lead to higher interest rates.

Credit Crisis.   Although rare, sometimes credit markets are so disrupted that it is virtually impossible for a firm to raise capital at reasonable rates. This happened in 2008 and 2009, before the U.S. Treasury and the Federal Reserve intervened to open up the capital markets. During such times, firms tend to cut back on growth plans; if they must raise capital, its cost can be extraordinarily high.

Market Risk Premium.   Investors' aversion to risk determines the market risk premium. Individual firms have no control over the RP_M, which affects the cost of equity and thus the WACC.

Tax Rates.   Tax rates, which are influenced by the president and set by Congress, have an important effect on the cost of capital. They are used when we calculate the after-tax cost of debt for use in the WACC. In addition, the lower tax rate on dividends and capital gains than on interest income favors financing with stock rather than bonds, as we discuss in detail in Chapter 15.

THREE FACTORS THE FIRM CAN CONTROL

A firm can affect its cost of capital through (1) its capital structure policy, (2) its dividend policy, and (3) its investment (capital budgeting) policy.

Capital Structure Policy.   In this chapter, we assume the firm has a given target capital structure, and we use weights based on that target to calculate its WACC. However, a firm can change its capital structure, and such a change can affect the cost of capital. For example, the after-tax cost of debt is lower than the cost of equity, so if the firm decides to use more debt and less common equity, then this increase in debt will tend to lower the WACC. However, an increased use of debt will increase the risk of debt and the equity, offsetting to some extent the effect due to a greater weighting of debt. In Chapter 15 we discuss this in more depth, and we demonstrate that the optimal capital structure is the one that minimizes the WACC, which maximizes the intrinsic value of the stock.

Dividend Policy. As we will see in Chapter 14, the percentage of earnings paid out in dividends may affect a stock's required rate of return, r_s. Also, if the payout ratio is so high that the firm must issue new stock to fund its capital budget, then the resulting flotation costs will also affect the WACC.

Investment Policy. When we estimate the cost of capital, we use as the starting point the required rates of return on the firm's outstanding stocks and bonds, which reflect the risks inherent in the existing assets. Therefore, we are implicitly assuming that new capital will be invested in assets with the same degree of risk as existing assets. This assumption is generally correct, because most firms invest in assets similar to those they currently use. However, the equal risk assumption is incorrect if a firm dramatically changes its investment policy. For example, if a company invests in an entirely new line of business, then its marginal cost of capital should reflect the risk of that new business. For example, we can see with hindsight that GE's huge investments in the TV and movie businesses, as well as its investment in mortgages, increased its risk and thus its cost of capital.

The following section explains how to adjust the cost of capital to reflect the risk of individual divisions and projects.

9-11b Adjusting the Cost of Capital for Risk: Divisions and Projects

As we have calculated it, the weighted average cost of capital reflects the average risk and overall capital structure of the entire firm. No adjustments are needed when using the WACC as the discount rate when estimating the value of a company by discounting its cash flows. However, adjustments for risk are often needed when evaluating a division or project. For example, what if a firm has divisions in several business lines that differ in risk? Or what if a company is considering a project that is much riskier than its typical project? It is not logical to use the overall cost of capital to discount divisional or project-specific cash flows that don't have the same risk as the company's average cash flows. The following sections explain how to adjust the cost of capital for divisions and for specific projects.

DIVISIONAL COSTS OF CAPITAL

Consider Starlight Sandwich Shops, a company with two divisions—a bakery operation and a chain of cafes. The bakery division is low-risk and has a 10% WACC. The cafe division is riskier and has a 14% WACC. Each division is approximately the same size, so Starlight's overall cost of capital is 12%. The bakery manager has a project with an 11% expected rate of return, and the cafe division manager has a project with a 13% expected return. Should these projects be accepted or rejected? Starlight will create value if it accepts the bakery's project, because its rate of return is greater than its cost of capital (11% > 10%), but the cafe project's rate of return is less than its cost of capital (13% < 14%), so it should reject that project. However, if management simply compared the two projects' returns with Starlight's 12% overall cost of capital, then the bakery's value-adding project would be rejected while the cafe's value-destroying project would be accepted.

Many firms use the CAPM to estimate the cost of capital for specific divisions. To begin, recall that the Security Market Line (SML) equation expresses the risk–return relationship as follows:

$$r_s = r_{RF} + (RP_M)b_i$$

As an example, consider the case of Huron Steel Company, an integrated steel producer operating in the Great Lakes region. For simplicity, assume that Huron has only one division and uses only equity capital, so its cost of equity is also its corporate cost of capital, or WACC. Huron's beta = b = 1.1, r_{RF} = 5%, and RP_M = 6%. Thus, Huron's cost of equity (and WACC) is 11.6%:

$$r_s = 5\% + (6\%)1.1 = 11.6\%$$

This suggests that investors should be willing to give Huron money to invest in new, average-risk projects if the company expects to earn 11.6% or more on this money. By "average risk" we mean projects having risk similar to the firm's existing division.

Now suppose Huron creates a new transportation division consisting of a fleet of barges to haul iron ore, and suppose barge operations typically have betas of 1.5 rather than 1.1. The barge division, with b = 1.5, has a 14.0% cost of capital:

$$r_{Barge} = 5\% + (6\%)1.5 = 14.0\%$$

On the other hand, if Huron adds a low-risk division, such as a new distribution center with a beta of only 0.5, then that division's cost of capital would be 8%:

$$r_{Center} = 5\% + (6\%)0.5 = 8.0\%$$

A firm itself may be regarded as a "portfolio of assets," and because the beta of a portfolio is a weighted average of the betas of its individual assets, adding the barge and distribution center divisions will change Huron's overall beta. The exact value of the new corporate beta would depend on the size of the investments in the new divisions relative to Huron's original steel operations. If 70% of Huron's total value ends up in the steel division, 20% in the barge division, and 10% in the distribution center, then its new corporate beta would be calculated as follows:

$$\text{New beta} = 0.7(1.1) + 0.2(1.5) + 0.1(0.5) = 1.12$$

Thus, investors in Huron's stock would require a return of

$$r_{Huron} = 5\% + (6\%)1.12 = 11.72\%$$

Even though investors require an overall return of 11.72%, they should expect a rate of return on projects in each division at least as high as the division's required return based on the SML. In particular, they should expect a return of at least 11.6% from the steel division, 14.0% from the barge division, and 8.0% from the distribution center.

Our example suggests a level of precision that is much higher than firms can obtain in the real world. Still, managers should be aware of this example'slogic, and they should strive to measure the required inputs as accurately as possible.

TECHNIQUES FOR MEASURING DIVISIONAL BETAS

In Chapter 6 we discussed the estimation of betas for stocks and indicated how difficult it is to measure beta precisely. Estimating divisional betas is much more difficult, primarily because divisions do not have their own publicly traded stock. Therefore, we must estimate the beta that the division would have if it were an independent, publicly traded company. Two approaches can be used to estimate divisional betas: the pure play method and the accounting beta method.

The Pure Play Method.   In the **pure play method**, the company tries to find the betas of several publicly held specialized companies in the same line of business as the division being evaluated, and it then averages those betas to determine the cost of capital for its own division. For example, suppose Huron found three companies devoted exclusively to operating barges, and suppose that Huron's management believes its barge division would be subject to the same risks as those firms. Then Huron could use the average beta of those firms as an estimate of its barge division's beta.[17]

The Accounting Beta Method.   As noted above, it may be impossible to find specialized publicly traded firms suitable for the pure play approach. If that is the case, we may be able to use the **accounting beta method**. Betas are normally found by regressing the returns of a particular company's *stock* against returns on a *stock market index*. However, we could run a regression of the division's *accounting return on assets* against the *average return on assets* for a large sample of companies, such as those included in the S&P 500. Betas determined in this way (that is, by using accounting data rather than stock market data) are called **accounting betas**.

ESTIMATING THE COST OF CAPITAL FOR INDIVIDUAL PROJECTS

In Chapter 11 we examine ways to estimate the risk inherent in individual projects, but at this point it is useful to consider how project risk is reflected in measures of the firm's cost of capital. First, although it is intuitively clear that riskier projects have a higher cost of capital, it is difficult to measure projects' relative risks. Also, note that three separate and distinct types of risk can be identified.

1. **Stand-alone risk**, which is the variability of the project's expected returns.
2. **Corporate**, or **within-firm**, **risk**, which is the variability the project contributes to the corporation's returns, giving consideration to the fact that the project represents only one asset of the firm's portfolio of assets and so some of its risk will be diversified away.
3. **Market**, or **beta**, **risk**, which is the risk of the project as seen by a well-diversified stockholder who owns many different stocks. A project's market risk is measured by its effect on the firm's overall beta coefficient.

Taking on a project with a high degree of either stand-alone or corporate risk will not necessarily increase the corporate beta. However, if the project has highly uncertain returns and if those returns are highly correlated with returns on the firm's other assets and with most other assets in the economy, then the project will have a high degree of all types of risk.

Of the three measures, market risk is theoretically the most relevant because of its direct effect on stock prices. Unfortunately, the market risk for a project is also the most difficult to estimate. In practice, most decision makers consider all three risk measures in a subjective manner.

---

[17]If the pure play firms employ different capital structures than that of Huron, then this must be addressed by adjusting the beta coefficients. See Chapter 15 for a discussion of this aspect of the pure play method. For a technique that can be used when pure play firms are not available, see Yatin Bhagwat and Michael Ehrhardt, "A Full Information Approach for Estimating Divisional Betas," *Financial Management,* Summer 1991, pp. 60–69.

The first step is to determine the divisional cost of capital before grouping divisional projects into subjective risk categories. Then, using the divisional WACC as a starting point, **risk-adjusted costs of capital** are developed for each category. For example, a firm might establish three risk classes—high, average, and low—and then assign average-risk projects the divisional cost of capital, higher-risk projects an above-average cost, and lower-risk projects a below-average cost. Thus, if a division's WACC were 10%, its managers might use 10% to evaluate average-risk projects in the division, 12% for high-risk projects, and 8% for low-risk projects. Although this approach is better than ignoring project risk, these adjustments are necessarily subjective and somewhat arbitrary. Unfortunately, given the data, there is no completely satisfactory way to specify exactly how much higher or lower we should go in setting risk-adjusted costs of capital.

9-12 Four Mistakes to Avoid

We often see managers and students make the following mistakes when estimating the cost of capital. Although we have discussed these errors previously at separate places in the chapter, they are worth repeating here.

1. *Never base the cost of debt on the coupon rate on a firm's existing debt.* The cost of debt must be based on the interest rate the firm would pay if it issued new debt today.
2. *When estimating the market risk premium for the CAPM method, never use the historical average return on stocks in conjunction with the current return on T-bonds.* The historical average return on bonds should be subtracted from the past average return on stocks to calculate the *historical market risk premium.* On the other hand, it is appropriate to subtract today's yield on T-bonds from an estimate of the expected future return on stocks to obtain the *forward-looking market risk premium.* A case can be made for using either the historical or the current risk premium, but it would be wrong to take the *historical* rate of return on stocks, subtract from it the *current* rate on T-bonds, and then use the difference as the market risk premium.
3. *Never use the current book value capital structure to obtain the weights when estimating the WACC.* Your first choice should be to use the firm's target capital structure for the weights. However, if you are an outside analyst and do not know the target weights, it would probably be best to estimate weights based on the current market values of the capital components. If the company's debt is not publicly traded, then it is reasonable to use the book value of debt to estimate the weights because book and market values of debt, especially short-term debt, are usually close to one another. However, stocks' market values in recent years have generally been at least 2–3 times their book values, so using book values for equity could lead to serious errors. The bottom line: If you don't know the target weights then use the market value, not the book value, of equity when calculating the WACC.
4. *Always remember that capital components are funds that come from investors.* If it's not from an investor, then it's not a capital component. Sometimes the argument is made that accounts payable and accruals should be included in the calculation of the WACC. However, these funds are not provided by investors, but instead, they arise from operating relationships with suppliers and employees. As such, the impact of accounts payable and accruals is incorporated into the calculations of free cash flows and project cash flows. Therefore, accounts payable and accruals should not be included as capital components when we calculate the WACC.

SELF-TEST

Name some factors that are generally beyond the firm's control but still affect its cost of capital.

What three policies under the firm's control affect its cost of capital?

Explain how a change in interest rates in the economy would be expected to affect each component of the weighted average cost of capital.

Based on the CAPM, how would one adjust the corporation's overall cost of capital to establish the required return for most projects in a low-risk division and in a high-risk division?

Describe the pure play and the accounting beta methods for estimating divisional betas.

What are the three types of risk to which projects are exposed? Which type of risk is theoretically the most relevant? Why?

Describe a procedure firms can use to establish costs of capital for projects with differing degrees of risk.

What four mistakes are commonly made when estimating the WACC?

SUMMARY

This chapter discussed how the cost of capital is developed for use in capital budgeting. The key points covered are listed below.

- The cost of capital used in capital budgeting is a **weighted average** of the types of capital the firm uses—typically long-term debt, short-term debt, preferred stock, and common equity.
- The **component cost of debt** is the **after-tax cost of new debt**. It is found by multiplying the interest rate paid on new debt by $1 - T$, where T is the firm's marginal tax rate: $r_d(1 - T)$.
- Most debt is raised directly from lenders without the use of investment bankers; hence no flotation costs are incurred. However, a **debt flotation cost adjustment** should be made if large flotation costs are incurred. We reduce the bond's issue price by the flotation expenses, reduce the bond's cash flows to reflect taxes, and then solve for the after-tax yield to maturity.
- The **component cost of preferred stock** is calculated as the preferred dividend divided by the net price the firm receives after deducting flotation costs: $r_{ps} = D_{ps}/[P_{ps}(1-F)]$. Flotation costs on preferred stock are usually fairly high, so we typically include the impact of flotation costs when estimating r_{ps}. Also note that if the preferred stock is convertible into common stock, then the true cost of the preferred stock will exceed the flotation-adjusted yield of the preferred dividend.
- The **cost of common equity**, r_s, also called the **cost of common stock**, is the rate of return required by the firm's stockholders.
- To use the **CAPM approach**, we (1) estimate the firm's beta, (2) multiply this beta by the market risk premium to obtain the firm's risk premium, and then (3) add the firm's risk premium to the risk-free rate to obtain its cost of common stock: $r_s = r_{PF} + (RP_M)b_i$.

- The best proxy for the **risk-free rate** is the yield on long-term T-bonds, with 10 years the maturity used most frequently.

- To use the **dividend-yield-plus-growth-rate approach**, which is also called the **discounted cash flow (DCF) approach**, add the firm's expected dividend growth rate to its expected dividend yield: $r_s = \hat{r} = D_1/P_0 + g$. **Web Extension 9A** shows how to estimate the DCF cost of equity (and the market risk premium) if dividends are not growing at a constant rate.

- The growth rate for use in the DCF model can be based on security analysts' **published forecasts**, on **historical growth rates** of earnings and dividends, or on the **retention growth model**, $g = (1 - \text{Payout})(\text{Return on equity})$.

- The **own-bond-yield-plus-judgmental-risk-premium approach** calls for adding a subjective risk premium of 3 to 5 percentage points to the interest rate on the firm's own long-term debt: $r_s = \text{Bond yield} + \text{Judgmental risk premium}$.

- When calculating the **cost of new common stock, r_e**, the DCF approach can be used to estimate the flotation cost. For a constant growth stock, the flotation-adjusted cost can be expressed as $r_s = \hat{r}_e = D_1/[P_0(1 - F)] + g$. Note that flotation costs cause r_e to be greater than r_s. We can find the difference between r_e and r_s and then add this differential to the CAPM estimate of r_s to find the CAPM estimate of r_e.

- Each firm has a **target capital structure**, which is defined as the mix of debt, preferred stock, and common equity that minimizes its **weighted average cost of capital (WACC)**:

$$\text{WACC} = w_d r_d(1 - T) + w_{std} r_{std}(1 - T) + w_{ps} r_{ps} + w_s r_s$$

- Various factors affect a firm's cost of capital. Some are determined by the financial environment, but the firm can influence others through its financing, investment, and dividend policies.

- Many firms estimate **divisional costs of capital** that reflect each division's risk and capital structure.

- The **pure play** and **accounting beta methods** can be used to estimate betas for large projects or for divisions.

- A project's **stand-alone risk** is the risk the project would have if it were the firm's only asset and if stockholders held only that one stock. Stand-alone risk is measured by the variability of the asset's expected returns.

- **Corporate**, or **within-firm**, **risk** reflects the effect of a project on the firm's risk, and it is measured by the project's effect on the firm's earnings variability.

- **Market**, or **beta**, **risk** reflects the effects of a project on stockholders' risk, assuming they hold diversified portfolios. Market risk is measured by the project's effect on the firm's beta coefficient.

- Most decision makers consider all three risk measures in a subjective manner and then classify projects into risk categories. Using the firm's WACC as a starting point, risk-adjusted costs of capital are developed for each category. The **risk-adjusted cost of capital** is the cost of capital appropriate for a given project, given its risk. The greater a project's risk, the higher its cost of capital.

The cost of capital as developed in this chapter is used in the next two chapters to evaluate potential capital budgeting projects, and it is used later in the text to determine the value of a corporation.

QUESTIONS

(9-1) Define each of the following terms:

    a. Weighted average cost of capital, WACC; after-tax cost of debt, $r_d(1 - T)$; after-tax cost of short-term debt, $r_{std}(1 - T)$

    b. Cost of preferred stock, r_{ps}; cost of common equity (or cost of common stock), r_s

    c. Target capital structure

    d. Flotation cost, F; cost of new external common equity, r_e

(9-2) How can the WACC be both an average cost and a marginal cost?

(9-3) How would each of the factors in the following table affect a firm's cost of debt, $r_d(1 - T)$; its cost of equity, r_s; and its weighted average cost of capital, WACC? Indicate by a plus (+), a minus (−), or a zero (0) if the factor would increase, reduce, or have an indeterminate effect on the item in question. Assume that all other factors are held constant. Be prepared to justify your answer, but recognize that several of the parts probably have no single correct answer; these questions are designed to stimulate thought and discussion.

	Effect on:		
	$r_d(1 - T)$	r_s	WACC
a. The corporate tax rate is lowered.			
b. The Federal Reserve tightens credit.			
c. The firm uses more debt.			
d. The firm doubles the amount of capital it raises during the year.			
e. The firm expands into a risky new area.			
f. Investors become more risk averse.			

(9-4) Distinguish between beta (i.e., market) risk, within-firm (i.e., corporate) risk, and stand-alone risk for a potential project. Of the three measures, which is theoretically the most relevant, and why?

(9-5) Suppose a firm estimates its overall cost of capital for the coming year to be 10%. What might be reasonable costs of capital for average-risk, high-risk, and low-risk projects?

SELF-TEST PROBLEM   Solution Appears in Appendix A

(ST-1)
WACC Longstreet Communications Inc. (LCI) has the following capital structure, which it considers to be optimal: debt = 25% (LCI has only long-term debt), preferred stock = 15%, and common stock = 60%. LCI's tax rate is 40%, and investors expect earnings and dividends to grow at a constant rate of 6% in the future. LCI paid a dividend of $3.70 per share last year (D_0), and its stock currently sells at a price of $60 per share. Ten-year Treasury bonds yield 6%, the market risk premium is 5%, and LCI's beta is 1.3. The following terms would apply to new security offerings.

Preferred: New preferred stock could be sold to the public at a price of $100 per share, with a dividend of $9. Flotation costs of $5 per share would be incurred.
Debt: Debt could be sold at an interest rate of 9%.
Common: New common equity will be raised only by retaining earnings.

    a. Find the component costs of debt, preferred stock, and common stock.
    b. What is the WACC?

PROBLEMS   Answers Appear in Appendix B

Easy Problems 1–8

(9-1)
After-Tax Cost of Debt

Calculate the after-tax cost of debt under each of the following conditions:

a. r_d of 13%, tax rate of 0%
b. r_d of 13%, tax rate of 20%
c. r_d of 13%, tax rate of 35%

(9-2)
After-Tax Cost of Debt

LL Incorporated's currently outstanding 11% coupon bonds have a yield to maturity of 8%. LL believes it could issue new bonds at par that would provide a similar yield to maturity. If its marginal tax rate is 35%, what is LL's after-tax cost of debt?

(9-3)
Cost of Preferred Stock

Duggins Veterinary Supplies can issue perpetual preferred stock at a price of $50 a share with an annual dividend of $4.50 a share. Ignoring flotation costs, what is the company's cost of preferred stock, r_{ps}?

(9-4)
Cost of Preferred Stock with Flotation Costs

Burnwood Tech plans to issue some $60 par preferred stock with a 6% dividend. A similar stock is selling on the market for $70. Burnwood must pay flotation costs of 5% of the issue price. What is the cost of the preferred stock?

(9-5)
Cost of Equity: DCF

Summerdahl Resort's common stock is currently trading at $36 a share. The stock is expected to pay a dividend of $3.00 a share at the end of the year (D_1 = $3.00), and the dividend is expected to grow at a constant rate of 5% a year. What is its cost of common equity?

(9-6)
Cost of Equity: CAPM

Booher Book Stores has a beta of 0.8. The yield on a 3-month T-bill is 4%, and the yield on a 10-year T-bond is 6%. The market risk premium is 5.5%, and the return on an average stock in the market last year was 15%. What is the estimated cost of common equity using the CAPM?

(9-7)
WACC

Shi Importers's balance sheet shows $300 million in debt, $50 million in preferred stock, and $250 million in total common equity. Shi's tax rate is 40%, r_d = 6%, r_{ps} = 5.8%, and r_s = 12%. If Shi has a target capital structure of 30% debt, 5% preferred stock, and 65% common stock, what is its WACC?

(9-8)
WACC

David Ortiz Motors has a target capital structure of 40% debt and 60% equity. The yield to maturity on the company's outstanding bonds is 9%, and the company's tax rate is 40%. Ortiz's CFO has calculated the company's WACC as 9.96%. What is the company's cost of equity capital?

Intermediate Problems 9–14

(9-9)
Bond Yield and After-Tax Cost of Debt

A company's 6% coupon rate, semiannual payment, $1,000 par value bond that matures in 30 years sells at a price of $515.16. The company's federal-plus-state tax rate is 40%. What is the firm's after-tax component cost of debt for purposes of calculating the WACC? (*Hint*: Base your answer on the *nominal* rate.)

(9-10)
Cost of Equity

The earnings, dividends, and stock price of Shelby Inc. are expected to grow at 7% per year in the future. Shelby's common stock sells for $23 per share, its last dividend was $2.00, and the company will pay a dividend of $2.14 at the end of the current year.

a. Using the discounted cash flow approach, what is its cost of equity?
b. If the firm's beta is 1.6, the risk-free rate is 9%, and the expected return on the market is 13%, then what would be the firm's cost of equity based on the CAPM approach?

c. If the firm's bonds earn a return of 12%, then what would be your estimate of r_s using the own-bond-yield-plus-judgmental-risk-premium approach? (*Hint:* Use the midpoint of the risk premium range.)

d. On the basis of the results of parts a through c, what would be your estimate of Shelby's cost of equity?

(9-11)
Cost of Equity

Radon Homes's current EPS is $6.50. It was $4.42 5years ago. The company pays out 40% of its earnings as dividends, and the stock sells for $36.

a. Calculate the historical growth rate in earnings. (*Hint:* This is a 5-year growth period.)

b. Calculate the *next* expected dividend per share, D_1. (*Hint:* $D_0 = 0.4(\$6.50) = \$2.60$.) Assume that the past growth rate will continue.

c. What is Radon's cost of equity, r_s?

(9-12)
Calculation of g and EPS

Spencer Supplies's stock is currently selling for $60 a share. The firm is expected to earn $5.40 per share this year and to pay a year-end dividend of $3.60.

a. If investors require a 9% return, what rate of growth must be expected for Spencer?

b. If Spencer reinvests earnings in projects with average returns equal to the stock's expected rate of return, then what will be next year's EPS? (*Hint:* $g = ROE \times$ Retention ratio.)

(9-13)
The Cost of Equity and Flotation Costs

Messman Manufacturing will issue common stock to the public for $30. The expected dividend and the growth in dividends are $3.00 per share and 5%, respectively. If the flotation cost is 10% of the issue's gross proceeds, what is the cost of external equity, r_e?

(9-14)
The Cost of Debt and Flotation Costs

Suppose a company will issue new 20-year debt with a par value of $1,000 and a coupon rate of 9%, paid annually. The tax rate is 40%. If the flotation cost is 2% of the issue proceeds, then what is the after-tax cost of debt? Disregard the tax shield from the amortization of flotation costs.

Challenging
Problems 15–17

(9-15)
WACC Estimation

On January 1, the total market value of the Tysseland Company was $60 million. During the year, the company plans to raise and invest $30 million in new projects. The firm's present market value capital structure, shown below, is considered to be optimal. There is no short-term debt.

Debt	$30,000,000
Common equity	30,000,000
Total capital	$60,000,000

New bonds will have an 8% coupon rate, and they will be sold at par. Common stock is currently selling at $30 a share. The stockholders' required rate of return is estimated to be 12%, consisting of a dividend yield of 4% and an expected constant growth rate of 8%. (The next expected dividend is $1.20, so the dividend yield is $1.20/\$30 = 4\%$.) The marginal tax rate is 40%.

a. In order to maintain the present capital structure, how much of the new investment must be financed by common equity?

b. Assuming there is sufficient cash flow for Tysseland to maintain its target capital structure without issuing additional shares of equity, what is its WACC?

c. Suppose now that there is not enough internal cash flow and the firm must issue new shares of stock. Qualitatively speaking, what will happen to the WACC? No numbers are required to answer this question.

(9-16)
Market Value Capital Structure

Suppose the Schoof Company has this *book value* balance sheet:

Current assets	$ 30,000,000	Current liabilities	$ 20,000,000
		Notes payable	$ 10,000,000
Fixed assets	70,000,000	Long-term debt	30,000,000
		Common stock (1 million shares)	1,000,000
		Retained earnings	39,000,000
Total assets	$100,000,000	Total liabilities and equity	$100,000,000

The notes payable are to banks, and the interest rate on this debt is 10%, the same as the rate on new bank loans. These bank loans are not used for seasonal financing but instead are part of the company's permanent capital structure. The long-term debt consists of 30,000 bonds, each with a par value of $1,000, an annual coupon interest rate of 6%, and a 20-year maturity. The going rate of interest on new long-term debt, r_d, is 10%, and this is the present yield to maturity on the bonds. The common stock sells at a price of $60 per share. Calculate the firm's *market value* capital structure.

(9-17)
WACC Estimation

The table below gives the balance sheet for Travellers Inn Inc. (TII), a company that was formed by merging a number of regional motel chains.

Travellers Inn: December 31, 2013 (Millions of Dollars)

Cash	$ 10	Accounts payable	$ 10
Accounts receivable	20	Accruals	10
Inventories	20	Short-term debt	5
Current assets	$ 50	Current liabilities	$ 25
Net fixed assets	50	Long-term debt	30
		Preferred stock	5
		Common equity	
		Common stock	$ 10
		Retained earnings	30
		Total common equity	$ 40
Total assets	$100	Total liabilities and equity	$100

The following facts also apply to TII.

(1) Short-term debt consists of bank loans that currently cost 10%, with interest payable quarterly. These loans are used to finance receivables and inventories on a seasonal basis, so bank loans are zero in the off-season.

(2) The long-term debt consists of 20-year, semiannual payment mortgage bonds with a coupon rate of 8%. Currently, these bonds provide a yield to investors of $r_d = 12\%$. If new bonds were sold, they would have a 12% yield to maturity.

(3) TII's perpetual preferred stock has a $100 par value, pays a quarterly dividend of $2, and has a yield to investors of 11%. New perpetual preferred stock would have

to provide the same yield to investors, and the company would incur a 5% flotation cost to sell it.

(4) The company has 4 million shares of common stock outstanding. $P_0 = \$20$, but the stock has recently traded in the price range from \$17 to \$23. $D_0 = \$1$ and $EPS_0 = \$2$. ROE based on average equity was 24% in 2012, but management expects to increase this return on equity to 30%; however, security analysts and investors generally are not aware of management's optimism in this regard.

(5) Betas, as reported by security analysts, range from 1.3 to 1.7; the T-bond rate is 10%; and RP_M is estimated by various brokerage houses to range from 4.5% to 5.5%. Some brokerage house analysts report forecasted growth dividend growth rates in the range of10% to 15% over the foreseeable future.

(6) TII's financial vice president recently polled some pension fund investment managers who hold TII's securities regarding what minimum rate of return on TII's common would make them willing to buy the common rather than TII bonds, given that the bonds yielded 12%. The responses suggested a risk premium over TII bonds of 4 to 6 percentage points.

(7) TII is in the 40% federal-plus-state tax bracket.

(8) TII's principal investment banker predicts a decline in interest rates, with r_d falling to 10% and the T-bond rate to 8%, although the bank acknowledges that an increase in the expected inflation rate could lead to an increase rather than a decrease in interest rates.

Assume that you were recently hired by TII as a financial analyst and that your boss, the treasurer, has asked you to estimate the company's WACC under the assumption that no new equity will be issued. Your cost of capital should be appropriate for use in evaluating projects that are in the same risk class as the assets TII now operates.

SPREADSHEET PROBLEM

(9-18)
Build a Model: WACC

r e s o u r c e

Start with the partial model in the file *Ch09 P18 Build a Model.xls* on the textbook's Web site. The stock of Gao Computing sells for \$50, and last year's dividend was \$2.10. A flotation cost of 10% would be required to issue new common stock. Gao's preferred stock pays a dividend of \$3.30 per share, and new preferred stock could be sold at a price to net the company \$30 per share. Security analysts are projecting that the common dividend will grow at a rate of 7% a year. The firm can issue additional long-term debt at an interest rate (or a before-tax cost) of 10%, and its marginal tax rate is 35%. The market risk premium is 6%, the risk-free rate is 6.5%, and Gao's beta is 0.83. In its cost-of-capital calculations, Gao uses a target capital structure with 45% debt, 5% preferred stock, and 50% common equity.

a. Calculate the cost of each capital component—in other words, the after-tax cost of debt, the cost of preferred stock (including flotation costs), and the cost of equity (ignoring flotation costs). Use both the DCF method and the CAPM method to find the cost of equity.

b. Calculate the cost of new stock using the DCF model.

c. What is the cost of new common stock based on the CAPM? (*Hint:* Find the difference between r_e and r_s as determined by the DCF method and then add that difference to the CAPM value for r_s.)

d. Assuming that Gao will not issue new equity and will continue to use the same target capital structure, what is the company's WACC?

e. Suppose Gao is evaluating three projects with the following characteristics.

(1) Each project has a cost of $1 million. They will all be financed using the target mix of long-term debt, preferred stock, and common equity. The cost of the common equity for each project should be based on the beta estimated for the project. All equity will come from reinvested earnings.

(2) Equity invested in Project A would have a beta of 0.5 and an expected return of 9.0%.

(3) Equity invested in Project B would have a beta of 1.0 and an expected return of 10.0%.

(4) Equity invested in Project C would have a beta of 2.0 and an expected return of 11.0%.

f. Analyze the company's situation, and explain why each project should be accepted or rejected.

THOMSON ONE   Business School Edition Problem

 THOMSON REUTERS   Use the Thomson ONE—Business School Edition online database to work this chapter's questions.

Calculating 3M's Cost of Capital

In this chapter we described how to estimate a company's WACC, which is the weighted average of its costs of debt, preferred stock, and common equity. Most of the data we need to do this can be found in Thomson ONE. Here, we walk through the steps used to calculate Minnesota Mining & Manufacturing's (MMM) WACC.

Thomson ONE—BSE Discussion Questions

1. As a first step, we need to estimate what percentage of MMM's capital comes from long-term debt, preferred stock, and common equity. If we click on FINANCIALS, we can see immediately from the balance sheet the amount of MMM's long-term debt and common equity (as of mid-2012, MMM had no preferred stock). Alternatively, you can click on FUNDAMENTAL RATIOS in the next row of tabs below and then select WORLD-SCOPE'S BALANCE SHEET RATIOS. Here, you will also find a recent measure of long-term debt as a percentage of total capital.

   Recall that the weights used in the WACC are based on the company's target capital structure. If we assume the company wants to maintain the same mix of capital that it currently has on its balance sheet, then what weights should you use to estimate the WACC for MMM? (In Chapter 15, we will see that we might arrive at different estimates for these weights if we assume that MMM bases its target capital structure on the market values, rather than the book values, of debt and equity.)

2. Once again, we can use the CAPM to estimate MMM's cost of equity. Thomson ONE provides various estimates of beta; select the measure that you believe is best and combine this with your estimates of the risk-free rate and the market risk premium to obtain an estimate of its cost of equity. (See the Thomson ONE exercise in Chapter 6 more details.) What is your estimate for the cost of equity? Why might it not make much sense to use the DCF approach to estimate MMM's cost of equity?

3. Next, we need to calculate MMM's cost of debt. Unfortunately, Thomson ONE doesn't provide a direct measure of the cost of debt. However, we can use different approaches to

estimate it. One approach is to take the company's long-term interest expense and divide it by the amount of long-term debt. This approach works only if the historical cost of debt equals the yield to maturity in today's market (that is, only if MMM's outstanding bonds are trading at close to par). This approach may produce misleading estimates in the years during which MMM issues a significant amount of new debt.

For example, if a company issues a lot of debt at the end of the year, then the full amount of debt will appear on the year-end balance sheet. However, we still may not see a sharp increase in interest expense on the annual income statement because the debt was outstanding for only a small portion of the entire year. When this situation occurs, the estimated cost of debt will likely understate the true cost of debt.

Another approach is to try to find this number in the notes to the company's annual report by accessing the company's home page and its Investor Relations section. Remember that you need the after-tax cost of debt to calculate a firm's WACC, so you will need MMM's average tax rate (which has been about 37% in recent years). What is your estimate of MMM's after-tax cost of debt?

4. Putting all this information together, what is your estimate of MMM's WACC? How confident are you in this estimate? Explain your answer.

MINI CASE

During the last few years, Harry Davis Industries has been too constrained by the high cost of capital to make many capital investments. Recently, though, capital costs have been declining, and the company has decided to look seriously at a major expansion program proposed by the marketing department. Assume that you are an assistant to Leigh Jones, the financial vice president. Your first task is to estimate Harry Davis's cost of capital. Jones has provided you with the following data, which she believes may be relevant to your task:

(1) The firm's tax rate is 40%.

(2) The current price of Harry Davis's 12% coupon, semiannual payment, noncallable bonds with 15 years remaining to maturity is $1,153.72. Harry Davis does not use short-term interest-bearing debt on a permanent basis. New bonds would be privately placed with no flotation cost.

(3) The current price of the firm's 10%, $100 par value, quarterly dividend, perpetual preferred stock is $116.95. Harry Davis would incur flotation costs equal to 5% of the proceeds on a new issue.

(4) Harry Davis's common stock is currently selling at $50 per share. Its last dividend (D_0) was $3.12, and dividends are expected to grow at a constant rate of 5.8% in the foreseeable future. Harry Davis's beta is 1.2, the yield on T-bonds is 5.6%, and the market risk premium is estimated to be 6%. For the own-bond-yield-plus-judgmental-risk-premium approach, the firm uses a 3.2% risk premium.

(5) Harry Davis's target capital structure is 30% long-term debt, 10% preferred stock, and 60% common equity.

To help you structure the task, Leigh Jones has asked you to answer the following questions.

a. (1) What sources of capital should be included when you estimate Harry Davis's weighted average cost of capital?

(2) Should the component costs be figured on a before-tax or an after-tax basis?

(3) Should the costs be historical (embedded) costs or new (marginal) costs?

b. What is the market interest rate on Harry Davis's debt, and what is the component cost of this debt for WACC purposes?

c. (1) What is the firm's cost of preferred stock?

(2 Harry Davis's preferred stock is riskier to investors than its debt, yet the preferred stock's yield to investors is lower than the yield to maturity on the debt. Does this suggest that you have made a mistake? (*Hint:* Think about taxes.)

d. (1) What are the two primary ways companies raise common equity?

(2) Why is there a cost associated with reinvested earnings?

(3) Harry Davis doesn't plan to issue new shares of common stock. Using the CAPM approach, what is Harry Davis's estimated cost of equity?

e. (1) What is the estimated cost of equity using the discounted cash flow (DCF) approach?

(2) Suppose the firm has historically earned 15% on equity (ROE) and has paid out 62% of earnings, and suppose investors expect similar values to obtain in the future. How could you use this information to estimate the future dividend growth rate, and what growth rate would you get? Is this consistent with the 5.8% growth rate given earlier?

(3) Could the DCF method be applied if the growth rate were not constant? How?

f. What is the cost of equity based on the own-bond-yield-plus-judgmental-risk-premium method?

g. What is your final estimate for the cost of equity, r_s?

h. What is Harry Davis's weighted average cost of capital (WACC)?

i. What factors influence a company's WACC?

j. Should the company use its overall WACC as the hurdle rate for each of its divisions?

k. What procedures can be used to estimate the risk-adjusted cost of capital for a particular division? What approaches are used to measure a division's beta?

l. Harry Davis is interested in establishing a new division that will focus primarily on developing new Internet-based projects. In trying to determine the cost of capital for this new division, you discover that specialized firms involved in similar projects have, on average, the following characteristics: (1) their capital structure is 10% debt and 90% common equity; (2) their cost of debt is typically 12%; and (3) they have a beta of 1.7. Given this information, what would your estimate be for the new division's cost of capital?

m. What are three types of project risk? How can each type of risk be considered when thinking about the new division's cost of capital?

n. Explain in words why new common stock that is raised externally has a higher percentage cost than equity that is raised internally by retaining earnings.

o. (1) Harry Davis estimates that if it issues new common stock, the flotation cost will be 15%. Harry Davis incorporates the flotation costs into the DCF approach. What is the estimated cost of newly issued common stock, taking into account the flotation cost?

(2) Suppose Harry Davis issues 30-year debt with a par value of $1,000 and a coupon rate of 10%, paid annually. If flotation costs are 2%, what is the after-tax cost of debt for the new bond issue?

p. What four common mistakes in estimating the WACC should Harry Davis avoid?

SELECTED ADDITIONAL CASES

The following cases from CengageCompose cover many of the concepts discussed in this chapter and are available at **compose.cengage.com**.

Klein-Brigham Series:
Case 42, "West Coast Semiconductor"; Case 54, "Ace Repair"; Case 55, "Premier Paint & Body"; Case 6, "Randolph Corporation"; Case 75, "The Western Company"; and Case 81, "Pressed Paper Products."

Brigham-Buzzard Series:
Case 5, "Powerline Network Corporation (Determining the Cost of Capital)."

© Adalberto Rios Szalay/Sexto Sol/Getty Images

CHAPTER **10**

The Basics of Capital Budgeting: Evaluating Cash Flows

N othing runs like a Deere, according to Deere & Co., the manufacturer of the iconic green tractors and agricultural equipment. Commonly known as John Deere, the company is indeed running fast with a multibillion dollar expansion. Some of the additional capacity will be overseas, as Deere announced plans to build seven new factories in the BRIC countries (Brazil, Russia, India, and China). Deere is making major upgrades to several of its domestic production facilities, including its Waterloo, Iowa, tractor factory.

Deere is projecting increased demand for its equipment based on global population growth and increased purchasing power from a larger worldwide middle class. Deere is not basing its plans on intuition. In the 2011 annual report, CEO Samuel R. Allen states that Deere focuses on "operating consistency and a disciplined approach to asset and cost management."

As you read this chapter, think about how capital budgeting methods are a vital part of asset selection and expansion decisions.

Sources: See the 2011 Deere & Company Annual Report, p. 3. Also see Bob Tita, "Deere Bets Big on Expanding Global Demand," *The Wall Street Journal*, May 17, 2012, p. B8.

Corporate Valuation and Capital Budgeting

© Rob Webb/Getty Images

You can calculate the cash flows (CF) for a project in much the same way as you do for a firm. When the project's cash flows are discounted at the appropriate risk-adjusted weighted average cost of capital ("r" for simplicity), the result is the project's value. When valuing an entire firm you discount its free cash flows at the overall weighted average cost of capital, but when valuing a project you discount its cash flows at the project's own risk-adjusted cost of capital. The firm's free cash flows are the total of all the net cash flows from its past projects. Thus, if a project is accepted and put into operation, it will provide cash flows that add to the firm's free cash flows and thus to the firm's value.

Subtracting the initial cost of the project from the discounted future expected cash flows gives the project's net present value (NPV). A project that has a positive NPV adds value to the firm. In fact, the firm's Market Value Added (MVA) is the sum of all its projects' NPVs. The key point, though, is that the process of evaluating projects, or capital budgeting, is critical to a firm's success.

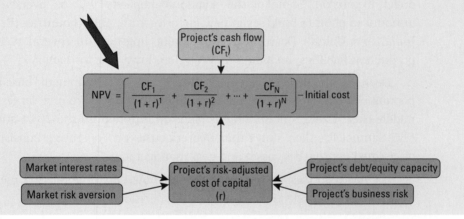

$$NPV = \left[\frac{CF_1}{(1 + r)^1} + \frac{CF_2}{(1 + r)^2} + \cdots + \frac{CF_N}{(1 + r)^N} \right] - \text{Initial cost}$$

© Cengage Learning 2014

resource

*The textbook's Web site contains an Excel file that will guide you through the chapter's calculations. The file for this chapter is **Ch10 Tool Kit.xls**, and we encourage you to open the file and follow along as you read the chapter.*

In Chapters 10 and 11, we discuss *capital budgeting.* Here *capital* refers to long-term assets used in production, and a *budget* is a plan that outlines projected expenditures during a future period. Thus, the *capital budget* is a summary of planned investments of assets that will last for more than a year, and **capital budgeting** is the whole process of analyzing projects and deciding which ones to accept and thus include in the capital budget. Chapter 10 explains the measures companies use to evaluate projects, including the measures' strengths and weaknesses. Chapter 10 also describes several other issues that arise in the capital budgeting process. Chapter 11 explains how to estimate cash flows and evaluate project risk.

10-1 An Overview of Capital Budgeting

A firm's ability to remain competitive and to survive depends on a constant flow of ideas for new products, improvements in existing products, and ways to operate more efficiently. Therefore, it is vital for a company to evaluate proposed projects accurately.

However, analyzing project proposals requires skill, effort, and time. For certain types of projects, an extremely detailed analysis may be warranted, whereas simpler procedures are adequate for other projects. Accordingly, firms generally categorize projects and analyze those in each category somewhat differently:

1. *Replacement needed to continue profitable operations.* An example would be replacing an essential pump on a profitable offshore oil platform. The platform manager could make this investment without an elaborate review process.
2. *Replacement to reduce costs.* An example would be the replacement of serviceable but obsolete equipment in order to lower costs. A fairly detailed analysis would be needed, with more detail required for larger expenditures.
3. *Expansion of existing products or markets.* These decisions require a forecast of growth in demand, so a more detailed analysis is required. Go/no-go decisions are generally made at a higher level in the organization than are replacement decisions.
4. *Expansion into new products or markets.* These investments involve strategic decisions that could change the fundamental nature of the business. A detailed analysis is required, and top officers make the final decision, possibly with board approval.
5. *Contraction decisions.* Especially during bad recessions, companies often find themselves with more capacity than they are likely to need. Rather than continue to operate plants at, say, 50% of capacity and incur losses as a result of excessive fixed costs, management decides to downsize. That generally requires payments to laid-off workers and additional costs for shutting down selected operations. These decisions are made at the board level.
6. *Safety and/or environmental projects.* Expenditures necessary to comply with environmental orders, labor agreements, or insurance policy terms fall into this category. How these projects are handled depends on their size, with small ones being treated much like the Category 1 projects and large ones requiring expenditures that might even cause the firm to abandon the line of business.
7. *Other.* This catch-all includes items such as office buildings, parking lots, and executive aircraft. How they are handled varies among companies.
8. *Mergers.* Buying a whole firm (or division) is different from buying a machine or building a new plant. Still, basic capital budgeting procedures are used when making merger decisions.

Relatively simple calculations, and only a few supporting documents, are required for most replacement decisions, especially maintenance investments in profitable plants. More detailed analyses are required as we move on to more complex expansion decisions, especially for investments in new products or areas. Also, within each category projects are grouped by their dollar costs: Larger investments require increasingly detailed analysis and approval at higher levels. Thus, a plant manager might be authorized to approve maintenance expenditures up to $10,000 using a simple payback analysis, but the full board of directors might have to approve decisions that involve either amounts greater than $1 million or expansions into new products or markets.

If a firm has capable and imaginative executives and employees, and if its incentive system is working properly, then many ideas for capital investment will be forthcoming. Some ideas will be good and should be funded, but others should be killed. Therefore, the following measures have been established for screening projects and deciding which to accept or reject:[1]

---

[1] One other rarely used measure, the Accounting Rate of Return, is covered in the chapter's *Excel Tool Kit* model and *Web Extension 10A*.

1. Net Present Value (NPV)
2. Internal Rate of Return (IRR)
3. Modified Internal Rate of Return (MIRR)
4. Profitability Index (PI)
5. Regular Payback
6. Discounted Payback

As we shall see, the NPV is the best single measure, primarily because it directly relates to the firm's central goal of maximizing intrinsic value. However, all of the measures provide some useful information, and all are used in practice.

SELF-TEST

Identify the major project classification categories, and explain how and why they are used.

List six procedures for screening projects and deciding which to accept or reject.

10-2 The First Step in Project Analysis

In the sections that follow, we will evaluate two projects that Guyton Products Company (GPC) is considering. GPC is a high-tech "lab-bench-to-market" development company that takes cutting-edge research advances and translates them into consumer products. GPC has recently licensed a nano-fabrication coating technology from a university that promises to significantly increase the efficiency with which solar energy can be harvested and stored as heat. GPC is considering using this technology in two different product lines. In the first, code-named "Project S" for "solid," the technology would be used to coat rock and concrete structures to be used as passive heat sinks and sources for energy-efficient residential and commercial buildings. In the second, code-named "Project L" for "liquid," it would be used to coat the collectors in a high-efficiency solar water heater. GPC must decide whether to undertake either of these two projects.

The first step in project analysis is to estimate the project's expected cash flows. We will explain cash flow estimation for Project L in Chapter 11, including the impact of depreciation, taxes, and salvage values. However, we want to focus now on the six evaluation measures, so we will specify the cash flows used in the following examples.[2]

Recall from Chapter 9 that a company's weighted average cost of capital (WACC) reflects the average risk of all the company's projects and that the appropriate cost of capital for a particular project may differ from the company's WACC. Chapter 11 explains how to estimate a project's risk-adjusted cost of capital, but for now assume that Projects L and S are equally risky and both have a 10% cost of capital.

Figure 10-1 shows the inputs for GPC's Projects S and L, including the projects' cost of capital and the time line of expected cash flows (with the initial cost shown at Year 0). Although Projects S and L are GPC's "solid" and "liquid" coating projects, you may also find it helpful to think of S and L as standing for *Short* and *Long*. Project S is a short-term project in the sense that its biggest cash inflows occur relatively soon; Project L has more total cash inflows, but its largest cash flows occur in the later years.

---

[2]We will see in Chapter 11 that project cash flows are, in fact, free cash flows as calculated in Chapter 3 and used in Chapter 7 to estimate corporate value.

FIGURE **10-1**

Cash Flows and Selected Evaluation Measures for Projects S and L (Millions of Dollars)

	A	B	C	D	E	F
19	Panel A: Inputs for Project Cash Flows and Cost of Capital, r					
20						
21	INPUTS:					
22	r = 10%					
23			Initial Cost and Expected Cash Flows			
24	Year	0	1	2	3	4
25	Project S	–$10,000	$5,300	$4,300	$1,874	$1,500
26	Project L	–$10,000	$1,900	$2,700	$2,345	$7,800
27						
28	Panel B: Summary of Selected Evaluation Measures					
29		Project S	Project L			
30	Net present value, NPV	$804.38	$1,048.02			
31	Internal rate of return, IRR	14.69%	13.79%			
32	Modified IRR, MIRR	12.15%	10.19%			
33	Profitability index, PI	1.08	1.10			
34	Payback	2.21	3.39			
35	Discounted payback	3.21	3.80			

resource

See *Ch10 Tool Kit.xls* on the textbook's Web site.

The second step in project analysis is to calculate the evaluation measures, which are shown in Panel B of Figure 10-1. The following sections explain how each measure is calculated.

S E L F - T E S T

What is the first step in project analysis?

10-3 Net Present Value (NPV)

The **net present value (NPV)** is defined as the present value of a project's expected cash flows (including its initial cost) discounted at the appropriate risk-adjusted rate. The NPV measures how much wealth the project contributes to shareholders. When deciding which projects to accept, NPV is generally regarded as the best single criterion.

10-3a Calculating NPV

We can calculate NPV with the following steps.

1. Calculate the present value of each cash flow discounted at the project's risk-adjusted cost of capital, which is r = 10% in our example.
2. The sum of the discounted cash flows is defined as the project's NPV.

The equation for the NPV, set up with input data for Project S, is

$$NPV = CF_0 + \frac{CF_1}{(1+r)^1} + \frac{CF_2}{(1+r)^2} + \cdots + \frac{CF_N}{(1+r)^N}$$

$$= \sum_{t=0}^{N} \frac{CF_t}{(1+r)^t}$$

(10-1)

Applying Equation 10-1 to Project S, we have

$$NPV_S = -\$10,000 + \frac{\$5,300}{(1.10)^1} + \frac{\$4,300}{(1.10)^2} + \frac{\$1,874}{(1.10)^3} + \frac{\$1,500}{(1.10)^4}$$

$$= -\$10,000 + \$4,818.18 + \$3,553.72 + \$1,407.96 + \$1,024.52$$

$$= \$804.38 \text{ million}$$

Here CF_t is the expected net cash flow at Time t, r is the project's risk-adjusted cost of capital (or WACC), and N is its life. Projects generally require an initial investment—for example, developing the product, buying the equipment needed to make it, building a factory, and stocking inventory. The initial investment is a negative cash flow. For Projects S and L, only CF_0 is negative; large projects often have outflows for several years before cash inflows begin.

Figure 10-2 shows the cash flow time line for Project S as taken from Figure 10-1. The initial cash flow is −$10,000, which is not discounted because it occurs at t = 0. The PV of each cash inflow and the sum of the PVs are shown in Column B. You could find the PVs of the cash flows with a calculator or with *Excel*, and the result would be the numbers in Column B. When we sum the PVs of the inflows and subtract the cost, the result is $804.38, which is NPV_S. The NPV for Project L, $1,048.02, can be found similarly, but there is a much easier way. The bottom section of Figure 10-2 shows how to use *Excel's* NPV function to calculate Project L's NPV. Notice that the NPV function uses the range of cash flows beginning with the Year 1 cash flow, not the Year 0 cash flow. Therefore, you must add the Year 0 cash flow to the result of the NPV function to calculate the net present value.

FIGURE 10-2

Finding the NPV for Projects S and L (Millions of Dollars)

	A	B	C	D	E	F
46	INPUTS:					
47	r =	10%				
48			Initial Cost and Expected Cash Flows			
49	Year	0	1	2	3	4
50	Project S	−$10,000	$5,300	$4,300	$1,874	$1,500
51		4,818.18	←←↵	↓	↓	↓
52		3,553.72	←←←←←← ←←↵	↓	↓	
53		1,407.96	←←←←←← ·←←←←←← ←←↵		↓	
54		1,024.52	←←←←←← ·←←←←←← ·←←←←←←	←←↵		
55	NPV_S =	$804.38	Long way:			
56			Sum the PVs of the CFs to find NPV			
57			Initial Cost and Expected Cash Flows			
58	Year	0	1	2	3	4
59	Project L	−$10,000	$1,900	$2,700	$2,345	$7,800
60	NPV_L =	$1,048.02	Short way: Use *Excel's* NPV function			
61			=NPV(B47,C59:F59)+B59			

r e s o u r c e

*See **Ch10 Tool Kit.xls** on the textbook's Web site.*

It is also possible to calculate the NPV with a financial calculator. As we discussed in Chapter 4, all calculators have a "cash flow register" that can be used to evaluate uneven cash flows such as those for Projects S and L. Equation 10-1 is programmed into these calculators, and all you need to do is enter the cash flows (with the correct signs) along with r = I/YR = 10. Once you have entered the data, press the NPV key to get the answer, 804.38, on the screen.[3]

10-3b Applying NPV as an Evaluation Measure

Before using these NPVs in the decision process, we need to know whether Projects S and L are **independent** or **mutually exclusive**. The cash flows for independent projects are not affected by other projects. For example, if Walmart were considering a new store in Boise and another in Atlanta, those projects would be independent. If both had positive NPVs, Walmart should accept both.

Mutually exclusive projects, on the other hand, are two different ways of accomplishing the same result, so if one project is accepted then the other must be rejected. A conveyor-belt system to move goods in a warehouse and a fleet of forklifts for the same purpose would be mutually exclusive—accepting one implies rejecting the other.

What should the decision be if Projects S and L are independent? In this case, both should be accepted because both have positive NPVs and thus add value to the firm. However, if they are mutually exclusive, then Project L should be chosen because it has the higher NPV and thus adds more value than S. We can summarize these criteria with the following rules:

1. *Independent projects:* If NPV exceeds zero, accept the project. Because S and L both have positive NPVs, accept them both if they are independent.
2. *Mutually exclusive projects:* Accept the project with the highest positive NPV. If no project has a positive NPV, then reject them all. If S and L are mutually exclusive, the NPV criterion would select L.

Projects must be either independent or mutually exclusive, so one or the other of these rules applies to every project.

S E L F - T E S T

Why is NPV the primary capital budgeting decision criterion?

What is the difference between "independent" and "mutually exclusive" projects?

Projects SS and LL have the following cash flows:

	End-of-Year Cash Flows			
	0	1	2	3
SS	−700	500	300	100
LL	−700	100	300	600

If the cost of capital is 10%, then what are the projects' NPVs? (**NPV$_{SS}$ = \$77.61; NPV$_{LL}$ = \$89.63**)

What project or set of projects would be in your capital budget if SS and LL were (a) independent or (b) mutually exclusive? (**Both; LL**)

10-4 Internal Rate of Return (IRR)

In Chapter 5 we discussed the yield to maturity on a bond, and we explained that if you hold a bond to maturity then you will earn the yield to maturity on your investment. The YTM is found as the discount rate that forces the present value of the cash inflows to

---

[3]The keystrokes for finding the NPV are shown for several calculators in the calculator tutorials we provide on the textbook's Web site.

equal the price of the bond. This same concept is used in capital budgeting when we calculate a project's **internal rate of return**, or **IRR**. A project's IRR is the discount rate that forces the PV of the expected future cash flows to equal the initial cash flow. This is equivalent to forcing the NPV to equal zero.

Why is the discount rate that causes a project's NPV to equal zero helpful as an evaluation measure? The reason is that the IRR is an estimate of the project's rate of return. If this return exceeds the cost of the funds used to finance the project, then the difference benefits the firm's stockholders. On the other hand, if the IRR is less than the cost of capital, stockholders must make up the shortfall.

10-4a Calculating the IRR

To calculate the IRR, begin with Equation 10-1 for the NPV, replace r in the denominator with the term "IRR," and choose a value of r so that the NPV is equal to zero. This transforms Equation 10-1 into Equation 10-2, the one used to find the IRR. The rate that forces NPV to equal zero is the IRR.[4]

$$NPV = CF_0 + \frac{CF_1}{(1 + IRR)^1} + \frac{CF_2}{(1 + IRR)^2} + \cdots + \frac{CF_N}{(1 + IRR)^N} = 0$$

$$= \sum_{t=0}^{N} \frac{CF_t}{(1 + IRR)^t} = 0$$

(10-2)

For Project S, we have

$$NPV_s = 0 = -\$10,000 + \frac{\$5,300}{(1 + IRR)^1} + \frac{\$4,300}{(1 + IRR)^2} + \frac{\$1,874}{(1 + IRR)^3} + \frac{\$1,500}{(1 + IRR)^4}$$

Figure 10-3 illustrates the process for finding the IRR of Project S.

Three procedures can be used to find the IRR:

resource

See *Ch10 Tool Kit.xls* on the textbook's Web site.

1. *Trial-and-error.* We could use a trial-and-error procedure: Try a discount rate, see if the equation solves to zero, and if it doesn't, try a different rate. Continue until you find the rate that forces the NPV to zero, and that rate will be the IRR. This procedure is rarely done by hand calculations, however. IRR usually is calculated using either a financial calculator or *Excel* (or some other computer program) as described below.
2. *Calculator solution.* Enter the cash flows into the calculator's cash flow register just as you did to find the NPV, and then press the calculator key labeled "IRR." Instantly, you get the internal rate of return. Here are the values for Projects S and L:

$$IRR_S = 14.686\%$$
$$IRR_L = 13.786\%$$

3. *Excel solution.* It is even easier to find IRRs using *Excel,* as Figure 10-3 shows for Project L. Notice that with *Excel's* IRR function, the range in the function includes the initial cash flow at Year 0. This is in contrast to the NPV function's range, which starts with the Year 1 cash flow. Be alert to this difference when you use these functions, because it is easy to mis-specify the range of inputs.

---

[4]For a large, complex project like an FPL power plant, costs are incurred for several years before cash inflows begin. That simply means that we have a number of negative cash flows before the positive cash flows begin.

FIGURE 10-3

Finding the IRR

	A	B	C	D	E	F
73	INPUTS:					
74			Initial Cost and Expected Cash Flows			
75	Year	0	1	2	3	4
76	Project S	−$10,000	$5,300	$4,300	$1,874	$1,500
77		4,621.33	←←↵	↓	↓	↓
78		3,269.26	←←←←←←	←←↵	↓	↓
79		1,242.34	←←←←←←	←←←←←←	←←↵	↓
80		867.07	←←←←←←	←←←←←←	←←←←←←	←←↵
81			Long way: Try a value for r, sum the PVs of the CFs to find NPV. If NPV is not zero, try another value for r. Or use Goal Seek to find the value of r that makes the NPV = 0.			
82	NPV$_S$ =	$0.00				
83						
84	IRR = r =	14.69%	Value of r that makes NPV = 0.			
85						
86			Initial Cost and Expected Cash Flows			
87	Year	0	1	2	3	4
88	Project L	−$10,000	$1,900	$2,700	$2,345	$7,800
89	IRR$_L$ =	13.79%	Short way: Use *Excel*'s IRR function =IRR(B88:F88)			
90						

10-4b A Potential Problem with the IRR: Multiple Internal Rates of Return[5]

If a project has a *normal* cash flow pattern, which is one or more cash outflows followed only by cash inflows (or the reverse, one or more cash inflows followed only by outflows), then the project can have only one positive real IRR. Here are some examples of normal cash flow patterns:

Normal: − + + +   or   − − + + +   or   + + − −

Notice that the sign of the cash flows only changes once for any of these examples, either from negative to positive or positive to negative.

However, some projects have cash flows with signs that change more than once. For example, consider a strip coal mine where the company first spends money to buy the property and prepare the site for mining. The mining company has positive inflows for several years, and then spends more money to return the land to its original condition. For this project, the cash flow sign goes from negative to positive and then changes again from positive to negative. This is a *nonnormal* cash flow pattern; here are some examples:

Nonnormal: − + + + −   or   − + + + − + + +

If a project's cash flows have a nonnormal pattern (i.e., the cash flows have more than one sign change), it is possible for the project to have more than one positive real IRR—that is, **multiple IRRs**.[6]

---

[5]This section is relatively technical, and some instructors may choose to omit it without loss of continuity.
[6]Equation 10-2 is a polynomial of degree n, so it has n different roots, or solutions. All except one of the roots are imaginary numbers when investments have normal cash flows (one or more cash outflows followed by cash inflows), so in the normal case only one value of IRR appears. However, the possibility of multiple real roots, and hence of multiple IRRs, arises when negative net cash flows occur after the project has been placed in operation.

To illustrate multiple IRRs, suppose a firm is considering a potential strip mine (Project M) that has a cost of $1.6 million and will produce a cash flow of $10 million at the end of Year 1; however, the firm must spend $10 million to restore the land to its original condition at the end of Year 2. Therefore, the project's expected net cash flows are as follows (in millions):

Year 0	End of Year 1	End of Year 2
Cash flows −$1.6	+$10	−$10

We can substitute these values into Equation 10-2 and then solve for the IRR:

$$\text{NPV} = \frac{-\$1.6 \text{ million}}{(1 + \text{IRR})^0} + \frac{\$10 \text{ million}}{(1 + \text{IRR})^1} + \frac{-\$10 \text{ million}}{(1 + \text{IRR})^2} = 0$$

resource

See **Ch10 Tool Kit.xls** on the textbook's Web site for all calculations.

For Project M's cash flows, the NPV equals 0 when IRR = 25%, but it also equals 0 when IRR = 400%.[7] Therefore, Project M has one IRR of 25% and another of 400%. Are either of these IRRs helpful in deciding whether to proceed with Project M? No! To see this, look at Figure 10-4, which shows Project M's NPV for different costs of capital. Notice that Project M has a negative NPV for costs of capital less than 25%. Therefore, Project M should be rejected for reasonable costs of capital.

When you evaluate a project, always look at the projected cash flows and count the number of times that the sign changes. If the sign changes more than once, don't even calculate the IRR, because it is at best useless and at worst misleading.

FIGURE 10-4

Graph for Multiple IRRs: Project M (Millions of Dollars

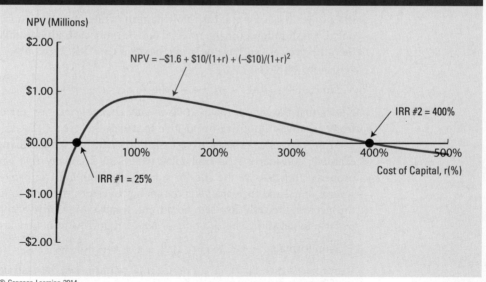

© Cengage Learning 2014

[7]If you attempt to find Project M's IRR with an HP calculator, you will get an error message, whereas TI calculators give only the IRR closest to zero. When you encounter either situation, you can find the approximate IRRs by first calculating NPVs using several different values for r = I/YR, constructing a graph with NPV on the vertical axis and cost of capital on the horizontal axis, and then visually determining approximately where NPV = 0. The intersection with the x-axis gives a rough idea of the IRRs' values. With some calculators and with *Excel*, you can find both IRRs by entering guesses, as we explain in our calculator and *Excel* tutorials.

10-4c Potential Problems When Using the IRR to Evaluate Mutually Exclusive Projects

Potential problems can arise when using the IRR to choose among mutually exclusive projects. Projects S and L are independent, but suppose for illustrative purposes that they are mutually exclusive. Their NPVs and IRRs are shown below:

	NPV	IRR
Project S	$804.38	14.69%
Project L	$1,048.02	13.79%

If using NPV as a decision criterion, Project L is preferred. But Project S is preferred if using IRR as a decision criterion. How do we resolve this conflict?

Resolving a Conflict between the IRR and NPV for Mutually Exclusive Projects: Pick the Project with the Highest NPV

Consider these two hypothetical games we offer our students in class. In Game 1, we offer to give a student $2 at the end of class if the student will give us $1 at the beginning. Assuming we can be trusted, Game 1 has a 100% rate of return. In Game 2, we offer to give a student $25 at the end of class in exchange for $20 at the beginning of class. The games are mutually exclusive and may not be repeated—a student can choose only one game and can play it only once. Which game would you choose? If you are like our students, you would choose Game 2 because your wealth goes up by $5, which is better than the $1 increase in wealth offered by Game 1. So even though Game 1 has a higher rate of return, people prefer more wealth to less wealth.

The same is true for the shareholders. If projects are mutually exclusive, managers should choose the project that provides the greatest increase in wealth (as measured by the NPV) even though it may not have the highest rate of return (as measured by the IRR). Therefore, if Projects S and L were mutually exclusive, managers would choose Project L because it has a higher NPV and generates more wealth for shareholders.

The Causes of Possible Conflicts between the IRR and NPV for Mutually Exclusive Projects: Timing and Scale Differences

Figure 10-5 illustrates the situation with a **net present value profile** for each project. This profile has a project's NPV plotted on the y-axis for different costs of capital. Notice the IRR for each project, which is the point at which the project has a zero NPV (it is also the place where the curve crosses the x-axis). As the figure shows, Project S has the largest IRR (the curve for Project S crosses the x-axis to the right of Project L's curve). Notice the NPV for each project when the cost of capital is 10%. Project L's NPV is above that of Project S.

The two NPV profile lines cross at a cost of capital of 12.247%, which is called the **crossover rate**. Find the crossover rate by calculating the IRR of the differences in the projects' cash flows, as demonstrated below:

	Year				
	0	1	2	3	4
Project S:	−$10,000	$5,300	$4,300	$1,874	$1,500
Project L:	−10,000	1,900	2,700	2,345	7,800
$\Delta = CF_S − CF_L$:	$0	$3,400	$1,600	−$471	−$6,300

IRR Δ = 12.274%

FIGURE **10-5**

NPV Profiles for Projects S and L

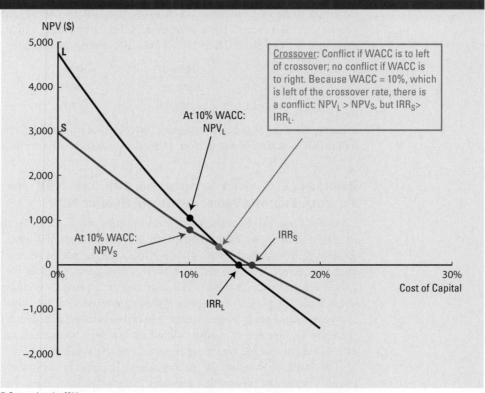

© Cengage Learning 2014

If the cost of capital is *less* than the crossover rate, Project L has the higher NPV. But if the cost of capital is *greater* than the crossover rate, Project S has the higher NPV.

Many projects don't have different rankings—if a project has a larger NPV, it usually has a higher IRR. But for projects whose rankings conflict, you must determine the source of the conflict. Note that in order for a conflict to exist, both projects must have positive NPVs and there must be a crossover rate. For a crossover rate to exist, the difference in cash flows between the two projects must have a normal pattern, as described in the previous section: The cash flows must have one and only one sign change. Therefore, a crossover rate only can exist for projects with positive NPVs if the cash flows have timing differences, size (or scale) differences, or some combination.[8] For example, consider the cash flows of Project Sooner and Project Later. Both have a 10% cost of capital; their cash flows are shown below:

| | Year | | | | |
	0	1	2	NPV	IRR
Project Sooner:	−$1,000	$1,020	$120	$26	12.7%
Project Later:	−$1,000	$120	$1,120	$35	12.0%
$\Delta = CF_S - CF_L$:	$0	$900	−$1,000		11.1%

---

[8]Also, if mutually exclusive projects have different lives (as opposed to different cash flow patterns over a common life), further complications arise; thus, for meaningful comparisons, some mutually exclusive projects must be evaluated over a common life. This point is discussed later in the chapter.

Both projects have the same scale (each requires an initial investment of $1,000), so the difference in their initial cost is zero. However, Project Sooner has most of its future cash flows in Year 1 and Project Later has most of its future cash flows in Year 2. This causes their difference in Year 1 to be positive and their difference in Year 2 to be negative. In other words, there is one and only one sign change, so a crossover rate exists. As this illustrates, projects with the same scale must have timing differences in future cash flows for there to be one and only one sign change.

What about a situation in which projects don't have timing differences but do have a scale difference? Projects Smaller and Larger each have a 10% cost of capital, and their cash flows are shown below:

| | Year | | | | |
	0	1	2	NPV	IRR
Smaller	−$90	$12	$112	$13	18.4%
Larger	−$1,000	$120	$1,120	$35	12.0%
$\Delta = CF_S - CF_L$	$910	−$108	−$1,008		11.3%

There are no timing differences in the future cash flows; in fact, Project Smaller's future cash flows are 10% of Project Larger's. However, there is a scale difference because Project Smaller's initial cost is much less than that of Project Larger. The scale difference causes the difference in the initial cash flow to be positive. However, the differences in the future cash flows are negative. This causes one and only one sign change, so a crossover rate exists.

10-4d Applying IRR as an Evaluation Measure

When using the IRR, it is important to distinguish between independent projects and mutually exclusive projects.

If you are evaluating an independent project with normal cash flows, then the NPV and IRR criteria always lead to the same accept/reject decision: If NPV says accept then IRR also says accept, and vice versa. To see why this is so, look at Figure 10-5 and notice (1) that the IRR says accept Project S if the cost of capital is less than (or to the left of) the IRR and (2) that if the cost of capital is less than the IRR, then the NPV must be positive. Thus, at any cost of capital less than 14.686%, Project S will be recommended by both the NPV and IRR criteria, but both methods reject the project if the cost of capital is greater than 14.686%. A similar statement can be made for Project L, or any other normal project, and we would always reach the same conclusion: For normal, independent projects, if the IRR says to accept it, then so will the NPV.

Now assume that Projects S and L are mutually exclusive rather than independent. Therefore, we can choose either S or L, or we can reject both, but we can't accept both. Now look at Figure 10-5 and note these points.

- $IRR_S > IRR_L$, so the IRR decision rule would say to accept Project S over Project L.
- As long as the cost of capital is *greater than* the crossover rate of 12.274%, both methods agree that Project S is better: $NPV_S > NPV_L$ and $IRR_S > IRR_L$. Therefore, if r is *greater* than the crossover rate, no conflict occurs.
- However, if the cost of capital is *less than* the crossover rate, a conflict arises: NPV ranks L higher, but IRR ranks S higher. In this situation, select the project with the highest NPV even if it has a lower IRR.

S E L F - T E S T

In what sense is a project's IRR similar to the YTM on a bond?

The cash flows for Projects SS and LL are as follows:

	End-of-Year Cash Flows			
	0	**1**	**2**	**3**
SS	−700	500	300	100
LL	−700	100	300	600

Assume that the firm's WACC = r = 10%. What are the two projects' IRRs? **(IRR$_{SS}$ = 18.0%; IRR$_{LL}$ = 15.6%)**

Which project would the IRR method select if the firm has a 10% cost of capital and the projects are (a) independent or (b) mutually exclusive? **(Both; SS)**

What condition regarding cash flows would cause more than one IRR to exist?

Project MM has the following cash flows:

	End-of-Year Cash Flows		
0	**1**	**2**	**3**
−$1,000	$2,000	$2,000	−$3,350

Calculate MM's NPV at discount rates of 0%, 10%, 12.2258%, 25%, 122.147%, and 150%. **(−$350; −$46; $0; $165; $0; −$94)**

What are MM's IRRs? **(12.23% and 122.15%)**

If the cost of capital were 10%, should the project be accepted or rejected? **(Rejected because NPV < 0)**

Describe in words how an NPV profile is constructed. How do you determine the intercepts for the x-axis and the y-axis?

What is the crossover rate, and how does it interact with the cost of capital to determine whether or not a conflict exists between NPV and IRR?

What two characteristics can lead to conflicts between the NPV and the IRR when evaluating mutually exclusive projects??

10-5 Modified Internal Rate of Return (MIRR)

Recall from Chapter 5 that an investor who purchases a bond and holds it to maturity (assuming no default) will receive the bond's yield to maturity (YTM) even if interest rates change. This happens because the realized rate of return on an investment is by definition the rate that sets the present value of the realized cash flows equal to the purchase price. However, the realized rate of return on the investment in the bond and the subsequent reinvestment of the coupons will not necessarily equal the YTM if interest rates change. Similar reasoning can be applied to a project—the project's expected return is equal to its IRR, but the expected return on the project and any reinvested cash flows is not necessarily equal to the IRR.

If a manager wishes to evaluate a project based on the return expected from the project and its reinvested cash flows, then the IRR overstates this return because it is more likely that the project's future cash flows can be reinvested at the cost of capital and not at the project's IRR. The **Modified IRR (MIRR)** is similar to the regular IRR, except it is based on the assumption that cash flows are reinvested at the WACC (or some other explicit

FIGURE 10-6

Finding the MIRR for Projects S and L

	A	B	C	D	E	F	G
293	INPUTS:						
294		r = 10%					
295			Initial Cost and Expected Cash Flows				
296	Year	0	1	2	3	4	
297	Project S	–$10,000	$5,300	$4,300	$1,874	$1,500	
298		↓	↓	↓	↳ → →	$2,061	
299		↓	↓	↳ → →	→ → → → →	$5,203	
300	Present Value of	↓	↳ → →	→ → → → →	→ → → → →	$7,054	
301	Negative CF (PV) =	–$10,000	Terminal Value of Positive CF (TV) =			$15,819	
302							
303	Calculator: N = 4, PV = –10000, PMT = 0, FV = 15819. Press I/YR to get:					MIRR$_S$ =	12.15%
304	*Excel* Rate function–Easier:		=RATE(F296,0,B301,F301)			MIRR$_S$ =	12.15%
305	*Excel* MIRR function–Easiest:		=MIRR(B297:F297,B294,B294)			MIRR$_S$ =	12.15%
306							
307	Year	0	1	2	3	4	
308	Project L	–$10,000	$1,900	$2,700	$2,345	$7,800	
309							
310	For Project L, using the MIRR function:		=MIRR(B308:F308,B294,B294)			MIRR$_L$ =	12.78%

Notes:

1. The terminal value (TV) is the future value of all positive cash flows. The present value (PV) is the present value of all negative cash flows.
2. Find the discount rate that forces the TV positive cash flows to equal the PV of negative cash flows. That discount rate is defined as the MIRR.

$$\text{PV of negative cash flows} = (\text{TV of positive cash flows})/(1 + \text{MIRR})^N$$

$$\$10,000 = \$15,819/(1 + \text{MIRR})^4$$

We can find the MIRR with a calculator or *Excel*.

rate if that is a more reasonable assumption). Refer to Figure 10-6 as you read the following steps that explain the MIRR's calculation.

1. Project S has just one outflow, a negative $10,000 at t = 0. Because it occurs at Time 0, it is not discounted, and its PV is –$10,000. If the project had additional outflows, we would find the PV at t = 0 for each one and then sum them for use in the MIRR calculation.

2. Next, we find the future value of each *inflow*, compounded at the WACC out to the "terminal year," which is the year the last inflow is received. We assume that cash flows are reinvested at the WACC. For Project S, the first cash flow, $5,300, is compounded at WACC = 10% for 3 years, and it grows to $7,054. The second inflow, $4,300, grows to $5,203, and the third inflow, $1,874, grows to $2,061. The last inflow, $1,500, is received at the end, so it is not compounded at all. The sum of the future values, $15,819, is called the "terminal value," or TV.

3. We now have the PV at t = 0 of all negative cash flows, –$10,000, and the TV at Year 4 of all positive cash flows, $15,819. There is some discount rate that will cause the PV of the terminal value to equal the cost. *That interest rate is defined as the Modified Internal Rate of Return (MIRR)*. In a calculator, enter N = 4, PV = –10000, PMT = 0, and FV = 15819. Then pressing the I/YR key yields the MIRR, 12.15%.

4. The MIRR can be found in a number of ways. Figure 10-6 illustrates how the MIRR is calculated: We compound each cash inflow, sum them to determine the TV, and then find the rate that causes the PV of the TV to equal the cost. That rate in this example is 12.15%. However, *Excel* and some of the better calculators have a built-in MIRR function that streamlines the process. We explain how to use the MIRR function in our calculator tutorials, and we explain how to find MIRR with *Excel* in this chapter's *Excel Tool Kit.*[9]

The MIRR has two significant advantages over the regular IRR. First, the MIRR assumes that cash flows are reinvested at the cost of capital (or some other explicit rate). Because reinvestment at the IRR is generally not correct, the MIRR is usually a better indicator of the rate of return on the project and its reinvested cash flows. Second, the MIRR eliminates the multiple IRR problem—there can never be more than one MIRR, and it can be compared with the cost of capital when deciding to accept or reject projects.

Our conclusion is that the MIRR is better than the regular IRR; however, this question remains: Is MIRR as good as the NPV? Here is our take on the situation.

- For *independent* projects, the NPV, IRR, and MIRR always reach the same accept–reject conclusion, so the three criteria are equally good when evaluating independent projects.
- However, if projects are *mutually exclusive* and if they differ in size, conflicts can arise. In such cases the NPV is best because it selects the project that maximizes value.[10]
- Our overall conclusions are that (1) the MIRR is superior to the regular IRR as an indicator of a project's "true" rate of return, but (2) NPV is better than either IRR or MIRR when choosing among competing projects. If managers want to know the expected rates of return on projects, it would be better to give them MIRRs than IRRs because MIRRs are more likely to be the rates that are actually earned if the projects' cash flows are reinvested in future projects.

---

[9]If we let COF_t and CIF_t denote cash outflows and inflows, respectively, then Equations 10-2a and 10-2b summarize the steps just described:

$$\sum_{t=0}^{N} \frac{COF_t}{(1+r)^t} = \frac{\sum_{t=0}^{N} CIF_t(1+r)^{N-t}}{(1+MIRR)^N}$$

10–2a

$$PV\ costs = \frac{TV}{(1+MIRR)^N}$$

10–2b

Also, note that there are alternative definitions for the MIRR. One difference relates to whether negative cash flows after the positive cash flows begin should be compounded and treated as part of the TV or discounted and treated as a cost. A related issue is whether negative and positive flows in a given year should be netted or treated separately. For more discussion, see David M. Shull, "Interpreting Rates of Return: A Modified Rate of Return Approach," *Financial Practice and Education,* Fall 1993, pp. 67–71.

[10]For projects of equal size but different lives, the MIRR will always lead to the same decision as the NPV if the MIRRs are both calculated using as the terminal year the life of the longer project. (Fill in zeros for the shorter project's missing cash flows.)

SELF-TEST

What's the primary difference between the MIRR and the regular IRR?

Projects A and B have the following cash flows:

	0	1	2
A	–$1,000	$1,150	$100
B	–$1,000	$100	$1,300

The cost of capital is 10%. What are the projects' IRRs, MIRRs, and NPVs? **(IRR$_A$ = 23.1%, IRR$_B$ = 19.1%; MIRR$_A$ = 16.8%, MIRR$_B$ = 18.7%; NPV$_A$ = $128.10, NPV$_B$ = $165.29)**

Which project would each method select? **(IRR: A; MIRR: B; NPV: B)**

10-6 Profitability Index (PI)

A fourth method used to evaluate projects is the **profitability index (PI)**:

$$\text{PI} = \frac{\text{PV of future cash flows}}{\text{Initial cost}} = \frac{\displaystyle\sum_{t=1}^{N} \frac{CF_t}{(1+r)^t}}{CF_0} \qquad (10\text{-}3)$$

Here CF_t represents the expected future cash flows and CF_0 represents the initial cost. The PI shows the *relative* profitability of any project, or the present value per dollar of initial cost. As we can see from Figure 10-7, the PI for Project S, based on a 10% cost of capital, is $10,804.38/$10,000 = 1.0804; the PI for Project L is 1.1048. Thus, Project S is expected to produce $1.0804 of present value for each $1 of investment whereas L should produce $1.1048 for each dollar invested.

A project is acceptable if its PI is greater than 1.0, and the higher the PI, the higher the project's ranking. Therefore, both S and L would be accepted by the PI criterion if they were independent, and L would be ranked ahead of S if they were mutually exclusive.

Mathematically, the NPV, IRR, MIRR, and PI methods will always lead to the same accept/reject decisions for *normal, independent* projects: If a project's NPV is positive, its IRR and MIRR will always exceed r and its PI will always be greater than 1.0. However, these methods can give conflicting rankings for *mutually exclusive* projects if the projects differ in size or in the timing of cash flows. If the PI ranking conflicts with the NPV, then the NPV ranking should be used.

FIGURE 10-7

Profitability Index (PI)

	A	B	C	D	E
332	**Project S:**		PI$_S$ = PV of future cash flows	÷	Initial cost
333			PI$_S$ = $10,804.38	÷	$10,000
334			PI$_S$ = 1.0804		
335					
336	**Project L:**		PI$_L$ = PV of future cash flows	÷	Initial cost
337			PI$_L$ = $11,048.02	÷	$10,000
338			PI$_L$ = 1.1048		

SELF-TEST

Explain how the PI is calculated. What does it measure?

A project has the following expected cash flows: $CF_0 = -\$500$, $CF_1 = \$200$, $CF_2 = \$200$, and $CF_3 = \$400$. If the project's cost of capital is 9%, what is the PI? **(1.32)**

10-7 Payback Period

NPV and IRR are the most commonly used methods today, but historically the first selection criterion was the **payback period**, defined as the number of years required to recover the funds invested in a project from its operating cash flows. Equation 10-4 is used for the calculation, and the process is diagrammed in Figure 10-8. We start with the project's cost, a negative number, and then add the cash inflow for each year until the cumulative cash flow turns positive. The payback year is the year *prior to* full recovery, plus a fraction equal to the shortfall at the end of the prior year divided by the cash flow during the year when full recovery occurs:[11]

$$\text{Payback} = \begin{array}{c}\text{Number of}\\\text{years prior to}\\\text{full recovery}\end{array} + \dfrac{\begin{array}{c}\text{Unrecovered cost}\\\text{at start of year}\end{array}}{\begin{array}{c}\text{Cash flow during}\\\text{full recovery year}\end{array}} \qquad (10\text{-}4)$$

FIGURE 10-8

Payback Period

	A	B	C	D	E	F	G
365	**Project S**	Year	0	1	2	3	4
366		Cash flow	−$10,000	$5,300	$4,300	$1,874	$1,500
367		Cumulative cash flow	−$10,000	−$4,700	−$400	$1,474	$2,974
368		Intermediate calculation for payback	—	—	—	2.21	3.98
369						↑	
370						Intermediate calculation:	
371	Manual calculation of Payback S = 2 + $400/$1,874 =		2.21		=IF(F367>0,E365+ABS(E367/F366),"—")		
372	*Excel* calculation of Payback S =		2.21			2.21	
373							
374	**Project L**	Year	0	1	2	3	4
375		Cash flow	−$10,000	$1,900	$2,700	$2,345	$7,800
376		Cumulative cash flow	−$10,000	−$8,100	−$5,400	−$3,055	$4,745
377							
378	Manual calculation of Payback L = 3 + $3,055/$7,800 =		3.39		Payback switches from negative to positive cash flow.		
379	Alternative *Excel* calculation of Payback L =						
380	=PERCENTRANK(C376:G376,0,6)*G374		3.39				

---

[11]Equation 10-4 assumes that cash flows come in uniformly during the full recovery year.

resource

*See **Ch10 Tool Kit.xls** on the textbook's Web site.*

The cash flows for Projects S and L, together with their paybacks, are shown in Figure 10-8.[12] The shorter the payback, the better the project. Therefore, if the firm requires a payback of 3 years or less, then S would be accepted but L would be rejected. If the projects were mutually exclusive, S would be ranked over L because of its shorter payback.

The regular payback has three flaws: (1) Dollars received in different years are all given the same weight—that is, the time value of money is ignored. (2) Cash flows beyond the payback year are given no consideration whatsoever, regardless of how large they might be. (3) Unlike the NPV or the IRR, which tell us how much wealth a project adds or how much a project's rate of return exceeds the cost of capital, the payback merely tells us how long it takes to recover our investment. There is no necessary relationship between a given payback period and investor wealth, so we don't know how to specify an acceptable payback. The firm might use 2 years, 3 years, or any other number as the minimum acceptable payback, but the choice is arbitrary.

To counter the first criticism, financial analysts developed the **discounted payback**, where cash flows are discounted at the WACC and then those discounted cash flows are used to find the payback. In Figure 10-9, we calculate the discounted paybacks for S and L, assuming both have a 10% cost of capital. Each inflow is divided by $(1 + r)^t = (1.10)^t$, where t is the year in which the cash flow occurs and r is the project's cost of capital, and then those PVs are used to find the payback. Project S's discounted payback is 3.21 years and L's is 3.80 years.

resource

*See **Ch10 Tool Kit.xls** on the textbook's Web site.*

Note that the payback is a "break-even" calculation in the sense that if cash flows come in at the expected rate, then the project will at least break even. However, because the regular payback doesn't consider the cost of capital, it doesn't specify the true break-even year. The discounted payback does consider capital costs, but it disregards cash flows

FIGURE 10-9

Discounted Payback

	A	B	C	D	E	F	G
393	Project WACC =	10%					
394	**Project S**		Year	0	1	2	3	4
395			Cash flow	−$10,000	$5,300	$4,300	$1,874	$1,500
396			Discounted cash flow	−$10,000	$4,818	$3,554	$1,408	$1,025
397			Cumulative discounted CF	−$10,000	−$5,182	−$1,628	−$220	$804
398								
399		Discounted Payback S = 3 + $220.14/$1,024.52 =		3.21		Switches from negative to		
400		*Excel* calculation of Discounted Payback S =				positive cash flow.		
401		=PERCENTRANK(C397:G397,0,6)*G394		3.21				
402								
403	**Project L**		Year	0	1	2	3	4
404			Cash flow	−$10,000	$1,900	$2,700	$2,345	$7,800
405			Discounted cash flow	−$10,000	$1,727	$2,231	$1,762	$5,328
406			Cumulative discounted CF	−$10,000	−$8,273	−$6,041	−$4,279	$1,048
407								
408		Discounted Payback L = 3 + $4,279.49/$5,327.50 =		3.80		Switches from negative to		
409		*Excel* calculation of Discounted Payback L =				positive cash flow.		
410		=PERCENTRANK(C406:G406,0,6)*G403		3.80				

[12]There is not an *Excel* function for payback. But if the cash flows are normal, then the PERCENTRANK function can be used to find payback, as illustrated in Figures 10-8 and 10-9.

poor decisions. Finally, there is no way to determine how short the payback periods must be to justify accepting a project.

Although the payback methods have faults as ranking criteria, they do provide information about *liquidity* and *risk*. The shorter the payback, other things held constant, the greater the project's liquidity. This factor is often important for smaller firms that don't have ready access to the capital markets. Also, cash flows expected in the distant future are generally riskier than near-term cash flows, so the payback period is also a risk indicator.

SELF-TEST

What two pieces of information does the payback method provide that are absent from the other capital budgeting decision methods?

What three flaws does the regular payback method have? Does the discounted payback method correct all of those flaws? Explain.

Project P has a cost of $1,000 and cash flows of $300 per year for 3 years plus another $1,000 in Year 4. The project's cost of capital is 15%. What are P's regular and discounted paybacks? **(3.10, 3.55)** *If the company requires a payback of 3 years or less, would the project be accepted? Would this be a good accept/reject decision, considering the NPV and/or the IRR?* **(NPV = $256.72, IRR = 24.78%)**?

10-8 How to Use the Different Capital Budgeting Methods

We have discussed six capital budgeting decision criteria: NPV, IRR, MIRR, PI, payback, and discounted payback. We compared these methods and highlighted their strengths and weaknesses. In the process, we may have created the impression that "sophisticated" firms should use only one method, the NPV. However, virtually all capital budgeting decisions are analyzed by computer, so it is easy to use all six methods. In making the accept–reject decision, most firms usually calculate and consider all six because each method provides a somewhat different piece of information about the decision.

10-8a A Comparison of the Methods

NPV is the single best criterion because it provides a direct measure of the value a project adds to shareholder wealth. IRR and MIRR measure profitability expressed as a percentage rate of return, which decision makers like to consider. The PI also measures profitability but in relation to the amount of the investment. Further, IRR, MIRR, and PI all contain information concerning a project's "safety margin." To illustrate, consider a firm, whose WACC is 10%, which must choose between these two mutually exclusive projects: SS (for small) has a cost of $10,000 and is expected to return $16,500 at the end of 1 year; LL (for large) has a cost of $100,000 and is expected to return $115,550 at the end of 1 year. SS has a huge IRR, 65%, while LL's IRR is a more modest 15.6%. The NPV paints a somewhat different picture: At the 10% cost of capital, SS's NPV is $5,000 while LL's is $5,045. By the NPV rule we would choose LL. However, SS's IRR indicates that it has a much larger margin for error: Even if its cash flow were 39% below the $16,500 forecast, the firm would still recover its $10,000 investment. On the other hand, if LL's inflows fell by only 13.5% from its forecasted $115,550, the firm would not recover its investment. Further, if neither project generated any cash flows at all, the firm would lose only $10,000 on SS but would lose $100,000 by accepting LL.

The modified IRR has all the virtues of the IRR, but it avoids the problem of multiple rates of return that can occur with the IRR. The MIRR also measures the expected return of the project and its reinvested cash flows, which provides additional insight into the project. So if decision makers want to know projects' rates of return, the MIRR is a better indicator than the regular IRR.

The PI tells a similar story to the IRR. Here PI_{LL} is only 1.05 while PI_{SS} is 1.50. As with the IRR, this indicates that Project SS's cash inflow could fall by a lot before it loses money, whereas a small decline in LL's cash flows would result in a loss.

Payback and discounted payback provide indications of a project's *liquidity* and *risk*. A long payback means that investment dollars will be locked up for a long time; hence the project is relatively illiquid. In addition, a long payback means that cash flows must be forecast far into the future, and that probably makes the project riskier than one with a shorter payback. A good analogy for this is bond valuation. An investor should never compare the yields to maturity on two bonds without also considering their terms to maturity, because a bond's risk is influenced significantly by its maturity. The same holds true for capital projects.

In summary, the different measures provide different types of useful information. It is easy to calculate all of them: Simply put the cost of capital and the cash flows into an *Excel* model like the one provided in this chapter's ***Tool Kit*** and the model will instantly calculate all six criteria. Therefore, most sophisticated companies consider all six measures when making capital budgeting decisions. For most decisions, the greatest weight should be given to the NPV, but it would be foolish to ignore the information provided by the other criteria.

10-8b The Decision Process: What Is the Source of a Project's NPV?

Just as it would be foolish to ignore these capital budgeting methods, it would also be foolish to make decisions based *solely* on them. One cannot know at Time 0 the exact cost of future capital or the exact future cash flows. These inputs are simply estimates, and if they turn out to be incorrect then so will be the calculated NPVs and IRRs. Thus, *quantitative methods provide valuable information, but they should not be used as the sole criteria for accept–reject decisions* in the capital budgeting process. Rather, managers should use quantitative methods in the decision-making process but should also consider the likelihood that actual results will differ from the forecasts. Qualitative factors, such as the chances of a tax increase, or a war, or a major product liability suit, should also be considered. In summary, *quantitative methods such as NPV and IRR should be considered as an aid to informed decisions but not as a substitute for sound managerial judgment.*

In this same vein, managers should ask sharp questions about any project that has a large NPV, a high IRR, or a high PI. In a perfectly competitive economy, there would be no positive-NPV projects—all companies would have the same opportunities, and competition would quickly eliminate any positive NPV. The existence of positive-NPV projects must be predicated on some imperfection in the marketplace, and the longer the life of the project, the longer that imperfection must last. Therefore, managers should be able to identify the imperfection and explain why it will persist before accepting that a project will really have a positive NPV. Valid explanations might include patents or proprietary technology, which is how pharmaceutical and software firms create positive-NPV projects. Pfizer's Lipitor (a cholesterol-reducing medicine) and Microsoft's Windows 7 operating system are examples. Companies can also create positive NPV by being the first entrant into a new market or by creating new products that meet some previously unidentified consumer needs. Post-it notes invented by 3M are an example. Similarly, Dell developed procedures for direct sales of microcomputers and, in the process, created projects with enormous NPV. Also, companies such as Southwest Airlines have trained and motivated their workers better than their competitors, and this has led to positive-NPV projects. In all of these cases, the companies developed some source of competitive advantage, and that advantage resulted in positive-NPV projects.

This discussion suggests three things: (1) If you can't identify the reason a project has a positive projected NPV, then its actual NPV will probably not be positive. (2) Positive-NPV projects don't just happen—they result from hard work to develop some competitive advantage. At the risk of oversimplification, the primary job of a manager is to find and develop areas of competitive advantage. (3) Some competitive advantages last longer than others, with their durability depending on competitors' ability to replicate them. Patents, the control of scarce resources, or large size in an industry where strong economies of scale exist can keep competitors at bay. However, it is relatively easy to replicate product features that cannot be patented. The bottom line is that managers should strive to develop nonreplicable sources of competitive advantage. If such an advantage cannot be demonstrated, then you should question projects with high NPV—especially if they have long lives.

10-8c Decision Criteria Used in Practice

Table 10-1 reports survey evidence and shows that a large majority of companies use NPV and IRR. As we suggested in the previous section, other methods are also used.

The table also reports the factors CEOs consider important in allocating capital within the firm. The ranking of projects by NPV is the factor that most CEOs consider important. Interestingly, CEOs also consider the manager who is proposing the project, both in terms of the manager's past success and the manager's confidence in the project. Confidence is often expressed through the range of possible outcomes for the project, with smaller ranges conveying more confidence. Chapter 11 explains how to estimate such confidence intervals.

TABLE 10-1

Capital Budgeting in Practice

Quantitative Measures Used by Companies	Percent Using	Factors Considered Important by CEOs when Allocating Capital within the Company	Percent Agreeing
NPV	75%	Project's ranking based on NPV	78.6%
IRR	76	Proposing manager's track record	71.3
Payback	57	Proposing manager's confidence in project	68.8
Discounted payback	29	Timing of project's cash flows	65.3
		Project's ability to protect market share	51.9
		Proposing division's track record	51.2

Sources: The percentages of companies using particular quantitative measures are from John R. Graham and Campbell R. Harvey, "The Theory and Practice of Corporate Finance: Evidence from the Field," *Journal of Financial Economics,* 2001, pp. 187–244. The percentages of CEOs agreeing with the capital allocation factors are from John R. Graham, Campbell R. Harvey, and Manju Puri, "Capital Allocation and Delegation of Decision Making Authority within Firms," NBER Working Paper 1730, 2011, **www.nber.org/papers/w17370**.

SELF-TEST

Describe the advantages and disadvantages of the six capital budgeting methods.

Should capital budgeting decisions be made solely on the basis of a project's NPV, with no regard to the other criteria? Explain your answer.

What are some possible reasons that a project might have a high NPV?

10-9 Other Issues in Capital Budgeting

Three other issues in capital budgeting are discussed in this section: (1) how to deal with mutually exclusive projects whose lives differ; (2) the potential advantage of terminating a project before the end of its physical life; and (3) the optimal capital budget when the cost of capital rises as the size of the capital budget increases.

10-9a Mutually Exclusive Projects with Unequal Lives

When choosing between two mutually exclusive alternatives with significantly different lives, an adjustment is necessary. For example, suppose a company is planning to modernize its production facilities and is considering either a conveyor system (Project C) or a fleet of forklift trucks (Project F) for moving materials. The first two sections of Figure 10-10 show the expected net cash flows, NPVs, and IRRs for these two mutually exclusive alternatives. We see that Project C, when discounted at the firm's 12% cost of capital, has the higher NPV and thus appears to be the better project.

resource

See Ch10 Tool Kit.xls on the textbook's Web site.

Although the NPVs shown in Figure 10-10 suggest that Project C should be selected, this analysis is incomplete, and the decision to choose Project C is actually incorrect. If we choose Project F, we will have an opportunity to make a similar investment in 3 years, and

FIGURE 10-10

Analysis of Projects C and F (r = 12%)

	A	B	C	D	E	F	G	H
438	WACC = r = **12.0%**							
439								
440	**Data on Project C, Conveyor System:**							
441	Year	**0**	**1**	**2**	**3**	**4**	**5**	**6**
442	Cash flows for C	−$40,000	$8,000	$14,000	$13,000	$12,000	$11,000	$10,000
443		NPV$_C$ =	$6,491		IRR$_C$ =	17.5%		
444								
445	**Data on Project F, Forklifts:**							
446	Year	**0**	**1**	**2**	**3**			
447	Cash flows for F	−$20,000	$7,000	$13,000	$12,000			
448		NPV$_F$ =	$5,155		IRR$_F$ =	25.2%		
449								
450	**Common Life Approach with F Repeated (Project FF):**							
451	Year	**0**	**1**	**2**	**3**	**4**	**5**	**6**
452	CF$_t$ for 1st F	−$20,000	$7,000	$13,000	$12,000			
453	CF$_t$ for 2nd F				−$20,000	$7,000	$13,000	$12,000
454	All CFs for FF	−$20,000	$7,000	$13,000	−$8,000	$7,000	$13,000	$12,000
455		NPV$_{FF}$ =	$8,824		IRR$_{FF}$ =	25.2%		

if cost and revenue conditions continue at the levels shown in Figure 10-10, then this second investment will also be profitable. However, if we choose Project C, we cannot make this second investment. Two approaches can be used to compare Projects C and F, as shown in Figure 10-10 and discussed next.

REPLACEMENT CHAINS

The key to the *replacement chain, or common life, approach* is to analyze both projects over an equal life. In our example, Project C has a 6-year life, so we assume that Project F will be repeated after 3 years and then analyze it over the same 6-year period. We can then calculate the NPV of C and compare it to the extended-life NPV of Project F. The NPV for Project C, as shown in Figure 10-10, is already based on the 6-year common life. For Project F, however, we must add in a second project to extend the overall life to 6 years. The time line for this extended project, denoted as "All CFs for FF," is shown in Figure 10-10. Here we assume (1) that Project F's cost and annual cash inflows will not change if the project is repeated in 3 years and (2) that the cost of capital will remain at 12%.

The NPV of this extended Project F is $8,824, and its IRR is 25.2%. (The IRR of two Project Fs is the same as the IRR for one Project F.) However, the $8,824 extended NPV of Project F is greater than Project C's $6,491 NPV, so Project F should be selected.

Alternatively, we could recognize that Project F has an NPV of $5,155 at Time 0 and a second NPV of that same amount at Time 3, find the PV of the second NPV at Time 0, and then sum the two to find Project F's extended-life NPV of $8,824.

EQUIVALENT ANNUAL ANNUITIES (EAA)

Electrical engineers designing power plants and distribution lines were the first to encounter the unequal life problem. They could install transformers and other equipment that had relatively low initial costs but short lives, or they could use equipment that had higher initial costs but longer lives. The services would be required into the indefinite future, so this was the issue: Which choice would result in a higher NPV in the long run? The engineers converted the annual cash flows under the alternative investments into a constant cash flow stream whose NPV was equal to, or equivalent to, the NPV of the initial stream. This was called the **equivalent annual annuity (EAA) method**. To apply the EAA method to Projects C and F, for each project find the constant payment streams that the projects' NPVs ($6,491 for C and $5,155 for F) would provide over their respective lives. Using a financial calculator for Project C, we enter N = 6, I/YR = 12, PV = −6491, and FV = 0. Then, when we press the PMT key, we find EAA$_C$ = $1,579. For Project F, we enter N = 3, I/YR = 12, PV = −5155, and FV = 0; solving for PMT, we find EAA$_F$ = $2,146. Project F would thus produce a higher cash flow stream over the 6 years, so it is the better project.

CONCLUSIONS ABOUT UNEQUAL LIVES

When should we worry about analysis of unequal lives? The unequal life issue (1) does not arise for independent projects but (2) can arise if mutually exclusive projects with significantly different lives are being compared. However, even for mutually exclusive projects, it is not always appropriate to extend the analysis to a common life. This should be done if and only if there is a high probability that the projects will actually be repeated at the end of their initial lives.

We should note several potentially serious weaknesses in this type of analysis. (1) If inflation occurs, then replacement equipment will have a higher price. Moreover, both sales prices and operating costs would probably change. Thus, the static conditions built into the analysis would be invalid. (2) Replacements that occur down the road would probably employ new technology, which in turn might change the cash flows. (3) It is difficult enough to estimate the lives of most projects, and even more so to estimate the lives of a series of projects. In view of these problems, no experienced financial analyst would be too concerned about comparing mutually exclusive projects with lives of, say, 8 years and 10 years. Given all the uncertainties in the estimation process, we would assume that such projects would, for all practical purposes, have the same life. Still, it is important to recognize that a problem exists if mutually exclusive projects have substantially different lives.

When we encounter situations with significant differences in project lives, we first use a computer spreadsheet to build expected inflation and/or possible efficiency gains directly into the cash flow estimates and then use the replacement chain approach. We prefer the replacement chain approach for two reasons. First, it is easier to explain to those who are responsible for approving capital budgets. Second, it is easier to build inflation and other modifications into a spreadsheet and then go on to make the replacement chain calculations.

10-9b Economic Life versus Physical Life

Projects are normally evaluated under the assumption that the firm will operate them over their full physical lives. However, this may not be the best plan—it may be better to terminate a project before the end of its potential life. For example, the cost of maintenance for trucks and machinery can become quite high if they are used for too many years, so it might be better to replace them before the end of their potential lives.

Figure 10-11 provides data for an asset with a physical life of 3 years. However, the project can be terminated at the end of any year and the asset sold at the indicated salvage values. All of the cash flows are after taxes, and the firm's cost of capital is 10%. The undiscounted cash flows are shown in Columns C and D in the upper part of the figure, and the present values of these flows are shown in Columns E and F. We find the project's NPV under different assumptions about how long it will be operated. If the project is operated for its full 3-year life, it will have a negative NPV. The NPV will be positive if it is operated for 2 years and then the asset is sold for a relatively high salvage value; the NPV will be negative if the asset is disposed after only 1 year of operation. Therefore, the project's optimal life is 2 years.

resource

See *Ch10 Tool Kit.xls* on the textbook's Web site.

This type of analysis is used to determine a project's **economic life**, which is the life that maximizes the NPV and thus shareholder wealth. For our project, the economic life is 2 years versus the 3-year **physical**, or **engineering, life**. Note that this analysis was based on the expected cash flows and the expected salvage values, and it should always be conducted as a part of the capital budgeting evaluation if salvage values are relatively high.

10-9c The Optimal Capital Budget

The **optimal capital budget** is defined as the set of projects that maximizes the value of the firm. Finance theory states that all independent projects with positive NPVs should be accepted, as should the mutually exclusive projects with the highest NPVs. Therefore, the optimal capital budget consists of that set of projects. However, two complications arise in practice: (1) The cost of capital might increase as the size of the capital budget increases, making it hard to know the proper discount rate to use when evaluating projects; and (2) sometimes firms set an upper limit on the size of their capital budgets, which is also known as *capital rationing*.

FIGURE 10-11

Economic Life versus Physical Life

	A	B	C	D	E	F	G
495	WACC = 10%				PVs of the Cash Flows		
496			Operating	Salvage	Operating	Salvage	
497		Year	Cash Flow	Value	Cash Flow	Value	
498		0	−$4,800				
499		1	2,000	$3,000	$1,818.18	$2,727.27	
500		2	2,000	1,650	1,652.89	1,363.64	
501		3	1,750	0	1,314.80	0.00	
502					PV of		PV of
503	NPV at Different Operating Lives:		Initial Cost	+	Operating	+	Salvage
504					Cash Flows		Value
505	Operate for 3 Years:						
506	NPV$_3$:	−$14.12	−$4,800	+	$4,785.88	+	$0.00
507	Operate for 2 Years:						
508	NPV$_2$:	$34.71	−$4,800	+	$3,471.07	+	$1,363.64
509	Operate for 1 Year:						
510	NPV$_1$:	−$254.55	−$4,800	+	$1,818.18	+	$2,727.27

Note: The project is profitable if and only if it is operated for just 2 years.

AN INCREASING COST OF CAPITAL

The cost of capital may increase as the capital budget increases—this is called an *increasing marginal cost of capital.* As we discussed in Chapter 9, flotation costs associated with issuing new equity can be quite high. This means that the cost of capital will increase once a company has invested all of its internally generated cash and must sell new common stock. In addition, once a firm has used up its normal credit lines and must seek additional debt capital, it may encounter an increase in its cost of debt. This means that a project might have a positive NPV if it is part of a $10 million capital budget, but the same project might have a negative NPV if it is part of a $20 million capital budget because the cost of capital might increase.

Fortunately, these problems rarely occur for most firms, especially those that are stable and well established. When a rising cost of capital is encountered, we would proceed as indicated below. You can look at Figure 10-12 as you read through our points.

- Find the IRR (or MIRR) on all potential projects, arrange them in rank order (along with their initial costs), and then plot them on a graph with the IRR on the vertical axis and the cumulative costs on the horizontal axis. The firm's data are shown in Figure 10-12, and the IRRs are plotted in the graph. The line is called the Investment Opportunity Schedule (IOS), and it shows the marginal return on capital.
- Next, determine how much capital can be raised before it is necessary to issue new common stock or go to higher-cost sources of debt, and identify the amounts of higher-cost capital. Use this information to calculate the WACC that corresponds to the different amounts of capital raised. In this example, the firm can raise $300 before the WACC rises, but the WACC increases as additional capital is raised. The

FIGURE 10-12

IOS and MCC Schedules

	A	B	C	D	E	F
517	**Investment Opportunity Schedule (IOS)**			**Marginal Cost of Capital (MCC)**		
518			**Highest to**	**Cumulative**	**Lowest to**	
519	**Projects**	**Cost**	**Lowest IRR**	**Cost**	**Highest WACC**	
520	A	$100	14.0%	$100		9.0%
521	B	$100	13.0%	$200		9.0%
522	C	$100	11.5%	$300		9.0%
523	D	$100	10.0%	$400		10.0%
524	E	$50	9.5%	$450		11.0%
525	F	$50	9.0%	$500		12.0%
526	G	$100	8.5%	$600		15.0%
527						
528	**MCC and IOS**		**MCC and IOS Schedules**			

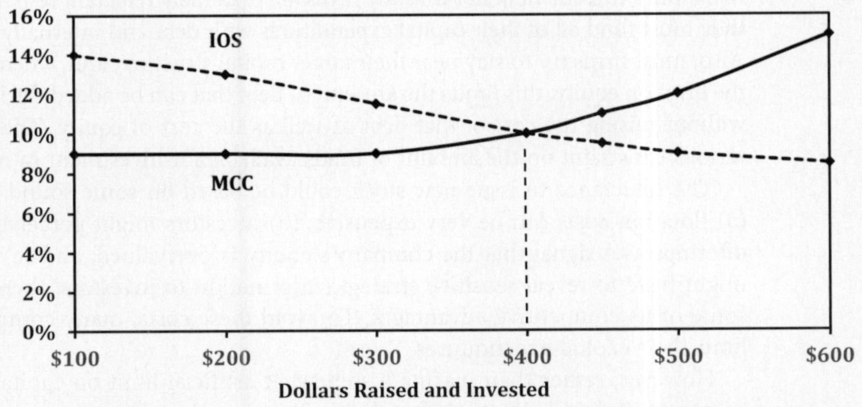

Note: Use WACC = 10% as the base rate for finding base risk-adjusted project WACCs.

resource

*See **Ch10 Tool Kit.xls** on the textbook's Web site.*

increasing WACC represents the marginal cost of capital, and its graph is called the Marginal Cost of Capital (MCC) schedule.

- The intersection of the IOS and MCC schedules indicates the amount of capital the firm should raise and invest, and it is analogous to the familiar marginal cost versus marginal revenue schedule discussed in introductory economics courses. In our example, the firm should have a capital budget of $400; if it uses a WACC of 10% then it will accept projects A, B, C, and D, which have a cumulative cost of $400. The 10% WACC should be used for average-risk projects, but it should be scaled up or down for more or less risky projects as discussed in Chapter 9.

Our example illustrates the case of a firm that cannot raise all the money it needs at a constant WACC. Firms should not try to be too precise with this process—the data are not good enough for precision—but they should be aware of the concept and get at least a rough idea of how raising additional capital will affect the WACC.

CAPITAL RATIONING

Armbrister Pyrotechnics, a manufacturer of fireworks and lasers for light shows, has identified 40 potential independent projects, of which 15 have a positive NPV based on the firm's 12% cost of capital. The total investment required to implement these 15 projects would be $75 million and so, according to finance theory, the optimal capital budget is $75 million. Thus, Armbrister should accept the 15 projects with positive NPVs and invest $75 million. However, Armbrister's management has imposed a limit of $50 million for capital expenditures during the upcoming year. Because of this restriction, the company must forgo a number of value-adding projects. This is an example of **capital rationing**, defined as a situation in which a firm limits its capital expenditures to an amount less than would be required to fund the optimal capital budget. Despite being at odds with finance theory, this practice is quite common.

Why would any company forgo value-adding projects? Here are some potential explanations, along with some suggestions for better ways to handle these situations.

1. *Reluctance to issue new stock.* Many firms are extremely reluctant to issue new stock, so they must fund all of their capital expenditures with debt and internally generated cash. Also, most firms try to stay near their target capital structure, and, when combined with the limit on equity, this limits the amount of debt that can be added during any one year without raising the cost of that debt as well as the cost of equity. The result can be a serious constraint on the amount of funds available for investment in new projects.

   The reluctance to issue new stock could be based on some sound reasons: (a) flotation costs can be very expensive; (b) investors might perceive new stock offerings as a signal that the company's equity is overvalued; and (c) the company might have to reveal sensitive strategic information to investors, thereby reducing some of its competitive advantages. To avoid these costs, many companies simply limit their capital expenditures.

   However, rather than placing a somewhat artificial limit on capital expenditures, companies might be better off explicitly incorporating the costs of raising external capital into their costs of capital along the lines shown in Figure 10-12. If there still are positive-NPV projects even with the higher cost of capital, then the company should go ahead and raise external equity and accept the projects.

2. *Constraints on nonmonetary resources.* Sometimes a firm simply doesn't have the necessary managerial, marketing, or engineering talent to immediately accept all positive-NPV projects. In other words, the potential projects may be independent from a demand standpoint but not from an internal standpoint, because accepting them all would raise the firm's costs. To avoid potential problems due to spreading existing talent too thin, many firms simply limit the capital budget to a size that can be accommodated by their current personnel.

   A better solution might be to employ a technique called **linear programming**. Each potential project has an expected NPV, and each potential project requires a certain level of support by different types of employees. A linear program can identify the set of projects that maximizes NPV *subject to the constraint* that the total amount of support required for these projects does not exceed the available resources.

3. *Controlling estimation bias.* Many managers become overly optimistic when estimating the cash flows for a project. Some firms try to control this estimation bias by requiring managers to use an unrealistically high cost of capital. Others try to control the bias by limiting the size of the capital budget. Neither solution is generally effective, because managers quickly learn the rules of the game and then increase their own estimates of project cash flows, which might have been biased upward to begin with.

A better solution is to implement a post-audit program and to link the accuracy of forecasts to the compensation of the managers who initiated the projects.

SELF-TEST

Briefly describe the replacement chain (common life) approach and differentiate it from the Equivalent Annual Annuity (EAA) approach.

Differentiate between a project's physical life and its economic life.

What factors can lead to an increasing marginal cost of capital? How might this affect capital budgeting?

What is capital rationing?

What are three explanations for capital rationing? How might firms otherwise handle these situations?

SUMMARY

This chapter has described six techniques used in capital budgeting analysis: NPV, IRR, MIRR, PI, payback, and discounted payback. Each approach provides a different piece of information, so in this age of computers, managers often look at all of them when evaluating projects. However, NPV is the best single measure, and almost all firms now use NPV. The key concepts covered in this chapter are listed below.

- **Capital budgeting** is the process of analyzing potential projects. Capital budgeting decisions are probably the most important ones that managers must make.
- The **net present value (NPV) method** discounts all cash flows at the project's cost of capital and then sums those cash flows. The project should be accepted if the NPV is positive because such a project increases shareholders' value.
- The **internal rate of return (IRR)** is defined as the discount rate that forces a project's NPV to equal zero. The project should be accepted if the IRR is greater than the cost of capital.
- The NPV and IRR methods make the same accept–reject decisions for **independent projects**, but if projects are **mutually exclusive** then ranking conflicts can arise. In such cases, the NPV method should generally be relied upon.
- It is possible for a project to have more than one IRR if the project's cash flows change signs more than once.
- Unlike the IRR, a project never has more than one **modified IRR (MIRR)**. MIRR requires finding the **terminal value (TV)** of the cash inflows, compounding them at the firm's cost of capital, and then determining the discount rate that forces the present value of the TV to equal the present value of the outflows.
- The **profitability index (PI)** is calculated by dividing the present value of cash inflows by the initial cost, so it measures relative profitability—that is, the amount of the present value per dollar of investment.
- The regular **payback period** is defined as the number of years required to recover a project's cost. The regular payback method has three flaws: It ignores cash flows beyond the payback period, it does not consider the time value of money, and it doesn't give a precise acceptance rule. The payback method does, however, provide an indication of a project's risk and liquidity, because it shows how long the invested capital will be tied up.
- The **discounted payback** is similar to the regular payback except that it discounts cash flows at the project's cost of capital. It considers the time value of money, but it still ignores cash flows beyond the payback period.

- The chapter's *Tool Kit Excel* model and *Web Extension 10A* describe another, but seldom-used, evaluation method—the **accounting rate of return**.
- If mutually exclusive projects have **unequal lives**, it may be necessary to adjust the analysis to put the projects on an equal-life basis. This can be done using the **replacement chain (common life) approach** or the **equivalent annual annuity (EAA) approach**.
- A project's true value may be greater than the NPV based on its **physical life** if it can be **terminated** at the end of its **economic life**.
- Flotation costs and increased risk associated with unusually large expansion programs can cause the **marginal cost of capital** to increase as the size of the capital budget increases.
- **Capital rationing** occurs when management places a constraint on the size of the firm's capital budget during a particular period.

QUESTIONS

(10-1) Define each of the following terms:

    a. Capital budgeting; regular payback period; discounted payback period
    b. Independent projects; mutually exclusive projects
    c. DCF techniques; net present value (NPV) method; internal rate of return (IRR) method; profitability index (PI)
    d. Modified internal rate of return (MIRR) method
    e. NPV profile; crossover rate
    f. Nonnormal cash flow projects; normal cash flow projects; multiple IRRs
    g. Reinvestment rate assumption
    h. Replacement chain; economic life; capital rationing; equivalent annual annuity (EAA)

(10-2) What types of projects require the least detailed and the most detailed analysis in the capital budgeting process?

(10-3) Explain why the NPV of a relatively long-term project, defined as one for which a high percentage of its cash flows are expected in the distant future, is more sensitive to changes in the cost of capital than is the NPV of a short-term project.

(10-4) When two mutually exclusive projects are being compared, explain why the short-term project might be ranked higher under the NPV criterion if the cost of capital is high whereas the long-term project might be deemed better if the cost of capital is low. Would changes in the cost of capital ever cause a change in the IRR ranking of two such projects? Why or why not?

(10-5) Suppose a firm is considering two mutually exclusive projects. One has a life of 6 years and the other a life of 10 years. Would the failure to employ some type of replacement chain analysis bias an NPV analysis against one of the projects? Explain.

SELF-TEST PROBLEM   Solution Appears in Appendix A

(ST-1)
Project Analysis

You are a financial analyst for the Hittle Company. The director of capital budgeting has asked you to analyze two proposed capital investments, Projects X and Y. Each project has a cost of $10,000, and the cost of capital for each is 12%. The projects' expected net cash flows are as follows:

	Expected Net Cash Flows	
Year	Project X	Project Y
0	−$10,000	−$10,000
1	6,500	3,500
2	3,000	3,500
3	3,000	3,500
4	1,000	3,500

a. Calculate each project's payback period, net present value (NPV), internal rate of return (IRR), modified internal rate of return (MIRR), and profitability index (PI).
b. Which project or projects should be accepted if they are independent?
c. Which project should be accepted if they are mutually exclusive?
d. How might a change in the cost of capital produce a conflict between the NPV and IRR rankings of these two projects? Would this conflict exist if r were 5%? (*Hint:* Plot the NPV profiles.)
e. Why does the conflict exist?

PROBLEMS   Answers Appear in Appendix B

Easy Problems 1–7

(10-1)
NPV
A project has an initial cost of $40,000, expected net cash inflows of $9,000 per year for 7 years, and a cost of capital of 11%. What is the project's NPV? (*Hint:* Begin by constructing a time line.)

(10-2)
IRR
Refer to Problem 10-1. What is the project's IRR?

(10-3)
MIRR
Refer to Problem 10-1. What is the project's MIRR?

(10-4)
Profitability Index
Refer to Problem 10-1. What is the project's PI?

(10-5)
Payback
Refer to Problem 10-1. What is the project's payback period?

(10-6)
Discounted Payback
Refer to Problem 10-1. What is the project's discounted payback period?

(10-7)
NPV
Your division is considering two investment projects, each of which requires an up-front expenditure of $15 million. You estimate that the investments will produce the following net cash flows:

Year	Project A	Project B
1	$ 5,000,000	$20,000,000
2	10,000,000	10,000,000
3	20,000,000	6,000,000

a. What are the two projects' net present values, assuming the cost of capital is 5%? 10%? 15%?
b. What are the two projects' IRRs at these same costs of capital?

(10-8)
NPVs, IRRs, and
MIRRs for Indepen-
dent Projects

Edelman Engineering is considering including two pieces of equipment, a truck and an overhead pulley system, in this year's capital budget. The projects are independent. The cash outlay for the truck is $17,100 and that for the pulley system is $22,430. The firm's cost of capital is 14%. After-tax cash flows, including depreciation, are as follows:

Year	Truck	Pulley
1	$5,100	$7,500
2	5,100	7,500
3	5,100	7,500
4	5,100	7,500
5	5,100	7,500

Calculate the IRR, the NPV, and the MIRR for each project, and indicate the correct accept–reject decision for each.

(10-9)
NPVs and IRRs for
Mutually Exclusive
Projects

Davis Industries must choose between a gas-powered and an electric-powered forklift truck for moving materials in its factory. Because both forklifts perform the same function, the firm will choose only one. (They are mutually exclusive investments.) The electric-powered truck will cost more, but it will be less expensive to operate; it will cost $22,000, whereas the gas-powered truck will cost $17,500. The cost of capital that applies to both investments is 12%. The life for both types of truck is estimated to be 6 years, during which time the net cash flows for the electric-powered truck will be $6,290 per year and those for the gas-powered truck will be $5,000 per year. Annual net cash flows include depreciation expenses. Calculate the NPV and IRR for each type of truck, and decide which to recommend.

(10-10)
Capital Budgeting
Methods

Project S has a cost of $10,000 and is expected to produce benefits (cash flows) of $3,000 per year for 5 years. Project L costs $25,000 and is expected to produce cash flows of $7,400 per year for 5 years. Calculate the two projects' NPVs, IRRs, MIRRs, and PIs, assuming a cost of capital of 12%. Which project would be selected, assuming they are mutually exclusive, using each ranking method? Which should actually be selected?

(10-11)
MIRR and NPV

Your company is considering two mutually exclusive projects, X and Y, whose costs and cash flows are shown below:

Year	X	Y
0	–$5,000	–$5,000
1	1,000	4,500
2	1,500	1,500
3	2,000	1,000
4	4,000	500

The projects are equally risky, and their cost of capital is 12%. You must make a recommendation, and you must base it on the modified IRR (MIRR). Which project has the higher MIRR?

(10-12)
NPV and IRR Analysis

After discovering a new gold vein in the Colorado mountains, CTC Mining Corporation must decide whether to go ahead and develop the deposit. The most cost-effective method of mining gold is sulfuric acid extraction, a process that could result in environmental damage.

Before proceeding with the extraction, CTC must spend $900,000 for new mining equipment and pay $165,000 for its installation. The gold mined will net the firm an estimated $350,000 each year for the 5-year life of the vein. CTC's cost of capital is 14%. For the purposes of this problem, assume that the cash inflows occur at the end of the year.

a. What are the project's NPV and IRR?
b. Should this project be undertaken if environmental impacts were not a consideration?
c. How should environmental effects be considered when evaluating this, or any other, project? How might these concepts affect the decision in part b?

(10-13)
NPV and IRR Analysis

Cummings Products is considering two mutually exclusive investments whose expected net cash flows are as follows:

	EXPECTED NET CASH FLOWS	
Year	Project A	Project B
0	−$400	−$650
1	−528	210
2	−219	210
3	−150	210
4	1,100	210
5	820	210
6	990	210
7	−325	210

a. Construct NPV profiles for Projects A and B.
b. What is each project's IRR?
c. If each project's cost of capital were 10%, which project, if either, should be selected? If the cost of capital were 17%, what would be the proper choice?
d. What is each project's MIRR at the cost of capital of 10%? At 17%? (*Hint:* Consider Period 7 as the end of Project B's life.)
e. What is the crossover rate, and what is its significance?

(10-14)
Timing Differences

The Ewert Exploration Company is considering two mutually exclusive plans for extracting oil on property for which it has mineral rights. Both plans call for the expenditure of $10 million to drill development wells. Under Plan A, all the oil will be extracted in 1 year, producing a cash flow at t = 1 of $12 million; under Plan B, cash flows will be $1.75 million per year for 20 years.

a. What are the annual incremental cash flows that will be available to Ewert Exploration if it undertakes Plan B rather than Plan A? (*Hint:* Subtract Plan A's flows from B's.)
b. If the company accepts Plan A and then invests the extra cash generated at the end of Year 1, what rate of return (reinvestment rate) would cause the cash flows from reinvestment to equal the cash flows from Plan B?
c. Suppose a firm's cost of capital is 10%. Is it logical to assume that the firm would take on all available independent projects (of average risk) with returns greater than 10%? Further, if all available projects with returns greater than 10% have been taken, would this mean that cash flows from past investments would have an opportunity cost of only 10%, because all the firm could do with these cash flows would be to replace money that has a cost of 10%? Finally, does this imply that the cost of capital is the correct rate to assume for the reinvestment of a project's cash flows?
d. Construct NPV profiles for Plans A and B, identify each project's IRR, and indicate the crossover rate.

(10-15)
Scale Differences

The Pinkerton Publishing Company is considering two mutually exclusive expansion plans. Plan A calls for the expenditure of $50 million on a large-scale, integrated plant that will provide an expected cash flow stream of $8 million per year for 20 years. Plan B calls for the expenditure of $15 million to build a somewhat less efficient, more labor-intensive plant that has an expected cash flow stream of $3.4 million per year for 20 years. The firm's cost of capital is 10%.

a. Calculate each project's NPV and IRR.
b. Set up a Project Δ by showing the cash flows that will exist if the firm goes with the large plant rather than the smaller plant. What are the NPV and the IRR for this Project Δ?
c. Graph the NPV profiles for Plan A, Plan B, and Project Δ.

(10-16)
Unequal Lives

Shao Airlines is considering the purchase of two alternative planes. Plane A has an expected life of 5 years, will cost $100 million, and will produce net cash flows of $30 million per year. Plane B has a life of 10 years, will cost $132 million, and will produce net cash flows of $25 million per year. Shao plans to serve the route for only 10 years. Inflation in operating costs, airplane costs, and fares is expected to be zero, and the company's cost of capital is 12%. By how much would the value of the company increase if it accepted the better project (plane)? What is the equivalent annual annuity for each plane?

(10-17)
Unequal Lives

The Perez Company has the opportunity to invest in one of two mutually exclusive machines that will produce a product it will need for the foreseeable future. Machine A costs $10 million but realizes after-tax inflows of $4 million per year for 4 years. After 4 years, the machine must be replaced. Machine B costs $15 million and realizes after-tax inflows of $3.5 million per year for 8 years, after which it must be replaced. Assume that machine prices are not expected to rise because inflation will be offset by cheaper components used in the machines. The cost of capital is 10%. By how much would the value of the company increase if it accepted the better machine? What is the equivalent annual annuity for each machine?

(10-18)
Unequal Lives

Filkins Fabric Company is considering the replacement of its old, fully depreciated knitting machine. Two new models are available: Machine 190-3, which has a cost of $190,000, a 3-year expected life, and after-tax cash flows (labor savings and depreciation) of $87,000 per year; and Machine 360-6, which has a cost of $360,000, a 6-year life, and after-tax cash flows of $98,300 per year. Knitting machine prices are not expected to rise, because inflation will be offset by cheaper components (microprocessors) used in the machines. Assume that Filkins's cost of capital is 14%. Should the firm replace its old knitting machine? If so, which new machine should it use? By how much would the value of the company increase if it accepted the better machine? What is the equivalent annual annuity for each machine?

Challenging
Problems 19–22

(10-19)
Multiple Rates of
Return

The Ulmer Uranium Company is deciding whether or not to open a strip mine whose net cost is $4.4 million. Net cash inflows are expected to be $27.7 million, all coming at the end of Year 1. The land must be returned to its natural state at a cost of $25 million, payable at the end of Year 2.

a. Plot the project's NPV profile.
b. Should the project be accepted if r = 8%? If r = 14%? Explain your reasoning.
c. Can you think of some other capital budgeting situations in which negative cash flows during or at the end of the project's life might lead to multiple IRRs?
d. What is the project's MIRR at r = 8%? At r = 14%? Does the MIRR method lead to the same accept–reject decision as the NPV method?

(10-20)
Present Value of
Costs

The Aubey Coffee Company is evaluating the within-plant distribution system for its new roasting, grinding, and packing plant. The two alternatives are (1) a conveyor system with a high initial cost but low annual operating costs, and (2) several forklift trucks, which cost less but have considerably higher operating costs. The decision to construct the plant has already been made, and the choice here will have no effect on the overall revenues of the project. The cost of capital for the plant is 8%, and the projects' expected net costs are listed in the following table:

Year	Expected Net Cost	
	Conveyor	Forklift
0	-$500,000	-$200,000
1	-120,000	-160,000
2	-120,000	-160,000
3	-120,000	-160,000
4	-120,000	-160,000
5	-20,000	-160,000

a. What is the IRR of each alternative?
b. What is the present value of the costs of each alternative? Which method should be chosen?

(10-21)
Payback, NPV, and
MIRR

Your division is considering two investment projects, each of which requires an up-front expenditure of $25 million. You estimate that the cost of capital is 10% and that the investments will produce the following after-tax cash flows (in millions of dollars):

Year	Project A	Project B
1	5	20
2	10	10
3	15	8
4	20	6

a. What is the regular payback period for each of the projects?
b. What is the discounted payback period for each of the projects?
c. If the two projects are independent and the cost of capital is 10%, which project or projects should the firm undertake?
d. If the two projects are mutually exclusive and the cost of capital is 5%, which project should the firm undertake?
e. If the two projects are mutually exclusive and the cost of capital is 15%, which project should the firm undertake?
f. What is the crossover rate?
g. If the cost of capital is 10%, what is the modified IRR (MIRR) of each project?

(10-22)
Economic Life

The Scampini Supplies Company recently purchased a new delivery truck. The new truck cost $22,500, and it is expected to generate net after-tax operating cash flows, including depreciation, of $6,250 per year. The truck has a 5-year expected life. The expected salvage values after tax adjustments for the truck are given below. The company's cost of capital is 10%.

Year	Annual Operating Cash Flow	Salvage Value
0	−$22,500	$22,500
1	6,250	17,500
2	6,250	14,000
3	6,250	11,000
4	6,250	5,000
5	6,250	0

a. Should the firm operate the truck until the end of its 5-year physical life? If not, then what is its optimal economic life?

b. Would the introduction of salvage values, in addition to operating cash flows, ever *reduce* the expected NPV and/or IRR of a project?

SPREADSHEET PROBLEM

(10-23)

Build a Model: Capital Budgeting Tools

resource

Start with the partial model in the file *Ch10 P23 Build a Model.xls* on the textbook's Web site. Gardial Fisheries is considering two mutually exclusive investments. The projects' expected net cash flows are as follows:

	Expected Net Cash Flows	
Year	Project A	Project B
0	−$375	−$575
1	−300	190
2	−200	190
3	−100	190
4	600	190
5	600	190
6	926	190
7	−200	0

a. If each project's cost of capital is 12%, which project should be selected? If the cost of capital is 18%, what project is the proper choice?

b. Construct NPV profiles for Projects A and B.

c. What is each project's IRR?

d. What is the crossover rate, and what is its significance?

e. What is each project's MIRR at a cost of capital of 12%? At r = 18%? (*Hint:* Consider Period 7 as the end of Project B's life.)

f. What is the regular payback period for these two projects?

g. At a cost of capital of 12%, what is the discounted payback period for these two projects?

h. What is the profitability index for each project if the cost of capital is 12%?

MINI CASE

You have just graduated from the MBA program of a large university, and one of your favorite courses was "Today's Entrepreneurs." In fact, you enjoyed it so much you have decided you want to "be your own boss." While you were in the master's program, your grandfather died and left you $1 million to do with as you please. You are not an inventor, and you do not have a trade skill that you can market; however, you have decided that you would like to purchase at least one established franchise in the fast-foods area, maybe two (if profitable). The problem is that you have never been one to stay with any project for too long, so you figure that your time frame is 3 years. After 3 years you will go on to something else.

You have narrowed your selection down to two choices: (1) Franchise L, Lisa's Soups, Salads, & Stuff, and (2) Franchise S, Sam's Fabulous Fried Chicken. The net cash flows shown below include the price you would receive for selling the franchise in Year 3 and the forecast of how each franchise will do over the 3-year period. Franchise L's cash flows will start off slowly but will increase rather quickly as people become more health-conscious, while Franchise S's cash flows will start off high but will trail off as other chicken competitors enter the marketplace and as people become more health-conscious and avoid fried foods. Franchise L serves breakfast and lunch whereas Franchise S serves only dinner, so it is possible for you to invest in both franchises. You see these franchises as perfect complements to one another: You could attract both the lunch and dinner crowds and the health-conscious and not-so-health-conscious crowds without the franchises directly competing against one another.

Here are the net cash flows (in thousands of dollars):

	Expected Net Cash Flows	
Year	Franchise L	Franchise S
0	−$100	−$100
1	10	70
2	60	50
3	80	20

Depreciation, salvage values, net working capital requirements, and tax effects are all included in these cash flows.

You also have made subjective risk assessments of each franchise and concluded that both franchises have risk characteristics that require a return of 10%. You must now determine whether one or both of the franchises should be accepted.

a. What is capital budgeting?
b. What is the difference between independent and mutually exclusive projects?
c. (1) Define the term *net present value (NPV)*. What is each franchise's NPV?
   (2) What is the rationale behind the NPV method? According to NPV, which franchise or franchises should be accepted if they are independent? Mutually exclusive?
   (3) Would the NPVs change if the cost of capital changed?
d. (1) Define the term *internal rate of return (IRR)*. What is each franchise's IRR?
   (2) How is the IRR on a project related to the YTM on a bond?
   (3) What is the logic behind the IRR method? According to IRR, which franchises should be accepted if they are independent? Mutually exclusive?
   (4) Would the franchises' IRRs change if the cost of capital changed?
e. (1) Draw NPV profiles for Franchises L and S. At what discount rate do the profiles cross?
   (2) Look at your NPV profile graph without referring to the actual NPVs and IRRs. Which franchise or franchises should be accepted if they are independent? Mutually exclusive? Explain. Are your answers correct at any cost of capital less than 23.6%?

f. What is the underlying cause of ranking conflicts between NPV and IRR?

g. Define the term *modified IRR (MIRR)*. Find the MIRRs for Franchises L and S.

h. What does the profitability index (PI) measure? What are the PIs of Franchises S and L?

i. (1) What is the payback period? Find the paybacks for Franchises L and S.

   (2) What is the rationale for the payback method? According to the payback criterion, which franchise or franchises should be accepted if the firm's maximum acceptable payback is 2 years and if Franchises L and S are independent? If they are mutually exclusive?

   (3) What is the difference between the regular and discounted payback periods?

   (4) What is the main disadvantage of discounted payback? Is the payback method of any real usefulness in capital budgeting decisions?

j. As a separate project (Project P), you are considering sponsorship of a pavilion at the upcoming World's Fair. The pavilion would cost $800,000, and it is expected to result in $5 million of incremental cash inflows during its single year of operation. However, it would then take another year, and $5 million of costs, to demolish the site and return it to its original condition. Thus, Project P's expected net cash flows look like this (in millions of dollars):

Year	Net Cash Flows
0	-$0.8
1	5.0
2	-5.0

The project is estimated to be of average risk, so its cost of capital is 10%.

   (1) What are normal and nonnormal cash flows?

   (2) What is Project P's NPV? What is its IRR? Its MIRR?

   (3) Draw Project P's NPV profile. Does Project P have normal or nonnormal cash flows? Should this project be accepted?

k. In an unrelated analysis, you have the opportunity to choose between the following two mutually exclusive projects, Project T (which lasts for two years) and Project F (which lasts for four years):

	Expected Net Cash Flows	
Year	Project T	Project F
0	-$100,000	-$100,000
1	60,000	33,500
2	60,000	33,500
3	___	33,500
4	___	33,500

The projects provide a necessary service, so whichever one is selected is expected to be repeated into the foreseeable future. Both projects have a 10% cost of capital.

   (1) What is each project's initial NPV without replication?

   (2) What is each project's equivalent annual annuity?

   (3) Apply the replacement chain approach to determine the projects' extended NPVs. Which project should be chosen?

   (4) Assume that the cost to replicate Project T in 2 years will increase to $105,000 due to inflation. How should the analysis be handled now, and which project should be chosen?

l. You are also considering another project that has a physical life of 3 years; that is, the machinery will be totally worn out after 3 years. However, if the project were terminated prior to the end of 3 years, the machinery would have a positive salvage value. Here are the project's estimated cash flows:

Year	Initial Investment and Operating Cash Flows	End-of-Year Net Salvage Value
0	−$5,000	$5,000
1	2,100	3,100
2	2,000	2,000
3	1,750	0

Using the 10% cost of capital, what is the project's NPV if it is operated for the full 3 years? Would the NPV change if the company planned to terminate the project at the end of Year 2? At the end of Year 1? What is the project's optimal (economic) life?

SELECTED ADDITIONAL CASES

The following cases from CengageCompose cover many of the concepts discussed in this chapter and are available at *compose.cengage.com*.

Klein-Brigham Series:
Case 11, "Chicago Valve Company."
Brigham-Buzzard Series:

Case 6, "Powerline Network Corporation (Basics of Capital Budgeting)."

Adalberto Rios Szalay/Sexto Sol/Getty Images

CHAPTER **11**

Cash Flow Estimation and Risk Analysis

Procter & Gamble, Unilever, and the Thales Group are among the many companies that understand the importance of cash flow estimation and risk analysis. For example, P&G conducts risk analysis on a wide variety of capital budgeting projects, from routine cost savings proposals at domestic facilities to cross-border facility location choices. P&G's Associate Director for Investment Analysis, Bob Hunt, says that risk analysis, especially the use of decision trees, "has been very useful in helping us break complex projects down into individual decision options, helping us understand the uncertainties, and ultimately helping us make superior decisions."

Unilever created its Decision Making Under Uncertainty (DMUU) approach to avoid overlooking risk during its project selection process. Unilever applies DMUU to conduct risk analysis for many types of projects, but especially when it must choose among multiple proposals.

Project evaluation is always difficult, but it is even more so when rapidly evolving technology is involved. For firms bidding for government and business contracts, the bidding process itself ramps up the already difficult task of project evaluation. The Thales Group competes in this market by providing communication systems for the defense and aerospace industries. Not only does Thales use risk analysis to better identify the expected levels and risks of project cash flows, but it also uses risk analysis to better understand and manage the risks associated with submitting bids for projects.

Keep these companies in mind as you read the chapter.

Source: Palisade Corporation is a leading developer of software for risk evaluation and decision analysis. For examples of companies using risk analysis, see the case analyses at **www.palisade.com/cases**.

Project Valuation, Cash Flows, and Risk Analysis

© Rob Webb/Getty Images

When we estimate a project's cash flows (CF) and then discount them at the project's risk-adjusted cost of capital, r, the result is the project's NPV, which tells us how much the project increases the firm's value. This chapter focuses on how to estimate the size and risk of a project's cash flows.

Note too that project cash flows, once a project has been accepted and placed in operation, are added to the firm's free cash flows from other sources. Therefore, projects' cash flows essentially determine the firm's free cash flows as discussed in Chapter 2 and thus form the basis for the firm's market value and stock price.

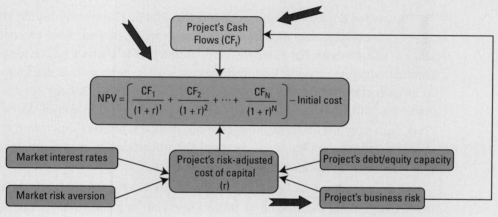

$$NPV = \left[\frac{CF_1}{(1+r)^1} + \frac{CF_2}{(1+r)^2} + \cdots + \frac{CF_N}{(1+r)^N} \right] - \text{Initial cost}$$

© Cengage Learning 2014

resource

The textbook's Web site contains an Excel file that will guide you through the chapter's calculations. The file for this chapter is **Ch11 Tool Kit.xls**, and we encourage you to open the file and follow along as you read the chapter.

Chapter 10 assumed that a project's cash flows had already been estimated. Now we cover cash flow estimation and identify the issues a manager faces in producing relevant and realistic cash flow estimates. In addition, cash flow estimates are just that: estimates! It is crucial for a manager to incorporate uncertainty into project analysis if a company is to make informed decisions regarding project selection. We begin with a discussion of procedures for estimating relevant and realistic cash flows.

11-1 Identifying Relevant Cash Flows

The most important—and difficult—step in capital budgeting is estimating a proposal's relevant **project cash flows**, which are the differences between the cash flows the firm will have if it implements the project versus the cash flows it will have if it rejects the project. These are called **incremental cash flows**:

$$\text{Incremental cash flows} = \frac{\text{Company's cash flows}}{\textit{with} \text{ the project}} - \frac{\text{Company's cash flows}}{\textit{without} \text{ the project}}$$

Estimating incremental cash flows might sound easy, but there are many potential pitfalls. In this section, we identify the key concepts that will help you avoid these pitfalls and then apply the concepts to an actual project to illustrate their application to cash flow estimation.

11-1a Cash Flow versus Accounting Income

We saw in Chapter 2 that free cash flow differs from accounting income: Free cash flow is cash flow that is available for distribution to investors, making free cash flow the basis of a firm's value. It is common in the practice of finance to speak of a firm's free cash flow and a project's cash flow (or net cash flow), but these are based on the same concepts. In fact, a project's cash flow is identical to the project's free cash flow, and a firm's total net cash flow from all projects is equal to the firm's free cash flow. We will follow the typical convention and refer to a project's free cash flow simply as project cash flow, but keep in mind that the two concepts are identical.[1]

Because net income is not equal to the cash flow available for distribution to investors, in the last chapter we discounted *net cash flows*, not accounting income, to find projects' NPVs. *For capital budgeting purposes it is the project's net cash flow, not its accounting income, which is relevant.* Therefore, when analyzing a proposed capital budgeting project, disregard the project's net income and focus exclusively on its net cash flow. Be especially alert to the following differences between cash flow and accounting income.

THE CASH FLOW EFFECT OF ASSET PURCHASES AND DEPRECIATION

Most projects require assets, and asset purchases represent *negative* cash flows. Even though the acquisition of assets results in a cash outflow, accountants do not show the purchase of fixed assets as a deduction from accounting income. Instead, they deduct a depreciation expense each year throughout the life of the asset. Depreciation shelters income from taxation, and this has an impact on cash flow, but depreciation itself is not a cash flow. Therefore, depreciation must be added back when estimating a project's operating cash flow.

Depreciation is the most common noncash charge, but there are many other noncash charges that might appear on a company's financial statements. Just as with depreciation, all other noncash charges should be added back when calculating a project's net cash flow.

CHANGES IN NET OPERATING WORKING CAPITAL

Normally, additional inventories are required to support a new operation, and expanded sales tie up additional funds in accounts receivable. However, payables and accruals increase as a result of the expansion, and this reduces the cash needed to finance inventories and receivables. The difference between the required increase in operating current assets and the increase in operating current liabilities is the change in net operating working capital. If this change is positive, as it generally is for expansion projects, then additional financing—beyond the cost of the fixed assets—will be needed.

Toward the end of a project's life, inventories will be used but not replaced, and receivables will be collected without corresponding replacements. As these changes occur the firm will receive cash inflows; as a result, the investment in net operating working capital will be returned by the end of the project's life.

---

[1]When the financial press refers to a firm's "net cash flow," it is almost always equal to the definition we provide in Chapter 2 (which simply adds back depreciation and any other noncash charges to net income). However, as we explained in Chapter 2, the net cash flow from operations (from the statement of cash flows) and the firm's free cash flow are much more useful measures of cash flow. When financial analysts within a company use the term "a project's net cash flow," they almost always calculate it as we do in this chapter, which is in essence the project's free cash flow. Thus, free cash flow means the same thing whether you calculate it for a firm or for a project. On the other hand, when the financial press talks about a firm's net cash flow or when an internal analyst talks about a project's net cash flow, those "net cash flows" are not the same.

INTEREST CHARGES ARE *NOT* INCLUDED IN PROJECT CASH FLOWS

Interest is a cash expense, so at first blush it would seem that interest on any debt used to finance a project should be deducted when we estimate the project's net cash flows. However, this is not correct. Recall from Chapter 10 that we discount a project's cash flows by its risk-adjusted cost of capital, which is a weighted average (WACC) of the costs of debt, preferred stock, and common equity, adjusted for the project's risk and debt capacity. This project cost of capital is the rate of return necessary to satisfy *all* of the firm's investors, including stockholders and debtholders. A common mistake made by many students and financial managers is to subtract interest payments when estimating a project's cash flows. This is a mistake because the cost of debt is already embedded in the cost of capital, so subtracting interest payments from the project's cash flows would amount to double-counting interest costs. Therefore, *you should not subtract interest expenses when finding a project's cash flows.*

11-1b Timing of Cash Flows: Yearly versus Other Periods

In theory, in capital budgeting analyses we should discount cash flows based on the exact moment when they occur. Therefore, one could argue that daily cash flows would be better than annual flows. However, it would be costly to estimate daily cash flows and laborious to analyze them. In general the analysis would be no better than one using annual flows because we simply can't make accurate forecasts of daily cash flows more than a couple of months into the future. Therefore, it is generally appropriate to assume that all cash flows occur at the end of the various years. For projects with highly predictable cash flows, such as constructing a building and then leasing it on a long-term basis (with monthly payments) to a financially sound tenant, we would analyze the project using monthly periods.

11-1c Expansion Projects and Replacement Projects

Two types of projects can be distinguished: (1) *expansion projects,* in which the firm makes an investment in, for example, a new Home Depot store in Seattle; and (2) *replacement projects*, in which the firm replaces existing assets, generally to reduce costs. In expansion projects, the cash expenditures on buildings, equipment, and required working capital are obviously incremental, as are the sales revenues and operating costs associated with the project. The incremental costs associated with replacement projects are not so obvious. For example, Home Depot might replace some of its delivery trucks to reduce fuel and maintenance expenses. Replacement analysis is complicated by the fact that most of the relevant cash flows are the cash flow differences between the existing project and the replacement project. For example, the fuel bill for a more efficient new truck might be $10,000 per year versus $15,000 for the old truck, and the $5,000 fuel savings would be an incremental cash flow associated with the replacement decision. We analyze an expansion and replacement decision later in the chapter.

11-1d Sunk Costs

A **sunk cost** is an outlay related to the project that was incurred in the past and that cannot be recovered in the future regardless of whether or not the project is accepted. Therefore, sunk costs are *not incremental costs* and thus are not relevant in a capital budgeting analysis.

To illustrate, suppose Home Depot spent $2 million to investigate sites for a potential new store in a given area. That $2 million is a sunk cost—the money is gone, and it won't come back regardless of whether or not a new store is built. Therefore, the $2 million should not be included in a capital budgeting decision. Improper treatment of sunk costs can lead to bad decisions. For example, suppose Home Depot completed the analysis for a new store and found that it must spend an additional (or incremental) $17 million to build and supply the store, on top of the $2 million already spent on the site study. Suppose the present value of future cash flows is $18 million. Should the project be accepted? If the sunk costs are mistakenly included, the NPV is −$2 million + (−$17 million) + $18 million = −$1 million and the project would be rejected. However, *that would be a bad decision*. The real issue is whether the *incremental* $17 million would result in enough *incremental* cash flow to produce a positive NPV. If the $2 million sunk cost were disregarded, as it should be, then the NPV on an incremental basis would be a *positive* $1 million.

11-1e Opportunity Costs Associated with Assets the Firm Already Owns

Another conceptual issue relates to **opportunity costs** related to assets the firm already owns. Continuing our example, suppose Home Depot (HD) owns land with a current market value of $2 million that can be used for the new store if it decides to build the store. If HD goes forward with the project, only another $15 million will be required, not the full $17 million, because it will not need to buy the required land. Does this mean that HD should use the $15 million incremental cost as the cost of the new store? The answer is definitely "no." If the new store is *not* built, then HD could sell the land and receive a cash flow of $2 million. This $2 million is an *opportunity cost*—it is cash that HD would not receive if the land is used for the new store. Therefore, the $2 million must be charged to the new project, and failing to do so would cause the new project's calculated NPV to be too high.

11-1f Externalities

Another conceptual issue relates to **externalities**, which are the effects of a project on other parts of the firm or on the environment. As explained in what follows, there are three types of externalities: negative within-firm externalities, positive within-firm externalities, and environmental externalities.

NEGATIVE WITHIN-FIRM EXTERNALITIES

If a retailer like Home Depot opens a new store that is close to its existing stores, then the new store might attract customers who would otherwise buy from the existing stores, reducing the old stores' cash flows. Therefore, the new store's incremental cash flow must be reduced by the amount of the cash flow lost by its other units. This type of externality is called **cannibalization**, because the new business eats into the company's existing business. Many businesses are subject to cannibalization. For example, each new iPod model cannibalizes existing models. Those lost cash flows should be considered, and that means charging them as a cost when analyzing new products.

Dealing properly with negative externalities requires careful thinking. If Apple decided not to come out with a new model of iPod because of cannibalization, another company might come out with a similar new model, causing Apple to lose sales on existing models.

Apple must examine the total situation, and this is definitely more than a simple, mechanical analysis. Experience and knowledge of the industry is required to make good decisions in most cases.

One of the best examples of a company getting into trouble as a result of not dealing correctly with cannibalization was IBM's response to the development of the first personal computers in the 1970s. IBM's mainframes dominated the computer industry, and they generated huge profits. IBM used its technology to enter the PC market, and initially it was the leading PC company. However, its top managers decided to deemphasize the PC division because they were afraid it would hurt the more profitable mainframe business. That decision opened the door for Apple, Dell, Hewlett Packard, Sony, and Chinese competitors to take PC business away from IBM. As a result, IBM went from being the most profitable firm in the world to one whose very survival was threatened. IBM's experience highlights that it is just as important to understand the industry and the long-run consequences of a given decision as it is to understand the theory of finance. Good judgment is an essential element for good financial decisions.

POSITIVE WITHIN-FIRM EXTERNALITIES

As we noted earlier, cannibalization occurs when a new product competes with an old one. However, a new project can also be *complementary* to an old one, in which case cash flows in the old operation will be *increased* when the new one is introduced. For example, Apple's iPod was a profitable product, but when Apple considered an investment in its music store it realized that the store would boost sales of iPods. So, even if an analysis of the proposed music store indicated a negative NPV, the analysis would not be complete unless the incremental cash flows that would occur in the iPod division were credited to the music store. Consideration of positive externalities often changes a project's NPV from negative to positive.

ENVIRONMENTAL EXTERNALITIES

The most common type of negative externality is a project's impact on the environment. Government rules and regulations constrain what companies can do, but firms have some flexibility in dealing with environmental issues. For example, suppose a manufacturer is studying a proposed new plant. The company could meet current environmental regulations at a cost of $1 million, but the plant would still emit fumes that would cause some bad will in its neighborhood. Those ill feelings would not show up in the cash flow analysis, but they should be considered. Perhaps a relatively small additional expenditure would reduce the emissions substantially, make the plant look good relative to other plants in the area, and provide goodwill that in the future would help the firm's sales and its negotiations with governmental agencies.

Of course, all firms' profits ultimately depend on the Earth remaining healthy, so companies have some incentive to do things that protect the environment even though those actions are not currently required. However, if one firm decides to take actions that are good for the environment but quite costly, then it must either raise its prices or suffer a decline in earnings. If its competitors decide to get by with less costly but environmentally unfriendly processes, they can price their products lower and make more money. Of course, the more environmentally friendly companies can advertise their environmental efforts, and this might—or might not—offset their higher costs. All this illustrates why government regulations are often necessary. Finance, politics, and the environment are all interconnected.

SELF-TEST

Why should companies use a project's net cash flows rather than accounting income when determining a project's NPV?

Explain the following terms: incremental cash flow, sunk cost, opportunity cost, externality, cannibalization, and complementary project.

Provide an example of a "good" externality—that is, one that increases a project's true NPV over what it would be if just its own cash flows were considered.

11-2 Analysis of an Expansion Project

In Chapter 10, we worked with the cash flows associated with one of Guyton Products Company's expansion projects. Recall that Project L is the application of a radically new liquid nano-coating technology to a new type of solar water heater module, which will be manufactured under a 4-year license from a university. In this section we show how these cash flows are estimated (we only show estimates for Project L in the chapter, but we also show estimates GPC's other project from Chapter 10, Project S, in *Ch11 Tool Kit.xls*). It's not clear how well the water heater will work, how strong demand for it will be, how long it will be before the product becomes obsolete, or whether the license can be renewed after the initial 4 years. Still, the water heater has the potential for being profitable, though it could also fail miserably. GPC is a relatively large company and this is one of many projects, so a failure would not bankrupt the firm but would hurt profits and the stock's price.

11-2a Base Case Inputs and Key Results

resource

See Ch11 Tool Kit.xls on the textbook's Web site.

We used *Excel* to do the analysis. We could have used a calculator and paper, but *Excel* is *much* easier when dealing with capital budgeting problems. You don't need to know *Excel* to understand our discussion, but if you plan to work in finance—or, really, in any business field—you must know how to use *Excel,* so we recommend that you open the *Excel Tool Kit* for this chapter and scroll through it as the textbook explains the analysis.

Figure 11-1 shows the Part 1 of the *Excel* model used in this analysis; see the first worksheet in *Ch11 Tool Kit.xls* named *1-Base-Case.* The base-case inputs are in the blue section. For example, the cost of required equipment to manufacture the water heaters is $7,750 and is shown in the blue input section. (All dollar values in Figure 11-1 and in our discussion here are reported in thousands, so the equipment actually costs $7,750,000.) The actual number-crunching takes place in Part 2 of the model, shown in Figure 11-2. Part 2 takes the inputs from the blue section of Figure 11-1 and generates the project's cash flows. Part 2 of the model also performs calculations of the project performance measures discussed in Chapter 10 and then reports those results in the orange section of Figure 11-1. This structure allows you (or your manager) to change and input and instantly see the impact on the reported performance measures.

We have saved these base-case inputs in *Ch11 Tool Kit.xls* with *Excel's* Scenario Manager. If you change some inputs but want to return to the original base-case inputs, you can select Data, What-If Analysis, Scenario Manager, pick the scenario named "Base-Case for Project L," and click Show. This will replace any changes with the original inputs. Scenario Manager is a very useful tool and we will have more to say about it later in this chapter.

FIGURE 11-1

Analysis of an Expansion Project: Inputs and Key Results (Thousands of Dollars)

	A	B	C	D	E	F	G	H	I
54	Part 1. Inputs and Key Results								
55									
56	Inputs				Base-Case		Key Results		
57	Equipment cost				$7,750		NPV		$1,048
58	Salvage value, equipment, Year 4				$639		IRR		13.79%
59	Opportunity cost				$0		MIRR		12.78%
60	Externalities (cannibalization)				$0		PI		1.10
61	Units sold, Year 1				10,000		Payback		3.39
62	Annual change in units sold, after Year 1				15%		Discounted payback		3.80
63	Sales price per unit, Year 1				$1.50				
64	Annual change in sales price, after Year 1				4%				
65	Variable cost per unit (VC), Year 1				$1.07				
66	Annual change in VC, after Year 1				3%				
67	Nonvariable cost (Non-VC), Year 1				$2,120				
68	Annual change in Non-VC, after Year 1				3%				
69	Project WACC				10%				
70	Tax rate				40%				
71	Working capital as % of next year's sales				15%				

11-2b Cash Flow Projections: Intermediate Calculations

Figure 11-2 shows Part 2 of the model. When setting up *Excel* models, we prefer to have more rows but shorter formulas. So instead of having very complicated formulas in the section for cash flow forecasts, we put intermediate calculations in a separate section. The blue section of Figure 11-2 shows these intermediate calculations for the GPC project, as we explain in the following sections.

resource

See Ch11 Tool Kit.xls on the textbook's Web site.

ANNUAL UNIT SALES, UNIT PRICES, UNIT COSTS, AND INFLATION

Rows 85–88 show annual unit sales, unit sale prices, unit variable costs, and nonvariable costs. These values are all projected to grow at the rates assumed in Part 1 of the model in Figure 11-1. If you ignore growth in prices and costs when estimating cash flows, you are likely to *underestimate* a project's value because the project's weighted average cost of capital (WACC) includes the impact of inflation. In other words, the estimated cash flows will be too low relative to the WACC, so the estimated net present value (NPV) also will be too low relative to the true NPV. To see that the WACC includes inflation, recall from Chapter 5 that the cost of debt includes an inflation premium. Also, the capital asset pricing model from Chapter 6 defines the cost of equity as the sum of the risk-free rate and a risk premium. Like the cost of debt, the risk-free rate also has an inflation premium. Therefore, if the WACC includes the impact of inflation, the estimated cash flows must also include inflation. It is theoretically possible to ignore inflation when estimating the cash flows but adjust the WACC so that it, too, doesn't incorporate inflation, but we have never seen this accomplished correctly in practice. Therefore, you should always include growth rates in prices and costs when estimating cash flows.

FIGURE 11-2

Analysis of an Expansion Project: Cash Flows and Performance Measures (Thousands of Dollars)

	A	B	C	D	E	F	G	H	I
83	Part 2. Cash Flows and Performance Measures								
84	**Intermediate Calculations**				0	1	2	3	4
85	Unit sales					10,000	11,500	13,225	15,209
86	Sales price per unit					$1.50	$1.56	$1.62	$1.69
87	Variable cost per unit (excl. depr.)					$1.07	$1.10	$1.14	$1.17
88	Nonvariable costs (excl. depr.)					$2,120	$2,184	$2,249	$2,317
89	Sales revenues = Units × Price/unit					$15,000	$17,940	$21,456	$25,662
90	$NOWC_t$ = 15%(Revenues$_{t+1}$)				$2,250	$2,691	$3,218	$3,849	$0
91	Basis for depreciation				$7,750				
92	Annual depreciation rate (MACRS)					33.33%	44.45%	14.81%	7.41%
93	Annual depreciation expense					$2,583	$3,445	$1,148	$574
94	Remaining undepreciated value					$5,167	$1,722	$574	$0
95	**Cash Flow Forecast**					Cash Flows at End of Year			
96					0	1	2	3	4
97	Sales revenues = Units × Price/unit					$15,000	$17,940	$21,456	$25,662
98	Variable costs = Units × Cost/unit					$10,700	$12,674	$15,013	$17,782
99	Nonvariable costs (excluding depr.)					$2,120	$2,184	$2,249	$2,317
100	Depreciation					$2,583	$3,445	$1,148	$574
101	Earnings before int. and taxes (EBIT)					−$403	−$363	$3,047	$4,988
102	Taxes on operating profit (40% rate)					−$161	−$145	$1,219	$1,995
103	Net operating profit after taxes					−$242	−$218	$1,828	$2,993
104	Add back depreciation					$2,583	$3,445	$1,148	$574
105	Equipment purchases				−$7,750				
106	Profit from salvage value								$639
107	Cash flow due to tax on salv. val.								−$256
108	Cash flow due to change in WC				−$2,250	−$441	−$527	−$631	$3,849
109	Opportunity cost, after taxes				$0	$0	$0	$0	S0
110	After-tax externalities					$0	$0	$0	S0
111	Project net cash flows: Time Line				−$10,000	$1,900	$2,700	$2,345	$7,800
112	**Project Evaluation Measures**								
113	NPV		$1,048	=NPV(E69,F111:I111)+E111					
114	IRR		13.79%	=IRR(E111:I111)					
115	MIRR		12.78%	=MIRR(E111:I111,E69,E69)					
116	Profitability index		1.10	=NPV(E69,F111:I111)/(-E111)					
117	Payback		3.39	=PERCENTRANK(E120:I120,0,6)*I119					
118	Disc. payback		3.80	=PERCENTRANK(E122:I122,0,6)*I119					
119	**Calculations for Payback**			Year:	0	1	2	3	4
120	Cumulative cash flows for payback				−$10,000	−$8,100	−$5,400	−$3,055	$4,745
121	Disc. cash flows for disc. payback				−$10,000	$1,727	$2,231	$1,762	$5,328
122	Cumulative discounted cash flows				−$10,000	−$8,273	−$6,041	−$4,279	$1,048

NET OPERATING WORKING CAPITAL (NOWC)

Virtually all projects require working capital, and this one is no exception. For example, raw materials must be purchased and replenished each year as they are used. In Part 1 (Figure 11-1) we assume that GPC must have an amount of net operating working capital on hand equal to 15% of the upcoming year's sales. For example, in Year 0, GPC must have 15%($15,000) = $2,250 in working capital on hand. As sales grow, so does the required working capital. Rows 89–90 show the annual sales revenues (the product of units sold and sales price) and the required working capital.

DEPRECIATION EXPENSE

Rows 91–94 report intermediate calculations related to depreciation, beginning with the depreciation basis, which is the cost of acquiring and installing a project. The basis for GPC's project is $7,750.[2] The depreciation expense for a year is the product of the basis and that year's depreciation rate. Depreciation rates depend on the type of property and its useful life. Even though GPC's project will operate for 4 years, it is classified as 3-year property for tax purposes. The depreciation rates in Row 92 are for 3-year property using the modified cost accelerated cost recovery system (MACRS); see Appendix 11A and the chapter's *Tool Kit* for more discussion of depreciation.[3] The remaining undepreciated value is equal to the original basis less the accumulated depreciation; this is called the book value of the asset and is used later in the model when calculating the tax on the salvage value.

resource
See **Ch11 Tool Kit.xls** on the textbook's Web site.

11-2c Cash Flow Projections: Estimating Net Operating Profit after Taxes (NOPAT)

The yellow section in the middle of Figure 11-2 shows the steps in calculating the project's net operating profit after taxes (NOPAT). Projected sales revenues are on Row 97. Annual variable unit costs are multiplied by the number of units sold to determine total variable costs, as shown on Row 98. Nonvariable costs are shown on Row 99, and depreciation expense is shown on Row 100. Subtracting variable costs, nonvariable costs, and depreciation from sales revenues results in operating profit, as shown on Row 101.

When discussing a company's income statement, operating profit often is called earnings before interest and taxes (EBIT). Remember, though, that we do not subtract interest when estimating a project's cash flows, because the project's WACC is the overall rate of return required by all the company's investors and not just shareholders. Therefore, the cash flows must also be the cash flows available to all investors and not just shareholders, so we do not subtract interest expense. We calculate taxes in Row 102 and subtract them to get the project's net operating profit after taxes (NOPAT) on Row 103. The project has negative earnings before interest and taxes in Years 1 and 2. When multiplied by the 40% tax rate, Row 102 shows negative taxes for Years 1 and 2. This negative tax is subtracted from EBIT and actually makes the after-tax operating profit larger than the pre-tax profit! For example, the Year 1 pre-tax profit is −$403 and the reported tax is −$161, leading to an after-tax profit of −$403 − (−$161) = −$242. In other words, it is as though the IRS is sending GPC a check for $161. How can this be correct?

Recall the basic concept underlying the relevant cash flows for project analysis—what are the company's cash flows with the project versus the company's cash flows without the project? Applying this concept, if GPC expects to have taxable income from other projects in excess of $403 in Year 1, then the project will shelter that income from $161 in taxes. Therefore, the project will generate $161 in cash flow for GPC in Year 1 due to the tax savings.[4]

---

[2]Regardless of whether accelerated or straight-line depreciation is used, the basis is not adjusted by the expected salvage value when calculating the depreciation expense that is used to determine taxable income. This is in contrast to the calculation of depreciation for purposes of financial reporting.

[3]MACRS assumes that property is placed in service in the middle of a year, so only one-half a year's depreciation is allowed in the first year. A final one-half year's depreciation is allowed in the fourth year.

[4]Even if GPC doesn't expect to have other taxable income in Year 1 but does have taxable income from the past two years, GPC can carryback the loss in Year 1 and receive a tax refund. If GPC doesn't have past taxable income, then we would report zero taxes for the project in Year 1 and carryforward the loss until GPC or the project does have taxable income.

11-2d Cash Flow Projections: Adjustments to NOPAT

Row 103 reports the project's NOPAT, but we must adjust NOPAT to determine the project's actual cash flows. In particular, we must account for depreciation, asset purchases and dispositions, changes in working capital, opportunity costs, externalities, and sunk costs.

ADJUSTMENTS TO DETERMINE CASH FLOWS: DEPRECIATION

The first step is to add back depreciation, which is a noncash expense. You might be wondering why we subtract depreciation on Row 100 only to add it back on Row 104, and the answer is due to depreciation's impact on taxes. If we had ignored the Year 1 depreciation of $2,583 when calculating NOPAT, the pre-tax income (EBIT) for Year 1 would have been $15,000 − $10,700 − $2,120 = $2,180 instead of −$403. Taxes would have been 40%($2,180) = $872 instead of −$161. This is a difference of $872 − (−$161) = $1,033. Cash flows should reflect the actual taxes, but we must add back the noncash depreciation expense to reflect the actual cash flow.[5]

ADJUSTMENTS TO DETERMINE CASH FLOWS: ASSET PURCHASES AND DISPOSITIONS

GPC purchased the asset at the beginning of the project for $7,750, which is a negative cash flow shown on Row 105. Had GPC purchased additional assets in other years, we would report those purchases, too.

GPC expects to salvage the investment at Year 4 for $639. In our example, GPC's project was fully depreciated by the end of the project, so the $639 salvage value is a taxable profit. At a 40% tax rate, GPC will owe 40%($639) = $256 in taxes, as shown on Row 107.

Suppose instead that GPC terminates operations before the equipment is fully depreciated. The after-tax salvage value depends on the price at which GPC can sell the equipment *and* on the book value of the equipment (i.e., the original basis less all previous depreciation charges). Suppose GPC terminates at Year 2, at which time the book value is $1,722, as shown on Row 94. We consider two cases, gains and losses. In the first case, the salvage value is $2,200 and so there is a reported gain of $2,200 − $1,722 = $478. This gain is taxed as ordinary income, so the tax is 40%($478) = $191. The after-tax cash flow is equal to the sales price less the tax: $2,200 − $191 = $2,009.

Now suppose the salvage value at Year 2 is only $500. In this case, there is a reported loss: $500 − $1,722 = −$1,222. This is treated as an ordinary expense, so its tax is 40% (−$1,222) = −$489. This "negative" tax acts as a credit if GPC has other taxable income, so the net after-tax cash flow is $500 − (−$489) = $989.

ADJUSTMENTS TO DETERMINE CASH FLOWS: WORKING CAPITAL

Row 90 shows the total amount of net operating working capital needed each year. Row 108 shows the incremental investment in working capital required each year. For example, at the start of the project, Cell E108 shows a cash flow of −$2,250 will be needed at the beginning of the project to support Year 1 sales. Row 90 shows working capital must increase from $2,250 to $2,691 to support Year 2 sales. Thus, GPC must invest $2,691 − $2,250 = $441 in working capital in Year 1, and this is shown as a negative number (because it is an investment) in Cell F108. Similar calculations are made for Years 2 and 3. At the end of Year 4, all of the

---

[5]Notice that the tax savings due to depreciation also may be calculated as the product of the tax rate and the depreciation expense: 40%($2,583) = $1,033.20. The numbers shown in the textbook are rounded, but the numbers used in the *Excel* model are not.

investments in working capital will be recovered. Inventories will be sold and not replaced, and all receivables will be collected by the end of Year 4. Total net working capital recovered at t = 4 is the sum of the initial investment at t = 0, $2,250, plus the additional investments during Years 1 through 3; the total is $3,849.

ADJUSTMENTS TO DETERMINE CASH FLOWS: SUNK COSTS, OPPORTUNITY COSTS, AND EXTERNALITIES

GPC's project doesn't have any sunk costs, opportunity costs, or externalities, but the following sections show how we would adjust the cash flows if GPC did have some of these issues.

Sunk Costs.   Suppose that last year GPC spent $1,500 on a marketing and feasibility study for the project. Should $1,500 be included in the project's cost? The answer is no. That money already has been spent and accepting or rejecting the project will not change that fact.

Opportunity Costs.   Now suppose the $7,750 equipment cost was based on the assumption that the project would use space in a building that GPC now owns but that the space could be leased to another company for $200 per year, after taxes, if the project is rejected. The $200 would be an *opportunity cost*, and it should be reflected in the cash flow calculations.

Externalities.   As noted earlier, the solar water heater project does not lead to any cannibalization effects. Suppose, however, that it would reduce the net after-tax cash flows of another GPC division by $50 per year and that no other firm could take on this project if GPC turns it down. In this case, we would use the cannibalization line at Row 110, deducting $50 each year. As a result, the project would have a lower NPV. On the other hand, if the project would cause additional inflows to some other GPC division because it was complementary to that other division's products (i.e., if a positive externality exists), then those after-tax inflows should be attributed to the water heater project and thus shown as a positive inflow on Row 110.

11-2e Evaluating Project Cash Flows

We sum Rows 103 to 110 to get the project's annual net cash flows, set up as a time line on Row 111. These cash flows are then used to calculate NPV, IRR, MIRR, PI, payback, and discounted payback, performance measures that are shown in the orange portion at the bottom of Figure 11-2.

PRELIMINARY EVALUATION OF THE BASE-CASE SCENARIO

Based on this analysis, the preliminary evaluation indicates that the project is acceptable. The NPV is $1,048, which is fairly large when compared to the initial investment of $10,000. Its IRR and MIRR are both greater than the 10% WACC, and the PI is larger than 1.0. The payback and discounted payback are almost as long as the project's life, which is somewhat concerning, and is something that needs to be explored by conducting a risk analysis of the project.

SCENARIO MANAGER

Excel's Scenario Manager is a very powerful and useful tool. We illustrate its use here as we examine two topics, the impact of forgetting to include inflation and the impact of accelerated depreciation versus straight-line depreciation. To use Scenario Manager in the worksheet named *1-Base-Case* in *Ch11 Tool Kit.xls,* Select Data, What-If Analysis, and Scenario Manager. There are five scenarios: (1) Base-Case for Project L but Forget Inflation, (2) Base-Case for Project L, (3) Project S, (4) MACRS Depreciation, and (5) Straight-Line Depreciation. The first three scenarios change the inputs in Rows 56–71. The last two scenarios change the depreciation rates in Row 92. This structure allows you to choose a set of inputs and then choose a depreciation method. Sometimes we include all the changing cells in each scenario, and sometimes we separate the scenarios into different groups as we did in this example.

The advantage of having all changing cells in each scenario is that you only have to select a single scenario to show all the desired inputs in the model. The disadvantage is that each scenario can get complicated by having many changing cells.

The advantage of having groups of scenarios is that you can focus on particular aspects of the analysis, such as the choice of depreciation methods. The disadvantage is that you must know which other scenarios are active in order to properly interpret your results.

For some models it makes sense to have only one group of scenarios in which each scenario has the same changing cells; for other models it makes sense to have different groups of scenarios.

The Impact of Inflation.   It is easy to overlook inflation, but it is important to include it. For example, had we forgotten to include inflation in the GPC example, the estimated NPV would have dropped from $1,048 to $225. You can see this by changing all the price and cost growth rates to zero and then looking at the NPV. An easy way to do this is with the Scenario Manager—just choose the scenario named "Base-Case for Project L but Forget Inflation." Forgetting to include inflation in a capital budgeting analysis typically causes the estimated NPV to be lower than the true NPV, which could cause a company to reject a project that it should have accepted. You can return to the original inputs by going back into Scenario Manager, selecting "Base-Case for Project L," and clicking on "Show."

Accelerated Depreciation versus Straight-Line Depreciation.   Congress permits firms to depreciate assets using either the straight-line method or an accelerated method. The results we have discussed thus far were based on accelerated depreciation. To see the impact of using straight-line depreciation, go to the Scenario Manager and select "Straight-Line Depreciation." Be sure that you have also selected "Base-Case for Project L." After selecting and showing these two scenarios, you will have a set of inputs for the base-case and straight-line deprecation rates.

The results indicate that the project's NPV is $921 when using straight-line depreciation, which is lower than the $1,048 NPV when using accelerated depreciation. In general, *profitable firms are better off using accelerated depreciation* because more depreciation is taken in the early years under the accelerated method, so taxes are lower in those years and higher in later years. Total depreciation, total cash flows, and total taxes are the same under both depreciation methods, but receiving the cash earlier under the accelerated method results in a higher NPV, IRR, and MIRR.

Suppose Congress wants to encourage companies to increase their capital expenditures and thereby boost economic growth and employment. What changes in depreciation regulations would have the desired effect? The answer is "Make accelerated depreciation even more accelerated." For example, if GPC could write off equipment at rates of 67%, 22%, 7%, and 4% rather than 33.33%, 44.45%, 14.81%, and 7.41%, then its early tax payments would be even lower, early cash flows would be even higher, and the project's NPV would exceed the value shown in Figure 11-2.[6]

Be sure to return the scenarios to "Base-Case for Project L" and "MACRS Depreciation."

---

[6]This is exactly what Congress did in 2008 and 2009, in response to the global economic crisis, by establishing a temporary "bonus" depreciation to stimulate investment. The depreciation in the first year is the regular accelerated depreciation plus a bonus of 50% of the original basis. This bonus was increased to 100% of the original basis for 2011, effectively allowing companies to fully expense certain capital expenditures in 2011. The bonus drops back to 50% for 2012. The provisions are set to expire at the end of 2012.

Project S.   Recall from Chapter 10 that GPC was also considering Project S, which used solid coatings. You can use the Scenario Manager to show this project by selecting the scenario "Project S," which will show the cash flows used in Chapter 10. Be sure to return the scenarios in the worksheet *1-Base-Case* to "Base-Case for Project L" and "MACRS Depreciation."

SELF-TEST

In what way is the setup for finding a project's cash flows similar to the projected income statements for a new, single-product firm? In what way would the two statements be different?

Would a project's NPV for a typical firm be higher or lower if the firm used accelerated rather than straight-line depreciation? Explain.

How could the analysis in Figure 11-2 be modified to consider cannibalization, opportunity costs, and sunk costs?

Why does net working capital appear with both negative and positive values in Figure 11-2?

11-3 Risk Analysis in Capital Budgeting[7]

Projects differ in risk, and risk should be reflected in capital budgeting decisions. There are three separate and distinct types of risk.

1. **Stand-alone risk** is a project's risk assuming (a) that it is the firm's only asset and (b) that each of the firm's stockholders holds only that one stock in his portfolio. Stand-alone risk is based on uncertainty about the project's expected cash flows. It is important to remember that *stand-alone risk ignores diversification by both the firm and its stockholders.*
2. **Within-firm risk** (also called **corporate risk**) is a project's risk to the corporation itself. Within-firm risk recognizes that the project is only one asset in the firm's portfolio of projects; hence some of its risk is eliminated by diversification within the firm. However, *within-firm risk ignores diversification by the firm's stockholders.* Within-firm risk is measured by the project's impact on uncertainty about the firm's future total cash flows.
3. **Market risk** (also called **beta risk**) is the risk of the project as seen by a well-diversified stockholder who recognizes that (a) the project is only one of the firm's projects and (b) the firm's stock is but one of her stocks. The project's market risk is measured by its effect on the firm's beta coefficient.

Taking on a project with a lot of stand-alone and/or corporate risk will not necessarily affect the firm's beta. However, if the project has high stand-alone risk and if its cash flows are highly correlated with cash flows on the firm's other assets and with cash flows of most other firms in the economy, then the project will have a high degree of all three types of risk. Market risk is, *theoretically*, the most relevant because it is the one that, according to the CAPM, is reflected in stock prices. Unfortunately, market risk is also the most difficult to measure, primarily because new projects don't have "market prices" that can be related to stock market returns.

---

[7]Some professors may choose to cover some of the risk sections and skip others. We offer a range of choices, and we tried to make the exposition clear enough that interested and self-motivated students can read these sections on their own if they are not assigned.

resource

See **Web Extension 11A** *on the textbook's Web site for a more detailed discussion on alternative methods for incorporating project risk into the capital budgeting decision process.*

Most decision makers conduct a *quantitative* analysis of stand-alone risk and then consider the other two types of risk in a *qualitative* manner. They classify projects into several categories; then, using the firm's overall WACC as a starting point, they assign a **risk-adjusted cost of capital** to each category. For example, a firm might establish three risk classes and then assign the corporate WACC to average-risk projects, add a 5% risk premium for higher-risk projects, and subtract 2% for low-risk projects. Under this setup, if the company's overall WACC were 10%, then 10% would be used to evaluate average-risk projects, 15% for high-risk projects, and 8% for low-risk projects. Although this approach is probably better than not making any risk adjustments, these adjustments are highly subjective and difficult to justify. Unfortunately, there's no perfect way to specify how high or low the risk adjustments should be.[8]

SELF-TEST

What are the three types of project risk?

Which type is theoretically the most relevant? Why?

Describe a type of classification scheme that firms often use to obtain risk-adjusted costs of capital.

11-4 Measuring Stand-Alone Risk

A project's stand-alone risk reflects uncertainty about its cash flows. The required dollars of investment, unit sales, sales prices, and operating costs as shown in Figure 11-1 for GPC's project are all subject to uncertainty. First-year sales are projected at 10,000 units to be sold at a price of $1.50 per unit (recall that all dollar values are reported in thousands). However, unit sales will almost certainly be somewhat higher or lower than 10,000, and the price will probably turn out to be different from the projected $1.50 per unit. Similarly, the other variables would probably differ from their indicated values. Indeed, *all the inputs are expected values, not known values, and actual values can and do vary from expected values.* That's what risk is all about!

Three techniques are used in practice to assess stand-alone risk: (1) sensitivity analysis, (2) scenario analysis, and (3) Monte Carlo simulation. We discuss them in the sections that follow.

SELF-TEST

What does a project's stand-alone risk reflect?

What three techniques are used to assess stand-alone risk?

11-5 Sensitivity Analysis

Intuitively, we know that a change in a key input variable such as units sold or the sales price will cause the NPV to change. **Sensitivity analysis** *measures the percentage change in NPV that results from a given percentage change in an input variable when other inputs are held at their expected values.* This is by far the most commonly used type of risk analysis. It begins with a base-case scenario in which the project's NPV is found using the base-case

---

[8]Note that the CAPM approach can be used for projects provided there are specialized publicly traded firms in the same business as that of the project under consideration. See the discussion in Chapter 10 regarding techniques for measuring divisional betas.

value for each input variable. GPC's base-case inputs were given in Figure 11-1, but it's easy to imagine changes in the inputs, and any changes would result in a different NPV.

11-5a Sensitivity Graph

When GPC's senior managers review a capital budgeting analysis, they are interested in the base-case NPV, but they always go on to ask a series of "what if" questions: "What if unit sales fall to 9,000?" "What if market conditions force us to price the product at $1.40, not $1.50?" "What if variable costs are higher than we have forecasted?" Sensitivity analysis is designed to provide answers to such questions. Each variable is increased or decreased by a specified percentage from its expected value, holding other variables constant at their base-case levels. Then the NPV is calculated using the changed input. Finally, the resulting set of NPVs is plotted to show how sensitive NPV is to changes in the different variables.

Figure 11-3 shows GPC's project's sensitivity graph for six key variables. The data below the graph give the NPVs based on different values of the inputs, and those NPVs were then plotted to make the graph. Figure 11-3 shows that, as unit sales and the sales price are increased, the project's NPV increases; in contrast, increases in variable costs, nonvariable costs, equipment

FIGURE 11-3

Sensitivity Graph for Solar Water Heater Project (Thousands of Dollars)

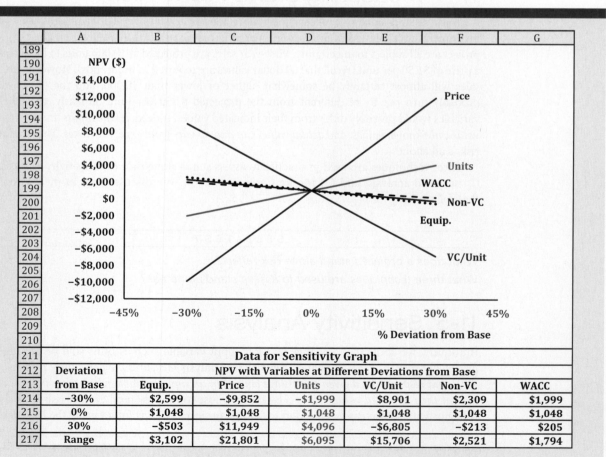

Deviation from Base	NPV with Variables at Different Deviations from Base					
	Equip.	Price	Units	VC/Unit	Non-VC	WACC
−30%	$2,599	−$9,852	−$1,999	$8,901	$2,309	$1,999
0%	$1,048	$1,048	$1,048	$1,048	$1,048	$1,048
30%	−$503	$11,949	$4,096	−$6,805	−$213	$205
Range	$3,102	$21,801	$6,095	$15,706	$2,521	$1,794

costs, and WACC lower the project's NPV. The slopes of the lines in the graph and the ranges in the table below the graph indicate how sensitive NPV is to each input: *The larger the range, the steeper the variable's slope, and the more sensitive the NPV is to this variable.* We see that NPV is extremely sensitive to changes in the sales price; fairly sensitive to changes in variable costs, units sold, and fixed costs; and not especially sensitive to changes in the equipment's cost and the WACC. Management should, of course, try especially hard to obtain accurate estimates of the variables that have the greatest impact on the NPV. See *2-Sens* in *Ch11 Tool Kit.xls* for all calculations.

resource

*See **Ch11 Tool Kit.xls** on the textbook's Web site.*

If we were comparing two projects, then the one with the steeper sensitivity lines would be riskier (other things held constant), because relatively small changes in the input variables would produce large changes in the NPV. Thus, sensitivity analysis provides useful insights into a project's risk.[9] Note, however, that even though NPV may be highly sensitive to certain variables, if those variables are not likely to change much from their expected values, then the project may not be very risky in spite of its high sensitivity. Also, if several of the inputs change at the same time, the combined effect on NPV can be much greater than sensitivity analysis suggests.

11-5b Tornado Diagrams

Tornado diagrams are another way to present results from sensitivity analysis. The first steps are to calculate the range of possible NPVs for each of the input variables being changed and then rank these ranges. In our example, the range for sales price per unit is the largest and the range for WACC is the smallest. The ranges for each variable are then plotted, with the largest range on top and the smallest range on the bottom. It is also helpful to plot a vertical line showing the base-case NPV. We present a tornado diagram in Figure 11-4. Notice that the diagram is like a tornado in the sense that it is widest at the top and smallest at the bottom; hence its name. The tornado diagram makes it immediately obvious which inputs have the greatest impact on NPV: sales price and variable costs in this case.

11-5c NPV Break-Even Analysis

resource

*See **Ch11 Tool Kit.xls** on the textbook's Web site.*

A special application of sensitivity analysis is called **NPV break-even analysis**. In a break-even analysis, we find the level of an input that produces an NPV of exactly zero. We used *Excel*'s Goal Seek feature to do this. See *Ch11 Tool Kit.xls* on the textbook's Web site for an explanation of how to use this *Excel* feature.

Table 11-1 shows the values of the inputs discussed previously that produce a zero NPV. For example, the number of units sold in Year 1 can drop to 9,868 before the project's NPV falls to zero. Break-even analysis is helpful in determining how bad things can get before the project has a negative NPV.

11-5d Extensions of Sensitivity Analysis

resource

*See **Ch11 Tool Kit.xls** on the textbook's Web site.*

In our examples, we showed how one output, NPV, varied with a change in a single input. Sensitivity analysis can easily be extended to show how multiple outputs, such as NPV and IRR, vary with a change in an input. See *Ch11 Tool Kit.xls* on the textbook's Web site for an example showing how to use *Excel*'s Data Table feature to present multiple outputs.

---

[9]Sensitivity analysis is tedious with a regular calculator but easy with a spreadsheet. We used the chapter's *Excel Tool Kit* to calculate the NPVs and then to draw the graph in Figure 11-3. To conduct such an analysis by hand would be quite time-consuming, and if the basic data were changed even slightly—say, the cost of the equipment was increased slightly—then all of the calculations would have to be redone. With a spreadsheet, we can simply type over the old input with the new one, and the analysis and the graph change instantaneously.

FIGURE 11-4

Tornado Diagram for Solar Water Heater Project: Range of Outcomes for Input Deviations from Base Case (Thousands of Dollars)

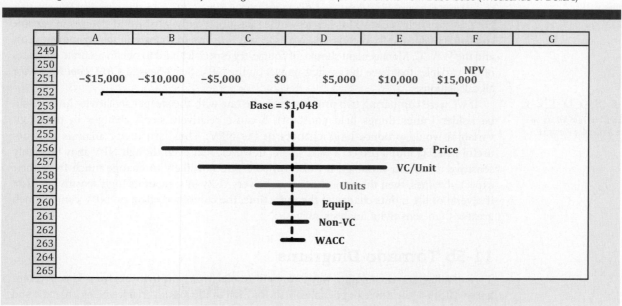

TABLE 11-1

NPV Break-Even Analysis (Thousands of Dollars)

Input	Input Value That Produces Zero NPV, Holding All Else Constant
Sales price per unit, Year 1	$1.457
Variable cost per unit (VC), Year 1	$1.113
Annual change in units sold after Year 1	7.40%
Units sold, Year 1	8,968
Nonvariable cost (Non-VC), Year 1	$2,649
Project WACC	13.79%

© Cengage Learning 2014

It is also possible to use a Data Table to show how a single output, such as NPV, varies for changes in two inputs, such as the number of units sold and the sales price per unit. See *Ch11 Tool Kit.xls* on the textbook's Web site for an example. However, when we examine the impact of a change in more than one input, we usually use scenario analysis, which is described in the following section.

S E L F - T E S T

What is sensitivity analysis?

Briefly explain the usefulness of a sensitivity graph.

Discuss the following statement: "A project may not be very risky in spite of its high sensitivity to certain variables."

11-6 Scenario Analysis

In the sensitivity analysis just described, we changed one variable at a time. However, it is useful to know what would happen to the project's NPV if several of the inputs turn out to be better or worse than expected, and this is what we do in a **scenario analysis**. Also, scenario analysis allows us to assign probabilities to the base (or most likely) case, the best case, and the worst case; then we can find the *expected value and standard deviation* of the project's NPV to get a better idea of the project's risk.

In a scenario analysis, we begin with the base-case scenario, which uses the most likely value for each input variable. We then ask marketing, engineering, and other operating managers to specify a worst-case scenario (low unit sales, low sales price, high variable costs, and so on) and a best-case scenario. Often, the best and worst cases are defined as having a 25% probability of occurring, with a 50% probability for the base-case conditions. Obviously, conditions could take on many more than three values, but such a scenario setup is useful to help get some idea of the project's riskiness.

*See **Ch11 Tool Kit.xls** on the textbook's Web site.*

After much discussion with the marketing staff, engineers, accountants, and other experts in the company, a set of worst-case and best-case values were determined for several key inputs. Figure 11-5, taken from worksheet *3a-Scen* of the chapter *Tool Kit* model, shows the probability and inputs assumed for the base-case, worst-case, and best-case scenarios, along with selected key results.

FIGURE 11-5

Inputs and Key Results for Each Scenario (Thousands of Dollars)

	A	B	C	D	E	F	G
34						Scenarios:	
35	Scenario Name				Base	Worst	Best
36	Probability of Scenario				50%	25%	25%
37	Inputs:						
38	Equipment cost				$7,750	$8,250	$7,250
39	Salvage value of equip. in Year 4				$639	$639	$639
40	Opportunity cost				$0	$0	$0
41	Externalities (cannibalization)				$0	$0	$0
42	Units sold, Year 1				10,000	8,500	11,500
43	% Δ in units sold, after Year 1				15%	5%	25%
44	Sales price per unit, Year 1				$1.50	$1.25	$1.75
45	% Δ in sales price, after Year 1				4%	4%	4%
46	Var. cost per unit (VC), Year 1				$1.07	$1.17	$0.97
47	% Δ in VC, after Year 1				3%	3%	3%
48	Nonvar. cost (Non-VC), Year 1				$2,120	$2,330	$1,910
49	% Δ in Non-VC, after Year 1				3%	3%	3%
50	Project WACC				10%	10%	10%
51	Tax rate				40%	50%	30%
52	NOWC as % of next year's sales				15%	15%	15%
53	Key Results:						
54				NPV	$1,048	–$7,543	$19,468
55				IRR	13.79%	–29.40%	62.41%
56				MIRR	12.78%	–22.23%	43.49%
57			Profitability index		1.10	0.23	2.90
58			Payback		3.39	Not found	1.83
59			Discounted payback		3.80	Not found	2.07

r e s o u r c e

See **Ch11 Tool Kit.xls** on
the textbook's Web site.

The project's cash flows and performance measures under each scenario are calculated; see *3a-Scen* in the *Tool Kit* for the calculations. The net cash flows for each scenario are shown in Figure 11-6, along with a probability distribution of the possible outcomes for NPV. If the project is highly successful, then a low initial investment, high sales price, high unit sales, and low production costs would combine to result in a very high NPV, $19,468. However, if things turn out badly, then the NPV would be a *negative* $7,543. This wide range of possibilities, and especially the large potential negative value, suggests that this is a risky project. If bad conditions materialize, the project will not bankrupt the company—this is just one project for a large company. Still, losing $7,543 (actually $7,543,000, as the units are thousands of dollars) would certainly hurt the company's value and the reputation of the project's manager.

If we multiply each scenario's probability by the NPV for that scenario and then sum the products, we will have the project's expected NPV of $3,505, as shown in Figure 11-6. Note that the *expected* NPV differs from the *base-case* NPV, which is the most likely outcome because it has a 50% probability. This is not an error—mathematically they are not equal.[10] We also calculate the standard deviation of the expected NPV; it is $9,861. Dividing the standard deviation by the expected NPV yields the **coefficient of variation**, 2.81, which is a measure of stand-alone risk. The coefficient of variation measures the amount of risk per dollar of NPV, so the coefficient of variation can be helpful when comparing the risk of projects with different NPVs. GPC's average project has a coefficient of variation of about 1.2, so the 2.81 indicates that this project is riskier than most of GPC's other typical projects.

GPC's corporate WACC is 9%, so that rate should be used to find the NPV of an average-risk project. However, the water heater project is riskier than average, so a higher discount rate should be used to find its NPV. There is no way to determine the precisely correct discount rate—this is a judgment call. Management decided to evaluate the project using a 10% rate.[11]

Note that the base-case results are the same in our sensitivity and scenario analyses, but in the scenario analysis the worst case is much worse than in the sensitivity analysis and the best case is much better. This is because in scenario analysis all of the variables are set at their best or worst levels, whereas in sensitivity analysis only one variable is adjusted and all the others are left at their base-case levels.

The project has a positive NPV, but its coefficient of variation (CV) is 2.81, which is more than double the 1.2 CV of an average project. With the higher risk, it is not clear if the project should be accepted or not. At this point, GPC's CEO will ask the CFO to investigate the risk further by performing a simulation analysis, as described in the next section.

---

[10]This result occurs for two reasons. First, although in this scenario analysis, the base-case input values happen to equal the average of the best- and worst-case values, this is by no means necessary. Best- and worst-case values need not be the same distance from the base case. Second, even though the base-case values are midway between the best- and worst-case values, in our model two uncertain variables, sales volume and sales price, are multiplied together to obtain dollar sales, and this process causes the NPV distribution to be skewed to the right. A large number multiplied by another large number produces a very big number, and this in turn causes the average value (or expected value) to increase.

[11]One could argue that the best-case scenario should be evaluated with a relatively low WACC, the worst-case scenario with a relatively high WACC, and the base case with the average corporate WACC. However, one could also argue that, at the time of the initial decision, we don't know what case will occur and hence a single rate should be used. Observe that, in the worst-case scenario, all of the cash flows are negative. If we used a high WACC because of this branch's risk, this would lower the PV of these negative cash flows, making the worst case much better than if we used the average WACC. Determining the "right" WACC to use in the analysis is not an easy task!

FIGURE 11-6

Scenario Analysis: Expected NPV and Its Risk (Thousands of Dollars)

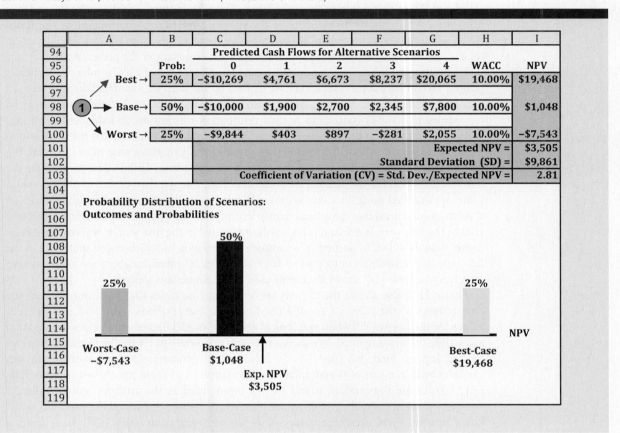

	A	B	C	D	E	F	G	H	I
94			Predicted Cash Flows for Alternative Scenarios						
95		Prob:	0	1	2	3	4	WACC	NPV
96	Best →	25%	−$10,269	$4,761	$6,673	$8,237	$20,065	10.00%	$19,468
97									
98	Base →	50%	−$10,000	$1,900	$2,700	$2,345	$7,800	10.00%	$1,048
99									
100	Worst →	25%	−$9,844	$403	$897	−$281	$2,055	10.00%	−$7,543
101							Expected NPV =		$3,505
102							Standard Deviation (SD) =		$9,861
103						Coefficient of Variation (CV) = Std. Dev./Expected NPV =			2.81

Probability Distribution of Scenarios: Outcomes and Probabilities

50%

25%   25%

Worst-Case   Base-Case   Best-Case   NPV
−$7,543 $1,048 $19,468

Exp. NPV
$3,505

SELF-TEST

What is scenario analysis?

Differentiate between sensitivity analysis and scenario analysis. What advantage does scenario analysis have over sensitivity analysis?

11-7 Monte Carlo Simulation[12]

Monte Carlo simulation ties together sensitivities, probability distributions, and correlations among the input variables. It grew out of work in the Manhattan Project to build the first atomic bomb and was so named because it utilized the mathematics of casino gambling. Although Monte Carlo simulation is considerably more complex than scenario analysis, simulation software packages make the process manageable. Many of these packages can be used as add-ins to *Excel* and other spreadsheet programs.

In a simulation analysis, a probability distribution is assigned to each input variable—sales in units, the sales price, the variable cost per unit, and so on. The computer begins by picking a random value for each variable from its probability distribution. Those values are then entered into the model, the project's NPV is calculated, and the NPV is stored in the

---

[12]This section is relatively technical, and some instructors may choose to skip it with no loss in continuity.

computer's memory. This is called a trial. After completing the first trial, a second set of input values is selected from the input variables' probability distributions, and a second NPV is calculated. This process is repeated many times. The NPVs from the trials can be charted on a histogram, which shows an estimate of the project's outcomes. The average of the trials' NPVs is interpreted as a measure of the project's expected NPV, with the standard deviation (or the coefficient of variation) of the trials' NPV as a measure of the project's risk.

Using this procedure, we conducted a simulation analysis of GPC's solar water heater project. To compare apples and apples, we focused on the same six variables that were allowed to change in the previously conducted scenario analysis. We assumed that each variable can be represented by its own continuous normal distribution with means and standard deviations that are consistent with the base-case scenario. For example, we assumed that the units sold in Year 1 come from a normal distribution with a mean equal to the base-case value of 10,000. We used the probabilities and outcomes of the three scenarios from Section 11-6 to estimate the standard deviation (all calculations are in the *Tool Kit*). The standard deviation of units sold is 1,061, as calculated using the scenario values. We made similar assumptions for all variables. In addition, we assumed that the annual change in unit sales will be positively correlated with unit sales in the first year: If demand is higher than expected in the first year, it will continue to be higher than expected. In particular, we assume a correlation of 0.65 between units sold in the first year and growth in units sold in later years. For all other variables, we assumed zero correlation. Figure 11-7 shows the inputs used in the simulation analysis.

Figure 11-7 also shows the current set of random variables that were drawn from the distributions at the time we created the figure for the textbook—you will see different values for the key results when you look at the *Excel* model because the values are updated every time the file is opened. We used a two-step procedure to create the random variables for the inputs. First, we used *Excel*'s functions to generate standard normal random variables with a mean of 0 and a standard deviation of 1; these are shown in Cells E38: E51.[13] To create the random values for the inputs used in the analysis, we multiplied a random standard normal variable by the standard deviation and added the expected value. For example, *Excel* drew the value −0.07 for first-year unit sales (Cell E42) from a standard normal distribution. We calculated the value for first-year unit sales to use in the current trial as 10,000 + 1,061(−0.07) = 9,927, which is shown in Cell F42.[14]

We used the inputs in Cells F38:F52 to generate cash flows and to calculate performance measures for the project (the calculations are in the *Tool Kit*). For the trial reported in Figure 11-7, the NPV is $15,121. We used a Data Table in the *Tool Kit* to generate additional trials. For each trial, the Data Table saved the value of the input variables and the value of the trial's NPV. Figure 11-8 presents selected results from the simulation for 10,000 trials. (The worksheet *4a-Sim100* in the *Tool Kit* shows only 100 trials; the worksheet *4b-Sim10000* has the ability to perform 10,000 simulations, but we have turned off the Data Table in that worksheet because simulating 10,000 trials reduces *Excel*'s speed when performing other calculations in the file.)

After running a simulation, the first thing we do is verify that the results are consistent with our assumptions. The resulting sample mean and standard deviation of units sold in the first year are 9,982 and 1,057, which are virtually identical to our assumptions in Figure 11-7. The same is true for all the other inputs, so we can be reasonably confident that the simulation is doing what we are asking. Figure 11-8 also reports summary statistics for the project's NPV. The mean is $1,120, which suggests that the project should be accepted. However, the range of outcomes is quite large, from a loss of $16,785 to a gain of

resource

See *Ch11 Tool Kit.xls* on the textbook's Web site.

---

[13]See the *Tool Kit* for detailed explanations on using *Excel* to generate random variables.
[14]There may be slight rounding differences because *Excel* doesn't round in intermediate steps. We used a slightly more complicated procedure to generate a random variable for the annual change in sales to ensure that it had 0.65 correlation with the first-year units sold. See the *Tool Kit* for details.

FIGURE 11-7

Inputs and Key Results for the Current Simulation Trial (Thousands of Dollars)

	A	B	C	D	E	F
33			**Inputs for Simulation**		**Random Variables Used in**	
34			**Probability Distributions**		**Current Simulation Trial**	
35			**Expected**	**Standard**	**Standard**	
36			**Value of**	**Deviation of**	**Normal**	**Value Used in**
37			**Input**	**Input**	**Random**	**Current Trial**
38	Equipment cost		$7,750	$354	−0.165	$7,692
39	Salvage value of equip. in Year 4		—	—	—	$639
40	Opportunity cost		—	—	—	$0
41	Externalities (cannibalization)		—	—	—	$0
42	Units sold, Year 1		$10,000	$1,061	−0.069	$9,927
43	% Δ in units sold, after Year 1		15.00%	7.07%	0.734	20.19%
44	Sales price per unit, Year 1		$1.50	$0.18	1.931	$1.84
45	% Δ in sales price, after Year 1		—	—	—	4.00%
46	Var. cost per unit (VC), Year 1		$1.07	$0.07	−1.087	$0.99
47	% Δ in VC, after Year 1		—	—	—	3.00%
48	Nonvar. cost (Non-VC), Year 1		$2,120	$148	0.514	$2,196
49	% Δ in Non-VC, after Year 1		—	—	—	3.00%
50	Project WACC		—	—	—	10.00%
51	Tax rate		40.00%	7.07%	−1.511	29.32%
52	NOWC as % of next year's sales		—	—	—	15.00%
53	Assumed correlation between units sold in Year 1 and annual change in					
54	units sold in later years:		$\rho = 65.00\%$			
55	**Key Results Based on Current Trial**					
56		NPV	$15,121			
57		IRR	53.23%			
58		MIRR	37.61%			
59		PI	2.45			
60		Payback	1.98			
61		Discounted payback	$2.25			

$26,406, so the project is clearly risky. The standard deviation of $5,132 indicates that losses could easily occur, which is consistent with this wide range of possible outcomes.[15] Figure 11-8 also reports a median NPV of $737, which means that half the time the project will have an NPV of less than $737. In fact, there is only 56.4% probability that the project will have a positive NPV.

A picture is worth a thousand words, and Figure 11-8 shows the probability distribution of the outcomes. Note that the distribution of outcomes is slightly skewed to the right. As the

---

[15]Note that the standard deviation of NPV in the simulation is much smaller than the standard deviation in the scenario analysis. In the scenario analysis, we assumed that all of the poor outcomes would occur together in the worst-case scenario and that all of the positive outcomes would occur together in the best-case scenario. In other words, we implicitly assumed that all of the risky variables were perfectly positively correlated. In the simulation, we assumed that the variables were independent (except for the correlation between unit sales and growth). The independence of variables in the simulation reduces the range of outcomes. For example, in the simulation, sometimes the sales price is high but the sales growth is low. In the scenario analysis, a high sales price is always coupled with high growth. Because the scenario analysis assumption of perfect correlation is unlikely, simulation may provide a better estimate of project risk. However, if the standard deviations and correlations used as inputs in the simulation are inaccurately estimated, then the simulation output will likewise be inaccurate.

FIGURE 11-8

Summary of Simulation Results (Thousands of Dollars)

	A	B	C	D	E	F	G	H	I
156	**Number of Trials 10,000**				**Input Variables**				
157					**% Δ in**	**Sales**	**Variable**	**Nonvar.**	
158				**Units**	**units sold,**	**price per**	**cost per**	**cost**	
159	**Summary Statistics for**		**Equip.**	**sold,**	**after**	**unit,**	**unit (VC),**	**(Non-VC),**	**Tax**
160	**Simulated Input Variables**		**cost**	**Year 1**	**Year 1**	**Year 1**	**Year 1**	**Year 1**	**rate**
161		**Average**	$7,750	9,982	15.0%	$1.50	$1.07	$2,122	39.9%
162		**Standard deviation**	$354	1,057	7.1%	$0.18	$0.07	$150	7.1%
163		**Maximum**	$9,072	14,005	45.0%	$2.15	$1.32	$2,682	68.7%
164		**Minimum**	$6,397	6,172	−13.97%	$0.81	$0.78	$1,549	13.5%
165	**Correlation with unit sales**				65.4%				
166	**Summary Statistics for**								
167	**Simulated Results**		**NPV**						
168		**Average**	$1,120						
169		**Standard deviation**	$5,132						
170		**Maximum**	$26,406						
171		**Minimum**	−$16,785						
172		**Median**	$737						
173	**Probability of NPV > 0**		56.4%						
174	**Coefficient of variation**		4.58						

figure shows, the potential downside losses are not as large as the potential upside gains. Our conclusion is that this is a very risky project, as indicated by the coefficient of variation, but it does have a positive expected NPV and the potential to be a "home run."

If the company decides to go ahead with the project, senior management should also identify possible contingency plans for responding to changes in market conditions. Senior managers always should consider qualitative factors in addition to the quantitative project analysis.

resource

See Ch11 Tool Kit.xls on the textbook's Web site.

SELF-TEST

What is Monte Carlo simulation?

11-8 Project Risk Conclusions

We have discussed the three types of risk normally considered in capital budgeting: stand-alone risk, within-firm (or corporate) risk, and market risk. However, two important questions remain: (1) Should firms care about stand-alone and corporate risk, given that finance theory says that market (beta) risk is the only relevant risk? (2) What do we do when the stand-alone, within-firm, and market risk assessments lead to different conclusions?

There are no easy answers to these questions. Strict adherents of the CAPM would argue that well-diversified investors are concerned only with market risk, that managers should be concerned only with maximizing stock price, and thus that market (beta) risk ought to be given virtually all the weight in capital budgeting decisions. However, we know that not all investors are well diversified, that the CAPM does not operate exactly as the theory says it should, and that measurement problems keep managers from having complete confidence in the CAPM inputs. In addition, the CAPM ignores bankruptcy costs, even though such costs can be substantial, and the probability of bankruptcy depends on a firm's corporate risk, not on its beta risk. Therefore, even well-diversified investors should want a firm's management to give at least some consideration to a project's corporate risk, and that means giving some consideration to stand-alone project risk.

Although it would be nice to reconcile these problems and to measure risk on some absolute scale, the best we can do in practice is to estimate risk in a somewhat nebulous, relative sense. For example, we can generally say with a fair degree of confidence that a particular project has more, less, or about the same stand-alone risk as the firm's average project. Then, because stand-alone and corporate risks generally are correlated, the project's stand-alone risk generally is a reasonably good measure of its corporate risk. Finally, assuming that market risk and corporate risk are correlated, as is true for most companies, a project with a relatively high or low corporate risk will also have a relatively high or low market risk. We wish we could be more specific, but one simply must use a lot of judgment when assessing projects' risks.

SELF-TEST

In theory, should a firm be equally concerned with stand-alone, corporate, and market risk? Would your answer be the same if we substituted "In practice" for "In theory"? Explain your answers.

If a project's stand-alone, corporate, and market risk are known to be highly correlated, would this make the task of evaluating the project's risk easier or harder? Explain.

11-9 Replacement Analysis

In the previous sections we assumed that the solar water heater project was an entirely new project, so all of its cash flows were incremental—they would occur if and only if the project were accepted. However, for replacement projects we must find the cash flow *differentials* between the new and old projects, and these differentials are the *incremental cash flows* that we must analyze.

We evaluate a replacement decision in Figure 11-9, which is set up much like Figures 11-1 and 11-2 but with data on both a new, highly efficient machine and data on the old machine. In Part I we show the key inputs in the analysis, including depreciation on the new and old machines. In Part II we find the cash flows the firm will have if it continues to use the old machine, and in Part III we find the cash flows if the firm replaces the old machine. Then, in Part IV, we subtract the old flows from the new to arrive at the *incremental cash flows*, and we evaluate those flows in Part V to find the NPV, IRR, and MIRR. Replacing the old machine appears to be a good decision.[16]

In some instances, replacements add capacity as well as lower operating costs. In this case, sales revenues in Part III would be increased, and if that leads to a need for more working capital, then this would be shown as a Time 0 expenditure along with a recovery at the end of the project's life. These changes would, of course, be reflected in the incremental cash flows on Row 52.

resource

See Ch11 Tool Kit.xls on the textbook's Web site.

---

[16]The same sort of risk analysis discussed in previous sections can be applied to replacement decisions.

FIGURE 11-9

Replacement Analysis

	A	B	C	D	E	F	G	H	I
15						Applies to:			
16	Part I. Inputs:				Both Machines	Old Machine	New Machine		
17	Cost of new machine						$2,000		
18	After-tax salvage value old machine					$400			
19	Sales revenues (fixed)				$2,500				
20	Annual operating costs except depr.					$1,200	$280		
21	Tax rate				40%				
22	WACC				10%				
23	Depreciation			1	2	3	4	Totals:	
24	Depr. rates (new machine)			33.33%	44.45%	14.81%	7.41%	100%	
25	Depreciation on new machine			$667	$889	$296	$148	$2,000	
26	Depreciation on old machine			$334	$333	$0	$0	$667	
27	Δ: Change in depreciation			$333	$556	$296	$148	$1,333	
28	Part II. Net Cash Flows before Replacement: Old Machine								
29					0	1	2	3	4
30	Sales revenues					$2,500	$2,500	$2,500	$2,500
31	Operating costs except depreciation					1,200	1,200	1,200	1,200
32	Depreciation					334	333	0	0
33	Total operating costs					$1,534	$1,533	$1,200	$1,200
34	Operating income					$966	$967	$1,300	$1,300
35	Taxes 40%					386	387	520	520
36	After-tax operating income					$580	$580	$780	$780
37	Add back depreciation					334	333	0	0
38	Net cash flows before replacement				$0	$914	$913	$780	$780
39	Part III. Net Cash Flows after Replacement: New Machine								
40					0	1	2	3	4
41	New machine cost:				−$2,000				
42	After-tax salvage value, old machine				$400				
43	Sales revenues					$2,500	$2,500	$2,500	$2,500
44	Operating costs except depreciation					$280	$280	$280	$280
45	Depreciation					$667	$889	$296	$148
46	Total operating costs					$947	$1,169	$576	$428
47	Operating income					$1,553	$1,331	$1,924	$2,072
48	Taxes 40%					$621	$532	$770	$829
49	After-tax operating income					$932	$799	$1,154	$1,243
50	Add back depreciation					$667	$889	$296	$148
51	Net cash flows after replacement				−$1,600	$1,599	$1,688	$1,450	$1,391
52	Part IV. Incremental CF: Row 51 − Row 38				−$1,600	$685	$774	$670	$611
53	Part V. Evaluation			NPV =	$584.02	IRR =	26.33%	MIRR =	18.90%

SELF-TEST

How are incremental cash flows found in a replacement analysis?

If you were analyzing a replacement project and suddenly learned that the old equipment could be sold for $1,000 rather than $400, would this new information make the replacement look better or worse? Explain.

In Figure 11-9 we assumed that output would remain stable if the old machine were replaced. Suppose output would double. How would this change be dealt with in the framework of Figure 11-9?

11-10 Real Options

According to traditional capital budgeting theory, a project's NPV is the present value of its expected future cash flows discounted at a rate that reflects the riskiness of those cash flows. Note, however, that this says nothing about actions taken *after* the project has been accepted and placed in operation that might lead to an increase in the cash flows. In other words, traditional capital budgeting theory assumes that a project is like a roulette wheel. A gambler can choose whether to spin the wheel, but once the wheel has been spun, nothing can be done to influence the outcome. Once the game begins, the outcome depends purely on chance, and no skill is involved.

Contrast roulette with a game such as poker. Chance plays a role in poker, and it continues to play a role after the initial deal because players receive additional cards throughout the game. However, poker players are able to respond to their opponents' actions, so skilled players usually win.

Capital budgeting decisions have more in common with poker than roulette because (1) chance plays a continuing role throughout the life of the project, but (2) managers can respond to changing market conditions and to competitors' actions. Opportunities to respond to changing circumstances are called **managerial options** (because they give managers a chance to influence the outcome of a project), **strategic options** (because they are often associated with large, strategic projects rather than routine maintenance projects), and **embedded options** (because they are a part of the project). Finally, they are called **real options** to differentiate them from financial options because they involve real, rather than financial, assets. The following sections describe projects with several types of real options.

11-10a Investment Timing Options

Conventional NPV analysis implicitly assumes that projects either will be accepted or rejected, which implies they will be undertaken now or never. In practice, however, companies sometimes have a third choice—delay the decision until later, when more information is available. Such **investment timing options** can dramatically affect a project's estimated profitability and risk, as we saw in our example of GPC's solar water heater project.

Keep in mind, though, that the *option to delay* is valuable only if it more than offsets any harm that might result from delaying. For example, while one company delays, some other company might establish a loyal customer base that makes it difficult for the first company to enter the market later. The option to delay is usually most valuable to firms with proprietary technology, patents, licenses, or other barriers to entry, because these factors lessen the threat of competition. The option to delay is valuable when market demand is uncertain, but it is also valuable during periods of volatile interest rates, because the ability to wait can allow firms to delay raising capital for a project until interest rates are lower.

11-10b Growth Options

A **growth option** allows a company to increase its capacity if market conditions are better than expected. There are several types of growth options. One lets a company *increase the capacity of an existing product line*. A "peaking unit" power plant illustrates this type of growth option. Such units have high variable costs and are used to produce additional power only if demand, thus prices, are high.

The second type of growth option allows a company to *expand into new geographic markets*. Many companies are investing in China, Eastern Europe, and Russia even though standard NPV analysis produces negative NPVs. However, if these developing markets really take off, the option to open more facilities could be quite valuable.

The third type of growth option is the opportunity to *add new products,* including complementary products and successive "generations" of the original product. Auto companies are losing money on their first electric autos, but the manufacturing skills and consumer recognition those cars will provide should help turn subsequent genera-tions of electric autos into moneymakers.

11-10c Abandonment Options

Consider the value of an **abandonment option**. Standard DCF analysis assumes that a project's assets will be used over a specified economic life. But even though some projects must be operated over their full economic life—in spite of deteriorating market conditions and hence lower than expected cash flows—other projects can be abandoned. Smart managers negotiate the right to abandon if a project turns out to be unsuccessful as a condition for undertaking the project.

Note, too, that some projects can be structured so that they provide the option to *reduce capacity* or *temporarily suspend operations*. Such options are common in the natural resources industry, including mining, oil, and timber, and they should be reflected in the analysis when NPVs are being estimated.

11-10d Flexibility Options

Many projects offer **flexibility options** that permit the firm to alter operations depending on how conditions change during the life of the project. Typically, either inputs or outputs (or both) can be changed. BMW's Spartanburg, South Carolina, auto assembly plant provides a good example of output flexibility. BMW needed the plant to produce sports coupes. If it built the plant configured to produce only these vehicles, the construction cost would be minimized. However, the company thought that later on it might want to switch production to some other vehicle type, and that would be difficult if the plant were designed just for coupes. Therefore, BMW decided to spend additional funds to construct a more flexible plant: one that could produce different types of vehicles should demand patterns shift. Sure enough, things did change. Demand for coupes dropped a bit and demand for sport-utility vehicles soared. But BMW was ready, and the Spartanburg plant began to produce hot-selling SUVs. The plant's cash flows were much higher than they would have been without the flexibility option that BMW "bought" by paying more to build a more flexible plant.

Electric power plants provide an example of input flexibility. Utilities can build plants that generate electricity by burning coal, oil, or natural gas. The prices of those fuels change over time in response to events in the Middle East, changing environmental policies, and weather conditions. Some years ago, virtually all power plants were designed to burn just one type of fuel, because this resulted in the lowest construction costs. However, as fuel cost volatility increased, power companies began to build higher-cost but more flexible plants, especially ones that could switch from oil to gas and back again depending on relative fuel prices.

11-10e Valuing Real Options

A full treatment of real option valuation is beyond the scope of this chapter, but there are some things we can say. First, if a project has an embedded real option, then management should at least recognize and articulate its existence. Second, we know that a financial option is more valuable if it has a long time until maturity or if the underlying asset is very risky. If either of these characteristics applies to a project's real option, then management should know that its value is probably relatively high. Third, management might be able to model the real option along the lines of a decision tree, as we illustrate in the following section.

SELF-TEST

Explain the relevance of the following statement: "Capital budgeting decisions have more in common with poker than roulette."

What are managerial options? Strategic options?

Identify some different types of real options and differentiate among them.

11-11 Phased Decisions and Decision Trees

Up to this point we have focused primarily on techniques for estimating a project's risk. Although this is an integral part of capital budgeting, managers are just as interested in *reducing* risk as in *measuring* it. One way to reduce risk is to structure projects so that expenditures can be made in stages over time rather than all at once. This gives managers the opportunity to reevaluate decisions using new information and then to either invest additional funds or terminate the project. This type of analysis involves the use of *decision trees*.

11-11a The Basic Decision Tree

resource

See *Ch11 Tool Kit.xls* on the textbook's Web site.

GPC's analysis of the solar water heater project thus far has assumed that the project cannot be abandoned once it goes into operation, even if the worst-case situation arises. However, GPC is considering the possibility of terminating (abandoning) the project at Year 2 if the demand is low. The net after-tax cash flow from salvage, legal fees, liquidation of working capital, and all other termination costs and revenues is $5,000. Using these assumptions, the GPC ran a new scenario analysis; the results are shown in Figure 11-10, which is a simple decision tree.

FIGURE **11-10**

Simple Decision Tree: Abandoning Project in Worst-Case Scenario

	A	B	C	D	E	F	G	H	I
123			Predicted Cash Flows for Alternative Scenarios						
124		Prob:	0	1	2	3	4	WACC	NPV
125	Best →	25%	−$10,269	$4,761	$6,673	$8,237	$20,065	10%	$19,468
126									
127	→Base→	50%	−$10,000	$1,900	$2,700	$2,345	$7,800	10%	$1,048
128									
129			−$9,844	$403	$897	−$281	$2,055		
130	Worst →	25%							
131			−$9,844	$403	$5,000	$0	$0	10%	−$5,345
132	If abandon, can liquidate for $5,000 at t = 2.								
133							Expected NPV =		$4,055
134							Standard Deviation (SD) =		$9,273
135				Coefficient of Variation (CV) = Std. Dev./Expected NPV =					2.29

Here we assume that, if the worst case materializes, then this will be recognized after the low Year-1 cash flow and GPC will abandon the project. Rather than continue realizing low cash flows in Years 2, 3, and 4, the company will shut down the operation and liquidate the project for $5,000 at t = 2. Now the expected NPV rises from $3,505 to $4,055 and the CV declines from 2.81 to 2.29. So, securing the right to abandon the project if things don't work out raised the project's expected return and lowered its risk. This will give you an approximate value, but keep in mind that you may not have a good estimate of the appropriate discount rate because the real option changes the risk, and hence the required return, of the project.[17]

11-11b Staged Decision Tree

After the management team thought about the decision-tree approach, other ideas for improving the project emerged. The marketing manager stated that he could undertake a study that would give the firm a better idea of demand for the product. If the marketing study found favorable responses to the product, the design engineer stated that she could build a prototype solar water heater to gauge consumer reactions to the actual product. After assessing consumer reactions, the company could either go ahead with the project or abandon it. This type of evaluation process is called a **staged decision tree** and is shown in Figure 11-11.

Decision trees such as the one in Figure 11-11 often are used to analyze multistage, or sequential, decisions. Each circle represents a decision point, also known as a **decision node**. The dollar value to the left of each decision node represents the net cash flow at that point, and the cash flows shown under t = 3, 4, 5, and 6 represent the cash inflows if the project is pushed on to completion. Each diagonal line leads to a **branch** of the decision tree, and each

FIGURE 11-11

Decision Tree with Multiple Decision Points

	A	B	C	D	E	F	G	H	I	J	K
144	Firm can abandon the project at t = 2									WACC =	10%
145	Time Periods, Cash Flows, Probabilities, and Decision Points									WACC =	10%
146	0		1		2	3	4	5	6	WACC =	10%
147	1st Invest	Prob.	2nd Invest	Prob.	3rd Invest	Inflow	Inflow	Inflow	Inflow	NPV	Joint Prob
148											
149				↗ 45%	−$10,269 ③	$4,761	$6,673	$8,237	$20,065	$15,534	36%
150				↑							
151		↗ 80%	−$500 ② →	40%	−$10,000 ③	$1,900	$2,700	$2,345	$7,800	$312	32%
152		↑		↓							
153	−$100 ①			↳ 15%	Stop ③	$0	$0	$0	$0	−$555	12%
154		↓									
155		↳ 20%	Stop ②			$0	$0	$0	$0	−$100	20%
156											100%
157								Expected NPV =		$5,606	
158								Standard Deviation (SD) =		$7,451	
159					Coefficient of Variation (CV) = Std. Dev./Expected NPV =					1.33	

[17]For more on real option valuation, see M. Amram and N. Kulatilaka, *Real Options: Managing Strategic Investment in an Uncertain World* (Boston: Harvard Business School Press, 1999); and H. Smit and L. Trigeorgis, *Strategic Investments: Real Options and Games* (Princeton, NJ: Princeton University Press, 2004).

branch has an estimated probability. For example, if the firm decides to "go" with the project at Decision Point 1, then it will spend $100,000 on the marketing study. Management estimates that there is a 0.8 probability that the study will produce *positive* results, leading to the decision to make an additional investment and thus move on to Decision Point 2, and a 0.2 probability that the marketing study will produce *negative* results, indicating that the project should be canceled after Stage 1. If the project is canceled, the cost to the company will be the $100,000 spent on the initial marketing study.

If the marketing study yields positive results, then the firm will spend $500,000 on the prototype water heater module at Decision Point 2. Management estimates (even before making the initial $100,000 investment) that there is a 45% probability of the pilot project yielding good results, a 40% probability of average results, and a 15% probability of bad results. If the prototype works well, then the firm will spend several millions more at Decision Point 3 to build a production plant, buy the necessary inventory, and commence operations. The operating cash flows over the project's 4-year life will be good, average, or bad, and these cash flows are shown under Years 3 through 6.

The column of joint probabilities in Figure 11-11 gives the probability of occurrence of each branch—and hence of each NPV. Each joint probability is obtained by multiplying together all the probabilities on that particular branch. For example, the probability that the company will, if Stage 1 is undertaken, move through Stages 2 and 3, and that a strong demand will produce the indicated cash flows, is $(0.8)(0.45) = 0.36 = 36.0\%$. There is a 32% probability of average results, a 12% probability of building the plant and then getting bad results, and a 20% probability of getting bad initial results and stopping after the marketing study. The NPV of the top (most favorable) branch as shown in Column J is $15,534, calculated as follows:

$$NPV = -\$100 - \frac{\$500}{(1.10)^1} - \frac{\$10,269}{(1.10)^2} + \frac{\$4,761}{(1.10)^3} + \frac{\$6,673}{(1.10)^4} + \frac{\$8,237}{(1.10)^5} + \frac{\$20,065}{(1.10)^6}$$
$$= \$15,534$$

The NPVs for the other branches are calculated similarly.[18]

The last column in Figure 11-11 gives the product of the NPV for each branch times the joint probability of that branch's occurring, and the sum of these products is the project's expected NPV. Based on the expectations used to create Figure 11-11 and a cost of capital of 10%, the project's expected NPV is $5,606, or $5.606 million.[19] In addition, the CV declines from 2.81 to 1.33, and the maximum anticipated loss is a manageable −$555,000. At this point, the solar water heater project looked good, and GPC's management decided to accept it.

As this example shows, decision-tree analysis requires managers to articulate explicitly the types of risk a project faces and to develop responses to potential scenarios. Note also that our example could be extended to cover many other types of decisions and could even be incorporated into a simulation analysis. All in all, decision-tree analysis is a valuable tool for analyzing project risks.[20]

---

[18]The calculations in *Excel* use nonrounded annual cash flows, so there may be small differences when calculating by hand with rounded annual cash flows.

[19]As we mentioned concerning the abandonment option, the presence of the real options in Figure 11-11 might cause the discount rate to change.

[20]In this example we glossed over an important issue: the appropriate cost of capital for the project. Adding decision nodes to a project clearly changes its risk, so we would expect the cost of capital for a project with few decision nodes to have a different risk than one with many nodes. If this is so then the projects should have different costs of capital. In fact, we might expect the cost of capital to change over time as the project moves to different stages, because the stages themselves differ in risk.

SELF-TEST

What is a decision tree? A branch? A node?

If a firm can structure a project such that expenditures can be made in stages rather than all at the beginning, how would this affect the project's risk and expected NPV? Explain.

SUMMARY

In this chapter, we developed a framework for analyzing a project's cash flows and its risk. The key concepts covered are listed below.

- The most important (and most difficult) step in analyzing a capital budgeting project is **estimating the incremental after-tax cash flows** the project will produce.
- A project's **net cash flow** is different from its accounting income. Project net cash flow reflects (1) cash outlays for fixed assets, (2) sales revenues, (3) operating costs, (4) the tax shield provided by depreciation, and (5) cash flows due to changes in net working capital. A project's net cash flow does *not* include interest payments, because they are accounted for by the discounting process. If we deducted interest and then discounted cash flows at the WACC, this would double-count interest charges.
- In determining incremental cash flows, **opportunity costs** (the cash flows forgone by using an asset) must be included, but **sunk costs** (cash outlays that have been made and that cannot be recouped) are not included. Any **externalities** (effects of a project on other parts of the firm) should also be reflected in the analysis. Externalities can be *positive* or *negative* and may be *environmental*.
- **Cannibalization** is an important type of externality that occurs when a new project leads to a reduction in sales of an existing product.
- **Tax laws** affect cash flow analysis in two ways: (1) taxes reduce operating cash flows, and (2) tax laws determine the depreciation expense that can be taken in each year.
- **Price level changes (inflation** or **deflation)** must be considered in project analysis. The best procedure is to build expected price changes into the cash flow estimates. Recognize that output prices and costs for a product can decline over time even though the economy is experiencing inflation.
- The chapter illustrates both **expansion projects**, in which the investment generates new sales, and **replacement projects**, where the primary purpose of the investment is to operate more efficiently and thus reduce costs.
- We discuss three types of risk: **Stand-alone risk, corporate** (or **within-firm) risk**, and **market** (or **beta) risk**. Stand-alone risk does not consider diversification at all; corporate risk considers risk among the firm's own assets; and market risk considers risk at the stockholder level, where stockholders' own diversification is considered.
- **Risk** is important because it affects the discount rate used in capital budgeting; in other words, a project's WACC depends on its risk.
- Assuming the CAPM holds true, **market risk** is the most important risk because (according to the CAPM) it is the risk that affects stock prices. However, usually *it is difficult to measure a project's market risk.*

- **Corporate risk** is important because it influences the firm's ability to use low-cost debt, to maintain smooth operations over time, and to avoid crises that might consume management's energy and disrupt its employees, customers, suppliers, and community. Also, a project's corporate risk is generally easier to measure than its market risk, and, because corporate and market risks are generally thought to be correlated, corporate risk can often serve as a proxy for market risk.

- **Stand-alone risk** is easier to measure than either market or corporate risk. Also, most of a firm's projects' cash flows are correlated with one another, and the firm's total cash flows are correlated with those of most other firms. These correlations mean that a project's stand-alone risk generally can be used as a proxy for hard-to-measure market and corporate risk. As a result, most risk analysis in capital budgeting focuses on stand-alone risk.

- **Sensitivity analysis** is a technique that shows how much a project's NPV will change in response to a given change in an input variable, such as sales, when all other factors are held constant.

- **Scenario analysis** is a risk analysis technique in which the best- and worst-case NPVs are compared with the project's base-case NPV.

- **Monte Carlo simulation** is a risk analysis technique that uses a computer to simulate future events and thereby estimate a project's profitability and riskiness.

- The **risk-adjusted discount rate**, or **project cost of capital**, is the rate used to evaluate a particular project. It is based on the corporate WACC, a value that is increased for projects that are riskier than the firm's average project and decreased for less risky projects.

- A **decision tree** shows how different decisions during a project's life can affect its value.

- A **staged decision tree** divides the analysis into different phases. At each phase a decision is made either to proceed or to stop the project. These decisions are represented on the decision trees by circles and are called **decision nodes**.

- Opportunities to respond to changing circumstances are called **real options** or **managerial options** because they give managers the option to influence the returns on a project. They are also called **strategic options** if they are associated with large, strategic projects rather than routine maintenance projects. Finally, they are also called "real" options because they involve "real" (or "physical") rather than "financial" assets. Many projects include a variety of these **embedded options** that can dramatically affect the true NPV.

- An **investment timing option** involves the possibility of delaying major expenditures until more information on likely outcomes is known. The opportunity to delay can dramatically change a project's estimated value.

- A **growth option** occurs if an investment creates the opportunity to make other potentially profitable investments that would not otherwise be possible. These include (1) options to expand the original project's output, (2) options to enter a new geographical market, and (3) options to introduce complementary products or successive generations of products.

- An **abandonment option** is the ability to discontinue a project if the operating cash flow turns out to be lower than expected. It reduces the risk of a project and increases its value. Instead of total abandonment, some options allow a company to reduce capacity or temporarily suspend operations.

- A **flexibility option** is the option to modify operations depending on how conditions develop during a project's life, especially the type of output produced or the inputs used.

QUESTIONS

(11-1)   Define each of the following terms:

   a. Project cash flow; accounting income
   b. Incremental cash flow; sunk cost; opportunity cost; externality; cannibalization; expansion project; replacement project
   c. Net operating working capital changes; salvage value
   d. Stand-alone risk; corporate (within-firm) risk; market (beta) risk
   e. Sensitivity analysis; scenario analysis; Monte Carlo simulation analysis
   f. Risk-adjusted discount rate; project cost of capital
   g. Decision tree; staged decision tree; decision node; branch
   h. Real options; managerial options; strategic options; embedded options
   i. Investment timing option; growth option; abandonment option; flexibility option

(11-2)   Operating cash flows, rather than accounting profits, are used in project analysis. What is the basis for this emphasis on cash flows as opposed to net income?

(11-3)   Why is it true, in general, that a failure to adjust expected cash flows for expected inflation biases the calculated NPV downward?

(11-4)   Explain why sunk costs should not be included in a capital budgeting analysis but opportunity costs and externalities should be included.

(11-5)   Explain how net operating working capital is recovered at the end of a project's life and why it is included in a capital budgeting analysis.

(11-6)   How do simulation analysis and scenario analysis differ in the way they treat very bad and very good outcomes? What does this imply about using each technique to evaluate project riskiness?

(11-7)   Why are interest charges not deducted when a project's cash flows are calculated for use in a capital budgeting analysis?

(11-8)   Most firms generate cash inflows every day, not just once at the end of the year. In capital budgeting, should we recognize this fact by estimating daily project cash flows and then using them in the analysis? If we do not, will this bias our results? If it does, would the NPV be biased up or down? Explain.

(11-9)   What are some differences in the analysis for a replacement project versus that for a new expansion project?

(11-10)   Distinguish among beta (or market) risk, within-firm (or corporate) risk, and stand-alone risk for a project being considered for inclusion in a firm's capital budget.

(11-11)   In theory, market risk should be the only "relevant" risk. However, companies focus as much on stand-alone risk as on market risk. What are the reasons for the focus on stand-alone risk?

SELF-TEST PROBLEMS   Solutions Appear in Appendix A

(ST-1)
New-Project Analysis

You have been asked by the president of the Farr Construction Company to evaluate the proposed acquisition of a new earth mover. The mover's basic price is $50,000, and it would cost another $10,000 to modify it for special use. Assume that the mover falls into the MACRS 3-year class (see Appendix 11A), that it would be sold after 3 years for $20,000, and that it would require an increase in net working capital (spare parts inventory) of $2,000 at the start of the project. This working capital will be recovered at

Year 3. The earth mover would have no effect on revenues, but it is expected to save the firm $20,000 per year in before-tax operating costs, mainly labor. The firm's marginal federal-plus-state tax rate is 40%.

    a. What are the Year-0 cash flows?
    b. What are the operating cash flows in Years 1, 2, and 3?
    c. What are the additional (nonoperating) cash flows in Year 3?
    d. If the project's cost of capital is 10%, should the earth mover be purchased?

(ST-2)
Corporate Risk Analysis

The staff of Porter Manufacturing has estimated the following net after-tax cash flows and probabilities for a new manufacturing process:

	Net After-Tax Cash Flows		
Year	P = 0.2	P = 0.6	P = 0.2
0	-$100,000	-$100,000	-$100,000
1	20,000	30,000	40,000
2	20,000	30,000	40,000
3	20,000	30,000	40,000
4	20,000	30,000	40,000
5	20,000	30,000	40,000
5*	0	20,000	30,000

Line 0 gives the cost of the process, Lines 1 through 5 give operating cash flows, and Line 5* contains the estimated salvage values. Porter's cost of capital for an average-risk project is 10%.

    a. Assume that the project has average risk. Find the project's expected NPV. (*Hint:* Use expected values for the net cash flow in each year.)
    b. Find the best-case and worst-case NPVs. What is the probability of occurrence of the worst case if the cash flows are perfectly dependent (perfectly positively correlated) over time? If they are independent over time?
    c. Assume that all the cash flows are perfectly positively correlated. That is, assume there are only three possible cash flow streams over time—the worst case, the most likely (or base) case, and the best case—with respective probabilities of 0.2, 0.6, and 0.2. These cases are represented by each of the columns in the table. Find the expected NPV, its standard deviation, and its coefficient of variation.

PROBLEMS   Answers Appear in Appendix B

Easy Problems 1–4

(11-1)
Investment Outlay

Talbot Industries is considering launching a new product. The new manufacturing equipment will cost $17 million, and production and sales will require an initial $5 million investment in net operating working capital. The company's tax rate is 40%.

    a. What is the initial investment outlay?
    b. The company spent and expensed $150,000 on research related to the new product last year. Would this change your answer? Explain.
    c. Rather than build a new manufacturing facility, the company plans to install the equipment in a building it owns but is not now using. The building could be sold for $1.5 million after taxes and real estate commissions. How would this affect your answer?

(11-2)
Operating Cash Flow

The financial staff of Cairn Communications has identified the following information for the first year of the roll-out of its new proposed service:

Projected sales	$18 million
Operating costs (not including depreciation)	$ 9 million
Depreciation	$ 4 million
Interest expense	$ 3 million

The company faces a 40% tax rate. What is the project's operating cash flow for the first year (t = 1)?

(11-3)
Net Salvage Value

Allen Air Lines must liquidate some equipment that is being replaced. The equipment originally cost $12 million, of which 75% has been depreciated. The used equipment can be sold today for $4 million, and its tax rate is 40%. What is the equipment's after-tax net salvage value?

(11-4)
Replacement Analysis

Although the Chen Company's milling machine is old, it is still in relatively good working order and would last for another 10 years. It is inefficient compared to modern standards, though, and so the company is considering replacing it. The new milling machine, at a cost of $110,000 delivered and installed, would also last for 10 years and would produce after-tax cash flows (labor savings and depreciation tax savings) of $19,000 per year. It would have zero salvage value at the end of its life. The firm's WACC is 10%, and its marginal tax rate is 35%. Should Chen buy the new machine?

Intermediate Problems 5–11

(11-5)
Depreciation Methods

Wendy's boss wants to use straight-line depreciation for the new expansion project because he said it will give higher net income in earlier years and give him a larger bonus. The project will last 4 years and requires $1,700,000 of equipment. The company could use either straight line or the 3-year MACRS accelerated method. Under straight-line depreciation, the cost of the equipment would be depreciated evenly over its 4-year life (ignore the half-year convention for the straight-line method). The applicable MACRS depreciation rates are 33.33%, 44.45%, 14.81%, and 7.41%, as discussed in Appendix 11A. The company's WACC is 10%, and its tax rate is 40%.

a. What would the depreciation expense be each year under each method?
b. Which depreciation method would produce the higher NPV, and how much higher would it be?
c. Why might Wendy's boss prefer straight-line depreciation?

(11-6)
New-Project Analysis

The Campbell Company is considering adding a robotic paint sprayer to its production line. The sprayer's base price is $1,080,000, and it would cost another $22,500 to install it. The machine falls into the MACRS 3-year class, and it would be sold after 3 years for $605,000. The MACRS rates for the first three years are 0.3333, 0.4445, and 0.1481. The machine would require an increase in net working capital (inventory) of $15,500. The sprayer would not change revenues, but it is expected to save the firm $380,000 per year in before-tax operating costs, mainly labor. Campbell's marginal tax rate is 35%.

a. What is the Year 0 net cash flow?
b. What are the net operating cash flows in Years 1, 2, and 3?
c. What is the additional Year-3 cash flow (i.e., the after-tax salvage and the return of working capital)?
d. If the project's cost of capital is 12%, should the machine be purchased?

(11-7)
New-Project Analysis

The president of the company you work for has asked you to evaluate the proposed acquisition of a new chromatograph for the firm's R&D department. The equipment's basic price is $70,000, and it would cost another $15,000 to modify it for special use by your firm. The chromatograph, which falls into the MACRS 3-year class, would be sold after 3 years for $30,000. The MACRS rates for the first three years are 0.3333, 0.4445, and 0.1481. Use of the equipment would require an increase in net working capital (spare parts inventory) of $4,000. The machine would have no effect on revenues, but it is expected to save the firm $25,000 per year in before-tax operating costs, mainly labor. The firm's marginal federal-plus-state tax rate is 40%.

    a. What is the Year-0 net cash flow?
    b. What are the net operating cash flows in Years 1, 2, and 3?
    c. What is the additional (nonoperating) cash flow in Year 3?
    d. If the project's cost of capital is 10%, should the chromatograph be purchased?

(11-8)
Inflation
Adjustments

The Rodriguez Company is considering an average-risk investment in a mineral water spring project that has a cost of $150,000. The project will produce 1,000 cases of mineral water per year indefinitely. The current sales price is $138 per case, and the current cost per case is $105. The firm is taxed at a rate of 34%. Both prices and costs are expected to rise at a rate of 6% per year. The firm uses only equity, and it has a cost of capital of 15%. Assume that cash flows consist only of after-tax profits, because the spring has an indefinite life and will not be depreciated.

    a. Should the firm accept the project? (*Hint:* The project is a growing perpetuity, so you must use the constant growth formula to find its NPV.)
    b. Suppose that total costs consisted of a fixed cost of $10,000 per year plus variable costs of $95 per unit and only the variable costs were expected to increase with inflation. Would this make the project better or worse? Continue to assume that the sales price will rise with inflation.

(11-9)
Replacement
Analysis

The Gilbert Instrument Corporation is considering replacing the wood steamer it currently uses to shape guitar sides. The steamer has 6 years of remaining life. If kept, the steamer will have depreciation expenses of $650 for five years and $325 for the sixth year. Its current book value is $3,575, and it can be sold on an Internet auction site for $4,150 at this time. If the old steamer is not replaced, it can be sold for $800 at the end of its useful life.

Gilbert is considering purchasing the *Side Steamer 3000*, a higher-end steamer, which costs $12,000 and has an estimated useful life of 6 years with an estimated salvage value of $1,500. This steamer falls into the MACRS 5-year class, so the applicable depreciation rates are 20.00%, 32.00%, 19.20%, 11.52%, 11.52%, and 5.76%. The new steamer is faster and allows for an output expansion, so sales would rise by $2,000 per year; the new machine's much greater efficiency would reduce operating expenses by $1,900 per year. To support the greater sales, the new machine would require that inventories increase by $2,900, but accounts payable would simultaneously increase by $700. Gilbert's marginal federal-plus-state tax rate is 40%, and its WACC is 15%. Should it replace the old steamer?

(11-10)
Replacement
Analysis

St. Johns River Shipyard's welding machine is 15 years old, fully depreciated, obsolete, and has no salvage value. However, even though it is obsolete, it is perfectly functional as originally designed and can be used for quite a while longer. A new welder will cost $182,500 and have an estimated life of 8 years with no salvage value. The new welder will be much more efficient, however, and this enhanced efficiency will increase earnings before depreciation from $27,000 to $74,000 per year. The new machine will be depreciated over its 5-year MACRS recovery period, so the applicable depreciation rates are 20.00%, 32.00%, 19.20%, 11.52%, 11.52%, and 5.76%. The applicable corporate tax rate is 40%, and the firm's WACC is 12%. Should the old welder be replaced by the new one?

Challenging Problems 11–17

(11-11)
Scenario Analysis

Shao Industries is considering a proposed project for its capital budget. The company estimates the project's NPV is $12 million. This estimate assumes that the economy and market conditions will be average over the next few years. The company's CFO, however, forecasts there is only a 50% chance that the economy will be average. Recognizing this uncertainty, she has also performed the following scenario analysis:

Economic Scenario	Probability of Outcome	NPV
Recession	0.05	−$70 million
Below average	0.20	−25 million
Average	0.50	12 million
Above average	0.20	20 million
Boom	0.05	30 million

What is the project's expected NPV, its standard deviation, and its coefficient of variation?

(11-12)
New-Project Analysis

Madison Manufacturing is considering a new machine that costs $350,000 and would reduce pre-tax manufacturing costs by $110,000 annually. Madison would use the 3-year MACRS method to depreciate the machine, and management thinks the machine would have a value of $33,000 at the end of its 5-year operating life. The applicable depreciation rates are 33.33%, 44.45%, 14.81%, and 7.42%, as discussed in Appendix 11A. Working capital would increase by $35,000 initially, but it would be recovered at the end of the project's 5-year life. Madison's marginal tax rate is 40%, and a 10% WACC is appropriate for the project.

a. Calculate the project's NPV, IRR, MIRR, and payback.
b. Assume management is unsure about the $110,000 cost savings—this figure could deviate by as much as plus or minus 20%. What would the NPV be under each of these extremes?
c. Suppose the CFO wants you to do a scenario analysis with different values for the cost savings, the machine's salvage value, and the working capital (WC) requirement. She asks you to use the following probabilities and values in the scenario analysis:

Scenario	Probability	Cost Savings	Salvage Value	WC
Worst case	0.35	$ 88,000	$28,000	$40,000
Base case	0.35	110,000	33,000	35,000
Best case	0.30	132,000	38,000	30,000

Calculate the project's expected NPV, its standard deviation, and its coefficient of variation. Would you recommend that the project be accepted?

(11-13)
Replacement Analysis

The Everly Equipment Company's flange-lipping machine was purchased 5 years ago for $55,000. It had an expected life of 10 years when it was bought and its remaining depreciation is $5,500 per year for each year of its remaining life. As the older flange-lippers are robust and useful machines, it can be sold for $20,000 at the end of its useful life.

A new high-efficiency, digital-controlled flange-lipper can be purchased for $120,000, including installation costs. During its 5-year life, it will reduce cash operating expenses by $30,000 per year, although it will not affect sales. At the end of its useful life, the high-efficiency machine is estimated to be worthless. MACRS depreciation will be used, and the machine will be depreciated over its 3-year class life rather than its 5-year economic life, so the applicable depreciation rates are 33.33%, 44.45%, 14.81%, and 7.41%.

The old machine can be sold today for $35,000. The firm's tax rate is 35%, and the appropriate WACC is 16%.

a. If the new flange-lipper is purchased, what is the amount of the initial cash flow at Year 0?
b. What are the incremental net cash flows that will occur at the end of Years 1 through 5?
c. What is the NPV of this project? Should Everly replace the flange-lipper?

(11-14)
Replacement Analysis

DeYoung Entertainment Enterprises is considering replacing the latex molding machine it uses to fabricate rubber chickens with a newer, more efficient model. The old machine has a book value of $450,000 and a remaining useful life of 5 years. The current machine would be worn out and worthless in 5 years, but DeYoung can sell it now to a Halloween mask manufacturer for $135,000. The old machine is being depreciated by $90,000 per year for each year of its remaining life.

The new machine has a purchase price of $775,000, an estimated useful life and MACRS class life of 5 years, and an estimated salvage value of $105,000. The applicable depreciation rates are 20.00%, 32.00%, 19.20%, 11.52%, 11.52%, and 5.76%. Being highly efficient, it is expected to economize on electric power usage, labor, and repair costs, and, most importantly, to reduce the number of defective chickens. In total, an annual savings of $185,000 will be realized if the new machine is installed. The company's marginal tax rate is 35%, and it has a 12% WACC.

a. What is the initial net cash flow if the new machine is purchased and the old one is replaced?
b. Calculate the annual depreciation allowances for both machines, and compute the change in the annual depreciation expense if the replacement is made.
c. What are the incremental net cash flows in Years 1 through 5?
d. Should the firm purchase the new machine? Support your answer.
e. In general, how would each of the following factors affect the investment decision, and how should each be treated?

(1) The expected life of the existing machine decreases.
(2) The WACC is not constant but is increasing as DeYoung adds more projects into its capital budget for the year.

(11-15)
Risky Cash Flows

The Bartram-Pulley Company (BPC) must decide between two mutually exclusive investment projects. Each project costs $6,750 and has an expected life of 3 years. Annual net cash flows from each project begin 1 year after the initial investment is made and have the following probability distributions:

Project A		Project B	
Probability	Net Cash Flows	Probability	Net Cash Flows
0.2	$6,000	0.2	$ 0
0.6	6,750	0.6	6,750
0.2	7,500	0.2	18,000

BPC has decided to evaluate the riskier project at a 12% rate and the less risky project at a 10% rate.

a. What is the expected value of the annual net cash flows from each project? What is the coefficient of variation (CV)? (*Hint:* $\sigma_B = \$5,798$ and $CV_B = 0.76$.)
b. What is the risk-adjusted NPV of each project?

c. If it were known that Project B is negatively correlated with other cash flows of the firm whereas Project A is positively correlated, how would this affect the decision? If Project B's cash flows were negatively correlated with gross domestic product (GDP), would that influence your assessment of its risk?

(11-16)
Simulation

Singleton Supplies Corporation (SSC) manufactures medical products for hospitals, clinics, and nursing homes. SSC may introduce a new type of X-ray scanner designed to identify certain types of cancers in their early stages. There are a number of uncertainties about the proposed project, but the following data are believed to be reasonably accurate.

Probability	Developmental Costs	Random Numbers
0.3	$2,000,000	00–29
0.4	4,000,000	30–69
0.3	6,000,000	70–99

Probability	Project Life	Random Numbers
0.2	3 years	00–19
0.6	8 years	20–79
0.2	13 years	80–99

Probability	Sales in Units	Random Numbers
0.2	100	00–19
0.6	200	20–79
0.2	300	80–99

Probability	Sales Price	Random Numbers
0.1	$13,000	00–09
0.8	13,500	10–89
0.1	14,000	90–99

Probability	Cost per Unit (Excluding Developmental Costs)	Random Numbers
0.3	$5,000	00–29
0.4	6,000	30–69
0.3	7,000	70–99

SSC uses a cost of capital of 15% to analyze average-risk projects, 12% for low-risk projects, and 18% for high-risk projects. These risk adjustments primarily reflect the uncertainty about each project's NPV and IRR as measured by their coefficients of variation. The firm is in the 40% federal-plus-state income tax bracket.

a. What is the expected IRR for the X-ray scanner project? Base your answer on the expected values of the variables. Also, assume the after-tax "profits" figure that you develop is equal to annual cash flows. All facilities are leased, so depreciation may be disregarded. Can you determine the value of σ_{IRR} short of actual simulation or complex statistical analysis?

b. Assume that SSC uses a 15% cost of capital for this project. What is the project's NPV? Could you estimate σ_{NPV} without either simulation or a complex statistical analysis?

c. Show the process by which a computer would perform a simulation analysis for this project. Use the random numbers 44, 17, 16, 58, 1; 79, 83, 86; and 19, 62, 6 to illustrate the process with the first computer run. Calculate the first-run NPV and IRR. Assume the cash flows for each year are independent of cash flows for other years. Also, assume the computer operates as follows: (1) A developmental cost and a project life are estimated for the first run using the first two random numbers. (2) Next, sales volume, sales price, and cost per unit are estimated using the next three random numbers and used to derive a cash flow for the first year. (3) Then, the next three random numbers are used to estimate sales volume, sales price, and cost per unit for the second year, hence the cash flow for the second year. (4) Cash flows for other years are developed similarly, on out to the first run's estimated life. (5) With the developmental cost and the cash flow stream established, NPV and IRR for the first run are derived and stored in the computer's memory. (6) The process is repeated to generate perhaps 500 other NPVs and IRRs. (7) Frequency distributions for NPV and IRR are plotted by the computer, and the distributions' means and standard deviations are calculated.

(11-17)
Decision Tree

The Yoran Yacht Company (YYC), a prominent sailboat builder in Newport, may design a new 30-foot sailboat based on the "winged" keels first introduced on the 12-meter yachts that raced for the America's Cup.

First, YYC would have to invest $10,000 at t = 0 for the design and model tank testing of the new boat. YYC's managers believe there is a 60% probability that this phase will be successful and the project will continue. If Stage 1 is not successful, the project will be abandoned with zero salvage value.

The next stage, if undertaken, would consist of making the molds and producing two prototype boats. This would cost $500,000 at t = 1. If the boats test well, YYC would go into production. If they do not, the molds and prototypes could be sold for $100,000. The managers estimate the probability is 80% that the boats will pass testing and that Stage 3 will be undertaken.

Stage 3 consists of converting an unused production line to produce the new design. This would cost $1 million at t = 2. If the economy is strong at this point, the net value of sales would be $3 million; if the economy is weak, the net value would be $1.5 million. Both net values occur at t = 3, and each state of the economy has a probability of 0.5. YYC's corporate cost of capital is 12%.

a. Assume this project has average risk. Construct a decision tree and determine the project's expected NPV.
b. Find the project's standard deviation of NPV and coefficient of variation of NPV. If YYC's average project had a CV of between 1.0 and 2.0, would this project be of high, low, or average stand-alone risk?

SPREADSHEET PROBLEM

(11-18)
Build a Model: Issues in Capital Budgeting

resource

Start with the partial model in the file *Ch11 P18 Build a Model.xls* on the textbook's Web site. Webmaster.com has developed a powerful new server that would be used for corporations' Internet activities. It would cost $10 million at Year 0 to buy the equipment necessary to manufacture the server. The project would require net working capital at the beginning of a year in an amount equal to 10% of the year's projected sales: $NOWC_0 = 10\%(Sales_1)$. The servers would sell for $24,000 per unit, and Webmasters believes that variable costs would amount to $17,500 per unit. After Year 1, the sales price and variable costs will increase at the inflation rate of 3%. The company's nonvariable costs would be $1 million at Year 1 and would increase with inflation.

The server project would have a life of 4 years. If the project is undertaken, it must be continued for the entire 4 years. Also, the project's returns are expected to be highly correlated with returns on the firm's other assets. The firm believes it could sell 1,000 units per year.

The equipment would be depreciated over a 5-year period, using MACRS rates. The estimated market value of the equipment at the end of the project's 4-year life is $500,000. Webmaster's federal-plus-state tax rate is 40%. Its cost of capital is 10% for average-risk projects, defined as projects with an NPV coefficient of variation between 0.8 and 1.2. Low-risk projects are evaluated with a WACC of 8% and high-risk projects at 13%.

a. Develop a spreadsheet model, and use it to find the project's NPV, IRR, and payback.
b. Conduct a sensitivity analysis to determine the sensitivity of NPV to changes in the sales price, variable costs per unit, and number of units sold. Set these variables' values at 10% and 20% above and below their base-case values. Include a graph in your analysis.
c. Conduct a scenario analysis. Assume that there is a 25% probability that best-case conditions, with each of the variables discussed in part b being 20% better than its base-case value, will occur. There is a 25% probability of worst-case conditions, with the variables 20% worse than base, and a 50% probability of base-case conditions.
d. If the project appears to be more or less risky than an average project, find its risk-adjusted NPV, IRR, and payback.
e. On the basis of information in the problem, would you recommend the project should be accepted?

MINI CASE

Shrieves Casting Company is considering adding a new line to its product mix, and the capital budgeting analysis is being conducted by Sidney Johnson, a recently graduated MBA. The production line would be set up in unused space in Shrieves's main plant. The machinery's invoice price would be approximately $200,000, another $10,000 in shipping charges would be required, and it would cost an additional $30,000 to install the equipment. The machinery has an economic life of 4 years, and Shrieves has obtained a special tax ruling that places the equipment in the MACRS 3-year class. The machinery is expected to have a salvage value of $25,000 after 4 years of use.

The new line would generate incremental sales of 1,250 units per year for 4 years at an incremental cost of $100 per unit in the first year, excluding depreciation. Each unit can be sold for $200 in the first year. The sales price and cost are both expected to increase by 3% per year due to inflation. Further, to handle the new line, the firm's net working capital would have to increase by an amount equal to 12% of sales revenues. The firm's tax rate is 40%, and its overall weighted average cost of capital is 10%.

a. Define "incremental cash flow."
  (1) Should you subtract interest expense or dividends when calculating project cash flow?
  (2) Suppose the firm spent $100,000 last year to rehabilitate the production line site. Should this be included in the analysis? Explain.
  (3) Now assume the plant space could be leased out to another firm at $25,000 per year. Should this be included in the analysis? If so, how?
  (4) Finally, assume that the new product line is expected to decrease sales of the firm's other lines by $50,000 per year. Should this be considered in the analysis? If so, how?

b. Disregard the assumptions in part a. What is Shrieves's depreciable basis? What are the annual depreciation expenses?

c. Calculate the annual sales revenues and costs (other than depreciation). Why is it important to include inflation when estimating cash flows?

d. Construct annual incremental operating cash flow statements.

e. Estimate the required net working capital for each year and the cash flow due to investments in net working capital.

f. Calculate the after-tax salvage cash flow.

g. Calculate the net cash flows for each year. Based on these cash flows, what are the project's NPV, IRR, MIRR, PI, payback, and discounted payback? Do these indicators suggest that the project should be undertaken?

h. What does the term "risk" mean in the context of capital budgeting; to what extent can risk be quantified; and, when risk is quantified, is the quantification based primarily on statistical analysis of historical data or on subjective, judgmental estimates?

i. (1) What are the three types of risk that are relevant in capital budgeting?

    (2) How is each of these risk types measured, and how do they relate to one another?

    (3) How is each type of risk used in the capital budgeting process?

j. (1) What is sensitivity analysis?

    (2) Perform a sensitivity analysis on the unit sales, salvage value, and cost of capital for the project. Assume each of these variables can vary from its base-case, or expected, value by ±10%, ±20%, and ±30%. Include a sensitivity diagram, and discuss the results.

    (3) What is the primary weakness of sensitivity analysis? What is its primary usefulness?

k. Assume that Sidney Johnson is confident in her estimates of all the variables that affect the project's cash flows except unit sales and sales price. If product acceptance is poor, unit sales would be only 900 units a year and the unit price would only be $160; a strong consumer response would produce sales of 1,600 units and a unit price of $240. Johnson believes there is a 25% chance of poor acceptance, a 25% chance of excellent acceptance, and a 50% chance of average acceptance (the base case).

    (1) What is scenario analysis?

    (2) What is the worst-case NPV? The best-case NPV?

    (3) Use the worst-, base-, and best-case NPVs and probabilities of occurrence to find the project's expected NPV, as well as the NPV's standard deviation and coefficient of variation.

l. Are there problems with scenario analysis? Define simulation analysis, and discuss its principal advantages and disadvantages.

m. (1) Assume Shrieves's average project has a coefficient of variation in the range of 0.2 to 0.4. Would the new line be classified as high risk, average risk, or low risk? What type of risk is being measured here?

    (2) Shrieves typically adds or subtracts 3 percentage points to the overall cost of capital to adjust for risk. Should the new line be accepted?

    (3) Are there any subjective risk factors that should be considered before the final decision is made?

n. What is a real option? What are some types of real options?

SELECTED ADDITIONAL CASES

The following cases from CengageCompose cover many of the concepts discussed in this chapter and are available at **compose.cengage.com**.

Klein-Brigham Series:
Case 12, "Indian River Citrus Company (A)"; Case 44, "Cranfield, Inc. (A)"; and Case 14, "Robert Montoya, Inc." focus on cash flow estimation. Case 13, "Indian River Citrus (B)"; Case 45, "Cranfield, Inc. (B)"; Case 58, "Tasty Foods (B)"; Case 60, "Heavenly Foods"; and Case 15, "Robert Montoya, Inc. (B)," illustrate project risk analysis. Cases 75, 76, and 77, "The Western Company (A and B)," are comprehensive cases.

Brigham-Buzzard Series:
Case 7, "Powerline Network Corporation (Risk and Real Options in Capital Budgeting)."

© lulu/fotolia.com

Appendix 11A

Tax Depreciation

Companies often calculate depreciation one way when figuring taxes and another way when reporting income to investors: Many use the **straight-line method** for stockholder reporting (or "book" purposes), but they use the fastest rate permitted by law for tax purposes. Under the straight-line method used for stockholder reporting, one normally takes the cost of the asset, subtracts its estimated salvage value, and divides the net amount by the asset's useful economic life. For example, consider an asset with a 5-year life that costs \$100,000 and has a \$12,500 salvage value; its annual straight-line depreciation charge is (\$100,000 − \$12,500)/5 = \$17,500. Note, however, as we stated earlier, salvage value is a factor in financial reporting but it is *not* considered for tax depreciation purposes.

For tax purposes, Congress changes the permissible tax depreciation methods from time to time. Prior to 1954, the straight-line method was required for tax purposes, but in 1954 **accelerated methods** (double-declining balance and sum-of-years'-digits) were permitted. Then, in 1981, the old accelerated methods were replaced by a simpler procedure known as the Accelerated Cost Recovery System (ACRS). The ACRS system was changed again in 1986 as a part of the Tax Reform Act, and it is now known as the **Modified Accelerated Cost Recovery System (MACRS)**; a 1993 tax law made further changes in this area.

Note that U.S. tax laws are complicated, and in this text we can provide only an overview of MACRS that will give you a basic understanding of the impact of depreciation on capital budgeting decisions. Further, the tax laws change so often that the numbers we present may be outdated before the book is published. Thus, when dealing with tax depreciation in real-world situations, always consult current Internal Revenue Service (IRS) publications or individuals with expertise in tax matters.

For tax purposes, the entire cost of an asset is expensed over its depreciable life. Historically, an asset's depreciable life was set equal to its estimated useful economic life; it was intended that an asset would be fully depreciated at approximately the same time that it reached the end of its useful economic life. However, MACRS totally abandoned that practice and set simple guidelines that created several classes of assets, each with a more-or-less arbitrarily prescribed life called a *recovery period* or *class life*. The MACRS class lives bear only a rough relationship to assets' expected useful economic lives. A major effect of the MACRS system has been to shorten the depreciable lives of assets, thus giving businesses larger tax deductions early in the assets' lives and thereby increasing the present value of the cash flows. Table 11A-1 describes the types of property that fit into the different class life groups, and Table 11A-2 sets forth the MACRS recovery allowance percentages (depreciation rates) for selected classes of investment property.

Consider Table 11A-1, which gives the MACRS class lives and the types of assets that fall into each category. Property in the 27.5- and 39-year categories (real estate) must be depreciated by the straight-line method, but 3-, 5-, 7-, and 10-year property (personal

TABLE **11A-1**

Major Classes and Asset Lives for MACRS

Class	Type of Property
3-year	Certain special manufacturing tools
5-year	Automobiles, light-duty trucks, computers, and certain special manufacturing equipment
7-year	Most industrial equipment, office furniture, and fixtures
10-year	Certain longer-lived types of equipment
27.5-year	Residential rental real property such as apartment buildings
39-year	All nonresidential real property, including commercial and industrial buildings

© Cengage Learning 2014

property) can be depreciated either by the accelerated method set forth in Table 11A-2 or by the straight-line method.[1]

As we saw earlier in the chapter, higher depreciation expenses result in lower taxes in the early years and hence lead to a higher present value of cash flows. Therefore, because firms have the choice of using straight-line rates or the accelerated rates shown in Table 11A-2, most elect to use the accelerated rates.

The yearly recovery allowance, or depreciation expense, is determined by multiplying each asset's *depreciable basis* by the applicable recovery percentage shown in Table 11A-2. You might be wondering why 4 years of deprecation rates are shown for property in the 3-year class. Under MACRS, the assumption is generally made that property is placed in service in the middle of the first year. Thus, for 3-year-class property, the recovery period begins in the middle of the year the asset is placed in service and ends 3 years later. The effect of the *half-year convention* is to extend the recovery period out one more year, so 3-year-class property is depreciated over 4 calendar years, 5-year property is depreciated over 6 calendar years, and so on. This convention is incorporated into Table 11A-2's recovery allowance percentages.[2]

SELF TEST

What do the acronyms ACRS and MACRS stand for? Briefly describe the tax depreciation system under MACRS.

---

[1]The Tax Code currently (for 2012) permits companies to *expense*, which is equivalent to depreciating over 1 year, up to $125,000 of equipment; see IRS Publication 946 for details. This is a benefit primarily for small companies. Thus, if a small company bought one asset worth up to $125,000, it could write the asset off in the year it was acquired. This is called "Section 179 expensing." We shall disregard this provision throughout the book. Also, Congress enacted the Job Creation and Worker Assistance Act of 2002 following the terrorist attacks on the World Trade Center and Pentagon. This act, among other things, temporarily changed how depreciation is charged for property acquired after September 10, 2001, and before September 11, 2004, and put in service before January 1, 2005. We shall disregard this provision throughout the book as well.

[2]The half-year convention also applies if the straight-line alternative is used, with half of one year's depreciation taken in the first year, a full year's depreciation taken in each of the remaining years of the asset's class life, and the remaining half-year's depreciation taken in the year following the end of the class life. You should recognize that virtually all companies have computerized depreciation systems. Each asset's depreciation pattern is programmed into the system at the time of its acquisition, and the computer aggregates the depreciation allowances for all assets when the accountants close the books and prepare financial statements and tax returns.

TABLE 11A-2

Recovery Allowance Percentage for Personal Property

Ownership Year	Class of Investment			
	3-Year	5-Year	7-Year	10-Year
1	33.33%	20.00%	14.29%	10.00%
2	44.45	32.00	24.49	18.00
3	14.81	19.20	17.49	14.40
4	7.41	11.52	12.49	11.52
5		11.52	8.93	9.22
6		5.76	8.92	7.37
7			8.93	6.55
8			4.46	6.55
9				6.56
10				6.55
11				3.28
	100%	100%	100%	100%

Notes:

1. We developed these recovery allowance percentages based on the 200% declining balance method prescribed by MACRS, with a switch to straight-line depreciation at some point in the asset's life. For example, consider the 5-year recovery allowance percentages. The straight-line percentage would be 20% per year, so the 200% declining balance multiplier is 2.0(20%) = 40% = 0.4. However, because the half-year convention applies, the MACRS percentage for Year 1 is 20%. For Year 2, there is 80% of the depreciable basis remaining to be depreciated, so the recovery allowance percentage is 0.40(80%) = 32%. In Year 3, 20% + 32% = 52% of the depreciation has been taken, leaving 48%, so the percentage is 0.4(48%) = 19.2%. In Year 4, the percentage is 0.4(28.8%) = 11.52%. After 4 years, straight-line depreciation exceeds the declining balance depreciation, so a switch is made to straight-line (which is permitted under the law). However, the half-year convention must also be applied at the end of the class life, and the remaining 17.28% of depreciation must be taken (amortized) over 1.5 years. Thus, the percentage in Year 5 is 17.28%/1.5 = 11.52%, and in Year 6 it is 17.28% − 11.52% = 5.76%. Although the tax tables carry the allowance percentages out to two decimal places, we have rounded to the nearest whole number for ease of illustration. See the worksheet *7. App. A* in the file *Ch11 Tool Kit.xls* on the textbook's Web site for the exact recovery percentages specified by the IRS.

2. Residential rental property (apartments) is depreciated over a 27.5-year life, whereas commercial and industrial structures are depreciated over 39 years. In both cases, straight-line depreciation must be used. The depreciation allowance for the first year is based, pro rata, on the month the asset was placed in service, with the remainder of the first year's depreciation being taken in the 28th or 40th year. A half-month convention is assumed; that is, an asset placed in service in February would receive 10.5 months of depreciation in the first year.

© Cengage Learning 2014

resource

See **Ch11 Tool Kit.xls** on the textbook's Web site for all calculations.

© lulu/fotolia.com

PART **5**

Corporate Valuation and Governance

Adalberto Rios Szalay/Sexto Sol/Getty Images

CHAPTER **12**

Corporate Valuation and Financial Planning

A survey of CFOs disclosed a paradox regarding financial planning. On one hand, almost all CFOs stated that financial planning is both important and highly useful for allocating resources. On the other hand, 45% also said that budgeting is "contentious, political, and time-consuming," and 53% went on to say that the budgeting process can encourage undesirable behavior among managers as they negotiate budgets to meet their own rather than the company's objectives. They also said that instead of basing growth and incentive compensation targets on an analysis of what markets and competitors are likely to do in the future, firms often set their targets at last year's levels plus a percentage increase, which is dangerous in a dynamic economy.

To resolve these issues, many companies use *demand-pull* budgeting, which links the budget to a sales forecast and updates the sales forecast to reflect changing economic conditions. This approach is often augmented with a *rolling forecast*, in which companies make 1-year and 5-year forecasts but then modify the 1-year forecast each month as new operating results become available.

Another survey shows that high-performance companies also focus on the links between forecasting, planning, and business strategy rather than on just cost management and cost accounting. According to John McMahan of the Hackett Group, such changes are leading to greater forecasting accuracy, higher employee morale, and better corporate performance. These issues are often thought of as "management" rather than "finance," but this is a false distinction. Much of finance is numbers-oriented, but as any CFO will tell you, his or her primary job is to help the firm as a whole achieve good results. The procedures discussed in this chapter can help firms improve their operations and results.

Sources: J. McCafferty, "Planning for the Best," *CFO*, February 2007, p. 24; and Don Durfee, "Alternative Budgeting," *CFO*, June 2006, p. 28.

Corporate Valuation and Financial Planning

© Rob Webb/Getty Images

The value of a firm is determined by the size, timing, and risk of its expected future free cash flows (FCF). Managers use projected financial statements to estimate the impact that different operating plans have on intrinsic value. Managers also use projected statements to identify deficits that must be financed in order to implement the operating plans. This chapter explains how to project financial statements that incorporate operating assumptions and financial policies.

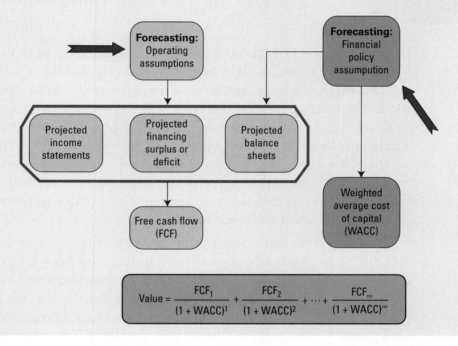

© Cengage Learning 2014

$$Value = \frac{FCF_1}{(1 + WACC)^1} + \frac{FCF_2}{(1 + WACC)^2} + \cdots + \frac{FCF_\infty}{(1 + WACC)^\infty}$$

resource

The textbook's Web site contains an Excel file that will guide you through the chapter's calculations. The file for this chapter is **Ch12 Tool Kit.xls**, and we encourage you to open the file and follow along as you read the chapter.

Our primary objective in this book is to explain how financial managers can make their companies more valuable. However, value creation is impossible unless the company has well-designed operating and financial plans. As Yogi Berra once said, "You've got to be careful if you don't know where you're going, because you might not get there."

A vital step in financial planning is to forecast financial statements, which are called **projected financial statements** or **pro forma financial statements**. Managers use projected financial statements in four ways: (1) By looking at projected statements, they can assess whether the firm's anticipated performance is in line with the firm's own general targets and with investors' expectations. (2) Pro forma statements can be used to estimate the effect of proposed operating changes, enabling managers to conduct "what if" analyses. (3) Managers use pro forma statements to anticipate the firm's future financing needs. (4) Managers forecast free cash flows under different operating plans, forecast their capital requirements, and then choose the plan that maximizes shareholder value. Security analysts make the same types of projections, forecasting future earnings, cash flows, and stock prices.

12-1 Overview of Financial Planning

The two most important components of financial planning are the operating plan and the financial plan.

12-1a The Operating Plan

As its name suggests, an operating plan provides detailed implementation guidance for a firm's operations, including the firm's choice of market segments, product lines, sales and marketing strategies, production processes, and logistics. An operating plan can be developed for any time horizon, but most companies use a 5-year horizon, with the plan being quite detailed for the first year but less and less specific for each succeeding year. The plan explains who is responsible for each particular function and when specific tasks are to be accomplished.

An important part of the operating plan is the forecast of sales, production costs, inventories, and other operating items. In fact, this part of the operating plan actually is a forecast of the company's expected free cash flow. (Recall from Chapter 2 that free cash flow is defined as net operating profit after taxes (NOPAT) minus the investment in total operating capital.)

Free cash flow is the primary source of a company's value. Using what-if analysis, managers can analyze different operating plans to estimate their impact on value. In addition, managers can apply sensitivity analysis, scenario analysis, and simulation to estimate the risk of different operating plans, which is an important part of risk management.

12-1b The Financial Plan

By definition, a company's operating assets can grow only by the purchase of additional assets. Therefore, a growing company must continually obtain cash to purchase new assets. Some of this cash might be generated internally by its operations, but some might have to come externally from shareholders or debtholders. This is the essence of financial planning—forecasting the additional sources of financing required to fund the operating plan.

There is a strong connection between financial planning and free cash flow. A company's operations generate the free cash flow, but the financial plan determines how the company will use the free cash flow. Recall from Chapter 2 that free cash flow can be used in five ways: (1) pay dividends, (2) repurchase stock, (3) pay the net after-tax interest on debt, (4) repay debt, or (5) purchase financial assets such as marketable securities. A company's financial plan must use free cash flow differently if FCF is negative than if FCF is positive.

If free cash flow is positive, the financial plan must identify how much FCF to allocate among its investors (shareholders or debtholders) and how much to put aside for future needs by purchasing marketable securities. If free cash flow is negative, either because the company is growing rapidly (which requires large investments in operating capital) or because the company has low NOPAT, then the total uses of free cash flow must also be negative. For example, instead of repurchasing stock, the company might have to issue stock; instead of repaying debt, the company might have to issue debt.

Therefore, the financial plan must incorporate (1) the company's dividend policy, which determines the targeted size and method of cash distributions to shareholders, and (2) the capital structure, which determines the targeted mix of debt and equity used to finance the firm, which in turn determines the relative mix of distributions to shareholders and payments to debtholders.

SELF-TEST

Briefly describe the key elements of an operating plan.

Identify the five uses of free cash flow and how these uses are related to a financial plan.

12-2 Financial Planning at MicroDrive, Inc.

As we described in Chapters 2 and 3, MicroDrive's operating performance and stock price have declined in recent years. As a result, MicroDrive's board recently installed a new management team: A new CEO, CFO, marketing manager, sales manager, inventory manager, and credit manager—only the production manager was retained. The new team met for a 3-day retreat with the goal of developing a plan to improve the company's performance.

One of the first steps was to develop forecasts based on the status quo to give the management team a better idea of where the company is now and where it will be if they don't make changes. The new CFO began by developing an *Excel* model to forecast the operating plan and the financial plan. Refer to ***Ch12 Tool Kit.xls*** as we explain MicroDrive's financial planning.

The CFO's first step was to examine the current and recent historical data. Figure 12-1 shows MicroDrive's most recent financial statements and selected additional data; see Chapters 2 and 3 for a full discussion of the process used to assess MicroDrive's current position and trends.

FIGURE 12-1

MicroDrive's Most Recent Financial Statements (Millions, Except for Per Share Data)

	A	B	C	D	E	F	G
15	**INCOME STATEMENTS**			**BALANCE SHEETS**			
16		**2012**	**2013**	*Assets*		**2012**	**2013**
17	Net sales	$ 4,760	$ 5,000	Cash	$ 60	$ 50	
18	COGS (excl. depr.)	3,560	3,800	ST Investments	40	-	
19	Depreciation	170	200	Accounts receivable	380	500	
20	Other operating expenses	480	500	Inventories	820	1,000	
21	EBIT	$ 550	$ 500	Total CA	$ 1,300	$ 1,550	
22	Interest expense	100	120	Net PP&E	1,700	2,000	
23	Pretax earnings	$ 450	$ 380	Total assets	$ 3,000	$ 3,550	
24	Taxes (40%)	180	152				
25	NI before pref. div.	$ 270	$ 228	*Liabilities and equity*			
26	Preferred div.	8	8	Accounts payable	$ 190	$ 200	
27	Net income	$ 262	$ 220	Accruals	280	300	
28				Notes payable	130	280	
29	*Other Data*			Total CL	$ 600	$ 780	
30	Common dividends	$48	$50	Long-term bonds	1,000	1,200	
31	Addition to RE	$214	$170	Total liabilities	$ 1,600	$ 1,980	
32	Tax rate	40%	40%	Preferred stock	100	100	
33	Shares of common stock	50	50	Common stock	500	500	
34	Earnings per share	$5.24	$4.40	Retained earnings	800	970	
35	Dividends per share	$0.96	$1.00	Total common equity	$ 1,300	$ 1,470	
36	Price per share	$40.00	$27.00	Total liabs. & equity	$ 3,000	$ 3,550	
37							

FIGURE 12-2

MicroDrive's Forecast: Inputs for the Status Quo Scenario

	A	B	C	D	E	F	G	H	I
60	**Status Quo**	Industry	MicroDrive		MicroDrive				
61	Inputs	Actual	Actual		Forecast				
62	*1. Operating Ratios*	2013	2012	2013	2014	2015	2016	2017	2018
63	Sales growth rate	5%	15%	5%	10%	8%	7%	5%	5%
64	COGS (excl. depr.) / Sales	76%	75%	76%	76%	76%	76%	76%	76%
65	Depreciation / Net PP&E	9%	10%	10%	10%	10%	10%	10%	10%
66	Other op. exp. / Sales	10%	10%	10%	10%	10%	10%	10%	10%
67	Cash / Sales	1%	1%	1%	1%	1%	1%	1%	1%
68	Acc. rec. / Sales	8%	8%	10%	10%	10%	10%	10%	10%
69	Inventory / Sales	15%	17%	20%	20%	20%	20%	20%	20%
70	Net PP&E / Sales	33%	36%	40%	40%	40%	40%	40%	40%
71	Acc. pay. / Sales	4%	4%	4%	4%	4%	4%	4%	4%
72	Accruals / Sales	7%	6%	6%	6%	6%	6%	6%	6%
73	Tax rate	40%	40%	40%	40%	40%	40%	40%	40%
74	*2. Capital Structure*	Actual Market Weights			Target Market Weights				
75	% Long-term debt	22%	31%	41%	28%	28%	28%	28%	28%
76	% Short-term debt	3%	4%	10%	2%	2%	2%	2%	2%
77	% Preferred stock	0%	3%	3%	3%	3%	3%	3%	3%
78	% Common stock	75%	62%	46%	67%	67%	67%	67%	67%
79	*3. Costs of Capital*				Forecast				
80	Rate on LT debt				9.0%	9%	9%	9%	9%
81	Rate on ST debt				10.0%	10%	10%	10%	10%
82	Rate on preferred stock (ignoring flotation costs)				8.0%	8%	8%	8%	8%
83	Cost of equity				13.58%	14%	14%	14%	14%
84	*4. Target Dividend Policy*		Actual						
85	Growth rate of dividends		11%	4.2%	5%	5%	5%	5%	5%

The CFO's second step was to choose a forecasting framework. Many companies, including MicroDrive, forecast their entire financial statements as part of the planning process. This approach is called **forecasted financial statements (FFS) method** of financial planning.

Figure 12-2 shows the inputs MicroDrive uses to forecast different scenarios for its operating plan and financial plan. The inputs are for the Status Quo scenario, which assumes most of MicroDrive's operating activities and financial policies remain unchanged. The figure shows actual values for industry peers (the silver section), actual values for MicroDrive's past two years, and forecasted values for MicroDrive's 5-year forecast. The blue section shows inputs for the first year and inputs for any subsequent years that differ from the previous year. Section 1 shows the ratios required to project the items required for an operating plan, Section 2 shows the inputs related to the capital structure, Section 3 shows the costs of the capital components, and Section 4 shows the target dividend policy. We will describe each of these sections as they are applied to the forecast, beginning with the forecast of operations.

12-3 Forecasting Operations

The first row in Section 1 of Figure 12-2 shows the forecast of the sales growth rate. After discussions with teams from marketing, sales, product development, and production, MicroDrive's CFO chose a growth rate of 10% for the next year. Keep in mind that this is just a preliminary estimate and that it is easy to make changes in the *Excel* model (after doing the hard work to build the model!). Notice that MicroDrive is forecasting sales growth to decline and level off by the end of the forecast. Recall from Chapter 7 that the growth rate for a company's sales and free cash flows must level off at some future date in order to apply the constant growth model at the forecast horizon. Had MicroDrive's managers projected nonconstant growth for more than five years, Figure 12-2 would need to be extended until growth does level out.

Other than sales growth, MicroDrive's managers assumed that the operating ratios for 2014 would remain constant for the entire forecast period. However, it would be quite easy for them to input changes in the future ratios, with one caveat. The operating ratios must level off by the end of the forecast period, or else the free cash flows *will not* be growing at a constant rate by the end of the forecast period even if sales *are* growing at a constant rate.

The following sections explain how MicroDrive uses the ratios in Figure 12-2 to forecast its operations. For convenience, the operating ratio inputs are repeated in Panel A of Figure 12-3; Panel B reports the resulting operating forecast.

12-3a Sales Revenues

Section B1 of Figure 12-3 shows the forecast of net sales based on the previous year's sales and the forecasted growth rate in sales. For example, the forecast of net sales for 2014 is $(1 + 0.10)(\$5,000) = \$5,500$.

12-3b Operating Assets

Section B2 of Figure 12-3 shows the forecast of operating assets. As noted earlier, MicroDrive's assets must increase if sales are to increase, and some types of assets grow proportionately to sales, including cash.

MicroDrive writes and deposits checks every day. Because its managers don't know exactly when all of the checks will clear, they can't predict exactly what the balance in their checking accounts will be on any given day. Therefore, they must maintain a balance of cash and cash equivalents (such as very short-term marketable securities) to avoid overdrawing their accounts. We discuss the issue of cash management in Chapter 16, but MicroDrive's CFO assumed that the cash required to support MicroDrive's operations is proportional to its sales. For example, the forecasted cash in 2014 is $1\%(2014 \text{ sales}) = 1\%(\$5,500) = \$55$. The CFO applied the same process to project cash in subsequent years.

Unless a company changes its credit policy or has a change in its customer base, accounts receivable should be proportional to sales. The CFO assumed that the credit policy and customers' paying patterns would remain constant and so projected accounts receivable as $10\%(\$5,500) = \$550$.

As sales increase, firms generally must carry more inventories. The CFO assumed here that inventory would be proportional to sales. (Chapter 16 will discuss inventory management in detail). The projected inventory is $20\%(\$5,500) = \$1,100$.

It might be reasonable to assume that cash, accounts receivable, and inventories will be proportional to sales, but will the amount of net property, plant, and equipment go up and down as sales go up and down? The correct answer could be either yes or no. When companies acquire PP&E, they often install more capacity than they currently need due to economies of scale in building capacity. Moreover, even if a plant is operating at its maximum-rated capacity, most companies can produce additional units by reducing

FIGURE 12-3

MicroDrive's Forecast of Operations for the Status Quo Scenario (Millions of Dollars, Except for Per Share Data)

	A	B	C	D	E	F	G	H	I
116	**Status Quo**	Industry	MicroDrive				MicroDrive		
117	**Panel A: Inputs**	Actual	Actual				Forecast		
118	***A1. Operating Ratios***	2013	2012	2013	2014	2015	2016	2017	2018
119	Sales growth rate	5%	15%	5%	10%	8%	7%	5%	5%
120	COGS (excl. depr.) / Sales	76%	75%	76%	76%	76%	76%	76%	76%
121	Depreciation / Net PP&E	9%	10%	10%	10%	10%	10%	10%	10%
122	Other op. exp. / Sales	10%	10%	10%	10%	10%	10%	10%	10%
123	Cash / Sales	1%	1%	1%	1%	1%	1%	1%	1%
124	Acc. rec. / Sales	8%	8%	10%	10%	10%	10%	10%	10%
125	Inventory / Sales	15%	17%	20%	20%	20%	20%	20%	20%
126	Net PP&E / Sales	33%	36%	40%	40%	40%	40%	40%	40%
127	Acc. pay. / Sales	4%	4%	4%	4%	4%	4%	4%	4%
128	Accruals / Sales	7%	6%	6%	6%	6%	6%	6%	6%
129	Tax rate	40%	40%	40%	40%	40%	40%	40%	40%
130	**Panel B: Results**			Actual			Forecast		
131	***B1. Sales Revenues***			2013	2014	2015	2016	2017	2018
132	Net sales			$5,000	$5,500	$5,940	$6,356	$6,674	$7,007
133	***B2. Operating Assets and Operating Liabilities***								
134	Cash			$50	$55	$59	$64	$67	$70
135	Accounts receivable			$500	$550	$594	$636	$667	$701
136	Inventories			$1,000	$1,100	$1,188	$1,271	$1,335	$1,401
137	Net PP&E			$2,000	$2,200	$2,376	$2,542	$2,669	$2,803
138	Accounts payable			$200	$220	$238	$254	$267	$280
139	Accruals			$300	$330	$356	$381	$400	$420
140	***B3. Operating Income***								
141	COGS (excl. depr.)			$3,800	$4,180	$4,514	$4,830	$5,072	$5,326
142	Depreciation			$200	$220	$238	$254	$267	$280
143	Other operating expenses			$500	$550	$594	$636	$667	$701
144	EBIT			$500	$550	$594	$636	$667	$701
145	Net operating profit after taxes			$300	$330	$356	$381	$400	$420
146	***B4. Free Cash Flows***								
147	Net operating working capital			$1,050	$1,155	$1,247	$1,335	$1,401	$1,472
148	Total operating capital			$3,050	$3,355	$3,623	$3,877	$4,071	$4,274
149	FCF = NOPAT − Δ op capital			−$260	$25	$88	$128	$207	$217
150	***B5. Estimated Intrinsic Value***								
151	Target WACC				11.0%	11.0%	11.0%	11.0%	11.0%
152	Return on invested capital			9.8%	9.8%	9.8%	9.8%	9.8%	9.8%
153	Growth in FCF					252%	45.1%	61.7%	5.0%
154									

155	**Horizon Value:**		Value of operations $2,719
156			+ ST investments $0
157	$HV_{2018} = \dfrac{FCF_{2018}(1+g_L)}{(WACC - g_L)} = $ $3,814		Estimated total intrinsic value $2,719
158			− All debt $1,480
159	**Value of Operations:**		− Preferred stock $100
160	Present value of HV $2,267		Estimated intrinsic value of equity $1,139
161	+ Present value of FCF $453		÷ Number of shares $50
162	Value of operations = $2,719		Estimated intrinsic stock price = $22.78

downtime for scheduled maintenance, by running machinery at a higher than optimal speed, or by adding a second or third shift. Therefore, at least in the short run, sales and net PP&E may not have a close relationship.

However, some companies do have a close relationship between sales and net PP&E, even in the short term. For example, new stores in many retail chains achieve the same sales during their first year as the chain's existing stores. The only way such retailers can grow (beyond inflation) is by adding new stores. Such companies therefore have a strong proportional relationship between fixed assets and sales.

Finally, in the long term there is a close relationship between sales and net PP&E for virtually all companies: Few companies can continue to increase sales unless they also add capacity. Therefore, it is reasonable to assume that the long-term ratio of net PP&E to sales will be constant.

For the first years in a forecast, managers generally build in the actual planned expenditures on plant and equipment. If those estimates are not available, it is generally best to assume a constant ratio of net PP&E to sales.

MicroDrive is a relatively large company and makes capital expenditures every year, so the CFO forecast net PP&E as a percent of sales. The projected net PP&E is 40%($5,500) = $2,200.

12-3c Operating Liabilities

Section B2 of Figure 12-3 shows the forecast of operating liabilities. Some types of liabilities grow proportionately to sales; these are called **spontaneous liabilities**, as we explain next.

As sales increase, so will purchases of raw materials, and those additional purchases will spontaneously lead to a higher level of accounts payable. MicroDrive's forecast of accounts payable in 2014 is 4%($5,500) = $220.

Higher sales require more labor, and higher sales normally result in higher taxable income and thus taxes. Therefore, accrued wages and taxes both increase as sales increase. The projection of accruals is 6%($5,500) = $330.

12-3d Operating Income

For most companies, the cost of goods sold (COGS) is highly correlated with sales, and MicroDrive is no exception. MicroDrive's forecast of COGS for 2014 is 76%($5,500) = $4,180.

Because depreciation depends on an asset's depreciable basis, as described in Chapter 11, it is more reasonable to forecast depreciation as a percent of net plant and equipment rather than of sales. MicroDrive's projection of depreciation in 2014 is 10%(2014 Net PP&E) = 10%($2,200) = $220.

MicroDrive's other operating expenses include items such as salaries of executives, insurance fees, and marketing costs. These items tend to be related to a company's size, which is related to sales. MicroDrive's projection is 10%($5,500) = $550.

Subtracting the COGS, depreciation, and other operating expenses from net sales gives the earnings before interest and taxes (EBIT). Recall from Chapter 2 that the net operating profit after taxes (NOPAT) is defined as EBIT(1 − T), where T is the tax rate.

12-3e Free Cash Flow (FCF)

Section B4 calculates free cash flow (FCF) using the process described in Chapter 2. The first row in Section B4 begins with a calculation of net operating capital (NOWC), which is defined as operating current assets minus operating current liabilities. Operating current assets is the sum of cash, accounts receivable, and inventories; operating current liabilities is the sum or accounts payable and accruals. The second row shows the forecast of total operating capital, which is NOWC plus net PP&E. All of the items required for these calculations were previously forecast in Section B2.

Recall from Chapter 2 that free cash flow is equal to NOPAT minus the investment in total operating capital; the forecast of NOPAT is in Section B3 and the forecast of total net operating capital is in the second row of Section B4.

12-3f Estimated Intrinsic Value

Section B5 begins with the estimated target WACC, calculated using the inputs from Sections 2 and 3 of Figure 12-2. These values are the same ones used in Chapter 9 to estimate MicroDrive's weighted average cost of capital, with the exception of the cost of preferred stock. To simplify the forecast of preferred dividends when projecting the income statement, MicroDrive's CFO decided to ignore flotation costs because they have a negligible impact on the WACC.

The weighted average cost of capital is calculated based on the target capital structure. MicroDrive's CFO decided to use the target capital structure for all scenarios, but to modify the projections later if the board decides to change the capital structure.

The second row in Section B5 of Figure 12-3 reports return on invested capital (ROIC) for easy comparison to the WACC. The third row shows the growth rate in FCF. Notice that the growth rate is very high in the early years of the forecast but then levels out at the sustainable growth rate of sales, 5%. Had it not done so, the forecast period would need to be extended until the growth in FCF became constant.

Using the estimated FCF, WACC, and long-term constant growth rate in FCF, Section B5 shows the calculation of the value of operations using the constant growth horizon value formula from Chapter 7. To find the value of operations, it is necessary to find the present value of the horizon value and the present value of the forecasted free cash flows, and then sum them, as shown at the lower-left corner of the figure.

The panel on the lower right of Section B5 estimates the intrinsic stock price using the approach in Chapter 7. For the Status Quo forecast, the estimated intrinsic value is $22.78. This estimate is about 16% lower than the price of $27 observed on December 31, 2013. What can account for this difference? First, keep in mind that MicroDrive's standard deviation of stock returns is about 49%, as estimated in Chapter 6. This high standard deviation makes the 16% difference between the estimated and actual stock price look pretty small. It could well be that the estimated intrinsic value would have been exactly equal to the actual stock price on a day during the week before or after December 31, 2013. Second, it could be that investors (who determine the price through their buying and selling activities) expect MicroDrive's performance in the future to be better than the Status Quo scenario.

We will have more to say about the operating forecast after completing the forecast of financial statements.

12-3g Enhancements to the Basic Model

Although the assumption that operating assets and operating liabilities grow proportionally to sales is a very good approximation for most companies, there are a few circumstances that might require more complicated modeling techniques. We describe four possible refinements in Section 12-7: economies of scale, nonlinear relationships, lumpy purchases of assets, and excess capacity adjustments. However, always keep in mind that additional complexity in a model might not be worth the incremental improvement in accuracy.

S E L F - T E S T

Which items comprise operating current assets? Why is it reasonable to assume that they grow proportionally to sales?

What are some reasons that net PP&E might grow proportionally to sales, and what are some reasons that it might not?

What are spontaneous liabilities?

12-4 Projecting MicroDrive's Financial Statements

A key output of a financial plan is the set of projected financial statements. The basic approach in projecting statements is a simple, three-step process: (1) forecast the operating items, (2) forecast the amounts of debt, equity, and dividends that are determined by the company's preliminary short-term financial policy, and (3) ensure that the company has sufficient but not excess financing to fund the operating plan.

Despite the simple process, projecting financial statements can be similar to peeling onions—but not because it smells bad and brings tears to your eyes! Just as there are many different onions (white, purple, large, small, sweet, sour, etc.), there are many different variations on the basic approach. And just as onions have many layers, a financial plan can have many layers of complexity. It would be impossible for us to cover all the different methods and details used when projecting financial statements, so we are going to focus on the straightforward method MicroDrive's CFO used, which is applicable to most companies.

Here are the three steps in this method:

1. MicroDrive will project all the operating items that are part of the operating plan.
2. For the initial forecast, MicroDrive's CFO applied the following preliminary short-term financial policy: (1) MicroDrive will not issue any long-term bonds, preferred stock, or common stock in the upcoming year; (2) MicroDrive will not pay off or increase notes payable; and (3) MicroDrive will increase regular dividends at the sustainable long-term growth rate discussed previously in the sales forecast.
3. If the short-term financial policies described in the second step do not provide sufficient additional financing to fund the additional operating assets needed by the operating plan described in the first step, MicroDrive will draw on a special line of credit. If the financial policies provide surplus financing, MicroDrive will pay a special dividend.

12-4a Forecast the Accounts from the Operating Plan

Figure 12-4 shows MicroDrive's projected financial statements for the Status Quo scenario for the upcoming year. MicroDrive's CFO forecast the operating plan in Section 12-3, so it is an easy matter to replicate the process and forecast the corresponding operating items on the financial statement accounts. Column C shows the most recent year, Column D shows the inputs from Figure 12-2, Columns E and F describe how the inputs are applied, and Column G shows the forecast for the upcoming year. Notice that the forecasts for the operating items in Figure 12-4 are identical to those in Figure 12-3.

FIGURE 12-4

MicroDrive's Projected Financial Statements (Millions of Dollars, Except for Per Share Data)

	A	B	C	D	E	F	G
201	**Status Quo**						
202	*1. Balance Sheets*		**Most Recent**				**Forecast**
203			2013	Input	Basis for 2014 Forecast		2014
204	*Assets*						
205	Cash		$50.0	1.00%	× 2014 Sales		$55.00
206	Accounts receivable		500.0	10.00%	× 2014 Sales		$550.00
207	Inventories		1,000.0	20.00%	× 2014 Sales		$1,100.00
208	Total current assets		$1,550.0				$1,705.00
209	Net PP&E		2,000.0	40.00%	× 2014 Sales		$2,200.00
210	Total assets (TA)		$3,550.0				$3,905.00
211	*Liabilities and equity*						
212	Accounts payable		$200.0	4.00%	× 2014 Sales		$220.00
213	Accruals		300.0	6.00%	× 2014 Sales		$330.00
214	Notes payable		280.0	Carry over from previous year			$280.00
215	Line of credit		0.0	Draw on LOC if financing deficit			$117.10
216	Total CL		$780.0				$947.10
217	Long-term bonds		1,200.0	Carry over from previous year			$1,200.00
218	Total liabilities		$1,980.0				$2,147.10
219	Preferred stock		$100.0	Carry over from previous year			$100.00
220	Common stock		500.0	Carry over from previous year			$500.00
221	Retained earnings		970.0	Old RE + Add. to RE			$1,158
222	Total common equity		$1,470.0				$1,658
223	Total liabs. & equity		$3,550.0				$3,905
224				Check: TA – Total Liab. & Eq. =			$0.00
225	*2. Income Statement*		**Most Recent**				**Forecast**
226			2013	Input	Basis for 2014 Forecast		2014
227	Net sales		$5,000.0	110%	× 2013 Sales		$5,500.00
228	COGS (excl. depr.)		3,800.0	76.00%	× 2014 Sales		$4,180.00
229	Depreciation		200.0	10.00%	× 2014 Net PP&E		$220.00
230	Other operating expenses		$500.0	10.00%	× 2014 Sales		$550.00
231	EBIT		$500.0				$550.00
232	Less: Interest on notes		20.0	10.00%	× Avg notes		$28.00
233	Interest on bonds		100.0	9.00%	× Avg bonds		$108.00
234	Interest on LOC		0.0	11.50%	× Beginning LOC		$0.00
235	Pretax earnings		$380.0				$414.00
236	Taxes (40%)		152.0	40.00%	× Pretax earnings		$165.60
237	NI before pref. div.		$228.0				$248.40
238	Preferred div.		8.0	8.00%	× Avg pref. stock		$8.00
239	Net income		$220.0				$240.40
240	Regular common dividends		$50.0	105%	× 2013 Dividend		$52.50
241	Special dividends		$0.0	Pay if financing surplus			$0.00
242	Addition to RE		$170.0	Net income – Dividends			$187.90
243							
244	*3. Elimination of the Financial Deficit or Surplus*						
245	Increase in spontaneous liabilities (accounts payable and accruals)						$50.00
246	+ Increase in notes payable, long-term bonds, preferred stock and common stock						$0.00
247	+ Net income minus regular common dividends						$187.90
248	Increase in financing						$237.90
249	– Increase in total assets						$355.00
250	Amount of deficit or surplus financing:						–$117.10
251	If deficit in financing (negative), draw on line of credit					Line of credit	$117.10
252	If surplus in financing (positive), pay special dividend					Special dividend	$0.00

12-4b Forecast Items Determined by the Preliminary Short-Term Financial Policy

MicroDrive has a target capital structure and target dividend growth, shown in Figure 12-2, Sections 2–4. Like most companies, MicroDrive is willing to deviate from those targets in the short term. For the purpose of this initial forecast, MicroDrive has a preliminary short-term financial policy that sets the projected values for notes payable, long-term debt, preferred stock, and common stock equal to their previous values. In other words, the preliminary short-term financial policy does not call for any change in these items. Keep in mind that financial planning is an iterative process—specify a plan, look at the results, modify if needed, and repeat the process until the plan is acceptable and achievable.

The pale silver rows with blue print in Figure 12-4 show the items determined by the preliminary short-term financial policy. Section 1 shows the projected balance sheets, with the projected values for notes payable, long-term debt, preferred stock, and common stock unchanged from their previous values. The basic approach for projecting financial statements would remain unchanged if the preliminary short-term financial policy had called for changes in these items, such as issuing new debt or equity. In fact, MicroDrive's CFO plans on presenting long-term recommendations to the board regarding the possibility of issuing additional common stock, preferred stock, or long-term bonds after the preliminary forecast has been analyzed.

Section 2 shows the projected income statement. The interest expense on notes payable is projected as the interest rate on notes payable multiplied by the average value of the notes payable outstanding during the year. For example, MicroDrive had $280 at the end of 2013 and projected $280 at the end of 2014, so the average balance during the year is $280 = ($280 + $280)/2. If MicroDrive's plans had called for borrowing an addition $40 in notes payable during the year (resulting in an end-of-year balance of $320), the average balance would have been $300 = ($280+ $320)/2. The same process is applied to long-term bonds and preferred stock.

Basing interest expense on the average amount of debt outstanding during the year implies that the debt is added (or repaid) smoothly during the year. However, if debt is not added until the last day of the year, that year's interest expense should be based on just the debt at the beginning of the year (i.e., the debt at the end of the previous year), because virtually no interest would have accrued on the new debt. On the other hand, if the new debt is added on the first day of the year, interest would accrue all year, so the interest expense should be based on the amount of debt shown at the end of the year.

MicroDrive's preliminary short-term financial policy calls for dividend growth of 5%.

The only items on the projected statements that have not been forecast by the operating plan or the preliminary short-term financial plan are the line of credit (LOC), interest on the LOC, and the item for special dividends. These are shown in dark red ink in the pale gray rows, and we explain them in the following section.

12-4c Identify and Eliminate the Financing Deficit or Surplus in the Projected Balance Sheets

At this point in the projection, it would be extremely unlikely for the balance sheets to balance because the increase in assets required by the operating plan probably is not equal to the increase in liabilities and financing caused by the operating plan and the preliminary short-term financial policy. There will be a financing deficit if the additional financing is less than the additional assets, and a financing surplus if the additional assets are greater than the additional financing. If there is a financing deficit, MicroDrive will not be able to afford its operating plan; if there is a financing surplus, MicroDrive must use it in some manner. Therefore, a realistic projection requires balance sheets that balance.

The first step in making the sheets balance is to identify the amount of financing surplus or deficit resulting from the operating plan and the preliminary short-term financial policy. The second step is to eliminate the deficit or surplus.

Preliminary additional financing comes from three sources: (1) spontaneous liabilities, (2) external financing (such as issuing new long-term bonds or common equity), and (3) internal financing (which is the amount of earnings that are reinvested rather than paid out as dividends). Following is an explanation of how to calculate the additional financing for MicroDrive.

Section 3 in Figure 12-4 begins by adding up the additional financing in the forecast relative to the previous year. For example, MicroDrive's spontaneous liabilities (accounts payable and accruals) went from a total of $500 to $550, an increase of $50. Due to MicroDrive's preliminary short-term financial policy, there were no changes in the external financing provided by notes payable, long-term bonds, preferred stock, or common stock. MicroDrive's preliminary policy calls for no changes in external financing, but it would be easy to modify this assumption. In fact, the CFO did make changes in external financing in a final plan that we discuss later. The preliminary amount of internal financing is the difference between net income and regular common dividends—this is the amount of earnings that are being reinvested. MicroDrive projects a total increase in financing of $237.9, as shown in Section 3 of Figure 12-4.

Is this enough financing, too much, or just right? To answer this question, start by calculating MicroDrive's projected increase in total assets: $355 = $3,905 − $3,550. The difference between MicroDrive's increase in financing and its increase in projected assets is $237.9 − $355 = −$117.1. This amount is negative because the increase in MicroDrive's projected assets is greater than the increase in MicroDrive's projected financing. Therefore, MicroDrive has a preliminary financing deficit—MicroDrive needs more financing to support its operating plan. Had this value been positive, MicroDrive would have had a financing surplus. How should a company handle a financing deficit or surplus?

There are an infinite number of answers to that question, which is why financial modeling can be complicated. MicroDrive's CFO chose a simple but effective answer—if there is a deficit, draw on a line of credit even though it has a high interest rate (the rate on the LOC is 1.5 percentage points higher than the rate on notes payable); if there is a surplus, pay a special dividend. Keep in mind that this is a preliminary plan and that MicroDrive might choose a different source of financing in its final plan.

The last two rows in Section 3 of Figure 12-4 apply this logic. The cell for the LOC in the balance sheet in Section 1 (Cell C215) is linked to the cell in Section 3 (G251). The next step is to estimate the interest expense on the LOC. MicroDrive's CFO made a simplifying assumption for the preliminary projection: The LOC will be drawn upon on the last day of the year. Therefore, the LOC will not accrue interest, so the interest expense on the LOC is equal to the interest rate multiplied by the balance of the LOC at the beginning of the year rather than the end of the year.

The CFO realizes that the projected interest expense will understate the true interest expense if MicroDrive draws on the LOC earlier in the year. However, the CFO wanted to keep the model simple for the preliminary presentations at the retreat. The CFO actually made more realistic (but more complex) assumptions in another model, which we describe later in the chapter.

Now that the hard work of projecting the financial statements is done, it is time for MicroDrive's managers to discuss the projections and formulate their plans.

SELF-TEST

How are operating items projected on financial statements?

How are preliminary levels of debt, preferred stock, common stock, and dividends projected?

What is the financing surplus or deficit? How is it calculated?

12-5 Analysis and Revision of the Preliminary Plan

After explaining the process used to forecast the statements in Figure 12-4, MicroDrive's CFO constructed a 5-year forecast based on the methods and assumptions of the 1-year forecast. Important inputs and key results are shown in Figure 12-5; the full forecast is shown in *Ch12 Tool Kit.xls.*

FIGURE 12-5

The Status Quo Scenario: Summary of Important Inputs and Key Results (Millions of Dollars, Except for Per Share Data)

	A	B	C	D	E	F	G	H
355	**Status Quo**	**Industry**				**MicroDrive**		
356	**Panel A: Inputs**	**Actual**	**Actual**				**Forecast**	
357	*A1. Operating Ratios*	**2013**	**2013**	**2014**	**2015**	**2016**	**2017**	**2018**
358	Sales growth rate	5%	*5%*	10%	8%	7%	5%	5%
359	COGS (excl. depr.) / Sales	76%	*76%*	76%	76%	76%	76%	76%
360	Inventory / Sales	15%	*20%*	20%	20%	20%	20%	20%
361	Net PP&E / Sales	33%	*40%*	40%	40%	40%	40%	40%
362	**Panel B: Key Results**	**Industry**				**MicroDrive**		
363		**Actual**	**Actual**				**Forecast**	
364	*B1. Operations*	**2013**	**2013**	**2014**	**2015**	**2016**	**2017**	**2018**
365	Free cash flow	NA	−$260	$25	$88	$128	$207	$217
366	Return on invested capital	15.0%	9.8%	9.8%	9.8%	9.8%	9.8%	9.8%
367	NOPAT/Sales	6.9%	6.0%	6.0%	6.0%	6.0%	6.0%	6.0%
368	Total op. capital / Sales	46.0%	61.0%	61.0%	61.0%	61.0%	61.0%	61.0%
369	Inventory turnover	5.0	4.0	4.0	4.0	4.0	4.0	4.0
370	Days sales outstanding	30.0	36.5	36.5	36.5	36.5	36.5	36.5
371	Fixed asset turnover	3.0	2.5	2.5	2.5	2.5	2.5	2.5
372	*B2. Financing*							
373	Total liabilities / TA	45.0%	55.8%	55.0%	53.5%	51.6%	49.0%	46.3%
374	Net income / Sales	6.2%	4.4%	4.4%	4.4%	4.4%	4.4%	4.6%
375	Return on assets (ROA)	11.0%	6.2%	6.2%	6.1%	6.2%	6.2%	6.4%
376	Return on equity (ROE)	19.0%	15.0%	14.5%	13.9%	13.4%	12.8%	12.4%
377	Times interest earned	10.0	4.2	4.0	4.0	4.1	4.2	4.5
378	Line of credit	NA	$0	$117	$182	$214	$173	$121
379	Payout ratio	35.0%	22.7%	21.8%	21.3%	20.7%	20.5%	20.0%
380	Regular dividends/share	NA	$1.00	$1.05	$1.10	$1.16	$1.22	$1.28
381	Special dividends/share	NA	$0.00	$0.00	$0.00	$0.00	$0.00	$0.00
382	Earnings per share	NA	$4.40	$4.81	$5.17	$5.58	$5.92	$6.38
383	*B3. Estimated intrinsic value*							
384	12/31/2013	Estimated value of operations =			$2,719			
385	12/31/2013	Estimated intrinsic stock price =			$22.78			

12-5a Analysis of the Preliminary Plan

Section B1 of Figure 12-5 shows key results from the operating plan for the Status Quo scenario. The good news is that FCF becomes positive, but the bad news is that the return on invested capital is much lower than the industry average and is lower than MicroDrive's cost of capital. Rows 367 and 368 show that MicroDrive has a lower NOPAT/Sales ratio than its peers and a higher Capital/Sales ratio. In other words, MicroDrive is less profitable and less efficient. Rows 369–371 show that MicroDrive carries too much inventory, collects more slowly from its customers, and utilizes its factories inefficiently.

The financial plan reflects the poor operating performance. The projected ratio of total liabilities to sales shows that MicroDrive will have more leverage than its peers and will need to borrow from the expensive line of credit. However, even higher leverage is not enough to boost MicroDrive's return on equity to the industry average.

The poor performance also is reflected in MicroDrive's estimated intrinsic stock value of $22.78, which is less than the current market price of $27. The management team concluded that unless they make changes soon, the market price will fall.

12-5b The Final Plan

The marketing and sales directors made the first suggestion. They felt they could boost sales growth to 12% in the next year and maintain sales growth of 6% in the post-forecast years. However, when the CFO input higher sales growth rates and left all other inputs unchanged, the intrinsic value *fell* by a small amount! (You should try this yourself in the model *Ch12 Tool Kit.xls* by selecting Data, What-If Analysis, Scenario Manager, and the scenario named Status Quo Except Higher Sales Growth.) The CFO explained that MicroDrive's return on invested capital was slightly lower than its cost of capital, so each additional dollar of sales is like adding a project that has small negative NPV.[1] Unless MicroDrive improves its ROIC, growth will not add value.

After much discussion, the management team concluded that, because of licensing fees and other costs, it was not feasible for the MicroDrive to reduce its COGS/Sales ratio in the next year. However, the director of R&D explained that the new products in the pipeline will have higher profit margins. If MicroDrive can fund some extra field tests, the new products can reach the market in a year and drive the ratio of COGS/Sales down to 75%.

The production, sales, and purchasing managers are jointly responsible for inventory in MicroDrive's supply chain. With some additional funding for technology to improve channels of information among suppliers and customers, MicroDrive can reduce inventory levels without hurting product availability. They estimated that the improved technology would push the Inventory/Sales ratio down to 17%.

The production and human resource managers stated that productivity could be increased with new training programs so that employees can better utilize the new production equipment that had been added the previous year. They estimated that the increased productivity would cause the ratio of PP&E/Sales to fall to 36% in the next two years.

Managers from accounting and finance estimated that the total cost for these improvement programs would be about $200 million.

---

[1]If the expected ROIC is less than the WACC, growth doesn't add value. The expected ROIC is defined as the projected NOPAT divided by the current level of total operating capital: Expected ROIC = $NOPAT_{t+1}$ / $Capital_t$.

The CFO entered these new inputs (except the cost to implement the new plans) into the model and named it the Final scenario. The results are shown in Figure 12-6. The value of operations increased from $3,814 million to $5,260 million. This is an increase of over $1.4 billion, well above the $200 million cost to implement the plans. Although the Final plan from the management retreat does not include the costs to implement the improvement plans, the CFO included these costs upon returning to headquarters.

Figure 12-6 shows that the ROIC improves to 12.7% by the second year, well above the WACC of 11%. Free cash flow becomes much larger, causing the estimated intrinsic stock price to increase to $51.20. With respect to financing, MicroDrive will not have to draw on its line of credit. In fact, the company will have extra cash available to distribute as a special dividend if the board chooses to do so.

The marketing and sales directors asked about the impact of growth in sales if the ROIC improves to 12.7%. The CFO input the higher growth rate and the model showed that increasing sales does increase value in scenarios that have the ROIC greater than the WACC (see the scenario named Final Except Higher Sales Growth in the *Tool Kit*).

FIGURE 12-6

The Final Scenario: Summary of Important Inputs and Key Results (Millions of Dollars, Except for Per Share Data)

	A	B	C	D	E	F	G	H
355	Final	Industry		MicroDrive				
356	Panel A: Inputs	Actual	Actual			Forecast		
357	A1. Operating Ratios	2013	2013	2014	2015	2016	2017	2018
358	Sales growth rate	5%	5%	10%	8%	7%	5%	5%
359	COGS (excl. depr.) / Sales	76%	76%	76%	75%	75%	75%	75%
360	Inventory / Sales	15%	20%	17%	17%	17%	17%	17%
361	Net PP&E / Sales	33%	40%	39%	36%	36%	36%	36%
362	Panel B: Key Results	Industry		MicroDrive				
363		Actual	Actual			Forecast		
364	B1. Operations	2013	2013	2014	2015	2016	2017	2018
365	Free cash flow	NA	−$260	$248	$334	$210	$285	$299
366	Return on invested capital	15.0%	9.8%	10.6%	12.7%	12.7%	12.7%	12.7%
367	NOPAT/Sales	6.9%	6.0%	6.1%	6.8%	6.8%	6.8%	6.8%
368	Total op. capital / Sales	46.0%	61.0%	57.0%	54.0%	54.0%	54.0%	54.0%
369	Inventory turnover	5.0	4.0	4.7	4.6	4.6	4.6	4.6
370	Days sales outstanding	30.0	36.5	36.5	36.5	36.5	36.5	36.5
371	Fixed asset turnover	3.0	2.5	2.6	2.8	2.8	2.8	2.8
372	B2. Financing							
373	Total liabilities / TA	45.0%	55.8%	55.1%	54.6%	52.0%	50.3%	48.6%
374	Net income / Sales	6.2%	4.4%	4.4%	5.3%	5.4%	5.5%	5.6%
375	Return on assets (ROA)	11.0%	6.2%	6.6%	8.3%	8.5%	8.6%	8.7%
376	Return on equity (ROE)	19.0%	15.0%	15.7%	19.5%	18.6%	18.1%	17.7%
377	Times interest earned	10.0	4.2	4.1	5.0	5.3	5.6	5.9
378	Line of credit	NA	$0	$0	$0	$0	$0	$0
379	Payout ratio	35.0%	22.7%	65.1%	77.1%	34.9%	53.2%	53.8%
380	Regular dividends/share	NA	$1.00	$3.17	$4.88	$2.41	$3.91	$4.19
381	Special dividends/share	NA	$0.00	$2.12	$3.78	$1.25	$2.69	$2.91
382	Earnings per share	NA	$4.40	$4.87	$6.33	$6.90	$7.34	$7.79
383	B3. Estimated intrinsic value							
384		12/31/2013	Estimated value of operations =		$4,140			
385		12/31/2013	Estimated intrinsic stock price =		$51.20			

12-5c The CFO's Model[2]

The CFO's final model, shown in the worksheet named *CFO Model* in the file *Ch12 Tool Kit.xls,* has several refinements to the basic model presented in the previous sections, including the incorporation of financing feedback and implementation of the target capital structure.

FINANCING FEEDBACK

The basic model assumed that no interest would accrue on the line of credit because the LOC would be added at the end of the year. However, if interest is calculated on the LOC's average balance during the year, which is more realistic, here is what happens:

1. The line of credit required to make the balance sheets balance is added to the balance sheet.
2. Interest expense increases due to the LOC.
3. Net income decreases because interest expenses are higher.
4. Internally generated financing decreases because net income decreases.
5. The financing deficit increases because internally generated financing decreases.
6. An additional amount of the LOC is added to the balance sheets to make them balance.
7. Go to step 2 and repeat the loop.

This loop is called *financing feedback* because the additional financing feeds back and causes a need for more additional financing. If programmed into *Excel,* there will be a circular reference. Sometimes *Excel* can handle this (if the iteration feature is enabled), but sometimes *Excel* freezes up. Fortunately, there is a simple way to modify the required line of credit by scaling it up so that no iterations are required. If this piques your interest, take a look at the *CFO Model* in the *Tool Kit.*

IMPLEMENTING THE TARGET CAPITAL STRUCTURE

The preliminary financial policy chosen by the CFO during the managers' retreat held external financing constant—with no additional borrowing or repayment of debt (other than the line of credit) and no new issues or repurchases of preferred stock or common stock. However, this ignores the target capital structure. Fortunately, there is a simple way to implement the target capital structure in the projected statements.

If MicroDrive implements its target capital structure, then it can find the current value of operations, as shown in Figure 12-3. Furthermore, MicroDrive also can estimate its value of operations for *each year* of the forecast, starting at the horizon and working backwards. For example, MicroDrive's horizon value from the final plan is $4,140 (to see this, select the Final scenario in the *Tool Kit* and look at the updated Figure 12-3). The value of operations at the horizon, 2018, is equal to the horizon value—this is the value of all FCF from 2019 and beyond discounted back to 2018. The value of operations at 2017, one year before the horizon, is equal to the value of all free cash flows beyond 2017, discounted at the WACC back to 2017. But we have already found the value of all FCF beyond 2018 discounted back to 2018 (which is equal to the value of operations at 2018), and we know the FCF of 2018. Therefore, we can discount the 2018 value of operations and the 2018 free cash flow back 1 year to get the 2017 value of operations: Value at 2017 = ($4,140 + $299)/(1 + 0.11) = $3,999. We can work our way back to the current date by repeating this process, providing estimates of the yearly values of operations.

[2]This section is relatively technical, and some instructors may choose to skip it with no loss in continuity.

We know the weights in the target capital structure for each year. For example, the target weight for long-term debt, w_d, is 28%. We can multiply this target weight by the value of operations each year to obtain the amount of long-term debt that conforms to the target capital structure. For example, in 2017 MicroDrive should have long-term debt of $1,120= 28%($3,999). Repeating this process for all the capital components each year provides the amounts of external funding that match the target capital structure.

The CFO's model implements a modified version of this procedure. Instead of setting the actual capital structure weights equal to the target weights in the first year of the forecast, the CFO allows the actual weights in the capital structure each year to move smoothly from the actual current values to the target values at the horizon. See the *CFO Model* in the *Tool Kit* for details.

S E L F - T E S T

Suppose a company's return on invested capital is less than its WACC. What happens to the value of operations if the sales growth rate increases? Explain your answer.

12-6 Additional Funds Needed (AFN) Equation Method

A complete financial plan includes projected financial statements, but the **additional funds needed (AFN) equation** method provides a simple way to get a ballpark estimate of the additional external financing that will be required. The AFN approach identifies the financing surplus or deficit in much the same way as we did in the previous sections: (1) Identify the amount of additional funding required by the additional assets due to growth in sales. (2) Identify the amount of spontaneous liabilities (which reduces the amount of external financing that is required to support the additional assets). (3) Identify the amount of funding generated internally from net income that will be available for reinvestment in the company after paying dividends. (4) Assume no new external financing (similar to the preliminary financial policy in the Status Quo scenario). The difference between the additional assets and the sum of spontaneous liabilities and reinvested net income is the amount of additional financing needed from external sources. Following are explanations and applications of these steps.

12-6a Required Increase in Assets

In a steady-state situation in which no excess capacity exists, the firm must have additional plant and equipment, more delivery trucks, higher inventories, and so forth if sales are to increase. In addition, more sales will lead to more accounts receivable, and those receivables must be financed from the time of the sale until they are collected. Therefore, both fixed and current assets must increase if sales are to increase. Of course, if assets are to increase, liabilities and equity must also increase by a like amount to make the balance sheet balance.

12-6b Spontaneous Liabilities

The first sources of expansion funding are the "spontaneous" increases that will occur in MicroDrive's accounts payable and accrued wages and taxes. The company's suppliers give it 10 days to pay for inventory purchases, and because purchases will increase with sales, accounts payable will automatically rise. For example, if sales rise by 10%, then inventory purchases will also rise by 10%, and this will cause accounts payable to rise spontaneously by the same 10%. Similarly, because the company pays workers every 2 weeks, more workers and a larger payroll will mean more accrued wages payable. Finally, higher expected income will mean more accrued income taxes, and its higher wage bill will mean more accrued withholding taxes. Normally no interest is paid on these spontaneous funds, but their amount is limited by credit terms, contracts with workers, and tax laws. Therefore, *spontaneous funds will thus be used to the extent possible, but there is little flexibility in their usage.*

12-6c Addition to Retained Earnings

The second source of funds for expansion comes from net income. Part of MicroDrive's profit will be paid out in dividends, but the remainder will be reinvested in operating assets, as shown in the Assets section of the balance sheet; a corresponding amount will be reported as an addition to retained earnings in the Liabilities and equity section of the balance sheet. There is some flexibility in the amount of funds that will be generated from new reinvested earnings because dividends can be increased or decreased, but if the firm plans to hold its dividend steady or to increase it at a target rate, as most do, then flexibility is limited.

12-6d Calculating Additional Funds Needed (AFN)

If we start with the required new assets and then subtract both spontaneous funds and additions to retained earnings, we are left with the additional funds needed, or AFN. The AFN must come from *external sources*; hence it is sometimes called EFN. The typical sources of external funds are bank loans, new long-term bonds, new preferred stock, and newly issued common stock. The mix of the external funds used should be consistent with the firm's financial policies, especially its target debt ratio.

12-6e Using MicroDrive's Data to Implement the AFN Equation Method

Equation 12-1 summarizes the logic underlying the AFN equation method. Figure 12-7 defines the notation in Equation 12-1 and applies it to identify MicroDrive's AFN. The **additional funds needed (AFN) equation** is:

$$
\begin{array}{ccccc}
\text{Required} & & \text{Increase in} & & \text{Increase in} & & & \text{Additional} \\
\text{increase} & - & \text{spontaneous} & - & \text{retained} & & = & \text{funds} \\
\text{in assets} & & \text{liabilities} & & \text{earnings} & & & \text{needed}
\end{array}
$$

$$
(A_0^*/S_0)\Delta S \;-\; (L_0^*/S_0)\Delta S \;-\; S_1 \times M \times \left(1 - \frac{\text{Payout}}{\text{Ratio}}\right) \;=\; \text{AFN} \qquad (12\text{-}1)
$$

We see from Part B of Figure 12-7 that for sales to increase by $500 million, MicroDrive must increase assets by $355 million. Therefore, liabilities and capital must also increase by $355 million. Of this total, $50 million will come from spontaneous liabilities, and another $187 million will come from new retained earnings. The remaining $118 million must be raised from external sources—probably some combination of short-term bank loans, long-term bonds, preferred stock, and common stock. Notice that the AFN from this model is very close to the surplus financing required in the Status Quo model for the projected financial statements because both methods assume that the operating ratios for MicroDrive will not change.

FIGURE **12-7**

Additional Funds Needed (AFN) (Millions of Dollars)

	A	B	C	D	E	F	G	H	I
397	*Part A. Inputs and Definitions*								
398	S_0:		Most recent year's sales =						$5,000
399	g:		Forecasted growth rate in sales =						10.00%
400	S_1:		Next year's sales: $S_0 \times (1 + g)$ =						$5,500
401	gS_0:		Change in sales = $S_1 - S_0 = \Delta S$ =						$500
402	A_0^*:		Most recent year's operating assets =						$3,550
403	A_0^* / S_0:		Required assets per dollar of sales =						71.00%
404	L_0^*:		Most recent year's spontaneous liabilities i.e., payables + accruals =						$500
405	L_0^* / S_0:		Spontaneous liabilities per dollar of sales =						10.00%
406	Profit margin (M):		Most recent profit margin = net income/sales =						4.40%
407	Payout ratio (POR):		Most recent year's dividends / net income = % of income paid out =						22.73%
408	*Part B. Additional Funds Needed (AFN) to Support Growth*								
409									
410	AFN	=	Required Increase in	–	Increase in Spon. Liab.		–	Addition to Retained	
411		=	$(A_0^*/S_0)\Delta S$	–	$(L_0^*/S_0)\Delta S$		–	$S_1 \times M \times (1 - POR)$	
412				–			–		
413		=	$(A_0^*/S_0)(gS_0)$	–	$(L_0^*/S_0)(gS_0)$		–	$(1+g)S_0 \times M \times (1 - POR)$	
414				–			–		
415		=	(0.710)($500)	–	(0.10)($500)		–	$5,500(0.044)(1 - 0.2273)$	
416		=	$355	–	$50.00		–	$187.00	
417	AFN =	$118.00							

12-6f Key Factors in the AFN Equation

The AFN equation shows that external financing requirements depend on five key factors.

1. **Sales growth (g)**. Rapidly growing companies require large increases in assets and a corresponding large amount of external financing, other things held constant.
2. **Capital intensity (A_0^*/S_0)**. The amount of assets required per dollar of sales, A_0^*/S_0, is the **capital intensity ratio**, which has a major effect on capital requirements. Companies with relatively high assets-to-sales ratios require a relatively large number of new assets for any given increase in sales; hence they have a greater need for external financing. If a firm can find a way to lower this ratio—for instance, by adopting a just-in-time inventory system, by going to two shifts in its manufacturing plants, or by outsourcing rather than manufacturing parts—then it can achieve a given level of growth with fewer assets and thus less new external capital.
3. **Spontaneous liabilities-to-sales ratio (L_0^*/S_0)**. If a company can increase its spontaneously generated liabilities, this will reduce its need for external financing. One way of raising this ratio is by paying suppliers in, say, 20 days rather than 10 days. Such a change may be possible but, as we shall see in Chapter 16, it would probably have serious adverse consequences.
4. **Profit margin (M = Net Income/Sales)**. The higher the profit margin, the more net income is available to support increases in assets—and hence the less the need for external financing. A firms' profit margin is normally as high as management can get it, but sometimes a change in operations can boost the sales price or reduce costs, thus raising the margin further. If so, this will permit a faster growth rate with less external capital.

5. **Payout ratio (POR = DPS/EPS).** The less of its income a company distributes as dividends, the larger its addition to retained earnings—hence the less its need for external capital. Companies typically like to keep their dividends stable or to increase them at a steady rate—stockholders like stable, dependable dividends, so such a dividend policy will generally lower the cost of equity and thus maximize the stock price. So even though reducing the dividend is one way a company can reduce its need for external capital, companies generally resort to this method only if they are under financial duress.

12-6g The Self-Supporting Growth Rate

One interesting question is: "What is the maximum growth rate the firm could achieve if it had no access to external capital?" This rate is called the *self-supporting growth rate*, and it can be found as the value of g that, when used in the AFN equation, results in an AFN of zero. We first replace ΔS in the AFN equation with gS_0 and S_1 with $(1+g)S_0$ so that the only unknown is g; we then solve for g to obtain the following equation for the self-supporting growth rate:

$$\text{Self-supporting } g = \frac{M(1-POR)(S_0)}{A_0{}^* - L_0{}^* - M(1-POR)(S_0)} \qquad (12\text{-}2)$$

The definitions of the terms used in this equation are shown in Figure 12-7.

If the firm has any positive earnings and pays out less than 100% in dividends, then it will have some additions to retained earnings, and those additions could be combined with spontaneous funds to enable the company to grow at some rate without having to raise external capital. As explained in the chapter's *Excel Tool Kit,* this value can be found either algebraically or with *Excel*'s Goal Seek function. For MicroDrive, the self-supporting growth rate is 5.9%; this means it could grow at that rate even if capital markets dried up completely, with everything else held constant.

r e s o u r c e

*See **Ch12 Tool Kit.xls** on the textbook's Web site for details.*

SELF-TEST

If all ratios are expected to remain constant, an equation can be used to forecast AFN. Write out the equation and briefly explain it.

Describe how the following factors affect external capital requirements: (1) payout ratio, (2) capital intensity, (3) profit margin.

In what sense do accounts payable and accruals provide "spontaneous funds" to a growing firm?

Is it possible for the calculated AFN to be negative? If so, what would this imply?

Refer to data in the MicroDrive example presented, but now assume that MicroDrive's growth rate in sales is forecasted to be 15% rather than 10%. If all ratios remain constant, what would the AFN be? **($205.6 million)**

12-7 Forecasting When the Ratios Change

The versions of the percent of sales forecasting model and the AFN method assumed that the forecasted items could be estimated as a percent of sales. This implies that each of the accounts for assets, spontaneous liabilities, and operating costs is proportional to sales. In graph form, this implies the type of relationship shown in Panel a of Figure 12-8,

FIGURE 12-8

Four Possible Ratio Relationships (Millions of Dollars)

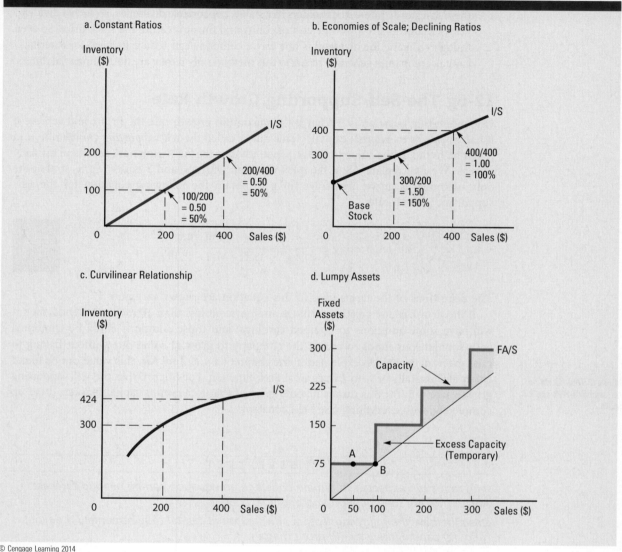

a. Constant Ratios

b. Economies of Scale; Declining Ratios

c. Curvilinear Relationship

d. Lumpy Assets

© Cengage Learning 2014

a relationship whose graph (1) is linear and (2) passes through the origin. Under those conditions, if the company's sales increase from $200 million to $400 million, or by 100%, then inventory will also increase by 100%, from $100 million to $200 million.

The assumption of constant ratios and identical growth rates is appropriate at times, but there are times when it is incorrect. We describe three such situations in the following sections.

12-7a Economies of Scale

There are economies of scale in the use of many kinds of assets, and when economies of scale occur, the ratios are likely to change over time as the size of the firm increases. For example, retailers often need to maintain base stocks of different inventory items even if current sales are quite low. As sales expand, inventories may then grow less rapidly than sales, so the ratio of inventory to sales (I/S) declines. This situation is depicted in Panel b of Figure 12-8. Here we see that the inventory/sales ratio is 1.5 (or 150%) when sales are $200 million but declines to 1.0 when sales climb to $400 million.

It is easy in *Excel* to incorporate this type of scale economy in the forecast. For example, the basic method forecasts inventory as: Inventory = m(Sales), where m is a constant. With economies of scale, forecast Inventory as: Inventory = b + m(Sales), where m and b are constants.

12-7b Nonlinear Relationships

The relationship in Panel b is linear, but nonlinear relationships often exist. Indeed, if the firm uses one popular model for establishing inventory levels (the Economic Ordering Quantity, or EOQ, model), its inventories will rise with the *square root* of sales. This situation is shown in Panel c of Figure 12-8, which shows a curved line whose slope decreases at higher sales levels. In this situation, very large increases in sales would require very little additional inventory. To incorporate this type of nonlinearity in *Excel,* for example, you could forecast inventory as a function of the square root of sales: Inventory = $m(\text{Sales}^{0.5})$.

12-7c Lumpy Assets and Excess Capacity

In many industries, technological considerations dictate that if a firm is to be competitive, it must add fixed assets in large, discrete units; such assets are often referred to as **lumpy assets**. In the paper industry, for example, there are strong economies of scale in basic paper mill equipment, so when a paper company expands capacity, it must do so in large, lumpy increments. This type of situation is depicted in Panel d of Figure 12-8. Here we assume that the minimum economically efficient plant has a cost of $75 million, and that such a plant can produce enough output to reach a sales level of $100 million. If the firm is to be competitive, it simply must have at least $75 million of fixed assets.

Lumpy assets have a major effect on the ratio of fixed assets to sales (FA/S) at different sales levels and, consequently, on financial requirements. At Point A in Panel d, which represents a sales level of $50 million, the fixed assets are $75 million and so the ratio FA/S = $75/$50 = 1.5. Sales can expand by $50 million, out to $100 million, with no additions to fixed assets. At that point, represented by Point B, the ratio FA/S = $75/$100 = 0.75. However, because the firm is operating at capacity (sales of $100 million), even a small increase in sales would require a doubling of plant capacity, so a small projected sales increase would bring with it a large financial requirement.[3]

If assets are lumpy and a firm makes a major purchase, the firm will have excess capacity, which means that sales can grow before the firm must add capacity. The level of full capacity sales is

---

[3]Several other points should be noted about Panel d of Figure 12-7. First, if the firm is operating at a sales level of $100 million or less, then any expansion that calls for a sales increase of more than $100 million would require a *doubling* of the firm's fixed assets. A much smaller percentage increase would be involved if the firm were large enough to be operating a number of plants. Second, firms generally go to multiple shifts and take other actions to minimize the need for new fixed asset capacity as they approach Point B. However, these efforts can only go so far, and eventually a fixed asset expansion will be required. Third, firms often arrange to share excess capacity with other firms in their industry. For example, the situation in the electric utility industry is very much like that depicted in Panel d. However, electric companies often build plants jointly, or they "take turns" building plants. Then they buy power from or sell power to other utilities to avoid building new plants that would be underutilized.

$$\text{Full capacity sales} = \frac{\text{Actual sales}}{\text{Percentage of capacity at which fixed assets were operated}} \qquad (12\text{-}3)$$

For example, consider MicroDrive and use the data from its financial statements in Figure 12-1, but now assume that excess capacity exists in fixed assets. Specifically, assume that fixed assets in 2013 were being utilized to only 96% of capacity. If fixed assets had been used to full capacity, then 2013 sales could have been as high as $3,125 million versus the $3,000 million in actual sales:

$$\text{Full capacity sales} = \frac{\text{Actual sales}}{\text{Percentage of capacity at which fixed assets were operated}}$$

$$= \frac{\$5,000 \text{ million}}{0.96} = \$5,208 \text{ million}$$

The target fixed assets/sales ratio can be defined in terms of the full capacity sales:

$$\text{Target fixed assets/Sales} = \frac{\text{Actual fixed assets}}{\text{Full capacity sales}} \qquad (12\text{-}4)$$

MicroDrive's target fixed assets/sales ratio should be 38.4% rather than 40%:

$$\text{Target fixed assets/Sales} = \frac{\text{Actual fixed assets}}{\text{Full capacity sales}}$$

$$= \frac{\$2,000}{\$5,208} = 0.384 = 38.4\%$$

The required level of fixed assets depends upon this target fixed assets/sales ratio:

$$\text{Required level of fixed assets} = \left(\frac{\text{Target fixed assets}}{\text{Sales}}\right)\left(\text{Projected sales}\right) \qquad (12\text{-}5)$$

Therefore, if MicroDrive's sales increase to $3,300 million, its fixed assets would have to increase to $1,056 million:

$$\text{Required level of fixed assets} = \left(\frac{\text{Target fixed assets}}{\text{Sales}}\right)\left(\text{Projected sales}\right)$$

$$= 0.384(\$5,500) = \$2,112 \text{ million}$$

We previously forecasted that MicroDrive would need to increase fixed assets at the same rate as sales, or by 10%. That meant an increase of $200 million, from $2,000 million to $2,200 million under the old assumption of no excess capacity. Under the new assumption of excess capacity, the actual required increase in fixed assets is only from $2,000 million to $2,112 million, which is an increase of $112 million. Thus, the capacity-adjusted forecast is less than the earlier forecast: $200 − $112 = $88 million. With a smaller fixed asset requirement, the projected AFN would decline from an estimated $118 million to $118 − $88 = $30 million.

Note also that when excess capacity exists, sales can grow to the capacity sales as calculated above with no increase in fixed assets, but sales beyond that level would require additions of fixed assets as in our example. The same situation could occur with respect to inventories, and the required additions would be determined in exactly the same manner as for fixed assets. Theoretically, the same situation could occur with other types of assets, but as a practical matter excess capacity normally exists only with respect to fixed assets and inventories.

SELF-TEST

How do economies of scale and lumpy assets affect financial forecasting?

SUMMARY

- The **forecasted financial statements (FFS) method** of financial planning forecasts the entire set of financial statements. It usually begins with a forecast of the firm's sales and then projects many items on the financial statements as a percent of sales.
- The **additional funds needed (AFN) equation** can be used to forecast additional external financing requirements, but only for one year ahead and only if all asset-to-sales ratios are identical, all spontaneous liabilities-to-sales ratios are identical, and all cost-to-sales ratios are identical.
- A firm can determine its **AFN** by estimating the amount of new assets necessary to support the forecasted level of sales and then subtracting from this amount the spontaneous funds that will be generated from operations.
- The higher a firm's **sales growth rate** and the higher its **payout ratio**, the greater will be its need for additional financing.
- There are two major applications of forecasted financial statements. First, the forecasted free cash flows can be used to estimate the impact that changes in operating plans have on the firm's estimated intrinsic value of operations and stock price. Second, the forecasted financing surplus or deficit allows the firm to identify its future financing needs.
- Adjustments must be made if **economies of scale** exist in the use of assets, if **excess capacity** exists, or if growth must occur in large increments (**lumpy assets**).
- **Excess capacity adjustments** can be used to forecast asset requirements in situations in which assets are not expected to grow at the same rate as sales.

QUESTIONS

(12-1)   Define each of the following terms:

a. Operating plan; financial plan
b. Spontaneous liabilities; profit margin; payout ratio
c. Additional funds needed (AFN); AFN equation; capital intensity ratio; self-supporting growth rate
d. Forecasted financial statement approach using percent of sales
e. Excess capacity; lumpy assets; economies of scale
f. Full capacity sales; target fixed assets/sales ratio; required level of fixed assets

(12-2) Some liability and net worth items increase spontaneously with increases in sales. Put a check (✓) by those items listed below that typically increase spontaneously:

Accounts payable	_____	Mortgage bonds	_____
Notes payable to banks	_____	Common stock	_____
Accrued wages	_____	Retained earnings	_____
Accrued taxes	_____		

(12-3) The following equation is sometimes used to forecast financial requirements:

$$AFN = (A_0^*/S_0)(\Delta S) - (L_0^*/S_0)(\Delta S) - MS_1(1 - POR)$$

What key assumption do we make when using this equation? Under what conditions might this assumption not hold true?

(12-4) Name five key factors that affect a firm's external financing requirements.

(12-5) What is meant by the term "self-supporting growth rate"? How is this rate related to the AFN equation, and how can that equation be used to calculate the self-supporting growth rate?

(12-6) Suppose a firm makes the policy changes listed below. If a change means that external, nonspontaneous financial requirements (AFN) will increase, indicate this by a (+); indicate a decrease by a (−); and indicate no effect or an indeterminate effect by a (0). Think in terms of the *immediate* effect on funds requirements.

a. The dividend payout ratio is increased. _____
b. The firm decides to pay all suppliers on delivery, rather than after a 30-day delay, to take advantage of discounts for rapid payment. _____
c. The firm begins to offer credit to its customers, whereas previously all sales had been on a cash basis. _____
d. The firm's profit margin is eroded by increased competition, although sales hold steady. _____
e. The firm sells its manufacturing plants for cash to a contractor and simultaneously signs an outsourcing contract to purchase from that contractor goods that the firm formerly produced. _____
f. The firm negotiates a new contract with its union that lowers its labor costs without affecting its output. _____

SELF-TEST PROBLEMS   Solutions Appear in Appendix A

(ST-1)
Self-Supporting
Growth Rate

The Barnsdale Corporation has the following ratios: $A_0^*/S_0 = 1.6$; $L_0^*/S_0 = 0.4$; profit margin = 0.10; and dividend payout ratio = 0.45, or 45%. Sales last year were $100 million. Assuming that these ratios will remain constant, use the AFN equation to determine the firm's self-supporting growth rate—in other words, the maximum growth rate Barnsdale can achieve without having to employ nonspontaneous external funds.

(ST-2)
AFN Equation

Refer to Problem ST-1, and suppose Barnsdale's financial consultants report (1) that the inventory turnover ratio (sales/inventory) is 3, compared with an industry average of 4, and (2) that Barnsdale could reduce inventories and thus raise its turnover ratio to 4 without affecting its sales, profit margin, or other asset turnover ratios. Under these conditions, use the AFN equation to determine the amount of additional funds Barnsdale would require during each of the next 2 years if sales grow at a rate of 20% per year.

(ST-3)

Excess Capacity

Van Auken Lumber's 2013 financial statements are shown below.

Van Auken Lumber: Balance Sheet as of December 31, 2013 (Thousands of Dollars)

Cash	$ 1,800	Accounts payable	$ 7,200
Receivables	10,800	Notes payable	3,472
Inventories	12,600	Line of credit	0
Total current assets	$25,200	Accruals	2,520
Net fixed assets	21,600	Total current liabilities	$13,192
		Mortgage bonds	5,000
		Common stock	2,000
		Retained earnings	26,608
Total assets	$46,800	Total liabilities and equity	$46,800

Van Auken Lumber: Income Statement for December 31, 2013 (Thousands of Dollars)

Sales	$36,000
Operating costs	30,783
Earnings before interest and taxes	$ 5,217
Interest	717
Pre-tax earnings	$ 4,500
Taxes (40%)	1,800
Net income	$ 2,700
Dividends (60%)	$ 1,620
Addition to retained earnings	$ 1,080

a. Assume that the company was operating at full capacity in 2013 with regard to all items *except* fixed assets, which in 2013 were being utilized to only 75% of capacity. By what percentage could 2014 sales increase over 2013 sales without the need for an increase in fixed assets?

b. Now suppose that 2014 sales increase by 25% over 2013 sales. Use the forecasted financial statement method to forecast a 12/31/14 balance sheet and 2014 income statement, assuming that (1) the historical ratios of operating costs/sales, cash/sales, receivables/sales, inventories/sales, accounts payable/sales, and accruals/sales remain constant; (2) Van Auken cannot sell any of its fixed assets; (3) any required financing is done at the *end* of 2014 as through a line of credit; (4) the firm earns no interest on its cash; and (5) the interest rate on all of its debt is 12%. Van Auken pays out 60% of its net income as dividends and has a tax rate of 40%. What is Van Auken's financing deficit or surplus? (*Hints:* Assume any additional financing through the line of credit will be drawn on the last day of the year. Therefore, the line of credit will not accrue interest expense during the year because any new line of credit is added at the end of the year; also, use the forecasted income statement to determine the addition to retained earnings for use in the balance sheet.)

PROBLEMS   Answers Appear in Appendix B

Easy Problems 1–3

(12-1)
AFN Equation

Broussard Skateboard's sales are expected to increase by 15% from $8 million in 2013 to $9.2 million in 2014. Its assets totaled $5 million at the end of 2013. Broussard is already at full capacity, so its assets must grow at the same rate as projected sales. At the end of 2013, current liabilities were $1.4 million, consisting of $450,000 of accounts payable, $500,000 of notes payable, and $450,000 of accruals. The after-tax profit margin is forecasted to be 6%, and the forecasted payout ratio is 40%. Use the AFN equation to forecast Broussard's additional funds needed for the coming year.

(12-2)
AFN Equation

Refer to Problem 12-1. What would be the additional funds needed if the company's year-end 2013 assets had been $7 million? Assume that all other numbers, including sales, are the same as in Problem 12-1 and that the company is operating at full capacity. Why is this AFN different from the one you found in Problem 12-1? Is the company's "capital intensity" ratio the same or different?

(12-3)
AFN Equation

Refer to Problem 12-1. Return to the assumption that the company had $5 million in assets at the end of 2013, but now assume that the company pays no dividends. Under these assumptions, what would be the additional funds needed for the coming year? Why is this AFN different from the one you found in Problem 12-1?

Intermediate
Problems 4–6

(12-4)
Sales Increase

Maggie's Muffins, Inc., generated $5,000,000 in sales during 2013, and its year-end total assets were $2,500,000. Also, at year-end 2013, current liabilities were $1,000,000, consisting of $300,000 of notes payable, $500,000 of accounts payable, and $200,000 of accruals. Looking ahead to 2014, the company estimates that its assets must increase at the same rate as sales, its spontaneous liabilities will increase at the same rate as sales, its profit margin will be 7%, and its payout ratio will be 80%. How large a sales increase can the company achieve without having to raise funds externally—that is, what is its self-supporting growth rate?

(12-5)
Long-Term Financing
Needed

At year-end 2013, Wallace Landscaping's total assets were $2.17 million and its accounts payable were $560,000. Sales, which in 2013 were $3.5 million, are expected to increase by 35% in 2014. Total assets and accounts payable are proportional to sales, and that relationship will be maintained. Wallace typically uses no current liabilities other than accounts payable. Common stock amounted to $625,000 in 2013, and retained earnings were $395,000. Wallace has arranged to sell $195,000 of new common stock in 2014 to meet some of its financing needs. The remainder of its financing needs will be met by issuing new long-term debt at the end of 2014. (Because the debt is added at the end of the year, there will be no additional interest expense due to the new debt.) Its net profit margin on sales is 5%, and 45% of earnings will be paid out as dividends.

a. What were Wallace's total long-term debt and total liabilities in 2013?
b. How much new long-term debt financing will be needed in 2014? (*Hint:* AFN − New stock = New long-term debt.)

(12-6)
Additional Funds
Needed

The Booth Company's sales are forecasted to double from $1,000 in 2013 to $2,000 in 2014. Here is the December 31, 2013, balance sheet:

Cash	$ 100	Accounts payable	$ 50
Accounts receivable	200	Notes payable	150
Inventories	200	Accruals	50
Net fixed assets	500	Long-term debt	400
		Common stock	100
		Retained earnings	250
Total assets	$1,000	Total liabilities and equity	$1,000

Booth's fixed assets were used to only 50% of capacity during 2013, but its current assets were at their proper levels in relation to sales. All assets except fixed assets must increase at the same rate as sales, and fixed assets would also have to increase at the same rate if the current excess capacity did not exist. Booth's after-tax profit margin is forecasted to be 5% and its payout ratio to be 60%. What is Booth's additional funds needed (AFN) for the coming year?

Challenging
Problems 7–9

(12-7)
Forecasted
Statements and
Ratios

Upton Computers makes bulk purchases of small computers, stocks them in conveniently located warehouses, ships them to its chain of retail stores, and has a staff to advise customers and help them set up their new computers. Upton's balance sheet as of December 31, 2013, is shown here (millions of dollars):

Cash	$ 3.5	Accounts payable	$ 9.0
Receivables	26.0	Notes payable	18.0
Inventories	58.0	Line of credit	0
Total current assets	$ 87.5	Accruals	8.5
Net fixed assets	35.0	Total current liabilities	$ 35.5
		Mortgage loan	6.0
		Common stock	15.0
		Retained earnings	66.0
Total assets	$122.5	Total liabilities and equity	$122.5

Sales for 2013 were $350 million and net income for the year was $10.5 million, so the firm's profit margin was 3.0%. Upton paid dividends of $4.2 million to common stockholders, so its payout ratio was 40%. Its tax rate was 40%, and it operated at full capacity. Assume that all assets/sales ratios, spontaneous liabilities/sales ratios, the profit margin, and the payout ratio remain constant in 2014.

a. If sales are projected to increase by $70 million, or 20%, during 2014, use the AFN equation to determine Upton's projected external capital requirements.

b. Using the AFN equation, determine Upton's self-supporting growth rate. That is, what is the maximum growth rate the firm can achieve without having to employ nonspontaneous external funds?

c. Use the forecasted financial statement method to forecast Upton's balance sheet for December 31, 2014. Assume that all additional external capital is raised as a line of credit at the end of the year and is reflected (because the debt is added at the end of the year, there will be no additional interest expense due to the new debt).

Assume Upton's profit margin and dividend payout ratio will be the same in 2014 as they were in 2013. What is the amount of the line of credit reported on the 2014 forecasted balance sheets? (*Hint:* You don't need to forecast the income statements because you are given the projected sales, profit margin, and dividend payout ratio; these figures allow you to calculate the 2014 addition to retained earnings for the balance sheet.)

(12-8)
Financing Deficit

Stevens Textiles's 2013 financial statements are shown here:

Balance Sheet as of December 31, 2013 (Thousands of Dollars)

Cash	$ 1,080	Accounts payable	$ 4,320
Receivables	6,480	Accruals	2,880
Inventories	9,000	Line of credit	0
Total current assets	$16,560	Notes payable	2,100
Net fixed assets	12,600	Total current liabilities	$ 9,300
		Mortgage bonds	3,500
		Common stock	3,500
		Retained earnings	12,860
Total assets	$29,160	Total liabilities and equity	$ 29,160

Income Statement for December 31, 2013 (Thousands of Dollars)

Sales	$36,000
Operating costs	32,440
Earnings before interest and taxes	$ 3,560
Interest	460
Pre-tax earnings	$ 3,100
Taxes (40%)	1,240
Net income	$ 1,860
Dividends (45%)	$ 837
Addition to retained earnings	$ 1,023

a. Suppose 2014 sales are projected to increase by 15% over 2013 sales. Use the forecasted financial statement method to forecast a balance sheet and income statement for December 31, 2014. The interest rate on all debt is 10%, and cash earns no interest income. Assume that all additional debt in the form of a line of credit is added at the end of the year, which means that you should base the forecasted interest expense on the balance of debt at the beginning of the year. Use the forecasted income statement to determine the addition to retained earnings. Assume that the company was operating at full capacity in 2013, that it cannot sell off any of its fixed assets, and that any required financing will be borrowed as notes payable. Also, assume that assets, spontaneous liabilities, and operating costs are expected to increase by the same percentage as sales. Determine the additional funds needed.

b. What is the resulting total forecasted amount of the line of credit?

c. In your answers to Parts a and b, you should not have charged any interest on the additional debt added during 2014 because it was assumed that the new debt was added at the end of the year. But now suppose that the new debt is added throughout the year. Don't do any calculations, but how would this change the answers to parts a and b?

(12-9)
Financing Deficit

Garlington Technologies Inc.'s 2013 financial statements are shown here:

Balance Sheet as of December 31, 2013

Cash	$ 180,000	Accounts payable	$ 360,000
Receivables	360,000	Notes payable	156,000
Inventories	720,000	Line of credit	0
Total current assets	$1,260,000	Accruals	180,000
Fixed assets	1,440,000	Total current liabilities	$ 696,000
		Common stock	1,800,000
		Retained earnings	204,000
Total assets	$2,700,000	Total liabilities and equity	$2,700,000

Income Statement for December 31, 2013

Sales	$3,600,000
Operating costs	3,279,720
EBIT	$ 320,280
Interest	18,280
Pre-tax earnings	$ 302,000
Taxes (40%)	120,800
Net income	$ 181,200
Dividends	$ 108,000

Suppose that in 2014 sales increase by 10% over 2013 sales and that 2014 dividends will increase to $112,000. Forecast the financial statements using the forecasted financial statement method. Assume the firm operated at full capacity in 2013. Use an interest rate of 13%, and assume that any new debt will be added at the end of the year (so forecast the interest expense based on the debt balance at the beginning of the year). Cash does not earn any interest income. Assume that the all new debt will be in the form of a line of credit.

SPREADSHEET PROBLEMS

(12-12)
Build a Model:
Forecasting Financial
Statements

resource

Start with the partial model in the file *Ch12 P10 Build a Model.xls* on the textbook's Web site, which contains the 2013 financial statements of Zieber Corporation. Forecast Zeiber's 2014 income statement and balance sheets. Use the following assumptions: (1) Sales grow by 6%. (2) The ratios of expenses to sales, depreciation to fixed assets, cash to sales, accounts receivable to sales, and inventories to sales will be the same in 2014 as in 2013. (3) Zeiber will not issue any new stock or new long-term bonds. (4) The interest rate is 11% for long-term debt and the interest expense on long-term debt is based on the average balance during the year. (5) No interest is earned on cash. (6) Dividends grow at an 8% rate. (6) Calculate the additional funds needed (AFN). If new financing is required, assume it will be raised by drawing on a line of credit with an interest rate of 12%. Assume that any draw on the line of credit will be made on the last day of the year, so there will be no additional interest expense for the new line of credit. If surplus funds are available, pay a special dividend.

a. What are the forecasted levels of the line of credit and special dividends?
b. Now assume that the growth in sales is only 3%. What are the forecasted levels of the line of credit and special dividends?

THOMSON ONE   Business School Edition Problem

 THOMSON REUTERS   Use the Thomson ONE—Business School Edition online database to work this chapter's questions.

Forecasting the Future Performance of Abercrombie & Fitch

Clothing retailer Abercrombie & Fitch enjoyed phenomenal success in the late 1990s. Between 1996 and 2000, its sales grew almost fourfold, from $335 million to more than $1.2 billion, and its stock price soared by more than 500%. More recently, however, its growth rate has begun to slow down, and Abercrombie has had a hard time meeting its quarterly earnings targets. These problems were compounded by the global recession in 2009 with the stock price in November 2009 falling by 90% from its high 1 year before. Abercrombie's struggles resulted from increased competition, a sluggish economy, and the challenges of staying ahead of the fashion curve.

Since 2009, the company's stock has rebounded strongly but questions remain about the firm's long-term growth prospects. Given the questions about Abercrombie's future growth rate, analysts have focused on the company's earnings reports. Thomson ONE provides a convenient and detailed summary of the company's recent earnings history along with a summary of analysts' earnings forecasts.

To access this information, we begin by entering the company's ticker symbol, ANF, on Thomson ONE's main screen and then selecting GO. This takes us to an overview of the company's recent performance. After checking out the overview, you should click on the tab labeled Estimates, near the top of your screen. Here you will find a wide range of information about the company's past and projected earnings.

Thomson ONE—BSE Discussion Questions

1. What are the mean and median forecasts for Abercrombie's earnings per share over the next fiscal year?
2. Based on analysts' forecasts, what is the firm's expected long-term growth rate in earnings?
3. Have analysts made any significant changes to their forecasted earnings for Abercrombie & Fitch in the past few months?
4. Historically, have Abercrombie's reported earnings generally met, exceeded, or fallen short of analysts' forecasted earnings?
5. How has Abercrombie's stock performed this year relative to the S&P 500?

MINI CASE

Hatfield Medical Supplies's stock price had been lagging its industry averages, so its board of directors brought in a new CEO, Jaiden Lee. Lee had brought in Ashley Novak, a finance MBA who had been working for a consulting company, to replace the old CFO, and Lee asked Ashley to develop the financial planning section of the strategic plan. In her previous job, Novak's primary task had been to help clients develop financial forecasts, and that was one reason Lee hired her.

Novak began by comparing Hatfield's financial ratios to the industry averages. If any ratio was substandard, she discussed it with the responsible manager to see what could be done to improve the situation. The following data show Hatfield's latest financial statements plus some ratios and other data that Novak plans to use in her analysis.

Hatfield Medical Supplies (Millions of Dollars Except Per Share Data)

Balance Sheet, 12/31/2013		Income Statement, Year Ending 2013	
Cash	$ 20	Sales	$2,000
Accts. rec.	280	Op. costs (excl. depr.)	1,800
Inventories	400	Depreciation	50
Total CA	$ 700	EBIT	$ 150
Net fixed assets	500	Interest	40
Total assets	$1,200	Pre-tax earnings	$ 110
		Taxes (40%)	44
Accts. pay. & accruals	$ 80	Net income	$ 66
Line of credit	$ 0		
Total CL	$ 80	Dividends	$ 20.0
Long-term debt	500	Add. to RE	$ 46.0
Total liabilities	$ 580	Common shares	10.0
Common stock	420	EPS	$ 6.60
Retained earnings	200	DPS	$ 2.00
Total common equ.	$ 620	Ending stock price	$52.80
Total liab. & equity	$1,200		

Selected Additional Data for 2013

	Hatfield	Industry		Hatfield	Industry
Op. costs/Sales	90.0%	88.0%	Total liability/Total assets	48.3%	36.7%
Depr./FA	10.0%	12.0%	Times interest earned	3.8	8.9
Cash/Sales	1.0%	1.0%	Return on assets (ROA)	5.5%	10.2%
Receivables/Sales	14.0%	11.0%	Profit margin (M)	3.30%	4.99%
Inventories/Sales	20.0%	15.0%	Sales/Assets	1.67	2.04
Fixed assets/Sales	25.0%	22.0%	Assets/Equity	1.94	1.58
Acc. pay. & accr./Sales	4.0%	4.0%	Return on equity (ROE)	10.6%	16.1%
Tax rate	40.0%	40.0%	P/E ratio	8.0	16.0
ROIC	8.0%	12.5%			
NOPAT/Sales	4.5%	5.6%			
Total op. capital/Sales	56.0%	45.0%			

a. Using Hatfield's data and its industry averages, how well run would you say Hatfield appears to be compared to other firms in its industry? What are its primary strengths and weaknesses? Be specific in your answer, and point to various ratios that support your position. Also, use the Du Pont equation (see Chapter 3) as one part of your analysis.

b. Use the AFN equation to estimate Hatfield's required new external capital for 2014 if the sales growth rate is 10%. Assume that the firm's 2013 ratios will remain the same in 2014. (*Hint:* Hatfield was operating at full capacity in 2013.)

c. Define the term capital intensity. Explain how a decline in capital intensity would affect the AFN, other things held constant. Would economies of scale combined with rapid growth affect capital intensity, other things held constant? Also, explain how changes in each of the following would affect AFN, holding other things constant: the growth rate, the amount of accounts payable, the profit margin, and the payout ratio.

d. Define the term self-supporting growth rate. What is Hatfield's self-supporting growth rate? Would the self-supporting growth rate be affected by a change in the capital intensity ratio or the other factors mentioned in the previous question? Other things held constant, would the calculated capital intensity ratio change over time if the company were growing and were also subject to economies of scale and/or lumpy assets?

e. Use the following assumptions to answer the questions below: (1) Operating ratios remain unchanged. (2) Sales will grow by 10%, 8%, 5%, and 5% for the next four years. (3) The target weighted average cost of capital (WACC) is 9%. This is the *No Change* scenario because operations remain unchanged.

   (1) For each of the next four years, forecast the following items: sales, cash, accounts receivable, inventories, net fixed assets, accounts payable & accruals, operating costs (excluding depreciation), depreciation, and earnings before interest and taxes (EBIT).

   (2) Using the previously forecasted items, calculate for each of the next four years the net operating profit after taxes (NOPAT), net operating working capital, total operating capital, free cash flow, (FCF), annual growth rate in FCF, and return on invested capital. What does the forecasted free cash flow in the first year imply about the need for external financing? Compare the forecasted ROIC with the WACC. What does this imply about how well the company is performing?

   (3) Assume that FCF will continue to grow at the growth rate for the last year in the forecast horizon (*Hint:* 5%). What is the horizon value at 2017? What is the present value of the horizon value? What is the present value of the forecasted FCF? (*Hint:* Use the free cash flows for 2014 through 2017.) What is the current value of operations? Using information from the 2013 financial statements, what is the current estimated intrinsic stock price?

f. Continue with the same assumptions for the *No Change* scenario from the previous question, but now forecast the balance sheet and income statements for 2014 (but not for the following three years) using the following preliminary financial policy. (1) Regular dividends will grow by 10%. (2) No additional long-term debt or common stock will be issued. (3) The interest rate on all debt is 8%. (4) Interest expense for long-term debt is based on the average balance during the year. (5) If the operating results and the preliminary financing plan cause a financing deficit, eliminate the deficit by drawing on a line of credit. The line of credit would be tapped on the last day of the year, so it would create no additional interest expenses for that year. (6) If there is a financing surplus, eliminate it by paying a special dividend. After forecasting the 2014 financial statements, answer the following questions.

(1) How much will Hatfield need to draw on the line of credit?

(2) What are some alternative ways than those in the preliminary financial policy that Hatfield might choose to eliminate the financing deficit?

g. Repeat the analysis performed the previous question but now assume that Hatfield is able to improve the following inputs: (1) reduce operating costs (excluding depreciation)/sales to 89.5% at a cost of $40 million, and (2) reduce inventories/sales to 16% at a cost of $10 million. This is the Improve scenario.

(1) Should Hatfield implement the plans? How much value would they add to the company?

(2) How much can Hatfield pay as a special dividend in the Improve scenario? What else might Hatfield do with the financing surplus?

SELECTED ADDITIONAL CASES

The following cases from TextChoice, *Cengage Learning's online library, cover many of the concepts discussed in this chapter and are available at* **http://www.textchoice2.com/casenet**.

Klein-Brigham Series:

Case 37, "Space-Age Materials, Inc."; Case 38, "Automated Banking Management, Inc."; Case 52, "Expert Systems"; and Case 69, "Medical Management Systems, Inc."

© Adalberto Rios Szalay/Sexto Sol/Getty Images

CHAPTER 13

Agency Conflicts and Corporate Governance

Citigroup CEO Vikram Pandit has had a wild ride regarding compensation. In 2007, Pandit sold his hedge fund to Citigroup and made a reported $167 million profit (the fund was shut down later due to poor performance). Citi appointed Pandit CEO in late 2007 and paid him about $1.2 million in cash and over $39 million in stocks and options during 2007 and 2008. But as the global economic crisis worsened, Pandit offered to take only $1 a year in salary and did so during 2009 and 2010.

The year 2011 was much better financially for Pandit, as he received a base salary of about $1.75 million and a retention bonus of over $23 million. Citi's board recommended that Pandit's salary be increased to $15 million at the 2012 board meeting. In addition, the board recommended a bonus plan in which Citi's top five executives could earn $18 million in 2012 if the combined 2011–2012 pretax income at Citi exceeded $12 billion.

Shareholders reacted angrily to these proposals and voted against the proposed compensation plans. What prompted such a reaction? It could have been that Citi earned $19.9 billion in pretax income in 2011, so the executives would still receive the proposed bonus even if Citi lost over $7 billion in pretax income in 2012!

Shareholder votes are nonbinding, and Citi's board ignored the vote. Shortly after, a large shareholder sued Citi's board for a breach of duty. Similar scenes are being played out at many other companies in the United States and overseas. Keep this example of corporate governance in mind as you read this chapter.

Source: Francesco Guerrera, "Citigroup's Pay Fiasco: Wake-Up Call for Board," *The Wall Street Journal,* April 24, 2012, p. C1.

Corporate Governance and Corporate Valuation

© Rob Webb/Getty Images

A company's managers make decisions that affect operations, financing, corporate culture, and many other organizational characteristics. These decisions affect the choices the company makes regarding operations and financing, which in turn affect free cash flow and risk.

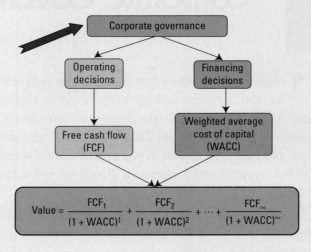

$$\text{Value} = \frac{\text{FCF}_1}{(1 + \text{WACC})^1} + \frac{\text{FCF}_2}{(1 + \text{WACC})^2} + \cdots + \frac{\text{FCF}_\infty}{(1 + \text{WACC})^\infty}$$

© Cengage Learning 2014

There is no conflict at a one-person company—the owner makes all the decisions, does all the work, reaps all the rewards, and suffers all the losses. This situation changes as the owner begins hiring employees because the employees don't fully share in the owner's rewards and losses. The situation becomes more complicated if the owner sells some shares of the company to an outsider, and even more complicated if the owner hires someone else to run the company. In this situation, there are many potential conflicts between owners, managers, employees, and creditors. These **agency conflicts** occur whenever owners authorize someone else to act on their behalf as their agents. The degree to which agency problems are minimized often depends on a company's **corporate governance**, which is the set of laws, rules, and procedures that influence the company's operations and the decisions its managers make. This chapter addresses these topics, beginning with agency conflicts.

13-1 Agency Conflicts

An **agency relationship** arises whenever someone, called a **principal**, hires someone else, called an **agent**, to perform some service, and the principal delegates decision-making authority to the agent. In companies, the primary agency relationships are between (1) stockholders and creditors, (2) inside owner/managers (managers who own a controlling interest in the company) and outside owners (who have no control), and (3) outside stockholders and hired managers.[1] These conflicts lead to **agency costs**, which are the reductions in a company's value due to agency conflicts. The following sections describe the agency conflicts, the costs, and methods to minimize the costs.

13-1a Conflicts between Stockholders and Creditors

Creditors have a claim on the firm's earnings stream, and they have a claim on its assets in the event of bankruptcy. However, stockholders have control (through the managers) of decisions that affect the firm's riskiness. Therefore, creditors allocate decision-making authority to someone else, creating a potential agency conflict.

Creditors lend funds at rates based on the firm's perceived risk at the time the credit is extended, which in turn is based on (1) the risk of the firm's existing assets, (2) expectations concerning the risk of future asset additions, (3) the existing capital structure, and (4) expectations concerning future capital structure changes. These are the primary determinants of the risk of the firm's cash flows, hence the safety of its debt.

Suppose the firm borrows money, then sells its relatively safe assets and invests the proceeds in assets for a large new project that is far riskier. The new project might be extremely profitable, but it also might lead to bankruptcy. If the risky project is successful, most of the benefits go to the stockholders, because creditors' returns are fixed at the original low-risk rate. However, if the project is unsuccessful, the bondholders take a loss. From the stockholders' point of view, this amounts to a game of "heads, I win; tails, you lose," which obviously is not good for the creditors. Thus, the increased risk due to the asset change will cause the required rate of return on the debt to increase, which in turn will cause the value of the outstanding debt to fall. This is called asset switching or "bait-and-switch."

A similar situation can occur if a company borrows and then issues additional debt, using the proceeds to repurchase some of its outstanding stock, thus increasing its financial leverage. If things go well, the stockholders will gain from the increased leverage. However, the value of the debt will probably decrease, because now there will be a larger amount of debt backed by the same amount of assets. In both the asset switch and the increased leverage situations, stockholders have the potential for gaining, but such gains are made at the expense of creditors.

There are two ways that lenders address the potential of asset switching or subsequent increases in leverage. First, creditors may charge a higher rate to protect themselves in case the company engages in activities which increase risk. However, if the company doesn't increase risk, then its weighted average cost of capital (WACC) will be higher than is justified by the company's risk. This higher WACC will reduce the company's intrinsic value (recall that intrinsic value is the present value of free cash flows discounted at the WACC). In addition, the company will reject projects that it otherwise would have accepted at the lower cost of capital. Therefore, this potential agency conflict has a cost, which is called an agency cost.

The second way that lenders address the potential agency problems is by writing detailed debt covenants specifying what actions the company can and cannot take. Many debt covenants have provisions that (1) prevent the company from increasing its debt ratios beyond a specified level, (2) prevent the company from repurchasing stock or paying dividends unless profits and retained earnings are above a certain level, and (3) require the company to maintain liquidity ratios above a specified level. These covenants

---

[1]One of the first, and most important, papers in finance and economics to address agency conflicts was written by Michael Jensen and William Meckling and entitled "Theory of the Firm: Managerial Behavior, Agency Costs and Ownership Structure," *Journal of Financial Economics*, Vol. 3, 1976, pp. 305–360.

can cause agency costs if they restrict a company from value-adding activities. For example, a company may not be able to accept an unexpected but particularly good investment opportunity if it requires temporarily adding debt above the level specified in the bond covenant. In addition, the costs incurred to write the covenant and monitor the company to verify compliance also are agency costs.

13-1b Conflicts between Inside Owner/Managers and Outside Owners

If a company's owner also runs the company, the owner/manager will presumably operate it so as to maximize his or her own welfare. This welfare obviously includes the increased wealth due to increasing the value of the company, but it also includes perquisites (or "perks") such as more leisure time, luxurious offices, executive assistants, expense accounts, limousines, corporate jets, and generous retirement plans. However, if the owner/manager incorporates the business and then sells some of the stock to outsiders, a potential conflict of interest immediately arises. Notice that the value of the perquisites still accrues to the owner/manager, but the cost of the perquisites is now partially born by the outsiders. This might even induce the owner/manager to increase consumption of the perquisites.

This agency problem causes outsiders to pay less for a share of the company and require a higher rate of return. This is exactly why dual class stock (see Chapter 1) that doesn't have voting rights has a lower price per share than voting stock.

13-1c Conflicts between Managers and Shareholders

Shareholders want companies to hire managers who are able and willing to take legal and ethical actions to maximize intrinsic stock prices.[2] This obviously requires managers with technical competence, but it also requires managers who are willing to put forth the extra effort necessary to identify and implement value-adding activities. However, managers are people, and people have both personal and corporate goals. Logically, therefore, managers can be expected to act in their own self-interests, and if their self-interests are not aligned with those of stockholders, then corporate value will not be maximized. There are six ways in which a manager's behavior might harm a firm's intrinsic value.

1. Managers might not expend the time and effort required to maximize firm value. Rather than focusing on corporate tasks, they might spend too much time on external activities, such as serving on boards of other companies, or on nonproductive activities, such as golf, gourmet meals, and travel.
2. Managers might use corporate resources on activities that benefit themselves rather than shareholders. For example, they might spend company money on such perquisites as lavish offices, memberships at country clubs, museum-quality art for corporate apartments, large personal staffs, and corporate jets. Because these perks are not actually cash payments to the managers, they are called **nonpecuniary benefits**.

---

[2]Notice that we said both legal and ethical actions. The accounting frauds perpetrated by Enron, WorldCom, and others that were uncovered in 2002 raised stock prices in the short run, but only because investors were misled about the companies' financial positions. Then, for example, when Enron finally revealed the correct financial information, the stocks tanked. Investors who bought shares based on the fraudulent financial statements lost tens of billions of dollars. Releasing false financial statements is illegal. Aggressive earnings management and the use of misleading accounting tricks to pump up reported earnings is unethical, and executives can go to jail as a result of their shenanigans. When we speak of taking actions to maximize stock prices, we mean making operational or financial changes designed to maximize intrinsic stock value, not fooling investors with false or misleading financial reports.

3. Managers might avoid making difficult but value-enhancing decisions that harm friends in the company. For example, a manager might not close a plant or terminate a project if the manager has personal relationships with those who are adversely affected by such decisions, even if termination is the economically sound action.

4. Managers might take on too much risk or they might not take on enough risk. For example, a company might have the opportunity to undertake a risky project with a positive NPV. If the project turns out badly, then the manager's reputation will be harmed and the manager might even be fired. Thus, a manager might choose to avoid risky projects even if they are desirable from a shareholder's point of view. On the other hand, a manager might take on projects with too much risk. Consider a project that is not living up to expectations. A manager might be tempted to invest even more money in the project rather than admit that the project is a failure. Or a manager might be willing to take on a second project with a negative NPV if it has even a slight chance of a very positive outcome, because hitting a home run with this second project might cover up the first project's poor performance. In other words, the manager might throw good money after bad.

5. If a company is generating positive free cash flow, a manager might "stockpile" it in the form of marketable securities instead of returning FCF to investors. This potentially harms investors because it prevents them from allocating these funds to other companies with good growth opportunities. Even worse, positive FCF often tempts a manager into paying too much for the acquisition of another company. In fact, most mergers and acquisitions end up as break-even deals, at best, for the acquiring company because the premiums paid for the targets are often very large.

   Why would a manager be reluctant to return cash to investors? First, extra cash on hand reduces the company's risk, which appeals to many managers. Second, a large distribution of cash to investors is an admission that the company doesn't have enough good investment opportunities. Slow growth is normal for a maturing company, but this isn't very exciting for a manager to admit. Third, there is a lot of glamour associated with making a large acquisition, and this can provide a large boost to a manager's ego. Fourth, compensation usually is higher for executives at larger companies; cash distributions to investors make a company smaller, not larger.

6. Managers might not release all the information that investors desire. Sometimes, they might withhold information to prevent competitors from gaining an advantage. Other times, they might try to avoid releasing bad news. For example, they might "massage" the data or "manage the earnings" so that the news doesn't look so bad. If investors are unsure about the quality of information managers provide, they tend to discount the company's expected free cash flows at a higher cost of capital, which reduces the company's intrinsic value.

If senior managers believe there is little chance they will be removed, we say that they are *entrenched*. Such a company faces a high risk of being poorly run, because entrenched managers are able to act in their own interests rather than in the interests of shareholders.

SELF-TEST

What are agency conflicts? What groups can have agency conflicts?

Name six types of managerial behaviors that can reduce a firm's intrinsic value.

r e s o u r c e

For excellent discussions of corporate governance, see the Web pages of CalPERS (the California Public Employees' Retirement System), www.calpers.org, *and TIAA-CREF (Teachers Insurance and Annuity Association College Retirement Equity Fund),* www.tiaa-cref.org.

13-2 Corporate Governance

Agency conflicts can decrease the value of stock owned by outside shareholders. Corporate governance can mitigate this loss in value. Corporate governance can be defined as the set of laws, rules, and procedures that influence a company's operations and the decisions its managers make. At the risk of oversimplification, most corporate governance provisions come in two forms, sticks and carrots. The primary stick is the *threat of removal,* either as a decision by the board of directors or as the result of a hostile takeover. If a firm's managers are maximizing the value of the resources entrusted to them, they need not fear the loss of their jobs. On the other hand, if managers are not maximizing value, they should be removed by their own boards of directors, by dissident stockholders, or by other companies seeking to profit by installing a better management team. The main carrot is *compensation.* Managers have greater incentives to maximize intrinsic stock value if their compensation is linked to the firm's performance rather than being strictly in the form of salary.

Almost all corporate governance provisions affect either the threat of removal or compensation. Some provisions are internal to a firm and are under its control.[3] These internal provisions and features can be divided into five areas: (1) monitoring and discipline by the board of directors, (2) charter provisions and bylaws that affect the likelihood of hostile takeovers, (3) compensation plans, (4) capital structure choices, and (5) accounting control systems. In addition to the corporate governance provisions that are under a firm's control, there are also environmental factors outside of a firm's control, such as the regulatory environment, block ownership patterns, competition in the product markets, the media, and litigation. Our discussion begins with the internal provisions.

13-2a Monitoring and Discipline by the Board of Directors

Shareholders are a corporation's owners, and they elect the board of directors to act as agents on their behalf. In the United States, it is the board's duty to monitor senior managers and discipline them if they do not act in the interests of shareholders, either by removal or by a reduction in compensation.[4] This is not necessarily the case outside the United States. For example, many companies in Europe are required to have employee representatives on the board. Also, many European and Asian companies have bank representatives on the board. But even in the United States, many boards fail to act in the shareholders' best interests. How can this be?

Consider the election process. The board of directors has a nominating committee. These directors choose the candidates for the open director positions, and the ballot for a board position usually lists only one candidate. Although outside candidates can run a "write-in" campaign, only those candidates named by the board's nominating committee are on the ballot.[5] At many companies, the CEO is also the chairman of the board and has considerable influence on this nominating committee. This means that in practice it often is the CEO who, in effect, nominates candidates for the board. High compensation and

---

[3]We have adapted this framework from the one provided by Stuart L. Gillan, "Recent Developments in Corporate Governance: An Overview," *Journal of Corporate Finance,* June 2006, pp. 381–402. Gillan provides an excellent discussion of the issues associated with corporate governance, and we highly recommend this article to the reader who is interested in an expanded discussion of the issues in this section.

[4]There are a few exceptions to this rule. For example, some states have laws allowing the board to consider the interests of other stakeholders, such as employees and members of the community.

[5]There is currently (early 2012) a movement under way to allow shareholders to nominate candidates for the board, but only time will tell whether this movement is successful.

prestige go with a position on the board of a major company, so board seats are prized possessions. Board members typically want to retain their positions, and they are grateful to whoever helped get them on the board. Thus, the nominating process often results in a board that is favorably disposed to the CEO.

At most companies, a candidate is elected simply by having a majority of votes cast. The proxy ballot usually lists all candidates, with a box for each candidate to check if the shareholder votes "For" the candidate and a box to check if the shareholder "Withholds" a vote on the candidate—you can't actually vote "No"; you can only withhold your vote. In theory, a candidate could be elected with a single "For" vote if all other votes were withheld. In practice, though, most shareholders either vote "For" or assign to management their right to vote (proxy is defined as the authority to act for another, which is why it is called a proxy statement). In practice, then, the nominated candidates virtually always receive a majority of votes and are thus elected.

Occasionally there is a "Just vote no" campaign in which a large investor (usually an institution such as a pension fund) urges stockholders to withhold their votes for one or more directors. Although such campaigns do not directly affect the director's election, they do provide a visible way for investors to express their dissatisfaction. Recent evidence shows that "Just vote no" campaigns at poorly performing firms lead to better performance and a greater probability that the CEO will be dismissed.[6]

Voting procedures also affect the ability of outsiders to gain positions on the board. If the charter specifies cumulative voting, then each shareholder is given a number of votes equal to his or her shares multiplied by the number of board seats up for election. For example, the holder of 100 shares of stock will receive 1,000 votes if 10 seats are to be filled. Then, the shareholder can distribute those votes however he or she sees fit. One hundred votes could be cast for each of 10 candidates, or all 1,000 votes could be cast for one candidate. If noncumulative voting is used, the hypothetical stockholder cannot concentrate votes in this way—no more than 100 votes can be cast for any one candidate.

With noncumulative voting, if management controls 51% of the shares, then they can fill every seat on the board, leaving dissident stockholders without any representation on the board. With cumulative voting, however, if 10 seats are to be filled, then dissidents could elect a representative, provided they have 10% plus 1 additional share of the stock.

Note also that bylaws specify whether the entire board is to be elected annually or if directors are to have staggered terms with, say, one-third of the seats to be filled each year and directors to serve 3-year terms. With staggered terms, fewer seats come up each year, making it harder for dissidents to gain representation on the board. Staggered boards are also called **classified boards**.

Many board members are "insiders"—that is, people who hold managerial positions within the company, such as the CFO. Because insiders report to the CEO, it may be difficult for them to oppose the CEO at a board meeting. To help mitigate this problem, several exchanges, such as the NYSE and NASDAQ, now require that listed companies have a majority of outside directors.

Some "outside" board members often have strong connections with the CEO through professional relationships, personal friendships, and consulting or other fee-generating activities. In fact, outsiders sometimes have very little expert business knowledge but have "celebrity" status from nonbusiness activities. Some companies also have **interlocking boards of directors**, where Company A's CEO sits on Company B's board and B's CEO sits on A's board. In these situations, even the outside directors are not truly independent and impartial.

---

[6]See Diane Del Guercio, Laura Seery, and Tracie Woidtke, "Do Boards Pay Attention When Institutional Investor Activists 'Just Vote No'?" *Journal of Financial Economics,* October 2008, pp. 84–103.

Large boards (those with more than about ten members) often are less effective than smaller boards. As anyone who has been on a committee can attest, individual participation tends to fall as committee size increases. Thus, there is a greater likelihood that members of a large board will be less active than those on smaller boards.

The compensation of board members has an impact on the board's effectiveness. When board members have exceptionally high compensation, the CEO also tends to have exceptionally high compensation. This suggests that such boards tend to be too lenient with the CEO.[7] The form of board compensation also affects board performance. Rather than compensating board members with only salary, many companies now include restricted stock grants or stock options in an effort to better align board members with stockholders.

Studies show that corporate governance usually improves if (1) the CEO is not also the chairman of the board, (2) the board has a majority of true outsiders who bring some type of business expertise to the board and are not too busy with other activities, (3) the board is not too large, and (4) board members are compensated appropriately (not too high and not all cash, but including exposure to equity risk through options or stock). The good news for the shareholder is that the boards at many companies have made significant improvements in these directions during the past decade. Fewer CEOs are also board chairmen and, as power has shifted from CEOs to boards as a whole, there has been a tendency to replace insiders with strong, independent outsiders. Today, the typical board has about one-third insiders and two-thirds outsiders, and most outsiders are truly independent. Moreover, board members are compensated primarily with stock or options rather than a straight salary. These changes clearly have decreased the patience of boards with poorly performing CEOs. Within the past several years the CEOs of Wachovia, Sprint Nextel, Gap, Hewlett-Packard, Home Depot, Citigroup, Pfizer, Ford, and Dynegy, to name just a few, have been removed by their boards. This would not have occurred 30 years ago.

13-2b Charter Provisions and Bylaws That Affect the Likelihood of Hostile Takeovers

Hostile takeovers usually occur when managers have not been willing or able to maximize the profit potential of the resources under their control. In such a situation, another company can acquire the poorly performing firm, replace its managers, increase free cash flow, and improve MVA. The following paragraphs describe some provisions that can be included in a corporate charter to make it harder for poorly performing managers to remain in control.[8]

A shareholder-friendly charter should ban **targeted share repurchases**, also known as **greenmail**. For example, suppose a company's stock is selling for $20 per share. Now a hostile bidder, or raider, who plans to replace management if the takeover is successful, buys 5% of the company's stock at the $20 price.[9] The raider then makes an offer to

---

[7]See I. E. Brick, O. Palmon, and J. Wald, "CEO Compensation, Director Compensation, and Firm Performance: Evidence of Cronyism?" *Journal of Corporate Finance,* June 2006, pp. 403–423.

[8]Some states have laws that go further than others to protect management. This is one reason that many companies are incorporated in manager-friendly Delaware. Some companies have even shifted their state of incorporation to Delaware because their managers felt that a hostile takeover attempt was likely. Note that a "shareholder-friendly charter" could and would waive the company's right to strong anti-takeover protection, even if the state allowed it.

[9]Someone can, under the law, acquire up to 5% of a firm's stock without announcing the acquisition. Once the 5% limit has been hit, the acquirer has 10 days to "announce" the acquisition by filing Schedule 13D with the SEC. Schedule 13D reports not only the acquirer's number of shares but also his or her intentions, such as a passive investment or a takeover. These reports are monitored closely, so as soon as one is filed, management is alerted to the possibility of an imminent takeover.

purchase the remainder of the stock for $30 per share. The company might offer to buy back the raider's stock at a price of, say, $35 per share. This is called a targeted share repurchase because the stock will be purchased only from the raider and not from any other shareholders. A raider who paid only $20 per share for the stock would be making a quick profit of $15 per share, which could easily total several hundred million dollars. As a part of the deal, the raider would sign a document promising not to attempt to take over the company for a specified number of years; hence the buyback also is called greenmail. Greenmail hurts shareholders in two ways. First, they are left with $20 stock when they could have received $30 per share. Second, the company purchased stock from the bidder at $35 per share, which represents a direct loss by the remaining shareholders of $15 for each repurchased share.

Managers who buy back stock in targeted repurchases typically argue that their firms are worth more than the raiders offered and that, in time, the "true value" will be revealed in the form of a much higher stock price. This situation might be true if a company were in the process of restructuring itself, or if new products with high potential were in the pipeline. But if the old management had been in power for a long time and had a history of making empty promises, then one should question whether the true purpose of the buyback was to protect stockholders or management.

Another characteristic of a stockholder-friendly charter is that it does not contain a **shareholder rights provision**, better described as a **poison pill**. These provisions give the shareholders of target firms the right to buy a specified number of shares in the company at a very low price if an outside group or firm acquires a specified percentage of the firm's stock. Therefore, if a potential acquirer tries to take over a company, its other shareholders will be entitled to purchase additional shares of stock at a bargain price, thus seriously diluting the holdings of the raider. For this reason, these clauses are called poison pills, because if they are in the charter, the acquirer will end up swallowing a poison pill if the acquisition is successful. Obviously, the existence of a poison pill makes a takeover more difficult, and this helps to entrench management.

A third management entrenchment tool is a **restricted voting rights** provision, which automatically cancels the voting rights of any shareholder who owns more than a specified amount of the company's stock. The board can grant voting rights to such a shareholder, but this is unlikely if that shareholder plans to take over the company.

13-2c Using Compensation to Align Managerial and Shareholder Interests

The typical CEO today receives a fixed salary, a cash bonus based on the firm's performance, and stock-based compensation, either in the form of stock grants or option grants. Cash bonuses often are based upon short-term operating factors, such as this year's growth in earnings per share, or medium-term operating performance, such as earnings growth over the past 3 years.

Stock-based compensation is often in the form of options. Chapter 8 explains option valuation in detail, but here we discuss how a standard **stock option compensation plan** works. Suppose IBM decides to grant an option to an employee, allowing her to purchase a specified number of IBM shares at a fixed price, called the **strike price** (or **exercise price**), regardless of the actual price of the stock. The strike price is usually set equal to the current stock price at the time the option is granted. Thus, if IBM's current price were $100, then the option would have an exercise price of $100. Options usually cannot be exercised until after some specified period (the **vesting period**), which is usually 1 to 5 years. Some grants have **cliff vesting**, which means that all the granted options vest at the

GLOBAL ECONOMIC CRISIS

© uniquely india/Getty Images

Would the U.S. Government Be an Effective Board Director?

In response to the global economic crisis that began with the recession of 2007, many governments are becoming major stakeholders in companies that had been publicly traded. For example, the U.S. government has invested billions in Fannie Mae and Freddie Mac, taking them into conservatorship and having a direct say in their leadership and operations, including the dismissal of former Fannie Mae CEO Daniel Mudd in 2008.

The U.S. government also made multibillion-dollar investments in banks (among them, Citigroup, Bank of America, JPMorgan Chase, and Wells Fargo), insurance companies, AIG (spectacularly), and auto companies (GM and Chrysler). Much of this has been in the form of preferred stock, which does not give the government any direct voting or decision-making authority. However, the government has certainly applied moral suasion, as evidenced by the removal of GM's former CEO Rick Wagoner. The government also imposed limits on executive compensation at firms receiving additional government funds.

For the most part, however, the government does not have voting rights with bailout recipients, nor does it have representation on their boards of directors. It will be interesting to see if this changes and if the government takes a more direct role in corporate governance.

Several large banks, including Citigroup, Goldman Sachs and JPMorgan Chase, have repaid the government's investments. In fact, about $70 billion of TARP funds have been repaid as of mid-2012; of course, there still is about $550 billion in TARP funding not yet repaid.

Sources: See **projects.nytimes.com/creditcrisis/recipients/ table** for updates on TARP recipients. See **http://projects. propublica.org/bailout/list** for a more comprehensive list that includes the bailouts funded through other programs, such as the bailout of Fannie Mae.

same date, such as 3 years after the grant. Other grants have **annual vesting**, which means that a certain percentage vests each year. For example, one-third of the options in the grant might vest each year. The options have an **expiration date**, usually 10 years after issue. For our IBM example, assume that the options have cliff vesting in 3 years and have an expiration date in 10 years. Thus, the employee can exercise the option 3 years after issue or wait as long as 10 years. Of course, the employee would not exercise unless IBM's stock is above the $100 exercise price, and if the price never rose above $100, the option would expire unexercised. However, if the stock price were above $100 on the expiration date, the option would surely be exercised.

Suppose the stock price had grown to $134 after 5 years, at which point the employee decided to exercise the option. She would buy stock from IBM for $100, so IBM would get only $100 for stock worth $134. The employee would (probably) sell the stock the same day she exercised the option and hence would receive in cash the $34 difference between the $134 stock price and the $100 exercise price. There are two important points to note in this example. First, most employees sell stock soon after exercising the option. Thus, the incentive effects of an option grant typically end when the option is exercised. Second, option pricing theory shows that it is not optimal to exercise a conventional call option on stock that does not pay dividends before the option expires: An investor is always better off selling the option in the marketplace rather than exercising it. But because employee stock options are not tradable, grantees often exercise the options well before they expire. For example, people often time the exercise of options to the purchase of a new home or some other large expenditure. But early exercise occurs not just for liquidity reasons, such as needing cash to purchase a house, but also because of behavioral reasons. For example, exercises occur more frequently after stock run-ups, which suggests that grantees view the stock as overpriced.

In theory, stock options should align a manager's interests with those of shareholders, influencing the manager to behave in a way that maximizes the company's value. But in practice there are two reasons why this does not always occur.

First, suppose a CEO granted options on 1 million shares. If we use the same stock prices as in our previous example, then the grantee would receive $34 for each option, or a total of $34 million. Keep in mind that this is in addition to an annual salary and cash bonuses. The logic behind employee options is that they motivate people to work harder and smarter, thus making the company more valuable and benefiting shareholders. But take a closer look at this example. If the risk-free rate is 5.5%, the market risk premium is 6%, and IBM's beta is 1.19, then the expected return, based on the CAPM, is 5.5% + 1.19(6%) = 12.64%. IBM's dividend yield is only 0.8%, so the expected annual price appreciation must be about 11.84% (12.64% − 0.8% = 11.84%). Now note that if IBM's stock price grew from $100 to $134 over 5 years, this would translate to an annual growth rate of only 6%, not the 11.84% shareholders expected. Thus, the executive would receive $34 million for helping run a company that performed below shareholders' expectations. As this example illustrates, standard stock options do not necessarily link executives' wealth with that of shareholders.

Second, and even worse, the events of the early 2000s showed that some executives were willing to illegally falsify financial statements in order to drive up stock prices just prior to exercising their stock options.[10] In some notable cases, the subsequent stock price drop and loss of investor confidence have forced firms into bankruptcy. Such behavior is certainly not in shareholders' best interests!

As a result, companies today are experimenting with different types of compensation plans that involve different vesting periods and different measures of performance. For example, from a legal standpoint it is more difficult to manipulate EVA (Economic Value Added) than earnings per share.[11] Therefore, many companies incorporate EVA-type measures in their compensation systems. Also, many companies have quit granting options and instead are granting restricted stock that cannot be sold until it has vested.

Just as "all ships rise in a rising tide," so too do most stocks rise in a bull market such as that of 2003–2007. In a strong market, even the stocks of companies whose performance ranks in the bottom 10% of their peer group can rise and thus trigger handsome executive bonuses. This situation is leading to compensation plans that are based on *relative* as opposed to *absolute* stock price performance. For example, some compensation plans have indexed options whose exercise prices depend on the performance of the market or a subset of competitors.

Finally, the empirical results from academic studies show that the correlation between executive compensation and corporate performance is mixed. Some studies suggest that the type of compensation plan used affects company performance, while others find little effect, if any. But we can say with certainty that managerial compensation plans will continue to receive lots of attention from researchers, the popular press, and boards of directors.

---

[10]Several academic studies show that option-based compensation leads to a greater likelihood of earnings restatements (which means having to refile financial statements with the SEC because there was a material error) and outright fraud. See A. Agrawal and S. Chadha, "Corporate Governance and Accounting Scandals," *Journal of Law and Economics,* 2006, pp. 371–406; N. Burns and S. Kedia, "The Impact of Performance-Based Compensation on Misreporting," *Journal of Financial Economics,* January 2006, pp. 35–67; and D. J. Denis, P. Hanouna, and A. Sarin, "Is There a Dark Side to Incentive Compensation?" *Journal of Corporate Finance,* June 2006, pp. 467–488.

[11]For a discussion of EVA, see Al Ehrbar, *EVA: The Real Key to Creating Wealth* (New York: John Wiley & Sons, 1998); and Pamela P. Peterson and David R. Peterson, *Company Performance and Measures of Value Added* (The Research Foundation of the Institute of Chartered Financial Analysts, 1996).

The Dodd-Frank Act and "Say on Pay"

© Rob Webb/Getty Images

The Dodd-Frank Act requires corporations to hold a non-binding vote to approve or reject the company's executive compensation plan. During 2011, the first proxy season in which the vote was required, shareholders approved about 92% of the proposals. As we write this in mid-2012, it is too early to say for sure, but already there are a number of companies whose shareholders have rejected the compensation plans, including Citigroup, WPP (a global advertising agency), Chiquita Brands International, Chesapeake Energy, Simon Property Group (a real estate developer with many shopping malls), International Game Technology, and American Eagle Outfitters.

In addition to say on pay, shareholders are also concerned with other issues, including political lobbying. The table below shows selected shareholder proposals in 2012.

	Number of proposals		Number of proposals
Board Issues		**Social Responsibility**	
Equal access to the proxy	13	Review political spending/lobbying	69
Independent board chairman	30	Climate change	7
Officer succession planning	2	Report on impact of fracturing	4
Takeover Defenses / Other		Report on sustainability	11
Right to call special meeting	29	Board diversity	4
Allow for written consent	31		
End supermajority vote requirement	23		
Repeal classified board	13		

Source: © 2012 MSCI. All rights reserved.

13-2d Capital Structure and Internal Control Systems

Capital structure decisions can affect managerial behavior. As the debt level increases, so does the probability of bankruptcy. This increased threat of bankruptcy affects managerial behavior in two ways. First, as discussed earlier in this chapter, managers may waste money on unnecessary expenditures and perquisites. This behavior is more likely when times are good and firms are flush with cash; it is less likely in the face of high debt levels and possible bankruptcy. Thus, high levels of debt tend to reduce managerial waste. Second, however, high levels of debt may also reduce a manager's willingness to undertake positive-NPV but risky projects. Most managers have their personal reputation and wealth tied to a single company. If that company has a lot of debt, then a particularly risky project, even if it has a positive NPV, may be just too risky for the manager to tolerate because a bad outcome could lead to bankruptcy and loss of the manager's job. Stockholders, on the other hand, are diversified and would want the manager to invest in positive-NPV projects even if they are risky. When managers forgo risky but value-adding projects, the resulting **underinvestment problem** reduces firm value. So increasing debt might increase firm value by reducing wasteful expenditures, but it also might reduce value by inducing underinvestment by managers. Empirical tests have not been able to establish exactly which effect dominates.

The Sarbanes-Oxley Act of 2002 and Corporate Governance

© Rob Webb/Getty Images

In 2002, Congress passed the Sarbanes-Oxley Act, known in the industry as SOX, as a measure to improve transparency in financial accounting and to prevent fraud. SOX consists of 11 chapters, or *titles*, which establish wide-ranging new regulations for auditors, CEOs and CFOs, boards of directors, investment analysts, and investment banks. These regulations are designed to ensure that (a) companies that perform audits are sufficiently independent of the companies that they audit, (b) a key executive in each company *personally* certifies that the financial statements are complete and accurate, (c) the board of directors' audit committee is relatively independent of management, (d) financial analysts are relatively independent of the companies they analyze, and (e) companies publicly and promptly release all important information about their financial condition. The individual titles are briefly summarized below.

Title I establishes the Public Company Accounting Oversight Board, whose charge is to oversee auditors and establish quality control and ethical standards for audits.

Title II requires that auditors be independent of the companies that they audit. Basically this means they can't provide consulting services to the companies they audit. The purpose is to remove financial incentives for auditors to help management cook the books.

Title III requires that the board of directors' audit committee must be composed of "independent" members. Section 302 requires that the CEO and CFO must review the annual and quarterly financial statements and reports and personally certify that they are complete and accurate. Penalties for certifying reports that executives know are false range up to a $5 million fine, 20 years in prison, or both. Under Section 304, if the financial statements turn out to be false and must be *restated,* then certain bonuses and equity-based compensation that executives earn must be reimbursed to the company.

Title IV's Section 401(a) requires prompt disclosure and more extensive reporting on off-balance sheet transactions. Section 404 requires that management evaluate its internal financial controls and report whether they are "effective." The external auditing firm must also indicate whether it agrees with management's evaluation of its internal controls. Section 409 requires that a company disclose to the public promptly and *in plain English* any material changes to its financial condition. Title IV also places restrictions on the loans that a company can make to its executives.

Title V addresses the relationship between financial analysts, the investment banks they work for, and the companies they cover. It requires that analysts and brokers who make stock recommendations disclose any conflicts of interest they might have concerning the stocks they recommend.

Titles VI and VII are technical in nature, dealing with the SEC's budget and powers and requiring that several studies be undertaken by the SEC.

Title VIII establishes penalties for destroying or falsifying audit records. It also provides "whistle-blower protection" for employees who report fraud.

Title IX increases the penalties for a variety of white-collar crimes associated with securities fraud, such as mail and wire fraud. Section 902 also makes it a crime to alter, destroy, or hide documents that might be used in an investigation. It also makes it a crime to conspire to do so.

Title X requires that the CEO sign the company's federal income tax return.

Title XI provides penalties for obstructing an investigation and grants the SEC authority to remove officers or directors from a company if they have committed fraud.

Internal control systems have become an increasingly important issue since the passage of the Sarbanes-Oxley Act of 2002. Section 404 of the act requires companies to establish effective internal control systems. The Securities and Exchange Commission, which is charged with the implementation of Sarbanes-Oxley, defines an effective internal control system as one that provides "reasonable assurance regarding the reliability of financial reporting and the preparation of financial statements for external purposes in accordance with generally accepted accounting principles." In other words, investors should be able to trust a company's reported financial statements.

13-2e Environmental Factors outside a Firm's Control

As noted earlier, corporate governance is also affected by environmental factors that are outside of a firm's control, including the regulatory/legal environment, block ownership patterns, competition in the product markets, the media, and litigation.

REGULATIONS AND LAWS

The regulatory/legal environment includes the agencies that regulate financial markets, such as the SEC. Even though the fines and penalties levied on firms for financial misrepresentation by the SEC are relatively small, the damage to a firm's reputation can have significant costs, leading to extremely large reductions in the firm's value.[12] Thus, the regulatory system has an enormous impact on corporate governance and firm value.

The regulatory/legal environment also includes the laws and legal system under which a company operates. These vary greatly from country to country. Studies show that firms located in countries with strong legal protection for investors have stronger corporate governance and that this is reflected in better access to financial markets, a lower cost of equity, increases in market liquidity, and less nonsystematic volatility in stock returns.[13]

BLOCK OWNERSHIP PATTERNS

Prior to the 1960s, most U.S. stock was owned by a large number of individual investors, each of whom owned a diversified portfolio of stocks. Because each individual owned a small amount of any given company's stock, there was little that he or she could do to influence its operations. Also, with such a small investment, it was not cost effective for the investor to monitor companies closely. Indeed, dissatisfied stockholders would typically just "vote with their feet" by selling the stock. This situation began to change as institutional investors such as pension funds and mutual funds gained control of larger and larger shares of investment capital—and as they then acquired larger and larger percentages of all outstanding stock. Given their large block holdings, it now makes sense for institutional investors to monitor management, and they have the clout to influence the board. In some cases, they have actually elected their own representatives to the board. For example, when TIAA-CREF, a huge private pension fund, became frustrated with the performance and leadership of Furr's/Bishop, a cafeteria chain, the fund led a fight that ousted the entire board and then elected a new board consisting only of outsiders.

In general, activist investors with large blocks in companies have been good for all shareholders. They have searched for firms with poor profitability and then replaced management with new teams that are well versed in value-based management techniques, thereby improving profitability. Not surprisingly, stock prices usually rise on the news that a well-known activist investor has taken a major position in an underperforming company.

Note that activist investors can improve performance even if they don't go so far as to take over a firm. More often, they either elect their own representatives to the board or simply point out the firm's problems to other board members. In such cases, boards often change their attitudes and become less tolerant when they realize that the management

[12]For example, see Jonathan M. Karpoff, D. Scott Lee, and Gerald S. Martin, "The Cost to Firms of Cooking the Books," *Journal of Financial and Quantitative Analysis,* September 2008, pp. 581–612.
[13]For example, see R. La Porta, F. Lopez-de-Silanes, A. Shleifer, and R. Vishny, "Legal Determinants of External Finance," *Journal of Finance,* January 1997, pp. 1131–1150; Hazem Daouk, Charles M. C. Lee, and David Ng, "Capital Market Governance: How Do Security Laws Affect Market Performance?" *Journal of Corporate Finance,* June 2006, pp. 560–593; and Li Jin and Stewart C. Myers, "R^2 Around the World: New Theory and New Tests," *Journal of Financial Economics,* February 2006, pp. 257–292.

team is not following the dictates of value-based management. Moreover, the firm's top managers recognize what will happen if they don't whip the company into shape, and they go about doing just that.

COMPETITION IN PRODUCT MARKETS

The degree of competition in a firm's product market has an impact on its corporate governance. For example, companies in industries with lots of competition don't have the luxury of tolerating poorly performing CEOs. As might be expected, CEO turnover is higher in competitive industries than in those with less competition.[14] When most firms in an industry are similar, you might expect it to be easier to find a qualified replacement from another firm for a poorly performing CEO. This is exactly what the evidence shows: As industry homogeneity increases, so does the incidence of CEO turnover.[15]

THE MEDIA AND LITIGATION

Corporate governance, especially compensation, is a hot topic in the media. The media can have a positive impact by discovering or reporting corporate problems, such as the Enron scandal. Another example is the extensive coverage that was given to option backdating, in which the exercise prices of executive stock options were set *after* the options officially were granted. Because the exercise prices were set at the lowest stock price during the quarter in which the options were granted, the options were in-the-money and more valuable when their "official" lives began. Several CEOs have already lost their jobs over this practice, and more firings are likely.

However, the media can also hurt corporate governance by focusing too much attention on a CEO. Such "superstar" CEOs often command excessive compensation packages and spend too much time on activities outside the company, resulting in too much pay for too little performance.[16]

In addition to penalties and fines from regulatory bodies such as the SEC, civil litigation also occurs when companies are suspected of fraud. Research indicates that such suits lead to improvements in corporate governance.[17]

SELF-TEST

What are the two primary forms of corporate governance provisions that correspond to the stick and the carrot?

What factors improve the effectiveness of a board of directors?

What are three provisions in many corporate charters that deter takeovers?

Describe how a typical stock option plan works. What are some problems with a typical stock option plan?

---

[14]See M. De Fond and C. Park, "The Effect of Competition on CEO Turnover," *Journal of Accounting and Economics,* Vol. 27, 1999, pp. 35–56; and T. Fee and C. Hadlock, "Management Turnover and Product Market Competition: Empirical Evidence from the U.S. Newspaper Industry," *Journal of Business,* April 2000, pp. 205–243.

[15]See R. Parrino, "CEO Turnover and Outside Succession: A Cross-Sectional Analysis," *Journal of Financial Economics,* Vol. 46, 1997, pp. 165–197.

[16]See U. Malmendier and G. A. Tate, "Superstar CEOs," *Quarterly Journal of Economics,* November 2009, pp. 1593–1638.

[17]For example, see D. B. Farber, "Restoring Trust after Fraud: Does Corporate Governance Matter?" *Accounting Review,* April 2005, pp. 539–561; and Stephen P. Ferris, Tomas Jandik, Robert M. Lawless, and Anil Makhija, "Derivative Lawsuits as a Corporate Governance Mechanism: Empirical Evidence on Board Changes Surrounding Filings," *Journal of Financial and Quantitative Analysis,* March 2007, pp. 143–166.

International Corporate Governance

© Rob Webb/Getty Images

Corporate governance includes the following factors: (1) the likelihood that a poorly performing firm can be taken over; (2) whether the board of directors is dominated by insiders or outsiders; (3) the extent to which most of the stock is held by a few large "blockholders" versus many small shareholders; and (4) the size and form of executive compensation. An interesting study compared corporate governance in Germany, Japan, and the United States.

First, note from the accompanying table that the threat of a takeover serves as a stick in the United States but not in Japan or Germany. This threat, which reduces management entrenchment, should benefit shareholders in the United States relative to the other two countries. Second, German and Japanese boards are larger than those in the United States. Japanese boards consist primarily of insiders, unlike German and American boards, which have similar inside/outside mixes. It should be noted, though, that the boards of most large German corporations include representatives of labor, whereas U.S. boards represent only shareholders. Thus, it would appear that U.S. boards, with a higher percentage of outsiders, would have interests most closely aligned with those of shareholders.

German and Japanese firms are also more likely to be controlled by large blocks of stock than those in the United States. Although institutional investors such as pension and mutual funds are increasingly important in the United States, block ownership is still less prevalent than in Germany and Japan. In both Germany and Japan, banks often own large blocks of stock, something that is not permitted by law in the United States, and corporations also own large blocks of stock in other corporations. In Japan, combinations of companies, called **keiretsus**, have cross-ownership of stock among the member companies, and these interlocking blocks distort the definition of an outside board member. For example, when the performance of a company in a keiretsu deteriorates, new directors are often appointed from the staffs of other members of the keiretsu. Such appointees might be classified officially as insiders, but they represent interests other than those of the troubled company's CEO.

In general, large blockholders are better able to monitor management than are small investors, so one might expect the blockholder factor to favor German and Japanese shareholders. However, these blockholders have other relationships with the company that might be detrimental to outside shareholders. For example, if one company buys from another, transfer pricing might be used to shift wealth to a favored company, or a company might be forced to buy from a sister company in spite of the availability of lower-cost resources from outside the group.

Executive compensation packages differ dramatically across the three countries, with U.S. executives receiving by far the highest compensation. However, compensation plans are remarkably similar in terms of how sensitive total compensation is to corporate performance.

Which country's system of corporate governance is best from the standpoint of a shareholder whose goal is stock price maximization? There is no definitive answer. U.S. stocks have had the best performance in recent years. Moreover, German and Japanese companies are slowly moving toward the U.S. system with respect to size of compensation, and compensation plans in all three countries are being linked ever more closely to performance. At the same time, however, U.S. companies are moving toward the others in the sense of having larger ownership blocks; because those blocks are primarily held by pension and mutual funds (rather than banks and related corporations), they better represent the interests of shareholders.

Source: Steven N. Kaplan, "Top Executive Incentives in Germany, Japan, and the USA: A Comparison," in *Executive Compensation and Shareholder Value,* Jennifer Carpenter and David Yermack, eds. (Boston: Kluwer Academic Publishers, 1999), pp. 3–12. Reprinted with kind permission from Springer Science+Business Media B.V.

(continued)

International Characteristics of Corporate Governance

	Germany	Japan	United States
Threat of a takeover	Moderate	Low	High
Board of directors			
Size of board	26	21	14
Percent insiders	27%	91%	33%
Percent outsiders	73%	9%	67%
Are large blocks of stock typically owned by			
A controlling family?	Yes	No	No
Another corporation?	Yes	Yes	No
A bank?	Yes	Yes	No
Executive compensation			
Amount of compensation	Moderate	Low	High
Sensitivity to performance	Low to moderate	Low to moderate	Low to moderate

13-3 Employee Stock Ownership Plans (ESOPs)

Studies show that 90% of the employees who receive stock under option plans sell the stock as soon as they exercise their options, so the plans motivate employees only for a limited period.[18] Moreover, many companies limit their stock option plans to key managers and executives. To help provide long-term productivity gains and improve retirement incomes for all employees, Congress authorized the use of **Employee Stock Ownership Plans (ESOPs)**. Today almost 10,000 privately held companies and about 330 publicly held firms have ESOPs, accounting for over 10 million workers. Typically, the ESOP's major asset is shares of the common stock of the company that created it, and of the 10,000 total ESOPs, about half of them actually own a majority of their company's stock.

WWW

See **www.esopassociation .org** *for updates on ESOP statistics.*

To illustrate how an ESOP works, consider Gallagher & Abbott Inc. (G&A), a construction company located in Knoxville, Tennessee. G&A's simplified balance sheet is shown below:

G&A's Balance Sheet Prior to ESOP (Millions of Dollars)

Assets		Liabilities and Equity	
Cash	$ 10	Debt	$100
Other	190	Equity (1 million shares)	100
Total	$200	Total	$200

[18]See Gary Laufman, "To Have and Have Not," *CFO,* March 1998, pp. 58–66.

Now G&A creates an ESOP, which is a new legal entity. The company issues 500,000 shares of new stock at $100 per share, or $50 million in total, which it sells to the ESOP. The company's employees are the ESOP's stockholders, and each employee receives an ownership interest based on the size of his or her salary and years of service. The ESOP borrows the $50 million to buy the newly issued stock.[19] Financial institutions are willing to lend the ESOP the money because G&A signs a guarantee for the loan. Here is the company's new balance sheet:

G&A's Balance Sheet after the ESOP (Millions of Dollars)

Assets		Liabilities and Equity	
Cash	$ 60	Debt[a]	$ 100
Other	190	Equity (1.5 million shares)	150
Total	$ 250	Total	$ 250

[a]The company has guaranteed the ESOP's loan, and it has promised to make payments to the ESOP sufficient to retire the loan, but this does not show up on the balance sheet.

The company now has an additional $50 million of cash and $50 million more of book equity, but it has a de facto liability owing to its guarantee of the ESOP's debt. It could use the cash to finance an expansion, but many companies use the cash to repurchase their own common stock, so we assume that G&A will do likewise. The company's new balance sheets, and that of the ESOP, are shown below:

G&A's Balance Sheet after the ESOP and Share Repurchase (Millions of Dollars)

Assets		Liabilities and Equity	
Cash	$ 10	Debt	$100
Other	190	Equity (1 million shares)	150
		Treasury stock	(50)
Total	$ 200	Total	$200

ESOP's Initial Balance Sheet (Millions of Dollars)

Assets		Liabilities and Equity	
G&A stock	$50	Debt	$50
		Equity	0
Total	$50	Total	$50

Note that although the company's balance sheet looks exactly as it did initially, there is actually a huge difference—the company has guaranteed the ESOP's debt and hence it has an off–balance sheet liability of $50 million. Moreover, because the ESOP has no equity,

---

[19]Our description is simplified. Technically, the stock would be placed in a suspense account and then be allocated to employees as the debt is repaid.

the guarantee is very real indeed. Finally, observe that operating assets have not been increased at all, but the total debt outstanding supported by those assets has increased by $50 million.[20]

If this were the whole story, then there would be no reason to have an ESOP. However, G&A has promised to make payments to the ESOP in sufficient amounts to enable the ESOP to pay interest and principal charges on the debt, amortizing it over 15 years. Thus, after 15 years, the debt will be paid off and the ESOP's equity holders (the employees) will have equity with a book value of $50 million and a market value that could be much higher if G&A's stock increases, as it should over time. Then, as employees retire, the ESOP will distribute a pro rata amount of the G&A stock to each employee, who can then use it as a part of his or her retirement plan.

An ESOP is clearly beneficial for employees, but why would a company want to establish one? There are five primary reasons.

1. Congress passed the enabling legislation in hopes of enhancing employees' productivity and thus making the economy more efficient. In theory, employees who have equity in the enterprise will work harder and smarter. Note too that if employees are more productive and creative then this will benefit outside shareholders, because productivity enhancements that benefit ESOP shareholders also benefit outside shareholders.

2. The ESOP represents additional compensation to employees: in our example, there is a $50 million (or more) transfer of wealth from existing shareholders to employees over the 15-year period. Presumably, if the ESOP were not created then some other form of compensation would have been required, and that alternative compensation might not have the secondary benefit of enhancing productivity. Also note that the ESOP's payments to employees (as opposed to the payment by the company) come primarily at retirement, and Congress wanted to boost retirement incomes.

3. Depending on when an employee's rights to the ESOP are vested, the ESOP may help the firm retain employees.

4. There are strong tax incentives that encourage a company to form an ESOP. First, Congress decreed that when the ESOP owns 50% or more of the company's common stock, financial institutions that lend money to ESOPs can exclude from taxable income 50% of the interest they receive on the loan. This improves the financial institutions' after-tax returns, which allows them to lend to ESOPs at below-market rates. Therefore, a company that establishes an ESOP can borrow through the ESOP at a lower rate than would otherwise be available—in our example, the $50 million of debt would be at a reduced rate.

   There is also a second tax advantage. If the company were to borrow directly, it could deduct interest but not principal payments from its taxable income. However, companies typically make the required payments to their ESOPs in the form of cash dividends. Dividends are not normally deductible from taxable income, but *cash dividends paid on ESOP stock are deductible if the dividends are paid to plan participants or are used to repay the loan.* Thus, companies whose ESOPs own 50% of their stock can in effect borrow on ESOP loans at subsidized rates and then deduct both the interest and principal payments made on the loans. American Airlines and Publix Supermarkets are two of the many firms that have used ESOPs to obtain this benefit, along with motivating employees by giving them an equity interest in the enterprise.

---

[20]We assumed that the company used the $50 million paid to it by the ESOP to repurchase common stock and thus to increase its de facto debt. It could have used the $50 million to retire debt, in which case its true debt ratio would remain unchanged, or it could have used the money to support an expansion.

5. A less desirable use of ESOPs is to help companies avoid being acquired by another company. The company's CEO, or someone appointed by the CEO, typically acts as trustee for its ESOP, and the trustee is supposed to vote the ESOP's shares according to the will of the plan participants. Moreover, the participants, who are the company's employees, usually oppose takeovers because they frequently involve labor cutbacks. Therefore, if an ESOP owns a significant percentage of the company's shares, then management has a powerful tool for warding off takeovers. This is not good for outside stockholders.

Are ESOPs good for a company's shareholders? In theory, ESOPs motivate employees by providing them with an ownership interest. That should increase productivity and thereby enhance stock values. Moreover, tax incentives mitigate the costs associated with some ESOPs. However, an ESOP can be used to help entrench management, and that could hurt stockholders. How do the pros and cons balance out? The empirical evidence is not entirely clear, but certain findings are worth noting. First, if an ESOP is established to help defend against a takeover, then the firm's stock price typically falls when plans for the ESOP are announced. The market does not like the prospect of entrenching management and having to give up the premium normally associated with a takeover. However, if the ESOP is established for tax purposes and/or to motivate employees, the stock price generally goes up at the time of the announcement. In these cases, the company typically has a subsequent improvement in sales per employee and other long-term performance measures, which stimulates the stock price. Indeed, a study showed that companies with ESOPs enjoyed a 26% average annual stock return compared to a return of only 19% for peer companies without ESOPs.[21] It thus appears that ESOPs, if used appropriately, can be a powerful tool for creating shareholder value.

SELF-TEST

What are ESOPs? What are some of their advantages and disadvantages?

SUMMARY

- An **agency relationship** arises whenever an individual or group, called a **principal**, hires someone called an **agent** to perform some service and the principal delegates decision-making power to the agent.
- Important agency relationships include those between stockholders and creditors, owner/managers and outside shareholders, and stockholders and managers.
- An **agency conflict** refers to a conflict between principals and agents. For example, managers, as agents, may pay themselves excessive salaries, obtain unreasonably large stock options, and the like, at the expense of the principals, the stockholders.
- **Agency costs** are the reductions in a company's value due to actions by agents, including the costs principals incur (such as monitoring costs) in trying to modify their agents' behaviors.
- **Corporate governance** involves the manner in which shareholders' objectives are implemented, and it is reflected in a company's policies and actions.
- The two primary mechanisms used in corporate governance are (1) the threat of removal of a poorly performing CEO and (2) the type of plan used to compensate executives and managers.

---

[21]See Daniel Eisenberg, "No ESOP Fable," *Time,* May 10, 1999, p. 95.

- Poorly performing managers can be removed either by a takeover or by the company's own board of directors. Provisions in the corporate charter affect the difficulty of a successful takeover, and the composition of the board of directors affects the likelihood of a manager being removed by the board.
- **Managerial entrenchment** is most likely when a company has a weak board of directors coupled with strong anti-takeover provisions in its corporate charter. In this situation, the likelihood that badly performing senior managers will be fired is low.
- **Nonpecuniary benefits** are noncash perks such as lavish offices, memberships at country clubs, corporate jets, foreign junkets, and the like. Some of these expenditures may be cost effective, but others are wasteful and simply reduce profits. Such fat is almost always cut after a hostile takeover.
- **Targeted share repurchases**, also known as **greenmail**, occur when a company buys back stock from a potential acquirer at a price higher than the market price. In return, the potential acquirer agrees not to attempt to take over the company.
- **Shareholder rights provisions**, also known as **poison pills**, allow existing shareholders to purchase additional shares of stock at a price lower than the market value if a potential acquirer purchases a controlling stake in the company.
- A **restricted voting rights** provision automatically deprives a shareholder of voting rights if he or she owns more than a specified amount of stock.
- **Interlocking boards of directors** occur when the CEO of Company A sits on the board of Company B and B's CEO sits on A's board.
- A **stock option** provides for the purchase of a share of stock at a fixed price, called the **exercise price**, no matter what the actual price of the stock is. Stock options have an **expiration date**, after which they cannot be exercised.
- An **Employee Stock Ownership Plan (ESOP)** is a plan that facilitates employees' ownership of stock in the company for which they work.

QUESTIONS

(13-1)   Define each of the following terms:

    a. Agent; principal; agency relationship
    b. Agency cost
    c. Basic types of agency conflicts
    d. Managerial entrenchment; nonpecuniary benefits
    e. Greenmail; poison pills; restricted voting rights
    f. Stock option; ESOP

(13-2)   What is the possible agency conflict between inside owner/managers and outside shareholders?

(13-3)   What are some possible agency conflicts between borrowers and lenders?

(13-4)   What are some actions an entrenched management might take that would harm shareholders?

(13-5)   How is it possible for an employee stock option to be valuable even if the firm's stock price fails to meet shareholders' expectations?

MINI CASE

Suppose you decide (as did Steve Jobs and Mark Zuckerberg) to start a company. Your product is a software platform that integrates a wide range of media devices, including laptop computers, desktop computers, digital video recorders, and cell phones. Your initial market is the student body at your university. Once you have established your company and set up procedures for operating it, you plan to expand to other colleges in the area, and eventually to go nationwide. At some point, hopefully sooner rather than later, you plan to go public with an IPO, and then to buy a yacht and take off for the South Pacific to indulge in your passion for underwater photography. With these issues in mind, you need to answer for yourself, and potential investors, the following questions.

a. What is an agency relationship? When you first begin operations, assuming you are the only employee and only your money is invested in the business, would any agency conflicts exist? Explain your answer.

b. If you expanded and hired additional people to help you, might that give rise to agency problems?

c. Suppose you need additional capital to expand and you sell some stock to outside investors. If you maintain enough stock to control the company, what type of agency conflict might occur?

d. Suppose your company raises funds from outside lenders. What type of agency costs might occur? How might lenders mitigate the agency costs?

e. Suppose your company is very successful and you cash out most of your stock and turn the company over to an elected board of directors. Neither you nor any other stockholders own a controlling interest (this is the situation at most public companies). List six potential managerial behaviors that can harm a firm's value.

f. What is corporate governance? List five corporate governance provisions that are internal to a firm and are under its control.

g. What characteristics of the board of directors usually lead to effective corporate governance?

h. List three provisions in the corporate charter that affect takeovers.

i. Briefly describe the use of stock options in a compensation plan. What are some potential problems with stock options as a form of compensation?

j. What is block ownership? How does it affect corporate governance?

k. Briefly explain how regulatory agencies and legal systems affect corporate governance.

© Adalberto Rios Szalay/Sexto Sol/Getty Images

CHAPTER **15**

Capital Structure Decisions

A bankruptcy and a liquidity crisis are very different. An *economic* bankruptcy means that the market value of a company's assets (which is determined by the cash flows those assets are expected to produce) is less than the amount owed to creditors. A *legal* bankruptcy occurs when a company files in bankruptcy court for protection from its creditors until it can arrange an orderly reorganization or liquidation. A *liquidity crisis* occurs when a company doesn't have access to enough cash to make payments to creditors as the payments come due in the near future. In normal times, a strong company (one whose market value of assets far exceeds the amount owed to creditors) can usually borrow money in the short-term credit markets to meet any urgent liquidity needs. Thus, a liquidity crisis usually doesn't trigger a bankruptcy.

However, 2008 and the 2009 were anything but usual. Many companies had loaded up on debt during the boom years prior to 2007, and much of that was short-term debt. When the mortgage crisis began in late 2007 and spread like wildfire through the financial sector, many financial institutions virtually stopped providing short-term credit as they tried to stave off their own bankruptcies. As a result, many nonfinancial companies faced liquidity crises. Even worse, consumer demand began to drop and investors' risk aversion began to rise, leading to falling market values of assets and triggering economic and legal bankruptcy for many companies.

The economic crisis drove many companies into bankruptcy, including Lehman Brothers, Washington Mutual, General Motors, Chrysler, Pilgrim's Pride, and Circuit City. Many other companies scrambled to reduce their liquidity problems. For example, Black & Decker issued about $350 million in 5-year notes and used the proceeds to pay off some of its commercial paper. Even though the interest rate on Black & Decker's 5-year notes was higher than the rates on its commercial paper, B&D did not have to repay the note for five years, whereas it had to refinance the commercial paper each time it came due.

As you read the chapter, think of these companies that suffered or failed because they mismanaged their capital structure decisions.

Sources: See **www.bankruptcydata.com** and the Black & Decker press release of April 23, 2009.

Corporate Valuation and Capital Structure

© Rob Webb/Getty Images

A firm's financing choices obviously have a direct effect on the weighted average cost of capital (WACC). Financing choices also have an indirect effect on the costs of debt and equity because they change the risk and required returns of debt and equity. Financing choices can also affect free cash flows if the probability of bankruptcy becomes high. This chapter focuses on the debt–equity choice and its effect on value.

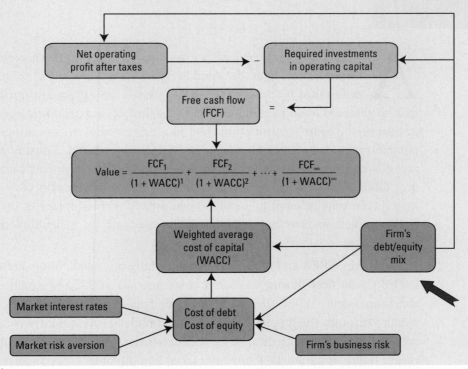

© Cengage Learning 2014

r e s o u r c e

*The textbook's Web site contains an Excel file that will guide you through the chapter's calculations. The file for this chapter is **Ch15 Tool Kit.xls**, and we encourage you to open the file and follow along as you read the chapter.*

As explained in Chapters 12 and 13, growth in sales requires growth in operating capital, and this often requires that external funds be raised through a combination of equity and debt. The firm's mixture of debt and equity is called its **capital structure**. Although actual levels of debt and equity may vary somewhat over time, most firms try to keep their financing mix close to a **target capital structure**. A firm's **capital structure decision** includes its choice of a target capital structure, the average maturity of its debt, and the specific types of financing it decides to use at any particular time. As with operating decisions, managers should make capital structure decisions that are designed to maximize the firm's intrinsic value.

15-1 An Overview of Capital Structure

The value of a firm's operations is the present value of its expected future free cash flows (FCF) discounted at its weighted average cost of capital (WACC):

$$V_{op} = \sum_{t=1}^{\infty} \frac{FCF_t}{(1 + WACC)^t}$$

(15-1)

The WACC of a firm financed only by debt and common stock depends on the percentages of debt and common stock (w_d and w_s), the cost of debt (r_d), the cost of stock (r_s), and the corporate tax rate (T):

$$WACC = w_d(1 - T)r_d + w_s r_s$$

(15-2)

As these equations show, the only way any decision can change the value of operations is by changing either expected free cash flows or the cost of capital. As you read the chapter, think about the ways the capital structure choices can affect FCF or the WACC.

For the average company in the S&P 500, the ratio of long-term debt to equity was about 108% in the spring of 2012. This means that the typical company had about $1.08 in debt for every dollar of equity. However, Table 15-1 shows that there are wide divergences in the average ratios for different business sectors and for different companies within a sector. For example, the technology sector has a very low average ratio (11%) while the utilities sector has a much higher ratio (79%). Even so, within each sector there are some companies with low levels of debt and others with high levels. For example, the average debt ratio for the consumer/noncyclical sector is 57%, but in this sector Starbucks has a ratio of 11% while Kellogg has a ratio of 206%. Why do we see such variation across companies and business sectors? Can a company make itself more valuable through its choice of debt ratio? We address those questions in the rest of this chapter, beginning with a description of business risk and financial risk.

TABLE 15-1

Long-Term Debt-to-Equity Ratios for Selected Firms and Industries

Sector and Company	Long-Term Debt-to-Equity Ratio	Sector and Company	Long-Term Debt-to-Equity Ratio
Technology	**11%**	**Capital Goods**	**57%**
Microsoft (MSFT)	17	Winnebago Industries (WGO)	0
Ricoh (RICOF.PK)	64	Caterpillar Inc. (CAT)	168
Energy	**11**	**Consumer/Noncyclical**	**57**
ExxonMobil (XOM)	6	Starbucks (SBUX)	11
Chesapeake Energy (CHK)	79	Kellogg Company (K)	206
Transportation	**49**	**Services**	**49**
United Parcel Service (UPS)	149	Waste Management (WM)	160
United Airlines (UAL)	748	Republic Services (RSG)	89
Basic Materials	**19**	**Utilities**	**79**
Anglo American PLC (AAUKYN.MX)	30	GenOn Energy, Inc. (GEN)	82
Century Aluminum (CENX)	24	CMS Energy (CMS)	208

Source: For updates on a company's ratio, go to **www.reuters.com** and enter the ticker symbol for a stock quote. Click on Financials tab for updates on the sector ratio.

SELF-TEST

What are some ways in which the capital structure decisions can affect the value of operations?

15-2 Business Risk and Financial Risk

Business risk and financial risk combine to determine the total risk of a firm's future return on equity, as we explain in the next sections.

15-2a Business Risk and Operating Leverage

Business risk is the risk a firm's common stockholders would face if the firm had no debt. In other words, it is the risk inherent in the firm's operations, which arises from uncertainty about future operating profits and capital requirements.

Business risk depends on a number of factors, beginning with variability in product demand and production costs. If a high percentage of a firm's costs are fixed and hence do not decline when demand falls, then the firm has high *operating leverage,* which increases its business risk.

A high degree of **operating leverage** implies that a relatively small change in sales results in a relatively large change in EBIT, net operating profits after taxes (NOPAT), return on invested capital (ROIC), return on assets (ROA), and return on equity (ROE). Other things held constant, the higher a firm's fixed costs, the greater its operating leverage. Higher fixed costs are generally associated with (1) highly automated, capital intensive firms; (2) businesses that employ highly skilled workers who must be retained and paid even when sales are low; and (3) firms with high product development costs that must be maintained to complete ongoing R&D projects.

To illustrate the relative impact of fixed versus variable costs, consider Strasburg Electronics Company, a manufacturer of components used in cell phones. Strasburg is considering several different operating technologies and several different financing alternatives. We will analyze its financing choices in the next section, but for now we will focus on its operating plans.

Strasburg is comparing two plans, each requiring a capital investment of $200 million; assume for now that Strasburg will finance its choice entirely with equity. Each plan is expected to produce 110 million units (Q) per year at a sales price (P) of $2 per unit. As shown in Figure 15-1, Plan A's technology requires a smaller annual fixed cost (F) than Plan U's, but Plan A has higher variable costs (V). (We denote the second plan with U because it has no financial leverage, and we denote the third plan with L because it does have financial leverage; Plan L is discussed in the next section.) Figure 15-1 also shows the projected income statements and selected performance measures for the first year. Notice that Plan U's performance measures are superior to Plan A's if the expected sales occur.

Notice that the projections in Figure 15-1 are based on the 110 million units expected to be sold. But what if demand is lower than expected? It often is useful to know how far sales can fall before operating profits become negative. The **operating break-even point** occurs when earnings before interest and taxes (EBIT) equal zero:[1]

---

[1]This definition of the break-even point does not include any fixed financial costs because it focuses on operating profits. We could also examine net income, in which case a firm with debt would have negative net income even at the operating break-even point. We introduce financial costs shortly.

FIGURE 15-1

Illustration of Operating and Financial Leverage (Millions of Dollars and Millions of Units, Except Per Unit Data)

	A	B	C	D	E
17	**1. Input Data**		**Plan A**	**Plan U**	**Plan L**
18	Required operating current assets		$3	$3	$3
19	Required long-term assets		$199	$199	$199
20	Resulting operating current liabilities		$2	$2	$2
21	Total assets		$202	$202	$202
22	Required capital (TA – Op. CL)		$200	$200	$200
23	Book equity		$200	$200	$150
24	Debt		$0	$0	$50
25	Interest rate		8%	8%	8%
26	Sales price (P)		$2.00	$2.00	$2.00
27	Tax rate (T)		40%	40%	40%
28	Expected units sold (Q)		110	110	110
29	Fixed costs (F)		$20	$60	$60
30	Variable costs (V)		$1.50	$1.00	$1.00
31	**2. Income Statements**		**Plan A**	**Plan U**	**Plan L**
32	Sales revenue (P x Q)		$220.0	$220.0	$220.0
33	Fixed costs		20.0	60.0	60.0
34	Variable costs (V x Q)		165.0	110.0	110.0
35	EBIT		$35.0	$50.0	$50.0
36	Interest		0.0	0.0	4.0
37	EBT		$35.0	$50.0	$46.0
38	Tax		14.0	20.0	18.4
39	Net income		$21.0	$30.0	$27.6
40	**3. Key Performance Measures**		**Plan A**	**Plan U**	**Plan L**
41	NOPAT = EBIT(1 – T)		$21.0	$30.0	$30.0
42	ROIC = NOPAT/Capital		10.5%	15.0%	15.0%
43	ROA = NI/Total assets		10.4%	14.9%	13.7%
44	ROE = NI/Equity		10.5%	15.0%	18.4%

Note:

ROA is not exactly equal to ROE for the Plan L or Plan U because total assets are not quite equal to equity for these plans. This is because the operating current liabilities, such as accounts payable and accruals, reduce the required capital investment of equity.

$$EBIT = PQ - VQ - F = 0 \qquad (15\text{-}3)$$

If we solve for the break-even quantity, Q_{BE}, we get this expression:

$$Q_{BE} = \frac{F}{P - V} \qquad (15\text{-}4)$$

The break-even quantities for Plans A and U are

$$\text{Plan A: } Q_{BE} = \frac{\$20 \text{ million}}{\$2.00 - \$1.50} = 40 \text{ million units}$$

$$\text{Plan U: } Q_{BE} = \frac{\$60 \text{ million}}{\$2.00 - \$1.00} = 60 \text{ million units}$$

FIGURE 15-2

Operating Leverage and Financial Leverage

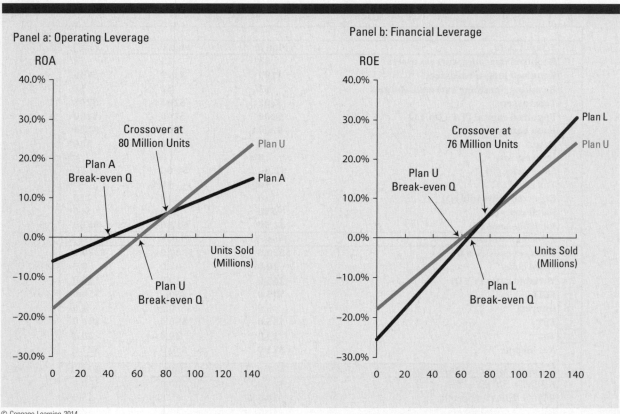

© Cengage Learning 2014

Plan A will be profitable if unit sales are above 40 million, whereas Plan U requires sales of 60 million units before it is profitable. This difference occurs because Plan U has higher fixed costs, so more units must be sold to cover these fixed costs. Panel a of Figure 15-2 illustrates the operating profitability of these two plans for different levels of unit sales. Because these companies have no debt, the return on assets measures operating profitability; we report ROA instead of EBIT to facilitate comparisons when we discuss financial risk in the next section.

Suppose sales are at 80 million units. In this case, the ROA is identical for each plan. As unit sales begin to climb above 80 million, both plans increase in profitability, but ROA increases more for Plan U than for Plan A. If sales fall below 80 million, then both plans become less profitable, but ROA decreases more for Plan U than for Plan A. This illustrates that the combination of higher fixed costs and lower variable costs of Plan U magnifies its gain or loss relative to Plan A. In other words, because Plan U has higher operating leverage, it also has greater business risk.

15-2b Financial Risk and Financial Leverage

Financial risk is the additional risk placed on the common stockholders as a result of the decision to finance with debt.[2] Conceptually, stockholders face a certain amount of risk

---

[2]Preferred stock also adds to financial risk. To simplify matters, we examine only debt and common equity in this chapter.

that is inherent in a firm's operations—this is its business risk, which is defined as the uncertainty in projections of future EBIT, NOPAT, and ROIC. If a firm uses debt (financial leverage), then the business risk is concentrated on the common stockholders. To illustrate, suppose ten people decide to form a corporation to manufacture flash memory drives. There is a certain amount of business risk in the operation. If the firm is capitalized only with common equity and if each person buys 10% of the stock, then each investor shares equally in the business risk. However, suppose the firm is capitalized with 50% debt and 50% equity, with five of the investors putting up their money by purchasing debt and the other five putting up their money by purchasing equity. In this case, the five debtholders are paid before the five stockholders, so *virtually all* of the business risk is borne by the stockholders. Thus, the use of debt, or **financial leverage**, concentrates business risk on stockholders.[3]

To illustrate the impact of financial risk, we can extend the Strasburg Electronics example. Strasburg initially decided to use the technology of Plan U, which is unlevered (financed with all equity), but now it's considering financing the technology with $150 million of equity and $50 million of debt at an 8% interest rate, as shown for Plan L in Figure 15-1 (recall that L denotes leverage). Compare Plans U and L. Notice that the ROIC of 15% is the same for the two plans because the financing choice doesn't affect operations. Plan L has lower net income ($27.6 million versus $30 million) because it must pay interest, but it has a higher ROE (18.4%) because the net income is shared over a smaller equity base.[4]

But there is more to the story than just a higher ROE with financial leverage. Just as operating leverage adds risk, so does financial leverage. We used the Data Table feature in the file **Ch15 Tool Kit.xls** to generate performance measures for plans U and L at different levels of unit sales. Panel b of Figure 15-2 shows the ROE of Plan L versus quantity sold.

When the quantity sold is 76 million, both plans have an ROIC of 4.8% (see the **Tool Kit** for the calculations). The after-tax cost of debt also is 8%(1 – 0.40) = 4.8%, which is no coincidence. As ROIC increases above 4.8%, the ROE increases for each plan, but more for Plan L than for Plan U. However, if ROIC falls below 4.8%, then the ROE falls further for Plan L than for Plan U. Thus, financial leverage magnifies the ROE for good or ill, depending on the ROIC, and so increases the risk of a levered firm relative to an unlevered firm.

We see, then, that using leverage has both good and bad effects: If expected ROIC is greater than the after-tax cost of debt, then higher leverage increases expected ROE but also increases risk.

SELF-TEST

What is business risk, and how can it be measured?

What are some determinants of business risk?

How does operating leverage affect business risk?

What is financial risk, and how does it arise?

Explain this statement: "Using leverage has both good and bad effects."

A firm has fixed operating costs of $100,000 and variable costs of $4 per unit. If it sells the product for $6 per unit, what is the break-even quantity? **(50,000)**

---

[3]Holders of corporate debt generally do bear some business risk, because they may lose some of their investment if the firm goes bankrupt. We discuss this in more depth later in the chapter.

[4]Recall that Strasburg has $202 million in total assets, all of which are operating assets. With $2 million in operating current liabilities, Strasburg has $202 – $2 = $200 million in operating capital, which must be financed with a combination of debt and equity.

15-3 Capital Structure Theory

In the previous section, we showed how capital structure choices affect a firm's ROE and its risk. For a number of reasons, we would expect capital structures to vary considerably across industries. For example, pharmaceutical companies generally have very different capital structures than airline companies. Moreover, capital structures vary among firms within a given industry. What factors explain these differences? In an attempt to answer this question, academics and practitioners have developed a number of theories, and the theories have been subjected to many empirical tests. The following sections examine several of these theories.[5]

15-3a Modigliani and Miller: No Taxes

Modern capital structure theory began in 1958, when Professors Franco Modigliani and Merton Miller (hereafter MM) published what has been called the most influential finance article ever written.[6] MM's study was based on some strong assumptions, which included the following:

1. There are no brokerage costs.
2. There are no taxes.
3. There are no bankruptcy costs.
4. Investors can borrow at the same rate as corporations.
5. All investors have the same information as management about the firm's future investment opportunities.
6. EBIT is not affected by the use of debt.

Modigliani and Miller imagined two hypothetical portfolios. The first contains all the equity of an unlevered firm, so the portfolio's value is V_U, the value of an unlevered firm. Because the firm has no growth (which means it does not need to invest in any new net assets) and because it pays no taxes, the firm can pay out all of its EBIT in the form of dividends. Therefore, the cash flow from owning this first portfolio is equal to EBIT.

Now consider a second firm that is identical to the unlevered firm *except* that it is partially financed with debt. The second portfolio contains all of the levered firm's stock (S_L) and debt (D), so the portfolio's value is V_L, the total value of the levered firm. If the interest rate is r_d, then the levered firm pays out interest in the amount $r_d D$. Because the firm is not growing and pays no taxes, it can pay out dividends in the amount EBIT − $r_d D$. If you owned all of the firm's debt and equity, your cash flow would be equal to the sum of the interest and dividends: $r_d D + (EBIT − r_d D) = EBIT$. Therefore, the cash flow from owning this second portfolio is equal to EBIT.

---

[5]For additional discussion of capital structure theories, see John C. Easterwood and Palani-Rajan Kadapakkam, "The Role of Private and Public Debt in Corporate Capital Structures," *Financial Management*, Autumn 1991, pp. 49–57; Gerald T. Garvey, "Leveraging the Underinvestment Problem: How High Debt and Management Shareholdings Solve the Agency Costs of Free Cash Flow," *Journal of Financial Research*, Summer 1992, pp. 149–166; Milton Harris and Artur Raviv, "Capital Structure and the Informational Role of Debt," *Journal of Finance*, June 1990, pp. 321–349; and Ronen Israel, "Capital Structure and the Market for Corporate Control: The Defensive Role of Debt Financing," *Journal of Finance*, September 1991, pp. 1391–1409.
[6]Franco Modigliani and Merton H. Miller, "The Cost of Capital, Corporation Finance, and the Theory of Investment," *American Economic Review*, June 1958, pp. 261–297. Modigliani and Miller each won a Nobel Prize for their work.

Notice that the cash flow of each portfolio is equal to EBIT. Thus, MM concluded that two portfolios producing the same cash flows must have the same value:[7]

$$V_L = V_U = S_L + D \tag{15-5}$$

Given their assumptions, MM proved that a firm's value is unaffected by its capital structure.

Recall that the WACC is a combination of the cost of debt and the relatively higher cost of equity, r_s. As leverage increases, more weight is given to low-cost debt but equity becomes riskier, which drives up r_s. Under MM's assumptions, r_s increases by exactly enough to keep the WACC constant. Put another way: If MM's assumptions are correct, then it doesn't matter how a firm finances its operations and so capital structure decisions are irrelevant.

Even though some of their assumptions are obviously unrealistic, MM's irrelevance result is extremely important. By indicating the conditions under which capital structure is irrelevant, MM also provided us with clues about what is required for capital structure to be relevant and hence to affect a firm's value. The work of MM marked the beginning of modern capital structure research, and subsequent research has focused on relaxing the MM assumptions in order to develop a more realistic theory of capital structure.

Modigliani and Miller's thought process was just as important as their conclusion. It seems simple now, but their idea that two portfolios with identical cash flows must also have identical values changed the entire financial world because it led to the development of options and derivatives. It is no surprise that Modigliani and Miller received Nobel awards for their work.

15-3b Modigliani and Miller II: The Effect of Corporate Taxes

In 1963, MM published a follow-up paper in which they relaxed the assumption that there are no corporate taxes.[8] The Tax Code allows corporations to deduct interest payments as an expense, but dividend payments to stockholders are not deductible. The differential treatment encourages corporations to use debt in their capital structures. This means that interest payments reduce the taxes a corporation pays, and if a corporation pays less to the government, then more of its cash flow is available for investors. In other words, the tax deductibility of the interest payments shields the firm's pre-tax income.

To illustrate, look at Figure 15-1 and see that Plan U (with no debt) pays taxes of $20, but Plan L (with leverage) pays taxes of only $18.40. What happens to the difference of $1.60 = $20 − $18.40? Notice that Plan U has $30 of net income for shareholders, but Plan U has $4 of interest for debtholders and $27.60 of net income for shareholders for a combined total of $31.60, which is exactly $1.60 more than Plan U. With more cash flows available for investors, a levered firm's total value should be greater than that of an unlevered firm, and this is what MM showed.

---

[7]They actually showed that if the values of the two portfolios differed, then an investor could engage in riskless arbitrage: The investor could create a trading strategy (buying one portfolio and selling the other short) that had no risk, required none of the investor's own cash, and resulted in a positive cash flow for the investor. This would be such a desirable strategy that everyone would try to implement it. But if everyone tries to buy the same portfolio, its price will be driven up by market demand, and if everyone tries to short sell a portfolio, its price will be driven down. The net result of the trading activity would be to change the portfolio's values until they were equal and no more arbitrage was possible.

[8]Franco Modigliani and Merton H. Miller, "Corporate Income Taxes and the Cost of Capital: A Correction," *American Economic Review,* June 1963, pp. 433–443.

Yogi Berra on the MM Proposition

© Rob Webb/Getty Images

When a waitress asked Yogi Berra, Baseball Hall of Fame catcher for the New York Yankees, whether he wanted his pizza cut into four pieces or eight, Yogi replied: "Better make it four. I don't think I can eat eight."[a]

Yogi's quip helps convey the basic insight of Modigliani and Miller. The firm's choice of leverage "slices" the distribution of future cash flows in a way that is like slicing a pizza. MM recognized that holding a company's investment activities fixed is like fixing the size of the pizza; no information costs means that everyone sees the same pizza; no taxes means the IRS gets none of the pie; and no "contracting costs" means nothing sticks to the knife.

So, just as the substance of Yogi's meal is unaffected by whether the pizza is sliced into four pieces or eight, the economic substance of the firm is unaffected by whether the liability side of the balance sheet is sliced to include more or less debt—at least under the MM assumptions.

[a]Lee Green, *Sportswit* (New York: Fawcett Crest, 1984), p. 228.

Source: "Yogi Berra on the MM Proposition," Michael J. Barclay, Clifford W. Smith, and Ross L. Watts. Copyright © 1995 by *Journal of Applied Corporate Finance*. Reproduced with permission of John Wiley & Sons, Ltd.

As in their earlier paper, MM introduced a second important way of looking at the effect of capital structure: The value of a levered firm is the value of an otherwise identical unlevered firm plus the value of any "side effects." While others have expanded on this idea by considering other side effects, MM focused on the tax shield:

$$V_L = V_U + \text{Value of side effects} = V_U + \text{Present value of tax shield} \qquad (15\text{-}6)$$

Under their assumptions, they showed that the present value of the tax shield is equal to the corporate tax rate, T, multiplied by the amount of debt, D:

$$V_L = V_U + TD \qquad (15\text{-}7)$$

With a tax rate of about 40%, this implies that every dollar of debt adds about 40 cents of value to the firm, and this leads to the conclusion that the optimal capital structure is virtually 100% debt. MM also showed that the cost of equity, r_s, increases as leverage increases but that it doesn't increase quite as fast as it would if there were no taxes. As a result, under MM with corporate taxes the WACC falls as debt is added.

15-3c Miller: The Effect of Corporate and Personal Taxes

Merton Miller (this time without Modigliani) later brought in the effects of personal taxes.[9] The income from bonds is generally interest, which is taxed as personal income at rates (T_d) going up to 35%, while income from stocks generally comes partly from dividends and partly from capital gains. Long-term capital gains are taxed at a rate of 15%, and this tax is deferred until the stock is sold and the gain realized. If stock is held

---

[9]See Merton H. Miller, "Debt and Taxes," *Journal of Finance*, May 1977, pp. 261–275.

until the owner dies, no capital gains tax whatsoever must be paid. So, on average, returns on stocks are taxed at lower effective rates (T_s) than returns on debt.[10]

Because of the tax situation, Miller argued that investors are willing to accept relatively low before-tax returns on stock relative to the before-tax returns on bonds. (The situation here is similar to that with tax-exempt municipal bonds as discussed in Chapter 5 and preferred stocks held by corporate investors as discussed in Chapter 7.) For example, an investor might require a return of 10% on Strasburg's bonds, and if stock income were taxed at the same rate as bond income, the required rate of return on Strasburg's stock might be 16% because of the stock's greater risk. However, in view of the favorable treatment of income on the stock, investors might be willing to accept a before-tax return of only 14% on the stock.

Thus, as Miller pointed out, (1) the *deductibility of interest* favors the use of debt financing, but (2) the *more favorable tax treatment of income from stock* lowers the required rate of return on stock and thus favors the use of equity financing.

Miller showed that the net impact of corporate and personal taxes is given by this equation:

$$V_L = V_U + \left[1 - \frac{(1 - T_c)(1 - T_s)}{(1 - T_d)}\right]D \qquad \text{(15-8)}$$

Here T_c is the corporate tax rate, T_s is the personal tax rate on income from stocks, and T_d is the tax rate on income from debt. Miller argued that the marginal tax rates on stock and debt balance out in such a way that the bracketed term in Equation 15-8 is zero and so $V_L = V_U$, but most observers believe there is still a tax advantage to debt if reasonable values of tax rates are assumed. For example, if the marginal corporate tax rate is 40%, the marginal rate on debt is 30%, and the marginal rate on stock is 12%, then the advantage of debt financing is

$$V_L = V_U + \left[1 - \frac{(1 - 0.40)(1 - 0.12)}{(1 - 0.30)}\right]D$$
$$= V_U + 0.25D \qquad \text{(15-8a)}$$

Thus it appears that the presence of personal taxes reduces but does not completely eliminate the advantage of debt financing.

15-3d Trade-Off Theory

The results of Modigliani and Miller also depend on the assumption that there are no **bankruptcy costs**. However, bankruptcy can be quite costly. Firms in bankruptcy have very high legal and accounting expenses, and they also have a hard time retaining customers, suppliers, and employees. Moreover, bankruptcy often forces a firm to liquidate or sell assets

---

[10]The Tax Code isn't quite as simple as this. An increasing number of investors face the Alternative Minimum Tax (AMT); see **Web Extension 2A** for a discussion. The AMT imposes a 28% tax rate on most income and an effective rate of 22% on long-term capital gains and dividends. Under the AMT there is still a spread between the tax rates on interest income and stock income, but the spread is narrower. See Leonard Burman, William Gale, Greg Leiserson, and Jeffrey Rohaly, "The AMT: What's Wrong and How to Fix It," *National Tax Journal*, September 2007, pp. 385–405.

for less than they would be worth if the firm were to continue operating. For example, if a steel manufacturer goes out of business it might be hard to find buyers for the company's blast furnaces. Such assets are often illiquid because they are configured to a company's individual needs and also because they are difficult to disassemble and move.

Note, too, that the *threat of bankruptcy,* not just bankruptcy per se, causes many of these same problems. Key employees jump ship, suppliers refuse to grant credit, customers seek more stable suppliers, and lenders demand higher interest rates and impose more restrictive loan covenants if potential bankruptcy looms. Therefore, even the threat of bankruptcy can cause free cash flows to fall, causing further declines in a company's value.

Bankruptcy-related problems are most likely to arise when a firm includes a great deal of debt in its capital structure. Therefore, bankruptcy costs discourage firms from pushing their use of debt to excessive levels.

Bankruptcy-related costs have two components: (1) the probability of financial distress and (2) the costs that would be incurred if financial distress does occur. Firms whose earnings are more volatile, all else equal, face a greater chance of bankruptcy and should therefore use less debt than more stable firms. This is consistent with our earlier point that firms with high operating leverage, and thus greater business risk, should limit their use of financial leverage. Likewise, firms that would face high costs in the event of financial distress should rely less heavily on debt. For example, firms whose assets are illiquid and thus would have to be sold at "fire sale" prices should limit their use of debt financing.

The preceding arguments led to the development of what is called the trade-off theory of leverage, in which firms trade off the benefits of debt financing (favorable corporate tax treatment) against higher interest rates and bankruptcy costs. In essence, the **trade-off theory** says that the value of a levered firm is equal to the value of an unlevered firm plus the value of any side effects, which include the tax shield and the expected costs due to financial distress. A summary of the trade-off theory is expressed graphically in Figure 15-3, and a list of observations about the figure follows here.

1. Under the assumptions of the MM model with corporate taxes, a firm's value increases linearly for every dollar of debt. The line labeled "MM Result Incorporating the Effects of Corporate Taxation" in Figure 15-3 expresses the relationship between value and debt under those assumptions.
2. There is some threshold level of debt, labeled D_1 in Figure 15-3, below which the probability of bankruptcy is so low as to be immaterial. Beyond D_1, however, expected bankruptcy-related costs become increasingly important, and they reduce the tax benefits of debt at an increasing rate. In the range from D_1 to D_2, expected bankruptcy-related costs reduce but do not completely offset the tax benefits of debt, so the stock price rises (but at a decreasing rate) as the debt ratio increases. However, beyond D_2, expected bankruptcy-related costs exceed the tax benefits, so from this point on increasing the debt ratio lowers the value of the stock. Therefore, D_2 is the optimal capital structure. Of course, D_1 and D_2 vary from firm to firm, depending on their business risks and bankruptcy costs.
3. Although theoretical and empirical work confirms the general shape of the curve in Figure 15-3, this graph must be taken as an approximation and not as a precisely defined function.

15-3e Signaling Theory

MM assumed that investors have the same information about a firm's prospects as its managers—this is called **symmetric information**. However, managers in fact often have better information than outside investors. This is called **asymmetric information**, and it has

FIGURE 15-3

Effect of Financial Leverage on Value

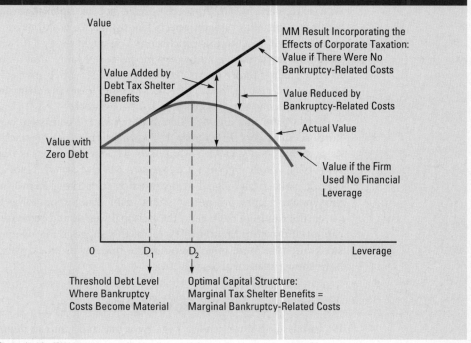

Value

Value with
Zero Debt

MM Result Incorporating the
Effects of Corporate Taxation:
Value if There Were No
Bankruptcy-Related Costs

Value Added by
Debt Tax Shelter
Benefits

Value Reduced by
Bankruptcy-Related Costs

Actual Value

Value if the Firm
Used No Financial
Leverage

0   D_1 D_2 Leverage

Threshold Debt Level
Where Bankruptcy
Costs Become Material

Optimal Capital Structure:
Marginal Tax Shelter Benefits =
Marginal Bankruptcy-Related Costs

© Cengage Learning 2014

an important effect on the optimal capital structure. To see why, consider two situations, one in which the company's managers know that its prospects are extremely positive (Firm P) and one in which the managers know that the future looks negative (Firm N).

Suppose, for example, that Firm P's R&D labs have just discovered a cure for the common cold. Firm P can't provide investors with any details about the product because that might give competitors an advantage. But if they don't provide details, then investors will underestimate the value of the discovery. Given the inability to provide accurate, verifiable information to the market, how should Firm P's management raise the needed capital?

Suppose Firm P issues stock. When profits from the new product start flowing in, the price of the stock would rise sharply and the purchasers of the new stock would make a bonanza. The current stockholders (including the managers) would also do well, but not as well as they would have done if the company had not sold stock before the price increased, because then they would not have had to share the benefits of the new product with the new stockholders. Therefore, *we should expect a firm with very positive prospects to avoid selling stock and instead to raise required new capital by other means, including debt usage beyond the normal target capital structure.*[11]

Now let's consider Firm N. Suppose its managers have information that new orders are off sharply because a competitor has installed new technology that has improved its products' quality. Firm N must upgrade its own facilities, at a high cost, just to maintain its current sales. As a result, its return on investment will fall (but not by as much as if it took no action, which would lead to a 100% loss through bankruptcy). How should Firm N raise the needed capital? Here the situation is just the reverse of that facing Firm P,

---

[11]It would be illegal for Firm P's managers to personally purchase more shares on the basis of their inside knowledge of the new product.

which did not want to sell stock so as to avoid having to share the benefits of future developments. *A firm with negative prospects would want to sell stock, which would mean bringing in new investors to share the losses!*[12] The conclusion from all this is that firms with extremely bright prospects prefer not to finance through new stock offerings, whereas firms with poor prospects like to finance with outside equity. How should you, as an investor, react to this conclusion? You ought to say: "If I see that a company plans to issue new stock, this should worry me because I know that management would not want to issue stock if future prospects looked good. However, management *would* want to issue stock if things looked bad. Therefore, I should lower my estimate of the firm's value, other things held constant, if it plans to issue new stock."

If you gave this answer, then your views are consistent with those of sophisticated portfolio managers. In a nutshell: *The announcement of a stock offering is generally taken as a* **signal** *that the firm's prospects as seen by its own management are not good; conversely, a debt offering is taken as a positive signal.* Notice that Firm N's managers cannot make a false signal to investors by mimicking Firm P and issuing debt. With its unfavorable future prospects, issuing debt could soon force Firm N into bankruptcy. Given the resulting damage to the personal wealth and reputations of N's managers, they cannot afford to mimic Firm P. All of this suggests that when a firm announces a new stock offering, more often than not the price of its stock will decline. Empirical studies have shown that this is indeed true.

15-3f Reserve Borrowing Capacity

Because issuing stock sends a negative signal and tends to depress the stock price even if the company's true prospects are bright, a company should try to maintain a **reserve borrowing capacity** so that debt can be used if an especially good investment opportunity comes along. This means that *firms should, in normal times, use more equity and less debt than is suggested by the tax benefit–bankruptcy cost trade-off model depicted in Figure 15-3.*

15-3g The Pecking Order Hypothesis

The presence of flotation costs and asymmetric information may cause a firm to raise capital according to a **pecking order**. In this situation, a firm first raises capital internally by reinvesting its net income and selling its short-term marketable securities. When that supply of funds has been exhausted, the firm will issue debt and perhaps preferred stock. Only as a last resort will the firm issue common stock.[13]

15-3h Using Debt Financing to Constrain Managers

Agency problems may arise if managers and shareholders have different objectives. Such conflicts are particularly likely when the firm's managers have too much cash at their disposal. Managers often use excess cash to finance pet projects or for perquisites such as nicer offices, corporate jets, and sky boxes at sports arenas—none of which have much to do with maximizing stock prices. Even worse, managers might be tempted to pay too much for an acquisition, something that could cost shareholders hundreds of millions of dollars. By contrast, managers with limited "excess cash flow" are less able to make wasteful expenditures.

---

[12]Of course, Firm N would have to make certain disclosures when it offered new shares to the public, but it might be able to meet the legal requirements without fully disclosing management's worst fears.

[13]For more information, see Jonathon Baskin, "An Empirical Investigation of the Pecking Order Hypothesis," *Financial Management,* Spring 1989, pp. 26–35.

Firms can reduce excess cash flow in a variety of ways. One way is to funnel some of it back to shareholders through higher dividends or stock repurchases. Another alternative is to shift the capital structure toward more debt in the hope that higher debt service requirements will force managers to be more disciplined. If debt is not serviced as required then the firm will be forced into bankruptcy, in which case its managers would likely lose their jobs. Therefore, a manager is less likely to buy an expensive new corporate jet if the firm has large debt service requirements that could cost the manager his or her job. In short, high levels of debt **bond the cash flow**, because much of it is precommitted to servicing the debt.

A **leveraged buyout (LBO)** is one way to bond cash flow. In an LBO, a large amount of debt and a small amount of cash are used to finance the purchase of a company's shares, after which the firm "goes private." The first wave of LBOs was in the mid-1980s; private equity funds led the buyouts of the late 1990s and early 2000s. Many of these LBOs were specifically designed to reduce corporate waste. As noted, high debt payments force managers to conserve cash by eliminating unnecessary expenditures.

Of course, increasing debt and reducing the available cash flow has its downside: It increases the risk of bankruptcy. Ben Bernanke, current (mid-2012) chairman of the Fed, has argued that adding debt to a firm's capital structure is like putting a dagger into the steering wheel of a car.[14] The dagger—which points toward your stomach—motivates you to drive more carefully, but you may get stabbed if someone runs into you—even if you are being careful. The analogy applies to corporations in the following sense: Higher debt forces managers to be more careful with shareholders' money, but even well-run firms could face bankruptcy (get stabbed) if some event beyond their control occurs: a war, an earthquake, a strike, or a recession. To complete the analogy, the capital structure decision comes down to deciding how long a dagger stockholders should use to keep managers in line.

Finally, too much debt may overly constrain managers. A large portion of a manager's personal wealth and reputation is tied to a single company, so managers are not well diversified. When faced with a positive-NPV project that is risky, a manager may decide that it's not worth taking on the risk even though well-diversified stockholders would find the risk acceptable. As previously mentioned, this is an underinvestment problem. The more debt the firm has, the greater the likelihood of financial distress and thus the greater the likelihood that managers will forgo risky projects even if they have positive NPVs.

15-3i The Investment Opportunity Set and Reserve Borrowing Capacity

Bankruptcy and financial distress are costly, and, as just reiterated, this can discourage highly levered firms from undertaking risky new investments. If potential new investments, although risky, have positive net present values, then high levels of debt can be doubly costly—the expected financial distress and bankruptcy costs are high, and the firm loses potential value by not making some potentially profitable investments. On the other hand, if a firm has very few profitable investment opportunities then high levels of debt can keep managers from wasting money by investing in poor projects. For such companies, increases in the debt ratio can actually increase the value of the firm.

Thus, in addition to the tax, signaling, bankruptcy, and managerial constraint effects discussed previously, the firm's optimal capital structure is related to its set of investment opportunities. Firms with many profitable opportunities should maintain their ability to

---

[14]See Ben Bernanke, "Is There Too Much Corporate Debt?" *Federal Reserve Bank of Philadelphia Business Review,* September/October 1989, pp. 3–13.

invest by using low levels of debt, which is also consistent with maintaining reserve borrowing capacity. Firms with few profitable investment opportunities should use high levels of debt (which have high interest payments) to impose managerial constraint.[15]

15-3j The Market Timing Theory

If markets are efficient, then security prices should reflect all available information; hence they are neither underpriced nor overpriced (except during the time it takes prices to move to a new equilibrium caused by the release of new information). The *market timing theory* states that managers don't believe this and supposes instead that stock prices and interest rates are sometimes either too low or too high relative to their true fundamental values. In particular, the theory suggests that managers issue equity when they believe stock market prices are abnormally high and issue debt when they believe interest rates are abnormally low. In other words, they try to time the market.[16] Notice that this differs from signaling theory because no asymmetric information is involved. These managers aren't basing their beliefs on insider information, just on a different opinion than the market consensus.

SELF-TEST

Why does the MM theory with corporate taxes lead to 100% debt?

Explain how asymmetric information and signals affect capital structure decisions.

What is meant by reserve borrowing capacity, and why is it important to firms?

How can the use of debt serve to discipline managers?

15-4 Capital Structure Evidence and Implications

There have been hundreds, perhaps even thousands, of papers testing the capital structure theories described in the previous section. We can cover only the highlights here, beginning with the empirical evidence.[17]

15-4a Empirical Evidence

There are thousands of papers that test the theories of capital structure in the previous section. Here is a brief summary of their findings.

THE TRADE-OFF BETWEEN TAX BENEFITS AND BANKRUPTCY COSTS

Recent studies by Professors Van Binsbergen, Graham, and Yang and by Professor Korteweg suggest that the average net benefits of leverage (i.e., the value of the tax shield

---

[15]See Michael J. Barclay and Clifford W. Smith, Jr., "The Capital Structure Puzzle: Another Look at the Evidence," *Journal of Applied Corporate Finance,* Spring 1999, pp. 8–20.

[16]See Malcolm Baker and Jeffrey Wurgler, "Market Timing and Capital Structure," *Journal of Finance,* February 2002, pp. 1–32.

[17]This section also draws heavily from Barclay and Smith, "The Capital Structure Puzzle," cited in footnote 19; Jay Ritter, ed., *Recent Developments in Corporate Finance* (Northampton, MA: Edward Elgar Publishing Inc., 2005); and a presentation by Jay Ritter at the 2003 FMA meeting, "The Windows of Opportunity Theory of Capital Structure."

less the expected cost of financial distress) make up about 3% to 6% of a levered firm's value.[18] To put this into perspective, let's look at the impact of debt on an average company's value. The average company is financed with about 25% to 35% debt, so let's suppose that the company has $25 debt and $75 of equity, just to keep the arithmetic simple. The total net benefit of debt would be about $5, based on the recent research. This implies that each dollar of debt added (on average) about $0.20 of value ($5/$25 = 0.2) to the company. The first dollar of debt adds a bigger net benefit because bankruptcy risk is low when debt is low. By the time the 25th dollar of debt is added, its incremental net benefit was close to zero—the incremental expected costs of financial distress were about equal to the incremental expected tax shield.

These studies also showed that the net benefits of debt increase slowly until reaching the optimal level, but decline rapidly thereafter. In other words, it isn't very costly to be somewhat below the optimal level of debt, but it is costly to exceed it.

A particularly interesting study by Professors Mehotra, Mikkelson, and Partch examined the capital structure of firms that were spun off from their parent companies.[19] The financing choices of existing firms might be influenced by their past financing choices and by the costs of moving from one capital structure to another, but because spin-offs are newly created companies, managers can choose a capital structure without regard to these issues. The study found that more profitable firms (which have a lower expected probability of bankruptcy) and more asset-intensive firms (which have better collateral and thus a lower cost of bankruptcy should one occur) have higher levels of debt.

These findings support the trade-off theory.

A Dynamic Trade-Off Theory

However, there is also evidence that is inconsistent with the static optimal target capital structure implied by the trade-off theory. For example, stock prices are volatile, which frequently causes a firm's actual market-based debt ratio to deviate from its target. However, such deviations don't cause firms to immediately return to their target by issuing or repurchasing securities. Instead, Professors Flannery and Rangan show that firms tend to make a partial adjustment each year, moving about 30% of the way toward their target capital structure. In a more recent study, Professors Faulkender, Flannery, Hankins, and Smith show that the speed of adjustment depends on a company's cash flows—companies with high cash flows adjust by about 50%. This effect is even more pronounced if the company's leverage exceeds its target—high cash flow companies in this situation have a 70% speed of adjustment. This is consistent with the idea that it is more costly to exceed the target debt ratio than to be lower than the target.[20]

Market Timing

If a stock price has a big run-up, which reduces the debt ratio, then the trade-off theory suggests that the firm should issue debt to return to its target. However, firms tend to do the opposite, issuing stock after big run-ups. This is much more consistent with the market timing theory, with managers trying to time the market by issuing stock when

[18]See Jules H. Van Binsbergen, John H. Graham, and Jie Yang, "The Cost of Debt," *Journal of Finance*, Vol. 65, No. 6, December, 2010, pp. 2089–2135; also see Arthur Korteweg, "The Net Benefits to Leverage," *Journal of Finance*, Vol. 65, No. 6, December, 2010, pp. 2137–2169.

[19]See V. Mehotra, W. Mikkelson, and M. Partch, "The Design of Financial Policies in Corporate Spin-offs," *Review of Financial Studies*, Winter 2003, pp. 1359–1388.

[20]See Mark Flannery and Kasturi Rangan, "Partial Adjustment toward Target Capital Structures," *Journal of Financial Economics*, Vol. 79, 2006, pp. 469–506. Also see Michael Faulkender, Mark Flannery, Kristine Hankins, and Jason Smith, "Cash Flows and Leverage," *Journal of Financial Economics*, Vol. 103, 2012, pp. 632–646.

they perceive the market to be overvalued. Furthermore, firms tend to issue debt when stock prices and interest rates are low. The maturity of the issued debt seems to reflect an attempt to time interest rates: Firms tend to issue short-term debt if the term structure is upward sloping but long-term debt if the term structure is flat. Again, these facts suggest that managers try to time the market.

SIGNALING AND THE PECKING ORDER

Firms issue equity much less frequently than debt. On the surface, this seems to support both the pecking order hypothesis and the signaling hypothesis. The pecking order hypothesis predicts that firms with a high level of informational asymmetry, which causes equity issuances to be costly, should issue debt before issuing equity. Yet we often see the opposite, with high-growth firms (which usually have greater informational asymmetry) issuing more equity than debt. Also, many highly profitable firms could afford to issue debt (which comes before equity in the pecking order) but instead choose to issue equity. With respect to the signaling hypothesis, consider the case of firms that have large increases in earnings that were unanticipated by the market. If managers have superior information, then they will anticipate these upcoming performance improvements and issue debt before the increase. Such firms do, in fact, tend to issue debt slightly more frequently than other firms, but the difference isn't economically meaningful.

RESERVE BORROWING CAPACITY

Many firms have less debt than might be expected, and many have large amounts of short-term investments. This is especially true for firms with high market/book ratios (which indicate many growth options as well as informational asymmetry). This behavior is consistent with the hypothesis that investment opportunities influence attempts to maintain reserve borrowing capacity. It is also consistent with tax considerations, because low-growth firms (which have more debt) are more likely to benefit from the tax shield. This behavior is not consistent with the pecking order hypothesis, where low-growth firms (which often have high free cash flow) would be able to avoid issuing debt by raising funds internally.

SUMMARY OF EMPIRICAL TESTS

To summarize these results, it appears that firms try to capture debt's tax benefits while avoiding financial distress costs. However, they also allow their debt ratios to deviate from the static optimal target ratio implied by the trade-off theory. In fact, Professors DeAngelo, DeAngelo, and Whited extend the dynamic trade-off model by showing that firms often deliberately issue debt to take advantage of unexpected investment opportunities, even if this causes them to exceed their target debt ratio.[21] Firms often maintain reserve borrowing capacity, especially firms with many growth opportunities or problems with informational asymmetry.[22] There is a little evidence that firms

---

[21]See Harry DeAngelo, Linda DeAngelo, and Toni Whited, "Capital Structure Dynamics and Transitory Debt," *Journal of Financial Economics,* Vol. 99, 2011, pp. 235–261.

[22]For more on empirical tests of capital structure theory, see Gregor Andrade and Steven Kaplan, "How Costly Is Financial (Not Economic) Distress? Evidence from Highly Leveraged Transactions That Became Distressed," *Journal of Finance,* Vol. 53, 1998, pp. 1443–1493; Malcolm Baker, Robin Greenwood, and Jeffrey Wurgler, "The Maturity of Debt Issues and Predictable Variation in Bond Returns," *Journal of Financial Economics,* November 2003, pp. 261–291; Murray Z. Frank and Vidhan K. Goyal, "Testing the Pecking Order Theory of Capital Structure," *Journal of Financial Economics,* February 2003, pp. 217–248; and Michael Long and Ileen Malitz, "The Investment-Financing Nexus: Some Empirical Evidence," *Midland Corporate Finance Journal,* Fall 1985, pp. 53–59.

follow a pecking order and use security issuances as signals, but there is some evidence in support of the market timing theory.

15-4b Implications for Managers

Managers should explicitly consider tax benefits when making capital structure decisions. Tax benefits obviously are more valuable for firms with high tax rates. Firms can utilize tax loss carryforwards and carrybacks, but the time value of money means that tax benefits are more valuable for firms with stable, positive pre-tax income. Therefore, a firm whose sales are relatively stable can safely take on more debt and incur higher fixed charges than a company with volatile sales. Other things being equal, a firm with less operating leverage is better able to employ financial leverage because it will have less business risk and less volatile earnings.

Managers should also consider the expected cost of financial distress, which depends on the probability and cost of distress. Notice that stable sales and lower operating leverage provide tax benefits but also reduce the *probability* of financial distress. One *cost* of financial distress comes from lost investment opportunities. Firms with profitable investment opportunities need to be able to fund them, either by holding higher levels of marketable securities or by maintaining excess borrowing capacity.

Another cost of financial distress is the possibility of being forced to sell assets to meet liquidity needs. General-purpose assets that can be used by many businesses are relatively liquid and make good collateral, in contrast to special-purpose assets. Thus, real estate companies are usually highly leveraged, whereas companies involved in technological research are not.

Asymmetric information also has a bearing on capital structure decisions. For example, suppose a firm has just successfully completed an R&D program, and it forecasts higher earnings in the immediate future. However, the new earnings are not yet anticipated by investors and hence are not reflected in the stock price. This company should not issue stock—it should finance with debt until the higher earnings materialize and are reflected in the stock price. Then it could issue common stock, retire the debt, and return to its target capital structure.

Managers should consider conditions in the stock and bond markets. For example, during a recent credit crunch, the junk bond market dried up and there was simply no market at a "reasonable" interest rate for any new long-term bonds rated below BBB. Therefore, low-rated companies in need of capital were forced to go to the stock market or to the short-term debt market, regardless of their target capital structures. When conditions eased, however, these companies sold bonds to get their capital structures back on target.

Finally, managers should always consider lenders' and rating agencies' attitudes. For example, Moody's and Standard & Poor's recently told one large utility that its bonds would be downgraded if it issued more debt. This influenced the utility's decision to finance its expansion with common equity. This doesn't mean that managers should never increase debt if it will cause their bond rating to fall, but managers should always factor this into their decision making.[23]

---

[23]For some insights into how practicing financial managers view the capital structure decision, see John Graham and Campbell Harvey, "The Theory and Practice of Corporate Finance: Evidence from the Field," *Journal of Financial Economics,* Vol. 60, 2001, pp. 187–243; Ravindra R. Kamath, "Long-Term Financing Decisions: Views and Practices of Financial Managers of NYSE Firms," *Financial Review,* May 1997, pp. 331–356; and Edgar Norton, "Factors Affecting Capital Structure Decisions," *Financial Review,* August 1991, pp. 431–446.

SELF-TEST

Which capital structure theories does the empirical evidence seem to support?

What issues should managers consider when making capital structure decisions?

15-5 Estimating the Optimal Capital Structure

Managers should choose the capital structure that maximizes shareholders' wealth. The basic approach is to consider a trial capital structure, based on the market values of the debt and equity, and then estimate the wealth of the shareholders under this capital structure. This approach is repeated until an optimal capital structure is identified. There are several steps in the analysis of each potential capital structure: (1) Estimate the interest rate the firm will pay. (2) Estimate the cost of equity. (3) Estimate the weighted average cost of capital. (4) Estimate the value of operations, which is the present value of free cash flows discounted by the new WACC. The objective is to find the amount of debt financing that maximizes the value of operations. As we will show, this capital structure maximizes both shareholder wealth and the intrinsic stock price. The following sections explain each of these steps, using the company we considered earlier, Strasburg Electronics.

15-5a The Current Value and Capital Structure of Strasburg

In Section 15-2 Strasburg was examining several different capital structure plans. Strasburg implemented Plan L, the one with high operating leverage and $50 million in debt financing. The plan has been in place for a year, and Strasburg's stock price is now $20 per share. With 10 million shares, Strasburg's market value of equity is $20(10) = $200 million. Strasburg has no short-term investments, so Strasburg's total enterprise value is the sum of its debt and equity: V = $50 + $200 = $250 million. In terms of market values, Strasburg's capital structure has 20% debt (w_d = $50/$250 = 0.20) and 80% equity (w_s = $200/$250 = 0.80). These calculations are reported in Figure 15-4 along with other input data.

Is this the optimal capital structure? We will address the question in more detail later, but for now let's focus on understanding Strasburg's current valuation, beginning with its cost of capital. Strasburg has a beta of 1.25. We can use the Capital Asset Pricing Model (CAPM) to estimate the cost of equity. The risk-free rate, r_{RF}, is 6.3% and the market risk premium, RP_M, is 6%, so the cost of equity is

$$r_s = r_{RF} + b(RP_M) = 6.3\% + 1.25(6\%) = 13.8\%$$

The weighted average cost of capital is

$$\begin{aligned} WACC &= w_d(1-T)r_d + w_s r_s \\ &= 20\%(1-0.40)(8\%) + 80\%(13.8\%) \\ &= 12\% \end{aligned}$$

As shown in Figure 15-3, Plan L has a NOPAT of $30 million. Strasburg expects zero growth, which means there are no required investments in capital. Therefore, FCF is equal to NOPAT. Using the constant growth formula, the value of operations is

$$V_{op} = \frac{FCF(1+g)}{WACC-g} = \frac{\$30(1+0)}{0.12-0} = \$250$$

FIGURE 15-4

Strasburg's Current Value and Capital Structure (Millions of Dollars, Except for Per Share Data)

	A	B	C	D	E
109	Input Data:		Capital Structure:		
110	Tax rate	40.00%	Market value of equity (S = P x n)		$200
111	Debt (D)	$50.00	Total value (V = D + S)		$250
112	# of shares (n)	10.00	% financed with debt (w_d = D/V)		20%
113	Stock price (P)	$20.00	% financed with stock (w_s = S/V)		80%
114	NOPAT	$30.00			
115	Free Cash Flow (FCF)[a]	$30.00			
116	Growth rate in FCF[a]	0.00%			
117	Cost of Capital:		Estimated Intrinsic Value:		
118	Cost of debt (r_d)	8.00%	Value of operations:		
119	Beta (b)	1.25	V_{op} = [FCF(1+g)]/(WACC−g)		$250.00
120	Risk-free rate (r_{RF})	6.30%	+ Value of ST investments		$0.00
121	Mkt. risk prem. (RP_M)	6.00%	Estimated total intrinsic value		$250.00
122	Cost of equity:		− Debt		$50.00
123	$r_s = r_{RF} + b(RP_M)$	13.80%	Estimated intrinsic value of equity		$200.00
124	WACC	12.00%	÷ Number of shares		10.00
125			Estimated intrinsic price per share		$20.00

Note:

[a] Strasburg's sales, earnings, and assets are not growing, so it does not need investments in operating capital. Therefore, FCF = NOPAT(1 − T). The growth in FCF also is 0.

Figure 15-4 illustrates the calculation of the intrinsic stock price. For Strasburg, the intrinsic stock price and the market price are each equal to $20. Can Strasburg increase its value by changing its capital structure? The next sections answer that question.

15-5b Estimating the Weighted Average Cost of Capital (WACC) for Different Levels of Debt

Following is a description of the steps to estimate the weighted average cost of capital for different levels of debt.

ESTIMATING THE COST OF DEBT (r_d)

The CFO asked Strasburg's investment bankers to estimate the cost of debt at different capital structures. The investment bankers began by analyzing industry conditions and prospects. They appraised Strasburg's business risk based on its past financial statements and its current technology and customer base. The bankers also forecasted financial statements with different capital structures and analyzed such key ratios as the current ratio and the times-interest-earned ratio. Finally, they factored in current conditions in the financial markets, including interest rates paid by firms in Strasburg's industry. Based on their analysis and judgment, they estimated interest rates at various capital structures as shown in Row 2 of Figure 15-5, starting with a 7.7% cost of debt for the first dollar of debt.[24] This rate increases to 16% if the firm

---

[24]For a description of a technique for estimating the cost of debt, see Jules H. Van Binsbergen, John H. Graham, and Jie Yang, "An Empirical Model of Optimal Capital Structure," *Journal of Applied Corporate Finance*, Vol. 23, No. 4, Fall, 2011, pp. 34–59. They also provide an approach for estimating the optimal capital structure that explicitly incorporates the tax benefits of debt net of the financial distress costs and other costs.

FIGURE 15-5

Estimating Strasburg's Optimal Capital Structure (Millions of Dollars)

	A	B	C	D	E	F	G	H
140		Percent of Firm Financed with Debt (w_d)						
141		0%	10%	20%	30%	40%	50%	60%
142	1. w_s	100.00%	90.00%	80.00%	70.00%	60.00%	50.00%	40.00%
143	2. r_d	7.70%	7.80%	8.00%	8.50%	9.90%	12.00%	16.00%
144	3. b	1.09	1.16	1.25	1.37	1.52	1.74	2.07
145	4. r_s	12.82%	13.26%	13.80%	14.50%	15.43%	16.73%	18.69%
146	5. r_d (1−T)	4.62%	4.68%	4.80%	5.10%	5.94%	7.20%	9.60%
147	6. WACC	12.82%	12.40%	12.00%	11.68%	11.63%	11.97%	13.24%
148	7. V_{op}	$233.98	$241.96	$250.00	$256.87	$257.86	$250.68	$226.65
149	8. Debt	$0.00	$24.20	$50.00	$77.06	$103.14	$125.34	$135.99
150	9. Equity	$233.98	$217.76	$200.00	$179.81	$154.72	$125.34	$90.66
151	10. # shares	12.72	11.34	10.00	8.69	7.44	6.25	5.13
152	11. Stock price	$18.40	$19.20	$20.00	$20.69	$20.79	$20.07	$17.66
153	12. Net income	$30.00	$28.87	$27.60	$26.07	$23.87	$20.98	$16.95
154	13. EPS	$2.36	$2.54	$2.76	$3.00	$3.21	$3.36	$3.30

Notes:

1. The percent financed with equity is: $w_s = 1 − w_d$.
2. The interest rate on debt, r_d, is obtained from investment bankers.
3. Beta is estimated using Hamada's formula, the unlevered beta of 1.09, and a tax rate of 40%: $b = b_U [1 + (1 − T)(w_d/w_s)]$.
4. The cost of equity is estimated using the CAPM formula with a risk-free rate of 6.3% and a market risk premium of 6%: $r_s = r_{RF} + b(RP_M)$.
5. The after-tax cost of debt is: $r_d(1 − T)$, where T = 40%.
6. The weighted average cost of capital is calculated as $WACC = w_d r_d(1 − T) + w_s r_s$.
7. The value of the firm's operations is calculated as $V_{op} = [FCF(1 + g)] / (WACC − g)$, where FCF = $30 million and g = 0.
8. Debt = $w_d × V_{op}$.
9. The intrinsic value of equity after the recapitalization and repurchase is $S_{Post} = V_{op} − Debt = w_s × V_{op}$.
10. The number of shares after the recap has been completed is found using this equation: $n_{Post} = n_{Prior} × [(V_{opNew} − D_{New}) / (V_{opNew} − D_{Old})]$.
    The subscript "Old" indicates values from the original capital structure, where $w_d = 20\%$; the subscript "New" indicates values at the current capital structure after the recap and repurchase; and the subscript "Post" indicates values after the recap and repurchase.
11. The price after the recap and repurchase is $P_{Post} = S_{Post}/n_{Post}$, but we can also find the price as $P_{Post} = (V_{opNew} − D_{Old})/n_{Prior}$.
12. EBIT is $50 million; see Figure 15-1. Net income is $NI = (EBIT − r_d D)(1 − T)$.
13. Earnings per share is $EPS = NI/n_{Post}$.

finances 60% of its capital structure with debt. Strasburg's current situation is in Column D and is shown in blue. (We will explain all the rows in Figure 15-5 in the following discussion.)

ESTIMATING THE COST OF EQUITY (r_s) USING THE HAMADA EQUATION

An increase in the debt ratio also increases the risk faced by shareholders, and this has an effect on the cost of equity, r_s. Recall from Chapter 6 that a stock's beta is the relevant measure of risk for diversified investors. Moreover, it has been demonstrated, both theoretically and empirically, that beta increases with financial leverage. The Hamada equation specifies the effect of financial leverage on beta:[25]

$$b = b_U[1 + (1−T)(D/S)] \qquad (15\text{-}9)$$

[25]See Robert S. Hamada, "Portfolio Analysis, Market Equilibrium, and Corporation Finance," *Journal of Finance*, March 1969, pp. 13–31. For a comprehensive framework, see Robert A. Taggart, Jr., "Consistent Valuation and Cost of Capital Expressions with Corporate and Personal Taxes," *Financial Management*, Autumn 1991, pp. 8–20.

Here D is the market value of the debt and S is the market value of the equity. The **Hamada equation** shows how increases in the market value debt/equity ratio increase beta. Here b_U is the firm's **unlevered beta** coefficient—that is, the beta it would have if it had no debt. In that case, beta would depend entirely on business risk and thus be a measure of the firm's "basic business risk."

Sometimes it is more convenient to work with the percentages of debt and equity at which the firm is financed (w_d and w_s) rather than the dollar values of D and S. Notice that w_d and w_s are defined as $D/(D + S)$ and $S/(D + S)$, respectively. This means that the ratio w_d/w_s is equal to the ratio D/S. Substituting these values gives us another form of Hamada's formula:

$$b = b_U[1 + (1 - T)(w_d/w_s)] \qquad \text{(15-9a)}$$

Often we know the current capital structure and beta but wish to know the unlevered beta. We find this by rearranging Equation 15-9a as follows:

$$b_U = b/[1 + (1 - T)(w_d/w_s)] \qquad \text{(15-10)}$$

For Strasburg, the unlevered beta is

$$b_U = 1.25/[1 + (1 - 0.40)(0.20/0.80)]$$

$$= 1.087$$

Using this unlevered beta, we can then apply Hamada's formula in Equation 15-9a to determine estimates of Strasburg's beta for different capital structures. These results are reported in Line 3 of Figure 15-5.

Recall from Section 15.2 that the risk-free rate is 6.3% and the market risk premium is 6%. We can use the CAPM and the previously estimated betas to estimate Strasburg's cost of equity for different capital structures (which cause Strasburg's beta to change). These results are shown in Line 4 of Figure 15-5. As expected, Strasburg's cost of equity increases as its debt increases. Figure 15-6 graphs Strasburg's required return on equity at different debt ratios. Observe that the cost of equity consists of the 6.3% risk-free rate, a constant premium for business risk in the amount of $RP_M(b_U) = 6.522\%$, and a premium for financial risk in the amount of $RP_M(b - b_U)$ that starts at zero (because $b = b_U$ for zero debt) but rises at an increasing rate as the debt ratio increases.

The Weighted Average Cost of Capital at Different Levels of Debt

Line 6 of Figure 15-5 shows Strasburg's weighted average cost of capital, WACC, at different capital structures. As the debt ratio increases, the costs of both debt and equity rise, at first slowly but then at an accelerating rate. Eventually, the increasing costs of these two components offset the fact that more debt (which is still less costly than equity) is being used. At 40% debt, Strasburg's WACC hits a minimum of 11.63%; Column F is the capital structure with the minimum WACC. Notice that the WACC begins to increase for capital structures with more than 40% debt. Figure 15-7 shows how the WACC changes as debt increases.

Also note that, even though the component cost of equity is always higher than that of debt, only using debt would not maximize value. If Strasburg were to issue more than 40% debt, then the costs of both debt and equity would increase in such a way that the overall WACC would increase, because the cost of debt would increase by more than the cost of equity.

FIGURE 15-6

Strasburg's Required Rate of Return on Equity at Different Debt Levels

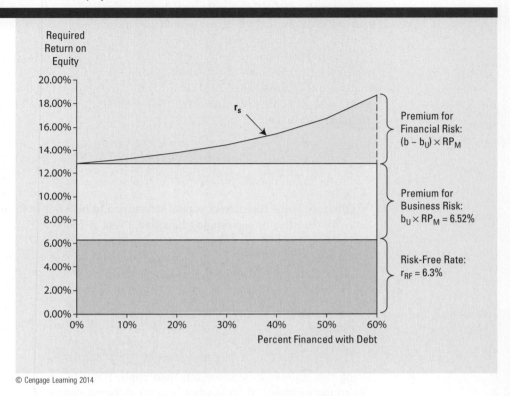

© Cengage Learning 2014

FIGURE 15-7

Effects of Capital Structure on the Cost of Capital

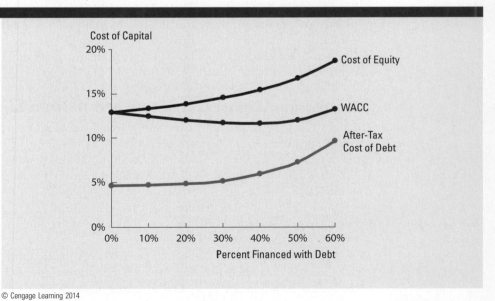

© Cengage Learning 2014

15-5c Estimating the Firm's Value

As we showed previously, Strasburg currently has a $250 million intrinsic value of operations: w_d = 20%, WACC = 12%, FCF = $30 million, and zero growth in FCF. Using the same approach as in Section 15-2, we can use the data in Figure 15-5 to estimate Strasburg's value of operations at different capital structures; these results are reported in Line 7 of Figure 15-5 and are graphed in Figure 15-8.[26] The maximum value of $257.86 million occurs at a capital structure with 40% debt, which also is the capital structure that minimizes the WACC.

Notice that the value of the firm initially increases but then begins to fall. As discussed earlier, the value initially rises because the WACC initially falls. But the rising costs of equity and debt eventually cause the WACC to increase, causing the value of the firm to fall. Notice how flat the curve is around the optimal level of debt. Thus, it doesn't make a great deal of difference whether Strasburg's capital structure has 30% debt or 40% debt. Also, notice that the maximum value is about 10% greater than the value with no debt. Although this example is for a single company, the results are typical: The optimal capital structure can add 2% to 15% more value relative to zero debt, and there is a fairly wide range of w_d (from about 20% to 50%) over which value changes very little.

Figures 15-5 and 15-8 also show the values of debt and equity for each capital structure. The value of debt is found by multiplying the value of operations by the percentage of the firm that is financed by debt: Debt = $w_d \times V_{op}$. The intrinsic value of equity is found in a

FIGURE 15-8

Effects of Capital Structure on the Value of Operations

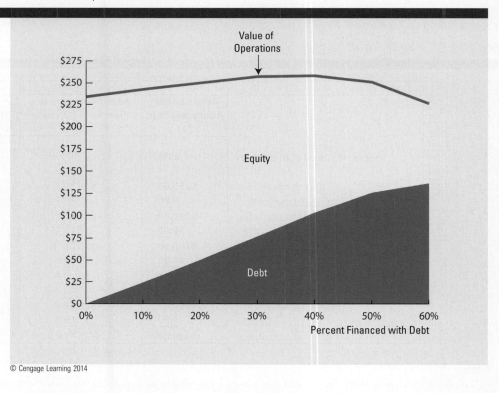

© Cengage Learning 2014

---

[26]In this analysis we assume that Strasburg's expected EBIT and FCF are constant for the various capital structures. In a more refined analysis, we might try to estimate any possible declines in FCF at high levels of debt as the threat of bankruptcy becomes imminent.

similar manner: $S = V_{op} - \text{Debt} = w_s \times V_{op}$. Even though the intrinsic value of equity falls as debt increases, the wealth of shareholders is maximized at the maximum value of operations, as we explain in the next section.

SELF-TEST

What happens to the costs of debt and equity when the leverage increases? Explain.

Use the Hamada equation to calculate the unlevered beta for JAB Industries, assuming the following data: Levered beta = b = 1.4; T = 40%; w_d = 45%. **(0.939)**

Suppose r_{RF} = 6% and RP_M = 5%. What would be the cost of equity for JAB Industries if it had no debt? **(10.7%)** *If w_d were 45%?* **(13.0%)**

15-6 Anatomy of a Recapitalization

Strasburg should **recapitalize**, meaning that it should issue enough additional debt to optimize its capital structure, and then use the debt proceeds to repurchase stock. As shown in Figure 15-5, a capital structure with 40% debt is optimal. But before tackling the **recap**, as it is commonly called, let's consider the sequence of events, starting with the situation before Strasburg issues any additional debt. Figure 15-4 shows the valuation analysis of Strasburg at a capital structure consisting of 20% debt and 80% equity. These results are repeated in Column 1 of Figure 15-9, along with the shareholder wealth, which consists entirely of $200 million in stock before the repurchase. The next step is to examine the impact of Strasburg's debt issuance.

FIGURE 15-9

Anatomy of a Recapitalization (Millions, Except for Per Share Data)

	A	B	C	D	E
			Before Issuing Additional Debt (1)	**After Debt Issue, but Prior to Repurchase** (2)	**Post Repurchase** (3)
325					
326					
327					
328					
329		Percent financed with debt: w_d	20%	40%	40%
330					
331		Value of operations	$250.00	$257.86	$257.86
332		+ Value of ST investments	0.00	53.14	0.00
333		Estimated total intrinsic value	$250.00	$311.00	$257.86
334		− Debt	50.00	103.14	103.14
335		Estimated intrinsic value of equity	$200.00	$207.86	$154.72
336		÷ Number of shares	10.00	10.00	7.44
337		Estimated intrinsic price per share	$20.00	$20.79	$20.79
338					
339		Value of stock	$200.00	$207.86	$154.72
340		+ Cash distributed in repurchase	0.00	0.00	53.14
341		Wealth of shareholders	$200.00	$207.86	$207.86

Notes:
1. The value of ST investments in Column 2 is equal to the amount of cash raised by issuing additional debt but that has not been used to repurchase shares: ST investments = $D_{New} - D_{Old}$.
2. The value of ST investments in Column 3 is zero because the funds have been used to repurchase shares of stock.
3. The number of shares in Column 3 reflects the shares repurchased: $n_{Post} = n_{Prior} - (Cash_{Rep}/P_{Prior}) = n_{Prior} - [(D_{New} - D_{Old})/P_{Prior}]$.

15-6a Strasburg Issues New Debt but Has Not Yet Repurchased Stock

The next step in the recap is to issue debt and announce the firm's intent to repurchase stock with the newly issued debt. At the optimal capital structure of 40% debt, the value of the firm's operations is $257.86 million, as calculated in Figure 15-5 and repeated in Column 2 of Figure 15-9. This value of operations is greater than the $250 million value of operations for w_d = 20% because the WACC is lower. Notice that Strasburg raised its debt from $50 million to $103.14 million, an increase of $53.14 million. Because Column 2 reports data prior to the repurchase, Strasburg has short-term investments in the amount of $53.14 million, the amount that was raised in the debt issuance but that has not yet been used to repurchase stock.[27] As Figure 15-9 shows, Strasburg's intrinsic value of equity is $207.86 million.

Because Strasburg has not yet repurchased any stock, it still has 10 million shares outstanding. Therefore, the price per share after the debt issue but prior to the repurchase is

$$P_{Prior} = S_{Prior}/n_{Prior}$$
$$= \$207.86/10 = \$20.79$$

Column 2 of Figure 15-9 summarizes these calculations and also shows the wealth of the shareholders. The shareholders own Strasburg's equity, which is worth $207.86 million. Strasburg has not yet made any cash distributions to shareholders, so the total wealth of shareholders is $207.86 million. The new wealth of $207.86 million is greater than the initial wealth of $200 million, so the recapitalization has added value to Strasburg's shareholders. Notice also that the recapitalization caused the intrinsic stock price to increase from $20.00 to $20.79.

Summarizing these results, we see that the issuance of debt and the resulting change in the optimal capital structure caused (1) the WACC to decrease, (2) the value of operations to increase, (3) shareholder wealth to increase, and (4) the stock price to increase.

15-6b Strasburg Repurchases Stock

What happens to the stock price during the repurchase? In Chapter 14 we discuss repurchases and note that a repurchase does not change the stock price. It is true that the additional debt will change the WACC and the stock price prior to the repurchase (P_{Prior}), but the subsequent repurchase itself will not affect the post-repurchase stock price (P_{Post}).[28] Therefore, $P_{Post} = P_{Prior}$. (Keep in mind that P_{Prior} is the price immediately prior to the repurchase, not the price prior to the event that led to the cash available for the repurchase, such as the issuance of debt in this example.)

Strasburg uses the entire amount of cash raised by the debt issue to repurchase stock. The total cash raised is equal to $D_{New} - D_{Old}$. The number of shares repurchased is equal to the cash raised by issuing debt divided by the repurchase price:

$$\text{Number of shares repurchased} = \frac{D_{New} - D_{Old}}{P_{Prior}} \qquad (15\text{-}11)$$

---

[27]These calculations are shown in the *Excel* file **Ch15 Tool Kit.xls** on the textbook's Web site. The values reported in the text are rounded, but the values used in calculations in the spreadsheet are not rounded.

[28]As we discuss in Chapter 14, a stock repurchase may be a signal of a company's future prospects or it may be the way a company "announces" a change in capital structure, and either of these situations could have an impact on estimated free cash flows or WACC. However, neither situation applies to Strasburg.

Strasburg repurchases ($103.14 − $50)/$20.79 = 2.56 million shares of stock.

The number of remaining shares after the repurchase, n_{Post}, is equal to the initial number of shares minus the number that is repurchased:

$$n_{Post} = \text{Number of outstanding shares remaining after the repurchase}$$
$$= n_{Prior} - \text{Number of shares repurchased}$$
$$= n_{Prior} - \frac{D_{New} - D_{Old}}{P_{Prior}} \qquad \text{(15-12)}$$

For Strasburg, the number of remaining shares after the repurchase is

$$n_{Post} = n_{Prior} - (D_{New} - D_{Old})/P_{Prior}$$
$$= 10 - (\$103.14 - \$50)/\$20.79$$
$$= 7.44 \text{ million}$$

Column 3 of Figure 15-9 summarizes these post-repurchase results. The repurchase doesn't change the value of operations, which remains at $257.86 million. However, the short-term investments are sold and the cash is used to repurchase stock. Strasburg is left with no short-term investments, so the intrinsic value of equity is:

$$S_{Post} = \$257.86 - \$103.14 = \$154.72 \text{ million}$$

After the repurchase, Strasburg has 7.44 million shares of stock. We can verify that the intrinsic stock price has not changed:[29]

$$P_{Post} = S_{Post}/n_{Post} = \$154.72/7.44 = \$20.79$$

Shareholders now own an equity position in the company worth only $154.72 million, but they have received a cash distribution in the amount of $53.14 million, so their total wealth is equal to the value of their equity plus the amount of cash they received: $154.72 + $53.14 = $207.86.

Here are some points worth noting. As shown in Column 3 of Figure 15-9, the change in capital structure clearly added wealth to the shareholders, increased the price per share, and increased the cash (in the form of short-term investments) temporarily held by the company. However, the repurchase itself did not affect shareholder wealth or the price per share. The repurchase did reduce the cash held by the company and the number of shares outstanding, but shareholder wealth stayed constant. After the repurchase, shareholders directly own the funds used in the repurchase; before the repurchase, shareholders indirectly own the funds. In either case, shareholders own the funds. The repurchase simply takes them out of the company's account and puts them into the shareholders' personal accounts.

The approach we've described here is based on the corporate valuation model, and it will always provide the correct value for S_{Post}, n_{Post}, and P_{Post}. However, there is a quicker way to calculate these values if the firm has no short-term investments either before or after the recap (other than the temporary short-term investments held between the time debt was issued and shares repurchased). After the recap is completed, the percentage of equity in the capital structure, based on market values, is equal to $1 - w_d$ if the firm holds no other short-term investments. Therefore, the value of equity after the repurchase is

$$S_{Post} = V_{opNew}(1 - w_d) \qquad \text{(15-13)}$$

---

[29]There may be a small rounding difference due to using rounded numbers in intermediate steps. See the *Excel* file ***Ch15 Tool Kit.xls*** for the exact calculations.

where we use the subscript "New" to indicate the value of operations at the new capital structure and the subscript "Post" to indicate the post-repurchase intrinsic value of equity.

The post-repurchase number of shares can be found using this equation:

$$n_{Post} = n_{Prior}\left[\frac{V_{opNew} - D_{New}}{V_{opNew} - D_{Old}}\right] \tag{15-14}$$

Given the value of equity and the number of shares, it is straightforward to calculate the intrinsic price per share as $P_{Post} = S_{Post}/n_{Post}$. But we can also calculate the post-repurchase price using

$$P_{Post} = \frac{V_{opNew} - D_{Old}}{n_{Prior}} \tag{15-15}$$

Figure 15-5 reports the number of shares and the intrinsic price per share in Lines 10–11. Notice that the number of shares goes down as debt goes up because the debt proceeds are used to buy back stock. Notice also that the capital structure that maximizes stock price, $w_d = 40\%$, is the same capital structure that optimizes the WACC and the value of operations.

Figure 15-5 also reports the earnings per share for the different levels of debt. Figure 15-10 graphs the intrinsic price per share and the earnings per share. Notice that the maximum earnings per share is at 50% debt even though the optimal capital structure is at 40% debt. This means that maximizing EPS will not maximize shareholder wealth.

FIGURE 15-10

Effects of Capital Structure on Stock Price and Earnings per Share

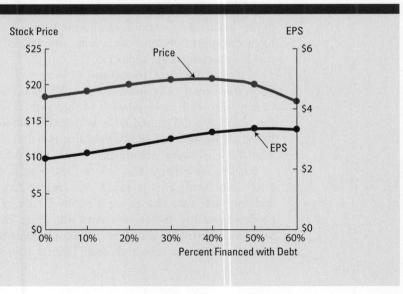

© Cengage Learning 2014

THEGLOBAL ECONOMIC CRISIS

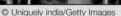

© Uniquely india/Getty Images

Deleveraging

Many households, nonfinancial businesses, and financial institutions loaded up on easy credit during the run-up to the global economic crisis and found themselves with too much debt during the recession that began in 2007. The process of reducing debt is called *deleveraging*, and it is painful for individuals and the economy.

The debt-to-income ratio for households increased from around 80%–90% during the 1990s to a peak of 133% in 2007. To deleverage, many households cut spending on consumer goods and paid off some of their debt. This belt-tightening is difficult for the individual households, but it also is difficult for the economy because decreased spending leads to economic contraction and job losses. Other households deleveraged by declaring bankruptcy, with over 1.5 million people filing in 2010.

Like individuals, businesses can deleverage by paying off debt or by declaring bankruptcy, and many did so during this global economic crisis. But businesses can also deleverage by issuing equity. For example, Dunkin' Brands Group, owner of the Dunkin' Donuts and Baskin-Robbins brands, issued $427 million in stock in July 2011, part of which was used to pay down debt. And Wells Fargo and Morgan Stanley issued over $12 billion in stock in May of 2009. A problem with deleveraging via stock issuances is that the stock price usually has been beaten down so much by the time of deleveraging that the new investors get a larger stake in the company, which dilutes the existing stockholders. But the bottom line is that dilution is better than bankruptcy!

Sources: Reuven Glick and Kevin J. Lansing, "U.S. Household Deleveraging and Future Consumption Growth," FRBSF Economic Letter, May 15, 2009, **www.frbsf.org/ publications/economics/letter/2009/el2009-16.pdf**; and BankruptcyAction.com, **www.bankruptcyaction.com/ USbankstats.htm**, May 2009.

15-6c Recapitalization: A Post-Mortem

In Chapter 12, we saw how a company can increase its value by improving its operations. There is good news and bad news regarding this connection. The good news is that small improvements in operations can lead to huge increases in value. The bad news is that it's often difficult to improve operations, especially if the company is already well managed and is in a competitive industry.

If instead you seek to increase a firm's value by changing its capital structure, we again have good news and bad news. The good news is that changing capital structure is easy—just call an investment banker and issue debt (or issue equity if the firm has too much debt). The bad news is that this will add only a relatively small amount of value. Of course, any additional value is better than none, so it's hard to understand why there are some mature firms with zero debt.

Finally, some firms have more debt than is optimal and should recapitalize to a lower debt level. This is called *deleveraging*. We can use exactly the same approach and the same formulas as we used for Strasburg. The difference is that the debt will go down and the number of shares will go up. In other words, the company will issue new shares of stock and then use the proceeds to pay off debt, resulting in a capital structure with less debt and lower interest payments.

SELF-TEST

*A firm's value of operations is equal to $800 million after a recapitalization (the firm had no debt before the recap). The firm raised $200 million in new debt and used this to buy back stock. The firm had no short-term investments before or after the recap. After the recap, w_d = 25%. The firm had 10 million shares before the recap. What is S (the value of equity after the recap)? **($600 million)** What is P (the stock price after the recap)? **($80/share)** What is n (the number of remaining shares after the recap)? **(7.5 million)***

SUMMARY

This chapter examined the effects of financial leverage on stock prices, earnings per share, and the cost of capital. The key concepts covered are listed below.

- A firm's **optimal capital structure** is the mix of debt and equity that maximizes the stock price. At any point in time, management has a specific **target capital structure** in mind, presumably the optimal one, but this target may change over time.

- Several factors influence a firm's capital structure. These include its (1) **business risk,** (2) **tax position,** (3) need for **financial flexibility,** (4) **managerial conservatism or aggressiveness,** and (5) **growth opportunities.**

- **Business risk** is the risk inherent in the firm's operations if it uses no debt. A firm will have little business risk if the demand for its products is stable, if the prices of its inputs and products remain relatively constant, if it can adjust its prices freely if costs increase, and if a high percentage of its costs are variable and hence will decrease if sales decrease. Other things the same, the lower a firm's business risk, the higher its optimal debt ratio.

- **Financial leverage** is the extent to which fixed-income securities (debt and preferred stock) are used in a firm's capital structure. **Financial risk** is the added risk borne by stockholders as a result of financial leverage.

- **Operating leverage** is the extent to which fixed costs are used in a firm's operations. In business terminology, a high degree of operating leverage, other factors held constant, implies that a relatively small change in sales results in a large change in ROIC. *Web Extension 15A* describes additional measures of operating and financial leverage.

- If there are no corporate or personal taxes, Modigliani and Miller showed that the value of a levered firm is equal to the value of an otherwise identical but unlevered firm:

$$V_L = V_U$$

- If there are only corporate taxes, Modigliani and Miller showed that a firm's value increases as it adds debt due to the interest rate deductibility of debt:

$$V_L = V_U + TD$$

- If there are personal and corporate taxes, Miller showed that

$$V_L = V_U + \left[1 - \frac{(1-T_c)(1-T_s)}{(1-T_d)}\right]D$$

- The **Hamada equation** shows the effect of financial leverage on beta as follows:

$$b = b_U[1 + (1-T)(D/S)]$$

Firms can use their current beta, tax rate, and debt/equity ratio to derive their **unlevered beta, b_U,** as follows:

$$b_U = b/[1 + (1-T)(D/S)] = b/[1 + (1-T)(w_d/w_s)]$$

- The **trade-off theory** of capital structure states that debt initially adds value because interest is tax deductible but that debt also brings costs associated with actual or potential bankruptcy. The optimal capital structure strikes a balance between the tax benefits of debt and the costs associated with bankruptcy.
- A firm's decision to use debt versus stock to raise new capital sends a **signal** to investors. A stock issue is viewed as a negative signal, whereas a debt issuance is a positive (or at least a neutral) signal. As a result, companies try to avoid having to issue stock by maintaining a **reserve borrowing capacity**, and this means using less debt in "normal" times than the trade-off theory would suggest.
- A firm's owners may decide to use a relatively large amount of debt to constrain the managers. A *high debt ratio raises the threat of bankruptcy,* which not only carries a cost but also forces managers to be more careful and less wasteful with shareholders' money. Many of the corporate takeovers and leveraged buyouts in recent years were designed to improve efficiency by reducing the cash flow available to managers.

QUESTIONS

(15-1)   Define each of the following terms:

a. Capital structure; business risk; financial risk
b. Operating leverage; financial leverage; break-even point
c. Reserve borrowing capacity

(15-2)   What term refers to the uncertainty inherent in projections of future ROIC?

(15-3)   Firms with relatively high nonfinancial fixed costs are said to have a high degree of what?

(15-4)   "One type of leverage affects both EBIT and EPS. The other type affects only EPS." Explain this statement.

(15-5)   Why is the following statement true? "Other things being the same, firms with relatively stable sales are able to carry relatively high debt ratios."

(15-6)   Why do public utility companies usually have capital structures that are different from those of retail firms?

(15-7)   Why is EBIT generally considered to be independent of financial leverage? Why might EBIT be influenced by financial leverage at high debt levels?

(15-8)   If a firm went from zero debt to successively higher levels of debt, why would you expect its stock price to first rise, then hit a peak, and then begin to decline?

SELF-TEST PROBLEMS   Solutions Appear in Appendix A

(ST-1)

Optimal Capital
Structure

The Rogers Company is currently in this situation: (1) EBIT = $4.7 million; (2) tax rate, T = 40%; (3) value of debt, D = $2 million; (4) r_d = 10%; (5) r_s = 15%; (6) shares of stock outstanding, n = 600,000; and stock price, P = $30. The firm's market is stable and it expects no growth, so all earnings are paid out as dividends. The debt consists of perpetual bonds.

a. What is the total market value of the firm's stock, S, and the firm's total market value, V?
b. What is the firm's weighted average cost of capital?
c. Suppose the firm can increase its debt so that its capital structure has 50% debt, based on market values (it will issue debt and buy back stock). At this level of debt, its cost of equity rises to 18.5% and its interest rate on all debt will rise to 12% (it will have to call and refund the old debt). What is the WACC under this capital structure? What is the total value? How much debt will it issue, and what is the stock price after the repurchase? How many shares will remain outstanding after the repurchase?

(ST-2)
Hamada Equation

Lighter Industrial Corporation (LIC) is considering a large-scale recapitalization. Currently, LIC is financed with 25% debt and 75% equity. LIC is considering increasing its level of debt until it is financed with 60% debt and 40% equity. The beta on its common stock at the current level of debt is 1.5, the risk-free rate is 6%, the market risk premium is 4%, and LIC faces a 40% federal-plus-state tax rate.

a. What is LIC's current cost of equity?
b. What is LIC's unlevered beta?
c. What will be the new beta and new cost of equity if LIC recapitalizes?

PROBLEMS   Answers Appear in Appendix B

Easy Problems 1–6

(15-1)
Break-even Quantity

Shapland Inc. has fixed operating costs of $500,000 and variable costs of $50 per unit. If it sells the product for $75 per unit, what is the break-even quantity?

(15-2)
Unlevered Beta

Counts Accounting has a beta of 1.15. The tax rate is 40%, and Counts is financed with 20% debt. What is Counts's unlevered beta?

(15-3)
Premium for Financial Risk

Ethier Enterprise has an unlevered beta of 1.0. Ethier is financed with 50% debt and has a levered beta of 1.6. If the risk-free rate is 5.5% and the market risk premium is 6%, how much is the additional premium that Ethier's shareholders require to be compensated for financial risk?

(15-4)
Value of Equity after Recapitalization

Nichols Corporation's value of operations is equal to $500 million after a recapitalization (the firm had no debt before the recap). It raised $200 million in new debt and used this to buy back stock. Nichols had no short-term investments before or after the recap. After the recap, $w_d = 40\%$. What is S (the value of equity after the recap)?

(15-5)
Stock Price after Recapitalization

Lee Manufacturing's value of operations is equal to $900 million after a recapitalization (the firm had no debt before the recap). Lee raised $300 million in new debt and used this to buy back stock. Lee had no short-term investments before or after the recap. After the recap, $w_d = 1/3$. The firm had 30 million shares before the recap. What is P (the stock price after the recap)?

(15-6)
Shares Remaining after Recapitalization

Dye Trucking raised $150 million in new debt and used this to buy back stock. After the recap, Dye's stock price is $7.50. If Dye had 60 million shares of stock before the recap, how many shares does it have after the recap?

Intermediate Problems 7–8

(15-7)
Break-even Point

Schweser Satellites Inc. produces satellite earth stations that sell for $100,000 each. The firm's fixed costs, F, are $2 million, 50 earth stations are produced and sold each year, profits total $500,000, and the firm's assets (all equity financed) are $5 million. The firm estimates that it can change its production process, adding $4 million to investment and $500,000 to fixed operating costs. This change will (1) reduce variable costs per unit by $10,000 and (2) increase output by 20 units, but (3) the sales price on all units will have to be lowered to $95,000 to permit sales of the additional output. The firm has tax loss carryforwards that render its tax rate zero, its cost of equity is 16%, and it uses no debt.

a. What is the incremental profit? To get a rough idea of the project's profitability, what is the project's expected rate of return for the next year (defined as the incremental profit divided by the investment)? Should the firm make the investment? Why or why not?
b. Would the firm's break-even point increase or decrease if it made the change?
c. Would the new situation expose the firm to more or less business risk than the old one?

(15-8)
Capital Structure Analysis

The Rivoli Company has no debt outstanding, and its financial position is given by the following data:

Assets (Market value = Book value)	$3,000,000
EBIT	$ 500,000
Cost of equity, r_s	10%
Stock price, P_0	$ 15
Shares outstanding, n_0	200,000
Tax rate, T (federal-plus-state)	40%

The firm is considering selling bonds and simultaneously repurchasing some of its stock. If it moves to a capital structure with 30% debt based on market values, its cost of equity, r_s, will increase to 11% to reflect the increased risk. Bonds can be sold at a cost, r_d, of 7%. Rivoli is a no-growth firm. Hence, all its earnings are paid out as dividends. Earnings are expected to be constant over time.

a. What effect would this use of leverage have on the value of the firm?
b. What would be the price of Rivoli's stock?
c. What happens to the firm's earnings per share after the recapitalization?
d. The $500,000 EBIT given previously is actually the expected value from the following probability distribution:

Probability	EBIT
0.10	($ 100,000)
0.20	200,000
0.40	500,000
0.20	800,000
0.10	1,100,000

Determine the times-interest-earned ratio for each probability. What is the probability of not covering the interest payment at the 30% debt level?

Challenging Problems 9–11

(15-9)
Capital Structure Analysis

Pettit Printing Company has a total market value of $100 million, consisting of 1 million shares selling for $50 per share and $50 million of 10% perpetual bonds now selling at par. The company's EBIT is $13.24 million, and its tax rate is 15%. Pettit can change its capital structure by either increasing its debt to 70% (based on market values) or decreasing it to 30%. If it decides to *increase* its use of leverage, it must call its old bonds and issue new ones with a 12% coupon. If it decides to *decrease* its leverage, it will call its old bonds and replace them with new 8% coupon bonds. The company will sell or repurchase stock at the new equilibrium price to complete the capital structure change.

The firm pays out all earnings as dividends; hence its stock is a zero-growth stock. Its current cost of equity, r_s, is 14%. If it increases leverage, r_s will be 16%. If it decreases leverage, r_s will be 13%. What is the firm's WACC and total corporate value under each capital structure?

(15-10)
Optimal Capital Structure with Hamada

Beckman Engineering and Associates (BEA) is considering a change in its capital structure. BEA currently has $20 million in debt carrying a rate of 8%, and its stock price is $40 per share with 2 million shares outstanding. BEA is a zero-growth firm and pays out all of its earnings as dividends. The firm's EBIT is $14.933 million, and it faces a 40% federal-plus-state tax rate. The market risk premium is 4%, and the risk-free rate is 6%. BEA is considering increasing its debt level to a capital structure with 40% debt, based on market values, and repurchasing shares with the extra money that it borrows. BEA will have to retire the old debt in order to issue new debt, and the rate on the new debt will be 9%. BEA has a beta of 1.0.

a. What is BEA's unlevered beta? Use market value D/S (which is the same as w_d/w_s) when unlevering.
b. What are BEA's new beta and cost of equity if it has 40% debt?
c. What are BEA's WACC and total value of the firm with 40% debt?

(15-11)
WACC and Optimal Capital Structure

F. Pierce Products Inc. is considering changing its capital structure. F. Pierce currently has no debt and no preferred stock, but it would like to add some debt to take advantage of low interest rates and the tax shield. Its investment banker has indicated that the pre-tax cost of debt under various possible capital structures would be as follows:

Market Debt-to-Value Ratio (w_d)	Market Equity-to-Value Ratio (w_s)	Market Debt-to-Equity Ratio (D/S)	Before-Tax Cost of Debt (r_d)
0.0	1.0	0.00	6.0%
0.2	0.8	0.25	7.0
0.4	0.6	0.67	8.0
0.6	0.4	1.50	9.0
0.8	0.2	4.00	10.0

F. Pierce uses the CAPM to estimate its cost of common equity, r_s and at the time of the analysis the risk-free rate is 5%, the market risk premium is 6%, and the company's tax rate is 40%. F. Pierce estimates that its beta now (which is "unlevered" because it currently has no debt) is 0.8. Based on this information, what is the firm's optimal capital structure, and what would be the weighted average cost of capital at the optimal capital structure?

SPREADSHEET PROBLEM

(15-12)
Build a Model: WACC and Optimal Capital Structure

resource

Start with the partial model in the file *Ch15 P12 Build a Model.xls* on the textbook's Web site. Reacher Technology has consulted with investment bankers and determined the interest rate it would pay for different capital structures, as shown in the following table. Data for the risk-free rate, the market risk premium, an estimate of Reacher's unlevered beta, and the tax rate are also shown. Based on this information, what is the firm's optimal capital structure, and what is the weighted average cost of capital at the optimal structure?

Percent Financed with Debt (w_d)	Before-Tax Cost Debt (r_d)	Input Data	
0%	6.0%	Risk-free rate	4.5%
10	6.1	Market risk premium	5.5%
20	7.0	Unlevered beta	0.8
30	8.0	Tax rate	40.0%
40	10.0		
50	12.5		
60	15.5		
70	18.0		

THOMSON ONE   Business School Edition Problem

 THOMSON REUTERS   Use the Thomson ONE—Business School Edition online database to work this chapter's questions.

Exploring the Capital Structures for Three Global Auto Companies

The following discussion questions demonstrate how we can evaluate the capital structures for three global automobile companies: Ford (F), BMW (BMW), and Toyota (J:TYMO). As you gather information on these companies, be mindful of the currencies in which these companies' financial data are reported.

Thomson ONE—BSE Discussion Questions

1. For an overall picture of each company's capital structure, it is helpful to see a chart that summarizes the company's capital structure over the past decade. To obtain this chart, choose a company to start with and select Financials. Next, select More>Thomson Reports & Charts>Capital Structure. This should generate a chart that plots the company's long-term debt, common equity, and total current liabilities over the past decade. What, if any, are the major trends that emerge from looking at these charts? Do these companies tend to have relatively high or relatively low levels of debt? Do these companies have significant levels of current liabilities? Have their capital structures changed over time?

2. To obtain more details about the companies' capital structures over the past 5 years, select Financials>Financial Ratios>Thomson Ratios. From here you can select Annual Ratios and/or 5Yr Average Ratios Report. In each case, you can scroll down and look for Leverage Ratios. Here you will find a variety of leverage ratios for the past 5 years. (Notice that these two pages offer different information. The Annual Ratios page offers year-end leverage ratios, whereas the 5Yr Average Ratios Report offers the average ratio over the previous 5 years for each calendar date. In other words, the 5Yr Average Ratios Report smooths the changes in capital structure over the reporting period.) Do these ratios suggest that the company has significantly changed its capital structure over the past 5 years? If so, what factors could possibly explain this shift? (Financial statements might be

useful for detecting any shifts that may have led to the company's changing capital structure. You may also consult the company's annual report to see if there is any discussion and/or explanation for these changes. Both the historical financial statements and annual report information can be found via Thomson ONE).

3. Repeat this procedure for the other auto companies. Do you find similar capital structures for each of the three companies? Do you find that the capital structures have moved in the same direction over the past 5 years, or have the different companies changed their capital structures in different ways over the past 5 years?

4. The financial ratios investigated thus far are based on book values of debt and equity. Determine whether using the market value of equity (market capitalization found on the Overview page) makes a significant difference in the most recent year's "LT Debt Pct Common Equity" and "Total Debt Pct Total Assets." (*Note:* "LT Debt" is defined by Thomson ONE as the "Long Term Debt" listed on the balance sheet, while "Total Debt" is defined as "Long Term Debt" plus "ST Debt & Current Portion Due LT Debt.") Are there big differences between the capital structures measured on a book or market basis?

5. You can also use Thomson ONE to search for companies with either very large or very small debt ratios. For example, if you want to find the top 50 companies with the highest debt ratio, select: Screening & Targeting > Companies > Step 1: All Companies > Step 2 Database: Thomson Financial > Categories: Ratios > Leverage. From here, select "LT Debt Pct Total Cap 5 Yr. Avg." (This will focus in on the average capital structure over the past 5 years, which may give us a better indication of the company's long-run target capital structure.) Once you click on SELECT, you should see the Search Expression Builder screen. From here, go to Rank and select the top 50 by typing "50" in the box below rank. Next click in the Expression box below and highlight the expression that was created and copy it by using the Control and the C button together. Now, back under Step 3, click on Add Item > Custom Criteria and paste the expression you copied into the box (using Shift Insert). Then click Add and then Search. You can easily change this to also select the bottom 50 (or perhaps the bottom 5% or 10%). Take a close look at the resulting firms by clicking on Search. Do you observe any differences between the types of firms that have high debt levels and the types of firms that have low debt levels? Are these patterns similar to what you expect after reading the chapter? (As a quick review, you may want to look at the average capital structures for different industries, which are summarized in the text.) *Note:* The searches are cumulative, so that if you ask for the top 10% of the database and follow that by asking for the bottom 5%, you will be shown the bottom 5% of the top 10%. In other words, you would only see a small subset of the firms you are asking for. Hence, *when beginning a new search, clear all existing searches first.*

6. From the submenu just above the list of firms, you may choose a number of options. "List" displays a list of the firms and allows you to access a firm report. "Profiles" provides key information about the firms, such as ticker, country, exchange, and industry code. "Financials" gives a couple of key financial figures (expressed in U.S. dollars) from the firms' balance sheets and income statements. "Market Data" includes the firms' market capitalization, current price, P/E ratio, EPS, and so forth. "Report Writer" allows you to create customized company reports.

MINI CASE

Assume you have just been hired as a business manager of PizzaPalace, a regional pizza restaurant chain. The company's EBIT was $50 million last year and is not expected to grow. The firm is currently financed with all equity, and it has 10 million shares outstanding. When you took your corporate finance course, your instructor stated that most firms' owners would be financially better off if the firms used some debt. When you suggested this to your new boss, he encouraged you to pursue the idea. As a first step, assume that you obtained from the firm's investment banker the following estimated costs of debt for the firm at different capital structures:

Percent Financed with Debt, w_d	r_d
0%	—
20	8.0%
30	8.5
40	10.0
50	12.0

If the company were to recapitalize, then debt would be issued and the funds received would be used to repurchase stock. PizzaPalace is in the 40% state-plus-federal corporate tax bracket, its beta is 1.0, the risk-free rate is 6%, and the market risk premium is 6%.

a. Using the free cash flow valuation model, show the only avenues by which capital structure can affect value.
b. (1) What is business risk? What factors influence a firm's business risk?
   (2) What is operating leverage, and how does it affect a firm's business risk? Show the operating break-even point if a company has fixed costs of $200, a sales price of $15, and variable costs of $10.
c. Now, to develop an example that can be presented to PizzaPalace's management to illustrate the effects of financial leverage, consider two hypothetical firms: Firm U, which uses no debt financing, and Firm L, which uses $10,000 of 12% debt. Both firms have $20,000 in assets, a 40% tax rate, and an expected EBIT of $3,000.
   (1) Construct partial income statements, which start with EBIT, for the two firms.
   (2) Now calculate ROE for both firms.
   (3) What does this example illustrate about the impact of financial leverage on ROE?
d. Explain the difference between financial risk and business risk.
e. What happens to ROE for Firm U and Firm L if EBIT falls to $2,000? What does this imply about the impact of leverage on risk and return?
f. What does capital structure theory attempt to do? What lessons can be learned from capital structure theory? Be sure to address the MM models.
g. What does the empirical evidence say about capital structure theory? What are the implications for managers?
h. With the preceding points in mind, now consider the optimal capital structure for PizzaPalace.
   (1) For each capital structure under consideration, calculate the levered beta, the cost of equity, and the WACC.
   (2) Now calculate the corporate value for each capital structure.

i. Describe the recapitalization process and apply it to PizzaPalace. Calculate the resulting value of the debt that will be issued, the resulting market value of equity, the price per share, the number of shares repurchased, and the remaining shares. Considering only the capital structures under analysis, what is PizzaPalace's optimal capital structure?

SELECTED ADDITIONAL CASES

The following cases from CengageCompose cover many of the concepts discussed in this chapter and are available at **compose.cengage.com**.

Klein-Brigham Series:
Case 9, "Kleen Kar, Inc."; Case 43, "Mountain Springs, Inc."; and Case 57, "Greta Cosmetics, Inc.," each present a situation similar to the Strasburg example in the text. Case 74, "The Western Company," and Case 99, "Moore Plumbing Supply," explore capital structure policies.

Brigham-Buzzard Series:
Case 8, "Powerline Network Corporation (Operating Leverage, Financial Leverage, and the Optimal Capital Structure)."

© lulu/fotolia.com

PART **7**

Managing Global Operations

© Adalberto Rios Szalay/Sexto Sol/Getty Images

CHAPTER 16

Supply Chains and Working Capital Management

W hat do Southwest Airlines, Apple, Qualcomm, and Family Dollar Stores have in common? Each led its industry in the latest *CFO Magazine* annual survey of working capital management, which covered the 1,000 largest U.S. publicly traded firms. Each company is rated on its "days of working capital," which is the amount of net operating working capital required per dollar of daily sales:

$$\text{Days of working capital (DWC)} = \frac{\text{Receivables} + \text{Inventory} - \text{Payables}}{\text{Average daily sales}}$$

The median industry ratio varies significantly. For example, the median in the computer and peripherals industry is 43, but the median in machinery is 82. The median airline holds zero days of working capital—its payables are as large as its combined receivables and inventory. But even within an industry, there is considerable variation. For example, Family Dollar has 16 days but Nordstrom has 79.

After being burned in the recent recession, many companies are holding record amounts of cash and have been accused by analysts of losing their focus on working capital. Not so with Thomson Reuters, a world leader in the news and data businesses, however. Thomson Reuters doesn't have much inventory and is hampered in reducing its receivables because it operates in so many different countries, so instead it focused on standardizing its global accounts payable policies and improved its DSO (days sales outstanding) by 3 days. When asked about the cash that other companies could possibly wring out of their working capital, Thomson Reuters's CFO Bob Daleo said, "Instead of giving it to their vendors and customers, why don't they give it back to their shareholders?" Keep this in mind as you read this chapter.

Sources: See David Katz, "Easing the Squeeze: The 2011 Working Capital Scorecard," *CFO,* July/August 2011, at the Web site **www.cfo.com/article.cfm/14586631/c_2984340/?f=archives**; for the rankings, see **www.cfo.com/media/pdf/1107WCcharts.pdf**.

Corporate Valuation and Working Capital Management

© Rob Webb/Getty Images

Superior working capital management can dramatically reduce required investments in operating capital, which can lead, in turn, to larger free cash flows and greater firm value.

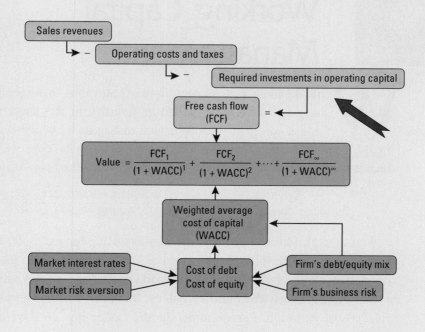

© Cengage Learning 2014

r e s o u r c e

The textbook's Web site contains an Excel *file that will guide you through the chapter's calculations. The file for this chapter is* **Ch16 Tool Kit.xls,** *and we encourage you to open the file and follow along as you read the chapter.*

Working capital management involves two basic questions: (1) What is the appropriate amount of working capital, both in total and for each specific account, and (2) how should working capital be financed? Note that sound working capital management goes beyond finance. Indeed, improving the firm's working capital position generally comes from improvements in the operating divisions. For example, experts in logistics, operations management, and information technology often work with engineers and production specialists to develop ways to speed up the manufacturing process and thus reduce the goods-in-process inventory. Similarly, marketing managers and logistics experts cooperate to develop better ways to deliver the firm's products to customers. Finance comes into play in evaluating how effective the firm's operating departments are relative to other firms in its industry and also in evaluating the profitability of alternative proposals for improving working capital management. In addition, financial managers decide how much cash their companies should keep on hand and how much short-term financing should be used to finance their working capital.

16-1 Overview of Working Capital Management

Consider some of the activities involved in a company's supply chain. The company places an order with a supplier. The supplier ships the order and bills the company. The company either pays immediately or waits, in which case the unpaid amount is called an account payable. The newly arrived shipment goes into inventory until it is needed. If the supplier shipped finished products, the company will distribute the goods to its warehouses or retail facilities. If instead the supplier shipped components or raw materials, the company will use the shipment in a manufacturing or assembly process, putting the final product into its finished goods inventory. Items from the finished goods inventory will be shipped either directly to customers or to warehouses for later shipments. When a customer purchases the product, the company bills the customer and often offers the customer credit. If the customer doesn't pay immediately, the unpaid balance is called an account receivable. During this process, the company has been accruing unpaid wages (because the company doesn't pay its employees daily) and unpaid taxes (because the company doesn't pay the IRS daily).

Several current assets and current liabilities are involved in this process—cash is spent (when paying suppliers, employees, taxes, etc.) and collected (when customers pay), accounts receivable are created and collected, inventory ebbs and flows, accounts payable are generated and paid, and accruals accumulate until paid. Notice that these are the same operating current assets (cash, accounts receivable, and inventories) and operating current liabilities (accounts payable and accruals) that are used in calculating **net operating working capital (NOWC)**, which is defined as operating current assets minus operating current liabilities.

In addition to operating current assets and operating current liabilities, there are two other current accounts related to working capital management: short-term investments and short-term debt. We discuss each current asset and liability later in the chapter, but it will be helpful if we first distinguish between cash and short-term investments because this can be a source of confusion.

Many dictionaries define cash as currency (coins and bills) and demand deposit accounts (such as a checking account at a bank). Most companies have very little currency on hand, and most have relatively small checking accounts. However, most companies own a wide variety of short-term financial assets. For example, Apple and Microsoft own: (1) checking accounts, (2) U.S. Treasury and agency securities, (3) certificates of deposits and time deposits, (4) commercial paper, (5) money market funds and other mutual funds (with low price volatility), (6) short-term or floating-rate corporate and municipal notes and bonds, and (7) and floating-rate preferred stock. Most of these holdings can be converted into cash very quickly at prices identical or very close to their book values, so sometimes they are called cash equivalents.

Some of these financial assets are held to support current ongoing operations and some are held for future purposes, and this is the distinction we make when defining cash and short-term investments. In particular, we define cash as the total value of the short-term financial assets that are held to support ongoing operations because this is the definition of cash that is required to be consistent with the definition of cash used to calculate NOWC (which is used, in turn, to calculate free cash flow and the intrinsic value of the company). We define short-term investments as the total value of short-term financial assets held for future purposes. Keep these distinctions in mind when we discuss cash management and short-term investments later in the chapter.

We normally use the term NOWC, but the term *working capital* is also used for slightly different purposes, so be aware of this when you see it in the financial press. For example, the financial press defines **working capital**, sometimes called *gross working capital,* as current assets used in operations.[1] The press also defines **net working capital** as all current assets minus all current liabilities.

16-2 Using and Financing Operating Current Assets

Operating current assets (CA) are used to support sales. Having too much invested in operating CA is inefficient, but having too little might constrain sales. Many companies have seasonal, growing sales, so they have seasonal growing operating CA, which has an implication for the pattern of financing that companies choose. The next sections address these issues.

16-2a Efficient Use of Operating Current Assets

Most companies can influence their ratios of operating current assets to sales. Some companies choose a relaxed policy and hold a lot of cash, receivables, and inventories relative to sales. This is a **relaxed policy**. On the other hand, if a firm has a **restricted policy**, holdings of current assets are minimized and we say that the firm's policy is *tight* or *"lean-and-mean."* A **moderate policy** lies between the two extremes.

We can use the Du Pont equation to demonstrate how working capital management affects the return on equity:

$$\text{ROE} = \text{Profit margin} \times \text{Total assets turnover} \times \text{Equity multiplier}$$
$$= \frac{\text{Net income}}{\text{Sales}} \times \frac{\text{Sales}}{\text{Assets}} \times \frac{\text{Assets}}{\text{Equity}}$$

A relaxed policy means a high level of assets and hence a low total assets turnover ratio; this results in a low ROE, other things held constant. Conversely, a restricted policy results in low current assets, a high turnover, and hence a relatively high ROE. However, the restricted policy exposes the firm to risk, because shortages can lead to work stoppages, unhappy customers, and serious long-run problems. The moderate policy falls between the two extremes. The optimal strategy is the one that management believes will maximize the firm's long-run free cash flow and thus the stock's intrinsic value.

Note that changing technologies can lead to changes in the optimal policy. For example, if a new technology makes it possible for a manufacturer to produce a given product in 5 rather than 10 days, then work-in-progress inventories can be cut in half. Similarly, many retailers have inventory management systems that use bar codes on all merchandise. These codes are read at the cash register; this information is transmitted electronically to a computer that adjusts the remaining stock of the item; and the computer automatically places an order with the supplier's computer when the stock falls to a specified level. This process lowers the "safety stocks" that would otherwise be necessary to avoid running out of stock. Such systems have dramatically lowered inventories and thus boosted profits.

---

[1]The term "working capital" originated with the old Yankee peddler, who would load his wagon with pots and pans and then take off to peddle his wares. His horse and wagon were his fixed assets, while his merchandise was sold, or turned over at a profit, and thus was called his *working capital.*

16-2b Financing Operating Current Assets

Investments in operating current assets must be financed, and the primary sources of funds include bank loans, credit from suppliers (accounts payable), accrued liabilities, long-term debt, and common equity. Each of those sources has advantages and disadvantages, so a firm must decide which sources are best for it.

To begin, note that most businesses experience seasonal and/or cyclical fluctuations. For example, construction firms tend to peak in the summer, retailers peak around Christmas, and the manufacturers who supply both construction companies and retailers follow related patterns. Similarly, the sales of virtually all businesses increase when the economy is strong, so they increase operating current assets during booms but let inventories and receivables fall during recessions. However, current assets rarely drop to zero—companies maintain some **permanent operating current assets**, which are the operating current assets needed even at the low point of the business cycle. For a growing firm in a growing economy, permanent current assets tend to increase over time. Also, as sales increase during a cyclical upswing, current assets are increased; these extra current assets are defined as **temporary operating current assets** as opposed to permanent current assets. The way permanent and temporary current assets are financed is called the firm's **operating current assets financing policy**. Three alternative policies are discussed next.

MATURITY MATCHING, OR "SELF-LIQUIDATING," APPROACH

The **maturity matching**, or **"self-liquidating," approach** calls for matching asset and liability maturities as shown in Panel a of Figure 16-1. All of the fixed assets plus the permanent current assets are financed with long-term capital, but temporary current assets are financed with short-term debt. Inventory expected to be sold in 30 days would be financed with a 30-day bank loan; a machine expected to last for 5 years would be financed with a 5-year loan; a 20-year building would be financed with a 20-year mortgage bond; and so on. Actually, two factors prevent exact maturity matching, uncertain asset lives and equity financing. For example, a firm might finance inventories with a 30-day bank loan, expecting to sell the inventories and use the cash to retire the loan. But if sales are slow, then the "life" of the inventories would exceed the original 30-day estimate and the cash from sales would not be forthcoming, perhaps causing the firm problems in paying off the loan when it comes due. In addition, some common equity financing must be used, and common equity has no maturity. Still, if a firm attempts to match or come close to matching asset and liability maturities, this is defined as a *moderate current asset financing policy*.

AGGRESSIVE APPROACH

Panel b of Figure 16-1 illustrates the situation for a more aggressive firm that finances some of its permanent assets with short-term debt. Note that we used the term "relatively" in the title for Panel b because there can be different *degrees* of aggressiveness. For example, the dashed line in Panel b could have been drawn *below* the line designating fixed assets, indicating that all of the current assets—both permanent and temporary— and part of the fixed assets were financed with short-term credit. This policy would be a highly aggressive and the firm would be subject to dangers from loan renewal as well as rising interest rate problems. However, short-term interest rates are generally lower than long-term rates, and some firms are willing to gamble by using a large amount of low-cost, short-term debt in hopes of earning higher profits.

A possible reason for adopting the aggressive policy is to take advantage of an upward sloping yield curve, for which short-term rates are lower than long-term rates. However,

FIGURE 16-1

Alternative Operating Current Assets Financing Policies

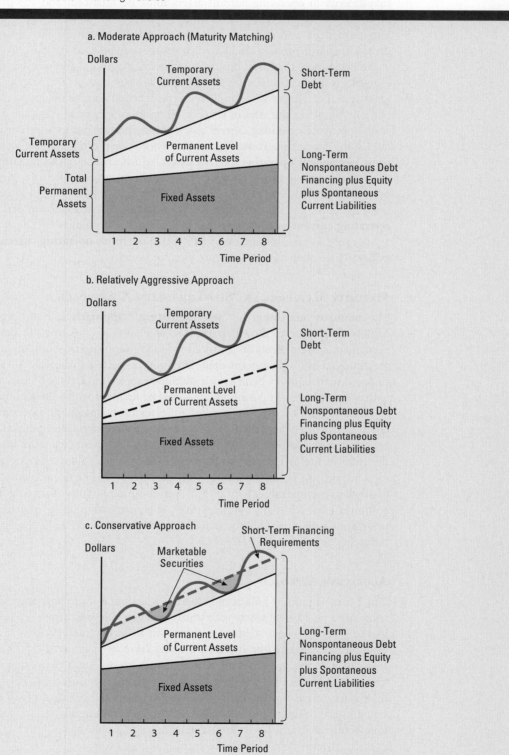

© Cengage Learning 2014

as many firms learned during the financial crisis of 2009, a strategy of financing long-term assets with short-term debt is really quite risky. As an illustration, suppose a company borrowed $1 million on a 1-year basis and used the funds to buy machinery that would lower labor costs by $200,000 per year for 10 years.[2] Cash flows from the equipment would not be sufficient to pay off the loan at the end of only one year, so the loan would have to be renewed. If the economy were in a recession like that of 2009, the lender might refuse to renew the loan, and that could lead to bankruptcy. Had the firm matched maturities and financed the equipment with a 10-year loan, then the annual loan payments would have been lower and better matched with the cash flows, and the loan renewal problem would not have arisen.

Under some circumstances, even maturity matching can be risky, as many firms that thought they were conservatively financed learned in 2009. If a firm borrowed on a 30-day bank loan to finance inventories that it expected to sell within 30 days but then sales dropped, as they did for many firms in 2009, the funds needed to pay off the maturing bank loan might not be available. Then the bank might not extend the loan, and if it did not, then the firm could be forced into bankruptcy. This happened to many firms in 2009, and it was exacerbated by the banks' own problems. The banks lost billions on mortgages, mortgage-backed bonds, and other bad investments, which led them to restrict credit to their normal business customers in order to conserve their own cash.

CONSERVATIVE APPROACH

Panel c of the figure shows the dashed line *above* the line designating permanent current assets, indicating that long-term capital is used to finance all permanent assets and also to meet some seasonal needs. In this situation, the firm uses a small amount of short-term credit to meet its peak requirements, but it also meets a part of its seasonal needs by "storing liquidity" in the form of marketable securities. The humps above the dashed line represent short-term financings, while the troughs below the dashed line represent short-term security holdings. This conservative financing policy is fairly safe, and the wisdom of using it was demonstrated in 2009—when credit dried up, firms with adequate cash holdings were able to operate more effectively than those that were forced to cut back their operations because they couldn't order new inventories or pay their normal workforce.

CHOOSING AMONG THE APPROACHES

Because the yield curve is normally upward sloping, *the cost of short-term debt is generally lower than that of long-term debt.* However, *short-term debt is riskier for the borrowing firm* for two reasons: (1) If a firm borrows on a long-term basis then its interest costs will be relatively stable over time, but if it uses short-term credit, then its interest expense can fluctuate widely—perhaps reaching such high levels that profits are extinguished.[3] (2) If a firm borrows heavily on a short-term basis, then a temporary recession may adversely affect its financial ratios and render it unable to repay its debt. Recognizing this fact, the lender may not renew the loan if the borrower's financial position is weak, which could force the borrower into bankruptcy.

---

[2] We are oversimplifying here. Few lenders would explicitly lend money for 1 year to finance a 10-year asset. What would actually happen is that the firm would borrow on a 1-year basis for "general corporate purposes" and then actually use the money to purchase the 10-year machinery.

[3] The prime interest rate—the rate banks charge very good customers—hit 21% in the early 1980s. This produced a level of business bankruptcies that was not seen again until 2009. The primary reason for the very high interest rate was that the inflation rate was up to 13%, and high inflation must be compensated by high interest rates. Also, the Federal Reserve was tightening credit in order to hold down inflation, and it was encouraging banks to restrict their lending.

Note also that *short-term loans can generally be negotiated much faster* than long-term loans. Lenders need to make a thorough financial examination before extending long-term credit, and the loan agreement must be spelled out in great detail because a lot can happen during the life of a 10- to 20-year loan.

Finally, *short-term debt generally offers greater flexibility.* If the firm thinks that interest rates are abnormally high and due for a decline, it may prefer short-term credit because prepayment penalties are often attached to long-term debt. Also, if its needs for funds are seasonal or cyclical, then the firm may not want to commit itself to long-term debt because of its underwriting costs and possible prepayment penalties. Finally, long-term loan agreements generally contain provisions, or *covenants,* that constrain the firm's future actions in order to protect the lender, whereas short-term credit agreements generally have fewer restrictions.

All things considered, it is not possible to state that either long-term or short-term financing is generally better. The firm's specific conditions will affect its decision, as will the risk preferences of managers. Optimistic and/or aggressive managers will lean more toward short-term credit to gain an interest cost advantage, whereas more conservative managers will lean toward long-term financing to avoid potential renewal problems. The factors discussed here should be considered, but the final decision will reflect managers' personal preferences and subjective judgments.

SELF-TEST

Identify and explain three alternative current asset investment policies.

Use the Du Pont equation to show how working capital policy can affect a firm's expected ROE.

What are the reasons for not wanting to hold too little working capital? For not wanting to hold too much?

Differentiate between permanent operating current assets and temporary operating current assets.

What does maturity matching mean, and what is the logic behind this policy?

What are some advantages and disadvantages of short-term versus long-term debt?

16-3 The Cash Conversion Cycle

All firms follow a "working capital cycle" in which they purchase or produce inventory, hold it for a time, and then sell it and receive cash. This process is known as the **cash conversion cycle (CCC).**

16-3a Calculating the Target CCC

Assume that Great Basin Medical Equipment (GBM), a start-up business, buys orthopedic devices from a manufacturer in China and sells them through distributors in the United States, Canada, and Mexico. Its business plan calls for it to purchase $10,000,000 of merchandise at the start of each month and sell it within 50 days. The company will have 40 days to pay its suppliers, and it will give its customers 60 days to pay for their purchases. GBM expects to just break even during its first few years and so its monthly sales will be $10,000,000, the same as its purchases (or cost of goods sold). For simplicity, assume that there are no administrative costs. Also, any funds required to support operations will be obtained from the bank, and those loans must be repaid as soon as cash becomes available.

This information can be used to calculate GBM's target, or theoretical, cash conversion cycle, which "nets out" the three time periods described below.

1. **Inventory conversion period**. For GBM, this is the 50 days it expects to take to sell the equipment, converting it from equipment to accounts receivable.[4]
2. **Average collection period (ACP)**. This is the length of time customers are given to pay for goods following a sale. The ACP is also called the *days sales outstanding* (DSO). GBM's business plan calls for an ACP of 60 days based on its 60-day credit terms. This is also called the *receivables conversion period*, as it is supposed to take 60 days to collect and thus convert receivables to cash.
3. **Payables deferral period**. This is the length of time GBM's suppliers give it to pay for its purchases, which in our example is 40 days.

On Day 1, GBM expects to buy merchandise, and it expects to sell the goods and thus convert them to accounts receivable within 50 days. It should then take 60 days to collect the receivables, making a total of 110 days between receiving merchandise and collecting cash. However, GBM is able to defer its own payments for only 40 days.

We can combine these three periods to find the theoretical, or target, cash conversion cycle, shown below as an equation and diagrammed in Figure 16-2.

$$\begin{array}{ccccccc} \text{Inventory} & & \text{Average} & & \text{Payables} & & \text{Cash} \\ \text{conversion} & + & \text{collection} & - & \text{deferral} & = & \text{conversion} \\ \text{period} & & \text{period} & & \text{period} & & \text{cycle} \end{array} \qquad (16\text{-}1)$$

$$50 \quad + \quad 60 \quad - \quad 40 \quad = \quad 70 \text{ days}$$

FIGURE 16-2

The Cash Conversion Cycle

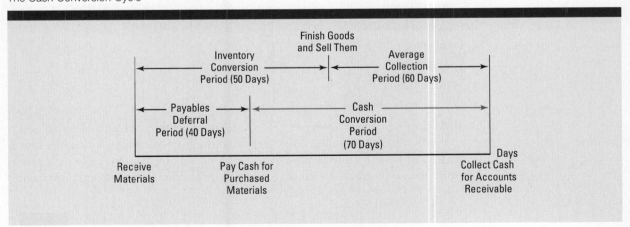

[4] If GBM were a manufacturer, the inventory conversion period would be the time required to convert raw materials into finished goods and then to sell those goods.

Although GBM is supposed to pay its suppliers $10,000,000 after 40 days, it does not expect to receive any cash until 50 + 60 = 110 days into the cycle. Therefore, it will have to borrow the $10,000,000 cost of the merchandise from its bank on Day 40, and it does not expect to be able to repay the loan until it collects on Day 110. Thus, for 110 − 40 = 70 days—which is the theoretical cash conversion cycle (CCC)—it will owe the bank $10,000,000 and it will be paying interest on this debt. The shorter the cash conversion cycle the better, because a shorter CCC means lower interest charges.

Observe that if GBM could sell goods faster, collect receivables faster, or defer its payables longer without hurting sales or increasing operating costs, then its CCC would decline, its expected interest charges would be reduced, and its expected profits and stock price would increase.

16-3b Calculating the Actual CCC from Financial Statements

So far we have illustrated the CCC from a theoretical standpoint. However, in practice we would generally calculate the CCC based on the firm's financial statements, and the actual CCC would almost certainly differ from the theoretical value because of real-world complexities such as shipping delays, sales slowdowns, and slow-paying customers. Moreover, a firm such as GBM would be continually starting new cycles before the earlier ones ended, and this too would muddy the waters.

To see how the CCC is calculated in practice, assume that GBM has been in business for several years and is in a stable position, placing orders, making sales, receiving payments, and making its own payments on a recurring basis. The following data were taken from its latest financial statements:

Selected Items from GBM's Financial Statements (Millions of Dollars)

Annual sales	$1,216.7
Cost of goods sold	1,013.9
Inventories	140.0
Accounts receivable	445.0
Accounts payable	115.0

Thus, GBM's net operating working capital due to inventory, receivables, and payables is $140 + $445 − $115 = $470 million, and that amount must be financed—in GBM's case, through bank loans at a 10% interest rate. Therefore, its interest expense is $47 million per year.

We can analyze the situation more closely. First, consider the inventory conversion period:

$$\text{Inventory conversion period} = \frac{\text{Inventory}}{\text{Cost of goods sold per day}} \qquad (16\text{-}2)$$

$$= \frac{\$140.0}{\$1,013.9/365} = 50.4 \text{ days}$$

Thus, it takes GBM an average of 50.4 days to sell its merchandise, which is very close to the 50 days called for in the business plan. Note also that inventory is carried at cost, which explains why the denominator in Equation 16-2 is the cost of goods sold per day, not daily sales.

The average collection period (or days sales outstanding) is calculated next:

$$\text{Average collection period} = \text{ACP(or DSO)} = \frac{\text{Receivables}}{\text{Sales}/365} \quad (16\text{-}3)$$

$$= \frac{\$445.0}{\$1,216.7/365} = 133.5 \text{ days}$$

Thus, it takes GBM 133.5 days after a sale to receive cash, not the 60 days called for in its business plan. Because receivables are recorded at the sales price, we use daily sales (rather than the cost of goods sold per day) in the denominator for the ACP.

The payables deferral period is found as follows, again using daily cost of goods sold in the denominator because payables are recorded at cost:

$$\frac{\text{Payables}}{\text{deferral period}} = \frac{\text{Payables}}{\text{Purchases per day}} = \frac{\text{Payables}}{\text{Cost of goods sold}/365} \quad (16\text{-}4)$$

$$= \frac{\$115.0}{\$1,013.9/365} = 41.4 \text{ days}$$

GBM is supposed to pay its suppliers after 40 days, but it actually pays on average just after Day 41. This slight delay is normal, because mail delays and time for checks to be cashed generally slow payments down a bit.

We can now combine the three periods to calculate GBM's actual cash conversion cycle:

$$\text{Cash conversion cycle(CCC)} = 50.4 \text{ days} + 133.5 \text{ days} - 41.4 \text{ days} = 142.5 \text{ days}$$

resource

*See **Ch16 Tool Kit.xls** on the textbook's Web site for details.*

Figure 16-3 summarizes all of these calculations and then analyzes why the actual CCC exceeds the theoretical CCC by such a large amount. It is clear from the figure that the firm's inventory control is working as expected in that sales match the inflow of new inventory items quite well. Also, its own payments match reasonably well the terms under which it buys. However, its accounts receivable are much higher than they should be, indicating that customers are not paying on time. In fact, they are paying 73.5 days late, which is increasing GBM's working capital. Because working capital must be financed, the collections delay is lowering the firm's profits and presumably hurting its stock price.

When the CFO reviewed the situation, she discovered that GBM's customers—doctors, hospitals, and clinics—were themselves reimbursed by insurance companies and government units, and those organizations were paying late. The credit manager was doing everything he could to collect faster, but the customers said that they just could not make their own payments until they themselves were paid. If GBM wanted to keep making sales, it seemed that it would have to accept late-paying customers. However, the CFO wondered if collections might come in faster if GBM offered substantial discounts for early payments. We will take up this issue later in the chapter.

FIGURE **16-3**

Summary of the Cash Conversion Cycle (Millions of Dollars)

	A	B	C	D	E	F	G
9	Panel a. Target CCC: Based on Planned Conditions						
10	Cash Conversion Cycle (CCC)	=	Planned Inventory Conversion Period (ICP)	+	Credit Terms Offered to Our Customers	−	Credit Terms Our Supplier Offers Us
11		=	50.0	+	60.0	−	40.0
12	Target CCC	=	70.0				
13	Panel b. Actual CCC: Based on Financial Statements						
14							
15	Sales	$1,216.7					
16	COGS	$1,013.9					
17	Inventories	$140.0					
18	Receivables	$445.0					
19	Payables	$115.0					
20	Days/year	365					
21	Actual CCC	=	Inventory ÷ (COGS/365)	+	Receivables ÷ (Sales/365)		Payables ÷ (COGS/365)
22		=	$140 ÷ ($1,013.9/365)	+	$445 ÷ ($1,216.7/365)		$115 ÷ ($1,013.9/365)
23		=	50.4	+	133.5		41.4
24	Actual CCC	=	142.5				
25	Panel c. Actual versus Target Components						
26			ICP		ACP		PDP
27	Actual − Target	=	50.4 - 50.0		133.5 - 60.0		41.4 - 40.0
28		=	0.4	+	73.5	−	1.4
29	% Difference	=	0.8%		122.5%		3.5%
30	Evaluation	=	OK		VERY BAD		OK

Note:

GBM's inventories are in line with its plans, and it is paying its suppliers nearly on time. However, some of its customers are paying quite late, so its average collection period (or DSO) is 133.5 days even though all customers are supposed to pay by Day 60.

16-3c Benefits of Reducing the CCC

As we have seen, GBM currently has a CCC of 142.5 days, which results in $470 million being tied up in net operating working capital. Assuming that its cost of debt to carry working capital is 10%, this means that the firm is incurring interest charges of $47 million per year to carry its working capital. Now suppose the company can speed up its sales enough to reduce the inventory conversion period from 50.4 to 35.0 days. In addition, it begins to offer discounts for early payment and thereby reduces its average collection period to 40 days. Finally, assume that it could negotiate a change in its own payment terms from 40 to 50 days. The "New" column of Figure 16-4 shows the net effects of these improvements: a 117.5-day reduction in the cash conversion cycle and a reduction in net operating working capital from $470.0 to $91.7 million, which saves $37.8 million of interest.

Recall also that free cash flow (FCF) is equal to NOPAT minus the net new investment in operating capital. Therefore, if working capital *decreases* by a given amount

FIGURE 16-4

Benefits from Reducing the Cash Conversion Cycle (Millions of Dollars)

	A	B	C	D	E	F	G
39					Old (Actual)		New (Target)
40	Inventory conversion period (ICP, days)				50.4		35.0
41	Average collection period (ACP, days)				133.5		40.0
42	Payable deferral period (PDP, days)				−41.4		−50.0
43	Cash Collection Cycle (CCC, days)				142.5		25.0
44							
45	Reduction in CCC					117.5	
46							
47	Effects of the CCC Reduction						
48	Annual sales				$1,216.7		$1,216.7
49	Costs of goods sold (COGS)				$1,013.9		$1,013.9
50	Inventory = Actual Old, New = new ICP(COGS/365)				$140.0		$97.2
51	Receivables = Actual Old, New = new ACP(Sales/365)				$445.0		$133.3
52	Payables = Actual Old, New = new PDP(COGS/365)				−$115.0		−$138.9
53	Net operating WC = Inv + Receivables − Payables				$470.0		$91.7
54							
55	Reduction in NOWC					$378.3	
56	Reduction in interest expense @ 10%					$37.8	

while other things remain constant, then FCF *increases* by that same amount—$378.3 million in the GBM example. If sales remained constant in the following years, then this reduction in working capital would simply be a one-time cash inflow. However, suppose sales grow in future years. When a company improves its working capital management, the components (inventory conversion period, collection period, and payments period) usually remain at their improved levels, which means the NOWC-to-Sales ratio remains at its new level. With an improved NOWC-to-Sales ratio, less working capital will be required to support future sales, leading to higher annual FCFs than would have otherwise existed.

Thus, an improvement in working capital management creates a large one-time increase in FCF at the time of the improvement as well as higher FCF in future years. Therefore, an improvement in working capital management is a gift that keeps on giving.

These benefits can add substantial value to the company. Professors Hyun-Han Shin and Luc Soenen studied more than 2,900 companies over a 20-year period, finding a strong relationship between a company's cash conversion cycle and its stock performance.[5] For an average company, a 10-day improvement in its CCC was associated with an increase in pre-tax operating profit margin from 12.76% to 13.02%. Moreover, companies with cash conversion cycles 10 days shorter than the average for their industry had annual stock returns that were 1.7 percentage points higher than the average company. Given results like these, it's no wonder firms place so much emphasis on working capital management![6]

---

[5]Hyun-Han Shin and Luc Soenen, "Efficiency of Working Capital Management and Corporate Profitability," *Financial Practice and Education,* Fall/Winter 1998, pp. 37–45.

[6]For more on the CCC, see James A. Gentry, R. Vaidyanathan, and Hei Wai Lee, "A Weighted Cash Conversion Cycle," *Financial Management,* Spring 1990, pp. 90–99.

Some Firms Operate with Negative Working Capital!

© Rob Webb/Getty Images

Some firms are able to operate with zero or even negative net working capital. Dell Computer and Amazon are examples. When customers order computers from Dell's Web site or books from Amazon, they must provide a credit card number. Dell and Amazon then receive next-day cash, even before the product is shipped and even before they have paid their own suppliers. This results in a negative CCC, which means that working capital *provides* cash rather than *uses* it.

In order to grow, companies normally need cash for working capital. However, if the CCC is negative then growth in sales *provides* cash rather than *uses* it. This cash can be invested in plant and equipment, research and development, or for any other corporate purpose. Analysts recognize this point when they value Dell and Amazon, and it certainly helps their stock prices.

SELF-TEST

Define the following terms: inventory conversion period, average collection period, and payables deferral period. Give the equation for each term.

What is the cash conversion cycle? What is its equation?

What should a firm's goal be regarding the cash conversion cycle, holding other things constant? Explain your answer.

What are some actions a firm can take to shorten its cash conversion cycle?

A company has $20 million of inventory, $5 million of receivables, and $4 million of payables. Its annual sales revenue is $80 million, and its cost of goods sold is $60 million. What is its CCC? **(120.15)**

16-4 The Cash Budget

resource

*See **Ch16 Tool Kit.xls** on the textbook's Web site for details.*

Firms must forecast their cash flows. If they are likely to need additional cash, then they should line up funds well in advance. Yet if they are likely to generate surplus cash, then they should plan for its productive use. The primary forecasting tool is the cash budget, illustrated in Figure 16-5, which is taken from the chapter's *Excel **Tool Kit*** model. The illustrative company is Educational Products Corporation (EPC), which supplies educational materials to schools and retailers in the Midwest. Sales are cyclical, peaking in September and then declining for the balance of the year.

16-4a Monthly Cash Budgets

Cash budgets can be of any length, but EPC and most companies use a monthly cash budget, such as the one in Figure 16-5, but set up for 12 months. We used only 6 months for the purpose of illustration. The monthly budget is used for longer-range planning, but a daily cash budget is also prepared at the start of each month to provide a more precise picture of the daily cash flows for use in scheduling actual payments on a day-by-day basis.

The cash budget focuses on cash flows, but it also includes information on forecasted sales, credit policy, and inventory management. Because the statement is a forecast and

FIGURE 16-5

EPC's Cash Budget, July–December 2014 (Millions of Dollars)

	A	B	C	D	E	F	G	H	I	J	K	L	M	N
144	**Base Case**					May	June	July	August	Sept	Oct	Nov	Dec	Jan
145	*Forecasted gross sales (manual inputs):*					$200	$250	$300	$400	$500	$350	$250	$200	$200
146	Adjustment: % deviation from forecast					0%	0%	0%	0%	0%	0%	0%	0%	0%
147	Adjusted gross sales forecast					$200	$250	$300	$400	$500	$350	$250	$200	$200
148	*Collections on sales:*													
149	During sales' month: 0.2 (Sales)(1 – discount %)							$58.8	$78.4	$98.0	$68.6	$49.0	$39.2	
150	During 2nd month: 0.7 (prior month's sales)							$175.0	$210.0	$280.0	$350.0	$245.0	$175.0	
151	Due in 3rd month: 0.1 (sales 2 months ago)							$20.0	$25.0	$30.0	$40.0	$50.0	$35.0	
152	Less bad debts (BD% × Sales 2 months ago)							$0.0	$0.0	$0.0	$0.0	$0.0	$0.0	
153	Total collections							$253.8	$313.4	$408.0	$458.6	$344.0	$249.2	
154	*Purchases: 60% of next month's sales*					$180.0	$240.0	$300.0	$210.0	$150.0	$120.0	$120.0		
155	*Payments*													
156	Pmt for last month's purchases (30 days of credit)							$180.0	$240.0	$300.0	$210.0	$150.0	$120.0	
157	Wages and salaries							$30.0	$40.0	$50.0	$40.0	$30.0	$30.0	
158	Lease payments							$30.0	$30.0	$30.0	$30.0	$30.0	$30.0	
159	Other payments (interest on LT bonds, dividends, etc.)							$30.0	$30.0	$30.0	$30.0	$30.0	$30.0	
160	Taxes									$30.0			$30.0	
161	Payment for plant construction									$150.0				
162	Total payments							$270.0	$340.0	$590.0	$310.0	$240.0	$240.0	
163	*Net cash flows:*													
164	Assumed <u>excess</u> cash on hand at start of forecast period							$0.0						
165	Net cash flow (NCF): Total collections – Total payments							–$16.2	–$26.6	–$182.0	$148.6	$104.0	$9.2	
166	Cumulative NCF: Prior month cum plus this month's NCF							–$16.2	–$42.8	–$224.8	–$76.2	$27.8	$37.0	
167	*Cash surplus (or loan requirement)*													
168	Target cash balance							$10.0	$10.0	$10.0	$10.0	$10.0	$10.0	
169	Surplus cash or loan needed: Cum NCF – Target cash							–$26.2	–$52.8	–$234.8	–$86.2	$17.8	$27.0	
170	Max required loan (most <u>negative</u> on Row 169)		$234.8											
171	Max investable funds (most <u>positive</u> on Row 169)		$27.0											

Notes:

1. Although the budget period is July through December, sales and purchases data for May and June are needed to determine collections and payments during July and August.

2. Firms can both borrow and pay off commercial loans on a daily basis, so the $26.2 million loan needed for July would likely be gradually borrowed as needed on a daily basis, and during October the $234.8 million loan that presumably existed at the beginning of the month would be reduced daily to the $86.2 million ending balance—which, in turn, would be completely paid off sometime during November.

3. The data in the figure are for EPC's base-case forecast. Data for alternative scenarios are shown in the chapter's *Excel Tool Kit* model.

not a report on historical results, actual results could vary from the figures given. Therefore, the cash budget is generally set up as an expected, or base-case, forecast, but it is created with a model that makes it easy to generate alternative forecasts to see what would happen under different conditions.

Figure 16-5 begins with a forecast of sales for each month on Row 145. Then, on Row 146, it shows possible percentage deviations from the forecasted sales. Because we are showing the base-case forecast, no adjustments are made, but the model is set up to show the effects if sales increase or decrease and so result in "adjusted sales" that are above or below the forecasted levels.

The company sells on terms of "2/10, net 60." This means that a 2% discount is given if payment is made within 10 days; otherwise, the full amount is due in 60 days. However, like most companies, EPC finds that some customers pay late. Experience shows that 20% of customers pay during the month of the sale and take the discount. Another 70% pay during the month immediately following the sale, and 10% are late, paying in the second month after the sale.[7]

The statement (Line 154) next shows forecasted materials purchases, which equal 60% of the following month's sales. EPC buys on terms of net 30, meaning that it receives no discounts and is required to pay for its purchases within 30 days of the purchase date. The purchases information is followed by forecasted payments for materials, labor, leases, other payments such as dividends and interest on long-term bonds, taxes (due in September and December), and a payment of $150 million in September for a new plant that is being constructed.

When the total forecasted payments are subtracted from the forecasted collections, the result is the expected net cash gain or loss for each month. This gain or loss is added to or subtracted from the excess cash on hand at the start of the forecast (which we assume was zero), and the result—the *cumulative net cash flow*—is the amount of cash the firm would have on hand at the end of the month if it neither borrowed nor invested.

EPC's target cash balance is $10 million, and it plans either to borrow to meet this target or to invest surplus funds if it generates more cash than it needs. How the target cash balance is determined is discussed later in the chapter, but EPC believes that it needs $10 million.

By subtracting the target cash balance from the cumulative cash flow, we calculate the *loan needed or surplus cash*, as shown on Row 169. A negative number indicates that we need a loan, whereas a positive number indicates that we forecast surplus cash that is available for investment or other uses.

We total the net cash flows on Row 165 and show the cumulative total on Row 166. Cell M166 shows that the cumulative for the forecast period is $37 million. Because this number is positive, it indicates that EPC's cumulative cash flow is positive. Also, note that EPC borrows on a basis that allows it to borrow or repay loans on a daily basis. Thus, it would borrow a total of $26.2 million in July, increasing the loan daily, and would continue to build up the loan through September. Then, when its cash flows turn positive in October, it would start repaying the loan on a daily basis and completely pay it off sometime in November, assuming that everything works out as forecasted.

Note that our cash budget is incomplete in that it shows neither interest paid on the working capital loans nor interest earned on the positive cash balances. These amounts could be added to the budget simply by adding rows and including them. Similarly, if the firm makes quarterly dividend payments, principal payments on its long-term bonds, or any other payments, or if it has investment income, then those cash flows also could be added to the statement. In our simplified statement, we just lumped all such payments into "other payments."

Under the base-case forecast, the CFO will need to arrange a line of credit so that the firm can borrow up to $234.8 million, increasing the loan over time as funds are needed and repaying it later when cash flows become positive. The treasurer would show the cash budget to the bankers when negotiating for the line of credit. Lenders would want to know how much the firm expects to need, when the funds will be needed, and when the loan will be repaid. The lenders—and EPC's top executives—would question the treasurer

---

[7]Because we are using a monthly forecast instead of a daily forecast, we assume that all purchases are made on the first day of the month. Thus, discounted payments are received in the month of the sale, regular payments are received in the month after the sale, and late payments are received two months after the sale. Obviously, a daily budget would be more accurate. Also, a negligible percentage of sales results in bad debts. The low bad-debt losses evident here result from EPC's careful screening of customers and its generally tight credit policies. However, the cash budget model is able to show the effects of bad debts, so EPC's CFO could show top management how cash flows would be affected if the firm relaxed its credit policy in order to stimulate sales or if the recession worsened and more customers were forced to delay payments.

about the budget, and they would want to know how the forecasts would be affected if sales were higher or lower than those projected, how changes in customers' payment times would affect the forecasts, and the like. The focus would be on these two questions: *How accurate is the forecast likely to be? What would be the effects of significant errors?* The first question could best be answered by examining historical forecasts, and the second by running different scenarios as we do in the *Excel Tool Kit* model.

resource

See **Ch16 Tool Kit.xls** on the textbook's Web site for details.

No matter how hard we try, no forecast will ever be exactly correct, and this includes cash budgets. You can imagine the bank's reaction if the company negotiated a loan of $235 million and then came back a few months later saying that it had underestimated its requirements and needed to boost the loan to say $260 million. The banker might refuse, thinking the company was not well managed. Therefore, EPC's treasurer would undoubtedly want to build a cushion into the line of credit—say, a maximum commitment of $260 million rather than the forecasted requirement of $234.8 million. However, as we discuss later in the chapter, banks charge commitment fees for guaranteed lines of credit; thus, the higher the cushion built into the line of credit, the more costly the credit will be. This is another reason why it is important to develop accurate forecasts.

16-4b Cash Budgets versus Income Statements and Free Cash Flows

If you look at the cash budget, it looks similar to an income statement. However, the two statements are quite different. Here are some key differences: (1) In an income statement, the focus would be on sales, not collections. (2) An income statement would show accrued taxes, wages, and so forth, not the actual payments. (3) An income statement would show depreciation as an expense, but it would not show expenditures on new fixed assets. (4) An income statement would show a cost for goods purchased when those goods were sold, not for when they were ordered or paid.

These are obviously large differences, so it would be a big mistake to confuse a cash budget with an income statement. Also, the cash flows shown on the cash budget are different from the firm's free cash flows, because FCF reflects after-tax operating income and the investments required to maintain future operations whereas the cash budget reflects only the actual cash inflows and outflows during a particular period.

The bottom line is that cash budgets, income statements, and free cash flows are all important and are related to one another, but they are also quite different. Each is designed for a specific purpose, and the main purpose of the cash budget is to forecast the firm's liquidity position, not its profitability.

16-4c Daily Cash Budgets

resource

See **Ch16 Tool Kit.xls** on the textbook's Web site for details.

Note that if cash inflows and outflows do not occur uniformly during each month, then the actual funds needed might be quite different from the indicated amounts. The data in Figure 16-5 show the situation on the last day of each month, and we see that the maximum projected loan during the forecast period is $234.8 million. Yet if all payments had to be made on the 1st of the month but most collections came on the 30th, then EPC would have to make $270 million of payments in July before it received the $253.8 million from collections. In that case, the firm would need to borrow about $270 million in July, not the $26.2 million shown in Figure 16-5. This would make the bank unhappy—perhaps so unhappy that it would not extend the requested credit. A daily cash budget would have revealed this situation.

Figure 16-5 was prepared using *Excel*, which makes it easy to change the assumptions. In the ***Tool Kit*** model we examine the cash flow effects of changes in sales, in customers' payment patterns, and so forth. Also, the effects of changes in credit policy and inventory management could be examined through the cash budget.

SELF-TEST

How could the cash budget be used when negotiating the terms of a bank loan?

How would a shift from a tight credit policy to a relaxed policy be likely to affect a firm's cash budget?

How would the cash budget be affected if our firm's suppliers offered us terms of "2/10, net 30," rather than "net 30," and we decided to take the discount?

Suppose a firm's cash flows do not occur uniformly throughout the month. What effect would this have on the accuracy of the forecasted borrowing requirements based on a monthly cash budget? How could the firm deal with this problem?

16-5 Cash Management and the Target Cash Balance

Companies need cash to pay for expenses related to daily ongoing operations, including labor, raw materials, utility bills, and taxes. Companies also need cash for several other predictable purposes, including major purchases and payments to investors (interest payments, principal payments, and dividend payments). Following are the issues that companies consider when deciding how much cash to hold in support of ongoing operations. We discuss major purchases and payments to investors in Section 16-10.

16-5a Routine (but Uncertain) Operating Transactions

Cash balances are necessary in business operations. Payments must be made in cash, and receipts are deposited in the cash account. Cash balances associated with routine payments and collections are known as **transactions balances**. Cash inflows and outflows are unpredictable, and the degree of predictability varies among firms and industries. Therefore, firms need to hold some cash to meet random, unforeseen fluctuations in inflows and outflows. These "safety stocks" are called **precautionary balances**, and the less predictable the firm's cash flows, the larger such balances should be. Research confirms this and shows that companies with volatile cash flows do in fact hold higher cash balances.[8]

In addition to holding cash for transactions and precautionary reasons, it is essential that the firm have sufficient cash to take **trade discounts**. Suppliers frequently offer customers discounts for early payment of bills. As we will see later in this chapter, the cost of not taking discounts is sometimes very high, so firms should have enough cash to permit payment of bills in time to take advantage of discounts.

Many companies have a line of credit to cover unexpected cash needs; we discuss lines of credit in Section 16-12.

---

[8]See Tim Opler, Lee Pinkowitz, René Stulz, and Rohan Williamson, "The Determinants and Implications of Corporate Cash Holdings," *Journal of Financial Economics,* 1999, pp. 3–46.

16-5b Compensating Balances

A bank makes money by lending out funds that have been deposited with it, so the larger its deposits, the better the bank's profit position. If a bank is providing services to a customer, then it may require that customer to leave a minimum balance on deposit to help offset the costs of providing those services. Also, banks may require borrowers to hold their transactions deposits at the bank. Both types of deposits are called **compensating balances**. In a 1979 survey, 84.7% of responding companies reported they were required to maintain compensating balances to help pay for bank services; only 13.3% reported paying direct fees for banking services.[9] By 1996, those findings were reversed: Only 28% paid for bank services with compensating balances, while 83% paid direct fees.[10] Although the use of compensating balances to pay for services has declined, these balances improve a firm's relationship with its bank and are still a reason why some companies hold additional cash.

SELF-TEST

Why is cash management important?

What are the primary motives for holding cash?

16-6 Cash Management Techniques

In terms of dollar volume, most business is conducted by large firms, many of which operate nationally or globally. They collect cash from many sources and make payments from a number of different cities or even countries. For example, companies such as IBM, General Electric, and Hewlett-Packard have manufacturing plants all around the world, even more sales offices, and bank accounts in virtually every city in which they do business. Their collection centers follow sales patterns. However, while some disbursements are made from local offices, most are made in the cities where manufacturing occurs or from the home office. Thus, a major corporation might have hundreds or even thousands of bank accounts located in cities all over the globe, but there is no reason to think that inflows and outflows will balance in each account. Therefore, a system must be in place to transfer funds from where they come in to where they are needed, to arrange loans to cover net corporate shortfalls, and to invest net corporate surpluses without delay. Some commonly used techniques for accomplishing these tasks are discussed next.[11]

16-6a Synchronizing Cash Flow

If you as an individual were to receive income once a year, then you would probably put it in the bank, draw down your account periodically, and have an average balance for the year equal to about half of your annual income. If instead you received income weekly and paid rent, tuition, and other charges on a daily basis, then your average bank balance

---

[9]See Lawrence J. Gitman, E. A. Moses, and I. T. White, "An Assessment of Corporate Cash Management Practices," *Financial Management,* Spring 1979, pp. 32–41.

[10]See Charles E. Maxwell, Lawrence J. Gitman, and Stephanie A. M. Smith, "Working Capital Management and Financial-Service Consumption Preferences of US and Foreign Firms: A Comparison of 1979 and 1996 Preferences," *Financial Practice and Education,* Fall/Winter 1998, pp. 46–52.

[11]For more information on cash management, see Bruce J. Summers, "Clearing and Payment Systems: The Role of the Central Bank," *Federal Reserve Bulletin*, February 1991, pp. 81–91.

would still be about half of your periodic receipts and thus only 1/52 as large as if you received income only once annually.

Exactly the same situation holds for businesses: By timing their cash receipts to coincide with their cash outlays, firms can hold their transactions balances to a minimum. Recognizing this fact, firms such as utilities, oil companies, and credit card companies arrange to bill customers—and to pay their own bills—on regular "billing cycles" throughout the month. This **synchronization of cash flows** provides cash when it is needed and thus enables firms to reduce their average cash balances.

16-6b Speeding Up the Check-Clearing Process

When a customer writes and mails a check, the funds are not available to the receiving firm until the **check-clearing process** has been completed. First, the check must be delivered through the mail. Checks received from customers in distant cities are especially subject to mail delays.

When a customer's check is written on one bank and a company deposits the check in another bank, the company's bank must verify that the check is valid before the payee can use those funds. Checks are generally cleared through the Federal Reserve System or through a clearinghouse set up by the banks in a particular city.[12] Before 2004, this process sometimes took 2 to 5 days. But with the passage of a federal law in 2004 known as "Check 21," banks can exchange digital images of checks. This means that most checks now clear in a single day.

16-6c Using Float

Float is defined as the difference between the balance shown in a firm's (or individual's) checkbook and the balance on the bank's records. Suppose a firm writes, on average, checks in the amount of $5,000 each day, and suppose it takes 6 days for these checks to clear and be deducted from the firm's bank account. This will cause the firm's own checkbook to show a balance that is $30,000 smaller than the balance on the bank's records; this difference is called **disbursement float**. Now suppose the firm also receives checks in the amount of $5,000 daily but that it loses 4 days while those checks are being deposited and cleared. This will result in $20,000 of **collections float**. In total, the firm's **net float**—the difference between the $30,000 positive disbursement float and the $20,000 negative collections float—will be $10,000. In sum, collections float is bad, disbursement float is good, and positive net float is even better.

Delays that cause float will occur because it takes time for checks to (1) travel through the mail (mail float), (2) be processed by the receiving firm (processing float), and (3) clear through the banking system (clearing, or availability, float). Basically, the size of a firm's net float is a function of its ability to speed up collections on checks it receives and to slow down collections on checks it writes. Efficient firms go to great lengths to speed up the processing of incoming checks, thus putting the funds to work faster, and they try to stretch their own payments out as long as possible, sometimes by disbursing checks from banks in remote locations.

---

[12]For example, suppose a check for $100 is written on Bank A and deposited at Bank B. Bank B will usually contact either the Federal Reserve System or a clearinghouse to which both banks belong. The Fed or the clearinghouse will then verify with Bank A that the check is valid and that the account has sufficient funds to cover the check. Bank A's account with the Fed or the clearinghouse is then reduced by $100, and Bank B's account is increased by $100. Of course, if the check is deposited in the same bank on which it was drawn, that bank merely transfers funds by bookkeeping entries from one depositor to another.

Your Check Isn't in the Mail

© Rob Webb/Getty Images

Issuing payroll checks to thousands of employees is expensive—in both the time and resources it takes the company to print, process, and deliver the checks, and in the time it takes the employee to deposit or cash the check. Paper checks cost a company between $1 and $2 each, and multiply that by thousands of employees, some of whom are paid weekly or biweekly, it adds up to a lot of money every year. Direct deposit of payroll checks into the employee's checking account reduces these costs, but there are still many employees, especially seasonal, temporary, part-time, or young employees, who don't have a checking account.

A growing solution to high check costs and the needs of these "unbanked" employees is the payroll debit card. Companies, in partnership with a bank, issue the employee a debit card that is automatically filled each payday. The employee either uses the debit card to make purchases or withdraws cash at an ATM. The cost to load a debit card is around $0.20, and so saves the companies 80% to 90% of the cost to print a check, and saves the unbanked employee from paying the frequently usurious check-cashing fees that can be 10% or more. In fact, because debit card transactions that are processed as a credit card result in fees to the merchant, there is a small amount of money available to provide a rebate to the employer. For example, Premier Pay Cards offers a 0.1% rebate to the employer on certain purchases the employee makes with the debit card.

Although the use of a debit card for payroll eliminates the float that would occur with check-based pay, for many companies the reduced processing costs and increased employee satisfaction more than outweigh the reduction in float.

Sources: "The End of the Paycheck," *Fortune Small Business Magazine*, December 5, 2006, and **www.premierpaycards.com**.

16-6d Speeding Up Collections

Two major techniques are used to speed collections and to get funds where they are needed: lockboxes and electronic transfers.

LOCKBOXES

A **lockbox system** is one of the oldest cash management tools. In a lockbox system, incoming checks are sent to post office boxes rather than to the firm's corporate headquarters. For example, a firm headquartered in New York City might have its West Coast customers send their payments to a post office box in San Francisco, its customers in the Southwest send their checks to Dallas, and so on, rather than having all checks sent to New York City. Several times a day, a local bank will empty the lockbox and deposit the checks into the company's local account. The bank then provides the firm with a daily record of the receipts collected, usually via an electronic data transmission system in a format that permits online updating of the firm's accounts receivable records.

A lockbox system reduces the time required to receive incoming checks, to deposit them, and to get them cleared through the banking system and available for use. Lockbox services can make funds available as many as 2 to 5 days faster than via the "regular" system.

PAYMENT BY WIRE OR AUTOMATIC DEBIT

Firms are increasingly demanding payments of larger bills by wire or by automatic electronic debits. Under an electronic debit system, funds are automatically deducted from one account and added to another. This is, of course, the ultimate in speeding up a collection process, and computer technology is making such a process increasingly feasible and efficient, even for retail transactions.

SELF-TEST

What is float? How do firms use float to increase cash management efficiency?

What are some methods firms can use to accelerate receipts?

16-7 Inventory Management

Inventory management techniques are covered in depth in production management courses. Still, financial managers have a responsibility for raising the capital needed to carry inventory and for overseeing the firm's overall profitability, so it is appropriate that we cover the financial aspects of inventory management here.

The twin goals of inventory management are (1) ensuring that the inventories needed to sustain operations are available, while (2) holding the costs of ordering and carrying inventories to the lowest possible level. In analyzing improvements in the cash conversion cycle, we identified some of the cash flows associated with a reduction in inventory. In addition to the points made earlier, lower inventory levels reduce costs due to storage and handling, insurance, property taxes, spoilage, and obsolescence.

Before the computer age, companies used simple inventory control techniques such as the "red line" system, where a red line was drawn around the inside of a bin holding inventory items; when the actual stock declined to the level where the red line showed, inventory would be reordered. Now computers have taken over, and supply chains have been established that provide inventory items just before they are needed—the *just-in-time* system. For example, consider Trane Corporation, which makes air conditioners and currently uses just-in-time procedures. In the past, Trane produced parts on a steady basis, stored them as inventory, and had them ready whenever the company received an order for a batch of air conditioners. However, the company's inventory eventually covered an area equal to three football fields, and it still could take as long as 15 days to fill an order. To make matters worse, occasionally some of the necessary components simply could not be located; in other instances, the components were located but found to have been damaged from long storage.

Then Trane adopted a new inventory policy—it began producing components only after receiving an order and then sending the parts directly from the machines that make them to the final assembly line. The net effect: Inventories fell nearly 40% even as sales were increasing by 30%.

Such improvements in inventory management can free up considerable amounts of cash. For example, suppose a company has sales of $120 million and an inventory turnover ratio of 3. This means the company has an inventory level of

$$\text{Inventory} = \text{Sales}/(\text{Inventory turnover ratio})$$
$$= \$120/3 = \$40 \text{ million}$$

If the company can improve its inventory turnover ratio to 4, then its inventory will fall to

$$\text{Inventory} = \$120/4 = \$30 \text{ million}$$

This $10 million reduction in inventory boosts free cash flow by $10 million.

However, there are costs associated with holding too little inventory, and these costs can be severe. If a business lowers its inventories, then it must reorder frequently, which increases ordering costs. Even worse, if stocks become depleted then firms can miss out on profitable sales and also suffer lost goodwill, which may lead to lower future sales.

Supply Chain Management

© Rob Webb/Getty Images

Herman Miller Inc. manufactures a wide variety of office furniture, and a typical order from a single customer might require work at five different plants. Each plant uses components from different suppliers, and each plant works on orders for many customers. Imagine all the coordination this requires. The sales force generates the order, the purchasing department orders components from suppliers, and the suppliers must order materials from their own suppliers. The suppliers make and then ship the components to Herman Miller, the factory builds the products, the different products are gathered together to complete the order, and then the order is shipped to the customer. If one part of that process malfunctions, then the order will be delayed, inventory will pile up, extra costs to expedite the order will be incurred, and the customer's goodwill will be damaged, hurting future growth.

To prevent such consequences, many companies employ supply chain management (SCM). The key element in SCM is sharing information all the way back from the retailer where the product is sold, to the company's own plant, then back to the firm's suppliers, and even back to the suppliers' suppliers. SCM requires special computer software, but even more important, it requires cooperation among the different companies and departments in the supply chain. This culture of open communication is often difficult for companies, because they are reluctant to divulge operating information. For example, EMC Corp., a manufacturer of data storage systems, has become deeply involved in the design processes and financial controls of its key suppliers. Many of EMC's suppliers were initially wary of these new relationships. However, SCM has been a win–win proposition, resulting in higher profits for both EMC and its suppliers.

The same is true at many other companies. After implementing SCM, Herman Miller was able to reduce its days of inventory on hand by a week and to cut 2 weeks off delivery times to customers. It was also able to operate its plants at a 20% higher volume without additional capital expenditures, because downtime due to inventory shortages was virtually eliminated. As another example, Heineken USA can now get beer from its Dutch breweries to its customers' shelves in less than 6 weeks, compared with 10 to 12 weeks before implementing SCM. As these and other companies have found, SCM increases free cash flows, and that leads to more profits and higher stock prices.

Sources: Elaine L. Appleton, "Supply Chain Brain," *CFO,* July 1997, pp. 51–54; and Kris Frieswick, "Up Close and Virtual," *CFO,* April 1998, pp. 87–91.

Therefore, it is important to have enough inventory on hand to meet customer demands but not so much as to incur the costs we discussed previously. Inventory optimization models have been developed, but the best approach—and the one most firms today are following—is to use supply chain management and monitor the system closely.[13]

SELF-TEST

What are some costs associated with high inventories? With low inventories?

What is a "supply chain," and how are supply chains related to just-in-time inventory procedures?

A company has $20 million in sales and an inventory turnover ratio of 2.0. If it can reduce its inventory and improve its inventory turnover ratio to 2.5 with no loss in sales, by how much will FCF increase? **($2 million)**

---

[13]For additional insights into the problems of inventory management, see Richard A. Followill, Michael Schellenger, and Patrick H. Marchard, "Economic Order Quantities, Volume Discounts, and Wealth Maximization," *The Financial Review*, February 1990, pp. 143–152.

16-8 Receivables Management

Firms would, in general, rather sell for cash than on credit, but competitive pressures force most firms to offer credit for substantial purchases, especially to other businesses. Thus, goods are shipped, inventories are reduced, and an **account receivable** is created.[14] Eventually, the customer will pay the account, at which time (1) the firm will receive cash and (2) its receivables will decline. Carrying receivables has both direct and indirect costs, but selling on credit also has an important benefit: increased sales.

Receivables management begins with the firm's credit policy, but a monitoring system is also important to keep tabs on whether the terms of credit are being observed. Corrective action is often needed, and the only way to know whether the situation is getting out of hand is with a good receivables control system.[15]

16-8a Credit Policy

The success or failure of a business depends primarily on the demand for its products—as a rule, high sales lead to larger profits and a higher stock price. Sales, in turn, depend on a number of factors: Some, like the state of the economy, are exogenous, but others are under the firm's control. The major controllable factors are sales prices, product quality, advertising, and the firm's **credit policy**. Credit policy, in turn, consists of the following four variables.

1. *Credit period.* A firm might sell on terms of "net 30," which means that the customer must pay within 30 days.
2. *Discounts.* If the credit terms are stated as "2/10, net 30," then buyers may deduct 2% of the purchase price if payment is made within 10 days; otherwise, the full amount must be paid within 30 days. Thus, these terms allow a discount to be taken.
3. *Credit standards.* How much financial strength must a customer show to qualify for credit? Lower credit standards boost sales, but they also increase bad debts.
4. *Collection policy.* How tough or lax is a company in attempting to collect slow-paying accounts? A tough policy may speed up collections, but it might also anger customers and cause them to take their business elsewhere.

The credit manager is responsible for administering the firm's credit policy. However, because of the pervasive importance of credit, the credit policy itself is normally established by the executive committee, which usually consists of the president plus the vice presidents of finance, marketing, and production.

16-8b The Accumulation of Receivables

The total amount of accounts receivable outstanding at any given time is determined by two factors: (1) the credit sales per day and (2) the average length of time it takes to collect cash on accounts receivable:

---

[14]Whenever goods are sold on credit, two accounts are created—an asset item entitled *accounts receivable* appears on the books of the selling firm, and a liability item called *accounts payable* appears on the books of the purchaser. At this point, we are analyzing the transaction from the viewpoint of the seller, so we are concentrating on the variables under its control (i.e., the receivables). We examine the transaction from the viewpoint of the purchaser later in this chapter, where we discuss accounts payable as a source of funds and consider their cost.

[15]For more on credit policy and receivables management, see Shehzad L. Mian and Clifford W. Smith, "Extending Trade Credit and Financing Receivables," *Journal of Applied Corporate Finance,* Spring 1994, pp. 75–84; and Paul D. Adams, Steve B. Wyatt, and Yong H. Kim, "A Contingent Claims Analysis of Trade Credit," *Financial Management,* Autumn 1992, pp. 104–112.

$$\underset{\text{receivable}}{\text{Accounts}} = \underset{\text{per day}}{\text{Credit sales}} \times \underset{\text{collection period}}{\text{Length of}} \tag{16-5}$$

For example, suppose Boston Lumber Company (BLC), a wholesale distributor of lumber products, opens a warehouse on January 1 and, starting the first day, makes sales of $1,000 each day. For simplicity, we assume that all sales are on credit and that customers are given 10 days to pay. At the end of the first day, accounts receivable will be $1,000; they will rise to $2,000 by the end of the second day; and by January 10, they will have risen to 10($1,000) = $10,000. On January 11, another $1,000 will be added to receivables, but payments for sales made on January 1 will be collected and thus will reduce receivables by $1,000, so total accounts receivable will remain constant at $10,000. Once the firm's operations have stabilized, the following situation will exist:

$$\begin{aligned}\underset{\text{receivable}}{\text{Accounts}} &= \underset{\text{per day}}{\text{Credit sales}} \times \underset{\text{collection period}}{\text{Length of}}\\ &= \quad \$1,000 \quad \times \quad \text{10 days} \quad = \$10,000\end{aligned}$$

If either credit sales or the collection period changes, these changes will be reflected in the accounts receivable balance.

16-8c Monitoring the Receivables Position

Both investors and bank loan officers should pay close attention to accounts receivable, because what you see on a financial statement is not necessarily what you end up getting. To see why, consider how the accounting system operates. When a credit sale is made, these events occur: (1) inventories are reduced by the cost of goods sold, (2) accounts receivable are increased by the sales price, and (3) the difference is reported as a profit, which is adjusted for taxes and then added to the previous retained earnings balance. If the sale is for cash, then the cash from the sale has actually been received by the firm and the scenario just described is completely valid. If the sale is on credit, however, then the firm will not receive the cash from the sale unless and until the account is collected. Firms have been known to encourage "sales" to weak customers in order to report high current profits. This could boost the firm's stock price—but only for a short time. Eventually, credit losses will lower earnings, at which time the stock price will fall. This is another example of how differences between a firm's stock price and its intrinsic value can arise, and it is something that security analysts must keep in mind.

An analysis along the lines suggested in the following sections will detect any such questionable practice, and it will also help a firm's management learn of problems that might be arising. Such early detection helps both investors and bankers avoid losses, and it also helps a firm's management maximize intrinsic values.

DAYS SALES OUTSTANDING (DSO)

Suppose Super Sets Inc., a television manufacturer, sells 200,000 television sets a year at a price of $198 each. Assume that all sales are on credit under the terms 2/10, net 30. Finally, assume that 70% of the customers take the discount and pay on Day 10 and that the other 30% pay on Day 30.[16]

---

[16]Unless otherwise noted, we assume throughout that payments are made either on the *last day* for taking discounts or on the *last day* of the credit period. It would be foolish to pay on (say) the 5th day or on the 20th day if the credit terms were 2/10, net 30.

Supply Chain Finance

© Rob Webb/Getty Images

In our global economy, companies purchase parts and materials from suppliers located all over the world. For small and mid-size suppliers, especially those in less developed economies, selling to international customers can lead to cash flow problems. First, many suppliers have no way of knowing when their invoices have been approved by their customers. Second, they have no way of knowing when they will actually receive payment from their customers. With a 4–5-month lag between the time an order is received and the time the payment occurs, many suppliers resort to expensive local financing that can add as much as 4% to their costs. Even worse, some suppliers go out of business, which reduces competition and ultimately leads to higher prices.

Although most companies work very hard with their suppliers to improve their supply chain operations—which is at the heart of supply management—a recent poll shows that only 13% actively use supply chain finance (SCF) techniques. However, that figure is likely

to rise in the near future. For example, Big Lots joined a Web-based service operated by PrimeRevenue that works like this: First, invoices received by Big Lots are posted to the system as soon as they are approved. The supplier doesn't need specialized software but can check its invoices using a Web browser. Second, the supplier has the option of selling the approved invoices at a discount to financial institutions and banks that have access to the PrimeRevenue network. A further advantage to the supplier is that it receives cash within a day of the invoices' approval. In addition, the effective interest rate built into the discounted price is based on the credit rating of Big Lots, not that of the supplier.

As Big Lots treasurer Jared Poff puts it, this allows vendors to "compete on their ability to make the product and not on their ability to access financing."

Source: Kate O'Sullivan, "Financing the Chain," *CFO,* February 2007, pp. 46–53.

Super Sets's **days sales outstanding (DSO)**, sometimes called the *average collection period (ACP),* is 16 days:

$$DSO = ACP = 0.7(10 \text{ days}) + 0.3(30 \text{ days}) = 16 \text{ days}$$

Super Sets's *average daily sales (ADS)* is $108,493:

$$ADS = \frac{\text{Annual sales}}{365} = \frac{(\text{Units sold})(\text{Sales price})}{365} \tag{16-6}$$

$$= \frac{200,000(\$198)}{365} = \frac{\$39,600,000}{365} = \$108,493$$

Super Sets's accounts receivable—assuming a constant, uniform rate of sales throughout the year—will at any point in time be $1,735,888:

$$\text{Receivables} = (DSO)(ADS) \tag{16-7}$$

$$= (\$108,493)(16) = \$1,735,888$$

Note that DSO, or average collection period, is a measure of the average length of time it takes the firm's customers to pay off their credit purchases. Super Sets's DSO is 16 days versus an industry average of 25 days, so either Super Sets has a higher percentage of discount customers or else its credit department is exceptionally good at ensuring prompt payment.

Finally, note that you can derive both the annual sales and the receivables balance from the firm's financial statements, so you can calculate DSO as follows:

$$\text{DSO} = \frac{\text{Receivables}}{\text{Sales per day}} = \frac{\$1,735,888}{\$108,493} = 16 \text{ days}$$

The DSO can also be compared with the firm's own credit terms. For example, suppose Super Sets's DSO had been averaging 35 days. With a 35-day DSO, some customers obviously are taking more than 30 days to pay their bills. In fact, if many customers are paying by Day 10 to take advantage of the discount, then the others must be taking, on average, *much* longer than 35 days. A way to check this possibility is to use an aging schedule, as described next.

AGING SCHEDULES

An **aging schedule** breaks down a firm's receivables by age of account. Table 16-1 shows the December 31, 2013, aging schedules of two television manufacturers, Super Sets and Wonder Vision. Both firms offer the same credit terms, and they have the same total receivables. Super Sets's aging schedule indicates that all of its customers pay on time: 70% pay by Day 10 and 30% pay by Day 30. In contrast, Wonder Vision's schedule, which is more typical, shows that many of its customers are not paying on time: 27% of its receivables are more than 30 days old, even though Wonder Vision's credit terms call for full payment by Day 30.

Aging schedules cannot be constructed from the type of summary data reported in financial statements; rather, they must be developed from the firm's accounts receivable ledger. However, well-run firms have computerized accounts receivable records, so it is easy to determine the age of each invoice, to sort electronically by age categories, and thus to generate an aging schedule.

Management should constantly monitor both the DSO and the aging schedule to detect any trends, to see how the firm's collections experience compares with its credit terms, and to see how effectively the credit department is operating in comparison with other firms in the industry. If the DSO starts to lengthen or the aging schedule begins to

TABLE 16-1

Aging Schedules

| Age of Account (Days) | Super Sets | | Wonder Vision | |
	Value of Account	Percentage of Total Value	Value of Account	Percentage of Total Value
0–10	$1,215,122	70%	$ 815,867	47%
11–30	520,766	30	451,331	26
31–45	0	0	260,383	15
46–60	0	0	173,589	10
Over 60	0	0	34,718	2
Total receivables	$1,735,888	100%	$1,735,888	100%

© Cengage Learning 2014

show an increasing percentage of past-due accounts, then the credit manager should examine why these changes are occurring.

Although increases in the DSO and the aging schedule are warning signs, this does not necessarily indicate the firm's credit policy has weakened. If a firm experiences sharp seasonal variations or if it is growing rapidly, then both the aging schedule and the DSO may be distorted. To see this point, note that the DSO is calculated as follows:

$$DSO = \frac{\text{Accounts receivable}}{\text{Annual sales}/365}$$

Receivables at any point in time reflect sales in the past 1 or 2 months, but sales as shown in the denominator are for the past 12 months. Therefore, a seasonal increase in sales will increase the numerator more than the denominator and hence will raise the DSO, even if customers continue to pay just as quickly as before. Similar problems arise with the aging schedule, because if sales are rising then the percentage in the 0–10-day category will be high, and the reverse will occur if sales are falling. Therefore, a change in either the DSO or the aging schedule should be taken as a signal to investigate further; it is not necessarily a sign that the firm's credit policy has weakened.

SELF-TEST

Explain how a new firm's receivables balance is built up over time.

Define days sales outstanding (DSO). What can be learned from it? How is it affected by sales fluctuations?

What is an aging schedule? What can be learned from it? How is it affected by sales fluctuations?

A company has annual sales of $730 million. If its DSO is 35, what is its average accounts receivables balance? **($70 million)**

16-9 Accruals and Accounts Payable (Trade Credit)

Recall that net operating working capital is equal to operating current assets minus operating current liabilities. The previous sections discussed the management of operating current assets (cash, inventory, and accounts receivable), and the following sections discuss the two major types of operating current liabilities: accruals and accounts payable.[17]

16-9a Accruals

Firms generally pay employees on a weekly, biweekly, or monthly basis, so the balance sheet will typically show some accrued wages. Similarly, the firm's own estimated income taxes, employment and income taxes withheld from employees, and sales taxes collected are generally paid on a weekly, monthly, or quarterly basis. Therefore, the balance sheet will typically show some accrued taxes along with accrued wages.

These **accruals** can be thought of as short-term, interest-free loans from employees and taxing authorities, and they increase automatically (that is, *spontaneously*) as a firm's

---

[17]For more on accounts payable management, see James A. Gentry and Jesus M. De La Garza, "Monitoring Accounts Payables," *Financial Review*, November 1990, pp. 559–576.

A Wag of the Finger or Tip of the Hat? The Colbert Report and Small Business Payment Terms

© Rob Webb/Getty Images

On February 17, 2011, The Colbert Report featured an interview with Jeffrey Leonard. During a spirited exchange with Stephen Colbert, Leonard accused many large businesses of imposing onerous payment terms on their small suppliers. According to Leonard, when Cisco Systems sells to the U.S. government, Cisco receives its payment in 30 days, the standard credit terms used by the federal government. Yet Cisco changed its own credit policy in 2010 to "net 60," meaning that Cisco's suppliers don't get paid for 60 days. In other words, many small companies essentially are helping Cisco finance its working capital, even though Cisco has over $39 billion in cash. Cisco isn't alone in delaying its payments: Dell, Walmart, and AB InBev (the owner of Anheuser-Busch) also pay slower than 30 days.

Colbert and Leonard agreed on the facts but interpreted them differently. Leonard suggested that the government should help small businesses by requiring its own supplier companies to offer their vendors the same terms as the government does. Colbert, however, suggested (perhaps with tongue-in-cheek) that this was just the natural result of free markets and that no government interference was warranted.

You be the judge. When big companies legally take what they can from smaller companies, should they receive a wag of the finger or a tip of the hat?

Sources: **www.washingtonmonthly.com/features/2011/ 1101.leonard.html; www.colbertnation.com/the-colbert-report-videos/374633/february-17-2011/jeffrey-leonard;** and **www.allbusiness.com/company-activities-management/ management- benchmarking/15472247-1.html**.

operations expand. However, a firm cannot ordinarily control its accruals: The timing of wage payments is set by economic forces and industry norms, and tax payment dates are established by law. Thus, firms generally use all the accruals they can, but they have little control over the levels of these accounts.

16-9b Accounts Payable (Trade Credit)

Firms generally make purchases from other firms on credit, recording the debt as an *account payable*. Accounts payable, or **trade credit**, is the largest single operating current liability, representing about 40% of the current liabilities for an average nonfinancial corporation. The percentage is somewhat larger for smaller firms: Because small companies often have difficulty obtaining financing from other sources, they rely especially heavily on trade credit.

Trade credit is a spontaneous source of financing in the sense that it arises from ordinary business transactions. For example, suppose a firm makes average purchases of $2,000 a day on terms of net 30, meaning that it must pay for goods 30 days after the invoice date. On average, it will owe 30 times $2,000, or $60,000, to its suppliers. If its sales, and consequently its purchases, were to double, then its accounts payable would also double, to $120,000. So simply by growing, the firm would spontaneously generate an additional $60,000 of financing. Similarly, if the terms under which the firm buys were extended from 30 to 40 days, then its accounts payable would expand from $60,000 to $80,000 even with no growth in sales. Thus, both expanding sales and lengthening the credit period generate additional amounts of financing via trade credit.

16-9c The Cost of Trade Credit

Firms that sell on credit have a *credit policy* that includes their *terms of credit.* For example, Microchip Electronics sells on terms of 2/10, net 30: It gives customers a 2% discount if they pay within 10 days of the invoice date, but the full invoice amount is due and payable within 30 days if the discount is not taken.

The "true price" of Microchip's products is the net price, or 0.98 times the list price, because any customer can purchase an item at that price as long as payment is made within 10 days. Now consider Personal Computer Company (PCC), which buys its memory chips from Microchip. One chip is listed at $100, so its "true" price to PCC is $98. Now if PCC wants an additional 20 days of credit beyond the 10-day discount period, it must incur a finance charge of $2 per chip for that credit. Thus, the $100 list price consists of two components:

$$\text{List price} = \$98 \text{ true price} + \$2 \text{ finance charge}$$

The question PCC must ask before it turns down the discount to obtain the additional 20 days of credit is this: Could credit be obtained at a lower cost from a bank or some other lender?

Now assume that PCC buys $11,923,333 of memory chips from Microchip each year at the net, or true, price. This amounts to $11,923,333/365 = $32,666.67 per day. For simplicity, assume that Microchip is PCC's only supplier. If PCC decides not to take the additional 20 days of trade credit—that is, if it pays on the 10th day and takes the discount—then its payables will average 10($32,666.67) = $326,667. Thus, PCC will be receiving $326,667 of credit from Microchip.

Now suppose PCC decides to take the additional 20 days credit and so must pay the full list price. Because PCC will now pay on the 30th day, its accounts payable will increase to 30($32,666.67) = $980,000.[18] Microchip will now be supplying PCC with an additional $980,000 − $326,667 = $653,333 of credit, which PCC could use to build up its cash account, to pay off debt, to expand inventories, or even to extend credit to its own customers, hence increasing its own accounts receivable.

Thus the additional trade credit offered by Microchip has a cost: PCC must pay a finance charge equal to the 2% discount it is forgoing. PCC buys $11,923,333 of chips at the true price, so the added finance charge would increase the total cost to $11,923,333/0.98 = $12,166,666. Therefore, the annual financing cost is $12,166,666 − $11,923,333 = $243,333. Dividing the $243,333 financing cost by the $653,333 of additional credit, we calculate the nominal annual cost rate of the additional trade credit to be 37.2%:

$$\text{Nominal annual costs} = \frac{\$243,333}{\$653,333} = 37.2\%$$

If PCC can borrow from its bank (or some other source) at an interest rate less than 37.2%, then it should take the 2% discount and forgo the additional trade credit.

The following equation can be used to calculate the nominal cost (on an annual basis) of not taking discounts, illustrated with terms of 2/10, net 30:

$$\text{Nominal cost of trade credit} = \text{Cost per period} \times \text{Number of periods per year}$$

---

[18]A question arises here: Should accounts payable reflect gross purchases or purchases net of discounts? Generally accepted accounting principles permit either treatment if the difference is not material, but if the discount is material, then the transaction must be recorded net of discounts, or at "true" prices. Then, the higher payment that results from not taking discounts is reported as an expense called "discounts lost." Therefore, *we show accounts payable net of discounts even if the company does not expect to take discounts.*

$$\begin{array}{c} \text{Nominal cost} \\ \text{of trade credit} \end{array} = \dfrac{\text{Discount percentage}}{100 - \begin{array}{c}\text{Discount}\\\text{percentage}\end{array}} \times \dfrac{365}{\begin{array}{c}\text{Days credit is}\\\text{outstanding}\end{array} - \begin{array}{c}\text{Discount}\\\text{period}\end{array}} \qquad (16\text{-}8)$$

$$= \frac{2}{98} \times \frac{365}{20} = 2.04\% \times 18.25 = 37.2\%$$

The numerator of the first term, Discount percentage, is the cost per dollar of credit, while the denominator, 100 − Discount percentage, represents the funds made available by not taking the discount. Thus, the first term, 2.04%, is the cost per period for the trade credit. The denominator of the second term is the number of days of extra credit obtained by not taking the discount, so the entire second term shows how many times each year the cost is incurred—18.25 times in this example.

This nominal annual cost formula does not consider the compounding of interest. In terms of effective annual interest, the cost of trade credit is even higher:

$$\text{Effective annual rate} = (1.0204)^{18.25} - 1.0 = 1.4459 - 1.0 = 44.6\%$$

Thus, the 37.2% nominal cost calculated with Equation 16-8 actually understates the true cost.

Note, however, that the calculated cost of trade credit can be reduced by paying late. Thus, if PCC could get away with paying in 60 days rather than the specified 30 days, then the effective credit period would become 60 − 10 = 50 days, the number of times the discount would be lost would fall to 365/50 = 7.3, and the nominal cost would drop from 37.2% to 2.04% × 7.3 = 14.9%. Then the effective annual rate would drop from 44.6% to 15.9%:

$$\text{Effective annual rate} = (1.0204)^{7.3} - 1.0 = 1.1589 - 1.0 = 15.9\%$$

In periods of excess capacity, firms may be able to get away with deliberately paying late, or **stretching accounts payable**. However, they will also suffer a variety of problems associated with being a "slow payer." These problems are discussed later in the chapter.

r e s o u r c e

*See **Ch16 Tool Kit.xls** on the textbook's Web site for details.*

The costs of the additional trade credit from forgoing discounts under some other purchase terms are taken from the chapter's *Excel **Tool Kit*** model and shown here as Figure 16-6. As these numbers indicate, the cost of not taking discounts can be substantial.

FIGURE 16-6

Varying Credit Terms and Their Associated Costs

	A	B	C	D	E	F
277	Days in year: 365				Cost of additional credit	
278						
279	**Credit terms**	**Discount**	**Discount period**	**Net period**	**Nominal**	**Effective**
280	1/10, net 20	1%	10	20	36.87%	44.32%
281	1/10, net 30	1%	10	30	18.43%	20.13%
282	1/10, net 90	1%	10	90	4.61%	4.69%
283	2/10, net 20	2%	10	20	74.49%	109.05%
284	2/10, net 30	2%	10	30	37.24%	44.59%
285	3/15, net 45	3%	15	45	37.63%	44.86%

On the basis of the preceding discussion, trade credit can be divided into two components: (1) **free trade credit**, which involves credit received during the discount period, and (2) **costly trade credit**, which involves credit in excess of the free trade credit and whose cost is an implicit one based on the forgone discounts. *Firms should always use the free component, but they should use the costly component only after analyzing the cost of this capital to make sure it is less than the cost of funds that could be obtained from other sources.* Under the terms of trade found in most industries, the costly component is relatively expensive, so stronger firms generally avoid using it.

Note, though, that firms sometimes offer favorable credit terms in order to stimulate sales. For example, suppose a firm has been selling on terms of 2/10, net 30, with a nominal cost of 37.24%, but a recession has reduced sales and the firm now has excess capacity. It wants to boost the sales of its product without cutting the list price, so it might offer terms of 1/10, net 90, which implies a nominal cost of additional credit of only 4.61%. In this situation, its customers would probably be wise to take the additional credit and reduce their reliance on banks and other lenders. So, turning down discounts is not always a bad decision.

SELF-TEST

What are accruals? How much control do managers have over accruals?

What is trade credit?

What's the difference between free trade credit and costly trade credit?

How does the cost of costly trade credit generally compare with the cost of short-term bank loans?

A company buys on terms of 2/12, net 28. What is its nominal cost of trade credit? **(46.6%)** *The effective cost?* **(58.5%)**

16-10 Managing Short-Term Investments

Short-term investments include short-term financial assets such as U.S. Treasury securities, U.S. agency securities, certificates of deposits, time deposits, and commercial paper. There are three reasons companies hold short-term investments: (1) for liquidation just prior to scheduled transactions, (2) for unexpected opportunities, and (3) to reduce the company's risk.

Some future transaction dates and amounts are known with a high degree of certainty. For example, a company knows the dates on which it will need cash to make interest, principal, and dividend payments; if a company has decided to make a major purchase, such as a new machine or even a new factory, the company knows the dates on which it will pay for the purchase. A company's payment isn't complete until the funds have been deducted from the company's bank account and credited to the depositor's bank account. Because a company doesn't actually need a balance in the bank account until the payment is deducted, most companies try to keep their bank account balances (which pay zero or very low interest rates) as low as possible until the day the payment is deducted. For example, if a company has a scheduled dividend payment, the company is likely to hold the amount needed for the payment in the form short-term investments such as T-bills or other interest-paying short-term securities. The company will liquidate these short-term investments and deposit the proceeds into its bank accounts just prior to the required payment date.

Short-term investments that are designated for making scheduled payments, such as those just described, are temporary in the sense that a company acquires these short-term investments and plans to hold them for a specific period and for a particular use. The following sections describe short-term investments that are less transitory.

Some companies hold short-term investments even though they haven't planned a specific use for them and even though the rate of return on short-term investments is very low. For example, some companies compete in businesses that have growth opportunities that arise unexpectedly. If such a company doesn't have stable cash flows or ready access to credit markets (perhaps because the company is small or doesn't have a high credit rating), it might not be able to take advantage of an unexpected opportunity. Therefore, the company might hold short-term investments, which are **speculative balances** in the sense that the company speculates that it will have an opportunity to use them and subsequently earn much more than the rate on short-term investments. Studies show that such firms do hold relatively high levels of marketable securities. In contrast, cash holdings are less important to large firms with high credit ratings, because they have quick and inexpensive access to capital markets. As expected, such firms hold relatively low levels of cash.[19]

Holding short-term investments reduces a company's risk of facing a liquidity crisis, such as the ones that occurred during the economic downturn and credit crunch of the 2007 recession. A stockpile of short-term investments also reduces transaction costs due to issuing securities because the investments can be liquidated instead.

Although there are good reasons many companies hold short-term investments, there are too many companies holding too much cash. As we write this in mid-2012, U.S. nonfinancial companies hold about $1.2 trillion in cash, making up about 6% of their total assets. Some companies, such as Apple and Microsoft, have much larger cash to assets ratios. Even with the uncertain economic environment, it is hard to believe that investors would not benefit by cash distributions instead of cash stockpiles.

SELF-TEST

Why might a company hold low-yielding marketable securities when it could earn a much higher return on operating assets?

16-11 Short-Term Financing

The three possible short-term financing policies described earlier in the chapter were distinguished by the relative amounts of short-term debt used under each policy. The aggressive policy called for the greatest use of short-term debt, and the conservative policy called for using the least; maturity matching fell in between. Although short-term credit is generally riskier than long-term credit, using short-term funds does have some significant advantages. The pros and cons of short-term financing are considered in this section.

16-11a Advantages of Short-Term Financing

First, a short-term loan can be obtained much faster than long-term credit. Lenders will insist on a more thorough financial examination before extending long-term credit, and the loan agreement will have to be spelled out in considerable detail because a lot can

---

[19]See the study by Opler, Pinkowitz, Stulz, and Williamson cited in footnote 9.

happen during the life of a 10- to 20-year loan. Therefore, if funds are needed in a hurry, the firm should look to the short-term markets.

Second, if its needs for funds are seasonal or cyclical, then a firm may not want to commit itself to long-term debt. There are three reasons for this: (1) Flotation costs are higher for long-term debt than for short-term credit. (2) Although long-term debt can be repaid early (provided the loan agreement includes a prepayment provision), prepayment penalties can be expensive. Accordingly, if a firm thinks its need for funds will diminish in the near future, it should choose short-term debt. (3) Long-term loan agreements always contain provisions, or covenants, that constrain the firm's future actions. Short-term credit agreements are generally less restrictive.

The third advantage is that, because the yield curve is normally upward sloping, interest rates are generally lower on short-term debt. Thus, under normal conditions, interest costs at the time the funds are obtained will be lower if the firm borrows on a short-term rather than a long-term basis.

16-11b Disadvantages of Short-Term Debt

Even though short-term rates are often lower than long-term rates, using short-term credit is riskier for two reasons: (1) If a firm borrows on a long-term basis then its interest costs will be relatively stable over time, but if it uses short-term credit, then its interest expense will fluctuate widely, at times going quite high. For example, the rate banks charged large corporations for short-term debt more than tripled over a 2-year period in the 1980s, rising from 6.25% to 21%. Many firms that had borrowed heavily on a short-term basis simply could not meet their rising interest costs; as a result, bankruptcies hit record levels during that period. (2) If a firm borrows heavily on a short-term basis, a temporary recession may render it unable to repay this debt. If the borrower is in a weak financial position, then the lender may not extend the loan, which could force the firm into bankruptcy.

SELF-TEST

What are the advantages and disadvantages of short-term debt compared with long-term debt?

16-12 Short-Term Bank Loans

Loans from commercial banks generally appear on balance sheets as notes payable. A bank's importance is actually greater than it appears from the dollar amounts shown on balance sheets because banks provide *nonspontaneous* funds. As a firm's financing needs increase, it requests additional funds from its bank. If the request is denied, the firm may be forced to abandon attractive growth opportunities. The key features of bank loans are discussed in the following paragraphs.

16-12a Maturity

Although banks do make longer-term loans, *the bulk of their lending is on a short-term basis*—about two-thirds of all bank loans mature in a year or less. Bank loans to businesses are frequently written as 90-day notes, so the loan must be repaid or renewed at the end of 90 days. Of course, if a borrower's financial position has deteriorated, then the bank may refuse to renew the loan. This can mean serious trouble for the borrower.

16-12b Promissory Notes

When a bank loan is approved, the agreement is executed by signing a **promissory note**. The note specifies (1) the amount borrowed, (2) the interest rate, (3) the repayment schedule, which can call for either a lump sum or a series of installments, (4) any collateral that might have to be put up as security for the loan, and (5) any other terms and conditions to which the bank and the borrower have agreed. When the note is signed, the bank credits the borrower's checking account with the funds; hence both cash and notes payable increase on the borrower's balance sheet.

16-12c Compensating Balances

Banks sometimes require borrowers to maintain an average demand deposit (checking account) balance of 10% to 20% of the loan's face amount. This is called a compensating balance, and such balances raise the effective interest rate on the loans. For example, if a firm needs $80,000 to pay off outstanding obligations but it must maintain a 20% compensating balance, then it must borrow $100,000 to obtain a usable $80,000. If the stated annual interest rate is 8%, the effective cost is actually 10%: $8,000 interest divided by $80,000 of usable funds equals 10%.[20]

As we noted earlier in the chapter, recent surveys indicate that compensating balances are much less common now than earlier. In fact, compensating balances are now illegal in many states. Despite this trend, some small banks in states where compensating balances are legal still require their customers to maintain them.

16-12d Informal Line of Credit

A **line of credit** is an informal agreement between a bank and a borrower indicating the maximum credit the bank will extend to the borrower. For example, on December 31, a bank loan officer might indicate to a financial manager that the bank regards the firm as being "good" for up to $80,000 during the forthcoming year, provided the borrower's financial condition does not deteriorate. If on January 10 the financial manager signs a 90-day promissory note for $15,000, this would be called "taking down" $15,000 of the total line of credit. This amount would be credited to the firm's checking account at the bank, and the firm could borrow additional amounts up to a total of $80,000 outstanding at any one time.

16-12e Revolving Credit Agreement

A **revolving credit agreement** is a formal line of credit often used by large firms. To illustrate, suppose in 2013 Texas Petroleum Company negotiated a revolving credit agreement for $100 million with a group of banks. The banks were formally committed for 4 years to lend the firm up to $100 million if the funds were needed. Texas Petroleum, in turn, paid an annual commitment fee of 0.25% on the unused balance of the commitment to compensate the banks for making the commitment. Thus, if Texas Petroleum did not take down any of the $100 million commitment during a year, it would still be required to pay a $250,000 annual fee, normally in monthly installments of $20,833.33. If it borrowed $50 million on the first day of the agreement, then the unused portion of the line of credit would fall to $50 million and the annual fee would fall to $125,000. Of course, interest would also have to be paid on

---

[20]Note, however, that the compensating balance may be set as a minimum monthly *average,* and if the firm would maintain this average anyway then the compensating balance requirement would not raise the effective interest rate. Also, note that these loan compensating balances are *added to* any compensating balances that the firm's bank may require for services performed, such as clearing checks.

the money Texas Petroleum actually borrowed. As a general rule, the interest rate on "revolvers" is pegged to the London Interbank Offered Rate (LIBOR), the T-bill rate, or some other market rate, so the cost of the loan varies over time as interest rates change. The interest that Texas Petroleum must pay was set at the prime lending rate plus 1.0%.

Observe that a revolving credit agreement is similar to an informal line of credit but has an important difference: The bank has a *legal obligation* to honor a revolving credit agreement, and it receives a commitment fee. Neither the legal obligation nor the fee exists under the informal line of credit.

Often a line of credit will have a **cleanup clause** that requires the borrower to reduce the loan balance to zero at least once a year. Keep in mind that a line of credit typically is designed to help finance seasonal or cyclical peaks in operations, not as a source of permanent capital. For example, our cash budget for Educational Products Corporation showed negative flows from July through September but positive flows from October through December. Also, the cumulative net cash flow goes positive in November, indicating that the firm could pay off its loan at that time. If the cumulative flows were always negative, this would indicate that the firm was using its credit lines as a permanent source of financing.

16-12f Costs of Bank Loans

The costs of bank loans vary for different types of borrowers at any given point in time and for all borrowers over time. Interest rates are higher for riskier borrowers, and rates are also higher on smaller loans because of the fixed costs involved in making and servicing loans. If a firm can qualify for "prime credit" because of its size and financial strength, it can borrow at the **prime rate**, which at one time was the lowest rate banks charged. Rates on other loans are generally scaled up from the prime rate. Loans to large, strong customers are made at rates tied to LIBOR and the costs of such loans are generally well below prime:

Rates on May 22, 2012	
Prime	3.25%
1-Year LIBOR	1.07%

The rate to smaller, riskier borrowers is generally stated something like "prime plus 1.0%"; but for a larger borrower it is generally stated as something like "LIBOR plus 1.5%."

Bank rates vary widely over time depending on economic conditions and Federal Reserve policy. When the economy is weak, loan demand is usually slack, inflation is low, and the Fed makes plenty of money available to the system. As a result, rates on all types of loans are relatively low. Conversely, when the economy is booming, loan demand is typically strong, the Fed restricts the money supply to fight inflation, and the result is high interest rates. As an indication of the kinds of fluctuations that can occur, the prime rate during 1980 rose from 11% to 21% in just 4 months; during 1994, it rose from 6% to 9%.

CALCULATING BANKS' INTEREST CHARGES: REGULAR (OR "SIMPLE") INTEREST

Banks calculate interest in several different ways. In this section, we explain the procedure used for most business loans. For illustration purposes, we assume a loan of $10,000 at the prime rate, currently 3.25%, with a 360-day year. Interest must be paid monthly, and the principal is payable "on demand" if and when the bank wants to end the loan. Such a loan is called a **regular interest** loan or a **simple interest** loan.

We begin by dividing the nominal interest rate (3.25% in this case) by 360 to obtain the rate per day. This rate is expressed as a *decimal fraction*, not as a percentage:

$$\text{Simple interest rate per day} = \frac{\text{Nominal rate}}{\text{Days in year}}$$
$$= 0.0325/360 = 0.000090278$$

To find the monthly interest payment, the daily rate is multiplied by the amount of the loan, and then by the number of days during the payment period. For our illustrative loan, the daily interest charge would be $0.902777778, and the total for a 30-day month would be $27.08:

$$\text{Interest charge for month} = (\text{Rate per day})(\text{Amount of loan})(\text{Days in month})$$
$$= (0.000090278)(\$10,000)(30 \text{ days}) = \$27.08$$

The *effective interest rate* on a loan depends on how frequently interest must be paid—the more frequently interest is paid, the higher the effective rate. If interest is paid once per year, then the nominal rate is also the effective rate. However, if interest must be paid monthly, then the effective rate is $(1 + 0.0325/12)^{12} - 1 = 3.2989\%$.

CALCULATING BANKS' INTEREST CHARGES: ADD-ON INTEREST

Banks and other lenders typically use **add-on interest** for automobiles and other types of installment loans. The term *add-on* means that the interest is calculated and then added to the amount borrowed to determine the loan's face value. To illustrate, suppose you borrow $10,000 on an add-on basis at a nominal rate of 7.25% to buy a car, with the loan to be repaid in 12 monthly installments. At a 7.25% add-on rate, you would make total interest payments of $10,000(0.0725) = $725. However, because the loan is paid off in monthly installments, you would have the use of the full $10,000 for only the first month; then the outstanding balance would decline until, during the last month, only 1/12 of the original loan was still outstanding.

To find the annual percentage rate (APR), we first find the payment per month, $10,725/12 = $893.75. With a financial calculator, enter N = 12, PV = 10000, PMT = −893.75, and FV = 0; then press I/YR to obtain 1.093585%. This is a monthly rate, so multiply by 12 to get 13.12%, which is the APR the bank would report to the borrower. This is quite a bit above the 7.25% rate, and the effective rate on an add-on loan is even higher. The effective annual rate is $(1.010936)^{12} - 1 = 13.94\%$. All in all, add-on interest loans can be very costly.

SELF-TEST

What is a promissory note, and what are some terms that are normally included in promissory notes?

What is a line of credit? A revolving credit agreement?

What's the difference between simple interest and add-on interest?

Explain how a firm that expects to need funds during the coming year might make sure that the needed funds will be available.

How does the cost of costly trade credit generally compare with the cost of short-term bank loans?

If a firm borrowed $500,000 at a rate of 10% simple interest with monthly interest payments and a 365-day year, what would be the required interest payment for a 30-day month? **($4,109.59)** *If interest must be paid monthly, what would be the effective annual rate?* **(10.47%)**

If this loan had been made on a 10% add-on basis, payable in 12 end-of-month installments, what would be the monthly payment amount? **($45,833.33)** *What is the annual percentage rate?* **(17.97%)** *The effective annual rate?* **(19.53%)**

WWW

For updates on the outstanding balances of commercial paper, go to **www.federalreserve.gov/econresdata/releases/statisticsdata.htm** and check out the volume statistics for Commercial Paper and the weekly releases for Assets and Liabilities of Commercial Banks in the United States.

WWW

For current rates, see **www.federalreserve.gov/econresdata/releases/statisticsdata.htm** and look at the Daily Releases for Selected Interest Rates.

16-13 Commercial Paper

Commercial paper is a type of unsecured promissory note issued by large, strong firms and sold primarily to other business firms, to insurance companies, to pension funds, to money market mutual funds, and to banks. In May 2012, there was approximately $1.2 trillion of commercial paper outstanding, versus nearly $1.4 trillion of commercial and industrial bank loans. Most, but not all, commercial paper outstanding is issued by financial institutions.

16-13a Maturity and Cost

Maturities of commercial paper generally vary from 1 day to 9 months, with an average of about 5 months.[21] The interest rate on commercial paper fluctuates with supply and demand conditions—it is determined in the marketplace, varying daily as conditions change. Recently, commercial paper rates have ranged from 1.5 to 3.5 percentage points below the stated prime rate and up to half of a percentage point above the T-bill rate. For example, in May 2012, the average rate on 3-month commercial paper was 0.20%, the prime rate was 3.25%, and the 3-month T-bill rate was 0.09%.

16-13b Use of Commercial Paper

The use of commercial paper is restricted to a comparatively small number of very large companies that are exceptionally good credit risks. Dealers prefer to handle the paper of firms whose net worth is $100 million or more and whose annual borrowing exceeds $10 million. One potential problem with commercial paper is that a debtor who has a temporary financial difficulty may receive little help because commercial paper dealings are generally less personal than are bank relationships. Thus, banks are generally more able and willing to help a good customer weather a temporary storm than is a commercial paper dealer. On the other hand, using commercial paper permits a corporation to tap a wide range of credit sources, including financial institutions outside its own area and industrial corporations across the country, and this can reduce interest costs.

SELF-TEST

What is commercial paper?

What types of companies can use commercial paper to meet their short-term financing needs?

How does the cost of commercial paper compare with the cost of short-term bank loans? With the cost of Treasury bills?

16-14 Use of Security in Short-Term Financing

Thus far, we have not addressed the question of whether or not short-term loans should be secured. Commercial paper is never secured, but other types of loans can be secured if this is deemed necessary or desirable. Other things held constant, it is better to borrow on

---

[21]The maximum maturity without SEC registration is 270 days. Also, commercial paper can be sold only to "sophisticated" investors; otherwise, SEC registration would be required even for maturities of 270 days or less.

an unsecured basis because the bookkeeping costs of **secured loans** are often high. However, firms often find that they can borrow only if they put up some type of collateral to protect the lender or that, by using security, they can borrow at a much lower rate.

Companies can employ several different kinds of collateral, including marketable stocks or bonds, land or buildings, equipment, inventory, and accounts receivable. Marketable securities make excellent collateral, but few firms that need loans also hold portfolios of stocks and bonds. Similarly, real property (land and buildings) and equipment are good forms of collateral, but they are generally used as security for long-term loans rather than for working capital loans. Therefore, most secured short-term business borrowing involves the use of accounts receivable and inventories as collateral.

resource

For a more detailed discussion of secured financing, see **Web Extension 16A** *on the textbook's Web site.*

Consider the case of a Chicago hardware dealer who requested a $200,000 bank loan to modernize and expand his store. After examining the business's financial statements, his bank indicated that it would lend him a maximum of $100,000 and that the effective interest rate would be 9%. The owner had a substantial personal portfolio of stocks, and he offered to put up $300,000 of high-quality stocks to support the $200,000 loan. The bank then granted the full $200,000 loan at the prime rate of 3.25%. The store owner might also have used his inventories or receivables as security for the loan, but processing costs would have been high.[22]

SELF-TEST

What is a secured loan?

What are some types of current assets that are pledged as security for short-term loans?

SUMMARY

This chapter discussed working capital management and short-term financing. The key concepts covered are listed below.

- **Working capital** refers to current assets used in operations, and **net working capital** is defined as current assets minus all current liabilities. **Net operating working capital** is defined as operating current assets minus operating current liabilities.
- Under a **relaxed working capital policy**, a firm would hold relatively large amounts of each type of current asset. Under a **restricted working capital policy**, the firm would hold minimal amounts of these items.
- A **moderate** approach to short-term financing involves matching, to the extent possible, the maturities of assets and liabilities, so that temporary operating current assets are financed with short-term debt and permanent operating current assets and fixed assets are financed with long-term debt or equity. Under an **aggressive** approach, some permanent operating current assets, and perhaps even some fixed assets, are financed with short-term debt. A **conservative** approach would be to use long-term sources to finance all permanent operating capital and some of the temporary operating current assets.

---

[22]The term "asset-based financing" is often used as a synonym for "secured financing." In recent years, accounts receivable have been used as security for long-term bonds, permitting corporations to borrow from lenders such as pension funds rather than just from banks and other traditional short-term lenders.

- **Permanent operating current assets** are the operating current assets the firm holds even during slack times, whereas **temporary operating current assets** are the additional operating current assets needed during seasonal or cyclical peaks. The methods used to finance permanent and temporary operating current assets define the firm's **short-term financing policy**.

- The **inventory conversion period** is the average time required to convert materials into finished goods and then to sell those goods:

$$\text{Inventory conversion period} = \text{Inventory} \div \text{Cost of goods sold per day}$$

- The **average collection period** is the average length of time required to convert the firm's receivables into cash—that is, to collect cash following a sale:

$$\text{Average collection period} = \text{DSO} = \text{Receivables} \div (\text{Sales}/365)$$

- The **payables deferral period** is the average length of time between the purchase of materials and labor and the payment of cash for them:

$$\text{Payables deferral period} = \text{Payables} \div \text{Cost of goods sold per day}$$

- The **cash conversion cycle (CCC)** is the length of time between the firm's actual cash expenditures to pay for productive resources (materials and labor) and its own cash receipts from the sale of products (that is, the length of time between paying for labor and materials and collecting on receivables):

$$
\begin{matrix}
\text{Cash} & & \text{Inventory} & & \text{Average} & & \text{Payables} \\
\text{conversion} & = & \text{conversion} & + & \text{collection} & - & \text{deferral} \\
\text{cycle} & & \text{period} & & \text{period} & & \text{period}
\end{matrix}
$$

- A **cash budget** is a schedule showing projected cash inflows and outflows over some period. The cash budget is used to predict cash surpluses and deficits, and it is the primary cash management planning tool.

- The **primary goal of cash management** is to minimize the amount of cash the firm must hold for conducting its normal business activities while at the same time maintaining a sufficient cash reserve to take discounts, pay bills promptly, and meet any unexpected cash needs.

- The **transactions balance** is the cash necessary to conduct routine day-to-day business; **precautionary balances** are cash reserves held to meet random, unforeseen needs. A **compensating balance** is a minimum checking account balance that a bank requires as compensation either for services provided or as part of a loan agreement.

- The twin goals of **inventory management** are (1) to ensure that the inventories needed to sustain operations are available, but (2) to hold the costs of ordering and carrying inventories to the lowest possible level.

- When a firm sells goods to a customer on credit, an **account receivable** is created.

- A firm can use an **aging schedule** and the **days sales outstanding (DSO)** to monitor its receivables balance and to help avoid an increase in bad debts.

- A firm's **credit policy** consists of four elements: (1) credit period, (2) discounts given for early payment, (3) credit standards, and (4) collection policy.

- **Accounts payable**, or **trade credit**, arises spontaneously as a result of credit purchases. Firms should use all the **free trade credit** they can obtain, but they should use **costly trade credit** only if it is less expensive than other forms of short-term debt. Suppliers often offer discounts to customers who pay within a stated period. The following equation may be used to calculate the nominal cost, on an annual basis, of not taking such discounts:

$$\text{Nominal annual cost of trade credit} = \frac{\text{Discount percentage}}{100 - \text{Discount percentage}} \times \frac{365}{\text{Days credit is outstanding} - \text{Discount period}}$$

- The advantages of short-term credit are (1) the **speed** with which short-term loans can be arranged, (2) increased *flexibility,* and (3) generally *lower interest rates* than with long-term credit. The principal disadvantage of short-term credit is the *extra risk* the borrower must bear because (1) the lender can demand payment on short notice, and (2) the cost of the loan will increase if interest rates rise.
- **Bank loans** are an important source of short-term credit. When a bank loan is approved, a **promissory note** is signed. It specifies: (1) the amount borrowed, (2) the percentage interest rate, (3) the repayment schedule, (4) the collateral, and (5) any other conditions to which the parties have agreed.
- Banks sometimes require borrowers to maintain **compensating balances**, which are deposit requirements set at between 10% and 20% of the loan amount. Compensating balances raise the effective interest rate on bank loans.
- A **line of credit** is an informal agreement between the bank and the borrower indicating the maximum amount of credit the bank will extend to the borrower.
- A **revolving credit agreement** is a formal line of credit often used by large firms; it involves a **commitment fee**.
- A **simple interest** loan is one in which interest must be paid monthly and the principal is payable "on demand" if and when the bank wants to end the loan.
- An **add-on interest loan** is one in which interest is calculated and added to the funds received to determine the face amount of the installment loan.
- **Commercial paper** is unsecured short-term debt issued by large, financially strong corporations. Although the cost of commercial paper is lower than the cost of bank loans, it can be used only by large firms with exceptionally strong credit ratings.
- Sometimes a borrower will find it is necessary to borrow on a **secured basis**, in which case the borrower pledges assets such as real estate, securities, equipment, inventories, or accounts receivable as collateral for the loan. For a more detailed discussion of secured financing, see *Web Extension 16A*.

QUESTIONS

(16-1) Define each of the following terms:

a. Working capital; net working capital; net operating working capital
b. Relaxed policy; restricted policy; moderate policy
c. Permanent operating current assets; temporary operating current assets
d. Moderate (maturity matching) financing policy; aggressive financing policy; conservative financing policy
e. Inventory conversion period; average collection period; payables deferral period; cash conversion cycle
f. Cash budget; target cash balance
g. Transactions balances; compensating balances; precautionary balances
h. Trade discounts
i. Credit policy; credit period; credit standards; collection policy; cash discounts
j. Account receivable; days sales outstanding; aging schedule
k. Accruals; trade credit

l. Stretching accounts payable; free trade credit; costly trade credit

m. Promissory note; line of credit; revolving credit agreement

n. Commercial paper; secured loan

(16-2) What are the two principal reasons for holding cash? Can a firm estimate its target cash balance by summing the cash held to satisfy each of the two reasons?

(16-3) Is it true that, when one firm sells to another on credit, the seller records the transaction as an account receivable while the buyer records it as an account payable and that, disregarding discounts, the receivable typically exceeds the payable by the amount of profit on the sale?

(16-4) What are the four elements of a firm's credit policy? To what extent can firms set their own credit policies as opposed to accepting policies that are dictated by their competitors?

(16-5) What are the advantages of matching the maturities of assets and liabilities? What are the disadvantages?

(16-6) From the standpoint of the borrower, is long-term or short-term credit riskier? Explain. Would it ever make sense to borrow on a short-term basis if short-term rates were above long-term rates?

(16-7) Discuss this statement: "Firms can control their accruals within fairly wide limits."

(16-8) Is it true that most firms are able to obtain some free trade credit and that additional trade credit is often available, but at a cost? Explain.

(16-9) What kinds of firms use commercial paper?

SELF-TEST PROBLEMS   Solutions Appear in Appendix A

(ST-1)
Working Capital
Policy

The Calgary Company is attempting to establish a current assets policy. Fixed assets are $600,000, and the firm plans to maintain a 50% debt-to-assets ratio. Calgary has no operating current liabilities. The interest rate is 10% on all debt. Three alternative current asset policies are under consideration: 40%, 50%, and 60% of projected sales. The company expects to earn 15% before interest and taxes on sales of $3 million. Calgary's effective federal-plus-state tax rate is 40%. What is the expected return on equity under each asset policy?

(ST-2)
Current Asset
Financing

Vanderheiden Press Inc. and the Herrenhouse Publishing Company had the following balance sheets as of December 31, 2013 (thousands of dollars):

	Vanderheiden Press	Herrenhouse Publishing
Current assets	$100,000	$ 80,000
Fixed assets (net)	100,000	120,000
Total assets	$200,000	$200,000
Current liabilities	$ 20,000	$ 80,000
Long-term debt	80,000	20,000
Common stock	50,000	50,000
Retained earnings	50,000	50,000
Total liabilities and equity	$200,000	$200,000

Earnings before interest and taxes for both firms are $30 million, and the effective federal-plus-state tax rate is 40%.

    a. What is the return on equity for each firm if the interest rate on current liabilities is 10% and the rate on long-term debt is 13%?

    b. Assume that the short-term rate rises to 20%, that the rate on new long-term debt rises to 16%, and that the rate on existing long-term debt remains unchanged. What would be the return on equity for Vanderheiden Press and Herrenhouse Publishing under these conditions?

    c. Which company is in a riskier position? Why?

PROBLEMS　　Answers Appear in Appendix B

Easy Problems 1–5

(16-1)
Cash Management

Williams & Sons last year reported sales of $10 million and an inventory turnover ratio of 2. The company is now adopting a new inventory system. If the new system is able to reduce the firm's inventory level and increase the firm's inventory turnover ratio to 5 while maintaining the same level of sales, how much cash will be freed up?

(16-2)
Receivables Investment

Medwig Corporation has a DSO of 17 days. The company averages $3,500 in credit sales each day. What is the company's average accounts receivable?

(16-3)
Cost of Trade Credit

What is the nominal and effective cost of trade credit under the credit terms of 3/15, net 30?

(16-4)
Cost of Trade Credit

A large retailer obtains merchandise under the credit terms of 1/15, net 45, but routinely takes 60 days to pay its bills. (Because the retailer is an important customer, suppliers allow the firm to stretch its credit terms.) What is the retailer's effective cost of trade credit?

(16-5)
Accounts Payable

A chain of appliance stores, APP Corporation, purchases inventory with a net price of $500,000 each day. The company purchases the inventory under the credit terms of 2/15, net 40. APP always takes the discount but takes the full 15 days to pay its bills. What is the average accounts payable for APP?

Intermediate Problems 6–12

(16-6)
Receivables Investment

Snider Industries sells on terms of 2/10, net 45. Total sales for the year are $1,500,000. Thirty percent of customers pay on the 10th day and take discounts; the other 70% pay, on average, 50 days after their purchases.

    a. What is the days sales outstanding?

    b. What is the average amount of receivables?

    c. What would happen to average receivables if Snider toughened its collection policy with the result that all nondiscount customers paid on the 45th day?

(16-7)
Cost of Trade Credit

Calculate the nominal annual cost of nonfree trade credit under each of the following terms. Assume that payment is made either on the discount date or on the due date.

    a. 1/15, net 20

    b. 2/10, net 60

    c. 3/10, net 45

    d. 2/10, net 45

    e. 2/15, net 40

(16-8)
Cost of Trade Credit

a. If a firm buys under terms of 3/15, net 45, but actually pays on the 20th day and *still takes the discount,* what is the nominal cost of its nonfree trade credit?

b. Does it receive more or less credit than it would if it paid within 15 days?

(16-9)
Cost of Trade Credit

Grunewald Industries sells on terms of 2/10, net 40. Gross sales last year were $4,562,500 and accounts receivable averaged $437,500. Half of Grunewald's customers paid on the 10th day and took discounts. What are the nominal and effective costs of trade credit to Grunewald's nondiscount customers? (*Hint:* Calculate daily sales based on a 365-day year, then calculate average receivables of discount customers, and then find the DSO for the nondiscount customers.)

(16-10)
Effective Cost of
Trade Credit

The D.J. Masson Corporation needs to raise $500,000 for 1 year to supply working capital to a new store. Masson buys from its suppliers on terms of 3/10, net 90, and it currently pays on the 10th day and takes discounts. However, it could forgo the discounts, pay on the 90th day, and thereby obtain the needed $500,000 in the form of costly trade credit. What is the effective annual interest rate of this trade credit?

(16-11)
Cash Conversion
Cycle

Negus Enterprises has an inventory conversion period of 50 days, an average collection period of 35 days, and a payables deferral period of 25 days. Assume that cost of goods sold is 80% of sales.

a. What is the length of the firm's cash conversion cycle?

b. If Negus's annual sales are $4,380,000 and all sales are on credit, what is the firm's investment in accounts receivable?

c. How many times per year does Negus Enterprises turn over its inventory?

(16-12)
Working Capital
Cash Flow Cycle

Strickler Technology is considering changes in its working capital policies to improve its cash flow cycle. Strickler's sales last year were $3,250,000 (all on credit), and its net profit margin was 7%. Its inventory turnover was 6.0 times during the year, and its DSO was 41 days. Its annual cost of goods sold was $1,800,000. The firm had fixed assets totaling $535,000. Strickler's payables deferral period is 45 days.

a. Calculate Strickler's cash conversion cycle.

b. Assuming Strickler holds negligible amounts of cash and marketable securities, calculate its total assets turnover and ROA.

c. Suppose Strickler's managers believe the annual inventory turnover can be raised to 9 times without affecting sales. What would Strickler's cash conversion cycle, total assets turnover, and ROA have been if the inventory turnover had been 9 for the year?

Challenging
Problems 13–17

(16-13)
Working Capital
Policy

Payne Products's sales last year were an anemic $1.6 million, but with an improved product mix it expects sales growth to be 25% this year, and Payne would like to determine the effect of various current assets policies on its financial performance. Payne has $1 million of fixed assets and intends to keep its debt ratio at its historical level of 60%. Payne's debt interest rate is currently 8%. You are to evaluate three different current asset policies: (1) a tight policy in which current assets are 45% of projected sales, (2) a moderate policy with 50% of sales tied up in current assets, and (3) a relaxed policy requiring current assets of 60% of sales. Earnings before interest and taxes is expected to be 12% of sales. Payne's tax rate is 40%.

a. What is the expected return on equity under each current asset level?

b. In this problem, we have assumed that the level of expected sales is independent of current asset policy. Is this a valid assumption? Why or why not?

c. How would the overall riskiness of the firm vary under each policy?

(16-14)
Cash Budgeting

Dorothy Koehl recently leased space in the Southside Mall and opened a new business, Koehl's Doll Shop. Business has been good, but Koehl frequently runs out of cash. This has necessitated late payment on certain orders, which is beginning to cause a problem with suppliers. Koehl plans to borrow from the bank to have cash ready as needed, but first she needs a forecast of how much she should borrow. Accordingly, she has asked you to prepare a cash budget for the critical period around Christmas, when needs will be especially high.

Sales are made on a cash basis only. Koehl's purchases must be paid for during the following month. Koehl pays herself a salary of $4,800 per month, and the rent is $2,000 per month. In addition, she must make a tax payment of $12,000 in December. The current cash on hand (on December 1) is $400, but Koehl has agreed to maintain an average bank balance of $6,000—this is her target cash balance. (Disregard the amount in the cash register, which is insignificant because Koehl keeps only a small amount on hand in order to lessen the chances of robbery.)

The estimated sales and purchases for December, January, and February are shown below. Purchases during November amounted to $140,000.

	Sales	Purchases
December	$160,000	$40,000
January	40,000	40,000
February	60,000	40,000

a. Prepare a cash budget for December, January, and February.
b. Suppose that Koehl starts selling on a credit basis on December 1, giving customers 30 days to pay. All customers accept these terms, and all other facts in the problem are unchanged. What would the company's loan requirements be at the end of December in this case? (*Hint:* The calculations required to answer this part are minimal.)

(16-15)
Cash Discounts

Suppose a firm makes purchases of $3.65 million per year under terms of 2/10, net 30, and takes discounts.

a. What is the average amount of accounts payable net of discounts? (Assume the $3.65 million of purchases is net of discounts—that is, gross purchases are $3,724,489.80, discounts are $74,489.80, and net purchases are $3.65 million.)
b. Is there a cost of the trade credit the firm uses?
c. If the firm did not take discounts but did pay on the due date, what would be its average payables and the cost of this nonfree trade credit?
d. What would be the firm's cost of not taking discounts if it could stretch its payments to 40 days?

(16-16)
Trade Credit

The Thompson Corporation projects an increase in sales from $1.5 million to $2 million, but it needs an additional $300,000 of current assets to support this expansion. Thompson can finance the expansion by no longer taking discounts, thus increasing accounts payable. Thompson purchases under terms of 2/10, net 30, but it can delay payment for an additional 35 days—paying in 65 days and thus becoming 35 days past due—without a penalty because its suppliers currently have excess capacity. What is the effective, or equivalent, annual cost of the trade credit?

(16-17)
Bank Financing

The Raattama Corporation had sales of $3.5 million last year, and it earned a 5% return (after taxes) on sales. Recently, the company has fallen behind in its accounts payable. Although its terms of purchase are net 30 days, its accounts payable represents 60 days' purchases. The company's treasurer is seeking to increase bank borrowing in order to become current in meeting its trade obligations (that is, to have 30 days' payables outstanding). The company's balance sheet is as follows (in thousands of dollars):

Cash	$ 100	Accounts payable	$ 600
Accounts receivable	300	Bank loans	700
Inventory	1,400	Accruals	200
Current assets	$1,800	Current liabilities	$1,500
Land and buildings	600	Mortgage on real estate	700
Equipment	600	Common stock, $0.10 par	300
		Retained earnings	500
Total assets	$3,000	Total liabilities and equity	$3,000

a. How much bank financing is needed to eliminate the past-due accounts payable?
b. Assume that the bank will lend the firm the amount calculated in part a. The terms of the loan offered are 8%, simple interest, and the bank uses a 360-day year for the interest calculation. What is the interest charge for 1 month? (Assume there are 30 days in a month.)
c. Now ignore part b and assume that the bank will lend the firm the amount calculated in part a. The terms of the loan are 7.5%, add-on interest, to be repaid in 12 monthly installments.
(1) What is the total loan amount?
(2) What are the monthly installments?
(3) What is the APR of the loan?
(4) What is the effective rate of the loan?
d. Would you, as a bank loan officer, make this loan? Why or why not?

SPREADSHEET PROBLEM

(16-18)
Build a Model: Cash Budgeting

resource

Start with the partial model in the file *Ch16 P18 Build a Model.xls* on the textbook's Web site. Rusty Spears, CEO of Rusty's Renovations, a custom building and repair company, is preparing documentation for a line of credit request from his commercial banker. Among the required documents is a detailed sales forecast for parts of 2014 and 2015:

	Sales	Labor and Raw Materials
May 2014	$60,000	$75,000
June	100,000	90,000
July	130,000	95,000
August	120,000	70,000
September	100,000	60,000
October	80,000	50,000
November	60,000	20,000
December	40,000	20,000
January 2015	30,000	NA

Estimates obtained from the credit and collection department are as follows: collections within the month of sale, 15%; collections during the month following the sale, 65%; collections the second month following the sale, 20%. Payments for labor and raw materials are typically made during the month following the one in which these costs were incurred. Total costs for labor and raw materials are estimated for each month as shown in the table.

General and administrative salaries will amount to approximately $15,000 a month; lease payments under long-term lease contracts will be $5,000 a month; depreciation charges will be $7,500 a month; miscellaneous expenses will be $2,000 a month; income tax payments of $25,000 will be due in both September and December; and a progress payment of $80,000 on a new office suite must be paid in October. Cash on hand on July 1 will amount to $60,000, and a minimum cash balance of $40,000 will be maintained throughout the cash budget period.

a. Prepare a monthly cash budget for the last 6 months of 2014.
b. Prepare an estimate of the required financing (or excess funds)—that is, the amount of money Rusty's Renovations will need to borrow (or will have available to invest)—for each month during that period.
c. Assume that receipts from sales come in uniformly during the month (i.e., cash receipts come in at the rate of 1/30 each day) but that all outflows are paid on the 5th of the month. Will this have an effect on the cash budget—in other words, would the cash budget you have prepared be valid under these assumptions? If not, what can be done to make a valid estimate of peak financing requirements? No calculations are required, although calculations can be used to illustrate the effects.
d. Rusty's Renovations produces on a seasonal basis, just ahead of sales. Without making any calculations, discuss how the company's current ratio and debt ratio would vary during the year assuming all financial requirements were met by short-term bank loans. Could changes in these ratios affect the firm's ability to obtain bank credit? Why or why not?
e. If its customers began to pay late, this would slow down collections and thus increase the required loan amount. Also, if sales dropped off, this would have an effect on the required loan amount. Perform a sensitivity analysis that shows the effects of these two factors on the maximum loan requirement.

MINI CASE

Karen Johnson, CFO for Raucous Roasters (RR), a specialty coffee manufacturer, is rethinking her company's working capital policy in light of a recent scare she faced when RR's corporate banker, citing a nationwide credit crunch, balked at renewing RR's line of credit. Had the line of credit not been renewed, RR would not have been able to make payroll, potentially forcing the company out of business. Although the line of credit was ultimately renewed, the scare has forced Johnson to examine carefully each component of RR's working capital to make sure it is needed, with the goal of determining whether the line of credit can be eliminated entirely. In addition to (possibly) freeing RR from the need for a line of credit, Johnson is well aware that reducing working capital can also add value to a company by improving its EVA (Economic Value Added). In her corporate finance course Johnson learned that EVA is calculated by taking net operating profit after taxes (NOPAT) and then subtracting the dollar cost of all the capital the firm uses:

$$EVA = NOPAT - \text{Capital costs}$$
$$= EBIT(1 - T) - WACC(\text{Total capital employed})$$

If EVA is positive, then the firm's management is creating value. On the other hand, if EVA is negative, then the firm is not covering its cost of capital and stockholders' value is being eroded. If RR could generate its current level of sales with fewer assets, it would need less capital. This would, other things held constant, lower capital costs and increase its EVA.

Historically, RR has done little to examine working capital, mainly because of poor communication among business functions. In the past, the production manager resisted Johnson's efforts to question his holdings of raw materials, the marketing manager resisted questions about finished goods, the sales staff resisted questions about credit policy (which affects accounts receivable), and the treasurer did not want to talk about the cash and securities balances. However, with the recent credit scare, this resistance became unacceptable and Johnson has undertaken a company-wide examination of cash, marketable securities, inventory, and accounts receivable levels.

Johnson also knows that decisions about working capital cannot be made in a vacuum. For example, if inventories could be lowered without adversely affecting operations, then less capital would be required, the dollar cost of capital would decline, and EVA would increase. However, lower raw materials inventories might lead to production slowdowns and higher costs, and lower finished goods inventories might lead to stock-outs and loss of sales. So, before inventories are changed, it will be necessary to study operating as well as financial effects. The situation is the same with regard to cash and receivables. Johnson has begun her investigation by collecting the ratios shown below. (The partial cash budget shown after the ratios is used later in this mini case.)

a. Johnson plans to use the preceding ratios as the starting point for discussions with RR's operating team. She wants everyone to think about the pros and cons of changing each type of current asset and how changes would interact to affect profits and EVA. Based on the data, does RR seem to be following a relaxed, moderate, or restricted working capital policy?

b. How can one distinguish between a relaxed but rational working capital policy and a situation in which a firm simply has excessive current assets because it is inefficient? Does RR's working capital policy seem appropriate?

c. Calculate the firm's cash conversion cycle given that annual sales are $660,000 and cost of goods sold represents 90% of sales. Assume a 365-day year.

d. What might RR do to reduce its cash without harming operations?

e. In an attempt to better understand RR's cash position, Johnson developed a cash budget for the first 2 months of the year. She has the figures for the other months, but they are not shown. Should depreciation expense be explicitly included in the cash budget? Why or why not?

f. In her preliminary cash budget, Johnson has assumed that all sales are collected and thus that RR has no bad debts. Is this realistic? If not, how would bad debts be dealt with in a cash budgeting sense? (*Hint:* Bad debts will affect collections but not purchases.)

g. Johnson's cash budget for the entire year, although not given here, is based heavily on her forecast for monthly sales. Sales are expected to be extremely low between May and September but then to increase dramatically in the fall and winter. November is typically the firm's best month, when RR ships its holiday blend of coffee. Johnson's forecasted cash budget indicates that the company's cash holdings will exceed the targeted cash balance every month except for October and November, when shipments will be high but collections will not be coming in until later. Based on the ratios shown earlier, does it appear that RR's target cash balance is appropriate? In addition to possibly lowering the target cash balance, what actions might RR take to better improve its cash management policies, and how might that affect its EVA?

	RR	Industry
Current	1.75	2.25
Quick	0.92	1.16
Total liabilities/assets	58.76%	50.00%
Turnover of cash and securities	16.67	22.22
Days sales outstanding (365-day basis)	45.63	32.00
Inventory turnover	10.80	20.00
Fixed assets turnover	7.75	13.22
Total assets turnover	2.60	3.00
Profit margin on sales	2.07%	3.50%
Return on equity (ROE)	10.45%	21.00%
Payables deferral period	30.00	33.00

Cash Budget (Thousands of Dollars)	Nov	Dec	Jan	Feb	Mar	Apr
Sales Forecast						
(1) Sales (gross)	$71,218.00	$68,212.00	$65,213.00	$52,475.00	$42,909.00	$30,524.00
Collections						
(2) During month of sale: (0.2)(0.98)(month's sales)			12,781.75	10,285.10		
(3) During first month after sale: (0.7)(previous month's sales)			47,748.40	45,649.10		
(4) During second month after sale: (0.1)(sales 2 months ago)			7,121.80	6,821.20		
(5) Total collections (Lines 2 + 3 + 4)			$67,651.95	$62,755.40		
Purchases						
(6) (0.85)(forecasted sales 2 months from now)		$44,603.75	$36,472.65	$25,945.40		
Payments						
(7) Payments (1-month lag)			44,603.75	36,472.65		
(8) Wages and salaries			6,690.56	5,470.90		
(9) Rent			2,500.00	2,500.00		
(10) Taxes						
(11) Total payments			$53,794.31	$44,443.55		
NCFs						
(12) Cash on hand at start of forecast			$ 3,000.00			
(13) NCF: Collections − Payments. = Line 5 − Line 11			$13,857.64	$18,311.85		
(14) Cum NCF: Prior + this mos. NCF			$16,857.64	$ 35169.49		
Cash Surplus (or Loan Requirement)						
(15) Target cash balance			1,500.00	1,500.00		
(16) Surplus cash or loan needed			$15,357.64	$33,669.49		

h. What reasons might RR have for maintaining a relatively high amount of cash?

i. Is there any reason to think that RR may be holding too much inventory? If so, how would that affect EVA and ROE?

j. If the company reduces its inventory without adversely affecting sales, what effect should this have on the company's cash position (1) in the short run and (2) in the long run? Explain in terms of the cash budget and the balance sheet.

k. Johnson knows that RR sells on the same credit terms as other firms in its industry. Use the ratios presented earlier to explain whether RR's customers pay more or less promptly than those of its competitors. If there are differences, does that suggest RR should tighten or loosen its credit policy? What four variables make up a firm's credit policy, and in what direction should each be changed by RR?

l. Does RR face any risks if it tightens its credit policy?

m. If the company reduces its DSO without seriously affecting sales, what effect would this have on its cash position (1) in the short run and (2) in the long run? Answer in terms of the cash budget and the balance sheet. What effect should this have on EVA in the long run?

n. In addition to improving the management of its current assets, RR is also reviewing the ways in which it finances its current assets. Is it likely that RR could make significantly greater use of accruals?

o. Assume that RR purchases $200,000 (net of discounts) of materials on terms of 1/10, net 30, but that it can get away with paying on the 40th day if it chooses not to take discounts. How much free trade credit can the company get from its equipment supplier, how much costly trade credit can it get, and what is the nominal annual interest rate of the costly credit? Should RR take discounts?

p. RR tries to match the maturity of its assets and liabilities. Describe how RR could adopt either a more aggressive or a more conservative financing policy.

q. What are the advantages and disadvantages of using short-term debt as a source of financing?

r. Would it be feasible for RR to finance with commercial paper?

SELECTED ADDITIONAL CASES

The following cases from CengageCompose cover many of the concepts discussed in this chapter and are available at **compose.cengage.com**.

Klein-Brigham Series:
Case 29, "Office Mates, Inc.," which illustrates how changes in current asset policy affect expected profitability and risk; Case 32, "Alpine Wear, Inc.," which illustrates the mechanics of the cash budget and the rationale behind its use; Case 50, "Toy World, Inc.," and Case 66, "Sorenson Stove Company," which deal with cash budgeting; Case 33, "Upscale Toddlers, Inc.," which deals with credit policy changes; and Case 34, "Texas Rose Company," which focuses on receivables management.

Brigham-Buzzard Series:
Case 11, "Powerline Network Corporation (Working Capital Management)."

© Adalberto Rios Szalay/Sexto Sol/Getty Images

CHAPTER 20

Hybrid Financing: Preferred Stock, Warrants, and Convertibles

T he U.S. government's responses to the global economic crisis were conducted through a wide variety of different programs administered by the Treasury Department, the Federal Reserve, the Federal Deposit Insurance Corporation, and Congress. Each program had a different emphasis, but many of the programs provided cash to troubled companies in exchange for newly issued securities that were (and still are) owned by the U.S. government. In addition to loans, these securities included preferred stock and warrants that are convertible into common stock.

For example, the Treasury bought about $67 billion in preferred stock from AIG, some of which was later converted to noncumulative preferred stock and common stock. The Treasury bought preferred stock and warrants from hundreds of financial institutions, including Bank of America, Citigroup, and JPMorgan Chase. The Treasury also made loans to GM and Chrysler. Some of the loans were replaced with stock as a part of the automakers' subsequent bankruptcy settlements.

Two questions arise. First, has the government made profitable investments? No—the government's daily TARP update estimates that the total lifetime cost of the programs will be about $43 billion. The U.S. financial system and economy have not (yet) collapsed as badly as they did in the Great Depression, so perhaps the money was well spent.

Second, how much control will the government exert on the companies in which it has invested? Preferred stock does not allow its owners to vote, so the government does not have any direct representation for those investments. The government owns over $50 billion in the common stock of AIG and GM, but no government employees are on GM's board.

As you read this chapter, think about the government's investments in preferred stock and warrants, and decide for yourself whether they were good investments.

Source: For updates and the status of the government TARP and stimulus **www.treasury. gov/initiatives/financial-stability/briefing-room/reports/105/Pages/default.aspx**

r e s o u r c e

The textbook's Web site contains an Excel file that will guide you through the chapter's calculations. The file for this chapter is **Ch20 Tool Kit.xls**, and we encourage you to open the file and follow along as you read the chapter.

In previous chapters, we examined common stocks and various types of long-term debt. In this chapter, we examine three other securities used to raise long-term capital: (1) *preferred stock*, which is a hybrid security that represents a cross between debt and common equity, (2) *warrants*, which are derivative securities issued by firms to facilitate the issuance of some other type of security, and (3) *convertibles*, which combine the features of debt (or preferred stock) and warrants.

20-1 Preferred Stock

Preferred stock is a hybrid—it is similar to bonds in some respects and to common stock in other ways. Accountants classify preferred stock as equity; hence they show it on the balance sheet as an equity account. However, from a financial perspective preferred stock lies somewhere between debt and common equity: It imposes a fixed charge and thus increases the firm's financial leverage, yet omitting the preferred dividend does not force a company into bankruptcy. Also, unlike interest on debt, preferred dividends are not deductible by the issuing corporation, so preferred stock has a higher cost of capital than does debt. We first describe the basic features of preferred stock, after which we discuss the types of preferred stock and the advantages and disadvantages of preferred stock.

20-1a Basic Features

Preferred stock has a par (or liquidating) value, often either $25 or $100. The dividend is stated as either a percentage of par, as so many dollars per share, or both ways. For example, several years ago Klondike Paper Company sold 150,000 shares of $100 par value perpetual preferred stock for a total of $15 million. This preferred stock had a stated annual dividend of $12 per share, so the preferred dividend yield was $12/$100 = 0.12, or 12%, at the time of issue. The dividend was set when the stock was issued; it will not be changed in the future. Therefore, if the required rate of return on preferred, r_{ps}, changes from 12% after the issue date—as it did—then the market price of the preferred stock will go up or down. Currently, r_{ps} for Klondike Paper's preferred is 9%, and the price of the preferred has risen from $100 to $12/0.09 = $133.33.

If the preferred dividend is not earned, the company does not have to pay it. However, most preferred issues are **cumulative**, meaning that the cumulative total of unpaid preferred dividends must be paid before dividends can be paid on the common stock. Unpaid preferred dividends are called **arrearages**. Dividends in arrears do not earn interest; thus, arrearages do not grow in a compound interest sense, they only grow from additional nonpayments of the preferred dividend. Also, many preferred stocks accrue arrearages for only a limited number of years—so that, for example, the cumulative feature may cease after 3 years. However, the dividends in arrears continue in force until they are paid.

Preferred stock normally has no voting rights. However, most preferred issues stipulate that the preferred stockholders can elect a minority of the directors—say, three out of ten—if the preferred dividend is passed (omitted). Some preferreds even entitle their holders to elect a majority of the board.

Although nonpayment of preferred dividends will not trigger bankruptcy, corporations issue preferred stock with every intention of paying the dividend. Even if passing the dividend does not give the preferred stockholders control of the company, failure to pay a preferred dividend precludes payment of common dividends. In addition, passing the

The Romance Had No Chemistry, But It Had a Lot of Preferred Stock!

© Rob Webb/Getty Images

On April 1, 2009, Dow Chemical Company merged with Rohm & Haas after a bitter dispute over the interpretation of their previous merger agreement. So even though the two companies make chemicals, there apparently wasn't much chemistry by the time the merger was completed.

To raise cash for the $78.97 per share purchase of Rohm & Haas's outstanding shares, Dow borrowed over $9 billion from Citibank and also issued $4 billion in convertible preferred stock to Berkshire Hathaway and The Kuwait Investment Authority.

The Haas Family Trusts and Paulson & Company were large shareholders in Rohm & Haas. As part of the deal, they sold their shares to Dow with one hand and bought $3 billion in preferred stock from Dow with the other. This preferred stock pays a cash dividend of 7%. It also pays an 8% "dividend" that either can be cash or additional shares of the preferred stock, with the choice left to Dow; this is called a payment-in-kind (PIK) dividend.

These terms mean that Dow can conserve cash if it runs into difficult times. Dow can pay the 8% in additional stock and Dow can even defer payment of the 7% cash dividend without risk of bankruptcy. But if this happens, a troubled marriage is likely to cause even more grief.

Source: 8-K reports from the SEC filed on March 12, 2009 and April 1, 2009.

W W W

For updates, go to **http://finance.yahoo.com** *and get quotes for AA-P, Alcoa's 3.75% preferred stock. For an updated bond yield, use the bond screener and search for Alcoa bonds.*

dividend makes it difficult to raise capital by selling bonds and virtually impossible to sell more preferred or common stock except at rock-bottom prices. However, having preferred stock outstanding does give a firm the chance to overcome its difficulties: If bonds had been used instead of preferred stock, a company could be forced into bankruptcy before it could straighten out its problems. Thus, *from the viewpoint of the issuing corporation, preferred stock is less risky than bonds.*

For an investor, however, preferred stock is riskier than bonds: (1) preferred stockholders' claims are subordinated to those of bondholders in the event of liquidation, and (2) bondholders are more likely to continue receiving income during hard times than are preferred stockholders. Accordingly, investors require a higher after-tax rate of return on a given firm's preferred stock than on its bonds. However, because 70% of preferred dividends is exempt from corporate taxes, preferred stock is attractive to corporate investors. Indeed, high-grade preferred stock, on average, sells on a lower pre-tax yield basis than high-grade bonds. As an example, Alcoa has preferred stock with an annual dividend of $3.75 (a 3.75% rate applied to $100 par value). In June 2012, Alcoa's preferred stock had a price of $82.50, for a market yield of about $3.75/$82.50 = 4.55%. Alcoa's long-term bonds that mature in 2037 provided a yield of 5.86%, which is 1.31 percentage points *more* than its preferred, even though preferred stock is riskier than debt. The tax treatment accounted for this differential; the *after-tax yield* to corporate investors was greater on the preferred stock than on the bonds because 70% of the dividend may be excluded from taxation by a corporate investor.[1]

About half of all preferred stock issued in recent years has been convertible into common stock. We discuss convertibles in Section 20-3.

---

[1]For example, the after-tax yield on an 8.1% bond to a corporate investor in the 34% marginal tax rate bracket is 8.1%(1 − T) = 5.3%. The after-tax yield on a 7.0% preferred stock is 7.0%(1 − Effective T) = 7.0%[1 − (0.30)(0.34)] = 6.3%. Also, note that tax law prevents arbitrage. If a firm issues debt and uses the proceeds to purchase another firm's preferred stock, then the 70% dividend exclusion is voided.

Some preferred stocks are similar to perpetual bonds in that they have no maturity date, but most new issues now have specified maturities. For example, many preferred shares have a sinking fund provision that calls for the retirement of 2% of the issue each year, meaning the issue will "mature" in a maximum of 50 years. Also, many preferred issues are callable by the issuing corporation, which can also limit the life of the preferred.[2]

Nonconvertible preferred stock is virtually all owned by corporations, which can take advantage of the 70% dividend exclusion to obtain a higher after-tax yield on preferred stock than on bonds. Individuals should not own preferred stocks (except convertible preferreds)—they can get higher yields on safer bonds, so it is not logical for them to hold preferreds.[3] As a result of this ownership pattern, the volume of preferred stock financing is geared to the supply of money in the hands of corporate investors. When the supply of such money is plentiful, the prices of preferred stocks are bid up, their yields fall, and investment bankers suggest that companies in need of financing consider issuing preferred stock.

For issuers, preferred stock has a tax *disadvantage* relative to debt: Interest expense is deductible, but preferred dividends are not. Still, firms with low tax rates may have an incentive to issue preferred stock that can be bought by high-tax-rate corporate investors, who can take advantage of the 70% dividend exclusion. If a firm has a lower tax rate than potential corporate buyers, then the firm might be better off issuing preferred stock than debt. The key here is that the tax advantage to a high-tax-rate corporation is greater than the tax disadvantage to a low-tax-rate issuer. As an illustration, assume that risk differentials between debt and preferred would require an issuer to set the interest rate on new debt at 10% and the dividend yield on new preferred stock 2% higher, or at 12% in a no-tax world. However, when taxes are considered, a corporate buyer with a high tax rate—say, 40%—might be willing to buy the preferred stock if it has an 8% before-tax yield. This would produce an 8%(1 − Effective T) = 8%[1 − 0.30(0.40)] = 7.04% after-tax return on the preferred versus 10%(1 − 0.40) = 6.0% on the debt. If the issuer has a low tax rate—say, 10%—then its after-tax costs would be 10%(1 − T) = 10%(0.90) = 9% on the bonds and 8% on the preferred. Thus, the security with lower risk to the issuer, preferred stock, also has a lower cost. Such situations can make preferred stock a logical financing choice.[4]

---

[2]Prior to the late 1970s, virtually all preferred stock was perpetual and almost no issues had sinking funds or call provisions. Then insurance company regulators, worried about the unrealized losses the companies had been incurring on preferred holdings as a result of rising interest rates, made changes essentially mandating that insurance companies buy only limited life preferreds. From that time on, virtually no new preferred has been perpetual. This example illustrates the way securities change as a result of changes in the economic environment.

[3]Since 2003, qualified dividends received by individuals are taxed at a capital gains rate rather than as ordinary income. This makes preferred stock more attractive relative to bonds, putting individual investors in much the same boat as corporations. For example, a corporation in the 35% tax bracket with a 70% dividend exclusion faces a (0.35)(1 − 0.70) = 10.5% tax rate on dividend income as compared to a 35% rate on interest income. Most individuals face a dividend tax rate of 15%, and high income earners would face a 35% tax on ordinary income. Thus there is a tax advantage for dividend income for both individuals and corporations, although the advantage is larger for corporations.

Also, some financially engineered preferred stock has "dividends" that the paying company can deduct for tax purposes in the same way that interest payments are deductible. Therefore, the company is able to pay a higher rate on such preferred stock, making it potentially attractive to individual investors. These securities trade under a variety of colorful names, including MIPS (Modified Income Preferred Securities), QUIPS (Quarterly Income Preferred Securities), TOPrS (Trust Originated Preferred Stock), and QUIDS (Quarterly Income Debt Securities). However, dividends from these hybrid securities are not subject to the 70% corporate exclusion and are taxed as ordinary income for individual investors.

[4]For more on preferred stock, see Arthur L. Houston Jr. and Carol Olson Houston, "Financing with Preferred Stock," *Financial Management,* Autumn 1990, pp. 42–54; and Michael J. Alderson and Donald R. Fraser, "Financial Innovations and Excesses Revisited: The Case of Auction Rate Preferred Stock," *Financial Management,* Summer 1993, pp. 61–75.

Hybrids Aren't Only for Corporations

© Rob Webb/Getty Images

The Cooperative Regions of Organic Producer Pools (CROPP) markets organic produce under such brand names as Organic Valley and Organic Prairie and is a supplier to Stonyfield, maker of organic yogurt. CROPP is not a corporation or a partnership. It is a cooperative, which is an organization that provides services for its owner/members. In this case, CROPP purchases produce from its members, processes the produce, and then resells it. Profits are redistributed to the owner/members as dividends.

With the beginnings of the financial recovery and an overall increase in the demand for organic products, CROPP's sales grew 18% in 2009 to over $600 million. High growth requires investments in operating assets, causing CROPP to need $14 million in additional external financing. CROPP decided to raise the funds by issuing preferred stock to members and non-members. CROPP had successfully issued preferred stock in the past and this issue was a $50 par, 6% cumulative dividend, non-

voting preferred stock, and was sold for $50 per share. CROPP chose not to use an investment banker for this issue; the co-op's investor relations manager was in charge of marketing and selling the preferred stock and CROPP saved quite a bit of money in fees with issuance costs totaling about 4.5% rather than the 7% or more charged by an investment bank.

Unlike preferred stock issued by corporations, dividends on preferred stock issued by a Section 521 cooperative such as CROPP can be deducted from its pre-tax income, and the dividend recipient treats it as ordinary income for tax purposes. Therefore this preferred stock is treated like perpetual debt for tax purposes. Why then would CROPP issue preferred stock rather than debt? The simple reason is that preferred stock is non-recourse. If CROPP misses a dividend payment, the dividend accrues, but the preferred stockholder cannot force CROPP into bankruptcy. This flexibility is valuable, especially in an industry as volatile as farming.

20-1b Other Types of Preferred Stock

In addition to "plain vanilla" preferred stock, there are two other variations: adjustable rate and market auction preferred stock.

ADJUSTABLE RATE PREFERRED STOCK

Instead of paying fixed dividends, **adjustable rate preferred stock (ARP)** has dividends tied to the rate on Treasury securities. ARPs are issued mainly by utilities and large commercial banks. When ARPs were first developed, they were touted as nearly perfect short-term corporate investments because (1) only 30% of the dividends are taxable to corporations, and (2) the floating-rate feature was supposed to keep the issue trading at near par. The new security proved to be popular as a short-term investment for firms with idle cash, so mutual funds that held ARPs sprouted like weeds (and shares of these funds, in turn, were purchased by corporations). However, the ARPs still had some price volatility due to (1) changes in the riskiness of the issuers (some big banks that had issued ARPs, such as Continental Illinois, ran into serious loan default problems) and (2) fluctuations in Treasury yields between dividend rate adjustment dates. Therefore, the ARPs had too much price instability to be held in the liquid asset portfolios of many corporate investors.

MARKET AUCTION PREFERRED STOCK

In 1984, investment bankers introduced **money market preferred stock**, which is also called **market auction preferred stock**.[5] Here the underwriter conducts an auction on the

---

[5]Confusingly, market auction preferred stock is frequently referred to as *auction-rate preferred* stock and with the acronym ARP as well.

issue every 7 weeks. (To get the 70% exclusion from taxable income, buyers must hold the stock for at least 46 days.) Holders who want to sell their shares can put them up for auction at par value. Buyers then submit bids in the form of the yields they are willing to accept over the next 7-week period. The yield set on the issue for the coming period is the lowest yield sufficient to sell all the shares being offered at that auction. The buyers pay the sellers the par value; hence holders are virtually assured that their shares can be sold at par. The issuer then must pay a dividend rate over the next 7-week period as determined by the auction. From the holder's standpoint, market auction preferred is a low-risk, largely tax-exempt, 7-week maturity security that can be sold between auction dates at close to par.

In practice, things may not go quite so smoothly. If there are few potential buyers, then an excessively high yield might be required to clear the market. To protect the issuing firms or mutual funds from high dividend payments, the securities have a cap on the allowable dividend yield. If the market-clearing yield is higher than this cap, then the next dividend yield will be set equal to this cap rate, but the auction will fail and the owners of the securities who wish to sell will not be able to do so. This happened in February 2008, and many market auction preferred stockholders were left holding securities they wanted to liquidate.

20-1c Advantages and Disadvantages of Preferred Stock

There are both advantages and disadvantages to financing with preferred stock. Here are the major advantages from the issuer's standpoint.

1. In contrast to bonds, the obligation to pay preferred dividends is not firm, and passing (not paying) a preferred dividend cannot force a firm into bankruptcy.
2. By issuing preferred stock, the firm avoids the dilution of common equity that occurs when common stock is sold.
3. Because preferred stock sometimes has no maturity and because preferred sinking fund payments (if present) are typically spread over a long period, preferred issues reduce the cash flow drain from repayment of principal that occurs with debt issues.

There are two major disadvantages, as follows.

1. Preferred stock dividends are not normally deductible to the issuer, so the after-tax cost of preferred is typically higher than the after-tax cost of debt. However, the tax advantage of preferreds to corporate purchasers lowers its pre-tax cost and thus its effective cost.
2. Although preferred dividends can be passed, investors expect them to be paid and firms intend to pay them if conditions permit. Thus, preferred dividends are considered to be a fixed cost. As a result, their use—like that of debt—increases financial risk and hence the cost of common equity.

SELF-TEST

Should preferred stock be classified as equity or debt? Explain.

Who are the major purchasers of nonconvertible preferred stock? Why?

Briefly explain the mechanics of adjustable rate and market auction preferred stock.

What are the advantages and disadvantages of preferred stock to the issuer?

A company's preferred stock has a pre-tax dividend yield of 7%, and its debt has a pre-tax yield of 8%. If an investor is in the 34% marginal tax bracket, what are the after-tax yields of the preferred stock and debt? **(6.29% and 5.28%)**

20-2 Warrants

A **warrant** is a certificate issued by a company that gives the holder the right to buy a stated number of shares of the company's stock at a specified price for some specified length of time. Generally, warrants are issued along with debt, and they are used to induce investors to buy long-term debt with a lower coupon rate than would otherwise be required. For example, when Infomatics Corporation, a rapidly growing high-tech company, wanted to sell $50 million of 20-year bonds in 2013, the company's investment bankers informed the financial vice president that the bonds would be difficult to sell and that a coupon rate of 10% would be required. However, as an alternative the bankers suggested that investors might be willing to buy the bonds with a coupon rate of only 8% if the company would offer 20 warrants with each $1,000 bond, each warrant entitling the holder to buy one share of common stock at a strike price (also called an *exercise price*) of $22 per share. The stock was selling for $20 per share at the time, and the warrants would expire in the year 2023 if they had not been exercised previously.

Why would investors be willing to buy Infomatics's bonds at a yield of only 8% in a 10% market just because warrants were also offered as part of the package? It's because the warrants are long-term *call options* that allow holders to buy the firm's common stock at the strike price regardless of how high the market price climbs. The value of this option offsets the low interest rate on the bonds and makes the package of low-yield bonds plus warrants attractive to investors. (See Chapter 8 for a discussion of options.)

20-2a Initial Market Price of a Bond with Warrants

If the Infomatics bonds had been issued as straight debt, they would have carried a 10% interest rate. However, with warrants attached, the bonds were sold to yield 8%. Someone buying the bonds at their $1,000 initial offering price would thus be receiving a package consisting of an 8%, 20-year bond plus 20 warrants. Because the going interest rate on bonds as risky as those of Infomatics was 10%, we can find the straight-debt value of the bonds, assuming an annual coupon for ease of illustration, as follows:

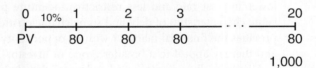

Using a financial calculator, input N = 20, I/YR = 10, PMT = 80, and FV = 1000. Then press the PV key to obtain the bond's value of $829.73, or approximately $830. Thus, a person buying the bonds in the initial underwriting would pay $1,000 and receive in exchange a straight bond worth about $830 plus 20 warrants that are presumably worth about $1,000 − $830 = $170:

$$\frac{\text{Price paid for}}{\text{bond with warrants}} = \frac{\text{Straight-debt}}{\text{value of bond}} + \frac{\text{Value of}}{\text{warrants}} \qquad \text{(20-1)}$$

$$\$1,000 = \$830 + \$170$$

Because investors receive 20 warrants with each bond, each warrant has an implied value of $170/20 = $8.50.

The key issue in setting the terms of a bond-with-warrants deal is valuing the warrants. The straight-debt value can be estimated quite accurately, as we have shown. However, it is more difficult to estimate the value of the warrants. The Black-Scholes option pricing model

(OPM), discussed in Chapter 8, can be used to find the value of a call option. There is a temptation to use this model to find the value of a warrant, because call options are similar to warrants in many respects: Both give the investor the right to buy a share of stock at a fixed strike price on or before the expiration date. However, there are major differences between call options and warrants. When call options are exercised, the stock provided to the option holder comes from the secondary market, but when warrants are exercised, the stock provided to the warrant holders is either newly issued shares or treasury stock the company has previously purchased. This means that the exercise of warrants dilutes the value of the original equity, which could cause the value of the original warrant to differ from the value of a similar call option. Also, call options typically have a life of just a few months, whereas warrants often have lives of 10 years or more. Finally, the Black-Scholes model assumes that the underlying stock pays no dividend, which is not unreasonable over a short period but is unreasonable for 5 or 10 years. Therefore, investment bankers cannot use the original Black-Scholes model to determine the value of warrants.

Even though the original Black-Scholes model cannot be used to determine a precise value for a warrant, there are more sophisticated models that work reasonably well.[6] In addition, investment bankers can simply contact portfolio managers of mutual funds, pension funds, and other organizations that would be interested in buying the securities to get an indication of how many they would buy at different prices. In effect, the bankers hold a presale auction and determine the set of terms that will just clear the market. If they do this job properly then they will, in effect, be letting the market determine the value of the warrants.

20-2b Use of Warrants in Financing

Warrants generally are used by small, rapidly growing firms as **sweeteners** when they sell debt or preferred stock. Such firms frequently are regarded by investors as being highly risky, so their bonds can be sold only at extremely high coupon rates and with very restrictive indenture provisions. To avoid such restrictions, firms like Infomatics often offer warrants along with the bonds.

Getting warrants along with bonds enables investors to share in the company's growth, assuming it does in fact grow and prosper. Therefore, investors are willing to accept a lower interest rate and less restrictive indenture provisions. A bond with warrants has some characteristics of debt and some characteristics of equity. It is a hybrid security that provides the financial manager with an opportunity to expand the firm's mix of securities and thereby appeal to a broader group of investors.

Virtually all warrants issued today are **detachable**. In other words, after a bond with attached warrants is sold, the warrants can be detached and traded separately from the bond.

---

[6]For example, see John C. Hull, *Options, Futures, and Other Derivatives*, 8th ed. (Boston: Prentice-Hall, 2012). Hull shows that if there are m warrants outstanding, each of which can be converted into γ shares of common stock at an exercise price of X, as well as n shares of common stock outstanding, then the price ω of a warrant is given by this modification of the Black-Scholes option pricing formula from Chapter 8:

$$\omega = \left(\frac{n\gamma}{n+m\gamma} \right) \left[S^* N(d_1^*) - Xe^{-r_{RF}(T-t)} N(d_2^*) \right] \text{ where } d_1^* = \frac{\ln(S^*/X) + (r_{RF} + \sigma_Q^2/2)(T-t)}{\sigma_Q \sqrt{T-t}}$$

Here $d_2^* = d_1^* - \sigma_Q(T-t)^{1/2}$ and $S^* = S + m\omega/n$, where S is the underlying stock price, T is the maturity date, r_{RF} is the risk free rate, σ_Q is the volatility of the stock and the warrants together, and $N(\cdot)$ is the cumulative normal distribution function. See Chapter 8 for more on the Black-Scholes option pricing formula. If $\gamma = 1$ and n is very much larger than m, so that the number of warrants issued is very small compared to the number of shares of stock outstanding, then this simplifies to the standard Black-Scholes option pricing formula.

Further, even after the warrants have been exercised, the bond (with its low coupon rate) remains outstanding.

The strike price on warrants is generally set some 20% to 30% above the market price of the stock on the date the bond is issued. If the firm grows and prospers, causing its stock price to rise above the strike price at which shares may be purchased, warrant holders could exercise their warrants and buy stock at the stated price. However, without some incentive, warrants would never be exercised prior to maturity—their value in the open market would be greater than their value if exercised, so holders would sell warrants rather than exercise them. There are three conditions that cause holders to exercise their warrants: (1) Warrant holders will surely exercise and buy stock if the warrants are about to expire and the market price of the stock is above the exercise price. (2) Warrant holders will exercise voluntarily if the company raises the dividend on the common stock by a sufficient amount. No dividend is earned on the warrant, so it provides no current income. However, if the common stock pays a high dividend, then it provides an attractive dividend yield but limits stock price growth. This induces warrant holders to exercise their option to buy the stock. (3) Warrants sometimes have stepped-up strike prices (also called stepped-up exercise prices), which prod owners into exercising them. For example, Williamson Scientific Company has warrants outstanding with a strike price of $25 until December 31, 2016, at which time the strike price rises to $30. If the price of the common stock is over $25 just before December 31, 2016, many warrant holders will exercise their options before the stepped-up price takes effect and the value of the warrants falls.

Another desirable feature of warrants is that they generally bring in funds only if funds are needed. If the company grows, it will probably need new equity capital. At the same time, growth will cause the price of the stock to rise and the warrants to be exercised; hence the firm will obtain the cash it needs. If the company is not successful and it cannot profitably employ additional money, then the price of its stock will probably not rise enough to induce exercise of the warrants.

20-2c The Component Cost of Bonds with Warrants

When Infomatics issued its bonds with warrants, the firm received $1,000 for each bond. The pre-tax cost of debt would have been 10% if no warrants had been attached, but each Infomatics bond has 20 warrants, each of which entitles its holder to buy one share of stock for $22. The presence of warrants also allows Infomatics to pay only 8% interest on the bonds, obligating it to pay $80 interest for 20 years plus $1,000 at the end of 20 years. What is the percentage cost of each $1,000 bond with warrants? As we shall see, the cost is well above the 8% coupon rate on the bonds.

The best way to approach this analysis is to break the $1,000 into two components, one consisting of an $830 bond and the other consisting of $170 of warrants. Thus, the $1,000 bond-with-warrants package consists of $830/$1,000 = 0.83 = 83% straight debt and $170/$1,000 = 0.17 = 17% warrant. Our objective is to find the cost of capital for the straight bonds and the cost of capital for the warrant, and then weight them to derive the cost of capital for the bond-with-warrants package.

The pre-tax cost of debt is 10% because this is the pre-tax cost of debt for a straight bond, so our task is to estimate the cost of capital for a warrant. Estimating the cost of capital for a warrant is fairly complicated, but we can use the following procedure to obtain a reasonable approximation.[7] The basic idea is to estimate the firm's expected cost of satisfying the warrant holders at the time the warrants expire. To do this, we need to

---

[7]For an exact solution, see P. Daves and M. Ehrhardt, "Convertible Securities, Employee Stock Options, and the Cost of Equity," *The Financial Review*, Vol. 42, 2007, pp. 267–288.

estimate the value the firm, the value of the debt, the intrinsic value of equity, and the stock price at the time of expiration.

Assume that the total value of Infomatics's operations and investments, which is $250 million immediately after issuing the bonds with warrants, is expected to grow at 9% per year. When the warrants are due to expire in 10 years, the total value of Infomatics is expected to be $250(1.09)^{10} = $591.841 million.

Infomatics will receive $22 per warrant when exercised; with 1 million warrants, this creates a $22 million cash flow to Infomatics. The total value of Infomatics will be equal to the value of operations plus the value of this cash. This will make the total value of Infomatics equal to $591.841 + $22 = $613.841 million.

When the warrants expire, the bonds will have 10 years remaining until maturity with a fixed coupon payment of $80. If the expected market interest rate is still 10%, then the time line of cash flows will be

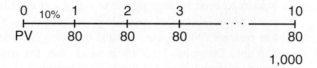

Using a financial calculator, input N = 10, I/YR = 10, PMT = 80, and FV = 1000; then press the PV key to obtain the bond's value, $877.11. The total value of all of the bonds is 50,000($877.11) = $43.856 million.

The intrinsic value of equity is equal to the total value of the firm minus the value of debt: $613.841 − $43.856 = $569.985 million.

Infomatics had 10 million shares outstanding prior to the warrants' exercise, so it will have 11 million after the 1 million options are exercised. The previous warrant holders will now own 1/11 of the equity, for a total of $569.985(1/11) = $51.82 million dollars. We can also estimate the predicted intrinsic stock price, which is equal to the intrinsic value of equity divided by the number of shares: $569.985/11 = $51.82 per share.[8] These calculations are summarized in Table 20-1.

To find the component cost of the warrants, consider that Infomatics will have to issue one share of stock worth $51.82 for each warrant exercised and, in return, Infomatics will receive the strike price, $22. Thus, a purchaser of the bonds with warrants, if she holds the complete package, would expect to realize a profit in Year 10 of $51.82 − $22 = $29.82 for each warrant exercised.[9] Because each bond has 20 warrants attached and because each warrant entitles the holder to buy one share of common stock, it follows that warrant holders will have an expected cash flow of 20($29.82) = $596.40 per bond at the end of Year 10. Here is a time line of the expected cash flow stream to a warrant holder:

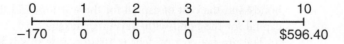

---

[8]If the stock price had been less than the strike price of $22 at expiration, then the warrants would not have been exercised. Based on the expected growth in the firm's value, there is little chance that the stock price will not be greater than $22.

[9]It is not strictly accurate to say that the expected profit from the warrant position is the expected stock price less the strike price: $29.82 = $51.82 − $22. This is because if the stock price drops below the strike price, in this case $22, then the warrant profit is $0, regardless of how low the stock price goes. Thus, the expected payoff will be somewhat more than $29.82. Although this expectation can be calculated using options techniques similar to those in Chapter 8, it is beyond the scope of this chapter. However, if there is a very small probability that the stock price will drop below the exercise price, then $29.82 is very close to the true expected payoff.

TABLE 20-1

Valuation Analysis after Exercise of Warrants in 10 Years (Millions of Dollars, Except for Per Share Data)

	Warrants Are Exercised
Expected value of operations and investments[a]	$ 591.841
Plus new cash from exercise of warrants[b]	22.000
Total value of firm	$ 613.841
Minus value of bonds	43.856
Value remaining for shareholders	$ 569.985
Divided by shares outstanding[c]	11
Price per share	$ 51.82

[a]The value of operations and investments is expected to grow from its current $250 million at a rate of 9%: $250(1.09)^{10} = $591.841 million.

[b]The warrants will be exercised only if the stock price at expiration is above $22. If the stock price is less than $22, then the warrants will expire worthless and there will be no new capital. Our calculations show that the expected stock price is much greater than $22, so the warrants are expected to be exercised.

[c] Before the warrants are exercised, there are 10 million shares of stock. After the warrants are exercised, there will be 10 + 1 = 11 million shares outstanding.

© Cengage Learning 2014

The IRR of this stream is 13.35%, which is an approximation of the warrant holder's expected return on the warrants (r_w) in the bond with warrants. The overall pre-tax cost of capital for the bonds with warrants is the weighted average of the cost of straight debt and the cost of warrants:

$$\text{Pre-tax cost of bonds with warrants} = r_d(\$830/\$1,000) + r_w(\$170/\$1,000)$$

$$= 10\%(0.83) + 13.35\%(0.17) = 10.57\%$$

The cost of the warrants is higher than the cost of debt because warrants are riskier than debt; in fact, the cost of warrants is greater than the cost of equity because warrants also are riskier than equity. Thus, the cost of capital for a bond with warrants is weighted between the cost of debt and the much higher cost of equity. This means the overall cost of capital for the bonds with warrants will be greater than the cost of straight debt and will be much higher than the 8% coupon rate on the bonds-with-warrants package.[10]

Bonds with warrants and preferred stock with warrants have become an important source of funding for companies during the global economic crisis. But as our example shows, this form of financing has a much higher cost of capital than its low coupon and preferred dividend might lead you to think.[11]

---

[10]In order to estimate the after-tax cost of capital, the after-tax cost of each component must be estimated. The after-tax cost of the warrant is the same as the pre-tax cost because warrants do not affect the issuer's tax liability. This is not true for the bond component. Because the straight bond is worth only $830 at the time of issue, it has an original issue discount (OID). This means that the after-tax cost of debt is not exactly equal to $r_d(1 - T)$. For long-term bonds, such as the one in this example, the difference is small enough to be neglected. See **Web Extension 5A** on the textbook's Web site for a general discussion of the after-tax cost of debt for zero coupon bonds and OID bonds. The **Ch20 Tool Kit.xls** calculates the after-tax cost of Infomatics's bond component, which is 6.3% rather than 10%(1 − 0.40) = 6%, assuming a 40% tax rate.

[11]For more on warrant pricing, see Michael C. Ehrhardt and Ronald E. Shrieves, "The Impact of Warrants and Convertible Securities on the Systematic Risk of Common Equity," *Financial Review*, November 1995, pp. 843–856; Beni Lauterbach and Paul Schultz, "Pricing Warrants: An Empirical Study of the Black-Scholes Model and Its Alternatives," *Journal of Finance*, September 1990, pp. 1181–1209; David C. Leonard and Michael E. Solt, "On Using the Black-Scholes Model to Value Warrants," *Journal of Financial Research*, Summer 1990, pp. 81–92; and Katherine L. Phelps, William T. Moore, and Rodney L. Roenfeldt, "Equity Valuation Effects of Warrant-Debt Financing," *Journal of Financial Research*, Summer 1991, pp. 93–103.

What is a warrant?

Describe how a new bond issue with warrants is valued.

How are warrants used in corporate financing?

The use of warrants lowers the coupon rate on the corresponding debt issue. Does this mean that the component cost of a debt-plus-warrants package is less than the cost of straight debt? Explain.

Shanton Corporation could issue 15-year straight debt at a rate of 8%. Instead, Shanton issues 15-year debt with a coupon rate of 6%, but each bond has 25 warrants attached. The bonds can be issued at par ($1,000 per bond). Assuming annual interest payments, what is the implied value of each warrant? **($6.85)**

20-3 Convertible Securities

Convertible securities are bonds or preferred stocks that, under specified terms and conditions, can be exchanged for (that is, converted into) common stock at the option of the holder. Unlike the exercise of warrants, which brings in additional funds to the firm, conversion does not provide new capital; debt (or preferred stock) is simply replaced on the balance sheet by common stock. Of course, reducing the debt or preferred stock will improve the firm's financial strength and make it easier to raise additional capital, but that requires a separate action.

20-3a Conversion Ratio and Conversion Price

resource

*See **Ch20 Tool Kit.xls** on the textbook's Web site for details.*

The **conversion ratio**, **CR**, for a convertible security is defined as the number of shares of stock a bondholder will receive upon conversion. The **conversion price**, P_c, is defined as the effective price investors pay for the common stock when conversion occurs. The relationship between the conversion ratio and the conversion price can be illustrated by Silicon Valley Software Company's convertible debentures issued at their $1,000 par value in July of 2013. At any time prior to maturity on July 15, 2033, a debenture holder can exchange a bond for 18 shares of common stock. Therefore, the conversion ratio, CR, is 18. The bond cost a purchaser $1,000, the par value, when it was issued. Dividing the $1,000 par value by the 18 shares received gives a conversion price of $55.56 a share:

$$\text{Conversion price} = P_c = \frac{\text{Par value of bond given up}}{\text{Shares received}} \qquad (20\text{-}2)$$

$$= \frac{\$1,000}{\text{CR}} = \frac{\$1,000}{18} = \$55.56$$

Conversely, by solving for CR, we obtain the conversion ratio:

$$\text{Conversion ratio} = \text{CR} = \frac{\$1,000}{P_c} \qquad (20\text{-}3)$$

$$= \frac{\$1,000}{\$55.56} = 18 \text{ shares}$$

Once CR is set, the value of P_c is established, and vice versa.

Like a warrant's exercise price, the conversion price is typically set some 20% to 30% above the prevailing market price of the common stock on the issue date. Generally, the conversion price and conversion ratio are fixed for the life of the bond, with the exception of protection against dilutive actions the company might take, including stock splits, stock dividends, and the sale of common stock at prices below the conversion price.[12]

The typical protective provision states that if the stock is split or if a stock dividend is declared, the conversion price must be lowered by the percentage amount of the stock dividend or split. For example, if Silicon Valley Software (SVS) were to have a 2-for-1 stock split, then the conversion ratio would automatically be adjusted from 18 to 36 and the conversion price lowered from $55.56 to $27.73. Also, if SVS sells common stock at a price below the conversion price, then the conversion price must be lowered (and the conversion ratio raised) to the price at which the new stock is issued. If protection were not contained in the contract, then a company could always prevent conversion by the use of stock splits and stock dividends. Warrants have similar protection against dilution.

However, this standard protection against dilution from selling new stock at prices below the conversion price can get a company into trouble. For example, SVS's stock was selling for $35 per share at the time the convertible was issued. Now suppose that the market went sour and the stock price dropped to $15 per share. If SVS needs new equity to support operations, a new common stock sale would require the company to lower the conversion price on the convertible debentures from $55.56 to $15. What impact would this have on the existing shareholders?

First, think about the value of a convertible bond as consisting of a straight bond and an option to convert. Reducing the conversion price is like reducing the strike price on an option, which would make the option to convert much more valuable. Second, recall the approach taken by the free cash flow valuation model to determine the value of equity—start with the value of operations, add the value of any nonoperating assets (like T-bills), and subtract the value of any debt, including convertible bonds. We can estimate the value of equity at the original conversion price and compare it to the value of equity at the new conversion price. At the new conversion price, the value of the convertible bond goes up, so the value of equity goes down, causing a transfer of wealth from the existing shareholders to the convertible bond-holders. Therefore, the protective reset feature on the conversion price makes it very costly for existing shareholders to raise additional equity in the times when new equity is needed.

20-3b The Component Cost of Convertibles

resource

See **Ch20 Tool Kit.xls** on the textbook's Web site for details.

resource

For a more detailed discussion of call strategies, see **Web Extension 20A** on the textbook's Web site.

In the spring of 2013, Silicon Valley Software was evaluating the use of the convertible bond issue described earlier. The issue would consist of 20-year convertible bonds that would sell at a price of $1,000 per bond; this $1,000 would also be the bond's par (and maturity) value. The bonds would pay an 8% annual coupon interest rate, which is $80 per year. Each bond would be convertible into 18 shares of stock, so the conversion price would be $1,000/18 = $55.56. Its stock price was $35. If the bonds were not made convertible then they would have to provide a yield of 10%, given their risk and the general level of interest rates. The convertible bonds would not be callable for 10 years, after which they could be called at a price of $1,050, with this price declining by $5 per year thereafter. If, after 10 years, the conversion value exceeded the call price by at least 20%, management would probably call the bonds.

---

[12]Some convertible bonds have a stepped-up conversion price. For example, a convertible bond might be convertible into 12 shares for the first 10 years, into 11 shares for the next 10, and 10 shares for the remainder of its life. This has the effect of increasing the conversion price over time, so that the holder of a convertible bond won't get rewarded if the stock price grows slowly.

SVS's cost of equity is 13%, with a 4% dividend yield and expected capital gain of 9% per year (Silicon Valley Software is a high risk company with low dividends and occasional stock repurchases, so its stock price has a high expected growth rate).

Figure 20-1 shows the expectations of both an average investor and the company. Refer to the figure as you consider the following points.

1. The horizontal dashed line at $1,000 represents the par (and maturity) value. Also, $1,000 is the price at which the bond is initially offered to the public.
2. The bond is protected against a call for 10 years. It is initially callable at a price of $1,050; the call price declines thereafter by $5 per year, as shown by the pink line in Figure 20-1.

FIGURE **20-1**

Silicon Valley Software: Convertible Bond Model

	Year	Straight-Bond Value, B_t	Conversion Value, C_t	Maturity (Par) Value	Market Value	Floor Value	Premium	Call Price
447	0	$830	$630	$1,000	$1,000	$830	$170	N/A
448	1	$833	$687	$1,000	$1,017	$833	$184	N/A
449	2	$836	$749	$1,000	$1,038	$836	$202	N/A
450	3	$840	$816	$1,000	$1,063	$840	$224	N/A
451	4	$844	$889	$1,000	$1,094	$889	$205	N/A
452	5	$848	$969	$1,000	$1,132	$969	$163	N/A
453	6	$853	$1,057	$1,000	$1,178	$1,057	$122	N/A
454	7	$858	$1,152	$1,000	$1,235	$1,152	$83	N/A
455	8	$864	$1,255	$1,000	$1,304	$1,255	$49	N/A
456	9	$870	$1,368	$1,000	$1,388	$1,368	$20	N/A
457	10	$877	$1,491	$1,000	$1,491	$1,491	$0	$1,050
458	11	$885	$1,626	$1,000	$1,626	$1,626	$0	$1,045
467	20	$1,000	$3,531	$1,000	$3,531	$3,531	$0	$1,000

3. Because the convertible has an 8% coupon rate and because the yield on a nonconvertible bond of similar risk is 10%, it follows that the expected "straight-bond" value of the convertible, B_t, must be less than par. At the time of issue and assuming an annual coupon, B_0 is $830:

$$\begin{array}{c}\text{Straight-debt value} \\ \text{at time of issue}\end{array} = B_0 = \sum_{t=1}^{N} \frac{\text{Coupon interest}}{(1 + r_d)^t} + \frac{\text{Maturity value}}{(1 + r_d)^N} \qquad (20\text{-}4)$$

$$= \sum_{t=1}^{20} \frac{\$80}{(1.10)^t} + \frac{\$1,000}{(1.10)^{20}} = \$830$$

Note, however, that the bond's straight-debt value must be $1,000 at maturity, so the straight-debt value rises over time; this is plotted by the brown line in Figure 20-1.

4. The bond's initial **conversion value, C_t,** or the value of the stock an investor would receive if the bonds were converted at t = 0, is $P_0(CR) = \$35(18 \text{ shares}) = \$630$. Because the stock price is expected to grow at a 9% rate, the conversion value should rise over time. For example, in Year 5 it should be $P_5(CR) = \$35(1.09)^5(18) = \$969$. The expected conversion value is shown by the green line in Figure 20-1.

5. If the market price dropped below the straight-bond value, then those who wanted bonds would recognize the bargain and buy the convertible as a bond. Similarly, if the market price dropped below the conversion value, people would buy the convertibles, exercise them to get stock, and then sell the stock at a profit. Therefore, the higher of the bond value and conversion value curves in the graph represents a *floor price* for the bond. In Figure 20-1, the floor price is represented by the red line.

6. The convertible bond's market price will exceed the straight-bond value because the option to convert is worth something—an 8% bond with conversion possibilities is worth more than an 8% bond without this option. The convertible's price will also exceed its conversion value because holding the convertible is equivalent to holding a call option and, prior to expiration, the option's true value is higher than its exercise (or conversion) value. Without using financial engineering models, we cannot say exactly where the market value line will lie, but as a rule it will be above the floor, as shown by the blue line in Figure 20-1.

7. If the stock price continues to increase, then it becomes more and more likely that the bond will be converted. As this likelihood increases, the market value line will begin to converge with the conversion value line.

After the bond becomes callable, its market value cannot exceed the higher of the conversion value and the call price without exposing investors to the danger of a call. For example, suppose that 10 years after issue (when the bonds become callable) the market value of the bond is $1,600, the conversion value is $1,500, and the call price is $1,050. If the company called the bonds the day after you bought one for $1,600, you would choose to convert them to stock worth only $1,500 (rather than let the company buy the bond from you at the $1,050 call price), so you would suffer a loss of $100. Recognizing this danger, you and other investors would refuse to pay a premium over the higher of the call price or the conversion value after the bond becomes callable. Therefore, in Figure 20-1, we assume that the market value line hits the conversion value line in Year 10, when the bond becomes callable.

8. In our example, the call-protection period ends in 10 years. At this time, the expected stock price is so high that the conversion value is almost certainly going to be greater than the call price; hence we assume that the bond will be converted immediately prior to the company calling the bond, which would happen in 10 years.

9. The expected market value at Year 10 is $35(1.09)^{10}(18) = \$1,491$. An investor can find the expected rate of return on the convertible bond, r_c, by finding the IRR of the following cash flow stream:

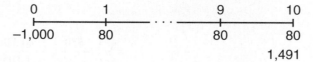

With a financial calculator, we set N = 10, PV = −1000, PMT = 80, and FV = 1491; we then solve for I/YR = r_c = IRR = 10.94%.[13]

10. A convertible bond is riskier than straight debt but less risky than stock, so its cost of capital should be somewhere between the cost of straight debt and the cost of equity. This is true in our example: $r_d = 10\%$, $r_c = 10.94\%$, and $r_s = 13\%$.[14]

20-3c Use of Convertibles in Financing

Convertibles have two important advantages from the issuer's standpoint: (1) Convertibles, like bonds with warrants, offer a company the chance to sell debt with a low coupon rate in exchange for giving bondholders a chance to participate in the company's success if it does well. (2) In a sense, convertibles provide a way to sell common stock at prices higher than those currently prevailing. Some companies actually want to sell common stock, not debt, but feel that the price of their stock is temporarily depressed. Management may know, for example, that earnings are depressed because of start-up costs associated with a new project, but they expect earnings to rise sharply during the next year or so, pulling the price of the stock up with them. Thus, if the company sold stock now, it would be giving up more shares than necessary to raise a given amount of capital. However, if it set the conversion price 20% to 30% above the present market price of the stock, then 20% to 30% fewer shares would be given up when the bonds were converted than if stock were sold directly at the current time. Note, however, that management is counting on the stock's price to rise above the conversion price, thus making the bonds attractive in conversion. If earnings do not rise and pull the stock price up, so that conversion does *not* occur, then the company will be saddled with debt in the face of low earnings, which could be disastrous.

---

[13]As in the case with warrants, the expected conversion value is not precisely equal to the expected stock price multiplied by the conversion ratio. Here is the reason. If after 10 years the stock price happens to be low, so that the conversion value is less than the call price, then the bondholders would not choose to convert—instead, they would surrender their bonds if the company called them. In this example, conversion does not occur if the stock price is less than $1,050/18 = \$58.33$ after 10 years. Because the company makes a call in order to force conversion, it won't call the bonds if the stock price is less than $58.33. So when the stock price is low, the bondholders will keep the bonds, whose value will depend primarily on interest rates at that time. Finding the expected value in this situation is a difficult problem (and is beyond the scope of this text). However, if the expected stock price is much greater than the conversion price when the bonds are called (in this case, $35[1.09]^{10}$ = $82.86 is much more than $58.33), then the difference between the true expected conversion value and the conversion value that we calculated using the expected stock price will be very small. Therefore, we can approximate the component cost reasonably accurately with the approach used in the example.

[14]To find the after-tax cost of the convertible, you can replace the pre-tax coupons with the after-tax coupons paid by the company. If the corporate tax rate is 40%, then we have N = 10, PV = −1000, PMT = 80(1 − 0.40) = 48, and FV = 1491; we solve for I/YR = $r_{c,AT}$ = 8.16%. Notice that this after-tax cost is not equal to $r_c(1 - T)$.

How can the company be sure that conversion will occur if the price of the stock rises above the conversion price? Typically, convertibles contain a call provision that enables the issuing firm to force holders to convert. Suppose the conversion price is $50, the conversion ratio is 20, the market price of the common stock has risen to $60, and the call price on a convertible bond is $1,050. If the company calls the bond, bondholders can either convert into common stock with a market value of 20($60) = $1,200 or allow the company to redeem the bond for $1,050. Naturally, bondholders prefer $1,200 to $1,050, so conversion would occur. The call provision thus gives the company a way to force conversion, provided the market price of the stock is greater than the conversion price. Note, however, that most convertibles have a fairly long period of call protection—10 years is typical. Therefore, if the company wants to be able to force conversion early, it will have to set a short call-protection period. This will, in turn, require that it set a higher coupon rate or a lower conversion price.

From the standpoint of the issuer, convertibles have three important disadvantages: (1) Even though the use of a convertible bond may give the company the opportunity to sell stock at a price higher than the current price, if the stock greatly increases in price, then the firm would be better off if it had used straight debt (in spite of its higher cost) and then later sold common stock and refunded the debt. (2) Convertibles typically have a low coupon interest rate, and the advantage of this low-cost debt will be lost when conversion occurs. (3) If the company truly wants to raise equity capital and if the price of the stock does not rise sufficiently after the bond is issued, then the company will be stuck with debt.

20-3d Convertibles and Agency Costs

A potential agency conflict between bondholders and stockholders is asset substitution, also known as "bait and switch." Suppose a company has been investing in low-risk projects, and because risk is low, bondholders charge a low interest rate. What happens if the company is considering a very risky but highly profitable venture that potential lenders don't know about? The company might decide to raise low-interest-rate debt without revealing that the funds will be invested in a risky project. After the funds have been raised and the investment is made, the value of the debt should fall because its interest rate will be too low to compensate debtholders for the high risk they bear. This is a "heads I win, tails you lose" situation, and it results in a wealth transfer from bondholders to stockholders.

Let's use some numbers to illustrate this scenario. The value of a company, based on the present value of its future free cash flows, is $800 million. It has $300 million of debt, based on market values. Therefore, its equity is worth $800 − $300 = $500 million. The company now undertakes some projects with high but risky expected returns, and its expected NPV remains unchanged. In other words, the actual NPV will probably end up much higher or much lower than under the old situation, but the firm still has the same expected value. Even though its total value is still $800 million, the value of the debt falls because its risk has increased. Note that the debtholders don't benefit if the venture's value is higher than expected, because the most they can receive is the contracted coupon and the principal repayment. However, they will suffer if the value of the projects turns out to be lower than expected, because they might not receive the full value of their contracted payments. In other words, risk doesn't give them any upside potential but does expose them to downside losses, so the bondholders' expected value must decline.

With a constant total firm value, if the value of the debt falls from $300 to $200 million, then the value of equity must increase from $500 to $800 − $200 = $600 million. Thus, the bait-and-switch tactic causes a wealth transfer of $100 million from debtholders to stockholders.

If debtholders think a company might employ the bait-and-switch tactic, they will charge a higher interest rate, and this higher interest rate is an agency cost. Debtholders will charge this higher rate even if the company has no intention of engaging in bait-and-switch behavior, because they can't know the company's true intentions. Therefore, they assume the worst and charge a higher interest rate.

Convertible securities are one way to mitigate this type of agency cost. Suppose the debt is convertible and the company does take on the high-risk project. If the value of the company turns out to be higher than expected, then bondholders can convert their debt to equity and benefit from the successful investment. Therefore, bondholders are willing to charge a lower interest rate on convertibles, and this serves to minimize the agency costs.

Note that if a company does not engage in bait-and-switch behavior by swapping low-risk projects for high-risk projects, then the chance of "hitting a home run" is reduced. Because there is less chance of a home run, the convertible bond is less likely to be converted. In this situation, the convertible bonds are actually similar to nonconvertible debt, except that they carry a lower interest rate.

Now consider a different agency cost, one due to asymmetric information between the managers and potential new stockholders. Suppose a firm's managers know that its future prospects are not as good as the market believes, which means the current stock price is too high. Acting in the interests of existing stockholders, managers can issue stock at the current high price. When the poor future prospects are eventually revealed, the stock price will fall, causing a transfer of wealth from the new shareholders to old shareholders.

To illustrate this, suppose the market estimates an $800 million present value of future free cash flows. For simplicity, assume the firm has no nonoperating assets and no debt, so the total value of both the firm and the equity is $800 million. However, its managers know the market has overestimated the future free cash flows and that the true value is only $700 million. When investors eventually discover this, the value of the company will drop to $700 million. But before this happens, suppose the company raises $200 million of new equity. The company uses this new cash to invest in projects with a present value of $200 million, which shouldn't be too hard, because these projects have a zero NPV. Right after the new stock is sold, the company will have a market value of $800 + $200 = $1,000 million, based on the market's overly optimistic estimate of the company's future prospects. Observe that the new shareholders own 20% of the company ($200/$1,000 = 0.20) and the original shareholders own 80%.

As time passes, the market will realize that the previously estimated value of $800 million for the company's original set of projects was too high and that these projects are worth only $700 million. The new projects are still worth $200 million, so the total value of the company will fall to $700 + $200 = $900 million. The original shareholders' value is now 80% of $900 million, which is $720 million. Note that this is $20 million *more* than it would have been if the company had issued no new stock. The new shareholders' value is now 0.20($900) = $180 million, which is $20 million *less* than their original investment. The net effect is a $20 million wealth transfer from the new shareholders to the original shareholders.

Because potential shareholders know this might occur, they interpret an issue of new stock as a signal of poor future prospects, which causes the stock price to fall. Note also that this will occur even for companies whose future prospects are actually quite good, because the market has no way of distinguishing between companies with good versus poor prospects.

A company with good future prospects might want to issue equity, but it knows the market will interpret this as a negative signal. One way to obtain equity and yet avoid this signaling effect is to issue convertible bonds. Because the company knows its true future prospects are better than the market anticipates, it knows the bonds will likely end up being converted to equity. Thus, a company in this situation is issuing equity "through the back door" when it issues convertible debt.

In summary, convertibles are logical securities to use in at least two situations. First, if a company would like to finance with straight debt but lenders are afraid the funds will be invested in a manner that increases the firm's risk profile, then convertibles are a good choice. Second, if a company wants to issue stock but thinks such a move would cause investors to interpret a stock offering as a signal of tough times ahead, then again convertibles would be a good choice.[15]

SELF-TEST

What is a conversion ratio? A conversion price? A straight-bond value?

What is meant by a convertible's floor value?

What are the advantages and disadvantages of convertibles to issuers? To investors?

How do convertibles reduce agency costs?

A convertible bond has a par value of $1,000 and a conversion price of $25. The stock currently trades for $22 a share. What are the bond's conversion ratio and conversion value at t = 0? **(40, $880)**

20-4 A Final Comparison of Warrants and Convertibles

Convertible debt can be thought of as straight debt with nondetachable warrants. Thus, at first blush, it might appear that debt with warrants and convertible debt are more or less interchangeable. However, a closer look reveals one major and several minor differences between these two securities.[16] First, as we discussed previously, the exercise of warrants brings in new equity capital, whereas the conversion of convertibles results only in an accounting transfer.

A second difference involves flexibility. Most convertibles contain a call provision that allows the issuer either to refund the debt or to force conversion, depending on the relationship between the conversion value and call price. However, most warrants are not callable, so firms must wait until maturity for the warrants to generate new equity capital. Generally, maturities also differ between warrants and convertibles. Warrants typically have much shorter maturities than convertibles, and warrants typically expire before their

---

[15]See Craig M. Lewis, Richard J. Rogalski, and James K. Seward, "Understanding the Design of Convertible Debt," *Journal of Applied Corporate Finance,* Vol. 11, No. 1, Spring 1998, pp. 45–53. For more insights into convertible pricing and use, see Paul Asquith and David W. Mullins Jr., "Convertible Debt: Corporate Call Policy and Voluntary Conversion," *Journal of Finance,* September 1991, pp. 1273–1289; Randall S. Billingsley and David M. Smith, "Why Do Firms Issue Convertible Debt?" *Financial Management,* Summer 1996, pp. 93–99; Douglas R. Emery, Mai E. Iskandor-Datta, and Jong-Chul Rhim, "Capital Structure Management as a Motivation for Calling Convertible Debt," *Journal of Financial Research,* Spring 1994, pp. 91–104; T. Harikumar, P. Kadapak-kam, and Ronald F. Singer, "Convertible Debt and Investment Incentives," *Journal of Financial Research,* Spring 1994, pp. 15–29; and V. Sivarama Krishnan and Ramesh P. Rao, "Financial Distress Costs and Delayed Calls of Convertible Bonds," *Financial Review,* November 1996, pp. 913–925.

[16]For a more detailed comparison of warrants and convertibles, see Michael S. Long and Stephen F. Sefcik, "Participation Financing: A Comparison of the Characteristics of Convertible Debt and Straight Bonds Issued in Conjunction with Warrants," *Financial Management,* Autumn 1990, pp. 23–34.

accompanying debt matures. Warrants also provide for fewer future common shares than do convertibles, because with convertibles all of the debt is converted to stock, whereas debt remains outstanding when warrants are exercised. Together, these facts suggest that debt-plus-warrant issuers are actually more interested in selling debt than in selling equity.

In general, firms that issue debt with warrants are smaller and riskier than those that issue convertibles. One possible rationale for the use of option securities, especially the use of debt with warrants by small firms, is the difficulty investors have in assessing the risk of small companies. If a start-up with a new, untested product seeks debt financing, then it's difficult for potential lenders to judge the riskiness of the venture and so it's difficult to set a fair interest rate. Under these circumstances, many potential investors will be reluctant to invest, making it necessary to set a very high interest rate to attract debt capital. By issuing debt with warrants, investors obtain a package that offers upside potential to offset the risks of loss.

Finally, there is a significant difference in issuance costs between debt with warrants and convertible debt. Bonds with warrants typically require issuance costs that are about 1.2 percentage points more than the flotation costs for convertibles. In general, bond-with-warrant financings have underwriting fees that approximate the weighted average of the fees associated with debt and equity issues, whereas underwriting costs for convertibles are more like those associated with straight debt.

SELF-TEST

What are some differences between debt-with-warrant financing and convertible debt?

Explain how bonds with warrants might help small, risky firms sell debt securities.

20-5 Reporting Earnings When Warrants or Convertibles Are Outstanding

If warrants or convertibles are outstanding, the Financial Accounting Standard Board requires that a firm report basic earnings per share and diluted earnings per share.[17]

1. *Basic EPS* is calculated as earnings available to common stockholders divided by the average number of shares actually outstanding during the period.
2. *Diluted EPS* is calculated as the earnings that would have been available to common shareholders divided by the average number of shares that would have been outstanding if "dilutive" securities had been converted. The rules governing the calculation of diluted EPS are quite complex; here we present a simple illustration using convertible bonds. If the bonds had been converted at the beginning of the

---

[17]FAS 128 was issued in February of 1997. It simplified the calculations required by firms, made U.S. standards more consistent with international standards, and required the presentation of both basic EPS and diluted EPS for those firms with significant amounts of convertible securities. In addition, it replaced a measure called *primary EPS* with basic EPS. In general, the calculation of primary EPS required the company to estimate whether or not a security was "likely to be converted in the near future" and to base the calculation of EPS on the assumption that those securities would in fact have been converted. In June 2008 the FASB issued FSP APB 14-1, which (although not changing how EPS is reported under FAS 128) requires that convertibles be split into their implied equity and debt components for accounting purposes, in much the same way as we analyze them in this chapter.

accounting period, then the firm's interest payments would have been lower because it would not have had to pay interest on the bonds, and this would have caused earnings to be higher. But the number of outstanding shares of stock also would have increased because of the conversion. If the higher earnings and higher number of shares caused EPS to fall, then the convertible bonds would be defined as dilutive securities because their conversion would decrease (or dilute) EPS. All convertible securities with a net dilutive effect are included when calculating diluted EPS. Therefore, this definition means that diluted EPS always will be lower than basic EPS. In essence, the diluted EPS measure is an attempt to show how the presence of convertible securities reduces common shareholders' claims on the firm.

Under SEC rules, firms are required to report both basic and diluted EPS. For firms with large amounts of option securities outstanding, there can be a substantial difference between the basic and diluted EPS figures. This makes it easier for investors to compare the performance of U.S. firms with their foreign counterparts, which tend to use basic EPS.

SELF-TEST

What are the three possible methods for reporting EPS when warrants and convertibles are outstanding?

Which methods are most used in practice?

Why should investors be concerned about a firm's outstanding warrants and convertibles?

SUMMARY

Although common stock and long-term debt provide most of the capital used by corporations, companies also use several forms of "hybrid securities." The hybrids include preferred stock, convertibles, and warrants, and they generally have some characteristics of debt and some of equity. The key concepts covered are listed below.

- **Preferred stock** is a hybrid—it is similar to bonds in some respects and to common stock in other ways.
- **Adjustable rate preferred stocks (ARPs)** pay dividends tied to the rate on Treasury securities. **Market auction (money market) preferred stocks** are low-risk, largely tax-exempt securities of 7-week maturity that can be sold between auction dates at close to par.
- A **warrant** is a long-term call option issued along with a bond. Warrants are generally detachable from the bond, and they trade separately in the market. When warrants are exercised, the firm receives additional equity capital, and the original bonds remain outstanding.
- A **convertible** security is a bond or preferred stock that can be exchanged for common stock at the option of the holder. When a security is converted, debt or preferred stock is replaced with common stock, and no money changes hands.
- Warrant and convertible issues generally are structured so that the **strike price** (also called the **exercise price**) or **conversion price** is 20% to 30% above the stock's price at time of issue.

- Although both warrants and convertibles are option securities, there are several differences between the two, including separability, impact when exercised, callability, maturity, and flotation costs.
- Warrants and convertibles are **sweeteners** used to make the underlying debt or preferred stock issue more attractive to investors. Although the coupon rate or dividend yield is lower when options are part of the issue, the overall cost of the issue is higher than the cost of straight debt or preferred, because option-related securities are riskier.
- For a more detailed discussion of call strategies see **Web Extension 20A** on the textbook's Web site.

QUESTIONS

(20-1) Define each of the following terms.

    a. Preferred stock
    b. Cumulative dividends; arrearages
    c. Warrant; detachable warrant
    d. Stepped-up price
    e. Convertible security
    f. Conversion ratio; conversion price; conversion value
    g. Sweetener

(20-2) Is preferred stock more like bonds or common stock? Explain.

(20-3) What effect does the trend in stock prices (subsequent to issue) have on a firm's ability to raise funds through (a) convertibles and (b) warrants?

(20-4) If a firm expects to have additional financial requirements in the future, would you recommend that it use convertibles or bonds with warrants? What factors would influence your decision?

(20-5) How does a firm's dividend policy affect each of the following?

    a. The value of its long-term warrants
    b. The likelihood that its convertible bonds will be converted
    c. The likelihood that its warrants will be exercised

(20-6) Evaluate the following statement: "Issuing convertible securities is a means by which a firm can sell common stock for more than the existing market price."

(20-7) Suppose a company simultaneously issues $50 million of convertible bonds with a coupon rate of 10% and $50 million of straight bonds with a coupon rate of 14%. Both bonds have the same maturity. Does the convertible issue's lower coupon rate suggest that it is less risky than the straight bond? Is the cost of capital lower on the convertible than on the straight bond? Explain.

SELF-TEST PROBLEM   Solution Appears in Appendix A

(ST-1)
Warrants

Connor Company recently issued two types of bonds. The first issue consisted of 10-year straight debt with a 6% annual coupon. The second issue consisted of 10-year bonds with a 4.5% annual coupon and attached warrants. Both issues sold at their $1,000 par values. What is the implied value of the warrants attached to each bond?

PROBLEMS   Answers Appear in Appendix B

Easy Problems 1–2

(20-1)
Warrants

Neubert Enterprises recently issued $1,000 par value 15-year bonds with a 5% coupon paid annually and warrants attached. These bonds are currently trading for $1,000. Neubert also has outstanding $1,000 par value 15-year straight debt with a 7% coupon paid annually, also trading for $1,000. What is the implied value of the warrants attached to each bond?

(20-2)
Convertibles

Breuer Investment's convertible bonds have a $1,000 par value and a conversion price of $50 a share. What is the convertible issue's conversion ratio?

Intermediate Problems 3–4

(20-3)
Warrants

Maese Industries Inc. has warrants outstanding that permit the holders to purchase 1 share of stock per warrant at a price of $25.

a. Calculate the exercise value of the firm's warrants if the common sells at each of the following prices: (1) $20, (2) $25, (3) $30, (4) $100. (*Hint:* A warrant's exercise value is the difference between the stock price and the purchase price specified by the warrant if the warrant were to be exercised.)

b. Assume the firm's stock now sells for $20 per share. The company wants to sell some 20-year, $1,000 par value bonds with interest paid annually. Each bond will have attached 50 warrants, each exercisable into 1 share of stock at an exercise price of $25. The firm's straight bonds yield 12%. Assume that each warrant will have a market value of $3 when the stock sells at $20. What coupon interest rate, and dollar coupon, must the company set on the bonds with warrants if they are to clear the market? (*Hint:* The convertible bond should have an initial price of $1,000.)

(20-4)
Convertible Premiums

The Tsetsekos Company was planning to finance an expansion. The principal executives of the company all agreed that an industrial company such as theirs should finance growth by means of common stock rather than by debt. However, they felt that the current $42 per share price of the company's common stock did not reflect its true worth, so they decided to sell a convertible security. They considered a convertible debenture but feared the burden of fixed interest charges if the common stock did not rise enough in price to make conversion attractive. They decided on an issue of convertible preferred stock, which would pay a dividend of $2.10 per share.

a. The conversion ratio will be 1.0; that is, each share of convertible preferred can be converted into a single share of common. Therefore, the convertible's par value (and also the issue price) will be equal to the conversion price, which in turn will be determined as a premium (i.e., the percentage by which the conversion price exceeds the stock price) over the current market price of the common stock. What will the conversion price be if it is set at a 10% premium? At a 30% premium?

b. Should the preferred stock include a call provision? Why or why not?

Challenging Problems 5–7

(20-5)
Convertible Bond Analysis

Fifteen years ago, Roop Industries sold $400 million of convertible bonds. The bonds had a 40-year maturity, a 5.75% coupon rate, and paid interest annually. They were sold at their $1,000 par value. The conversion price was set at $62.75, and the common stock price was $55 per share. The bonds were subordinated debentures and were given an

A rating; straight nonconvertible debentures of the same quality yielded about 8.75% at the time Roop's bonds were issued.

a. Calculate the premium on the bonds—that is, the percentage excess of the conversion price over the stock price at the time of issue.
b. What is Roop's annual before-tax interest savings on the convertible issue versus a straight-debt issue?
c. At the time the bonds were issued, what was the value per bond of the conversion feature?
d. Suppose the price of Roop's common stock fell from $55 on the day the bonds were issued to $32.75 now, 15 years after the issue date (also assume the stock price never exceeded $62.75). Assume interest rates remained constant. What is the current price of the straight-bond portion of the convertible bond? What is the current value if a bondholder converts a bond? Do you think it is likely that the bonds will be converted? Why or why not?
e. The bonds originally sold for $1,000. If interest rates on A-rated bonds had remained constant at 8.75% and if the stock price had fallen to $32.75, then what do you think would have happened to the price of the convertible bonds? (Assume no change in the standard deviation of stock returns.)
f. Now suppose that the price of Roop's common stock had fallen from $55 on the day the bonds were issued to $32.75 at present, 15 years after the issue. Suppose also that the interest rate on similar straight debt had fallen from 8.75% to 5.75%. Under these conditions, what is the current price of the straight-bond portion of the convertible bond? What is the current value if a bondholder converts a bond? What do you think would have happened to the price of the bonds?

(20-6)
Warrant/Convertible Decisions

The Howland Carpet Company has grown rapidly during the past 5 years. Recently, its commercial bank urged the company to consider increasing its permanent financing. Its bank loan under a line of credit has risen to $250,000, carrying an 8% interest rate. Howland has been 30 to 60 days late in paying trade creditors.

Discussions with an investment banker have resulted in the decision to raise $500,000 at this time. Investment bankers have assured the firm that the following alternatives are feasible (flotation costs will be ignored).

- *Alternative 1:* Sell common stock at $8.
- *Alternative 2:* Sell convertible bonds at an 8% coupon, convertible into 100 shares of common stock for each $1,000 bond (i.e., the conversion price is $10 per share).
- *Alternative 3:* Sell debentures at an 8% coupon, each $1,000 bond carrying 100 warrants to buy common stock at $10.

John L. Howland, the president, owns 80% of the common stock and wishes to maintain control of the company. There are 100,000 shares outstanding. The following are extracts of Howland's latest financial statements:

Balance Sheet

		Current liabilities	$400,000
		Common stock, par $1	100,000
		Retained earnings	50,000
Total assets	$550,000	Total claims	$550,000

Income Statement

Sales	$1,100,000
All costs except interest	990,000
EBIT	$ 110,000
Interest	20,000
EBT	$ 90,000
Taxes (40%)	36,000
Net income	$ 54,000
Shares outstanding	100,000
Earnings per share	$ 0.54
Price/earnings ratio	15.83
Market price of stock	$ 8.55

a. Show the new balance sheet under each alternative. For Alternatives 2 and 3, show the balance sheet after conversion of the bonds or exercise of the warrants. Assume that half of the funds raised will be used to pay off the bank loan and half to increase total assets.

b. Show Mr. Howland's control position under each alternative, assuming that he does not purchase additional shares.

c. What is the effect on earnings per share of each alternative, assuming that profits before interest and taxes will be 20% of total assets?

d. What will be the debt ratio (TL/TA) under each alternative?

e. Which of the three alternatives would you recommend to Howland, and why?

(20-7)
Convertible Bond Analysis

Niendorf Incorporated needs to raise $25 million to construct production facilities for a new type of USB memory device. The firm's straight nonconvertible debentures currently yield 9%. Its stock sells for $23 per share, has an expected constant growth rate of 6%, and has an expected dividend yield of 7%, for a total expected return on equity of 13%. Investment bankers have tentatively proposed that the firm raise the $25 million by issuing convertible debentures. These convertibles would have a $1,000 par value, carry a coupon rate of 8%, have a 20-year maturity, and be convertible into 35 shares of stock. Coupon payments would be made annually. The bonds would be noncallable for 5 years, after which they would be callable at a price of $1,075; this call price would decline by $5 per year in Year 6 and each year thereafter. For simplicity, assume that the bonds may be called or converted only at the end of a year, immediately after the coupon and dividend payments. Also assume that management would call eligible bonds if the conversion value exceeded 20% of par value (not 20% of call price).

a. At what year do you expect the bonds will be forced into conversion with a call? What is the bond's value in conversion when it is converted at this time? What is the cash flow to the bondholder when it is converted at this time? (*Hint:* The cash flow includes the conversion value and the coupon payment, because the conversion occurs immediately after the coupon is paid.)

b. What is the expected rate of return (i.e., the before-tax component cost) on the proposed convertible issue?

SPREADSHEET PROBLEM

(20-8)
Build a Model: Convertible Bond Analysis

resource

Start with the partial model in the file *Ch20 P08 Build a Model.xls* on the textbook's Web site. Maggie's Magazines (MM) has straight nonconvertible bonds that currently yield 9%. MM's stock sells for $22 per share, has an expected constant growth rate of 6%, and has a dividend yield of 4%. MM plans on issuing convertible bonds that will have a $1,000 par value, a coupon rate of 8%, a 20-year maturity, and a conversion ratio of 32 (i.e., each bond could be convertible into 32 shares of stock). Coupon payments will be made annually. The bonds will be noncallable for 5 years, after which they will be callable at a price of $1,090; this call price would decline by $6 per year in Year 6 and each year thereafter. For simplicity, assume that the bonds may be called or converted only at the end of a year, immediately after the coupon and dividend payments. Management will call the bonds when their conversion value exceeds 25% of their par value (not their call price).

a. For each year, calculate (1) the anticipated stock price, (2) the anticipated conversion value, (3) the anticipated straight-bond price, and (4) the cash flow to the investor assuming conversion occurs. At what year do you expect the bonds will be forced into conversion with a call? What is the bond's value in conversion when it is converted at this time? What is the cash flow to the bondholder when it is converted at this time? (*Hint:* The cash flow includes the conversion value and the coupon payment, because the conversion occurs immediately after the coupon is paid.)

b. What is the expected rate of return (i.e., the before-tax component cost) on the proposed convertible issue?

c. Assume that the convertible bondholders require a 9% rate of return. If the coupon rate remains unchanged, then what conversion ratio will give a bond price of $1,000?

MINI CASE

Paul Duncan, financial manager of EduSoft Inc., is facing a dilemma. The firm was founded 5 years ago to provide educational software for the rapidly expanding primary and secondary school markets. Although EduSoft has done well, the firm's founder believes an industry shakeout is imminent. To survive, EduSoft must grab market share now, and this will require a large infusion of new capital.

Because he expects earnings to continue rising sharply and looks for the stock price to follow suit, Mr. Duncan does not think it would be wise to issue new common stock at this time. On the other hand, interest rates are currently high by historical standards, and the firm's B rating means that interest payments on a new debt issue would be prohibitive. Thus, he has narrowed his choice of financing alternatives to (1) preferred stock, (2) bonds with warrants, or (3) convertible bonds.

As Duncan's assistant, you have been asked to help in the decision process by answering the following questions.

a. How does preferred stock differ from both common equity and debt? Is preferred stock more risky than common stock? What is floating rate preferred stock?

b. How can knowledge of call options help a financial manager to better understand warrants and convertibles?

c. Mr. Duncan has decided to eliminate preferred stock as one of the alternatives and focus on the others. EduSoft's investment banker estimates that EduSoft could issue a bond-with-warrants package consisting of a 20-year bond and 27 warrants. Each warrant would have a strike price of $25 and 10 years until expiration. It is estimated that each warrant, when detached and traded separately, would have a value of $5. The coupon on a similar bond but without warrants would be 10%.

(1) What coupon rate should be set on the bond with warrants if the total package is to sell at par ($1,000)?

(2) When would you expect the warrants to be exercised? What is a stepped-up exercise price?

(3) Will the warrants bring in additional capital when exercised? If EduSoft issues 100,000 bond-with-warrant packages, how much cash will EduSoft receive when

the warrants are exercised? How many shares of stock will be outstanding after the warrants are exercised? (EduSoft currently has 20 million shares outstanding.)

(4) Because the presence of warrants results in a lower coupon rate on the accompanying debt issue, shouldn't all debt be issued with warrants? To answer this, estimate the anticipated stock price in 10 years when the warrants are expected to be exercised, and then estimate the return to the holders of the bond-with-warrants packages. Use the corporate valuation model to estimate the expected stock price in 10 years. Assume that EduSoft's current value of operations is $500 million and it is expected to grow at 8% per year.

(5) How would you expect the cost of the bond with warrants to compare with the cost of straight debt? With the cost of common stock (which is 13.4%)?

(6) If the corporate tax rate is 40%, what is the after-tax cost of the bond with warrants?

d. As an alternative to the bond with warrants, Mr. Duncan is considering convertible bonds. The firm's investment bankers estimate that EduSoft could sell a 20-year, 8.5% coupon (paid annually), callable convertible bond for its $1,000 par value, whereas a straight-debt issue would require a 10% coupon (paid annually). The convertibles would be call protected for 5 years, the call price would be $1,100, and the company would probably call the bonds as soon as possible after their conversion value exceeds $1,200. Note, though, that the call must occur on an issue-date anniversary. EduSoft's current stock price is $20, its last dividend was $1, and the dividend is expected to grow at a constant 8% rate. The convertible could be converted into 40 shares of EduSoft stock at the owner's option.

(1) What conversion price is built into the bond?

(2) What is the convertible's straight-debt value? What is the implied value of the convertibility feature?

(3) What is the formula for the bond's expected conversion value in any year? What is its conversion value at Year 0? At Year 10?

(4) What is meant by the "floor value" of a convertible? What is the convertible's expected floor value at Year 0? At Year 10?

(5) Assume that EduSoft intends to force conversion by calling the bond as soon as possible after its conversion value exceeds 20% above its par value, or 1.2($1,000) = $1,200. When is the issue expected to be called? (*Hint:* Recall that the call must be made on an anniversary date of the issue.)

(6) What is the expected cost of capital for the convertible to EduSoft? Does this cost appear to be consistent with the riskiness of the issue?

(7) What is the after-tax cost of the convertible bond?

e. Mr. Duncan believes that the costs of both the bond with warrants and the convertible bond are close enough to call them even and that the costs are consistent with the risks involved. Thus, he will make his decision based on other factors. What are some of the factors that he should consider?

f. How do convertible bonds help reduce agency costs?

SELECTED ADDITIONAL CASES

The following cases from CengageCompose cover many of the concepts discussed in this chapter and are available at **compose.cengage.com**.

Klein-Brigham Series:
Case 27, "Virginia May Chocolate Company," which illustrates convertible bond valuation, and Case 98, "Levinger Organic Snack," which illustrates the use of convertibles and warrants.

© lulu/fotolia.com

Strategic Finance in a Dynamic Environment

© Adalberto Rios Szalay/Sexto Sol/Getty Images

CHAPTER **21**

Dynamic Capital Structures

Take a look at the two charts below. The first shows the ratio of total debt to book capital (as measured by book values from financial statements) for Hewlett-Packard (HPQ) and Procter & Gamble (PG). The second shows the ratio of total debt to total market capitalization (the sum of the market value of equity and the book value of debt).

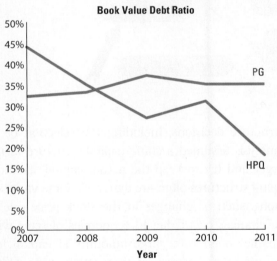

© Cengage Learning 2014

Notice that P&G has kept a very stable capital structure as measured by either ratio. In contrast, Hewlett-Packard's debt ratios have been volatile and have declined by substantial amounts. In theory, companies have target debt ratios. In practice, debt ratios are dynamic—some companies have a target but adjust to it slowly, other companies deliberately deviate from their target to take advantage of unexpected opportunities, and others change targets frequently. Think about the dynamic nature of Hewlett-Packard's capital structure as you read this chapter.

Corporate Valuation and Capital Structure Decisions

© Rob Webb/Getty Images

A firm's financing choices obviously have a direct effect on its weighted average cost of capital (WACC). Financing choices also have an indirect effect because they change the risk and required return of debt and equity. This chapter focuses on the debt–equity choice and its effect on value in a dynamic environment.

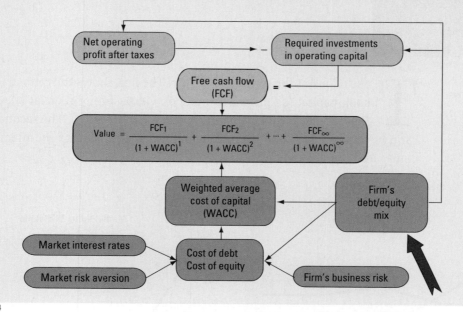

© Cengage Learning 2014

Chapter 15 described capital structure decisions, including the selection of an optimal capital structure. The analysis assumed a static capital structure in the sense that managers have a target and try to keep the actual capital structure equal to the target. However, capital structures often are dynamic. Some variation occurs without managerial actions, such as changes in the stock price due to overall market conditions. Some changes occur due to economies of scale with respect to raising capital—companies often raise large amounts of capital less frequently instead of small amounts often because of transaction costs. Other changes occur as companies deliberately deviate from their target to take advantage of unexpected opportunities. The first part of the chapter provides a general framework for analyzing capital structure effects on value, including applications for familiar cases, such as the Modigliani and Miller models. The second part shows how to evaluate companies with dynamic capital structures.

21-1 The Impact of Growth and Tax Shields on Value

Before addressing issues arising from dynamic capital structures, we need a framework for analyzing the impact of capital structure on a levered firm's value, V_L. The most general conceptual framework is to start with the value of an unlevered but

r e s o u r c e

*The textbook's Web site contains an Excel file that will guide you through the chapter's calculations. The file for this chapter is **Ch21 Tool Kit.xls**, and we encourage you to open the file and follow along as you read the chapter.*

otherwise identical firm, V_U, and adjust the unlevered value for any side effects due to leverage:

$$V_L = V_U + \text{Value of side effects} \qquad (21\text{-}1)$$

The value of an unlevered firm is the present value of its free cash flows (FCF) discounted at the weighted average cost of capital (WACC). For an unlevered firm, the WACC is the unlevered cost of equity: $\text{WACC} = r_{sU}$. If growth in FCF is expected to be constant at the rate g, then the free cash flow corporate valuation model from Chapter 7 shows that

$$V_U = \frac{FCF_1}{r_{sU} - g} \qquad (21\text{-}2)$$

In Chapter 15, we discussed some of the side effects of leverage, including benefits due to deductibility of interest expenses and costs due to financial distress. We will focus on the tax benefits now and address the costs of financial distress later.

The tax benefits are the annual tax savings (also called tax shields), TS_t, which are the annual reductions in taxes resulting from the deductibility of interest expenses. If r_d is the interest rate on debt, D_t is the amount of debt, and T is the tax rate, then the tax saving due to deducting interest expense is:

$$TS_t = r_d\, D_t\, T = (\text{Interest expense})(T) \qquad (21\text{-}3)$$

Each year a levered company can deduct its interest expenses, so the value of the levered firm is equal to the value of the unlevered firm plus the gain from leverage, which is the present value of the interest tax savings, also known as the **interest tax shield**:

$$V_L = V_U + V_{\text{Tax shield}} \qquad (21\text{-}1a)$$

The value of the tax shield is the present value of all of the interest tax savings (TS), discounted at the appropriate rate, r_{TS}:

$$V_{\text{Tax shield}} = \sum_{t=1}^{\infty} \frac{TS_t}{(1 + r_{TS})^t} = \sum_{t=1}^{\infty} \frac{r_d T D_t}{(1 + r_{TS})^t} \qquad (21\text{-}4)$$

If free cash flows grow at a constant rate and the proportions of debt and equity in the capital structure remain constant, then the annual tax savings grow at a constant rate. Using the constant growth model, the present value of these growing tax savings is

$$V_{\text{Tax shield}} = \frac{r_d T D_1}{r_{TS} - g} \qquad (21\text{-}5)$$

Substituting Equations 21-2 and 21-5 into Equation 21-1a yields a valuation expression that separately identifies the impact of leverage and growth on value:

$$V_L = V_U + \left(\frac{r_d}{r_{TS} - g}\right) TD_1 \qquad (21\text{-}6)$$

With considerable algebra, the levered cost of equity (r_{sL}) can be expressed in terms of: (1) the unlevered cost of equity; (2) the capital structure weights (w_d is the percentage of the firm financed with debt and w_s is the percentage financed with common stock); (3) the cost of debt (r_d); and (4) the discount rate for the tax shield.

$$r_{sL} = r_{sU} + (r_{sU} - r_d)\frac{w_d}{w_s} - (r_{sU} - r_{TS})\left[\frac{r_d T}{r_{TS} - g}\right]\frac{w_d}{w_s} \qquad (21\text{-}7)$$

The ratio of w_d/w_s is also equal to the ratio D/S, where S is the value of the stock. For some problems it is easier to use the ratio of D/S if you have already calculated D and S; in other problems, you might have a target capital structure, so it is easier to use the ratio w_s/w_s. We usually use the ratio that saves calculations and time, so be aware of this as you read the chapter and work problems.

Surprisingly, Equation 21-7 shows that growth actually can cause the levered cost of equity to be *less* than the unlevered cost of equity if $r_{TS} < r_{sU}$ and the last term is very large.[1] This could happen for combinations of rapid growth and low discount rate for the tax shield that cause the value of the tax shield to be very large. However, it is unlikely for such combinations to occur, because it would mean that high-growth firms would tend to have larger amounts of debt than low-growth firms. But this is not consistent either with intuition or observations in the market: High-growth firms actually tend to have lower levels of debt. Regardless of the growth rate, firms with more debt should have a higher cost of equity than firms with no debt. It is worth mentioning now that growth cannot cause the levered cost of equity to be lower than the unlevered cost of equity if $r_{TS} = r_{sU}$. We will use this finding later in the chapter when we discuss dynamic capital structures.

With a little more algebra, we can express a company's beta as a function of the unlevered beta of stock, b_U, the beta of the debt, b_D, and the beta of the tax shield, b_{TS}; the betas of the debt and the tax shield reflect the systematic risk of debt and the tax shield. The levered beta of a company is:

$$b = b_U + (b_U - b_D)\frac{w_d}{w_s} - (b_U - b_{TS})\left[\frac{r_d T}{r_{TS} - g}\right]\frac{w_d}{w_s} \qquad (21\text{-}8)$$

Observe that Equation 21-8 includes the term b_D. If corporate debt is not riskless, then its beta, b_D, may not be zero. If we assume that bonds lie on the Security Market Line, then a bond's required return, r_d, can be expressed as $r_d = r_{RF} + b_D RP_M$. Solving for b_D then gives $b_D = (r_d - r_{RF})/RP_M$.

---

[1] See Michael C. Ehrhardt and Phillip R. Daves, "Corporate Valuation: The Combined Impact of Growth and the Tax Shield of Debt on the Cost of Capital and Systematic Risk," *Journal of Applied Finance*, Fall/Winter 2002, pp. 31–38.

Armed with this general framework, let's examine some special cases, including the Modigliani and Miller models from Chapter 15 and a new model, the compressed adjusted present value (APV) model.

What is the value of an unlevered firm?

What is the tax shield due to debt in the capital structure?

How does the value of a levered firm compare to the value of an unlevered firm that is otherwise identical?

21-2 The Modigliani and Miller Models and the Compressed Adjusted Present Value (APV) Model

Recall from Chapter 15 that Modigliani and Miller (MM) developed a model of capital structure based on the assumption of zero growth and no risk of bankruptcy. In addition, they assumed that the appropriate discount rate for the tax shield is $r_{TS} = r_d$. They made this assumption because the annual tax savings are proportional to the annual debt, which implies that the tax savings have the same risk as debt. MM examined two situations, one with no taxes and one with corporate taxes.

21-2a Modigliani and Miller: No Taxes

In addition to the previous assumptions, MM's first model assumed no taxes. We show a proof of their model in Section 21-6, but here are three of their results:

$$V_L = V_U = FCF/r_{sU} \tag{21-9}$$

and

$$r_{sL} = r_{sU} + (r_{sU} - r_d)(w_d/w_s) \tag{21-10}$$

The Hamada adjustment that we discussed in Chapter 15 becomes:

$$b = b_U[1 + (w_d/w_s)] \tag{21-11}$$

21-2b Modigliani and Miller: Corporate Taxes

When MM include corporate taxes (but keep all their previous assumptions), their models become:

$$V_L = V_U + TD = FCF/r_{sU} + TD \tag{21-12}$$

and

$$r_{sL} = r_{sU} + (r_{sU} - r_d)(1 - T)(w_d/w_s)$$

(21-13)

The Hamada model is shown below:

$$b = b_U[1 + (1 - T)(w_d/w_s)]$$

(21-14)

Again, these three equations are exactly equal to the corresponding equations for the general framework (Equations 21-6, 21-7, and 21-8) if $g = 0$, $r_{TS} = r_d$.

21-2c The Compressed Adjusted Present Value Model (APV)

The compressed **adjusted present value (APV) model** allows non-zero growth and risky debt with a nonzero beta.[2] It also differs from the MM models in its assumption regarding the appropriate discount rate for the tax shield. In particular, it assumes that $r_{TS} = r_{sU}$. Here is the logic behind that choice.

A fundamental concept in finance is that the appropriate discount rate is the rate of return that investors require to compensate them for risk. So what is the risk of the tax shield? If the company will always get to deduct interest expenses, then the tax shield has no risk and should be discounted at the risk-free rate. However, corporate debt is not risk-free—firms do occasionally default on their loans if cash flows from operations are so low that the firm's value is less than the debt's value. Even if a company doesn't default on its debt, a company might not be able to use tax savings from interest deductions in the current year if it has a pre-tax operating loss. Therefore, the future tax savings are not risk-free and hence should be discounted using a higher rate than the risk-free rate.

How much higher should the discount rate be? The risk that the company will not be able to use future interest rate deductions stems from the risk of its pre-tax operating profit. This suggests that the unlevered cost of equity, which reflects the risk of operations, should be an upper limit for the required return on the tax shield.

Based on the previous logic, r_{TS} should be between the risk-free rate and the unlevered cost of equity. As we previously showed, the cost of levered equity can be less than the cost of unlevered equity unless $r_{TS} = r_{sU}$. Therefore, the compressed APV assumes that $r_{TS} = r_{sU}$.[3] Substituting this into the general valuation model in Equation 21-6, we get:

$$V_L = V_U + \left(\frac{r_d TD_1}{r_{sU} - g}\right)$$

(21-15)

---

[2]For a discussion of the *compressed APV* valuation method, which assumes that $r_{TS} = r_{sU}$, see Steven N. Kaplan and Richard S. Ruback, "The Valuation of Cash Flow Forecasts: An Empirical Analysis," *Journal of Finance,* September 1995, pp. 1059–1093. For evidence showing the effectiveness of the adjusted present value approach, see S. N. Kaplan and R. S. Ruback, "The Market Pricing of Cash Flow Forecasts: Discounted Cash Flow vs. the Method of 'Comparables,'" *Journal of Applied Corporate Finance,* Winter 1996, pp. 45–60.

[3]It is called the *compressed* APV because it is not necessary to separate the NOPAT and the interest expenses because all cash flows are discounted at the unlevered cost of equity. This means you can define the cash flow as net income minus required investments in operating capital. However, we usually keep interest expenses separate from free cash flow so that we can more easily identify the impact on value due to operations versus leverage.

Notice that the gain from leverage (the second term in Equation 21-15) can be larger or smaller than the gain from leverage in the MM model with taxes, depending on the fraction $r_d/(r_{sU} - g)$. If the cost of debt is low relative to the spread between the unlevered cost of equity and the growth rate, then a growing tax shield is very valuable. On the other hand, if growth is very low (or zero), then fraction $r_d/(r_{sU} - g)$ is less than 1, which means that the gain from leverage is bigger in the MM model than in the APV model. This makes sense, because the MM model discounts the tax savings at the relatively low cost of debt, r_d, while the APV model discounts the tax savings at the relatively high unlevered cost of equity, r_{sU}.

Substituting that $r_{TS} = r_{sU}$ into Equation 21-7 shows that the levered cost of equity is:

$$r_{sL} = r_{sU} + (r_{sU} - r_d)(w_d/w_s) \tag{21-16}$$

Although the derivation of Equation 21-16 reflects corporate taxes and growth, neither of these expressions includes the corporate tax rate or the growth rate. This means that the expression for the levered required rate of return, Equation 21-16, is exactly the same as MM's expression for the levered required rate of return *without taxes*, Equation 21-10. The reason the tax rate and the growth rate drop out of these two expressions is that the growing tax shield is discounted at the unlevered cost of equity, r_{sU}, not at the cost of debt as in the MM model. The tax rate drops out because no matter how high the level of T, the total risk of the firm will not be changed—the unlevered cash flows and the tax shield are discounted at the same rate. The growth rate drops out for the same reason—an increasing debt level will not change the risk of the entire firm no matter what rate of growth prevails.

Substituting $r_{TS} = r_{sU}$ into Equation 21-8 shows the levered beta:

$$b = b_U + (b_U - b_D)(w_d/w_s) \tag{21-17}$$

If the systematic risk of debt is small enough to neglect, then the relationship between the levered beta and the unlevered beta is:

$$b = b_U[1 + (w_d/w_s)] \tag{21-17a}$$

This expression for the levered beta is exactly the same as Hamada's formula in Equation 21-11 (and 21-14 but *without taxes*).

21-2d Illustration of the Models

resource

See *Ch21 Tool Kit.xls* on the textbook's Web site for all calculations.

To illustrate the models, we will examine the impact of leverage on Fredrickson Water Company, an established firm that supplies water to residential customers in several no-growth upstate New York communities. Following is some information about the company.

THE EXAMPLE COMPANY

Following are the required data for the analysis.

1. Fredrickson currently has no debt.
2. Expected EBIT = $2.4 million.
3. Fredrickson is in a no-growth situation, so g = 0.
4. If Fredrickson begins to use debt, it can borrow at a rate r_d = 8%. This borrowing rate is constant—it does not increase regardless of the amount of debt used. Any money raised by selling debt would be used to repurchase common stock, so *Fredrickson's assets would remain constant.*
5. The business risk inherent in Fredrickson's assets, and thus in its EBIT, is such that its beta is 0.80; this is called the unlevered beta, b_U, because Fredrickson has no debt. The risk-free rate is 8%, and the market risk premium (RP_M) is 5%. Using the Capital Asset Pricing Model (CAPM), Fredrickson's required rate of return on stock, r_{sU}, is 12% if no debt is used:

$$r_{sU} = r_{RF} + b_U(RP_M) = 8\% + 0.80(5\%) = 12\%$$

MM WITH ZERO TAXES

To begin, assume that there are no taxes and so T = 0%. Free cash flow is defined as NOPAT less required investments in capital. With zero growth, Frederickson doesn't require any investments in capital. NOPAT is defined as EBIT(1 – T), but no taxes mean that FCF is equal to EBIT.

Using Equation 21-9, Fredrickson's value is $20 million (no matter how much debt it has):

$$V_L = V_U = \frac{FCF}{r_{sU}} = \frac{EBIT}{r_{sU}} = \frac{\$2.4 \text{ million}}{0.12} = \$20.0 \text{ million}$$

If Fredrickson uses $10 million of debt, then the value of its stock, S, must be $10 million:

$$V_L = S + D$$

$$S = V - D = \$20 \text{ million} - \$10 \text{ million} = \$10 \text{ million}$$

With $10 million in debt and $10 million in stock, Frederickson would be financed with capital structure weights of w_d = 50% and w_s = 50%.

We can also find Fredrickson's cost of equity, r_{sL}, and its WACC at a debt level of $10 million. First, we use Equation 21-10 to find r_{sL}, Fredrickson's levered cost of equity:

$$r_{sL} = r_{sU} + (r_{sU} - r_d)(w_d/w_s)$$

$$= 12\% + (12\% - 8\%)(0.5/0.5)$$

$$= 12\% + 4.0\% = 16.0\%$$

Now we can find the company's weighted average cost of capital:

$$WACC = w_d(r_d)(1 - T) + w_s r_{sL}$$

$$= 0.5(8\%)(1.0) + 0.5(16.0\%) = 12.0\%$$

Fredrickson's value based on the MM model without taxes at various debt levels is shown in Panel a in Figure 21-1. Panel b reports the cost of equity and WACC. Here we see that, in an MM world without taxes, financial leverage simply does not matter: *The value of the firm and its overall cost of capital are both independent of the amount of debt.*

FIGURE 21-1

Effects of Leverage (Millions of Dollars Except Percentages)

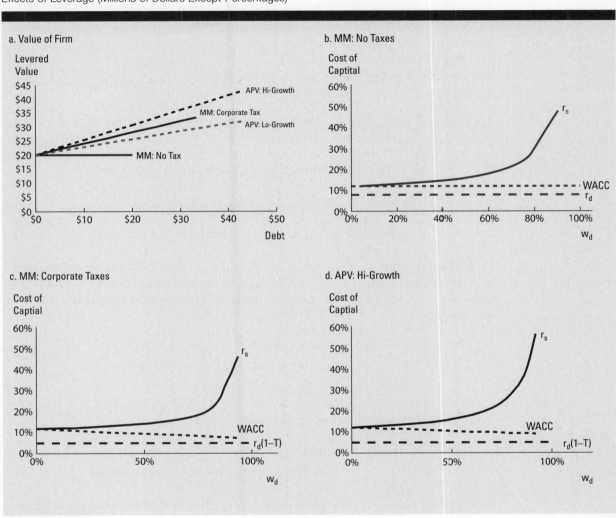

© Cengage Learning 2014

MM WITH CORPORATE TAXES

To illustrate the MM model with corporate taxes, assume that all of the previous conditions hold except for the following changes:

1. Expected EBIT = $4 million.[4]
2. Fredrickson has a 40% federal-plus-state tax rate, so T = 40%.

---

[4]If we had left Fredrickson's EBIT at $2.4 million, then introducing corporate taxes would have reduced the firm's value from $20 million to $12 million:

$$v_U = \frac{EBIT(1-T)}{r_{sU}} = \frac{\$2.4 \text{ million } (0.6)}{0.12} = \$12.0 \text{ million}$$

Corporate taxes reduce the amount of operating income available to investors in an unlevered firm by the factor $(1-T)$, so the value of the firm would be reduced by the same amount, holding r_{sU} constant.

Other things held constant, the introduction of corporate taxes would lower Fredrickson's net income and hence its value, so we increased EBIT from $2.4 million to $4 million to facilitate comparisons between the two models.

When Fredrickson has zero debt but pays taxes, Equation 21-12 can be used to find its current zero debt value:

$$v_U = \frac{EBIT(1-T)}{r_{sU}} + TD = \frac{\$4 \text{ million}(0.6)}{0.12} + \$0 = \$20 \text{ million}$$

If Fredrickson now uses $10 million of debt in a world with taxes, we see that its total market value rises from $20 to $24 million:

$$V_L = V_U + TD = \$20 \text{ million} + 0.4(\$10 \text{ million}) = \$24 \text{ million}$$

Therefore, the implied value of Fredrickson's equity is $14 million:

$$S = V - D = \$24 \text{ million} - \$10 \text{ million} = \$14 \text{ million}$$

We can also find Fredrickson's cost of equity, r_{sL}, and its WACC at a debt level of $10 million, which is equivalent to capital structure weights of $w_d = \$10/\$24 = 41.67\%$ and $w_s = 58.33\%$. First, we use Equation 21-13 to find r_{sL}, the levered cost of equity:

$$
\begin{aligned}
r_{sL} &= r_{sU} + (r_{sU} - r_d)(1-T)(w_d/w_s) \\
&= 12\% + (12\% - 8\%)(0.6)(0.4167/0.5833) \\
&= 12\% + 1.71\% = 13.71\%
\end{aligned}
$$

The company's weighted average cost of capital is then

$$
\begin{aligned}
WACC &= w_d(r_d)(1-T) + w_s r_{sL} \\
&= (0.4167)(8\%)(0.6) + 0.5833(13.71\%) = 10.0\%
\end{aligned}
$$

Note that we can also find the levered beta and then the levered cost of equity. First, we apply Hamada's equation to find the levered beta:

$$
\begin{aligned}
b &= b_U[1 + (1-T)(w_d/w_s)] \\
&= 0.80[1 + (1-0.4)(0.4167/0.5833)] \\
&= 1.1429
\end{aligned}
$$

Applying the CAPM then yields the levered cost of equity as

$$r_{sL} = r_{RF} + b(RP_M) = 8\% + 1.1429(5\%) = 0.1371 = 13.71\%$$

Observe that this is the same levered cost of equity that we obtained directly using Equation 21-13.

Fredrickson's value at various debt levels with corporate taxes is shown in Panel a of Figure 21-1; Panel c show the cost of equity and the WACC. In an MM world with corporate taxes, financial leverage does matter: The value of the firm is maximized—and its overall cost of capital is minimized—if it uses almost 100%

debt financing. The increase in value is due solely to the tax deductibility of interest payments, which lowers both the cost of debt and the equity risk premium by $(1 - T)$.[5]

APV: HI-GROWTH AND LO-GROWTH

This section illustrates the compressed adjusted present value model in a Hi-Growth scenario and a Lo-Growth scenario. Assume that all of the previous conditions hold except for the following changes:

1. Required investment in operating capital = $0.60 million.
2. Hi-Growth scenario: Expected EBIT = $3 million and constant growth rate = 6%.[6]
3. Lo-Growth scenario: Expected EBIT = $4.83 million and constant growth rate = 0.5%.

Fredrickson's expected free cash flow in the Hi-Growth scenario is:

$$FCF = \$3(1 - 0.4) - \$0.60 = \$1.2 \text{ million}.$$

Frederickson's unlevered value is $20 million:

$$V_U = \frac{FCF}{r_{sU} - g} = \frac{\$1.2 \text{ million}}{0.12 - 0.6} = \$20.0 \text{ million}$$

With $10 million in debt financing, we use Equation 21-15 to estimate the levered value:

$$V_L = \$20 + \left(\frac{0.08(0.4)(\$10)}{0.12 - 0.06} \right) = \$20 + \$5.33 = \$25.33$$

The capital structure weights are $w_d = \$10/(\$25.33) = 39.48\%$ and $w_s = 60.52\%$. Using Equation 21-16, the levered cost of equity is

$$r_{sL} = 12\% + (12\% - 8\%)(0.3948/0.6052) = 14.61\%$$

The WACC is:

$$WACC = (0.3948)(8\%)(1 - 0.4) + 0.6052(14.61\%) = 10.74\%$$

---

[5]In the limit case where the firm used 100% debt financing, the bondholders would own the entire company and so would bear all the business risk. (Up until this point, MM assume that stockholders bear all the risk.) If the bondholders bear all the risk, then the capitalization rate on the debt should be equal to the equity capitalization rate at zero debt, $r_d = r_{sU} = 12\%$.

The income stream to the stockholders in the all-equity case was $4,000 000(1 - T) = $2,400,000, and the value of the firm was

$$V_U = \frac{\$2,400,000}{0.12} = \$20,000,000$$

With all debt, the entire $4,000,000 of EBIT would be used to pay interest charges: r_d would be 12%, so I = 0.12(Debt) = $4,000,000. Taxes would be zero, so the investors (bondholders) would get the entire $4,000,000 of operating income (they would not have to share it with the government). Thus, the value of the firm at 100% debt would be

$$V_L = \frac{\$4,000,000}{0.12} = \$33,333,333 = D$$

There is, of course, a transition problem in all this. Modigliani and Miller assume that $r_d = 8\%$ regardless of how much debt the firm has until debt reaches 100%, at which point r_d jumps to 12%, the cost of equity. As we shall see later in the chapter, r_d actually rises as the risk of financial distress increases.

[6]We made these changes so that the unlevered value would remain at $20 million.

We repeated all calculations for the Lo-Growth scenario; see ***Ch21 Tool Kit.xls*** for the calculations. Look at Panel a in Figure 21-1, which shows the value of the firm at different levels of debt for the MM model with no taxes, the MM model with taxes, and the two APV scenarios. With zero taxes, there is no tax shield and the value of a levered firm is the same as the value of an unlevered firm. For the MM model with corporate taxes, the value increases as debt increases, but it tops out at around $33 million. At this level of debt, virtually all operating earnings are being used to pay interest. For the APV scenarios, the value steadily increases as debt is added. For the Lo-Growth scenario, its value is less than the MM model with taxes because the APV model discounts the tax savings at the relatively high unlevered cost of equity whereas the MM model discounts tax savings at the much lower cost of debt.

Panels b, c, and d show the levered cost of equity, the WACC and the cost of debt for the two MM models and for the Hi-Growth APV scenario. With zero taxes (Panel b), the cost of equity goes up just fast enough to keep the WACC constant. However, when taxes are considered (Panels c and d), the combination of the after-tax cost of debt and the levered cost of equity results in a decrease in the WACC as more debt is added. The WACC falls faster for the MM model in Panel c than in the APV model in Panel d because the MM model discounts the tax savings at the relatively low cost of debt.

THE LEVERED BETA VERSUS THE UNLEVERED BETA

We have examined three models: (1) MM: No tax, (2) MM: Tax, and (3) APV. Each of the models has different implications for the levered cost of equity and the levered beta.

SELF-TEST

Is there an optimal capital structure under the MM zero-tax model?

What is the optimal capital structure under the MM model with corporate taxes?

Why do taxes result in a "gain from leverage" in the MM model with corporate taxes?

How does growth affect the value of the tax shield?

How will your estimates of the levered cost of equity be biased if you use the MM or Hamada models when growth is present?

An unlevered firm has a value of $100 million. An otherwise identical but levered firm has $30 million in debt. Under the MM zero-tax model, what is the value of the levered firm? **($100 million)** *Under the MM corporate tax model, what is the value of a levered firm if the corporate tax rate is 40%?* **($112 million)**

An unlevered firm has a value of $100 million. An otherwise identical but levered firm has $30 million in debt. Both firms are growing at a constant rate of 5%, the corporate tax rate is 40%, the cost of debt is 6%, and the unlevered cost of equity is 8% (assume r_{sU} is the appropriate discount rate for the tax shield). What is the value of the levered firm? **($124 million)** *What is the value of the stock?* **($94 million)** *What is the levered cost of equity?* **(8.64%)**

21-3 Dynamic Capital Structures and the Adjusted Present Value (APV) Model

A dynamic capital structure implies that a company's capital structure weights are changing over time. What impact does that have on a company's value? We can't use the dividend growth model or the free cash flow valuation model to answer that question—both models assume that the rates used to discount future cash flows (the required return on stock in the dividend growth model and the weighted average cost of capital in the free cash flow valuation model) are constant over time, but these rates definitely change if the capital structure changes. Therefore, a different approach must be used. Fortunately, the adjusted present value model is ideally suited for such situations.

21-3a An Overview of the APV Model for Dynamic Capital Structures

Even for dynamic capital structures, the value of operations can be broken into the portions due to unlevered operations and the tax shield

$$V_{\text{Operations}} = V_{\text{Unlevered}} + V_{\text{Tax shield}}$$

(21-1b)

To estimate the unlevered value of operations, $V_{\text{Unlevered}}$, we need the projected free cash flows and the unlevered cost of equity, r_{sU}. It is straightforward to estimate the projected free cash flows, as shown in Chapter 12. It can be a bit more complicated to estimate the unlevered cost of equity. If the company being analyzed currently has no debt, then its current cost of equity *is* the unlevered cost of equity. If the company already has some debt, then we need to unlever its current cost of equity. As mentioned previously, the Hamada equation is based on the MM model with corporate taxes, which discounts the tax savings at the cost of debt and which assumes zero growth, which makes the Hamada equation inappropriate for applications of the APV model. Instead, we use Equation 21-17 (or 21-17a if we neglect the systematic risk of debt). Given the estimated FCF and unlevered cost of equity, the unlevered value of operations is the present value of the firm's free cash flows discounted at the unlevered cost of equity:

$$V_{\text{Unlevered}} = \sum_{t=1}^{\infty} \frac{\text{FCF}_t}{(1 + r_{sU})^t}$$

(21-18)

As described earlier, the compressed APV discounts the tax savings at the unlevered cost of equity, so the value of the tax shield is:

$$V_{\text{Tax shield}} = \sum_{t=1}^{\infty} \frac{\text{TS}_t}{(1 + r_{sU})^t}$$

(21-19)

Application of the APV model to a dynamic capital structure still requires that the capital structure must eventually stabilize. It also requires that the FCF and TS eventually must grow at a constant rate, which allows us to find the horizon values using an approach similar to the ones we used in Chapter 7 for the nonconstant dividend model and the free cash flow corporate valuation model. Recall that those approaches explicitly projected the values for years with nonconstant growth rates, estimated the horizon value at the end of the nonconstant growth period, and then calculated the present value of the horizon value and the cash flows during the forecast period.

21-3b Application of the APV Model in a Dynamic Capital Structure

We illustrate the APV model with the following example. Mencer's Outdoor Gear (MEG) borrowed heavily and is reducing its debt over the next 3 years to a sustainable level. MEG has forecast free cash flows, interest expenses, and the tax savings due to the deductibility of interest expense for the next three years, as shown below:

	1	2	3
Free cash flow	$1,000	$1,200	$1,350
Interest expense	$ 800	$ 600	$ 400
Tax savings (T = 40%)	$ 320	$ 240	$ 160

The FCF and interest expenses are expected to grow at a constant rate of 4% after Year 3. MEG's unlevered cost of equity 10% and its tax rate is 40%.

THE UNLEVERED VALUE OF OPERATIONS

The horizon value of an unlevered firm at Year N ($HV_{U,N}$) is the value of all free cash flows beyond the horizon discounted back to the horizon at the unlevered cost of equity. Because FCF grows at a constant rate of g_L in the post-horizon period, we can use the constant growth formula:

$$\text{Horizon value of unlevered firm} = HV_{U,N} = \frac{FCF_{N+1}}{r_{sU} - g_L} = \frac{FCF_N(1 + g_L)}{r_{sU} - g_L} \qquad (21\text{-}20)$$

For Mencer, the horizon value of operations is:

$$HV_{U,3} = \frac{\$1,350(1 + 0.04)}{0.10 - 0.04} = \$23,400$$

This is the value of all free cash flows from Year 4 and beyond discounted back to Year 3.

The next step is to calculate the present value of the horizon value and the present values of all the free cash flows during the forecast period. Their sum is the current unlevered value of operations:

$$
\begin{aligned}
V_{\text{Unlevered}} &= \sum_{t=1}^{N} \frac{FCF_t}{(1 + r_{sU})^t} + \frac{HV_{U,N}}{(1 + r_{sU})^N} \\
&= \left[\frac{FCF_1}{(1 + r_{sU})^1} + \frac{FCF_2}{(1 + r_{sU})^2} + \cdots + \frac{FCF_N}{(1 + r_{sU})^N} \right] + \frac{[(TS_{N+1})/(r_{sU} - g_L)]}{(1 + r_{sU})^N}
\end{aligned}
\qquad (21\text{-}21)
$$

For Mencer's Outdoor Gear, the unlevered value of operations is:

$$V_{\text{Unlevered}} = \left[\frac{\$1,000}{(1.10)^1} + \frac{\$1,200}{(1.10)^2} + \frac{\$1,350}{(1.10)^3} \right] + \frac{\$23,400}{(1.10)^3}$$

$$= \$2,915.10 + \$17,580.77 = \$20,495.87$$

MEG's unlevered value of operations is $20,495.87. This would be the value of the company if it had no debt or nonoperating assets.

THE VALUE OF THE TAX SHIELD

The horizon value of the tax shield, $HV_{TS,N}$, is the value of all tax savings beyond the horizon, discounted back to the horizon:

$$\frac{\text{Horizon value of}}{\text{tax shield}} = HV_{TS,N} = \frac{TS_{N+1}}{r_{sU} - g_L} = \frac{TS_N(1 + g_L)}{r_{sU} - g_L} \qquad (21\text{-}22)$$

For Mencer's, the horizon value of the tax shield is:

$$HV_{TS,3} = \frac{160(1 + 0.04)}{0.10 - 0.04} = \$2,773.33$$

This is the value of all tax savings from Year 4 and beyond discounted back to Year 3.

The next step is to calculate the present value of the horizon value and the present values of all the tax savings during the forecast period. Their sum is the current value of the tax shield:

$$V_{\text{Tax shield}} = \sum_{t=1}^{N} \frac{TS_t}{(1 + r_{sU})^t} + \frac{HV_{TS,N}}{(1 + r_{sU})^N}$$

$$= \left[\frac{TS_1}{(1 + r_{sU})^1} + \frac{TS_2}{(1 + r_{sU})^2} + \cdots + \frac{TS_N}{(1 + r_{sU})^N} \right] + \frac{\left[(FCF_{N+1}) / (r_{sU} - g_L) \right]}{(1 + r_{sU})^1} \qquad (21\text{-}23)$$

For MEG, the value of the tax shield is:

$$V_{\text{Tax shield}} = \left[\frac{\$320}{(1.10)^1} + \frac{\$240}{(1.10)^2} + \frac{\$160}{(1.10)^3} \right] + \frac{\$2,773.33}{(1.10)^3}$$

$$= \$609.47 + \$2,083.64 = \$2,693.11$$

THE LEVERED VALUE OF OPERATIONS

The horizon value of the tax shield, $HV_{TS,N}$, is the value of all tax savings beyond the horizon, discounted back to the horizon:

$$V_{\text{Operations}} = V_{\text{Unlevered}} + V_{\text{Tax shield}}$$

$$= \$20,495.87 + \$2,693.11$$

$$= \$23,189$$

The APV approach gives the same answer as the dividend growth model and the free cash flow valuation model if the capital structure is constant. In a dynamic situation with a nonconstant capital structure, however, only the APV approach gives the correct value.

SELF-TEST

Why is the adjusted present value approach appropriate for situations with a changing capital structure?

Describe the steps required to apply the APV approach.

A company forecasts free cash flow of $400 at Year 1, $600 at Year 2; after Year 2, the FCF grow at a constant rate of 5%. The company forecasts the tax savings from interest deductions as $200 in Year 1, $100 in Year 2; after Year 2, the tax savings grow at a constant rate of 5%. The unlevered cost of equity is 9%. What is the horizon value of operations at Year 2? **($15,750.0)** *What is the current unlevered value of operations?* **($14,128.4)** *What is the horizon value of the tax shield at Year 2?* **($2,625.0)** *What is the current value of the tax shield?* **($2,477.1)** *What is the levered value of operations at Year 0?* **($16,605.5)**

21-4 Risky Debt and Equity as an Option

In the previous sections, we evaluated equity and debt using the standard discounted cash flow techniques. However, we learned in Chapter 11 that if there is an opportunity for management to make a change as a result of new information after a project or investment has been started, then there might be an option component to the project or investment being evaluated. This is the case with equity. To see why, consider Kunkel Inc., a small manufacturer of electronic wiring harnesses and instrumentation located in Minot, North Dakota. Kunkel's current value (debt plus equity) is $20 million, and its debt consists of $10 million face value of 5-year zero coupon bonds. What decision does management make when the debt comes due? In most cases, it would pay the $10 million that is due. But what if the company has done poorly and the firm is worth only $9 million? In that case, the firm is technically bankrupt, because its value is less than the amount of debt due. Management will choose to default on the loan; in this case, the firm will be liquidated or sold for $9 million, the debtholders will get all $9 million, and the stockholders will get nothing. Of course, if the firm is worth $10 million or more then management will choose to repay the loan. The ability to make this decision—to pay or not to pay—looks very much like an option, and the techniques we developed in Chapter 8 can be used to value it.

21-4a Using the Black-Scholes Option Pricing Model to Value Equity

To put this decision into an option context, suppose P is Kunkel's total value when the debt matures. Then, if the debt is paid off, Kunkel's stockholders will receive the equivalent of P − $10 million if P > $10 million.[7] They will receive nothing if P ≤ $10 million because management will default on the bond and the bondholders will take over the company. These facts can be summarized as follows:

$$\text{Payoff to stockholders} = \text{MAX}(P - \$10 \text{ million}, 0)$$

This is exactly the same payoff as a European call option on the total value (P) of the firm with a strike price equal to the face value of the debt, $10 million. We can use the Black-Scholes option pricing model from Chapter 8 to determine the value of this asset.

resource

*See **Ch21 Tool Kit.xls** on the textbook's Web site for all calculations.*

---

[7]Actually, rather than receive cash of P − $10 million, the stockholders will keep the company (which is worth P − $10 million) rather than turn it over to the bondholders.

Recall from Chapter 8 that the value of a call option depends on five factors: the price of the underlying asset, the strike price, the risk-free rate, the time to expiration, and the volatility of the market value of the underlying asset. Here the underlying asset is the total value of the firm. If we assume that volatility is 40% and that the risk-free rate is 6%, then the inputs for the Black-Scholes model are as follows:

$$P = \$20 \text{ million}$$
$$X = \$10 \text{ million}$$
$$t = 5 \text{ years}$$
$$r_{RF} = 6\%$$
$$\sigma = 40\%$$

The value of a European call option, as shown in Chapter 8, is

$$V = P[(N(d_1)] - Xe^{-r_{RF}t}[N(d_2)] \qquad \text{(21-24)}$$

where

$$d_1 = \frac{\ln(P/X) + (r_{RF}+\sigma^2/2)t}{\sigma\sqrt{t}} \qquad \text{(21-25)}$$

and

$$d_2 = d_1 - \sigma\sqrt{t} \qquad \text{(21-26)}$$

For Kunkel Inc.,

$$d_1 = \frac{\ln(20/10) + (0.06 + 0.40^2/2)5}{0.40\sqrt{5}} = 1.5576$$

$$d_2 = 1.5576 - 0.40\sqrt{5} = 0.6632$$

Using the *Excel* NORMSDIST function gives $N(d_1) = N(1.5576) = 0.9403$, $N(d_2) = N(0.6632) = 0.7464$, and $V = \$20(0.9403) - \$10e^{-0.06(5)}(0.7464) = \$13.28$ million. So Kunkel's equity is worth \$13.28 million, and its debt must be worth what is left over: \$20 − \$13.28 = \$6.72 million. Because this is 5-year, zero coupon debt, its yield must be

$$\text{Yield on debt} = \left(\frac{10}{6.72}\right)^{1/5} - 1 = 0.0827 = 8.27\%$$

Thus, when Kunkel issued the debt, it received \$6.72 million and the yield on the debt was 8.27%. Notice that the yield on the debt, 8.27%, is greater than the 6% risk-free rate. This is because the firm might default if its value falls enough, so the bonds are risky. Note also that the yield on the debt depends on the value of the option and hence on the riskiness of the firm. The debt will have a lower value—and a higher yield—the more the option is worth.

21-4b Managerial Incentives

The only decision an investor in a stock option can make, once the option is purchased, is whether and when to exercise it. However, this restriction does not apply to equity when it is viewed as an option on the total value of the firm. Management has some leeway to affect the riskiness of the firm through its capital budgeting and investment decisions, and it can affect the amount of capital invested in the firm through its dividend policy.

21-4c Capital Budgeting Decisions

When Kunkel issued the $10 million face value debt discussed previously, the yield was determined in part by Kunkel's riskiness, which in turn was determined in part by what management intended to do with the $6.72 million it raised. We know from our analysis in Chapter 8 that options are worth more when volatility is higher. This means that if Kunkel's management can find a way to increase its riskiness without decreasing the total value of the firm, then doing so will increase the equity's value while decreasing the debt's value. Management can accomplish this by selecting risky rather than safe investment projects. Table 21-1 shows the value of equity, the value of debt, and the yield on debt for a range of possible volatilities. See *Ch21 Tool Kit.xls* for the calculations.

Kunkel's current volatility is 40%, so its equity is worth $13.28 million and its debt is worth $6.72 million. But if, after incurring the debt, management undertakes projects that increase its riskiness from a volatility of 40% to a volatility of 80%, then the value of Kunkel's equity will increase by $2.53 million to $15.81 million and the value of its debt will decrease by the same amount. This 19% increase in the value of the equity represents a transfer of wealth from bondholders to stockholders. A corresponding transfer of wealth from stockholders to bondholders would occur if Kunkel undertook projects that were safer than originally planned. Table 21-1 shows that if management undertakes safe projects and drives the volatility down to 30%, then stockholders will lose (and bondholders will gain) $0.45 million.[4]

Such a strategy of investing borrowed funds in risky assets is called **bait and switch** because the firm obtains the money by promising one investment policy and then switching to another policy. The bait-and-switch problem is more severe when a firm's value is low relative to its level of debt. If Kunkel's total value is $20 million, then doubling its volatility from 40% to 80%

TABLE 21-1

The Value of Kunkel's Debt and Equity for Various Levels of Volatility (Millions of Dollars)

r e s o u r c e

See Ch21 Tool Kit.xls on the textbook's Web site for all calculations.

Standard Deviation	Equity	Proceeds from Debt	Debt Yield
20%	$12.62	$7.38	6.25%
30	12.83	7.17	6.89
40	**13.28**	**6.72**	**8.27**
50	13.86	6.14	10.25
60	14.51	5.49	12.74
70	15.17	4.83	15.66
80	15.81	4.19	18.99
90	16.41	3.59	22.74
100	16.96	3.04	26.92
110	17.46	2.54	31.56
120	17.90	2.10	36.68

© Cengage Learning 2014

TABLE 21-2

Debt and Equity Values for Various Levels of Volatility When the Firm's Total
Value is $10 Million (Millions of Dollars)

Standard Deviation	Equity	Value of Debt	Debt Yield
20%	$3.16	$6.84	7.90%
30	3.80	6.20	10.02
40	**4.46**	**5.54**	**12.52**
50	5.10	4.90	15.35
60	5.72	4.28	18.49
70	6.30	3.70	21.98
80	6.83	3.17	25.81
90	7.31	2.69	30.04
100	7.74	2.26	34.68
110	8.13	1.87	39.77
120	8.46	1.54	45.36

© Cengage Learning 2014

increases its equity value by 19%. But if Kunkel had done poorly in recent years and its total value were only $10 million, then the impact of increasing volatility would be much greater. Table 21-2 shows that if Kunkel's total value were only $10 million and it issued $10 million face value of 5-year, zero coupon debt, then its equity would be worth $4.46 million at a volatility of 40%. Doubling the volatility to 80% would increase the value of the equity to $6.83 million, or by 53%. The incentive for management to "roll the dice" with borrowed funds can be enormous, and if management owns many stock options, then their payoff from rolling the dice is even greater than the payoff to stockholders!

Bondholders are aware of these incentives and write covenants into debt issues that restrict management's ability to invest in riskier projects than originally promised. However, their attempts to protect themselves are not always successful, as the failures of Enron, Lehman Brothers, and AIG demonstrate. The combination of a risky industry, high levels of debt, and option-based compensation has proven to be very dangerous.

21-4d Equity with Risky Coupon Debt

We have analyzed the simple case when a firm has zero coupon debt outstanding. The analysis becomes much more complicated when a firm has debt that requires periodic interest payments, because then management can decide whether to default on each interest payment date. For example, suppose Kunkel's $10 million of debt is a 1-year, 8% loan with semiannual payments. The scheduled payments are $400,000 in 6 months, and then $10.4 million at the end of the year. If management makes the scheduled $400,000 interest payment, then the stockholders will acquire the right to make the next payment of $10.4 million. If it does not make the $400,000 payment, then by defaulting the stockholders lose the right to make that next payment and hence lose the firm.[8] In other words, at the beginning of the year the stockholders have an option to

---

[8]Bankruptcy is far more complicated than our example suggests. As a firm approaches default it can take a number of actions, and even after filing for bankruptcy the stockholders can substantially delay a takeover by bondholders, during which time the value of the firm can deteriorate further. As a result, stockholders can often extract concessions from bondholders in situations where it would seem that the bondholders should get all of the firm's value. Bankruptcy is discussed in more detail in Chapter 24.

purchase an option. The option they own has an exercise price of $400,000 and it expires in 6 months, and if they exercise it, they will acquire an option to purchase the entire firm for $10.4 million in another 6 months.

If the debt were 2-year debt, then there would be four decision points for management and the stockholders' position would be like an option on an option on an option on an option! These types of options are called **compound options**, and techniques for valuing them are beyond the scope of this book. However, the incentives discussed previously for the case when a firm has risky zero coupon debt still apply when the firm has periodic interest payments to make.[9]

SELF-TEST

Discuss how equity can be viewed as an option. Who has the option and what decision can they make?

Why would management want to increase the riskiness of the firm? Why would this make bondholders unhappy?

What can bondholders do to limit management's ability to bait and switch?

21-5 Introducing Personal Taxes: The Miller Model

Although MM included *corporate taxes* in the second version of their model, they did not extend the model to include *personal taxes*. However, in his presidential address to the American Finance Association, Merton Miller presented a model to show how leverage affects firms' values when both personal and corporate taxes are taken into account.[10]

21-5a The Miller Model

To explain Miller's model, we begin by defining T_c as the corporate tax rate, T_s as the personal tax rate on income from stocks, and T_d as the personal tax rate on income from debt. Note that stock returns are expected to come partly as dividends and partly as capital gains, so T_s is a weighted average of the effective tax rates on dividends and capital gains. However, essentially all debt income comes from interest, which is effectively taxed at investors' top rates; thus T_d is higher than T_s.

With personal taxes included and under the same set of assumptions used in the earlier MM models, the value of an unlevered firm is found as follows:

$$V_U = \frac{EBIT(1 - T_c)}{r_{sU}}$$

$$= \frac{EBIT(1 - T_c)(1 - T_s)}{r_{sU}(1 - T_s)}$$

(21-27)

---

[9]For more on viewing equity as an option, see D. Galai and R. Masulis, "The Option Pricing Model and the Risk Factor of Stock," *Journal of Financial Economics*, Vol. 3, 1976, pp. 53–81. For a discussion on compound options, see Robert Geske, "The Valuation of Corporate Liabilities as Compound Options," *Journal of Financial and Quantitative Analysis*, June 1984, pp. 541–552.

[10]See Merton H. Miller, "Debt and Taxes," *Journal of Finance*, May 1977, pp. 261–275.

The $(1 - T_s)$ term takes account of personal taxes. Note that, in order to find the value of the unlevered firm, we can either discount pre-personal-tax cash flows at the pre-personal-tax rate of r_{sU} or discount after-personal-tax cash flows at the after-personal-tax rate of $r_{sU}(1 - T_s)$. Therefore, the numerator in the second line of Equation 21-27 shows how much of the firm's operating income is left after the unlevered firm pays corporate income taxes and its stockholders subsequently pay personal taxes on their equity income. Note also that the discount rate, r_{sU}, in Equation 21-27 is not necessarily equal to the discount rate in Equation 21-12. The r_{sU} from Equation 21-12 is the required discount rate in a world with corporate taxes but no personal taxes; the r_{sU} in Equation 21-27 is the required discount rate in a world with both corporate and personal taxes.

21-5b Derivation of the Miller Model

To begin, we partition the levered firm's annual cash flows, CF_L, into those going to stockholders and those going to bondholders *after* corporate and personal taxes:

$$CF_L = \text{Net CF to stockholders} + \text{Net CF to bondholders}$$

$$= (EBIT - I)(1 - T_c)(1 - T_s) + I(1 - T_d) \qquad (21\text{-}28)$$

where I is the annual interest payment. Equation 21-28 can be rearranged as follows:

$$CF_L = [EBIT(1 - T_c)(1 - T_s)] - [I(1 - T_c)(1 - T_s)] + [I(1 - T_d)] \qquad (21\text{-}28a)$$

The first term in Equation 21-28a is identical to the after-personal-tax cash flow of an unlevered firm as shown in the numerator of Equation 21-27, and its present value is found by discounting the perpetual cash flow by $r_{sU}(1 - T_s)$.

The second and third terms reflect leverage and result from the cash flows associated with debt financing, which under the MM assumptions are riskless (because the firm's debt is riskless under those assumptions). We can either discount pre-personal-tax interest payments at the pre-personal-tax rate of r_d or discount after-personal-tax interest payments at the after-personal-tax rate of $r_d(1 - T_d)$. Because they are after-personal-tax cash flows to debtholders, the present value of the last two right-hand terms in Equation 21-28a can be obtained by discounting at the after-personal-tax cost of debt, $r_d(1 - T_d)$. Combining the present values of the three terms, we obtain this value for the levered firm:

$$V_L = \frac{EBIT(1 - T_c)(1 - T_s)}{r_{sU}(1 - T_s)} - \frac{I(1 - T_c)(1 - T_s)}{r_d(1 - T_d)} + \frac{I(1 - T_d)}{r_d(1 - T_d)} \qquad (21\text{-}29)$$

The first right-hand term in Equation 21-29 is identical to V_U in Equation 21-27. Recognizing this and consolidating the second two terms, we obtain

$$V_L = V_U + \left[1 - \frac{(1 - T_c)(1 - T_s)}{(1 - T_d)}\right]\left[\frac{I(1 - T_d)}{r_d(1 - T_d)}\right] \qquad (21\text{-}29a)$$

Now recognize that the after-tax perpetual interest payment divided by the after-tax required rate of return on debt, $I(1 - T_d)/r_d(1 - T_d)$, is equal to the market value of the perpetual debt, D:

$$D = \frac{I}{r_d} = \frac{I(1 - T_d)}{r_d(1 - T_d)} \qquad (21\text{-}30)$$

Substituting D into Equation 21-29a and rearranging, we obtain the following expression, which is called the **Miller model**:

$$\text{Miller model: } V_L = V_U + \left[1 - \frac{(1 - T_c)(1 - T_s)}{(1 - T_d)}\right] D \qquad (21\text{-}31)$$

The Miller model provides an estimate of the value of a levered firm in a world with both corporate and personal taxes.

The Miller model has several important implications, as follows.

1. The term in brackets,

$$\left[1 - \frac{(1 - T_c)(1 - T_s)}{(1 - T_d)}\right]$$

when multiplied by D, represents the gain from leverage. The bracketed term thus replaces the corporate tax rate, T, in the earlier MM model with corporate taxes $(V_L = V_U + TD)$.
2. If we ignore all taxes (i.e., if $T_c = T_s = T_d = 0$), then the bracketed term is zero, so in this case Equation 21-31 is the same as the original MM model without taxes.
3. If we ignore personal taxes (i.e., if $T_s = T_d = 0$), then the bracketed term reduces to $[1 - (1 - T_c)] = T_c$, so in this case Equation 21-31 is the same as the MM model with corporate taxes.
4. If the effective personal tax rates on stock and bond incomes were equal (i.e., if $T_s = T_d$), then $(1 - T_s)$ and $(1 - T_d)$ would cancel and so the bracketed term would again reduce to T_c.
5. If $(1 - T_c)(1 - T_s) = (1 - T_d)$, then the bracketed term would be zero and so the value of using leverage would also be zero. This implies that the tax advantage of debt to the firm would be exactly offset by the personal tax advantage of equity. Under this condition, capital structure would have no effect on a firm's value or its cost of capital, so we would be back to MM's original zero-tax proposition.

21-5c Application of the Miller Model

Because taxes on capital gains are lower than on ordinary income and can be deferred, the effective tax rate on stock income is normally less than that on bond income. This being the case, what would the Miller model predict as the gain from leverage? To answer this question, assume the tax rate on corporate income is $T_c = 34\%$, the effective rate on bond income is $T_d = 28\%$, and the effective rate on stock income is $T_s = 15\%$. Using these values in the Miller model, we find that a levered firm's value exceeds that of an unlevered firm by 22% of the market value of corporate debt:

$$\text{Gain from leverage} = \left[1 - \frac{(1-T_c)(1-T_s)}{(1-T_d)}\right]D$$

$$= \left[1 - \frac{(1-0.34)(1-0.15)}{(1-0.28)}\right]D$$

$$= (1 - 0.78)D$$

$$= 0.22D$$

Note that the MM model with corporate taxes would indicate a gain from leverage of $T_c(D) = 0.34D$, or 34% of the amount of corporate debt. Thus, with these assumed tax rates, adding personal taxes to the model lowers, but does not eliminate, the benefit from corporate debt. In general, whenever the effective tax rate on income from stock is less than the effective rate on income from bonds, the Miller model produces a lower gain from leverage than is produced by the MM model with taxes.

In his paper, Miller argued that firms in the aggregate would issue a mix of debt and equity securities such that the before-tax yields on corporate securities and the personal tax rates of the investors who bought these securities would adjust until equilibrium was reached. At equilibrium, $(1 - T_d)$ would equal $(1 - T_c)(1 - T_s)$ and so, as we noted in item 5 above, the tax advantage of debt to the firm would be exactly offset by personal taxation and thus capital structure would have no effect on a firm's value or its cost of capital. Hence, according to Miller, the conclusions derived from the original MM zero-tax model are correct!

Others have extended and tested Miller's analysis. Generally, these extensions question Miller's conclusion that there is no advantage to the use of corporate debt. In fact, Equation 21-31 shows that both T_c and T_s must be less than T_d if there is to be zero gain from leverage. For most U.S. corporations and investors, the effective tax rate on income from stock is less than the rate on income from bonds; that is, $T_s < T_d$. However, many corporate bonds are held by tax-exempt institutions, and in those cases T_c is generally greater than T_d. Also, for those high-tax-bracket individuals with $T_d > T_c$, T_s may be large enough that $(1 - T_c)(1 - T_s)$ is less than $(1 - T_d)$; in this case there would be an advantage to using corporate debt. Still, Miller's work does show that personal taxes offset some of the benefits of corporate debt. This means that the tax advantages of corporate debt are less than were implied by the earlier MM model, which considered only corporate taxes.

As we discuss in the next section, both the MM and the Miller models are based on strong but unrealistic assumptions, so we should regard our examples as indicating the general effects of leverage on a firm's value and not a precise relationship.

SELF-TEST

How does the Miller model differ from the MM model with corporate taxes?

What are the implications of the Miller model if $T_c = T_s = T_d = 0$? If $T_s = T_d = 0$?

Considering the current tax structure in the United States, what is the primary implication of the Miller model?

An unlevered firm has a value of $100 million. An otherwise identical but levered firm has $30 million in debt. Use the Miller model to calculate the value of a levered firm if the corporate tax rate is 40%, the personal tax rate on equity is 15%, and the personal tax rate on debt is 35%. **($106.46 million)**

21-6 Capital Structure Theory: Arbitrage Proofs of the Modigliani-Miller Theorems

Until 1958, capital structure theory consisted of loose assertions about investor behavior rather than carefully constructed models that could be tested by formal statistical analysis. In what has been called the most influential set of financial papers ever published, Franco Modigliani and Merton Miller (MM) addressed capital structure in a rigorous, scientific fashion, and they set off a chain of research that continues to this day.[11]

21-6a Assumptions

As we explain in this chapter, MM employed the concept of **arbitrage** to develop their theory. Arbitrage occurs if two similar assets—in this case, levered and unlevered stocks—sell at different prices. Arbitrageurs will buy the undervalued stock and simultaneously sell the overvalued stock, earning a profit in the process, and will continue doing so until market forces of supply and demand cause the prices of the two assets to be equal. For arbitrage to work, the assets must be equivalent, or nearly so. MM show that, under their assumptions, levered and unlevered stocks are sufficiently similar for the arbitrage process to operate.

No one, not even MM, believes their assumptions are sufficiently correct that their models will hold exactly in the real world. However, their models do show how money can be made through arbitrage if one can find ways around problems with the assumptions. Though some of them were later relaxed, here are the initial MM assumptions.

1. There are *no taxes*, either personal or corporate.
2. Business risk can be measured by σ_{EBIT}, and firms with the same degree of business risk are said to be in a *homogeneous risk class*.
3. All present and prospective investors have identical estimates of each firm's future EBIT; that is, investors have *homogeneous expectations* about expected future corporate earnings and the riskiness of those earnings.
4. Stocks and bonds are traded in *perfect capital markets*. This assumption implies, among other things, (a) that there are no brokerage costs and (b) that investors (both individuals and institutions) can borrow at the same rate as corporations.
5. *Debt is riskless*. This applies to both firms and investors, so the interest rate on all debt is the risk-free rate. Further, this situation holds regardless of how much debt a firm (or individual) uses.
6. All cash flows are *perpetuities*. This means that growth is zero, expected EBIT is constant, and all bonds are perpetuities with no maturity dates.

---

[11]See Franco Modigliani and Merton H. Miller, "The Cost of Capital, Corporation Finance and the Theory of Investment," *American Economic Review*, June 1958, pp. 261–297; "The Cost of Capital, Corporation Finance and the Theory of Investment: Reply," *American Economic Review*, September 1958, pp. 655–669; "Taxes and the Cost of Capital: A Correction," *American Economic Review*, June 1963, pp. 433–443; and "Reply," *American Economic Review*, June 1965, pp. 524–527. In a survey of Financial Management Association members, the original MM article was judged to have had the greatest impact on the field of finance of any work ever published. See Philip L. Cooley and J. Louis Heck, "Significant Contributions to Finance Literature," *Financial Management*, Tenth Anniversary Issue, 1981, pp. 23–33. Note that both Modigliani and Miller won Nobel Prizes—Modigliani in 1985 and Miller in 1990.

21-6b MM without Taxes

MM first analyzed leverage under the assumption that there are no corporate or personal income taxes. On the basis of their assumptions, they stated and algebraically proved two propositions.[12]

PROPOSITION I

The value of any firm is established by capitalizing its expected net operating income (EBIT) at a constant rate (r_{sU}) that is based on the firm's risk class:

$$V_L = V_U = \frac{EBIT}{WACC} = \frac{EBIT}{r_{sU}} \tag{21-32}$$

Here the subscript L designates a levered firm and U designates an unlevered firm. Both firms are assumed to be in the same business risk class, and r_{sU} is the required rate of return for an unlevered (i.e., all-equity) firm of this risk class when there are no taxes. For our purposes, it is easiest to think in terms of a single firm that has the option of financing either with all equity or with some combination of debt and equity. Hence, L designates a firm that uses some amount of debt and U designates a firm that uses no debt.

As established by Equation 21-32, V is a constant; therefore, *under the MM model, if there are no taxes then the value of the firm is independent of its leverage.* As we shall see, this also implies the following statements.

1. The weighted average cost of capital, WACC, is completely independent of a firm's capital structure.
2. Regardless of the amount of debt a firm uses, its WACC is equal to the cost of equity that it would have if it used no debt.

PROPOSITION II

When there are no taxes, the cost of equity to a levered firm, r_{sL}, is equal to (1) the cost of equity to an unlevered firm in the same risk class, r_{sU}, plus (2) a risk premium whose size depends on (a) the difference between an unlevered firm's costs of debt and equity and (b) the amount of debt used:

$$r_{sL} = r_{sU} + \text{Risk premium} = r_{sU} + (r_{sU} - r_d)(D/S) \tag{21-33}$$

Here D is the market value of the firm's debt, S is the market value of its equity, and r_d is the constant cost of debt. Equation 21-33 states that, *as debt increases, the cost of equity rises in a mathematically precise manner* (even though the cost of debt does not rise).

Taken together, the two MM propositions imply that using more debt in the capital structure will not increase the value of the firm, because the benefits of cheaper debt will be exactly offset by an increase in the riskiness of the equity and hence in its cost. Thus, MM argue that, *in a world without taxes, both the value of a firm and its WACC would be unaffected by its capital structure.*

---

[12]Modigliani and Miller actually stated and proved three propositions, but the third one is not material to our discussion here.

21-6c MM's Arbitrage Proof

Propositions I and II are important because they showed for the first time that any valuation effects due to the use of debt must arise from taxes or other market frictions. The technique that MM used to prove these propositions is equally important, however, so we discuss it in detail here. They used an *arbitrage proof* to support their propositions, and this proof technique was later used in the development of option pricing models that revolutionized the securities industry.[13] Modigliani and Miller showed that, under their assumptions, if two companies differed only (1) in the way they were financed and (2) in their total market values, then investors would sell shares of the higher-valued firm, buy those of the lower-valued firm, and continue this process until the companies had exactly the same market value. To illustrate, assume that two firms, L and U, are identical in all important respects except that Firm L has $4,000,000 of 7.5% debt while Firm U uses only equity. Both firms have EBIT = $900,000, and σ_{EBIT} is the same for both firms, so they are in the same business risk class.

Modigliani and Miller assumed that all firms are in a zero-growth situation. In other words, EBIT is expected to remain constant; this will occur if ROE is constant, all earnings are paid out as dividends, and there are no taxes. Under the constant EBIT assumption, the total market value of the common stock, S, is the present value of a perpetuity, which is found as follows:

$$S = \frac{\text{Dividends}}{r_{sL}} = \frac{\text{Net income}}{r_{sL}} = \frac{\text{EBIT} - r_d D}{r_{sL}} \tag{21-34}$$

Equation 21-34 is merely the value of a perpetuity, where the numerator is the net income available to common stockholders (all of which is paid out as dividends) and the denominator is the cost of common equity. Since there are no taxes, the numerator is not multiplied by $(1 - T)$, as it was when we calculated NOPAT in Chapters 2 and 13.

Assume that initially, *before any arbitrage occurs*, both firms have the same equity capitalization rate (that is, required rate of return on equity): $r_{sU} = r_{sL} = 10\%$. Under this condition, according to Equation 21-34, the following situation would exist.

FIRM U

$$\text{Value of Firm U's stock} = S_U = \frac{\text{EBIT} - r_d D}{r_{sU}}$$

$$= \frac{\$900,000 - \$0}{0.10} = \$9,000,000$$

$$\text{Total market value of Firm U} = V_U = D_U + S_U = \$0 + \$9,000,000$$

$$= \$9,000,000$$

---

[13]By *arbitrage* we mean the simultaneous buying and selling of essentially identical assets that sell at different prices. The buying increases the price of the undervalued asset, and the selling decreases the price of the overvalued asset. Arbitrage operations will continue until prices have adjusted to the point where the arbitrageur can no longer earn a profit, at which point the market is in equilibrium. In the absence of transaction costs, equilibrium requires that the prices of the two assets be equal.

FIRM L

$$\text{Value of Firm L's stock} = S_L = \frac{\text{EBIT} - r_d D}{r_{sL}}$$

$$= \frac{\$900,000 - 0.075(\$4,000,000)}{0.10} = \frac{\$600,000}{0.10}$$

$$= \$6,000,000$$

$$\text{Total market value of Firm L} = V_L = D_L + S_L = \$4,000,000 + \$6,000,000$$
$$= \$10,000,000$$

Thus, before arbitrage (and assuming that $r_{sU} = r_{sL}$, which implies that capital structure has no effect on the cost of equity), the value of the levered Firm L exceeds that of the unlevered Firm U.

Modigliani and Miller argued that this result is a disequilibrium that cannot persist. To see why, suppose you owned 10% of L's stock and so the market value of your investment was $0.10(\$6,000,000) = \$600,000$. According to MM, you could increase your income without increasing your exposure to risk. For example, you could (1) sell your stock in L for $600,000, (2) borrow an amount equal to 10% of L's debt ($400,000), and then (3) buy 10% of U's stock for $900,000. Note that you would receive $1,000,000 from the sale of your 10% of L's stock plus your borrowing, and you would be spending only $900,000 on U's stock. Hence you would have an extra $100,000, which you could invest in riskless debt to yield 7.5%, or $7,500 annually.

Now consider your income positions:

Old Portfolio		New Portfolio	
10% of L's $600,000 equity income	$60,000	10% of U's $900,000 equity income	$90,000
		Less 7.5% interest on $400,000 loan	(30,000)
		Plus 7.5% interest on extra $100,000	7,500
Total income	$60,000	Total income	$67,500

Thus, your net income from common stock would be exactly the same as before, $60,000, but you would have $100,000 left over for investment in riskless debt and this would increase your income by $7,500. Therefore, the total return on your $600,000 net worth would rise to $67,500. And your risk, according to MM, would be the same as before, because you would have simply substituted $400,000 of "homemade" leverage for your 10% share of Firm L's $4 million of corporate leverage. Thus, neither your "effective" debt nor your risk would have changed. Therefore, you would have increased your income without raising your risk, which is obviously desirable.

Modigliani and Miller argued that this arbitrage process would actually occur, with sales of L's stock driving its price down and purchases of U's stock driving its price up, until the market values of the two firms were equal. Until this equality was established, gains could be obtained by switching from one stock to the other; hence the profit motive would force equality to be reached. When equilibrium is established, the values of Firms L and U must be equal, which is what Proposition I states. If their values are equal, then Equation 21-32 implies that WACC = r_{sU}. Because there are no taxes, we have

$$WACC = [D/(D + S)]r_d + [S/(D + S)]r_{sL}$$

and a little algebra then yields

$$r_{sL} = r_{sU} + (r_{sU} - r_d)(D/S)$$

which is what Proposition II states. Thus, according to MM, both a firm's value and its WACC must be independent of capital structure.

Note that each of the assumptions listed at the beginning of this section is necessary for the arbitrage proof to work exactly. For example, if the companies did not have identical business risk or if transaction costs were significant, then the arbitrage process could not be invoked. We discuss other implications of the assumptions later in the chapter.

21-6d Arbitrage with Short Sales

Even if you did not own any stock in L, you still could reap benefits if U and L did not have the same total market value. Your first step would be to sell short $600,000 of stock in L. To do this, your broker would let you borrow stock in L from another client. Your broker would then sell the stock for you and give you the proceeds, or $600,000 in cash. You would supplement this $600,000 by borrowing $400,000. With the $1 million total, you would buy 10% of the stock in U for $900,000 and have $100,000 remaining.

Your position would then consist of $100,000 in cash and two portfolios. The first portfolio would contain $900,000 of stock in U, which would generate $90,000 of income. Because you would own the stock, we'll call it the "long" portfolio. The other portfolio would consist of $600,000 of stock in L and $400,000 of debt. The value of this portfolio is $1 million, and it would generate $60,000 of dividends and $30,000 of interest. However, you would not own this second portfolio—you would "owe" it. Because you borrowed the $400,000, you would owe the $30,000 in interest. And because you borrowed the stock in L, you would "owe the stock" to the client from whom it was borrowed. Therefore, you would have to pay your broker the $60,000 of dividends paid by L, which the broker would then pass on to the client from whom the stock was borrowed. Thus your net cash flow from the second portfolio would be a negative $90,000. Because you would "owe" this portfolio, we'll call it the "short" portfolio.

Where would you get the $90,000 that you must pay on the short portfolio? The good news is that this is exactly the amount of cash flow generated by your long portfolio. Because the cash flows generated by each portfolio are the same, the short portfolio "replicates" the long portfolio.

Here is the bottom line. You started out with no money of your own. By selling L short, borrowing $400,000, and purchasing stock in U, you ended up with $100,000 in cash plus the two portfolios. The portfolios mirror one another, so their net cash flow is zero. This is perfect arbitrage: You invest none of your own money, you have no risk, you have no future negative cash flows, but you end up with cash in your pocket.

Not surprisingly, many traders would want to do this. The selling pressure on L would cause its price to fall, and the buying pressure on U would cause its price to rise, until the two companies' values were equal. To put it another way, *if the long and short replicating portfolios have the same cash flows, then arbitrage will force them to have the same value.*

This is one of the most important ideas in modern finance. Not only does it give us insights into capital structure, but it is the fundamental building block underlying the valuation of real and financial options and derivatives as discussed in Chapters 8 and 23. Without the concept of arbitrage, the options and derivatives markets we have today simply would not exist.

21-6e MM with Corporate Taxes

Modigliani and Miller's original work, published in 1958, assumed zero taxes. In 1963, they published a second article that incorporated corporate taxes. With corporate income taxes, they concluded that leverage will increase a firm's value. This occurs because interest is a tax-deductible expense; hence more of a levered firm's operating income flows through to investors.

Later in this chapter we present a proof of the MM propositions when personal taxes as well as corporate taxes are allowed. The situation when there are corporate taxes but no personal taxes is a special instance of the situation with both personal and corporate taxes, so we only present results in this case.

PROPOSITION I

The value of a levered firm is equal to the value of an unlevered firm in the same risk class (V_U) *plus* the value of the tax shield ($V_{Tax\ shield}$) due to the tax deductibility of interest expenses. The value of the tax shield, which is often called *the gain from leverage*, is the present value of the annual tax savings. The annual tax saving is equal to the interest payment multiplied by the tax rate, T:

$$\text{Annual tax saving} = r_d D(T)$$

Modigliani and Miller assume a no-growth firm, so the present value of the annual tax saving is the present value of a perpetuity. They assume that the appropriate discount rate for the tax shield is the interest rate on debt, so the value of the tax shield is

$$V_{Tax\ shield} = \frac{r_d D(T)}{r_d} = TD$$

Therefore, the value of a levered firm is

$$V_L = V_U + V_{Tax\ shield}$$
$$= V_U + TD$$

(21-35)

The important point here is that, when corporate taxes are introduced, the value of the levered firm exceeds that of the unlevered firm by the amount TD. Because the gain from leverage increases as debt increases, this implies that a firm's value is maximized at 100% debt financing.

Because all cash flows are assumed to be perpetuities, the value of the unlevered firm can be found by using Equation 21-34 and incorporating taxes. With zero debt (D = $0), the value of the firm is its equity value:

$$V_U = S = \frac{EBIT(1-T)}{r_{sU}}$$

(21-36)

Note that the discount rate, r_{sU}, is not necessarily equal to the discount rate in Equation 21-1. The r_{sU} from Equation 21-32 is the required discount rate in a world with no taxes, whereas the r_{sU} in Equation 21-36 is the required discount rate in a world with taxes.

Proposition II

The cost of equity to a levered firm is equal to (1) the cost of equity to an unlevered firm in the same risk class plus (2) a risk premium whose size depends on (a) the difference between the costs of equity and debt to an unlevered firm, (b) the amount of financial leverage used, and (c) the corporate tax rate:

$$r_{sL} = r_{sU} + (r_{sU} - r_d)(1 - T)(D/S) \qquad \text{(21-37)}$$

Observe that Equation 21-37 is identical to the corresponding without-tax Equation 21-33 except for the term $(1 - T)$, which appears only in Equation 21-37. Because $(1 - T)$ is less than 1, corporate taxes cause the cost of equity to rise less rapidly with leverage than it would in the absence of taxes. Proposition II, coupled with the reduction (due to taxes) in the effective cost of debt, is what produces the Proposition I result—namely, that the firm's value increases as its leverage increases.

As shown in Chapter 15, Professor Robert Hamada extended the MM analysis to define the relationship between a firm's beta, b, and the amount of leverage it has. The beta of an unlevered firm is denoted by b_U, and Hamada's equation is

$$b = b_U[1 + (1 - T)(D/S)] \qquad \text{(21-38)}$$

Note that beta, like the cost of stock shown in Equation 21-6, increases with leverage.

SELF-TEST

Is there an optimal capital structure under the MM zero-tax model?

What is the optimal capital structure under the MM model with corporate taxes?

How does the Proposition I equation differ between the two models?

How does the Proposition II equation differ between the two models?

Why do taxes result in a "gain from leverage" in the MM model with corporate taxes?

SUMMARY

In this chapter we discussed a variety of topics related to capital structure decisions. The key concepts covered are listed below.

- The most general approach to analyzing capital structure effects expresses the levered value of a company as the combination of its unlevered value and the value of side effects due to leverage:

$$V_L = V_U + \text{Value of side effects}$$

- MM stated that the primary benefit of debt stems from the **tax deductibility of interest payments.** The present value of the tax savings due to interest expense deductibility is called the **tax shield**. If we ignore other side effects, the value of an unlevered firm is:

$$V_L = V_U + V_{\text{Tax shield}}$$

- In 1958, **Franco Modigliani and Merton Miller (M)** proved, under a restrictive set of assumptions including zero taxes, that capital structure is irrelevant; thus, according to the original MM article, a firm's value is not affected by its financing mix.
- Modigliani and Miller later added **corporate taxes** to their model and reached the conclusion that capital structure does matter. Indeed, their model led to the conclusion that firms should use 100% debt financing.
- Later, Miller extended the theory to include **personal taxes**. The introduction of personal taxes reduces, but does not eliminate, the benefits of debt financing. Thus, the **Miller model** also leads to 100% debt financing.
- The compressed **adjusted present value (PV)** model incorporates nonconstant growth and assumes that the tax savings should be discounted at the unlevered cost of equity.
- The levered cost of equity and the levered beta are different in the APV model than in the MM and Hamada models. In the APV model, the relationships are:

$$r_{sL} = r_{sU} + (r_{sU} - r_d)\left(\frac{w_d}{w_s}\right)$$

and

$$b = b_U + (b_U = b_D)\left(\frac{w_d}{w_s}\right)$$

- When debt is risky, management may choose to default. If the debt is zero coupon debt, then this makes equity like an option on the value of the firm with a strike price equal to the face value of the debt. If the debt has periodic interest payments, then the equity is like an option on an option, or a **compound option**.
- When a firm has risky debt and equity is like an option, management has an incentive to increase the firm's risk in order to increase the equity value at the expense of the debt value. This is called **bait and switch**.

QUESTIONS

(21-1) Define each of the following terms:

     a. MM Proposition I without taxes and with corporate taxes
     b. MM Proposition II without taxes and with corporate taxes
     c. Miller model
     d. Adjusted present value (APV) model
     e. Value of debt tax shield
     f. Equity as an option

(21-2) Explain, in your own words, how MM uses the arbitrage process to prove the validity of Proposition I. Also, list the major MM assumptions and explain why each of these assumptions is necessary in the arbitrage proof.

(21-3) A utility company is allowed to charge prices high enough to cover all costs, including its cost of capital. Public service commissions are supposed to take actions that stimulate companies to operate as efficiently as possible in order to keep costs, and hence prices, as low as possible. Some time ago, AT&T's debt ratio was about 33%. Some individuals (Myron J. Gordon, in particular) argued that a higher debt ratio would lower AT&T's cost of capital and permit it to charge lower rates for telephone service. Gordon thought an optimal debt ratio for AT&T was about 50%. Do the theories presented in the chapter support or refute Gordon's position?

(21-4) Modigliani and Miller assumed that firms do not grow. How does positive growth change their conclusions about the value of the levered firm and its cost of capital?

(21-5) Your firm's CEO has just learned about options and how your firm's equity can be viewed as an option. Why might he want to increase the riskiness of the firm, and why might the bondholders be unhappy about this?

SELF-TEST PROBLEM   Solution Appears in Appendix A

(ST-1)
Value of a Levered
Firm

Menendez Corporation forecasts free cash flow of $100 at Year 1 and $120 at Year 2; after Year 2, the FCF is expected to grow at a constant rate of 4%. The company has a tax rate of 40% and $500 in debt at an interest rate of 5%. The company plans to hold debt steady until after Year 2, after which the debt (and tax savings) will grow at a constant rate of 4%. The unlevered cost of equity is 8%.

a. What is the horizon value of operations at Year 2?
b. What is the current unlevered value of operations?
c. What is the tax savings for Year 1 and Year 2 (*Hint:* They are identical because the debt doesn't change.)
d. What is the horizon value of the tax shield at Year 2?
e. What is the current value of the tax shield?
f. What is the levered value of operations at Year 0?

PROBLEMS   Answers Appear in Appendix B

Easy Problems 1–4

(21-1)
MM Model with
Zero Taxes

An unlevered firm has a value of $500 million. An otherwise identical but levered firm has $50 million in debt. Under the MM zero-tax model, what is the value of the levered firm?

(21-2)
MM Model with
Corporate Taxes

An unlevered firm has a value of $800 million. An otherwise identical but levered firm has $60 million in debt at a 5% interest rate. Its cost of debt is 5% and its unlevered cost of equity is 11%. No growth is expected. Assuming the corporate tax rate is 35%, use the MM model with corporate taxes to determine the value of the levered firm.

(21-3)
Miller Model with
Corporate and
Personal Taxes

An unlevered firm has a value of $600 million. An otherwise identical but levered firm has $240 million in debt. Under the Miller model, what is the value of the levered firm if the corporate tax rate is 34%, the personal tax rate on equity is 10%, and the personal tax rate on debt is 35%?

(21-4)
APV Model with
Constant Growth

An unlevered firm has a value of $800 million. An otherwise identical but levered firm has $60 million in debt at a 5% interest rate. Its cost of debt is 5% and its unlevered cost of equity is 11%. After Year 1, free cash flows and tax savings are expected to grow at a constant rate of 3%. Assuming the corporate tax rate is 35%, use the compressed adjusted present value model to determine the value of the levered firm. (*Hint:* The interest expense at Year 1 is based on the current level of debt.)

Intermediate
Problems 5–8

(21-5)
Business and
Financial Risk—MM
Model

Air Tampa has just been incorporated, and its board of directors is grappling with the question of optimal capital structure. The company plans to offer commuter air services between Tampa and smaller surrounding cities. Jaxair has been around for a few years, and it has about the same basic business risk as Air Tampa would have. Jaxair's market-determined beta is 1.8, and it has a current market value debt ratio (total debt to total assets) of 50% and a federal-plus-state tax rate of 40%. Air Tampa expects to be only marginally profitable at start-up; hence its tax rate would only be 25%. Air Tampa's owners expect that the total book and market value of the firm's stock, if it uses zero debt, would be $10 million. Air Tampa's CFO believes that the MM and Hamada formulas for the value of a levered firm and the levered firm's cost of capital should be used. (These are given in Equations 21-12, 21-13, and 21-14.)

a. Estimate the beta of an unlevered firm in the commuter airline business based on Jaxair's market-determined beta. (*Hint:* This is a levered beta; use Equation 21-14 and solve for b_U.)
b. Now assume that $r_d = r_{RF} = 10\%$ and that the market risk premium $RP_M = 5\%$. Find the required rate of return on equity for an unlevered commuter airline.
c. Air Tampa is considering three capital structures: (1) $2 million debt, (2) $4 million debt, and (3) $6 million debt. Estimate Air Tampa's r_s for these debt levels.
d. Calculate Air Tampa's r_s at $6 million debt while assuming its federal-plus-state tax rate is now 40%. Compare this with your corresponding answer to part c. (*Hint:* The increase in the tax rate causes V_U to drop to $8 million.)

(21-6)
MM without Taxes

Companies U and L are identical in every respect except that U is unlevered while L has $10 million of 5% bonds outstanding. Assume that (1) there are no corporate or personal taxes, (2) all of the other MM assumptions are met, (3) EBIT is $2 million, and (4) the cost of equity to Company U is 10%.

a. What value would MM estimate for each firm?
b. What is r_s for Firm U? For Firm L?
c. Find S_L, and then show that $S_L + D = V_L = \$20$ million.
d. What is the WACC for Firm U? For Firm L?
e. Suppose $V_U = \$20$ million and $V_L = \$22$ million. According to MM, are these values consistent with equilibrium? If not, explain the process by which equilibrium would be restored.

(21-7)
MM with Corporate Taxes

Companies U and L are identical in every respect except that U is unlevered while L has $10 million of 5% bonds outstanding. Assume that (1) all of the MM assumptions are met, (2) both firms are subject to a 40% federal-plus-state corporate tax rate, (3) EBIT is $2 million, and (4) the unlevered cost of equity is 10%.

a. What value would MM now estimate for each firm? (*Hint:* Use Proposition I.)
b. What is r_s for Firm U? For Firm L?
c. Find S_L, and then show that $S_L + D = V_L$ results in the same value as obtained in part a.
d. What is the WACC for Firm U? For Firm L?

(21-8)
Miller Model

Companies U and L are identical in every respect except that U is unlevered while L has $10 million of 5% bonds outstanding. Both firms have an EBIT of $2 million. Assume that all of the MM assumptions are met.

a. Suppose that both firms are subject to a 40% federal-plus-state corporate tax rate, investors in both firms face a tax rate of $T_d = 28\%$ on debt income and $T_s = 20\%$ (on average) on stock income, and the appropriate required pre-personal-tax rate r_{sU} is 10%. What is the value of the unlevered firm, V_U? What is the value of the levered firm, V_L? What is the gain from leverage?
b. Now keep the other assumptions (D = $10 million, $r_d = 5\%$, EBIT = $2 million, and $r_{sU} = 10\%$) but set $T_c = T_s = T_d = 0$. What is the value of the unlevered firm, V_U? What is the value of the levered firm, V_L? What is the gain from leverage?

c. Keep the other assumptions (D = $10 million, r_d = 5%, EBIT = $2 million, and r_{sU} = 10%), but now suppose T_s = T_d = 0 and T_c= 40%. What is the value of the unlevered firm, V_U? What is the value of the levered firm, V_L? What is the gain from leverage?

d. Keep the other assumptions (D = $10 million, r_d = 5%, EBIT = $2 million, and r_{sU} = 10%), but now suppose that T_d = 28%, T_s = 28%, and T_c = 40%. Now what are the value of the levered firm and the gain from leverage?

Challenging
Problems 9–12

(21-9)
Adjusted Present
Value

Schwarzentraub Industries' expected free cash flow for the year is $500,000; in the future, free cash flow is expected to grow at a rate of 9%. The company currently has no debt, and its cost of equity is 13%. Its tax rate is 40%. (*Hint:* Use Equations 21-15 and 21-16.)

a. Find V_U.

b. Find V_L and r_{sL} if Schwarzentraub uses $5 million in debt with a cost of 7%. Use the APV model that allows for growth.

c. Based on V_U from part a, find V_L and r_{sL} using the MM model (with taxes) if Schwarzentraub uses $5 million in 7% debt.

d. Explain the difference between your answers to parts b and c.

(21-10)
MM with and without
Taxes

International Associates (IA) is about to commence operations as an international trading company. The firm will have book assets of $10 million, and it expects to earn a 16% return on these assets before taxes. However, because of certain tax arrangements with foreign governments, IA will not pay any taxes; that is, its tax rate will be zero. Management is trying to decide how to raise the required $10 million. It is known that the capitalization rate r_U for an all-equity firm in this business is 11%, and IA can borrow at a rate r_d = 6%. Assume that the MM assumptions apply.

a. According to MM, what will be the value of IA if it uses no debt? If it uses $6 million of 6% debt?

b. What are the values of the WACC and r_s at debt levels of D = $0, D = $6 million, and D = $10 million? What effect does leverage have on firm value? Why?

c. Assume the initial facts of the problem (r_d = 6%, EBIT = $1.6 million, r_{sU} = 11%), but now assume that a 40% federal-plus-state corporate tax rate exists. Use the MM formulas to find the new market values for IA with zero debt and with $6 million of debt.

d. What are the values of the WACC and r_s at debt levels of D = $0, D = $6 million, and D = $10 million if we assume a 40% corporate tax rate? Plot the relationship between the value of the firm and the debt ratio as well as that between capital costs and the debt ratio.

e. What is the maximum dollar amount of debt financing that can be used? What is the value of the firm at this debt level? What is the cost of this debt?

f. How would each of the following factors tend to change the values you plotted in your graph?

(1) The interest rate on debt increases as the debt ratio rises.

(2) At higher levels of debt, the probability of financial distress rises.

(21-11)
Equity Viewed
as an Option

A. Fethe Inc. is a custom manufacturer of guitars, mandolins, and other stringed instruments and is located near Knoxville, Tennessee. Fethe's current value of operations, which is also its value of debt plus equity, is estimated to be $5 million. Fethe has $2 million face value, zero coupon debt that is due in 2 years. The risk-free rate is 6%, and the standard deviation of returns for companies similar to Fethe is 50%. Fethe's owners view their equity investment as an option and they would like to know the value of their investment.

a. Using the Black-Scholes option pricing model, how much is Fethe's equity worth?
b. How much is the debt worth today? What is its yield?
c. How would the equity value and the yield on the debt change if Fethe's managers could use risk management techniques to reduce its volatility to 30%? Can you explain this?

(21-12)
Compressed APV with Nonconstant Growth

Sheldon Corporation projects the following free cash flows (FCFs) and interest expenses for the next 3 years, after which FCF and interest expenses are expected to grow at a constant 7% rate. Sheldon's unlevered cost of equity is 13% its tax rate is 40%.

	Year		
	1	2	3
Free cash flow ($ millions)	$20	$30	$40
Interest expense ($ millions)	$ 8	$ 9	$10

a. What is Sheldon's unlevered horizon value of operations at Year 3?
b. What is the current unlevered value of operations?
c. What is horizon value of the tax shield at Year 3?
d. What is the current value of the tax shield?
e. What is the current total value of the company?

SPREADSHEET PROBLEMS

(21-13)
Build a Model: Equity Viewed as an Option

resource

Higgs Bassoon Corporation is a custom manufacturer of bassoons and other wind instruments. Its current value of operations, which is also its value of debt plus equity, is estimated to be $200 million. Higgs has zero coupon debt outstanding that matures in 3 years with $110 million face value. The risk-free rate is 5%, and the standard deviation of returns for similar companies is 60%. The owners of Higgs Bassoon view their equity investment as an option and would like to know its value. Start with the partial model in the file *Ch21 P13 Build a Model.xls* on the textbook's Web site and answer the following questions.

a. Using the Black-Scholes option pricing model, how much is the equity worth?
b. How much is the debt worth today? What is its yield?
c. How would the equity value change if Fethe's managers could use risk management techniques to reduce its volatility to 45%? Can you explain this?
d. Graph the cost of debt versus the face value of debt for values of the face value from $10 to $160 million.
e. Graph the values of debt and equity for volatilities from 0.10 to 0.90 when the face value of the debt is $100 million.

(21-14)
Build a Model: Compressed Adjusted Value Model

Start with the partial model in the file *Ch21 P14 Build a Model.xls* on the textbook's Web site. Kasperov Corporation has an unlevered cost of equity of 12% and is taxed at a 40% rate. The 4-year forecasts of free cash flow and interest expenses are shown below. Free cash flow and interest expenses are expected to grow at a 5% rate starting after Year 4. Answer the following questions.

INPUTS (In Millions)		Projected		
Year:	1	2	3	4
Free cash flow	$200	$280	$320	$340
Interest expense	$100	$120	$120	$140

a. Calculate the estimated horizon value of unlevered operations at Year 4 (i.e., immediately after the Year-4 free cash flow).
b. Calculate the current value of unlevered operations.
c. Calculate the estimated horizon value of the tax shield at Year 4 (i.e., immediately after the Year-4 free cash flow).
d. Calculate the current value of the tax shield.
e. Calculate the current total value.

MINI CASE

David Lyons, CEO of Lyons Solar Technologies, is concerned about his firm's level of debt financing. The company uses short-term debt to finance its temporary working capital needs, but it does not use any permanent (long-term) debt. Other solar technology companies average about 30% debt, and Mr. Lyons wonders why they use so much more debt and how it affects stock prices. To gain some insights into the matter, he poses the following questions to you, his recently hired assistant.

a. Who were Modigliani and Miller (MM), and what assumptions are embedded in the MM and Miller models?
b. Assume that Firms U and L are in the same risk class and that both have EBIT = $500,000. Firm U uses no debt financing, and its cost of equity is r_{sU} = 14%. Firm L has $1 million of debt outstanding at a cost of r_d = 8%. There are no taxes. Assume that the MM assumptions hold.
   (1) Find V, S, r_s, and WACC for Firms U and L.
   (2) Graph (a) the relationships between capital costs and leverage as measured by D/V and (b) the relationship between V and D.
c. Now assume that Firms L and U are both subject to a 40% corporate tax rate. Using the data given in part b, repeat the analysis called for in b(1) and b(2) under the MM model with taxes.
d. Suppose investors are subject to the following tax rates: T_d = 30% and T_s = 12%.
   (1) According to the Miller model, what is the gain from leverage?
   (2) How does this gain compare with the gain in the MM model with corporate taxes?
   (3) What does the Miller model imply about the effect of corporate debt on the value of the firm; that is, how do personal taxes affect the situation?
e. What capital structure policy recommendations do the three theories (MM without taxes, MM with corporate taxes, and Miller) suggest to financial managers? Empirically, do firms appear to follow any one of these guidelines?
f. Suppose that Firms U and L are growing at a constant rate of 7% and that the investment in net operating assets required to support this growth is 10% of EBIT. Use the compressed adjusted present value (APV) model to estimate the value of U and L. Also estimate the levered cost of equity and the weighted average cost of capital.
g. Suppose the expected free cash flow for Year 1 is $250,000 but it is expected to grow unevenly over the next 3 years: FCF2 = $290,000 and FCF3 = $320,000, after which it will grow at a constant rate of 7%. The expected interest expense at Year 1 is $80,000,

but it is expected to grow over the next couple of years before the capital structure becomes constant: Interest expense at Year 2 will be $95,000, at Year 3 it will be $120,000 and it will grow at 7% thereafter. What is the estimated horizon unlevered value of operations (i.e., the value at Year 3 immediately after the FCF at Year 3)? What is the current unlevered value of operations? What is the horizon value of the tax shield at Year 3? What is the current value of the tax shield? What is the current total value? The tax rate and unlevered cost of equity remain at 40% and 14%, respectively.

h. Suppose there is a large probability that L will default on its debt. For the purpose of this example, assume that the value of L's operations is $4 million (the value of its debt plus equity). Assume also that its debt consists of 1-year, zero coupon bonds with a face value of $2 million. Finally, assume that L's volatility, σ, is 0.60 and that the risk-free rate r_{RF} is 6%.

i. What is the value of L's stock for volatilities between 0.20 and 0.95? What incentives might the manager of L have if she understands this relationship? What might debtholders do in response?

SELECTED ADDITIONAL CASES

The following cases from CengageCompose cover many of the concepts discussed in this chapter and are available at **compose.cengage.com**.

Klein-Brigham Series:

Case 7, "Seattle Steel Products"; Case 9, "Kleen Kar, Inc."; Case 10, "Aspeon Sparkling Water"; Case 43, "Mountain Springs"; Case 57, "Greta Cosmetics"; Case 74, "The Western Company"; Case 83, "Armstrong Production Company"; and Case 99, "Moore Plumbing Supply Company," focus on capital structure theory. Case 8, "Johnson Window Company," and Case 56, "Isle Marine Boat Company," cover operating and financial leverage.

Brigham-Buzzard Series:

Case 8, "Powerline Network Corporation," covers operating leverage, financial leverage, and the optimal capital structure.

© Adalberto Rios Szalay/Sexto Sol/Getty Images

CHAPTER **22**

Mergers and Corporate Control

On January 28, 2005, Procter & Gamble (P&G) bid almost $55 billion to acquire Gillette in a friendly merger. When the deal was completed on October 1, 2005, it created the world's largest consumer goods company, making the merger the biggest of the year.

Combining Gillette and P&G has already produced several winners. When the deal was announced, Gillette's shareholders saw the value of their stock rise by more than 17%. One particular winner was Gillette's largest shareholder, Warren Buffett, who owned roughly 96 million shares. Other winners included Gillette's senior executives, who saw the value of their stock and stock options increase, and the investment banks that helped put the deal together. Estimates suggest that Goldman Sachs, Merrill Lynch, and UBS each received $30 million from the transaction.

Although many applauded the deal, others believe that P&G will have to work hard to justify the price it paid for Gillette. Moreover, as we point out in this chapter, the track record for acquiring firms in large deals has not always been good. However, as we write this in July 2012, P&G's stock has outperformed the S&P 500 by an annual rate of about 1 percentage point even though P&G's beta is less than 1, making this merger a success story. Keep the P&G–Gillette merger in mind as you read this chapter.

resource

The textbook's Web site contains an Excel file that will guide you through the chapter's calculations. The file for this chapter is **Ch22 Tool Kit.xls**, and we encourage you to open the file and follow along as you read the chapter.

Most corporate growth occurs by *internal expansion*, which takes place when a firm's existing divisions grow through normal capital budgeting activities. However, the most dramatic examples of growth result from mergers, the first topic covered in this chapter. Other actions that alter corporate control are divestitures—conditions change over time, causing firms to sell off, or divest, major divisions to other firms that can better utilize the divested assets. A *holding company* is a form of organization in which one corporation controls other companies by owning some, or all, of their stocks.

22-1 Rationale for Mergers

Many reasons have been proposed by financial managers and theorists to account for the high level of U.S. merger activity. The primary motives behind corporate **mergers** are presented in this section.[1]

22-1a Synergy

The primary motivation for most mergers is to increase the value of the combined enterprise. If Companies A and B merge to form Company C and if C's value exceeds that of A and B taken together, then **synergy** is said to exist, and such a merger should be beneficial to both A's and B's stockholders.[2] Synergistic effects can arise from five sources: (1) *operating economies*, which result from economies of scale in management, marketing, production, or distribution; (2) *financial economies*, including lower transaction costs and better coverage by security analysts; (3) *tax effects*, in which case the combined enterprise pays less in taxes than the separate firms would pay; (4) *differential efficiency*, which implies that the management of one firm is more efficient and that the weaker firm's assets will be more productive after the merger; and (5) *increased market power* due to reduced competition. Operating and financial economies are socially desirable, as are mergers that increase managerial efficiency, but mergers that reduce competition are socially undesirable and illegal.[3]

Expected synergies are not always realized. For example, when AOL acquired Time Warner, it believed that Time Warner's extensive content library could be sold to AOL's Internet subscribers and that AOL subscribers could be shifted over to Time Warner's cable system. When the merger was announced, the new management estimated that such synergies would increase operating income by $1 billion per year. However, things didn't work out as expected, and in 2002 Time Warner had to write off about $100 billion in lost value associated with the merger.

---

[1]As we use the term, *merger* means any combination that forms one economic unit from two or more previous ones. For legal purposes, there are distinctions among the various ways these combinations can occur, but our focus is on the fundamental economic and financial aspects of mergers.

[2]If synergy exists, then the whole is greater than the sum of the parts. Synergy is also called the "2 plus 2 equals 5 effect." The distribution of the synergistic gain between A's and B's stockholders is determined by negotiation. This point is discussed later in the chapter.

[3]In the 1880s and 1890s, many mergers occurred in the United States, and some of them were directed toward gaining market power rather than increasing efficiency. As a result, Congress passed a series of acts designed to ensure that mergers are not used to reduce competition. The principal acts include the Sherman Act (1890), the Clayton Act (1914), and the Celler Act (1950). These acts make it illegal for firms to combine if the combination tends to lessen competition. The acts are enforced by the antitrust division of the Justice Department and by the Federal Trade Commission.

Merrill Lynch (ML) was facing bankruptcy in late 2008, so federal officials encouraged Bank of America (BoA) to save ML from bankruptcy by acquiring it, creating one of the world's largest (if not the largest) financial conglomerate. But BoA tried to back out of the deal as it learned more about ML's situation. Under pressure from the government, BoA went through with the merger and almost immediately reported over $21 billion in associated losses.

As these examples illustrate, often it is blemishes, not synergies, that materialize after a merger.

22-1b Tax Considerations

Tax considerations have stimulated a number of mergers. For example, a profitable firm in the highest tax bracket could acquire a firm with large accumulated tax losses. These losses could then be turned into immediate tax savings rather than carried forward and used in the future.[4]

Also, mergers can serve as a way of minimizing taxes when disposing of excess cash. For example, if a firm has a shortage of internal investment opportunities compared with its free cash flow, it could (1) pay an extra dividend, (2) invest in marketable securities, (3) repurchase its own stock, or (4) purchase another firm. If it pays an extra dividend, its stockholders would have to pay immediate taxes on the distribution. Marketable securities often provide a good temporary parking place for money, but they generally earn a rate of return less than that required by stockholders. A stock repurchase might result in a capital gain for the selling stockholders. However, using surplus cash to acquire another firm would avoid all these problems, and this has motivated a number of mergers. Still, as we discuss later, the tax savings are often less than the premium paid in the acquisition. Thus, mergers motivated only by tax considerations often reduce the acquiring shareholders' wealth.

22-1c Purchase of Assets below Their Replacement Cost

Sometimes a firm will be touted as an acquisition candidate because the cost of replacing its assets is considerably higher than its market value. This is especially true in the natural resources industry; for example, an oil company's reserves might be worth more on paper than the company's stock. (Of course, converting paper value to monetary value isn't always as easy as it sounds.)

22-1d Diversification

Managers often cite diversification as a reason for mergers. They contend that diversification helps stabilize a firm's earnings and thus benefits its owners. Stabilization of earnings is certainly beneficial to employees, suppliers, and customers, but its value to stockholders is less certain. Why should Firm A acquire Firm B to stabilize earnings when stockholders can simply buy the stocks of both firms? Indeed, research suggests that in most cases diversification does not increase the firm's value. In fact, many studies find that diversified firms are worth significantly *less* than the sum of their individual parts.[5]

Of course, if you were the owner-manager of a closely held firm, it might be nearly impossible to sell part of your stock to diversify. Also, selling your stock would probably

---

[4]Mergers undertaken only to use accumulated tax losses would probably be challenged by the IRS. In recent years, Congress has made it increasingly difficult for firms to pass along tax savings after mergers.
[5]See, for example, Philip Berger and Eli Ofek, "Diversification's Effect on Firm Value," *Journal of Financial Economics*, 1995, pp. 37–65; and Larry Lang and René Stulz, "Tobin's Q, Corporate Diversification, and Firm Performance," *Journal of Political Economy*, December 1994, pp. 1248–1280.

lead to a large capital gains tax. So, a diversification merger might be the best way to achieve personal diversification for a privately held firm.

22-1e Managers' Personal Incentives

Financial economists like to think that business decisions are based only on economic considerations, especially maximization of firms' values. However, many business decisions are based more on managers' personal motivations than on economic analyses. Business leaders like power, and more power is attached to running a larger corporation than a smaller one. Most likely, no executive would admit that his or her ego was the primary reason behind a merger, but egos do play a prominent role in many mergers.[6]

It has also been observed that executive salaries are highly correlated with company size—the bigger the company, the higher the salaries of its top officers. This, too, could obviously cause unnecessary acquisitions.

Personal considerations deter as well as motivate mergers. After most takeovers, some managers of the acquired companies lose their jobs, or at least their autonomy. Therefore, managers who own less than 51% of their firms' stock look to devices that will lessen the chances of a takeover, and a merger can serve as such a device. In 2005, for example, MCI's board of directors, over the objection of large shareholders, turned down repeated acquisition offers from Qwest, at the time the nation's fourth-largest local phone company, in favor of substantially smaller offers from Verizon, the nation's largest phone company. MCI's management viewed Verizon as a stronger, more stable partner than Qwest even though Qwest's bid was at times 20% higher than Verizon's. In response to management's refusal to accept the higher bid, the holders of some 28% of MCI's stock withheld their votes to re-elect the board of directors as a protest. Nonetheless, management proceeded with the Verizon merger negotiations, and the two companies merged in June of 2006. In such cases, management always argues that synergy, not a desire to protect their own jobs, is the motivation for the choice. However, it is difficult to rationalize rejecting a 20% larger bid for undocumented synergies, and some observers suspect that this merger—like many others—was ultimately designed to benefit managers rather than shareholders.

22-1f Breakup Value

Some takeover specialists estimate a company's **breakup value**, which is the value of the individual parts of the firm if they were sold off separately. If this value is higher than the firm's current market value, then a takeover specialist could acquire the firm at or even above its current market value, sell it off in pieces, and earn a profit.

SELF-TEST

Define synergy. Is synergy a valid rationale for mergers? Describe several situations that might produce synergistic gains.

Suppose your firm could purchase another firm for only half of its replacement value. Would that be a sufficient justification for the acquisition? Why or why not?

Discuss the pros and cons of diversification as a rationale for mergers.

What is breakup value?

---

[6]See Randall Morck, Andrei Shleifer, and Robert W. Vishny, "Do Managerial Objectives Drive Bad Acquisitions?" *Journal of Finance*, March 1990, pp. 31–48.

22-2 Types of Mergers

Economists classify mergers into four types: (1) horizontal, (2) vertical, (3) congeneric, and (4) conglomerate. A **horizontal merger** occurs when one firm combines with another in its same line of business—the 2005 Sprint–Nextel merger is an example as is the 2009 Wachovia–Wells Fargo merger. An example of a **vertical merger** would be a steel producer's acquisition of one of its own suppliers, such as an iron or coal mining firm, or an oil producer's acquisition of a petrochemical firm that uses oil as a raw material. *Congeneric* means "allied in nature or action"; hence a **congeneric merger** involves related enterprises but not producers of the same product (horizontal) or firms in a producer–supplier relationship (vertical). The AOL and Time Warner merger is an example. A **conglomerate merger** occurs when unrelated enterprises combine.

Operating economies (and also anticompetitive effects) are at least partially dependent on the type of merger involved. Vertical and horizontal mergers generally provide the greatest synergistic operating benefits, but they are also the ones most likely to be attacked by the Department of Justice as being anticompetitive.[7] In any event, it is useful to think of these economic classifications when analyzing prospective mergers.

SELF-TEST

What are the four types of mergers?

22-3 Level of Merger Activity

Five principal "merger waves" have occurred in the United States. The first was in the late 1800s, when consolidations occurred in the oil, steel, tobacco, and other basic industries. The second was in the 1920s, when the stock market boom helped financial promoters consolidate firms in a number of industries, including utilities, communications, and autos. The third was in the 1960s, when conglomerate mergers were the rage. The fourth occurred in the 1980s, when LBO firms and others began using junk bonds to finance all manner of acquisitions. The fifth, which involves strategic alliances designed to enable firms to compete better in the global economy, lasted throughout the 1990s. Some speculate that the 2000s were a sixth wave, driven by private equity.

As shown in Table 22-1, some huge mergers have occurred. Most recent mergers have been strategic in nature—companies are merging to gain economies of scale or scope and thus be better able to compete in the world economy. Indeed, many recent mergers have involved companies in the financial, defense, media, computer, telecommunications, and health care industries, all of which are experiencing structural changes and intense competition.

In the 1980s, cash was the preferred method of payment, because large cash payments could convince even the most reluctant shareholder to approve the deal. However, the cash was generally obtained by borrowing, leaving the consolidated company with a heavy debt burden, which often led to difficulties. Through the mid-2000s, stock replaced borrowed cash as the merger currency for two reasons: (1) Many of the 1980s mergers were financed with junk bonds that later went into default. These defaults, along with the

---

[7]For interesting insights into antitrust regulations and mergers, see B. Espen Eckbo, "Mergers and the Value of Antitrust Deterrence," *Journal of Finance,* July 1992, pp. 1005–1029.

TABLE 22-1

The Ten Largest Completed Mergers Worldwide through December 31, 2011

Buyer	Target	Completion Date	Value (Billions of U.S. Dollars)
Vodafone AirTouch	Mannesmann	April 12, 2000	$161
Pfizer	Warner-Lambert	June 19, 2000	116
America Online	Time Warner	January 11, 2001	106
RFS Holdings	ABN-AMRO Holding	October 5, 2007	99
Exxon	Mobil	November 30, 1999	81
Glaxo Wellcome	SmithKline Beecham	December 27, 2000	74
Royal Dutch Petroleum	Shell Transport and Trading	July 20, 2005	74
ATT	BellSouth	December 29, 2006	73
SBC Communications	Ameritech	October 8, 1999	72
VodafoneGroup	AirTouch	June 30, 1999	69

Sources: "A Look at the Top 10 Global Mergers," *Associated Press Newswires,* January 11, 2001; *The Wall Street Journal,* "Year-End Review of Markets and Finance World-Wide Deals," various issues.

demise of Drexel Burnham, the leading junk bond dealer, have made it difficult to arrange debt-financed mergers. (2) Many of the mergers during that time were for strategic reasons, such as Eli Lilly's $6.5 billion acquisition of ImClone Systems in 2008. Most of these mergers have been friendly, and stock swaps are easier to arrange in friendly mergers than in hostile ones. Global merger activity has declined significantly since the 2007–2008 financial crisis and subsequent recession, and much of the activity that took place from 2009 to 2011 again consisted of cash deals, such as the 2011 $2.2 billion acquisition of Novell by the private IT company, Attachmate.

There has also been an increase in cross-border mergers. For example, in 2011 the Swiss automation technology company ABB acquired Baldor Electric Company, a U.S.-based industrial motors manufacturer. Also in early 2011, Pepsico acquired a 66% interest in the Russian food company, Wimm-Bill-Dann Foods, and purchased the remaining shares in late 2011.

SELF-TEST

What major "merger waves" have occurred in the United States?

22-4 Hostile versus Friendly Takeovers

In the vast majority of merger situations, one firm (generally the larger of the two) simply decides to buy another company, negotiates a price with the management of the target firm, and then acquires the target company. Occasionally, the acquired firm will initiate the action, but it is much more common for a firm to seek companies to acquire than to seek to be acquired. Following convention, we call a company that seeks to acquire another firm the **acquiring company** and the one that it seeks to acquire the **target company**.

Once an acquiring company has identified a possible target, it must (1) establish a suitable price, or range of prices, and (2) decide on the terms of payment—will it offer cash, its own common stock, bonds, or some combination? Next, the acquiring firm's managers must decide how to approach the target company's managers. If the acquiring firm has reason to believe that the target's management will approve the merger, then one CEO will contact the other, propose a merger, and then try to work out suitable terms. If an agreement is reached, then the two management groups will issue statements to their stockholders indicating that they approve the merger, and the target firm's management will recommend to its stockholders that they agree to the merger. Generally, the stockholders are asked to *tender* (or send in) their shares to a designated financial institution, along with a signed power of attorney that transfers ownership of the shares to the acquiring firm. The target firm's stockholders then receive the specified payment, either common stock of the acquiring company (in which case the target company's stockholders become stockholders of the acquiring company), cash, bonds, or some mix of cash and securities. This is a **friendly merger**. Kraft's acquisition of the British firm Cadbury in 2010 is an example of a friendly merger, even though Cadbury initially rejected an earlier offer by Kraft for being too low.

Often, however, the target company's management resists the merger. Perhaps they feel that the price offered is too low or perhaps they simply want to keep their jobs. Regardless of the reasons, in this case the acquiring firm's offer is said to be **hostile** rather than friendly, and the acquiring firm must make a direct appeal to the target firm's stockholders. In a hostile merger, the acquiring company will again make a **tender offer**, and again it will ask the stockholders of the target firm to tender their shares in exchange for the offered price. This time, though, the target firm's managers will urge stockholders not to tender their shares, generally stating that the price offered (cash, bonds, or stocks in the acquiring firm) is too low. For example, in late 2010 the board of directors for the biotech company Genzyme refused to consider a $69 per share offer from French pharmaceutical giant Sanofi. To encourage the board to actively consider the offer, Sanofi appealed directly to Genzyme's shareholders with a tender offer at $69 per share. The tender offer got the attention of Genzyme's board and in early 2011, Sanofi increased the cash component of the offer to $74 and added a security called a contingent value right (CVR) to the mix. The CVR would pay up to $14 per share more to the selling shareholders, depending on performance of one of Genzyme's drugs, and the merger was finally approved by management.[8]

Although most mergers are friendly, there are cases in which high-profile firms have attempted hostile takeovers. For example, Wachovia, before its acquisition by Wells Fargo during the financial crisis in 2008, defeated a hostile bid by SunTrust and was acquired, instead, by First Union. Looking overseas, Olivetti successfully conducted a hostile takeover of Telecom Italia, and, in another hostile telecommunications merger, Britain's Vodafone AirTouch acquired its German rival, Mannesmann AG.

Perhaps not surprisingly, hostile bids often fail. However, an all-cash offer that is high enough will generally overcome any resistance by the target firm's management. A hostile merger often begins with a "preemptive" or "blowout" bid. The idea is to offer such a high premium over the pre-announcement price that (a) no other bidders will be willing to jump into the fray and (b) the target company's board cannot simply reject the bid. If a hostile bid is eventually accepted by the target's board, then the deal ends up as "friendly," despite any acrimony during the hostile phase.

---

[8]See **www.bloomberg.com/news/2011-02-16/sanofi-aventis-agrees-to-buy-genzyme-for-74-a-share-in-19-2-billion-deal.html** for more information on the Sanofi-Genzyme acquisition.

What is the difference between a hostile and a friendly merger?

22-5 Merger Regulation

Prior to the mid-1960s, friendly acquisitions generally took place as simple exchange-of-stock mergers, and a proxy fight was the primary weapon used in hostile control battles. In the mid-1960s, however, corporate raiders began to operate differently. First, it took a long time to mount a proxy fight—raiders had to first request a list of the target company's stockholders, be refused, and then get a court order forcing management to turn over the list. During that time, the target's management could think through and then implement a strategy to fend off the raider. As a result, management won most proxy fights.

Then raiders thought, "If we could bring the decision to a head quickly, before management can take countermeasures, it would greatly increase our probability of success." That led the raiders to turn from proxy fights to tender offers, which had a much shorter response time. For example, the stockholders of a company whose stock was selling for $20 might be offered $27 per share and be given 2 weeks to accept. The raider, meanwhile, would have accumulated a substantial block of the shares in open market purchases, and additional shares might have been purchased by institutional friends of the raider who promised to tender their shares in exchange for the tip that a raid was to occur.

Faced with a well-planned raid, managements were generally overwhelmed. The stock might actually be worth more than the offered price, but management simply did not have time to get this message across to stockholders or to find a competing bidder. This situation seemed unfair, so Congress passed the Williams Act in 1968. This law had two main objectives: (1) to regulate the way acquiring firms can structure takeover offers and (2) to force acquiring firms to disclose more information about their offers. In essence, Congress wanted to put target managements in a better position to defend against hostile offers. Additionally, Congress believed that shareholders needed easier access to information about tender offers—including information on any securities that might be offered in lieu of cash—in order to make rational tender-versus-don't-tender decisions.

The Williams Act placed the following four restrictions on acquiring firms: (1) Acquirers must disclose their current holdings and future intentions within 10 days of amassing at least 5% of a company's stock. (2) Acquirers must disclose the source of the funds to be used in the acquisition. (3) The target firm's shareholders must be allowed at least 20 days to tender their shares; that is, the offer must be "open" for at least 20 days. (4) If the acquiring firm increases the offer price during the 20-day open period, then all shareholders who tendered prior to the new offer must receive the higher price. In total, these restrictions were intended to reduce the acquiring firm's ability to surprise management and to stampede target shareholders into accepting an inadequate offer. Prior to the Williams Act, offers were generally made on a first-come, first-served basis, and they were often accompanied by an implicit threat to lower the bid price after 50% of the shares were in hand. The legislation also gave the target more time to mount a defense, and it gave rival bidders and white knights a chance to enter the fray and thus help a target's stockholders obtain a better price.

Many states have also passed laws designed to protect firms in their states from hostile takeovers. In 1987 the U.S. Supreme Court upheld an Indiana law that radically changed the rules of the takeover game. Specifically, the Indiana law first defined "control shares" as enough shares to give an investor 20% of the vote. It went on to state that when an investor buys control shares, those shares can be voted only after approval by a majority of "disinterested shareholders," defined as those who are neither officers nor inside directors of the company nor associates of the raider. The law also gives the buyer of control shares the right to insist that a shareholders' meeting be called within 50 days to decide whether the shares may be voted. The Indiana law dealt a major blow to raiders, mainly because it slows down the action and thus gives the target firm time to mount a defense. Delaware (the state in which most large companies are incorporated) later passed a similar bill, as did New York and a number of other important states.

State laws also have some features that protect target stockholders from their own managers. Included are limits on the use of golden parachutes, onerous debt financing plans, and some types of takeover defenses. Because these laws do not regulate tender offers per se but rather govern the practices of firms in the state, they have withstood all legal challenges to date. But when companies such as IBM offer 100% premiums for companies such as Lotus, it is hard for any defense to hold them off.

SELF-TEST

Is there a need to regulate mergers? Explain.

Do the states play a role in merger regulation, or is it all done at the national level? Explain.

22-6 Overview of Merger Analysis

An acquiring firm must answer two questions. First, how much would the target be worth after being incorporated into the acquirer? Notice that this may be quite different from the target's current value, which does not reflect any post-merger synergies or tax benefits. Second, how much should the acquirer offer for the target? A low price is obviously better for the acquirer, but the target won't take the offer if it is too low. However, a higher offer price could scare off potential rival bidders. Later sections discuss setting the offer's price and structure (cash versus stock), but for now we focus on estimating the post-merger value of the target.

There are two basic approaches used in merger valuation: discounted cash flow (DCF) techniques and market multiple analysis.[9] Survey evidence shows that 49.3% of firms use only discounted cash flow techniques, 33.3% use both DCF and market multiples, and 12.0% use only market multiples. The market multiple approach assumes that a target is directly comparable to the average firm in its industry. Therefore, this procedure provides at best a ballpark estimate. Because the market multiple approach is less accurate and less frequently used than DCF approaches, we will focus on DCF methods.[10]

---

[9]See Chapter 7 for an explanation of market multiple analysis.

[10]For recent survey evidence on merger valuation methods, see Tarun K. Mukherjee, Halil Kiymaz, and H. Kent Baker, "Merger Motives and Target Valuation: A Survey of Evidence from CFOs," *Journal of Applied Finance*, Fall/Winter 2004, pp. 7–23. For evidence on the effectiveness of market multiples and DCF approaches, see S. N. Kaplan and R. S. Ruback, "The Market Pricing of Cash Flow Forecasts: Discounted Cash Flow vs. the Method of 'Comparables,'" *Journal of Applied Corporate Finance*, Winter 1996, pp. 45–60. Also see Samuel C. Weaver, Robert S. Harris, Daniel W. Bielinski, and Kenneth F. MacKenzie, "Merger and Acquisition Valuation," *Financial Management*, Summer 1991, pp. 85–96; and Nancy Mohan, M. Fall Ainina, Daniel Kaufman, and Bernard J. Winger, "Acquisition/Divestiture Valuation Practices in Major U.S. Firms," *Financial Practice and Education*, Spring 1991, pp. 73–81.

There are three widely used DCF methods: (1) the corporate free cash flow valuation method, (2) the adjusted present value method, and (3) the equity residual method, which is also called the "free cash flow to equity" method. Chapter 7 explained the corporate valuation model, Chapter 21 explained the adjusted present value model, and Section 22-7 explains the equity residual model. Section 22-8 provides a numerical illustration for a company with a constant capital structure and shows that all three models, when properly applied, produce identical valuations if the capital structure is held constant. However, in many situations, there will be a nonconstant capital structure in years immediately following the merger. For example, this often occurs if an acquisition is financed with a temporarily high level of debt that will be reduced to a sustainable level as the merger is digested. In such situations, it is extremely difficult to apply the corporate valuation model or the equity residual model correctly because the cost of equity and the cost of capital are changing as the capital structure changes. Fortunately, the adjusted present value model is ideally suited for such situations, as we illustrate in Section 22-10.

SELF-TEST

What are the two questions that an acquirer must answer?

What are four methods for estimating a target's value?

22-7 The Free Cash Flow to Equity (FCFE) Approach

Free cash flow is the cash flow available for distribution to *all* investors. In contrast, **free cash flow to equity (FCFE)** is the cash flow available for distribution to *common shareholders*. Because FCFE is available for distribution only to shareholders, it should be discounted at the levered cost of equity, r_{sL}. Therefore, the **free cash flow to equity approach**, also called the **equity residual model**, discounts the projected FCFEs at the cost of equity to determine the value of the equity from operations.

Because FCFE is the cash flow available for distribution to shareholders, it may be used to pay common dividends, repurchase stock, purchase financial assets, or some combination of these uses. In other words, the uses of FCFE include all those of FCF except for distributions to debtholders. Therefore, one way to calculate FCFE is to start with FCF and reduce it by the net after-tax distributions to debtholders:

$$
\begin{aligned}
\text{FCFE} &= \frac{\text{Free}}{\text{cash flow}} - \frac{\text{After-tax}}{\text{interest expense}} - \frac{\text{Principal}}{\text{payments}} + \frac{\text{Newly issued}}{\text{debt}} \\
&= \frac{\text{Free}}{\text{cash flow}} - \frac{\text{Interest}}{\text{expense}} + \frac{\text{Interest}}{\text{tax shield}} + \frac{\text{Net change}}{\text{in debt}}
\end{aligned}
\tag{22-1}
$$

Alternatively, the FCFE can be calculated as

$$
\text{FCFE} = \text{Net income} - \frac{\text{Net investment in}}{\text{operating capital}} + \frac{\text{Net change}}{\text{in debt}}
\tag{22-1a}
$$

Both calculations provide the same value for FCFE, but Equation 22-1 is used more often because analysts don't always estimate the net income for a target after it has been acquired.

Given projections of FCFE, the value of a firm's equity due to operations, V_{FCFE}, is

$$V_{FCFE} = \sum_{t=1}^{\infty} \frac{FCFE_t}{(1 + r_{sL})^t} \tag{22-2}$$

If we assume constant growth beyond the horizon, then the horizon value of the value of equity due to operations, $HV_{FCFE,N}$, is

$$HV_{FCFE,N} = \frac{FCFE_{N+1}}{r_{sL} - g} = \frac{FCFE_N(1 + g)}{r_{sL} - g} \tag{22-3}$$

The value of equity due to operations is the present value of the horizon value and the FCFE during the forecast period:

$$V_{FCFE} = \sum_{t=1}^{N} \frac{FCFE_t}{(1 + r_{sL})^t} + \frac{HV_{FCFE,\,N}}{(1 + r_{sL})^N} \tag{22-4}$$

The total value of a company's equity, S, is the value of the equity from operations plus the value of any nonoperating assets:

$$S = V_{FCFE} + \text{Nonoperating assets} \tag{22-5}$$

To get a per share price, simply divide the total value of equity by the shares outstanding.[11] Like the corporate valuation model, the FCFE model can be applied only when the capital structure is constant.

Table 22-2 summarizes the three cash flow valuation methods and their assumptions.

SELF-TEST

What cash flows are discounted in the FCFE model, and what is the discount rate?

How do the FCFE, corporate FCF valuation, and APV models differ? How are they similar?

---

[11]The FCFE model is similar to the dividend growth model in that cash flows are discounted at the cost of equity. The cash flows in the FCFE model are those that are generated from operations, while the cash flows in the dividend growth model (i.e., the dividends) also contain cash flows due to interest earned on nonoperating assets.

© Cengage Learning 2014

TABLE 22-2

Summary of Cash Flow Approaches

	Approach		
	Corporate FCF Valuation Model	**Free Cash Flow to Equity Model**	**APV Model**
Cash flow definition	FCF = NOPAT − Net investment in operating capital	FCFE = FCF − Interest expense + Interest tax shield + Net change in debt	(1) FCF and (2) Interest tax savings
Discount rate	WACC	r_{sL} = Cost of equity	r_{sU} = Unlevered cost of equity
Result of present value calculation	Value of operations	Value of equity due to operations	(1) Value of unlevered operations and (2) Value of the tax shield; together, these are the value of operations
How to get equity value	Value of operations + Value of nonoperating assets − Value of debt	Value of equity due to operations + Value of nonoperating assets	Value of operations + Value of nonoperating assets − Value of debt
Assumption about capital structure during forecast period	Capital structure is constant	Capital structure is constant	None
Requirement for analyst to project interest expense	No interest expense projections needed	Projected interest expense must be based on the assumed capital structure	Interest expense projections are unconstrained
Assumption at horizon	FCF grows at constant rate g	FCFE grows at constant rate g	FCF and interest tax savings grow at constant rate g

22-8 Illustration of the Three Valuation Approaches for a Constant Capital Structure

To illustrate the three valuation approaches, consider Caldwell Inc., a large technology company, as it evaluates the potential acquisition of Tutwiler Controls. If the acquisition takes place, it will occur on January 1, 2014, and so each valuation will be as of that date and will be based on the capital structure and synergies expected after the acquisition. Tutwiler currently has a $62.5 million market value of equity and $27 million in debt, for a total market value of $89.5 million. Thus, Tutwiler's capital structure consists of $27/($62.5 + $27) = 30.17% debt. Caldwell intends to finance the acquisition with this same proportion of debt and plans to maintain this constant capital structure throughout the projection period and thereafter. Tutwiler is a publicly traded company, and its market-determined pre-merger beta was 1.2. Given a risk-free rate of 7% and a 5% market risk premium, the Capital Asset Pricing Model produces a pre-merger required rate of return on equity, r_{sL}, of

$$r_{sL} = r_{RF} + b(RP_M)$$
$$= 7\% + 1.2(5\%) = 13\%$$

Tutwiler's cost of debt is 9%. Its WACC is

$$\begin{aligned}
\text{WACC} &= w_d(1-T)r_d + w_s r_{sL} \\
&= 0.3017(0.60)(9\%) + 0.6983(13\%) \\
&= 10.707\%
\end{aligned}$$

How much would Tutwiler be worth to Caldwell after the merger? The following sections illustrate the application of the corporate valuation model, the APV model, and the FCFE model. All three models produce an identical value of equity, but keep in mind this is only because the capital structure is constant. If the capital structure were to change during the projection period before becoming stable, then only the APV model could be used. Section 22-10 illustrates the APV in the case of a nonconstant capital structure.

22-8a Projecting Post-Merger Cash Flows

The first order of business is to estimate the post-merger cash flows that Tutwiler will produce. This is by far the most important task in any merger analysis. In a **pure financial merger**, defined as one in which no operating synergies are expected, the incremental post-merger cash flows are simply the target firm's expected cash flows. In an **operating merger**, in which the two firms' operations are to be integrated, forecasting future cash flows is obviously more difficult, because potential synergies must be estimated. People from marketing, production, human resources, and accounting play leading roles here, with financial managers focusing on financing the acquisition and performing an analysis designed to determine whether the projected cash flows are worth the cost. In this chapter, we take the projections as given and concentrate on how they are analyzed. See **Web Extension 22A**, available on the textbook's Web site, for a discussion that focuses on projecting financial statements in a merger analysis.

resource

See *Ch22 Tool Kit.xls* for details.

Table 22-3 shows the post-merger projections for Tutwiler, taking into account all expected synergies and maintaining a constant capital structure. Both Caldwell and Tutwiler are in the 40% marginal federal-plus-state tax bracket. The cost of debt after the acquisition will remain at 9%. The projections assume that growth in the post-horizon period will be 6%.

Panel A of Table 22-3 shows selected items from the projected financial statements. Panel B shows the calculations for free cash flow, which is used in the corporate FCF valuation model. Row 9 shows net operating profit after taxes (NOPAT), which is equal to EBIT(1 − T). Row 10 shows the net investment in operating capital, which is the annual change in the total net operating capital in Row 8. Free cash flow, shown in Row 11, is equal to NOPAT less the net investment in operating capital. Panel C shows the cash flows that will be used in the APV model. In particular, Row 13 shows the annual tax shield, which is equal to the interest expense multiplied by the tax rate. Panel D provides the calculations for FCFE, based upon Equation 22-1.

Of course, the post-merger cash flows are extremely difficult to estimate, and in merger valuations—just as in capital budgeting analysis—sensitivity, scenario, and simulation analyses should be conducted.[12] Indeed, in a friendly merger the acquiring firm would send a team consisting of literally dozens of financial analysts, accountants, engineers, and so forth to the target firm's headquarters. They would go over its books, estimate required

---

[12]We purposely kept the cash flows simple in order to focus on key analytical issues. In actual merger valuations, the cash flows would be much more complex, normally including such items as tax loss carryforwards, tax effects of plant and equipment valuation adjustments, and cash flows from the sale of some of the subsidiary's assets.

TABLE 22-3

Post-Merger Projections for the Tutwiler Subsidiary (Millions of Dollars)

	1/1/14	12/31/14	12/31/15	12/31/16	12/31/17	12/31/18
Panel A: Selected Items from Projected Financial Statements[a]						
1. Net sales		$105.0	$126.0	$151.0	$174.0	$191.0
2. Cost of goods sold		80.0	94.0	113.0	129.3	142.0
3. Selling and administrative expenses		10.0	12.0	13.0	15.0	16.0
4. Depreciation		8.0	8.0	9.0	9.0	10.0
5. EBIT		$ 7.0	$ 12.0	$ 16.0	$ 20.7	$ 23.0
6 Interest expense[b]		3.0	3.2	3.5	3.7	3.9
7 Debt[c]	$ 33.2	35.8	38.7	41.1	43.6	46.2
8. Total net operating capital	116.0	117.0	121.0	125.0	131.0	138.0
Panel B: Corporate Valuation Model Cash Flows						
9. NOPAT = EBIT(1 − T)		$ 4.2	$ 7.2	$ 9.6	$ 12.4	$ 13.8
10. Less net investment in operating capital		1.0	4.0	4.0	6.0	7.0
11. Free cash flow		$ 3.2	$ 3.2	$ 5.6	$ 6.4	$ 6.8
Panel C: APV Model Cash Flows						
12. Free cash flow		$ 3.2	$ 3.2	$ 5.6	$ 6.4	$ 6.8
13. Interest tax saving = Interest(T)		$ 1.2	$ 1.3	$ 1.4	$ 1.5	$ 1.6
Panel D: FCFE Model Cash Flows						
14. Free cash flow		$ 3.2	$ 3.2	$ 5.6	$ 6.4	$ 6.8
15. Less A-T interest = Interest(1 − T)		1.8	1.9	2.1	2.2	2.4
16. Plus change in debt[d]	6.2	2.6	2.9	2.5	2.5	2.6
17. FCFE	$ 6.2	$ 4.0	$ 4.1	$ 6.0	$ 6.7	$ 7.1

Notes:
[a]Rounded figures are presented here, but the full nonrounded values are used in all calculations. The tax rate is 40%.
[b]Interest payments are based on Tutwiler's existing debt, new debt to be issued to finance the acquisition, and additional debt required to finance annual growth.
[c]Debt is existing debt plus additional debt required to maintain a constant capital structure. Caldwell will increase Tutwiler's debt by $6.2 million, from $27 million to $33.2 million, at the time of the acquisition in order to keep the capital structure constant. This increase occurs because the post-merger synergies make Tutwiler more valuable to Caldwell than it was on a stand-alone basis. Therefore, it can support more dollars of debt and still maintain the constant debt ratio.
[d]The increase in debt at the time of acquisition is a source of free cash flow to equity.

© Cengage Learning 2014

maintenance expenditures, set values on assets such as real estate and petroleum reserves, and the like. Such an investigation, which is one example of **due diligence**, is an essential part of any merger analysis.

Following are valuations of Tutwiler using all three methods, beginning with the corporate valuation model.

22-8b Valuation Using the Corporate FCF Valuation Model

Because Caldwell does not plan on changing Tutwiler's capital structure, the post-merger WACC will be equal to the pre-merger WACC of 10.707% that we calculated previously. Tutwiler's free cash flows are shown in Row 11 of Table 22-3. The horizon value of

r e s o u r c e

See **Ch22 Tool Kit.xls** on the textbook's Web site for all calculations. Note that rounded intermediate values are shown in the text, but all calculations are performed in Excel using nonrounded values.

Tutwiler's operations as of 2018 can be calculated with the constant growth formula that we used in Chapter 13:

$$HV_{Operations,\,2018} = \frac{FCF_{2019}}{WACC - g_L} = \frac{FCF_{2018}(1 + g_L)}{WACC - g_L}$$

$$= \frac{\$6.800(1.06)}{0.10707 - 0.06} = \$153.1 \text{ million}$$

The value of operations as of January 1, 2014, is the present value of the cash flows in the forecast period and the horizon value:

$$V_{Operations} = \frac{\$3.2}{(1 + 0.10707)^1} + \frac{\$3.2}{(1 + 0.10707)^2} + \frac{\$5.6}{(1 + 0.10707)^3}$$

$$+ \frac{\$6.4}{(1 + 0.10707)^4} + \frac{\$6.8 + \$153.1}{(1 + 0.10707)^5}$$

$$= \$110.1$$

There are no nonoperating assets, so the value of equity to Caldwell if Tutwiler is acquired is equal to the value of operations less the value of Tutwiler's debt:[13]

$$\$110.1 - \$27 = \$83.1 \text{ million}$$

22-8c Valuation Using the APV Approach

The APV approach requires an estimate of Tutwiler's unlevered cost of equity. As shown in Chapter 21, the levered cost of equity is:

$$r_{sL} = r_{sU} + (r_{sU} - r_d)(w_d/w_s) \tag{22-6}$$

Inputting Tutwiler's capital structure, cost of equity, and cost of debt, Equation 22-6 can be rearranged to estimate the unlevered cost of equity:

$$r_{sU} = w_s r_{sL} + w_d r_d \tag{22-6a}$$

$$= 0.6983(13\%) + 0.3017(9\%)$$
$$= 11.793\%$$

In other words, if Tutwiler had no debt, its cost of equity would be 11.793%.[14]

Instead of directly estimating the unlevered cost of equity, we can estimate the unlevered beta, b_U, and then calculate the unlevered cost of equity. Chapter 21 shows an expression for the unlevered beta.

$$b = b_U + (b_U - b_D)(w_d/w_s) \tag{22-7}$$

where b_D is the beta of the debt.

---

[13]Notice that we subtract the $27 million value of Tutwiler's debt, not the $33.2 million of debt supported *after* the merger, because $27 million is the amount that must be paid off or assumed by Caldwell.

[14]Notice that we do not use the Hamada equation to unlever beta because the Hamada equation assumes zero growth.

Notice that this is different from the Hamada formula in Chapter 15. First, the Hamada formula assumes zero growth, but 22-7 incorporates growth. Second, the Hamada formula assumes away risky debt. But if the CAPM is used to estimate the risk of equity, then the CAPM must be used to estimate the risk of debt, otherwise we would be comparing apples to oranges.

To estimate the beta on debt due to systematic risk, we can start with the observed cost of debt and solve the CAPM for the implied beta on debt:

$$b_D = (r_d - r_{RF})/RP_M$$
$$= (0.09 - 0.07)/0.05$$
$$= 0.4$$

Rearranging Equation 22-7, Tutwiler's unlevered beta is:

$$b_U = [b + b_D(w_d/w_s)]/[1 + (w_d/w_s)]$$
$$= [1.2 + 0.4(0.3017/0.6983)]/[1 + (0.3017/0.6983)]$$
$$= 0.9586$$

Using the CAPM, the unlevered cost of equity is:

$$r_{sL} = r_{RF} + b(RP_M)$$
$$= 7\% + 0.9586(5\%) = 11.79\%$$

This is exactly the same value previously estimated. Because this alternative approach requires that we assume the CAPM is the correct model, and because it takes extra steps, we usually use the first method shown in Equations 22-6 and 22-6a.

The horizon value of Tutwiler's unlevered cash flows ($HV_{U,2018}$) and tax shield ($HV_{TS,2018}$) can be calculated using the constant growth formula with the unlevered cost of equity as the discount rate, as shown in Chapter 21:[15]

$$HV_{U,2018} = \frac{FCF_{2019}}{r_{sU} - g_L} = \frac{FCF_{2018}(1 + g_L)}{r_{sU} - g_L} = \frac{\$6.800(1.06)}{0.11793 - 0.06} = \$124.4 \text{ million}$$

$$HV_{TS,2018} = \frac{TS_{2019}}{r_{sU} - g_L} = \frac{TS_{2018}(1 + g_L)}{r_{sU} - g_L} = \frac{\$1.57(1.06)}{0.11793 - 0.06} = \$28.7 \text{ million}$$

The sum of the two horizon values is $124.4 + $28.7 = $153.1 million. This is the horizon value of operations, which is the same as the horizon value calculation we reached with the corporate FCF valuation model.

Row 11 in Table 22-3 shows the projected free cash flows. The unlevered value of operations is calculated as the present value of the free cash flows during the forecast period and the horizon value of the free cash flows:

$$V_{Unlevered} = \frac{\$3.2}{(1 + 0.11793)^1} + \frac{\$3.2}{(1 + 0.11793)^2} + \frac{\$5.6}{(1 + 0.11793)^3}$$

$$+ \frac{\$6.4}{(1 + 0.11793)^4} + \frac{\$6.8 + \$124.4}{(1 + 0.11793)^5}$$

$$= \$88.7 \text{ million}$$

This shows that Tutwiler's operations would be worth $88.7 million if it had no debt.

---

[15]Note that we report two decimal places for the 2018 tax shield even though Table 22-3 reports only one decimal place. All calculations are performed in *Excel*, which uses the full nonrounded values.

Row 13 shows the yearly interest tax savings. The value of the tax shield is calculated as the present value of the yearly tax savings and the horizon value of the tax shield:

$$V_{\text{Tax shield}} = \frac{\$1.2}{(1 + 0.11793)^1} + \frac{\$1.3}{(1 + 0.11793)^2} + \frac{\$1.4}{(1 + 0.11793)^3}$$

$$+ \frac{\$1.5}{(1 + 0.11793)^4} + \frac{\$1.57 + \$28.7}{(1 + 0.11793)^5}$$

$$= \$21.4 \text{ million}$$

resource

See Ch22 Tool Kit.xls on the textbook's Web site for all calculations. Note that rounded intermediate values are shown in the text, but all calculations are performed in Excel using nonrounded values.

Thus, Tutwiler's operations would be worth only $88.7 million if it had no debt, but its capital structure contributes $21.4 million in value due to the tax deductibility of its interest payments. Because Tutwiler has no nonoperating assets, the total value of the firm is the sum of the unlevered value of operations, $88.7 million, and the value of the tax shield, $21.4 million, for a total of $110.1 million. The value of the equity is this total value less Tutwiler's outstanding debt of $27 million: $110.1 − $27 = $83.1 million. Note that this is the same value we obtained using the corporate valuation model.

22-8d Valuation Using the FCFE Model

The horizon value of Tutwiler's free cash flows to equity can be calculated using the constant growth formula of Equation 22-3:[16]

$$HV_{\text{FCFE}, 2018} = \frac{FCF_{2018}(1 + g_L)}{r_{sL} - g_L} = \frac{\$7.06(1.06)}{0.13 - 0.06} = \$106.9 \text{ million}$$

Notice that this horizon value is different from the APV and corporate FCF valuation horizon values. That is because the FCFE horizon value is only for equity, whereas the other two horizon values are for the total value of operations. If the 2018 debt of $46.2 million shown in Row 7 of Table 22-3 is added to the $HV_{\text{FCFE},2018}$, the result is the same $153.1 million horizon value of operations obtained with the corporate valuation model and APV model.

Row 17 in Table 22-3 shows the yearly projections of FCFE. When discounted at the 13% cost of equity, the present value of these yearly FCFEs and the horizon value is the value of equity due to operations, which is $83.1 million:[17]

$$V_{\text{FCFE}} = \$6.2 + \frac{\$4.0}{(1 + 0.13)^1} + \frac{\$4.1}{(1 + 0.13)^2} + \frac{\$6.0}{(1 + 0.13)^3}$$

$$+ \frac{\$6.7}{(1 + 0.13)^4} + \frac{\$7.1 + \$106.9}{(1 + 0.13)^5}$$

$$= \$83.1 \text{ million}$$

If Tutwiler had any nonoperating assets, we would add them to V_{FCFE} to determine the total value of equity. Because Tutwiler has no nonoperating assets, its total equity value is

---

[16]Note that we report two decimal places for the 2018 FCFE even though Table 22-3 reports only one decimal place. All calculations are performed in *Excel*, which uses the full nonrounded values.

[17]Row 16 in Table 22-3 shows that debt is forecast to increase from its pre-merger $27 million to $33.2 million at the acquisition date. This is because Tutwiler is more valuable after the merger, so it can support more dollars of debt while still maintaining 30% debt in its capital structure. The increase in debt of $33.2 − $27 = $6.2 million is a FCFE that is immediately available to Caldwell and so is not discounted.

equal to the V_{FCFE} of $83.1 million. Notice that this is the same value given by the corporate valuation model and the APV approach.

All three models agree that the estimated equity value is $83.1 million, which is more than the $62.5 million current market value of Tutwiler's equity. This means that Tutwiler is more valuable as a part of Caldwell than as a stand-alone corporation being run by its current managers.

resource

See **Ch22 Tool Kit.xls,** on the textbook's Web site for complete calculations and **Web Extension 22A** for a more detailed explanation.

SELF-TEST

Why is the adjusted present value approach appropriate for situations with a changing capital structure?

Describe the steps required to apply the APV approach.

How do the FCFE, APV, and corporate valuation approaches differ from one another?

22-9 Setting the Bid Price

Under the acquisition plan, Caldwell would assume Tutwiler's debt and would also take on additional short-term debt as necessary to complete the purchase. The valuation models show that $83.1 million is the most it should pay for Tutwiler's stock. If it paid more, then Caldwell's own value would be diluted. On the other hand, if it could get Tutwiler for less than $83.1 million, Caldwell's stockholders would gain value. Therefore, Caldwell should bid something less than $83.1 million when it makes an offer for Tutwiler.

Now consider the target company. As stated earlier, Tutwiler's value of equity as an independent operating company is $62.5 million. If Tutwiler were acquired at a price greater than $62.5 million, then its stockholders would gain value, whereas they would lose value at any lower price.

The difference between $62.5 million and $83.1 million, or $20.6 million, represents **synergistic benefits** expected from the merger. If there were no synergistic benefits, the maximum bid would be the current value of the target company. The greater the synergistic gains, the greater the gap between the target's current price and the maximum the acquiring company could pay.

The issue of how to divide the synergistic benefits is critically important. Obviously, both parties would want to get the best deal possible. In our example, if it knew the maximum price Caldwell could pay, Tutwiler's management would argue for a price close to $83.1 million. Caldwell, on the other hand, would try to get Tutwiler at a price as close to $62.5 million as possible.

Where, within the range of $62.5 to $83.1 million, will the actual price be set? The answer depends on a number of factors, including whether Caldwell offers to pay with cash or securities, the negotiating skills of the two management teams, and, most importantly, the bargaining positions of the two parties as determined by fundamental economic conditions. Let's first consider bargaining power and then examine the mechanics of a cash offer versus a stock offer.

22-9a Relative Bargaining Power

To illustrate the relative bargaining power of the target and the acquirer, assume there are many companies similar to Tutwiler that Caldwell could acquire, but suppose that no company other than Caldwell could gain synergies by acquiring Tutwiler. In this case,

Caldwell would probably make a relatively low, take-it-or-leave-it offer, and Tutwiler would probably take it because some gain is better than none. On the other hand, if Tutwiler has some unique technology or other asset that many companies want, then once Caldwell announces its offer, others would probably make competing bids and the final price would probably be close to (or even above) $83.1 million. A price above $83.1 million presumably would be paid by some other company with a better synergistic fit or with a management that is more optimistic about Tutwiler's cash flow potential.

Caldwell would, of course, want to keep its maximum bid secret, and it would plan its bidding strategy carefully. If Caldwell thought other bidders would emerge or that Tutwiler's management might resist in order to preserve their jobs, Caldwell might make a high preemptive bid in hopes of scaring off competing bids or management resistance. On the other hand, it might make a lowball bid in hopes of "stealing" the company.[18]

22-9b Cash Offers versus Stock Offers

Most target stockholders prefer to sell their shares for cash rather than to exchange them for stock in the post-merger company. Following is a brief description of each payment method.

CASH OFFERS

Tutwiler's pre-merger equity is worth $62.5 million. With 10 million shares outstanding, Tutwiler's stock price is $62.5/10 = $6.25. If the synergies are realized, then Tutwiler's equity will be worth $83.1 million to Caldwell, so $83.1/10 = $8.31 is the maximum price per share that Caldwell should be willing to pay to Tutwiler's stockholders. For example, Caldwell might offer $7.75 cash for each share of Tutwiler stock.

STOCK OFFERS

In a stock offer, Tutwiler's stockholders exchange their Tutwiler shares for new shares in the post-merger company, which will be named CaldwellTutwiler. Targets typically prefer cash offers to stock offers, all else equal, but taxation of the offer prevents all else from being equal. We discuss taxation in more detail in Section 22-11, but for now you should know that stock offerings are taxed more favorably than cash offerings. In this case, perhaps Caldwell should offer a package worth $7.50 per share. With 10 million outstanding Tutwiler shares, the Tutwiler shareholders must end up owning $7.50 × 10 million = $75 million worth of stock in the post-merger company.

Suppose Caldwell has 20 million shares of stock outstanding (n_{Old}) prior to the merger and the stock price per share is $15. Then the total pre-merger value of Caldwell's equity is $15 × 20 million = $300 million. As calculated previously, the post-merger value of Tutwiler to Caldwell is $83.1 million. Therefore, the total post-merger value of CaldwellTutwiler will be $300 + $83.1 = $383.1 million.

After the merger, Tutwiler's former stockholders should own $75/$383.1 = 0.196 = 19.58% of the post-merger CaldwellTutwiler. With 20 million Caldwell shares outstanding, Caldwell must issue enough new shares, n_{New}, to the Tutwiler stockholders (in exchange

---

[13]For an interesting discussion of the aftereffects of losing a bidding contest, see Mark L. Mitchell and Kenneth Lehn, "Do Bad Bidders Become Good Targets?" *Journal of Applied Corporate Finance,* Summer 1990, pp. 60–69.

for the Tutwiler shares) so that Tutwiler's former stockholders will own 19.6% of the shares of CaldwellTutwiler:

$$\text{Percent required by target stockholders} = \frac{n_{New}}{n_{New} + n_{Old}}$$

$$19.58\% = \frac{n_{New}}{n_{New} + 20}$$

$$n_{New} = \frac{20 \times 0.1958}{1 - 0.1958} = 4.87 \text{ million}$$

Tutwiler's former stockholders will exchange 10 million shares of stock in Tutwiler for 4.87 million shares of stock in the combined CaldwellTutwiler. Thus, the exchange ratio is 4.87/10 = 0.487.

After the merger, there will be 4.87 million new shares for a total of 24.87 million shares. With a combined intrinsic equity value of $383.1 million, the resulting price per share will be $383.1/24.87 = $15.40. The total value owned by Tutwiler's shareholders is this price multiplied by their shares: $15.40 × 4.87 million = $75 million. Also notice that the price will increase from $15.00 per share before the merger to $15.40 after the merger, so the merger will benefit Caldwell's shareholders if the synergies are realized.

SELF-TEST

Explain the issues involved in setting the bid price.

22-10 Analysis When There Is a Permanent Change in Capital Structure

Tutwiler currently has equity worth $62.5 million and debt of $27 million, giving it a capital structure financed with about 30% debt: $27.0/($62.5 + $27.0) = 0.302 = 30.2%. Suppose Caldwell has decided to increase Tutwiler's debt from 30% to 50% over the next 5 years and to maintain the capital structure at that level from 2018 on. How would this affect Tutwiler's valuation? The free cash flows will not change, but the interest tax shield, the WACC, and the bid price will all change.[19] At a 30% debt level, the interest rate on Tutwiler's debt was 9%. However, at a 50% debt level, Tutwiler is more risky, and its interest rate would rise to 9.5% to reflect this additional risk. Because the capital structure is changing, we will use only the APV for this analysis.

22-10a The Effect on the Tax Shield

It is reasonable to assume that Caldwell will use more debt during the first 5 years of the acquisition if its long-run target capital structure is 50% debt. With more debt and a higher interest rate, the interest payments will be higher than those shown in Table 22-3,

---

[19]We are assuming for simplicity that Tutwiler has no more expected bankruptcy costs at 50% debt than at 30% debt. If Tutwiler's risk of bankruptcy and hence its expected bankruptcy costs are larger at this higher level of debt, then its projected free cash flows should be reduced by these expected costs. In practice it is extremely difficult to estimate expected bankruptcy costs. However, these costs can be significant and should be considered when a high degree of leverage is being used.

thus increasing the tax savings shown in Line 15. The interest payments and tax savings with more debt and a higher interest rate are projected as follows:

resource

For more information on projecting financial statements, see **Web Extension 22A** *and* **Ch22 Tool Kit.xls** *on the textbook's Web site.*

	2014	2015	2016	2017	2018
Interest	$5.00	$6.00	$7.00	$7.50	$8.30
Interest tax savings	2.00	2.40	2.80	3.00	3.32

In these projections, Tutwiler will reach its target capital structure of 50% debt and 50% equity by the start of 2018.[20]

22-10b The Effect on the Bid Price

The new capital structure would affect the maximum bid price by changing the value of Tutwiler to Caldwell. Based on the new tax shields, the unlevered and tax shield horizon values in 2018 are calculated as

$$HV_{U,2018} = \frac{FCF_{2019}}{r_{sU} - g} = \frac{FCF_{2018}(1 + g)}{r_{sU} - g} = \frac{\$6.800(1.06)}{0.11793 - 0.06} = \$124.4$$

$$HV_{TS,2018} = \frac{TS_{2019}}{r_{sU} - g} = \frac{TS_{2018}(1 + g)}{r_{sU} - g} = \frac{\$3.32(1.06)}{0.11793 - 0.06} = \$60.7$$

Based on the new interest payments and horizon values, the cash flows to be discounted at the unlevered cost of equity are as follows:

	2014	2015	2016	2017	2018
Free cash flow	$3.2	$3.2	$5.6	$6.4	$ 6.8
Unlevered horizon value					124.4
FCF plus horizon value	$3.2	$3.2	$5.6	$6.4	$131.2
Interest tax saving	2.0	2.4	2.8	3.0	3.3
Tax shield horizon value					$ 60.7
TS$_t$ plus horizon value	$2.0	$2.4	$2.8	$3.0	$ 64.0

The present value of the free cash flows and their horizon value is $88.7 million, just as it was under the 30% debt policy; the unlevered value of operations is not impacted by the change in capital structure:

$$V_{Unlevered} = \frac{\$3.2}{(1 + 0.11793)^1} + \frac{\$3.2}{(1 + 0.11793)^2} + \frac{\$5.6}{(1 + 0.11793)^3}$$

$$+ \frac{\$6.4}{(1 + 0.11793)^4} + \frac{\$6.8 + \$124.4}{(1 + 0.11793)^5}$$

$$= \$88.7 \text{ million}$$

---

[20]The last year's projected interest expense must be consistent with the assumed capital structure in order to use the relation $TS_{N+1} = TS_N(1 + g)$ in calculating the tax shield horizon value.

The present value of the tax shields and their horizon value is $44.3 million, which is $22.9 million more than the value of the tax shield under the 30% debt policy:

$$V_{\text{Tax shield}} = \frac{\$2.0}{(1 + 0.11793)^1} + \frac{\$2.4}{(1 + 0.11793)^2} + \frac{\$2.8}{(1 + 0.11793)^3}$$

$$+ \frac{\$3.0}{(1 + 0.11793)^4} + \frac{\$3.3 + \$60.7}{(1 + 0.11793)^5}$$

$$= \$44.3 \text{ million}$$

Thus, Tutwiler is worth almost $23 million more to Caldwell if it is financed with 50% rather than 30% debt because of the added value of the tax shields.

The value of operations under the new 50% debt policy is the sum of the unlevered value of operations and the value of the tax shields, or $133.0 million. There are no nonoperating assets to add, and subtracting the debt of $27 million leaves the value of Tutwiler's equity at $106.0 million. Because Tutwiler has 10 million shares outstanding, the maximum amount Caldwell should be willing to pay per share, given a post-merger target capital structure of 50% debt, is $10.60. This is more than the $8.31 maximum price if the capital structure had 30% debt. The difference, $2.29 per share, reflects the added value of the interest tax shields under the higher-debt plan.

SELF-TEST

How does a change in capital structure affect the valuation analysis?

22-11 Taxes and the Structure of the Takeover Bid

In a merger, the acquiring firm can either buy the target's assets or buy shares of stock directly from the target's shareholders. If the offer is for the target's assets then the target's board of directors will make a recommendation to the shareholders, who will vote either to accept or reject the offer. If they accept the offer, the payment goes directly to the target corporation, which pays off any debt not assumed by the acquiring firm, pays any corporate taxes that are due, and then distributes the remainder of the payment to the shareholders, often in the form of a liquidating dividend. In this situation, the target firm is usually dissolved and no longer continues to exist as a separate legal entity, although its assets and work force may continue to function as a division or as a wholly owned subsidiary of the acquiring firm. The acquisition of assets is a common form of takeover for small and medium-sized firms, especially those that are not publicly traded. A major advantage of this method compared with the acquisition of the target's stock is that the acquiring firm simply acquires assets and is not saddled with any hidden liabilities. In contrast, if the acquiring firm buys the target's stock, then it is responsible for any legal contingencies against the target, even for those that might have occurred prior to the takeover.

An offer for a target's stock rather than its assets can be made either directly to the shareholders, as is typical in a hostile takeover, or indirectly through the board of directors, which in a friendly deal makes a recommendation to the shareholders to accept the offer. In a successful offer, the acquiring firm will end up owning a controlling interest or perhaps even all of the target's stock. Sometimes the target retains its identity as a separate legal entity and is operated as a subsidiary of the acquiring firm, and sometimes its corporate status is dissolved and it is operated as one of the acquiring firm's divisions.

Tempest in a Teapot?

© Rob Webb/Getty Images

In 2001, amid a flurry of warnings and lobbying, the Financial Accounting Standards Board (FASB) in its Statement 141 eliminated the use of pooling for merger accounting, requiring that purchase accounting be used instead. Because the change would otherwise have required that all purchased goodwill be amortized and reported earnings be reduced, the FASB also issued Statement 142, which eliminated the regular amortization of purchased goodwill, replacing it with an "impairment test." The impairment test requires that companies evaluate annually their purchased goodwill and write it down if its value has declined. This impairment test resulted in Time Warner's unprecedented 2002 write-down of $54 billion of goodwill associated with the AOL merger.

So what exactly is the effect of the change? First and foremost, the change does *nothing* to the firm's actual cash flows. Purchased goodwill may still be amortized for federal income tax purposes, so the change does not affect the actual taxes a company pays, nor does it affect the

company's operating cash flows. However, it does affect the earnings that companies report to their shareholders. Firms that used to have large goodwill charges from past acquisitions have seen their reported earnings increase because they no longer have to amortize the remaining goodwill. Firms whose acquisitions have fared badly, such as Time Warner, must make large write-downs. Executives facing boosted earnings hope—and executives facing a write-down fear—that investors will not see through these accounting changes. However, evidence suggests that investors realize that a company's assets have deteriorated long before the write-down actually occurs, and they build this information into the price of the stock. For example, Time Warner's announcement of its $54 billion charge in January 2002 resulted in only a blip in its stock price at that time, even though the write-down totaled more than a third of its market value. The market had recognized the decline in value months earlier, and by the time of the announcement Time Warner had already lost more than $100 billion in market value.

The payment offered by the acquiring firm can be in the form of cash, stock of the acquiring firm, debt of the acquiring firm, or some combination. The structure of the bid affects (1) the capital structure of the post-merger firm, (2) the tax treatment of both the acquiring firm and the target's stockholders, (3) the ability of the target firm's stockholders to benefit from future merger-related gains, and (4) the types of federal and state regulations to which the acquiring firm will be subjected.

The tax consequences of the merger depend on whether it is classified as a *taxable offer* or a *nontaxable offer*.[21] In general, a nontaxable offer is one in which the form of payment is predominately stock, although the application of this simple principle is much more complicated in practice. The Internal Revenue Code views a mostly stock merger as an exchange rather than a sale, making it a nontaxable event. However, if the offer includes a significant amount of cash or bonds, then the IRS views it as a sale, and it is a taxable transaction just like any other sale.

In a nontaxable deal, target shareholders who receive shares of the acquiring company's stock do not have to pay any taxes at the time of the merger. When they eventually sell their stock in the acquiring company, they must pay a tax on the gain. The amount of the gain is the sales price of their stock in the acquiring company minus the price at which they purchased their original stock in the target company.[22] In a taxable offer, the gain

---

[21]For more details, see J. Fred Weston, Mark L. Mitchell, and Harold Mulherin, *Takeovers, Restructuring, and Corporate Governance*, 4th ed. (Upper Saddle River, NJ: Prentice-Hall, 2004), especially Chapter 4. Also see Kenneth E. Anderson, Thomas R. Pope, and John L. Kramer, eds., *Prentice Hall's Federal Taxation: Corporations, Partnerships, Estates, and Trusts*, 2006 ed. (Upper Saddle River, NJ: Prentice-Hall, 2006), especially Chapter 7.

[22]This is a capital gain if it has been at least 1 year since they purchased their original stock in the target.

between the offer price and the original purchase price of the target stock is taxed in the year of the merger.[23]

All other things equal, stockholders prefer nontaxable offers, because they may then postpone taxes on their gains. Furthermore, if the target firm's stockholders receive stock, they will benefit from any synergistic gains produced by the merger. Most target shareholders are thus willing to give up their stock for a lower price in a nontaxable offer than in a taxable one. As a result, one might expect nontaxable bids to dominate. However, this is not the case: Roughly half of all mergers have been taxable. The reason for this is explained in the following paragraphs.

The form of the payment also has tax consequences for the acquiring and target firms. To illustrate, consider the following situation. The target firm has assets with a book value of $100 million, but these assets have an appraised value of $150 million. The offer by the acquiring firm is worth $225 million. If it is a nontaxable offer, then after the merger the acquiring firm simply adds the $100 million book value of the target's assets to its own assets and continues to depreciate them according to their previous depreciation schedules. To keep the example simple, we assume the target has no debt.

The situation is more complicated for a taxable offer, and the treatment is different depending on whether the offer is for the target's assets or for its stock. If the acquiring firm offers $225 million for the target's assets, then the target firm must pay a tax on the gain of $225 − $100 = $125 million. Assuming a corporate tax rate of 40%, this tax is 0.40 ($125) = $50 million. This leaves the target with $225 − $50 = $175 million to distribute to its shareholders upon liquidation. Adding insult to injury, the target's shareholders must also pay individual taxes on any of their own gains.[24] This is truly a taxable transaction, with taxes assessed at both the corporate and individual levels!

In contrast to the tax disadvantages for the target and its shareholders, the acquiring firm receives two major tax advantages. First, it records the acquired assets at their appraised value and depreciates them accordingly. Thus, it will depreciate $150 million of assets in this taxable transaction versus only $100 million in a nontaxable transaction. Second, it will create $75 million in a new asset account called **goodwill**, which is the difference between the purchase price of $225 million and the appraised value of $150 million. Tax laws that took effect in 1993 permit companies to amortize this goodwill over 15 years using the straight-line method and also to deduct the amortization from taxable income. The net effect is that the full purchase price of $225 million can be written off in a taxable merger versus only the original book value of $100 million in a nontaxable transaction.

Now suppose the acquiring firm offers $225 million for the target's stock, rather than just its assets as in the preceding example, in a taxable offer. After completing the merger, the acquiring firm must choose between two tax treatments. Under the first alternative, it will record the assets at their book value of $100 million and continue depreciating them using their current schedules. This treatment does not create any goodwill. Under the second alternative, it will record the assets at their appraised value of $150 million and create $75 million of goodwill. As described earlier for the asset purchase, this allows the acquiring firm to effectively depreciate the entire purchase price of $225 million for tax purposes. However, there will also be an immediate tax liability on the $125 million gain, just as when the firm purchased assets.[25]

---

[23]Even in nontaxable deals, taxes must be paid in the year of the merger by any stockholders who receive cash.
[24]Our example assumes that the target is a publicly owned firm, which means that it must be a "C corporation" for tax purposes. However, if it is privately held then it might be an "S corporation," in which case only the stockholders would be taxed. This helps smaller firms to use mergers as an exit strategy.
[25]Technically speaking, it is the target firm that is responsible for this tax on the write-up. Keep in mind, however, that the acquiring firm previously purchased the stock in the target and so, in reality, must bear the brunt of the tax.

FIGURE 22-1

Merger Tax Effects

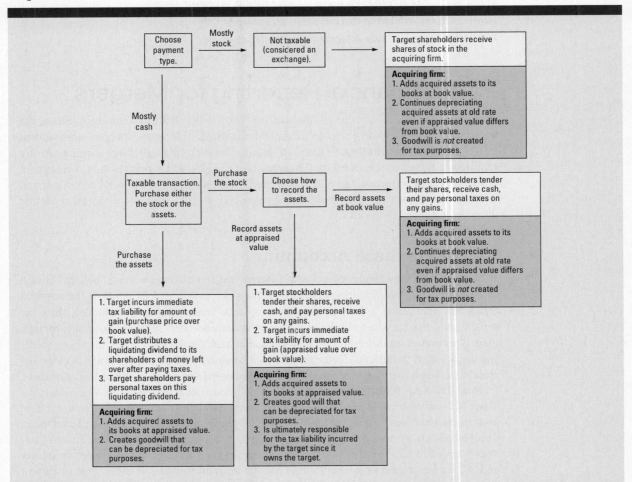

Note: These are actual cash tax effects. However, the tax effects reported to shareholders will be different because shareholder statements must conform to GAAP conventions, not to federal Tax Code conventions. For example, purchased goodwill can no longer be deducted for shareholder reporting under GAAP, even though it is still deductible for federal tax purposes. See the box entitled "Tempest in a Teapot?" which deals with changes in the accounting treatment of mergers and goodwill.

© Cengage Learning 2014

Therefore, many companies choose not to mark up the assets. Figure 22-1 illustrates the tax implications for the various types of transactions.

If you think this is complicated, you are right! At this point, you should know enough to talk with specialized accountants and lawyers or be ready to delve into tax accounting texts, but merger taxation is too complex a subject to be covered thoroughly in a general finance textbook.

Securities laws also have an effect on the offer's construction. The SEC has oversight over the issuance of new securities, including stock or debt issued in connection with a merger. Therefore, whenever a corporation bids for control of another firm through the exchange of equity or debt, the entire process must take place under the scrutiny of the Securities and Exchange Commission. The time required for such reviews allows target managements to implement defensive tactics and other firms to make competing offers; as a result, nearly all hostile tender offers are for cash rather than securities.

SELF-TEST

What are some alternative ways of structuring takeover bids?

How do taxes influence the payment structure?

How do securities laws affect the payment structure?

22-12 Financial Reporting for Mergers

Although a detailed discussion of financial reporting is best left to accounting courses, the accounting implications of mergers cannot be ignored. Currently, mergers are handled using **purchase accounting**.[26] Keep in mind, however, that all large companies are required to keep two sets of books. The first is for the IRS, and it reflects the tax treatment of mergers as described in the previous section. The second is for financial reporting, and it reflects the treatment described here. As you will see, the rules for financial reporting differ from those for the IRS.

22-12a Purchase Accounting

Table 22-4 illustrates purchase accounting. Here, Firm A is assumed to have "bought" Firm B using the stock of the acquiring company. If the price paid is exactly equal to the acquired firm's *net asset value*, which is defined as its total assets minus its liabilities, then the consolidated balance sheet will be as if the two statements were merged. Normally, though, there is an important difference. If the price paid *exceeds* the net asset value, then asset values will be increased to reflect the price actually paid, whereas if the price paid is *less* than the net asset value, then assets must be written down when preparing the consolidated balance sheet.

Note that Firm B's net asset value is $30, which is also its reported common equity value. This $30 book value could be equal to the market value (which is determined by investors based on the firm's earning power), but book value could also be more or less than the market value. Three situations are considered in Table 22-4. First, in Column 3 we assume that Firm A gives stock worth $20 for Firm B. Thus, B's assets as reported on its balance sheet were overvalued, and A pays less than B's net asset value. The overvaluation could be in either fixed or current assets; an appraisal would be made, but we assume it is fixed assets that are overvalued. Accordingly, we reduce B's fixed assets and also its common equity by $10 before constructing the consolidated balance sheet shown in Column 3. Next, in Column 4, we assume that A pays exactly the net asset value for B. In this case, the financial statements are simply combined.

Finally, in Column 5 we assume that A pays more than the net asset value for B: $50 is paid for $30 of net assets. This excess is assumed to be partly attributable to undervalued assets (land, buildings, machinery, and inventories) and so, to reflect this undervaluation, current and fixed assets are each increased by $5. In addition, we assume that $10 of the $20 excess of market value over book value is due to a superior sales organization or to some other intangible factor, and we post this excess as goodwill. Firm B's common equity is increased by $20, the sum of the increases in current and fixed assets plus goodwill, and this markup is also reflected in Firm A's post-merger equity account.[27]

---

[26]Recall that in 2001, the Financial Accounting Standards Board (FASB) issued Statement 141, which eliminated the use of *pooling* accounting.

[27]This example assumes that additional debt was not issued to help finance the acquisition. If the acquisition were totally debt financed, then the post-merger balance sheet would show an increase in debt rather than an increase in the equity account. If it were financed by a mix of debt and equity, both accounts would increase. If the acquisition were paid for with cash on hand, then current assets would decrease by the amount paid and the equity account would not increase.

TABLE 22-4

Accounting for Mergers: Firm A Acquires Firm B with Stock

	Firm A (1)	Firm B (2)	Post-Merger: Firm A		
			$20 Paid[a] (3)	$30 Paid[a] (4)	$50 Paid[a] (5)
Current assets	$ 50	$25	$ 75	$ 75	$ 80[b]
Fixed assets	50	25	65[c]	75	80[b]
Goodwill[d]	0	0	0	0	10[d]
Total assets	$100	$50	$140	$150	$170
Liabilities	$ 40	$20	$ 60	$ 60	$ 60
Equity	60	30	80[e]	90	110[f]
Total claims	$100	$50	$140	$150	$170

[a]The price paid is the *net asset value*—that is, total assets minus liabilities.

[b]Here we assume that Firm B's current and fixed assets are both increased to $30.

[c]Here we assume that Firm B's fixed assets are written down from $25 to $15 before constructing the consolidated balance sheet.

[d]*Goodwill* refers to the excess paid for a firm above the appraised value of the physical assets purchased. Goodwill represents payment both for intangibles such as patents and for "organization value," such as that associated with having an effective sales force. Beginning in 2001, purchased goodwill such as this may not be amortized for financial statement reporting purposes.

[e]Firm B's common equity is reduced by $10 prior to consolidation to reflect the fixed asset write-off.

[f]Firm B's equity is increased to $50 to reflect the above-book purchase price.

© Cengage Learning 2014

22-12b Income Statement Effects

A merger can have a significant effect on reported profits. If asset values are increased, as they often are under a purchase, then this must be reflected in higher depreciation charges (and also in a higher cost of goods sold if inventories are written up). This, in turn, will further reduce reported profits. Prior to 2001, goodwill was also amortized over its expected life. Now, however, goodwill is subject to an "annual impairment test." If the fair market value of the goodwill has declined over the year, then the amount of the decline must be charged to earnings. If not, then there is no charge, but gains in goodwill cannot be added to earnings.

resource

See Ch22 Tool Kit.xls on the textbook's Web site for details.

Table 22-5 illustrates the income statement effects of the write-up of current and fixed assets. We assume A purchased B for $50, creating $10 of goodwill and $10 of higher physical asset value. As Column 3 indicates, the asset markups cause reported profits to be lower than the sum of the individual companies' reported profits.

The asset markup is also reflected in earnings per share. In our hypothetical merger, we assume that nine shares exist in the consolidated firm. (Six of these shares went to A's stockholders, and three went to B's.) The merged company's EPS is $2.33, whereas each of the individual companies' EPS was $2.40.

SELF-TEST

What is purchase accounting for mergers?

What is goodwill? What impact does goodwill have on the firm's balance sheet? On its income statement?

TABLE 22-5

Income Statement Effects

	Pre-Merger		Post-Merger: Firm A
	Firm A (1)	Firm B (2)	Merged (3)
Sales	$100.0	$ 50.0	$150.0
Operating costs	72.0	36.0	109.0[a]
Operating income	$ 28.0	$ 14.0	$ 41.0[a]
Interest (10%)	4.0	2.0	6.0
Taxable income	$ 24.0	$ 12.0	$ 35.0
Taxes (40%)	9.6	4.8	14.0
Net income	$ 14.4	$ 7.2	$ 21.0
EPS[b]	$ 2.40	$ 2.40	$ 2.33

[a]Operating costs are $1 higher than they otherwise would be; this reflects the higher reported costs (depreciation and cost of goods sold) caused by the physical asset markup at the time of purchase.

[b]Before the merger, Firm A had six shares and Firm B had three shares. Firm A gives one of its shares for each of Firm B's, so A has nine shares outstanding after the merger.

© Cengage Learning 2014

22-13 Analysis for a "True Consolidation"

Most of our analysis in the preceding sections assumed that one firm plans to acquire another. However, in many situations it is hard to identify an "acquirer" and a "target"—the merger appears to be a true "merger of equals," as was the case with the Exxon–Mobil and First Union–Wachovia mergers. In such cases, how is the analysis handled?

The first step is to estimate the value of the combined enterprise, incorporating any synergies, tax effects, or capital structure changes. The second step is to decide how to allocate the new company's stock between the two sets of old stockholders. Because of synergy, one would normally expect the consolidated value to exceed the sum of the pre-announcement values of the two companies. For example, Company A might have had a pre-merger equity value of $10 billion, found as (Number of shares)(Price per share), and Company B might have had a pre-merger value of $15 billion. If the post-merger value of new Company AB is estimated to be $30 billion, then that value must be allocated. Company A's stockholders must receive enough shares to give them a projected value of at least $10 billion, and Company B's stockholders must receive at least $15 billion. But how will the remaining $5 billion of synergistically induced value be divided?

This is a key issue, requiring intense negotiation between the two management groups. There is no rule or formula to apply, but one basis for the allocation is the relative pre-announcement values of the two companies. For example, in our hypothetical merger of A and B to form AB, the companies might agree to give $10/$25 = 40% of the new stock to A's stockholders and 60% to B's stockholders. Unless a case could be made for giving a higher percentage of the shares to one of the companies because it was responsible for more of the synergistic value, then the pre-merger value proportions would seem to be a "fair" solution. In any event, the pre-merger proportions will probably be given the greatest weight in reaching the final decision.

It should also be noted that control of the consolidated company is always an issue. Generally, the companies hold a press conference and announce that the CEO of one firm will be chairman of the new company, that the other CEO will be president, that the new board will consist of directors from both old boards, and that power will be shared. With huge mergers such as those we have been seeing lately, there is plenty of power to be shared.

SELF-TEST

How does merger analysis differ in the case of a large company acquiring a smaller one versus a "true merger of equals"?

Do you think the same guidelines for allocating synergistic gains would be used in both types of mergers?

22-14 The Role of Investment Bankers

Investment bankers are involved with mergers in a number of ways: (1) they help arrange mergers, (2) they help target companies develop and implement defensive tactics, (3) they help value target companies, (4) they help finance mergers, and (5) they invest in the stocks of potential merger candidates.

22-14a Arranging Mergers

The major investment banking firms have merger and acquisition groups that operate within their corporate finance departments. (Corporate finance departments offer advice, as opposed to underwriting or brokerage services, to business firms.) Members of these groups identify firms with excess cash that might want to buy other firms, companies that might be willing to be bought, and firms that might, for a number of reasons, be attractive to others. Sometimes dissident stockholders of firms with poor track records work with investment bankers to oust management by helping to arrange a merger.

22-14b Developing Defensive Tactics

Target firms that do not want to be acquired generally enlist the help of an investment banking firm along with a law firm that specializes in mergers. Defenses include such tactics as (1) changing the bylaws so that only one-third of the directors are elected each year and/or so that a 75% approval (a *super majority*) rather than a simple majority is required to approve a merger, (2) trying to convince the target firm's stockholders that the price being offered is too low, (3) raising antitrust issues in the hope that the Justice Department will intervene, (4) repurchasing stock in the open market in an effort to push the price above that being offered by the potential acquirer, (5) finding a **white knight** who is acceptable to the target firm's management to compete with the potential acquirer, and (6) finding a **white squire** who is friendly to current management and can buy enough of the target firm's shares to block the merger.

22-14c Establishing a Fair Value

If a friendly merger is being worked out between two firms' managements, then it is important to document that the agreed-upon price is a fair one; otherwise, the stockholders of either company may sue to block the merger. Therefore, in most large mergers, each side will hire an investment banking firm to evaluate the target company and to help establish the fair price. Even if the merger is not friendly, investment bankers may still be asked to help establish a price. If a surprise tender offer is to be made, then the acquiring firm will want to know the lowest price at which it might be able to acquire the stock while the target firm may seek help in "proving" that the price being offered is too low.

22-14d Financing Mergers

To be successful in the mergers and acquisitions (M&A) business, an investment banker must be able to offer a financing package to clients—whether they are acquirers who need capital to take over companies or target companies trying to finance stock repurchase plans or other defenses against takeovers. In fact, the fees that investment banks generate through issuing merger-related debt often dwarf their other merger-related fees.

22-14e Arbitrage Operations

Arbitrage generally means simultaneously buying and selling the same commodity or security in two different markets at different prices and pocketing a risk-free return. However, the major brokerage houses, as well as some wealthy private investors, are engaged in a different type of arbitrage called *risk arbitrage*. The *arbitrageurs*, or "arbs," speculate in the stocks of companies that are likely takeover targets. Vast amounts of capital are required to speculate in a large number of securities and thus reduce risk, and also to make money on narrow spreads. Yet the large investment bankers have the wherewithal to play this game. To be successful, arbs must be able to sniff out likely targets, assess the probability of offers reaching fruition, and move in and out of the market quickly and with low transaction costs.

SELF-TEST

What are some defensive tactics that firms can use to resist hostile takeovers?

What is the difference between pure arbitrage and risk arbitrage?

22-15 Who Wins: The Empirical Evidence

The magnitude of the merger market raises two questions: (1) Do corporate acquisitions create value? (2) If so, how is the value shared between the parties?

Most researchers agree that takeovers increase the wealth of the shareholders of target firms, otherwise they would not agree to the offer. However, there is a debate as to whether mergers benefit the acquiring firm's shareholders. In particular, managements of acquiring firms may be motivated by factors other than maximizing shareholder wealth. For example, they may want to merge merely to increase the size of the corporations they manage, because increased size usually brings larger salaries plus job security, perquisites, power, and prestige.

The question of who gains from corporate acquisitions can be tested by examining the stock price changes that occur around the time of a merger or takeover announcement. Changes in the stock prices of the acquiring and target firms represent market participants' beliefs about the value created by the merger and about how that value will be

Merger Mistakes

© Rob Webb/Getty Images

Academics have long known that acquiring firms' shareholders rarely reap the benefits of mergers. However, this important information never seemed to make it up to the offices of corporate America's decision makers; the 1990s saw bad deal after bad deal and with no apparent learning on the part of acquisitive executives. *BusinessWeek* published an analysis of 302 large mergers from 1995 to 2001, and it found that 61% of them led to losses by the acquiring firms' shareholders. Indeed, those losing shareholders' returns during the first post-merger year averaged 25 percentage points less than the returns on other companies in their industry. The average returns for all the merging companies, both winners and losers, were 4.3% below industry averages and 9.2% below the S&P 500.

The article cited four common mistakes:

1. The acquiring firms often overpaid. Generally, the acquirers gave away all of the synergies from the mergers to the acquired firms' shareholders, and then some.

2. Management overestimated the synergies (cost savings and revenue gains) that would result from the merger.

3. Management took too long to integrate operations between the merged companies. This irritated customers and employees alike, and it postponed any gains from the integration.

4. Some companies cut costs too deeply at the expense of maintaining sales and production infrastructures.

The worst performance came from companies that paid for their acquisitions with stock. The best performance, albeit a paltry 0.3% better than industry averages, came from companies that used cash for their acquisitions. On the bright side, the shareholders of the companies that were acquired fared quite well, earning on average 19.3% more than their industry peers, and all of those gains came in the two weeks surrounding the merger announcement.

Source: David Henry, "Mergers: Why Most Big Deals Don't Pay Off," *BusinessWeek*, October 14, 2002, pp. 60–70.

---

divided between the target and acquiring firms' shareholders. Therefore, examining a large sample of stock price movements can shed light on the issue of who gains from mergers.

One cannot simply examine stock prices around merger announcement dates, because other factors influence stock prices. For example, if a merger was announced on a day when the entire market advanced, then a rise in the target firm's price would not necessarily signify that the merger was expected to create value. In other words, did the event (in this case, a merger announcement) cause a change in value? Hence, studies examine *abnormal returns* associated with merger announcements, where abnormal returns are defined as that part of a stock price change caused by factors other than changes in the general stock market. Some research defines abnormal returns as the return not explained by an asset pricing model, such as the CAPM or the Fama-French 3-Factor model, as we described in Chapter 6.

Event studies have examined both acquiring and target firms' stock price responses to mergers and tender offers. Jointly, they have covered nearly every acquisition involving publicly traded firms from the early 1960s to the present, and they are remarkably consistent in their results: On average, the stock prices of target firms increase by about 30% in hostile tender offers, whereas in friendly mergers the average increase is about 20%. However, for both hostile and friendly deals, the stock prices of acquiring firms, on average, remain constant. Thus, the event study evidence strongly indicates (1) that acquisitions do create value but (2) that shareholders of target firms reap virtually all the benefits.

The event study evidence suggests that mergers benefit targets but not acquirers—and hence that an acquiring firm's stockholders should be skeptical of its managers' plans for acquisitions. This evidence cannot be dismissed out of hand, but neither is it entirely convincing. There are undoubtedly many good mergers, just as there are many poorly conceived ones. Like most of finance, merger decisions should be studied carefully, and it is best not to judge the outcome of a specific merger until the actual results start to come in.

SELF-TEST

Explain how researchers can study the effects of mergers on shareholder wealth.

Do mergers create value? If so, who profits from this value?

Do the research results discussed in this section seem logical? Explain.

22-16 Corporate Alliances

Mergers are one way for two companies to join forces, but many companies are striking cooperative deals, called **corporate**, or **strategic**, **alliances**, which stop far short of merging. Whereas mergers combine all of the assets of the firms involved, as well as their ownership and managerial expertise, alliances allow firms to create combinations that focus on specific business lines that offer the most potential synergies. These alliances take many forms, from simple marketing agreements to joint ownership of worldwide operations.

One form of corporate alliance is the **joint venture**, in which parts of companies are joined to achieve specific, limited objectives. A joint venture is controlled by a management team consisting of representatives of the two (or more) parent companies. A study of 345 corporate alliances found that the stock prices of both partners in an alliance tended to increase when the alliance was announced, with an average abnormal return of about 0.64% on the day of the announcement.[28] About 43% of the alliances were marketing agreements, 14% were R&D agreements, 11% were for licensing technology, 7% for technology transfers, and 25% were for some combination of these four reasons. Although most alliances were for marketing agreements, the market reacted most favorably when the alliance was for technology sharing between two firms in the same industry. The study also found that the typical alliance lasted at least 5 years and that the allied firms had better operating performance than their industry peers during this period.

SELF-TEST

What is the difference between a merger and a corporate alliance?

What is a joint venture? Give some reasons why joint ventures may be advantageous to the parties involved.

22-17 Divestitures

There are four types of **divestitures**. A **sale to another firm** generally involves the sale of an entire division or unit, usually for cash but sometimes for stock in the acquiring firm. In a **spin-off**, the firm's existing stockholders are given new stock representing separate

---

[28]See Su Han Chan, John W. Kensinger, Arthur J. Keown, and John D. Martin, "When Do Strategic Alliances Create Shareholder Value?" *Journal of Applied Corporate Finance,* Winter 1999, pp. 82–87.

ownership rights in the division that was divested. The division establishes its own board of directors and officers, and it becomes a separate company. The stockholders end up owning shares of two firms instead of one, but no cash has been transferred. In a **carve-out,** a minority interest in a corporate subsidiary is sold to new shareholders, so the parent gains new equity financing yet retains control. In a **liquidation**, the assets of a division are sold off piecemeal to many purchasers rather than as an single operating entity to one purchaser. To illustrate the different types of divestitures, we now present some examples.

In 2011, Ralcorp Holdings proposed splitting the company into a Post Foods piece and a private-label business. The reason for the spin-off was to allow the two divisions to focus on their different product markets and also to allow ConAgra, which had been pursuing Ralcorp for its private-label business, to make a more limited acquisition. In 2009, Time Warner announced that it planned to spin off AOL, the dissolution of a merger that had never worked. And in 2008, Cadbury Schweppes decided to focus on its chocolate and candy businesses, so it spun off soft-drink brands into a separately traded company, the Dr Pepper Snapple Group.

As these examples illustrate, the reasons for divestitures vary widely. Sometimes the market feels more comfortable when firms "stick to their knitting," as the Cadbury Schweppes divestiture illustrates. Sometimes companies need cash either to finance expansion in their primary business lines or to reduce a large debt burden, and divestitures can be used to raise this cash; for example, AMD spun off its manufacturing operations in 2009. The divestitures also show that running a business is a dynamic process—conditions change, corporate strategies change in response, and consequently firms alter their asset portfolios by acquisitions and/or divestitures. Some divestitures are designed to unload losing assets that would otherwise drag the company down, such as Time Warner's planned spin-off of AOL.

In general, the empirical evidence shows that the market reacts favorably to divestitures, with the divesting company typically having a small increase in stock price on the day of the announcement. The announcement-day returns are largest for companies that "undo" previous conglomerate mergers by divesting businesses in unrelated areas.[29] Studies also show that divestitures generally lead to superior operating performance for both the parent and the divested company.[30]

SELF-TEST

What are some types of divestitures?

What are some motives for divestitures?

22-18 Holding Companies

Holding companies date from 1889, when New Jersey became the first state to pass a law permitting corporations to be formed for the sole purpose of owning the stocks of other companies. Many of the advantages and disadvantages of holding companies are identical

---

[29]For details, see Jeffrey W. Allen, Scott L. Lummer, John J. McConnell, and Debra K. Reed, "Can Takeover Losses Explain Spin-off Gains?" *Journal of Financial and Quantitative Analysis,* December 1995, pp. 465–485.

[30]See Shane A. Johnson, Daniel P. Klein, and Verne L. Thibodeaux, "The Effects of Spin-offs on Corporate Investment and Performance," *Journal of Financial Research,* Summer 1996, pp. 293–307. Also see Steven Kaplan and Michael S. Weisbach, "The Success of Acquisitions: Evidence from Divestitures," *Journal of Finance,* March 1992, pp. 107–138.

to those of any large-scale organization. Whether a company is organized on a divisional basis or with subsidiaries kept as separate companies does not affect the basic reasons for conducting a large-scale, multiproduct, multiplant operation.

22-18a Advantages and Disadvantages of Holding Companies

There are two principal advantages of a holding company.

1. *Control with fractional ownership.* Through a holding company operation, a firm may buy 5%, 10%, or 50% of the stock of another corporation. Such fractional ownership may be sufficient to give the holding company effective working control over the operations of the company in which it has acquired stock ownership. Working control is often considered to entail more than 25% of the common stock, but it can be as low as 10% if the stock is widely distributed. One financier says that the attitude of management is more important than the number of shares owned: "If management thinks you can control the company, then you do." In addition, control on a very slim margin can be held through relationships with large stockholders outside the holding company group.

2. *Isolation of risks.* Because the various **operating companies** in a holding company system are separate legal entities, the obligations of any one unit are separate from those of the other units. Therefore, catastrophic losses incurred by one unit of the holding company system may not be translatable into claims on the assets of the other units. However, we should note that while this is a customary generalization, it is not always valid. First, the **parent company** may feel obligated to make good on the subsidiary's debts, even though it is not legally bound to do so, in order to keep its good name and to retain customers. Second, a parent company may feel obligated to supply capital to an affiliate in order to protect its initial investment. And third, when lending to one of the units of a holding company system, an astute loan officer may require a guarantee by the parent holding company. To some degree, then, the assets in the various elements of a holding company are not really separate.

The main disadvantage of a holding company involves *partial multiple taxation.* Provided the holding company owns at least 80% of a subsidiary's voting stock, the IRS permits the filing of consolidated returns, in which case dividends received by the parent are not taxed. However, if less than 80% of the stock is owned, then tax returns cannot be consolidated. Firms that own more than 20% but less than 80% of another corporation can deduct 80% of the dividends received, whereas firms that own less than 20% may deduct only 70% of the dividends received. This partial double taxation somewhat offsets the benefits of holding company control with limited ownership, but whether the tax penalty is sufficient to offset other possible advantages varies from case to case.

22-18b Holding Companies as a Leveraging Device

The holding company vehicle has been used to obtain huge degrees of financial leverage. In the 1920s, several tiers of holding companies were established in the electric utility, railroad, and other industries. In those days, an operating company at the bottom of the pyramid might have $100 million of assets, financed by $50 million of debt and $50 million of equity. Then, a first-tier holding company might own the stock of the operating firm as its only asset and be financed with $25 million of debt and $25 million of equity. A second-tier holding company, which owned the stock of the first-tier company, might be financed with $12.5 million of debt and $12.5 million of equity. Such systems were extended to five or six levels. With six holding companies, $100 million of operating assets could be controlled at the top by only $0.78 million of equity, and the operating assets would have to provide enough cash income to support $99.22 million of debt. *Such a holding company system is highly leveraged—its consolidated debt ratio is 99.22%, even though each of the individual components shows only a 50% debt/assets ratio.* Because of this consolidated leverage, even a small decline in profits at the operating company level could bring the whole system down like a house of cards. This situation existed in the electric utility industry in the 1920s, and the Depression of the 1930s wreaked such havoc with the holding companies that federal legislation was enacted that constrained holding companies in that industry.

SELF-TEST

What is a holding company?

What are some of the advantages of holding companies? Identify a disadvantage.

SUMMARY

- A **merger** occurs when two firms combine to form a single company. The primary motives for mergers are (1) synergy, (2) tax considerations, (3) purchase of assets below their replacement costs, (4) diversification, (5) gaining control over a larger enterprise, and (6) breakup value.
- Mergers can provide economic benefits through **economies of scale** and through putting assets in the hands of more efficient managers. However, mergers also have the potential for reducing competition, and for this reason they are carefully regulated by government agencies.
- In most mergers, one company (the **acquiring company**) initiates action to take over another (the **target company**).
- A **horizontal merger** occurs when two firms in the same line of business combine.
- A **vertical merger** combines a firm with one of its customers or suppliers.
- A **congeneric merger** involves firms in related industries but where no customer–supplier relationship exists.
- A **conglomerate merger** occurs when firms in totally different industries combine.
- In a **friendly merger**, the managements of both firms approve the merger, whereas in a **hostile merger**, the target firm's management opposes it.
- An **operating merger** is one in which the operations of the two firms are combined. A **financial merger** is one in which the firms continue to operate separately; hence no operating economies are expected.
- In a typical **merger analysis**, the key issues to be resolved are (1) the price to be paid for the target firm and (2) the employment/control situation. If the merger is a consolidation of two relatively equal firms, at issue is the percentage of ownership that each merger partner's shareholders will receive.
- Four methods are commonly used to determine the value of the target firm: (1) **market multiple analysis**, (2) the **corporate valuation model**, (3) the **free cash flow to equity (FCFE) model**, and (4) the **adjusted present value (APV) model**. The three cash flow models give the same value if implemented correctly, but the APV

model is the easiest to implement correctly and should be used when the capital structure is changing.

- **Purchase accounting** treats mergers as a purchase and is used for financial reporting.
- A **joint venture** is a **corporate alliance** in which two or more companies combine some of their resources to achieve a specific, limited objective.
- A **divestiture** is the sale of some of a company's operating assets. A divestiture may involve (1) selling an operating unit to another firm, (2) **spinning off** a unit as a separate company, (3) **carving out** a unit by selling a minority interest, or (4) the outright **liquidation** of a unit's assets.
- The reasons for divestiture include (1) settling antitrust suits, (2) improving the transparency of the resulting companies so that investors can more easily evaluate them, (3) enabling management to concentrate on a particular type of activity, and (4) raising the capital needed to strengthen the corporation's core business.
- A **holding company** is a corporation that owns sufficient stock in another firm to control it. The holding company is also known as the **parent company**, and the companies that it controls are called **subsidiaries**, or **operating companies**.
- Holding company operations are advantageous because (1) control can often be obtained for a smaller cash outlay, (2) risks may be segregated, and (3) regulated companies can operate separate subsidiaries for their regulated and unregulated businesses.
- A major disadvantage to holding companies is the possibility of income being taxed at the subsidiary and at the parent.

QUESTIONS

(22-1)   Define each of the following terms:

a. Synergy; merger
b. Horizontal merger; vertical merger; congeneric merger; conglomerate merger
c. Friendly merger; hostile merger; defensive merger; tender offer; target company; breakup value; acquiring company
d. Operating merger; financial merger
e. Free cash flow to equity
f. Purchase accounting
g. White knight; proxy fight
h. Joint venture; corporate alliance
i. Divestiture; spin-off
j. Holding company; operating company; parent company
k. Arbitrage; risk arbitrage

(22-2)   Four economic classifications of mergers are (1) horizontal, (2) vertical, (3) conglomerate, and (4) congeneric. Explain the significance of these terms in merger analysis with regard to (a) the likelihood of governmental intervention and (b) possibilities for operating synergy.

(22-3)   Firm A wants to acquire Firm B. Firm B's management agrees that the merger is a good idea. Might a tender offer be used? Why or why not?

(22-4)   Distinguish between operating mergers and financial mergers.

(22-5)   Distinguish between the APV, FCFE, and corporate valuation models.

SELF-TEST PROBLEM   Solution Appears in Appendix A

(ST-1)
Valuation

Red Valley Breweries is considering an acquisition of Flagg Markets. Flagg currently has a cost of equity of 10%; 25% of its financing is in the form of 6% debt, and the rest is in common equity. Its federal-plus-state tax rate is 40%. After the acquisition, Red Valley expects Flagg to have the following FCFs and interest payments for the next 3 years (in millions):

	Year 1	Year 2	Year 3
FCF	$10.00	$20.00	$25.00
Interest expense	28.00	24.00	20.28

After this, the free cash flows are expected to grow at a constant rate of 5%, and the capital structure will stabilize at 35% debt with an interest rate of 7%.

a. What is Flagg's unlevered cost of equity? What are its levered cost of equity and cost of capital for the post-horizon period?

b. Using the adjusted present value approach, what is Flagg's value of operations to Red Valley?

PROBLEMS   Answers Appear in Appendix B

The following information is required to work Problems 22-1 through 22-4.

Hastings Corporation is interested in acquiring Vandell Corporation. Vandell has 1 million shares outstanding and a target capital structure consisting of 30% debt. Vandell's debt interest rate is 8%. Assume that the risk-free rate of interest is 5% and the market risk premium is 6%. Both Vandell and Hastings face a 40% tax rate.

Easy Problem 1

(22-1)
Valuation

Vandell's free cash flow (FCF_0) is $2 million per year and is expected to grow at a constant rate of 5% a year; its beta is 1.4. What is the value of Vandell's operations? If Vandell has $10.82 million in debt, what is the current value of Vandell's stock? (*Hint:* Use the corporate valuation model from Chapter 7.)

Intermediate Problems 2–3

(22-2)
Merger Valuation

Hastings estimates that if it acquires Vandell, interest payments will be $1.5 million per year for 3 years, after which the current target capital structure of 30% debt will be maintained. Interest in the fourth year will be $1.472 million, after which interest and the tax shield will grow at 5%. Synergies will cause the free cash flows to be $2.5 million, $2.9 million, $3.4 million, and $3.57 million in Years 1 through 4, respectively, after which the free cash flows will grow at a 5% rate. What is the unlevered value of Vandell, and what is the value of its tax shields? What is the per share value of Vandell to Hastings Corporation? Assume that Vandell now has $10.82 million in debt.

(22-3)
Merger Bid

On the basis of your answers to Problems 22-1 and 22-2, indicate the range of possible prices that Hastings could bid for each share of Vandell common stock in an acquisition.

Challenging Problems 4–6

(22-4)
Merger Valuation with Change in Capital Structure

Assuming the same information as for Problem 22-2, suppose Hastings will increase Vandell's level of debt at the end of Year 3 to $30.6 million so that the target capital structure is now 45% debt. Assume that with this higher level of debt the interest rate would be 8.5%, and assume that interest payments in Year 4 are based on the new debt level from the end of Year 3 and a new interest rate. Again, free cash flows and tax shields are projected to grow at 5% after Year 4. What are the values of the unlevered firm and the tax shield, and what is the maximum price that Hastings would bid for Vandell now?

(22-5)
Merger Analysis

Marston Marble Corporation is considering a merger with the Conroy Concrete Company. Conroy is a publicly traded company, and its beta is 1.30. Conroy has been barely profitable, so it has paid an average of only 20% in taxes during the last several years. In addition, it uses little debt; its target ratio is just 25%, with the cost of debt 9%.

If the acquisition were made, Marston would operate Conroy as a separate, wholly owned subsidiary. Marston would pay taxes on a consolidated basis, and the tax rate would therefore increase to 35%. Marston also would increase the debt capitalization in the Conroy subsidiary to $w_d = 40\%$, for a total of $22.27 million in debt by the end of Year 4, and pay 9.5% on the debt. Marston's acquisition department estimates that Conroy, if acquired, would generate the following free cash flows and interest expenses (in millions of dollars) in Years 1–5:

Year	Free Cash Flows	Interest Expense
1	$1.30	$1.2
2	1.50	1.7
3	1.75	2.8
4	2.00	2.1
5	2.12	?

In Year 5, Conroy's interest expense would be based on its beginning-of-year (that is, the end-of-Year-4) debt, and in subsequent years both interest expense and free cash flows are projected to grow at a rate of 6%.

These cash flows include all acquisition effects. Marston's cost of equity is 10.5%, its beta is 1.0, and its cost of debt is 9.5%. The risk-free rate is 6%, and the market risk premium is 4.5%.

a. What is the value of Conroy's unlevered operations, and what is the value of Conroy's tax shields under the proposed merger and financing arrangements?
b. What is the dollar value of Conroy's operations? If Conroy has $10 million in debt outstanding, how much would Marston be willing to pay for Conroy?

(22-6)
Merger Valuation with Change in Capital Structure

VolWorld Communications Inc., a large telecommunications company, is evaluating the possible acquisition of Bulldog Cable Company (BCC), a regional cable company. VolWorld's analysts project the following post-merger data for BCC (in thousands of dollars, with a year end of December 31):

	2013	2014	2015	2016	2017	2018
Net sales		$450	$518	$ 555	$ 600	$ 643
Selling and administrative expense		45	53	60	68	73
Interest		40	45	47	52	54
Total net operating capital	$800	850	930	1,005	1,075	1,150

Tax rate after merger: 35%
Cost of goods sold as a percent of sales: 65%
BCC's pre-merger beta: 1.40
Risk-free rate: 6%
Market risk premium: 4%
Terminal growth rate of free cash flows: 7%

If the acquisition is made, it will occur on January 1, 2014. All cash flows shown in the income statements are assumed to occur at the end of the year. BCC currently has a capital structure of 40% debt, which costs 10%, but over the next 4 years VolWorld would increase that to 50%, and the target capital structure would be reached by the start of 2018. BCC, if independent, would pay taxes at 20%, but its income would be taxed at 35% if it were consolidated. BCC's current market-determined beta is 1.4. The cost of goods sold is expected to be 65% of sales.

a. What is the unlevered cost of equity for BCC?
b. What are the free cash flows and interest tax shields for the first 5 years?
c. What is BCC's horizon value of interest tax shields and unlevered horizon value?
d. What is the value of BCC's equity to VolWorld's shareholders if BCC has $300,000 in debt outstanding now?

SPREADSHEET PROBLEM

(22-7)

Build a Model: Merger Analysis

resource

Start with the partial model in the file *Ch22 P07 Build a Model.xls* on the textbook's Web site. Wansley Portal Inc., a large Internet service provider, is evaluating the possible acquisition of Alabama Connections Company (ACC), a regional Internet service provider. Wansley's analysts project the following post-merger data for ACC (in thousands of dollars):

	2014	2015	2016	2017	2018
Net sales	$500	$600	$700	$760	$806
Selling and administrative expense	60	70	80	90	96
Interest	30	40	45	60	74

If the acquisition is made, it will occur on January 1, 2014. All cash flows shown in the income statements are assumed to occur at the end of the year. ACC currently has a capital structure of 30% debt, which costs 9%, but Wansley would increase that over time to 40%, costing 10%, if the acquisition were made. ACC, if independent, would pay taxes at 30%, but its income would be taxed at 35% if it were consolidated. ACC's current market-determined beta is 1.4. The cost of goods sold, which includes depreciation, is expected to be 65% of sales, but it could vary somewhat. Required gross investment in operating capital is approximately equal to the depreciation charged, so there will be no investment in net operating capital. The risk-free rate is 7%, and the market risk premium is 6.5%. Wansley currently has $400,000 in debt outstanding.

a. What is the unlevered cost of equity?
b. What are the horizon value of the tax shields and the horizon value of the unlevered operations? What are the value of ACC's operations and the value of ACC's equity to Wansley's shareholders?

MINI CASE

Hager's Home Repair Company, a regional hardware chain that specializes in "do it yourself" materials and equipment rentals, is cash rich because of several consecutive good years. One of the alternative uses for the excess funds is an acquisition. Doug Zona, Hager's treasurer and your boss, has been asked to place a value on a potential target,

Lyons Lighting (LL), a chain that operates in several adjacent states, and he has enlisted your help.

The table below indicates Zona's estimates of LL's earnings potential if it came under Hager's management (in millions of dollars). The interest expense listed here includes the interest (1) on LL's existing debt, which is $55 million at a rate of 9%, and (2) on new debt expected to be issued over time to help finance expansion within the new "L division," the code name given to the target firm. If acquired, LL will face a 40% tax rate.

Security analysts estimate LL's beta to be 1.3. The acquisition would not change Lyons's capital structure, which is 20% debt. Zona realizes that Lyons Lighting's business plan also requires certain levels of operating capital and that the annual investment could be significant. The required levels of total net operating capital are listed in the table.

Zona estimates the risk-free rate to be 7% and the market risk premium to be 4%. He also estimates that free cash flows after 2018 will grow at a constant rate of 6%. Following are projections for sales and other items.

	2013	2014	2015	2016	2017	2018
Net sales		$ 60.00	$ 90.00	$112.50	$127.50	$139.70
Cost of goods sold (60%)		36.00	54.00	67.50	76.50	83.80
Selling/administrative expense		4.50	6.00	7.50	9.00	11.00
Interest expense		5.00	6.50	6.50	7.00	8.16
Total net operating capital	$150.00	150.00	157.50	163.50	168.00	173.00

Hager's management is new to the merger game, so Zona has been asked to answer some basic questions about mergers as well as to perform the merger analysis. To structure the task, Zona has developed the following questions, which you must answer and then defend to Hager's board.

a. Several reasons have been proposed to justify mergers. Among the more prominent are (1) tax considerations, (2) risk reduction, (3) control, (4) purchase of assets at below replacement cost, (5) synergy, and (6) globalization. In general, which of the reasons are economically justifiable? Which are not? Which fit the situation at hand? Explain.
b. Briefly describe the differences between a hostile merger and a friendly merger.
c. What are the steps in valuing a merger?
d. Use the data developed in the table to construct the L division's free cash flows for 2014 through 2018. Why are we identifying interest expense separately when it is not normally included in calculating free cash flows or in a capital budgeting cash flow analysis? Why is investment in net operating capital included when calculating the free cash flow?
e. Conceptually, what is the appropriate discount rate to apply to the cash flows developed in part c? What is your actual estimate of this discount rate?
f. What is the estimated horizon, or continuing, value of the acquisition; that is, what is the estimated value of the L division's cash flows beyond 2018? What is LL's value to Hager's shareholders? Suppose another firm were evaluating LL as an acquisition candidate. Would it obtain the same value? Explain.
g. Assume that LL has 20 million shares outstanding. These shares are traded relatively infrequently, but the last trade (made several weeks ago) was at a price of $11 per share. Should Hager's make an offer for Lyons Lighting? If so, how much should it offer per share?

h. How would the analysis be different if Hager's intended to recapitalize LL with 40% debt costing 10% at the end of 4 years? This amounts to $221.6 million in debt as of the end of 2017.

i. There has been considerable research undertaken to determine whether mergers really create value and, if so, how this value is shared between the parties involved. What are the results of this research?

j. What method is used to account for mergers?

k. What merger-related activities are undertaken by investment bankers?

l. What are the major types of divestitures? What motivates firms to divest assets?

m. What are holding companies? What are their advantages and disadvantages?

SELECTED ADDITIONAL CASES

The following cases from CengageCompose cover many of the concepts discussed in this chapter and are available at **compose.cengage.com**.

Klein-Brigham Series:
Case 40, "Nina's Fashions, Inc."; Case 53, "Nero's Pasta, Inc."; and Case 70, "Computer Concepts/CompuTech."

© Adalberto Rios Szalay/Sexto Sol/Getty Images

CHAPTER **23**

Enterprise Risk Management

O n April 13, 2012, JPMorgan Chase CEO Jamie Dimon called rumors of impending trading losses a "tempest in a teapot." Three months later, it looked like the tempest could exceed $9 billion in losses, making it a pretty big teapot!

Banks make loans to businesses, and JPMorgan is no exception. Many of its borrowers were exposed to difficult global economic conditions, including the Eurozone crises, which in turn exposed JPMorgan to risk. To offset potential losses on commercial lending, JPMorgan's Chief Investment Office in London took short positions on selected indexes that would pay off if some large companies, including some of their customers, defaulted on bank loans.[1] This is a classic hedge—if borrowers defaulted, JPMorgan's commercial lending group would lose money, but the London office would make money, and vice versa.

However, that is not the end of the story. The London office also took long positions on derivatives based on a broader credit index, the CDX.NA.IG.9. (Long positions meant that JPMorgan made commitments to buy at a fixed price.) Their intentions were to reduce expenses but also to hedge their short positions in the selected indexes, betting that the selected indexes were temporarily mispriced relative to the IG.9. JPMorgan continued to take long positions on the IG.9 during late 2011 and early 2012, until it became the biggest trader in this segment of the market. In fact, it is likely that JPMorgan's own trading activities artificially drove down the IG.9's price.

The low price of the IG.9 attracted hedge funds, and what goes down must come up. As the IG.9 price increased, JPMorgan began to lose money on its long positions and started liquidating some if its positions to prevent even bigger losses in the future. As we write this in July 2012, the fallout from this failed strategy has just begun—a big drop in JPMorgan's stock price, regulatory concerns over hedging versus speculation, and talk of clawing back JPMorgan's 2011 executive bonuses. Keep this episode in mind as you read the rest of the chapter.

---

[1]These indexes were actually composed of credit default swaps, so JPMorgan was going short in a derivative based on other derivatives.

Corporate Valuation and Risk Management

© Rob Webb/Getty Images

All companies are exposed to risk from volatility in product prices, demand, input costs, and other sources of business risk, such as the risk stemming from the choice of production technology. Many companies also are exposed to risk from volatility in exchange rates and interest rates. Risk management can reduce firm risk, preventing catastrophes and leading to a lower cost of capital. In some instances, derivatives such as swaps can reduce the effective interest rate paid by a corporation, again reducing its cost of capital.

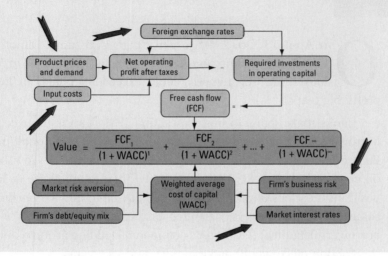

© Cengage Learning 2014

resource

The textbook's Web site contains an Excel file that will guide you through the chapter's calculations. The file for this chapter is *Ch23 Tool Kit.xls,* and we encourage you to open the file and follow along as you read the chapter.

Defining risk management is simple: Identify events that could have adverse consequences and then take actions to prevent or minimize the damage caused by these events. Applying risk management is more difficult, but it is vital for a company's success, and perhaps even its survival. In this chapter we explain how risk management adds value to a corporation, describe an enterprise risk management framework, identify different categories of risks, explain how to measure selected risks, and show how to manage those risks.[2] We also illustrate how companies can use **derivatives**, which are securities whose values are determined by the market price of some other asset, to manage certain types of risk.

23-1 Reasons to Manage Risk

Will reducing risk make a company more valuable? Consider Plastic Inc., which manufactures dashboards, interior door panels, and other plastic components used by auto companies. Petroleum is the key feedstock for plastic and thus makes up a large

---

[2]For excellent overviews of risk management, see Kenneth A. Froot, David S. Scharfstein, and Jeremy Stein, "A Framework for Risk Management," *Journal of Applied Corporate Finance,* Fall 1994, pp. 22–32; Brian Nocco and Rene Stultz, "Enterprise Risk Management, Theory and Practice," *Journal of Applied Corporate Finance,* Fall 2006, pp. 8–20; Walter Dolde, "The Trajectory of Corporate Financial Risk Management," *Journal of Applied Corporate Finance,* Fall 1993, pp. 33–41; and Marshall Blake and Nelda Mahady, "How Mid-Sized Companies Manage Risk," *Journal of Applied Corporate Finance,* Spring 1991, pp. 59–65.

percentage of its costs. Plastic has a 3-year contract with an auto company to deliver 500,000 door panels each year at a price of $20 each. When the company recently signed this contract, oil sold for $100 per barrel and was expected to stay at that level for the next 3 years. If oil prices fell during this time, Plastic would have higher than expected profits and free cash flows, but if oil prices rose, profits would fall. Because Plastic's value depends on its profits and free cash flows, a change in the price of oil would cause stockholders to earn either more or less than they anticipated.

Now suppose that, shortly after signing the contract with its door panel supplier, Plastic announces that it plans to lock in a 3-year supply of oil at a guaranteed price of $100 per barrel *and* that the cost of this guarantee is zero. Would that cause its stock price to rise? At first glance, it seems the answer should be "yes," but that might not be correct. Recall that the value of a stock depends on the present value of its expected future free cash flows, discounted at the weighted average cost of capital (WACC). Locking in the cost of oil will cause an increase in Plastic's stock price if and only if (1) it causes the expected future free cash flows to increase or (2) it causes the WACC to decline.

Consider first the free cash flows. Before the announcement of guaranteed oil costs, investors had formed an estimate of the expected future free cash flows based on an expected oil price of $100 per barrel. Locking in the cost of oil at $100 per barrel will lower the *risk* of the expected future free cash flows, but it might not change the expected *size* of these cash flows because investors already expected a price of $100 per barrel. Of course, smaller than expected cash flows can disrupt a firm's operation and that disruption can, in turn, adversely affect cash flows.

Now what about the WACC? It will change only if locking in the cost of oil causes a change either in the cost of debt or equity or in the target capital structure. If the foreseeable increases in the price of oil are not enough to increase the threat of bankruptcy, then Plastic's cost of debt should not change and neither should its target capital structure. Regarding the cost of equity, recall from Chapter 6 that most investors hold well-diversified portfolios, which means that the cost of equity should depend only on systematic risk. Moreover, even though an increase in oil prices would have a negative effect on Plastic's stock price, it would not have a negative effect on all stocks. Indeed, oil producers should have higher than expected returns and stock prices. Assuming that Plastic's investors hold well-diversified portfolios that include stocks of oil-producing companies, we should have little reason to expect its cost of equity to decrease. The bottom line is this: If Plastic's expected future cash flows and WACC will not change significantly as a consequence of eliminating the risk of oil price increases, then neither should the value of its stock.

We discuss futures contracts and hedging in detail in the next section, but for now let's assume that Plastic has *not* locked in oil prices. Therefore, if oil prices increase, its stock price will fall. However, if its stockholders know this, they can build portfolios that contain oil futures whose values will rise or fall with oil prices and thus offset changes in the price of Plastic's stock. By choosing the correct amount of futures contracts, investors can thus "hedge" their portfolios and completely eliminate the risk due to changes in oil prices. There will be a cost to hedging, but that cost to large investors should be about the same as the cost to Plastic. Because stockholders can hedge away oil price risk themselves, why should they pay a higher price for Plastic's stock just because the company itself hedged away that risk?

The previous points notwithstanding, companies clearly believe that active risk management is important. A 1998 survey reported that 83% of firms with market values greater than $1.2 billion engage in risk management.[3] A more recent 2005 survey of CFOs

[3]See Gordon M. Bodnar, Gregory S. Hayt, and Richard C. Marston, "1998 Wharton Survey of Financial Risk Management by U.S. Non-Financial Firms," *Financial Management,* Winter, 1998, pp. 70–91.

reported that 90% of the international and domestic firms responding considered risk in the planning process. The average of the estimates of the contribution that risk management made to the market value of the firm was 3.8%.[4] There are many reasons why companies manage their risks.

1. *Debt capacity.* Risk management can reduce the volatility of cash flows, which decreases the probability of bankruptcy. As we discussed in Chapter 15, firms with lower operating risks can use more debt, and this can lead to higher stock prices due to the interest tax savings.
2. *Maintaining the optimal capital budget over time.* Recall from Chapter 15 that firms are reluctant to raise external equity because of high flotation costs and market pressure. This means that the capital budget must generally be financed with a combination of debt and internally generated funds. In bad years, internal cash flows may be too low to support the optimal capital budget, causing firms to either slow investment below the optimal rate or else incur the high costs associated with external equity. By smoothing out the cash flows, risk management can alleviate this problem. This issue is most relevant for firms with large growth opportunities. A study by Professors Gerald Gay and Jouahn Nam found that such firms do in fact use derivatives more than low-growth firms.[5] Thus, maintaining an optimal capital budget is an important determinant of firms' risk management practices.
3. *Financial distress.* The stages of financial distress can range from stockholder concern and higher interest rates on debt to customer defections and bankruptcy. Any serious level of financial distress causes a firm to have lower cash flows than expected. Risk management can reduce the likelihood of low cash flows and hence of financial distress.
4. *Comparative advantages in hedging.* Most investors cannot hedge as efficiently as a company. First, firms generally incur lower transaction costs because of their larger volume of hedging activities. Second, there is the problem of asymmetric information: Managers know more about the firm's risk exposure than do outside investors, so managers can create more effective hedges. And third, effective risk management requires specialized skills and knowledge that firms are more likely to have.
5. *Borrowing costs.* As discussed later in the chapter, firms can sometimes reduce input costs—especially the interest rate on debt—through the use of derivative instruments called *swaps.* Any such cost reduction adds value to the firm.
6. *Tax effects.* The present value of taxes paid by companies with volatile earnings is higher than the present value of taxes paid by stable companies; this is because of the treatment of tax credits and the rules governing corporate loss carryforwards and carrybacks. Moreover, if volatile earnings cause a company to declare bankruptcy, then the company usually completely loses its tax loss carryforwards. Therefore, using risk management to stabilize earnings can reduce the present value of a company's tax burden.
7. *Compensation systems.* Many compensation systems establish "floors" and "ceilings" on bonuses and also reward managers for meeting targets. To illustrate, suppose a firm's compensation system calls for a manager to receive no bonus if net income is below $1 million, a bonus of $10,000 if income is between $1 million and $2 million, or a bonus of $20,000 if income is $2 million or more. The manager will also receive an additional $10,000 if actual income is at least 90% of the forecasted level, which is

[4]See Henri Servaes, Ane Tamayo, and Peter Tufano, "The Theory and Practice of Corporate Risk Management," *Journal of Applied Corporate Finance,* Fall, 2009, pp. 60–78.
[5]See Gerald D. Gay and Jouahn Nam, "The Underinvestment Problem and Corporate Derivatives Use," *Financial Management,* Winter, 1998, pp. 53–69.

$1 million. Now consider the following two situations. First, if income is stable at $2 million each year then the manager receives a $30,000 bonus each year, for a 2-year total of $60,000. However, if income is zero the first year and $4 million the second, the manager gets no bonus the first year and $30,000 the second, for a 2-year total of $30,000. So, even though the company has the same total income ($4 million) over the two years, the manager's bonus is higher if earnings are stable. Therefore, even if hedging does not add much value for stockholders, it may still benefit managers.

There are regulatory and economically driven reasons to manage risk. The following section describes a typical enterprise risk management framework.

SELF-TEST

Explain why finance theory, combined with well-diversified investors and "homemade hedging," might suggest that risk management should not add much value to a company.

List and explain some reasons companies might employ risk management techniques.

23-2 An Overview of Enterprise Risk Management

The practice of enterprise risk management has evolved considerably over the last 20 years, due to advances in technology and regulatory changes. To better explain the framework for risk enterprise risk management, we begin with a brief history of risk management.

One of the earliest used tools in risk management is a futures contract, which is an agreement in which a buyer pledges to purchase a specific quantity of an item at a specific price on a specific future date from a seller who has pledged to provide the item at the agreed-upon terms. Written records show that commodity futures contracts were used and traded over 4,000 years ago in India, so risk management has been around a very long time. In the United States, grain traders used futures contracts as far back as the early 1800s.[6]

The history of insurance also dates back hundreds of years, with maritime insurance offered in Genoa in the 1300s and fire insurance offered in London in 1680, not long after the Great Fire of London. In fact, Benjamin Franklin and the Union Fire Company began a fire insurance company in 1752.

As the previous examples illustrate, commodity futures contracts and insurance have been used worldwide for centuries. At the risk of oversimplification, not much new happened until the 1970s, probably because several sources of risk (interest rates, currency exchange rates, and oil prices) had been relatively stable, and perhaps because models for options and other derivatives had not yet been developed. However, the 1970s saw the end of the monetary gold standard (which dramatically increased foreign exchange rate volatility), runaway inflation in the United States, and a reversal in bargaining power between OPEC and oil companies during the Yom Kippur War between Egypt and Israel

---

[6]For a thorough treatment of the history of enterprise risk management, see Betty Simkins and Steven A. Ramirez, "Enterprise-Wide Risk Management and Corporate Governance, *Loyola University Chicago Law Journal*, Vol. 39, 2008, pp. 571–594.

in 1973. These events, combined with the acceleration of international competition, exposed companies to much more risk than in the previous decades. In turn, these sources of risk made stocks, bonds, and other investments much more volatile.

With the development of pricing models for derivatives, most companies began to actively manage their exposures to interest rates, exchange rates, and a wide variety of commodities. However, few companies employed a systematic approach to risk management. Instead, most companies had a risk management group in charge of insurance-related issues, but different groups in charge of managing each of the other specific risks. For example, one group might manage foreign exchange risk and another might manage commodity risk.

The impetus for a more comprehensive and systematic approach to risk management came from several sources, including corporate bribery scandals in the 1970s, the S&L crisis in the early 1980s, the accounting scandals in the early 2000s (including Enron and WorldCom), and the banking crisis in the late 2000s. All of these events had several common factors, including accounting systems that lacked insufficient controls to identify improper activities.

Regulators responded to each of these crises in an effort to assign blame and prevent the next crisis. In 1977, Congress passed the Foreign Corrupt Practices Act (FCPA) to prevent corporate bribery, and one of its provisions requires companies to have an accounting system that can identify funds used for bribery. In the mid-1980s, a Congressional committee examined the S&L failures and found that some of the failed financial institutions had fraudulent financial statements. In addition to criticizing accounting standards, this committee hinted that Congress and the SEC would impose additional regulatory controls if the accounting profession did not take actions to prevent similar frauds. In 2002, Congress passed the Sarbanes-Oxley (SOX) Act to prevent accounting scandals like those that occurred at Enron, Arthur Andersen, and Tyco. Section 404 of SOX requires senior management to include a section in the annual report that addresses the internal control system, including the system's framework and an assessment of its ability to detect fraud.

In response to stinging criticism from Congress, five major accounting organizations formed the Committee of Sponsoring Organizations (COSO) and released several reports, including one in 1992 that provided a framework for an internal control system designed to prevent fraudulent accounting. The framework for the COSO accounting internal control system satisfied the reporting requirements made by the Foreign Corrupt Practices Act (FCPA) and SOX, so many companies adopted the framework. In 2004, COSO also issued a framework for enterprise risk management, which broadened the scope of the original internal control framework. Because many companies were already using the framework for internal controls, some adopted versions of the broader framework for enterprise risk management. Today, the COSO framework and similar frameworks are widely used.

COSO defines **enterprise risk management (ERM)** as follows:

> Enterprise risk management is a *process*, effected by an entity's *board of directors*, management and other personnel, applied in *strategy setting* and across the *enterprise*, designed to identify *potential events* that may affect the entity, and manage risk to be within its *risk appetite*, to provide reasonable *assurance* regarding the achievement of entity objectives.[7]

Notice how this definition differs from the traditional compartmentalization of risk management. The COSO framework is inclusive, starting with the board of directors in addition to managers and other employees; COSO is broad in defining risk, ranging from strategic choices to specific events; COSO is unambiguous, with the company explicitly

---

[7]We added the italics for emphasis. See page 2 of COSO, "Summary of Enterprise Risk Management—Integrated Framework," 2004, **www.coso.org/documents/coso_erm_executivesummary.pdf**.

choosing an acceptable level of risk; and COSO is transparent, requiring monitoring and reporting.

Before we describe ERM frameworks in more detail, you should know about the Basel Accords, another big regulatory wave that has had an impact on risk management. The Basel Committee, headquartered in Switzerland, is composed of the heads of the central banks from well-developed economies. In the past 25 years, the Committee has introduced three major accords designed to control risk in the global financial system, Basel I (1988), Basel II (2004), and Basel III (introduced in 2010 and revised in 2011). There are similarities in all three accords, but we focus on Basel III because it is the most recent.

The essence of banking is raising funds (from sales of stock, issuances of debt, borrowing through short-term loans, and taking deposits) and then investing the funds in assets (such as business loans and derivatives). A bank experiences financial distress when its assets' cash flows and values aren't sufficient to cover its obligations to its creditors. To prevent a bank from experiencing financial distress (and then passing its problems on to taxpayers and the global financial system), Basel III seeks to ensure that a bank is not financed with too much debt relative to the risk of its assets. In addition to regulations regarding the types and proportions of capital a bank must maintain relative to its assets' risks, Basel III also requires adequate internal control systems to supervise a bank's risk and goes on to suggest particular techniques for measuring risk. We will describe several of these measures later in the chapter, including *value at risk* and *expected shortfall*.

SELF-TEST

Describe some regulatory actions that have influenced the evolution of risk management.

Define enterprise risk management.

23-3 A Framework for Enterprise Risk Management

No single framework is applicable to all companies, but the COSO framework (including modified versions) is widely used, so it provides an excellent example of an ERM framework.[8]

23-3a The Committee of Sponsoring Organizations' (COSO) Framework for Enterprise Risk Management (ERM)

COSO designed its enterprise risk management framework with three dimensions. The first dimension is the organizational level. The COSO framework applies ERM at all levels

---

[8]For more on the COSO framework, see The Committee of Sponsoring Organizations of the Treadway Commission, *Enterprise Risk Management—Integrated Framework,* 2004, available at **www.coso.org/guidance.htm**. A summary of the framework is available for free at the same Web site. Another widely used framework is ISO 3100:2009, published by the International Organization for Standardization (ISO), headquartered in Switzerland. For an ERM framework that is consistent with COSO and ISO, see **www.theirm.org/documents/SARM_FINAL.pdf**, a report that is authored jointly by three major UK risk management associations.

of an organization, including the corporate level, division levels, business units, and subsidiaries.

The second dimension is the category of objectives. Each organizational level should define its objectives in each of four categories: (1) *strategic objectives,* which are based on the company's mission and overall goals; (2) *operating objectives,* which focus on the selection, implementation, and ongoing execution of projects and other applications of corporate resources; (3) *reporting objectives,* which seek to disseminate accurate and up-to-date information to decision-makers inside the company and stakeholders outside the company (such as investors and regulators); and (4) *compliance objectives,* which seek to ensure the company complies with laws and regulatory requirements.

The third dimension is the process of risk management for an objective at a particular level within the organization. The risk management process for each objective has eight components, which we discuss in the following section.

23-3b The Components of the COSO Enterprise Risk Management Framework

The eight components of the COSO ERM process define the way in which an organization approaches and applies risk management.

COMPONENTS 1 AND 2: INTERNAL ENVIRONMENT AND OBJECTIVE SETTING

The first two components are related to a company's culture and mission, including the company's workplace environment, attitude towards risk, and goal-setting process. An important part of these processes is the identification of the amount of risk that a company is willing to take, which often is called the *risk appetite.*

COMPONENT 3: EVENT IDENTIFICATION

You can't manage a source of risk if you don't recognize it. A **risky event** is defined as any uncertain outcome that affects a company's previously defined objectives.[9] For example, risky events include increases in the prices of raw materials, an explosion at a factory, or a loss of customers to a competitor. To prevent overlooking risky events, ERM systems typically define categories and then identify the potential events within those categories. We will take a much closer look at risk categories later.

COMPONENT 4: RISK ASSESSMENT

After identifying a risk, a company should assess the risk. We will describe risk assessment in more detail later, but it always includes estimating both the probability that the event will occur and the resulting impact on the company's objectives. For example, an event might be an increase in interest rates, which would affect a company's cost when it issues debt. To assess this risk, the company would begin by forecasting the probabilities of different interest rates at the time it plans to issue the debt, and then estimate the cost of issuing debt at the different interest rates. As another example, an event might be a fire at a warehouse. In this case, a company would estimate the probability of a fire and the resulting cost. The insurance industry often uses the terms *loss frequency* and *loss severity* (the dollar value of each loss) for these concepts.

---

[9]COSO defines risk as an event that negatively affects an objective, and an opportunity as an event the can positively affect an objective. We don't make that distinction—we define risk as uncertainty, which can result in positive or negative outcomes.

COMPONENT 5: RISK RESPONSE

After identifying and assessing a risky event, the next steps are to choose a response to the risk and implement that choice. There are several different types of responses, including these:

TOTALLY AVOID THE ACTIVITY THAT GIVES RISE TO THE RISK.　　For example, a company might discontinue a product or service line because the risks outweigh the rewards. This often is the case with pharmaceutical products that have potentially harmful side effects or global expansion into countries with civil unrest.

REDUCE THE PROBABILITY OF OCCURRENCE OF AN ADVERSE EVENT.　　The expected loss arising from any risk is a function of both the probability of occurrence and the dollar loss if the adverse event occurs. In some instances, it is possible to reduce the probability that an adverse event will occur. For example, the probability that a fire will occur can be reduced by instituting a fire prevention program, by replacing old electrical wiring, and by using fire-resistant materials in areas with the greatest fire potential.

REDUCE THE MAGNITUDE OF THE LOSS ASSOCIATED WITH AN ADVERSE EVENT.　　In some instances, companies can take actions to reduce losses even if the event occurs. Continuing with the previous example, the dollar cost associated with a fire can be reduced by such actions as installing sprinkler systems, designing facilities with self-contained fire zones, and locating facilities close to a fire station.

TRANSFER THE RISK TO AN INSURANCE COMPANY.　　Often, it is advantageous to insure against risk by transferring it to an insurance company. Even though an insured item's expected loss is the same for its owner and for the insurance company, the insurance company benefits from diversification. For example, an insurance company might provide coverage for tractors, harvesters, and other types of agricultural equipment, which often cost several hundred thousand dollars or more. If the insurance company has a large number of customers, it can predict quite accurately the amounts it will pay in claims and then can set premiums high enough to pay the claims and provide the return required by its investors. In addition, insurance companies can themselves insure parts of their risk by purchasing reinsurance from another insurance company. Therefore, the potential loss of a harvester might be quite risky to a farmer, but it may not be risky to a large insurance company.

However, just because something can be insured does not mean that a company should insure it. In many instances, it might be better for the company to *self-insure*, which means bearing the risk directly rather than paying another party to bear it. In fact, many large companies choose to self-insure, or to insure only the part of an asset's loss that exceeds a certain amount, which is equivalent to an individual who has a large deductible on car or home insurance.

Insurance typically excludes acts of war or terrorism, but this became a major issue after the September 11, 2001, attacks on the World Trade Center and the Pentagon. Unless possible terrorist targets—including large malls, office buildings, oil refineries, airlines, and ships—can be insured against attacks, lenders may refuse to provide mortgage financing, and that would crimp the economy. Private insurance companies are reluctant to insure these projects, at least without charging prohibitive premiums, so the federal government has been asked to step in and provide terrorist insurance. However, losses due to terrorist attacks are potentially so large that they could bankrupt even strong insurance companies. Therefore, Congress passed the Terrorism Risk Insurance Act

(TRIA) in 2002 and extended it in 2007 through 2014. Under the TRIA, the federal government and private insurers will share the cost of benefits paid on insured losses caused by terrorists.

TRANSFER THE FUNCTION THAT PRODUCES THE RISK TO A THIRD PARTY.   For example, suppose a furniture manufacturer is concerned about potential liabilities arising from its ownership of a fleet of trucks used to transfer products from its manufacturing plant to various points across the country. One way to eliminate this risk would be to contract with a trucking company to do the shipping, thus passing the risks to a third party.

SHARE OR ELIMINATE THE RISK BY USING DERIVATIVE CONTRACTS.   Many companies use derivative contracts to reduce or eliminate an event's risk. For example, a cereal company may use corn or wheat futures to hedge against increases in grain prices. Similarly, financial derivatives can be used to reduce risks that arise from changes in interest rates and exchange rates. As we will describe later, the risk doesn't disappear—it is just taken on by the other party in the derivative contract.

ACCEPT THE RISK.   In some instances, a company will decide to accept a risk because the expected benefits are greater than the expected costs and because the risk doesn't exceed the company's risk appetite. Indeed, accepting risk is the nature of most businesses—if they were riskless, then investors would expect to receive a return only equal to the risk-free rate. Also, some stand-alone risks may be quite large, but they may not contribute much to the total corporate risk if they are not highly correlated with the company's other risks.

COMPONENTS 6, 7, AND 8: CONTROL ACTIVITIES, INFORMATION AND COMMUNICATION, AND MONITORING

The last three components focus on ensuring that risky events are in fact being treated according to the responses that were previously chosen—it doesn't do much good to develop strategies and tactics if employees don't follow them! For example, a single rogue trader lost €4.9 billion in 2008 at the French bank Societe Generale, and another lost £1.5 billion in 2011 at the London branch of UBS (headquartered in Switzerland).

SELF-TEST

Define a risk event.

What are the two stages in risk assessment?

Describe some possible risk responses.

Should a firm insure itself against all of the insurable risks it faces? Explain.

23-4 Categories of Risk Events

Before addressing alternative risk responses to specific risk events, it will be helpful to describe ways to categorize risk.

23-4a Major Categories

Following is a typical list of major categories that are representative of those at several organizations.[10]

1. *Strategy and reputation.* A company's strategic choices simultaneously influence and respond to its competitors' actions, corporate social responsibilities, the public's perception of its activities, and its reputation among suppliers, peers, and customers. ERM addresses the risk inherent in these strategic choices.

2. *Control and compliance.* This category includes risk events related to regulatory requirements, litigation risks, intellectual property rights, reporting accuracy, and internal control systems.

3. *Hazards.* These include fires, floods, riots, acts of terrorism, and other natural or man-made disasters. Notice that hazards only have negative outcomes—an earthquake might destroy a factory, but it isn't going to build one.

4. *Human resources.* Success often depends upon a company's employees. ERM addresses risk events related to employees, including recruiting, succession planning, employee health, and employee safety.

5. *Operations.* A company's operations include supply chains, manufacturing facilities, existing product lines, and business processes. Risk events include supply chain disruptions, equipment failures, product recalls, and changes in customer demand.

6. *Technology.* Technology changes rapidly and is a major source of risk, including risk events related to innovations, technological failures, and IT reliability and security.

7. *Financial management.* This category includes risk events related to (1) foreign exchange risk, (2) commodity price risk, (3) interest rate risk, (4) project selection risk (including major capital expenditures, mergers, and acquisitions), (5) liquidity risk, (6) customer credit risk, and (7) portfolio risk (the risk that a portfolio of financial assets will decrease in value). For the remainder of the chapter, we will focus on the risk events related to financial management, but first we need to describe several other ways to think about risk.

23-4b Dimensions of Risk

Sometimes it is helpful to think about risk events based on different dimensions. For example, several risk management systems classify risk by whether is driven by external forces or by internal decisions and activities. This is especially helpful in risk identification because it forces managers to look at a broader range of risk events.

Sometimes it is useful to classify risk by whether it is a pure risk that only has a downside (e.g., a hazard, such as a fire) or a speculative risk that has potential positive as well as negative outcomes (e.g., the exchange rate between dollars and euros can go up or down, which would have a big impact on the cash flows of U.S. importers). Most pure risks can be reduced or eliminated with insurance products.

When choosing among different risk responses, it is helpful to determine whether the source of risk is linear or nonlinear. For example, consider an agricultural company with access to a low-cost source of water for irrigation. The company grows corn and can

---

[10]To see the way that several organizations have categorized risk and the ways that surveyors categorize risk, see the following: Mark L. Frigo and Hans Læssøe, "Strategic Risk Management at the LEGO Group," *Strategic Finance*, February, 2012, pp. 27–35; Henri Servaes, Ane Tamayo, and Peter Tufano, "The Theory and Practice of Corporate Risk Management," *Journal of Applied Corporate Finance*, Fall, 2009, pp. 60–78; Celina Rogers, *The Risk Management Imperative*, (Boston: CFO Publishing LLC), 2010, **http://secure.cfo.com/whitepapers/index .cfm/download/14521624**; Casualty Actuarial Society, *Overview of Risk Management*, 2003, **www.casact.org/ research/erm/overview.pdf**; and the sources cited in footnote 12.

predict its costs and the size of its harvest, but it is exposed to volatility in the price of corn. Notice that this is a linear risk—the company loses money when prices are low and makes money when they are high. We discuss the details later, but the company can enter into derivative contracts that provide positive cash flows when prices are low but create negative cash flows when prices are high. The derivative also has a linear payout, but its payouts are opposite those of the company. The combination of the company's internally generated cash flows from the harvest and its externally generated cash flows from the derivative can reduce or eliminate the company's risk.

In contrast, consider a company in the oil exploration and extraction industry.[11] The company will incur fixed costs and negative cash flows associated with continuing operations when oil prices are too low to justify additional exploration. When oil prices are high, the company incurs fixed costs and also variable costs associated with expanded exploration and extraction. However, when oil prices are high, the company will generate enough positive cash flow to cover its fixed costs and also the new variable costs associated with the additional exploration and extraction. Therefore, the company is exposed to nonlinear risk—it needs additional cash flow to support its ongoing operations only when oil prices are low but not when prices are high. In this situation, the company might be willing to buy a derivative that pays out only when oil prices are low. In other words, the company reduces its nonlinear risk with a nonlinear hedging strategy.

SELF-TEST

List and define the different major categories of risk events.

Should a firm insure itself against all of the insurable risks it faces? Explain.

Explain the difference between a linear risk and a nonlinear risk.

23-5 Foreign Exchange (FX) Risk

Foreign exchange (FX) risk occurs when a company's cash flows are affected by changes in currency exchange rates. This can occur if a company imports materials from other countries or sells its products in other countries. Some smaller companies manage FX risk for each transaction, but most large companies aggregate their transactions and manage their exposures centrally. For example, if one division is selling goods denominated in Canadian dollars and another division is purchasing goods denominated in Canadian dollars, the company would net out the two transactions and just manage any remaining exposure.

The primary tool used to manage FX risk is a **forward contract**, which is an agreement in which one party agrees to buy an item at a specific price on a specific future date and another party agrees to sell the item at the agreed upon terms. *Goods are actually delivered under forward contracts.* In the case of foreign exchange, the goods are the amount of foreign currency specified in the contract, paid for with the other currency specified in the contract.

Most FX trading is directly between two parties using customized contracts with unique amounts and dates—there is no central market with standardized contracts. Unless both parties are morally and financially strong, there is a danger that one party

---

[11]See Kenneth A. Froot, David S. Scharfstein, and Jeremy Stein, "A Framework for Risk Management," *Journal of Applied Corporate Finance*, Fall 1994, pp. 22–32; also see the paper by Servais et al, cited in footnote 14.

will default on the contract—this is called **counterparty risk**. Major banks often act as counterparties for their customers. For example, a bank might agree to buy euros in 30 days at a price of 1.24 dollars per euro from one customer and agree to sell euros in 30 days at a price of 1.25 dollars per euro to another customer. Depending on the change in the euro exchange rate, the bank will make money on one of the contracts and lose money on the other, netting only the spread on the difference in prices. This matching of contracts allows banks to reduce their net exposure to exchange rate volatility, but the bank is still exposed to counterparty risk from the customers.

Because there is no central market, trading in FX is an OTC (over the counter) transaction. The amount of currency to be delivered is called the notional amount. At the end of 2011, there was a total of about $30 *trillion* in the notional value of forward contracts outstanding globally.

The failure to manage counterparty risk was one of the causes of the 2007 global financial crisis. For example, Lehman Brothers was a counterparty to many other financial institutions in a variety of derivative contracts, so Lehman's failure caused distress at financial institutions throughout the world.

To illustrate how foreign exchange contracts are used, suppose GE arranges to buy electric motors from a European manufacturer on terms that call for GE to pay 10 million euros in 180 days. GE would not want to give up the free trade credit, but if the euro appreciated against the dollar during the next 6 months then the dollar cost of the 10 million euros would rise. GE could hedge the transaction by buying a forward contract under which it agreed to buy the 10 million euros in 180 days at a fixed dollar price, which would lock in the dollar cost of the motors. This transaction would probably be conducted through a money center bank, which would try to find a European company that needed dollars in 6 months.

W W W

See the Quarterly Review from the Bank of International Settlements, **www .bis.org/publ/qtrpdf/r_ qt1206.htm**.

SELF-TEST

What is a forward contract?

Explain how a company can use forward contracts to eliminate FX risk.

What is counterparty risk?

W W W

See the CME Group's Web site, **www.cmegroup.com**, for a wealth of information on the operation and history of the exchange.

23-6 Commodity Price Risk

Many companies use or produce commodities, including agricultural products, energy, metals, and lumber. Because commodity prices can be quite volatile, many companies manage their exposure to commodity price risk. Before describing specific ways to manage commodity price risk, we begin with a brief overview of futures markets in the United States to illustrate some key concepts.

23-6a An Overview of Futures Markets

As we noted earlier, Midwest farmers in the early 1800s were concerned about the price they would receive for their wheat when they sold it in the fall, and millers were concerned about the price they would have to pay. Each party soon realized that the risks they faced could be reduced if they established a price earlier in the year. Accordingly, mill agents began going out to the Wheat Belt with contracts that called for the farmers to deliver grain at a predetermined price, and both parties benefited from the transaction in the sense that their risks were reduced. The farmers could concentrate on growing their crop without worrying about the price of grain, and the millers could concentrate on their milling operations.

These early agreements were between two parties who arranged the transactions themselves. Soon, though, intermediaries came into the picture. The Chicago Board of Trade, founded in 1848, was an early marketplace where *futures dealers* helped make a market in futures contracts.

A **futures contract** is similar to a forward contract in that two parties are involved, with one party taking a long position (which obligates the party to buy the underlying asset) and the other party taking a short position (which obligates the party to sell the asset). However, there are three key differences. First, futures contracts are marked-to-market on a daily basis, meaning that gains and losses are recognized daily and money must be put up to cover losses. This greatly reduces the risk of default that exists with forward contracts because daily price changes are usually smaller than the cumulative change over the contract's life. For example, if a corn futures contract has a price of $7.00 per bushel and the price goes up to $7.10 the next day, a party with a short position must pay the $0.10 difference, and a party with a long position would receive the difference. This marking-to-market occurs daily until the delivery date. To see that this procedure does in fact lock in the price, suppose that the price doesn't change again. On the delivery date, the party with the short position would sell corn at the current price of $7.10. Because the short seller had already paid $0.10 from daily marking-to-market, the short seller's net cash flow is $7.00. The party with the long position would have to buy corn at the current price of $7.10, but because the purchaser had already received $0.10 from cumulative daily marking-to-market, the net purchase price would be $7.00.

The second major difference between a forward contract and a futures contract is that physical delivery of the underlying asset in a futures contract is virtually never taken—the two parties simply settle up with cash for the difference between the contracted price and the actual price on the expiration date. The third difference is that futures contracts are generally standardized instruments that are traded on exchanges, whereas forward contracts are usually tailor-made, negotiated between two parties, and not traded after they have been signed.

The needs of farmers and millers allowed a **natural hedge**, defined as a situation in which aggregate risk can be reduced by derivatives transactions between two parties. Natural hedges occur when futures are traded between cotton farmers and cotton mills, copper mines and copper fabricators, importers and foreign manufacturers for currency exchange rates, electric utilities and coal mines, and oil producers and oil users. In all such situations, hedging reduces aggregate risk and thus benefits the economy.

There are two basic types of hedges: (1) **long hedges**, in which futures contracts are *bought* (obligating the hedger to purchase the underlying asset), providing protection against price increases, and (2) **short hedges**, where a firm or individual *sells* futures contracts (obligating the hedger to sell the underlying asset), providing protection against falling prices.

Not all participants in the futures markets are hedgers. **Speculation** involves betting on future price movements, and futures are used instead of the commodities because of the leverage inherent in the contract. For example, a speculator might buy corn for $7 a bushel. If corn goes up to $7.70, the speculator has a 10% return (assuming rats don't eat the corn before it can be sold). Now consider a futures contract for 5,000 bushels at $7 per bushel. The exchange requires an investor to put up a **margin requirement** to ensure that the investor will not renege on the daily marking to market. However, the margin is quite small relative to the size of a contract—the margin is only $2,700, but the total amount of corn is valued at $35,000 = $7(5,000).[12] If the price goes up to $7.70, the profit is

W W W

For current margin requirements, go to **www .cmegroup.com**, *and select Performance Bond/ Margins under the Featured Links section. The T-bond futures contract is Product Code 17.*

---

[12]This is the margin requirement for hedgers. Speculators have a higher margin requirement.

$3,500 = (\$7.70 - \$7.00)(5,000)$. The rate of return on the invested margin is 140% = \$3,500/\$2,500. Of course, any losses on the contract also would be magnified.

At first blush, one might think that the appearance of speculators would increase risk, but this is not necessarily true. Speculators add capital and players to the market. Thus, to the extent that speculators broaden the market and make hedging possible, they help decrease risk for those who seek to avoid it. Unlike the natural hedge, however, risk is not eliminated. Instead, it is transferred from the hedgers to the speculators.

Today, futures contracts are available on hundreds of real and financial assets traded on dozens of U.S. and international exchanges, the largest of which are the Chicago Board of Trade (CBOT) and the Chicago Mercantile Exchange (CME), both of which are now part of the CME Group. Futures contracts are divided into two classes, **commodity futures** and **financial futures**. Commodity futures include oil, various grains, oilseeds, livestock, meats, fibers, metals, and wood. Financial futures, which were first traded in 1975, include Treasury bills, notes, bonds, certificates of deposit, Eurodollar deposits, foreign currencies, and stock indexes. We describe how financial futures can reduce interest rate risk in a later section.

23-6b Using Futures Contracts to Reduce Commodity Price Exposure

We will use Porter Electronics, which uses large quantities of copper, as well as several precious metals, to illustrate inventory hedging. Suppose that in May 2013, Porter foresaw a need for 100,000 pounds of copper in March 2014 for use in fulfilling a fixed-price contract to supply solar power cells to the U.S. government. Porter's managers are concerned that a strike by Chilean copper miners might occur, which would raise the price of copper in world markets and possibly turn Porter's expected profit into a loss.

Porter could go ahead and buy the copper it will need to fulfill the contract, but it would have to borrow money to pay for the copper and then pay for storage. As an alternative, the company could hedge against increasing copper prices in the futures market. The New York Commodity Exchange trades standard copper futures contracts of 25,000 pounds each. Thus, Porter could buy four contracts (go long) for delivery in March 2014. Assume these contracts were trading in May for about \$4.10 per pound and that the spot price at that date was about \$4.08 per pound. If copper prices rose appreciably over the next 10 months, then the value of Porter's long position in copper futures would increase, thus offsetting some of the price increase in the commodity itself. Of course, if copper prices fell, then Porter would lose money on its futures contracts, but the company would be buying the copper on the spot market at a cheaper price, so it would make a higher than anticipated profit on its sale of solar cells. Thus, hedging in the copper futures market locks in the cost of raw materials and removes some risk to which the firm would otherwise be exposed.

Many other companies, such as Alcoa with aluminum and Archer Daniels Midland with grains, routinely use the futures markets to reduce the risks associated with price volatility.

23-6c Options on Futures

Futures contracts and options are similar to one another—so similar that people often confuse the two. Therefore, it is useful to compare the two instruments. A *futures contract* is a definite agreement on the part of one party to buy something on a specific date and at a specific price, and the other party agrees to sell on the same terms. No matter how low or how high the price goes, the two parties must settle the contract at the agreed-upon price and the losses of one party must exactly equal to the gains of the other. In addition, a dollar increase in the futures price has exactly the opposite effect of a dollar decrease in the futures price. A hedge constructed using futures contracts is called a *symmetric hedge* because of this feature; the payoff from an increase in the futures price is exactly opposite the payoff from a decrease in the futures price. For this reason, symmetric hedges are typically used to provide a fixed transaction price at some date in the future and are ideal for managing a risk that is linear.

For example, suppose an agricultural company has access to a source of low-cost water for irrigation. The company can predict its costs and the size of its harvest but is exposed to price risk. The company could sell futures contracts (take a long position, which obligates it to sell corn) for delivery when the corn is harvested in 6 months. If the corn price (and hence the corn futures price) decreases over the 6 months, then the company will receive less when selling the corn but will make up the difference when closing out the futures contract. If instead the corn price increases, then the company will make more money when selling the corn in 6 months but will lose money when closing out the futures contract. In this way the ending value of the position doesn't depend on the corn price in 6 months, and so the amount received for selling the corn in 6 months is locked in.

An *option*, on the other hand, gives someone the right to buy (call) or sell (put) an asset, but the holder of the option does not have to complete the transaction. The payoff from a hedge constructed using options will be different from a futures hedge because of this option feature. As discussed in Chapter 8, the payoff from a call option increases as the price of the underlying asset increases, but if the underlying asset price decreases, then the most the option holder can lose is the amount invested in the option. That is, upside gains are unlimited but downside losses are capped at the amount invested in the option. For this reason, an option is said to create an *asymmetric hedge*—it hedges price changes in one direction more than price changes in the other. As such, options are ideal for managing nonlinear risks.

For example, suppose the agricultural company did not have access to irrigation but operated many farms in different states. A widespread drought would reduce the size of the harvest but probably would cause the price of corn to increase due to the lower supply. If this happened, the company's revenues would fall but would not be eliminated—the higher corn price would partially compensate for the smaller harvest. This means the company faces nonlinear risk with respect to corn prices. Instead of going long in a futures contract, the company might buy a put option on a corn futures contract, giving the company the right to sell a futures contract at a fixed price. If the price of corn decreased, the value of the put option would increase, and the profits on the option would offset the loss from selling the corn at the lower price. However, if corn prices increased, then the investor would let the put option expire and simply sell its smaller harvest at the higher price.

SELF-TEST

How does a futures contract differ from a forward contract?

What is a "natural hedge"? Give some examples of natural hedges.

Suppose a company knows the quantity of a commodity that it will produce. Describe how it might hedge using a futures contract.

23-7 Interest Rate Risk

Interest rates can be quite volatile, exposing a company to interest rate risk, especially if the company is planning to issue debt or if the company has floating rate debt. The following sections describe these two situations.

23-7a Using Futures Contracts to Manage the Risk of Debt Issuances

To illustrate, assume that Carson Foods is considering in July a plan to issue $10,000,000 of 20-year bonds in December to finance a capital expenditure program. The interest rate would be 9% paid semiannually if the bonds were issued today, and at that rate the project would have a positive NPV. However, interest rates may rise, and when the issue is actually sold, which would increase Carson's financing costs. Carson can protect itself against a rise in rates by hedging in the futures market using an interest rate futures contract.

INTEREST RATES FUTURES

To illustrate how interest rate futures work, consider the CBOT's contract on Treasury bonds. The basic contract is for $100,000 of a hypothetical 6% coupon, semiannual payment Treasury bond with 20 years to maturity.[13] Table 23-1 shows Treasury bond futures data from the Chicago Board of Trade.

The first column of Table 23-1 shows the delivery month and year. Column 2 shows the last price of the day, also called the *settlement* price, and the next column shows the change in price from the previous day. For example, the settlement price for the December 2012 contract, 149'28, means 149 plus $^{28}/_{32}$, or 149.8750%, of par. The change was 0'13, which means the December 2012 contract's last price of the day was $^{13}/_{32}$ higher than the previous day's last trade, which must have been at 149'15. The next three columns show the opening, high, and low prices for the day. Column 7 shows the day's estimated trading volume. Notice that most of the trading occurs in the contract with

TABLE 23-1

Futures Prices (Treasury Bonds: $100,000; Pts. 32nds of 100%)

Delivery Month (1)	Settle (2)	Change (3)	Open (4)	High (5)	Low (6)	Estimated Volume (7)	Open Interest (8)
Sep 2012	148'29	0'12	148'17	149'08	148'17	333490	623580
Dec 2012	149'28	0'13	149'28	149'28	149'28	124	3194
Mar 2013	150'08	0'25	150'08	150'08	150'08	0	1

Source: The Wall Street Journal Online, **www.wsj.com**, settlement prices for July 5, 2012.

[13]The coupon rate on the hypothetical bond was changed to 6% from 8% in March 2000. The CBOT contract doesn't specify a 20-year bond but instead allows delivery of any noncallable bond with a remaining maturity greater than 15 years (or callable bond that is not callable for at least 15 years) and less than 25 years. Rather than simply deliver a bond, which might have an interest rate other than 6%, the actual bond price is adjusted by a conversion feature to make it equivalent to a 6% bond that is trading at par. Because the average maturity of bonds that are eligible for delivery is about 20 years, we use a 20-year maturity for the hypothetical bond in the futures contract. For even longer maturity hedging, the CBOT also has the Ultra T-Bond contract, which allows for delivery of a Treasury bond of at least 25 years to maturity.

the nearest delivery date. Finally, Column 8 shows the "open interest," which is the number of contracts outstanding.

To illustrate, we focus on the Treasury bonds for December delivery. The settlement price was 149.8750% of the $100,000 contract value. Thus, the price at which one could buy $100,000 face value of 6%, 20-year Treasury bonds to be delivered in December was 149.8750% ($100,000) = $149,875.0.

The contract price increased by $^{13}/_{32}$ of 1% of $100,000 from the previous day's price, so if you had bought the contract yesterday, you would have made $406.25 = ($^{13}/_{32}$)(0.01) ($100,000). There were 3,194 contracts outstanding, representing a total value of about 3,194($149,875.0) = $478,700,750.

Note that the contract increased by $^{13}/_{32}$ of a percent on this particular day. Why would the value of the bond futures contract increase? Bond prices increase when interest rates fall, so interest rates must have fallen on that day. Moreover, we can calculate the implied rate inherent in the futures price. Recall that the contract relates to a hypothetical 20-year, semiannual payment, 6% coupon bond. The settlement price was 149.8750% of par, so a $1,000 par bond would have a price of 149.8750% ($1,000) = $1,498.750. We can solve for r_d by using the following equation:

See **Ch23 Tool Kit.xls** on the textbook's Web site for all calculations.

$$\sum_{t=1}^{40} \frac{\$30}{(1 + r_d/2)^t} + \frac{\$1,000}{(1 + r_d/2)^{40}} = \$1,498.75$$

Using a financial calculator, input N = 40, PV = −1498.75, PMT = 30, and FV = 1000; then solve for I/YR = 1.37163%. This is the semiannual rate, which is equivalent to a nominal annual rate of 2.7433%, or approximately 2.74%.

The previous day's last (settlement) price was 149'15, or 149.46875%, for a bond price of $1,494.6875 = 149.46875%($1,000). Setting N = 40, PV = −1494.6875, PMT = 30, and FV = 1000 and then solving for I/YR = 1.381848 implies an annual yield of 2.7637%, or approximately 2.76%. Therefore, interest rates fell from $2.76% to 2.74%. This was only 2 basis points, but that was enough to increase the value of the contract by $406.25.

In July 2012, when the data in Table 23-1 were gathered, the yield on a 20-year T-bond was about 2.28%. But as we just calculated, the implied yield on the December 2012 futures contract was about 2.74%. The December yield reflects investors' beliefs as to what the interest rate level will be in December: The marginal trader in the futures market was predicting a 46-basis-point increase in yields between July and December. That prediction could, of course, turn out to be incorrect.

For example, suppose that 3 months later, in October, implied yields in the futures market had fallen by 50 basis points from the earlier levels—say, from 2.74% to 2.24%. Inputting N = 40, I/YR = 2.24/2 = 1.12, PMT = 30, and FV = 1000 and then solving for PV = −1603.4503 shows that the December contract would be worth about $160,345.03 in September if implied yields fell by 50 basis points. Thus, the contract's value would have increased by $160,345.03 − $149,875.00 ≈ $10,470.

HEDGING WITH TREASURY BOND FUTURES CONTRACTS

Recall that Carson Foods plans to issue $10,000,000 of 9% semiannual 20-year bonds in December and would like to protect itself from a possible increase in interest rates by using T-bond futures contracts. Rising interest rates cause bond prices to fall, and thus decrease the value of bond futures contracts. Therefore, Carson can guard against an *increase* in interest rates by taking a short position on a T-bond futures contract—if rates go up, Carson will receive a cash flow from the futures contract equal to the original futures price less the now-lower futures price.

resource

See *Ch23 Tool Kit.xls* on the textbook's Web site for all calculations.

Carson would choose a futures contract on the security most similar to the one it plans to issue, long-term bonds, and so would probably hedge with December Treasury bond futures. In the previous section, we calculated the price of a contract, which was $149,875.00. Because Carson plans to issue $10,000,000 of bonds and because each contract is worth $149,875.00, Carson will sell $10,000,000/$149,875.00 = 66.722 ≈ 67 contracts for delivery in December.[14] The total value of the contracts is 67($149,875.00) = $10,041,625.00, which is very close to the value of the bonds Carson wants to issue.

Now suppose that in December, when Carson issues its bonds, renewed fears of inflation push interest rates up by 100 basis points. What would the bond proceeds be if Carson still tried to issue 9% coupon bonds when the market requires a 10% rate of return? We can find the total value of the offering with a financial calculator, inputting N = 40, I/YR = 5, PMT = −450000, and FV = −10000000 and then solving for PV = 9142046. Therefore, bonds with a 9% coupon, based upon its original plans, would bring proceeds of only $9,142,046, because investors now require a 10% return. Because Carson would have to issue $10 million worth of bonds at a 10% rate, Carson's cost would go up by $857,954 = $10,000,000 − $9,142,046 as a result of delaying the financing.

Alternatively, we can estimate Carson's cost of delaying by calculating the present value of the incremental payments Carson must make. The increase in interest rates from 9% to 10% would cause the semiannual coupon payments to go up from $45 to $50 on a per-bond basis. For 10,000 bonds, the total incremental semiannual coupon payments are $50,000 = ($50 − $45)(10,000). We can find the present value of these incremental payments by, inputting N = 40, I/YR = 5, PMT = −50000, and FV = 0 and then solving for PV = −857954 = −$857,954, which is the same cost found by the first method. Mathematically, this is true because a little bit of algebra will show that the two methods use the same formula. Intuitively, this is because the first method identifies the difference between an asset's par value and its market value given a change in interest rates. This difference can be thought of as the extra amount of value that would need to be added to bring the market value up to par. One way to add value would be to increase the payments, which is what the second approach does.

Either way we calculate it, Carson incurs a cost of $857,954 due to the increase in rates. However, the increase in interest rates would also bring about a change in the value of Carson's short position in the futures contract. When interest rates increase, the value of the futures contract will fall. If the interest rate on the futures contract also increased by the same full percentage point, from 2.7637% to 3.7637%, then the new contract value can be found by inputting N = 40, I/YR = 3.7637/2 = 1.88185, PMT = −3000, and FV = −100000 and then solving for PV = 131231.030 per contract. With 67 contracts, the total value of the position is thus $8,792,479 = 67($131,231.030). Carson would then close its position in the futures market by repurchasing for $8,792,479 the contracts that it earlier sold for $10,041,625, giving it a profit of $1,249,146.

Thus, Carson would offset the loss on the bond issue if we ignore commissions and the opportunity cost of the margin money. In fact, in our example Carson more than offsets the loss, pocketing an additional $298,756 = $1,156,710 − $857,954.[15] Of course, if interest

[14]Carson will have to put up a margin of 67($2,700) = $180,900 and also pay brokerage commissions.
[15]Carson would have to pay taxes on the profit from the futures contract, so the after-tax value of the future's transaction can be found by multiplying the pretax profit by (1 − T). However, Carson would get to deduct the larger additional coupon payments from its income. To find the present value of the after-tax additional coupon payments, we multiply the additional pretax coupons by (1 − T) and calculate the present value. This gives the same result as first finding the present value of the additional pretax coupons and then multiplying the present value by (1 − T). In other words, the pretax cost of delaying and the pretax profit from the futures contract should be multiplied by (1 − T) to estimate the after-tax effectiveness of the hedge.

rates had fallen, then Carson would have lost on its futures position, but this loss would have been offset because Carson could now sell its bonds with a lower coupon.

If futures contracts existed on Carson's own debt and if interest rates moved identically in the spot and futures markets, then the firm could construct a perfect hedge in which gains on the futures contract would exactly offset losses on the bonds. In reality, it is virtually impossible to construct perfect hedges, because in most cases the underlying asset is not identical to the futures asset; and even when the assets are identical, prices (and interest rates) may not move exactly together in the spot and futures markets.[16]

Observe also that if Carson had been planning an equity offering and if its stock tended to move fairly closely with one of the stock indexes, then the company could have hedged against falling stock prices by selling the index future. Even better, if options on Carson's stock were traded in the options market, then it could use options rather than futures to hedge against falling stock prices.

The futures and options markets permit flexibility in the timing of financial transactions: The firm can be protected, at least partially, against changes that occur between the time a decision is reached and the time the transaction is completed. However, this protection has a cost—the firm must pay commissions. Whether or not the protection is worth the cost is a matter of judgment. The decision to hedge also depends on management's risk aversion and on the company's strength and ability to assume the risk in question.[17]

23-7b Using Interest Rate Swaps: Managing Floating versus Fixed Rates

Suppose that Company S has a 20-year, $100 million floating-rate bond outstanding and that Company F has a $100 million, 20-year, fixed-rate issue outstanding. Thus, each company has an obligation to make a stream of interest payments, but one payment stream is fixed while the other will vary as interest rates change in the future. This situation is shown in the top part of Figure 23-1.

Now suppose that Company S has stable cash flows and wants to lock in its cost of debt. Company F has cash flows that fluctuate with the economy, rising when the economy is strong and falling when it is weak. Recognizing that interest rates also move up and down with the economy, Company F has concluded it would be better off with variable-rate debt. Suppose the companies agreed to swap their payment obligations. The bottom half of Figure 23-1 shows that the net cash flows for Company S are at a fixed rate and those for Company F are based on a floating rate. Company S would now have to make fixed payments, which are consistent with its stable cash inflows, and Company F would have a floating obligation, which for it is less risky.

A **swap** is just what the name implies—two parties agree to swap something, generally obligations to make specified payment streams.

---

[16]In this example, Carson hedged a 20-year bond with a T-bond futures contract. Rather than simply matching on maturity, it would be more accurate to match on duration (see **Web Extension 5C**, available on the textbook's Web site, for a discussion of duration). A matching duration in the futures contracts could be accomplished by taking positions in the T-bond futures contract and in another financial futures contract, such as the 10-Year Treasury note contract. Because Carson's bond had a 20-year maturity, matching on maturity instead of duration provided a good hedge. If Carson's bond had a different maturity, then it would be essential to match on duration.

[17]For additional insights into the use of financial futures for hedging, see Mark G. Castelino, Jack C. Francis, and Avner Wolf, "Cross-Hedging: Basis Risk and Choice of the Optimal Hedging Vehicle," *The Financial Review*, May 1991, pp. 179–210.

FIGURE 23-1

Cash Flows under a Swap

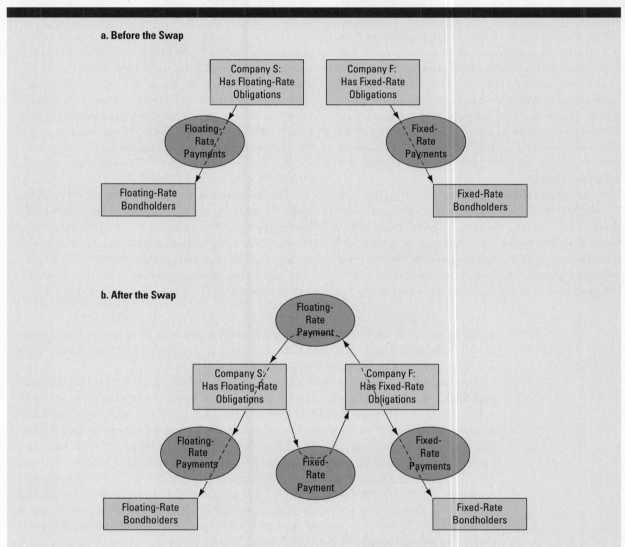

a. Before the Swap

b. After the Swap

Note: In Panel a, Company S must make floating-rate payments out of its own internal cash flows; but in Panel b, it uses the floating payments from Company F to pay its bondholders. Company F has a reversed position. After the swap, S has de facto fixed payments, which are consistent with its stable internal flows, and F has floating payments, which are consistent with its fluctuating flows.

© Cengage Learning 2014

The previous example illustrates how swaps can reduce risks by allowing each company to match the variability of its interest payments with that of its cash flows. However, there are also situations in which swaps can reduce both the risk and the effective cost of debt. For example, Antron Corporation, which has a high credit rating, can issue either floating-rate debt at LIBOR + 1% or fixed-rate debt at 10%.[18] Bosworth Industries is less creditworthy, so its cost for floating-rate debt is LIBOR + 1.5% and its fixed-rate cost is 10.4%. Owing to the nature of Antron's operations, its CFO has decided that the firm

---

[18]LIBOR stands for the London Interbank Offered Rate, the rate charged on interbank dollar loans in the Eurodollar market.

The Game of Truth or LIBOR

© Rob Webb/Getty Images

LIBOR stands for the London Interbank Offered Rate, the rate banks charge one another for loans in the Eurodollar market. LIBOR might possibly be the most important number that is reported in financial markets because many derivative contracts base payments on LIBOR. Some analysts estimate that there are over $300 trillion dollars of derivatives linked to LIBOR. Because LIBOR is such a widely used rate, you might think that it is reported with the utmost care and accuracy. Wrong!

The largest banks in London report to Thomson Reuters the rates they charge one another on loans. Each day Thomson Reuters collects these rates, throws out the highest and lowest percentiles, and uses the middle 50% to calculate the average rate, which it reports to the rest of the world. That part of the process is clear, but how do the banks define the

rates that they report? It turns out that some of them just pick a number. On June 27, 2012, Barclays admitted that it had been fined £290 million by U.S. and U.K. regulators for knowingly reporting untrue rates. Barclays reported low rates at times to disguise how risky other banks viewed Barclays, according to its own emails. In addition, some emails suggest that Barclays manipulated LIBOR to profit on trades. In the wake of this news, Barclays's CEO and other senior executives were forced to resign.

The Barclays case could be just the beginning of a much bigger scandal because other financial institutions may have engaged in the same behavior. In July 2012, analysts speculated that additional civil damages will be cost banks billions, and there could be criminal charges based on investigations by the U.S. Justice Department.

would be better off with fixed-rate debt; meanwhile, Bosworth's CFO prefers floating-rate debt. Paradoxically, both firms can benefit by issuing the type of debt they do not want and then swapping their payment obligations.

First, each company will issue an identical amount of debt, which is called the **notional principal**. Even though Antron wants fixed-rate debt, it issues floating-rate debt at LIBOR + 1%, and Bosworth issues fixed-rate debt at 10.4%. Next, the two companies enter into an interest rate swap.[19] Assume the debt maturities are 5 years, which means the length of this swap will also be 5 years. By convention, the floating-rate payments of most swaps are based on LIBOR, with the fixed rate adjusted upward or downward to reflect credit risk and the term structure. The riskier the company that will receive the floating-rate payments, the higher the fixed-rate payment it must make. In our example, Antron will be receiving floating-rate payments from Bosworth, and those payments will be set at LIBOR multiplied by the notional principal. Then, payments will be adjusted every 6 months to reflect changes in the LIBOR rate.

The fixed payment that Antron must make to Bosworth is set (that is, "fixed") for the duration of the swap at the time the contract is signed, and it depends primarily on two factors: (1) the level of fixed interest rates at the time of the agreement and (2) the relative creditworthiness of the two companies.

In our example, assume interest rates and creditworthiness are such that 8.95% is the appropriate fixed swap rate for Antron, so it will make 8.95% fixed-rate payments to Bosworth. In turn, Bosworth will pay the LIBOR rate to Antron. Table 23-2 shows the net rates paid by each participant, and Figure 23-2 graphs the flows. Note that Antron ends up making fixed payments, which it desires, but because of the swap the rate paid is 9.95% versus the 10% rate it would have paid had it issued fixed-rate debt directly. At the same time, the swap leaves Bosworth with floating-rate debt, which it wants, but at a rate of

---

[19]Such transactions are generally arranged by large money center banks, and payments are made to the bank, which in turn pays the interest on the original loans. The bank assumes the credit risk and guarantees the payments should one of the parties default. For its services, the bank receives a percentage of the payments as its fee.

TABLE 23-2

Anatomy of an Interest Rate Swap

Antron's Payments: Borrows Floating, Swaps for Fixed		Bosworth's Payments: Borrows Fixed, Swaps for Floating	
Payment to lender	−(LIBOR + 1%)	Payment to lender	−10.40% fixed
Payment from Bosworth	+LIBOR	Payment from Antron	+8.95% fixed
Payment to Bosworth	−8.95% fixed	Payment to Antron	−LIBOR
Net payment by Antron	−9.95% fixed	Net payment by Bosworth	−(LIBOR + 1.45%)

© Cengage Learning 2014

FIGURE 23-2

The Antron/Bosworth Swap

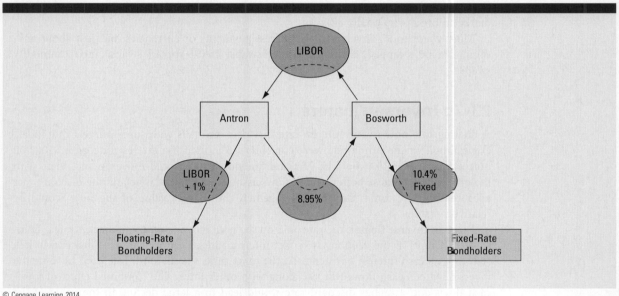

© Cengage Learning 2014

LIBOR + 1.45% versus the LIBOR + 1.50% it would have paid on directly issued floating-rate debt. As this example illustrates, swaps can sometimes lower the interest rate paid by each party.

Currency swaps are special types of interest rate swaps. To illustrate, suppose Company A, an American firm, had issued $100 million of dollar-denominated bonds in the United States to fund an investment in Germany. Meanwhile, Company G, a German firm, had issued $100 million of euro-denominated bonds in Germany to make an investment in the United States. Company A would earn euros but be required to make payments in dollars, and Company G would be in the opposite situation. Thus, both companies would be exposed to exchange rate risk. However, both companies' risks would be eliminated if they swapped payment obligations.

Originally, swaps were arranged between companies by money center banks, which would match up counterparties. Such matching still occurs, but today most swaps are between companies and banks, with the banks then taking steps to ensure that their own risks are hedged. For example, Citibank might arrange a swap with Company A. Company A would agree to make specified payments in euros to Citibank, while Citibank made dollar payments to Company A. Citibank would charge a fee for setting up the swap, and those charges would reflect the creditworthiness of Company A. To protect itself against exchange rate movements, the bank would hedge its position, either by lining up a European company that needed to make dollar payments or else by using currency futures.[20]

Major changes have occurred over time in the swaps market. First, standardized contracts have been developed for the most common types of swaps, which has had two effects: (1) Standardized contracts lower the time and effort involved in arranging swaps, and this lowers transactions costs. (2) The development of standardized contracts has led to a secondary market for swaps, which has increased the liquidity and efficiency of the swaps market. A number of international banks now make markets in swaps and offer quotes on several standard types. Also, as noted previously, the banks now take counterparty positions in swaps, so it is not necessary to find another firm with mirror-image needs before a swap transaction can be completed. The bank would generally find a final counterparty for the swap at a later date, so its positioning helps make the swap market more operationally efficient.

Most swaps today involve either interest payments or currencies, but just about anything can be swapped, including equity swaps, credit spread swaps, and commodity swaps.[21]

23-7c Inverse Floaters

A floating-rate note has an interest rate that rises and falls with some interest rate index. For example, if the prime rate were currently 8.5%, then the interest rate on a $100,000 note at prime plus 1% would be 9.5% and the note's rate would move up and down with the prime rate. Because both the cash flows associated with the note and the discount rate used to value it would rise and fall together, the market value of the note would be relatively stable.

With an **inverse floater**, the rate paid on the note moves *counter* to market rates. Thus, if interest rates in the economy rise, the interest rate paid on an inverse floater will fall, reducing its cash interest payments. At the same time, the discount rate used to value the inverse floater's cash flows will rise along with other rates. The combined effect of lower cash flows and a higher discount rate would lead to a large decline in the value of the inverse floater. Thus, inverse floaters are exceptionally vulnerable to increases in interest rates. Of course, if interest rates fall then the value of an inverse floater will soar.

Could an inverse floater be used for hedging purposes? The answer is "yes, perhaps quite effectively." These securities have a magnified effect, so not many are required to hedge a given position. However, because they are so volatile, they could make what is supposed to be a hedged position quite risky.

---

[20]For more information on swaps, see Keith C. Brown and Donald J. Smith, "Default Risk and Innovations in the Design of Interest Rate Swaps," *Financial Management,* Summer 1993, pp. 94–105; Robert Einzig and Bruce Lange, "Swaps at Transamerica: Applications and Analysis," *Journal of Applied Corporate Finance,* Winter 1990, pp. 48–58; John F. Marshall, Vipul K. Bansal, Anthony F. Herbst, and Alan L. Tucker, "Hedging Business Cycle Risk with Macro Swaps and Options," *Journal of Applied Corporate Finance,* Winter 1992, pp. 103–108; and Laurie S. Goodman, "The Uses of Interest Rate Swaps in Managing Corporate Liabilities," *Journal of Applied Corporate Finance,* Winter 1990, pp. 35–47.

[21]In an equity swap, the cash flow based on an equity index is swapped for some other cash flow. In a commodity swap, the swapped cash flow is based on commodity prices. In a credit swap, the cash flow usually is based on the spread between a risky bond and a U.S. Treasury bond.

SELF-TEST

Explain how a company can use Treasury bond futures to hedge against rising interest rates.

What is an interest rate swap? Describe the mechanics of a fixed-rate to floating-rate swap.

A Treasury bond futures contract is selling for 94′16. What is the implied annual yield? **(6.5%)**

Messman Corporation issues fixed-rate debt at a rate of 9.00%. Messman agrees to an interest rate swap in which it pays LIBOR to Moore Inc. and Moore pays 8.75% to Messman. What is Messman's resulting net payment? **(LIBOR + 0.25%)**

23-8 Project Selection Risks

A project is any corporate undertaking that uses corporate assets such as cash, factories, buildings, equipment, IT infrastructure, intellectual property, and people. A successful project creates value by generating a return that is commensurate with the size and risk of the assets invested in the project. Perhaps the most important factor for a company's success is its ability to select value-adding projects and avoid value-destroying projects.

23-8a Using Monte Carlo Simulation to Evaluate Project Risk

When evaluating a potential project, a company should assess the project qualitatively and quantitatively using the three-step approach we described in Chapters 10 and 11: (1) forecast the project's future cash flows, (2) estimate the value of the cash flows, and (3) analyze the risk of the cash flows.[22] Small projects, such as the replacement of a single machine, require less analysis than large projects, which include major capital expenditures, product line extensions, new products, geographic expansion, acquisitions, and mergers.

For larger projects, it is absolutely vital to conduct a thorough risk analysis, including sensitivity analysis and scenario analysis, as described in Chapter 11. Very large projects require even more risk analysis, including Monte Carlo simulation, which is widely used in enterprise risk management—you can't manage a risk very well if you can't measure it!

We repeat here some of the results from the simulation analysis in Chapter 11, and we include some new results. Recall that the analysis in Chapter 11 was for the application of a radically new liquid nano-coating technology to a new type of solar water heater module. We projected cash flows for the project, calculated NPV and other evaluation measures, performed a sensitivity analysis, and did a scenario analysis; see Section 11-2 for the basic analysis and Sections 11-5 and 11-6 for the sensitivity and scenario analyses.

We conducted a Monte Carlo simulation analysis in Section 11-7. Recall that in a simulation analysis, a probability distribution is assigned to each input variable—sales in units, the sales price, the variable cost per unit, and so on. The computer begins by picking a random value for each variable from its probability distribution. Those values are then entered into the model, the project's NPV (and any other measures) is calculated, and the NPV is stored in the computer's memory. This is called a trial. After completing the first

---

[22]Recall from Chapter 10 that cash flow evaluation methods include the net present value (NPV), the internal rate of return (IRR), the modified internal rate of return (MIRR), the profitability index (PI), the payback period, and the discounted payback period.

trial, a second set of input values is selected from the input variables' probability distributions, and a second NPV is calculated. This process is repeated until there are enough observations that the estimated NPV and any other outcome measures are stable.

We replicated the simulation analysis from Chapter 11 with 10,000 iterations; see *Ch23 Tool Kit.xls* and look in the worksheet *Simulation*. Figure 23-3 reports the estimated evaluation measures from Chapter 11 and some additional measures. The measures from Chapter 11 for NPV include its average, standard deviation, maximum, minimum, median, and the probability that the NPV will be positive. Based on these measures, the project has a positive expected NPV and will break even about 57% of the time.

In addition to the evaluation measures from Chapter 11, enterprise risk management systems often use another measure called **value at risk (VaR)**. Using the trials from the simulation analysis, the company specifies a threshold, such as the bottom 1% or 5% of

FIGURE 23-3

An Example of Monte Carlo Simulation Applied to Project Analysis (Thousands of Dollars)

	O	P	Q		R	S	T	U
165		**Number of Trials =**	**10,000**					
166		**Summary Statistics for**						
167		**Simulated Results**	**NPV**					
168		**Average**	$1,180			**NPV at 5th percentile**		−$6,616
169		**Standard deviation**	$5,182		**Average NPV below 5th percentile**			−$8,823
170		**Maximum**	$32,413			**NPV at 1st percentile**		−$10,043
171		**Minimum**	−$18,962		**Average NPV below 1st percentile**			−$11,945
172		**Median**	$831				**Skewness**	0.42
173		**Probability of NPV > 0**	57.1%					
174		**Coefficient of variation**	4.39					
175								
176								
177								
178		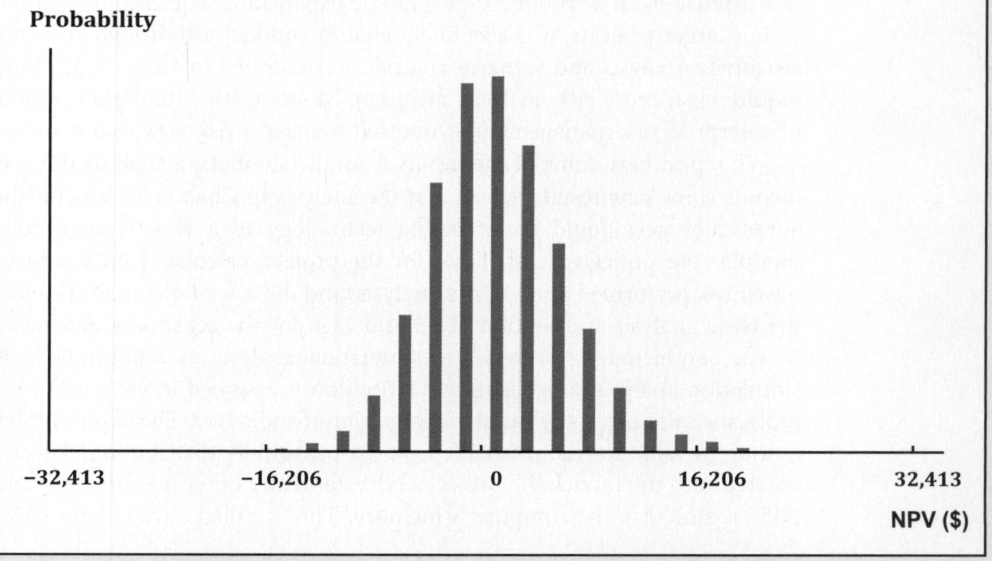 **Probability**						

	−32,413	−16,206	0	16,206	32,413

NPV ($)

outcomes. The basic idea is to measure the value of the project if things go badly. For example, Figure 23-3 shows that there is a 5% chance that the project will lose $6.6 million or more (the values are reported in thousands) and a 1% chance that the project will lose $10.0 million or more.

The VaR measures are helpful, but they don't measure the extent of possible losses if things go badly. A measure that many companies now apply is the **conditional value at risk (CVaR)**; it is also called the **expected shortfall**, the expected tail loss (ETL), and the average value at risk (AVaR). The CVaR measures the average NPV of all outcomes below the threshold—it is the average NPV conditional upon the NPV being less than the threshold value.[23] For example, the CVaR for the 1% threshold is −$11.9 million. The VaR shows that there is a 1% chance of losing more than $10.0 million, and CVaR shows that there is a 1% chance of an expected loss of $11.9 million. Notice that the VaR calculation is not affected by the size of the losses below the threshold—it just tells you size of the loss at the threshold percentile. In contrast, the CVaR takes into account the size of the losses below the threshold—it shows the expected loss if things go badly.

Many companies now are applying simulation when they analyze mergers and acquisition. In addition to the quantitative output from a simulation analysis, the process of identifying sources of risk can help companies avoid costly mistakes.

23-8b Using Monte Carlo Simulation to Evaluate Financing Risks

Companies use simulation for purposes other than project analysis. For example, the Danish maker of the popular plastic building-brick toys, the LEGO Group, also uses simulation in its budgeting process to show the possible outcomes. CFO Hans Læssøe reports that simulation analysis revealed that sales volatility has a much bigger impact than top managers previously understood.[24]

Simulation also is helpful when a company prepares a cash budget such as the one we described in Chapter 16. Rather than just showing the expected short-term financing requirements, simulation can show the probabilities of a larger financing requirement, allowing companies to plan for previously unexpected credit needs.

23-8c Using Monte Carlo Simulation to Evaluate Portfolio Risks

Many companies are exposed to portfolio risk, which is the risk that a portfolio of financial assets will decrease in value. For example, many companies offer pension plans to their employees. Defined benefit plans have a portfolio of stocks, bonds, and other financial assets that is used to support promised pension benefits to its employees. Such companies are exposed to significant portfolio risk—if the value of the pension assets portfolio drops too much relative to the value of the promised pension benefits, then the company will have to use its other resources to make additional contributions to the plan.

Most financial institutions are also exposed to portfolio risk because they own financial assets and have financial liabilities. Simulation is a widely used tool for measuring a bank's portfolio risk. In fact, the Basel II and III accords require banks to report their VaR and

---

[23]This definition is correct when applying CVaR to the outcomes from a Monte Carlo simulation because there is an equal probability of each outcome. It is a little more complicated to calculate CVaR from a given probability distribution than it is from the outcomes of a simulation.

[24]See the paper by Mark Frigo and Hans Læssøe cited in footnote 14.

the Basel Committee is presently (2012) considering requiring banks to also report the expected shortfall (the CVar).

When the trading and risk management groups at financial institutions use VaR (or CVaR), they usually measure it over a very short time horizon because they want to know how much they might lose overnight or within a couple of days.

SELF-TEST

What is Monte Carlo simulation?

What is value at risk, VaR? What is conditional value at risk, CVaR?

23-9 Managing Credit Risks

Nonfinancial companies are exposed to risk if they extend credit to their customers, and financial institutions are exposed to credit risk when they lend to their customers. Following are some key concepts in the management of credit risk.

23-9a Managing Credit Risk at Nonfinancial Companies

As we described in Chapter 16, when a company sells a product to a customer but does not require immediate payment, an account receivable is created. There are three primary tools that companies use to manage this credit risk.

First, a company evaluates its customers before extending credit. The company can do its own evaluation or purchase an evaluation from a third party. If the customer is an individual, credit evaluations are available from several companies, including as Equifax, Experian, and TransUnion. Each of these companies provides a numerical score, with the FICO score being the most widely used. The score ranges from 300 to 850, with lower scores indicating that the customer is more likely to default.

When the customer is another company, the evaluation is conducted using many of the same ratios and analyses we described in Chapter 3. In addition, some companies create their own credit scoring models based on past experience or statistical models (such as discriminate analysis).

A company can mitigate its credit risk by selling its accounts receivable to a third party in a process called factoring. Of course, the price a company receives from selling its receivables depends on the receivables' risk, with riskier receivables purchased for much less than their nominal value. A company can also buy insurance for some or all of its receivables. Many companies, including the LEGO Group, use simulation to estimate the risk of their receivables so that they can better negotiate with insurers.

23-9b Managing Credit Risk at Financial Institutions

WWW

See the Markit Group Limited's Web site for updates on CDS data. Free registration allows access to a variety of current data, including indexes: www .markit.com/en/.

In addition to the same techniques used at nonfinancial corporations (credit scoring models and simulation), many financial institutions use credit default swaps (CDS). Even though CDS are called swaps, they are like insurance. For example, an investor (which might be a financial institution) might purchase a CDS by making an annual payment to a counterparty to insure a particular bond or other security against default; if the bond defaults, the counterparty pays the purchaser the amount of the defaulted bond that was insured.

The CDS "price" is quoted in basis points and is called the CDS spread. For example, the spread on Telefonica SA, a large telecommunications company headquartered in Madrid, was about 480 basis points in July 2012. An easy way to interpret the reported basis point spread is that it would be the annual fee in dollars (or euros) to protect $10,000 (or euros) of the bond. Therefore, it would cost €480 per year to insure €10,000 of Telefonica's bonds.

To protect €10 million of Telefonica's debt, a buyer would pay €480,000 = 0.048(€10 million) per year. In contrast, the spread on Nestlé SA was only 36 basis points, so insuring €10 million of Nestlé's debt would cost only $36,000 per year. If the investors owned the bonds, then the purchase of the CDS would reduce the investor's risk.

There is an active secondary market for CDS and it is not necessary to own the underlying security. In fact, most participants in the CDS market don't own the underlying securities. For example, a speculator might purchase a CDS on Telefonica for 480 basis points but only purchase coverage for 1 month, which would be a payment of €40,000 = €480,000/12. Now suppose the Eurozone's problems immediately worsened and drove Telefonica's CDS spread up to 504 basis points. The investor could liquidate the position by selling 1-month credit protection for €42,000 = €504,000/12 and use the previously purchased CDS to offset the newly sold CDS. The investor's profit would be €2,000.

In addition to CDS for individual securities, there are CDS for indices. For example, the CDX.NA.IG is an index of 125 CDS for North American investment-grade debt. The index's movements are correlated with the overall level of default for many commercial loans—the index goes when default rates increase. Therefore, a U.S. bank can protect itself from increasing default rates in its loan portfolio by taking short positions in the CDX.NA.IG, which pay off if the index goes up. This is a situation in which the CDS help reduce a financial institution's risk.

Recall from the opening vignette that JPMorgan took *long* positions in a particular series of the CDX.NA.IG, which certainly wasn't to hedge its loan portfolios. JPMorgan explained that it was to hedge other derivatives that were hedging its loan portfolio, which sounds very complicated—no wonder it didn't work!

When banks and other major financial institutions take positions in swaps and CDS, they are themselves exposed to various risks, especially if their counterparties cannot meet their obligations. Furthermore, swaps are off–balance sheet transactions, making it impossible to tell just how large the swap market is or who has what obligation. Some estimate that the notional value of all CDS is over $25 trillion. As we write this in the summer of 2012, the SEC and the Commodity Futures Trading Commission (CFTC) were working on the implementation of provisions in Title VII of the 2010 Dodd-Frank Act to improve transparency in the swaps markets. In a major breakthrough, the SEC and the CFTC were able to agree on a definition for swaps. Perhaps by the time you read this even more progress will have been made.

Credit default swaps are traded on government debt as well as corporate debt. Before 2008, a CDS on a 5-year U.S. Treasury bond was trading at less than 7 basis points, which would be a $7 annual fee to protect $10,000 of the bond. The CDS price increased to almost 100 basis points in 2009, and is currently (July 2012) trading around 46 basis points. Figure 23-4 shows the prices for the U.S. and selected European countries, some which have adopted the euro (Germany, France, Italy, Spain, and Portugal) and some which have not. The extremely high prices for Eurozone debt indicate the problems facing these countries.

SELF-TEST

Describe some ways to manage credit risk at a nonfinancial company.

What are credit default swaps?

FIGURE 23-4

Credit Default Swap Spreads for Sovereign Debt (July 20, 2012)

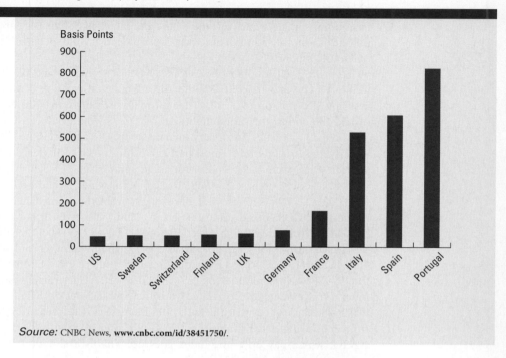

Source: CNBC News, **www.cnbc.com/id/38451750/.**

23-10 Risk and Human Safety

Risk management decisions, like all corporate decisions, should begin with a cost–benefit analysis for each feasible alternative. For example, suppose it would cost $50,000 per year to conduct a comprehensive fire safety training program for all personnel in a high-risk plant. Presumably, this program would reduce the expected value of future fire losses. An alternative to the training program would be to place $50,000 annually in a reserve fund set aside to cover future fire losses. Both alternatives involve expected cash flows, and from an economic standpoint the choice should be made on the basis of the lowest present value of future costs.

However, suppose a fire occurs and a life is lost. In situations involving safety and health, the trade-off between expected profits and expected losses is not sufficient for making sound decisions. Companies must always consider the impact their decisions have on the safety of their employees and customers. Ignoring safety and health is an ethical mistake, but it also is a business mistake because many companies have been forced out of business or suffered debilitating losses when they produced unsafe products.

SELF-TEST

Describe a situation in risk management that involves ethical as well as financial issues.

SUMMARY

The key concepts in enterprise risk management are listed below.

- **Enterprise risk management (ERM)** includes risk identification, risk assessment, and risk responses.
- A **derivative** is a security whose value is determined by the market price or interest rate of some other security.
- There are several reasons **risk management** might increase the value of a firm. Risk management allows corporations (1) to increase their **use of debt,** (2) to maintain their **capital budget** over time, (3) to avoid costs associated with **financial distress,** (4) to utilize their **comparative advantages in hedging** relative to the hedging ability of individual investors, (5) to reduce both the risks and costs of borrowing by using **swaps,** and (6) to reduce the **higher taxes** that result from fluctuating earnings. Managers may also want to stabilize earnings in order to boost their own compensation.
- Risk responses include: (1) avoiding the activity, (2) reducing the probability of occurrence of an adverse event, (3) reducing the magnitude of the loss associated with an adverse event, (4) transferring the risk to an insurance company, (5) transferring the function that produces the risk to a third party, (6) sharing the risk by purchasing a derivative contract.
- Major categories of risk include: (1) strategy and reputation, (2) control and compliance, (3) hazards, (4) human resources, (5) operation, (6) technology, and (7) financial management.
- Types of financial risk include: (1) foreign exchange risk, (2) commodity price risk, (3) interest rate risk, (4) project selection risk, (5) liquidity risk, (6) customer credit risk, and (7) portfolio risk.
- A **hedge** is a transaction that lowers risk. A **natural hedge** is a transaction between two **counterparties** whose risks are mirror images of each other.
- A **futures contract** is a standardized contract that is traded on an exchange and is marked-to-market daily, although physical delivery of the underlying asset usually does not occur.
- Under a **forward contract**, one party agrees to buy a commodity at a specific price and a specific future date and the other party agrees to make the sale; delivery does occur.
- A **swap** is an exchange of cash payment obligations. Swaps occur because the parties involved prefer the other's payment stream.
- **Financial futures** permit firms to create hedge positions to protect themselves against fluctuating interest rates, stock prices, and exchange rates.
- **Commodity futures** can be used to hedge against input price increases.
- **Long hedges** involve buying futures contracts to guard against price increases.
- **Short hedges** involve selling futures contracts to guard against price declines.
- **Symmetric hedges** protect against price increases and price decreases. Futures contracts are frequently used for symmetric hedges.
- **Asymmetric hedges** protect against price movements in one direction more than movements in another. Options are frequently used for asymmetric hedges.
- A **perfect hedge** occurs when the gain or loss on the hedged transaction exactly offsets the loss or gain on the unhedged position.

QUESTIONS

(23-1)   Define each of the following terms:

    a. Derivatives
    b. Enterprise risk management
    c. Financial futures; forward contract
    d. Hedging; natural hedge; long hedge; short hedge; perfect hedge; symmetric hedge; asymmetric hedge
    e. Swap; structured note
    f. Commodity futures

(23-2)   Give two reasons stockholders might be indifferent between owning the stock of a firm with volatile cash flows and that of a firm with stable cash flows.

(23-3)   List six reasons why risk management might increase the value of a firm.

(23-4)   Discuss some of the techniques available to reduce risk exposures.

(23-5)   Explain how the futures markets can be used to reduce interest rate risk and input price risk.

(23-6)   How can swaps be used to reduce the risks associated with debt contracts?

SELF-TEST PROBLEM   Solution Appears in Appendix A

(ST-1)

Hedging

It is now March, and the current cost of debt for Wansley Construction is 12%. Wansley plans to issue $5 million in 20-year bonds (with coupons paid semiannually) in September, but it's afraid that rates will climb even higher before then. The following data are available:

Futures Prices: Treasury Bonds—$100,000; Pts. 32nds of 100%

Delivery Month (1)	Open (2)	High (3)	Low (4)	Settle (5)	Change (6)
Mar	96'28	97'13	97'22	98'05	+7
June	98'03	98'03	97'13	97'25	+8
Sept	97'03	97'17	97'03	97'13	+8

a. What is the implied interest rate on the September contract?
b. Construct a hedge for Wansley.
c. Assume all interest rates rise by 1 percentage point. What is the dollar value of Wansley's increased cost of issuing debt? What is Wansley's gain from the futures contract?

PROBLEMS   Answers Appear in Appendix B

Easy Problems 1–2

(23-1)

Swaps

Zhao Automotive issues fixed-rate debt at a rate of 7.00%. Zhao agrees to an interest rate swap in which it pays LIBOR to Lee Financial and Lee pays 6.8% to Zhao. What is Zhao's resulting net payment?

(23-2)

Futures

A Treasury bond futures contract has a settlement price of 89'08. What is the implied annual yield?

(23-3)   What is the implied interest rate on a Treasury bond ($100,000) futures contract that
Futures   settled at 100'16? If interest rates increased by 1%, what would be the contract's new value?

(23-4)   Carter Enterprises can issue floating-rate debt at LIBOR + 2% or fixed-rate debt at 10%. Brence
Swaps   Manufacturing can issue floating-rate debt at LIBOR + 3.1% or fixed-rate debt at 11%. Suppose
Carter issues floating-rate debt and Brence issues fixed-rate debt. They are considering a swap
in which Carter makes a fixed-rate payment of 7.95% to Brence and Brence makes a payment
of LIBOR to Carter. What are the net payments of Carter and Brence if they engage in the
swap? Would Carter be better off if it issued fixed-rate debt or if it issued floating-rate debt and
engaged in the swap? Would Brence be better off if it issued floating-rate debt or if it issued
fixed-rate debt and engaged in the swap? Explain your answers.

Challenging
Problem 5

(23-5)   The Zinn Company plans to issue $10,000,000 of 20-year bonds in June to help finance a
Hedging   new research and development laboratory. The bonds will pay interest semiannually. It is
now November, and the current cost of debt to the high-risk biotech company is 11%.
However, the firm's financial manager is concerned that interest rates will climb even
higher in coming months. The following data are available:

Futures Prices: Treasury Bonds—$100,000; Pts. 32nds of 100%

Delivery Month (1)	Open (2)	High (3)	Low (4)	Settle (5)	Change (6)	Open Interest (7)
Dec	94'28	95'13	94'22	95'05	+0'07	591,944
Mar	96'03	96'03	95'13	95'25	+0'08	120,353
June	95'03	95'17	95'03	95'17	+0'08	13,597

a. Use the given data to create a hedge against rising interest rates.
b. Assume that interest rates in general increase by 200 basis points. How well did your
   hedge perform?
c. What is a perfect hedge? Are any real-world hedges perfect? Explain.

SPREADSHEET PROBLEM

(23-6)   Start with the partial model in the file *Ch23 P06 Build a Model.xls* on the textbook's Web
Build a Model: site. Use the information and data below.
Hedging   F. Pierce Products Inc. is financing a new manufacturing facility with the issue in
March of $20,000,000 of 20-year bonds with semiannual interest payments. It is now
October, and if Pierce were to issue the bonds now, the yield would be 10% because of
Pierce's high risk. Pierce's CFO is concerned that interest rates will climb even higher in
resource   coming months and is considering hedging the bond issue. The following data are available:

Futures Prices: Treasury Bonds—$100,000; Pts. 32nds of 100%

Delivery Month (1)	Open (2)	High (3)	Low (4)	Settle (5)	Change (6)	Open Interest (7)
Dec	93'28	94'13	93'22	94'05	+0'06	723,946
Mar	95'03	95'03	94'13	94'25	+0'07	97,254

a. Create a hedge with the futures contract for Pierce's planned March debt offering of $20 million using the March Treasury Bond futures contract. What is the implied yield on the bond underlying the futures contract?
b. Suppose that interest rates fall by 300 basis points. What are the dollar savings from issuing the debt at the new interest rate? What is the dollar change in value of the futures position? What is the total dollar value change of the hedged position?
c. Create a graph showing the effectiveness of the hedge if the change in interest rates, in basis points, is −300, −200, −100, 0, 100, 200, or 300. Show the dollar cost (or savings) from issuing the debt at the new interest rates, the dollar change in value of the futures position, and the total dollar value change.

MINI CASE

Assume you have just been hired as a financial analyst by Tennessee Sunshine Inc., a mid-sized Tennessee company that specializes in creating exotic sauces from imported fruits and vegetables. The firm's CEO, Bill Stooksbury, recently returned from an industry corporate executive conference in San Francisco, and one of the sessions he attended was on the pressing need for companies to institute enterprise risk management programs. Because no one at Tennessee Sunshine is familiar with the basics of enterprise risk management, Stooksbury has asked you to prepare a brief report that the firm's executives could use to gain at least a cursory understanding of the topics.

To begin, you gathered some outside materials on derivatives and risk management and used these materials to draft a list of pertinent questions that need to be answered. In fact, one possible approach to the paper is to use a question-and-answer format. Now that the questions have been drafted, you have to develop the answers.

a. Why might stockholders be indifferent to whether or not a firm reduces the volatility of its cash flows?
b. What are six reasons risk management might increase the value of a corporation?
c. What is COSO? How does COSO define enterprise risk management?
d. Describe the eight components of the COSO ERM framework.
e. Describe some of the risks events within the following major categories of risk: (1) strategy and reputation, (2) control and compliance, (3) hazards, (4) human resources, (5) operations, (6) technology, and (7) financial management.
f. What are some actions that companies can take to minimize or reduce risk exposures?
g. What are forward contracts? How can they be used to manage foreign exchange risk?
h. Describe how commodity futures markets can be used to reduce input price risk.
i. It is January, and Tennessee Sunshine is considering issuing $5 million in bonds in June to raise capital for an expansion. Currently, the firm can issue 20-year bonds with a 7% coupon (with interest paid semiannually), but interest rates are on the rise and Stooksbury is concerned that long-term interest rates might rise by as much as 1% before June. You looked online and found that June T-bond futures are trading at 111'25. What are the risks of not hedging, and how might TS hedge this exposure? In your analysis, consider what would happen if interest rates all increased by 1%.
j. What is a swap? Suppose two firms have different credit ratings. Firm Hi can borrow fixed at 11% and floating at LIBOR + 1%. Firm Lo can borrow fixed at 11.4% and floating at LIBOR + 1.5%. Describe a floating versus fixed interest rate swap between firms Hi and Lo in which Lo also makes a "side payment" of 45 basis points to Firm L.

© lulu/fotolia.com

Solutions to Self-Test Problems

CHAPTER 2

ST-1 a.

EBIT	$5,000,000
Interest	1,000,000
EBT	$4,000,000
Taxes (40%)	1,600,000
Net income	$2,400,000

b.
$$NCF = NI + DEP \text{ and } AMORT$$
$$= \$2,400,000 + \$1,000,000 = \$3,400,000$$

c.
$$NOPAT = EBIT(1 - T)$$
$$= \$5,000,000(0.6)$$
$$= \$3,000,000$$

d.
$$NOWC = \text{Operating current assets} - \text{Operating current liabilities}$$
$$= (\text{Cash} + \text{Accounts receivable} + \text{Inventory})$$
$$-(\text{Accounts payable} + \text{Accruals})$$
$$= \$14,000,000 - \$4,000,000$$
$$= \$10,000,000$$

$$\text{Total net operating capital} = NOWC + \text{Operating long-term assets}$$
$$= \$10,000,000 + \$15,000,000$$
$$= \$25,000,000$$

e.
$$FCF = NOPAT - \text{Net investment in operating capital}$$
$$= \$3,000,000 - (\$25,000,000 - \$24,000,000)$$
$$= \$2,000,000$$

f.
$$ROIC = NOPAT/\text{Total net operating capital})$$
$$= \$3,000,000/\$25,000,000$$
$$= 12\%$$

g.
$$EVA = NOPAT - (\text{Total net operating capital})(\text{After-tax cost of capital})$$
$$= \$5,000,000(0.6) - (\$25,000,000)(0.10)$$
$$= \$3,000,000 - \$2,500,000 = \$500,000$$

CHAPTER 3

ST-1 Argent has $120 million in debt. With $150 million in total liabilities and $210 million in total common equity, Argent has $150 + $210 = $360 million in total liabilities and equity. Therefore, Argent also has $360 million in total assets (because balance sheets must balance). Argent's debt-to-assets ratio is:

$$\text{Debt-to-assets} = \frac{\text{Total debt}}{\text{Total assets}} = \frac{\$120}{\$360} = 33.33\%$$

Argent's debt-to-equity ratio is:

$$\text{Debt-to-equity} = \frac{\text{Total debt}}{\text{Total common equity}}$$

$$= \frac{\$120}{\$210} = 57.14\%$$

ST-2   a.   In answering questions such as this, always begin by writing down the relevant definitional equations and then start filling in numbers. Note that the extra zeros indicating millions have been deleted in the calculations below.

(1)
$$\text{DSO} = \frac{\text{Accounts receivable}}{\text{Sales}/365}$$

$$40.55 = \frac{\text{AR}}{\text{Sales}/365}$$

$$\text{AR} = 40.55(\$2.7397) = \$111.1 \text{ million}$$

(2) $\text{Quick ratio} = \dfrac{\text{Current assets} - \text{Inventories}}{\text{Current liabilities}} = 2.0$

$$= \frac{\text{Cash and marketable securities} + \text{AR}}{\text{Current liabilities}} = 2.0$$

$$2.0 = \frac{\$100.0 + \$111.1}{\text{Current liabilities}}$$

$$\text{Current liabilities} = (\$100.0 + \$111.1)/2 = \$105.5 \text{ million}$$

(3) $\text{Current ratio} = \dfrac{\text{Current assets}}{\text{Current liabilities}} = 3.0$

$$= \frac{\text{Current assets}}{\$105.5} = 3.0$$

$$\text{Current assets} = 3.0(\$105.5) = \$316.50 \text{ million}$$

(4) $\text{Total assets} = \text{Current assets} + \text{Fixed assets}$

$$= \$316.5 + \$283.5 = \$600 \text{ million}$$

(5) $\text{ROA} = \text{Profit margin} \times \text{Total assets turnover}$

$$= \frac{\text{Net income}}{\text{Sales}} \times \frac{\text{Sales}}{\text{Total assets}}$$

$$= \frac{\$50}{\$1,000} \times \frac{\$1,000}{\$600}$$

$$= 0.05 \times 1.667 = 0.083333 = 8.3333\%$$

(6)
$$\text{ROE} = \text{ROA} \times \frac{\text{Assets}}{\text{Equity}}$$

$$12.0\% = 8.3333\% \times \frac{\$600}{\text{Equity}}$$

$$\text{Equity} = \frac{(8.3333\%)(\$600)}{12.0\%}$$

$$= \$416.67 \text{ million}$$

(7)   Total assets = Total claims = $600 million
Current liabilities + Long-term debt + Equity = $600 million
$105.5 + Long-term debt + $416.67 = $600 million
Long-term debt = $600 − $105.5 − $416.67 = $77.83 million

Note: We could also have found equity as follows:

$$\text{ROE} = \frac{\text{Net income}}{\text{Equity}}$$

$$12.0\% = \frac{\$50}{\text{Equity}}$$

$$\text{Equity} = \$50/0.12$$

$$= \$416.67 \text{ million}$$

Then we could have gone on to find long-term debt.

CHAPTER 4

ST-1   a. 0   8%   1   2   3   4
           |―――|―――|―――――――|―――――――|
              −1,000   FV = ?

$1,000 is being compounded for 3 years, so your balance at Year 4 is $1,259.71:

$$FV_N = PV(1 + I)^N = \$1,000(1 + 0.08)^3 = \$1,259.71$$

Alternatively, using a financial calculator, input N = 3, I/YR = 8, PV = −1000, and PMT = 0; then solve for FV = $1,259.71.

b. 0   2%   4   8   12   16
    |―+―+―+―+―+―+―+―+―+―+―+―+―|
        −1,000   FV = ?

There are 12 compounding periods from Quarter 4 to Quarter 16.

$$FV_N = PV\left(1 + \frac{I_{NOM}}{M}\right)^{NM} = FV_{12} = \$1,000(1.02)^{12} = \$1,268.24$$

Alternatively, using a financial calculator, input N = 12, I/YR = 2, PV = −1000, and PMT = 0; then solve for FV = $1,268.24.

c. 0   8%   1   2   3   4
    |―――|―――|―――――――|―――――――|
             250   250   250   250
                                           FV = ?

$$FVA_4 = \$250\left[\frac{(1 + 0.08)^4}{0.08} - \frac{1}{0.08}\right] = \$1,126.53$$

Using a financial calculator, input N = 4, I/YR = 8, PV = 0, and PMT = −250; then solve for FV = $1,126.53.

d. 0   8%   1   2   3   4
    |―――|―――|―――――――|―――――――|
              ?   ?   ?   ?
                                           FV = 1,259.71

$$\text{PMT}\left[\frac{(1 + 0.08)^4}{0.08} - \frac{1}{0.08}\right] = \$1,259.71$$

$$\text{PMT}(4.5061) = \$1,259.71$$

Using a financial calculator, input N = 4, I/YR = 8, PV = 0, and FV = 1259.71; then solve for PMT = −$279.56.

ST-2 a. Set up a time line like the one in the preceding problem:

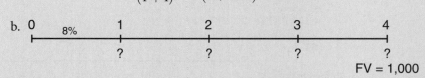

Note that your deposit will grow for 3 years at 8%. The deposit at Year 1 is the PV, and the FV is $1,000. Here is the solution:

$$N = 3, I/YR = 8, PMT = 0, FV = 1000; \text{ then } PV = 793.83.$$

Alternatively,

$$PV = \frac{FV_N}{(1+I)^N} = \frac{\$1,000}{(1+0.08)^3} = \$793.83$$

b.

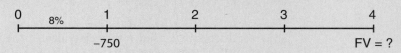

Here we are dealing with a 4-year annuity whose first payment occurs 1 year from today and whose future value must equal $1,000. Here is the solution: N = 4; I/YR = 8; PV = 0; FV = 1000; then PMT = $221.92. Alternatively,

$$PMT\left[\frac{(1+0.08)^4}{0.08} - \frac{1}{0.08}\right] = \$1,000$$
$$PMT(4.5061) = \$1,000$$
$$PMT = \$221.92$$

c. This problem can be approached in several ways. Perhaps the simplest is to ask this question: "If I received $750 1 year from now and deposited it to earn 8%, would I have the required $1,000 4 years from now?" The answer is "no":

```
0      8%    1           2           3           4
|------------+-----------+-----------+-----------|
           −750                              FV = ?
```

$$FV_3 = \$750(1.08)(1.08)(1.08) = \$944.78$$

This indicates that you should let your father make the payments rather than accept the lump sum of $750.

You could also compare the $750 with the PV of the payments:

```
0      8%    1           2           3           4
|------------+-----------+-----------+-----------|
          221.92       221.92      221.92      221.92
```

$$N = 4, I/YR = 8, PMT = -221.92, FV = 0; \text{ then } PV = 735.03.$$

Alternatively,

$$PVA_4 = \$221.92\left[\frac{1}{0.08} - \frac{1}{(0.08)(1+0.08)^4}\right] = \$735.03$$

This is less than the $750 lump sum offer, so your initial reaction might be to accept the lump sum of $750. However, it would be a mistake to do so. The problem is that, when you found the $735.03 PV of the annuity, you were finding the value of the annuity *today*. You were comparing $735.03 today with the lump sum of $750 in 1 year. This is, of course, invalid. What you should have done was take the $735.03, recognize that this is the PV of an annuity as of today, multiply $735.03 by 1.08 to get $793.83, and compare this $793.83 with the lump sum of $750. You would then take your father's offer to make the payments rather than take the lump sum 1 year from now.

d.

0	1	2	3	4
I = ?				
	−750			1,000

$N = 3, PV = -750, PMT = 0, FV = 1000$; then $I/YR = 10.0642\%$.

e.

0	1	2	3	4
I = ?				
	186.29	186.29	186.29	186.29
				FV = 1,000

$N = 4, PV = 0, PMT = -186.29, FV = 1000$; then $I/YR = 19.9997\%$.

You might be able to find a borrower willing to offer you a 20% interest rate, but there would be some risk involved—he or she might not actually pay you your $1,000!

f.

0 8%	1	2	3	4
	400	?	?	?
				FV = 1,000

Find the future value of the original $400 deposit:

$$FV_6 = PV(1 + I)^6 = 400(1 + 0.04)^6 = \$400(1.2653) = \$506.12.$$

This means that, at Year 4, you need an additional sum of $493.88: $1,000.00 − $506.12 = $493.88. This amount will be accumulated by making 6 equal payments that earn 8% compounded semiannually, or 4% each 6 months: $N = 6$, $I/YR = 4, PV = 0, FV = 493.88$; then $PMT = \$74.46$. Alternatively,

$$PMT\left[\frac{(1 + 0.04)^6}{0.04} - \frac{1}{0.04}\right] = \$493.88$$

$$PMT(6.6330) = \$493.88$$

$$PMT = \$74.46$$

g.

$$EFF\% = \left(1 + \frac{I_{NOM}}{M}\right)^M - 1.0$$

$$= \left(1 + \frac{0.08}{2}\right)^2 - 1.0$$

$$= 1.0816 - 1 = 0.0816 = 8.16\%$$

ST-3   Bank A's effective annual rate is 8.24%:

$$EFF\% = \left(1 + \frac{0.08}{4}\right)^4 - 1.0$$

$$= 1.0824 - 1 = 0.0824 = 8.24\%$$

Now Bank B must have the same effective annual rate:

$$\left(1+\frac{I}{12}\right)^{12}-1.0 = 0.0824$$

$$\left(1+\frac{I}{12}\right)^{12} = 1.0824$$

$$1+\frac{I}{12} = (1.0824)^{1/12}$$

$$1+\frac{I}{12} = 1.00662$$

$$\frac{I}{12} = 0.00662$$

$$I = 0.07944 = 7.94\%$$

Thus, the two banks have different quoted rates—Bank A's quoted rate is 8%, whereas Bank B's quoted rate is 7.94%—yet both banks have the same effective annual rate of 8.24%. The difference in their quoted rates is due to the difference in compounding frequency.

CHAPTER 5

ST-1 a. Pennington's bonds were sold at par; therefore, the original YTM equaled the coupon rate of 12%.

b.

$$V_B = \sum_{t=1}^{50}\frac{\$120/2}{\left(1+\frac{0.10}{2}\right)^t} + \frac{\$1,000}{\left(1+\frac{1.10}{2}\right)^{50}}$$

$$= \$60\left[\frac{1}{0.05}-\frac{1}{0.05(1+0.05)^{50}}\right] + \frac{\$1,000}{(1+0.05)^{50}}$$

$$= \$1,182.56$$

Alternatively, with a financial calculator, input the following: N = 50, I/YR = 5, PMT = 60, and FV = 1000; solve for PV = – $1,182.56.

c.
$$\text{Current yield} = \text{Annual coupon payment} \div \text{Price}$$
$$= \$120/\$1,182.56$$
$$= 0.1015 = 10.15\%$$
$$\text{Capital gains yield} = \text{Total yield} - \text{Current yield}$$
$$= 10\% - 10.15\% = -0.15\%$$
$$\text{Total yield} = \text{Current yield} + \text{Capital gains yield}$$
$$= 10.15\% + (-0.15\%) = 10.00\%$$

d.
$$\$916.42 = \sum_{t=1}^{13}\frac{\$60}{(1+r_d/2)^t} + \frac{\$1000}{(1+r_d/2)^{13}}$$

With a financial calculator, input the following: N = 13, PV = –916.42, PMT = 60, and FV = 1000; then solve for = I/YR = r_d/2 = 7.00%. Therefore, r_d = 14.00%.

$$\text{Current yield} = \$120/\$916.42 = 13.09\%$$
$$\text{Capital gains yield} = 14\% - 13.09\% = \underline{0.91\%}$$
$$\text{Total yield} = 14.00\%$$

e. The following time line illustrates the years to maturity of the bond:

1/1/13   6/30/13   12/31/13   6/30/14   12/31/14   12/31/19

3/1/13

Thus, on March 1, 2013, there were 13⅔ periods left before the bond matured. Bond traders actually use the following procedure to determine the price of the bond.

(1) Find the price of the bond immediately after the next coupon is paid on June 30, 2013:

$$V_B = \$60\left[\frac{1}{0.0775} - \frac{1}{0.0775(1 + 0.0775)^{13}}\right] + \frac{\$1,000}{(1 + 0.0775)^{13}}$$

$$= \$859.76$$

Using a financial calculator, input N = 13, I/YR = 7.75, PMT = 60, and FV = 1000; then solve for PV = −$859.76.

(2) Add the coupon, $60, to the bond price to get the total value, TV, of the bond on the next interest payment date: TV = $859.76 + $60.00 = $919.76.

(3) Discount this total value back to the purchase date:

$$\text{Value at purchase date (March 1, 2013)} = \frac{\$919.76}{(1 + 0.0775)^{(4/6)}}$$

$$= \$875.11$$

Using a financial calculator, input N = 4/6, I/YR = 7.75, PMT = 0, and FV = 919.76; then solve for PV = $875.11.

(4) Therefore, you would have written a check for $875.11 to complete the transaction. Of this amount, $20 = (⅓)($60) would represent accrued interest and $855.11 would represent the bond's basic value. This breakdown would affect both your taxes and those of the seller.

(5) This problem could be solved *very* easily using a spreadsheet or a financial calculator with a bond valuation function.

CHAPTER 6

ST-1 a. The average rate of return for each stock is calculated simply by averaging the returns over the 5-year period. The average return for Stock A is

$$\bar{r}_{\text{Avg A}} = (-18\% + 44\% - 22\% + 22\% + 34\%)/5$$

$$= 12\%$$

The realized rate of return on a portfolio made up of Stock A and Stock B would be calculated by finding the average return in each year as

$$\bar{r}_{A,t}(\% \text{ of Stock A}) + \bar{r}_{B,t}(\% \text{ of Stock B})$$

Then average these annual returns:

Year	Portfolio AB's Return, $\bar{r}_{AB}$
2009	−21%
2010	34
2011	−13
2012	15
2013	45
	$\bar{r}_{\text{Avg AB}} = 12\%$

b. The standard deviation of returns is estimated as follows:

$$\text{Estimated } \sigma = S = \sqrt{\dfrac{\sum\limits_{t=1}^{T}(\bar{r}_t - \bar{r}_{Avg})^2}{T-1}}$$

For Stock A, the estimated σ is about 30%:

$$\sigma_A = \sqrt{\dfrac{\begin{array}{c}(-0.18-0.12)^2+(0.44-0.12)^2+(-0.22-0.12)^2+\\(0.22-0.12)^2+(0.34-0.12)^2\end{array}}{5-1}}$$

$$= 0.30265 \approx 30\%$$

The standard deviations of returns for Stock B and for the portfolio are similarly determined, and they are as follows:

	Stock A	Stock B	Portfolio AB
Standard deviation	30%	30%	29%

c. Because the risk reduction from diversification is small (σ_{AB} falls only from 30% to 29%), the most likely value of the correlation coefficient is 0.8. If the correlation coefficient were −0.8, then the risk reduction would be much larger. In fact, the correlation coefficient between Stocks A and B is 0.8.

d. If more randomly selected stocks were added to a portfolio, σ_P would decline to somewhere in the vicinity of 20%. The value of σ_P would remain constant only if the correlation coefficient were +1.0, which is most unlikely. The value of σ_P would decline to zero only if $\rho = -1.0$ for some pair of stocks or some pair of portfolios.

ST-2 a. $b = (0.6)(0.70) + (0.25)(0.90) + (0.1)(1.30) + (0.05)(1.50)$

$= 0.42 + 0.225 + 0.13 + 0.075 = 0.85$

b. $r_{RF} = 6\%;\ RP_M = 5\%;\ b = 0.85$

$r_p = 6\% + (5\%)(0.85)$

$= 10.25\%$

c. $b_N = (0.5)(0.70) + (0.25)(0.90) + (0.1)(1.30) + (0.15)(1.50)$

$= 0.35 + 0.225 + 0.13 + 0.225$

$= 0.93$

$r = 6\% + (5\%)(0.93)$
$= 10.65\%$

CHAPTER 7

ST-1 The first step is to solve for g, the unknown variable, in the constant growth equation. Because D_1 is unknown but D_0 is known, substitute $D_0(1+g)$ as follows:

$$\hat{P}_0 = P_0 = \dfrac{D_1}{r_s - g} = \dfrac{D_0(1+g)}{r_s - g}$$

$$\$36 = \dfrac{\$2.40(1+g)}{0.12 - g}.$$

Solving for g, we find the growth rate to be 5%:

$$\$4.32 - \$36g = \$2.40 + \$2.40g$$
$$\$38.4g = \$1.92$$
$$g = 0.05 = 5\%$$

The next step is to use the growth rate to project the stock price 5 years hence:

$$\hat{P}_5 = \frac{D_0(1+g)^6}{r_s - g}$$
$$= \frac{\$2.40(1.05)^6}{0.12 - 0.05}$$
$$= \$45.95$$

(Alternatively, $\hat{P}_5 = \$36(1.05)^5 = \$45.95$.) Therefore, Ewald Company's expected stock price 5 years from now, $\hat{P}_5$, is \$45.95.

ST-2   a.   (1) Calculate the PV of the dividends paid during the supernormal growth period:

$$D_1 = \$1.1500(1.15) = \$1.3225$$
$$D_2 = \$1.3225(1.15) = \$1.5209$$
$$D_3 = \$1.5209(1.13) = \$1.7186$$

$$\text{PV of Div} = \$1.3225/(1.12) + \$1.5209/(1.12)^2 + \$1.7186/(1.12)^3$$
$$= \$3.6167 \approx \$3.62$$

(2) Find the PV of Snyder's stock price at the end of Year 3:

$$\hat{P}_3 = \frac{D_4}{r_s - g} = \frac{D_3(1+g)}{r_s - g}$$
$$= \frac{\$1.7186(1.06)}{0.12 - 0.06}$$
$$= \$30.36$$
$$\text{PV of } \hat{P}_3 = \$30.36/(1.12)^3 = \$21.61$$

(3) Sum the two components to find the value of the stock today:

$$\hat{P}_0 = \$3.62 + \$21.61 = \$25.23$$

Alternatively, the cash flows can be placed on a time line as follows:

Enter the cash flows into the cash flow register (CF$_0$ = 0, CF$_1$ = 1.3225, CF$_2$ = 1.5209, CF$_3$ = 32.0803) and I/YR = 12; then press the NPV key to obtain $\hat{P}_0$ = \$25.23.

b. $\hat{P}_1 = \$1.5209/(1.12) + \$1.7186/(1.12)^2 + \$30.36/(1.12)^2$

$= \$26.9311 \approx \$26.93$

(Calculator solution: \$26.93.)

$\hat{P}_2 = \$1.7186/(1.12) + \$30.36/(1.12)$

$= \$28.6429 \approx \$28.64$

(Calculator solution: \$28.64.)

Year	Dividend Yield	+	Capital Gains Yield	=	Total Return
1	$\dfrac{\$1.3225}{\$25.23} \approx 5.24\%$	+	$\dfrac{\$26.93 - \$25.23}{\$25.23} \approx 6.74\%$	$\approx$	12%
2	$\dfrac{\$1.5209}{\$26.93} \approx 5.65\%$	+	$\dfrac{\$28.64 - \$26.93}{\$26.93} \approx 6.35\%$	$\approx$	12%
3	$\dfrac{\$1.7186}{\$28.64} \approx 6.00\%$	+	$\dfrac{\$30.36 - \$28.64}{\$28.64} \approx 6.00\%$	$\approx$	12%

ST-3   a. $V_{op} = \dfrac{FCF(1+g)}{WACC - g} = \dfrac{\$100,000(1 + 0.07)}{0.11 - 0.07} = \$2,675,000$

b.   Total value = Value of operations + Value of nonoperating assets

$= \$2,675,000 + \$325,000 = \$3,000,000$

c.   Value of equity = Total value − Value of debt

$= \$3,000,000 - \$1,000,000 = \$2,000,000$

d.   Price per share = Value of equity ÷ Number of shares

$= \$2,000,000/50,000 = \$40$

CHAPTER 8

ST-1   The option will pay off \$60 − \$42 = \$18 if the stock price is up. The option pays off nothing (\$0) if the stock price is down. Find the number of shares in the hedge portfolio:

$$N = \frac{C_u - C_d}{P_u - P_d} = \frac{\$18 - \$0}{\$60 - \$30} = 0.60$$

With 0.6 shares, the stock's payoff will be either 0.6(\$60) = \$36 or 0.6(\$30) = \$18. The portfolio's payoff will be \$36 − \$18 = \$18, or \$18 − 0 = \$18.

The present value of \$18 at the daily compounded risk-free rate is PV = \$18 / $[1 + (0.05/365)]^{365}$ = \$17.12. Or use a financial calculator and enter N = 365, I/YR = 5/365, PMT = 0, and FV = −18; solve for PV = 17.12. The option price is the current value of the stock in the portfolio minus the PV of the payoff:

$$V = 0.6(\$40) - \$17.12 = \$6.88$$

ST-2

$$d_1 = \frac{\ln(P/X) + [r_{RF} + (\sigma^2/2)]t}{\sigma\sqrt{t}} :$$

$$= \frac{\ln(\$22/\$20) + [0.05 + (0.49/2)](0.5)}{0.7\sqrt{0.5}}$$

$$= 0.4906$$

$$d_2 = d_1 - \sigma(t)^{0.5} = 0.4906 - 0.7(0.5)^{0.5} = -0.0044$$

$N(d_1) = 0.6881$ (from *Excel* NORMSDIST function)

$N(d_2) = 0.4982$ (from *Excel* NORMSDIST function)

$$V = P[N(d_1)] - Xe^{-r_{RF}t}[N(d_2)]$$

$$= \$22(0.6881) - \$20e^{(-0.05)(0.5)}(0.4982)$$

$$= \$5.42$$

CHAPTER 9

ST-1 a. Component costs are as follows:
- **Debt at r_d = 9%:**

$$r_d(1 - T) = 9\%(0.6) = 5.4\%$$

- **Preferred with F = 5%:**

$$r_{ps} = \frac{\text{Preferred dividend}}{P_{ps}(1 - F)} = \frac{\$9}{\$100(0.95)} = 9.5\%.$$

- **Common with DCF:**

$$r_s = \frac{D_1}{P_0} + g = \frac{\$3.922}{\$60} + 6\% = 12.5\%.$$

- **Common with CAPM:**

$$r_s = 6\% + 1.3(5\%) = 12.5\%$$

b. $WACC = w_d r_d(1 - T) + w_{ps} r_{ps} + w_s r_s$

$$= 0.25(9\%)(1 - T) + 0.15(9.5\%) + 0.60(12.5\%)$$

$$= 10.275\%$$

CHAPTER 10

ST-1 a. **Payback:**

To determine the payback, construct the cumulative cash flows for each project as follows.

	Cumulative Cash Flows	
Year	Project X	Project Y
0	−$10,000	−$10,000
1	−3,500	−6,500
2	−500	−3,000
3	2,500	500
4	3,500	4,000

$$\text{Payback}_X = 2 + \frac{\$500}{\$3,000} = 2.17 \text{years}$$

$$\text{Payback}_Y = 2 + \frac{\$3,000}{\$3,500} = 2.86 \text{years}$$

Net present value (NPV):

$$\text{NPV}_X = -\$10,000 + \frac{\$6,500}{(1.12)^1} + \frac{\$3,000}{(1.12)^2} + \frac{\$3,000}{(1.12)^3} + \frac{\$1,000}{(1.12)^4} = \$966.01$$

$$\text{NPV}_Y = -\$10,000 + \frac{\$3,500}{(1.12)^1} + \frac{\$3,500}{(1.12)^2} + \frac{\$3,500}{(1.12)^3} + \frac{\$3,500}{(1.12)^4} = \$630.72$$

Alternatively, using a financial calculator, input the cash flows into the cash flow register, enter I/YR = 12, and then press the NPV key to obtain $\text{NPV}_X = \$966.01$ and $\text{NPV}_Y = \$630.72$.

Internal rate of return (IRR):
To solve for each project's IRR, find the discount rates that equate each NPV to zero:

$$\text{IRR}_X = 18.0\%$$

$$\text{IRR}_Y = 15.0\%$$

Modified Internal Rate of Return (MIRR):

To obtain each project's MIRR, begin by finding each project's terminal value (TV) of cash inflows:

$$\text{TV}_X = \$6,500(1.12)^3 + \$3,000(1.12)^2 + \$3,000(1.12)^1 + \$1,000 = \$17,255.23$$

$$\text{TV}_Y = \$3,500(1.12)^3 + \$3,500(1.12)^2 + \$3,500(1.12)^1 + \$3,500 = \$16,727.65$$

Now, each project's MIRR is the discount rate that equates the PV of the TV to each project's cost, $10,000:

$$\text{MIRR}_X = 14.61\%$$

$$\text{MIRR}_Y = 13.73\%$$

Profitability index (PI):
To obtain each project's PI, divide its present value of future cash flows by its initial cost. The PV of future cash flows can be found from the NPV calculated earlier:

$$\text{PV}_X = \text{NPV}_X + \text{Cost of X} = \$966.01 + \$10,000 = \$10,966.01$$

$$\text{PV}_Y = \text{NPV}_Y + \text{Cost of Y} = \$630.72 + \$10,000 = \$10,630.72$$

$$\text{PI}_X = \text{PV}_X / \text{Cost of X} = \$10,966.01 / \$10,000 = 1.097$$

$$\text{PI}_Y = \text{PV}_Y / \text{Cost of Y} = \$10,630.72 / \$10,000 = 1.063$$

b.   The following table summarizes the project rankings by each method:

	Project That Ranks Higher
Payback	X
NPV	X
IRR	X
MIRR	X

Note that all methods rank Project X over Project Y. Because both projects are acceptable under the NPV, IRR, and MIRR criteria, both should be accepted if they are independent.

c. In this case, we would choose the project with the higher NPV at r = 12%, or Project X.

d. To determine the effects of changing the cost of capital, plot the NPV profiles of each project. The crossover rate occurs at about 6% to 7% (6.2%). See the graph below.

If the firm's cost of capital is less than 6.2%, then a conflict exists because $NPV_Y > NPV_X$ but $IRR_X > IRR_Y$. Therefore, if r were 5% then a conflict would exist. Note, however, that when r = 5.0% we have $MIRR_X = 10.64\%$ and $MIRR_Y = 10.83\%$; hence, the modified IRR ranks the projects correctly even if r is to the left of the crossover point.

e. The conflict in decision rules for the NPV and IRR criteria is due to the differences in the timing patterns of the projects' cash flows. Notice that Y's cash flows are bigger than X's in the latter years. Because the present value of a long-term cash flow falls more than the present value of a short-term cash flow if the cost of capital increases, Y has a relatively high NPV when the cost of capital is low, but a relatively low NPV when the cost of capital is high.

NPV Profiles for Projects X and Y

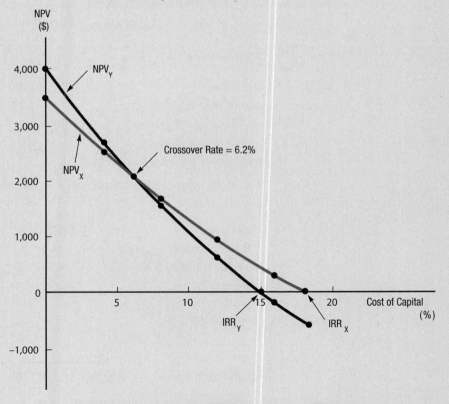

Cost of Capital	NPV$_X$	NPV$_Y$
0%	$3,500	
4	2,545	
8	1,707	
12	966	
16	307	

CHAPTER 11

ST-1   a. **Estimated Investment Requirements:**

Price	−$50,000
Modification	−10,000
Change in net working capital	−2,000
Total investment	−$62,000

      b. **Operating Cash Flows:**

	Year 1	Year 2	Year 3
1. After-tax cost savings[a]	$12,000	$12,000	$12,000
2. Depreciation[b]	19,998	26,670	8,886
3. Depreciation tax savings[c]	7,999	10,668	3,554
Operating cash flow (1 + 3)	$19,999	$22,668	$15,554

[a]$20,000(1 − T).

[b]Depreciable basis = $60,000; the MACRS percentage allowances are 0.3333, 0.4445, and 0.1481 in Years 1, 2, and 3, respectively; hence, depreciation in Year 1 = 0.3333($60,000) = $19,998, Year 2 = 0.4445 ($60,000) = $26,670, and Year 3 = 0.1481 ($60,000) = $8,886. There will remain $4,446, or 7.41%, undepreciated after Year 3; it would normally be taken in Year 4.

[c]Depreciation tax savings = T(Depreciation) = 0.4($19,998) = $7,999.2 in Year 1, and so forth.

      c. **Termination Cash Flow:**

Salvage value	$20,000
Tax on salvage value[a]	−6,222
Net working capital recovery	2,000
Termination cash flow	$15,778

[a]Calculation of tax on salvage value:

$$\text{Book value} = \text{Depreciation basis} - \text{Accumulated depreciation}$$
$$= \$60,000 - \$55,554 = \$4,446$$

Sales price	$20,000
Less book value	4,446
Taxable income	$15,554
Tax at 40%	$ 6,222

ST-2   d. **Project NPV:**

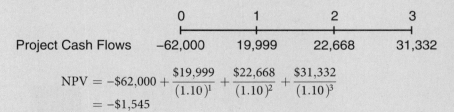

	0	1	2	3
Project Cash Flows	−62,000	19,999	22,668	31,332

$$NPV = -\$62,000 + \frac{\$19,999}{(1.10)^1} + \frac{\$22,668}{(1.10)^2} + \frac{\$31,332}{(1.10)^3}$$
$$= -\$1,545$$

Alternatively, using a financial calculator, input the cash flows into the cash flow register, enter I/YR = 10, and then press the NPV key to obtain

NPV = -$1,545. Because the earth mover has a negative NPV, it should not be purchased. We rounded all cash flows to integers. If you use *Excel* and do not round, you should get $1,544.23.

ST-2   a.   First, find the expected cash flows:

Year	Expected Cash Flows				
0	0.2(-$100,000)	+ 0.6(-$100,000)	+ 0.2(-$100,000)	=	-$100,000
1	0.2($20,000)	+ 0.6($30,000)	+ 0.2($40,000)	=	$ 30,000
2	0.2($20,000)	+ 0.6($30,000)	+ 0.2($40,000)	=	$ 30,000
3	0.2($20,000)	+ 0.6($30,000)	+ 0.2($40,000)	=	$ 30,000
4	0.2($20,000)	+ 0.6($30,000)	+ 0.2($40,000)	=	$ 30,000
5	0.2($20,000)	+ 0.6($30,000)	+ 0.2($40,000)	=	$ 30,000
5*	0.2($0)	+ 0.6($20,000)	+ 0.2($30,000)	=	$ 18,000

```
0        1        2        3        4        5
|--10%---+--------+--------+--------+--------+
-$100,000  30,000   30,000   30,000   30,000   48,000
```

Next, determine the NPV based on the expected cash flows:

$$NPV = -\$100,000 + \frac{\$30,000}{(1.10)^1} + \frac{\$30,000}{(1.10)^2} + \frac{\$30,000}{(1.10)^3}$$

$$+ \frac{\$30,000}{(1.10)^4} + \frac{\$48,000}{(1.10)^5} = \$24,900$$

Alternatively, using a financial calculator, input the cash flows in the cash flow register, enter I/YR = 10, and then press the NPV key to obtain NPV = $24,900.

b.   For the worst case, the cash flow values from the cash flow column farthest on the left are used to calculate NPV:

```
0        1        2        3        4        5
|--10%---+--------+--------+--------+--------+
-$100,000  20,000   20,000   20,000   20,000   20,000
```

$$NPV = -\$100,000 + \frac{\$20,000}{(1.10)^1} + \frac{\$20,000}{(1.10)^2} + \frac{\$20,000}{(1.10)^3}$$

$$+ \frac{\$20,000}{(1.10)^4} + \frac{\$20,000}{(1.10)^5} = -\$24,184$$

Similarly, for the best case, use the values from the column farthest on the right. Here the NPV is $70,259.

If the cash flows are perfectly dependent, then the low cash flow in the first year will mean a low cash flow in every year. Thus, the probability of the worst case occurring is the probability of getting the $20,000 net cash flow in Year 1, or 20%. If the cash flows are independent, then the cash flow in each year can be low, high, or average and so the probability of getting all low cash flows will be

$$(0.2)(0.2)(0.2)(0.2)(0.2) = 0.2^5 = 0.00032 = 0.032\%$$

c. The base-case NPV is found using the most likely cash flows and is equal to $26,142. This value differs from the expected NPV of $24,900 because the Year-5 cash flows are not symmetric. Under these conditions, the NPV distribution is as follows:

P	NPV
0.2	-$24,184
0.6	26,142
0.2	70,259

Thus, the expected NPV is 0.2(-$24,184) + 0.6($26,142) + 0.2($70,259) = $24,900. As is always the case, the expected NPV is the same as the NPV of the expected cash flows found in part a. The standard deviation is $29,904:

$$\sigma_{NPV}^2 = 0.2(-\$24,184 - \$24,900)^2 + 0.6(\$26,142 - \$24,900)^2$$
$$+0.2(\$70,259 - \$24,900)^2$$
$$= \$894,261,126$$
$$\sigma_{NPV} = \sqrt{\$894,261,126} = \$29,904.$$

The coefficient of variation, CV, is $29,904/$24,900 = 1.20.

CHAPTER 12

ST-1 To solve this problem, we first define ΔS as the change in sales and g as the growth rate in sales. Then we use the three following equations:

$$\Delta S = S_0 g$$
$$S_1 = S_0(1 + g)$$
$$AFN = (A^*/S_0)(\Delta S) - (L^*/S_0)(\Delta S) - MS_1(1 - \text{Payout ratio})$$

Set AFN = 0; substitute in known values for A^*/S_0, L^*/S_0, M, d, and S_0, and then solve for g:

$$0 = 1.6(\$100g) - 0.4(\$100g) - 0.10[\$100(1 + g)](0.55)$$
$$= \$160g - \$40g - 0.055(\$100 + \$100g)$$
$$= \$160g - \$40g - \$5.5 - \$5.5g$$
$$\$114.5g = \$5.5$$
$$g = \$5.5/\$114.5 = 0.048 = 4.8\%$$
$$= \text{Maximum growth rate without external financing}$$

ST-2 Assets consist of cash, marketable securities, receivables, inventories, and fixed assets. Therefore, we can break the A^*/S_0 ratio into its components—cash/sales, inventories/sales, and so forth. Then,

$$\frac{A^*}{S_0} = \frac{A^* - \text{Inventories}}{S_0} + \frac{\text{Inventories}}{S_0} = 1.6$$

We know that the inventory turnover ratio is sales/inventories = 3 times, so inventories/sales = 1/3 = 0.3333. Further, if the inventory turnover ratio can be increased to 4 times, then the inventory/sales ratio will fall to 1/4 = 0.25, a difference of 0.3333 − 0.2500 = 0.0833. This, in turn, causes the A^*/S_0 ratio to fall from A^*/S_0 = 1.6 to A^*/S_0 = 1.6 − 0.0833 = 1.5167. This change has two effects: First, it changes the AFN equation, and second, it means that Barnsdale currently has excessive inventories. Because it is costly to hold excess inventories, Barnsdale will want to reduce its inventory holdings by not replacing inventories until the excess amounts have been used. We can account for this by setting up the revised AFN equation (using the new A^*/S_0 ratio), estimating the funds that will be needed next year if no excess inventories are currently on hand, and then subtracting out the excess inventories that are currently on hand:

Present Conditions:

$$\frac{\text{Sales}}{\text{Inventories}} = \frac{\$100}{\text{Inventories}} = 3$$

so

$$\text{Inventories} = \$100/3 = \$33.3 \text{ million at present}$$

New Conditions:

$$\frac{\text{Sales}}{\text{Inventories}} = \frac{\$100}{\text{Inventories}} = 4$$

so

$$\text{New level of inventories} = \$100/4 = \$25 \text{ million}$$

Therefore,

$$\text{Excess inventories} = \$33.3 - \$25 = \$8.3 \text{ million}$$

Forecast of Funds Needed, First Year:

$$\Delta S \text{ in first year} = 0.2(\$100 \text{ million}) = \$20 \text{ million}$$
$$\text{AFN} = 1.5167(\$20) - 0.4(\$20) - 0.1(0.55)(\$120) - \$8.3$$
$$= \$30.3 - \$8 - \$6.6 - \$8.3$$
$$= \$7.4 \text{ million}$$

- **Forecast of Funds Needed, Second Year:**

$$\Delta S \text{ in second year} = gS_1 = 0.2(\$120 \text{ million}) = \$24 \text{ million}$$
$$\text{AFN} = 1.5167(\$24) - 0.4(\$24) - 0.1(0.55)(\$144)$$
$$= \$36.4 - \$9.6 - \$7.9$$
$$= \$18.9 \text{ million}$$

ST-3 a. Full capacity sales $= \dfrac{\text{Current sales}}{\substack{\text{Percentage of capacity at which} \\ \text{FA were operated}}} = \dfrac{\$36,000}{0.75} = \$48,000$

Percentage increase $= \dfrac{\text{New sales} - \text{Old sales}}{\text{Old sales}} = \dfrac{\$48,000 - \$36,000}{\$36,000} = 0.33$

$$= 33\%$$

Therefore, sales could expand by 33% before Van Auken Lumber would need to add fixed assets.

b. Van Auken Lumber: Projected Income Statement for December 31, 2014 (Thousands of Dollars)

	2013	Forecast Basis	2014
Sales	$36,000	$1.25(Sales_{13})$	$ 45,000
Operating costs	30,783	$85.508\%(Sales_{14})$	38,479
EBIT	$ 5,217		$ 6,521
Interest	717	$12\%(Debt_{13})$	1,017
EBT	$ 4,500		$ 5,504
Taxes (40%)	1,800		2,202
Net income	$ 2,700		$ 3,302
Dividends (60%)	$ 1,620		$ 1,981
Additions to RE	$ 1,080		$ 1,321

Van Auken Lumber: Projected Balance Sheet for December 31, 2014 (Thousands of Dollars)

	2013	Percent of 2014 Sales	Additions	2014	LOC	2014 after AFN
Cash	$ 1,800	5%		$ 2,250		$ 2,250
Receivables	10,800	30		13,500		13,500
Inventories	12,600	35		15,750		15,750
Total current assets	$25,200			$31,500		$31,500
Net fixed assets	21,600			21,600[a]		21,600
Total assets	$46,800			$53,100		$53,100
Accounts payable	$ 7,200	20		$ 9,000		$ 9,000
Notes payable	3,472			3,472		3,472
Line of credit	0			0	2,549	2,549
Accruals	2,520	7		3,150		3,150
Total current liabilities	$13,192			$15,622		$ 18,171
Mortgage bonds	5,000			5,000		5,000
Common stock	2,000			2,000		2,000
Retained earnings	26,608		1,321[b]	27,929		27,929
Total liabilities and equity	$46,800			$50,551		$53,100
Financing deficit =				$ 2,549		

[a]From part a we know that sales can increase by 33% before additions to fixed assets are needed.
[b]See income statement.

CHAPTER 14

ST-1   a.

Capital investments	$6,000,000
Projected net income	$5,000,000
Required equity = 60%(Capital inv.)	$3,600,000
Available residual	$1,400,000
Shares outstanding	1,000,000

DPS = $1,400/1,000,000 shares = $1.40

b. EPS = $5,000,000/1,000,000 shares = $5.00

Payout ratio = DPS/EPS = $1.4/$5 = 28%, or

Total dividends ÷ NI = $1,400,000/$5,000,000 = 28%

ST-2 a.

Value of operations	$2,100
+ Value of ST investments	$100
Total intrinsic value of firm	$2,200
− Debt	$ 200
− Preferred stock	$ 0
Intrinsic value of equity	$2,000
÷ Number of shares	100
Intrinsic price per share	$ 20

b.

Value of operations	$2,100
+ Value of ST investments	$ 0
Total intrinsic value of firm	$2,100
− Debt	$ 200
− Preferred stock	$ 0
Intrinsic value of equity	$1,900
÷ Number of shares	100
Intrinsic price per share	$ 19

c. The price before the repurchase, during the repurchase, and after the repurchase doesn't change. So the number of shares after the repurchase is the value of equity after the repurchase divided by the original price: n_{Post} = $1,900/$20 = 95.

Value of operations	$2,100
+ Value of ST investments	$ 0
Total intrinsic value of firm	$2,100
− Debt	$ 200
− Preferred stock	$ 0
Intrinsic value of equity	$1,900
÷ Number of shares	95
Intrinsic price per share	$ 20

CHAPTER 15

ST-1 a. $S = P(n) = \$30(600,000) = \$18,000,000$

$V = D + S = \$2000,000 + \$18,000,000 = \$20,000,000$

b. $w_d = D/V = \$2,000,000/\$20,000,000 = 0.10$

$w_s = S/V = \$18,000,000/\$20,000,000 = 0.90$

$WACC = w_d r_d (1 - T) + w_s r_s$
$= (0.10)(10\%)(0.60) + (0.90)(15\%) = 14.1\%$

c. $WACC = (0.50)(12\%)(0.60) + (0.50)(18.5\%) = 12.85\%$

Since g = 0, it follows that FCF = NOPAT.

$$V_{opNew} = FCF/WACC = EBIT(1-T)/0.1285 = \$4,700,000(0.60)/0.1285$$
$$= \$21,945,525.292$$

$$D = w_d(V_{op}) = 0.50(\$21,945,525.292) = \$10,972,762.646$$

Since it started with \$2 million debt, it will issue

$$D_{New} - D_{Old} = \$8,972,762.646 = \$10,972,762.646 - \$2,000,000.$$

$$S_{Post} = V_{opNew} - D_{New} = \$21,945,525.292 - \$10,972,762.646 = \$10,972,762.646$$

$$\left(\text{Alternatively, } S_{Post} = w_s(V_{opNew}) = 0.50(\$21,945,525.292) = \$10,972,762.646.\right)$$

$$n_{Post} = n_{Prior}\left[\frac{V_{opNew} - D_{New}}{V_{opNew} - D_{Old}}\right]$$

$$= 600,000\left[\frac{\$21,945,525.292 - \$10,972,762.646}{\$21,945,525.292 - \$2,000,000}\right]$$

$$= 600,000\left[\frac{\$10,972,762.646}{\$19,945,525.292}\right]$$

$$= 330,082$$

$$P_{Post} = (V_{opNew} - D_{Old})/n_{Prior}$$

$$= (\$21,945,525.292 - \$2,000,000)/600,000$$

$$= \$33.2425$$

Alternatively, after issuing debt and before repurchasing stock, the firm's equity, S_{Prior}, is worth $V_{opNew} + (D_{New} - D_{Old}) - D_{New} = \$21,945,525.292 + \$8,972,762.646 - \$10,972,762.646 = \$19,945,525.29$. The stock price prior to the repurchase is $P_{Prior} = S_{Prior}/n_{Prior} = \$19,945,525.29/600,000 = \$33.242542$. The firm used the proceeds of the new debt, \$8,972,762.646, to repurchase X shares of stock at a price of \$33.242542 per share. The number of shares it will repurchase is $X = \$8,972,762.646/\$33.242542 = 269,918.07$. Thus, there are $600,000 - 269,918.07 = 330,082$ shares remaining. As a check, the stock price should equal the market value of equity (S) divided by the number of shares: $P_0 = \$10,972,762.646/330,082 = \$33.2425$.

ST-2   a.   LIC's current cost of equity is
$$r_s = 6\% + 1.5(4\%) = 12\%$$

   b.   LIC's unlevered beta is
$$b_U = 1.5/[1 + (1 - 0.40)(25\%/75\%)] = 1.5/1.2 = 1.25$$

   c.   LIC's levered beta at D/S = 60%/40% = 1.5 is
$$b = 1.25[1 + (1 - 0.40)(60/40)] = 2.375$$

   LIC's new cost of capital will be
$$r_s = 6\% + (2.375)(4\%) = 15.5\%$$

CHAPTER 16

ST-1   The Calgary Company: Alternative Balance Sheets

	Restricted (40%)	Moderate (50%)	Relaxed (60%)
Current assets (% of sales)	$1,200,000	$1,500,000	$1,800,000
Fixed assets	600,000	600,000	600,000
Total assets	$1,800,000	$2,100,000	$2,400,000
Debt	$ 900,000	$1,050,000	$1,200,000
Equity	900,000	1,050,000	1,200,000
Total liabilities and equity	$1,800,000	$2,100,000	$2,400,000

The Calgary Company: Alternative Income Statements

	Restricted	Moderate	Relaxed
Sales	$3,000,000	$3,000,000	$3,000,000
EBIT	450,000	450,000	450,000
Interest (10%)	90,000	105,000	120,000
Earnings before taxes	$ 360,000	$ 345,000	$ 330,000
Taxes (40%)	144,000	138,000	132,000
Net income	$ 216,000	$ 207,000	$ 198,000
ROE	24.0%	19.7%	16.5%

ST-2   a.   a and b.

**Income Statements for Year Ended December 31, 2013
(Thousands of Dollars)**

	Vanderheiden Press		Herrenhouse Publishing	
	a	b	a	b
EBIT	$ 30,000	$ 30,000	$ 30,000	$ 30,000
Interest	12,400	14,400	10,600	18,600
Taxable income	$ 17,600	$ 15,600	$ 19,400	$ 11,400
Taxes (40%)	7,040	6,240	7,760	4,560
Net income	$ 10,560	$ 9,360	$ 11,640	$ 6,840
Equity	$100,000	$100,000	$100,000	$100,000
Return on equity	10.56%	9.36%	11.64%	6.84%

The Vanderheiden Press has a higher ROE when short-term interest rates are high, whereas Herrenhouse Publishing does better when rates are lower.

c.   Herrenhouse's position is riskier. First, its profits and return on equity are much more volatile than Vanderheiden's. Second, Herrenhouse must renew its large short-term loan every year, and if the renewal comes up at a time when money is tight or when its business is depressed or both, then Herrenhouse could be denied credit, which could put it out of business.

CHAPTER 17

ST-1
$$\frac{\text{Euros}}{\text{C\$}} = \frac{\text{Euros}}{\text{US\$}} \times \frac{\text{US\$}}{\text{C\$}}$$

$$= \frac{0.98}{\$1} \times \frac{\$1}{1.5} = \frac{0.98}{1.5} = 0.6533 \text{ euros per Canadian dollar}$$

CHAPTER 18

ST-1 a. Proceeds per share $= (1 - 0.07)(20) = \$18.60$.

Required proceeds after direct costs: \$30 million + \$800,000 = \$30.8 million.

Number of shares = \$30.8 million/\$18.60 per share = 1.656 million shares.

  b. Amount left on table = (Closing price − offer price)(Number of shares)

$$= (\$22 - \$20)(1.656 \text{ million}) = \$3.312 \text{ million}.$$

  c. Underwriting cost $= 0.07(\$20)(1.656) = \$2.318$ million.

Total costs $= \$0.800 + \$2.318 + \$3.312 = \$6.430$ million.

CHAPTER 19

ST-1 a. **Cost of Leasing:**

	Year 0	Year 1	Year 2	Year 3	Year 4
Lease payment	−$10,000	−$10,000	−$10,000	−$10,000	$0
Payment tax savings	4,000	4,000	4,000	4,000	0
Net cash flow	−$ 6,000	− $ 6,000	−$ 6,000	−$ 6,000	$0
PV of leasing @ 6% =	−$22,038				

  b. **Cost of Owning:**

In our solution, we will consider the \$40,000 cost as a Year-0 outflow rather than including all the financing cash flows. The net effect is the same because the PV of the financing flows, when discounted at the after-tax cost of debt, is the cost of the asset.

	Year 0	Year 1	Year 2	Year 3	Year 4
Net purchase price	−$40,000				
Maintenance cost		−$1,000	−$1,000	−$1,000	−$1,000
Maintenance tax savings		400	400	400	400
Depreciation tax savings		5,280	7,200	2,400	1,120
Residual value					10,000
Residual value tax					−4,000
Net cash flow	−$40,000	$4,680	$6,600	$1,800	$6,520
PV of owning @ 6% =	−$23,035				

Since the present value of leasing is better than the present value of owning, the truck should be leased. Specifically, the NAL is −$22,038 − (−$23,035) = $997.

c. Use the cost of debt because most cash flows are fixed by contract and thus are relatively certain; therefore, lease cash flows have about the same risk as the firm's debt. Also, leasing is considered as a substitute for debt. Use an after-tax cost rate to account for interest tax deductibility.

CHAPTER 20

ST-1 First issue: 10-year straight bonds with a 6% coupon.

Second issue: 10-year bonds with 4.5% annual coupon with warrants. Both bonds issued at par $1,000. Value of warrants = ?

First issue: $N = 10$, $PV = -1000$, $PMT = 60$, and $FV = 1000$; then solve for $I/YR = r_d = 6\%$. (Since it sold for par, we should know that $r_d = 6\%$.)

Second issue: $\$1,000 = \text{Bond} + \text{Warrants}$. This bond should be evaluated at 6% (since we know the first issue sold at par) in order to determine its present value: $N = 10$, $I/YR = r_d = 6$, $PMT = 45$, and $FV = 1000$; then solve for $PV = \$889.60$.

The value of the warrants can be determined as the difference between $1,000 and the second bond's present value:

$$\text{Value of warrants} = \$1,000 - \$889.6 = \$110.40.$$

CHAPTER 21

ST-1 a. $HV_{U,2} = \left[FCF_2(1 + g_L)\right]/(r_{sU} - g_L) = [\$120(1.04)]/0.08 - 0.4) = \$3,120$

b. $V_U = FCF_1/(1 + r_{sU}) + \left(FCF_2 + HV_{U,2}\right)/(1 + r_{sU})^2$
$$= (100/1.08) + (\$120 + \$3,120)/(1.08)^2 = \$2,870.37$$

c. $TS_1 = r_d D\ T = 0.05(\$500)(0.4) = \$10.$

$TS_2 = TS_1 = \$10.$

d. $HV_{TS,2} = \left[TS_2(1 + g_L)\right]/(r_{sU} - g_L) = [\$10(1.04)]/0.08 - 0.4) = \$260.$

e. $V_{\text{Tax shield}} = TS_1/(1 + r_{sU}) + \left(TS_2 + HV_{TS,2}\right)/(1 + r_{sU})^2$
$$= (10/1.08) + (\$10 + \$260)/(1.08)^2 = \$240.74.$$

f. $V_{op} = V_U + V_{\text{Tax shield}} = \$2,870.37 + \$240.74 = \$3,111.11$

CHAPTER 22

ST-1 a. The unlevered cost of equity based on the pre-merger required rate of return and pre-merger capital structure is

$$r_{sU} = w_d r_d + w_s r_{sL}$$
$$= 0.25(6\%) + 0.75(10\%)$$
$$= 9\%$$

The post-horizon levered cost of equity is

$$r_{sL} = r_{sU} + (r_{sU} - r_d)(D/S)$$
$$= 9\% + (9\% - 7\%)(0.35/0.65)$$
$$= 10.077\%$$

$$WACC = w_d r_d (1 - T) + w_s r_s$$
$$= 0.35(7\%)(1 - 0.40) + 0.65(10.077\%)$$
$$= 8.02\%$$

b. The horizon value of unlevered operations is

$$HV_{U,3} = FCF_3(1 + g)/(r_{sU} - g)$$
$$= [\$25(1.05)]/(0.09 - 0.05)$$
$$= \$656.250 \text{ million}$$

$$\text{Unlevered } V_{ops} = \frac{\$10}{(1.09)^1} + \frac{\$20}{(1.09)^2} + \frac{\$25 + \$656.25}{(1.09)^3}$$
$$= \$552.058 \text{ million}$$

Tax shields in Years 1 through 3 are

$$\text{Tax shield} = \text{Interest} \times T$$
$$TS_1 = \$28.00(0.40) = \$11.200 \text{ million}$$
$$TS_2 = \$24.00(0.40) = \$9.600 \text{ million}$$
$$TS_3 = \$20.28(0.40) = \$8.112 \text{ million}$$

$$HV_{TS,3} = TS_3(1 + g)/(r_{sU} - g)$$
$$= [\$8.112(1.05)]/(0.09 - 0.05)$$
$$= \$212.940 \text{ million}$$

$$\text{Value of tax shield} = \frac{\$11.2}{(1.09)^1} + \frac{\$9.6}{(1.09)^2} + \frac{\$8.112 + \$212.940}{(1.09)^3}$$
$$= \$189.048 \text{ million}$$

$$\text{Total value} = \text{Unlevered } V_{ops} + \text{Value of tax shield}$$
$$= \$552.058 + \$189.048$$
$$= \$741.106.$$

CHAPTER 23

ST-1   a. The hypothetical bond in the futures contract has an annual coupon of 6% (paid semiannually) and a maturity of 20 years. At a price of 97'13 (this is the percent of par), a $1,000 par bond would have a price of $1,000(97 + 13/32)/100 = \$974.0625. To find the yield: N = 40, PMT = 30, FV = 1000, PV = −974.0625; then I = 3.1143% per 6 months. The nominal annual yield is 2(3.1143%) = 6.2286%.

b. In this situation, the firm would be hurt if interest rates were to rise by September, so it would use a short hedge or sell futures contracts. Because futures contracts are for $100,000 in Treasury bonds, the value of a futures contract is $97,406.25 and the firm must sell $5,000,000/$97,406.25 = 51.33 ≈ 51 contracts to cover the planned $5,000,000 September bond issue. Because futures maturing in June are selling for 97 13/32 of par, the value of Wansley's futures is about 51($97,406.25) = $4,967,718.75. Should interest rates rise by September, Wansley will be able to repurchase the futures contracts at a lower cost, which will help offset their loss from financing at the higher interest rate. Thus, the firm has hedged against rising interest rates.

c. The firm would now pay 13% on the bonds. With a 12% coupon rate, the PV of the new issue is only \$4,646,361.83 (N = 40, I = 13/2 = 6.5, PMT = -0.12/2(5000000) = -300000, FV = -5000000; then solve for PV). Therefore, the new bond issue would bring in only \$4,646,361.83, so the cost of the bond issue that is due to rising rates is \$5,000,000 - \$4,646,361.83 = \$353,638.17.

However, the value of the short futures position began at \$4,967,718.75. Now, if interest rates increased by 1 percentage point, then the yield on the futures would go up to 7.2286% (7.2286 = 6.2286 + 1). To find the value of the futures contract, enter N = 40, I = 7.2286/2 = 3.6143 (from part a), PMT = 3000, and FV = 100000; then solve for PV = \$87,111.04 per contract. With 51 contracts, the value of the futures position is \$4,442,663.04. (*Note:* If you don't round off in any previous calculations, then the PV comes to \$4,442,668.38.)

Because Wansley Company sold the futures contracts for \$4,967,718.75 and will, in effect, buy them back at \$4,442,668.04, the firm would make a profit of \$4,967,718.75 - \$4,442,668.04 = \$525,050.71 profit on the transaction (if we ignore transaction costs).

Thus, the firm gained \$525,050.71 on its futures position, but lost \$353,638.17 on its underlying bond issue. On net, it gained \$525,050.71 - \$353,638.17 = \$171,412.54.

CHAPTER 24

ST-1   a.   Distribution to priority claimants (millions of dollars):

Total proceeds from the sale of assets	\$1,150
Less:	
1. First mortgage (paid from sale of fixed assets)	700
2. Second mortgage (paid from sale of fixed assets after satisfying first mortgage: \$750 - \$700 = \$50)	50
3. Fees and expenses of bankruptcy	1
4. Wages due to workers	60
5. Taxes due	90
Funds available for distribution to general creditors	\$ 249

b. Distribution to general creditors (millions of dollars):

General Creditor Claims	Amount of Claim	Pro Rata Distribution[a]	Distribution after Subordinate Adjustment[b]	% of Original Claim Received
Unsatisfied second mortgage	$ 350	$ 60	$ 60	28%[c]
Accounts payable	100	17	17	17
Notes payable	300	52	86	29
Debentures	500	86	86	17
Subordinated debentures	200	34	0	0
Total	$1,450	$249	$249	

Notes:

[a]Pro rata distribution: $249/$1,450 = 0.172 = 17.2%.

[b]Subordinated debentures are subordinated to notes payable. Unsatisfied portion of notes payable is greater than subordinated debenture distribution, so subordinated debentures receive $0.

[c]Includes $50 from sale of fixed assets received in priority distribution.

Total distribution to second mortgage holders: $50 + $60 = $110 million.

Total distribution to holders of notes payable: $86 million.

Total distribution to holders of subordinated debentures: $0 million.

Total distribution to common stockholders: $0 million.

CHAPTER 25

ST-1   a. For Security A:

P_A	r_A	$P_A r_A$	$(r_A - \hat{r}_A)$	$(r_A - \hat{r}_A)^2$	$P_A(r_A - \hat{r}_A)^2$
0.1	−10%	−1.0%	−25%	625	62.5
0.2	5	1.0	−10	100	20.0
0.4	15	6.0	0	0	0.0
0.2	25	5.0	10	100	20.0
0.1	40	4.0	25	625	62.5
		$\hat{r}_A$ = 15.0%			$\sigma_A = \sqrt{165.0} = 12.8\%$

b.
$$w_A = \frac{\sigma_B(\sigma_B - \rho_{AB}\sigma_A)}{\sigma_A^2 + \sigma_B^2 - 2\rho_{AB}\sigma_A\sigma_B}$$

$$= \frac{25.7[25.7 - (-0.5)(12.8)]}{(12.8)^2 + (25.7)^2 - 2(-0.5)(12.8)(25.7)}$$

$$= \frac{824.97}{1,153.29} = 0.7153.$$

or 71.53% invested in A and 28.47% invested in B.

c.
$$\sigma_p = \sqrt{(w_A\sigma_A)^2 + (1-w_A)^2(\sigma_B)^2 + 2w_A(1-w_A)\rho_{AB}\sigma_A\sigma_B}$$

$$= \sqrt{(0.75)^2(12.8)^2 + (0.25)^2(25.7)^2 + 2(0.75)(0.25)(-0.5)(12.8)(25.7)}$$

$$= \sqrt{92.16 + 41.28 - 61.68}$$

$$= \sqrt{71.76} = 8.47\% \text{ when } w_A = 75\%$$

$$\sigma_p = \sqrt{(0.7153)^2(12.8)^2 + (0.2847)^2(25.7)^2 + 2(0.7153)(0.2847)(-0.5)(12.8)(25.7)}$$

$$= 8.38\% \text{ when } w_A = 71.53\% \text{ (this is the minimum } \sigma_P)$$

$$\sigma_p = \sqrt{(0.5)^2(12.8)^2 + (0.5)^2(25.7)^2 + 2(0.5)(0.5)(-0.5)(12.8)(25.7)}$$

$$= 11.3\% \text{ when } w_A = 50\%$$

$$\sigma_p = \sqrt{(0.25)^2(12.8)^2 + (0.75)^2(25.7)^2 + 2(0.25)(0.75)(-0.5)(12.8)(25.7)}$$

$$= 17.89\% \text{ when } w_A = 25\%$$

% in A	% in B	$\hat{r}_p$	σ_p
100.00%	0.00%	15.00%	12.8%
75.00	25.00	16.25	8.5
71.53	28.47	16.42	8.4
50.00	50.00	17.50	11.1
25.00	75.00	18.75	17.9
0.00	100.00	20.00	25.7

Calculations for preceding table:

$$
\begin{aligned}
\hat{r}_p &= w_A(\hat{r}_A) + (1-w_A)(\hat{r}_B) \\
&= 0.75(15) + (0.25)(20) &&= 16.25\% &&\text{when } w_A &&= 75\% \\
&= 0.7153(15) + 0.2847(20) &&= 16.42\% &&\text{when } w_{A0} &&= 71.53\% \\
&= 0.5(15) + 0.5(20) &&= 17.50\% &&\text{when } w_A &&= 50\% \\
&= 0.25(15) + 0.75(20) &&= 18.75\% &&\text{when } w_A &&= 25\%
\end{aligned}
$$

d.   See graph below.

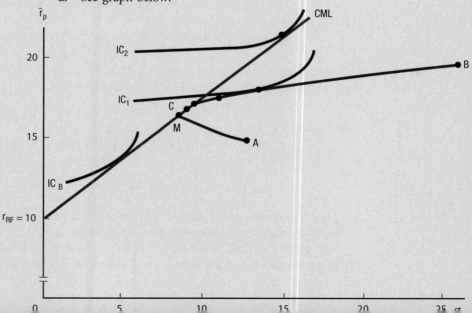

e.   See indifference curve IC_1 in the preceding graph. At the point where $\hat{r}_p = 18\%$, $\sigma_p = 13.5\%$.

$$\hat{r}_p = w_A(\hat{r}_A) + (1 - w_A)(\hat{r}_B)$$
$$18 = w_A(15) + (1 - w_A)(20)$$
$$= 15w_A + 20 - 20w_A$$
$$5w_A = 2$$
$$w_A = 0.4 \text{ or } 40\%.$$

Therefore, to an approximation, your optimal portfolio would have 40% in A and 60% in B, with $\hat{r}_P = 18\%$ and $\sigma_p = 13.5\%$. (We could get an exact σ_p by using $w_A = 0.4$ in the equation for σ_p.)

f.   The existence of the riskless asset would enable you to go to the CAPM. We would draw in the CML as shown on the graph in part d. Now you would hold a portfolio of stocks, borrowing on margin to hold more stocks than your net worth, and move to a higher indifference curve, IC_2.

You can put all of your money into the riskless asset, all in A, all in B, or some in each security. The most logical choices are (1) hold a portfolio of A and B plus some of the riskless asset, (2) hold only a portfolio of A and B, or (3) hold a portfolio of A and B and borrow to leverage the portfolio, assuming you can borrow at the riskless rate.

Reading from the graph, we see that your $\hat{r}_p$ at the point of tangency between your IC_2 and the CML is about 22%. We can use this information to find out how much you invest in the market portfolio and how much you invest in the riskless asset. (It will turn out that you have a *negative* investment in the riskless asset, which means that you borrow rather than lend at the risk-free rate.)

$$\hat{r}_p = w_{RF}(r_{RF}) + (1 - w_{RF})(\hat{r}_M)$$
$$22 = w_{RF}(10) + (1 - w_{RF})(16.8)$$
$$= 10w_{RF} + 16.8 - 16.8w_{RF}$$
$$-6.8w_{RF} = 5.2$$
$$w_{RF} = -0.76 \text{ or } -76\% \text{ (which means that you borrow)}$$
$$1 - w_{RF} = 1.0 - (-0.76)$$
$$= +1.76 \text{ or } 176\% \text{ in the market portfolio}$$

Hence this investor, with $200,000 of net worth, buys stock with a value of $200,000(1.76) = $352,000 and borrows $152,000.

The risk of this leveraged portfolio is

$$\sigma_p = \sqrt{(-0.76)^2(0)^2 + (1.76)^2(8.5)^2 + 2(-0.76)(1.76)(0)(8.5)(0)}$$
$$= \sqrt{(1.76)^2(8.5)^2}$$
$$= (1.76)(8.5) = 15\%$$

Your indifference curve suggests that you are not very risk averse. A risk-averse investor would have a steep indifference curve (visualize a set of steep curves that were tangent to CML to the left of Point C). This investor would hold some of A and B, combined to form portfolio M, and some of the riskless asset.

g. Given your assumed indifference curve, you would, when the riskless asset becomes available, change your portfolio from the one found in part e (with $\hat{r}_p = 18\%$ and $\sigma_p = 13.5\%$) to one with $\hat{r}_p \approx 22.0\%$ and $\sigma_p \approx 15.00\%$.

h.
$$r_A = r_{RF} + (r_M - r_{RF})b_A$$
$$15 = 10 + (16.8 - 10)b_A$$
$$= 10 + (6.8)b_A.$$
$$b_A = 0.74.$$
$$20 = 10 + (6.8)b_B$$
$$b_B = 1.47$$

Note that the 16.8% value for r_M was approximated from the graph. Also, this solution *assumes* that you can borrow at $r_{RF} = 10\%$. This is a basic—but questionable—CAPM assumption. If the borrowing rate is *above* r_{RF}, then the CML would turn down to the right of Point M.

CHAPTER 26

ST-1   a. NPV of each demand scenario:

		Future Cash Flows		NPV This	Probability
0	Probability	Year 1	Year 2	Scenario	× NPV
		$13	$13	$13.13	$3.28
	25%				
−$8	50%	$7	$7	$3.38	$1.69
	25%				
		$1	$1	−$6.37	−$1.59
			Expected NPV of future CFs =		$3.38

NPV under high-demand scenario:
$$NPV = -\$8 + \frac{\$13}{(1 + 0.15)^1} + \frac{\$13}{(1 + 0.15)^2} = \$13.13$$

NPV under medium-demand scenario:
$$NPV = -\$8 + \frac{\$7}{(1 + 0.15)^1} + \frac{\$7}{(1 - 0.15)^2} = \$3.38$$

NPV under low-demand scenario:
$$NPV = -\$8 + \frac{\$1}{(1 + 0.15)^1} + \frac{\$1}{(1 + 0.15)^2} = -\$6.37$$

Expected NPV = 0.25($13.13) + 0.50($3.38) + 0.25(−$6.37) = $3.38 million.

b. NPV of operating cash flows if the additional project is implemented only when optimal:

Probability	Future Operating Cash Flows (Discount at WACC)				NPV This Scenario	Probability × NPV
	Year 1	Year 2	Year 3	Year 4		
25%	$13	$13	$13	$13	$37.11	$9.28
50%	$7	$7	$7	$7	$19.98	$9.99
25%	$1	$1	$0	$0	$1.63	$0.41

Expected NPV of future operating CFs = $19.68

Probability	Future Operating Cash Flows (Discount at WACC)				NPV This Scenario	Probability × NPV
	Year 1	Year 2	Year 3	Year 4		
25%	$13	$13	$13	$13	$37.11	$9.28
50%	$7	$7	$7	$7	$19.98	$9.99
25%	$1	$1	$0	$0	$1.63	$0.41

Expected NPV of future operating CFs = $19.68

NPV of operating cash flows under high-demand scenario:

$$\text{NPV} = \frac{\$13}{(1+0.15)^1} + \frac{\$13}{(1+0.15)^2} + \frac{\$13}{(1+0.15)^3} + \frac{\$13}{(1+0.15)^4} = \$37.11$$

NPV of operating cash flows under medium-demand scenario:

$$\text{NPV} = \frac{\$7}{(1+0.15)^1} + \frac{\$7}{(1+0.15)^2} + \frac{\$7}{(1+0.15)^3} + \frac{\$7}{(1+0.15)^4} = \$19.98$$

NPV of operating cash flows under low-demand scenario:

$$\text{NPV} = \frac{\$1}{(1+0.15)^1} + \frac{\$1}{(1+0.15)^2} = \$1.63$$

$$
\begin{aligned}
\text{Expected NPV of operating cash flows} &= 0.25(\$37.11) + 0.50(\$19.98) \\
&\quad + 0.25(\$1.63) \\
&= \$19.68 \text{ million}
\end{aligned}
$$

Find NPV of costs, discounted at risk-free rate:

0	Probability	Year 1	Year 2	NPV This Scenario	Probability × NPV
		$0	−$8	−$15.12	−$3.78
	25%				
−$8	50% ⟶	$0	−$8	−$15.12	−$7.56
	25%				
		$0	$0	−$8.00	−$2.00

Expected NPV of future operating CFs = $\boxed{-\$13.34}$

NPV of costs under high-demand scenario:

$$NPV = -\$8 + \frac{\$0}{(1 + 0.06)^1} + \frac{-\$8}{(1 + 0.06)^2} = -\$15.12$$

NPV of costs under medium-demand scenario:

$$NPV = -\$8 + \frac{\$0}{(1 + 0.06)^1} + \frac{-\$8}{(1 + 0.06)^2} = -\$15.12$$

NPV of costs under low-demand scenario:

$$NPV = -\$8 + \frac{\$0}{(1 + 0.06)^1} + \frac{\$0}{(1 + 0.06)^2} = -\$8.00$$

$$\text{Expected NPV of costs} = 0.25(-\$15.12) + 0.50(-\$15.12) + 0.25(-\$8.00)$$
$$= -\$13.34 \text{ million}$$

$$\begin{array}{c} \text{Expected NPV} \\ \text{of project} \end{array} = \begin{array}{c} \text{Expected NPV of} \\ \text{operating cash flows} \end{array} - \begin{array}{c} \text{Expected NPV} \\ \text{of costs} \end{array}$$

$$= \$19.68 - \$13.34 = \$6.34$$

c.   Find the expected NPV of the additional project's operating cash flows, which is analogous to the "stock price" in the Black-Scholes model:

0	Probability	Year 1	Year 2	Year 3	Year 4	NPV of This Scenario	Probability × NPV
		$0	$0	$13	$13	$15.98	$4.00
	25%						
	50% ⟶	$0	$0	$7	$7	$8.60	$4.30
	25%						
		$0	$0	$1	$1	$1.23	$0.31

Expected NPV future operating CFs = $\boxed{\$8.60}$

NPV of operating cash flows under high-demand scenario:

$$NPV = \frac{\$0}{(1 + 0.15)^1} + \frac{\$0}{(1 + 0.15)^2} + \frac{\$13}{(1 + 0.15)^3} + \frac{\$13}{(1 + 0.15)^4} = \$15.98$$

NPV of operating cash flows under medium-demand scenario:

$$NPV = \frac{\$0}{(1 + 0.15)^1} + \frac{\$0}{(1 + 0.15)^2} + \frac{\$7}{(1 + 0.15)^3} + \frac{\$7}{(1 + 0.15)^4} = \$8.60$$

NPV of operating cash flows under low-demand scenario:

$$NPV = \frac{\$0}{(1 + 0.15)^1} + \frac{\$0}{(1 + 0.15)^2} + \frac{\$1}{(1 + 0.15)^3} + \frac{\$1}{(1 + 0.15)^4} = \$1.23$$

$$\begin{aligned} \text{Expected NPV of additional project's operating cash flows} \quad &= \quad 0.25(\$15.98) + 0.50(\$8.60) \\ &\quad + 0.25(\$1.23) \\ &= \quad \$8.60 \text{ million} \end{aligned}$$

The inputs for the Black-Scholes model are: $r_{RF} = 0.06$, $X = 8$, $P = 8.6$, $t = 2$, and $\sigma^2 = 0.150$. Using these inputs, the value of the option, V, is

$$d_1 = \frac{\ln(P/X) + \left[r_{RF} + \dfrac{\sigma^2}{2}\right] \times t}{\sigma\sqrt{t}} = \frac{\ln(8.6/8) + \left[0.06 + \dfrac{0.150}{2}\right] \times 2}{\sqrt{0.15}\sqrt{2}} = 0.62499$$

$$d_2 = d_1 - \sigma\sqrt{t} = 0.62499 - \sqrt{0.15}\sqrt{2} = 0.07727$$

Use *Excel*'s NORMSDIST function to calculate $N(d_1)$ and $N(d_2)$:

$$N(d_1) = 0.73401$$
$$N(d_2) = 0.53079$$

$$V = P[N(d_1)] - Xe^{-r_{RF}t}[N(d_2)] = 8.6(0.73401) - 8e^{-0.06(2)}(0.53079) = \$2.55 \text{ million}$$

The total value is the value of the original project (from part a) and the value of the growth option:

$$\text{Total value} = \$3.38 + \$2.55 = \$5.93 \text{ million}$$

Answers to End-of-Chapter Problems

We present here some intermediate steps and final answers to selected end-of-chapter problems. Please note that your answer may differ slightly from ours because of rounding differences. Also, although we hope not, some of the problems may have more than one correct solution, depending on what assumptions are made when working the problem. Finally, many of the problems involve some verbal discussion as well as numerical calculations; this verbal material is not presented here.

2-1 5.8%.

2-2 25%.

2-3 $3,000,000.

2-4 $2,000,000.

2-5 $3,600,000.

2-6 $25,000,000.

2-7 Tax = $107,855;
NI = $222,145;
Marginal tax rate = 39%;
Average tax rate = 33.8%.

2-8 a. Tax = $3,575,000.
b. Tax = $350,000.
c. Tax = $105,000.

2-9 AT&T bond = 4.875%;
AT&T preferred stock =5.37%;
Florida bond = 5%.

2-10 NI = $450,000;
NCF = $650,000.

2-11 a. $2,400,000.
b. NI = $0;
NCF = $3,000,000.
c. NI = $1,350,000;
NCF = $2,100,000.

2-12 a. NOPAT = $756 million.
b. $NOWC_{12}$ = $3.0 billion;
$NOWC_{13}$ = $3.3 billion.
c. Op. $capital_{12}$ = $6.5 billion;
Op. $capital_{13}$ = $7.15 billion.
d. FCF = $106 million.

e. ROIC = 10.57%.
f. Answers in millions:
A-T int. = $72.
Inc. in debt = −$284.
Div. = $220.
Rep. stock = $88.
Purch. ST inv. = $10.

2-13 Refund = $120,000.
Future taxes = $0; $0;
$40,000; $60,000; $60,000.

3-1 AR = $400,000.

3-2 Debt ratio = 15%.

3-3 M/B = 10.

3-4 P/E = 16.0.

3-5 ROE = 12%.

3-6 S/TA = 2.4; TA/E = 1.67.

3-7 CL = $2,000,000;
Inv = $1,000,000.

3-8 Net profit margin = 3.33%;
L/A = 42.86%.
Debt ratio = 21.43%.

3-9 $262,500; 1.19.

3-10 TIE = 4.13.

3-11 Sales = $600,000;
COGS = $450,000;
Cash = $28,000;
AR = $60,000;

Inv. = \$120,000;
FA = \$192,000.
AP = \$110,000;
Common stock = \$140,000;

3-12   Sales = \$2,580,000.

3-13   a. Current ratio = 2.01;
        DSO = 77 days;
        Inv TO = 5.67;
        FA turnover = 5.56;
        TA turnover = 1.75;
        PM = 1.5%;
        ROA = 2.6%;
        ROE = 6.4%;
        Debt ratio = 33%.
        L/TA = 59%.

3-14   Quick ratio = 0.8;
        CA/CL = 2.3;
        Inv. TO = 4.2;
        DSO = 37 days;
        FA TO = 10.0;
        TA TO = 2.3;
        ROA = 5.9%;
        ROE = 13.1%;
        PM = 2.5%;
        Debt ratio = 27.5%.
        L/TA = 54.8%.
        PE ratio = 5.0;
        P/CF ratio = 2.0;
        M/B ratio = 0.65.

4-1 FV_5 = \$16,105.10.

4-2   PV = \$1,292.10.

4-3   I/YR = 8.01%.

4-4   N = 11.01 years.

4-5   N = 11 years.

4-6 FVA_5 = \$1,725.22;
        $FVA_{5\ Due}$ = \$1,845.99.

4-7   PV = \$923.98;
        FV = \$1,466.24.

4-8   PMT = \$444.89;
        EAR = 12.6825%.

4-9   a. \$530.
        b. \$561.80.
        c. \$471.70.
        d. \$445.00.

4-10   a. \$895.42.
        b. \$1,552.92.
        c. \$279.20.
        d. \$160.99.

4-11   a. N = 10.24 ≈ 10 years.
        b. N = 7.27 ≈ 7 years.
        c. N = 4.19 ≈ 4 years.
        d. N = 1.00 ≈ 1 year.

4-12   a. \$6,374.97.
        b. \$1,105.13.
        c. \$2,000.00.
        d. (1) \$7,012.46.
           (2) \$1,160.38.
           (3) \$2,000.00.

4-13   a. \$2,457.83.
        b. \$865.90.
        c. \$2,000.00.
        d. (1) \$2,703.61.
           (2) \$909.19.
           (3) \$2,000.00.

4-14   a. PV_A = \$1,251.25.
           PV_B = \$1,300.32.
        b. PV_A = \$1,600.
           PV_B = \$1,600.

4-15   a. 7%.
        b. 7%.
        c. 9%.
        d. 15%.

4-16   a. \$881.17.
        b. \$895.42.
        c. \$903.06.
        d. \$908.35.

4-17   a. \$279.20.
        b. \$276.84.
        c. \$443.72.

4-18   a. \$5,272.32.
        b. \$5,374.07.

4-19   a. Universal, EAR = 7%;
           Regional, EAR = 6.14%.

4-20   a. PMT = \$6,594.94;
           $Interest_1$ = \$2,500;
           $Interest_2$ = \$2,090.51.
        b. \$13,189.87.
        c. \$8,137.27.

4-21   a. I = 14.87% ≈ 15%.

4-22 $I = 7.18\%$.

4-23 $I = 9\%$.

4-24 a. \$33,872.11.
 b. (1) \$26,243.16.
  (2) \$0.

4-25 $N = 14.77 \approx 15$ years.

4-26 6 years; \$1,106.01.

4-27 (1) \$1,428.57.
 (2) \$714.29.

4-28 \$893.26.

4-29 \$984.88.

4-30 57.18%.

4-31 a. \$1,432.02.
 b. \$93.07.

4-32 $I_{NOM} = 15.19\%$.

4-33 PMT = \$36,949.61.

4-34 First PMT = \$9,736.96.

5-1 \$928.39.

5-2 12.48%.

5-3 8.55%.

5-4 7%; 7.33%.

5-5 2.5%.

5-6 0.3%.

5-7 \$1,085.80.

5-8 YTM = 6.62%; YTC = 6.49%.

5-9 a. 5%: $V_L = \$1,518.98$;
  $V_S = \$1,047.62$.
  8%: $V_L = \$1,171.19$;
  $V_S = \$1,018.52$.
  12%: $V_L = \$863.78$;
  $V_S = \$982.14$.

5-10 a. YTM at \$829 = 13.98%;
  YTM at \$1,104 = 6.50%.

5-11 14.82%.

5-12 a. 10.37%.
 b. 10.91%.
 c. −0.54%.
 d. 10.15%.

5-13 8.65%.

5-14 10.78%.

5-15 YTC = 6.47%.

5-16 a. 10-year, 10% coupon = 6.75%;
  10-year zero = 9.75%;
  5-year zero = 4.76%;
  30-year zero = 32.19%;
  \$100 perpetuity = 14.29%.

5-17 $C_0 = \$1,012.79$; $Z_0 = \$693.04$;
  $C_1 = \$1,010.02$; $Z_1 = \$759.57$;
  $C_2 = \$1,006.98$; $Z_2 = \$832.49$;
  $C_3 = \$1,003.65$; $Z_3 = \$912.41$;
  $C_4 = \$1,000.00$; $Z_4 = \$1,000.00$.

5-18 5.8%.

5-19 1.5%.

5-20 6.0%.

5-21 a. \$1,251.22.
 b. \$898.94.

5-22 a. 8.02%.
 b. 7.59%.

5-23 a. $r_1 = 9.20\%$; $r_5 = 7.20\%$.

6-1 $b = 1.08$.

6-2 $r_s = 10.40\%$.

6-3 $r_M = 12\%$; $r_{sB} = 16.9\%$.

6-4 15.96%.

6-5 $\hat{r} = 11.40\%$; $\sigma = 26.69\%$.

6-6 a. $\hat{r}_M = 13.5\%$; $\hat{r}_j = 11.6\%$.
 b. $\sigma_M = 3.85\%$; $\sigma_j = 6.22\%$.

6-7 a. $b_A = 1.40$.
 b. $r_A = 15\%$.

6-8 a. $r_i = 14.8\%$.
 b. (1) $r_M = 13\%$; $r_i = 15.8\%$.
  (2) $r_M = 11\%$; $r_i = 13.8\%$.
 c. (1) $r_i = 17.6\%$.
  (2) $r_i = 13.4\%$.

6-9 $b_N = 1.25$.

6-10 $b_p = 0.7625$; $r_p = 12.1\%$.

6-11 $b_N = 1.1250$.

6-12 4.5%.

6-13 a. $\bar{r}_A = 11.80\%$; $\bar{r}_B = 11.80\%$.
 b. $\bar{r}_p = 11.80\%$
 c. $\sigma_A = 25.3\%$; $\sigma_B = 24.3\%$;
  $\sigma_p = 16.3\%$.

6-14 a. $b_X = 1.3471$; $b_Y = 0.6508$.
      b. $r_X = 12.7355\%$; $r_Y = 9.254\%$.
      c. $r_p = 12.04\%$.

7-1 $D_1 = \$1.5750$; $D_3 = \$1.7364$;
      $D_5 = \$2.1011$.

7-2 $\hat{P}_0 = \$21.43$.

7-3 $\hat{P}_1 = \$24.20$; $\hat{r}_s = 16.00\%$.

7-4 $r_{ps} = 10\%$.

7-5 $\$50.50$.

7-6 $V_{op} = \$6,000,000$.

7-7 V_{op} at 2016 = $\$15,000$
      (Million of $\$$).

7-8 $g = 9\%$.

7-9 $\hat{P}_3 = \$43.08$.

7-10 a. 11.67%.
      b. 8.75%.
      c. 7.00%.
      d. 5.00%.

7-11 $32.00.

7-12 $25.03.

7-13 $\hat{P}_0 = \$10.76$.

7-14 a. $125.
      b. $83.33.

7-15 a. 7%.
      b. 5%.
      c. 12%.

7-16 a. (1) $15.83.
         (2) $23.08.
         (3) $39.38.
         (4) $110.00.
      b. (1) Undefined.

7-17 a. $HV_2 = \$2,700,000$.
      b. $2,303,571.43.

7-18 a. $713.33 million.
      b. $527.89 million.
      c. $43.79.

7-19 a. $1.79
      b. PV = $3.97.
      c. $18.74.
      d. $22.71.

7-20 a. $2.01, $2.31, $2.66, $3.06, $3.52.
      b. $\hat{P}_0 = \$39.42$.
      c. $D_1/P_0 = 5.10\%$;
         $D_6/P_5 = 7.00\%$.

7-21 $\hat{P}_0 = \$78.35$.

8-1 $5; $2.

8-2 $27.00; $37.00.

8-3 $1.67.

8-4 $3.70.

8-5 $1.90.

8-6 $2.39.

8-7 $1.91.

9-1   a. 13%.
      b. 10.4%.
      c. 8.45%.

9-2   5.2%.

9-3   9%.

9-4   5.41%.

9-5   13.33%.

9-6   10.4%.

9-7   9.17%.

9-8   13%.

9-9   7.2%.

9-10 a. 16.3%.
      b. 15.4%.
      c. 16%.

9-11 a. 8%.
      b. $2.81.
      c. 15.81%.

9-12 a. $g = 3\%$.
      b. $EPS_1 = \$5.562$.

9-13 16.1%.

9-14 $(1 - T)r_d = 5.57\%$.

9-15 a. $15,000,000.
      b. 8.4%.

9-16 Short-term debt = 11.14%;
      Long-term debt = 22.03%;
      Common equity = 66.83%.

9-17 $w_{std} = 0\%$; $w_d = 20\%$;
$w_{ps} = 4\%$; $w_s = 76\%$;
r_d(After-tax) = 7.2%;
$r_{ps} = 11.6\%$; $r_s \approx 17.5\%$.

10-1 NPV = $2,409.77.

10-2 IRR = 12.84%.

10-3 MIRR = 11.93%.

10-4 PI = 1.06.

10-5 4.44 years.

10-6 6.44 years.

10-7 a.   5%: $NPV_A = \$16,108,952$;
$NPV_B = \$18,300,939$.

10%: $NPV_A = \$12,836,213$;
$NPV_B = \$15,954,170$.

15%: $NPV_A = \$10,059,587$;
$NPV_B = \$13,897,838$.

b. $IRR_A = 43.97\%$; $IRR_B = 82.03\%$

10-8 $NPV_T = \$409$; $IRR_T = 15\%$;
$MIRR_T = 14.54\%$; Accept.
$NPV_P = \$3,318$; $IRR_P = 20\%$;
$MIRR_P = 17.19\%$; Accept.

10-9 $NPV_E = \$3,861$; $IRR_E = 18\%$;
$NPV_G = \$3,057$; $IRR_G = 18\%$;
Purchase electric-powered forklift
because it has a higher NPV.

10-10 $NPV_S = \$814.33$;
$NPV_L = \$1,675.34$;
$IRR_S = 15.24\%$;
$IRR_L = 14.67\%$;
$MIRR_S = 13.77\%$;
$MIRR_L = 13.46\%$;
$PI_S = 1.081$; $PI_L = 1.067$.

10-11 $MIRR_X = 17.49\%$;
$MIRR_Y = 18.39\%$.

10-12 a. NPV = $136,578;
IRR = 19.22%.

10-13 b. $IRR_A = 20.7\%$;
$IRR_B = 25.8\%$.
c. 10%: $NPV_A = \$478.83$;
$NPV_B = \$372.37$.
17%: $NPV_A = \$133.76$;
$NPV_B = \$173.70$.

d. (1) $MIRR_A = 14.91\%$;
$MIRR_B = 17.35\%$.
(2) $MIRR_A = 18.76\%$;
$MIRR_B = 21.03\%$.
e. Crossover rate = 14.76%.

10-14 a. $0; −$10,250,000;
$1,750,000.
b. 16.07%.

10-15 a. $NPV_A = \$18,108,510$;
$NPV_B = \$13,946,117$;
$IRR_A = 15.03\%$; $IRR_B = 22.26\%$.
b. $NPV_\Delta = \$4,162,393$;
$IRR_\Delta = 11.71\%$.

10-16 Extended $NPV_A = \$12.76$ million;
Extended $NPV_B = \$9.26$ million.
$EAA_A = \$2.26$ million;
$EAA_B = \$1.64$ million.

10-17 Extended $NPV_A = \$4.51$ million.
$EAA_A = \$0.85$ million;
$EAA_B = \$0.69$ million.

10-18 NPV of 360-6 = $22,256.
Extended NPV of 190-3 = $20,070.
EAA of 360-6 = $5,723.30;
EAA of 190-3 = $5,161.02.

10-19 d. 7.61%; 15.58%.

10-20 a. Undefined.
b. $NPV_C = −\$911,067$;
$NPV_F = −\$838,834$.

10-21 a. A = 2.67 years;
B = 1.5 years.
b. A = 3.07 years;
B = 1.825 years.
c. $NPV_A = \$12,739,908$; $IRR_A = 27.27\%$;
$NPV_B = \$11,554,880$; $IRR_B = 36.15\%$;
Choose both.
d. $NPV_A = \$18,243,813$;
$NPV_B = \$14,964,829$;
Choose A.
e. $NPV_A = \$8,207,071$; $NPV_B = \$8,643,390$;
Choose B.
f. 13.53%.
g. $MIRR_A = 21.93\%$;
$MIRR_B = 20.96\%$.

10-22 a. 3 years; $NPV_3 = \$1,307$.
b. No.

11-1 a. $22,000,000.
   b. No.
   c. Charge it against project and add $1.5 million to initial investment outlay.

11-2 $7,000,000.

11-3 $3,600,000.

11-4 NPV = $6,746.78

11-5 a. Straight Line: $425,000 per year.
   MACRS: $566,610; $755,650; $251,770; $125,970.
   b. MACRS, $27,043.62 higher.

11-6 a. −$1,118,000.
   b. $375,612; $418,521; $304,148.
   c. $437,343.
   d. NPV = $78,790; Purchase.

11-7 a. −$89,000
   b. $26,332; $30,113; $20,035.
   c. $24,519.
   d. NPV = −$6,700;
      Don't purchase.

11-8 a. NPV = $106,520.

11-9 NPV of replace = $2,083.51.

11-10 NPV of replace = $11,468.48.

11-11 E(NPV) = $3 million;
   σ_{NPV} = $23.622 million;
   CV_{NPV} = 7.874.

11-12 a. NPV = $15,732;
      IRR = 11.64%;
      MIRR = 10.88%; Payback = 3.75 years.
   b. $65,770; −$34,307.
   c. E(NPV) = $13,041;
      σ_{NPV} = $43,289;
      CV = 3.32.

11-13 a. −$87,625.
   b. $31,574; $36,244; $23,795; $20,687; $4,575.
   c. -$4,623.

11-14 a. −$529,750.
   b. New depreciation: $155,000; $248,000; $148,800; $89,280; $89,280.
   c. Net incremental cash flows: $143,000; $175,550; $140,830; $119,998; $203,872.
   d. NPV = $30,059.

11-15 a. Expected CF_A = $6,750;
      Expected CF_B = $7,650;
      CV_A = 0.0703.
   b. NPV_A = $10,036;
      NPV_B = $11,624.

11-16 a. E(IRR) ≈ 15.3%.
   b. $38,589.

11-17 a. $117,779.
   b. σ_{NPV} = $445,060;
      CV_{NPV} = 3.78.

12-1 AFN = $283,800.

12-2 AFN = $583,800.

12-3 AFN = $63,000.

12-4 ΔS = $202,312.

12-5 a. $590,000; $1,150,000.
   b. $238,563.

12-6 AFN = $360.

12-7 a. $13.44 million.
   b. 6.38%.
   c. LOC = $13.44 million.

12-8 a. Total assets = $ 33,534 (thousands);
      Deficit = $2,128 (thousands).
   b. LOC = $4,228 (thousands).

12-9 LOC = $128,783.

14-1 Payout = 33.33%.

14-2 Payout = 20%.

14-3 Payout = 52%.

14-4 V_{op} = $175 million;
   n = 8.75 million.

14-5 P_0 = $80.

14-6 $6,900,000.

14-7 n = 4,000; EPS = $5.00;
   DPS = $1.50; P = $40.00.

14-8 D_0 = $4.25.

14-9 Payout = 17.89%.

14-10 a. (1) $2,808,000.
      (2) $3.34 Million.
      (3) $7,855,000.
      (4) Regular = $2,808,000;
           Extra = $5,047,000.

14-11 a. $10,500,000.
b. DPS = $0.50; Payout
= 4.55%.
c. $9,000,000.
d. No.
e. 40%.
f. $1,500,000.
g. $12,875,143.

14-12 a. $848 million.
b. $450 million.
c. $30.
d. 1 million; 14 million.
e. $420 million; $30.

15-1 20,000.

15-2 1.0.

15-3 3.6%.

15-4 $300 million.

15-5 $30.

15-6 40 million.

15-7 a. ΔProfit = $850,000;
Return = 21.25% > r_s = 15%.
b. $Q_{BE,Old}$ = 40;
$Q_{BE,New}$ = 45.45.

15-8 a. V = $3,348,214.
b. $16.74.
c. $1.84.
d. 10%.

15-9 30% debt:
WACC = 11.14%;
V = $101.023 million.

50% debt:
WACC = 11.25%;
V = $100 million.

70% debt:
WACC = 11.94%;
V = $94.255 million.

15-10 a. 0.870.
b. b = 1.218; r_s = 10.872%.
c. WACC = 8.683%;
V = $103.188 million.

15-11 WACC at optimal debt level: 8.89%.

16-1 $3,000,000.

16-2 AR = $59,500.

16-3 r_{NOM} = 75.26%;
EAR = 109.84%.

16-4 EAR = 8.49%.

16-5 $7,500,000.

16-6 a. DSO = 38 days.
b. AR = $156,164.
c. AR = $141,781.

16-7 a. 73.74%.
b. 14.90%.
c. 32.25%.
d. 21.28%.
e. 29.80%.

16-8 a. 45.15%.

16-9 Nominal cost = 14.90%;
Effective cost = 15.89%.

16-10 14.91%.

16-11 a. 60 days.
b. $420,000.
c. 7.3.

16-12 a. 56.8 days.
b. (1) 2.7082.
(2) 18.96%.
c. (1) 36.6 days.
(2) 2.95.
(3) 20.68%.

16-13 a. ROE_T = 11.75%;
ROE_M = 10.80%;
ROE_R = 9.16%.

16-14 a. Feb. surplus = $2,000.
b. $164,400.

16-15 a. $100,000.
b. (1) $300,000.
(2) Nominal cost = 37.24%;
Effective cost = 44.59%.
c. Nominal cost = 24.83%;
Effective cost = 27.86%.

16-16 a. 14.35%.

16-17 a. $300,000.
b. $2,000.
c. (1) $322,500.
(2) $26,875.
(3) 13.57%.
(4) 14.44%.

17-1   12.358 yen per peso.

17-2 f_t = $0.00907.

17-3   1 euro = $0.9091 or
        $1 = 1.1 euros.

17-4   0.6667 euros per dollar.

17-5   1.5152 SFr.

17-6   2.4 Swiss francs per pound.

17-7 $r_{NOM-U.S.}$ = 4.6%.

17-8   117 pesos.

17-9   +$500,000.

17-10 $24,500.

17-11   a. $1,658,925.
        b. $$1,646,091.
        c. $2,000,000.

17-12   b. f_t = 1.3990 dollars per Swiss franc; discount.

17-13 $322 million.

17-14   a. $89,357; 20%.
        b. 1,039.90 won per U.S. dollar and 1029.95
           won per U.S. dollar.
        c. 78,150,661 won; 18.85%.

18-1   a. $700,000.
        b. $3,700,000.
        c. −$2,300,000.

18-2   964,115 shares.

18-3   10,000 shares at $20 per share.

18-4   a. $$22,016,893; $ 40.03per share.
        b. Abercrombie: D/A 30.43%;
           P/E 15.91; M/B 2.19; ROE 13.8%; P/FCF
           21.47
           Gunter: D/A 20.00%;
           P/E 15.02; M/B 2.35; ROE 15.7%; P/FCF
           18.50.
           B&C: D/A 18.18%%;
           P/E 15.40; M/B 2.22; ROE 14.4%; P/FCF
           20.02.
        c. Price based on: Abercrombie P/E $41.36;
           Gunter P/E $39.04.
           Price based on: Abercrombie M/B $39.38;
           Gunter M/B $42.30.
           Price based on: Abercrombie P/FCF
           $42.94; Gunter P/FCF $37.01.

18-5 $14.74; $13.708 million.

18-6   a. After-tax call cost = $2,640,000.
        b. Flotation cost = $1,600,000.
        c. $1,920,000; $768,000.
        d. $3,472,000.
        e. New tax savings = $16,000;
           Lost tax savings = $19,200.
        f. $360,000.
        g. PV = $9,109,413.
        h. $5,637,413.

18-7   a. NPV = $2,717,128.

19-1   a. (1) 50%.
           (2) 60%.
           (3) 50%.

19-2   Cost of owning = −$127;
        Cost of leasing = −$128;
        NAL = −$1.

19-3   a. Energen: Debt/TA = 50%;
           Hastings: Debt/TA = 33%.
        b. TA = $200.

19-4   a. NAL = $108,147.

19-5   a. PV of leasing = −667,261;
           PV of owning =
           −$713,300;
           NAL = $46,039
        b. $245,703.

20-1 $182.16.

20-2   20 shares.

20-3   a. (1) $0.
           (2) $0.
           (3) $5.
           (4) $75.
        b. 10%; $100.

20-4   Premium = 10%: $46.20;
        Premium = 30%: $54.60.

20-5   a. 14.1%.
        b. $12 million before tax.
        c. $331.89.
        d. Value as a straight bond = $699.25; Value
           in conversion = $521.91.
        e. Value as a straight bond = $1,000.00; Value
           in conversion = $521.91.

20-6   a. Plan 1, 49%; Plan 2, 53%;
           Plan 3, 53%.

b. Plan 1, $0.59; Plan 2, $0.64;
   Plan 3, $0.88.
c. Plan 1, 19%; Plan 2, 19%;
   Plan 3, 50%.

20-7 a. Year = 7;
        CV_7 = $1,210.422;
        CF_7 = $1,290.422.
     b. 10.20%.

21-1 $500 million.

21-2 $821 million.

21-3 $620.68 million.

21-4 $813.125 million.

21-5 a. b_U = 1.125.
     b. r_{sU} = 15.625%.
     c. 16.62%; 18.04%; 20.23%.
     d. 20.23%.

21-6 a. V_U = V_L = $20 million.
     b. r_{sU} = 10%; r_{sL} = 15%.
     c. S_L = $10 million.
     d. $WACC_U$ = 10%;
        $WACC_L$ = 10%.

21-7 a. V_U = $12 million;
        V_L = $16 million.
     b. r_{sU} = 10%; r_{sL} = 15%.
     c. S_L = $6 million.
     d. $WACC_U$ = 10%;
        $WACC_L$ = 7.5%.

21-8 a. V_U = $12 million;
        V_L = $15.33 million;
        $3.33 million.
     b. V_L = V_U = $20 million; $0.
     c. V_U = $12 million;
        V_L = $16 million;
        $4 million.
     d. V_U = $12 million;
        V_L = $16 million;
        $4 million.

21-9 a. V_U = $12.5 million.
     b. V_L = $16 million; r_{sL} = 15.7%.
     c. V_L = $14.5 million; r_{sL} = 14.9%.

21-10 a. V_U = V_L = $14,545,455.
      b. At D = $6 million:
         r_{sL} = 14.51%;
         WACC = 11.0%.
      c. V_U = $8,727,273;
         V_L = $11,127,273.

d. At D = $6 million:
   r_{sL} = 14.51%;
   WACC = 8.63%.
e. D = V = $14,545,455.

21-11 a. V = $3.29 million.
      b. D = $1.71 million; Yield = 8.1%.
      c. V = $3.23 million; D = $1.77 million;
         Yield = 6.3%.

21-12 a. $713.33 million.
      b. $563.29 million.
      c. $71.33 million.
      d. $57.86 million.
      e. $621.15 million.

22-1 P_0 = $25.26.

22-2 P_0 = $41.54.

22-3 $25.26 to $41.54.

22-4 Value of equity = $46.30 million.

22-5 a. $V_{op\ Unlevered}$ = $32.02 million;
        $V_{Tax\ shields}$ = $11.50 million.
     b. V_{op} = $43.52 million;
        max = $33.52 million.

22-6 a. 10.96%.
     b. (All in millions)
        FCF_1 = $23.12,
        TS_1 = $14.00;
        FCF_3 = $12.26,
        TS_3 = $16.45;
        FCF_5 = $23.83,
        TS_5 = $18.90.
     c. HV_{TS} = $510.68 million;
        HV_U = $643.89 million.
     d. Value of equity = $508.57 million.

23-1 Net payment = LIBOR + 0.2%.

23-2 r_d = 7.01%.

23-3 r_d = 5.96%;
     Futures = $89,748.42.

23-4 Net to Carter = 9.95% fixed;
     Net to Brence = LIBOR + 3.05% floating.

23-5 a. Sell 105 contracts.
     b. Bond = −$1,414,552.69;
        Futures = $1,951,497.45;
        Net = +$536,944.76.

24-1 AP = $375,000;
      NP = $750,000;
      SD = $750,000; Stockholders = $343,750.

24-2 a. Total assets: $327 million.
      b. Income: $7 million.
      c. Before, $15.6 million;
         After, $13.0 million.
      d. Before, 35.7%;
         After, 64.2%.

24-3 a. $0.
      b. First mortgage holders, $300,000; Second
         mortgage holders, $100,000 plus $12,700
         as a general claimant.
      c. Trustee's expenses, $50,000;
         Wages due, $30,000;
         Taxes due, $40,000.
      d. *Before subordination*
         Accounts payable = $6,350;
         Notes payable = $22,860;
         Second mortgage = $12,700 + $100,000;
         Debentures = $25,400;
         Sub. debentures = $12,700.
         After subordination
         Notes payable = $35,560;
         Sub. debentures = $0.

24-4 a. $0 for stockholders.
      b. AP = 24%; NP = 100%; WP = 100%;
         TP = 100%; Mortgage = 85%; Subordinated
         debentures = 9%; Trustee = 100%.

25-1 1.4.

25-2 12%.

25-3 16.2%; 45.9%.

25-4 a. $r_i = r_{RF} + (r_M - r_{RF}) \dfrac{\rho_{iM} \sigma_i}{\sigma_M}$

25-5 a. b = 0.56.
      b. X: 10.6%; 13.1%.
         M: 12.1%; 22.6%.
      c. 8.6%.

25-6 a. b = 0.62.

26-1 a. $1.074 million.
      b. $2.96 million.

26-2 a. $4.6795 million.
      b. $3.208 million.

26-3 a. −$19 million.
      b. $9.0981 million.

26-4 a. −$2.113 million.
      b. $1.973 million.
      c. −$70,222.
      d. $565,090.
      e. $1.116 million.

26-5 a. $2,562.
      b. E[NPV] = $9,786; Value of growth
         option = $7,224.

26-6 P = $18.646 million;
      X = $20 million; t = 1;
      r_{RF} = 0.08; σ^2 = 0.0687;
      V = $2.028 million.

26-7 P = $10.479 million;
      X = $9 million; t = 2;
      r_{RF} = 0.06; σ^2 = 0.0111;
      V = $2.514 million.

26-8 P = $18,646;
      X = $20,000; t = 2;
      V = $5,009.

Appendix C

Selected Equations

CHAPTER 1

$$\text{Value} = \frac{\text{FCF}_1}{(1 + \text{WACC})^1} + \frac{\text{FCF}_2}{(1 + \text{WACC})^2} + \frac{\text{FCF}_3}{(1 + \text{WACC})^3} + \cdots + \frac{\text{FCF}_\infty}{(1 + \text{WACC})^\infty}$$

CHAPTER 2

EBIT = Earnings before interest and taxes = Sales revenues − Operating costs

EBITDA = Earnings before interest, taxes, depreciation, and amortization
= EBIT + Depreciation + Amortization

Net cash flow = Net income + Depreciation and amortization

NOWC = Net operating working capital

= Operating current assets − Operating current liabilities

$$= \left(\begin{array}{c} \text{Cash} + \text{Accounts receivable} \\ + \text{Inventories} \end{array} \right) - \left(\begin{array}{c} \text{Accounts payable} \\ + \text{Accruals} \end{array} \right)$$

Total net operating capital = Net operating working capital + Operating long-term assets

NOPAT = Net operating profit after taxes = EBIT(1 − Tax rate)

Free cash flow (FCF) = NOPAT − Net investment in operating capital

$$= \text{NOPAT} - \left(\begin{array}{c} \text{CashCurrent year's total} \\ \text{net operating capital} \end{array} - \begin{array}{c} \text{Previous year's total} \\ \text{net operating capital} \end{array} \right)$$

$$\text{FCF} = \text{Operating cash flow} - \begin{array}{c} \text{Gross investment} \\ \text{in operating capital} \end{array}$$

$$\text{Return on invested capital (ROIC)} = \frac{\text{NOPAT}}{\text{Total net operating capital}}$$

MVA = Market value of stock − Equity capital supplied by shareholders

= (Shares outstanding)(Stock price) − Total common equity

MVA = Total market value − Total investor-supplied capital

$$= \left(\begin{array}{c} \text{Market value of stock} \\ + \text{Market value of debt} \end{array} \right) - \text{Total investor-supplied capital}$$

$$EVA = \left(\begin{array}{c} \text{Net operating profit} \\ \text{after taxes (NOPAT)} \end{array} \right) - \left(\begin{array}{c} \text{After-tax dollar cost of capital} \\ \text{used to support operations} \end{array} \right)$$

$$= EBIT(1 - \text{Tax rate}) - (\text{Total net operating capital})(WACC)$$

$$EVA = (\text{Total net operating capital})(ROIC - WACC)$$

CHAPTER 3

$$\text{Current ratio} = \frac{\text{Current assets}}{\text{Current liabilities}}$$

$$\text{Quick, or acid test, ratio} = \frac{\text{Current assets} - \text{Inventories}}{\text{Current liabilities}}$$

$$\text{Inventory turnover ratio} = \frac{\text{Cost of Goods Sold}}{\text{Inventories}}$$

$$DSO = \text{Days sales outstanding} = \frac{\text{Receivables}}{\text{Average sales per day}} = \frac{\text{Receivables}}{\text{Annual sales}/365}$$

$$\text{Fixed assets turnover ratio} = \frac{\text{Sales}}{\text{Net fixed assets}}$$

$$\text{Total assets turnover ratio} = \frac{\text{Sales}}{\text{Total assets}}$$

$$\text{Debt ratio} = \frac{\text{Total debt}}{\text{Total assets}}$$

$$\text{Liabilities-to-assets ratio} = \frac{\text{Total liabilities}}{\text{Total assets}}$$

$$\text{Market debt ratio} = \frac{\text{Total debt}}{\text{Total debt} + \text{Market value of equity}}$$

$$\text{Debt-to-equity ratio} = \frac{\text{Total debt}}{\text{Total common equity}}$$

$$\text{Equity multiplier} = \frac{\text{Total assets}}{\text{Common equity}}$$

$$\text{Times-interest-earned (TIE) ratio} = \frac{EBIT}{\text{Interest charges}}$$

$$\text{EBITDA coverage ratio} = \frac{\text{EBITDA} + \text{Lease payments}}{\text{Interest} + \text{Principal payments} + \text{Lease payments}}$$

$$\text{Net profit margin} = \frac{\text{Net income available to common stockholders}}{\text{Sales}}$$

$$\text{Operating profit margin} = \frac{EBIT}{\text{Sales}}$$

$$\text{Gross profit margin} = \frac{\text{Sales} - \text{Cost of goods sold}}{\text{Sales}}$$

$$\text{Return on total assets (ROA)} = \frac{\text{Net income available to common stockholders}}{\text{Total assets}}$$

$$\text{Basic earning power (BEP) ratio} = \frac{\text{EBIT}}{\text{Total assets}}$$

$$\text{ROA} = \text{Profit margin} \times \text{Total assets turnover} = \frac{\text{Net income}}{\text{Sales}} \times \frac{\text{Sales}}{\text{Total assets}}$$

$$\text{Return on common equity (ROE)} = \frac{\text{Net income available to common stockholders}}{\text{Common equity}}$$

$$\text{ROE} = \text{ROA} \times \text{Equity multiplier}$$

$$= \text{Profit margin} \times \text{Total assets turnover} \times \text{Equity multiplier}$$

$$= \frac{\text{Net income}}{\text{Sales}} \times \frac{\text{Sales}}{\text{Total assets}} \times \frac{\text{Total assets}}{\text{Common equity}}$$

$$\text{Price/earnings (P/E) ratio} = \frac{\text{Price per share}}{\text{Earnings per share}}$$

$$\text{Price/cash flow ratio} = \frac{\text{Price per share}}{\text{Cash flow per share}}$$

$$\text{Book value per share} = \frac{\text{Common equity}}{\text{Shares outstanding}}$$

$$\text{Market/book (M/B) ratio} = \frac{\text{Market price per share}}{\text{Book value per share}}$$

CHAPTER 4

$$FV_N = PV(1 + I)^N$$

$$PV = \frac{FV_N}{(1 + I)^N}$$

$$FVA_N = PMT\left[\frac{(1 + I)^N}{I} - \frac{1}{I}\right] = PMT\left[\frac{(1 + I)^N - 1}{I}\right]$$

$$FVA_{due} = FVA_{ordinary}(1 + I)$$

$$PVA_N = PMT\left[\frac{1}{I} - \frac{1}{I(1 + I)^N}\right] = PMT\left[\frac{1 - \frac{1}{(1 + I)^N}}{I}\right]$$

$$PVA_{Due} = PVA_{Ordinary}(1 + I)$$

$$PV \text{ of a perpetuity} = \frac{PMT}{I}$$

$$PV_{\text{Uneven stream}} = \sum_{t=1}^{N} \frac{CF_t}{(1 + I)^t}$$

$$FV_{\text{Uneven stream}} = \sum_{t=1}^{N} CF_t(1 + I)^{N-t}$$

$$I_{PER} = \frac{I_{NOM}}{M}$$

$$APR = (I_{PER})M$$

Number of periods = NM

$$FV_N = PV(1 + I_{PER})^{\text{Number of periods}} = PV\left(1 + \frac{I_{NOM}}{M}\right)^{MN}$$

$$EFF\% = \left(1 + \frac{I_{NOM}}{M}\right)^M - 1.0$$

CHAPTER 5

$$V_B = \sum_{t=1}^{N} \frac{INT}{(1 + r_d)^t} + \frac{M}{(1 + r_d)^N}$$

Semiannual payments: $V_B = \displaystyle\sum_{t=1}^{2N} \frac{INT/2}{(1 + r_d/2)^t} + \frac{M}{(1 + r_d/2)^{2N}}$

Yield to maturity: Bond price $= \displaystyle\sum_{t=1}^{N} \frac{INT}{(1 + YTM)^t} + \frac{M}{(1 + YTM)^N}$

Price of callable bond (if called at N) $= \displaystyle\sum_{t=1}^{N} \frac{INT}{(1 + r_d)^t} + \frac{\text{Call price}}{(1 + r_d)^N}$

$$\text{Current yield} = \frac{\text{Annual interest}}{\text{Bond's current price}}$$

Current yield + Capital gains yield = Yield to maturity

$$r_d = r^* + IP + DRP + LP + MRP$$

$$r_{RF} = r^* + IP$$

$$r_d = r_{RF} + DRP + LP + MRP$$

$$IP_N = \frac{I_1 + I_2 + \cdots + I_N}{N}$$

CHAPTER 6

$$\text{Expected rate of return} = \hat{r} = \sum_{i=1}^{n} P_i r_i$$

$$\text{Historical average, } \bar{r}_{Avg} = \frac{\displaystyle\sum_{t=1}^{T} \bar{r}_t}{T}$$

$$\text{Variance} = \sigma^2 = \sum_{i=1}^{n} (r_i - \hat{r})^2 P_i$$

$$\text{Standard deviation} = \sigma = \sqrt{\sum_{i=1}^{n} (r_i - \hat{r})^2 P_i}$$

Historical estimated $\sigma = S = \sqrt{\dfrac{\sum\limits_{t=1}^{T} (\bar{r}_t - \bar{r}_{Avg})^2}{T-1}}$

$\hat{r}_p = \sum\limits_{i=1}^{n} w_i \hat{r}_i$

$\sigma_P = \sqrt{\sum\limits_{i=1}^{n} (r_{pi} - \hat{r}_p)^2 P_i}$

Estimated $\rho = R = \dfrac{\sum\limits_{t=1}^{T} (\bar{r}_{i,j} - \bar{r}_{i,Avg})(\bar{r}_{j,t} - \bar{r}_{j,Avg})}{\sqrt{\sum\limits_{t=1}^{T} (\bar{r}_{i,t} - \bar{r}_{i,Avg})^2 \sum\limits_{t=1}^{T} (\bar{r}_{j,t} - \bar{r}_{j,Avg})^2}}$

$COV_{iM} = \rho_{iM} \sigma_i \sigma_M$

$b_i = \left(\dfrac{\sigma_i}{\sigma_M}\right)\rho_{iM} = \dfrac{COV_{iM}}{\sigma_M^2}$

$b_p = \sum\limits_{i=1}^{n} w_i b_i$

Required return on stock market $= r_M$

Market risk premium $= RP_M = r_M - r_{RF}$

$RP_i = (r_M - r_{RF})b_i = (RP_M)b_i$

$SML = r_i = r_{RF} + (r_M - r_{RF})b_i = r_{RF} + RP_M b_i$

CHAPTER 7

$\hat{P}_0 = $ PV of expected future dividends $= \sum\limits_{t=1}^{\infty} \dfrac{D_t}{(1+r_s)^t}$

Constant growth: $\hat{P}_0 = \dfrac{D_0(1+g)}{r_s - g} = \dfrac{D_1}{r_s - g}$

$\hat{r}_s = \dfrac{D_1}{P_0} + g$

Capital gains yield $= \dfrac{\hat{P}_1 - P_0}{P_0}$

Dividend yield $= \dfrac{D_1}{P_0}$

For a zero growth stock, $\hat{P}_0 = \dfrac{D}{r_s}$

Horizon value of stock $=$ Terminal value $= \hat{P}_N = \dfrac{D_{N+1}}{r_s - g_L} = \dfrac{D_N(1+g_L)}{r_s - g_L}$

$$V_{ps} = \frac{D_{ps}}{r_{ps}}$$

$$\hat{r}_{ps} = \frac{D_{ps}}{V_{ps}}$$

$\bar{r}_s$ = Actual dividend yield + Actual capital gains yield

V_{op} = Value of operations

     = PV of expected future free cash flows

$$= \sum_{t=1}^{\infty} \frac{FCF_1}{(1+WACC)^t}$$

Horizon value of operations: $V_{op(\text{at time } N)} = \dfrac{FCF_{N+1}}{WACC - g_L} = \dfrac{FCF_N(1 + g_L)}{WACC - g_L}$

Total entity value = V_{op} + Value of nonoperating assets

Value of equity = Total entity value − Preferred stock − Debt

CHAPTER 8

Exercise value = MAX[Current price of stock − Strike price, 0]

Number of stock shares in hedged portfolio = $N = \dfrac{C_u - C_d}{P_u - P_d}$

$V_C = P[N(d_1)] - Xe^{-r_{RF}t}[N(d_2)]$

$$d_1 = \frac{\ln(P/X) + [r_{RF} + (\sigma^2/2)]t}{\sigma\sqrt{t}}$$

$d_2 = d_1 - \sigma\sqrt{t}$

Put–call parity: Put option = $V_C - P + Xe^{-r_{RF}t}$

V of put = $P[N(d_1) - 1] - Xe^{-r_{RF}t}[N(d_2)-1]$

CHAPTER 9

After-tax component cost of debt = $r_d(1 - T)$

$$M(1-F) = \sum_{t=1}^{N} \frac{INT(1 - T)}{[1 + r_d(1 - T)]^t} + \frac{M}{[1 + r_d(1 - T)]^N}$$

$$r_{ps} = \frac{D_{ps}}{P_{ps}(1 - F)}$$

Market equilibrium: $\dfrac{\text{Expected}}{\text{rate of return}} = \hat{r}_M = \dfrac{D_1}{P_0} + g = r_{RF} + RP_M = r_M = \dfrac{\text{Required}}{\text{rate of return}}$

Note: D_1, P_0, and g are for the market, not an individual company.

$$r_M = \hat{r}_M = \frac{D_1}{P_0} + g$$

Note: g is long-term growth rate in total dividends for the market and D_1 and P_0 are for the market, not an individual company.

CAPM: $r_s = r_{RF} + b_i(RP_M)$

DCF: $r_s = \hat{r}_s = \frac{D_1}{P_0} +$ Expected g in dividends per share

Own-bond yield-plus-judgmental-risk-premium: $r_s = \begin{matrix} \text{Company's own} \\ \text{bond yield} \end{matrix} + \begin{matrix} \text{Judgemental} \\ \text{risk premium} \end{matrix}$

g = (Retention rate)(ROE) = (1.0 − Payout rate)(ROE)

$$r_e = \hat{r}_e = \frac{D_1}{P_0(1 - F)} + g$$

$$WACC = w_d r_d (1 - T) + w_{ps} r_{ps} + w_s r_s$$

CHAPTER 10

$$NPV = CF_0 + \frac{CF_1}{(1+r)^1} + \frac{CF_2}{(1+r)^2} + \cdots + \frac{CF_N}{(1+r)^N}$$

$$= \sum_{t=0}^{N} \frac{CF_t}{(1+r)^t}$$

$$IRR: CF_0 + \frac{CF_1}{(1+IRR)^1} + \frac{CF_2}{(1+IRR)^2} + \cdots + \frac{CF_N}{(1+IRR)^N} = 0$$

$$NPV = \sum_{t=0}^{N} \frac{CF_t}{(1+IRR)^t} = 0$$

MIRR: PV of costs = PV of terminal value

$$\sum_{t=0}^{N} \frac{COF_t}{(1+r)^t} = \frac{\sum_{t=0}^{N} CIF_t(1+r)^{N-t}}{(1+MIRR)^N}$$

$$PV \text{ of costs} = \frac{\text{Terminal value}}{(1+MIRR)^N}$$

$$PI = \frac{PV \text{ of future cash flows}}{\text{initial cost}} = \frac{\sum_{t=1}^{N} \frac{CF_t}{(1+r)^t}}{CF_0}$$

$$\text{Payback} = \begin{matrix} \text{Number of} \\ \text{years prior to} \\ \text{full recovery} \end{matrix} + \frac{\begin{matrix} \text{Uncovered cost} \\ \text{at start of year} \end{matrix}}{\begin{matrix} \text{Cash flow during} \\ \text{full recovery year} \end{matrix}}$$

CHAPTER 11

$$\text{Project cash flow} = \text{FCF} = \begin{matrix}\text{Investment outlay} \\ \text{cash flow}\end{matrix} + \begin{matrix}\text{Operating} \\ \text{cash flow}\end{matrix} + \begin{matrix}\text{NOWC} \\ \text{cash flow}\end{matrix} + \begin{matrix}\text{Salvage} \\ \text{cash flow}\end{matrix}$$

$$\text{Expected NPV} = \sum_{i=1}^{n} P_i\,(NPV_i)$$

$$\sigma_{NPV} = \sqrt{\sum_{i=1}^{n} P_i\,(NPV_i - \text{Expected NPV})^2}$$

$$CV_{NPV} = \frac{\sigma_{NPV}}{E(NPV)}$$

CHAPTER 12

$$\begin{matrix}\text{Additional} \\ \text{funds} \\ \text{needed}\end{matrix} = \begin{matrix}\text{Required} \\ \text{asset} \\ \text{increase}\end{matrix} - \begin{matrix}\text{Spontaneous} \\ \text{liability} \\ \text{increase}\end{matrix} - \begin{matrix}\text{Increase in} \\ \text{retained} \\ \text{earnings}\end{matrix}$$

$$\text{AFN} = (A^*/S_0)\Delta S - (L^*/S_0)\Delta S - MS_1(1 - \text{Payout ratio})$$

$$\begin{matrix}\text{Full} \\ \text{capacity} \\ \text{sales}\end{matrix} = \frac{\text{Actual sales}}{\begin{matrix}\text{Percentage of capacity} \\ \text{at which fixed assets} \\ \text{were operated}\end{matrix}}$$

$$\text{Target fixed assets/Sales} = \frac{\text{Actual fixed assets}}{\text{Full capacity sales}}$$

$$\begin{matrix}\text{Required level} \\ \text{of fixed assets}\end{matrix} = (\text{Target fixed assets/Sales})(\text{Projected sales})$$

CHAPTER 14

$$\text{Residual distribution} = \text{Net income} - [(\text{Target equity ratio})(\text{Total capital budget})]$$

$$\text{Number of shares repurchased} = n_{Prior} - n_{Post} = \frac{Cash_{Rep}}{P_{Prior}}$$

$$n_{Post} = n_{Prior} - \frac{Cash_{Rep}}{P_{Prior}} = n_{Prior} - \frac{Cash_{Rep}}{S_{Prior}/n_{Prior}} = n_{Prior}\left(1 - \frac{Cash_{Rep}}{S_{Prior}}\right)$$

CHAPTER 15

$$V_{op} = \sum_{t=1}^{\infty} \frac{FCF_t}{(1 + WACC)^t}$$

$$WACC = w_d(1 - T)r_d + w_s r_s$$

$$ROIC = \frac{NOPAT}{Capital} = \frac{EBIT(1 - T)}{Capital}$$

$$EBIT = PQ - VQ - F$$

$$Q_{BE} = \frac{F}{P - V}$$

$$V_L = S_L + D$$

MM, no taxes: $V_L = V_U$

MM, corporate taxes: $V_L = V_U + TD$

Miller, corporate and personal taxes: $V_L = V_U + \left[1 - \frac{(1 - T_c)(1 - T_s)}{(1 - T_d)}\right] D$

$$b = b_U[1 + (1 - T)(D/S)] = b_U[1 + (1 - T)(w_d/w_s)]$$

$$b_U = b/[1 + (1 - T)(D/S)] = b/[1 + (1 - T)(w_d/w_s)]$$

$$r_s = r_{RF} + RP_M(b)$$

$$r_s = r_{RF} + \text{Premium for business risk} + \text{Premium for financial risk}$$

If $g = 0$: $V_{op} = \dfrac{FCF}{WACC} = \dfrac{NOPAT}{WACC} = \dfrac{EBIT(1 - T)}{WACC}$

Total corporate value $= V_{op} + \text{Value of short-term investments}$

$S = \text{Total corporate value} - \text{Value of all debt}$

$$D = w_d V_{op}$$

$$S = (1 - w_d)V_{op}$$

Cash raised by issuing debt $= D - D_0$

$$P_{Prior} = S_{Prior}/n_{Prior}$$

$$P_{Post} = P_{Prior}$$

$$n_{Post} = n_{Prior}\left[\frac{V_{opNew} - D_{New}}{V_{opNew} - D_{Old}}\right]$$

$$n_{Post} = n_{Prior} - (D_{New} - D_{Old})/P_{Prior}$$

$$P_{Post} = \frac{V_{opNew} - D_{Old}}{n_{Prior}}$$

$$NI = (EBIT - r_d D)(1 - T)$$

$$EPS = NI/n$$

CHAPTER 16

$$\text{Inventory conversion period} = \frac{\text{Inventory}}{(\text{Cost of goods sold})/365}$$

$$\text{Receivables collection period} = DSO = \frac{\text{Receivables}}{\text{Sales}/365}$$

$$\text{Payables deferral period} = \frac{\text{Payables}}{(\text{Cost of goods sold})/365}$$

$$\begin{matrix} \text{Cash} \\ \text{conversion} \\ \text{cycle} \end{matrix} = \begin{matrix} \text{Inventory} \\ \text{conversion} \\ \text{period} \end{matrix} + \begin{matrix} \text{Average} \\ \text{collection} \\ \text{period} \end{matrix} - \begin{matrix} \text{Payables} \\ \text{deferral} \\ \text{period} \end{matrix}$$

$$\begin{array}{c} \text{Accounts} \\ \text{receivable} \end{array} = \begin{array}{c} \text{Credit sales} \\ \text{per day} \end{array} \times \begin{array}{c} \text{Length of} \\ \text{collection period} \end{array}$$

$$\text{ADS} = \frac{(\text{Units sold})(\text{Sales price})}{365} = \frac{\text{Annual sales}}{365}$$

$$\text{Receivables} = (\text{ADS})(\text{DSO})$$

$$\begin{array}{c} \text{Nominal annual cost} \\ \text{of trade credit} \end{array} = \frac{\text{Discount percentage}}{100 - \begin{array}{c} \text{Discount} \\ \text{percentage} \end{array}} \times \frac{365}{\begin{array}{c} \text{Days credit is} \\ \text{outstanding} \end{array} - \begin{array}{c} \text{Discount} \\ \text{period} \end{array}}$$

CHAPTER 17

$$\begin{array}{c} \text{Single-period interest} \\ \text{rate parity} \end{array} : \frac{\text{Forward exchange rate}}{\text{Spot exchange rate}} = \frac{1 + r_h}{1 + r_f}$$

$$\begin{array}{c} \text{Expected t-year} \\ \text{forward exchange rate} \end{array} = (\text{Spot rate})\left(\frac{1 + r_h}{1 + r_f}\right)^t$$

$$P_h = (P_f)(\text{Spot rate})$$

$$\text{Spot rate} = \frac{P_h}{P_f}$$

CHAPTER 18

$$\text{Amount left on table} = (\text{Closing price} - \text{Offer price})(\text{Number of shares})$$

CHAPTER 19

$$\text{NAL} = \text{PV of leasing} - \text{PV of owning}$$

CHAPTER 20

$$\begin{array}{c} \text{Price paid for} \\ \text{bond with warrants} \end{array} = \begin{array}{c} \text{Straight-debt} \\ \text{value of bond} \end{array} + \begin{array}{c} \text{Value of} \\ \text{warrants} \end{array}$$

$$\text{Conversion price} = P_c = \frac{\text{Par value of bond given up}}{\text{Shares received}}$$

$$= \frac{\text{Par value of bond given up}}{\text{CR}}$$

$$\text{Conversion ratio} = \text{CR} = \frac{\text{Par value of bond given up}}{P_c}$$

CHAPTER 21

MM, no taxes ($T = 0$ and $g = 0$):

$$V_L = V_U = \frac{EBIT}{WACC} = \frac{EBIT}{r_{sU}}$$

$$r_{sL} = r_{sU} + \text{Risk premium} = r_{sU} + (r_{sU} - r_d)(D/S)$$

MM, corporate taxes ($r_{TS} = rd$ and $g = 0$):

$$V_L = V_U + TD$$

$$V_U = S = \frac{EBIT(1 - T)}{r_{sU}}$$

$$r_{sL} = r_{sU} + (r_{sU} - r_d)(1 - T)(D/S)$$

Miller, personal taxes taxes ($r_{TS} = rd$ and $g = 0$):

$$V_U = \frac{EBIT(1 - T_c)}{r_{sU}} = \frac{EBIT(1 - T_c)(1 - T_s)}{r_{sU}(1 - T_s)}$$

$$CF_L = (EBIT - I)(1 - T_c)(1 - T_s) + I(1 - T_d)$$

$$V_L = V_U + \left[1 - \frac{(1 - T_c)(1 - T_s)}{(1 - T_d)}\right] D$$

Adjusted present value approach ($g = $ constant):

Tax savings = (Interest expense)(Tax rate)

Value of operations = $V_{op} = V_{Unlevered} + V_{Tax\ shield}$

$$V_L = V_U + V_{Tax\ shield}$$

$$V_{Tax\ shield} = \frac{r_d TD}{r_{TS} - g}$$

$$V_L = V_U + \left(\frac{r_d}{r_{TS} - g}\right) TD$$

Compressed adjusted present value approach ($r_{TS} = r_{sU}$ and $g = $ constant):

$$V_L = V_U + \left(\frac{r_d TD}{r_{sU} - g}\right)$$

$$r_{sL} = r_{sU} + (r_{sU} - r_d)\frac{D}{S}$$

$$b = b_U + (b_U - b_D)\frac{D}{S}$$

$$r_{sU} = w_s r_{sL} + w_d r_d$$

Compressed adjusted present value approach $(r_{TS} = rs_U)$:

$$\text{Horizon value of unlevered firm} = HV_{U,N} = \frac{FCF_{N+1}}{r_{sU} - g} = \frac{FCF_N(1 + g)}{r_{sU} - g}$$

$$\text{Horizon value of tax shield} = HV_{TS,N} = \frac{TS_{N+1}}{r_{sU} - g} = \frac{TS_N(1 + g)}{r_{sU} - g}$$

$$V_{Unlevered} = \sum_{t=1}^{N} \frac{FCF_t}{(1 + r_{sU})^t} + \frac{HV_{U,N}}{(1 + r_{sU})^N}$$

$$V_{Tax\ shield} = \sum_{t=1}^{N} \frac{TS_t}{(1 + r_{sU})^t} + \frac{HV_{TS,N}}{(1 + r_{sU})^N}$$

CHAPTER 22

$$FCFE = \text{Free cash flow} - \text{After-tax interest expense} - \text{Principal payments} + \text{Newly issued debt}$$

$$= \text{Free cash flow} - \text{Interest expense} + \text{Interest tax shield} + \text{Net change in debt}$$

$$FCFE = \text{Net income} - \text{Net investment in operating capital} + \text{Net change in debt}$$

$$HV_{FCFE,N} = \frac{FCFE_{N+1}}{r_{sL} - g} = \frac{FCFE_N(1 + g)}{r_{sL} - g}$$

$$V_{FCFE} = \sum_{t=1}^{N} \frac{FCFE_t}{(1 + r_{sL})^t} + \frac{HV_{FCFE,N}}{(1 + r_{sL})^N}$$

$$S = V_{FCFE} + \text{Nonoperating assets}$$

$$\frac{\text{Total value of shares to target shareholders}}{\text{Total post-merger value of equity}} = \frac{\text{Percent required by target stockholders}}{} = \frac{n_{New}}{n_{New} + n_{Old}}$$

CHAPTER 25

$$\hat{r}_p = w_A \hat{r}_A + (1 - w_A)\hat{r}_B$$

$$\text{Portfolio SD} = \sigma_P = \sqrt{w_A^2 \sigma_A^2 + (1 - w_A)^2 \sigma_B^2 + 2w_A(1 - w_A)\rho_{AB}\sigma_A\sigma_B}$$

$$\text{Minimum-risk portfolio: } w_A = \frac{\sigma_B(\sigma_B - \rho_{AB}\sigma_A)}{\sigma_A^2 + \sigma_B^2 - 2\rho_{AB}\sigma_A\sigma_B}$$

$$\hat{r}_p = \sum_{i=1}^{N} (w_i \hat{r}_i)$$

$$\sigma_p^2 = \sum_{i=1}^{N} \sum_{j=1}^{N} \left(w_i \, w_j \, \sigma_i \, \sigma_j \, \rho_{ij} \right)$$

$$\sigma_p^2 = \sum_{i=1}^{N} w_i^2 \, \sigma_i^2 + \sum_{i=1}^{N} \sum_{\substack{j=1 \\ j \neq i}}^{N} w_i \, \sigma_i \, w_j \, \sigma_j \, \rho_{ij}$$

$$\sigma_p = \sqrt{\left(1 - w_{RF}\right)^2 \sigma_M^2} = \left(1 - w_{RF}\right)\sigma_M$$

$$\text{CML: } \hat{r}_p = r_{RF} + \left(\frac{\hat{r}_M - r_{RF}}{\sigma_M} \right)\sigma_p$$

$$r_i = r_{RF} + \frac{(r_M - r_{RF})}{\sigma_M} \left(\frac{\text{Cov}(r_i, r_M)}{\sigma_M} \right) = r_{RF} + (r_M - r_{RF}) \left(\frac{\text{Cov}(r_i, r_M)}{\sigma_M^2} \right)$$

$$b_i = \frac{\text{Covariance between stock i and the market}}{\text{Variance of market returns}} = \frac{\text{Cov}(r_i, r_M)}{\sigma_M^2} = \frac{\rho_{iM}\sigma_i\sigma_M}{\sigma_M^2} = \rho_{iM}\left(\frac{\sigma_i}{\sigma_M} \right)$$

$$\text{SML} = r_i = r_{RF} + (r_M - r_{RF})b_i = r_{RF} + (RP_M)b_i$$

$$\sigma_i^2 = b_i^2 \sigma_M^2 + \sigma_{e_i}{}^2$$

$$\text{APT: } r_i = r_{RF} + (r_1 - r_{RF})b_{i1} + \cdots + (r_j - r_{RF})b_{ij}$$

CHAPTER 26

$$CV = \frac{\sigma \, (\text{PV of future CF})}{E \, (\text{PV of future CF})}$$

Variance of project's rate of return: $\sigma^2 = \dfrac{\ln (CV^2 + 1)}{t}$

© lulu/fotolia.com

Values of the Areas under the Standard Normal Distribution Function

TABLE D-1

Values of the Areas under the Standard Normal Distribution Function

Z	0.00	0.01	0.02	0.03	0.04	0.05	0.06	0.07	0.08	0.09
0.0	.0000	.0040	.0080	.0120	.0160	.0199	.0239	.0279	.0319	.0359
0.1	.0398	.0438	.0478	.0517	.0557	.0596	.0636	.0675	.0714	.0753
0.2	.0793	.0832	.0871	.0910	.0948	.0987	.1026	.1064	.1103	.1141
0.3	.1179	.1217	.1255	.1293	.1331	.1368	.1406	.1443	.1480	.1517
0.4	.1554	.1591	.1628	.1664	.1700	.1736	.1772	.1808	.1844	.1879
0.5	.1915	.1950	.1985	.2019	.2054	.2088	.2123	.2157	.2190	.2224
0.6	.2257	.2291	.2324	.2357	.2389	.2422	.2454	.2486	.2517	.2549
0.7	.2580	.2611	.2642	.2673	.2704	.2734	.2764	.2794	.2823	.2852
0.8	.2881	.2910	.2939	.2967	.2995	.3023	.3051	.3078	.3106	.3133
0.9	.3159	.3186	.3212	.3238	.3264	.3289	.3315	.3340	.3365	.3389
1.0	.3413	.3438	.3461	.3485	.3508	.3531	.3554	.3577	.3599	.3621
1.1	.3643	.3665	.3686	.3708	.3729	.3749	.3770	.3790	.3810	.3830
1.2	.3849	.3869	.3888	.3907	.3925	.3944	.3962	.3980	.3997	.4015
1.3	.4032	.4049	.4066	.4082	.4099	.4115	.4131	.4147	.4162	.4177
1.4	.4192	.4207	.4222	.4236	.4251	.4265	.4279	.4292	.4306	.4319
1.5	.4332	.4345	.4357	.4370	.4382	.4394	.4406	.4418	.4429	.4441
1.6	.4452	.4463	.4474	.4484	.4495	.4505	.4515	.4525	.4535	.4545
1.7	.4554	.4564	.4573	.4582	.4591	.4599	.4608	.4616	.4625	.4633
1.8	.4641	.4649	.4656	.4664	.4671	.4678	.4686	.4693	.4699	.4706
1.9	.4713	.4719	.4726	.4732	.4738	.4744	.4750	.4756	.4761	.4767
2.0	.4773	.4778	.4783	.4788	.4793	.4798	.4803	.4808	.4812	.4817
2.1	.4821	.4826	.4830	.4834	.4838	.4842	.4846	.4850	.4854	.4857
2.2	.4861	.4864	.4868	.4871	.4875	.4878	.4881	.4884	.4887	.4890
2.3	.4893	.4896	.4898	.4901	.4904	.4906	.4909	.4911	.4913	.4916
2.4	.4918	.4920	.4922	.4925	.4927	.4929	.4931	.4932	.4934	.4936
2.5	.4938	.4940	.4941	.4943	.4945	.4946	.4948	.4949	.4951	.4952
2.6	.4953	.4955	.4956	.4957	.4959	.4960	.4961	.4962	.4963	.4964
2.7	.4965	.4966	.4967	.4968	.4969	.4970	.4971	.4972	.4973	.4974
2.8	.4974	.4975	.4976	.4977	.4977	.4978	.4979	.4979	.4980	.4981
2.9	.4981	.4982	.4982	.4982	.4984	.4984	.4985	.4985	.4986	.4986
3.0	.4987	.4987	.4987	.4988	.4988	.4989	.4989	.4989	.4990	.4990

© lulu/fotolia.com

Glossary

A

abandonment option   Allows a company to reduce the capacity of its output in response to changing market conditions. This includes the option to contract production or abandon a project if market conditions deteriorate too much.

absolute priority doctrine   States that claims must be paid in strict accordance with the priority of each claim, regardless of the consequence to other claimants.

account receivable   Created when a good is shipped or a service is performed, and payment for that good is made on a credit basis, not on a cash basis.

accounting income   Income as defined by Generally Accepted Accounting Principles (GAAP).

accounting profit   A firm's net income as reported on its income statement.

acquiring company   A company that seeks to acquire another firm.

actual, or realized, rate of return, $\bar{r}_s$ The rate of return that was actually realized at the end of some holding period.

additional funds needed (AFN)   Those funds required from external sources to increase the firm's assets to support a sales increase. A sales increase will normally require an increase in assets. However, some of this increase is usually offset by a spontaneous increase in liabilities as well as by earnings retained in the firm. Those funds that are required but not generated internally must be obtained from external sources.

add-on basis installment loan   Interest is calculated over the life of the loan and then added on to the loan amount. This total amount is paid in equal installments. This raises the effective cost of the loan.

agency cost or problem   An expense, either direct or indirect, that is borne by a principal as a result of having delegated authority to an agent. An example is the costs borne by shareholders to encourage managers to maximize a firm's stock price rather than act in their own self-interests. These costs may also arise from lost efficiency and the expense of monitoring management to ensure that debtholders' rights are protected.

agency debt   Debt issued by federal agencies. Agency debt is not officially backed by the full faith and credit of the U.S. government, but investors assume that the government implicitly guarantees this debt, so these bonds carry interest rates only slightly higher than Treasury bonds.

aggressive short-term financing policy   Refers to a policy in which a firm finances all of its fixed assets with long-term capital but part of its permanent current assets with short-term, nonspontaneous credit.

aging schedule   Breaks down accounts receivable according to how long they have been outstanding. This gives the firm a more complete picture of the structure of accounts receivable than that provided by days sales outstanding.

alternative minimum tax (AMT)   A provision of the U.S. Tax Code that requires profitable firms to pay at least some taxes if such taxes are greater than the amount due under standard tax accounting.

amortization   A noncash charge against intangible assets, such as goodwill.

amortization schedule   A table that breaks down the periodic fixed payment of an installment loan into its principal and interest components.

amortized loan   A loan that is repaid in equal periodic amounts (or "killed off") over time.

anchoring bias   Occurs when predictions of future events are influenced too heavily by recent events.

annual report   A report issued annually by a corporation to its stockholders. It contains basic financial statements as well as management's opinion of the past year's operations and the firm's future prospects.

annual vesting   A certain percentage of the options in a grant vest each year. For example, one-third of the options in the grant might vest each year.

annuity   A series of payments of a fixed amount for a specified number of periods.

annuity due   An annuity with payments occurring at the beginning of each period.

APR   The nominal annual interest rate is also called the annual percentage rate, or APR.

arbitrage   The simultaneous buying and selling of the same commodity or security in two different markets at different prices, thus yielding a risk-free return.

Arbitrage Pricing Theory (APT)   An approach to measuring the equilibrium risk–return relationship for a given stock as a function of multiple factors, rather than the single factor (the market return) used by the CAPM. The APT is based on complex mathematical and statistical theory, and it can account for several factors (such as GNP and the level of inflation) in determining the required return for a particular stock.

arrearages   Preferred dividends that have not been paid and hence are "in arrears."

asset management ratios   A set of ratios that measure how effectively a firm is managing its assets.

assignment   An informal procedure for liquidating debts that transfers title to a debtor's assets to a third person, known as an assignee or trustee.

asymmetric information theory   Assumes managers have more complete information than investors and leads to a preferred "pecking order" of financing: (1) retained earnings, followed by (2) debt, and then (3) new common stock. Also known as signaling theory.

average tax rate   Calculated by taking the total amount of tax paid divided by taxable income.

B

balance sheet   A statement of the firm's financial position at a specific point in time. The firm's assets are listed on the left-hand side of the balance sheet; the right-hand side shows its liabilities and equity, or the claims against these assets.

banker's acceptance   Created when an importer's bank promises to accept a postdated check written to an exporter even if there are insufficient funds in the importer's account. If the bank is strong, then this financial instrument virtually eliminates credit risk.

Bankruptcy Reform Act of 1978   Enacted to speed up and streamline bankruptcy proceedings. This law represented a shift to a relative priority doctrine of creditors' claims.

basic earning power (BEP) ratio   Calculated by dividing earnings before interest and taxes by total assets. This ratio shows the raw earning power of the firm's assets before the influence of taxes and leverage.

behavioral finance   A field of study that analyzes investor behavior as a result of psychological traits. It does not assume that investors necessarily behave rationally.

benchmarking   When a firm compares its ratios to other leading companies in the same industry.

best efforts arrangement   A type of contract with an investment banker when issuing stock. In a best efforts sale, the investment banker is only committed to making every effort to sell the stock at the offering price. In this case, the issuing firm bears the risk that the new issue will not be fully subscribed.

beta coefficient, b   A measure of the amount of risk that an individual stock contributes to a well-diversified portfolio.

bird-in-the-hand theory   Assumes that investors value a dollar of dividends more highly than a dollar of expected capital gains, because a certain dividend is less risky than a possible capital gain. This theory implies that a high-dividend stock has a higher price and lower required return, all else held equal.

Black-Scholes option pricing model   A model to estimate the value of a call option. It is widely used by options traders.

bond   A promissory note issued by a business or a governmental unit.

bond insurance   Protects investors against default by the issuer and provides credit enhancement to the bond issue.

book value per share   Common equity divided by the number of shares outstanding.

break-even point   The level of unit sales at which costs equal revenues.

breakup value   A firm's value if its assets are sold off in pieces.

business risk   The risk inherent in the operations of the firm, prior to the financing decision. Thus, business risk is the uncertainty inherent in future operating income or earnings before interest and taxes. Business risk is caused by many factors; two of the most important are sales variability and operating leverage.

C

call option   An option that allows the holder to buy the asset at some predetermined price within a specified period of time.

call provision   Gives the issuing corporation the right to call the bonds for redemption. The call provision generally states that if the bonds are called then the company must pay the bondholders an amount greater than the par value, or a call premium. Most bonds contain a call provision.

capacity option   Allows a company to change the capacity of its output in response to changing market conditions. This includes the option to contract or expand production. It also includes the option to abandon a project if market conditions deteriorate too much.

Capital Asset Pricing Model (CAPM)   A model based on the proposition that any stock's required rate of return is equal to the risk-free rate of return plus a risk premium reflecting only the risk remaining after diversification. The CAPM equation is $r_i = r_{RF} + b_i(r_M - r_{RF})$.

capital budget   Outlines the planned expenditures on fixed assets.

capital budgeting   The whole process of analyzing projects and deciding whether they should be included in the capital budget.

capital gain (loss)   The profit (loss) from the sale of a capital asset for more (less) than its purchase price.

capital gains yield   Results from changing prices and is calculated as $(P_1 - P_0)/P_0$, where P_0 is the beginning-of-period price and P_1 is the end-of-period price.

capital intensity ratio   The dollar amount of assets required to produce a dollar of sales. The capital intensity ratio is the reciprocal of the total assets turnover ratio.

capital market   Capital markets are the financial markets for long-term debt and corporate stocks. The New York Stock Exchange is an example of a capital market.

capital rationing   Occurs when management places a constraint on the size of the firm's capital budget during a particular period.

capital structure   The manner in which a firm's assets are financed; that is, the right side of the balance sheet. Capital structure is normally expressed as the percentage of each type of capital used by the firm such as debt, preferred stock, and common equity.

capitalizing   Incorporating the lease provisions into the balance sheet by reporting the leased asset under fixed assets and reporting the present value of future lease payments as debt.

cash budget   A schedule showing cash flows (receipts, disbursements, and cash balances) for a firm over a specified period.

cash conversion cycle   The length of time between the firm's actual cash expenditures on productive resources (materials and labor) and its own cash receipts from the sale of products (that is, the length of time between paying for labor and materials and collecting on receivables). Thus, the cash conversion cycle equals the length of time the firm has funds tied up in current assets.

cash discounts   The amount by which a seller is willing to reduce the invoice price in order to be paid immediately, rather than in the future. A cash discount might be 2/10, net 30, which means a 2% discount if the bill is paid within 10 days and otherwise the entire amount is due within 30 days.

CDO, collateralized debt obligation   Created when large numbers of mortgages are bundled into pools to create new securities that are then sliced into tranches; the tranches are recombined and re-divided into securities called CDOs.

CDS, credit default swap   Derivative in which a counterparty pays if a specified debt instrument goes into default; similar to insurance on a bond.

Chapter 11 bankruptcy   The 11th chapter of the bankruptcy statutes, regulates reorganization in a bankruptcy.

Chapter 7 bankruptcy   The 7th chapter of the bankruptcy statutes, regulates liquidation in a bankruptcy.

characteristic line   Obtained by regressing the historical returns on a particular stock against the historical returns on the general stock market. The slope of the characteristic line is the stock's beta, which measures the amount by which the stock's expected return increases for a given increase in the expected return on the market.

charter   The legal document that is filed with the state to incorporate a company.

check-clearing process   When a customer's check is written upon one bank and a company deposits the check in its own bank, the company's bank must verify that the check is valid before the company can use those funds. Checks are generally cleared through the Federal Reserve System or through a clearinghouse set up by the banks in a particular city.

classified boards   A board of directors with staggered terms. For example, a board with one-third of the seats filled each year and directors serving three-year terms.

classified stock   Sometimes created by a firm to meet special needs and circumstances. Generally, when special classifications of stock are used, one type is designated "Class A," another as "Class B," and so on. For example, Class A might be entitled to receive dividends before dividends can be paid on Class B stock. Class B might have the exclusive right to vote.

cleanup clause   A clause in a line of credit that requires the borrower to reduce the loan balance to zero at least once a year.

clientele effect   The attraction of companies with specific dividend policies to those investors whose needs are best served by those policies. Thus, companies with high dividends will have a clientele of investors with low marginal tax rates and strong desires for current income. Conversely, companies with low dividends will have a clientele of investors with high marginal tax rates and little need for current income.

cliff vesting   All the options in a grant vest on the same date.

closely held corporation   Refers to companies that are so small that their common stocks are not actively traded; they are owned by only a few people, usually the companies' managers.

coefficient of variation, CV   Equal to the standard deviation divided by the expected return; it is a standardized risk measure that allows comparisons between investments having different expected returns and standard deviations.

collection policy   The procedure for collecting accounts receivable. A change in collection policy will affect sales, days sales outstanding, bad debt losses, and the percentage of customers taking discounts.

collections float   Float created while funds from customers' checks are being deposited and cleared through the check collection process.

combination lease   Combines some aspects of both operating and financial leases. For example, a financial lease that contains a cancellation clause—normally associated with operating leases—is a combination lease.

commercial paper   Unsecured, short-term promissory notes of large firms, usually issued in denominations of $100,000 or more and having an interest rate somewhat below the prime rate.

commodity futures   Futures contracts that involve the sale or purchase of various commodities, including grains, oilseeds, livestock, meats, fiber, metals, and wood.

common stockholders' equity (net worth)   The capital supplied by common stockholders—capital stock, paid-in capital, retained earnings, and (occasionally) certain reserves. Paid-in capital is the difference between the stock's par value and what stockholders paid when they bought newly issued shares.

comparative ratio analysis Compares a firm's own ratios to other leading companies in the same industry. This technique is also known as benchmarking.

compensating balance (CB) A minimum checking account balance that a firm must maintain with a bank to compensate the bank for services rendered or for making a loan; generally equal to 10%–20% of the loans outstanding.

composition Creditors voluntarily reduce their fixed claims on the debtor by accepting a lower principal amount, reducing the interest rate on the debt, accepting equity in place of debt, or some combination of these changes.

compounding The process of finding the future value of a single payment or series of payments.

computer/telephone network A computer/ telephone network, such as NASDAQ, consists of all the facilities that provide for security transactions not conducted at a physical location exchange. These facilities are, basically, the communications networks that link buyers and sellers.

conditional value at risk (CVaR) The average portfolio value (or loss) conditional upon the portfolio value being less than a specified threshold value (or threshold percentile). It can also be defined as the average NPV conditional upon the NPV being less than a specified threshold value (or threshold percentile). It is also called the expected shortfall (ES).

congeneric merger Involves firms that are interrelated but do not have identical lines of business. One example is Prudential's acquisition of Bache & Company.

conglomerate merger Occurs when unrelated enterprises combine, such as Mobil Oil and Montgomery Ward.

conservative short-term financing policy Refers to using permanent capital to finance all permanent asset requirements as well as to meet some or all of the seasonal demands.

consol A type of perpetuity. Consols were originally bonds issued by England in the mid-1700s to consolidate past debt.

continuous probability distribution Contains an infinite number of outcomes and is graphed from $-\infty$ and $+\infty$.

conversion price The effective price per share of stock if conversion occurs; the par value of the convertible security divided by the conversion ratio.

conversion ratio The number of shares of common stock received upon conversion of one convertible security.

conversion value The value of the stock that the investor would receive if conversion occurred; the market price per share times the conversion ratio.

convertible bond Security that is convertible into shares of common stock, at a fixed price, at the option of the bondholder.

convertible currency A currency that can be traded in the currency markets and can be redeemed at current market rates.

convertible security Bonds or preferred stocks that can be exchanged for (converted into) common stock, under specific terms, at the option of the holder. Unlike the exercise of warrants, conversion of a convertible security does not provide additional capital to the issuer.

corporate alliance A cooperative deal that stops short of a merger; also called a strategic alliance.

corporate bond Debt issued by corporations and exposed to default risk. Different corporate bonds have different levels of default risk, depending on the issuing company's characteristics and on the terms of the specific bond.

corporate governance The set of rules that controls a company's behavior toward its directors, managers, employees, shareholders, creditors, customers, competitors, and community.

corporate valuation model Defines the total value of a company as the present value of its expected free cash flows discounted at the weighted average cost of capital (i.e., the value of operations) plus the value of nonoperating assets such as T-bills.

corporation A corporation is a legal entity created by a state. The corporation is separate and distinct from its owners and managers.

correlation The tendency of two variables to move together.

correlation coefficient, ρ (rho) A standardized measure of how two random variables covary. A correlation coefficient (ρ) of +1.0 means that the two variables move up and down in perfect synchronization, whereas a coefficient of −1.0 means the variables always move in opposite directions. A correlation coefficient of zero suggests that the two variables are not related to one another; that is, they are independent.

cost of common stock, r_s The return required by the firm's common stockholders. It is usually calculated using Capital Asset Pricing Model or the dividend growth model.

cost of new external common equity, r_e A project financed with external equity must earn a higher rate of return because it must cover the flotation costs. Thus, the cost of new common equity is higher than that of common equity raised internally by reinvesting earnings.

cost of preferred stock, r_{ps} The return required by the firm's preferred stockholders. The cost of preferred stock, r_{ps}, is the cost to the firm of issuing new preferred stock. For perpetual preferred, it is the preferred dividend, D_{ps}, divided by the net issuing price, P_n.

costly trade credit Credit taken (in excess of free trade credit) whose cost is equal to the discount lost.

coupon interest rate Stated rate of interest on a bond; defined as the coupon payment divided by the par value.

coupon payment Dollar amount of interest paid to each bondholder on the interest payment dates.

coverage ratio Similar to the times-interest-earned ratio, but it recognizes that many firms lease assets and also must make sinking fund payments. It is found by adding earnings before interest, taxes, depreciation, amortization (EBITDA), and lease payments and then dividing this total by interest charges, lease payments,

and sinking fund payments over 1 − T (where T is the tax rate).

cramdown Reorganization plans that are mandated by the bankruptcy court and binding on all parties.

credit period The length of time for which credit is extended. If the credit period is lengthened, then sales will generally increase, as will accounts receivable. This will increase the firm's financing needs and possibly increase bad debt losses. A shortening of the credit period will have the opposite effect.

credit policy The firm's policy on granting and collecting credit. There are four elements of credit policy, or credit policy variables: credit period, credit standards, collection policy, and discounts.

credit standards The financial strength and creditworthiness that qualifies a customer for a firm's regular credit terms.

credit terms Statements of the credit period and any discounts offered—for example, 2/10, net 30.

cross rate The exchange rate between two non-U.S. currencies.

crossover rate The cost of capital at which the NPV profiles for two projects intersect.

cumulative preferred dividends A protective feature on preferred stock that requires all past preferred dividends to be paid before any common dividends can be paid.

currency appreciation Occurs to a particular currency when it increases in value relative to another particular currency. For example, if the exchange rate of 1.0 dollar per euro changes to 1.1 dollars per euro, then euro has appreciated against the dollar by 10%.

currency depreciation Occurs to a particular currency when it decreases in value relative to another particular currency. For example, if the exchange rate of 1.0 dollar per euro changes to 0.9 dollars per euro, then euro has depreciated against the dollar by 10%.

current ratio Indicates the extent to which current liabilities are covered by those assets expected to be converted to cash in the near future; it is found by dividing current assets by current liabilities.

current yield (on a bond)   The annual coupon payment divided by the current market price.

D

days sales outstanding (DSO)   Used to appraise accounts receivable and indicates the length of time the firm must wait after making a sale before receiving cash. It is found by dividing receivables by average sales per day.

DCF (discounted cash flow) techniques   The net present value (NPV) and internal rate of return (IRR) techniques are discounted cash flow (DCF) evaluation techniques. These are called DCF methods because they explicitly recognize the time value of money.

dealer market   In a dealer market, a dealer holds an inventory of the security and makes a market by offering to buy or sell. Others who wish to buy or sell can see the offers made by the dealers and can contact the dealer of their choice to arrange a transaction.

debenture   An unsecured bond; as such, it provides no lien against specific property as security for the obligation. Debenture holders are therefore general creditors whose claims are protected by property not otherwise pledged.

debt ratio   The ratio of total debt to total assets, it measures the percentage of funds provided by investors other than preferred or common shareholders.

debt-to-equity ratio   Ratio of debt divided by equity.

decision trees   A form of scenario analysis in which different actions are taken in different scenarios.

declaration date   The date on which a firm's directors issue a statement declaring a dividend.

default risk   The risk that a borrower may not pay the interest and/or principal on a loan when it becomes due. If the issuer defaults, investors receive less than the promised return on the bond. Default risk is influenced by the financial strength of the issuer and also by the terms of the bond contract, especially whether collateral has been pledged to

secure the bond. The greater the default risk, the higher the bond's yield to maturity.

default risk premium (DRP)   The premium added to the real risk-free rate to compensate investors for the risk that a borrower may fail to pay the interest and/or principal on a loan when they become due.

defensive merger   Occurs when one company acquires another to help ward off a hostile merger attempt.

depreciation   A noncash charge against tangible assets, such as buildings or machines. It is taken for the purpose of showing an asset's estimated dollar cost of the capital equipment used up in the production process.

derivatives   Claims whose value depends on what happens to the value of some other asset. Futures and options are two important types of derivatives, and their values depend on what happens to the prices of other assets. Therefore, the value of a derivative security is derived from the value of an underlying real asset or other security.

detachable warrant   A warrant that can be detached and traded separately from the underlying security. Most warrants are detachable.

devaluation   The lowering, by governmental action, of the price of its currency relative to another currency. For example, in 1967 the British pound was devalued from $2.80 per pound to $2.50 per pound.

development bond   A tax-exempt bond sold by state and local governments whose proceeds are made available to corporations for specific uses deemed (by Congress) to be in the public interest.

direct quotation   When discussing exchange rates, the number of units of home currency required to purchase one unit of a foreign currency.

disbursement float   Float created before checks written by a firm have cleared and been deducted from the firm's account; disbursement float causes the firm's own checkbook balance to be smaller than the balance on the bank's records.

discount bond   Bond prices and interest rates are inversely related; that is, they tend to move in the opposite direction from one another. A fixed-rate bond will sell at par when its coupon interest rate is equal to the going rate of interest, r_d. When the going rate of interest is above the coupon rate, a fixed-rate bond will sell at a "discount" below its par value. If current interest rates are below the coupon rate, a fixed-rate bond will sell at a "premium" above its par value.

discount interest   Interest that is calculated on the face amount of a loan but is paid in advance.

discount on forward rate   Occurs when the forward exchange rate differs from the spot rate. When the forward rate is below the spot rate, the forward rate is said to be at a discount.

discounted cash flow (DCF) method   A method of valuing a business that involves the application of capital budgeting procedures to an entire firm rather than to a single project.

discounted payback period   The number of years it takes a firm to recover its project investment based on discounted cash flows.

discounting   The process of finding the present value of a single payment or series of payments.

distribution policy   The policy that sets the level of distributions and the form of the distributions (dividends and stock repurchases).

diversifiable risk   Refers to that part of a security's total risk associated with random events not affecting the market as a whole. This risk can be eliminated by proper diversification. Also known as company-specific risk.

divestiture   The opposite of an acquisition. That is, a company sells a portion of its assets—often a whole division—to another firm or individual.

dividend irrelevance theory   Holds that dividend policy has no effect on either the price of a firm's stock or its cost of capital.

dividend reinvestment plan (DRIP)   Allows stockholders to automatically purchase shares of common stock of the paying corporation in lieu of receiving cash dividends. There are two types of plans: one involves only stock that is already outstanding; the other involves newly issued stock. In the first type, the dividends of all participants are pooled and the stock is purchased on the open market. Participants

benefit from lower transaction costs. In the second type, the company issues new shares to the participants. Thus, the company issues stock in lieu of the cash dividend.

dividend yield   Defined as either the end-of-period dividend divided by the beginning-of-period price or as the ratio of the current dividend to the current price. Valuation formulas use the former definition.

DuPont chart   A chart designed to show the relationships among return on investment, asset turnover, the profit margin, and leverage.

DuPont equation   A formula showing that the rate of return on equity can be found as the profit margin multiplied by the product of total assets turnover and the equity multiplier.

E

EBITDA   Earnings before interest, taxes, depreciation, and amortization.

ECN   In an ECN (electronic communications network), orders from potential buyers and sellers are automatically matched and the transaction is automatically completed.

economic life   The number of years a project should be operated to maximize its net present value; often less than the maximum potential life.

Economic Value Added (EVA)   A method used to measure a firm's true profitability. EVA is found by taking the firm's after-tax operating profit and subtracting the annual cost of all the capital a firm uses. If the firm generates a positive EVA, its management has created value for its shareholders. If the EVA is negative, management has destroyed shareholder value.

effective (or equivalent) annual rate (EAR or EFF%)   The effective annual rate is the rate that, under annual compounding, would have produced the same future value at the end of 1 year as was produced by more frequent compounding, say quarterly. If the compounding occurs annually, then the effective annual rate and the nominal rate are the same. If compounding occurs more frequently, then the effective annual rate is greater than the nominal rate.

efficient frontier   The set of efficient portfolios out of the full set of potential portfolios. On a graph, the efficient frontier constitutes the boundary line of the set of potential portfolios.

Efficient Markets Hypothesis (EMH)   States (1) that stocks are always in equilibrium and (2) that it is impossible for an investor to consistently "beat the market." The EMH assumes that all important information regarding a stock is reflected in the price of that stock.

efficient portfolio   Provides the highest expected return for any degree of risk. The efficient portfolio also provides the lowest degree of risk for any expected return.

embedded options   Options that are a part of another project. Also called real options, managerial options, and strategic options.

enterprise risk management (ERM)   A process that includes risk identification, risk assessment, and risk responses. ERM requires the participation of all levels within an organization.

entrenchment   Occurs when a company has such a weak board of directors and has such strong anti-takeover provisions in its corporate charter that senior managers feel there is little chance of being removed.

equilibrium   The condition under which the intrinsic value of a security is equal to its price; also, when a security's expected return is equal to its required return.

equity risk premium RP_M; Expected market return minus the risk-free rate; also called market risk premium or equity premium

ESOP (employee stock ownership plan)   A type of retirement plan in which employees own stock in the company.

euro   The currency used by nations in the European Monetary Union.

Eurobond   Any bond sold in some country other than the one in whose currency the bond is denominated. Thus, a U.S. firm selling dollar bonds in Switzerland is selling Eurobonds.

Eurodollar   A U.S. dollar on deposit in a foreign bank or a foreign branch of a U.S. bank. Eurodollars are used to conduct transactions throughout Europe and the rest of the world.

exchange rate   Specifies the number of units of a given currency that can be purchased for one unit of another currency.

exchange rate risk   Refers to the fluctuation in exchange rates between currencies over time.

ex-dividend date   The date when the right to the dividend leaves the stock. This date was established by stockbrokers to avoid confusion, and it is four business days prior to the holder-of-record date. If the stock sale is made prior to the ex-dividend date, then the dividend is paid to the buyer; if the stock is bought on or after the ex-dividend date, the dividend is paid to the seller.

exercise price   The price stated in the option contract at which the security can be bought (or sold). Also called the strike price.

exercise value   Equal to the current price of the stock (underlying the option) minus the strike price of the option.

expectations theory   States that the slope of the yield curve depends on expectations about future inflation rates and interest rates. Thus, if the annual rate of inflation and future interest rates are expected to increase, then the yield curve will be upward sloping; the curve will be downward sloping if the annual rates are expected to decrease.

expected rate of return, $\hat{r}_s$ The rate of return expected on a stock given its current price and expected future cash flows. If the stock is in equilibrium, the required rate of return will equal the expected rate of return.

expected shortfall (ES)   The average portfolio value conditional upon the portfolio value being less than a specified threshold value (or threshold percentile). It can also be defined as the average NPV conditional upon the NPV being less than a specified threshold value (or threshold percentile). It is also called the conditional value at risk (CVaR).

extension   A form of debt restructuring in which creditors postpone the dates of required interest or principal payments, or both.

extra dividend A dividend paid, in addition to the regular dividend, when earnings permit. Firms with volatile earnings may have a low regular dividend that can be maintained even in years of low profit (or high capital investment) but is supplemented by an extra dividend when excess funds are available.

F

fairness The standard of fairness states that claims must be recognized in the order of their legal and contractual priority. In simpler terms, the reorganization must be fair to all parties.

Fama-French three-factor model Includes one factor for the excess market return (the market return minus the risk-free rate), a second factor for size (defined as the return on a portfolio of small firms minus the return on a portfolio of big firms), and a third factor for the book-to-market effect (defined as the return on a portfolio of firms with a high book-to-market ratio minus the return on a portfolio of firms with a low book-to-market ratio).

FASB Financial Accounting Standards Board.

FASB Statement 13 The Financial Accounting Standards Board statement that spells out the conditions under which a lease must be capitalized and the specific procedures to follow.

feasibility The standard of feasibility states that there must be a reasonably high probability of successful rehabilitation and profitable future operations.

feasible set Represents all portfolios that can be constructed from a given set of stocks; also known as the attainable set.

financial distress costs Incurred when a leveraged firm facing a decline in earnings is forced to take actions to avoid bankruptcy. These costs may be the result of delays in the liquidation of assets, legal fees, the effects on product quality from cutting costs, and evasive actions by suppliers and customers.

financial futures Provide for the purchase or sale of a financial asset at some time in the future, but at a price that is established today. Financial futures exist for Treasury bills, Treasury notes and bonds, certificates of deposit, Eurodollar deposits, foreign currencies, and stock indexes.

financial intermediary Intermediary that buys securities with funds that it obtains by issuing its own securities. An example is a common stock mutual fund that buys common stocks with funds obtained by issuing shares in the mutual fund.

financial lease Covers the entire expected life of the equipment; does not provide for maintenance service, is not cancellable, and is fully amortized.

financial leverage The extent to which fixed-income securities (debt and preferred stock) are used in a firm's capital structure. If a high percentage of a firm's capital structure is in the form of debt and preferred stock, then the firm is said to have a high degree of financial leverage.

financial merger A merger in which the companies will not be operated as a single unit and for which no operating economies are expected.

financial risk The risk added by the use of debt financing. Debt financing increases the variability of earnings before taxes (but after interest); thus, along with business risk, it contributes to the uncertainty of net income and earnings per share. Business risk plus financial risk equals total corporate risk.

financial service corporation A corporation that offers a wide range of financial services such as brokerage operations, insurance, and commercial banking.

financing deficit The shortfall of spontaneous liabilities, planned change in external financing (total changes of debt, preferred stock, and common stock from the preliminary financing plan), and internal funds (net income less planned dividends) relative to additional assets required by the operating plan.

financing feedback Circularity created when additional debt causes additional interest expense, which reduces the addition to retained earnings, which in turn requires a higher level of debt, which causes still more interest expense, causing the cycle to be repeated.

financing surplus The excess of spontaneous liabilities, planned change in external financing (total changes of debt, preferred stock, and common stock from the preliminary financing plan), and internal funds (net income less planned dividends) relative to additional assets required by the operating plan.

fixed assets turnover ratio   The ratio of sales to net fixed assets; it measures how effectively the firm uses its plant and equipment.

fixed exchange rate system   The system in effect from the end of World War II until August 1971. Under the system, the U.S. dollar was linked to gold at the rate of $35 per ounce, and other currencies were then tied to the dollar.

floating exchange rates   The system currently in effect, where the forces of supply and demand are allowed to determine currency prices with little government intervention.

floating-rate bond   A bond whose coupon payment may vary over time. The coupon rate is usually linked to the rate on some other security, such as a Treasury security, or to some other rate, such as the prime rate or LIBOR.

flotation cost, F   Those costs occurring when a company issues a new security, including fees to an investment banker and legal fees.

forecasted financial statements approach   A method of forecasting financial statements to determine the additional funds needed. Many items on the income statement and balance sheets are assumed to increase proportionally with sales. As sales increase, these items that are tied to sales also increase, and the values of these items for a particular year are estimated as percentages of the forecasted sales for that year.

foreign bond   A bond sold by a foreign borrower but denominated in the currency of the country in which the issue is sold. Thus, a U.S. firm selling bonds denominated in Swiss francs in Switzerland is selling foreign bonds.

foreign exchange (FX) risk   The risk that a change in a currency exchange rate might adversely affect a company.

foreign trade deficit   A deficit that occurs when businesses and individuals in the United States import more goods from foreign countries than are exported.

forward contract   A contract to buy or sell some item at some time in the future at a price established when the contract is entered into.

forward exchange rate   The prevailing exchange rate for exchange (delivery) at some agreed-upon future date, which is usually 30, 90, or 180 days from the day the transaction is negotiated.

founders' shares   Stock owned by the firm's founders that have sole voting rights but restricted dividends for a specified number of years.

free cash flow (FCF)   The cash flow actually available for distribution to all investors after the company has made all investments in fixed assets and working capital necessary to sustain ongoing operations.

free cash flow valuation model   Defines the total value of a company as the present value of its expected free cash flows discounted at the weighted average cost of capital (i.e., the value of operations) plus the value of nonoperating assets such as T-bills.

free trade credit   Credit received during the discount period.

friendly merger   Occurs when the target company's management agrees to the merger and recommends that shareholders approve the deal.

fundamental value or price   Value or price that incorporates all relevant information regarding expected future cash flows and risk.

FVA_N   The future value of a stream of annuity payments, where N is the number of payments of the annuity.

$FVIFA_{I,N}$ The future value interest factor for an ordinary annuity of N periodic payments paying I percent interest per period.

$FVIF_{I,N}$ The future value interest factor for a lump sum left in an account for N periods paying I percent interest per period.

FV_N   The future value of an initial single cash flow, where N is the number of periods the initial cash flow is compounded.

G

GAAP, Generally Accepted Accounting Principles.   A set of standards for financial reporting established by the accounting profession.

going public   The act of selling stock to the public at large by a closely held corporation or its principal stockholders.

golden parachute   A payment made to executives who are forced out when a merger takes place.

greenmail   Targeted share repurchases that occur when a company buys back stock from a potential acquirer at a higher than fair-market price. In return, the potential acquirer agrees not to attempt to take over the company.

gross profit margin   Ratio of gross profit (sales minus cost of goods sold) divided by sales.

growth option   Occurs if an investment creates the opportunity to make other potentially profitable investments that would not otherwise be possible, including options to expand output, to enter a new geographical market, and to introduce complementary products or successive generations of products.

GSE (government-sponsored entity) debt   Debt issued by government-sponsored entities (GSEs) such as the Tennessee Valley Authority or the Small Business Administration; not officially backed by the full faith and credit of the U.S. government.

guideline lease   Meets all of the Internal Revenue Service (IRS) requirements for a genuine lease. If a lease meets the IRS guidelines, the IRS allows the lessor to deduct the asset's depreciation and allows the lessee to deduct the lease payments. Also called a tax-oriented lease.

H

Hamada equation   Shows the effect of debt on the beta coefficient—increases in debt increase beta, and decreases in debt reduce beta.

hard currencies   Currencies considered to be convertible because the nation that issues them allows them to be traded in the currency markets and is willing to redeem them at market rates.

hedging   A transaction that lowers a firm's risk of damage due to fluctuating commodity prices, interest rates, and exchange rates.

herding instinct   When one group of investors does well, other investors begin to emulate them, acting like a herd of sheep.

holder-of-record date   If a company lists the stockholder as an owner on the holder-of-record date, then the stockholder receives the dividend.

holding company   A corporation formed for the sole purpose of owning stocks in other companies. A holding company differs from a stock mutual fund in that holding companies own sufficient stock in their operating companies to exercise effective working control.

holdout   A problematic characteristic of informal reorganizations whereby all of the involved parties do not agree to the voluntary plan. Holdouts are usually made by creditors in an effort to receive full payment on claims.

horizon value of operations   The value of operations at the end of the explicit forecast period. It is equal to the present value of all free cash flows beyond the forecast period, discounted back to the end of the forecast period at the weighted average cost of capital.

horizontal merger   A merger between two companies in the same line of business.

hostile merger   Occurs when the management of the target company resists the offer.

hurdle rate   The project cost of capital, or discount rate. It is the rate used to discount future cash flows in the net present value method or to compare with the internal rate of return.

I

improper accumulation   The retention of earnings by a business for the purpose of enabling stockholders to avoid personal income taxes on dividends.

income bond   Pays interest only if the interest is earned. These securities cannot bankrupt a company, but from an investor's standpoint, they are riskier than "regular" bonds.

income statement   Summarizes the firm's revenues and expenses over an accounting period. Net sales are shown at the top of each statement, after which various costs, including income taxes, are subtracted to obtain the net income available to common stockholders. The bottom of the statement reports earnings and dividends per share.

incremental cash flow   Those cash flows that arise solely from the asset that is being evaluated.

indentures   A legal document that spells out the rights of both bondholders and the issuing corporation.

independent projects   Projects that can be accepted or rejected individually.

indexed, or purchasing power, bond   The interest rate of such a bond is based on an inflation index such as the consumer price index (CPI), so the interest paid rises automatically when the inflation rate rises, thus protecting the bondholders against inflation.

indifference curve   The risk–return trade-off function for a particular investor; reflects that investor's attitude toward risk. An investor would be indifferent between any pair of assets on the same indifference curve. In risk–return space, the greater the slope of the indifference curve, the greater is the investor's risk aversion.

indirect quotation   When discussing exchange rates, the number of units of foreign currency that can be purchased for one unit of home currency.

inflation premium (IP)   The premium added to the real risk-free rate of interest to compensate for the expected loss of purchasing power. The inflation premium is the average rate of inflation expected over the life of the security.

informal debt restructuring   An agreement between a troubled firm and its creditors to change existing debt terms. An extension postpones the required payment date; a composition is a reduction in creditor claims.

information content, or signaling, hypothesis   A theory that holds that investors regard dividend changes as "signals" of management forecasts. Thus, when dividends are raised, this is viewed by investors as recognition by management of future earnings increases. Therefore, if a firm's stock price increases with a dividend increase, the reason may not be investor preference for dividends but rather expectations of higher future earnings. Conversely, a dividend reduction may signal that management is forecasting poor earnings in the future.

initial public offering (IPO)   Occurs when a closely held corporation or its principal stockholders sell stock to the public at large.

initial public offering (IPO) market   Going public is the act of selling stock to the public at large by a closely held corporation or its principal stockholders, and this market is often termed the initial public offering market.

I_{NOM} The nominal, or quoted, interest rate.

insiders   The officers, directors, and major stockholders of a firm.

interest coverage ratio   Also called the times-interest-earned (TIE) ratio; determined by dividing earnings before interest and taxes by the interest expense.

interest rate parity   Holds that investors should expect to earn the same return in all countries after adjusting for risk.

interest rate risk   Arises from the fact that bond prices decline when interest rates rise. Under these circumstances, selling a bond prior to maturity will result in a capital loss; the longer the term to maturity, the larger the loss.

interlocking boards of directors   Occur when the CEO of Company A sits on the board of Company B while B's CEO sits on A's board.

internal rate of return (IRR) method   The discount rate that equates the present value of the expected future cash inflows and outflows. IRR measures the rate of return on a project, but it assumes that all cash flows can be reinvested at the IRR rate.

international bond   Any bond sold outside of the country of the borrower. There are two types of international bonds: Eurobonds and foreign bonds.

intrinsic value or price   Value or price that incorporates all relevant information regarding expected future cash flows and risk.

inventory conversion period   The average length of time to convert materials into finished goods and then to sell them; calculated by dividing total inventory by daily costs of goods sold.

inventory turnover ratio   Cost of goods sold divided by inventories.

inverted (abnormal) yield curve   A downward-sloping yield curve.

investment bank   A firm that assists in the design of an issuing firm's corporate securities and in the sale of the new securities to investors in the primary market.

investment grade bond   Securities with ratings of Baa/BBB or above.

investment timing option   Gives companies the option to delay a project rather than implement it immediately. This option to wait allows a company to reduce the uncertainty of market conditions before it decides to implement the project.

investor-supplied capital   Total amount of short-term debt, long-term debt, preferred stock, and total common equity shown on a balance sheet. It is the amount of financing that investors have provided to a company. It also called total investor-supplied capital.

investor-supplied operating capital   The total amount of short-term debt, long-term debt, preferred stock, and total common equity shown on a balance sheet, less the amount of short-term investments shown on the balance sheet. It is the amount of financing used in operations that investors have provided to a company. It also called total investor-supplied operating capital.

J

Jensen's alpha   Measures the vertical distance of a portfolio's return above or below the Security Market Line; first suggested by Professor Michael Jensen, it became popular because of its ease of calculation.

joint venture   Involves the joining together of parts of companies to accomplish specific, limited objectives. Joint ventures are controlled by the combined management of the two (or more) parent companies.

junk bond   High-risk, high-yield bond issued to finance leveraged buyouts, mergers, or troubled companies.

L

lessee   The party leasing the property.

lessee's analysis   Involves determining whether leasing an asset is less costly than buying the asset. The lessee will compare the present value cost of

leasing the asset with the present value cost of purchasing the asset (assuming the funds to purchase the asset are obtained through a loan). If the present value cost of the lease is less than the present value cost of purchasing, then the asset should be leased. The lessee can also analyze the lease using the IRR approach or the equivalent loan method.

lessor   The party receiving the payments from the lease (that is, the owner of the property).

lessor's analysis   Involves determining the rate of return on the proposed lease. If the internal rate of return of the lease cash flows exceeds the lessor's opportunity cost of capital, then the lease is a good investment. This is equivalent to analyzing whether the net present value of the lease is positive.

leveraged buyout (LBO)   A transaction in which a firm's publicly owned stock is acquired in a mostly debt-financed tender offer, resulting in a privately owned, highly leveraged firm. Often, the firm's own management initiates the LBO.

leveraged lease   The lessor borrows a portion of the funds needed to buy the equipment to be leased.

liabilities to assets ratio   The ratio of total liabilities to total assets, it measures the percentage of funds provided by creditors.

LIBOR   London Interbank Offered Rate; the rate that U.K. banks charge one another.

limited liability partnership   A limited liability partnership (LLP), sometimes called a limited liability company (LLC), combines the limited liability advantage of a corporation with the tax advantages of a partnership.

limited partnership   A partnership in which limited partners' liabilities, investment returns, and control are limited; general partners have unlimited liability and control.

line of credit   An arrangement in which a bank agrees to lend up to a specified maximum amount of funds during a designated period.

liquidation in bankruptcy   The sale of the assets of a firm and the distribution of the proceeds to the creditors and owners in a specific priority.

liquidity Liquidity refers to a firm's cash and marketable securities position and to its ability to meet maturing obligations. A liquid asset is any asset that can be quickly sold and converted to cash at its "fair" value. Active markets provide liquidity.

liquidity premium (LP) A liquidity premium is added to the real risk-free rate of interest, in addition to other premiums, if a security is not liquid.

liquidity ratio A ratio that shows the relationship of a firm's cash and other current assets to its current liabilities.

lockbox plan A cash management tool in which incoming checks for a firm are sent to post office boxes rather than to corporate headquarters. Several times a day, a local bank will collect the contents of the lockbox and deposit the checks into the company's local account.

long hedges Occur when futures contracts are bought in anticipation of (or to guard against) price increases.

low-regular-dividend-plus-extras policy Dividend policy in which a company announces a low regular dividend that it is sure can be maintained; if extra funds are available, the company pays a specially designated extra dividend or repurchases shares of stock.

lumpy assets Those assets that cannot be acquired smoothly and instead require large, discrete additions. For example, an electric utility that is operating at full capacity cannot add a small amount of generating capacity, at least not economically.

M

managerial options Options that give opportunities to managers to respond to changing market conditions. Also called real options.

margin requirement The margin is the percentage of a stock's price that an investor has borrowed in order to purchase the stock. The Securities and Exchange Commission sets margin requirements, which is the maximum percentage of debt that can be used to purchase a stock.

marginal tax rate The tax rate on the last unit of income.

market multiple method Multiplies a market-determined ratio (called a multiple) to some value of the target firm to estimate the target's value. The market multiple can be based on net income, earnings per share, sales, book value, or number of subscribers.

market portfolio A portfolio consisting of all stocks.

market risk That part of a security's total risk that cannot be eliminated by diversification; measured by the beta coefficient.

market risk premium, RP_M The difference between the expected return on the market and the risk-free rate.

Market Value Added (MVA) The difference between the market value of the firm (that is, the sum of the market value of common equity, the market value of debt, and the market value of preferred stock) and the book value of the firm's common equity, debt, and preferred stock. If the book values of debt and preferred stock are equal to their market values, then MVA is also equal to the difference between the market value of equity and the amount of equity capital that investors supplied.

market value ratios Relate the firm's stock price to its earnings and book value per share.

marketable securities Can be converted to cash on very short notice and provide at least a modest return.

maturity date The date when the bond's par value is repaid to the bondholder. Maturity dates generally range from 10 to 40 years from the time of issue.

maturity matching short-term financing policy A policy that matches asset and liability maturities. It is also referred to as the moderate, or self-liquidating, approach.

maturity risk premium (MRP) The premium that must be added to the real risk-free rate of interest to compensate for interest rate risk, which depends on a bond's maturity. Interest rate risk arises from the fact that bond prices decline when interest rates rise. Under these circumstances, selling a bond prior to maturity will result in a capital loss; the longer the term to maturity, the larger the loss.

merger The joining of two firms to form a single firm.

Miller model Introduces the effect of personal taxes into the valuation of a levered firm, which reduces the advantage of corporate debt financing.

MM Proposition I with corporate taxes $V_L = V_U + TD$. Thus, firm value increases with leverage and the optimal capital structure is virtually all debt.

MM Proposition I without taxes $V_L = V_U = EBIT/r_{sU}$. Since both EBIT and r_{sU} are constant, firm value is also constant and capital structure is irrelevant.

MM Proposition II with corporate taxes $r_{sL} = r_{sU} + (r_{sU} - r_d)(1 - T)(D/S)$. Here the increase in equity costs is less than the zero-tax case, and the increasing use of lower-cost debt causes the firm's cost of capital to decrease. In this case, the optimal capital structure is virtually all debt.

MM Proposition II without taxes $r_{sL} = r_{sU} + (r_{sU} - r_d)(D/S)$. Thus, r_s increases in a precise way as leverage increases. In fact, this increase is just sufficient to offset the increased use of lower-cost debt.

moderate net operating working capital policy A policy that matches asset and liability maturities. It is also referred to as maturity matching or the self-liquidating approach.

Modified Internal Rate of Return (MIRR) method Assumes that cash flows from all projects are reinvested at the cost of capital, not at the project's own IRR. This makes the modified internal rate of return a better indicator of a project's true profitability.

money market A financial market for debt securities with maturities of less than 1 year (short-term). The New York money market is the world's largest.

money market fund A mutual fund that invests in short-term debt instruments and offers investors check-writing privileges; thus, it amounts to an interest-bearing checking account.

Monte Carlo simulation analysis A risk analysis technique in which a computer is used to simulate probable future events and thus to estimate the likely profitability and risk of a project.

mortgage bond A bond for which a corporation pledges certain assets as security. All such bonds are written subject to an indenture.

multinational (or global) corporation A corporation that operates in two or more countries.

municipal bond Issued by state and local governments. The interest earned on most municipal bonds is exempt from federal taxes and also from state taxes if the holder is a resident of the issuing state.

municipal bond insurance An insurance company guarantees to pay the coupon and principal payments should the issuer of the bond (the municipality) default. This reduces the risk to investors who are willing to accept a lower coupon rate for an insured bond issue compared to an uninsured issue.

mutual fund A corporation that sells shares in the fund and uses the proceeds to buy stocks, long-term bonds, or short-term debt instruments. The resulting dividends, interest, and capital gains are distributed to the fund's shareholders after the deduction of operating expenses. Some funds specialize in certain types of securities, such as growth stocks, international stocks, or municipal bonds.

mutually exclusive projects Projects that cannot be performed at the same time. A company could choose either Project 1 or Project 2, or it can reject both, but it cannot accept both projects.

N

National Association of Securities Dealers (NASD) An industry group primarily concerned with the operation of the over-the-counter (OTC) market.

natural hedge A transaction between two counterparties where both parties' risks are reduced.

net advantage to leasing (NAL) The dollar value of the lease to the lessee. It is the net present value of leasing minus the net present value of owning.

net cash flow The sum of net income plus noncash adjustments.

net float The difference between a firm's disbursement float and collections float.

net operating working capital (NOWC) Operating current assets minus operating current liabilities. Operating current assets are the current assets used to support operations, such as cash, accounts receivable, and inventory. They do not include short-term investments. Operating current liabilities are the current liabilities that are a natural consequence of the firm's operations, such as accounts payable and accruals. They do not include notes payable or any other short-term debt that charges interest.

net present value (NPV) method   The present value of the project's expected future cash flows, discounted at the appropriate cost of capital. NPV is a direct measure of the value of the project to shareholders.

net working capital   Current assets minus current liabilities.

new issue market   The market for stock of companies that go public.

nominal (quoted) interest rate, I_{NOM}   The rate of interest stated in a contract. If the compounding occurs annually, the effective annual rate and the nominal rate are the same. If compounding occurs more frequently, the effective annual rate is greater than the nominal rate. The nominal annual interest rate is also called the annual percentage rate, or APR.

nominal rate of return, r_n   Includes an inflation adjustment (premium). Thus, if nominal rates of return are used in the capital budgeting process, then the net cash flows must also be nominal.

nominal risk-free rate of interest, r_{RF}   The real risk-free rate plus a premium for expected inflation. The short-term nominal risk-free rate is usually approximated by the U.S. Treasury bill rate, and the long-term nominal risk-free rate is approximated by the rate on U.S. Treasury bonds.

nonnormal cash flow projects   Projects with a large cash outflow either sometime during or at the end of their lives. A common problem encountered when evaluating projects with nonnormal cash flows is multiple internal rates of return.

nonoperating assets   Include investments in marketable securities and noncontrolling interests in the stock of other companies.

nonpecuniary benefits   Perks that are not actual cash payments, such as lavish offices, memberships at country clubs, corporate jets, and excessively large staffs.

NOPAT (net operating profit after taxes)   The amount of profit a company would generate if it had no debt and no financial assets.

normal cash flow project   A project with one or more cash outflows (costs) followed by a series of cash inflows.

normal yield curve   When the yield curve slopes upward it is said to be "normal," because it is like this most of the time.

O

off–balance sheet financing   A financing technique in which a firm uses partnerships and other arrangements to (in effect) borrow money while not reporting the liability on its balance sheet. For example, for many years neither leased assets nor the liabilities under lease contracts appeared on the lessees' balance sheets. To correct this problem, the Financial Accounting Standards Board issued FASB Statement 13.

open outcry auction   A method of matching buyers and sellers in which the buyers and sellers are face to face, all stating a price at which they will buy or sell.

operating capital   The sum of net operating working capital and operating long-term assets, such as net plant and equipment. Operating capital also is equal to the net amount of capital raised from investors. This is the amount of interest-bearing debt plus preferred stock plus common equity minus short-term investments. Also called total net operating capital, net operating capital, or net operating assets.

operating company   A company controlled by a holding company.

operating current assets   The current assets used to support operations, such as cash, accounts receivable, and inventory. It does not include short-term investments.

operating current liabilities   The current liabilities that are a natural consequence of the firm's operations, such as accounts payable and accruals. It does not include notes payable or any other short-term debt that charges interest.

operating lease   Provides for both financing and maintenance. Generally, the operating lease

---

---

contract is written for a period considerably shorter than the expected life of the leased equipment and contains a cancellation clause; sometimes called a service lease.

operating leverage The extent to which fixed costs are used in a firm's operations. If a high percentage of a firm's total costs are fixed costs, then the firm is said to have a high degree of operating leverage. Operating leverage is a measure of one element of business risk but does not include the second major element, sales variability.

operating merger Occurs when the operations of two companies are integrated with the expectation of obtaining synergistic gains. These may occur in response to economies of scale, management efficiency, or a host of other factors.

operating profit margin Ratio of earnings before interest and taxes divided by sales.

opportunity cost A cash flow that a firm must forgo in order to accept a project. For example, if the project requires the use of a building that could otherwise be sold, then the market value of the building is an opportunity cost of the project.

opportunity cost rate The rate of return available on the best alternative investment of similar risk.

optimal distribution policy The distribution policy that maximizes the value of the firm by choosing the optimal level and form of distributions (dividends and stock repurchases).

optimal dividend policy The dividend policy that strikes a balance between current dividends and future growth and maximizes the firm's stock price.

optimal portfolio The point at which the efficient set of portfolios—the efficient frontier—is just tangent to the investor's indifference curve. This point marks the highest level of satisfaction an investor can attain given the set of potential portfolios.

option A contract that gives its holder the right to buy or sell an asset at some predetermined price within a specified period of time.

ordinary (deferred) annuity An annuity with a fixed number of equal payments occurring at the end of each period.

original issue discount (OID) bond In general, any bond originally offered at a price that is significantly below its par value.

P

par value The nominal or face value of a stock or bond. The par value of a bond generally represents the amount of money that the firm borrows and promises to repay at some future date. The par value of a bond is often $1,000, but it can be $5,000 or more.

parent company Another name for a holding company. A parent company will often have control over many subsidiaries.

partnership A partnership exists when two or more persons associate to conduct a business.

payables deferral period The average length of time between a firm's purchase of materials and labor and the payment of cash for them. It is calculated by dividing accounts payable by credit purchases per day (i.e., cost of goods sold ÷ 365).

payback period The number of years it takes a firm to recover its project investment. Payback does not capture a project's entire cash flow stream and is thus not the preferred evaluation method. Note, however, that the payback does measure a project's liquidity, so many firms use it as a risk measure.

payment date The date on which a firm actually mails dividend checks.

payment, PMT Equal to the dollar amount of an equal or constant cash flow (an annuity).

pegged exchange rates Rates that are fixed against a major currency such as the U.S. dollar. Consequently, the values of the pegged currencies move together over time.

perfect hedge A hedge in which the gain or loss on the hedged transaction exactly offsets the loss or gain on the unhedged position.

periodic rate, I_{PER} The rate charged by a lender or paid by a borrower each period. It can be a rate per year, per 6-month period, per quarter, per month, per day, or per any other time interval (usually 1 year or less).

permanent net operating working capital The NOWC required when the economy is weak and seasonal sales are at their low point. Thus, this level of NOWC always requires financing and can be regarded as permanent.

perpetuity A series of payments of a fixed amount that continue indefinitely.

physical location exchanges Exchanges, such as the New York Stock Exchange, that facilitate trading of securities at a particular location.

plug technique Technique used in financial forecasting to "plug" in enough new liabilities or assets to make the balance sheets balance.

poison pills Shareholder rights provisions that allow existing shareholders in a company to purchase additional shares of stock at a lower-than-market value if a potential acquirer purchases a controlling stake in the company.

political risk Refers to the possibility of expropriation and the unanticipated restriction of cash flows to the parent by a foreign government.

pooling of interests A method of accounting for a merger in which the consolidated balance sheet is constructed by simply adding together the balance sheets of the merged companies. This is no longer allowed.

portfolio A group of individual assets held in combination. An asset that would be relatively risky if held in isolation may have little or no risk if held in a well-diversified portfolio.

post-audit The final aspect of the capital budgeting process. The post-audit is a feedback process in which the actual results are compared with those predicted in the original capital budgeting analysis. The post-audit has several purposes, of which the most important are to improve forecasts and operations.

precautionary balance A cash balance held in reserve for random, unforeseen fluctuations in cash inflows and outflows.

preemptive right Gives the current shareholders the right to purchase any new shares issued in proportion to their current holdings. The preemptive right enables current owners to maintain their proportionate share of ownership and control of the business.

preferred stock A hybrid security that is similar to bonds in some respects and to common stock in other respects. Preferred dividends are similar to interest payments on bonds in that they are fixed in amount and generally must be paid before common stock dividends can be paid. If the preferred dividend is not earned, the directors can omit it without throwing the company into bankruptcy.

premium bond Bond prices and interest rates are inversely related; that is, they tend to move in the opposite direction from one another. A fixed-rate bond will sell at par when its coupon interest rate is equal to the going rate of interest, r_d. When the going rate of interest is above the coupon rate, a fixed-rate bond will sell at a "discount" below its par value. If current interest rates are below the coupon rate, a fixed-rate bond will sell at a "premium" above its par value.

premium on forward rate Occurs when the forward exchange rate differs from the spot rate. When the forward rate is above the spot rate, it is said to be at a premium.

prepackaged bankruptcy (or pre-pack) A type of reorganization that combines the advantages of informal workouts and formal Chapter 11 reorganization.

pre-tax earnings or income The amount of earnings (or income) that is subject to taxes. It is also equal to earnings before interest and taxes (EBIT) less the interest expense. It is sometimes called earnings before taxes (EBT)

price/cash flow ratio Calculated by dividing price per share by cash flow per share. This shows how much investors are willing to pay per dollar of cash flow.

price/earnings (P/E) ratio Calculated by dividing price per share by earnings per share. This shows how much investors are willing to pay per dollar of reported profits.

price/EBITDA ratio The ratio of price per share divided by per share earnings before interest, depreciation, and amortization.

primary market Markets in which newly issued securities are sold for the first time.

priority of claims in liquidation   Established in Chapter 7 of the Bankruptcy Act. It specifies the order in which the debtor's assets are distributed among the creditors.

private markets   Markets in which transactions are worked out directly between two parties and structured in any manner that appeals to them. Bank loans and private placements of debt with insurance companies are examples of private market transactions.

private placement   The sale of stock to only one or a few investors, usually institutional investors. The advantages of private placements are lower flotation costs and greater speed, since the shares issued are not subject to Securities and Exchange Commission registration.

probability distribution   A listing, chart, or graph of all possible outcomes, such as expected rates of return, with a probability assigned to each outcome.

professional corporation (PC)   Has most of the benefits of incorporation but the participants are not relieved of professional (malpractice) liability; known in some states as a professional association (PA).

profit margin on sales   Calculated by dividing net income by sales; gives the profit per dollar of sales.

profitability index   Found by dividing the project's present value of future cash flows by its initial cost. A profitability index greater than 1 is equivalent to a project's having positive net present value.

profitability ratios   Ratios that show the combined effects of liquidity, asset management, and debt on operations.

progressive tax   A tax system in which the higher one's income, the larger the percentage paid in taxes.

project cash flows   The incremental cash flows of a proposed project.

project cost of capital   The risk-adjusted discount rate for that project.

project financing   Financing method in which the project's creditors do not have full recourse against the borrowers; the lenders and lessors must be paid from the project's cash flows and equity.

projected (pro forma) financial statement   Shows how an actual statement would look if certain assumptions are realized.

promissory note   A document specifying the terms and conditions of a loan, including the amount, interest rate, and repayment schedule.

proprietorship   A business owned by one individual.

prospectus   Summarizes information about a new security issue and the issuing company.

proxy   A document giving one person the authority to act for another, typically the power to vote shares of common stock.

proxy fight   An attempt to take over a company in which an outside group solicits existing shareholders' proxies, which are authorizations to vote shares in a shareholders' meeting, in an effort to overthrow management and take control of the business.

public markets   Markets in which standardized contracts are traded on organized exchanges. Securities that are issued in public markets, such as common stock and corporate bonds, are ultimately held by a large number of individuals.

public offering   An offer of new common stock to the general public.

publicly owned corporation   Corporation in which the stock is owned by a large number of investors, most of whom are not active in management.

purchase accounting   A method of accounting for a merger in which the merger is handled as a purchase. In this method, the acquiring firm is assumed to have "bought" the acquired company in much the same way it would buy any capital asset.

purchasing power parity   Implies that the level of exchange rates adjusts so that identical goods cost the same in different countries. Sometimes referred to as the "law of one price."

put option   Allows the holder to sell the asset at some predetermined price within a specified period of time.

PV   The value today of a future payment, or stream of payments, discounted at the appropriate rate of interest. PV is also the beginning amount that will grow to some future value.

PVA_N   The value today of a future stream of N equal payments at the end of each period (an ordinary annuity).

PVIFA$_{I,N}$ The present value interest factor for an ordinary annuity of N periodic payments discounted at I percent interest per period.

PVIF$_{I,N}$ The present value interest factor for a lump sum received N periods in the future discounted at I percent per period.

Q

quick, or acid test, ratio Found by taking current assets less inventories and then dividing by current liabilities.

R

real options Occur when managers can influence the size and risk of a project's cash flows by taking different actions during the project's life. They are referred to as real options because they deal with real as opposed to financial assets. They are also called managerial options because they give opportunities to managers to respond to changing market conditions. Sometimes they are called strategic options because they often deal with strategic issues. Finally, they are also called embedded options because they are a part of another project.

real rate of return, r$_r$ Contains no adjustment for expected inflation. If net cash flows from a project do not include inflation adjustments, then the cash flows should be discounted at the real cost of capital. In a similar manner, the internal rate of return resulting from real net cash flows should be compared with the real cost of capital.

real risk-free rate of interest, r* The interest rate on a risk-free security in an economy with zero inflation. The real risk-free rate could also be called the pure rate of interest since it is the rate of interest that would exist on very short-term, default-free U.S. Treasury securities if the expected rate of inflation were zero.

realized rate of return, r̄ The actual return an investor receives on his or her investment. It can be quite different from the expected return.

receivables collection period The average length of time required to convert a firm's receivables into cash. It is calculated by dividing accounts receivable by sales per day.

red herring (preliminary) prospectus A preliminary prospectus that may be distributed to potential buyers prior to approval of the registration statement by the Securities and Exchange Commission. After the registration has become effective, the securities—accompanied by the prospectus—may be offered for sale.

redeemable bond Gives investors the right to sell the bonds back to the corporation at a price that is usually close to the par value. If interest rates rise, then investors can redeem the bonds and reinvest at the higher rates.

refunding Occurs when a company issues debt at current low rates and uses the proceeds to repurchase one of its existing high–coupon rate debt issues. Often these are callable issues, which means the company can purchase the debt at a call price lower than the market price.

registration statement Required by the Securities and Exchange Commission before a company's securities can be offered to the public. This statement is used to summarize various financial and legal information about the company.

reinvestment rate risk Occurs when a short-term debt security must be "rolled over." If interest rates have fallen then the reinvestment of principal will be at a lower rate, with correspondingly lower interest payments and ending value.

relative priority doctrine More flexible than absolute priority. Gives a more balanced consideration to all claimants in a bankruptcy reorganization than does the absolute priority doctrine.

relaxed net operating working capital policy A policy under which relatively large amounts of cash, marketable securities, and inventories are carried and under which sales are stimulated by a liberal credit policy, resulting in a high level of receivables.

reorganization in bankruptcy A court-approved attempt to keep a company alive by changing its capital structure in lieu of liquidation. A reorganization must adhere to the standards of fairness and feasibility.

repatriation of earnings The cash flow, usually in the form of dividends or royalties, from the foreign branch or subsidiary to the parent company. These cash flows must be converted to the currency of the parent and thus are subject to future exchange rate changes. A foreign government may restrict the amount of cash that may be repatriated.

replacement chain (common life) approach A method of comparing mutually exclusive projects that have unequal lives. Each project is replicated so that they will both terminate in a common year. If projects with lives of 3 years and 5 years are being evaluated, then the 3-year project would be replicated 5 times and the 5-year project replicated 3 times; thus, both projects would terminate in 15 years.

required rate of return, r_s The minimum acceptable rate of return, considering both its risk and the returns available on other investments.

reserve borrowing capacity Exists when a firm uses less debt under "normal" conditions than called for by the trade-off theory. This allows the firm some flexibility to use debt in the future when additional capital is needed.

residual distribution model In this model, firms should pay dividends only when more earnings are available than needed to support the optimal capital budget.

residual value The market value of the leased property at the expiration of the lease. The estimate of the residual value is one of the key elements in lease analysis.

restricted net operating working capital policy A policy under which holdings of cash, securities, inventories, and receivables are minimized.

restricted voting rights A provision that automatically deprives a shareholder of voting rights if the shareholder owns more than a specified amount of stock.

retained earnings The portion of the firm's earnings that have been saved rather than paid out as dividends.

retiree health benefits A major issue for employers because of the escalating costs of health care and a recent FASB ruling forcing companies to accrue the retiree health care liability rather than expensing the cash flows as they occur.

return on common equity (ROE) Found by dividing net income by common equity.

return on invested capital (ROIC) Net operating profit after taxes divided by the operating capital.

return on total assets (ROA) The ratio of net income to total assets.

revaluation Occurs when the relative price of a currency is increased. It is the opposite of devaluation.

revenue bonds Type of municipal bonds that are secured by the revenues derived from projects such as roads and bridges, airports, water and sewage systems, and not-for-profit health care facilities.

reverse split Situation in which shareholders exchange a particular number of shares of stock for a smaller number of new shares.

revolving credit agreement A formal, committed line of credit extended by a bank or other lending institution.

rights offering Occurs when a corporation sells a new issue of common stock to its existing stockholders. Each stockholder receives a certificate, called a stock purchase right, giving the stockholder the option to purchase a specified number of the new shares. The rights are issued in proportion to the amount of stock that each shareholder currently owns.

risk arbitrage The practice of purchasing stock in companies (in the context of mergers) that may become takeover targets.

risk aversion A risk-averse investor dislikes risk and requires a higher rate of return as an inducement to buy riskier securities.

risk premium for Stock i, RP_i The extra return that an investor requires to hold risky Stock i instead of a risk-free asset.

risk-adjusted discount rate Incorporates the risk of the project's cash flows. The cost of capital to the firm reflects the average risk of the firm's existing projects. Thus, new projects that are riskier than existing projects should have a higher risk-adjusted discount rate. Conversely, projects with less risk should have a lower risk-adjusted discount rate.

risky event An uncertain outcome that adversely affects a company's objectives.

roadshow Before an IPO, the senior management team and the investment banker make presentations to potential investors. They make three to five presentations daily over a 2-week period in 10 to 20 cities.

S

S corporation A small corporation that, under Subchapter S of the Internal Revenue Code, elects to be taxed as a proprietorship or a partnership yet retains limited liability and other benefits of the corporate form of organization.

safety stock Inventory held to guard against larger-than-normal sales and/or shipping delays.

sale-and-leaseback A type of financial lease in which the firm owning the property sells it to another firm, often a financial institution, while simultaneously entering into an agreement to lease the property back from the firm.

salvage value The market value of an asset after its useful life.

scenario analysis A shorter version of simulation analysis that uses only a few outcomes. Often the outcomes are for three scenarios: optimistic, pessimistic, and most likely.

seasonal effects on ratios Seasonal factors can distort ratio analysis. At certain times of the year, a firm may have excessive inventories in preparation of a "season" of high demand. Therefore, an inventory turnover ratio taken at this time will be radically different than one taken after the season.

secondary market Markets in which securities are resold after initial issue in the primary market. The New York Stock Exchange is an example.

secured loan A loan backed by collateral, which is often in the form of inventories or receivables.

Securities and Exchange Commission (SEC) A government agency that regulates the sales of new securities and the operations of securities exchanges. The SEC, along with other government agencies and self-regulation, helps ensure stable markets, sound brokerage firms, and the absence of stock manipulation.

securitization The process whereby financial instruments that were previously thinly traded are converted to a form that creates greater liquidity. Securitization also applies to the situation where specific assets are pledged as collateral for securities, thus creating asset-backed securities. One example of the former is junk bonds; an example of the latter is mortgage-backed securities.

Security Market Line (SML) Represents, in a graphical form, the relationship between the risk of an asset as measured by its beta and the required rates of return for individual securities. The SML equation is one of the key results of the CAPM: $r_i = r_{RF} + b_i(r_M - r_{RF})$.

semistrong form of market efficiency States that current market prices reflect all publicly available information. Therefore, the only way to gain abnormal returns on a stock is to possess inside information about the company's stock.

sensitivity analysis Indicates exactly how much net present value will change in response to a given change in an input variable, other things held constant. Sensitivity analysis is sometimes called "what if" analysis because it answers this type of question.

shareholder rights provision Also known as a poison pill, it allows existing shareholders to purchase additional shares of stock at a price that is lower than the market value if a potential acquirer purchases a controlling stake in the company.

shelf registration Frequently, companies will file a master registration statement and then update it with a short-form statement just before an offering. This procedure is termed shelf registration because companies put new securities "on the shelf" and then later sell them when the market is right.

short hedges Occur when futures contracts are sold to guard against price declines.

simple interest The situation when interest is not compounded; that is, interest is not earned on interest. Also called regular interest. Divide the nominal interest rate by 365 and multiply by the number of days the funds are borrowed to find the interest for the term borrowed.

sinking fund Facilitates the orderly retirement of a bond issue. This can be achieved in one of two ways: (1) the company can call in for redemption (at par value) a certain percentage of bonds each year, or (2) the company may buy the required amount of bonds on the open market.

social value   Projects of not-for-profit businesses are expected to provide a social value in addition to an economic value.

soft currencies   Currencies of countries that set the exchange rate but do not allow their currencies to be traded on world markets.

special dividend   A dividend paid, in addition to the regular dividend, when earnings permit. Firms with volatile earnings may have a low regular dividend that can be maintained even in years of low profit (or high capital investment) but is supplemented by an extra dividend when excess funds are available.

speculative balances   Funds held by a firm in order to have cash for taking advantage of bargain purchases or growth opportunities.

spin-off   Occurs when a holding company distributes the stock of one of the operating companies to its shareholders, thus passing control from the holding company to the shareholders directly.

spontaneous liabilities   Liabilities which grow with sales, such as accounts payable and accruals.

spot rate   The exchange rate that applies to "on the spot" trades or, more precisely, to exchanges that occur two days following the day of trade (in other words, current exchanges).

spread, underwriting   The difference between the price at which an underwriter sells the stock in an initial public offering and the proceeds that the underwriter passes on to the issuing firm; the fee collected by the underwriter. It is often about 7% of the offering price.

spread, yield   The difference between the yield of a bond relative to another bond with less risk.

stakeholders   All parties that have an interest, financial or otherwise, in a not-for-profit business.

stand-alone risk   The risk an investor takes by holding only one asset.

standard deviation, σ   A statistical measure of the variability of a set of observations. It is the square root of the variance.

statement of cash flows   Reports the impact of a firm's operating, investing, and financing activities on cash flows over an accounting period.

statement of stockholders' equity   Statement showing the beginning stockholders' equity, any changes due to stock issues/repurchases, the amount of net income that is retained, and the ending stockholders' equity.

stepped-up strike (or exercise) price   A provision in a warrant that increases the strike price over time. This provision is included to encourage owners to exercise their warrants.

stock dividend   Increases the number of shares outstanding but at a slower rate than splits. Current shareholders receive additional shares on some proportional basis. Thus, a holder of 100 shares would receive 5 additional shares at no cost if a 5% stock dividend were declared.

stock option   Allows its owner to purchase a share of stock at a fixed price, called the strike price or the exercise price, no matter what the actual price of the stock is. Stock options always have an expiration date, after which they cannot be exercised.

stock repurchase   Occurs when a firm repurchases its own stock. These shares of stock are then referred to as treasury stock.

stock split   Current shareholders are given some number (or fraction) of shares for each stock share owned. Thus, in a 3-for-1 split, each shareholder would receive three new shares in exchange for each old share, thereby tripling the number of shares outstanding. Stock splits usually occur when the stock price is outside of the optimal trading range.

strategic options   Options that often deal with strategic issues. Also called real options, embedded options, and managerial options.

stretching accounts payable   The practice of deliberately paying accounts late.

strike (or exercise) price   The price stated in the option contract at which the security can be bought (or sold).

strong form of market efficiency   Assumes that all information pertaining to a stock, whether public or inside information, is reflected in current market prices. Thus, no investors would be able to earn abnormal returns in the stock market.

structured note   A debt obligation derived from another debt obligation. Permits a partitioning of risks to give investors what they want.

subordinated debenture   Debentures that have claims on assets, in the event of bankruptcy, only after senior debt (as named in the subordinated debt's indenture) has been paid off. Subordinated debentures may be subordinated to designated notes payable or to all other debt.

sunk cost   A cost that has already occurred and is not affected by the capital project decision. Sunk costs are not relevant to capital budgeting decisions.

swap   An exchange of cash payment obligations. Usually occurs because the parties involved prefer someone else's payment pattern or type.

sweetener   A feature that makes a security more attractive to some investors, thereby inducing them to accept a lower current yield. Convertible features and warrants are examples of sweeteners.

synchronization of cash flows   Occurs when firms are able to time cash receipts to coincide with cash requirements.

synergy   Occurs when the whole is greater than the sum of its parts. When applied to mergers, a synergistic merger occurs when the post-merger earnings exceed the sum of the separate companies' pre-merger earnings.

T

takeover   An action whereby a person or group succeeds in ousting a firm's management and taking control of the company.

target capital structure   The relative amount of debt, preferred stock, and common equity that the firm desires. The weighted average cost of capital should be based on these target weights.

target cash balance   The desired cash balance that a firm plans to maintain in order to conduct business.

target company   A firm that another company seeks to acquire.

target distribution ratio   Percentage of net income distributed to shareholders through cash dividends or stock repurchases.

target payout ratio   Percentage of net income paid as a cash dividend.

targeted share repurchases   Also known as greenmail, occurs when a company buys back stock from a potential acquirer at a price that is higher than the market price. In return, the potential acquirer agrees not to attempt to take over the company.

tax loss carryback and carryforward   Ordinary corporate operating losses can be carried backward for 2 years or forward for 20 years to offset taxable income in a given year.

tax preference theory   Proposes that investors prefer capital gains over dividends, because capital gains taxes can be deferred into the future but taxes on dividends must be paid as the dividends are received.

taxable income   Gross income less a set of exemptions and deductions that are spelled out in the instructions to the tax forms that individuals must file.

technical analysts   Stock analysts who believe that past trends or patterns in stock prices can be used to predict future stock prices.

TED spread   The 3-month LIBOR rate minus the 3-month T-bill rate. It is a measure of risk aversion and measures the extra compensation that banks require to induce them to lend to one another.

temporary net operating working capital   The NOWC required above the permanent level when the economy is strong and/or seasonal sales are high.

tender offer   The offer of one firm to buy the stock of another by going directly to the stockholders, frequently over the opposition of the target company's management.

term structure of interest rates   The relationship between yield to maturity and term to maturity for bonds of a single risk class.

terminal value   Value of operations at the end of the explicit forecast period; equal to the present value of all free cash flows beyond the forecast period, discounted back to the end of the forecast period at the weighted average cost of capital.

99788888889878888888887888888888888888888888888888888888

time line A graphical representation used to show the timing of cash flows.

times-interest-earned (TIE) ratio Determined by dividing earnings before interest and taxes by the interest charges. This ratio measures the extent to which operating income can decline before the firm is unable to meet its annual interest costs.

total assets turnover ratio Measures the turnover of all the firm's assets; it is calculated by dividing sales by total assets.

trade credit Debt arising from credit sales and recorded as an account receivable by the seller and as an account payable by the buyer.

trade deficit Occurs when a country imports more goods from abroad than it exports.

trade discounts Price reductions that suppliers offer customers for early payment of bills.

trade-off model The addition of financial distress and agency costs to either the MM tax model or the Miller model. In this model, the optimal capital structure can be visualized as a trade-off between the benefit of debt (the interest tax shelter) and the costs of debt (financial distress and agency costs).

transactions balance The cash balance associated with payments and collections; the balance necessary for day-to-day operations.

Treasury bond Bonds issued by the federal government; sometimes called T-bonds or government bonds. Treasury bonds have no default risk.

trend analysis An analysis of a firm's financial ratios over time. It is used to estimate the likelihood of improvement or deterioration in its financial situation.

U

underinvestment problem A type of agency problem in which high debt can cause managers to forgo positive NPV projects unless they are extremely safe.

underwritten arrangement Contract between a firm and an investment banker when stock is issued. An investment banker agrees to buy the entire issue at a set price and then resells the stock at the offering price. Thus, the risk of selling the issue rests with the investment banker.

V

value at risk (VaR) The dollar value that defines a specified percentile in the probability distribution of portfolio's loss or a project's NPV. For example, if the specified percentile is 5%, a VaR of −$1 million means that there is a 5% probability that the portfolio will lose $1 million or more.

value of operations (V_{op}) The present value of all expected future free cash flows when discounted at the weighted average cost of capital.

variance, σ^2 A measure of the distribution's variability. It is the sum of the squared deviations about the expected value.

venture capitalist The manager of a venture capital fund. The fund raises most of its capital from institutional investors and invests in start-up companies in exchange for equity.

vertical merger Occurs when a company acquires another firm that is "upstream" or "downstream"; for example, an automobile manufacturer acquires a steel producer.

vesting If employees have the rights to receive pension benefits even if they leave the company prior to retirement, their rights are said to be vested.

vesting period Period during which employee stock options cannot be exercised.

W

warrant A call option, issued by a company, that allows the holder to buy a stated number of shares of stock from the company at a specified price. Warrants are generally distributed with debt, or preferred stock, to induce investors to buy those securities at lower cost.

weak form of market efficiency Assumes that all information contained in past price movements is fully reflected in current market prices. Thus, information about recent trends in a stock's price is of no use in selecting a stock.

weighted average cost of capital (WACC) The weighted average of the after-tax component costs of capital—debt, preferred stock, and common equity. Each weighting factor is the proportion of that type of capital in the optimal, or target, capital structure.

white knight A friendly competing bidder that a target management likes better than the company making a hostile offer; the target solicits a merger with the white knight as a preferable alternative.

window dressing Techniques employed by firms to make their financial statements look better than they really are.

working capital A firm's investment in short-term assets—cash, marketable securities, inventory, and accounts receivable.

workout Voluntary reorganization plans arranged between creditors and generally sound companies experiencing temporary financial difficulties. Workouts typically require some restructuring of the firm's debt.

Y

Yankee bonds Bond issued by a foreign borrower denominated in dollars and sold in the United States under SEC regulations.

yield curve The curve that results when yield to maturity is plotted on the y-axis with term to maturity on the x-axis.

yield to call (YTC) The rate of interest earned on a bond if it is called. If current interest rates are well below an outstanding callable bond's coupon rate, then the YTC may be a more relevant estimate of expected return than the YTM because the bond is likely to be called.

yield to maturity (YTM) The rate of interest earned on a bond if it is held to maturity.

Z

zero coupon bond Pays no coupons at all but is offered at a substantial discount below its par value and hence provides capital appreciation rather than interest income.

© lulu/fotolia.com

Name Index

A

Abreo, Leslie, 760
Adams, Paul D., 654n
Aeppel, Timothy, 357n
Agrawal, A., 533
Ainina, M. Fall, 875n
Alderson, Michael J., 802n
Allen, Jeffrey W., 899n
Allen, Samuel R., 397
Allen, Woody, 141
Altman, Edward I., 944n, 950n
Amram, Martha, 466n, 1029n
Anderson, Kenneth E., 889n
Andrade, Gregor, 606n
Appleton, Elaine L., 653
Ashcraft, Adam B., 43n
Asquith, Paul, 557n, 817n

B

Baker, H. Kent, 578n, 741n, 875n
Baker, Malcolm, 604n, 606n
Bansal, Vipul K., 932n
Barberis, Nicholas, 274
Barclay, Michael J., 604n
Bauguess, Scott, 744n
Benartzi, Shlomo, 558n
Beranek, William, 952n
Berger, Philip, 869n
Berk, Jonathan, 276n
Bernanke, Ben, 603
Berra, Yogi, 598
Bertrand, Marianne, 171
Betker, Brian L., 957n
Bhagwat, Yatin, 384n
Bielinski, Daniel W., 875n
Billingsley, Randall S., 817n
Black, Fischer, 345
Blake, Marshall, 910n
Blume, Marshall, 997, 997n, 999, 999n
Bodnar, Gordon M., 911n
Boehmer, Robert, 952n
Bonaparte, Napoleon, 963
Born, Jeffrey A., 558n

C

Branson, Richard (Sir), 771
Brav, Alon, 576n
Brennan, Michael, 1029n
Brick, I. E., 530
Brook, Yaron, 558n
Brooks, Robert, 294n
Brown, Keith C., 932n
Bruner, Robert E., 371
Bubnys, Edward L., 1004n
Buffett, Warren, 41, 578n, 867
Bunge, Jacob, 30, 729
Burman, Leonard, 555n, 599n

Cameron, Doug, 30
Campbell, John Y., 249n, 273n
Carbaugh, Robert, 692
Carell, Steve, 771
Cassidy, John, 43n
Castelino, Mark G., 928n
Chadha, S., 533
Chan, Louis K.C., 249n
Chance, Don, 346, 347n
Chang, Rosita P., 555n, 709n
Chapman, Brandyn, 357
Charlton, William, Jr., 558n
Chatterjee, Sris, 957n
Cherney, Mike, 748
Chiang, Raymond C., 762n
Clements, Jonathan, 269n
Colbert, Stephen, 659
Constantinides, George, 274n, 744n
Cook, Timothy, 547
Cooley, Philip L., 852n
Cooney, John W., 744n
Copeland, Thomas E., 1003n
Cruise, Tom, 37
Crum, Roy, 681
Cyr, Billy, 357

D

Daleo, Bob, 631
Daniel, Kent, 275n

1121

© lulu/fotolia.com

Subject Index